Contemporary Literary Criticism

Literary and Cultural Studies

Contemporary Literary Criticism

Literary and Cultural Studies

fourth edition

Robert Con Davis
Ronald Schleifer
University of Oklahoma

 LONGMAN

An imprint of Addison Wesley Longman, Inc.

New York • Reading, Massachusetts • Menlo Park, California • Harlow, England
Don Mills, Ontario • Sydney • Mexico City • Madrid • Amsterdam

Editor-in-Chief: Patricia Rossi
Senior Editor: Lisa Moore
Supplements Editor: Donna Campion
Marketing Manager: John Holdcroft
Project Manager: Robert Ginsberg
Design Manager and Text Designer: John Callahan
Cover Designer: Sandra Watanabe
Cover Illustration: from *Perspective* by Jan Vredeman de Vries, Dover Publications, Inc., 1968
Art Studio: ElectraGraphics, Inc.
Photo Researcher: Sandy Schneider
Production Manager: Valerie A. Vargas
Manufacturing Manager: Hilda Koparanian
Electronic Page Makeup: Jim Sullivan
Printer and Binder: RR Donnelley & Sons Company
Cover Printer: Coral Graphic Services, Inc.

For permission to use copyrighted material, grateful acknowledgment is made to the copyright holders on pp. 728–729, which are hereby made part of this copyright page.

Library of Congress Cataloging-in-Publication Data

Contemporary literary criticism: literary and cultural studies.—
    4th ed. / [edited by] Robert Con Davis, Ronald Schleifer.
        p.   cm.
    Includes bibliographical references and index.
    ISBN 0-8013-3002-5
    1. Criticism—History—20th century. I. Davis, Robert Con, date.
    II. Schleifer, Ronald.
PN94.C67   1998
801′.95′0904—dc21   97-37648
                                           CIP

Please visit our website at http://longman.awl.com

ISBN 0-8013-3002-5

2345678910—DOC –020100

Contents

v

Preface

READING *CONTEMPORARY LITERARY CRITICISM*

This book is intended to help readers to explore and interrogate contemporary literary criticism and theory. To that end, it provides the immediate background for current criticism with essays that attempt to trace the definitions and history of criticism and theory.

In our General Introduction we have attempted to offer a short overview of contemporary literary and cultural criticism by presenting a short historical and formal definition of literature and raising some of the implications, worked out in our introductions and selections throughout this book, of juxtaposing formal and historical questions that arise in interpretation.

Parts I and II examine the ways that contemporary criticism has taught us to reexamine and critique the practice of literary studies in terms of the nature of "literature," the "ethics" of criticism, the profession of intellectual (or "theoretical") study, the formation of literary canons, and the place and efficacy of literary study in the world. The book then presents criticism in terms of six major areas of concern that illustrate particular critical questions or systems of thought—rhetorical, structuralist, poststructuralist, psychological, historical, and gender-based—and a final section that raises explicitly the relationships between interpretation and cultural life. This is not an inclusive listing of contemporary approaches to reading literature—it presents little that deals with traditional literary analysis (such as explicit examples of "New Critical" literary criticism) or more traditional literary history or, at another extreme, the remarkable outpouring of studies of "popular" culture. And it touches little on the rich recent work demonstrating the relationship between reading and writing. But the nine areas covered are arguably major areas of concern that suggest and connect with many of the others and are likely to spawn other developments in the new century.

We imagine, in fact, that one possible way of using this text is to begin with a chronological reading of the part introductions. By doing so the student can follow an integrated discussion and a kind of intellectual history of contemporary thought about literature and discourse in general. To this end we have extensively interrelated the discussions across parts of the book. The General Introduction, as we said, examines the history and definition of "literature" and discusses contemporary criticism and the "humanities" in relation to the concept of the "human sciences." And in subsequent introductions, we emphasize the role of critique in literary studies and the possibilities of reading literary and other cultural texts in terms of ethics as well as aesthetics. These possibilities, we think, help expand literary to "cultural" studies. The last introduction in many ways sums up all the other part introductions, and the introductions together comprise a history—a coherent narrative and survey—of contemporary critical thought.

THE STRUCTURE OF THE BOOK

Within each part, the essays are designed to raise questions about one another, and the "framing" sections—the introductions to "What Is Literary Studies?" (Part I) and "What Is Literary Theory?" (Part II) and the gesture toward a conclusion in "Cultural Studies" (Part IX)—are especially designed to present various kinds of debate about crucial issues concerning the definition, functioning, and value of literary criticism. Thus, "What Is Literary Studies?" offers the argument over whether literature is "disinterested" or "interested" and whether its study is best understood as formal or historical. "What Is Literary Theory?" offers the argument, clearly seen in the juxtaposition of Aijaz Ahmad and Edward Said, about the *value* of literary theory. We also discuss the definition of "culture," the nature of knowledge, and the relationship between understanding and social action.

In other words, the essays of this book are closely interrelated as "contests," as Said says, over "forms and values," and the framing sections attempt to make that interrelationship clear. There are two other ways we have attempted to emphasize this. Each part introduction ends with a list of further reading. These alternative readings address the concerns of that section from a different vantage point. (In the Introduction to "Feminism and Gender Studies" (Part VII) we even give a close reading of Annette Kuhn's "The Body and Cinema: Some Problems for Feminism," which is not included in our book, in part to suggest an important text for further reading.) Moreover, each part introduction provides cross-references to essays in other parts of the book. In this way, students and instructors can choose to follow a thematic rather than paradigmatic exploration of contemporary literary studies. But more than this, each part introduction also offers an overview of the history and concerns governing the essays contained in it, which aims, as far as possible, to relate that section to the others. Just as, earlier in the preface, we attempted to relate our discussion of ways of reading criticism to the two definitions of teaching Felman examines in "Psychology and Psychoanalysis" (Part VI)—and then offered a short list of essays in the book that help define her approach—so the part introductions offer discursive relationships among the parts themselves.

THE STRUCTURE OF THE SECTIONS

A significant feature of this book is the manner in which each part is structured. First of all, we have chosen one essay of each section (in "What Is Literary Studies?" [Part I] and "What Is Literary Theory?" [Part II], the first two essays) to provide an especially clear and basic description of the school or approach of the whole part.

Northrop Frye, Paul de Man, J. Hillis Miller, Stanley Fish, Jonathan Culler, Slavoj Žižek, Raymond Williams, Diana Fuss, and Dick Hebdige each provide an introduction to a way of thinking about literature—ways of performing, enacting, criticism—that helps to situate the essays that follow in each section. Even when we begin with more "classical" statements—Ferdinand de Saussure's technical but illuminating attempt to reorient students to language study, Jacques Lacan's attempt to rethink psychoanalysis in terms of discourse, Mikhail Bakhtin's innovative attempt to relate meaning and historical materialism—the next essay performs this duty of introduction. In Part I, the opening essay has a conspicuous function. T. S. Eliot's famous "Tradition and the Individual Talent" begins *Contemporary Literary Criticism* by reminding us that "criticism is as inevitable as breathing," and our Introduction to "What Is Literary Studies?" (Part I) aims at situating contemporary criticism in relation to modernism and American New Criticism so that students will get a sense of the historicity of criticism and a sense, too, of the ways that critical activity has attempted to negotiate a position for itself between formal and historical analyses. There and throughout this book, our aim is to allow students to comprehend the very existence of literary criticism as a dialogue in relation to the intellectual world it finds itself in and to grasp its sense of the *stakes* of that activity.

NEW TO THIS EDITION

In this edition, we have redesigned *Contemporary Literary Criticism* by adding thirteen new essays (including the essay by Bakhtin, which appeared in the second edition). We retained the organizational structure of the third edition. Our overriding aim in these changes was to make the major issues shaping literary studies today—sometimes issues which by their very nature aim at making "common sense" difficult—accessible to students of this exciting area of intellectual life. Thus, *Contemporary Literary Criticism* offers alternative tables of contents in the cross-referenced essays in the introductions. Many colleagues who offered suggestions and criticism based on their use of the earlier editions expressed a need for such guides for students and classes, and we hope that these innovations will prove useful.

The fourth edition has a complicated relationship with the previous editions, especially the second edition. That book was the result of our collaboration (after R. C. Davis developed the first edition on his own), and our ongoing collaboration with *Contemporary Literary Criticism* led us to write *Criticism and Culture: The Role of Critique in Modern Literary Theory* (Longman, 1991). *Criticism and Culture*, closely based upon our work on the second edition of *Contemporary Literary Criticism*, attempts to develop a sense of the cultural work of literary criticism in the twentieth century. What we learned from working on *Criticism and Culture* had great influence on the third edition of *Contemporary Literary Criticism*, where we developed the nine section titles we have retained for this fourth edition. The changes from the second edition to the third were extensive, and we have found with some gratification that the directions we had then imagined were shaping contemporary literary and cultural studies have, in fact, remained the most exciting and important areas in contemporary criticism. Thus, the changes in the fourth edition are more modest. We have

- added thirteen new essays, including work by Mikhail Bakhtin, bell hooks, Cornel West, and Slavoj Žižek

- emphasized, more than earlier editions, the work in postcolonial studies, with the addition of essays by Gauri Viswanathan and by Aijaz Ahmad

- added an essay that surveys the intellectual and pedagogical implications of new technologies of discourse, "Hypertext and the Dreams of a New Culture" by Stuart Moulthrop

- substantially reworked the section on Feminism and Gender Studies and added several essays in other sections that emphasize feminist approaches to criticism, so that the fourth edition includes new essays by Teresa de Laurentis, Nancy Armstrong, Diana Fuss, Cora Kaplan, and Judith Butler

- continued the integration of critical approaches across the topics organizing the book so that feminist, psychoanalytic, philosophical, and other ways of reading inform all the sections of the book

- and, finally, tried to foreground, both in our selections and in our introductions, the basic task that seems critical to literary studies as we enter the new century, the juxtaposition and integration of historical understanding and formal analysis in the study of language, literature, and culture.

All of these issues, we believe, were present in the earlier editions. We have attempted here to make them clearer and more precise for students of criticism.

READING LITERARY CRITICISM

We noted in earlier editions the difficulties that teachers of criticism see some students encounter, even while other students have few difficulties from the beginning, do well in class and on papers, and clearly enjoy studying criticism. In some ways, the "difficulties" of criticism—its esoteric vocabularies, its high allusiveness, the intricacies of its argument—are a little less apparent when its scope is widened, as it is in the fourth edition, to take in forms of culture more familiar to late-twentieth-century students. Still, the difficulty of critique remains in this edition: the problem of questioning the self-evident, of trying to imagine, in encounters with literary and other forms of cultural discourse, the world being different from the familiar one. Thus, a central problem we noted that makes criticism "difficult"—namely, an approach that isolates it from other activities of interpretation we all habitually pursue—is still evident here. To really "work," criticism must be related to something else, and it can be thus related only when it is conceived as an activity, a doing in the human sciences, which, as we argue in the General Introduction, opens onto the largest questions about the relationships of people to culture. Interpretive criticism—of literature, of social and cultural institutions, of personal relations—is one of the more important things a literate person can do.

Thus, students who do well with this material not only recognize criticism as essentially an activity to be performed but also understand its importance. Other students tend to regard criticism as simply a body of knowledge to be learned, in which failure is always lurking so that each new critical position or school they encounter could be something to confuse and confound them. They imagine that successful completion of the course means getting through it unscathed, "mastering" criticism, but basically remaining untouched by the critical positions they have examined, their own views on literature still intact. In "Psychoanalysis and Education" in "Psychology and Psychoanalysis," (Part VI), Shoshana Felman discusses these two versions of "learning." They are related, as she demonstrates, to Jonathan Culler's discussion of "Convention and Meaning" in "Deconstruction and Poststructualism" (Part V) and tutored by the recent turn in psychology and psychoanalysis discussed by Teresa de Lauretis, Jacques Lacan, Catherine Belsey, Michael Warner, and others throughout this book. Felman presents a "performative" version of learning that encourages students to view a course in criticism as a tour on which they will explore a number of worlds from the "inside." In this version of education, students should be able to learn from literary rhetoric, as Barbara Johnson suggests, to apprehend the function of rhetoric in the most pressing controversies of our society.

When they read Louis Marin's structural analysis of Disneyland, in another example, as much as possible they should "become" structuralists and see the world of experience of capable of being subjected to "textual" analysis. When they read poststructuralism, they should come to know a text as decentered by the play of difference and learn to read by undoing the fixation of hierarchical authority. As Marxist critics, they should try to understand a text as situated within an ideological superstructure in relation to a historical and "material" base, while as feminist or gender critics, they should self-consciously read with a sense of the overwhelming importance of gender in relation to the understanding of personal and cultural experience.

In other words, "becoming" a critic is making the assumptions particular critics make about literature and culture in their reading and understanding. Learning (and "doing") criticism, like learning to play the piano, is something one practices to do. Students may eventually reject some or all of the critical schools presented in this book. But while studying each area of concern, they can try to see it as one of its adherents might view it, as in fact a central concern of understanding our world and a central concern of attempting to affect the world we live in. Becoming a "member" of the critical school we are studying constitutes a methodological wager that valuable insight can be gained from a sympathetic entry into a critical system, as opposed to an "objective" scrutiny of a foreign object.

At the beginning of this book, in "What Is Literary Studies?" (Part I) and "What Is Literary Theory?" (Part II), we present essays that examine the most fundamental assumptions of literary studies in order to situate the practice of criticism in the larger social contexts presented throughout the book—in the classroom, in the profession, in society at large, and even in the larger world outside Western Anglo-American society. But even these macrocosmic approaches to criticism—these broad "stances"—are positions to be assumed by students. At the book's end, in "Cultural Studies" (Part IX), we try to offer a range of discussions of the ways in which the study of literary (and, in James Clifford's ethnographic study of missionary work, "sacred") discourse can raise questions about culture and society that have been more or less implicit throughout all the essays. Cultural studies at its best, we believe, fulfills the most ambitious promises of literary studies. It allows us to see criticism not as a set of monuments to worship but as a set of activities undertaken with others who have made a record of their explorations in literary studies in order to establish a critical stance, an articulation of value, and a call to action. In this way, criticism may become something that one tries out, tries on, lives in, and lives through. It is an experience that one actively engages in rather than a difficulty that one avoids or fends off.

ACKNOWLEDGMENTS

This book derives largely from our experience teaching literary criticism in undergraduate and graduate courses at the University of Oklahoma, the University of Tulsa, and Knox College. Additionally, we were enriched by, and this book has benefited from, discussions about contemporary criticism with faculty and students at the University of Washington; Wichita State University; the University of Kansas; Georgia Institute of Technology; Eastern Michigan University; the Southern Illinois University at Edwardsville; Texas Tech University; the University of Northern Colorado; and places as far away as the University of Otago in Dunedin, New Zealand; the University of Haifa; Rome; Moscow; and Utrecht. This fourth edition has also been greatly improved by the help and good advice of a host of people who have used the earlier editions. Many of these people were friends and colleagues, but at least equal in number were the many who simply wrote to discuss their experiences of using the book in class.

A large number of people assisted in the preparation of this edition of *Contemporary Literary Criticism*. An old debt, and chief among our debts, is to the late Gordon T. R. Anderson of Longman, USA. In the first two editions, he was instrumental in developing this text, and the strong guidance he gave to higher education throughout the United States in his work at Longman is a lasting legacy of his wisdom and generosity. Kathy Schurawich and David Fox of Longman saw the third edition through publication and gave important assistance. The fourth edition, amid changing schedules and editorial locales, benefited greatly from the advice of Virginia Blanford and Lisa Moore at Longman. Their patience and good humor made our job a pleasure rather than a task. Our wives, Julie Davis and Nancy Mergler, were equally helpful and patient during the revision of the book. Noah Mathew Davis was born just as we began thinking about this new edition, and it is to him, along with Cyrus and Benjamin Schleifer and Joshua Michael Davis, that we dedicate this fourth edition of the book.

Many colleagues and friends at the University of Oklahoma made suggestions, read material, lent books, and endlessly discussed how the earlier editions could be improved. They include Eve Tavor Bannet, Richard Barney, Hunter Cadzow, Daniel Cottom, David Gross, Susan Kates, David Mair, Henry McDonald, Catherine Hobbs, and Alan Velie. We also consulted widely, and we received timely and important suggestions from Nancy Armstrong (Brown University), Philip Barnard (University of Kansas), members of the Bible and Culture Collective, Linda Brigham (Kansas State University), Bruce Clark (Texas Tech University), Jonathan Culler (Cornell University), Stanley Fish (Duke University), Elizabeth Hinds (University of Northern Colorado), Robert Markley (West Virginia University), Patrick McGee (Louisiana State University), Mary Janell Metzger (Western Washington State), J. Hillis Miller (University of California, Irvine), Gita Rajan (Fairfield University), Herman Rapaport (Wayne State University), Russell Reising (University of Toledo), Isaiah Smithson (Southern Illinois University), Gary Lee Stonum (Case Western Reserve University), Daphna Vulcan-Erdinast (University of Haifa), Michael Sexson (Montana State University), and Nancy West. Laurie Finke (Kenyon College) spent many hours working with us on the fourth edition.

Also, several colleagues and graduate students wrote some of the biographical headnotes for the critics in this book, as follows: Dorie Glickman: *T. S. Eliot;* Justin Everett: *Northrop Frye;* Brad Will: *Cornel West* and *bell hooks;* Brian Cowlishaw: *Gauri Viswanathan* and *Nancy Armstrong;* Richard Barney: *Paul de Man* and *Michael Warner;* Amie Doughty: *Aijaz Ahmad;* Vinay Dharwadker: *Edward Said;* Kate Myers: *Patrocinio Schweickart* and *Shoshana Felman;* Karen Sheriff: *Barbara Johnson, Diana Fuss,* and *Stuart Hall;* Bridget Roussell: *Stuart Moulthrop;* Pamela Liggett: *Ferdinand de Saussure;* Samantha Ward: *Teresa de Lauretis;* Scott Kelley: *Louis Marin* and *James Clifford;* James Comas: *Michel Foucault;* Susan Williams: *Jonathan Culler;* Scott LaMascus: *Jacques Derrida;* Stephanie Gross: *Catherine Belsey;* Elizabeth Hinds: *Jacques Lacan* and (with Thomas Bowden) *Mikhail Bakhtin;* Meredith Jones: *Slavoj Žižek;* Katherine Patterson: *Laura Mulvey;* David Gross: *Raymond Williams;* Hunter Cadzow: *Stephen Greenblatt;* Mitchell Lewis: *Cora Kaplan* and *Dick Hebdige;* Jennifer McClinton: *Judith Butler;* Thom Conroy: *Donna Haraway.* We also thank Brian Cowlishaw for coordinating the work on the headnotes for the twelve new contributors to the fourth edition, and Roger Cook for updating biographical information for the earlier headnotes. Roger served as our assistant in readying the fourth edition for press, and his cheerful help greatly aided the completion of this edition, as did the work of Bonner J. Slayton and Susan Kendrick.

Our thanks to all of you.

ROBERT CON DAVIS
RONALD SCHLEIFER

the "humanities" is an area of knowledge that examines unique human events. Every "object" of humanistic study—Chaucer's *Canterbury Tales*, the Battle of Waterloo, Locke's *Treatise on Human Nature*, Picasso's *Guernica*, Mozart's *Hunt Quartet*, even Newton's *Principia* and Darwin's *Origin of Species*—is a unique event that occurred only once and, in a manner of speaking, can be studied only through description and paraphrase. As the linguist Louis Hjelmslev notes, according to this traditional view, "humanistic, as opposed to natural phenomena, are non-recurrent and for that very reason cannot, like natural phenomena, be subjected to exact and generalizing treatment." "In the field of the humanities," he goes on, "consequently, there would have to be a different method [from science]—namely, mere description, which would be nearer to poetry than to exact science—or, at any event, a method that restricts itself to a discursive form of presentation in which the phenomena pass by, one by one, without being interpreted through a system."

This "method," Hjelmslev suggests, is "history" in its most chronological manifestation. Since the "objects" of humanistic study are unique, they can be cataloged only in chronological order. Because of this, the humanities have traditionally been "historical" studies: the history of philosophy, the history of art, history itself, the history of science, literary history, and so forth. Northrop Frye says the same thing about critical practice in "The Function of Criticism at the Present Time" (in "What Is Literary Studies?" [Part I]): "Literature being as yet unorganized by criticism, it still appears as a huge aggregate or miscellaneous pile of creative efforts. The only organizing principle so far discovered in it is chronology, and when we see the miscellaneous pile strung out along a chronological line, some coherence is given to it by the linear factors in tradition [chronologically conceived]."

Implicit in Frye's and Hjelmslev's remarks is the possibility that the humanities could "reorient" itself and adopt a more scientific model for its study. Instead of following what Frye calls "naive induction," the humanities could be subject to the attempt, as Hjelmslev says, "to rise above the level of mere primitive description to that of a systematic, exact, and generalizing science, in the theory of which all events (possible combinations of elements) are foreseen and the conditions for their realization established." Such a discipline would attempt to account for the objects of humanistic study in terms of the systematic relationships among them (e.g., Frye's attempt to understand genre—poetry, fiction, drama, etc.—as a system governing "literature") or among the elements that combine to constitute those objects rather than their chronological description. In this case, the "humanities" could be conceived as the "human sciences." In such a conception, criticism would take its place among the social sciences rather than the natural sciences. In fact, such a division can be seen in the social sciences themselves. In the *Course in General Linguistics*, for instance, Ferdinand de Saussure specifically distinguishes between two methods of studying economics—economic history and the "synchronic" study of the economic system at any particular moment. Most of the social sciences, in contemporary practice, are divided in this fashion. Psychology, for instance, encompasses the analysis of unique case histories of "clinical" psychology (such as the Sherlock Holmes case Slavoj Žižek analyzes in "Psychology and Psychoanalysis" [Part VI]) and the analysis of the general functioning of mental activity in "experimental" psychology. Anthropology encompasses both the study of unique cultures and, as in Claude Lévi-Strauss's work, the "general" functioning of aspects of culture. Even an earth science such as geology studies both the historical development and the synchronic composition of geological formations.

Literary study also can be seen to offer two "methods" of study—literary history and more or less systematizing criticism. What allows the systemization of criticism, however, is the common and "recurrent" element of traditional humanistic study, the fact that, as Hjelmslev notes, all the humanities deal in the study of language and discourse. Discourse, moreover, is common to the social sciences in general, and consequently a systematic criticism could be a more general theory of discourse, a more general study of cultural (i.e., discursive) formations. Criticism can transform itself into being the "human sciences" that would study the functioning and creation of a host of "discourses" within society (including, of course, "literary" discourse). Such a human science would attempt to describe what distinguishes literature from other language uses and what literature shares with them. It would attempt, as many have already attempted, to situate literary practice within other cultural practices, including linguistics, teaching, politics, psychology, philosophy, ideology, sociology—and even the "professional" debates within literary studies themselves. All of these areas intersect with the instances of literary and cultural studies that are examined in the various essays of this book.

We are suggesting that the study of criticism can profitably be situated as a part—and a leading part—of the study of culture. A more complete justification for this expansion would necessarily involve a discussion of the definition of the term "culture" beyond what we can offer here. (See our book *Criticism and Culture: The Role of Critique in Modern Literary Theory.*) "Culture," Raymond Williams notes in *Keywords,* is "one of the two or three most complicated words in the English language." In another book, *Culture,* Williams says that "'cultural practice' and 'cultural production' are not simply derived from an otherwise constituted social order but are themselves major elements in its constitution." In this conception, culture is not some "informing spirit" within society. Rather, Williams writes, it is "the *signifying system* through which necessarily . . . a social system is communicated, reproduced, experienced and explored."

Williams's definitions are not the only valid description of culture, but it is clear from his ideas that literary studies conceived as a systematized critical activity—a criticism that studies "signifying systems" in a more or less systematic, exact, and generalizing way—is in a position to direct its methods and observations to the widest area of the production of meanings, to cultural activities as specific signifying practices and as a general area of inquiry. A strong argument can be made—Williams in *The Long Revolution* and in this book critics as different as Cornel West, bell hooks, Paul de Man, Edward Said, Catherine Belsey, Nancy Armstrong, and Shoshana Felman also make this argument—that the texts that we customarily call "literature" constitute a privileged site where the most important social, psychological, and cultural forces combine and contend. In this way, the attention to discourse, to language in all its manifestations, in its production and in its reception, is a "natural" focus of literary studies and a "natural" outgrowth of criticism. One result of such a possibility has been the recent turn, in critical activity, to the examination of the institution of literary study in the academy. In books like Robert Scholes's *Textual Power,* Richard

Ohmann's *English in America,* Gerald Graff's *Professing Literature* and *Beyond the Culture Wars,* Jonathan Culler's *Framing the Sign: Criticism and Its Institutions,* Frank Lentricchia's *Criticism and Social Change,* as well as a host of feminist, postcolonial, and African-American studies, the very nature of the study of literature is being examined in relation to other cultural practices. We are attempting in this book to include as much as possible this wider conception of critical practice focused upon cultural critique as an important informing force within contemporary literary criticism. This is apparent in the fact that many of the contributors—Cornel West, Edward Said, Stuart Moulthrop, Jacques Derrida, Michel Foucault, Judith Butler, James Clifford, Donna Haraway—do not conceive of themselves to be (at least primarily) literary critics.

LITERATURE AS AN INSTITUTION

The concept and existence of privileged forms of verbal discourse that go beyond the pragmatic function of communication seem to have been a part of all organized human societies. Ancient Chinese culture, for instance, developed the term *wen,* which referred to "patterned" or rhymed language, what we might call "literary language" or "poetry." But *wen* also referred to patterns or markings on natural objects, to inherited cultural traditions, and to the order of the cosmos. Chinese ideas about patterned discourse played an important role in ancient Japanese culture, and the earliest anthology of Japanese verse, dating from the eighth century, demonstrates the strong Chinese influence of codified ideas about poetry. Similarly, Classical Greek culture coined the term "poetry" (from the Greek *poesis,* meaning "to make") and, in Plato and Aristotle, developed a sophisticated sense of what would be called "literature" today. But even earlier pre-Classical Greek commentaries on poetry and poets, handed down mostly in fragments, suggest that the poet's discourse was a privileged mode of linguistic activity. These commentaries describe the divine origin of such discourse; its power to arouse emotions of pleasure, distress, or anger; and its special status in preserving personal glory and social values. In ancient India, as we know from commentaries that predate Plato and Aristotle by more than a thousand years, the practice and appreciation of patterned discourse was deeply integrated into the activities of daily life. Thus, *Ayurveda,* the Indian science of medicine, believed that a perfectly structured couplet could clean the air and heal the sick. But even in less expansive societies than ancient China, Greece, or India, in smaller tribes and villages and in societies without writing, the patterned discourses of myth and poetry are ubiquitous within social formations. Native American cultures, for example, consistently distinguish between sacred and secular narratives, and different tribes carefully define the subject matter and the manner of telling of sacred tales.

This survey, adapted from Ronald Schleifer's definition of "literature" in the *Encyclopedia Americana,* concludes with a catalog of six definitions of "literature." These definitions can be identified or associated with particular arguments about literature exampled throughout *Contemporary Literary Criticism.* They include T. S. Eliot's emphasis on the universal and philosophical focus of literature; Matthew Arnold's definition of its disinterested and expressive nature; the scientific-linguistic definitions of literature that grow out of structuralism; the emphasis on its religious and metaphysical power that J. Hillis Miller and James Clifford describe; definitions of the conventional and generic nature of literary forms, elaborately classified in the Renaissance, implicit in Barbara Johnson's study of lyrics and in Slavoj Žižek's study of mystery narratives; and finally, examinations of the ways that literature helps us to understand historical and ideological formations of particular cultures, such as those of Raymond Williams, Nancy Armstrong, Cora Kaplan, and several others in this book.

But even as peoples have classified and revered certain kinds of linguistic production from time immemorial, the term "literature" itself is of a much more recent origin, arising, in its present meaning, during the Enlightenment of the seventeenth and eighteenth centuries in the West. The earliest use of the term "literature" in English, Raymond Williams tells us, occurred in the fourteenth century, borrowed from French and Latin, and it described polite learning through reading. For this reason, literary studies has come to have the role, most often a privileged one, of transmitting definitions and understandings of culture and knowledge from one age to another. Gerald Graff and J. Hillis Miller both discuss this role of literary studies in "What Is Literary Studies?" (Part I) and "What Is Literary Theory?" (Part II) in this book; Gauri Viswanathan and Aijaz Ahmad offer historical critiques of its role. Often that institutional role, as Robert Hodge notes in *Literature as Discourse,* takes the form of defining a "regime of literature" whose initial task is to separate "literature" from "non-literature" and then make the many designations among poem, novel, play, short story, and so on substantiate and support the initial separation and bolster the institution of literature as a category and practice in culture. Aristotle made this distinction when he ranked the study of literature above the study of history, owing to literature's ability to discover that which is representative and exemplary among history's supposed mere records of what has happened. The narrow definition of "literature" as fine and artistic writing, as Williams notes in *Keywords,* dates only to the nineteenth century. In *The English Novel,* Williams also defines literature as that which exists on the foundation of an essential (though temporally specific) "structure of feeling that is lived and experienced," a realm of actual experience that must be in place before the elaborations of culture and literature. In time, Williams believes, those structures get "arranged as [the] institutions" of culture such as art and literature.

The definition of "literature" as a cultural and social institution is a useful and also a persistent one. But, as we have seen, it is not the only way to view literature. Even in Williams's comments there are overtones of a different view. While Williams clearly treats literature as a cultural and social institution, his concept of a "structure of feeling"—in the understanding of it that Aijaz Ahmad discusses in "Literary Theory and 'Third World Literature': Some Contexts" in "What Is Literary Theory?" (Part II) and Stuart Hall presents in "Cultural Studies: Two Paradigms" in "Cultural Studies" (Part IX)—posits a natural progression from the essential (noncultural) foundations of "feeling" and, in a recurrent topic of this book, of "experience." To the extent that "literature" is an organized outgrowth of "experience" and "feeling," these things must function sufficiently to stipulate the program for the way culture and society must be. In this sense, "literature" is not a constructed institution but an expression of the ways the world and the human experience of it *are*. "The study of English Literature is accepted by most of its practitioners," Chris Baldick notes in *The Social Mission of English Criticism: 1848–1932*, "as a 'natural' activity without an identifiable historical genesis." "It is only history," as Baldick goes on, "which can challenge any assumption of 'timelessness' about literature as an institution." Baldick is opposing history to the "timelessness" of literary "form" and "formalism" that express universal and "essential" human experiences. The opposition between the formal and historical study of literature—implicit in the "systematizing" and "historical" approaches to literary study we mentioned in relation to Hjelmslev and, indeed, in the "transcultural" (e.g., its presence in "all organized human societies") and historical definitions of literature we are presenting here—is examined throughout the essays that introduce the sections of this book, but especially in the Introduction to "What Is Literary Studies?" (Part I). Williams advances the historical critique of literature Baldick is articulating, and the recurring references to him throughout the essays in various sections of *Contemporary Literary Criticism* attest to the influence of his work. That is, Williams's conception of "structures of feeling" emphasizes not only the "natural" self-evidence of *feeling* but the very socially and historically determined *structures* that give rise to feeling. In an important sense, the phrase "structures of feeling," gathering together historically determined mechanisms and seeming "timeless" experience, is an oxymoron that combines the different impulses and definitions of "literature."

The definition of literature-as-institution remains confusing in part because of the equally persistent view of literature as a realm in its own right, a view glimpsed fleetingly in Williams's *The English Novel*. If literature as a total body or as a tradition is seen, in fact, as "presumably coherent in and of itself," as Graff describes this position in "The Humanist Myth" (in "What Is Literary Studies?" [Part I]), then one conclusion to draw is that the study of literature through criticism would most likely distort or loosen that coherence, "murdering" to dissect, in Wordsworth's famous description of rational analysis. The corollary to the view of literature "in and of itself" (literature viewed as a privileged aesthetic or "disinterested" realm, largely separate from particular historical cultural formations) is that literature will be appreciated best in concert with the recognition that, in Graff's words, "literature teaches itself." As implemented in literary studies in the United States, this credo has meant that, as he explains, "great literary works can be freed from the institutional and professional encumbrances that come between students or laymen and the potency of the work itself." (Viswanathan's counterhistory of literary studies emphasizes, literally, the *politics* imbedded in pedagogy.)

This view—which Graff is explaining and not propounding—is problematic particularly in light of the fact that, as Baldick notes, "the real content of the school and college subject which goes under the name 'English Literature' is not literature in the primary sense, but *criticism*." Baldick's point is not a theoretical one but a practical observation that "every student in British education [and U.S. education, as well] is required to compose, not tragic dramas, but essays in criticism." All literary courses are perforce criticism courses in that ordinarily in literature courses (as opposed to creative writing courses) students write essays about the material and do not try to write within the genre they are studying. Literature may be, as Terry Eagleton writes, "non-prag-matic discourse" in the specific sense that it "serves no immediate practical purpose, but it is to be taken as referring to a general state of affairs." Even as "non-pragmatic discourse," however, literature is always studied in the discourse about literature that students can enact when they speak to each other and when they write. Practically speaking, there will be no access to the "work itself" or "literature itself," whatever form that could take: as Frye says, "all the arts are dumb." The idea of studying Shake-speare or interpreting the Bible begins to sound presumptuous compared to the activity of participating in the critical discourse about these texts.

A pragmatic and probably defensible definition of literature is the *functional* one that Eagleton offers when he says that literature is the "number of ways in which peo-ple *relate themselves* to writing." Those strategies of relating, played out in the con-flicts of theme and form among and within literary texts, create the patterned effects of what is commonly called "texture" in literature. If we accept this functional defini-tion, then we must probably forget the "illusion" forever, as Eagleton goes on, "that the category 'literature' is 'objective.'" Remember that this institutional definition of "literature" is functional by dint of being utterly provisional and specific to the time, place, and occasion for defining it in such a way. It is no wonder, as Robert Scholes argues in *Textual Power,* that the teaching of literary texts now means the teaching of the "cultural text," too.

There is one dimension of the definition of literature that draws assent from most quarters, the idea of literature as the vehicle and transmitter of cultural values. "Liter-ature," Eagleton says bluntly, "in the meaning of the word we have inherited, *is* an ideology." He means that as a form of representation, literature reflects the cultural hierarchies that organize the ways in which the world is understood and even experi-enced. Those hierarchies are ordered by certain values that constitute a specific social ideology. His claiming this is not so different from countless other claims about val-ues in modern literary studies. Eagleton specifically quotes George Gordon, professor of English literature at Oxford in the early twentieth century, as saying in his inau-gural lecture that "England is sick, and . . . English literature must save it. The Churches (as I understand) having failed, and social remedies being slow, English lit-erature has now a triple function: still, I suppose, to delight and instruct us, but also, and above all, to save our souls and heal the State." With startling candor, Gordon at once views literature as a communicator of value and as a privileged institution in its effect on culture. Matthew Arnold, F. R. Leavis, Lionel Trilling, Gayatri Chakravorty Spivak, and many others make a similar claim, if not so extreme, for literature's ability to articulate and transmit cultural value. Gauri Viswanathan, in "Lessons of History" in "What Is Literary Studies?" (Part I), a chapter excerpted from *Masks of Conquest,* explicitly traces historically the assumption that literature "transmits" cultural value; she focuses on the establishment of literary studies in India during the nineteenth century (i.e., contemporaneously with Arnold) as part of Britain's imperial program. In the 1920s and 1930s, Leavis claimed that literature was the only medium that could effectively transmit value in the modern, industrialized world in which social institutions are in constant and irreversible transition, and even decay. Lionel Trilling, too, believed that only literature and its study would allow us to glimpse anything like the "whole" of human experience, the "whole" person—the rational, emotional, sacred, and profane dimensions of being human.

From a contemporary perspective, we still find the claim that literature and literary studies have a privileged grasp of the materials and forms of culture. It is often advanced that the power of literature and literary studies is made possible by a certain sophisticated flexibility, even a certain lack of focus and commitment, in literature regarding any particular dimension of cultural encounter. Literature's broad engagement with culture and cultures may account both for its power and for the frequent difficulty of organizing the findings and methods of literary studies. ("Literature," in Irving Howe's famous statement, "is difficult to organize.") The paradox here is that a certain *lack* of precision in the cultural positioning of literature as a total enterprise—a lack of fixed grounding—may explain both the strength and weakness of literary studies as a cultural agent.

For example, in current discussions of cultural studies and multiculturalism there is often considerable questioning about the aims and methods of inquiry and the apparent loss in modern culture of consensus about the value of traditional cultural goals. Whenever such cultural discourse breaks down and even basic questions of value remain unsettled, as Samuel Weber writes, the "process of *granting*" cultural validity and recognition becomes the focus of attention. "If such a development can be seen today as a characteristic of much modern thought," Weber goes on, "it is no accident that the field of literary studies" is one of the "privileged arenas" for discussion. Weber argues that it is privileged particularly owing to a strategic *lack* of grounding in literature. As Weber writes, "the object that defines this field of study—'literature'— has traditionally been distinguished from other 'objects' of study precisely by a certain *lack* of objectivity. . . . And such a lack of objectivity has, from Plato onward, confronted the study of literature (or of art in general) with the problem of its *legitimation,* and hence, with its status as, and in regard to, *institution(s)*." This is another way of saying, as Eagleton does, that literature "has the most intimate relations to questions of social power." If this is true, one can begin to see why literature and literary studies have played such a large role in the development of cultural critique and cultural studies.

CRITICISM AND CRITIQUE

A student who stays with these issues long enough will see that the process of such exploration has been a part of the Western understanding and interpretation of texts since the time of Greek First Philosophy and the Enlightenment of the eighteenth century. This understanding often takes the form not only of understanding a particular text but of understanding our own working assumptions as we interpret texts. That is, the issue of literature's definition is always tied up with the concomitant issue of *how* to read, "practices" of reading. If "literature" as a concept has a history that plays different roles in different historical settings while maintaining at least a family of characteristics or resemblances that allow its recognition across those settings, the very process of reading also has a history, and that history is closely connected to the value imputed to "literature," the value of literacy. In *The Use of Poetry and the Use of Criticism* (1933), Eliot makes the revealing comment about Dr. Samuel Johnson, the great English critic of the eighteenth century, that "had he lived a generation later, he would have been obliged to look more deeply into the foundations [of his critical practices], and so would have been unable to leave us an example of what criticism ought to be for a civilization which, being settled, has no need, while it lasts, to enquire into the function of its parts." Dr. Johnson, in other words, would have been compelled to interrogate his own assumptions in the *practice* of interpretation. In this comment, Eliot also makes the assumption that some ages have the characteristic of being more "critical." He further advances that there is the specialized activity in criticism of looking "more deeply into the foundations" of our understanding, of being theoretically self-conscious about the criticism we practice. This questioning of assumptions at the "foundations" of critical practices—the assumptions we make about the nature of texts and the efficacy of our methods—is the particular activity that we are calling *critique*. The questioning that belongs to critique can be distinguished from the different questioning about what texts say and how they say it. This second questioning involves actually interpreting the work and goes under the name of *criticism*. Criticism studies what texts say and how they say it, while critique studies the often-unnoticed assumptions within the reading practices of criticism that govern the practices of reading and the definitions of the "object" of reading. This is true when the "object" of critical reading is "literature," but it is also true when criticism "reads" nonliterary texts such as film; historical narratives; psychological narratives; philosophical ideas; social relationships of gender, race, and class; other, "non-Western" cultures; and even the "theories" of criticism and culture themselves. This list describes most of the essays in this book, and in most of these essays one will find both the reading of criticism and the questioning of critique.

After we finished the second edition of *Contemporary Literary Criticism*, we continued to think about the distinction between criticism and critique and what we saw as the need for scholars to be clear about the significance of emphasizing one or another of these forms of understanding. Focusing especially on the practice of critique since the ancient Greeks, the great attempts at critique in the eighteenth century, and the many practices of modern criticism, we decided to mark out for students and scholars of criticism and theory the historical path critique has taken to become, among other things, literary and cultural criticism and cultural studies. We also saw that mapping out this path in the history of criticism and theory could help students to understand what criticism is and how it has developed. We wrote *Criticism and Culture: The Role of Critique in Modern Literary Theory* specifically to discuss these questions for students and scholars. In that book, arising from our work together on the second edition of *Contemporary Literary Criticism*, we explored the interactions between philosophical critique and cultural theory and the many practical hybrids (schools of criticism) that have come from that encounter. Thus, the second edition of *Contemporary Literary Criticism* led us to the writing of *Criticism and Culture*, and that book and the perspectives we developed in it have strongly influenced the approach we have taken to the third, and now the fourth, edition of *Contemporary Literary Criticism*.

Most of all, but in addition to many other concerns, we would like students to see two related phenomena we examined in our book: the *institutional* dimension of criticism and the *transformative* potential of critique. Again, these related phenomena are emphases (not necessarily pure examples) of the opposition between formalism and historicism that we develop throughout the section introductions in this edition of *Contemporary Literary Criticism*. The last chapter of our book *Criticism and Culture*, "Notes Towards a Definition of Cultural Studies," implicitly addresses the complex relationship between formalism and historicism by analyzing instituted cultural formations and bringing the intelligence of that analysis to bear in order to transform cultural institutions, what we call "the institutional and transformative concerns of cultural studies." Specifically, our discussion of the "subjects" and "objects" of cultural studies implicitly corresponds to historical practices of reading and (more or less) formal definitions of literature and offers a nice parallel to this opposition. (Many of the new selections in the fourth edition, including those of bell hooks, Teresa de Lauretis, Slavoj Žižek, Mikhail Bakhtin, and Diana Fuss, also emphasize the relation between subjectivity and objectivity in terms of the relationship between historicism and formalism.) Such complexity, as we argue, can be found throughout our cultural history. Plato and Aristotle, for example, thought a good deal in their literary and cultural criticism about the *forms* poetry can take, and they made important critical distinctions about dramatic genres—comedy, tragedy, the different kinds of heroes and characters appropriate to each, and so on. But they also focused on the ethical and historical implications of using various forms of dramatic and narrative poetry—how poetry could help or hinder governance of the state and affect impressionable children, for instance. Still, especially in Plato's criticism, the emphasis on institutions is clear in his strong rejection of the *historically* transformative potential of critique and a decision to develop, instead, practices supportive of existing educational and governmental goals and institutional practices that, in their self-evidence, seem *transhistorical*. Plato, in effect, chose to practice criticism over critique.

In the eighteenth century, Immanuel Kant helped to define the nature of critique as a practice and projected a separate realm for the aesthetic effects of literary and other kinds of art. Kant distinguished between analytical and synthetic thinking and created the foundation for a purely aesthetic dimension of critical understanding. He effectively created programmatic ways of thinking about criticism and critique and laid the foundations for many developments in subsequent criticism and theory. Especially influential was his idea about the free play of the imagination and the realm of aesthetics that can be understood in relation to analytical thinking. In the nineteenth century, for example, the French scholar Hippolyte Taine exploited the distinction between formal criticism and historical critique in his definition of an inner human core of personality and character that supposedly exists separate from the "outer" world subject to change and transformation. Taine succeeded in constructing a historical model for understanding literary and cultural texts that assumed the existence of pure ethnic traits that can be elaborated and manifested in literature. His assumptions about the existence of "pure" ethnic and national character traits serve the institutional ends of criticism and can, by the way, be shown to have racist implications. His accomplishment, nonetheless, was to define a line of historical criticism that continues through the present. Still, the "purity" of his historical categories shows also how easily historicism and formalism contaminate one another.

In the twentieth century, dating from early manifestoes of modernism and formalism—which we discuss in the introductions to "What Is Literary Studies?" (Part I) and "Structuralism and Semiotics" (Part IV)—through the most recent work in gender and cultural theory, there is a large turn of interest toward exploring the transformative potential of critique, a sustained and massive interrogation of the protocols of formal and textual relations, both in how to define texts and in how to interpret them in relation to culture. The questions continually being asked are these: What constitutes a text? What are its boundaries? What constitutes reading? What readerly competence is required to interpret a text? What constitutes a persuasive or "valid" interpretation of a text? In the history of modern criticism, this interrogation of the assumptions of literary and cultural practices has been answered in various ways, but the overriding consideration has always been how we are to understand the connections of criticism, critique, and culture in terms of the relationships among them as practices.

PRACTICES OF READING

These questions about the nature of cultural texts (including practical and historical definitions of "literature" we have touched upon here) and of various practices of reading are precisely what we take up in our selections in this collection and in the introductions we have written. In this fourth edition, we are choosing to emphasize the complex relationship between historical and transhistorical forms of understanding. We have chosen works that address these important questions in a coherent fashion. We assume that our readers—undergraduate or graduate students, or simply readers interested in criticism and culture—are not passive onlookers, tourists, moving easily and quickly over the terrain of modern critical thought. We take them to be actively interested in the question of what criticism has been as it serves institutional ends and how critique may change and transform those ends—in short, how literary and cultural texts interact as the focus and agent of forms of knowledge and different kinds of historical activity.

Even readers inexperienced in the practice of criticism and theory soon will note that the essays in this book tend to fall within two categories and deploy two modes of understanding. Take "Interpreting the *Variorum*" by Stanley Fish (in "Rhetoric and Reader Response" [Part III]). At certain moments, Fish finds productive ways of interpreting texts. He reads a poem and determines what words, sentences, and images mean, and then he posits a likely reading of a line in that poem. At the next moment, he finds his interpretation undercut by the implications of interpretations in later lines of the same poem. This process of gaining and losing ground in interpretation happens several times, and Fish begins to question whether the poem as a whole can ever make sense in precisely the way its individual lines seem to. At a certain point, this questioning leads him to seek explanations for the way the poem works differently from what was described by the explanations he started with. While he makes use of strategies of critique in this essay, he generally interprets the poem according to more or less formal rules and assumptions that he already has in mind, or that he learned from someone else, or that he established in other essays. In effect, in this act of reading and interpretation he is performing what we are calling *criticism*. When Fish begins to question his own procedures and look for new ones—that is, when he begins to look for fundamentally new ways of understanding or even conceiving of the poem (as Eliot claims Dr. Johnson was unable to do)—he has begun doing what we call *critique*.

The next discovery awaiting the inexperienced reader of criticism and theory, in other words, is that some of the essays in this book lean more toward criticism and that some are closer to critique. Stuart Moulthrop's "Rhizome and Resistance: Hypertext and the Dream of a New Culture," Slavoj Žižek's "Two Ways to Avoid the Real of Desire," and Diana Fuss's "Reading Like a Feminist," one can argue, have important moments of critique but are on the whole criticism. Each one lucidly explains and applies critical notions that have already been established and are, in some sense, already generally known to be useful or "true." Eliot's "Tradition and the Individual Talent," Gauri Viswanathan's "Lessons of History," Aijaz Ahmad's "Literary Theory and 'Third World Literature,'" Donna Haraway's "A Cyborg Manifesto," and even Cora Kaplan's "Pandora's Box: Subjectivity, Class and Sexuality in Socialist Feminist Criticism" lean more toward being exploratory critiques—tending more toward interrogation and the testing of the limits of understanding and the potential for discovering new grounds of explanation. This distinction between institutional criticism and transformative critique parallels J. Hillis Miller's distinction between "canny" and "uncanny" criticism, the first being institutional and the second being transformative. Both sets of concepts can be traced back, further, to Claude Lévi-Strauss's different but related distinction between the rational and institutionally oriented "engineer" and the innovating and experimental "*bricoleur*," or tinker. (In Lévi-Strauss's work, however, a genuinely transformative potential is not present in either term.) When Teresa de Lauretis analyzes semiotics in order to define and allow us to rethink the category of (historical) "experience," when Jacques Derrida analyzes the principle of reason in order to allow us to rethink the university as an institution, when Shoshana Felman analyzes psychoanalysis in order to allow us to rethink teaching as an institution, when Dick Hebdige analyzes the "genealogy" of the idea of "culture" in order to allow us to rethink the relationship between historical events and understanding, when Michael Warner analyzes psychoanalytic definitions of homosexuality in order to demonstrate the contradictions and unspoken assumptions in purportedly "objective" and ahistorical descriptions of psychological development, they are all engaging in practices of reading whose aim is not simply *formal* "analysis," but also the examination of the modes of *historical* understanding that allow certain institutions to exist with an eye to imagining the possibility of transforming those institutions. These activities of critique, as we shall see in a moment, lend themselves to the particular "difficulties" of contemporary literary criticism by developing practices of reading that are different from what we have been taught.

By foregrounding the distinction between criticism and critique, exploring this distinction in relation to different versions of formalism and historicism, and by choosing the particular essays that appear in this book, we have intended to provide a set of categories for understanding directions in criticism at an early stage of study. Among these are two "basic" categories: definitions of objects of study ("literature," "ideas," "culture," the "agent" or "subject" of experience, etc.) and practices of reading in the processes of study (including such things as "feeling," "experience," and even "difficulty"). These two categories are fully integrated—reading defines objects and objects call for particular reading—but they correspond to the *provisional* opposition between criticism and critique in the analysis and transformation of cultural institutions just as the examples of, say, Northrop Frye's and Donna Haraway's practices of reading define a *provisional* opposition. We hope our readers will actively use the terms "criticism" and "critique"— as well as many of the other useful terms the writers in this book develop—as tools with which to teach themselves about criticism and theory and to discover for themselves the historical situation of contemporary literary and cultural criticism.

THE DIFFICULTY OF CRITICISM

The questioning of self-evident truths and the development of procedures that examine the historically particular ends that may be contained in seemingly "disinterested" and "objective" forms of knowledge—two projects that critique pursues in examining objects of knowledge and the methods used to examine them—lead to forms of density and seeming obscurity in much contemporary literary criticism. As Roland Barthes says in *S/Z,* the texts of criticism are often "readerly" in their reliance on the participation of the reader for completion rather than offering the "writerly" contextual explanations that characterizes much nineteenth-century literature. (The "writerliness" that Barthes sees is a characteristic of the seemingly stable subject of experience and knowledge of nineteenth-century middle-class culture.) In other words, it has become a commonplace of contemporary thought that much contemporary criticism and cultural critique—Paul de Man's literary studies, semiotics in general, Derrida's "deconstructive" philosophy, the psychoanalysis of Lacan, Bakhtin's neologisms (e.g., "dialogism"), Haraway's postmodern interdisciplinarity, even Williams's clear prose when he asks us to question self-evident truths—should be difficult to follow. But what does it mean exactly for a critical text to be difficult? For one thing, since they did not write in the tradition of New Critical "objective" close readings, these critics are frequently maddeningly elliptical, especially in wordplay. As George Steiner remarks about such "difficult" writers, it can seem as though "at certain levels, we are not meant to understand at all, and our interpretation, indeed our reading itself, is an intrusion." "For whom"—and here Steiner could be referring to many contemporary critical texts—are they "composing [their] cryptograms?"

In this essay, "On Difficulty," Steiner examines why the reading of contemporary criticism should be this difficult. In response, he has suggested that resistance to reading occasioned by *modernist* literature and contemporary criticism can be understood as belonging to one or more of the following four categories of "difficulty"—impediments that, if not properly understood, can block access to reading a particular text. The first, in Steiner's terms, is *contingent difficulty*. This is the problem one faces when there are things—words or references—in a poem or text that cannot be identified, that the reader simply does not know. In Saussure's discussion of linguistics, for instance, he mentions the "diachronic" study of language. A reader who does not know that term must look it up in a dictionary. Similarly, readers who do not know references to critics or critical positions—the New Criticism de Man mentions; the "airy insouciance of postaxiological criticism" Edward Said mentions; or simply the work of Wayne Booth, whom Patricinio Schweickart describes without specifically locating within the debates in the literary studies—can easily become lost and feel as if they are overhearing a discussion in another language. Moreover, if these contingent difficulties are not identified, their accumulation can finally prevent students from grasping the central import of an argument. The point is, however, that "contingent difficulties" can be completely overcome by briefly consulting a reference book, a footnote, or a teacher.

Steiner calls the second difficulty of reading *modal difficulty*. This kind of difficulty is more trouble to overcome than contingent difficulties. Modal difficulty occurs when one is not familiar with or cannot follow the form, or mode, something comes in. Some people have a "modal difficulty" with MTV: they simply cannot follow and process the quick visual cuts from scene to scene, which is significantly different from the longer scenes in films and television from the 1950s and 60s. Such "cuts" are the mode of presentation of music videos. Other modal difficulties are the fragmented language of much modernist poetry, T. S. Eliot's famous lack of transitions, for instance. In contemporary literary criticism this can be seen in the shorthand allusiveness in many of the essays here, such as the vague suggestion (for those who are new to this work) that Derrida, say, has a particular interlocutor in mind (such as the critics mentioned in a footnote) or the polemical mode of Bakhtin's refutation of Russian Formalism (only implicitly present in his discussion). Such "modal difficulty" (like contingent difficulty) can be remedied through learning and practice. The difficulties of the modalities of understanding can be overcome through practice, for example, in learning to use a new language that has a different number or division of tenses from English, or even learning that the English concepts of "language" and "speech" are reoriented across three terms in French (*langue, parole, langage*), in order to rethink these concepts in relation to one another. Thus people can "learn" to follow MTV or the seemingly strange argumentative forms of contemporary criticism. As James Clifford suggests in "The Translation of Cultures" (in "Cultural Studies" [Part IX]), modal difficulties call for "deep translation" and "intercultural translation" that are "part of the creative interpenetration of two cultures, a liberation and revivification of meanings latent in each" in order "to grasp a moving language."

The third difficulty Steiner describes is *tactical difficulty*. This kind of difficulty is a formidable resistance to received methods of reading that one brings to literature or criticism. Unlike contingent or modal difficulties, which are occasioned by the fact that writers simply use facts and modes of discourse different from those of their readers so that the writers themselves will not be aware of the "difficulties" their language produces, "tactical difficulties" are tactics writers use to produce certain effects in their readers. That effect is to situate their readers in such a way that the "easy" and usual ways they understand language and experience no longer effectively account for that experience and language. The *uses* of the "performative" aspects of language that Shoshana Felman and Jonathan Culler discuss—the aspects of language that is better understood as an act occurring at a particular historical moment rather than conveying transhistorical information—are examples of such "tactics" insofar as they are designed to create interpersonal relationships (including relationships of "confusion") rather than to impart knowledge. Thus, Lacan's *purpose* is as much to overpower with a strange (contingently difficult) vocabulary as it is to convey information. The *agenda* of many contemporary critics—the *agenda* of critique itself as we have described it—is as much to *reorient* understanding as it is to convey or provoke understanding, and this purpose, in feminism, Marxism, psychoanalysis, and other schools of criticism, presents a conception of "understanding" that is tactically different from what we have been taught. Felman, in her psychoanalytic discussion of teaching, discusses this different conception of knowledge. And insofar as the difference between literature and criticism has become a problem that is explored in contemporary criticism—and we should add now that this problem of categorization is a "modal difficulty" insofar as it raises the question of whether we are in the "mode" of art or of knowledge—then the tactics or purpose of questioning the self-evident opposition between literature and criticism (or, in the terms of the Introduction to Part II, aesthetics and ethics) is itself a "tactical" performance that is part of the *critical* project of "reorientation" pursued by much contemporary criticism. (Such questioning can be seen in the essays by de Man, Schweickart, Johnson, Žižek, Greenblatt, Kaplan, and others here.) If critique questions the self-evident—including the self-evident validity of standard argumentation—than a tactic to achieve this end is to make the self-evident strange. Such a difficulty is not "overcome" in the same way contingent or modal difficulties are overcome: the aim is the historical critique of reorienting understanding.

Steiner calls his final form of difficulty (a version of the "resistance" to reading de Man describes) *ontological difficulty.* An "ontological difficulty" is the hardest of all to deal with, and many times readers must simply accept this type of difficulty as insurmountable. It is not simply confusion over contingent facts or modes of understanding or even the attempt to produce reorientations in readers. Rather, "ontological difficulties" involve trying to see and feel the world from a perspective other than one's own—perhaps through eyes of women, or members of ethic minorities, or people subject to colonialism. (Patrocinio Schweickart discusses the ways that the views of middle-class men are situated as the "normal" and "natural" perspective.) Sometimes the gap between perspectives is quite great and virtually unbridgeable. J. Hillis Miller, in "The Search for Grounds in Literary Study" (in "What Is Literary Theory?" [Part II]), begins with literary presentations of such "ontological difficulties"—presentations of what seems to be a sort of breach within "reality" in Maurice Blanchot, George Eliot, and Wallace Stevens, all texts that he says seem "irreducibly strange, inexplicable, perhaps even mad." He goes on, in this essay, to describe the ways criticism has attempted to account for and tame such uncanny experiences. The scandal presented by contemporary criticism, which goes to the heart of the ontological difficulty, can be described as a radical division, a *split*—the "devastating experience," Miller describes, "of a transformation of the scene which leaves it nevertheless exactly the same."

The pervasive figure of a "split" or contradiction in contemporary criticism and understanding indicates a sense of a fundamental division within texts, specifically as regards their involvement in the abstract formalism of "aesthetic" moments, but also in the concrete sense that the forms of literature, culture, and knowledge we "experience" occur at, and are in part determined by, particular historical moments. Most current theories of textuality, for example, do not emphasize criticism as attempting a unified "reading," or even see a text as defined by "meaning" or "content." They see, instead, a process, a "split" twofold process between textual and cultural "product" and "production" that reaches stability or wholeness only (if at all) at particular moments. This interpretive model, encompassing order and a large measure of disorder, poses a serious threat to the empirically based tradition of interpretation as a transparent and focusable lens through which a detached critical investigator peers into a stable text. From the viewpoint of much contemporary criticism, in fact, the notion of a detached ("disinterested") observer no longer exists (or exists, again, only "momentarily"). Rather, contemporary criticism posits involvement between critic and text and believes that an ontological fault line, time itself, runs through and creates a radical split in all knowledge, making both what we know and how we know it—the transhistorical forms of knowledge and the historically contingent methods that isolate and investigate the objects of knowledge—irremediably problematic. Contemporary criticism, in this regard, is "difficult" because it questions definitions of "literature" and methods of "reading." What the New Critics were accustomed to calling "unity" and "wholeness" in form, as concepts central to interpretation, have become the problem of "interpretation" to be discussed rather than the goal toward which interpretation moves.

In global shifts such as these—dislocating and potentially painful shifts in which sense and nonsense, the essential and the contingent, literature and culture, are seen to switch places—we witness ourselves moving from one paradigm to the other, from a world that already made sense to a world that is just now making sense. This revolution in criticism and the resultant shift in the way we understand literature and wider forms of cultural discourse pose an ontological difficulty of the highest order. This difficulty, more than any other, explains both the challenge and the excitement of (and also the occasional hostility toward) contemporary literary and cultural studies.

REFERENCES AND FURTHER READING

Abrams, M. H., *The Mirror and the Lamp: Romantic Theory and the Critical Tradition* (New York: Oxford University Press, 1953).

———, *Natural Supernaturalism: Tradition and Revolution in Romantic Literature* (New York: Norton, 1971).

———, "Rationality and Imagination in Cultural History: A Reply to Wayne Booth," in *Critical Inquiry*, 2 (1976), 247–64.

Arnold, Matthew, *Arnold: Poetry and Prose*, ed. John Bryson (London: Hart-Davis, 1954).

Baldick, Chris, *The Social Mission of English Criticism: 1848–1932* (Oxford: Clarendon, 1987).

Barthes, Roland, *S/Z,* trans. Richard Miller (New York: Hill and Wang, 1985).

Bloom, Harold, *The Western Canon: The Books and School of the Ages* (New York: Harcourt Brace, 1994).

Culler, Jonathan, *Framing the Sign: Criticism and Its Institutions* (Norman: University of Oklahoma Press, 1988).

Davis, Robert Con, and Ronald Schleifer, *Criticism and Culture: The Role of Critique in Modern Literary Theory* (London: Longman, 1991).

Deleuze, Gilles, and Félix Guattari, *A Thousand Plateaus: Capitalism and Schizophrenia* (Minneapolis: University of Minnesota Press, 1987).

Derrida, Jacques, *Limited, Inc.* (Evanston, IL: Northwestern University Press, 1988).

Eagleton, Terry, *Literary Theory: An Introduction* (Minneapolis: University of Minnesota Press, 1983).

Eliot, T. S., *The Use of Poetry and the Use of Criticism: Studies in the Relation of Criticism to Poetry in England* (Cambridge, MA: Harvard University Press, 1933).

Fish, Stanley Eugene, *Professional Correctness: Literary Studies and Political Change* (New York: Oxford University Press, 1995).

Frye, Northrop, *Anatomy of Criticism: Four Essays* (Princeton, NJ: Princeton University Press, 1957).

Gallop, Jane, *The Daughter's Seduction* (Ithaca, NY: Cornell University Press, 1982).

Gilligan, Carol, *In a Different Voice* (Cambridge, MA: Harvard University Press, 1982).

Graff, Gerald, *Beyond the Culture Wars: How Teaching the Conflicts Can Revitalize American Education* (New York: Norton, 1992).

———, *Literature Against Itself: Literary Ideas in Modern Society* (Chicago: University of Chicago Press, 1979).

———, *Professing Literature* (Chicago: University of Chicago Press, 1987).

Guillory, John, *Cultural Capital: The Problem of Literary Canon Formation* (Chicago: University of Chicago Press, 1993).

Hjelmslev, Louis, *Prolegomena to a Theory of Language,* trans. Francis Whitfield (Madison: University of Wisconsin Press, 1961).

Hodge, Robert, *Literature as Discourse* (Baltimore: Johns Hopkins University Press, 1990).

Lentricchia, Frank, *Criticism and Social Change* (Chicago: University of Chicago Press, 1983).

Miller, J. Hillis, *Illustration* (Cambridge, MA: Harvard University Press, 1992).

———, "Steven's Rock and Criticism as Cure," in *Georgia Review,* 31 (1977), 44–60.

Ohmann, Richard, *English in America* (New York: Oxford University Press, 1976).

Ryan, Michael, *Marxism and Deconstruction: A Critical Articulation* (Baltimore: Johns Hopkins University Press, 1982).

Said, Edward, *Culture and Imperialism* (New York: Knopf, 1993).

Schleifer, Ronald, "The Poison of Ink: Post-War Literary Criticism," in *New Orleans Review,* 8 (1981), 241–49.

———, "Literature," in *Encyclopedia Americana,* fifteenth edition. 1995.

Scholes, Robert, *Textual Power* (New Haven, CT: Yale University Press, 1985).

Sontag, Susan, *Against Interpretation* (New York: Dell, 1966).

Sosnoski, James, *Token Professionals and Master Critics: A Critique of Orthodoxy in Literary Studies* (Albany: State University of New York Press, 1994).

Spivak, Gayatri Chakravorty, *Outside of the Teaching Machine* (New York: Routledge, 1993).

Steiner, George, *On Difficulty and Other Essays* (New York: Oxford University Press, 1978).

Weber, Samuel, *Institution and Interpretation* (Minneapolis: University of Minnesota Press, 1987).

Williams, Raymond, *Culture* (London: Verso, 1981).

———, *The English Novel: From Dickens to Lawrence* (New York: Oxford University Press, 1970).

———, *Keywords* (London: Fontana, 1986).

———, *The Long Revolution* (New York: Columbia University Press, 1961).

PART I

What Is Literary Studies?

Questions about the nature of literary studies—what it is, how it works, and what it accomplishes—consistently draw people into controversy these days as frequently as discussions of politics and religion. Certainly readers have always discussed and even argued the meaning and significance of books and plays, and such spirited discussion goes on today as much as ever. The discussion that takes places in literary studies, however, is more specialized than casual talk about whether one likes a particular text or what one likes to read generally. Literary studies tends to be focused not on immediate and passing responses to a particular work, a novel, a play, a poem, but on larger issues about the kinds of literary texts that exist, how they work, and how they work in relation to each other. Contemporary literary critics are known for trying to work out detailed and sometimes technical strategies to answer these questions, for trying to read texts accurately and well, and for trying to relate the meaning they find in texts to other parts of cultural and social life.

Frequently in the background of literary studies, and even in the foreground as of late, is the additional, elusive possibility of producing information and knowledge with quasi-scientific validity—the attempt to identify trends in national literatures, for example, or isolate phases of development in literature worldwide, and especially to describe literary texts and their effects with near-quantitative precision and accuracy. Throughout this century, in fact, the "formal" study of literature, wherein scholars try to study at close range the actual form literature takes and how it works, has been the main and dominant aim of literary studies. Extreme rigor in methodology and the repeatability of findings and of effect are goals that the scholarly world attributes primarily to science. In current criticism, we see this impulse toward extreme rigor especially as scholars describe and study the reading process and also how literature as a body of knowledge relates to other areas of culture—in Reader-Response criticism, structuralism, and cultural studies. (Louis Hjelmslev, whom we quoted in the General Introduction distinguishing between the sciences and the humanities, was a *structural* linguist.) At the same time, others in literary studies still have a strong humanistic orientation and are offended at the intrusion of scientific methods in literary studies for fear that the humanities will be merely trying to ape or mimic science. The goal remains for many in literary studies, however, to see criticism produce reliable, accurate, and replicable conclusions (approaching the results of scientific inquiry) about the nature of texts and the nature of literary experience.

We see a typical example of critical inquiry in the way or ways in which literary criticism defines its objects of study—literature and culture. Assume for a moment, as many literary critics have, that the definitions of literature and culture determine in advance the actual methods of study, the *kinds* of questions readers and students bring to their experience of literature. This assumption says that what we bring to literary study determines, to a degree, what we will find. A case in point in this section is the article by Gauri Viswanathan. In her essay, she makes an assumption about the way we study literature when she draws the contrast between definitions of literature and practices of literary studies in England and India in the nineteenth century. She argues that the British confined themselves to "formal," literary concerns, while the Indians were more aware of historical determinants. The opposition between the "formal" study of literature in England and its "historical" study in India has implications for Indian culture, as she demonstrates, that go far beyond the most immediate concerns of literary studies. Those new to literary studies will be surprised as they read Viswanathan and learn the extent to which this conflict gets played out in cultural and social events far removed from literary study narrowly conceived. Viswanathan shows that the opposition between formalism, or the rules by which texts operate, and historicism, or the reflection of historical meaning in literary texts, makes us question whether we should be focused on the historical background and context for a literary text or on the internal operations of the text itself. In actual practice, the difficulty of deciding between these options creates what Viswanathan calls the multiplication of "cultural and literary forms." Ultimately, this multiplication of "cultural and literary forms" means that there are quite different and conflicting claims—advanced from different positions of principle and belief—about what a text says and means.

This distinction between "formal" and "historical" definitions of literary study governs the essays in this section and, indeed, throughout this book. In fact, we could say that literary studies is shaped by the relationship between the formal analyses of aesthetics and the historical analyses of the "contents"—the politics, psychology, language, ideas, and more general "ethos"—that literary works represent. When Matthew Arnold articulated the "function of criticism" and the "burden" or import of literature to convey values to subsequent generations he was trying to describe such a relationship.

The study of literature in institutions of higher learning from Arnold's time forward has recurrently struggled with finding some satisfying relationship between these two "tasks" of literary study. Gerald Graff's contribution to this section traces part of this story. The formal study of literature, represented here in the essays by T. S. Eliot and Northrop Frye—both of whom, in their different ways, are seeking an aesthetic, self-contained world of "literature"—follow Colin McCabe's description of Renaissance conceptions of language that tended to remove "'attention from the situation of utterance and located all significance in the logic of language [Eliot's "ideal order" of works of art and Frye's "verbal universe"], which was determined by non-linguistic considerations.'" The historical study of literature has a very different premise—as we can see in Graff's call to teach the "conflicts" among definitions of literature and literary studies, in Cornel West's claim that cultural critics are "attuned to political conflict and struggle" and that such attention should be contrasted with "black formalism," and in Viswanathan's examination of the history of literary studies in relation to British colonialism in India. The historical perspective in literary study fosters the assumption that literature is not "disinterested" and "useless," as Frye asserts, but that it has social and political consequences in terms of political and social institutions, including the institutions that, as Graff says, "organize literature." The historically informed approach assumes that cultural products and institutions are, from a certain *historical* vantage, always "interested." (We discuss the issue of "interest" and its various meanings in the Introduction to Part II.)

LITERARY CRITICISM

The "organization" of literature that Graff mentions is one of the meanings of the term "criticism." (Frye describes the need for establishing criticism as a "properly organized science.") Literary studies, however, is not confined to literary criticism. Frye, Graff, and Viswanathan all distinguish "criticism"—which analyzes particular literary works and larger literary forms such as genres, themes, and even patterns of language as in Frye's "theory of imagery"—from highly "organized" approaches to literature. Another approach could be "philology," which Frye describes as rigorously studying the development of national languages in relation to literature and other cultural forms, or the humanist "belle lettrist" appreciations Graff describes, which articulate more or less personal and idiosyncratic responses to literature and the self-evident "truths" in the Arnoldian tradition—an "appreciation" that can move outside of the bounds of "literary studies" altogether.

   Students of literary and cultural studies find that they are significantly advanced in their work by coming to terms with "criticism" as a concept as early in their studies as possible. There is no surer division between the casual reader of texts or observer of culture and the serious student than the willingness to engage the task of understanding in its self-consciously critical dimensions. In this regard, a necessary component of criticism as the study of literature and other forms of discourse and language involves giving self-conscious attention to the methods of understanding. Literary criticism, as opposed to the more general and, as Northrop Frye says, the more "philosophical" study of aesthetics, aims at developing, as we noted in the General Introduction to this book, definitions of "literature" and methods of "reading." If criticism "is as inevitable as breathing," as Eliot says, and "we should be none the worse for articulating what passes in our minds when we read a book and feel an emotion about it, for criticizing our own minds in the work of criticism," then others throughout this book provides different and usually complementary definitions of criticism. Criticism, Frye argues in "The Function of Criticism at the Present Time," speaks *for* literature, which, like the "data" that are the object of scientific discourse, remains in itself "dumb."

   Frye goes on to say that the aim or function of criticism is to discover what literary texts—and "literature" itself—"actually mean as a whole," and it should pursue this task as systematically as other "sciences"—such as mathematics or history. This attention to the "wholeness" of what we study in literature marks Frye as a formalist, since formalism—from the New Critical formalism we discuss later in this section to the structuralist formalism discussed in "Structuralism and Semiotics" (Part IV)—attempts to describe various relations between the part and the whole of meaningful phenomena. Frye argues that criticism "preserves the scientific and systematic element in [literary] research" in order for literary studies as a whole to make "an immediately significant contribution to culture." Roland Barthes, in his essay "What Is Criticism?" in "Structuralism and Semiotics" (Part IV), argues that criticism is "essentially an activity" that "must include in its discourse . . . an implicit reflection on itself." Its aim is "not to *discover* the work in question but on the contrary to *cover* it as completely as possible by its own language." Criticism, Elaine Showalter has argued in discussing specifically *feminist* criticism, is positioned between "ideology and the liberal ideal of disinterestedness," *between* the formal and historical definitions of literary and cultural studies we are describing. Here again, criticism studies both "reading" and "literature," but they come together for Showalter—as they do for many in this book—"to make the leap to a new conceptual vantage point" to focus on "the essential question of difference"—"differences" among texts but also "differences" of value and discrimination within texts.

Frye joins Eliot and Barthes (and to a lesser extent Showalter) to say that criticism is a kind of formalism that seeks out a "conceptual vantage point" so that it can deal "with literature in terms of a specific conceptual framework." Frye describes *one* particular "conceptual framework" based upon grand "archetypal" patterns of significance (discussed in the Introduction to "Psychology and Psychoanalysis" [Part VI]), while Viswanathan, Graff, and others in *Contemporary Literary Criticism* describe different ones, such as the frameworks of colonial history, institutional history, Marxism, psychoanalysis, different kinds of feminism, and so on. Graff, in "The Humanist Myth," writes a *history* of the relations among these vantages or "frameworks." His point is that the "humanist myth" concerning literature—beginning, in important ways, in Matthew Arnold's attempt to define "The Function of Criticism at the Present Time" in 1865—assumed that "*literature teaches itself.*" "Practical criticism"—criticism that takes as its task the close scrutiny or explication of particular literary texts—often seems to be versions of literature "teaching itself." But as the detailed interpretations of texts in this book explicitly show—interpretations such as Louis Marin's "semiotic" reading of Disneyland, Stephen Greenblatt's "New Historicist" reading of Shakespeare's *Henry IV,* Nancy Armstrong's reading of *Alice in Wonderland,* or Slavoj Žižek's reading of Conan Doyle in relation to Freud and Lacan—approaches to practical criticism always carry "silent" assumptions and presuppositions about the nature of reading, the definition of literature, and the cultural work of literary and discursive analyses.

The assumption that literature teaches itself—thus implying that criticism has a very limited use—is clear in Arnold's description of the aim of criticism "to see the object as in itself it *really* is" (emphasis added). With this task accomplished, the critic can then aspire to present "the best that is known and thought in the world." Graff's point is that the seeming *self-evident truths* of the liberal humanist tradition, most fully articulated in what Graff calls "Arnoldian humanism," presuppose a particular "conceptual framework," or theory, even when that tradition claims to be simply disinterested, simply an attempted "reading," simply encompassing and promoting the best that is known and thought. Barthes describes the "guilty silence" of this tradition, which he says, "is not to be blamed for its prejudices but for the fact that it conceals them, masks them under the moral alibi of rigor and objectivity," and Viswanathan makes this especially clear in the case of the self-conscious *uses* of literary education by the colonial administrators of India for explicit political purposes.

Implicit in the juxtaposition Viswanathan presents is the suggestion that "disinterestedness" as an ideal of self-understanding could be dispensed with in the critical practices of oppressed colonial people—people who have no interest in maintaining the pretense of being objective. Likewise, when Cornel West advances that there is a "prevailing crisis in the humanities," he is interpreting contemporary Western culture historically. His "reading" of contemporary culture reveals both *internal* and *external* "decolonization," a series of historical and ideological shifts away from the mentality, worldview, and values that produced colonialism to begin with. This shift is reshaping how intellectuals and others view the world. West's version of cultural studies in this analysis demonstrates a particular *kind* of criticism that cuts across many traditional boundaries of inquiry. His own criticism is at once historical and political, and as such it "must simply know much more than a professional literary critical training [normally] provides."

In these definitions of criticism, these critics, and many others throughout this book, are attempting to create a broader sense of "culture" and "cultural studies" than even Arnold presents in *Culture and Anarchy.* There he defines the concept of culture as the "great help out of our present difficulties; culture being a pursuit of our total perfection by means of getting to know, on all the matters which most concern us, the best which has been thought and said in the world; and, through this knowledge, turning a stream of fresh and free thought upon our stock notions and habits."

Almost half a century earlier, Walt Whitman was able to look ahead and see, too, that "the word of the modern . . . is the word Culture." Similarly, Eliot, who like Whitman saw "culture" as a construction of modern society and not as a "natural" outgrowth of anything, defines culture in the Western tradition as shaped by "the mind of Europe." (Dick Hebdige offers a "genealogy" of the term "culture" in "Cultural Studies" [Part IX] that traces its uses in recent history.) Frye ends his essay by alluding to both Eliot and Arnold: "I even think," he writes, "that the consolidation of literature by criticism into the verbal universe was one of the things that Matthew Arnold meant by culture." Throughout *Contemporary Literary Criticism* critics create a broader sense of "culture" by emphasizing even more than Arnold, as West, Graff, and Viswanathan do, the specific, historical impact of cultural work (as opposed to Eliot's *universal historical sense*). Edward Said says in "The Politics of Knowledge" (in "What Is Literary Theory?" [Part II]) that such work is both *interested* and *unprovincial.* In his history of the relationship between ideas about literature and the professional institution of those ideas, Graff emphasizes this double and seemingly self-contradictory task in his attempt to trace "questions about the nature and cultural functions of literature" that literary criticism more generally pursues.

CRITICISM AND THE QUESTION OF HISTORY

J. Hillis Miller in "The Search for Grounds in Literary Study" (in "What Is Literary Theory?" [Part II]) focuses his discussion around Arnold and contemporary understandings of Arnold's critical practice in order to isolate an "imperial" element in literary criticism. Miller argues that, beginning in the eighteenth century at least, literary criticism has attempted to address wider areas of cultural practice beyond literature. The study of literature "has been weighted down in our culture with the burden of carrying from generation to generation the whole freight of the values of that culture, what Matthew Arnold called 'the best that is known and thought in the world.'" Similarly, Viswanathan cites Lionel Gossman's contention that "given the fact that there is no greater distinguishing feature than the uniquely human ability to manipulate symbolic systems, language and literature acquire an importance exceeding that of even science and technology."

Miller questions why literature should be so conceived and so valued. Gossman offers a "formal" explanation in terms of the "distinguishing feature" of literature, but Miller—and, for that matter, Arnold—offer historical answers in terms of the transformation of social values and social life. (Arnold argues that literature has come to define spiritual values that were formerly the province of religion.) Thus, Miller asks what historical events in the eighteenth or nineteenth centuries might have contributed to the idea of literature and this practice of literary studies that comes to us from Matthew Arnold. In this section, West proposes the "crisis" in the "European age" (stretching from 1492 to 1945) and the end of European dominance in world culture; Graff suggests that the "professionalization" of literary studies at the end of the nineteenth century has elevated the importance of literature; Viswanathan suggests that "the Western encounter with alien cultural and literary forms" during the centuries of imperial colonialism accounts for attributing so much to literature. All of these things—imperialism, professionalism, and the "crisis" of modern Western Enlightenment culture—seem to culminate or come to self-conscious self-questioning in the late nineteenth century, the time of Arnold.

Many of the essays throughout *Contemporary Literary Criticism,* but especially those in "What Is Literary Theory?," raise questions about the *interest* of criticism. Who is served by the forms criticism has taken? Who is left out? How do silent assumptions about the nature of "reading," "literature," "culture," "self-evidence," and "rigor and objectivity" affect people in particular places—in the classroom, in India, or Melanesia, in jail, at the national convention for the Modern Language Association, in the particular self-concepts and social concepts created by gender, race, and class? (These are all "places" described in different essays in this book.) Who is served when literary studies is understood as either a species of formalism or a species of history? Who is served when criticism is conceived as either simply commentary on literature (a method of reading) or a conceptual framework that allows a text to be considered "literary" (the definition of "literature")? One goal of this book is to specify and localize different contexts in which reading and literature are defined, to help describe what Showalter has called "the essential question of difference" in terms of encounters with alien cultural and literary forms. (An important aspect of studying literature, even when confined to literature written in one country, is the encounter with "aliens" who lived in historical times very different from our own. In *The French Lieutenant's Woman,* John Fowles defines literature as presenting a world different from our own, but possible.)

As opposed to "formal" definitions—which define issues once and for all in terms of "distinguishing features," or necessary attributes—"historical" definitions tend to present no universal truths but only local significance. This opposition makes clear why there is so much debate and controversy in literary criticism. Criticism is the modest and *formal* activity of creating a situation in which the best that is known and thought can have wide currency (Frye's description of criticism's job is "to get as many people in contact with the best that has been and is being thought and said"). Criticism also has the imperial and *historical* "burden" of maintaining cultural values in general (Frye's description of the "verbal universe, in which life and reality are inside literature" and which only the methods of criticism can help us to understand; but also Viswanathan's description of the burden of transforming the people of India into abstract Platonic political subjects). In fact, as the subtitle of this book ("Literary and Cultural Studies") suggests, the very *function* of criticism has become more self-reflexive in recent time. Contemporary criticism has expanded its horizon to include a vast array of historical questions that heretofore seemed outside, or only implicit within, its purview—questions of local and global politics, semantics, possibilities of cross-disciplinary work, the philosophy of language, the role of historically situated readers in the activity of interpretation, sexual and social relations, what West calls "the recovery and revisioning of American history [but also literary and cultural "histories"] in light of those on its underside," as well as the nature of literary study—its responsibilities and its very objects of study.

Such expansion has occasioned much controversy and debate, exacerbating rather than resolving the contradiction within the field (or "fields") of literary studies and the anxiety about its practice. The exploration of wider cultural questions has come in recent times to be called "cultural studies," and it has often met tremendous opposition, not only within the academy but in the popular press as well. It is Graff's argument that literary studies should explore rather than cover up its own contradictions and controversies, and it is also the argument of West and Viswanathan that literary studies should explore rather than cover up its involvement with larger historical and social contradictions and controversies. (Stanley Fish makes a similar argument on the level of rhetoric and interpretation in "Rhetoric and Reader Response" [Part III] when he argues that, in reading interpretations of literature that are at odds with one another, the controversy *itself* can be "regarded as evidence, not of an ambiguity that must be removed, but of an ambiguity that readers have always experienced.")

ELIOT, FORMALISM, AND THE TRADITION OF "NEW CRITICISM"

Criticism defined in the mode of "historicism" defines much of contemporary literary criticism. In the spirit of such historicism, we, too, emphasize repeatedly in this book analysis of the specific context, in social and cultural terms, that encompasses every attempt at criticism. As we convey at several points in this book, there is no single universal criticism or transhistorical approach to literary and cultural study. None has been discovered and none will yet be found. We say this because we believe that social and cultural contexts frame all critical analysis. The essays in this section tend to comment on the social and cultural frames in relation to the study of literary form—the internal patterning of poetry, fiction, and drama—earlier in the nineteenth and twentieth centuries. This work goes under the general name of "formalism"—the "black formalism" West mentions or the rhetorical formalism Viswanathan mentions.

A particular school of this movement, mentioned by West and Graff, is called the New Criticism. (Even Frye is responding to the detailed attention New Critical formalism brought to *particular* poems when he asserts that criticism should study the "whole" of literature.) The New Criticism was influential in America from the late 1930s through the late 1950s and still has an impact in the final years of the twentieth century. Formalism and the New Criticism, in turn, were very much governed by the movement in the arts that occurred in the first thirty years of the twentieth century that early in that period came to be called Modernism. So much of contemporary literary criticism is a self-conscious response to the related movements of Modernism and New Criticism—not only the "historicist" responses of Reader-Response criticism, the New Historicism, gender studies, and cultural studies, but even the less historical approaches of semiotics, poststructuralism, and psychoanalysis—that it is necessary to look closely at these movements in order to understand a significant global context of contemporary criticism. In other words, it is the self-proclaimed "universal," "impersonal," and "objective" criticism of Modernism and New Criticism that much contemporary literary criticism is responding to and reacting against. In part this is the reason we begin the book with Eliot's essay, which is an important critical statement of literary Modernism.

Here we want to offer examples of Eliot's modernist sense of literature and culture and the formal treatments of literature which follow from that sense. Eliot is a central figure in literary Modernism; in many ways Modernism in the Anglo-American world is contemporaneous with Eliot, dating from the early twentieth century and the influence of the French Symbolist poetry of Baudelaire, Mallarmé, Valéry, and others. Modernism is a body of literature and criticism as well as a critical perspective—or, rather, several related perspectives—that produced some of the great writers and critics of our age. Sometimes Modernism is said to have begun at the turn of the century with Conrad and Yeats, sometimes that it is most clearly delineated as a post–World War I phenomenon best represented by the publication of James Joyce's *Ulysses* and T. S. Eliot's *The Waste Land* in 1922. By some accounts, the movement ended in the mid-1930s. According to others, it went on until World War II; and some, Fredric Jameson among them, note that contemporary postmodernism is simply another version of Modernism. (Important feminist rereadings of literary Modernism by Shari Benstock, Bonnie Kime Scott, and others offer a historical "revisioning" of Modernism, to use West's term.) In any case, the height of modernist fervor was surely Virginia Woolf's assurance in 1924 that "in or about December, 1910, human character changed." Woolf explained that "all human relations have shifted—those between masters and servants, husbands and wives, parents and children. And when human relations change there is at the same time a change in religion, conduct, politics, and literature." But even a decade earlier, D. H. Lawrence had described a similarly radical reconception of human character "as representing some greater, inhuman will." Like Woolf—and like Eliot in the essay included here—Lawrence presents an antiromantic, antiexpressionist conception of human character in literature, a conception of the subject which, as Eliot says, is "impersonal" and a conception of literature as something other than "expressive." Their conception is owing to the *forms* of literature and experience rather than the narrowest sense of "personal," "human" significance.

Modernism responded to huge historical dislocations at the turn of the twentieth century, the second industrial revolution, the growth of democratic institutions in Europe, the great scientific and technological changes in Europe and America, the conquering of much of the world by European imperialism, the Great War (resulting in large part from all these things) that devastated much of Europe. The rhetoric of "high" Modernism—at least among its mostly male, middle-class spokespersons—is that of loss, apocalypse, and new beginnings: "Make it new!" was Ezra Pound's slogan for Modernism, articulated against the background of lost connections between the cultural past and present. For Modernism, there are no ordained or natural lines of order in the world; no cultural backdrop gives automatic meaning to a text; there is no providential plan according to which history and its outcomes are meaningfully situated. On the contrary, the disinheritance of modern culture is precisely the loss of belief in such traditional schemes as the Great Chain of Being. Pound and Eliot, in particular, do speak of grand cultural orders ("the mind of Europe," "tradition," "the past," and so on), but these are always distinctly human artifacts that must be reimagined for each poet and each culture.

The Modernists were involved in a serious reevaluation of the limits of literary form and of the possibilities for a new aesthetic in the arts generally—if not exactly new ways of being human, then at least a new paradigm of presentation for the products of twentieth-century culture. This aesthetic reevaluation took its place within the context of a serious questioning of the *subject* of experience and knowledge occasioned by the vast changes in the West in the early twentieth century. Henceforth, as Irving Babbitt said most forcefully, any romantic or sentimental tendencies in literature must be viewed as mere "emotional naturalism," a dissolving of real-world distinctions and a glossing over of important cultural demarcations. In place of nineteenth-century romantic "sloppiness," Babbitt said, is the emergent "modern spirit," "the positive and critical spirit, the spirit that refuses to take things on authority." Babbitt calls for a further movement away from supposedly "soft" and "uncritical" romanticism to "tough," "critical" modernism. It is a shift, as T. E. Hulme argued, into a contemporary version of the neoclassic sensibility and its modes of precise expression and carefully modulated sentiments. In short, Babbitt and Hulme call for the abandonment of romanticism and for the development of an emergent modern, antiromantic *formal* sensibility.

Eliot elaborates this process in "Tradition and the Individual Talent" when he argues that "past," "present," and "future" are not given facts or simple realities of experience but a *formal* arrangement of areas of disturbance and discontinuity in the midst of which the poet constructs art and culture in a collage. Similarly, in this period the semiotician Ferdinand de Saussure—Eliot's contemporary (see "Structuralism and Semiotics" [Part IV])—proposed that experience itself is a linguistic arrangement of "signified" and potential meanings, a rational and formal arrangement situated within a context of arbitrariness. Thus, cut off from the past, disinherited from it, the poet, the artist, or any user of language can choose to accept the imperative and responsibility to "make it new" or else remain without any operative sense of past or present culture at all. This modernist version of poetry suggests a highly rational (almost Augustan) practice, but it is poetic logic shown to exist in the irrational wasteland of modern culture, where the poet toils to make (actually *create*) cultural connections that otherwise would not exist. In other words, poetry introduces form into a cultural flux of the modern world that by definition cannot be well formed, or "finished," because it remains in transition.

The double task of Eliot's work in criticism as well as poetry—the presentation of rational objectivity alongside great subjective anxiety—is a defining articulation of literary Modernism. In addition, Eliot's work as a critic as well as a poet initiated what Leslie Fiedler describes as the "Age of Eliot," the American literary criticism of the 1940s and 1950s which, under the name of "New Criticism," explored linguistic and literary form as a way of creating the so-called objective sense that literature presents and examined the subjective "effects" such literary forms give rise to. Paul de Man defines the New Criticism in "The Resistance to Theory" (in "What Is Literary Theory?" [Part II]): "The perfect embodiment of the New Criticism," he writes, "remains, in many respects, the personality and the ideology of T. S. Eliot, a combination of original talent, traditional learning, verbal wit and moral earnestness, an Anglo-American blend of intellectual gentility not so repressed as not to afford tantalizing glimpses of darker psychic and political depths." This position, de Man goes on, assumes "the integrity of a social and historical self": it is based upon both the assertion of, but also a grave crisis in, "disinterested" subjects of experience and knowledge. (In the Introduction to Part IV we examine the closely related European phenomenon of Russian Formalism where, as we mentioned in the General Introduction, scientific objectivity goes hand in hand with explorations of "strangeness.")

Aijaz Ahmad, writing in a context of postcolonial studies quite different from the deconstructive criticism of de Man (in "What Is Literary Theory?" [Part II]), describes New Criticism in more historical terms. "When 'New Criticism' appeared on the horizon," he writes, "—with its fetishistic notions of the utter autonomy of each single literary work, and its post-Romantic idea of 'Literature' as a special kind of *language* which yields a special kind of knowledge—its practice of reified reading proved . . . extremely useful as a pedagogical tool in the American classroom precisely because it required of the student little knowledge of anything not strictly 'literary'— no history which was not predominantly literary history, no science of the social, no philosophy—except the procedures and precepts of literary formalism." Thus, Ahmad continues, "the favourite New Critical text was the short lyric, precisely because the lyric could be detached with comparatively greater ease from the larger body of texts, indeed from the world itself, to become the ground for analysis of compositional minutiae; the pedagogical advantage was, of course, that such analyses of short lyrics could fit rather neatly into one hour in the undergraduate classroom." Ahmad's comment repeats Frye's implicit complaint about the New Criticism in the selection here, namely, that it detaches particular works of literature from the larger body of texts of "literature" conceived as a whole. It also repeats West's explicit complaint that New Critical formalism "rests upon a fetishism of literature—a religious belief in the magical powers of a glorified set of particular cultural archives somehow autonomous and disconnected from other social practices." (In "Rhetoric and Reader Response" [Part III], Schweickart also complains of "the fetishized art object, the 'Verbal Icon,' of New Criticism.") In fact, in these comments we can understand Ahmad's repeated description of extreme formalism—including New Critical formalism—as the "technicist" practice of literary studies.

The New Criticism, whose *textual* strategies de Man personifies in the figure of Eliot and whose *social* implications Ahmad and West describe in the context of post–World War II decolonization, was firmly embedded in the "high" literary Modernism of Eliot, Pound, and Lawrence, a species of "American modernism" that Ahmad describes as "deeply conservative and elitist." A single orthodoxy for the New Criticism as a broad movement does not exist, but we can add to those characteristics mentioned by de Man and Ahmad several of the key tenets articulated by major Anglo-American critics from the 1930s through the 1950s, the period of the New Criticism's active development. In particular, the New Criticism tried to displace content in literary analysis and to treat a work's form in a manner analogous to empirical research. Also, the New Criticism tried to organize the larger, generic forms of literature in accord with the inner ordering of works as revealed in specific analyses or "close readings." In its objectivity, it defined the subject of (poetic) experience and knowledge formally and, thus, avoided the "Modernist" crisis of subjectivity; in its "close readings," it defined literature solely as impersonal aesthetic experience and avoided the crisis of cultural institutions everywhere apparent in Modernism. It accomplished both of these tasks by conceiving of literature (to one degree or another) as a self-sustaining "artifact," a "spatial form" in Joseph Frank's term, and of form as a self-contained "autonomous" entity. Perhaps most important was the New Critical reliance on "imagery" as a concept with which to define form.

Drawing heavily on the work of the modernist critics, New Critics like Cleanth Brooks made the literary image the primary material or constituent of form itself. Brooks's New Critical "close reading" of John Donne's poem "The Canonization," for instance, involves a preliminary identification of key images in a recurring pattern of opposition, or as he says, "tension." Only once this pattern of imagery is established do the New Critics attend to any interpretive considerations of form. Just as Eliot uses paradox and irony to pursue his argument in "Tradition and the Individual Talent," the New Critics posited paradox and irony as controlling figures, in effect, turning them into a kind of content. As Brooks says in *The Well-Wrought Urn*, paradox and irony actually reflect the structure of the imagination itself.

The definition of literary form is the largest difference between the "substantial" formalism of the New Criticism and the "functional" formalism of Russian Formalism (discussed in "Structuralism and Semiotics" [Part IV]). Whereas the Russian Formalists attempted merely to lay bare the operation of local devices, rejecting any authoritative and final interpretation of a work, the New Critics believed that a work can be read objectively and accurately in light of its actual structure or form. A work can, thus, have a single, or "correct," interpretation. W. K. Wimsatt and Monroe C.

Beardsley in "The Intentional Fallacy" stipulate the manner of reading a work the "right" way. They explain the interference and inaccuracies possible when authorial intentions become a consideration in close reading, which is, according to the New Critics, the "wrong" way to read. In "The Affective Fallacy," they also show how at the other extreme a reader's undisciplined "affective" responses to a text—the very *effects* that Reader-Response criticism studies and that Russian Formalism attempts to account for—may distort the correct apprehension and interpretation of images. In this thinking, the New Critics retrieved from romanticism the concept of aesthetic wholeness and unity as well as a unified or single interpretation of a work. They argued that a work, properly read, will always be unified by a set of reconceived tensions, as expressed in paradox and irony. In short, the New Critics assumed total coherence in a work that is unaffected by historical contexts.

CONTEMPORARY LITERARY CRITICISM

Criticism after the New Criticism has pursued aims very different from those of Eliot and the New Critics. In fact, the very "traditions" that are critiqued in this section, especially the New Criticism, pursued what Graff calls "the atomized empiricism of research and explication, which trusted that the accumulation of facts and interpretations about literature would somehow of itself add up to a coherent picture." (In "Structuralism and Semiotics" [Part IV], Barthes critiques a similar formalist "tradition" in criticism that was concerned with "rigor and objectivity" but in the narrow "establishment of facts.") West traces the collapse of New Critical formalism in the wake of social and political events after World War II and warns against the establishment of a "new black formalism" that may well govern the formation of an African-American literary canon. And Viswanathan examines the alternative functionings of formalism and historicism in the early development of literary studies in the early nineteenth century in England and India. Even Frye, in the *Anatomy of Criticism* (in which he republished "The Function of Criticism at the Present Time" as its "Polemical Introduction"), critiqued the New Criticism as a kind of "delicate learning"—appreciative, narrow, and, above all, certain and unself-conscious in the making of its own critical assumptions.

There is a high degree of self-consciousness in, among other areas, West's conception of the "cultural critic" and in the historical senses and contexts Graff and Viswanathan bring to literary studies. In *After the New Criticism,* Frank Lentricchia examines the crisis in criticism that the failure (or fulfillment) of the modernist tradition of New Criticism occasioned. A significant response to that crisis, as the various "schools" of criticism we examine in this book suggest, was to resubmit literature to self-conscious examination within the cultural and social contexts of its functioning. (A second response, in the cases of rhetorical and psychoanalytic criticism and in particular strains of poststructural criticism as in Foucault and Belsey, was analyses of the "constructed" nature of authors, characters, and reading subjects.) Such a reevaluation of literary studies, as we will see in Part II, requires that the autonomy of "aesthetics"—with its anonymous subject (or perspective of values), its transparent media, and its seeming separation from the world of controversy and culture—be replaced by "theory" and, on occasion, by aesthetics conceived within the context of theory. But it also required, as we will see as well, that "theory" itself address questions of social and political history.

RELATED ESSAYS IN *CONTEMPORARY LITERARY CRITICISM*

Aijaz Ahmad, "Literary Theory and 'Third World Literature': Some Contexts"
Teresa de Lauretis, "Semiotics and Experience"
Michel Foucault, "What Is an Author?"
Donna Haraway, "A Cyborg Manifesto: Science, Technology, and Socialist-Feminism in the Late Twentieth Century"
Dick Hebdige, "From Culture to Hegemony"
Cora Kaplan, "Pandora's Box: Subjectivity, Class and Sexuality in Socialist Feminist Criticism"
J. Hillis Miller, "The Search for Grounds in Literary Study"

REFERENCES AND FURTHER READING

Arnold, Matthew, *Arnold: Poetry and Prose,* ed. John Bryson (London: Hart-Davis, 1954).
Babbitt, Irving, *Rousseau and Romanticism* (New York: Houghton Mifflin, 1919).
Bennett, Tony, *Formalism and Marxism* (London: Methuen, 1979).
Benstock, Shari, *Women of the Left Bank: Paris, 1900–1940* (Austin: University of Texas Press, 1986).
Berman, Marshall, *All That Is Solid Melts into Air: The Experience of Modernity* (New York: Simon & Schuster, 1982).
Bloom, Harold, *The Western Canon: The Books and School of the Ages* (New York: Harcourt Brace, 1994).
Bradbury, Malcolm, and James McFarlane, *Modernism: 1890–1930* (New York: Penguin Books, 1976).
Brooker, Peter, ed., *Modernism/Postmodernism* (New York: Longman, 1992).
Brooks, Cleanth, "My Credo: Formalist Critics," in *Kenyon Review,* 13 (1951), 72–81.
———, *The Well-Wrought Urn* (New York: Harcourt, 1975).
———, and Robert Penn Warren, eds., *Understanding Poetry* (New York: Holt, 1983).
Conroy, Mark, *Modernism and Authority: Strategies of Legitimation in Flaubert and Conrad* (Baltimore: Johns Hopkins University Press, 1985).
Crane, R. S., et al., eds., *Critics and Criticism: Ancient and Modern* (Chicago: University of Chicago Press, 1957).
Culler, Jonathan, *Framing the Sign: Criticism and Its Institutions* (Norman: University of Oklahoma Press, 1988).
Eliot, T. S., *The Sacred Wood* (London: Methuen, 1920).
Ellmann, Richard, and Charles Feidelson, Jr., *The Modern Tradition: Backgrounds of Modern Literature* (New York: Oxford University Press, 1965).
Fish, Stanley Eugene, *Professional Correctness: Literary Studies and Political Change* (New York: Oxford University Press, 1995).
Frank, Joseph, *The Widening Gyre: Crisis and Mastery in Modern Literature* (New Brunswick, NJ: Rutgers University Press, 1963).
Frye, Northrop, *Anatomy of Criticism: Four Essays* (Princeton, NJ: Princeton University Press, 1957).

Graff, Gerald, *Beyond the Culture Wars: How Teaching the Conflicts Can Revitalize American Education* (New York: Norton, 1992).

———, *Literature Against Itself: Literary Ideas in Modern Society* (Chicago: University of Chicago Press, 1979).

———, *Professing Literature* (Chicago: University of Chicago Press, 1987).

Guillory, John, *Cultural Capital: The Problem of Literary Canon Formation* (Chicago: University of Chicago Press, 1993).

Hartman, Geoffrey H., *Criticism in the Wilderness: The Study of Literature Today* (New Haven, CT: Yale University Press, 1980).

Howe, Irving, ed., *Literary Modernism* (New York: Fawcett, 1967).

Kenner, Hugh, *A Homemade World: The American Modernist Writers* (New York: Morrow, 1975).

———, *The Pound Era* (Berkeley: University of California Press, 1971).

Kermode, Frank, and John Hollander, eds., *Modern British Literature* (New York: Morrow, 1975).

Lentricchia, Frank, *After the New Criticism* (Chicago: University of Chicago Press, 1980).

Lodge, David, ed., *Modern Criticism and Theory: A Reader* (White Plains, NY: Longman, 1988).

Miller, J. Hillis, *Poets of Reality* (Cambridge, MA: Harvard University Press, 1965).

Ortega y Gasset, José, *The Dehumanization of Art and Other Writings on Art, Culture, and Literature* (1948; rpt. Garden City, NY: Doubleday, 1956).

Pound, Ezra, *The ABC of Reading* (New Haven, CT: Yale University Press, 1934).

Ransom, John Crowe, *The New Criticism* (New York: New Directions, 1941).

Richards, I. A., *Practical Criticism* (New York: Harcourt, Brace, 1929).

———, *Principles of Literary Criticism* (New York: Harcourt, Brace, 1925).

Schleifer, Ronald, *Rhetoric and Death: The Language of Modernism and Postmodern Discourse Theory* (Urbana: University of Illinois Press, 1990).

Scholes, Robert, *Textual Power* (New Haven, CT: Yale University Press, 1985).

Scott, Bonnie Kime, *Refiguring Modernism* (Bloomington: Indiana University Press, 1995).

———, and Mary Lynn Broe, eds., *The Gender of Modernism: A Critical Anthology* (Bloomington: Indiana University Press, 1990).

Showalter, Elaine, "Feminist Criticism in the Wilderness," in *Critical Inquiry* 8 (1981), 179–205.

Sosnoski, James, *Token Professionals and Master Critics: A Critique of Orthodoxy in Literary Studies* (Albany: State University of New York Press, 1994).

Spender, Stephen, *The Struggle of the Modern* (Berkeley: University of California Press, 1963).

Spivak, Gayatri Chakravorty, *Outside of the Teaching Machine* (New York: Routledge, 1993).

Spurlin, William J., and William Fischer, *The New Criticism and Contemporary Literary Theory: Connections and Continuities* (New York: Garland, 1995).

Symons, Arthur, *The Symbolist Movement in Literature* (1899; rpt. New York: Dutton, 1958).

Wimsatt, W. K., *The Verbal Icon* (Lexington: University of Kentucky Press, 1954).

Winters, Yvor, *In Defense of Reason* (Denver: Swallow Press, 1947).

1

T. S. Eliot
1888–1965

T. S. (Thomas Stearns) Eliot is best known as a poet, but he is arguably a central modern critic writing in English. He had vast influence in several areas: he almost singlehandedly brought about the reappraisal of sixteenth- and seventeenth-century drama and metaphysical poetry; he demonstrated the necessity of reading American and English literature in relation to European and non-European (especially Oriental) traditions; he helped to formulate a modern way of reading and writing that eschewed romantic values and furthered an aesthetic of "hard, dry" images and sentiments. Eliot thus directed modern readers in what and how to read and how to understand literary texts. These achievements, along with the critical revolution signaled by his own poetry, make Eliot a modern critic of the first rank. His major works of criticism include *The Sacred Wood* (1920), *The Use of Poetry and the Use of Criticism* (1933), *Christianity and Culture* (1940), *Notes Towards a Definition of Culture* (1949), *Selected Essays* (1953), and *On Poetry and Poets* (1957).

Eliot directed his criticism as much toward professional literary critics as he did toward the general public. In "Tradition and the Individual Talent" (1919), an essay that could easily borrow Pope's title "Essay on Criticism," Eliot emphasizes the necessity of critical thinking—"criticism is as inevitable as breathing." This essay shows some of the furthest reaches of Elliot's theories and literary philosophy. He asserts the value of poetic creation as the process by which a whole culture locates itself in the present in relation to an acquired sense of the past. The past is an active force in the present, constituting "the presentness of the past," and is a channel of access to a cultural "mind" larger than any single poet's and ultimately decisive in determining the direction and import of all "significant" art in any age. These ideas had a direct influence on modernist criticism and literature, but—to a greater extent than is sometimes recognized—they also underlie some contemporary cultural theories, such as Reader-Response criticism and various approaches to audience-reception theory. Noteworthy for its coherence and cogency, this essay is perhaps Eliot's most important critical statement.

Tradition and the Individual Talent

I

In English writing we seldom speak of tradition, though we occasionally apply its name in deploring its absence. We cannot refer to "the tradition" or to "a tradition"; at most, we employ that adjective in saying that the poetry of So-and-so is "traditional" or even "too traditional." Seldom, perhaps, does the word appear except in a phrase of censure. If otherwise, it is vaguely approbative, with the implication, as to the work approved, of some pleasing archaeological reconstruction. You can hardly make the word agreeable to English ears without this comfortable reference to the reassuring science of archaeology. Certainly the word is not likely to appear in our appreciations of living or dead writers. Every nation, every race, has not only its own creative, but its own critical turn of mind; and is even more oblivious of the shortcomings and limitations of its critical habits than of those of its creative genius. We know, or think we know, from the enormous mass of critical writing that has appeared in the French language the critical method or habit of the French; we only conclude (we are such unconscious people) that the French are "more critical" than we, and sometimes even plume ourselves a little with the fact, as if the French were the less spontaneous. Perhaps they are; but we might remind ourselves that criticism is as inevitable as breathing, and that we should be none the worse for articulating what passes in our minds when we read a book and feel an emotion about it, for criticizing our own minds in their work of criticism. One of the facts that might come to light in this process is our tendency to insist, when we praise a poet, upon those aspects of his work in which he least resembles anyone else. In these aspects or parts of his work we pretend to find what is individual, what is the peculiar essence of the man. We dwell with satisfaction upon the poet's difference from his predecessors, especially his immediate predecessors; we endeavour to find something that can be isolated in order to be enjoyed. Whereas if we approach a poet without this prejudice we shall often find that not only the best, but the most individual parts of his work may be those in which the dead poets, his ancestors, assert their immortality most vigorously. And I do not mean the impressionable period of adolescence, but the period of full maturity.

Yet if the only form of tradition, of handing down, consisted in following the ways of the immediate generation before us in a blind or timid adherence to its successes, "tradition" should positively be discouraged. We have seen many such simple currents soon lost in the sand; and novelty is better than repetition. Tradition is a matter of much wider significance. It cannot be inherited, and if you want it you must obtain it by great labour. It involves, in the first place, the historical sense, which we may call nearly indispensable to anyone who would continue to be a poet beyond his twenty-fifth year; and the historical sense involves a perception, not only of the pastness of the past, but of its presence; the historical sense compels a man to write not merely with his own generation in his bones, but with a feeling that the whole of the literature of Europe from Homer and within it the whole of the literature of his own country has a simultaneous existence and composes a simultaneous order. This historical sense, which is a sense of the timeless as well as of the temporal and of the timeless and of the temporal together, is what makes a writer traditional. And it is at the same time what makes a writer most acutely conscious of his place in time, of his own contemporaneity.

No poet, no artist of any art, has his complete meaning alone. His significance, his appreciation is the appreciation of his relation to the dead poets and artists. You cannot value him alone; you must see him, for contrast and comparison, among the dead. I mean this as a principle of aesthetic, not merely historical, criticism. The necessity that he shall conform, that he shall cohere, is not onesided; what happens when a new work of art is created is something that happens simultaneously to all the works of art which preceded it. The existing monuments form an ideal order among themselves, which is modified by the introduction of the new (the really new) work of art among them. The existing order is complete before the new work arrives; for order to persist after the supervention of novelty, the whole existing order must be, if ever so slightly altered; and so the relations, proportions, values of each work of art towards the whole are readjusted; and this is conformity between the old and the new. Whoever has approved this idea of order, of the form of European, of English literature will not find it preposterous that the past should be altered by the present as much as the present is directed by the past. And the poet who is aware of this will be aware of great difficulties and responsibilities.

In a peculiar sense he will be aware also that he must inevitably be judged by the standards of the past. I say judged, not amputated, by them; not judged to be as good as, or worse or better than, the dead; and certainly not judged by the canons of dead critics. It is a judgment, a comparison, in which two things are measured by each other. To conform merely would be for the new work not really to conform at all; it would not be new, and would therefore not be a work of art. And we do not quite say that the new is more valuable because it fits in; but its fitting in is a test of its value—a test, it is true, which can only be slowly and cautiously applied, for we are none of us infallible judges of conformity. We say: it appears to conform, and is perhaps individual, or it appears individual, and may conform; but we are hardly likely to find that it is one and not the other.

To proceed to a more intelligible exposition of the relation of the poet to the past: he can neither take the past as a lump, an indiscriminate bolus, nor can he form himself wholly on one or two private admirations, nor can he form himself wholly upon one preferred period. The first course is inadmissible, the second is an important experience of youth, and the third is a pleasant and highly desirable supplement. The poet must be very conscious of the main current, which does not at all flow invariably through the most distinguished reputations. He must be quite aware of the obvious fact that art never improves, but that the material of art is never quite the same. He must be aware that the mind of Europe—the mind of his own country—a mind which he learns in time to be much more important than his own private mind—is a mind which changes, and that this change is a development which abandons nothing *en route,* which does not superannuate either Shakespeare, or Homer, or the rock drawing of the Magdalenian draughtsmen. That this development, refinement perhaps, complication certainly, is not from the point of view of the artist, any improvement. Perhaps not even an improvement from the point of view of the psychologist or not to the extent which we imagine; perhaps only in the end based upon a complication in economics and machinery. But the difference between the present and the past is that the conscious present is an awareness of the past in a way and to an extent which the past's awareness of itself cannot show.

Someone said: "The dead writers are remote from us because we *know* so much more than they did." Precisely, and they are that which we know.

I am alive to a usual objection to what is clearly part of my programme for the *métier* of poetry. The objection is that the doctrine requires a ridiculous amount of erudition (pedantry), a claim which can be rejected by appeal to the lives of poets in any pantheon. It will even be affirmed that much learning deadens or perverts poetic sensibility. While, however, we persist in believing that a poet ought to know as much as will not encroach upon his necessary receptivity and necessary laziness, it is not desirable to confine knowledge to whatever can be

put into a useful shape for examinations, drawing rooms, or the still more pretentious modes
of publicity. Some can absorb knowledge, the
more tardy must sweat for it. Shakespeare acquired more essential history from Plutarch
than most men could from the whole British
Museum. What is to be insisted upon is that the
poet must develop or procure the consciousness
of the past and that he should continue to develop this consciousness throughout his career.

What happens is a continual surrender of
himself as he is at the moment to something
which is more valuable. The progress of an artist
is a continual self-sacrifice, a continual extinction of personality.

There remains to define this process of depersonalization and its relation to the sense of tradition. It is in this depersonalization that art may
be said to approach the condition of science. I
therefore invite you to consider, as a suggestive
analogy, the action which takes place when a bit
of finely filiated platinum is introduced into a
chamber containing oxygen and sulphur dioxide.

II

Honest criticism and sensitive appreciation are
directed not upon the poet but upon the poetry. If
we attend to the confused cries of the newspaper
critics and the *susurrus* of popular repetition that
follows, we shall hear the names of poets in great
numbers; if we seek not Blue-book knowledge
but the enjoyment of poetry, and ask for a poem,
we shall seldom find it. I have tried to point out
the importance of the relation of the poem to
other poems by other authors, and suggested the
conception of poetry as a living whole of all the
poetry that has ever been written. The other aspect of this Impersonal theory of poetry is the relation of the poem to its author. And I hinted, by
an analogy, that the mind of the mature poet differs from that of the immature one not precisely
in any valuation of "personality," not being necessarily more interesting, or having "more to say,"
but rather by being a more finely perfected

medium in which special, or varied, feelings are at
liberty to enter into new combinations.

The analogy was that of the catalyst. When
the two gases previously mentioned are mixed in
the presence of a filament of platinum, they
form sulphurous acid. This combination takes
place only if the platinum is present; nevertheless the newly formed acid contains no trace of
platinum, and the platinum itself is apparently
unaffected: has remained inert, neutral, and un-
changed. The mind of the poet is the shred of
platinum. It may partly or exclusively operate
upon the experience of the man himself; but,
the more perfect the artist, the more completely
separate in him will be the man who suffers and
the mind which creates; the more perfectly will
the mind digest and transmute the passions
which are its material.

The experience, you will notice, the elements
which enter the presence of the transforming catalyst, are of two kinds: emotions and feelings.
The effect of a work of art upon the person who
enjoys it is an experience different in kind from
any experience not of art. It may be formed out
of one emotion, or may be a combination of several; and various feelings, inhering for the writer
in particular words or phrases or images, may be
added to compose the final result. Or great poetry may be made without the direct use of any
emotion whatever: composed out of feelings
solely. Canto XV of the *Inferno* (Brunetto Latini)
is a working up of the emotion evident in the situation; but the effect, though single as that of any
work of art, is obtained by considerable complexity of detail. The last quatrain[1] gives an image, a
feeling attaching to an image, which "came,"
which did not develop simply out of what precedes, but which was probably in suspension in
the poet's mind until the proper combination arrived for it to add itself to. The poet's mind is in
fact a receptacle for seizing and storing up numberless feelings, phrases, images, which remain
there until all the particles which can unite to
form a new compound are present together.

If you compare several representative passages
of the greatest poetry you see how great is the va-

riety of types of combination, and also how completely any semi-ethical criterion of "sublimity" misses the mark. For it is not the "greatness," the intensity, of the emotions, the components, but the intensity of the artistic process, the pressure, so to speak, under which the fusion takes place, that counts. The episode of Paolo and Francesca employs a definite emotion, but the intensity of the poetry is something quite different from whatever intensity in the supposed experience it may give the impression of. It is not more intense, furthermore, than Canto XXVI, the voyage of Ulysses, which has not the direct dependence upon an emotion. Great variety is possible in the process of transmutation of emotion: the murder of Agamemnon, or the agony of Othello, gives an artistic effect apparently closer to a possible original than the scenes from Dante. In the *Agamemnon,* the artistic emotion approximates to the emotion of an actual spectator; in *Othello* to the emotion of the protagonist himself. But the difference between art and the event is always absolute; the combination which is the murder of Agamemnon is probably as complex as that which is the voyage of Ulysses. In either case there has been a fusion of elements. The ode of Keats contains a number of feelings which have nothing particular to do with the nightingale, but which the nightingale, partly perhaps because of its reputation, served to bring together.

The point of view which I am struggling to attack is perhaps related to the metaphysical theory of the substantial unity of the soul: for my meaning is, that the poet has, not a "personality" to express, but a particular medium, which is only a medium and not a personality, in which impressions and experiences combine in peculiar and unexpected ways. Impressions and experiences which are important for the man may take no place in the poetry, and those which become important in the poetry may play quite a negligible part in the man, the personality.

I will quote a passage which is unfamiliar enough to be regarded with fresh attention in the light—or darkness—of these observations:

And now methinks I could e'en chide myself
For doating on her beauty, though her death
Shall be revenged after no common action.
Does the silkworm expend her yellow
    labours
For thee? For thee does she undo herself?
Are lordships sold to maintain ladyships
For the poor benefit of a bewildering
    minute?
Why does yon fellow falsify highways,
And put his life between the judge's lips,
To refine such a thing—keeps horse and men
To beat their valours for her? . . . [2]

In this passage (as is evident if it is taken in its context) there is a combination of positive and negative emotions: an intensely strong attraction towards beauty and an equally intense fascination by the ugliness which is contrasted with it and which destroys it. This balance of contrasted emotion is in the dramatic situation to which the speech is pertinent, but that situation alone is inadequate to it. This is, so to speak, the structural emotion, provided by the drama. But the whole effect, the dominant tone, is due to the fact that a number of floating feelings, having an affinity to this emotion by no means superficially evident, have combined with it to give us a new art emotion.

It is not in his personal emotions, the emotions provoked by particular events in his life, that the poet is in any way remarkable or interesting. His particular emotions may be simple, or crude, or flat. The emotion in his poetry will be a very complex thing, but not with the complexity of the emotions of people who have very complex or unusual emotions in life. One error, in fact, of eccentricity in poetry is to seek for new human emotions to express; and in this search for novelty in the wrong place it discovers the perverse. The business of the poet is not to find new emotions, but the use of ordinary ones and, in working them up into poetry, to express feelings which are not in actual emotions at all. And emotions which he has never experienced will serve his turn as well as those familiar to him. Consequently, we must believe that "emotion recollected in tranquility"[3] is an inexact formula. For it is neither emotion, nor recollection, nor, without distortion of meaning, tranquility. It is a concentration, and a new thing resulting from the concentration, of a very great number of experiences which to the practical and active person would not seem to be experiences at all; it is a concentration which does not happen consciously or of deliberation. These experiences are not "recollected," and they finally unite in an atmosphere which is "tranquil" only in that it is a passive attending upon the event. Of course this is not quite the whole story. There is a great deal, in the writing of poetry, which must be conscious and deliberate. In fact, the bad poet is usually unconscious where he ought to be conscious, and conscious where he ought to be unconscious. Both errors tend to make him "personal." Poetry is not a turning loose of emotion, but an escape from emotion; it is not the expression of personality, but an escape from personality. But, of course, only those who have personality and emotions know what it means to want to escape from these things.

III

ὁ δὲ νοῦς ἴνως θειότερόν τι καὶ ἀπαθές ἐστιν.[4]

This essay proposes to halt at the frontier of metaphysics or mysticism, and confine itself to such practical conclusions as can be applied by the responsible person interested in poetry. To divert interest from the poet to the poetry is a laudable aim: for it would conduce to a juster estimation of actual poetry, good and bad. There are many people who appreciate the expression of sincere emotion in verse, and there is a smaller number of people who can appreciate technical excellence. But very few know when there is an expression of *significant* emotion, emotion which has its life in the poem and not in the history of the poet. The emotion of art is impersonal. And the poet cannot reach this impersonality without surrendering himself wholly to the work to be done. And he is not likely to know what is to be done unless he believes in what is not merely the present, but the present moment of the past, unless he is conscious, not of what is dead, but of what is already living.

NOTES

1. In the translation of Dorothy L. Sayers:

    Then he turned round.
    And seemed like one of those who over the flat
    And open course in the fields beside Verona
    Run for the green cloth; and he seemed, at that,
    Not like a loser, but the winning runner.

2. Cyril Tourneur, *The Revenger's Tragedy* (1607), III, iv.

3. "Poetry is the spontaneous overflow of powerful feelings: it takes its origins from emotion recollected in tranquility." Wordsworth, Preface to *Lyrical Ballads* (1800).

4. "While the intellect is doubtless a thing more divine and is impassive." Aristotle, *De Anima*.

Northrop Frye
1912–1991

Northrop Frye's most acclaimed work is *Anatomy of Criticism* (1957), in which he introduced his systematic approach to literature. Among his other works are *The Well-Tempered Critic* (1963), *The Critical Path: An Essay on the Social Context of Literary Criticism* (1971); and *The Stubborn Structure: Essays on Criticism and Society* (1970). He also authored two books on Shakespeare: *Fools of Time: Studies in Shakespearean Tragedy* (1967) and *A Natural Perspective* (1965). His two in-depth studies of Romanticism are *Fearful Symmetry: A Study of William Blake* (1947) and *A Study of English Romanticism* (1968).

In his work Frye offers a concise, fully developed, and systematic approach to the study of literature. Unlike the preceding theories of formalism (which concentrate on the individual work) and historicism (emphasizing the author as creator), his method identifies the whole of literature as a culturally structured entity consisting of the entire canon of poems, dramas, and prose. Frye uses a mythological model to illustrate the morphology of literature: it consists of birth (melodrama), zenith (comedy), death (tragedy), and darkness (ironic literature).

In "The Function of Criticism at the Present Time" (1949), Frye considers it the responsibility of the critic to systematize the previously unorganized study of literature. As the shaper of intellectual tradition, the critic must organize the material within a critical framework that follows the natural contours of literature. Before criticism can exist as an organized system, it must thoroughly—even scientifically—classify literature, reconsidering the all-too-frequent use of unsupported value judgments by many writers in discussing literary works. To understand literature, says Frye, requires seeing it as a system of word-symbols, not unlike mathematics, which must be considered as part of its greater structure, separate from the world that gave rise to the ideas it depicts.

The Function of Criticism at the Present Time

The subject-matter of literary criticism is an art, and criticism is presumably an art too. This sounds as though criticism were a parasitic form of literary expression, an art based on pre-existing art, a second-hand imitation of creative power. The conception of the critic as a creator *manqué* is very popular, especially among artists. Yet the critic has specific jobs to do which the experience of literature has proved to be less ignoble. One obvious function of criticism is to mediate between the artist and his public. Art that tries to do without criticism is apt to get involved in either of two fallacies. One is the attempt to reach the public directly through "popular" art, the assumption being that criticism is artificial and public taste natural. Below this is a further assumption about natural taste which goes back to Rousseau. The opposite fallacy is the conception of art as a mystery, an initiation into an esoteric community. Here criticism is restricted to masonic signs of occult understanding, to significant exclamations and gestures and oblique cryptic comments. This fallacy is like the other one in assuming a rough correlation between the merit of art and the degree of public response to it, though the correlation it assumes is inverse. But art of this kind is cut off from society as a whole, not so much because it retreats from life—the usual charge against it—as because it rejects criticism.

On the other hand, a public that attempts to do without criticism, and asserts that it knows what it likes, brutalizes the arts. Rejection of criticism from the point of view of the public, or its guardians, is involved in all forms of censorship. Art is a continuously emancipating factor in society, and the critic, whose job it is to get as many people in contact with the best that has been and is being thought and said, is, at least ideally, the pioneer of education and the shaper of cultural tradition. There is no immediate correlation either way between the merits of art and its general reception. Shakespeare was more

popular than Webster, but not because he was a greater dramatist; W. H. Auden is less popular than Edgar Guest, but not because he is a better poet. But after the critic has been at work for a while, some positive correlation may begin to take shape. Most of Shakespeare's current popularity is due to critical publicity.

Why does criticism have to exist? The best and shortest answer is that it can talk, and all the arts are dumb. In painting, sculpture, or music it is easy enough to see that the art shows forth, and cannot say anything. And, although it sounds like a frantic paradox to say that the poet is inarticulate or speechless, literary works also are, for the critic, mute complexes of facts, like the data of science. Poetry is a *disinterested* use of words: it does not address a reader directly. When it does so, we feel that the poet has a certain distrust in the capacity of readers and critics to interpret his meaning without assistance, and has therefore stopped creating a poem and begun to talk. It is not merely tradition that impels a poet to invoke a Muse and protest that his utterance is involuntary. Nor is it mere paradox that causes Mr. MacLeish, in his famous "Ars Poetica," to apply the words "mute," "dumb," and "wordless" to a poem. The poet, as Mill saw in a wonderful flash of critical insight, is not heard, but overheard. The first assumption of criticism, and the assumption on which the autonomy of criticism rests, is not that the poet does not know what he is talking about, but that he cannot talk about what he knows, any more than the painter or composer can.

The poet may of course have some critical ability of his own, and so interpret his own work; but the Dante who writes a commentary on the first canto of the *Paradiso* is merely one more of Dante's critics. What he says has a peculiar interest, but not a peculiar authority. Poets are too often the most unreliable judges of the value or even the meaning of what they have written. When Ibsen maintains that *Emperor and Galilean* is his greatest play and that certain episodes in *Peer Gynt* are not allegorical, one can only say that Ibsen is an indifferent critic of Ibsen. Wordsworth's Preface to the *Lyrical Ballads* is a remarkable document, but as a piece of Wordsworthian criticism nobody would give it more than about a B plus. Critics of Shakespeare are often supposed to be ridiculed by the assertion that if Shakespeare were to come back from the dead he would not be able to understand their criticism and would accuse them of reading far more meaning into his work than he intended. This, though pure hypothesis, is likely enough: we have very little evidence of Shakespeare's interest in criticism, either of himself or of anyone else. But all that this means is that Shakespeare, though a great dramatist, was not also the greatest Shakespearean critic. Why should he be?

The notion that the poet is necessarily his own best interpreter is indissolubly linked with the conception of the critic as a parasite or jackal of literature. Once we admit that he has a specific field of activity, and that he has autonomy within that field, we are forced to concede that criticism deals with literature in terms of a specific conceptual framework. This framework is not that of literature itself, for this is the parasite theory again, but neither is it something outside literature, for in that case the autonomy of criticism would again disappear, and the whole subject would be assimilated to something else.

Here, however, we have arrived at another conception of criticism which is different from the one we started with. This autonomous organizing of literature may be criticism, but it is not the activity of mediating between the artist and his public which we at first ascribed to criticism. There is one kind of critic, evidently, who faces the public and another who is still as completely involved in literary values as the poet himself. We may call this latter type the critic proper, and the former the critical reader. It may sound like quibbling to imply such a distinction, but actually the whole question of whether the critic has a real function, independent both of the artist at his most explicit and of the public at its most discriminating, is involved in it.

Our present-day critical traditions are rooted in the age of Hazlitt and Arnold and Sainte-Beuve, who were, in terms of our distinction, critical readers. They represented, not another conceptual framework within literature, but the reading public at its most expert and judicious. They conceived it to be the task of a critic to exemplify how a man of taste uses and evaluates literature, and thus how literature is to be absorbed into society. The nineteenth century has bequeathed to us the conception of the *causerie,* the man of taste's reflections on works of literature, as the normal form of critical expression. I give one example of the difference between a critic and a critical reader which amounts to a head-on collision. In one of his curious, brilliant, scatter-brained footnotes to *Munera Pulveris,* John Ruskin says:

> Of Shakespeare's names I will afterwards speak at more length; they are curiously—often barbarously—mixed out of various traditions and languages. Three of the clearest in meaning have been already noticed. Desdemona—"δυσδαιμονία" *miserable fortune*—is also plain enough. Othello is, I believe, "the careful"; all the calamity of the tragedy arising from the single flaw and error in his magnificently collected strength. Ophelia, "serviceableness," the true, lost wife of Hamlet, is marked as having a Greek name by that of her brother, Laertes; and its signification is once exquisitely alluded to in that brother's last word of her, where her gentle preciousness is opposed to the uselessness of the churlish clergy: "*A ministering* angel shall my sister be, when thou liest howling."

On this passage Matthew Arnold comments as follows:

> Now, really, what a piece of extravagance all that is! I will not say that the meaning of Shakespeare's names (I put aside the question

as to the correctness of Mr. Ruskin's etymologies) has no effect at all, may be entirely lost sight of; but to give it that degree of prominence is to throw the reins to one's whim, to forget all moderation and proportion, to lose the balance of one's mind altogether. It is to show in one's criticism, to the highest excess, the note of provinciality.

Ruskin is a critic, perhaps the only important one that the Victorian age produced, and, whether he is right or wrong, what he is attempting is genuine criticism. He is trying to interpret Shakespeare in terms of a conceptual framework which belongs to the critic alone, and yet relates itself to the plays alone. Arnold is perfectly right in feeling that this is not the sort of material that the public critic can directly use. But he does not suspect the existence of criticism as we have defined it above. Here it is Arnold who is the provincial. Ruskin has learned his trade from the great iconological tradition which comes down through classical and biblical scholarship into Dante and Spenser, both of whom he knew how to read, and which is incorporated in the medieval cathedrals he had pored over in such detail. Arnold is assuming, as a universal law of nature, certain "plain sense" critical assumptions which were hardly heard of before Dryden's time and which can assuredly not survive the age of Freud and Jung and Frazer and Cassirer. What emerges from this is that the critic and critical reader are each better off when they know of one another's existence, and perhaps best off when their work forms different aspects of the same thing.

However, the *causerie* does not, or at least need not, involve any fallacy in the theory of criticism itself. The same cannot be said of the reaction against the *causerie* which has produced the leading twentieth-century substitute for criticism. This is the integrated system of religious, philosophical, and political ideas which takes in, as a matter of course, a critical attitude to literature. Thus Mr. Eliot defines his outlook as clas-

sical in literature, royalist in politics, anglo-catholic in religion; and it is clear that the third of these has been the spark-plug, the motivating power that drives the other two. Mr. Allen Tate describes his own critical attitude as "reactionary" in a sense intended to include political and philosophical overtones, and the same is true of Hulme's *Speculations,* which are primarily political speculations. Mr. Yvor Winters collects his criticism under the title "In Defence of Reason." What earthly business, one may inquire, has a literary critic to defend reason? He might as well be defending virtue. And so we could go through the list of Marxist, Thomist, Kierkegaardian, Freudian, Jungian, Spenglerian, or existential critics, all determined to substitute a critical attitude for criticism, all proposing, not to find a conceptual framework for criticism within literature, but to attach criticism to one of a miscellany of frameworks outside it. The axioms and postulates of criticism have to grow out of the art that the critic is dealing with. The first thing that the literary critic has to do is to read literature, to make an inductive survey of his own field and let his critical principles shape themselves solely out of his knowledge of that field. Critical principles cannot be taken over ready-made from theology, philosophy, politics, science, or any combination of these. Further, an inductive survey of his own field is equally essential for the critic of painting or of music, and so each art has its own criticism. Aesthetics, or the consideration of art as a whole, is not a form of criticism but a branch of philosophy. I state all this as dogma, but I think the experience of literature bears me out. To subordinate criticism to a critical attitude is to stereotype certain values in literature which can be related to the extra-literary source of the value-judgment. Mr. Eliot does not mean to say that Dante is a greater poet than Shakespeare or perhaps even Milton; yet he imposes on literature an extra-literary schematism, a sort of religio-political colour-filter, which makes Dante leap into prominence, shows Milton up as dark and faulty, and largely obliterates the outlines of Shakespeare. All that the genuine critic can do with this colour-filter is to murmur politely that it shows things in a new light and is indeed a most stimulating contribution to criticism.

If it is insisted that we cannot criticize literature until we have acquired a coherent philosophy of criticism with its centre of gravity in something else, the existence of criticism as a separate subject is still being denied. But there is one possibility further. If criticism exists, it must be, we have said, an examination of literature in terms of a conceptual framework derivable from an inductive survey of the literary field. The word "inductive" suggests some sort of scientific procedure. What if criticism is a science as well as an art? The writing of history is an art, but no one doubts that scientific principles are involved in the historian's treatment of evidence, and that the presence of this scientific element is what distinguishes history from legend. Is it also a scientific element in criticism which distinguishes it from *causerie* on the one hand, and the superimposed critical attitude on the other? For just as the presence of science changes the character of a subject from the casual to the causal, from the random and intuitive to the systematic, so it also safeguards the integrity of a subject from external invasions. So we may find in science a means of strengthening the fences of criticism against enclosure movements coming not only from religion and philosophy, but from the other sciences as well.

If criticism is a science, it is clearly a social science, which means that it should waste no time in trying to assimilate its methods to those of the natural sciences. Like psychology, it is directly concerned with the human mind, and will only confuse itself with statistical methodologies. I understand that there is a Ph.D. thesis somewhere that displays a list of Hardy's novels in the order of the percentages of gloom that they contain, but one does not feel that that sort of procedure should be encouraged. Yet as the field is narrowed to the social sciences the dis-

tinctions must be kept equally sharp. Thus there can be no such thing as a sociological "approach" to literature. There is no reason why a sociologist should not work exclusively on literary material, but if he does he should pay no attention to literary values. In this field Horatio Alger and the writer of the Elsie books are more important than Hawthorne or Melville, and a single issue of the *Ladies' Home Journal* is worth all of Henry James. The literary critic using sociological data is similarly under no obligation to respect sociological values.

It seems absurd to say that there *may* be a scientific element in criticism when there are dozens of learned journals based on the assumption that there is, and thousands of scholars engaged in a scientific procedure related to literary criticism. Either literary criticism is a science, or all these highly trained and intelligent people are wasting their time on a pseudoscience, one to be ranked with phrenology and election forecasting. Yet one is forced to wonder whether scholars as a whole are consciously aware that the assumptions on which their work is based are scientific ones. In the growing complication of secondary sources which constitutes literary scholarship, one misses, for the most part, that sense of systematic progressive consolidation which belongs to a science. Research begins in what is known as "background," and one would expect it, as it goes on, to organize the foreground as well. The digging up of relevant information about a poet should lead to a steady consolidating progress in the criticism of his poetry. One feels a certain failure of nerve in coming out of the background into the foreground, and research seems to prefer to become centrifugal, moving away from the works of art into more and more research projects. I have noticed this particularly in two fields in which I am interested, Blake and Spenser. For every critic of Spenser who is interested in knowing what, say, the fourth book of *The Faerie Queene* actually means as a whole, there are dozens who are interested primarily in how Spenser used Chaucer,

Malory, and Ariosto in putting it together. So far as I know there is no book devoted to an analysis of *The Faerie Queene* itself, though there are any number on its sources, and, of course, background. As for Blake, I have read a whole shelf of books on his poetry by critics who did not know what any of his major poems meant. The better ones were distinguishable only by the fact that they did not boast of their ignorance.

The reason for this is that research is ancillary to criticism, but the critic to whom the researcher should entrust his materials hardly exists. What passes for criticism is mainly the work of critical readers or spokesmen of various critical attitudes, and these make, in general, a random and haphazard use of scholarship. Such criticism is therefore often regarded by the researcher as a subjective and regressive dilettantism, interesting in its place, but not real work. On the other hand, the critical reader is apt to treat the researcher as Hamlet did the grave-digger, ignoring everything he throws out except an odd skull that he can pick up and moralize about. Yet unless research consolidates into a criticism which preserves the scientific and systematic element in research, the literary scholar will be debarred by his choice of profession from ever making an immediately significant contribution to culture. The absence of direction in research is, naturally, clearest on the very lowest levels of all, where it is only a spasmodic laying of unfertilized eggs in order to avoid an administrative axe. Here the research is characterized by a kind of desperate tentativeness, an implied hope that some synthesizing critical Messiah of the future will find it useful. A philologist can show the relationship of even the most minute study of dialect to his subject as a whole, because philology is a properly organized science. But the researcher who collects all a poet's references to the sea or God or beautiful women does not know who will find this useful or in what ways it could be used, because he has no theory of imagery.

I am not, obviously, saying that literary scholarship at present is doing the wrong thing or should be doing something else: I am saying that it should be possible to get a clearer and more systematic comprehension of what it is doing. Most literary scholarship could be described as prior criticism (the so-called "lower" criticism of biblical scholarship), the editing of texts and the collecting of relevant facts. Of the posterior (or "higher") criticism that is obviously the final cause of this work we have as yet no theory, no tradition, and above all no systematic organization. We have, of course, a good deal of the thing itself. There is even some good posterior criticism of Spenser, though most of it was written in the eighteenth century. And in every age the great scholar will do the right thing by the instinct of genius. But genius is rare, and scholarship is not.

Sciences normally begin in a state of naïve induction: they come immediately in contact with phenomena and take the things to be explained as their immediate data. Thus physics began by taking the immediate sensations of experience, classified as hot, cold, moist, and dry, as fundamental principles. Eventually physics turned inside out, and discovered that its real function was to explain what heat and moisture were. History began as chronicle; but the difference between the old chronicler and the modern historian is that to the chronicler the events he recorded were also the structure of history, whereas the historian sees these events as historical phenomena, to be explained in terms of a conceptual framework different in shape from them. Similarly each modern science has had to take what Bacon calls (though in another context) an inductive leap, occupying a new vantage ground from which it could see its former principles as new things to be explained. As long as astronomers regarded the movements of heavenly bodies as the *structure* of astronomy, they were compelled to regard their own point of view as fixed. Once they thought of movement as itself an explainable phenomenon, a mathematical theory of movement became the conceptual framework, and so the way was cleared for the heliocentric solar system and the law of gravitation. As long as biology thought of animal and vegetable forms of life as constituting its subject, the different branches of biology were largely efforts of cataloguing. As soon as it was the existence of forms of life themselves that had to be explained, the theory of evolution and the conceptions of protoplasm and the cell poured into biology and completely revitalized it.

It occurs to me that literary criticism is now in such a state of naïve induction as we find in a primitive science. Its materials, the masterpieces of literature, are not yet regarded as phenomena to be explained in terms of a conceptual framework which criticism alone possesses. They are still regarded as somehow constituting the framework or form of criticism as well. I suggest that it is time for criticism to leap to a new ground from which it can discover what the organizing or containing forms of its conceptual framework are. And no one can examine the present containing forms of criticism without being depressed by an overwhelming sense of unreality. Let me give one example.

In confronting any work of literature, one obvious containing form is the genre to which it belongs. And criticism, incredible as it may seem, has as yet no coherent conception of genres. The very word sticks out in an English sentence as the unpronounceable and alien thing it is. In poetry, the common-sense Greek division by methods of performance, which distinguishes poetry as lyric, epic, or dramatic according to whether it is sung, spoken, or shown forth, survives vestigially. On the whole it does not fit the facts of Western poetry, though in Joyce's *Portrait* there is an interesting and suggestive attempt made to re-define the terms. So, apart from a drama which belongs equally to prose, a handful of epics recognizable as such only because they are classical imitations, and a number of long poems also called epics because they are long, we are reduced to the ignoble and slovenly practice of calling almost the whole of poetry "lyric" because the Greeks had no other word for it. The Greeks did not need to develop

a classification of prose forms: we do, but have never done so. The circulating-library distinction between fiction and non-fiction, between books which are about things admitted not to be true and books which are about everything else, is apparently satisfactory to us. Asked what the forms of prose fiction are, the literary critic can only say, "well, er—the novel." Asked what form of prose fiction *Gulliver's Travels,* which is clearly not a novel, belongs to, there is not one critic in a hundred who could give a definite answer, and not one in a thousand who would regard the answer (which happens to be "Menippean satire") as essential to the critical treatment of the book. Asked what he is working on, the critic will invariably say that he is working on Donne, or Shelley's thought, or the period from 1640 to 1660, or give some other answer which implies that history, or philosophy, or literature itself, constitutes the structural basis of criticism. It would never occur to any critic to say, for instance, "I am working on the theory of genres." If he actually were interested in this, he would say that he was working on a "general" topic; and the work he would do would probably show the marks of naïve induction: that is, it would be an effort to classify and pigeon-hole instead of clarifying the tradition of the genre.

If we do not know how to handle even the genre, the most obvious of all critical conceptions, it is hardly likely that subtler instruments will be better understood. In any work of literature the characteristics of the language it is written in form an essential critical conception. To the philologist, literature is a function of language, its works linguistic documents, and to the philologist the phrase "English literature" makes sense. It ought not to make any sense at all to a literary critic. For while the philologist sees English literature as illustrating the organic growth of the English language, the literary critic can only see it as the miscellaneous pile of literary works that happened to get written in English. (I say in English, not in England, for the part of "English literature" that was written in Latin or Norman French has a way of dropping unobtrusively into other departments.) Language is an important secondary aspect of literature, but when magnified into a primary basis of classification it becomes absurdly arbitrary.

Critics, of course, maintain that they know this, and that they keep the linguistic categories only for convenience. But theoretical fictions have a way of becoming practical assumptions, and in no time the meaningless convenience of "English literature" expands into the meaningless inconvenience of the "history of English literature." Now, again, the historian must necessarily regard literature as an historical product and its works as historical documents. It is also quite true that the time a work was written in forms an essential critical conception. But again, to the literary critic, as such, the phrase "history of English literature" ought to mean nothing at all. If he doubts this, let him try writing one, and he will find himself confronted by an insoluble problem of form, or rather by an indissoluble amorphousness. The "history" part of his project is an abstract history, a bald chronicle of names and dates and works and influences, deprived of all the real historical interest that a real historian would give it, however much enlivened with discussions of "background." This chronicle is periodically interrupted by conventional judgments of value lugged in from another world, which confuse the history and yet are nothing by themselves. The *form* of literary history has not been discovered, and probably does not exist, and every successful one has been either a textbook or a *tour de force*. Linear time is not an exact enough category to catch literature, and all writers whatever are subtly belittled by a purely historical treatment.

Biography, a branch of history, presents a similar fallacy to the critic, for the biographer turns to a different job and a different kind of book when he turns to criticism. Again, the man who wrote the poem is one of the legitimate containing forms of criticism. But here we have to distinguish the poet *qua* poet, whose work is a single imaginative body, from the poet as man,

who is something else altogether. The latter involves us in what is known as the personal heresy, or rather the heroic fallacy. For a biographer, poetry is an emanation of a personality; for the literary critic it is not, and the problem is to detach it from the personality and consider it on impersonal merits. The no man's land between biography and criticism, the process by which a poet's impressions of his environment are transmuted into poetry, has to be viewed by biographer and critic from opposite points of view. The process is too complex ever to be completely unified, Lowes's *Road to Xanadu* being the kind of exception that goes a long way to prove the rule. In Johnson's *Lives of the Poets* a biographical narrative is followed by a critical analysis, and the break between them is so sharp that it is represented in the text by a space.

In all these cases, the same principle recurs. The critic is surrounded by biography, history, philosophy, and language. No one doubts that he has to familiarize himself with these subjects. But is his job only to be the jackal of the historian, the philologist, and the biographer, or can he use these subjects in his own way? If he is not to sell out to all his neighbours in turn, what is distinctive about his approach to the poet's life, the time when he lived, and the language he wrote? To ask this is to raise one of the problems involved in the whole question of what the containing forms of literature are as they take their place in the conceptual framework of criticism. This confronts me with the challenge to make my criticism of criticism constructive. All I have space to do is to outline what I think the first major steps should be.

We have to see what literature is, and try to distinguish the category of literature among all the books there are in the world. I do not know that criticism has made any serious effort to determine what literature is. Next, as discussed above, we should examine the containing forms of criticism, including the poet's life, his historical context, his language, and his thought, to see whether the critic can impose a unified critical form on these things, without giving place to or turning into a biographer, an historian, a philologist, or a philosopher. Next, we should establish the broad distinctions, such as that between prose and poetry, which are preparatory to working out a comprehensive theory of genres. I do not know that critics have clearly explained what the difference between prose and poetry, for instance, really is. Then we should try to see whether the critic, like his neighbours the historian and the philosopher, lives in his own universe. To the historian there is nothing that cannot be considered historically; to the philosopher nothing that cannot be considered philosophically. Does the critic aspire to contain all things in criticism, and so swallow history and philosophy in his own synthesis, or must he be forever the historian's and philosopher's pupil? If I have shown up Arnold in a poor light, I should say that he is the only one I know who suggests that criticism can be, like history and philosophy, a total attitude to experience. And finally, since criticism may obviously deal with anything in a poem from its superficial texture to its ultimate significance, the question arises whether there are different levels of meaning in literature, and, if so, whether they can be defined and classified.

It follows that arriving at value-judgments is not, as it is so often said to be, part of the immediate tactic of criticism. Criticism is not well enough organized as yet to know what the factors of value in a critical judgment are. For instance, as was indicated above in connection with Blake and Spenser, the question of the quality of a poet's thinking as revealed in the integration of his argument is an essential factor in a value-judgment, but many poets are exhaustively discussed in terms of value without this factor being considered. Contemporary judgments of value come mainly from either the critical reader or from the spokesman of a critical attitude. That is, they must be on the whole either unorganized and tentative, or over-organized and irrelevant. For no one can jump directly from research to a value-judgment. I give one melancholy instance. I recently read a study

of the sources of mythological allusions in some of the romantic poets, which showed that for the second part of *Faust* Goethe had used a miscellany of cribs, some of dubious authenticity. "I have now, I hope," said the author triumphantly at the end of his investigation, "given sufficient proof that the second part of *Faust* is not a great work of art." I do not deny the ultimate importance of the value-judgment. I would even consider the suggestion that the value-judgment is precisely what distinguishes the social from the natural science. But the more important it is, the more careful we should be about getting it solidly established.

What literature is may perhaps best be understood by an analogy. We shall have to labour the analogy, but that is due mainly to the novelty of the idea here presented. Mathematics appears to begin in the counting and measuring of objects, as a numerical commentary on the world. But the mathematician does not think of his subject as the counting and measuring of physical objects at all. For him it is an autonomous language, and there is a point at which it becomes in a measure independent of that common field of experience which we think of as the physical world, or as existence, or as reality, according to our mood. Many of its terms, such as irrational numbers, have no direct connection with the common field of experience, but depend for their meaning solely on the interrelations of the subject itself. Irrational numbers in mathematics may be compared to prepositions in verbal languages, which, unlike nouns and verbs, have no external symbolic reference. When we distinguish pure from applied mathematics, we are thinking of the former as a disinterested conception of numerical relationships, concerned more and more with its inner integrity, and less and less with its reference to external criteria.

Where, in that case, is pure mathematics going? We may gain a hint from the final chapter of Sir James Jeans' *Mysterious Universe,* which I choose because it shows some of the characteristics of the imaginative leap to a new conceptual framework already mentioned. There, the author speaks of the failure of physical cosmology in the nineteenth century to conceive of the universe as ultimately mechanical, and suggests that a mathematical approach to it may have better luck. The universe cannot be a machine, but it may be an interlocking set of mathematical formulas. What this means is surely that pure mathematics exists in a mathematical universe which is no longer a commentary on an "outside" world, but contains that world within itself. Mathematics is at first a form of understanding an objective world regarded as its content, but in the end it conceives of the content as being itself mathematical in form, so that when the conception of the mathematical universe is reached, form and content become the same thing.

Jeans was a mathematician, and thought of his mathematical universe as *the* universe. Doubtless it is, but it does not follow that the only way of conceiving it is mathematical. For we think also of literature at first as a commentary on an external "life" or "reality." But just as in mathematics we have to go from three apples to three, and from a square field to a square, so in reading Jane Austen we have to go from the faithful reflection of English society to the novel, and pass from literature as symbol to literature as an autonomous language. And just as mathematics exists in a mathematical universe which is at the circumference of the common field of experience, so literature exists in a verbal universe, which is not a commentary on life or reality, but contains life and reality in a system of verbal relationships. This conception of a verbal universe, in which life and reality are inside literature, and not outside it and being described or represented or approached or symbolized by it, seems to me the first postulate of a properly organized criticism.

It is vulgar for the critic to think of literature as a tiny palace of art looking out upon an inconceivably gigantic "life." "Life" should be for the critic only the seed-plot of literature, a vast mass of potential literary forms, only a few of which will grow up into the greater world of the verbal universe. Similar universes exist for all the arts. "We make to ourselves picture of facts," says Wittgenstein, but by pictures he means representative illustrations, which are not pictures. Pictures as pictures are themselves facts, and exist only in a pictorial universe. It is easy enough to say that while the stars in their courses may form the subject of a poem, they will still remain the stars in their courses, forever outside poetry. But this is pure regression to the common field of experience, and nothing more; for the more strenuously we try to conceive the stars in their courses in non-literary ways, the more assuredly we shall fall into the idioms and conventions of some other mental universe. The conception of a constant external reality acts as a kind of censor principle in the arts. Painting has been much bedevilled by it, and much of the freakishness of modern painting is clearly due to the energy of its revolt against the representational fallacy. Music on the other hand has remained fairly free of it: at least no one, so far as I know, insists that it is flying in the face of common sense for music to do anything but reproduce the sounds heard in external nature. In literature the chief function of representationalism is to neutralize its opposing fallacy of an "inner" or subjective reality.

These different universes are presumably different ways of conceiving the same universe. What we call the common field of experience is a provisional means of unifying them on the level of sense-perception, and it is natural to infer a higher unity, a sort of beautification of common sense. But it is not easy to find any human language capable of reaching such exalted heights. If it is true, as is being increasingly asserted, that metaphysics is a system of verbal constructions with no direct reference to external criteria by means of which its truth or falsehood may be tested, it follows that metaphysics forms part of the verbal universe. Theology postulates an ultimate reality in God, but it does not assume that man is capable of describing it in his own terms, nor does it claim to be itself such a description. In any case, if we assert this final unity too quickly we may injure the integrity of the different means of approaching it. It does not help a poet much to tell him that the function of literature is to empty itself into an ocean of superverbal significance, when the nature of that significance is unknown.

Pure mathematics, we have said, does not relate itself directly to the common field of experience, but indirectly, not to avoid it, but with the ultimate design of swallowing it. It thus presents the appearance of a series of hypothetical possibilities. It by-passes the confirmation from without which is the goal of applied mathematics, and seeks it only from within: its conclusions are related primarily to its own premises. Literature also proceeds by hypothetical possibilities. The poet, said Sidney, never affirmeth. He never says "this is so"; he says "let there be such a situation," and poetic truth, the validity of his conclusion, is to be tested primarily by its coherence with his original postulate. Of course, there is applied literature, just as there is applied mathematics, which we test historically, by its lifelikeness, or philosophically, by the cogency of its propositions. Literature, like mathematics, is constantly useful, a word which means having a continuing relationship to the common field of experience. But pure literature, like pure mathematics, is disinterested, or useless: it contains its own meaning. Any attempt to determine the category of literature must start with a distinction between the verbal form which is primarily itself and the verbal form which is primarily related to something else. The former is a complex verbal fact, the latter a complex of verbal symbols.

We have to use the mathematical analogy once more before we leave it. Literature is, of course, dependent on the haphazard and unpredictable appearance of creative genius. So actually is mathematics, but we hardly notice this because in mathematics a steady consolidating process goes on, and the work of its geniuses is absorbed in the evolving and expanding pattern of the mathematical universe. Literature being as yet unorganized by criticism, it still appears as a huge aggregate or miscellaneous pile of creative efforts. The only organizing principle so far discovered in it is chronology, and when we see the miscellaneous pile strung out along a chronological line, some coherence is given to it by the linear factors in tradition. We can trace an epic tradition by virtue of the fact that Virgil succeeded Homer, Dante Virgil, and Milton Dante. But, as already suggested, this is very far from being the best we can do. Criticism has still to develop a theory of literature which will see this aggregate within a verbal universe, as forms integrated within a total form. An epic, besides occurring at a certain point in time, is also something of a definitive statement of the poet's imaginative experience, whereas a lyric is usually a more fragmentary one. This suggests the image of a kind of radiating circle of literary experience in which the lyric is nearer to a periphery and the epic nearer to a centre. It is only an image, but the notion that literature, like any other form of knowledge, possesses a centre and a circumference seems reasonable enough.

If so, then literature is a single body, a vast organically growing form, and, though of course works of art do not improve, yet it may be possible for criticism to see literature as showing a progressive evolution in time, of a kind rather like what Newman postulates for Catholic dogma. One could collect remarks by the dozen from various critics, many of them quite misleading, to show that they are dimly aware, on some level of consciousness, of the possibility of a critical progress toward a total comprehension of literature which no critical history gives any hint of. When Mr. Eliot says that the whole tradition of Western poetry from Homer down ought to exist simultaneously in the poet's mind, the adverb suggests a transcending by criticism of the tyranny of historical categories. I even think that the consolidation of literature by criticism into the verbal universe was one of the things that Matthew Arnold meant by culture. To begin this process seems to me the function of criticism at the present time.

Cornel West
1953–

Cornel West is in the Afro-American Studies Department and the Department of Divinity at Harvard University. His works include *Prophesy Deliverance!* (1982), *Prophetic Fragments* (1988), *The Ethical Dimensions of Marxist Thought* (1991), *Breaking Bread: Insurgent Black Intellectual Life* (with bell hooks, 1991), and *Beyond Eurocentrism and Multiculturalism* (1993). With his eighth book, *Race Matters,* published on the first anniversary of the 1992 Los Angeles riots, West reached a popular audience beyond academic circles. That slim volume, like much of West's work, covers a broad range of topics. West said of himself in a 1993 interview published in *Essence,* "There are intellectuals who grapple with one idea for years, but that's not my style. I want to be a provocative intellectual who writes about many unsettling issues."

West confronts the current effort to reform the literary canon in "Black Critics and the Pitfalls of Canon Formation," taken from his 1993 book *Keeping Faith: Philosophy and Race in America.* West critiques the pluralist ideologies informing contemporary canon formation. He sees efforts to admit African-American texts into an expanded canon or the development of a separate African-American canon as not serving the interests of African-American literature. Pluralistic inclusion, which allows for the admission of select samples of African-American texts, limits African-American literary critics to considering those texts within a closed system, analyzing African-American texts only in relation to other African-American texts. West cites Jean Toomer, Ralph Ellison, James Baldwin, Toni Morrison, and Ishmael Reed as African-American authors whose contributions to literature as a whole have been overshadowed by the tendency of literary critics to view them solely in the context of African-American intellectual history rather than in the context of intellectual history in general. Rather than simple expansion of the canon, West calls for "a wholesale reconsideration of the canon already in place." Such a reconsideration would bring African-American texts out of the literary ghetto, permitting critical examination of African-American literature within a broader historical and political context, thereby enacting positive, transformative cultural action.

West implicates African-American literary critics in the development of a literary ghetto, showing that expansion of a pluralist canon serves the particular interests of the literary critics themselves rather than the general interest of African-American literature as a whole. The pluralist agenda situates African-American literature as yet another of a series of specializations of fields. Consequently, African-American literary critics are hired by English departments to serve as "academic superintendents" and thus are granted authority over African-American literature. West goes on to suggest that because this authority comes from a pluralist, ghettoizing system, it is in the interest of these critics to support and perpetuate this system. Rather than having a positive transformative effect, these critics have contributed to "the glacier shift from an African-American literature of racial confrontation . . . to one of cultural introspection."

Black Critics and the Pitfalls of Canon Formation

What does it mean to engage in canon formation at this historical moment? In what ways does the prevailing crisis in the humanities impede or enable new canon formations? And what role do the class and professional interests of the canonizers play in either the enlarging of a canon or the making of multiple, conflicting canons? I shall address these questions in the form of a critical self-inventory of my own intellectual activity as an African American cultural critic. This self-inventory shall consist of three moments. First, I shall locate my own cultural criticism against a particular historical reading of the contemporary crisis in the humanities. Second, I shall examine my own deeply ambiguous intellectual sentiments regarding the process of canon formation now afoot in African American literary criticism. And third, I shall put forward what I understand to be the appropriate role and function of oppositional cultural critics in regard to prevailing forms of canon formation in our time.

Any attempt to expand old canons or constitute new ones presupposes particular interpretations of the historical moment at which canonization is to take place. The major Western, male, literary canonizers of our century—T. S. Eliot, F. R. Leavis, F. O. Matthiessen, Cleanth Brooks, Northrop Frye, M. H. Abrams and Paul de Man—all assumed specific interpretations of why their canonizing efforts were required and how these efforts could play a positive role. Contemporary literary critics remain too preoccupied with the fascinating and ingenious ways

in which these canonizers reevaluated and readjusted the old canon. As a cultural critic, I would like to see more attention paid to the prevailing historical interpretations of the cultural crisis which prompts, guides and regulates the canonizing efforts. In this sense, attempts to revise or reconstitute literary canons rest upon prior—though often tacit—interpretive acts of rendering a canonical historical reading of the crisis that in part authorizes literary canons. So the first battle over literary canon formation has to do with one's historical interpretation of the crisis achieving canonical status.

For instance, the power of T. S. Eliot's canonizing efforts had as much to do with this canonical reading of the crisis of European civilization after the unprecedented carnage and dislocations of World War I as with his literary evaluations of the Metaphysicals and Dryden over Spenser and Milton or his nearly wholesale disapproval of Romantic and Victorian poetry. As the first moment of my own self-inventory as an African American cultural critic, I focus not on the kinds of texts to choose for an enlargement of the old canon or the making of a new one but rather on a historical reading of the present-day crisis of American civilization, an aspiring canonical historical reading that shapes the way in which literary canon formation itself ought to proceed and the kind of cultural archives that should constitute this formation. This reading is informed by a particular sense of history in which conflict, struggle and contestation are prominent. It accents the complex interplay of rhetorical practices (and their effects, for example, rational persuasion and intellectual pleasure) and the operations of power and authority (and their effects, for example, subordination and resistance).

My historical reading of the present cultural crisis begins with a distinctive feature of the twentieth century: the decolonization of the Third World associated with the historical agency of those oppressed and exploited, devalued and degraded by European civilization. This interpretive point of entry is in no way exhaustive—it does not treat other significant aspects of our time—yet neither is it merely arbitrary. Rather it is a world-historical process that has fundamentally changed not only our conceptions of ourselves and those constituted as "Others" (non-Europeans, women, gays, lesbians) but, more important, our understanding of how we have constructed and do construct conceptions of ourselves and others as selves, subjects and peoples. In short, the decolonization of the Third World has unleashed attitudes, values, sensibilities and perspectives with which we have yet fully to come to terms.

More specifically, the decolonization process signaled the end of the European age—an age that extends from 1492 to 1945. The eclipse of European domination and the dwarfing of European populations enabled the intellectual activities of demystifying European cultural hegemony and of deconstructing European philosophical edifices. In other words, as the prolonged period of European self-confidence came to an end with the emergence of the United States as the major world power after World War II, the reverberations and ramifications of the decline of European civilization could be felt in the upper reaches of the WASP elite institutions of higher learning—including its humanistic disciplines. The emergence of the first major subcultures of American non-WASP intellectuals as exemplified by the so-called New York intellectuals, the Abstract Expressionists and the bebop jazz artists constituted a major challenge to an American, male, WASP cultural elite loyal to an older and eroding European culture.

The first significant blow—a salutary one, I might add—was dealt when assimilated Jewish Americans entered the high echelons of the academy—especially Ivy league institutions. Lionel Trilling at Columbia, Oscar Handlin at Harvard and John Blum at Yale initiated the slow but sure undoing of male, WASP cultural homogeneity—that is, the snobbish gentility, tribal civility and institutional loyalty that circumscribed the relative consensus which rests upon the Arnoldian conception of culture and its concomitant canon. The genius of Lionel Trilling was to appropriate this conception for his own political and cultural purposes—thereby unraveling the old male WASP consensus yet erecting a new liberal academic consensus around the cold-war anticommunist rendition of the values of complexity, difficulty and modulation. In addition, the professionalization and specialization of teaching in the humanities that resulted from the postwar American economic boom promoted the close reading techniques of the New Critics—severed from their conservative and organicist anticapitalist (or anti-industrialist) ideology. Like Trilling's revisionist Arnoldian criticism, the New Critics' academic preoccupation with paradox, irony and ambiguity both helped to canonize modernist literature and provided new readers of literary studies with a formal rigor and intellectual vigor which buttressed beleaguered humanist self-images in an expanding, technocentric culture. The new programs of American studies provided one of the few discursive spaces—especially for second-generation immigrants with progressive sentiments—wherein critiques of the emerging liberal consensus could be put forward, and even this space was limited by the ebullient postwar American nationalism which partly fueled the new interdisciplinary endeavor and by the subsequent repressive atmosphere of McCarthyism, which discouraged explicit social criticism.

The sixties constitute the watershed period in my schematic sketch of our present cultural crisis. During that decade we witnessed the shattering of male, WASP, cultural homogeneity and the collapse of the short-lived liberal consensus. More pointedly, the inclusion of African Americans, Hispanic Americans, Asian Americans, Native Americans and American women in the academy repoliticized literary studies in a way that went against the grain of the old, male, WASP, cultural hegemony and the new, revisionist, liberal consensus. This repoliticizing of the humanities yielded disorienting intellectual polemics and inescapable ideological polarization. These polemics and this polarization focused primarily on the limits, blindnesses, and exclusions of the prevailing forms of gentility, civility, and loyalty as well as the accompanying notions of culture and canonicity.

The radical and thorough questioning of male, Euro-American, cultural elites by Americans of color, American women, and New Left white males highlighted three crucial processes in the life of the country. First, the reception of the traveling theories from continental Europe—especially the work of the Frankfurt School and French Marxisms, structuralisms and poststructuralisms. A distinctive feature of these theories was the degree to which they grappled with the devastation, decline and decay of European civilization since the defeat of fascism and the fall of the British and French empires in Asia and Africa. The American reception of these theories undoubtedly domesticated them for academic consumption. But the theories also internationalized American humanistic discourses so that they extended beyond the North Atlantic connection. For the first time, significant Latin American, African and Asian writers figured visibly in academic literary studies.

The second noteworthy process accelerated by the struggles of the sixties was the recovery and revisioning of American history in light of those on its underside. Marxist histories, new social histories, women's histories, histories of peoples of color, gay and lesbian histories, all made new demands of scholars in literary studies. Issues concerning texts in history and history in texts loomed large. The third process I shall note is the onslaught of forms of popular culture such as film and television on highbrow literate culture. American technology—under the aegis of capital—transformed the cultural sphere and everyday life of people and thereby questioned the very place, presence and power of the printed word.

The establishmentarian response in the humanities was to accommodate the new social forces. In order to avoid divisive infighting within departments and to overcome the incommensurability of discourses among colleagues, ideologies of pluralism emerged to mediate clashing methods and perspectives in structurally fragmented departments. These ideologies served both to contain and often conceal irresoluble conflict and to ensure slots for ambitious and upwardly mobile young professors who were anxiety-ridden about their professional-managerial class status and fascinated with their bold, transgressive rhetoric, given their relative political impotence and inactivity. Needless to say, conservative spokespersons both inside and especially outside the academy lamented what they perceived as an "assault on the life of the mind" and made nostalgic calls for a return to older forms of consensus. Contemporary reflections on ideologies of canon formation take their place within this context of cultural heterogeneity, political struggle and academic dissensus—a context which itself is a particular historical reading of our prevailing critical struggle for canonical status in the midst of the battle over literary canon formation.

Not surprisingly, attempts to justify and legitimate canon formation in African American literary criticism are made in the name of pluralism. In our present historical context (with its highly limited options), these efforts are worthy of critical support. Yet I remain suspicious of them for two basic reasons. First, they tend to direct the energies of African American critics toward scrutinizing and defending primarily African American literary texts for a new or emerging canon and away from demystifying the already existing canon. The mere addition of African American texts to the present canon without any explicit and persuasive account of how this addition leads us to see the canon anew reveals the worst of academic pluralist ideology. Serious African American literary canon formation cannot take place without a wholesale reconsideration of the canon already in place. This is so not because "existing monuments form an ideal order among themselves which is modified by the introduction of the new (the really new) work of art among them"—as T. S. Eliot posited in his influential essay "Tradition and the Individual Talent." Rather the interdependence of the canonical and noncanonical as well as the interplay of the old canonical texts and the new canonical ones again require us to examine the crucial role of our historical readings of the current crisis that acknowledges this interdependence and promotes this interplay. Mere preoccupation with African American literary texts—already marginalized and ghettoized in literary studies—which leads toward a marginal and ghetto status in an enlarged canon or independent canon, forecloses this broader examination of the present crisis and thereby precludes action to transform it.

This foreclosure is neither fortuitous nor accidental. Rather it is symptomatic of the class interests of African American literary critics: they become the academic superintendents of a segment of an expanded canon or a separate canon. Such supervisory power over African American literary culture—including its significant consulting activities and sometimes patronage relations to powerful, white, academic critics and publishers—not only ensures slots for black literary scholars in highly competitive English departments. More important, these slots are themselves held up as evidence for the success of prevailing ideologies of pluralism. Such talk of success masks the ever-growing power of universities over American literary culture and, more specifically, the increasing authority of black literary professional managers over African American literary practices and products. This authority cannot but have a major impact on the kinds of literary texts produced—especially as African American literary programs increasingly produce the people who write the texts. It is fortunate that Richard Wright, Ann Petry and Ralph Ellison did not labor under such authority. In fact, I would go as far as to postulate that the glacier shift from an African American literature of racial confrontation during the four decades of the forties to the seventies to one of cultural introspection in our time is linked in some complex and mediated way to the existential needs and accommodating values of the black and white literary professional-managerial classes who assess and promote most of this literature.

Lest I be misunderstood I am not suggesting that literary studies would be better off without African American literary critics or with fewer of them. Nor am I arguing that canon formation among African American critics ought not to take place. Rather I am making three fundamental claims. First, that African American canon formation regulated by an ideology of pluralism is more an emblem of the prevailing crisis in contemporary humanistic studies than a creative response to it. Second, that this activity—despite its limited positive effects such as rendering visible African American literary texts of high quality—principally reproduces and reinforces prevailing forms of cultural authority in our professionalized supervision of literary products. Third, that black inclusion in these forms of cultural authority—with black literary critics overseeing a black canon—primarily serves the class interests of African American literary academic critics.

A brief glance at the history of African American literary criticism—including its present state—bears out these claims. Like most black literate intellectual activity in the Western world and especially in the United States, African American literary criticism has tended to take a defensive posture. That is, it has viewed itself as evidence of the humanity and intellectual capacity of black people that are often questioned by the dominant culture. This posture is understandably shot through with self-doubts and inferiority anxieties. And it often has resulted in bloated and exorbitant claims about black literary achievement. In stark contrast to black artistic practices in homiletics and music, in which blacks' self-confidence abounds owing to the vitality of rich and varied indigenous traditions, black literary artists and critics have proclaimed a Harlem Renaissance that never took place, novelistic breakthroughs that amounted to poignant yet narrow mediums of social protest (for example, *Native Son*) and literary movements that consist of talented though disparate women writers with little more than their gender and color in common. Such defensive posturing overlooks and downplays the grand contributions of the major twentieth-century African American literary artists—Jean Toomer, Ralph Ellison, James Baldwin (more his essays than his fiction), Toni Morrison and Ishmael Reed. Such diminishment takes place because these authors arbitrarily get lumped with a group of black writers or associated with a particular theme in African American intellectual history, which obscures their literary profundity and accents their less important aspects.

For instance, Toomer's ingenious modernist formal innovations and his chilling encounter with black southern culture in *Cane* are masked by associating him with the assertion of pride by the "new Negro" in the twenties. Ellison's existentialist blues novelistic practices, with their deep sources in African American music, folklore, Western literary humanism, and American pluralist ideology, are concealed by subsuming him under a "post-Wright school of black writing." Baldwin's masterful and memorable essays that mix Jamesian prose with black sermonic rhythms are similarly treated. Toni Morrison's

magic realist portrayal of forms of African American cultural disruption and transformation links her more closely to contemporary Latin American literary treatments of the arrested agency of colonized peoples than with American feminist preoccupations with self-fulfillment and sisterhood. Last, Ishmael Reed's bizarre and brilliant postmodernist stories fall well outside black literary lineages and genealogies. In short, it is difficult to imagine an African American canon formation that does not domesticate and dilute the literary power and historical significance of these major figures.

Recent developments in African American literary criticism that focus on the figurative language of the texts are indeed improvements over the flat content analyses, vague black aesthetic efforts and political didacticism of earlier critics of African American literature. Yet this new black formalism—under whose auspices African American literary canon formation will more than likely take place—overreacts to the limits of the older approaches and thereby captures only select rhetorical features of texts while dehistoricizing their form and content. It ignores the way in which issues of power, political struggle and cultural identity are inscribed within the formal structures of texts and thereby misses the implicit historical readings of the crisis that circumscribes the texts and to which the texts inescapably and subtly respond.

This new formalism goes even farther astray when it attempts, in the words of critic Henry Louis Gates, Jr., to "turn to the Black tradition itself to develop theories of criticism indigenous to our literature." It goes farther astray because it proceeds on the dubious notion that theories of criticism must be developed from literature itself—be it vernacular, oral or highbrow literature. To put it crudely, this notion rests upon a fetishism of literature—a religious belief in the magical powers of a glorified set of particular cultural archives somehow autonomous and disconnected from other social practices. Must film criticism develop only from film itself? Must jazz criticism emerge only from jazz itself? One set of distinctive cultural archives must never be reducible or intelligible in terms of another set of cultural archives—including criticism itself. Yet it is impossible to grasp the complexity and multidimensionality of a specific set of artistic practices without relating it to other broader cultural and political practices at a given historical moment. In this sense, the move African American literary critics have made from a preoccupation with Northrop Frye's myth structuralism (with its assumption of the autonomy of the literary universe) and Paul de Man's rigorous deconstructive criticism (with its guiding notion of the self-reflexive and self-contradictory rhetorics of literary texts) to the signifying activity of dynamic black vernacular literature is but a displacement of one kind of formalism for another; it is but a shift from Euro-American elitist formalism to African American populist formalism, and it continues to resist viewing political conflict and cultural contestation within the forms themselves.

The appropriate role and function of opposition cultural critics regarding current forms of canon formation are threefold. First, we must no longer be literary critics who presume that our cultivated gaze on literary objects—the reified objects of our compartmentalized and professionalized disciplines—yields solely or principally judgments about the literary properties of these objects. There is indeed an inescapable evaluative dimension to any valid cultural criticism. Yet the literary objects upon which we focus are themselves cultural responses to specific crises in particular historical moments. Because these crises and moments must themselves be mediated through textual constructs, the literary objects we examine are never merely literary, and attempts to see them as such constitute a dehistoricizing and depoliticizing of literary

texts that should be scrutinized for their ideological content, role and function. In this sense, canon formations that invoke the sole criterion of form—be it of the elitist or populist variety—are suspect.

Second, as cultural critics attuned to political conflict and struggle inscribed within the rhetorical enactments of texts, we should relate such conflict and struggle to larger institutional and structural battles occurring in and across societies, cultures and economies. This means that knowledge of sophisticated versions of historiography and refined perspectives of social theory are indispensable for a serious cultural critic. In other words—like the cultural critics of old—we must simply know much more than a professional literary critical training provides. The key here is not mere interdisciplinary work that traverses existing boundaries of disciplines but rather the more demanding efforts of pursuing dedisciplinizing modes of knowing that call into question the very boundaries of the disciplines themselves.

Finally, cultural critics should promote types of canon formation that serve as strategic weapons in the contemporary battle over how best to respond to the current crisis in one's society and culture. This view does not entail a crude, unidimensional, instrumental approach to literature; it simply acknowledges that so-called noninstrumental approaches are themselves always already implicated in the raging battle in one's society and culture. The fundamental question is not how one's canon can transcend this battle but rather how old or new canons, enlarged or conflicting canons, guide particular historical interpretations of this battle and enable individual and collective action within it. I simply hope that as canon formation proceeds among African American cultural critics and others we can try to avoid as much as possible the pitfalls I have sketched.

4

Gerald Graff
1937–

Gerald Graff was born in Chicago and received his Ph.D. from Stanford University in 1963. He has taught at Northwestern University and currently teaches at the University of Chicago. His major publications approach the conflicts within modern literary studies from a wide range of disciplines dealing with pedagogy, cultural studies, history, criticism, education, and literary theory. His writings include *Poetic Statements and Critical Dogma* (1970), *Criticism in the University* (1985), *Literature Against Itself: Literary Ideas in Modern Society* (1979), *Beyond the Culture Wars: How Teaching the Conflicts Can Revitalize American Education* (1992), and *Adventures of Huckleberry Finn: A Case Study* (1995).

Many of his articles, such as "Other Voices, Other Rooms: Organizing and Teaching the Humanities Conflict" (1990) and "Teach the Conflicts" (1990), also deal with the problems inherent in the multifaceted and often fractured humanities. *Professing Literature: An Institutional History* (1987), possibly Graff's best-known work, illuminates the history of the dissonance in literary instruction that has existed in the instruction of literature in American universities, "roughly from the Yale Report in 1828 . . . to the waning of New Criticism in the 1960s." In his "Introduction: The Humanist Myth," Graff traces the origin of the cycle of displacement and the inability of the academy to present a well-functioning (much less a cohesive) policy of literary instruction to "the union of Arnoldian humanism and scientific research which gave birth to academic literary studies." Graff writes of his agreement with Marxist critic Terry Eagleton, who in *Literary Theory* says that literary studies is used for ends other than the study of literature. Graff sees such study as reflective of whichever academic ideal holds sway at a given time. Graff also says, as does Michel Foucault, that the very boundaries and classifications that are articulated by literary studies also define them. Unlike Eagleton and Foucault, however, Graff refuses to brand the attempt at classification as an evil. He "sees nothing inherently self-undoing or illegitimate about all idealizations such as deconstructionists do," nor does he think deconstructive criticism can "distinguish between legitimate and illegitimate forms of institutional or rhetorical power." At the same time, Graff rejects Allan Bloom's and E. D. Hirsch's recollection of a sentimental golden age of literary study in the American academy. Thus, Graff chooses to be a centrist and study the past to point out the divisions that have existed for the purpose of generating discussion and, perhaps, discovering ways of sharing and understanding the differences that do exist.

The remainder of Graff's book addresses specific patterns of conflict that emerge between the "traditional" approach of the time and whichever counterapproaches appear. Graff deals with each in a manner that is fascinating and immediate. He is willing to explore the complaints of Latin students or the confusion in the speeches of many Modern Language Association presidents who were trying to come to grips with a rapidly changing field.

Introduction: The Humanist Myth

When a sufficient number of specialists are assembled on a college faculty, the subject of which each knows only a small part is said to be covered, and the academic department to which they all belong is regarded as fully manned. In ancient Ireland, if legend is to be trusted, there was a tower so high that it took two persons to see to the top of it. One would begin at the bottom and look up as far as sight could reach, the other would begin where the first left off, and see the rest of the way.

—John Erskine

It's hard to organize literature.

—Irving Howe

Professing Literature is a history of academic literary studies in the United States, roughly from the Yale Report of 1828, which assured the primacy of the classical over the vernacular languages in American colleges for another half-century, to the waning of the New Criticism in the 1960s and subsequent controversies over literary theory. Strictly speaking, there were no "academic literary studies" in America or anywhere else until the formation of language and literature departments in the last quarter of the nineteenth century. But the use of literature as a vehicle of education goes back to ancient times, and in America since the Colonial era literary texts had been studied in college classes in Greek and Latin, English grammar, and rhetoric and elocution. These early practices assumed a theory of the social function of literature that affected the shape of literature departments when they finally emerged.

But the idea that literature could or should be taught—rather than simply enjoyed or absorbed as part of the normal upbringing of gentlefolk—was a novel one, and no precedents existed for organizing such an enterprise. To "organize literature" is difficult under any circumstances, but particularly when it means reconstituting as a curriculum under more or less democratic conditions something that had previously been part of the socialization of a particular class. My account suggests that this project was never thought through in all its ramifications, but, if anything, early educators were more alert to its difficulties than we are today, since they had the advantage of a historical perspective that was lost once academic literary studies became established and complacent and once it no longer could remember a preacademic literary culture for comparison.

Any single-volume treatment of so vast a subject must omit some matters and reduce others to schematic proportions. Though I refer generically to "academic literary studies" and "the literature department," most of my evidence is drawn from research-oriented departments of English at major universities, and I make only occasional attempts to distinguish patterns in English from those in other modern language departments or departments of comparative literature. Perhaps I ought to have subtitled the book "A History of English Studies," but I decided that essential traits have been similar enough to warrant the broader label.

My account does not do justice to the small-college experience, however. And I suspect that some of the conditions I treat as chronic dilemmas will be seen as grounds for envy in institutions where literature, as distinct from composition, has become a luxury. I deal only in passing with the teaching of composition, though the pioneer work of William Riley Parker, Wallace Douglas, and Richard Ohmann has shown that without that enterprise the teaching of literature could never have achieved its central status, and none of the issues I discuss would matter very much. I have made only occasional mention of British universities, despite the influence they exerted on native developments.

The aim of my concluding chapter is not to examine recent controversies over literary theory in detail—something outside the scope of this kind of book—but to point out how these controversies echo old ones as far back as the beginnings of the profession. My aim here is also to suggest that literary theory can help illuminate old and new conflicts in ways that might infuse some welcome self-consciousness into literary studies. As I use the term, there is a sense in which all teachers of literature are "theorists" and have a stake in theoretical disputes. For that matter, there is a sense in which a literature department (and curriculum) is itself a theory, though it has been largely an incoherent theory, and this incoherence strengthens the impression that the department has no theory.

It is possible to defend the infusion of theory into the curriculum on traditional grounds, namely, that students need theoretical concepts in order to be able to make sense of literature and talk about it intelligently. We shall see that until recently, in fact, the word "theory" was embraced by educational traditionalists, in reaction against the atomized empiricism of research and explication, which trusted that the accumulation of facts and interpretations about literature would somehow of itself add up to a coherent picture. This is not to deny that much current theory amounts to a radical attack on

the premises and values of traditional literary humanism. But such attacks on traditional literary humanism raise the kinds of questions about the nature and cultural functions of literature that used to be the concern of traditional humanists, even as they reject the traditional humanistic answers to those questions as no longer sufficient. The real enemy of tradition is the kind of orthodox literary study that neglects theoretical questions about ends, values, and definitions in the hope that they will take care of themselves. It was the breakdown of agreement (or ostensible agreement) on these questions that inspired the current theory explosion and ensures, I think, that it will not be a passing fad.

When I first began this inquiry I vaguely assumed that the founders of academic literary studies must originally have had a shared idea of their rationale that had somehow got lost along the way. I imagined that this shared rationale had something to do with concepts like "humanism" and "cultural tradition," more or less in the sense associated with the name of Matthew Arnold. What I discovered, however, was that although the transmission of humanism and cultural tradition in the Matthew Arnold sense was indeed the official goal of the literature department, there were from the outset fundamental disagreements about how that goal should be pursued. Early educators who identified themselves with the Matthew Arnold view of literature and culture strenuously objected to the philological and historical literary scholarship that had qualified literary studies for departmental status in the new research university.

The union of Arnoldian humanism and scientific research which gave birth to academic literary studies was never free from strain. Traditional humanists argued that the compartmentalization of literature in narrowly specialized and disconnected "fields" and the glorification of quantitative "production" in research tended to undermine Arnold's ideal of broad general culture and his view of literature as a coherent criticism of life. The research fetish seemed only another example of that triumph of practical and technical "machinery" over ethical and cultural ends that Arnold had deplored in so many features of the modern world—and that seemed peculiarly unrestrained in the United States.

It is worth pondering that the kind of scholarship we now think of as traditionally humanistic was regarded as a subversive innovation by the traditionalists of an earlier era, whatever its roots may have been in the classical humanism of the Renaissance. It is also worth pondering that traditional humanists of the same era indicted research scholarship for many of the very same sins for which later traditionalists indicted the New Criticism and present day traditionalists indict literary theory: elevating esoteric, technocratic jargon over humanistic values, coming between literature itself and the student, turning literature into an elitist pastime for specialists. Whatever the sins of recent theory, those who blame the problems of the humanities on them—and on other post-1960 developments—only illustrate their own pet maxim that those who forget the past are condemned to repeat it. The solutions they propose—a return to a great tradition with no investigation of why that tradition has come to be questioned—figures only to send us yet one more time around what we will see has been an oft-repeated cycle.

Of course the research scholars who were the targets of the earliest criticism did not see matters the way their critics did. They too saw themselves as legitimate heirs of Matthew Arnold, and they dismissed their detractors as dilettantes and victims of mere nostalgia, as many of them were. Even so, a surprising number of these early research scholars could not help agreeing with their critics that there was a disturbing disparity between their traditional humanistic ideals and their professional practices. They spent much of their time at the early meetings of the Modern Language Association exhorting one another to do something about the disparity, though few of them went beyond ineffectual assertions, reiterated countless times by now, that teaching should be restored to equal importance with research, that the "general culture" of the undergraduate college should be reasserted against the specialization of the graduate school, and (above all) that literature itself should somehow be restored to primacy over scholarship and methodology. The very nature of this diagnosis led the critics of the profession to lapse into fatalism, blaming their problems on the inherent philistinism of American democracy, the inherent vulgarity of the modern age, or the incurable inferiority of their students.

The complaint that research and publication have displaced teaching has always resembled the parallel complaint that technology or bureaucracy has displaced more human or communal relations. Whatever its justifications, such a complaint leads nowhere, for it envisages no role for the professional interests of the scholar except to extinguish themselves. The diagnosis on which the complaint rests blames the problems of the institution on the process of professionalization itself, not distinguishing between professionalism as such and the specific forms professionalism has taken under the peculiar circumstances of the new university, forms which—it must be stressed—need not be the only forms possible. But however limited their value as present guides, these early critics can at least cure us of the delusion that academic literary studies at some point underwent a falling-away from genuine Arnoldian humanism.

Helping prop up this humanist myth, however, is the habit of thinking of institutions as if they were unmediated projections of the values, methods, and ideologies of major individuals and movements. This procedure is convenient and seems to accord with common sense, but it ignores, for one thing, the substantial changes that even the dominant critical values, methods, and ideologies may undergo when they become institutionalized in the form of scholarly fields, curricula, and pedagogy. "Professionalization" and "academicization" are not neutral principles of organization, but agents that transform the cultural and literary-critical "isms" fed into them, often to the point of subverting their original purpose, or so deflecting them that they become unrecognizable to outsiders. What goes in is not necessarily what comes out, and this is one reason why the things the institution seems self-evidently to stand for to insiders may scarcely register on outsiders.

In calling this book an institutional history, I mean to underscore that its concern is not only with particular scholarly and critical practices, but also with what has happened to those practices once they have become institutionalized in modern universities—in ways that are not the only possible ones. My emphasis, in other words, is not only on what "goes on" in the shape of individual scholarly accomplishments and trends, but on what "comes out" as an operational totality and how that totality is perceived, misperceived, or not perceived at all by outsiders. Most histories of criticism properly ignore such matters and concentrate on major figures and movements, but for this reason their results may not yield a safe basis for an institutional analysis. For even major figures and movements can fail to stamp their values on the institution as a whole. In large degree Arnoldian humanism has been the outlook of singular individuals, individuals who have exerted a powerful and still-present influence on students and followers, but who have repeatedly failed to make their values visibly characteristic of the totality. Without going into the complex history of the term, we can note that already by the turn of the century, "Humanist"—in its association with Irving Babbitt and his group—was the name of one particular professional faction, one

"field" among many, more or less estranged from the established ones. It is no accident that many of the exemplary Arnoldian humanists from Babbitt to Walter Jackson Bate have ended up as bitter critics of the profession.

Their failure does not seem to me a state of affairs to be lamented, since it is after all the inability of their Arnoldian humanism to become an effective umbrella concept that has gradually opened academic literary studies to a variety of competing views of literature, scholarship, and culture. The discouraging thing is not that such institutional conflicts have gone unresolved—unresolved conflict being just the sort of thing a democratic educational system should thrive on—but how little of the potential educational value of such conflicts the professional system has been able to turn into part of what it studies and teaches, instead of a source of paralysis. Not all the conflicts of literary studies have been so esoteric as to lack potential interest to outsiders, and even those that have a large esoteric dimension (like the current cold war between theorists and humanists) have a surprising way of exemplifying cultural conflicts of potentially general interest. But educational-cultural battles tend at present to be fought out only behind the scenes, as it were, in specialized journals, technical vocabularies, and private faculty meetings. They are exemplified rather than foregrounded by the department and the curriculum and thus do not become part of the context of the average student's education or the average professor's professional life.

The pretense that humanism and the cultural tradition preside over the various dispersed activities of literary studies is one of the things which has permitted ideological conflicts to be kept out of public view. But another powerful cause lies in the field-coverage model of departmental organization, which has conceived literature departments as aggregates arranged to cover an array of historical and generic literary fields.

The field-coverage principle accompanied the modernization and professionalization of education of the 1870s and 1880s, when schools and colleges organized themselves into departments corresponding to what were deemed to be the major subjects and research fields. For reasons having to do equally with ensuring humanistic breadth and facilitating specialized research, the literature department adopted the assumption that it would consider itself respectably staffed once it had amassed instructors competent to "cover" a more or less balanced spread of literary periods and genres, with a scattering of themes and special topics.

The field-coverage principle seems so innocuous as to be hardly worth looking at, and we have lived with it so long that we hardly even see it, but its consequences have been far reaching. Its great advantage was to make the department and the curriculum virtually self-regulating. By assigning each instructor a commonly understood role—to cover a predefined period or field—the principle created a system in which the job of instruction could proceed as if on automatic pilot, without the need for instructors to debate aims and methods. Assuming individual instructors were competently trained—and the system of graduate work which developed rapidly in America after the 1890s took care of that—instructors could be left on their own to get on with teaching and research, with little need for elaborate supervision and management.

The second advantage of the field-coverage principle was to give the institution enormous flexibility in assimilating new ideas, subjects, and methods. In the model of education that had preceded the modern school or university, where a primary goal was to enforce a Christian religious and social ideology, any innovation that challenged the prevailing way of doing things was disruptive and had to be excluded or expelled. In the coverage model, by contrast, innovation even of a threatening kind could be welcomed by simply *adding* another unit to the aggregate of fields

to be covered. Fierce resistance to innovation arose frequently, of course, but since all instructors were on their own, the absorption of innovation did not oblige pre-established habits to change, so that in the long run—and increasingly it was not a very long run—resistance tended to give way. It is only the field-coverage principle that explains how the literature department has managed to avoid incurring paralyzing clashes of ideology during a period when it has preserved much of its earlier traditional orientation while incorporating disruptive novelties such as contemporary literature, black studies, feminism, Marxism, and deconstruction.

The field-coverage principle made the modern educational machine friction free, for by making individuals functionally independent in the carrying out of their tasks it prevented conflicts from erupting which would otherwise have had to be confronted, debated, and worked through. An invisible hand—fortified by the faith that humanism in the Matthew Arnold sense pervaded all the branches of the department's and the profession's activities—saw to it that the sum of the parts added up to a coherent whole. Yet these very strengths of the field-coverage principle were also liabilities. By making the teaching staff and the curriculum self-regulating, the principle let instructors get on with the job of teaching and research in an efficient and untroubled way, but it also relieved them of the need to discuss the reasons they were doing what they were doing. Organizational structure left the faculty without the need to confer about matters of fundamental concern with colleagues in their own and other departments. Not that there was any lack of controversy, of course—this has always been plentiful enough—but controversy was curiously screened from students and outsiders. The tacit assumption has been that students should be exposed only to the *results* of professional controversies, not to the controversies themselves, which would presumably confuse or demoralize them. The curriculum has been determined by political trade-offs, while the clashing principles that might at least have made the process edifying have been removed from view.

The division of fields according to the least controversial principles made the department easy to administer but masked its most interesting conflicts and connections. To put it another way, the field-coverage principle enabled administrative organization to take the place of principled thought and discussion. The presence of an array of fully staffed fields made it unnecessary for anybody to have a theoretical idea of the department's goals in order for it to get on with its work. The grid of literary periods, genres, and themes in the catalog was a sufficiently clear expression of what the department was about.

Critics objected to the department's compartmentalization as if that in itself was the problem, but division of labor is necessary in any bureaucraticized system. It was not the compartmentalizations which created the problem but their disconnection, which rendered invisible the relations and contrasts that could have forced the meanings of the department's divisions into relief. Since the courses in periods and genres did not address one another, teachers tended not to raise the question of what connections or contrasts the different periods and genres might bear to one another, what was meant by a particular periodization or by "period" in general, or what it might mean to approach literature in a historical or generic (and later a "New Critical") way. It was as if categories existed in order to make it unnecessary to think about them and to recognize that they were the product of theoretical choices.

By organizing itself on a principle of systematic non-relationship in which all parties tacitly agreed not to ask how they might be connected or opposed, the department prevented potentially edifying conflicts from becoming part of what literary studies was about. Students (and instructors) were thus deprived of a means of situating themselves in relation to the cultural issues of their time. For students learn not just by exposure to individual instructors, but by sensing how the teaching aggregate hangs together or divides, so that to obscure these relations robs students of one of the central means of making sense of education and the cultural world. Latent conflicts of method and ideology that had divided the faculty from the first did not have to be confronted; it was up to each instructor (within increasingly flexible limits) to determine method and ideology without correlation with one another. Thus, even though conflicts over method and ideology were becoming more frequent and intense as the profession developed, the myth of shared humanistic values and purposes could always be maintained. Not only was there no need to ask what theoretical assumptions underlay these values, the illusion could be kept up that nobody had a theory.

This effect operated vertically as well as horizontally, as the methodologies of literary study became detached from the cultural rationales that originally had given point to them. This pattern of detachment, whereby methods become separated from their goals, first arose in the pre-professional era, but professionalization, with its multiplication of technical methodologies, greatly intensified it. Usually the blame falls on the inherent tendency of methodology itself to become a monster grinding out research and criticism without their producers knowing why they are producing it. Again, however, it is arguably not methodology that necessarily invites such routinization, but a system which, by isolating functions, separates methodology from the contexts and theories which would keep its justifications visible.

The field-coverage principle effected at the administrative level what the humanist myth perpetuated at the level of ideology. In combination, the two provided a solution to the problem of how to "organize literature" that removed the need for continued collective discussion. Just as the literature faculty was self-regulating as long as periodization predefined the functions of individuals, literature was self-interpreting as long as it remained an expression of humanism. Hence there arose a curriculum that expressed the faith that exposure to a more or less balanced array of periods, genres, and themes would add up in the mind of the student to an appreciation of humanism and the cultural tradition. More succinctly, the assumption implicit in the humanist myth and the field-coverage principle has been that *literature teaches itself.* Since the literary tradition is presumably coherent in and of itself, it should naturally dictate the way teachers collectively organize themselves. That literature teaches itself is not necessarily the conscious assumption of individual teachers (though many have embraced it, as we will see), but something presupposed by the overall structure.

Unfortunately the assumption has never proved true—but the dream still persists that it might, if the encumbrances of scholarship, criticism, or theory could somehow be prevented from getting in the way. One of the recurrent motifs in the present history is the appeal to "literature itself" against various forms of commentary *about* literature as a cure for institutional dilemmas. The hope is that salvation can be achieved if only the great literary works can be freed from the institutional and professional encumbrances that come between students or laymen and the potency of the work itself. For a long time it was positivistic scholarship that was the target of this view, then it became analytic criticism, and today it has become literary theory and various attempts to historicize literature. But the basic form of the "literature itself" argument remains the same, bespeaking the perennial wish to believe that if the quality of individual instruction is good and the right works are taught, the effect of the whole will take care of itself.

Literary studies have not yet found a way to institutionalize the lesson of recent criticism that no text is an island, that every work of literature is a rejoinder in a conversation or dialogue that it presupposes but may or may not mention explicitly. It is in this spirit that Robert Scholes argues, in his recent book, *Textual Power,* that to teach the literary text one must teach the "cultural text" as well. Many instructors already do so, but individual pedagogy alone can have only limited effects when it conflicts with institutional structure. The disconnection between the divisions that organize the literature department and the university tends to efface the larger cultural conversation to which works of literature refer. The cultural text tends to fall into the cracks separating periods, genres, and fields, criticism, creative writing, and composition. Nobody is responsible for it since it is nobody's field—or else someone is responsible for it only as one field among others.

One might expect traditionalists to show some sympathy with such a conservatively historical argument as this, yet the idea still remains powerful that students are best introduced to literature by being put in "direct" contact with texts themselves, with a minimum of contextualizing interference. Those who hold this view cling to it tenaciously, believing it has been validated by the historical experience they have lived through for the past thirty or forty years. They recall so vividly the disastrously mechanical kinds of contextualizing they were subjected to under the old positivistic literary history that when they hear words like "contextualize," "historicize," and "theorize," they envision students even more bored and disaffected than they were before the New Criticism put the old historicism out of its misery. But the remedy for a poor contextualizing of literature is not no contextualizing but better contextualizing. That did not arise out of the compromise between New Criticism and background study that resolved disciplinary controversies after World War II. Nobody can doubt that the turn to "close reading" at that time constituted an immense improvement over what came before, but it has proved to be a short-term solution whose costs are now increasingly apparent. By treating the contexts of literature as an extrinsic matter, however important, the compromise between New Critical and historical pedagogy that stabilized literature departments over the past three or four decades has only reinforced the inveterate assumption that these contexts will take care of themselves if a balanced spread of fields is represented, and thus that they do not need to be collectively worked out or organized. By treating the contexts of literature as an extrinsic affair, the New Criticism made it all the more unnecessary to worry about how those contexts might be organized institutionally. But without a context, the student's "direct" experience of literature itself tends to result either in uncertainty or facile acquiescence in an interpretive routine.

Current radical critiques of academic literary studies have effectively exposed the pretensions of "unproblematic" appeals to literature itself, and my analysis often echoes them. I agree with Terry Eagleton's argument, in *Literary Theory,* that literary studies have arbitrarily narrowed the concept of "literature," and that the goal should be to repair the disabling dislocation of literature "from other cultural and social practices." I echo Foucault in looking at the way seemingly neutral, disciplinary classifications and boundaries actually constitute the fields they organize. Like certain deconstructionists, I am concerned with the way idealizations such as "humanism" have functioned rhetorically to mask the conflicts that constituted them.

At the same time, I see nothing inherently self-undoing or illegitimate about all idealizations, as the deconstructionists do, and I doubt that all institutional patterns can be explained as effects of ideology, power, "logocentrism," or subjugation. Valuable as they are, these forms of critique seem to lack a criterion that would enable them to distinguish between legitimate and illegitimate forms of institutional or rhetorical power. Furthermore, they tend to accept the same working model of institutional history as the traditionalists, merely "reinscribing" it in an accusatory vocabulary. Like the Right, the Left mistakes pious wishes and pronouncements for institutional fact. A case in point is Eagleton's account of the rise and development of "English" as a project of "controlling and incorporating the working class" through the consolidation of the national literature.

There is some truth in this "social control" theory of academic literary studies, for many members of the founding generation did conceive these studies explicitly and openly as a means of reinstating cultural uniformity and thus controlling those unruly democratic elements that were entering higher education for the first time after the Civil War. What Eagleton describes in England was true in the United States as well, that "in the work of 'English' pioneers like F. D. Maurice and Charles Kingsley, the emphasis was on solidarity between the social classes, the cultivation of 'larger sympathies,' the instillation of national pride and the transmission of 'moral' values." But the question remains, how successfully was this nationalistic mission for literary studies carried out? Did the ideology of the founders remain "the distinctive hallmark of literary studies" down to the present, as Eagleton claims?

If their testimony can be taken seriously, those who most wanted the mission to succeed thought it had failed right from the start. The hope that the study of English would restore national leadership to the academic custodians of high culture disintegrated very clearly. On the one hand, high literary culture was increasingly marginal to the commercial and corporate interests dominating modern life, making laughable the pretensions of the literary elite to cultural leadership. On the other hand, even within the university the old elite was losing control—at least it complained bitterly that the new academic professionalism tended to place the interests of the research field above the interests of the nation. Underlying the animus of many early Arnoldian humanists against the professional research industry was the view that research sacrificed literature's potential as an instrument of socialization to the narrow interests of a professional clique. Although the turn of the century saw the imposition of a uniform canon of English literature, traditionalists complained that the curriculum had all but dissipated the civic potential of the canon by breaking it up into such disconnected fragments that students could get no clear sense of its unity. Far from being organized on a centralized logocentric model, the American university is itself something of a deconstructionist, proliferating a variety of disciplinary vocabularies that nobody can reduce to the common measure of any metalanguage. This in fact is one of the reasons why such institutions are so hard to change.

My evidence, in any case, suggests that professionalization not only failed to turn academic literary studies into the effective instrument of nationalist ideology some of the founders hoped they would be, but in some ways it subverted that ideology. Again, the American situation may have to be distinguished from that of France and England, where the traditional social elites were more powerful and more able to resist professionalization than were their counterparts in the United States. In the American university, the frustration of cultural nationalism is particularly obvious in the late and grudging academic recognition according to America's national literature, which was at first excluded from departments because it did not suit the prevailing research methods and then, when at last incorporated, proceeded to be so assimilated to those methods that its coherence as an expression of the national spirit was rendered all but invisible. Professional literary studies would not have encountered so many problems of identity had they not come into being at the

very moment when the principle of nationality, for most of the nineteenth century the major way of conceptualizing literature as a whole, was losing its effectiveness.

The point needs to be kept in mind when considering recent critiques of the canon. Unquestionably, the exclusion of blacks, women, and other heterodox traditions from the canon has had major ideological effects. What is prevented from "going in" to begin with can hardly have an effect on what comes out. But this is not to say that what comes out is ideologically of a piece. When critics like Jane Tompkins argue that the academic remaking of the American literature canon gave "the American people a conception of themselves and their history," they fail to ask whether the canon was ever taught homogeneously or effectively enough to convey a clear conception of the national spirit to students, much less to "the American people" as a whole. In order to specify the ideological effects of the canon, it should be necessary to do more than make inferences from the canonized texts and interpretations. Though recent reader-centered criticism has taught us that readers appropriate texts in heterogeneous ways, this lesson tends to be forgotten when the ideology of the canon is at stake.

Both the accusatory and the honorific view of literary studies—which turn out, curiously, to be the same view—rest on wishful thinking. They credit the institution with a more cohesive impact than it has ever achieved. Like other inventions of the Progressive Era, academic literary studies have combined class, ethnic, and gender prejudices with a genuinely democratic egalitarianism—that is what has made it possible for radical critics to find a home in them. Literary studies have been no beacon of political enlightenment, but they have not been an instrument of dominant ideology and social control either—or, if so, they have been a singularly inefficient one.

As I have told it, then, the story of academic literary studies in America is a tale not of triumphant humanism, nationalism, or any single professional model, but of a series of conflicts that have tended to be masked by their very failure to find visible institutional expression. This emphasis on conflicts is seen in the successive oppositions that organize my narrative: classicists versus modern-language scholars; research investigators versus generalists; historical scholars versus critics; New Humanists versus New Critics; academic critics versus literary journalists and culture critics; critics and scholars versus theorists. These controversies have seemed to me to possess greater richness and vitality than any of the conclusions they led to about the nature of literary studies as a discipline or the nature of literature as an object. Among the matters in dispute have been not just the nature of literature and the discipline, but whether there is—or needs to be—such a thing as a "discipline" of literary studies at all, or such a thing as "literature" in some univocal sense, as opposed to a variety of different literary and critical activities made coherent, if at all, only by their conflicts. If one conflict subsumes the others in my story, however, it is the one which has pitted scholars against critics. We tend to forget that until recently the terms were considered antithetical: scholars did research and dealt with verifiable facts, whereas critics presided over interpretations and values, which supposedly had no objective basis and therefore did not qualify for serious academic study. This state of affairs changed so rapidly that the implications of the change hardly had time to be assessed. Whereas "academic criticism" had been a contradiction in terms, it suddenly became a redundancy, as criticism, once the province of nonacademic journalists and men of letters, became (with impor-tant exceptions) virtually the monopoly of university departments.

Yet the old antagonism of scholar and critic did not disappear as much as it became submerged, after World War II, in an atmosphere where methodological and conceptual progress seemed more desirable than ideological confrontation. Many of the old issues reappeared under a realignment of the parties that has now set scholars and critics on the same side in opposition to theorists. Among these issues are the nature of literature (or whether it has a nature), the nature of literary interpretation and evaluation, the relation between the "intrinsic" domain of literature and the "extrinsic" ones of history, society, philosophy, and psychology, and above all, the issue of whether or in what way literature should be historicized and assimilated to social and political contexts.

Those who argue that the humanities have become disablingly incoherent seem to me right, but many of them fail to see that coherence can no longer be grounded on some restored consensus, whether it be traditional "basics," revolutionary ideological critique, or something else. In the final analysis, what academic literary studies have had to work with is not a coherent cultural tradition, but a series of conflicts that have remained unresolved, unacknowledged, and assumed to be outside the proper sphere of literary education. To bring these conflicts inside that sphere will mean thinking of literary education as part of a larger cultural history that includes the other humanities as well as the sciences even while acknowledging that terms like "humanities," "science," "culture," and "history" are contested.

Gauri Viswanathan

1950–

Gauri Viswanathan is a professor of English and comparative literature at Columbia University, where she also earned her Ph.D. Her publications in cultural and Asian studies includes "Raymond Williams and British Colonialism: The Limits of Metropolitan Cultural Theory" (1993); "English in a Literature Society" (1992); and perhaps her best-known work, *Masks of Conquest: Literary Study and British Rule in India* (1989), from which the following selection was taken.

"Lessons of History," the book's fifth chapter, details the shift in Indian English studies "from the rhetorical tradition of belles lettres to the historical study of literature." Warren Hastings attempted in the 1780s to popularize Charles Wilkins's translation of the *Bhagavad Gita,* but the poem was so different from Western epics that Western readers had no standards by which to judge the work. This confusion encouraged a new way of reading: rather than apply "imperishable standards" derived from Greek and Roman classics, readers could learn about Indian society from the texts themselves, then judge that society by its values and customs as revealed in the literature. The focus shifted from discovering the timeless beauty of the work to identifying in it historically specific social practices that were more or less worthy of emulation in the present. The British developed this new approach to deal with Indian texts, then later taught it to Indian subjects.

James Mill, a practitioner of a kind of utilitarian criticism, found Indian works such as the *Ramayana* and the *Mahabharata* to (falsely) reconcile contradictory moral stances under the aegis of Brahminism. What was needed, he argued, was to reseparate these moral elements, as well as to understand them literally and not allegorically. To mediate contradictory morals and to read allegorically as Indians did was, for Mill, to sanctify immorality; it was to pretend that the immorality plainly visible on the surface (for example, Draupadi's marrying five men) does *not* count, and that only the allegorical moral message (the union of Lakshmi with Vishnu, "of whom the five Pandavas are merely manifestations") *does* count. In contrast, analytical readings of the British kind would ostensibly teach self-improvement, ambition, and a critical, moral approach to life—the personality characteristics Adam Smith collectively called the impartial spectator.

Smith's view of the self assumes an internal division—a good self that monitors and improves a bad self; however, paradoxically, the historical approach to literature at the same time posits an inherently, wholly good Indian self that is only "thwarted from realizing itself by a despotic, corrupt political society" (namely, its own). The new British imperial approach to reading, then, fulfilled two objectives: "rousing Indians to a consciousness of the inconsistencies in the native system of society while simultaneously leading them to a recognition of the principles of order and justice in the Western [system]." The Indian reader was "taken *back* to a true self" which British government and Western texts exemplified. "By this logic, the good that England represented for India constituted the only valid content of instruction for its youth," and in this way, justifying colonial power on many levels while effacing the signs of its existence, English studies in India became an important part of the colonialist project. Viswanathan offers several examples from English exams written by Indians that demonstrate how very well students internalized the desired literary and historical attitudes.

Lessons of History

And so they who listened with rapture to the songs of the bards overran the provinces of those who were charmed with the fairy tale.

—*Asiatic Journal* (1831), 32:142

The orientation of literary study to the cultural heritage contained in a national past is a fairly new phenomenon, displacing an older rhetorical tradition. The inaugural lecture of A. J. Scott at University College, London, in 1848 is said to be the earliest instance of a formal academic plea for the study of literature as an expression of the culture of an age and as a reflection of society. By 1852 the historical study of English literature was firmly established in University College. In 1875 the alliance between literature and history was given institutional expression with the merging of the chair of English literature with that of history. Never very stable or clear on the point of the relationship between language and literature, English as a discipline became even more blurred and confused when a separate chair was created for English language in that same year.

The transition from the rhetorical tradition of belles lettres to the historical study of literature is explained as a displacement of Renaissance conceptions of language that "removed attention from the situation of utterance and located all significance in the logic of language, which was determined by nonlinguistic consid-

erations."[1] With the passing of the old rhetorical traditions, the study of literary genres gradually became oriented in literary history. Present-oriented and context-bound, the formal method of disputation gave way to the authority of preexisting structures of mind and society as the prime catalyst of knowledge. The choice was *against* a kind of intellectual inquiry directed toward the present in favor of one based on the authority of established usage, historical precedent, and social convention. The object of literary training is understood as twofold: first, to develop a historical awareness of the cultural moments in which those usages, precedents, and conventions are especially strong; and second, to reclaim those moments as exemplary instances of truth, coherence, and value.

Linking "this new historical and organic awareness of society" to the Romantic reaction against the Industrial Revolution and its impoverishment of cultural life, D. J. Palmer describes the emphasis on order, continuity, sequence, and moral purpose as an internal shift within English studies, "the immediate condition alike of a revivified approach to classical studies, and of a social philosophy such as Coleridge's to bind the present with the past."[2]

Described thus, the shift within English studies appears to have an inner logic and consistency, but the description is marked by a curious reticence to account for those external conditions that produce or require any such shift from present to past, from rhetoric to history. It is not clear how exactly the "logic of language" is determined by "nonlinguistic considerations" (at best an ambiguous phrase); it is even less clear why that should cause an alliance of literature with history. To explain this development solely in terms of widened conceptions of language, with the rhetorical study of argumentation giving way to the appreciation of style as cultural expression, is to confine discussion of the development of English studies to changes merely at the level of form.

To study the institutionalization of these shifts it is impossible to evade the political context of expanding territorial control and power in which the merging of literature and history was first seriously considered and then actively urged as a principle of study and criticism. Though the influence of the Western encounter with alien cultural and literary forms on the formation of nineteenth-century English studies is not the subject of this book or this chapter, it is still necessary to signal the partial history that results from the persistent disregard of Britain's colonial involvement in producing new articulations of literary functions, unless of course such study is somehow construed to be threatening to the integrity of the British intellectual, cultural, and social tradition as a source of literary judgments.[3]

I am aware that one of the problems involved in pursuing this line of inquiry, where connections between confrontation with different cultures and societies and redefinitions of literary value are not that readily established empirically, is that of confusing the logical with the historical. That is to say, in an effort to understand the relations between English studies and colonialism there is always the danger of claiming an overriding determinism in the relation. To proceed from this assumption and draw conclusions from it is to ignore entirely that the relations may be largely historical; that is, that they

occur in the form that they do, not because they are locked in a mutuality of cause-effect determination, but because the situations with which they were complicit produced such particular, detailed effects on subsequent action and policy that they render the history of English studies incomplete by itself, as is the study of colonial expansion, without reference to the mutually supportive role that each played in response to Britain's confrontation with peoples and cultures different from its own.

The reading of literature as an expression of culture and society has an opaque, textured history in British India. It dates back to the early Anglicist-Orientalist debates out of which emerged redefinitions of truth as the discovery of error. . . . [T]he relativization of cultures necessitated by the dialectical progression toward truth through error promoted literary study as intellectual exercise. English studies established itself in direct dialectical interplay with the Eastern tradition, taking the totality of Indian society and culture, its contradictions and anomalies, as a reference point for critical formulations that eventually fed into pedagogical practice. Given the fact that the British ruling in India were administrators and not literary critics, it is not surprising that the multiple realities of India with which they had to deal would force an expansion of the traditional framework within which literature was normally discussed to include other levels of India represented by its laws, religion, government, and social institutions.

Warren Hastings unwittingly opened the door to historical approaches to literature when he sought to popularize the translation of the *Bhagavad Gita* by Charles Wilkins, who had presented him with a copy of it in 1784, when he was governor-general of Bengal. Hastings had a difficult time reconciling the literati of the West to a poem so wholly different in structure, style, and substance from the classical models of Greece and Rome that centuries of study and imitation had consecrated. He attempted to win acceptance for the work by persuading Western literati to suspend for a while the "imperishable standards" of classical criticism:

> Might I, an unlettered man, venture to pre-scribe bounds to the latitude of criticism, I should exclude, in estimating the merit of such a production, all rules drawn from the ancient or modern literature of Europe, all ref-erences to such sentiments or manners as are become the standards of propriety for opinion and action in our own modes of life, and equally all appeals to our revealed tenets of re-ligion and moral duty. I should exclude them, as by no means applicable to the language, sentiments, manners, or morality appertain-ing to a system of society with which we have for ages been unconnected. . . . I would exact from every reader the allowance of obscurity, absurdity, barbarous habits, and a perverted morality. Where the reverse appears, I would have him receive it as much clear gain, and al-low it a merit proportioned to the disappoint-ment of a different expectation.[4]

Though Hastings' motive was to have the *Gita* read without undue comparisons to Western lit-erature, his argument had the effect of referring critics to that "system of society with which we have for ages been unconnected" to derive those principles empirically.

In the hands of a critic like James Mill, the derivation of standards of art by empirical meth-ods became a devastating rationale for evaluat-ing art not in relation to intrinsic properties, but in relation to a doctrine of utility that ap-proached works in terms of the social and reli-gious practice they threw open for examination.[5] To deploy his theory of historicist readings in practical criticism, Mill turned to William Jones as his foil. Jones' admiration for Indian litera-ture and the favorable comparisons with West-ern literature that he made on its behalf are witheringly dismissed by Mill as naive responses made solely at the level of form. Jones had pro-claimed Kalidas the Shakespeare of India and had himself undertaken the translation of *Shakuntala*. Admittedly, Mill's quarrel was not with the lyricism of the play; he even grudgingly conceded *Shakuntala* to be a perfect example of pastoral. His main objections were to Jones' be-lief that the features of pastoral, marked by "courtesy and urbanity, a love of poetry and elo-quence, and the practice of exalted virtues,"[6] were an adequate measure of a perfect society. For Mill, this was a woefully uncritical stance, evidence that Jones had succumbed to the se-ductive pleasures of a literary genre that ob-scured consciousness of the evil social practices prevalent at the time. Using Jones as a perfect example of an ahistorical reader, Mill set out to show that only a historicist reading truly re-vealed the meaning of pastoral: namely, that it is a literary form produced by nations in their in-fancy, when individuals remained so fettered by the tyranny of despotic government that social criticism of any kind had to give way to indul-gence in light romances. Mill's real message, of course, is that the more responsibility in govern-ment a people are given, the more occupied they will be with the business of state and the less prone, therefore, to pure fiction or poetry.

Mill read the lyricism and sentiment in In-dian drama as a mark of a self-indulgent society and that in turn as the product of a despotic state. Developing his theory of art simultane-ously with his theory of civilization, he main-tained that the quality of government is largely responsible for channeling the energies of the individual to work for the common good. In the ancient despotic states, the individual primarily strove for self-gratification, which became the value by which he lived. Everything that he did and produced, even his art, was a reflection of his incapacity to perceive a higher good or duty.

The social values that *Shakuntala* celebrates—superstition, extravagant belief, and arbitrary will—appeared to prove Mill's point. He inter-preted exaggeration in art as a reflection of in-consistencies in the laws and institutions of the society from which it springs and for which it is intended. A social practice that he found irreconcilable with the notions of a "refined" people is the marriage that takes place in the forest between the hero and heroine in *Shakuntala* or, in his words, "that kind of marriage which two lovers contract from the desire of amorous embraces."[7] Another custom sanctioned by Hindu society that figures in the plot of the play is the obeisance traditionally given the Brahmins. The cause of the heroine's misfortune is a Brahmin who lays a curse on her because she had neglected to receive him at the hermitage with the expected honors. Far from showing the Brahmin as an evil force whose power is to be resisted, the play merely uses his curse as a device to add a twist to the plot: "Surely no contrivance for such a purpose was ever less entitled to admiration than the curse of a Brahmen."[8] That is to say, the narrative contrivances in Sanskrit literature are not merely reflective of a childish imagination but have more sinister overtones, for they deliberately thwart reflection upon those same practices that are the source of the Indians' "degradation."

Oddly, Mill offered the kind of reading that, almost a century and a half later, Lévi-Strauss was to give in his studies of myth and culture. In much the same way that Mill interpreted the narrative structure of Indian drama as perpetuating the beliefs and practices of Hindu society, Lévi-Strauss read the structure of myth as a coded message by means of which a culture offers models of belief and action to its individual members.[9] In order to decode the message and probe the sources that give it form, the critical observer had first to break that form and recast the myth in a non-narrative mode. It is precisely in such an act that Lévi-Strauss believed the inherent contradictions of the social system are exposed.

Lévi-Strauss explains the power of myth in terms of a concept—that of mediation—that is useful in explaining the British disapproval of Indian literature on moral grounds. Essentially, mediation refers to the contrived resolution, by means of a tale or legend, of self-contradictions within a morality; for example, a society's practice of incest is mediated in the Oedipus myth by oracular prophecies and divine agencies. *Shakuntala* is replete with comparable instances of mediation, one of which is the aforementioned transformation of the Brahmin's curse from an ugly social fact to a narrative device that invokes religious mystery and awe. Other instances involve the attitude that the reader is expected to have toward King Dushyanta, who promises to send for his new bride, Shakuntala, and not only fails to do so, but rejects her when she appears at his court with his child. Were it not for yet another narrative contrivance, the lost ring, Dushyanta's callousness would have quite possibly been seen by the contemporary audience as a fairly accurate representation of the way royal personages treated women—a theme that a court dramatist like Kalidas could have pursued only with grave consequences to himself. The ring is brought into the story to offset this impression. Dushyanta is doomed by the Brahmin's curse to forget Shakuntala when it is lost. When it is found and the memory of her comes back to him, he is smitten by remorse for having rejected her. But such moments of awareness of personal guilt are not permitted to last long, and in mediating between actions and individual responsibility there is always the suggestion of external agency. The cause of her current misfortunes, Shakuntala explains to Dushyanta, is not the king or even the Brahmin who cursed her, but the sins of her past life.

The concept of mediation is also useful in explaining why the Hindu epics the *Ramayana* and the *Mahabharata* were regarded as problematic works and not readily assimilable as texts for instruction in Indian schools and colleges in British India. The contradictions in these two epics could not be explained away other than as the superimposition of Brahminical readings on what presumably originated as the heroic songs of the Kshatriyas (the second order in the caste hierarchy). A case in point is the polyandry of the heroine Draupadi in the *Mahabharata,* a practice that evidently existed in pre-Brahminical times but could not possibly have continued into the Brahminical era. British commentators explained the continuing presence of polyandry in the later versions as an attempt by the Brahmins to allegorize events in order to justify the epic as divine truth. The moral repugnance that would normally have been aroused in the reader by the literal fact of Draupadi marrying five men is mediated by a Brahminic interpretation that considers the marriage a symbolic union of the goddess Lakshmi with her consort Vishnu, of whom the five Pandavas are merely manifestations.

Ironically, it is the internal process of moralization in Indian literature—of assigning a deeper significance through allegory to a social custom that is otherwise distasteful—that struck the most discordant chords for British commentators, far more perhaps then the custom itself, for undesirable social practices, if understood as historical fact bound to a certain time and place, did not have the power to influence behavior and action in the same way that their transformation into abstract universal principles did. When allegorized, these social customs received a sanctity that prevented the reader from distinguishing a moral act from an immoral one. The Indian's insufficient sense of decency was directly attributed to the texts they read from their own tradition, which blurred distinctions between decency and indecency.[10] Morality became urgently linked to the development of a historical consciousness through which alone the reader would learn to sift fact from legend, for if it was true that "wild symbolic form and mysterious allegory formed a hieratic character in which events of the past were recorded,"[11] it was imperative to undo that form and recast it in another where the signs would be easily interpretable.

Accurate interpretation of signs therefore acquired a moral significance far surpassing any utilitarian function that might have otherwise been assigned. A great deal of research undertaken by Europeans on the historical basis of the two epics was motivated in large part by an urge to demystify and de-Brahminize them. Of the historians who were engaged in this task, J. Talboys Wheeler, who taught for some time at Presidency College, Madras, and in 1862 became assistant secretary to the government, most clearly and consciously aimed at separating fact from legend in the act of reconstructing India's past from the *Ramayana* and the *Mahabharata.* In telling the history of India from its literature, he deliberately set out to de-allegorize and to focus attention on the social practices themselves: "Every legend and tradition has been systematically Brahmanized for the purpose of bringing all the religious laws and usages of the different races of India into conformity with Brahmanical ideas. When stripped of these Brahmanical grafts and overgrowth, the legends and traditions will be found to furnish large illustrations of old Hindu civilization."[12] The large number of histories written by Englishmen that were part of the literature curriculum in Indian schools and colleges no doubt performed the same function, which was essentially analytic in nature. Among the histories of India prescribed for study were Marshman's *History of Bengal* and *History of India,* Murray's *History of India, with Readings from Mill and Other Authors,* and Henry Morris' *History of India.*[13] A point that British critics returned to with remarkable consistency was that as long as Indian youth were without a historical consciousness, they would remain shackled to the tyranny of forms. The curricular juxtaposition of historical texts with native literature was part of an effort to break through those forms; as a study in contrasting modes of explanation, the juxtaposition offered the means to developing an analytical cast of mind required for dismantling inherited structures and myths. If the genius of Sanskrit literature synthesized and harmonized disparate elements to fit a Brahminical conception, the whole thrust of historical instruction during the period of British rule was to break them down and force a steady gaze on each element in isolation. History was transformed into nothing less than the recasting of myth in a non-literary mode by means of which the discordancies of Hindu society were forced into the open.

Incidentally, one of the ways that nationalism sought to express itself in the 1870s and 1880s was by restoring allegorical readings to legends that were denounced by the British for their licentiousness. Often the inspiration for such readings came from commentaries produced in the Orientalist period, which defiantly transformed what Anglicists attacked as sensual images in Hindu art into representations of spirit:

> Whenever I look around me, in the vast region of Hindoo mythology, I discover piety in the garb of allegory: and I see Morality, at every turn, blended with every tale; and as far as I can rely on my own judgment, it appears the most complete and ample system of Moral Allegory that the world has ever produced. . . . We satisfactorily learn from the Geeta that it is not mere images, but the invisible spirit, that they thus worship.[14]

The theosophist and nationalist leader Annie Besant, for example, took the cue from her Orientalist predecessors by reading the tale of Lord Krishna (the "philanderer-god") stealing the clothes of maidens while they were bathing as an allegory about the nakedness of the soul approaching Supreme Being.[15] Such readings were a conscious revolt against a narrow British historicism threatening to break the continuity of a popular Hindu consciousness, whose strength lay in the ability to transcend the immediate and the particular and to bring together various segments of society through an appeal to the universal and the timeless.

Gandhi, however, went a little further back than Annie Besant, to the British representations themselves, and claimed that Europeans tended to look for deeper significances in Hindu customs and practices, which were then invariably equated with the obscene:

> It has remained for our Western visitors to acquaint us with the obscenity of many practices which we have hitherto innocently indulged in. It was in a missionary book that I first learnt that Shivalingam [a Hindu phallic symbol] had any obscene significance at all and even now when I see a Shivalingam neither the shape nor the association in which I see it suggests any obscenity. It was again in a missionary book that I learnt that the temples in Orissa were disfigured with obscenities. When I went to Puri, it was not without an effort that I was able to see those things. But I do know that the thousands who flock to the temple know nothing about the obscenity surrounding these figures.[16]

An important aspect of Gandhi's observation is that in the name of separating fact from legend, British readings had introduced a literalism that was paradoxically allegorical in effect, for it assumed that every sign had to have a meaning, whereas for Hindus this was not necessarily true. Instead, a sign could easily do no more than suggest another sign, which in turn might suggest yet another, and so on. The process could continue *ad infinitum* without ever getting beyond the act of signifying, which is perfectly consistent with the Hindu belief that all phenomena are multiple manifestations of a single entity that alone has meaning but is at the same time unknowable.

But the British argument was that there was no clearer proof of the childishness of the Indian mind than its inability to pierce through the outer layers of form. If Indians failed to perceive meanings, the argument went, it was not because the signs did not contain any, but because the Indians lacked the mental capacity to see that a concrete reality lay behind these signs that was both a cause and an explanation for them. The act of forcing meanings into the open comprised an important aspect of the British ideology of literary education, owing much to critical readings of the kind produced by James Mill.

In every respect, the historical orientation to literary study reverses the assumptions and rationale of Christian instruction or, at the very least, provides a new set of terms. One such inversion is concerned with conceptions of human nature. If, according to the doctrinal basis of Christianity, man is inherently depraved and in a state of original sin, the object of an education on Christian principles is to raise individuals from the state of bestial nature in which they are born, toward the spiritual good that is their eternal promise. Whatever distinguishes man from beasts becomes the instrument of his regeneration. As Lionel Gossman points out, given the fact that there is no greater distinguishing feature than the uniquely human ability to manipulate symbolic systems, language and literature acquire an importance exceeding that of even science and technology.[17] Early British arguments for literary instruction assumed a condition of innate depravity, and the rhetoric of dualism ensuing from that assumption demarcated a "cultivated" self formed by learning, language, and literature from a "natural" self still burdened by sin, willful pride, and vileness of temperament. Clerical attacks on Utilitarian principles in education emphasized the Christian progress toward the ideal self through literature, as in the following remarks, made to the commencement audience at Cambridge in 1826 by the Rev. Hugh James Rose, later to be principal of King's College, London: "[Literature] is not partial in its cultivation of the intellect, but tends at once to correct the taste, to strengthen the judgement, *to instruct us in the wisdom of men better and wiser than ourselves,* to exercise the reasoning faculties on subjects which demand and deserve their attention, and to show them the boundaries imposed on them by Providence" (emphasis mine).[18] Rose's remark assumes a gap between the reader and the text: the reader's deficiencies are understood as the result of an innately vile and depraved nature, while the text is designated as the superior agency to lead the malformed individual to a plane of superior moral being.

It is not necessary to limit ourselves to the most obvious instances where such distinctions were routinely made, such as in the missionary curriculum in literature, to gain some sense of the widespread prevalence of such characterizations of literary functions, presupposing a dualism of man's base self and his higher nature. Significantly, much the same characterization informed Adam Smith's understanding of the uses of literature to offset the ill-effects of a crass materialism produced by laissez-faire individualism. Smith's *Theory of Moral Sentiments* (1759) remained a central text in the Indian curriculum throughout the nineteenth century, both in government and missionary institutions—the Calcutta University Commission Report of 1919, for instance, still listed it as part of the prescribed course of studies. Though it was well over a century before his proposals were implemented, Adam Smith was evidently among the earliest thinkers to propose the study of selections from the works of English prose writers as a social and moral corrective for dangers that he believed were inherent in laissez-faire capitalism, particularly dangers associated with the potential for a morally corrupted concept of individualism.[19]

In *Moral Sentiments* Adam Smith argued the need for a broad academic program that would encourage and direct a process of self-evaluation and self-enlightenment. His work can be read as a systematic argument for the education of the man of intellect who is also a man of good conduct and virtue. Smith began by noting a principle inherent in man's nature, which he called the impartial spectator, that makes him responsive to how others think and behave. Those who are able to direct our sentiments are models of intellectual virtue: the "man of taste," for instance, "who distinguishes the minute and scarce perceptible differences of beauty and deformity" or the "experienced mathematician who unravels with case the most intricate and perplexed proportions."[20] Smith believed that through the admiration of the sentiments of these "others," these learning models, we come to realize the existence of intellectual virtues. The impartial spectator, the spectator within us, as Smith referred to him, "enters by sympathy into the sentiments of the master" and "views the object under the same agreeable aspect."[21] The task before us, Smith claimed, if we truly wish to realize the intellectual virtues, is to cultivate the impartial spectator within us, to develop the ability to place ourselves in the context of those sentiments. The study of literature, Smith argued, provides the formative structures that will determine the development of this spectator within. Through literature, he wrote, "we endeavour to examine our own conduct as we imagine any other fair and impartial spectator would examine it. If, upon placing ourselves in his situation, we thoroughly enter into all the passions and motives which influenced it, we approve of it, by sympathy with the approbation of this supposed equitable judge. If otherwise, we enter into his disapprobation, and condemn it."[22]

Smith's concept of the impartial spectator was embedded in the rationale of literary instruction, which presupposed a divided self-consciousness. Working strictly from within the Protestant tradition, Smith had written that "when I endeavour to examine my own conduct, when I endeavour to pass sentence upon it . . . either to approve or condemn it, it is evident that, in all such cases, I divide myself as it were into two persons; and that I, the examiner and judge, represents a different character from the other I, the person whose conduct is examined and judged of."[23] The first I becomes the half he called the "spectator"; the second person is the person whose conduct, "under the character of a spectator, I was endeavouring to form some opinion [of]."[24] This concept is of instrumental value in disengaging the individual from his natural self, in order that he might observe it critically from the viewpoint of the other, the impartial I.

But the historical emphasis, which comes uncannily close to reinforcing a conception of hu-man nature antithetical to Protestant premises, negates the dualism of nature (base)/spirit (elevated) and claims an innate goodness of Indian character that is thwarted from realizing itself by a despotic, corrupt political society. In what appears to be an abrupt reversal of the customary Western denigration of Oriental character, the basic difference between European and Oriental is claimed to be a feature not of character but of government. In an unprecedented affirmation of unity between the Eastern and the Western temperament, Indians are described in one assessment as ideally having the capacity for every virtue, having "great natural sagacity, quickness of apprehension, sound intellect, sound reasoning and eloquence of expression."[25] What prevented the Indian from realizing the potential for a common identity with Europeans, however, was the tendency toward despotic government in Oriental society, which had spread anarchy through internal administration, driving people to habits that degraded them and paralyzed "every principle intended by nature to promote the improvement of man."[26]

The ancient feudal system of Europe, on the other hand, was characterized in the same assessment as a society driven by antidespotic principles unknown in the East. "The forms of their government, the wisdom of their Statesmen, the brilliant deeds of their heroes and patriots, the effusion of their poets, and the principles of their philosophers" were purportedly built into the literary system of British schools, strengthening and stimulating the intellectual faculties to higher attainments.[27] For training in polity the youth of England had no better instructor than the history and literature of Greece and Rome, which contained enough themes to inspire them to heights of enthusiasm, heroic action, and noble passion. In contrast to the heroic fictions of the Europeans that provided an impulse to the habits and pursuits accounting for their elevated political order, the romances of the Indians, it was maintained, only encouraged indulgence and luxury. The contrast between the two strengthened the British conviction that the more dedicated to the celebration of high adventure and high exploits is an art form, the more roused the people would become to action and virtue and so to installing a form of government befitting such values. A circular definition prevailed. If strength was a prerequisite for fortification against the wild exercise of imagination, then imagination acquired a moral value when it was harnessed to the service of political organization. Unlike the inhabitants of India, the Europeans "did not convert the luxury of their imaginations into a means of weakening and effeminating their minds; but they used it as a prompter to activity and a stimulant to high enterprise."[28]

In British administrative discussions of Indian education, "right" motives for reading were vitally connected with the restructuring of society. The tradition of reading for pleasure was held responsible for preventing Oriental people from recognizing the extent to which the evils of their society were valorized in their literature, whose gorgeous texture and rich imagery were a seductive distraction from plot and theme.[29] Europeans, on the other hand, presumably read from other motives, which sprang from active engagement with the world. A mere glance at the art forms that had evolved in different societies of the West and the East was deemed sufficient to reveal the basic difference. While Eastern literature still continued to be dominated by the romance, which fed the mind on sensuous pleasure, Western literature had outgrown it, the European tradition of "restless ambition" never quite being congenial to its sustained expression. Not only did the epic spirit that was ushered in brace the mind and lift it to high thoughts, but the conflict the bards recorded provided the inspiring source of the Europeans' impulse to action and ambition and, ultimately, to conquest itself. And thus it could be said, as a writer for the *Asiatic Journal* candidly did, that "they who listened with rapture to the songs of the bards, overran the provinces of those who were charmed with the fairy tale."[30]

Such critical statements were paralleled by the judgment of those on the General Council of Public Instruction in Calcutta that the more politically enlightened a society, the more its laws could be expected to harmonize with and be reflected in literary form. One of the most forceful statements of this idea came from Charles Trevelyan, who argued that recognition of the standards of excellence in literature was one step toward establishment of "the Law" in the minds of Indians. In English literature he saw the merging of the aesthetic, the intellectual, and the moral, the means by which intellectual discernment of the rules of composition would lead the mind to an understanding and appreciation of the highest laws of the state or the moral principles that regulate and guide conduct.

The great harm done by Oriental literatures, Trevelyan implied, was that the laws represented therein were arbitrary and whimsical and the rules of composition equally so. By not allowing for prior individual reflection or understanding, they failed to give human actions a solid base and taught that man has no choice but to act arbitrarily. For Trevelyan, the cultural power of English literary study lay in its confirming that "knowledge and thought must precede action" and intellect and Christian morality act in concert in shaping man as a public being. By inducing colonial subjects to read literature as an expression of the culture of an age, the historical approach served the twin objectives of rousing Indians to a consciousness of the inconsistencies in the native system of society while simultaneously leading them to a recognition of the principles of order and justice in the Western.

In the presumed absence of comparable objects of admiration in their own history and literature, Indian youth were seen as pitiably doomed to a perpetual state of degradation. But it was a degradation that was portrayed as decidedly not intrinsic to their character but the result of despotic rule. If the Indian was made aware of the cause of his debasement, there was every likelihood that he would seek release from the bonds of a tyrannical system. As a warning lesson for Indians, C. E. Trevelyan pointed to the negative example of Arabs as a people who were so "confident in the riches of their native tongue, [they] disdained the study of any foreign idiom. If they had made themselves familiar with Greek and Roman literature, they might have suspected that their caliph was a traitor, and their prophet an impostor."[31] In the same breath, Trevelyan linked the awakening of the intellectual faculties through literary study to awareness of despotism: "The sword of the Saracens became less formidable when their youth was drawn away from the camp to the college, where the armies of the faithful presumed to read and reflect."[32] By arousing the dormant young Indian from the deep slumber of a tyrannical past to a full sense of the evils of his native political society, historical training acquired deeper, more refined, more exalted motives, reconstituting the object of instruction as the restoration of the Indian student to his original state of goodness.

The self-righteous justification for government intervention in this formulation is too obvious to require comment, but what is especially striking is the insistent reassurance that British education was not seeking to assimilate Indians to the European model by urging them to cast aside their Indian identity (and thus removing them from their native, "base" state, as Christian instruction attempted). Rather, the suggestion is that English education was designed, in a Platonist sense, to awaken the colonial subjects to a memory of their innate character, corrupted as it had become, again in a Platonist sense, through the feudalistic character of Oriental society. In this universalizing narrative, rescripted from a scenario furnished earlier by missionaries, the British government was refashioned as the ideal republic to which Indians must naturally aspire as a spontaneous expression of self, a state in which the British rulers won a figurative place as Platonic Guardians. The secular rewrit-

ing of the Christian account of sinful, fallen man identified natural self with an original, uncorrupted political order. As the British scenario envisioned it, through the catalytic agency of British intervention, specifically its laws and institutions, the educated Indian was taken *back* to a true self, not away from an (inherently corrupt) self toward an external, transcendental ideal such as implied in the missionary scheme of instruction.

By this logic, the good that England represented for India constituted the only valid content of instruction for its youth. But to perceive that good, as John Murdoch realized—with profound implications for curricular selection—Indian students required an active intellectual disposition capable of comparative distinctions. Murdoch, an official in the Madras Presidency who was commissioned to assess the importance of vernacular literature in relation to other school subjects, was baffled by the resentment to English rule by the mass of Indians he encountered. He was equally puzzled by the fact that there were no comparable records of popular hostility to earlier, more despotic governments. As he continued his project on Indian vernacular literature, he stumbled on a possible answer in an issue of the *Imperial Review* edited by William Hunter, later chairman of the Indian Education Commission. The British inability to understand native tolerance to earlier despotic rule, the article stated,

> overlooked the fact that the present generation of our Eastern subjects has not the means of instituting such a comparison. The greater part of them have had no experience of any dynasty but our own, and are not possessed of any historical information, wherewith to supply this lack of knowledge. . . . [The author then goes on to examine how British officials should respond.] All desire to falsify history or to present one-sided views is disclaimed. The amplest credit should be given to the various dynasties that have pre-

ceded us. At the same time, it seems practicable to show that, notwithstanding all our faults we have been a blessing to India. The *History of India* would be the best vehicle for such teaching, though it might also find a place, to some extent, in the general Reading Books.[33]

But as Murdoch further realized, mere comparison was not enough if it was not also accompanied by a constant reinforcement of British ideals to which Indian youth were expected to aspire. The political pitfalls of partial enlightenment are described by Murdoch in quasi-religious terms, and he concludes by urging instruction in the advantages of stable government not as an option but as public duty:

> We place in a boy's hands the histories of Greece and Rome, and hold up to his admiration the examples of those ancient patriots who have freed their country from domestic tyranny or a foreign yoke. The knowledge which we impart to him destroys the reverence which he would naturally feel for his own religion and its precepts. In its stead, we implant no other of a holier and purer kind. Can we wonder, then, at the harvest which we too frequently reap—disloyalty untempered by gratitude, a spurious and selfish patriotism, unchecked by religion and an overweening conceit of literary attainment supported by no corresponding dignity of character.[34]

The Indian Education Commission of 1882 took up the theme introduced by Murdoch of maintaining an appropriate balance between affirming British norms and preserving Indian self-respect. But it disagreed in the main with Murdoch's approbation of Morris' *History of India* as a suitable text for Indian schools and colleges, denouncing it as too overbearing and "denationalizing, the tenor of which went to magnify British power and to lower and degrade Indian men and manners."[35] Morris' *History* was replaced by William Hunter's *Indian People* as a text that was better geared to promoting loyalty to the government without coercing Indian students to believe they were only members of a great nation with certain duties toward it, thus robbing them of a sense of national character.[36]

English education, fighting to stave off the appearance of imposing an alien culture on native society, gained subtle redefinition as an instrument of authenticity. A historical consciousness was intended to bring the Indian in touch with himself, recovering his true essence and identity from the degradation to which it had become subject through native despotism. Far from alienating the Indian from his own culture, background, and traditions, English education gained the image of being an agency for restoring Indian youth to an essential self and, in turn, reinserting him into the course of Western civilization.

The examination questions following lessons in literature suggest a direction in British Indian classroom pedagogy closely paralleling the historical emphasis of critical readings such as those of James Mill. While the topics themselves may not seem extraordinary or innovative in the intellectual demands made on students to compare, analyze, and demonstrate with historical proof, they are quite distinctive when juxtaposed to the type of examination questions being asked in England, which tended by and large to consist of paraphrase, parsing, and direct explication. As D. J. Palmer points out in his history of English studies in England, the questions for students of an English class were constructed in the style of a catechism, consisting of four sections: History of the English Language, Principles and Practice of English Composition, Translations from Classical Authors into English, and Rhetoric. The focus on language, style, and rhetoric in the English curriculum is replicated in the examination questions. The compulsory question on Shakespeare, for example, was sometimes directed at his bad grammar: "Derive and conjugate the irregular verb to break, and state whether there is any grammatical error in the following: 'I have broke with her father, and his good will obtained'—Shakespeare." In general, the examination questions required short, descriptive, factual answers assessing appropriateness of style and language, as for example with these questions: "Who is the first distinguished writer of English prose: Point out the characteristic features of his style, and say in what respect it differs from that of Lord Clarendon"; "When is the translation of an idiomatic expression perfect?" "Why is D a perfect letter?"[37]

By contrast, the examination questions in the Indian curriculum are less oriented toward mechanical points of grammar and less frequently ask for direct explication of specific texts. They are also less confined to single texts and appear to encompass a broader perspective on intellectual and social history, demanding an overall critical assessment of literature as an expression of culture and society. Warnings were sounded constantly about the dangers of allowing Indian examination questions to drift in the direction of essay topics in British schools and colleges mechanically testing rote recall without critical understanding. Hodgson Pratt, an Inspector of Schools, irately asked in the Bengal Public Instruction Report of 1856–1857:

> . . . why should Greeschunder Chuckerbutty be expected to know "what circumstances enabled Shakespeare to exhibit an accurate knowledge of Greek Mythology," or "in what respect the Dramatic compositions called 'Mysteries' differ from those called 'Moralities,'" and other facts of a like nature? On the other hand, it is of very great importance, that he should see clearly the dangers of living with an open sewer running under the lower floor of his house, or the cruelty of marrying his children at an immature age, or the impolicy of exhausting the soil of his fields by the disregard of important principles

in Chemistry: and it is very important that his mind should comprehend the sublimity and beauty of the laws by which his own body and everything around him are governed; and that his heart should if possible, be awakened to the great facts and conclusions of Natural Theology.[38]

The comparative emphasis in the Indian curriculum is reflected in questions requiring students to commit themselves to critical judgment of the contradictory values to which their own societies adhered. In many instances the topics on which students were asked to write were worded in such a way as to predetermine the response. Missionary institutions in general posed more direct, less subtle questions than government schools did, as with the following: "On the disadvantages of Caste, and the benefits of its abolition"; "On the internal marks of Falsehood in the Hindu Shastras"; "On the Physical Errors of Hinduism"; "The best Contrast between Christianity and Hinduism, morally considered"; "Essay, illustrative of the manner in which the Law of the Hindu Caste is opposed to the Principles of Political Economy"; "The Evidences of the Antiquity of the New Testament, and the bearing of this question on the General Argument for the Truth of Christianity"; "On the Merits of Christianity, and the Demerits of Hinduism"; "On the inquiry, Whether the Savage State be the original state of Man, or not?"; "On the Exposure of the Sick on the Banks of the Ganges"; "On the Causes of Opposition to Christianity in India"; "On the History of the British Constitution"; "On the History of Bengal during the Muhammedan Period"; and "The Influence exerted on the Nations of Europe by the Maritime Discoveries of the Fifteenth Century."[39]

The questions in the government institutions shied away from direct reference to religion, but they were no less oriented toward making Indian youth conscious of the benefits of British rule, as with these topics: "The Effects upon India of the New Communication with Europe by means of Steam," "The Advantages India derives in regard to commerce, security of property, and the diffusion of knowledge, from its Connexion with England," and "The Diffusion of Knowledge through the Medium of the English Language in India."[40]

The answers that students wrote to these questions cannot be taken, of course, as indicative of their actual responses to the content of instruction. The nature of institutionalized education, with the pressure to compete for promotion and awards and prizes, is obviously too complex to permit us to read student essays categorically as personally felt, intellectually committed responses. Selections from student essays are not reproduced below as proof of either success or failure of the British ideology, but to indicate the degree of correspondence between the objectives of instruction and the internalization of what students clearly sensed as desirable responses to the content of instruction.

Rajnarain Bose, a student at Hindu College in Calcutta in 1843, was asked along with other classmates to gloss the following passage by Bacon:

He thought also, there was found in the mind of man an affection naturally bred and fortified, and furthered by discourse and doctrine, which did pervert the true proceeding towards active and operative knowledge.

This was a false estimation, that it should be as a diminution to the mind of man to be much conversant in experiences and particulars, subject to sense, and bound in matter, and which are laborious to search, ignoble to mediate, harsh to deliver, illiberal to practise, infinite as is supposed in number, and no ways accommodated to the glory of arts.

This opinion or state of mind received much credit and strength, by the school of Plato, who, thinking that particulars rather revived the notions, or excited the faculties of the mind, than merely informed; and having mingled his philosophy with superstition, which never favoureth the sense, extolleth too

much the understanding of man in the inward light thereof; and again Aristotle's school, which giveth the due to the sense in assertion, denieth it in practice much more than that of Plato.

For we see the schoolmen, Aristotle's successors, which were utterly ignorant of history, rested only upon agitation of wit; whereas Plato giveth good example of inquiry by induction and view of particulars; though in such a wandering manner as if of no force or fruit. So that he saw well that the supposition of the sufficiency of man's mind hath lost the means thereof.[41]

The passage was followed by several specific questions, including this one: "In what sense are the schoolmen here said to have been 'utterly ignorant of history'?" Though Bose's response did not specifically compare European medieval schoolmen with the classical scholars of India, the movement in his essay between specific descriptions of a historical past and generalizations with application to the present left a nebulous space where such identifications could be forged:

The schoolmen were utterly ignorant of history; i.e. the history of material nature. Men who were enamoured of theological and metaphysical inquiries, and pursued those inquiries with the greatest alacrity and application, cannot be expected to have much knowledge of natural science, and to pay much attention to its investigation. Their minds rested only upon "agitation of wit," i.e. upon wrangling and controversy on the subjects above-mentioned. Theological controversy was the chief employment of the learned in the middle ages. Any University who could puzzle and confound a rival one with their subtleties was declared victorious, and its renown was spread far and abroad. There were prizes given to the parties victorious in metaphysical disputations. These incitements had due effect upon the minds of students, and they devoted their whole attention and time to the study of theology and metaphysics, to the perusal of the huge volumes of St. Augustine, Thomas Aquinas and Duns Scotus. The sense in which the term "history" is used in this passage by Bacon, is countenanced by his division of the intellectual faculties of man and of human knowledge, in the second book of his advancement of learning. He there divides history into civil and natural history. . . . Plato saw well that if we suppose man's mind to be all-sufficient, and that it can pronounce with decision upon subjects beyond its reach, we must acknowledge on the other hand that it has not the means of doing so; for, as far as induction and view of particulars go, so far can man proceed with firm steps in his inquiries and speculation.[42]

Incidentally, Bacon was widely read in both government and missionary schools. His importance in the literary education of Indian students was so great that it was not uncommon to have students matriculating from schools possessing no knowledge other than that of Bacon's works, which were well represented in the curriculum. It was reported that James Ballantyne, a great Sanskrit scholar who had himself also translated Bacon into Sanskrit, taught English to his Brahmin students, not in the usual elementary spelling-book style followed in England, but by putting Bacon's *Novum Organon* into their hands as soon as they learned the letters of the English alphabet.[43] The selection of Bacon was particularly apt in light of the criticism that Indian literature was devoid of experimental science or natural philosophy. Condemning Hindu philosophers for being poets rather than experimental investigators with the will to submit phenomena to rigid analysis, a writer for the *Calcutta Christian Observer* dismissively characterized Hindus as half-witted mystics who "thought much and deeply, but

were ever fonder of chasing the phantoms of a speculative fancy than of following the indications of nature."[44] No one was more critical of this aspect of the Hindu mind than the Indian social reformer Rammohun Roy, whose Baconian intellect rebelled against the establishment of Sanskrit seminaries "similar in character to those which existed in Europe before the time of Lord Bacon," which could only be expected to "load the minds of youth with grammatical niceties and metaphysical distinctions of little or no practical use to the possessor or to society."[45]

From the British standpoint Bacon's relevance for India lay in the command over nature exerted by philosophy to deliver substantial material benefits. Through such command, philosophy was endowed with a pragmatic dimension that enabled it to be put to the service of mankind, with the alleviation of human suffering and the increase of human happiness being as much its province as the search for truth. The application to India is self-evident in the context of critiques of the Hindu spirit of philosophy, denounced as incapable of nurturing any but "ascetic gymnosophists," mystical casuists who prevented the advancement of man's physical well-being by teaching that all matter is delusion.[46]

Fondness for Baconian ideas of material progress appears periodically in essays Indian students were assigned to write. Nobinchunder Dass, a student at Hooghly College, Calcutta, was asked to respond to the topic "The Effects upon India of the new Communication with Europe by means of Steam." His essay universalizes the myth of progress through analogies of the British presence in India and the Roman conquest of Britain. The result, a tour de force of sustained moral earnestness, is nothing short of an apology for imperialism.

> Nothing tends so much to advance society, to humanize the manners, and to elevate men in the scale of civilization, as intercourse with different nations. It encourages commerce,

by supplying the wants of one country with the superfluities of another; the knowledge of one people may be made the common property of all by its means, what the people of the remotest regions discover or invent, can be communicated everywhere. In short, intercourse renders the earth, separated as it is into continents, islands, &c., by vast oceans, sometimes by insurmountable mountains, into one entire whole; and all mankind, as the members of one and the same family.

It was by carrying on an intercourse with the Greeks, that the Romans were enabled to improve in the liberal and mechanic arts. It was Greek philosophy that softened and polished the rough military manners of the Romans, and soothed them when misfortune compelled them to look for the opening of a communication between Asia and Europe, the people of the latter continent who, sunk in barbarism and ignorance, were then groaning under the pressure of tyranny and oppression, received from the hands of the Asiatics, who were their superiors in civilization, the blessings of social life and happiness. But those short days of Asiatic glory and superiority are gone, the stream of civilization has taken an opposite course; before, it flowed from Asia to Europe, now, but with more than its pristine vigour and rapidity, it flows from Europe into Asia.

The blessings that Europe now showers upon us are numerous and useful. Both in ancient and modern times Europe has been the seat of philosophy and civilization, but in consequence of there being no safe intercourse in ancient times, that civilization was confined to where it grew. But now that that obstacle is removed, an entire change has taken place in the circumstances of countries; whatever is now or has been gathered in Europe or in any part of the earth, receives an universal circulation.

England which is of all the countries of Europe nearest related to India by her present position in Asia, is particularly engaged in the cause of Indian improvement. She not only carries on commerce with India, but she is ardently employed in instructing the natives in the arts and sciences, in history and political economy, and, in fact, in every thing that is calculated to elevate their understanding, meliorate their condition, and increase their resources. . . .

The English are to us what the Romans were to the English; and as the English are the children of modern times, and command more resources and power than the Romans, we derive the greater advantage. The facility afforded to communication by the use of steam has enabled the English to govern our country with great prudence and vigilance, they do not appear to be at any time at the risk of forbearing in the glorious work which they have commenced, of improving the native mind and condition, but prosecute it with honour to themselves and favour to their subjects, till they are styled the regenerators of India.[47]

This essay strikingly demonstrates the extent to which the objectives of British instruction have been internalized by this student, regardless of whether the statements themselves provide an index to personal conviction. What specifically matters is the successful transference, from ruler to subject, of the view that India will not witness progress unless channels of communication are opened with the West. And the intellectual strategy that enables it is the conjoining of commercial expansion with culture and knowledge to suggest a reciprocal, symbiotic relationship. Without commerce, without territorial expansion, without intercourse between nations, writes Nobinchunder Dass, knowledge will remain frozen. The material classification of knowledge as property, which is alternatively possessed, appropriated, received, distributed, and redistributed, further strengthens the justificatory claims of commercial expansion: ". . . whatever is now or has been gathered in Europe or in any part of the earth, receives an universal circulation."

So complete is the identification of the subject with the ruler, so precisely realigned is his divided self-consciousness, that Nobinchunder Dass can refer to his fellow Indians distantly, even contemptuously, as "the natives." It is "their" understanding that must be improved; it is "their" condition and "their" resources that require remedy. In Nobinchunder Dass, Adam Smith's impartial spectator has found a congenial home: "The English are to us what the Romans were to the English." In this one sentence are redeemed years of lessons in history leading to this culminating moment of affirmation, the endorsement of the Macaulayan dream.

In yet another essay, Mahendra Lal Basak, a student at the General Assembly Institution in Calcutta, takes upon himself the Platonist project of awakening Indian youth to a memory of their innate character, corrupted by a retrograde indigenous society. His is as much of a universalizing narrative as Nobinchunder Dass':

> But alas! alas! our countrymen are still asleep—still sleeping the sleep of death. Rise up, ye sons of India, arise, see the glory of the Sun of Righteousness! Beauty is around you; life blooms before you; why, why will ye sleep the sleep of death? And shall we who have drunk in that beauty—shall we not awake our poor countrymen? Come what will, ours will be the part, the happy part of arousing the slumber of slumbering India.[48]

The British government is set up as the ideal republic to which Mahendra wants his countrymen to aspire for realization of their true selves, and it is through the catalytic agency of British intervention, specifically its laws and institutions, that Mahendra truly believes his fellow Indians *will* be returned to a true self.

In essays by students such as Mahendra Lal and Nobinchunder Dass, English education gains subtle redefinition as an instrument of authenticity. English literary instruction, with its pedagogical imperative of nurturing a historically minded youth, places the Indian reader in a position where he renews contact with himself, recovering his true essence and identity from the degradation to which it had become subject through native despotism. Far from alienating the reader from his own culture, background, and traditions, English literature, taught less as a branch of rhetoric than of history, sought to return him to an essential unity with himself and reinsert him into the course of development of civilized man. At the same time the removal of "false thinking" through English education cleared the path to a perception of the British government as a fair one promoting national prosperity and justice.[49]

NOTES

1. Colin McCabe, "Towards a Modern Trivium," p. 70.

2. D. J. Palmer, *The Rise of English Studies,* p. 42.

3. An intriguing discussion of the effect of the colonial encounter on redefinitions of literary forms is provided by Judith Wilt in "The Imperial Mouth," 618–628. Wilt argues that Western incursions into the unknown in Africa, India, and the Middle East produced a neurosis in the Victorian imagination about how the future would appear. That anxiety is reflected in works like H. G. Wells' *War of the Worlds* (1898), Bram Stoker's *Dracula* (1897), and Joseph Conrad's *Heart of Darkness* (1899), science fiction works that Wilt reads as mutations of Victorian gothic, the colonial encounter being the catalytic agent for such transformation.

4. "Warren Hastings' letter to Nathaniel Smith, Esq., of the Court of Directors, October 4, 1784," preface to *The Bhagvat Geeta, or Dialogues of Kreeshna and Arjoon,* trans. Charles Wilkins (London: C. Nourse, 1784), p. 7.

5. History for Mill was not a recital but a "methodical description of social phenomena and the laws which regulate them." Elie Halévy writes that "far from using the empirical knowledge which he obtained from the history of British India to determine inductively the necessary movement of progress from the barbarous state to civilization, he rather writes conjectural history and, in most cases, he

takes as a point of departure a definition of progress based on the constant facts of human nature and deduces from that what, in fact, the progress of Hindu society must have been." *The Growth of Philosophical Radicalism,* Mary Morris, trans. (London: Faber and Faber, 1928; reprint, 1952), p. 274.

6. William Jones, *Asiatic Researches,* 2:3; quoted by James Mill in *History of British India,* vol. 2, book 2, p. 111.

7. James Mill, *History of British India,* p. 37.

8. James Mill, *History of British India,* p. 39.

9. See Claude Lévi-Strauss, *Structural Anthropology,* translated from the French by Claire Jacobsen and Brooke Grundfest Shoepf (New York: Basic Books, 1963), particularly the essay "The Structural Study of Myth."

10. Great Britain, *Parliamentary Papers, 1852–53,* Evidence of J. Tucker, 32:349.

11. *Quarterly Review* (1832), 48:4.

12. J. Talboys Wheeler, *The History of India from the Earliest Ages,* p. 6.

13. Great Britain, *Parliamentary Papers, 1852–53,* 32, Appendix D.

14. Colonel "Hindoo" Stewart, *Vindication of the Hindoos, by a Bengal Officer* (London, 1808), p. 97, quoted in David Kopf, *British Orientalism and the Bengal Renaissance,* p. 141.

15. "Avataras: Four Lectures Delivered at the Theosophical Society, Madras 1899," in Ainslee T. Embree, ed., *The Hindu Tradition* (New York: Modern Library, 1965), pp. 322–324.

16. "Drain Inspector's Report," in *Collected Works of Mahatma Gandhi* (Ahmedabad: Navajivan Press, 1969), 34:546.

17. Lionel Gossman, "Literature and Education," *New Literary History* (Winter 1982), pp. 344–45. Gossman writes that "underpinning the central place of language and literature in the eighteenth-century college curriculum were certain ideas about the nature of man and of culture. One of these was that, as Herder put it, following Descartes over a century earlier, it is language—the ability to manipulate symbolic systems—that distinguishes man from the beasts (and not science or technology as we might tend to think). To learn to speak and write well was to be humanized. Protestants, especially, valued literacy and—more cautiously—literature as the instrument by which man might enter into the immediate presence of the Word of God in Holy Scripture and thus be freed from narrow, tra-

ditional, and—as they saw it—corrupt doctrines and practices. . . . The acquisition and use of correct literary models of expression was seen by Christians and *philosophes* alike as a defense against the constant threat of regression into the bestiality of our original condition . . . [and] the teaching of language and literature as a means of weaning young men from their natural beastliness. Seventeenth- and eighteenth-century teachers thus saw in polished language and literature an essential instrument for removing their pupils from natural origins, releasing them from the narrowness of an oral, largely peasant culture, presumed to be shut in on itself and enslaved to routine and superstition, and for introducing them to the larger view of a universal, human culture, spanning the ages and the nations."

18. Hugh James Rose, *The Tendency of Prevalent Opinions about Knowledge Considered* (Cambridge: Deighteon, and London: Rivington, 1826), p. 11, quoted in Alan Bacon, "English Literature Becomes a University Subject," p. 594.

19. For this insight I am indebted to Franklin Court's article, "Adam Smith and the Teaching of English Literature," pp. 325–341.

20. Adam Smith, *Theory of Moral Sentiments,* p. 214.

21. Adam Smith, *Theory of Moral Sentiments,* pp. 257–258.

22. Adam Smith, *Theory of Moral Sentiments,* p. 162.

23. Adam Smith, *Theory of Moral Sentiments,* p. 164.

24. Adam Smith, *Theory of Moral Sentiments,* p. 165.

25. "Facts Illustrative of the Character and Condition of the People of India," *Oriental Herald* (October 1828), 19:129.

26. "Facts Illustrative of the Character and Condition of the People of India," p. 127.

27. "Facts Illustrative of the Character and Condition of the People of India," p. 101.

28. "Philosophy of Fiction," p. 142.

29. "Philosophy of Fiction," p. 141. Oriental people were deemed to have "unfurnished, uncultivated, unreflecting, and unobservant minds," as a result of which their fictional characters were completely without interest.

30. "Philosophy of Fiction," *Asiatic Journal,* p. 142. The Asiatic tale on the other hand "lets the mind sit on a couch of luxury and indolence. . . . [The Asiatic tales of adventure] indicate a sympathy with fate, rather than a sympathy with an energy that defies fate and contends against destiny."

31. Charles Trevelyan, *On the Education of the People of India,* p. 192.

32. Charles Trevelyan, *On the Education of the People of India,* p. 192. Recorded accounts by English-educated Indians confirmed Trevelyan's assessment, as in the following statement by one recipient of English education, Chander Nath Bose: "English education tells us that we live under tyrannies more numerous and more radically mischievous than those, which produced the great revolution of '89. It tells us that, here in India, we have a social tyranny, a domestic tyranny, a tyranny of caste, a tyranny of custom, a religious tyranny, a clerical tyranny, a tyranny of thought over thought, of sentiment over sentiment. And it not only tells us of all these tyrannies, but makes us feel them with terrific intensity." "High Education in India: An Essay Read at the Bethune Society on the 25th April, 1878," quoted in Bruce McCully, *English Education and the Origins of Indian Nationalism,* p. 221.

33. John Murdoch, *Education in India,* pp. 104–105.

34. John Murdoch, *Education in India,* p. 17.

35. Education Commission, *Report by the Bombay Provincial Committee* (Calcutta: Superintendent of Government Printing, 1884), p. 235.

36. John Murdoch, *Education in India,* p. III. The selection of Hunter's text is understandable in light of the fact that the Commission that recommended it was headed by Hunter himself.

37. D. J. Palmer, *Rise of English Studies,* p. 22.

38. *Bengal Public Instruction Report for 1856–7,* Appendix A, p. 213, quoted in John Murdoch, *Education in India,* p. 44. There were numerous complaints that subjects like health, thrift, extravagance in marriage and funerals, and the role of women were not taught adequately by professors of English literature, who had "neither knowledge of the people nor sympathy with them." Consequently selections of readings to communicate informed attitudes to these issues were considered absolutely essential.

39. Great Britain, *Parliamentary Papers, 1852–53,* Appendix G, Statement of the Progress and Success of the General Assembly (now Free Church) Institution at Calcutta, 32:452–453.

40. Great Britain, *Parliamentary Papers, 1852–53,* Appendix N, General Report on Public Instruction in the Lower Provinces of the Bengal Presidency for 1843–1844, pp. 491–617.

41. Great Britain, *Parliamentary Papers, 1852–53,* Appendix N, Scholarship Examination Questions 1843: Literature, 32:573.

42. Great Britain, *Parliamentary Papers, 1853–53,* Appendix N, Hindoo College Answers, 32:587.

43. Great Britain, *Parliamentary Papers, 1852–53,* Evidence of Alexander Duff, 32:47.

44. *Calcutta Review* (1845), 3:13.

45. "Letter to His Excellency the Right Hon'ble William Pitt, Lord Amherst, 11 December 1823," in *Selected Works of Raja Rammohun Roy,* p. 301.

46. "Baconian Philosophy Applicable to the Mental Regeneration of India," *Calcutta Christian Observer* (January–December 1838), 7:124.

47. Great Britain, *Parliamentary Papers, 1852–53,* Appendix N, Hooghly College Essays, 32:594–595.

48. Great Britain, *Parliamentary Papers, 1852–53,* Extract from Mahendra Lal Basak's essay "The Influence of Sound General Knowledge on Hinduism," 32:450.

49. Great Britain, *Parliamentary Papers, 1852–53,* Evidence of George Norton, 32:105.

PART II

What Is Literary Theory?

Over the last two decades, "literary theory" has emerged as a cultural phenomenon of significant proportions. The work of theory can be described as providing the philosophical foundation, the aims, and the reason-for-being of criticism. Theory tries to explore the rationale for seeing literature and culture in a particular way, and theory is the place where assumptions about literature and culture are tested overtly and where changes in critical practices are first indicated. These are largely practical and necessary tasks. And yet there are reasons to see literary theory as a generally unsettling practice. Literary theory tends to be conflict-oriented in that it has the function and responsibility of critiquing existing critical systems and addressing the possibility of change. In this sense, literary theory is a constant indicator of changing future directions in literary and cultural studies and, thus, tends to be at the center of controversy in the arts. In his 1986 presidential address to the Modern Language Association, J. Hillis Miller described the "violence and irrationality" surrounding the "attacks on theory" even as theory seemed to "triumph" in the 1970s and 1980s as a noteworthy cultural development. He discussed the controversy over theory as linked to widespread reconsideration of the nature of knowledge and of aesthetic experience.

The current use of the broad and encompassing term "theory" in literary studies is curious in itself. In 1949, W. K. Wimsatt argued that literary art was too expansive to be encompassed within the study of aesthetics and required its own study in what he called "literary theory." "Literary theorists of our day," Wimsatt argued, "have been content to say little about 'beauty' or about any over-all aesthetic concept. In his most general formulation the literary theorist is likely to be content with something like 'human interest'" even though "disinterestedness, we remember, is something that Kant made a character of art." Nineteen forty-nine, we will remember from the previous section of this book, was the same year Northrop Frye called for the "scientific" study of literature in his essay "The Function of Criticism at the Present Time."

Wimsatt marks "theory" as an attempt to replace the aesthetic focus on the disinterested effects of art by focusing, to some degree, on the relationship between literary meaning and *interested* writers and readers. Wimsatt's term "theory," like Miller's use of the term, is connected with the problem of knowledge conceived as the object of disinterested scientific investigation. Jürgen Habermas describes this problem in his account of the term's origin. "The *theoros,*" he notes, "was the representative sent by Greek cities to public celebrations. Through *theoria,* that is through looking on, he abandoned himself to the sacred events. In philosophical language, *theoria* was transferred to contemplation of the cosmos." Similarly, Jacques Derrida, in "The Principle of Reason" ("Deconstruction and Poststructuralism" [Part V]), notes the relationship in the West between "knowledge" and "seeing" and attempts to construct knowledge at the extremes of objectification. Habermas, unlike Derrida, contrasts this "scientific" ("objective") conception of "theory" and its use in the nonscientific discourses of "historical-hermeneutic" practices in which theory involves the elaboration and testing of approaches to and perspectives on meaning. Habermas here is repeating the gesture made by Michel Foucault in "What Is an Author?" ("Deconstruction and Poststructuralism" [Part V]) when he distinguishes between scientific theorists who establish particular scientific practices and the initiators of "discursive practice" as broad areas of belief and ideology in the culture. Derrida calls for the questioning of "scientific normativity"—the assumptions behind what creates the "norms" of scientific as well as interpretative understanding—and for analyses of "the rhetoric, the rites, the modes of presentation and demonstration that [the sciences] continue to respect." (See also Donna Haraway's "A Cyborg Manifesto" in "Cultural Studies" [Part IX].)

The conception of "theory" as the exploration and testing of meaning is congruent with Wimsatt's "literary theory" and Frye's argument that criticism should take its place among the social sciences. That is, if theory makes understanding and not the world its object, it does so by examining understanding in aesthetic terms and also by examining the contexts (social and otherwise) for aesthetics and systems of understanding. For this reason, Miller in his presidential address defined "theory" as "the displacement in literary studies from a focus on the meaning of texts to a focus on the ways meaning is conveyed." As Barthes and others say of theory (Part IV), it is the furtherest extreme of language used to talk about language. Paul de Man adds a crucial element of theory, in this section, when he discusses its focus on referentiality as a problem rather than as something that reliably and unambiguously relates a reader to the "real world" of history and society. Frank Lentricchia describes "theory" in yet another way. "Theory," he writes, "is primarily a *process* of discovery of the lesson that I am calling historical; any single, formulable theory is a reduced version of the process, a frozen proposition which will tend to cover up the process it grew out of by projecting itself as an uncontingent [freestanding] system of ideas."

bell hooks in "Postmodern Blackness" also critiques the idea of theory and then goes on to recontextualize it within the social and political life of black writers and readers. In her designation of "postmodern theory," the relationship between "postmodernism" as a cultural movement and literary theory is a connection made as well by many of the authors in *Contemporary Literary Criticism*. This is a point to which we will return. Others see in theory a kind of coterie from which they have been excluded. In "Literary Theory and 'Third World Literature': Some Contexts," Aijaz Ahmad describes theory as having developed into a "full-scale technology." "Literary criticism in the English-speaking countries," at a particular moment in history, he goes on, "gave way to what came to be known as literary theory." Still others, as Edward Said suggests in the "academic" narrative at the beginning of "The Politics of Knowledge," see the development of theory in largely political terms, as an event taking place between the active engagement of a fully politicized "cultural studies"—the critique of culture and its products as belonging to a stage of social transformation—

and the old aesthetic of interpreting individual works for greater clarity and "appreciation" in a gesture associated with traditionalism.

All three of these writers must be distinguished from "traditionalist" criticisms of theory made by "the neutral humanists." Barbara Christian has described "the neutral humanists" as those "who see literature as pure expression and [who] will not admit to the obvious control of its production, value, and distribution by those who have power." She distinguishes herself from critics like E. D. Hirsh who describe "the Great Literary Theory Debate" (in Hirsh's words) as an "interest conflict" between those who seek to recover "primary interpretations"—namely, the intentional meanings of literary authors—and those who seek "secondary interpretation, or what Foucault calls '*resemanticizing* the text.'" In this debate, Hirsh sees the struggle between "the needs and interests of undergraduates" who presumably simply want to get to "know" literature and its authors—who simply want to achieve the "humane [and aesthetic] pleasure of particular books"—and "the institutional advantages of secondary interpretation in the sphere of professorial publication."

Throughout the debate over the meaning of theory, we can see the striking phenomenon of the past two decades in which "theory" as an independent term, as Martin Kreiswirth and Mark Cheetham have noted, "more and more appears . . . on its own, without delimiting modifiers, either before or after. No longer is the term wedded to antecedent adjectives, as in *critical theory, literary theory,* or *psychoanalytic theory.* No longer does it routinely drag behind trailing genitives—*of social action, of language,* etc." This is so because "theory" has come to designate critique—as J. Hillis Miller says in this section. "It is 'criticism' in the fundamental sense of 'critique,' discriminating, testing out, in this case a testing out of the medium of which the bridge between theory and practice is made." Even Wimsatt used the term "theory" in this way. "The mark of 'theory,'" Gerald Graff and Reginald Gibbons argue, "is inevitable at a moment when once-accepted definitions, categories, and disciplinary boundaries have become matters of debate and controversy." In this way, critique breaches the self-standing boundaries of knowledge. "While criticism . . . stands outside the object it criticizes, asserting norms against facts, and the dictates of reason against the unreasonableness of the world," Seyla Benhabib has argued, "critique refuses to stand outside its object and instead juxtaposes the immanent, normative self-understanding of its object to the material actuality of this object." Critique, then (as we suggested in the General Introduction), goes beyond the aesthetic consistency of knowledge, questioning its seeming simplicity, its generalizing wholeness, and even the modalities of its accuracy. This is what Barthes means by the "active role" of theory he describes in *The Grain of the Voice:* its aim "is to reveal as past what we still believe to be present: theory mortifies, and that is what makes it avant-garde."

THEORY, IDEOLOGY, AND THE AESTHETICS OF TRUTH

Literary theory arose, as Graff and Gibbons note, as an enactment of *critique*—the questioning of the assumptions behind patterns of understanding and personal aesthetic experience. Literary theory arose as the questioning of the assumptions governing the definition and understanding of "literature" itself (see the General Introduction). The form this critique has taken, to one degree or another, is to question the "disinterested" nature of personal aesthetic experience. Those who advance the cause of aesthetics claim that there are various defenses for aesthetic "disinterestedness." Aesthetics, first of all, is a recognizable phenomenon that is *self-consistent* (as a possible object of knowledge) and *self-evident* (unmediated by linguistic, psychological, or culturally specific forms). Moreover, aesthetic effects are *self-contained* and not affected by the status of the subject of (aesthetic) experience because aesthetics is an end in itself without ulterior motives, no purposes beyond itself. It is *disengaged* from both personal and cultural history.

The critique of aesthetics questions these assumptions. It questions the self-consistent and self-evident "truth" of aesthetics, and it questions the disengaged, disinterested "situation" of aesthetics. The key terms of this questioning and of this section of our book, along with "theory" and "aesthetics," are "ideology," "politics," and, implicitly along with these, "ethics." Paul de Man and J. Hillis Miller examine the "ideology" of aesthetics—what de Man has called "aesthetic ideology." By contrast, Aijaz Ahmad, Edward Said, and, to a lesser extent, bell hooks explore the "politics" of aesthetics and literary studies—what Said calls the "politics of knowledge" (a phrase that Derrida also uses). A central term in bell hooks's discourse, "postmodernism," which Ahmad also explores, has also been described by Hal Foster as part of an "anti-aesthetic." Together, these authors present a complex sense of the work of literary theory.

Such work consistently focuses on ideology and ethics. Ideology, as de Man says in "The Resistance to Theory," "is precisely the confusion of linguistic with natural reality, of reference with phenomenalism." Ideology takes as "natural" the product of human activity, precisely the realm of the self-evident and self-consistent. Catherine Belsey gives the most thorough discussion of ideology in *Contemporary Literary Criticism* in "Constructing the Subject: Deconstructing the Text" ("Deconstruction and Poststructuralism" [Part V]; but see also Mikhail Bakhtin's discussion in "Historical Criticism" [Part VII]). Ideology, she argues, "is not, therefore, to be thought of as a system of ideas in people's heads, nor as the expression at a higher level of real material relationships, but as the necessary condition of action within the social formation." It is the "condition of action" in this definition that links ideology to ethics. In the terms we have been pursuing here, ideology makes seemingly "disinterested" aesthetic experience—the object of the "humanist myth"—the *end* rather than the object of analysis. When such experience becomes the object of analysis, we have "theory." "The advent of theory," de Man says, signals "the break that is now so often being deplored and that sets it aside from literary history and from literary criticism, occurs with the introduction of linguistic terminology in the metalanguage about literature." Theory, he says, "upsets rooted ideologies by revealing the mechanics of their workings; it goes against a powerful philosophical tradition of which aesthetics is a prominent part; it upsets the established canon of literary works and blurs the borderlines between literary and non-literary discourse."

De Man pursues this thesis—in what is, as we note in the Introduction to Part V, a classic "deconstructive" argument—by exploding the self-consistent truth of the concepts he employs. "Intuition," he writes, "implies perception, consciousness, experi-

ence, and leads at once into the world of logic and of understanding with all its correlatives, among which aesthetics occupies a prominent place." Yet it is the aim of
theory precisely to analyze the self-consistency of "perception, consciousness, experience." De Man pursues such an analysis in "The Resistance to Theory" by arguing
that "a tension develops between methods of understanding and the knowledge
which those methods allow one to reach"—that is, a tension between the methods
of reading and definitions of literature we discussed in the General Introduction.
De Man negotiates this critical terrain, as he does throughout the closely argued essays that have been his contribution to literary scholarship, through a rigorous and ascetic mode of reasoning. In an essay by de Man, concepts are defined precisely in order to arrive at a situation where those definitions can no longer function. At the
beginning of "The Resistance to Theory," he defines teaching as a rigorously "cognitive process in which self and other are only tangentially and contiguously involved,"
only to argue by the end of the essay that "persuasion by *proof*"—the very model of
impersonal cognition—becomes an example of and "inseparable from" the "purely affective and intentional realm" of rhetoric. But rhetoric is always involved with the
contiguous involvement of self and other.

Moreover, in the piece here, de Man begins by asserting the "impossibility" of
defining "literary theory," even though throughout the essay he offers a number of
rigorously self-evident senses of "theory." He asserts, for instance, that theory possesses "impersonal consistency," that it is both "philosophical" yet beyond aesthetic
categories of philosophy to the extent that "literary theory may now well have become a legitimate concern of philosophy but it cannot be assimilated to it." Its basis
in linguistic analysis creates in de Man's work "the resistance to theory . . . a resistance
to the rhetoric and tropological dimension of language." "Theory" for de Man is
thoroughly *rhetorical*—a mode of "rhetorical reading," but as such it is "theory and
not theory at the same time, the universal theory of the impossibility of theory." In
this formulation, "self-consistency" breaks down, and he concludes that "nothing can
overcome the resistance to theory since theory *is* itself this resistance. The loftier the
aims and the better the methods of literary theory, the less possible it becomes." In
this paradox, de Man has followed the path of logic and precision to demonstrate the
"impossibility" of self-consistency. Literature is the *site* of these contradictions, where
both "aesthetic categories" and "mimetic" imitation—self-evident personal experience and self-consistent objects in the world—are "voided." That is, "the resistance to
theory is a resistance to the rhetorical or tropological dimension of language, a dimension which is perhaps more explicitly in the foreground in literature (broadly
conceived) than in other verbal manifestations or—to be somewhat less vague—
which can be revealed in any verbal event when it is read textually."

If de Man examines the "truth" of aesthetic self-consistency, then J. Hillis Miller
examines the "truth" of aesthetic self-evidence in "The Search for Grounds in Literary
Study." Miller begins from a viewpoint directly at odds with the unexamined assumption of the self-evident value of literary education whose history Gerald Graff
examines in "The Humanist Myth" ("What Is Literary Studies?" [Part I]). Miller describes four basic assumptions or "grounds" that govern literary study. These assumptions make understanding possible by "grounding" the infinite "play" of discourse—
what Michel Foucault calls "the cancerous and dangerous proliferation of

significations within a world where one is thrifty not only with one's resources and riches, but also with one's discourses and their significations." Foucault, in "What Is an Author?" ("Deconstruction and Poststructuralism" [Part V]), is describing the ways an "author" grounds such proliferation.

The "author" (or "author-function") is an aspect of one of the grounds Miller describes, fitting within the psychological grounding of discourse, which reduces the play of meanings to the conscious and unconscious intentions of the subject of discourse. This "ground" governs the varieties of contemporary psychoanalytic criticism exampled throughout this book. A second ground Miller describes is social, which reduces the play of meanings to articulations of more or less explicit social forces: the Marxist "base," Foucauldian "power" and social "function," feminist "phallologocentrism" and the "discursive organization" of society Michael Warner describes ("Feminism and Gender Studies" [Part VIII]), or most generally the rhetorical definition of language and literature as interpersonal communication implicit throughout "Rhetoric and Reader Response" (Part III). A third ground is language itself—the linguistics and rhetoric de Man describes—which reduces the play of meanings to the linguistic forms and structures analyzed by the linguistic methods of structuralist criticism. The final ground Miller describes is, as he says, "properly religious, metaphysical, or ontological, though hardly in a traditional or conventional way." This ground, in Miller's argument, is the basis of Derrida's unconventional (and even "anti-") metaphysics. Like the "anagogic" framework of Frye's vision of literature as a "verbal universe" (as he calls it in *Anatomy of Criticism*), this ground establishes an overriding vision of the whole of "discourse" or cultural life.

The point of Miller's discussion, however, is *ethical*. He—like Said, Graff, Derrida, Fuss, and many others writing today—wants to test grounds against the tasks they are set to perform. Most globally, he wants to test "literature" itself against the "whole freight of the values" of culture that traditional humanistic education claimed for it. (Gauri Viswanathan explores the spiritual and political aims of humanistic education in "What Is Literary Studies?" [Part I].) To this end, Miller describes the "imperialism" of each of the grounds he describes, their tendency to reduce and dismiss all other explanations—that is, to make each mode of understanding, in turn, a "base" to the superstructure and epiphenomena of other discursive formations. Along with this tendency, he also describes the blind resistance contemporary versions of these grounds—psychoanalytic, Marxist, structuralist, and deconstructive—have encountered in polemics that have reduced what Derrida describes as the loss of "all sense of proportion and control" among those attacking him and his followers ("Deconstruction and Poststructuralism" [Part V]). (Derrida also presents a thorough discussion of the term "ground" as Miller uses it, as does Diana Fuss in "Feminism and Gender Studies" [Part VIII].)

The two aspects of "grounds" Miller describes—the "self-evident" ability to account for everything by their adherents and the equally self-evident dismissal by those who do not subscribe to them—have ethical implications. These implications define the responsibility of criticism according to the larger aspects of human life, what Edward Said calls "the central factor of human work, the actual participation of peoples in the making of human life," and what Aijaz Ahmad calls, in a different register, "simple decency." When the study of literature is reducible to the study of language, then criticism becomes "scientific" and "objective" in relation to other cultural formations; it ceases to traffic in the cultural values Miller is describing and turns its attention to the linguistic conditions that allows such values to arise. At its worst, criticism becomes dry formalism, the "technicist" study of literature Ahmad describes. When it is reducible to the study of psychology, it becomes either a symptomatics, diagnosing particular authors or even particular eras in terms of "health" or, more usually, "disease," or it becomes a model for understanding based upon more or less autonomous subjects.

When it is reducible to the study of society, criticism becomes a program for social action—what Lentricchia calls in *Criticism and Social Change* "the production of knowledge to the ends of power." In this case, the study of literature recognizes cultural values, but those values themselves are defined only collectively and socially and, like the other grounding gestures, leave out or "marginalize" (as "false consciousness," "self-interest," or even "ideology") what they cannot describe as "basic." Literary study becomes the kind of "identity politics" Said describes or the "sad irony" bell hooks describes of "contemporary discourse which talks . . . [of the] recognition of Otherness . . . primarily to a specialized audience that shares a common language rooted in the very master narratives it claims to challenge." Finally, if the study of literature is expandable to one all-encompassing "anagogic" vision or another, it leads too readily to a preexisting vision of the world, to the "indeterminacies" of de Man's deconstructive readings, or Frye's Christian quest romance—or even Eliot's "mind of Europe," which is "much more important" than the poet's own private mind and only accessible, as Eliot says, to "those who have personality and emotions [and consequently] know what it means to want to escape from these things." In this case, theory reverts to what Cornel West calls in "Black Critics and the Pitfalls of Canon Formation" ("What Is Literary Studies?" [Part I]) "a fetishism" or "a religious belief" in something unassailable and autonomous.

Both imperialism and resistance are acts that call for ethical judgment, what Derrida describes as the questioning of the "values" that govern and authorize particular practices. Based on particular "grounds" of literary study, the theoretical approaches Miller describes account for only so much, while still claiming, as Raymond Williams says (in "Historical Criticism" [Part VII]), "to exhaust the full range of human practice, human energy, human intention (. . . that extraordinary range of variations, both practiced and imagined, of which human beings are and have shown themselves to be capable)." The job for ethics, in John Dewey's traditional terms, is to deal "with conduct in its entirety, with reference . . . to what makes it conduct, its *ends,* its real meaning." Its job, in Julia Kristeva's more contemporary sense, is no longer its "coercive, customary manner of ensuring the cohesiveness of a particular group." Now, she continues, "ethics crops up wherever a code (mores, social contract) must be shattered in order to give way to the free play of negativity, need, desire, pleasure, and *jouissance,* before being put together again." In both cases—of the "old" traditional humanism and the new sense of theoretical uprootings de Man describes in the contemporary debate—the issue can be and is being understood in terms of ethics rather than aesthetics. The emphasis here is on the place of value in human affairs and, more specifically, the relationship that ethics always attempts to understand between *particular* and *local* activities and more *general* principles by which to judge them.

THE ANTI-AESTHETICS OF "POSTMODERN" THEORY

In recent years, the kind of intellectual inquiry embodied in the term "theory"—the questioning of the overriding Enlightenment values of simplicity, accuracy, and generalizability—has often been associated with the term "postmodern." bell hooks makes this association in her essay, describing what she calls "postmodern critical writing" and "postmodern theory." On the one hand, this description is one of style: bell hooks describes her own creative writing as "reflective of a postmodern oppositional sensibility, work that is abstract, fragmented, non-linear narrative"—work, that is, embodying the contingent and modal "difficulties" we outlined in the General Introduction. Such a style—in language, architecture, the fine arts, television, even philosophical and political discourse—is characterized by what Jean-François Lyotard has called the reluctance to embrace "grand narratives" that have governed and conditioned knowledge and understanding. (In "Rhetoric and Reader Response" [Part III], Stuart Moulthrop cites Lyotard's contention that "postmodernism begins . . . with 'incredulity toward metanarratives.'") Fredric Jameson has described the "postmodern" avoidance of grand narrative as "pastiche," the juxtaposition of styles from different historical periods, different disciplinary discourses, different "modes" of articulation, without any overriding meaning or purpose governing that juxtaposition. In *Postmodernism; or The Cultural Logic of Late Capitalism,* he argues that

> pastiche is, like parody, the imitation of a peculiar or unique, idiosyncratic style, the wearing of a linguistic mask, speech in a dead language. But it is a neutral practice of such mimicry, without any of parody's ulterior motives, amputated of the satiric impulse, devoid of laughter and of any conviction that alongside the abnormal tongue you have momentarily borrowed, some healthy linguistic normality still exists. Pastiche is thus blank parody, a statue with blind eyeballs: it is to parody what that other interesting and historically original modern thing, the practice of a kind of blank irony, is to what Wayne Booth calls the "stable ironies" of the eighteenth century.

For Jameson, postmodern pastiche is a kind of "anti-style"—quite literally an "anti-aesthetic" insofar as aesthetic experience, as we have argued, is traditionally characterized as simple and coherent, "disinterested" experience that creates the sense of coherent subjects and objects of experience. As Hal Foster says, within the postmodern "the discourse or knowledge is affected no less: in the midst of the academic disciplines, Jameson writes, extraordinary new projects have emerged. 'Is the work of Michel Foucault, for example, to be called philosophy, history, social theory or political science?'"

The "irony" of postmodern style is "blank" insofar as it does not imply coherent objects and ideas—which are, as we have said, simple, accurate, and generalizing.

Neither does it imply coherent subjects of experience, who are unified and stable across time. As we shall see, the essays in "Deconstruction and Poststructuralism" (Part V) raise questions about the "objects" of knowledge, as do the essays of "Historical Criticism" (Part VII) and "Cultural Studies" (Part IX). The essays of "Psychology and Psychoanalysis" (Part VI) raise questions about the "subjects" of knowledge, while the essays of "Feminism and Gender Studies" (Part VIII) raise issues about subjects and objects. Those of "Rhetoric and Reader Response" (Part III) blur the traditional Enlightenment separation between subject and object, the "distancing" that is usually associated with aesthetic experience. In these arguments, issues of "style" become issues of "content," and the distinction between form and content that is so important for the universalizing formalism of Enlightenment thinking—its coherent subjects and objects of experience and the clear distinction between them—tends to break down within the category of "postmodern."

Both of these tendencies enact what bell hooks calls "postmodern critiques of essentialism," of universal, "once and for all" definitions of things (subjects and objects). The first essays of this section suggest such critiques in de Man's "deconstructive" argument we have described and in the "undecidability" among "grounds" for literary study Miller describes. Such critiques occur throughout this book (in Derrida and Foucault, in Felman and Haraway, in the blurring of "literary" and "non-literary" texts in Greenblatt, Armstrong, and Bakhtin), but Diana Fuss explores the issue of "essentialism" most explicitly in relation to feminism in "Reading Like a Feminist" ("Feminism and Gender Studies" [Part VIII]) by examining "the vexed relation between feminism and deconstruction." In this section, bell hooks examines the "vexed relation" between the experience of black Americans and contemporary "postmodern" theory. This is most clear, we think, when she considers the actual historical "subjects" of theory. "It never surprises me," she writes, "when black folks respond to the critique of essentialism, especially when it denies the validity of identity politics, by saying, 'Yeah, it's easy to give up identity, when you got one.' Should we not be suspicious of postmodern critiques of the 'subject,'" she continues, "when they surface at a historical moment when many subjugated people feel themselves coming to voice for the first time." Similarly, Ahmad contrasts the postcolonial critic Homi Bhabha, speaking from within the "material conditions of *post*modernity which presume the benefits of modernity," with those who live "where a majority of the population has been denied access to such benefits of 'modernity' as hospitals or better health insurance or even basic literacy."

These critics, like Edward Said in this section, are attempting to pose questions that are ethical insofar as ethics is the science of the *timely,* of what we called in the Introduction to Part I the *historical.* Speaking of the postmodern, Hal Foster argues that "the rubric 'anti-aesthetic' . . . is *not* intended as one more assertion of the negation of art or of representation as such. . . . [Postmodern] critics take for granted that we are never outside representation—or rather, never outside politics. Here then, 'anti-aesthetic' is the sign not of a modern nihilism . . . but rather of a critique which destructures the order of representations in order to reinscribe them." Such reinscription is ethical and political: it calls, as bell hooks and Ahmad do, for the recovery of "voice" and the enactment of "decency" within the timeliness and worldliness of work that Said describes.

THE ETHICS OF THEORY

De Man and Miller explore the intellectual "grounds" of theory, and the other selections in this section examine the historical activity of theory. Several years ago Mark Conroy reviewed a collection of Paul de Man's posthumous essays. In that review he asks, "can our present-day stars of gender studies, culture critique and socio- and psychocriticism even be practicing the same craft as [de Man]? Like the return of the repressed, the panoply of anthropological interests scorned by de Man now have possession of the debate." Conroy's insightful point is that precisely the realm of anthropological issues and interests scorned by de Man now are central to theoretical debate. "Although [de Man's] most recent piece is less than fifteen years old," Conroy continues, "the volume has an antiquarian feel, in tone and sensibility as much as in theoretical purport. The past from which these pages come is indeed another country from the one most critics now inhabit."

The stark contrast between the narrow textual focus of de Man's work and the great diversity of cultural studies today reveals much about contemporary directions in criticism and theory. And yet the concern with questioning Enlightenment assumptions about the relations between texts and the world—to make them *more* "worldly" in Said's sense of the word—unites de Man's and Miller's concerns with the work of contemporary cultural studies. What Miller calls "the linguistic moment in literature" addresses the same issues of values and power that we have been calling the "ethics" of interpretation and cultural criticism. Such a conception of "ethics" can be seen in the work of bell hooks (as well as in West and Viswanathan in Part I), and it informs Ahmad's survey of "theory" in relation to the politics of colonialism and imperialism. Said makes a similar "move from the realm of interpretation to the realm of world politics," although he sees that this is "risky." The risk is that "the real work, the hard work" of intellectual activity will be lost in "identity politics" if those "politics" address only the restricted interests of narrowly defined groups. What theoretical work needed, Said argues, "is nothing less than the reintegration of all those people and cultures, once confined and reduced to peripheral status, with the rest of the human race."

Such work is the activity of ethics. Aesthetics connects particular experiences to a general system of meaning in order to create regular relationships between feeling and meaning—some possibility of *disinterested* experience. Ethics is an archive of strategies for connecting particular and *interested* activities to a general system of values. The strategies of ethics are always complex and "impure" because ethics has traditionally and repeatedly been used as a weapon in warfare between peoples, a way of asserting dominance of one group over another—of asserting that particular and interested values are, in fact, general and disinterested. For example, when bell hooks resists the sway of "theory," her complaint is that any version of "theory" brings with it an ethical frame that puts it in service to a particular social class or group. This is why the question of *interests*—the "central question today" that Barbara Christian articulates, namely, "For whom are we doing what we are doing when we do literary criticism?"—is crucially a question of ethics. For bell hooks, "postmodern" theory works because, as she says, "It's not like I'm going to talk about writing and thinking about postmodernism with other academics and/or intellectuals and not discuss these ideas with underclass non-academic black folks who are family, friends and comrades.

Since I have not broken the ties that bind me to underclass poor black community, I have seen that knowledge, especially that which enhances daily life and strengthens our capacity to survive, can be shared." Similarly, for Ahmad twentieth-century, anti-colonial struggle concommitant with (and perhaps, in his analysis, conditioning) the rise of "theory" has had a powerful positive effect on institutions of knowledge. "Despite the havoc caused recently," he writes, "by the more mindless kinds of poststructuralism[,] for the first time in its history the metropolitan university is being forced, in some of its nooks and niches, to face issues of race and gender and empire in a way it has never done before." (Cornel West makes a similar argument in "What Is Literary Studies?" [Part I].)

Ethics, unlike aesthetics, does not do away with interests and the "politics" that accompanies values and commitments, but attempts to situate them, as Said says, within a broad view of the world. Unlike aesthetics, ethics remains, in Said's term, a form of "worldliness" (involving social relations) that relates to the values of human work, which is always local, interested, and always particular. "Worldliness" is also connected to work "by an appreciation not of some tiny, defensively constituted corner of the world, but of the large, many-windowed house of human culture as a whole." Reconsideration of the "ties between the text and the world" that Said describes as the larger work of "theory"—it is also, as we have suggested in the General Introduction, the larger of work of "cultural studies" in departments of literature and language—remains an "interested," ethical activity. Said ends his essay with the "central" ethical question of the very idea of "interests." "Who benefits from leveling attacks on the canon?" he asks. "Certainly not the disadvantaged person or class whose history, if you bother to read it at all, is full of evidence that popular resistance to injustice has always derived immense benefits from literature and culture in general. . . . The crucial lesson," he goes on, "is that great antiauthoritarian uprisings made their earliest advances, not by denying the humanitarian and universalist claims of the general dominant culture, but by attacking the adherents of that culture for failing to uphold their own declared standards, for failing to extend them to all, as opposed to a small fraction, of humanity." These are, he says, "the great revisionary gestures" of literary theory.

The domain of "theory," as we see, is a site of debate, "the contest for forms and values which any decent cultural work embodies, realizes, and contains." The contest of theory is an ethical enterprise. Among other things, that enterprise weighs methods of understanding against objects of knowledge. Literary theory makes criticism self-conscious and examines explicitly methods of reading and definitions of literature. Whatever else they do, all the articles in Part II perform these functions. The function of theory—both "partisan" and "global," "unprovincial" and "interested"—moves beyond commitments to feminism, deconstruction, psychoanalysis, a particular ideology, or a school of cultural studies. It is the function of theory to explore what is at stake in the contest for forms and values in literary and cultural studies.

RELATED ESSAYS IN *CONTEMPORARY LITERARY CRITICISM*

Mikhail Bakhtin, "Discourse in Life and Discourse in Art (Concerning Sociological Poetics)"

Jacques Derrida, "The Principle of Reason: The University in the Eyes of Its Pupils"

Shoshana Felman, "Psychoanalysis and Education: Teaching Terminable and Interminable"

Diana Fuss, "Reading Like a Feminist"

Donna Haraway, "A Cyborg Manifesto: Science, Technology, and Socialist-Feminism in the Late Twentieth Century"

Cornel West, "Black Critics and the Pitfalls of Canon Formation"

Raymond Williams, "Base and Superstructure in Marxist Cultural Theory"

REFERENCES AND FURTHER READING

Baldick, Chris, *Criticism and Literary Theory: 1890 to the Present* (New York: Longman, 1996).

Barthes, Roland, *The Grain of the Voice: Interviews 1962–1980,* trans. Linda Coverdale (New York: Hill and Wang, 1985).

Benhabib, Seyla, *Critique, Norm, and Utopia: A Study of the Foundations of Critical Theory* (New York: Columbia University Press, 1986).

Booker, M. Keith, *A Practical Introduction to Literary Theory and Criticism* (White Plains, NY: Longman, 1996).

Conroy, Mark, Review of Paul de Man, *Critical Writings, 1953–1978,* in *Criticism* 33 (1991), 395–402.

Dewey, John, *Outlines of a Critical Theory of Ethics,* in *Early Works,* vol. 3, ed. Jo Ann Boydaton (Carbondale: Southern Illinois University Press, 1969).

Donoghue, Denis, *The Pure Gold of Theory* (Cambridge, MA: Blackwell, 1992).

Eagleton, Mary, *Feminist Literary Theory: A Reader* (Cambridge, MA: Blackwell, 1996).

Easterlin, Nancy, and Barbara Riebling, *After Poststructuralism: Interdisciplinarity and Literary Theory* (Evanston, IL: Northwestern University Press, 1993).

Foster, Hal, "Postmodernism: A Preface," in *The Anti-Aesthetic: Essays on Postmodern Culture,* ed. Hal Foster (Port Townsend, WA: Bay Press, 1983), ix–xvi.

Graff, Gerald, and Reginald Gibbons, "Preface," in *Criticism in the University,* ed. Gerald Graff and Reginald Gibbons (Evanston: Northwestern University Press, 1985), 7–12.

Groden, Michael, and Martin Kreiswirth, *The Johns Hopkins Guide to Literary Theory and Criticism* (Baltimore: Johns Hopkins University Press, 1994).

Habermas, Jürgen, "Knowledge and Human Interests: A General Perspective," in *Knowledge and Human Interests,* trans. Jeremy Shapiro (Boston: Beacon Press, 1971).

Hirsch, E. D., "Back to History," in *Criticism in the University,* ed. Gerald Graff and Reginald Gibbons (Evanston, IL: Northwestern University Press, 1985). 189–97.

Hunter, Ian, "Aesthetics and Cultural Studies," in *Cultural Studies,* ed. Lawrence Grossberg, Cary Nelson, and Paula Treicher (New York: Routledge, 1992), 347–367.

Jameson, Fredric, *Postmodernism; or The Cultural Logic of Late Capitalism* (Durham, NC: Duke University Press, 1991).

Kreiswirth, Martin, and Mark Cheetham, "Introduction: 'Theory-Mad Beyond Redemption'(?)," in *Theory Between the Disciplines,* ed. Martin Kreiswirth and Mark Cheetham (Ann Arbor: University of Michigan Press, 1990), 1–16.

Kristeva, Julia, "The Ethics of Linguistics," in *Desire in Language,* trans. Thomas Gora, Alice Jardine, and Leon Roudiez (New York: Columbia University Press, 1980).

Leitch, Vincent B., *Cultural Criticism, Literary Theory, Poststructuralism* (New York: Columbia University Press, 1992).

Lentricchia, Frank, *Criticism and Social Change* (Chicago: University of Chicago Press, 1983).

————, "On Behalf of Theory," in *Criticism in the University,* ed. Gerald Graff and Reginald Gibbons (Evanston, IL: Northwestern University Press, 1985), 105–10.

Lyotard, Jean-François, *The Postmodern Condition: A Report On Knowledge* (Minneapolis: University of Minnesota Press, 1984).

————, *The Postmodern Explained: Correspondence, 1982–85* (Minneapolis: University of Minnesota Press, 1993).

McGee, Patrick, *Telling the Other: The Question of Value in Modern and Postmodern Writing* (Ithaca, NY: Cornell University Press, 1992).

Merod, Jim, *The Political Responsibility of the Critic* (Ithaca: Cornell University Press, 1987).

Miller, J. Hillis, *The Ethics of Reading* (New York: Columbia University Press, 1986).

————, "Presidential Address: The Triumph of Theory, the Resistance to Reading, and the Question of the Material Base," in *PMLA,* 102 (1987), 281–91.

Norris, Christopher, *Paul de Man: Deconstruction and the Critique of Aesthetic Ideology* (New York: Routledge, 1988).

Quinney, Laura, *Literary Power and the Criteria of Truth* (Gainesville: University Press of Florida, 1995).

Said, Edward, *The World, the Text, and the Critic* (Cambridge, MA: Harvard University Press, 1983).

Schleifer, Ronald, "The Advent of Theory and the Transformation of Journal Editing," *Editors' Notes: Bulletin of the Council of Editors of Learned Journals,* 1991, 10, no. 1: 38–45.

————, Robert Con Davis, and Nancy Mergler, *Culture and Cognition: The Boundaries of Literary and Scientific Understanding* (Ithaca: Cornell University Press, 1992).

Schwab, Gabriele, *The Mirror and the Killer-Queen: Otherness in Literary Language* (Bloomington: Indiana University Press, 1996).

Szondi, Peter, *Introduction to Literary Hermeneutics* (New York: Cambridge University Press, 1995).

W. K. Wimsatt, "The Domain of Criticism," (1949), reprinted in *The Verbal Icon* (Lexington: University of Kentucky Press, 1954), 221–32.

Paul de Man
1919–1983

Paul de Man was born in Antwerp and received a Ph.D. from Harvard University in 1960. At the time of his death, he was Sterling Professor of French and comparative literature at Yale University. In the course of his academic career—especially in its last decade—he became a major intellectual force in American literary studies. In large part, this was due to his early and articulate understanding of the importance of Continental philosophy to literary studies and the ease with which he moved between philosophy and literature and among English, French, and German texts. His major form was the philosophical-literary essay, written in a severe and difficult, yet rewarding style. All his books are collections of essays, including *Blindness and Insight: Essays in the Rhetoric of Contemporary Criticism* (1971, reprint 1983), *Allegories of Reading: Figural Language in Rousseau, Nietzsche, Rilke, and Proust* (1979), *The Rhetoric of Romanticism* (1984), and *The Resistance to Theory* (1986). Soon after his death, a number of articles he wrote for the collaborationist press of Nazi-occupied Belgium were discovered and reprinted. These articles, and the fact that he never made public references to his youthful activity, have occasioned a great deal of controversy and much rereading of his work.

Still, that work has been immensely important in literary criticism for the last twenty years. It most clearly articulated the literary implications of post–World War II Continental philosophy. In his early work, de Man described a kind of Sartrean existential approach to literature, and later he turned to the phenomenological criticism occasioned by Husserl and Heidegger. His major work since 1970, however, is marked by the influence of Nietzsche and poststructuralist thought—especially that of Jacques Derrida—and, with his Yale colleagues J. Hillis Miller and Geoffrey Hartman, he helped to define a distinctively American brand of deconstructive literary criticism.

The following essay, "The Resistance to Theory" (1982), is part of that effort, in that ultimately de Man defines the general project of literary theory in terms strongly resonant with Yale School deconstruction. First published near the end of his life, this piece offers a condensed survey of de Man's views concerning philosophy, language, literature, and rhetoric. He argues that during the 1960s, literary theory emerged when approaches to literary texts became based on linguistics rather than history or aesthetics. A focus on the specific dynamics of language, he claims, defines an integral and transhistorical way by which to articulate literature's function—a consequence that can explain more traditional critics' resistance. But since de Man describes language as a signifying system whose logical and grammatical dimensions are ineluctably undermined and destabilized by the rhetorical dimension of tropes or metaphors, literary theory itself becomes a self-divided project. On the one hand, its refined analytic techniques articulate, sometimes unwittingly, a critical process de Man summarizes as "reading," which documents how the unreliability of rhetorical tropes makes texts' meanings indeterminate. On the other hand, since this very linguistic feature threatens to unravel theory's own aspirations to formulate general literary principles, de Man claims that "resistance may be a built-in constituent of its discourse." Turning this paradoxical screw one notch further, he concludes that "technically correct rhetorical readings . . . are theory and not theory at the same time, the universal theory of the impossibility of theory." This is a dilemma without clear recourse, since, as de Man explains in his own devious trope, rejecting theory on this basis "would be like rejecting anatomy because it has failed to cure mortality."

The Resistance to Theory

This essay was not originally intended to address the question of teaching directly, although it was supposed to have a didactic and an educational function—which it failed to achieve. It was written at the request of the Committee on Research Activities of the Modern Language Association as a contribution to a collective volume entitled *Introduction to Scholarship in Modern Languages and Literatures.* I was asked to write the section on literary theory. Such essays are expected to follow a clearly determined program: they are supposed to provide the reader with a select but comprehensive list of the main trends and publications in the field, to synthesize and classify the main problematic areas and to lay out a critical and programmatic projection of the solutions which can be expected in the foreseeable future. All this with a keen awareness that, ten years later, someone will be asked to repeat the same exercise.

I found it difficult to live up, in minimal good faith, to the requirements of this program and could only try to explain, as concisely as possible, why the main theoretical interest of literary theory consists in the impossibility of its definition. The Committee rightly judged that

this was an inauspicious way to achieve the pedagogical objectives of the volume and commissioned another article. I thought their decision altogether justified, as well as interesting in its implications for the teaching of literature.

I tell this for two reasons. First, to explain the traces in the article of the original assignment which account for the awkwardness of trying to be more retrospective and more general than one can legitimately hope to be. But, second, because the predicament also reveals a question of general interest: that of the relationship between the scholarship (the key word in the title of the MLA volume), the theory, and the teaching of literature.

Overfacile opinion notwithstanding, teaching is not primarily an intersubjective relationship between people but a cognitive process in which self and other are only tangentially and contiguously involved. The only teaching worthy of the name is scholarly, not personal; analogies between teaching and various aspects of show business or guidance counseling are more often than not excuses for having abdicated the task. Scholarship has, in principle, to be eminently teachable. In the case of literature, such scholarship involves at least two complementary areas: historical and philological facts as the preparatory condition for understanding, and methods of reading or interpretation. The latter is admittedly an open discipline, which can, however, hope to evolve by rational means, despite internal crises, controversies and polemics. As a controlled reflection on the formation of method, theory rightly proves to be entirely compatible with teaching, and one can think of numerous important theoreticians who are or were also prominent scholars. A question arises only if a tension develops between methods of understanding and the knowledge which those methods allow one to reach. If there is indeed something about literature, as such, which allows for a discrepancy between truth and method, between *Wahrheit* and *Methode,* then scholarship and theory are no longer necessarily compatible; as a first casualty of this complication, the notion of "literature as such" as well as the clear distinction between history and interpretation can no longer be taken for granted. For a method that cannot be made to suit the "truth" of its object can only teach delusion. Various developments, not only in the contemporary scene but in the long and complicated history of literary and linguistic instruction, reveal symptoms that suggest that such a difficulty is an inherent focus of the discourse about literature. These uncertainties are manifest in the hostility directed at theory in the name of ethical and aesthetic values, as well as in the recuperative attempts of theoreticians to reassert their own subservience to these values. The most effective of these attacks will denounce theory as an obstacle to scholarship and, consequently, to teaching. It is worth examining whether, and why, this is the case. For if this is indeed so, then it is better to fail in teaching what should not be taught than to succeed in teaching what is not true.

A general statement about literary theory should not, in theory, start from pragmatic con-siderations. It should address such questions as the definition of literature (what is literature?) and discuss the distinction between literary and non-literary uses of language, as well as between literary and non-verbal forms of art. It should then proceed to the descriptive taxonomy of the various aspects and species of the literary genus and to the normative rules that are bound to follow from such a classification. Or, if one rejects a scholastic for a phenomenological model, one should attempt a phenomenology of the literary activity as writing, reading or both, or of the literary work as the product, the correlate of such an activity. Whatever the approach taken (and several other theoretically justifiable starting-points can be imagined) it is certain that considerable difficulties will arise at once, difficulties that cut so deep that even the most elementary task of scholarship, the delimitation of the corpus and the *état présent* of the question, is bound to end in confusion, not necessarily because the bibliography is so large but because it is impossible to fix its borderlines. Such predictable difficulties have not prevented many writers on literature from proceeding along theoretical rather than pragmatic lines, often with considerable success. It can be shown however that, in all cases, this success depends on the power of a system (philosophical, religious or ideological) that may well remain implicit but that determines an *a priori* conception of what is "literary" by starting out from the premises of the system rather than from the literary thing itself—if such a "thing" indeed exists. This last qualification is of course a real question which in fact accounts for the predictability of the difficulties just alluded to: if the condition of existence of an entity is itself particularly critical, then the theory of this entity is bound to fall back into the pragmatic. The difficult and inconclusive history of literary theory indicates that this is indeed the case for literature in an even more manifest manner than for other verbalized occurrences such as jokes, for example, or even dreams. The attempt to treat literature theoretically may as well resign itself to the fact that it has to start out from empirical considerations.

Pragmatically speaking, then, we know that there has been, over the last fifteen to twenty years, a strong interest in something called literary theory and that, in the United States, this interest has at times coincided with the importation and reception of foreign, mostly but not always continental, influences. We also know that this wave of interest now seems to be receding as some satiation or disappointment sets in after the initial enthusiasm. Such an ebb and flow is natural enough, but it remains interesting, in this case, because it makes the depth of the resistance to literary theory so manifest. It is a recurrent strategy of any anxiety to defuse what it considers threatening by magnification or minimization, by attributing to it claims to power of which it is bound to fall short. If a cat is called a tiger it can easily be dismissed as a paper tiger; the question remains however why one was so scared of the cat in the first place. The same tactic works in reverse: calling the cat a mouse and then deriding it for its pretense to be mighty. Rather than being drawn into this polemical whirlpool, it might be better to try to call the cat a cat and to document, however briefly, the contemporary version of the resistance to theory in this country.

The predominant trends in North American literary criticism, before the nineteen sixties, were certainly not averse to theory, if by theory one understands the rooting of literary exegesis and of critical evaluation in a system of some conceptual generality. Even the most intuitive, empirical and theoretically low-key writers on literature made use of a minimal set of concepts (tone, organic form, allusion, tradition, historical situation, etc.) of at least some general import. In several other cases, the interest in theory was publicly asserted and practiced. A broadly shared methodology, more or less overtly proclaimed, links together such influential text books of the era as *Understanding Poetry* (Brooks and Warren), *Theory of Literature* (Wellek and Warren) and *The Fields of Light* (Reuben Brower) or such theoretically oriented works as *The Mirror and the Lamp, Language as Gesture* and *The Verbal Icon*.

Yet, with the possible exception of Kenneth Burke and, in some respects, Northrop Frye, none of these authors would have considered themselves theoreticians in the post-1960 sense of the term, nor did their work provoke as strong reactions, positive or negative, as that of later theoreticians. There were polemics, no doubt, and differences in approach that cover a wide spectrum of divergencies, yet the fundamental curriculum of literary studies as well as the talent and training expected for them were not being seriously challenged. New Critical approaches experienced no difficulty fitting into the academic establishments without their practitioners having to betray their literary sensibilities in any way; several of its representatives pursued successful parallel careers as poets or novelists next to their academic functions. Nor did they experience difficulties with regard to a national tradition which, though certainly less tyrannical than its European counterparts, is nevertheless far from powerless. The perfect embodiment of the New Criticism remains, in many respects, the personality and the ideology of T. S. Eliot, a combination of original talent, traditional learning, verbal wit and moral earnestness, an Anglo-American blend of intellectual gentility not so repressed as not to afford tantalizing glimpses of darker psychic and political depths, but without breaking the surface of an ambivalent decorum that has its own complacencies and seductions. The normative principles of such a literary ambiance are cultural and ideological rather than theoretical, oriented towards the integrity of a social and historical self rather than towards the impersonal consistency that theory requires. Culture allows for, indeed advocates, a degree of cosmopolitanism, and the literary spirit of the American Academy of the fifties was anything but provincial. It had no difficulty appreciating and assimilating outstanding products of a kindred spirit that originated in Europe: Curtius, Auerbach, Croce, Spitzer, Alonso, Valéry and also, with the exception of some of his works, J. P. Sartre. The inclusion of Sartre in this list is important, for it indicates that the dominant cultural code we are trying to evoke cannot simply be assimilated to a political polarity of the left and the right, of the academic and non-academic, of Greenwich Village and Gambier, Ohio. Politically oriented and predominantly non-academic journals, of which the *Partisan Review* of the fifties remains the best example, did not (after due allowance is made for all proper reservations and distinctions) stand in any genuine opposition to the New Critical approaches. The broad, though negative, consensus that brings these extremely diverse trends and individuals together is their shared resistance to theory. This diagnosis is borne out by the arguments and complicities that have since come to light in a more articulate opposition to the common opponent.

The interest of these considerations would be at most anecdotal (the historical impact of twentieth-century literary discussion being so slight) if it were not for the theoretical implications of the resistance to theory. The local manifestations of this resistance are themselves systematic enough to warrant one's interest.

What is it that is being threatened by the approaches to literature that developed during the sixties and that now, under a variety of designations, make up the ill-defined and somewhat chaotic field of literary theory? These approaches cannot be simply equated with any particular method or country. Structuralism was not the only trend to dominate the stage, not even in France, and structuralism as well as semiology are inseparable from prior tendencies in the Slavic domain. In Germany, the main impulses have come from other directions, from the Frankfurt school and more orthodox Marx-

ists, from post-Husserlian phenomenology and post-Heideggerian hermeneutics, with only minor inroads made by structural analysis. All these trends have had their share of influence in the United States, in more or less productive combinations with nationally rooted concerns. Only a nationally or personally competitive view of history would wish to hierarchize such hard-to-label movements. The possibility of doing literary theory, which is by no means to be taken for granted, has itself become a consciously reflected-upon question and those who have progressed furthest in this question are the most controversial but also the best sources of information. This certainly includes several of the names loosely connected with structuralism, broadly enough defined to include Saussure, Jakobson and Barthes as well as Greimas and Althusser, that is to say, so broadly defined as to be no longer of use as a meaningful historical term.

Literary theory can be said to come into being when the approach to literary texts is no longer based on non-linguistic, that is to say historical and aesthetic, considerations or, to put it somewhat less crudely, when the object of discussion is no longer the meaning or the value but the modalities of production and of reception of meaning and of value prior to their establishment—the implication being that this establishment is problematic enough to require an autonomous discipline of critical investigation to consider its possibility and its status. Literary history, even when considered at the furthest remove from the platitudes of positivistic historicism, is still the history of an understanding of which the possibility is taken for granted. The question of the relationship between aesthetics and meaning is more complex, since aesthetics apparently has to do with the *effect* of meaning rather than with its content *per se*. But aesthetics is in fact, ever since its development just before and with Kant, a phenomenalism of a process of meaning and understanding, and it may be naive in that it postulates (as its name indicates) a phenomenology of art and of literature which may well be what is at issue. Aesthetics is part of a universal system of philosophy rather than a specific theory. In the nineteenth-century philosophical tradition, Nietzsche's challenge of the system erected by Kant, Hegel and their successors is a version of the general question of philosophy. Nietzsche's critique of metaphysics includes, or starts out from, the aesthetic, and the same could be argued for Heidegger. The invocation of prestigious philosophical names does not intimate that the present-day development of literary theory is a by-product of larger philosophical speculations. In some rare cases, a direct link may exist between philosophy and literary theory. More frequently, however, contemporary literary theory is a relatively autonomous version of questions that also surface, in a different context, in philosophy, though not necessarily in a clearer and more rigorous form. Philosophy, in England as well as on the Continent, is less freed from traditional patterns than it sometimes pretends to believe and the prominent, though never dominant, place of aesthetics among the main components of the system is a constitutive part of this system. It is therefore not surprising that contemporary literary theory came into being from outside philosophy and sometimes in conscious rebellion against the weight of its tradition. Literary theory may now well have become a legitimate concern of philosophy but it cannot be assimilated to it, either factually or theoretically. It contains a necessarily pragmatic moment that certainly weakens it as theory but that adds a subversive element of unpredictability and makes it something of a wild card in the serious game of the theoretical disciplines.

The advent of theory, the break that is now so often being deplored and that sets it aside from literary history and from literary criticism, occurs with the introduction of linguistic terminology in the metalanguage about literature. By linguistic terminology is meant a terminology that designates reference prior to designating the referent and takes into account, in the consider-

ation of the world, the referential function of language or, to be somewhat more specific, that considers reference as a function of language and not necessarily as an intuition. Intuition implies perception, consciousness, experience, and leads at once into the world of logic and of understanding with all its correlatives, among which aesthetics occupies a prominent place. The assumption that there can be a science of language which is not necessarily a logic leads to the development of a terminology which is not necessarily aesthetic. Contemporary literary theory comes into its own in such events as the application of Saussurian linguistics to literary texts.

The affinity between structural linguistics and literary texts is not as obvious as, with the hindsight of history, it now may seem. Peirce, Saussure, Sapir and Bloomfield were not originally concerned with literature at all but with the scientific foundations of linguistics. But the interest of philologists such as Roman Jakobson or literary critics such as Roland Barthes in semiology reveals the natural attraction of literature to a theory of linguistic signs. By considering language as a system of signs and of signification rather than as an established pattern of meanings, one displaces or even suspends the traditional barriers between literary and presumably non-literary uses of language and liberates the corpus from the secular weight of textual canonization. The results of the encounter between semiology and literature went considerably further than those of many other theoretical models—philological, psychological or classically epistemological—which writers on literature in quest of such models had tried out before. The responsiveness of literary texts to semiotic analysis is visible in that, whereas other approaches were unable to reach beyond observations that could be paraphrased or translated in terms of common knowledge, these analyses revealed patterns that could only be described in terms of their own, specifically linguistic, aspects. The linguistics of semiology and of literature apparently have something in common that only their shared perspective can detect and that pertains distinctively to them. The definition of this something, often referred to as literariness, has become the object of literary theory.

Literariness, however, is often misunderstood in a way that has provoked much of the confusion which dominates today's polemics. It is frequently assumed, for instance, that literariness is another word for, or another mode of, aesthetic response. The use, in conjunction with literariness, of such terms as style and stylistics, form or even "poetry" (as in "the poetry of grammar"), all of which carry strong aesthetic connotations, helps to foster this confusion, even among those who first put the term in circulation. Roland Barthes, for example, in an essay properly and revealingly dedicated to Roman Jakobson, speaks eloquently of the writer's quest for a perfect coincidence of the phonic properties of a word with its signifying function. "We would also wish to insist on the Cratylism of the name (and of the sign) in Proust. . . . Proust sees the relationship between signifier and signified as motivated, the one copying the other and representing in its material form the signified essence of the thing (and not the thing itself). . . . This realism (in the scholastic sense of the word), which conceives of names as the 'copy' of the ideas, has taken, in Proust, a radical form. But one may well ask whether it is not more or less consciously present in all writing and whether it is possible to be a writer without some sort of belief in the natural relationship between names and essences. The poetic function, in the widest sense of the word, would thus be defined by a Cratylian awareness of the sign, and the writer would be the conveyor of this secular myth which wants language to imitate the idea and which, contrary to the teachings of linguistic science, thinks of signs as motivated signs."[1] To the extent that Cratylism assumes a convergence of the phenomenal aspects of language, as sound, with its signifying function as referent, it is an aesthetically oriented conception; one could, in fact, without distortion, consider aesthetic theory, including its most systematic for-

mulation in Hegel, as the complete unfolding of the model of which the Cratylian conception of language is a version. Hegel's somewhat cryptic reference to Plato, in the *Aesthetics,* may well be interpreted in this sense. Barthes and Jakobson often seem to invite a purely aesthetic reading, yet there is a part of their statement that moves in the opposite direction. For the convergence of sound and meaning celebrated by Barthes in Proust and, as Gérard Genette has decisively shown,[2] later dismantled by Proust himself as a seductive temptation to mystified minds, is also considered here to be a mere *effect* which language can perfectly well achieve, but which bears no substantial relationship, by analogy or by ontologically grounded imitation, to anything beyond that particular effect. It is a rhetorical rather than an aesthetic function of language, an identifiable trope (paronomasis) that operates on the level of the signifier and contains no responsible pronouncement on the nature of the world—despite its powerful potential to create the opposite illusion. The phenomenality of the signifier, as sound, is unquestionably involved in the correspondence between the name and the thing named, but the link, the relationship between word and thing, is not phenomenal but conventional.

This gives the language considerable freedom from referential restraint, but it makes it epistemologically highly suspect and volatile, since its use can no longer be said to be determined by considerations of truth and falsehood, good and evil, beauty and ugliness, or pleasure and pain. Whenever this autonomous potential of language can be revealed by analysis, we are dealing with literariness and, in fact, with literature as the place where this negative knowledge about the reliability of linguistic utterance is made available. The ensuing foregrounding of material, phenomenal aspects of the signifier creates a strong illusion of aesthetic seduction at the very moment when the actual aesthetic function has been, at the very least, suspended. It is inevitable that semiology or similarly oriented methods be considered formalistic, in the sense of being aesthetically rather than semantically valorized, but the inevitability of such an interpretation does not make it less aberrant. Literature involves the voiding, rather than the affirmation, of aesthetic categories. One of the consequences of this is that, whereas we have traditionally been accustomed to reading literature by analogy with the plastic arts and with music, we now have to recognize the necessity of a non-perceptual, linguistic moment in painting and music, and learn to *read* pictures rather than to *imagine* meaning.

If literariness is not an aesthetic quality, it is also not primarily mimetic. Mimesis becomes one trope among others, language choosing to imitate a non-verbal entity just as paronomasis "imitates" a sound without any claim to identity (or reflection on difference) between the verbal and non-verbal elements. The most misleading representation of literariness, and also the most recurrent objection to contemporary literary theory, considers it as pure verbalism, as a denial of the reality principle in the name of absolute fictions, and for reasons that are said to be ethically and politically shameful. The attack reflects the anxiety of the aggressors rather than the guilt of the accused. By allowing for the necessity of a non-phenomenal linguistics, one frees the discourse on literature from naive oppositions between fiction and reality, which are themselves an offspring of an uncritically mimetic conception of art. In a genuine semiology as well as in other linguistically oriented theories, the referential function of language is not being denied—far from it; what is in question is its authority as a model for natural or phenomenal cognition. Literature is fiction not because it somehow refuses to acknowledge "reality," but because it is not *a priori* certain that language functions according to principles which are those, or which are *like* those, of the phenomenal world. It is therefore not *a priori* certain that literature is a reliable source of information about anything but its own language.

It would be unfortunate, for example, to confuse the materiality of the signifier with the materiality of what it signifies. This may seem obvious enough on the level of light and sound, but it is less so with regard to the more general phenomenality of space, time or especially of the self; no one in his right mind will try to grow grapes by the luminosity of the word "day," but it is very difficult not to conceive the pattern of one's past and future existence as in accordance with temporal and spatial schemes that belong to fictional narratives and not to the world. This does not mean that fictional narratives are not part of the world and of reality; their impact upon the world may well be all too strong for comfort. What we call ideology is precisely the confusion of linguistic with natural reality, of reference with phenomenalism. It follows that, more than any other mode of inquiry, including economics, the linguistics of literariness is a powerful and indispensable tool in the unmasking of ideological aberrations, as well as a determining factor in accounting for their occurrence. Those who reproach literary theory for being oblivious to social and historical (that is to say ideological) reality are merely stating their fear at having their own ideological mystifications exposed by the tool they are trying to discredit. They are, in short, very poor readers of Marx's *German Ideology*.

In these all too summary evocations of arguments that have been much more extensively and convincingly made by others, we begin to perceive some of the answers to the initial question: what is it about literary theory that is so threatening that it provokes such strong resistance and attacks? It upsets rooted ideologies by revealing the mechanics of their workings; it goes against a powerful philosophical tradition of which aesthetics is a prominent part; it upsets the established canon of literary works and blurs the borderlines between literary and non-literary discourse. By implication, it may also reveal the links between ideologies and philosophy. All this is ample enough reason for suspicion, but not a satisfying answer to the question. For it makes the tension between contemporary literary theory and the tradition of literary studies appear as a mere historical conflict between two modes of thought that happen to hold the stage at the same time. If the conflict is merely historical, in the literal sense, it is of limited theoretical interest, a passing squall in the intellectual weather of the world. As a matter of fact, the arguments in favor of the legitimacy of literary theory are so compelling that it seems useless to concern oneself with the conflict at all. Certainly, none of the objections to theory, presented again and again, always misinformed or based on crude misunderstandings of such terms as mimesis, fiction, reality, ideology, reference and, for that matter, relevance, can be said to be of genuine rhetorical interest.

It may well be, however, that the development of literary theory is itself overdetermined by complications inherent in its very project and unsettling with regard to its status as a scientific discipline. Resistance may be a built-in constituent of its discourse, in a manner that would be inconceivable in the natural sciences and unmentionable in the social sciences. It may well be, in other words, that the polemical opposition, the systematic nonunderstanding and misrepresentation, the unsubstantial but eternally recurrent objections, are the displaced symptoms of a resistance inherent in the theoretical enterprise itself. To claim that this would be sufficient reason not to envisage doing literary theory would be like rejecting anatomy because it has failed to cure mortality. The real debate of literary theory is not with its polemical opponents but rather with its own methodological assumptions and possibilities. Rather than asking why literary theory is threatening, we should perhaps ask why it has such difficulty going about its business and why it lapses so readily either into the language of self-justification and self-defense or else into the overcompensation of a programmatically euphoric utopianism. Such insecurity about its own project calls for self-analysis, if one is to understand the frustrations that attend upon its practitioners, even when they seem to dwell in serene methodological

self-assurance. And if these difficulties are indeed an integral part of the problem, then they will have to be, to some extent, a-historical in the temporal sense of the term. The way in which they are encountered on the present local literary scene as a resistance to the introduction of linguistic terminology in aesthetic and historical discourse about literature is only one particular version of a question that cannot be reduced to a specific historical situation and called modern, post-modern, post-classical or romantic (not even in Hegel's sense of the term), although its compulsive way of forcing itself upon us in the guise of a system of historical periodization is certainly part of its problematic nature. Such difficulties can be read in the text of literary theory at all times, at whatever historical moment one wishes to select. One of the main achievements of the present theoretical trends is to have restored some awareness of this fact. Classical, medieval and Renaissance literary theory is now often being read in a way that knows enough about what it is doing not to wish to call itself "modern."

We return, then, to the original question in an attempt to broaden the discussion enough to inscribe the polemics inside the question rather than having them determine it. The resistance to theory is a resistance to the use of language about language. It is therefore a resistance to language itself or to the possibility that language contains factors or functions that cannot be reduced to intuition. But we seem to assume all too readily that, when we refer to something called "language," we know what it is we are talking about, although there is probably no word to be found in the language that is as overdetermined, self-evasive, disfigured and disfiguring as "language." Even if we choose to consider it at a safe remove from any theoretical model, in the pragmatic history of "language," not as a concept, but as a didactic assignment that no human being can bypass, we soon find ourselves confronted by theoretical enigmas. The most familiar and general of all linguistic models, the classical *trivium,* which considers the science of language as consisting of grammar, rhetoric, and logic (or dialectics), is in fact a set of unresolved tensions powerful enough to have generated an infinitely prolonged discourse of endless frustration of which contemporary literary theory, even at its most self-assured, is one more chapter. The difficulties extend to the internal articulations between the constituent parts as well as the articulation of the field of language with the knowledge of the world in general, the link between the *trivium* and the *quadrivium,* which covers the non-verbal sciences of number (arithmetic), of space (geometry), of motion (astronomy), and of time (music). In the history of philosophy, this link is traditionally, as well as substantially, accomplished by way of logic, the area where the rigor of the linguistic discourse about itself matches up with the rigor of the mathematical discourse about the world. Seventeenth-century epistemology, for instance, at the moment when the relationship between philosophy and mathematics is particularly close, holds up the language of what it calls geometry (*mos geometricus*), and which in fact includes the homogeneous concatenation between space, time and number, as the sole model of coherence and economy. Reasoning *more geometrico* is said to be "almost the only mode of reasoning that is infallible, because it is the only one to adhere to the true method, whereas all other ones are by natural necessity in a degree of confusion of which only geometrical minds can be aware."[3] This is a clear instance of the interconnection between a science of the phenomenal world and a science of language conceived as definitional logic, the pre-condition for a correct axiomatic-deductive, synthetic reasoning. The possibility of thus circulating freely between logic and mathematics has its own complex and problematic history as well as its contemporary equivalences with a different logic and a different mathematics. What matters for our present argument is that this articulation of the sciences

of language with the mathematical sciences represents a particularly compelling version of a continuity between a theory of language, as logic, and the knowledge of the phenomenal world to which mathematics gives access. In such a system, the place of aesthetics is preordained and by no means alien, provided the priority of logic, in the model of the *trivium,* is not being questioned. For even if one assumes, for the sake of argument and against a great deal of historical evidence, that the link between logic and the natural sciences is secure, this leaves open the question, within the confines of the *trivium* itself, of the relationship between grammar, rhetoric and logic. And this is the point at which literariness, the use of language that foregrounds the rhetorical over the grammatical and the logical function, intervenes as a decisive but unsettling element which, in a variety of modes and aspects, disrupts the inner balance of the model and, consequently, its outward extension to the nonverbal world as well.

Logic and grammar seem to have a natural enough affinity for each other and, in the tradition of Cartesian linguistics, the grammarians of Port-Royal experienced little difficulty at being logicians as well. The same claim persists today in very different methods and terminologies that nevertheless maintain the same orientation toward the universality that logic shares with science. Replying to those who oppose the singularity of specific texts to the scientific generality of the semiotic project, A. J. Greimas disputes the right to use the dignity of "grammar" to describe a reading that would not be committed to universality. Those who have doubts about the semiotic method, he writes, "postulate the necessity of constructing a grammar for each particular text. But the essence (*le propre*) of a grammar is its ability to account for a large number of texts, and the metaphorical use of the term . . . fails to hide the fact that one has, in fact, given up on the semiotic project."[4] There is no doubt that what is here prudently called "a large number" implies the hope at least of a future model that would in fact be applicable to the generation of all texts. Again, it is not our present purpose to discuss the validity of this methodological optimism, but merely to offer it as an instance of the persistent symbiosis between grammar and logic. It is clear that, for Greimas as for the entire tradition to which he belongs, the grammatical and the logical functions of language are co-extensive. Grammar is an isotope of logic.

It follows that, as long as it remains grounded in grammar, any theory of language, including a literary one, does not threaten what we hold to be the underlying principle of all cognitive and aesthetic linguistic systems. Grammar stands in the service of logic which, in turn, allows for the passage to the knowledge of the world. The study of grammar, the first of the *artes liberales,* is the necessary pre-condition for scientific and humanistic knowledge. As long as it leaves this principle intact, there is nothing threatening about literary theory. The continuity between theory and phenomenalism is asserted and preserved by the system itself. Difficulties occur only when it is no longer possible to ignore the epistemological thrust of the rhetorical dimension of discourse, that is, when it is no longer possible to keep it in its place as a mere adjunct, a mere ornament within the semantic function.

The uncertain relationship between grammar and rhetoric (as opposed to that between grammar and logic) is apparent, in the history of the *trivium,* in the uncertain status of figures of speech or tropes, a component of language that straddles the disputed borderlines between the two areas. Tropes used to be part of the study of grammar but were also considered to be the semantic agent of the specific function (or effect) that rhetoric performs as persuasion as well as meaning. Tropes, unlike grammar, pertain primordially to language. They are text-producing functions that are not necessarily patterned on a non-verbal entity, whereas grammar is by definition capable of extra-linguistic generalization. The latent tension between rhetoric and grammar precipitates out in the problem of reading,

the process that necessarily partakes of both. It turns out that the resistance to theory is in fact a resistance to reading, a resistance that is perhaps at its most effective, in contemporary studies, in the methodologies that call themselves theories of reading but nevertheless avoid the function they claim as their object.

What is meant when we assert that the study of literary texts is necessarily dependent on an act of reading, or when we claim that this act is being systematically avoided? Certainly more than the tautology that one has to have read at least some parts, however small, of a text (or read some part, however small, of a text about this text) in order to be able to make a statement about it. Common as it may be, criticism by hearsay is only rarely held up as exemplary. To stress the by no means self-evident necessity of reading implies at least two things. First of all, it implies that literature is not a transparent message in which it can be taken for granted that the distinction between the message and the means of communication is clearly established. Second, and more problematically, it implies that the grammatical decoding of a text leaves a residue of indetermination that has to be, but cannot be, resolved by grammatical means, however extensively conceived. The extension of grammar to include para-figural dimensions is in fact the most remarkable and debatable strategy of contemporary semiology, especially in the study of syntagmatic and narrative structures. The codification of contextual elements well beyond the syntactical limits of the sentence leads to the systematic study of metaphrastic dimensions and has considerably refined and expanded the knowledge of textual codes. It is equally clear, however, that this extension is always strategically directed towards the replacement of rhetorical figures by grammatical codes. This tendency to replace a rhetorical by a grammatical terminology (to speak of hypotaxis, for instance, to designate anamorphic or metonymic tropes) is part of an explicit program, a program that is entirely admirable in its intent since it tends towards the mastering and the clarification of meaning. The replacement of a hermeneutic by a semiotic model, of interpretation by decoding, would represent, in view of the baffling historical instability of textual meanings (including, of course, those of canonical texts), a considerable progress. Much of the hesitation associated with "reading" could thus be dispelled.

The argument can be made, however, that no grammatical decoding, however, refined, could claim to reach the determining figural dimensions of a text. There are elements in all texts that are by no means ungrammatical, but whose semantic function is not grammatically definable, neither in themselves nor in context. Do we have to interpret the genitive in the title of Keats' unfinished epic *The Fall of Hyperion* as meaning "Hyperion's Fall," the case story of the defeat of an older by a newer power, the very recognizable story from which Keats indeed started out but from which he increasingly strayed away, or as "Hyperion Falling," the much less specific but more disquieting evocation of an actual process of falling, regardless of its beginning, its end or the identity of the entity to whom it befalls to be falling? This story is indeed told in the later fragment entitled *The Fall of Hyperion,* but it is told about a character who resembles Apollo rather than Hyperion, the same Apollo who, in the first version (called *Hyperion*), should definitely be triumphantly standing rather than falling if Keats had not been compelled to interrupt, for no apparent reason, the story of Apollo's triumph. Does the title tell us that Hyperion is fallen and that Apollo stands, or does it tell us that Hyperion and Apollo (and Keats, whom it is hard to distinguish, at times, from Apollo) are interchangeable in that all of them are necessarily and constantly falling? Both readings are grammatically correct, but it is impossible to decide from the context (the ensuing narrative) which version is the right one. The narrative context suits neither and both at the same time, and one is tempted to suggest that the fact that Keats was unable to complete either version manifests the impossi-

bility, for him as for us, of reading his own title. One could then read the word "Hyperion" in the title *The Fall of Hyperion* figurally, or, if one wishes, intertextually, as referring not to the historical or mythological character but as referring to the title of Keats' own earlier text *(Hyperion)*. But are we then telling the story of the failure of the first text as the success of the second, the Fall of *Hyperion* as the Triumph of *The Fall of Hyperion?* Manifestly, yes, but not quite, since the second text also fails to be concluded. Or are we telling the story of why all texts, as texts, can always be said to be falling? Manifestly yes, but not quite, either, since the story of the fall of the first version, as told in the second, applies to the first version only and could not legitimately be read as meaning also the fall of *The Fall of Hyperion*. The undecidability involves the figural or literal status of the proper name Hyperion as well as of the verb falling, and is thus a matter of figuration and not of grammar. In "Hyperion's Fall," the word "fall" is plainly figural, the representation of a figural fall, and we, as readers, read this fall standing up. But in "Hyperion Falling," this is not so clearly the case, for if Hyperion can be Apollo and Apollo can be Keats, then he can also be us and his figural (or symbolic) fall becomes his and our literal falling as well. The difference between the two readings is itself structured as a trope. And it matters a great deal how we read the title, as an exercise not only in semantics, but in what the text actually does to us. Faced with the ineluctable necessity to come to a decision, no grammatical or logical analysis can help us out. Just as Keats had to break off his narrative, the reader has to break off his understanding at the very moment when he is most directly engaged and summoned by the text. One could hardly expect to find solace in this "fearful symmetry" between the author's and reader's plight since, at this point, the symmetry is no longer a formal but an actual trap, and the question no longer "merely" theoretical.

This undoing of theory, this disturbance of the stable cognitive field that extends from grammar to logic to a general science of man and of the phenomenal world, can in its turn be made into a theoretical project of rhetorical analysis that will reveal the inadequacy of grammatical models of non-reading. Rhetoric, by its actively negative relationship to grammar and to logic, certainly undoes the claims of the *trivium* (and by extension, of language) to be an epistemologically stable construct. The resistance to theory is a resistance to the rhetorical or tropological dimension of language, a dimension which is perhaps more explicitly in the foreground in literature (broadly conceived) than in other verbal manifestations or—to be somewhat less vague—which can be revealed in any verbal event when it is read textually. Since grammar as well as figuration is an integral part of reading, it follows that reading will be a negative process in which the grammatical cognition is undone, at all times, by its rhetorical displacement. The model of the *trivium* contains within itself the pseudo-dialectic of its own undoing and its history tells the story of this dialectic.

This conclusion allows for a somewhat more systematic description of the contemporary theoretical scene. This scene is dominated by an increased stress on reading as a theoretical problem or, as it is sometimes erroneously phrased, by an increased stress on the reception rather than on the production of texts. It is in this area that the most fruitful exchanges have come about between writers and journals of various countries and that the most interesting dialogue has developed between literary theory and other disciplines, in the arts as well as in linguistics, philosophy and the social sciences. A straightforward *report* on the present state of literary theory in the United States would have to stress the emphasis on reading, a direction which is already present, moreover, in the New Critical tradition of the forties and the fifties. The methods are now more technical, but the contemporary interest in a poetics of literature is clearly linked, traditionally enough, to the problems of reading. And since the models that are being used certainly are no longer *simply* intentional and

centered on an identifiable self, nor *simply* hermeneutic in the postulation of a single originary, pre-figural and absolute text, it would appear that this concentration on reading would lead to the rediscovery of the theoretical difficulties associated with rhetoric. This is indeed the case, to some extent; but not quite. Perhaps the most instructive aspect of contemporary theory is the refinement of the techniques by which the threat inherent in rhetorical analysis is being avoided at the very moment when the efficacy of these techniques has progressed so far that the rhetorical obstacles to understanding can no longer be mistranslated in thematic and phenomenal commonplaces. The resistance to theory which, as we saw, is a resistance to reading, appears in its most rigorous and theoretically elaborated form among the theoreticians of reading who dominate the contemporary theoretical scene.

It would be a relatively easy, though lengthy, process to show that this is so for theoreticians of reading who, like Greimas or, on a more refined level, Riffaterre or, in a very different mode, H. R. Jauss or Wolfgang Iser—all of whom have a definite, though sometimes occult, influence on literary theory in this country—are committed to the use of grammatical models or, in the case of *Rezeptionsästhetik,* to traditional hermeneutic models that do not allow for the problematization of the phenomenalism of reading and therefore remain uncritically confined within a theory of literature rooted in aesthetics. Such an argument would be easy to make because, once a reader has become aware of the rhetorical dimensions of a text, he will not be amiss in finding textual instances that are irreducible to grammar or to historically determined meaning, provided only he is willing to acknowledge what he is bound to notice. The problem quickly becomes the more baffling one of having to account for the shared reluctance to acknowledge the obvious. But the argument would be lengthy because it has to involve a textual analysis that cannot avoid being somewhat elaborate; one can succinctly suggest the grammatical indetermination of a title such as *The Fall of Hyperion,* but to confront such an undecidable enigma with the critical reception and reading of Keats' text requires some space.

The demonstration is less easy (though perhaps less ponderous) in the case of the theoreticians of reading whose avoidance of rhetoric takes another turn. We have witnessed, in recent years, a strong interest in certain elements in language whose function is not only not dependent on any form of phenomenalism but on any form of cognition as well, and which thus excludes, or postpones, the consideration of tropes, ideologies, etc., from a reading that would be primarily performative. In some cases, a link is reintroduced between performance, grammar, logic, and stable referential meaning, and the resulting theories (as in the case of Ohmann) are not in essence distinct from those of avowed grammarians or semioticians. But the most astute practitioners of a speech act theory of reading avoid this relapse and rightly insist on the necessity to keep the actual performance of speech acts, which is conventional rather than cognitive, separate from its causes and effects— to keep, in their terminology, the illocutionary force separate from its perlocutionary function. Rhetoric, understood as persuasion, is forcefully banished (like Coriolanus) from the performative moment and exiled in the affective area of perlocution. Stanley Fish, in a masterful essay, convincingly makes this point.[5] What awakens one's suspicion about this conclusion is that it relegates persuasion, which is indeed inseparable from rhetoric, to a purely affective and intentional realm and makes no allowance for modes of persuasion which are no less rhetorical and no less at work in literary texts, but which are of the order of persuasion by *proof* rather than persuasion by seduction. Thus to empty rhetoric of its epistemological impact is possible only because its tropological, figural functions are being bypassed. It is as if, to return for a moment to the

model of the *trivium,* rhetoric could be isolated from the generality that grammar and logic have in common and considered as a mere correlative of an illusionary power. The equation of rhetoric with psychology rather than with epistemology opens up dreary prospects of pragmatic banality, all the drearier if compared to the brilliance of the performative analysis. Speech act theories of reading in fact repeat, in a much more effective way, the grammatization of the *trivium* at the expense of rhetoric. For the characterization of the performative as sheer convention reduces it in effect to a grammatical code among others. The relationship between trope and performance is actually closer but more disruptive than what is here being proposed. Nor is this relationship properly captured by reference to a supposedly "creative" aspect of performance, a notion with which Fish rightly takes issue. The performative power of language can be called positional, which differs considerably from conventional as well as from "creatively" (or, in the technical sense, intentionally) constitutive. Speech act oriented theories of reading read only to the extent that they prepare the way for the rhetorical reading they avoid.

But the same is still true even if a "truly" rhetorical reading that would stay clear of any undue phenomenalization or of any undue grammatical or performative codification of the text could be conceived—something which is not necessarily impossible and for which the aims and methods of literary theory should certainly strive. Such a reading would indeed appear as the methodical undoing of the grammatical construct and, in its systematic disarticulation of the *trivium,* will be theoretically sound as well as effective. Technically correct rhetorical readings may be boring, monotonous, predictable and unpleasant, but they are irrefutable. They are also totalizing (and potentially totalitarian) for since the structures and functions they expose do not lead to the knowledge of an entity (such as language) but are an unreliable process of knowledge production that prevents all entities, including linguistic entities, from coming into discourse as such, they are indeed universals, consistently defective models of language's impossibility to be a model language. They are, always in theory, the most elastic theoretical and dialectical model to end all models and they can rightly claim to contain within their own defective selves all the other defective models of reading-avoidance, referential, semiological, grammatical, performative, logical, or whatever. They are theory and not theory at the same time, the universal theory of the impossibility of theory. To the extent however that they are theory, that is to say teachable, generalizable and highly responsive to systematization, rhetorical readings, like the other kinds, still avoid and resist the reading they advocate. Nothing can overcome the resistance to theory since theory *is* itself this resistance. The loftier the aims and the better the methods of literary theory, the less possible it becomes. Yet literary theory is not in danger of going under; it cannot help but flourish, and the more it is resisted, the more it flourishes, since the language it speaks is the language of self-resistance. What remains impossible to decide is whether this flourishing is a triumph or a fall.

NOTES

1. Roland Barthes, "Proust et les noms," in *To Honor Roman Jakobson* (The Hague: Mouton, 1967), part I, pp. 157–58.

2. "Proust et le language indirect," in *Figures II* (Paris: Seuil, 1969).

3. Blaise Pascal, "De l'esprit géométrique et de l'art de persuader," in *Oeuvres complètes,* L. Lafuma, ed. (Paris: Seuil, 1963), pp. 349ff.

4. A. J. Greimas, *Du Sens* (Paris: Seuil, 1970), p. 13.

5. Stanley Fish, "How to Do Things with Austin and Searle: Speech Act Theory and Literary Criticism," in *MLN* 91 (1976), pp. 983–1025. See especially p. 1008.

7

J. Hillis Miller
1928–

J. Hillis Miller, a distinguished critic and scholar, received a Ph.D. from Harvard University in 1951. He taught for more than two decades at Johns Hopkins University and fourteen years at Yale University. He is now a distinguished professor of English and comparative literature at the University of California, Irvine. At Yale with Geoffrey Hartman and Paul de Man, Miller had been vital in introducing Continental literary studies and philosophy to the Anglo-American academic community, practicing versions of deconstructive and poststructuralist criticism. Miller's work has always been at the forefront of critical discourse in the United States; in fact, his career—including a formalist dissertation, books that approach texts from a phenomenological perspective, and his present work in deconstructive criticism—epitomizes postwar American literary studies. His major works include *Charles Dickens: The World of His Novels* (1958), *The Disappearance of God* (1963), *Poets of Reality: Six Twentieth-Century Writers* (1965), *The Form of Victorian Fiction* (1968), *Thomas Hardy: Distance and Desire* (1970), *Fiction and Repetition* (1982), *The Linguistic Moment* (1985), *The Ethics of Reading* (1987), *Hawthorne and History: Defacing It* (1991), *Theory Now and Then* (1991), *Versions of Pygmalion* (1990), *Ariadne's Thread: Story Lines* (1992), *Illustration* (1992), *Topographies* (1995), and *Reading Narrative* (1998).

The most striking aspect of Miller's work is his lucid faithfulness to the literary or critical texts he examines in the context of the most profound questions of the experience of those texts. Throughout his career, Miller has sought in many ways for such a "metaphysical" reading of literature, but never without maintaining a close sense of the literary texts themselves. As he wrote in *Fiction and Repetition,* "a theory is all too easy to refute or deny, but a reading can be controverted only by going through the difficult task of rereading the work in question and proposing an alternate reading."

In "The Search for Grounds in Literary Study" (1985) Miller specifically returns to Matthew Arnold in the kind of rereading he is calling for. In this essay, he is attempting to do several things simultaneously. First of all, he is trying to account for the *experience* of reading, to make sense of—or at least describe—the strange, uncanny experience reading sometimes gives rise to. Second, he is trying to articulate the unconscious assumptions that govern critical writing: he argues that there are four "grounds" upon which to base reading—linguistic, social, psychological, and ontological or metaphysical—and that various critics and schools of critics assume one or the other of these. Moreover, these grounds have two striking qualities: First, they are "imperialist," by which Miller means they tend to reduce all understanding to their own base. Second, they each occasion remarkable resistance, almost hysterical denial (in the Freudian sense of the word) beyond all proportion. A third aim of this essay is to question the larger "ground" of literary study, to ask why it is that literature, since Arnold's time, has been "burdened" with the weight of carrying and maintaining cultural values. For Miller, this is not a necessary aspect of literature, and one can, indeed, question why so many people have seen this as a function of criticism, what he calls the "scrupulously slow reading" that Nietzsche speaks of in his call "Back to the texts!"

The Search for Grounds in Literary Study

You ask me in what I think or have thought you going wrong: in this: that you would never take your assiette as something determined final and unchangeable for you and proceed to work away on the basis of that: but were always poking and patching and cobbling at the assiette itself—
—Matthew Arnold, *Letters to Clough*[1]

. . . perhaps one is a philologist still, that is to say, a teacher of slow reading [ein Lehrer des langsamen Lesens].
—Friedrich Nietzsche, "Preface" to *Daybreak*[2]

An important passage in George Eliot's *Daniel Deronda* (1876) speaks of the liability of the heroine, Gwendolen Harleth, to sudden, inexplicable fits of hysterical terror or of "spiritual dread." She has these fits when faced with open spaces: "Solitude in any wide scene impressed her with an undefined feeling of immeasurable existence aloof from her, in the midst of which she was helplessly incapable of asserting herself."[3]

A strange little paragraph by Maurice Blanchot entitled "Une scène primitive," "A Primitive Scene," and published just a century later, in 1976, describes a "similar" "experience," ascribed this time to a child of seven or eight standing at the window and looking at a wintry urban or suburban scene outside:

Ce qu'il voit, le jardin, les arbres d'hiver, le mur d'une maison; tandis qu'il voit, sans doute à la manière d'un enfant, son espace de jeu, il se lasse et lentement regarde en haut vers le ciel ordinaire, avec les nuages, la lumière grise, le jour terne et sans lointain. Ce qui se passe ensuite: le ciel, le *même* ciel, soudain ouvert, noir absolument et vide absolument, révélant (comme par la vitre brisée) une telle absence que tout s'y est depuis toujours et à jamais perdu, au point que s'y affirme et s'y dissipe le savoir vertigineux que rien est ce qu'il y a, et d'abord rien au-delà.

[What he saw, the garden, the winter trees, the wall of a house; while he looked, no doubt in the way a child does, at his play area, he got bored and slowly looked higher toward the ordinary sky, with the clouds, the grey light, the day flat and without distance. What happened then: the sky, the *same* sky, suddenly opened, black absolutely and empty absolutely, revealing (as if the window had been broken) such an absence that everything is since forever and for forever lost, to the point at which there was affirmed and dispersed there the vertiginous knowledge that nothing is what there is there, and especially nothing beyond.][4]

"Rien est ce qu'il y a, et d'abord rien au-delà": nothing is what there is there, and first of all nothing beyond. As in the case of Wallace

Stevens's "The Snow Man," where the listener and watcher in the snow, "nothing himself, beholds/Nothing that is not there and the nothing that is,"[5] the devastating experience of a transfiguration of the scene which leaves it nevertheless exactly the same, the *same* sky, is the confrontation of a nothing which somehow is, has being, and which absorbs into itself any beyond or transcendence. In this primitive scene, original and originating, for Blanchot's child, or possibly even for Blanchot as a child, the sky definitely does not open to reveal heavenly light or choirs of angels singing "Glory, glory, glory." If the effect on Gwendolen Harleth in Eliot's novel of confronting open space in solitude is sometimes hysterical outbursts, the effect on Blanchot's child of an opening of the sky which does not open is seemingly endless tears of a "ravaging joy [joie ravagéant]."

I take these details from *Daniel Deronda* and from Blanchot's little scene, quite arbitrarily, or almost quite arbitrarily, as parables for the terror or dread readers may experience when they confront a text which seems irreducibly strange, inexplicable, perhaps even mad, for example Blanchot's *Death Sentence* [*L'arrêt de mort*]. As long as we have not identified the law by which the text can be made reasonable, explicable, it is as if we have come face to face with an immeasurable existence aloof from us, perhaps malign, perhaps benign, in any case something we have not yet mastered and assimilated into what we already know. It is as if the sky had opened, while still remaining the same sky, for are not those words there on the page familiar and ordinary words, words in our own language or mother tongue, words whose meaning we know? And yet they have suddenly opened and become terrifying, inexplicable. On the one hand, our task as readers is to transfer to reading Henry James's injunction to the observer of life, the novice writer: "Try to be one of those on whom nothing is lost." A good reader, that is, especially notices oddnesses, gaps, anacoluthons, non sequiturs, apparently irrelevant details, in short, all the marks of the inexplicable, all the marks of

the unaccountable, perhaps of the mad, in a text. On the other hand, the reader's task is to reduce the inexplicable to the explicable, to find its reason, its law, its ground, to make the mad sane. The task of the reader, it will be seen, is not too different from the task of the psychoanalyst.

Current criticism tends to propose one or another of the three following grounds on the basis of which the anomalies of literature may be made lawful, the unaccountable accountable: society, the more or less hidden social or ideological pressures which impose themselves on literature and reveal themselves in oddnesses; individual psychology, the more or less hidden psychic pressures which impose themselves on a work of literature and make it odd, unaccountable; language, the more or less hidden rhetorical pressures, or pressures from some torsion within language itself as such, which impose themselves on the writer and make it impossible for his work to maintain itself as an absolutely lucid and reasonable account.

The stories or *récits* of Maurice Blanchot, as well as his criticism, propose a fourth possibility. Though this possibility is, in the case of Blanchot at least, exceedingly difficult to name in so many words, and though the whole task of the reader of Blanchot could be defined as a (perhaps impossible) attempt to make this definition clear to oneself or to others, it can be said that this fourth possibility for the disturber of narrative sanity and coherence, a disruptive energy neither society nor individual psychology nor language itself, is properly religious, metaphysical, or ontological, though hardly in a traditional or conventional way. To borrow a mode of locution familiar to readers of Blanchot it is an ontology without ontology. Nor is it to be defined simply as a species of negative theology. Blanchot gives to this "something" that enters into the words or between the words the names, among others, of it [*il*]; the thing [*la chose*]; dying [*mourir*]; the neutral [*le neutre*]; the nonpresence of the eternal return [*le retour éternel*]; writing [*écrire*]; the thought [*la pensée*]; the truth [*la verité*]; the other of the other [*l'autre de l'autre*]; meaning something encountered in our relations to other people, especially relations involving love, betrayal, and that ultimate betrayal by the other of our love for him or her, the death of the other. To list these names in this way cannot possibly convey very much, except possibly, in their multiplicity and incoherence, a glimpse of the inadequacy of any one of them and of the fact that all of them must in one way or another be figurative rather than literal. What sort of "thing" is it which cannot be pinned down and labelled with one single name, so that all names for it are improper, whether proper or generic? All Blanchot's writing is a patient, continual, long-maintained attempt to answer this question, the question posed by the experience recorded in "A Primitive Scene."

Two further features may be identified of my four proposed modes of rationalizing or accounting for or finding grounds for the irrational or unaccountable in any literary account.

The first feature seems obvious enough, though it is evaded often enough to need emphasizing. This is the exclusivity or imperialism of any one of the four. Each has a mode of explanation or of grounding the anomalous in literature which demands to exercise sovereign control over the others, to make the others find their ground in *it*. You cannot have all four at once or even any two of them without ultimately grounding, or rather without having already implicitly grounded, all but one in the single regal ur-explanation. Psychological explanations tend to see linguistic, religious, or social explanations as ultimately finding *their* cause in individual human psychology. Social explanations see human psychology, language, and religion as epiphenomena of underlying and determining social forces, the "real" conditions of class, production, consumption, exchange. Linguistic explanations tend to imply or even openly to assert that society, psychology, and religion are "all language," generated by language in the first place and ultimately to be explained by features of language. Metaphysical explana-

tions see society, psychology, and language as secondary, peripheral. Each of these modes of grounding explanation asserts that it is the true "principle of reason," the true *Satz vom Grund,* the others bogus, an abyss not a ground. Each asserts a jealous will to power over the others.

The second feature of these four modes of explaining oddnesses in literature is the strong resistance each of them seems to generate in those to whom they are proposed. The resistance, for example, to Sigmund Freud's assertion of a universal unconscious sexual etiology for neurosis is notorious, and that resistance has by no means subsided. In Marxist theory, for example that of Louis Althusser in *For Marx,* "ideology" is the name given to the imaginary structures, whereby men and women resist facing directly the real economic and social conditions of their existence. "Ideology, then," says Althusser, "is the expression of the relation between men and their 'world,' that is, the (overdetermined) unity of the real relation and the imaginary relation between them and their real conditions of existence."[6] There is a tremendous resistance to totalizing explanations which say, "It's all language," the resistance encountered, for example, by structuralism, semiotics, and by misunderstandings of so-called "deconstruction" today. Many people, finally, seem able to live on from day to day and year to year, even as readers of literature, without seeing religious or metaphysical questions as having any sort of force or substance. It is not the case that man is everywhere and universally a religious or metaphysical animal. George Eliot, speaking still of Gwendolen, describes eloquently the latter's resistance to two of my sovereign principles of grounding:

> She had no permanent consciousness of other fetters, or of more spiritual restraints, having always disliked whatever was presented to her under the name of religion, in the same way that some people dislike arithmetic and accounts: it had raised no other emotion in her, no alarm, no longing; so that the question

whether she believed it had not occurred to her, any more than it had occurred to her to inquire into the conditions of colonial property and banking, on which, as she had had many opportunities of knowing, the family fortune was dependent. (pp. 89–90)

Why this resistance to looking into things, including works of literature, all the way down to the bottom is so strong and so universal I shall not attempt here to explain. Perhaps it is inexplicable. Perhaps it is a general consensus that, as Conrad's Winnie Verloc in *The Secret Agent* puts it, "life doesn't stand much looking into."[7] It might be better not to know.

Is it legitimate to seek in literature a serious concern for such serious topics, to see works of literature as in one way or another interrogations of the ground, taking ground in the sense of a sustaining metaphysical foundation outside language, outside nature, and outside the human mind? The role granted to poetry or to "literature" within our culture and in particular within our colleges and universities today is curiously contradictory. The contradiction is an historical inheritance going back at least to Kant and to eighteenth-century aesthetic theory or "critical philosophy." The tradition comes down from the enlightenment through Romantic literary theory and later by way of such figures as Matthew Arnold (crucial to the development of the "humanities" in American higher education) to the New Criticism and the academic humanism of our own day. On the one hand the enjoyment of poetry is supposed to be the "disinterested" aesthetic contemplation of beautiful or sublime organic forms made of words. It is supposed to be "value free," without contamination by use of the poem for any cognitive, practical, ethical, or political purposes. Such appropriations, it is said, are a misuse of poetry. According to this aestheticizing assumption one ought to be able to read Dante and Milton, for example, or Aeschylus and Shelley, without raising either the question of the truth or falsity of their

philosophical and religious beliefs, or the question of the practical consequences of acting on those beliefs. Cleanth Brooks, for example, in a recent essay vigorously reaffirming the tenets of the New Criticism, presents *Paradise Lost* as a case in point: "Milton tells us in the opening lines of *Paradise Lost* that his purpose is to 'justify the ways of God to men,' and there is no reason to doubt that this was what he hoped to do. But what we actually have in the poem is a wonderful interconnected story of events in heaven and hell and upon earth, with grand and awesome scenes brilliantly painted and with heroic actions dramatically rendered. In short, generations of readers have found that the grandeur of the poem far exceeds any direct statement of theological views. The point is underscored by the fact that some readers who reject Milton's theology altogether nevertheless regard *Paradise Lost* as a great poem."[8]

On the other hand, literature has been weighted down in our culture with the burden of carrying from generation to generation the whole freight of the values of that culture, what Matthew Arnold called "the best that is known and thought in the world."[9] Cleanth Brooks elsewhere in his essay also reiterates this traditional assumption about literature. Walter Jackson Bate, in a recent polemical essay, sees specialization, including the New Criticism's specialization of close reading, as greatly weakening the humanities generally and departments of English in particular. Bate regrets the good old days (from 1930 to 1950) when departments of English taught everything under the sun but reading as such, in a modern reincarnation of the Renaissance ideal of *litterae humaniores*. The literature components of the humanities in our colleges and universities, and departments of English in particular, have with a good conscience undertaken, after hurrying through a soupçon of rhetoric and poetics, to teach theology, metaphysics, psychology, ethics, politics, social and intellectual history, even the history of science and natural history, in short,

"Allerleiwissenschaft," like Carlyle's Professor Diogenes Teufelsdröck.[10]

The implicit reasoning behind this apparently blatant contradiction may not be all that difficult to grasp, though the reasoning will only restate the contradiction. It is just because, and only because, works of literature are stable, self-contained, value-free objects of disinterested aesthetic contemplation that they can be trustworthy vehicles of the immense weight of values they carry from generation to generation uncontaminated by the distortions of gross reality. Just because the values are enshrined in works of literature, uninvested, not collecting interest, not put out to vulgar practical use, they remain pure, not used up, still free to be reappropriated for whatever use we may want to make of them. Has not Kant in the third critique, the *Critique of Judgment,* once and for all set works of art as reliable and indispensable middle member *(Mittelglied),* between cognition (pure reason, theory, the subject of the first critique) and ethics (practical reason, praxis, ethics, the subject of the second critique)? And has not Kant defined beauty, as embodied for example in a poem, as "the symbol of morality [*Symbol der Sittlichkeit*]"?[11] Both Bate and René Wellek, the latter in another outspoken polemical essay with the nice title of "Destroying Literary Studies," invoke Kant, or rather their understanding of Kant, as having settled these matters once and for all, as if there were no more need to worry about them, and as if our understanding of Kant, or rather theirs, could safely be taken for granted: ". . . Why not," asks Bate, "turn to David Hume, the greatest skeptic in the history of thought . . . and then turn to Kant, by whom so much of this is answered?" (p. 52); "One can doubt the very existence of aesthetic experience," says Wellek, "and refuse to recognize the distinctions, clearly formulated in Immanuel Kant's *Critique of Judgment,* between the good, the true, the useful, and the beautiful."[12] So much is at stake here that it is probably a good idea to go back and read Kant for ourselves, no

easy task to be sure, in order to be certain that he says what Bate and Wellek say he says.

When Matthew Arnold, the founding father, so to speak, of the American concept of the humanities, praises the virtues of disinterested contemplation, he is being faithful to the Kantian inheritance, no doubt by way of its somewhat vulgarizing distortions in Schiller. It was, and is, by no means necessary to have read Kant to be a Kantian of sorts. Arnold's full formulaic definition of criticism, in "The Function of Criticism at the Present Time" (1864), is "a disinterested endeavour to learn and propagate the best that is known and thought in the world."[13] He speaks elsewhere in the same essay of the "disinterested love of a free play of the mind on all subjects, for its own sake."[14] When Arnold, in a well-known statement in "The Study of Poetry" (1880) which has echoed down the decades as the implicit credo of many American departments of English, says: "The future of poetry is immense, because in poetry, where it is worthy of its high destinies, our race, as time goes on, will find an ever surer and surer stay," he goes on to make it clear that poetry is a "stay" just because it is detached from the question of its truth or falsity as fact. Poetry can therefore replace religion when the fact fails religion. Poetry is cut off from such questions, sequestered in a realm of disinterested fiction. Just for this reason poetry is a "stay," a firm resting place when all else gives way, like a building without a solid foundation. "There is not a creed which is not shaken," says Arnold in his melancholy litany, "not an accredited dogma which is not shown to be questionable, not a received tradition which does not threaten to dissolve. Our religion has materialized itself in the fact, in the supposed fact; it has attached its emotion to the fact, and now the fact is failing it. But for poetry the idea is everything; the rest is a world of illusion, of divine illusion. Poetry attaches its emotion to the idea; the idea *is* the fact."[15] The image here is that of a self-sustaining linguistic fiction or illusion which holds itself up by a kind of intrinsic magic of levitation over the abyss, like an aerial floating bridge over chaos, as long as one does not poke and patch at the assiette. This bridge or platform may therefore hold up also the ideas the poem contains and the readers who sustain themselves by these ideas.

Arnold had this double or even triple notion of the staying power of poetry already in mind when, in 1848 or 1849, many years before writing "The Study of Poetry," he wrote to Arthur Hugh Clough: "Those who cannot read G[ree]k sh[ou]ld read nothing but Milton and parts of Wordsworth: the state should see to it . . . ."[16] Most Freshman and Sophomore courses in American colleges and universities in "Major English Authors" are still conceived in the spirit of Arnold's categorical dictum. The uplifting moral value of reading Milton and parts of Wordsworth, so important that it should be enforced by the highest civil authority, is initially stylistic. Arnold opposes the solemn, elevated, composing "grand" style of Homer, or, failing that, of Milton and parts of Wordsworth, to the "confused multitudinousness" (ibid.) of Browning, Keats, and Tennyson, the Romantics and Victorians generally, excepting that part of Wordsworth. The occasion of Arnold's letter to Clough is the devastating effect on him of reading Keats's letters: "What a brute you were to tell me to read Keats's Letters. However it is over now: and reflexion resumes her power over agitation" (p. 96). From Keats Arnold turns to the Greeks, to Milton, and to those parts of Wordsworth to subdue his inner agitation as well as to protect himself from the agitation without.

Only secondary to the sustaining effect of the grand style as such are the "ideas" expressed in that style. A writer, says Arnold, "must begin with an Idea of the world in order not to be prevailed over by the world's multitudinousness" (ibid., p. 97). The Idea, so to speak, is the style, or the style is the Idea, since the grand style is nothing but the notion of composure, elevation, coherence, objectivity, that is, just the character-

istics of the grand style. This combination of grand elevated style and presupposed, preconceived, or preposited grand comprehensive Idea of the world (never mind whether it is empirically verifiable) not only composes and elevates the mind but also fences it off from the confused multitudinousness outside and the danger therefore of confused multitudinousness within. The latter, Arnold, in the "Preface" of 1853, calls "the dialogue of the mind with itself."[17] He associates it especially with the modern spirit, and fears it more than anything else. It is the dissolution of the mind's objectivity, calm, and unity with itself. This composing, lifting up, and fencing out through literature takes place, to borrow from one of the authors Arnold tells us exclusively to read, as God organizes chaos in the work of creation, or as Milton, at the beginning of *Paradise Lost,* prays that his interior chaos, likened to the unformed Abyss, may be illuminated, elevated, impregnated, and grounded by the Holy Spirit or heavenly muse: "Thou from the first/Was present, and with mighty wings outspread/Dove-like satst brooding on the vast Abyss/And madst it pregnant:/What in me is dark/Illumine, what is low raise and support" (*Paradise Lost,* I, 19–23).

It is only a step from Kant's image in paragraph 59 of the *Critique of Judgment* of art or poetry as *hypotyposis* [*Hypotypose*], indirect symbols of intuitions for which there is no direct expression,[18] to Hegel's assertion that sublime poetry, like parable, fable, and apologue, is characterized by the non-adequation and dissimilarity between symbol and symbolized, what he calls the *Sichnichtentsprechen beider,* the noncorrespondence of the two.[19] It is only another step beyond that to I. A. Richards' assertion, in *Principles of Literary Criticism,* with some help from Jeremy Bentham's theory of fictions, that the function of poetry is to produce an equilibrium among painfully conflicting impulses and thereby to provide fictive solutions to real psychological problems. Another step in this sequence (which is not even a progression, radicalizing or deepening, but a movement in place), takes us to Wallace Stevens's resonant formulation in the *Adagia* of what all these writers in somewhat different ways are saying: "The final belief is to believe in a fiction, which you know to be a fiction, there being nothing else. The exquisite truth is to know that it is a fiction and that you believe in it willingly."[20]

Proof that Matthew Arnold still plays an indispensable role within this sequence as the presumed base for a conservative humanism is a forceful recent article by Eugene Goodheart, "Arnold at the Present Time," with accompanying essays and responses by George Levine, Morris Dickstein, and Stuart M. Tave.[21] As is not surprising, the oppositions among these essays come down to a question of how one reads Arnold. If Goodheart grossly misrepresents "deconstruction" and the sort of "criticism as critique" I advocate (which is not surprising), he is also a bad reader or a non-reader of Arnold. Goodheart takes for granted the traditional misreading of Arnold which has been necessary to make him, as Goodheart puts it, "the inspiration of humanistic study in England and America" (p. 451). Levine, Dickstein, and Tave are, it happens, far better and more searching readers of Arnold. Adjudication of differences here is of course possibly only by a response to that call, "Back to the texts!," which must be performed again and again in literary study. Nothing previous critics have said can be taken for granted, however authoritative it may seem. Each reader must do again for himself the laborious task of a scrupulous slow reading, trying to find out what the texts actually say rather than imposing on them what she or he wants them to say or wishes they said. Advances in literary study are not made by the free invention of new conceptual or historical schemes (which always turn out to be old ones anew in any case), but by that grappling with the texts which always has to be done over once more by each new reader. In the case of Arnold the poetry and prose must be read together, not assumed to be discontinuous units or an early negative stage and a late affirmative stage negating the earlier negation. Far from offering a firm "assiette" to the sort of humanism Goodheart advocates, such a careful reading of Arnold will reveal him to be a nihilist writer through and through, nihilist in the precise sense in which Nietzsche or Heidegger defines the term: as a specifically historical designation of the moment within the development of Western metaphysics when the highest values devalue themselves and come to nothing as their transcendent base dissolves:[22] "There is not a creed which is not shaken, not an accredited dogma which is not shown to be questionable, not a received tradition which does not threaten to dissolve." "I am nothing and very probably never shall be anything," said Arnold in one of the letters to Clough.[23]

A house built on sand, in this case a humanistic tradition built on the shaky foundation of a misreading of Matthew Arnold, cannot stand firmly. To put this another way, the affirmations of Goodheart, Bate, Wellek, and others like them participate inevitably in the historical movement of nihilism ("the history of the next two centuries," Nietzsche called it)[24] which they contest. Most of all they do this in the act itself of contestation. "The question arises," says Heidegger in the section on nihilism in his *Nietzsche,* "whether the innermost essence of nihilism and the power of its dominion do not consist precisely in considering the nothing merely as a nullity [*nur für etwas Nichtiges*], considering nihilism as an apotheosis of the merely vacuous [*der blossen Leere*], as a negation [*eine Verneinung*] that can be set to rights at once by an energetic affirmation."[25]

In a brilliant essay on "The Principle of Reason: The University in the Eyes of its Pupils,"[26] Jacques Derrida identifies the way the modern university and the study of literature within it are based on the domination of the Leibnizian principle of reason, what in German is called "der Satz vom Grund," the notion that everything can and should be accounted for, *Omnis veritatis reddi ratio potest,* that nothing is without reason, *nihil est sine ratione.* Following Nietzsche and Heidegger, Derrida also argues that so-called nihilism is an historical moment which is "completely symmetrical to, thus dependent on, the principle of reason" (p. 15). Nihilism arises naturally and inevitably during a period, the era of technology, when the principle of universal accountability holds sway in the organization of society and of the universities accountable to that society. "For the principle of reason," says Derrida, "may have obscurantist and nihilist effects. They can be seen more or less everywhere, in Europe and America among those who believe they are defending philosophy, literature, and the humanities against these new modes of questioning that are also a new relation to language and tradition, a new affirmation, and new ways of taking responsibility. We can easily see on which side obscurantism and nihilism are lurking when on occasion great professors or representatives of prestigious institutions lose all sense of proportion and control; on such occasions they forget their principles that they claim to defend in their work and suddenly begin to heap insults, to say whatever comes into their heads on the subject of texts that they obviously have never opened or that they have encountered through a mediocre journalism that in other circumstances they would pretend to scorn" (p. 15). Obviously much is at stake here, and we must go carefully, looking before and after, testing the ground carefully, taking nothing for granted.

If such a tremendous burden is being placed on literature throughout all the period from Kant to academic humanists of our own day like Bate and Goodheart, it is of crucial importance to be sure that literature is able to bear the weight, or that it is a suitable instrument to perform its function. The question is too grave for its answer to be left untested. To raise the ques-

tion of the weight-bearing capacities of the medium of poetry is of course not the only thing criticism can do or ought to do, but I claim it is one all-important task of literary study. The question in question here is not of the thematic content of or the assertions made by works of literature but of the weight-bearing characteristics of the medium of literature, that is, of language. It is a question of what the language of poetry is and does. It is indeed solid enough and trustworthy enough to serve, according to the metaphor Kant proposes at the end of the introduction to the *Critique of Judgment,* as the fundamentally necessary bridge passing back and forth between pure cognition and moral action, between *theoria* and *praxis?* "The realm of the natural concept under the one legislation," says Kant, "and that of the concept of freedom under the other are entirely removed [*gänzlich abgesondert*] from all mutual influence [*wechselseitigen Einfluss*] which they might have on one another (each according to its fundamental laws) by the great gulf [*die grosse Kluft*] that separates the supersensible from phenomena [*das Übersinnliche von den Erscheinungen*]. The concept of freedom determines nothing in respect of the theoretical cognition of nature, and the internal concept determines nothing in respect of the practical laws of freedom. So far, then, it is not possible to throw a bridge from the one realm to the other [*eine Brücke von einem Gebiete zu dem andern hinüber zu schlagen*]."[27]

Art or the aesthetic experience is the only candidate for a possible bridge. The whole of the *Critique of Judgment* is written to test out the solidity, so to speak, of the planks by which this indispensable bridge from the realm of knowledge to the realm of moral action might be built, across the great gulf that separates them. If the "beauty" of the work of art is the sensible symbol of morality, it is, on the other hand, the sensible embodiment of the pure idea, what Hegel was to call, in a famous formulation, and in echo of Kant's word *Erscheinungen,* "the sensible shining forth of the idea [*das sinnliche 'scheinen' der Idee*]."[28] As Hegel elsewhere puts it, "art occupies the intermediate ground between the purely sensory and pure thought [*steht in der 'Mitte' zwischen der umittelbaren Sinnlichkeit und dem ideellen Gedanken*]" (Ibid., I, 60, my trans.). Whether Kant or Hegel establish satisfactorily the solidity of this ground, its adequacy as a bridge, is another question, one that a full reading of Kant's third *Kritik* and of Hegel's *Ästhetik* would be necessary to answer. That the answer is affirmative does not go without saying, nor of course that it is negative either. Others are at work on this task of re-reading Kant and Hegel.

The sort of interrogation for which I am calling is neither a work of "pure theory" nor a work of pure praxis, a series of explications. It is something between those two or preparatory to them, a clearing of the ground and an attempt to sink foundations. It is "criticism" in the fundamental sense of "critique," discriminating testing out, in this case a testing out of the medium of which the bridge between theory and practice is made. If criticism as critique is between theory and practice, it is also neither to be identified with hermeneutics, or the search for intentional meaning, on the one side, nor with poetics, or the theory of how texts have meaning, on the other side, though it is closely related to the latter. Critique, however, is a testing of the grounding of language in this or that particular text, not in the abstract or in abstraction from any particular case.

If this sort of investigation of the weight-bearing features of language is often an object of suspicion these days from the point of view of a certain traditional humanism, the humanism of *litterae humaniores,* it is also under attack from the other direction, from the point of view of those who see the central work of literary study as the reinsertion of the work of literature within its social context. The reproaches from the opposite political directions are strangely similar or symmetrical. They often come to the same thing or are couched in the same words. It is as if there were an unconscious alliance of the left and the right to suppress something which is the bad conscience of both a conservative humanism and a "radical" politicizing or sociologizing of the study of literature. A specific problematic is associated with the latter move, which attempts to put literature under the law of economy, under the laws of economic change and social power. I shall examine this problematic in detail elsewhere,[29] but it may be said here that the most resolute attempts to bracket linguistic considerations in the study of literature, to take the language of literature for granted and shift from the study of the relations of word with word to the study of the relations of words with things or with subjectivities, will only lead back in the end to the study of language. Any conceivable encounter with things or with subjectivities in literature or in discourse about literature must already have represented things and subjects in words, numbers, or other signs. Any conceivable representation of the relations of words to things, powers, persons, modes of production and exchange, juridical or political systems (or whatever name the presumably non-linguistic may be given) will turn out to be one or another figure of speech. As such, it will require a rhetorical interpretation, such as that given by Marx in *Capital* and in the *Grundrisse.* Among such figures are that of mimesis, mirroring reflection or representation. This turns out to be a species of metaphor. Another such figure is that of part to whole, work to surrounding and determining milieu, text to context, container to thing contained. This relation is one variety or another of synecdoche or of metonymy. Another figure of the relation of text to social context is that of anamorphosis or of ideology, which is a species of affirmation by denial, abnegation, what Freud called *Verneinung.* Sociologists of literature still all too often do no more than set some social fact side by side with some citation from a literary work and assert that the latter reflects the former, or is accounted for by it, or is determined by it, or is an intrinsic part of it, or is grounded in it. It is just in this place, in the interpretation of this asserted liaison, that the work of rhetorical analysis is indispensable. The necessary dialogue between those practicing poetics or rhetoric and sociologists of literature has scarcely begun. Conservative humanists and "radical" sociologists of literature have this at least in common: both tend to suppress, displace, or replace what I call the linguistic moment in literature.[30] Here too, however, denegation is affirmation. The covering over always leaves traces behind, tracks which may be followed back to those questions about language I am raising.

Kant, once more, in the "Preface" to the *Critique of Judgment* has admirably formulated the necessity of this work of critique: "For if such a system is one day to be completed [*einmal zu Stande kommen soll*] under the general name of metaphysic . . . , the soil for the edifice [*den Boden zu diesem Gebaude*] must be explored by critique [*die Kritik*] as deep down as the foundation [*die erste Grundlage*] of the faculty of principles independent of experience, in order that it may sink in no part [*damit es nicht an irgend einem Teile sinke*], for this would inevitably bring about the downfall [*Einsturz*] of the whole" (Eng. 4; Ger. 74–75). Elsewhere, in the *Critique of Pure Reason,* the same metaphor has already been posited as the foundation of the edifice of pure thought: "But though the following out of these considerations is what gives to philosophy its peculiar dignity, we must meantime occupy ourselves with a less resplendent [*nicht so glänzenden*], but still meritorious task, namely, to level the ground, and to render it sufficiently secure for moral edifices of these majestic dimensions [*den Boden zu jenen majestätischen sittlichen Gebäuden eben und baufest zu machen*]. For this ground has been honeycombed by subterranean workings [*allerlei Maulwurfsgänge:* all sorts of mole tunnels: Smith's translation effaces the figure] which rea-

son, in its confident but fruitless search for hidden treasures has carried out in all directions, and which threaten the security of the superstructures [*und die jenes Bauwerk unsicher machen*]."[31]

Which is critique? Is it groundbreaking to be distinguished from mole-tunnelling and a repair of it, as the second quotation claims, or is critique, as the first quotation affirms, the work of tunnelling itself, the underground search for bedrock which in that process hollows out the soil? Does this contradiction in Kant's formulations not have something to do with the fact that Kant uses a metaphor from art, or to put this another way, throws out a little artwork of his own in the form of an architectural metaphor, in order to define the work of criticism which is supposed to be a testing out of the very instrument of bridging of which the definition makes use? This is an example of a *mise en abyme* in the technical sense of placing within the larger sign system a miniature image of that larger one, a smaller one potentially within that, and so on, in a filling in and covering over of the abyss, gulf, or *Kluft* which is at the same time an opening of the abyss. Such a simultaneous opening and covering over is the regular law of the *mise en abyme.*

Have I not, finally, by an intrinsic and unavoidable necessity, done the same thing as Kant, with my images of bridges, tunnels, bedrock, pathways, and so on, and with my strategy of borrowing citations from Arnold, Kant, and the rest to describe obliquely my own enterprise? This somersaulting, self-constructing, self-undermining form of language, the throwing out of a bridge where no firm bedrock exists, in place of the bedrock, is a fundamental feature of what I call critique. Groundlevelling, it appears, becomes inevitably tunnelling down in search of bedrock, as, to quote Milton again, beneath the lowest deep a lower deep still opens.

I end by drawing several conclusions from what I have said, and by briefly relating what I have said to the question of genre. The first conclusion is a reiteration of my assertion that the stakes are so large in the present quarrels among students of literature that we must go slowly and circumspectly, testing the ground carefully and taking nothing for granted, returning once more to those founding texts of our modern tradition of literary study and reading them anew with patience and care. To put this another way, the teaching of philology, of that "slow reading" or *langsamen Lesen* for which Nietzsche calls, is still a fundamental responsibility of the humanities, at no time more needed than today. Second conclusion: Disagreements among students of literature can often be traced to often more covert disagreements about the presupposed ground of literature—whether that ground is assumed to be society, the self, language, or the "thing." One of these four presuppositions may be taken so for granted by a given critic that he is not even aware that it determines all his procedures and strategies of interpretation. Much will be gained by bringing the fundamental causes of these disagreements into the open. Third conclusion: Though the intellectual activity of ground-testing and of testing out the very idea of the ground or of the principle of reason, through slow reading, has a long and venerable tradition under the names of philology and of critical philosophy, nevertheless such testing has a peculiar role in the university. It is likely to seem subversive, threatening, outside the pale of what is a legitimate activity within the university, if research within the university, including research and teaching in the humanities, is all under the sovereign and unquestioned rule of the principle of reason. Nevertheless, moving forward to the necessary new affirmation and the new taking of responsibility for the humanities and within the humanities depends now, as it always has, on allowing that interrogation to take place.

This new taking of responsibility for language and literature, for the language of literature, which I am calling critique, has, finally, important implications for genre theory or for generic criticism. What I have said would imply not that generic classifications or distinctions and the use of these as a guide to interpretation and evaluation are illegitimate, without grounds, but that they are in a certain sense superficial. They do not go all the way to the ground, and the choice of a ground (or being chosen by one) may be more decisive for literary interpretation than generic distinctions and even determine those generic distinctions and their import. It is only on the grounds of a commitment to language, society, the self, or the "it," one or another of these, that generic distinctions make sense and have force. The choice of a ground determines both the definition of each genre and the implicit or explicit hierarchy among them. It is possible, it makes sense, to say "This is a lyric poem," or "This is a novel," and to proceed on the basis of that to follow certain interpretative procedures and ultimately to say, "This is a good lyric poem," or "This is a bad novel." Nevertheless, it is possible and makes sense to do these things only on the grounds of a prior commitment, perhaps one entirely implicit or even unthought, to founding assumptions about the ultimate ground on which all these genres are erected as so many different dwelling places or cultural forms for the human spirit to live in and use.

Beyond that, it might be added that what I am calling critique, in its double emphasis on rhetoric as the study of tropes, on the one hand, in a work of whatever genre, and, on the other hand, on the way any work of literature, of whatever genre, tells a story with beginning, middle, end, and underlying *logos* or *Grund* and at the same time interrupts or deconstructs that story—this double emphasis tends to break down generic distinctions and to recognize, for example, the fundamental role of tropes in novels, the way any lyric poem tells a story and can be interpreted as a narrative, or the way a work of philosophy may be read in terms of its tropological patterns or in terms of the story it tells. Much important criticism today goes against the grain of traditional generic distinctions, while at the same time perpetuating them in new ways in relation to one or another of my four grounds, just as many important works of recent primary literature do not fit easily into any one generic pigeon-hole.

NOTES

1. *The Letters of Matthew Arnold to Arthur Hugh Clough,* ed. H. F. Lowry (London and New York: Oxford University Press, 1932), 130.

2. Friedrich Nietzsche, *Daybreak: Thoughts on the Prejudices of Morality,* trans. R. J. Hollingdale (Cambridge: Cambridge University Press, 1982), 5, trans. slightly altered; German: Freidrich Nietzsche, *Morgenröte,* "Vorrede," *Werke in Drei Bänden,* ed. Karl Schlecta, I (Munich: Carl Hanser Verlag, 1966), 1016. Further citations will be from these editions.

3. George Eliot, *Daniel Deronda,* I, *Works,* Cabinet Edition (Edinburgh and London: William Blackwood and Sons, n. d.), chap. 6, p. 90. Further references will be to this volume of this edition.

4. In *Première Livraison* (1976), my trans.

5. Wallace Stevens, *The Collected Poems* (New York: Alfred A. Knopf, 1954), 10.

6. Louis Althusser, *For Marx,* trans. Ben Brewster (New York: Vintage Books, 1970), pp. 233–34.

7. Joseph Conrad, *The Secret Agent* (Garden City, N.Y.: Doubleday, Page, 1925), xiii.

8. Cleanth Brooks, "The Primacy of the Author," *The Missouri Review,* 6 (1982), 162.

9. Matthew Arnold, "The Function of Criticism at the Present Time," *Lectures and Essays in Criticism, The Complete Prose Works,* ed. R. H. Super, III (Ann Arbor: The University of Michigan Press, 1962), 270.

10. See Walter Jackson Bate, "The Crisis in English Studies," *Harvard Magazine,* 85, No. 1 (1982), 46–53, esp. pp. 46–47. For a vigorous reply to Bate's essay see Paul de Man, "The Return to Philology," *The Times Literary Supplement,* No. 4, 158 (Friday, December 10, 1982), 1355–56.

11. Immanuel Kant, paragraph 59, "Of Beauty as the Symbol of Morality," *Critique of Judgment,* trans. J. H. Bernard (New York: Hafner Publishing Company, 1951),

p. 196; German: *Kritik der Urteilskraft, Werkausgabe,* ed. Wilhelm Weischedel, X (Frankfurt am Main: Suhrkamp Verlag, 1979), 294.

12. René Wellek, "Destroying Literary Studies," *The New Criterion* (December 1983), 2.

13. Matthew Arnold, "The Function of Criticism at the Present Time," p. 282.

14. Ibid., p. 268.

15. Matthew Arnold, "The Study of Poetry," *English Literature and Irish Politics, The Complete Prose Works,* ed. R. H. Super, IX (Ann Arbor: The University of Michigan Press, 1973), 161.

16. *Letters to Clough,* p. 97.

17. Matthew Arnold, *Poems,* ed. Kenneth Allott (London: Longmans, Green and Co. Ltd., 1965), p. 591.

18. See Kant, *Critique of Judgment,* eds. cit.: Eng., pp. 197–98; Ger., pp. 295–297.

19. G. W. F. von Hegel, *Aesthetics: Lectures on Fine Art,* trans. T. M. Knox, I (New York: Oxford University Press, 1975), 378; *Vorlesungen über die Ästhetik,* I (Frankfurt am Main: Surhkamp, 1970), 486.

20. Wallace Stevens, *Opus Posthumous* (New York: Alfred A. Knopf, 1957), p. 163.

21. "The Function of Matthew Arnold at the Present Time," *Critical Inquiry,* 9 (1983), 451–516. Goodheart's essay, "Arnold at the Present Time," is on pp. 451–68.

22. See Friedrich Nietzsche, "European Nihilism," *The Will to Power,* trans. Walter Kaufmann and R. J. Hollingdale (New York: Vintage Books, 1968), pp. 5–82. These notes are dispersed in chronological order with the other notes traditionally making up *Der Wille zur Macht* in Nietzsche, "Aus dem Nachlass der Achtzigerjahre," *Werke in Drei Bänden,* III, 415–925. See also Martin Heidegger, "Nihilism," *Nietzsche,* trans. Frank A. Capuzzi, IV (San Francisco: Harper & Row, 1982); German: *Nietzsche,* II (Pfullingen: Verlag Günther Neske, 1961), 31–256; 335–98.

23. *Letters to Clough,* p. 135.

24. *The Will to Power,* p. 3.

25. Heidegger, "Nihilism," *Nietzsche,* IV, 21; German: *Nietzsche,* II, 53.

26. Trans. Catherine Porter and Edward P. Morris, *Diacritics,* 13 (1983), 3–20.

27. Kant, *Critique of Judgment,* Eng., p. 32; Ger., p. 106.

28. Hegel, *Ästhetik,* I, 151, my trans.

29. In "Economy," in *Penelope's Web: On the External Relations of Narrative,* forthcoming.

30. A book on nineteenth and twentieth-century poetry with that title is forthcoming from Princeton University Press [*The Linguistic Moment: From Wordsworth to Stevens.* Princeton, N.J.: Princeton University Press, 1985].

31. Immanuel Kant, *Critique of Pure Reason,* trans. Norman Kemp Smith (New York: St. Martin's Press, 1965), pp. 313–14; German: *Kritik der reinen Vernunft,* A (1781), p. 319; B (1787), pp. 375–76, *Werkausgabe,* ed. cit., III, 325–26. For a discussion of the image of the mole in Kant, Hegel, and Nietzsche see David Farrell Krell, "*Der Maulwurf: Die philosophische Wühlarbeit bei Kant, Hegel und Nietzsche*/The Mole: Philosophic Burrowings in Kant, Hegel, and Nietzsche," *Boundary,* 2, 9 and 10 (Spring/Fall, 1981), 155–79.

8

bell hooks

1952–

Recognizing that African-American women have been silenced within the discourses of both gender and race, bell hooks (who adopted the name of her maternal great-grandmother, a woman known for her willingness to speak her mind and "talk back") speaks from the junction of those two issues. She has worked to foreground issues of race within women's studies and issues of gender within African-American studies. Her works include *Ain't I a Woman: Black Women and Feminism* (1981), *Feminist Theory: From Margin to Center* (1984), *Talking Back: Thinking Feminist, Thinking Black* (1989), *Breaking Bread: Insurgent Black Intellectual Life* (with Cornel West, 1991), and *Black Looks: Race and Representation* (1992).

In "Postmodern Blackness," from *Yearning: Race, Gender and Cultural Politics* (1991), hooks critiques the exclusion of African Americans from postmodern discourse. This exclusion is particularly ironic given that the core issues of postmodernism—heterogeneity, the decentered subject, identity, and otherness—are the issues that face African Americans. Hooks suggests that African Americans are resistant to the postmodern critique of essentialism and the subsequent critiques of subject and identity because these critiques arrive just as African Americans are coming into positions as speaking subjects and are developing an increasingly strong African-American identity. The critique of essentialism appears to undermine the African-American community's sense of shared history and commonality, but hooks suggests instead that a critique of essentialism allows for recognition of multiple African-American identities through "emphasizing the significance of 'the authority of experience'" and recognizing "the way black identity has been specifically constituted in the experience of exile and struggle." hooks sees the postmodern critique of essentialism as key to the struggle against racism in that it challenges colonial, imperialist, white-supremacist stereotypes of African-American culture. hooks goes on to enact her own critique of essentialism, seeking to disrupt the notion that African Americans who are engaged in intellectual discourse are essentially disengaged from the nonacademic African-American community, suggesting that when it is made accessible to a wider, popular audience, postmodernism can enact positive, radical cultural change.

Postmodern Blackness

Postmodernist discourses are often exclusionary even as they call attention to, appropriate even, the experience of 'difference' and 'Otherness' to provide oppositional political meaning, legitimacy and immediacy when they are accused of lacking concrete relevance. Very few African-American intellectuals have talked or written about postmodernism. At a dinner party I talked about trying to grapple with the significance of postmodernism for contemporary black experience. It was one of those social gatherings where only one other black person was present. The setting quickly became a field of contestation. I was told by the other black person that I was wasting my time, that 'this stuff does not relate in any way to what's happening with black people'. Speaking in the presence of a group of white onlookers, staring at us as though this encounter were staged for their benefit, we engaged in a passionate discussion about black experience. Apparently, no one sympathized with my insistence that racism is perpetuated when blackness is associated solely with concrete gut level experience conceived as either opposing or having no connection to abstract thinking and the production of critical theory. The idea that there is no meaningful connection between black experience and critical thinking about aesthetics or culture must be continually interrogated.

My defense of postmodernism and its relevance to black folks sounded good, but I worried that I lacked conviction, largely because I approach the subject cautiously and with suspicion.

Disturbed not so much by the 'sense' of postmodernism but by the conventional language used when it is written or talked about and by those who speak it, I find myself on the outside of the discourse looking in. As a discursive practice it is dominated primarily by the voices of white male intellectuals and/or academic elites who speak to and about one another with coded familiarity. Reading and studying their writing to understand postmodernism in its multiple manifestations, I appreciate it but feel little inclination to ally myself with the academic hierarchy and exclusivity pervasive in the movement today.

Critical of most writing on postmodernism, I perhaps am more conscious of the way in which the focus on 'Otherness and difference' that is often alluded to in these works seems to have little concrete impact as an analysis or standpoint that might change the nature and direction of postmodernist theory. Since much of this theory has been constructed in reaction to and against high modernism, there is seldom any mention of black experience or writings by black people in this work, specifically black women (though in more recent work one may see a reference to Cornel West, the black male scholar who has most engaged postmodernist discourse). Even if an aspect of black culture is the subject of postmodern critical writing, the works cited will usually be those of black men. A work that comes immediately to mind is Andrew Ross's chapter 'Hip, and the long front of color' in *No Respect: Intellectuals and popular culture;* while it is an interesting reading, it constructs black culture as though black women have had no role in black cultural production. At the end of Meaghan Morris' discussion of postmodernism in her collection of essays *The Pirate's Fiancé: Feminism and postmodernism,* she provides a bibliography of works by women, identifying them as important contributions to a discourse on postmodernism that offer new insight as well as challenging male theoretical hegemony. Even though many of the works do not directly address postmodernism, they address similar concerns. There are no references to works by black women.

The failure to recognize a critical black presence in the culture and in most scholarship and writing on postmodernism compels a black reader, particularly a black female reader, to interrogate her interest in a subject where those who discuss and write about it seem not to know black women exist or even to consider the possibility that we might be somewhere writing or saying something that should be listened to, or producing art that should be seen, heard, approached with intellectual seriousness. This is especially the case with works that go on and on about the way in which postmodernist discourse has opened up a theoretical terrain where 'difference and Otherness' can be considered legitimate issues in the academy. Confronting both the absence of recognition of black female presence that much postmodernist theory re-inscribes and the resistance on the part of most black folks to hearing about real connection between postmodernism and black experience, I enter a discourse, a practice, where there may be no ready audience for my words, no clear listener, uncertain, then, that my voice can or will be heard.

During the sixties, the black power movement was influenced by perspectives that could easily be labeled modernist. Certainly many of the ways black folks addressed issues of identity conformed to a modernist universalizing agenda. There was little critique of patriarchy as a master narrative among black militants. Despite the fact that black power ideology reflected a modernist sensibility, these elements were soon rendered irrelevant as militant protest was stifled by a powerful, repressive postmodern state. The period directly after the black power movement was a time when major news magazines carried articles with cocky headlines like 'Whatever happened to Black America?' This response was an ironic reply to the aggressive, unmet demand by decentered, marginalized black subjects who had at least momentarily successfully demanded a hearing, who had made it possible for black liberation to be on the national political agenda. In the wake of the black power movement, after so many rebels were slaughtered and lost, many of these voices were silenced by a repressive

state; others became inarticulate. It has become necessary to find new avenues to transmit the messages of black liberation struggle, new ways to talk about racism and other politics of domination. Radical postmodernist practice, most powerfully conceptualized as a 'politics of difference', should incorporate the voices of displaced, marginalized, exploited and oppressed black people. It is sadly ironic that the contemporary discourse which talks the most about heterogeneity, the decentered subject, declaring breakthroughs that allow recognition of Otherness, still directs its critical voice primarily to a specialized audience that shares a common language rooted in the very master narratives it claims to challenge. If radical postmodernist thinking is to have a transformative impact, then a critical break with the notion of 'authority' as 'mastery over' must not simply be a rhetorical device. It must be reflected in habits of being, including styles of writing as well as chosen subject matter. Third world nationals, elites and white critics who passively absorb white supremacist thinking, and therefore never notice or look at black people on the streets or at their jobs, who render us invisible with their gaze in all areas of daily life, are not likely to produce liberatory theory that will challenge racist domination, or promote a breakdown in traditional ways of seeing and thinking about reality, ways of constructing aesthetic theory and practice. From a different standpoint, Robert Storr makes a similar critique in the global issue of *Art in America* when he asserts:

> To be sure, much postmodernist critical inquiry has centered precisely on the issues of 'difference' and 'Otherness'. On the purely theoretical plane the exploration of these concepts has produced some important results, but in the absence of any sustained research into what artists of color and others outside the mainstream might be up to, such discussions become rootless instead of radical. Endless second guessing about the latent

imperialism of intruding upon other cultures only compounded matters, preventing or excusing these theorists from investigating what black, Hispanic, Asian and Native American artists were actually doing.

Without adequate concrete knowledge of and contact with the non-white 'Other', white theorists may move in discursive theoretical directions that are threatening and potentially disruptive of that critical practice which would support radical liberation struggle.

The postmodern critique of 'identity', though relevant for renewed black liberation struggle, is often posed in ways that are problematic. Given a pervasive politic of white supremacy which seeks to prevent the formation of radical black subjectivity, we cannot cavalierly dismiss a concern with identity politics. Any critic exploring the radical potential of postmodernism as it relates to racial difference and racial domination would need to consider the implications of a critique of identity for oppressed groups. Many of us are struggling to find new strategies of resistance. We must engage decolonization as a critical practice if we are to have meaningful chances of survival even as we must simultaneously cope with the loss of political grounding which made radical activism more possible. I am thinking here about the postmodernist critique of essentialism as it pertains to the construction of 'identity' as one example.

Postmodern theory that is not seeking to simply appropriate the experience of 'Otherness' to enhance the discourse or to be radically chic should not separate the 'politics of difference' from the politics of racism. To take racism seriously one must consider the plight of underclass people of color, a vast majority of whom are black. For African-Americans our collective condition prior to the advent of postmodernism and perhaps more tragically expressed under current postmodern conditions has been and is characterized by continued displacement, profound alienation and despair. Writing about

blacks and postmodernism, Cornel West describes our collective plight:

> There is increasing class division and differentiation, creating on the one hand a significant black middle-class, highly anxiety-ridden, insecure, willing to be co-opted and incorporated into the powers that be, concerned with racism to the degree that it poses constraints on upward social mobility; and, on the other, a vast and growing black underclass, an underclass that embodies a kind of walking nihilism of pervasive drug addiction, pervasive alcoholism, pervasive homicide, and an exponential rise in suicide. Now because of the deindustrialization, we also have a devastated black industrial working class. We are talking here about tremendous hopelessness.

This hopelessness creates longing for insight and strategies for change that can renew spirits and reconstruct grounds for collective black liberation struggle. The overall impact of postmodernism is that many other groups now share with black folks a sense of deep alienation, despair, uncertainty, loss of a sense of grounding even if it is not informed by shared circumstance. Radical postmodernism calls attention to those shared sensibilities which cross the boundaries of class, gender, race, etc., that could be fertile ground for the construction of empathy—ties that would promote recognition of common commitments, and serve as a base for solidarity and coalition.

Yearning is the word that best describes a common psychological state shared by many of us, cutting across boundaries of race, class, gender and sexual practice. Specifically, in relation to the postmodernist reconstruction of 'master' narratives, the yearning that wells in the hearts and minds of those whom such narratives have silenced is the longing for critical voice. It is no accident that 'rap' has usurped the primary position of rhythm and blues music among young black folks as the most desired sound or that it

began as a form of 'testimony' for the underclass. It has enabled underclass black youth to
develop a critical voice, as a group of young
black men told me, a 'common literacy'. Rap
projects a critical voice, explaining, demanding,
urging. Working with this insight in his essay
'Putting the pop back into postmodernism',
Lawrence Grossberg comments:

> The postmodern sensibility appropriates
> practices as boasts that announce their own—
> and consequently our own—existence, like a
> rap song boasting of the imaginary (or real—
> it makes no difference) accomplishments of
> the rapper. They offer forms of empower-
> ment not only in the face of nihilism but pre-
> cisely through the forms of nihilism itself: an
> empowering nihilism, a moment of positivity
> through the production and structuring of af-
> fective relations.

Considering that it is as subject one comes to
voice, then the postmodernist focus on the critique of identity appears at first glance to
threaten and close down the possibility that this
discourse and practice will allow those who have
suffered the crippling effects of colonization and
domination to gain or regain a hearing. Even if
this sense of threat and the fear it evokes are
based on a misunderstanding of the postmodernist political project, they nevertheless shape
responses. It never surprises me when black
folks respond to the critique of essentialism, especially when it denies the validity of identity
politics, by saying, 'Yeah, it's easy to give up
identity, when you got one'. Should we not be
suspicious of postmodern critiques of the 'subject' when they surface at a historical moment
when many subjugated people feel themselves
coming to voice for the first time? Though an
apt and oftentimes appropriate comeback, it
does not really intervene in the discourse in a
way that alters and transforms.
Criticisms of directions in postmodern
thinking should not obscure insights it may of-

fer that open up our understanding of African-
American experience. The critique of essentialism encouraged by postmodernist thought is
useful for African-Americans concerned with reformulating outmoded notions of identity. We
have too long had imposed upon us from both
the outside and the inside a narrow, constricting
notion of blackness. Postmodern critiques of essentialism which challenge notions of universality and static over-determined identity within
mass culture and mass consciousness can open
up new possibilities for the construction of self
and the assertion of agency.
Employing a critique of essentialism allows
African-Americans to acknowledge the way in
which class mobility has altered collective black
experience so that racism does not necessarily
have the same impact on our lives. Such a critique allows us to affirm multiple black identities, varied black experience. It also challenges
colonial imperialist paradigms of black identity
which represent blackness one-dimensionally in
ways that reinforce and sustain white supremacy.
This discourse created the idea of the 'primitive'
and promoted the notion of an 'authentic' experience, seeing as 'natural' those expressions of
black life which conformed to a pre-existing pattern or stereotype. Abandoning essentialist notions would be a serious challenge to racism.
Contemporary African-American resistance
struggle must be rooted in a process of decolonization that continually opposes re-inscribing
notions of 'authentic' black identity. This critique should not be made synonymous with a
dismissal of the struggle of oppressed and exploited peoples to make ourselves subjects. Nor
should it deny that in certain circumstances this
experience affords us a privileged critical location
from which to speak. This is not a re-inscription
of modernist master narratives of authority
which privilege some voices by denying voice to
others. Part of our struggle for radical black subjectivity is the quest to find ways to construct self
and identity that are oppositional and liberatory.
The unwillingness to critique essentialism on the

part of many African-Americans is rooted in the fear that it will cause folks to lose sight of the specific history and experience of African-Americans and the unique sensibilities and culture that arise from that experience. An adequate response to this concern is to critique essentialism while emphasizing the significance of 'the authority of experience'. There is a radical difference between a repudiation of the idea that there is a black 'essence' and recognition of the way black identity has been specifically constituted in the experience of exile and struggle.

When black folks critique essentialism, we are empowered to recognize multiple experiences of black identity that are the lived conditions which make diverse cultural productions possible. When this diversity is ignored, it is easy to see black folks as falling into two categories: nationalist or assimilationist, black-identified or white-identified. Coming to terms with the impact of postmodernism for black experience, particularly as it changes our sense of identity, means that we must and can rearticulate the basis for collective bonding. Given the various crises facing African-Americans (economic, spiritual, escalating racial violence, etc.), we are compelled by circumstance to reassess our relationship to popular culture and resistance struggle. Many of us are as reluctant to face this task as many non-black postmodern thinkers who focus theoretically on the issue of 'difference' are to confront the issue of race and racism.

Music is the cultural product created by African-Americans that has most attracted postmodern theorists. It is rarely acknowledged that there is far greater censorship and restriction of other forms of cultural production by black folks—literary, critical writing, etc. Attempts on the part of editors and publishing houses to control and manipulate the representation of black culture, as well as the desire to promote the creation of products that will attract the widest audience, limit in a crippling and stifling way the kind of work many black folks feel we can do and still receive recognition. Using myself as an example, that creative writing I do which I consider to be most reflective of a postmodern oppositional sensibility, work that is abstract, fragmented, non-linear narrative, is constantly rejected by editors and publishers. It does not conform to the type of writing they think black women should be doing or the type of writing they believe will sell. Certainly I do not think I am the only black person engaged in forms of cultural production, especially experimental ones, who is constrained by the lack of an audience for certain kinds of work. It is important for postmodern thinkers and theorists to constitute themselves as an audience for such work. To do this they must assert power and privilege within the space of critical writing to open up the field so that it will be more inclusive. To change the exclusionary practice of postmodern critical discourse is to enact a postmodernism of resistance. Part of this intervention entails black intellectual participation in the discourse.

In his essay 'Postmodernism and Black America', Cornel West suggests that black intellectuals 'are marginal—usually languishing at the interface of Black and white cultures or thoroughly ensconced in Euro-American settings'. He cannot see this group as potential producers of radical postmodernist thought. While I generally agree with this assessment, black intellectuals must proceed with the understanding that we are not condemned to the margins. The way we work and what we do can determine whether or not what we produce will be meaningful to a wider audience, one that includes all classes of black people. West suggests that black intellectuals lack 'any organic link with most of Black life' and that this 'diminishes their value to Black resistance'. This statement bears traces of essentialism. Perhaps we need to focus more on those black intellectuals, however rare our presence, who do not feel this lack and whose work is primarily directed towards the enhancement of black critical consciousness and the strengthening of our collective capacity to engage in meaningful resistance struggle. Theoretical ideas and critical thinking need not be transmitted solely in written work or solely in the academy. While I work in a predominantly white institution, I remain intimately and passionately engaged with black community. It's not like I'm going to talk about writing and thinking about postmodernism with other academics and/or intellectuals and not discuss these ideas with underclass non-academic black folks who are family, friends and comrades. Since I have not broken the ties that bind me to underclass poor black community, I have seen that knowledge, especially that which enhances daily life and strengthens our capacity to survive, can be shared. It means that critics, writers and academics have to give the same critical attention to nurturing and cultivating our ties to black community that we give to writing articles, teaching and lecturing. Here again I am really talking about cultivating habits of being that reinforce awareness that knowledge can be disseminated and shared on a number of fronts. The extent to which knowledge is made available, accessible, etc., depends on the nature of one's political commitments.

Postmodern culture with its decentered subject can be the space where ties are severed or it can provide the occasion for new and varied forms of bonding. To some extent, ruptures, surfaces, contextuality, and a host of other happenings create gaps that make space for oppositional practices which no longer require intellectuals to be confined by narrow separate spheres with no meaningful connection to the world of the everyday. Much postmodern engagement with culture emerges from the yearning to do intellectual work that connects with habits of being, forms of artistic expression and aesthetics that inform the daily life of writers and scholars as well as a mass population. On the terrain of culture, one can participate in critical dialogue with the uneducated poor, the black underclass who are thinking about aesthetics. One can talk about what we are seeing, thinking or listening to; a space is there for critical exchange. It's exciting to think, write, talk about and create art that reflects passionate engagement with popular culture, because this may very well be 'the' central future location of resistance struggle, a meeting place where new and radical happenings can occur.

9

Aijaz Ahmad
1945–

A native of India, Aijaz Ahmad lived in Pakistan for many years before returning to India, where he is now a professorial fellow at the Centre of Contemporary Studies, Nehru Memorial Museum and Library, New Delhi. He is the editor of *Ghazals of Ghalib: Version from the Urdu* (1971) and the author of many critical articles, including most recently "Reconstructing Derrida: 'Spectres of Marx' and Deconstructive Politics" (1994) and "The Politics of Literary Postcoloniality" (1995). In 1992, Ahmad published *In Theory: Classes, Nations, Literatures,* which sparked enough interest that the journal *Public Culture* devoted its fall 1993 issue to nine essays debating the book.

"Literary Theory and 'Third World Literature': Some Contexts" is the first chapter of *In Theory,* and it opens with the argument that third world literature is a construct of the metropolitan universities, which were under pressure to devise "a new set of categories within the larger conceptual category of Literature." The focus of this new category was nationalism, while "the rich history of our opposition and radical cultural productions" was (intentionally or unintentionally) subverted. From this broad introduction of his text, Ahmad moves to explaining the "backgrounds and contexts of contemporary literary theory itself" to help explain the genesis of third world literature. He notes that the Algerian Revolution and the Vietnam War helped contribute to "four consequences for the teaching of literature" at universities: black literature gained a place; women's studies programs were organized; Marxism and the New Left appeared; and the issues of colonialism and nationalism were addressed. It is this last "consequence" that is Ahmad's main concern. The attention given to colonialism and imperialism at universities was not, he argues, the result of Marxist pressures, but instead arose from "already existing nationalist premises and predispositions." The focus of third world literature was on the dichotomy between imperialism and nationalism—"Colonial Discourse"—and looked toward the past instead of the future. The result is that cultural nationalism is the "constitutive ideology" around which issues of third world literature are raised. For Ahmad, the danger for third world literature—and any other "radicalism"—is that of "embourgeoisement."

Literary Theory and 'Third World Literature': Some Contexts

The issue of assembling and professionalizing a new area of literature, namely 'Third World Literature', has arisen primarily in the metropolitan university, in England and North America for the most part, which is responding to quite specific kinds of pressures by appropriating particular kinds of texts, and by devising a new set of categories within the larger conceptual category of Literature as such. We may begin, then, by summarizing some of the pressures—literary, cultural, political pressures—as well as the general ideological conjuncture which impels them—and, through them, *us*—first to speak of a unitary category of Third World Literature and then to reproduce that very ideology, on an extended scale, in all we think and say about that category.[1] The directly political contexts . . . gave rise to the Three Worlds Theory in the first place, before it became a literary-critical matter. . . . The pressures and paradoxes I examine in this chapter, and also in the next, take institutional and pedagogical forms. Through these forms, I trace lineages of particular intelligentsias and then connect the practices of these intelligentsias with their largely unrecognized global determinations in order, precisely, to prepare a theoretical ground for examining the fairly widespread proposition that nationalism of one kind or another is the determinate ideological imperative in the cultural productions of the 'Third World' in the era of colonialism and imperialism. . . .

I might add that I had initially felt reluctant to speak of these matters in the context of Indian debates because this matter of 'Third World Literature' is connected, really, with the context of the metropolitan university and the teaching of Literature in *that* situation, but it has been necessary to engage with these questions here for obvious reasons. So fundamental and even genetic is the Indian university's relation with—indeed, dependence upon—its British and American counterparts that knowledges produced there become immediately effective here, in a relation of imperial dominance, shaping even the way we think of ourselves. So, in examining the pressures which impel the metropolitan university to devise new categories for conceptualizing cultural productions in our part of the world, I am speaking also of pressures which are exerted *by* the metropolitan university upon the already-subordinated Indian university. Nowhere is this parasitic intellectual dependence of the Indian university upon its metropolitan counterparts so obvious as in the teaching of English. And, typically, this dependence tends to be greater at the higher, more elite levels of English teaching in India: the more privileged universities, the handful of the elite colleges, those among the university faculties who are the most lavishly armed with degrees, foreign experience, lists of publications, academic ambitions. It is with disorientations of elite scholarship in our institutions that I am here implicitly most concerned.

In declaring nationalism to be the main political imperative of our era, the theoretical positions of 'Third World Literature' and 'Colonial Discourse Analysis' would tend to subvert, with overt intent or not, the rich history of our oppositional and radical cultural productions, which have more often than not come out of communist political practice and, more broadly, from inside a political culture deeply marked by Marxism. What we need to do is to build vastly better knowledges on the basis of that heritage; to revert, instead, from the Marxist critique of class, colony and empire to the emptiness of a Third-Worldist nationalism is politically and theoretically a regression. Inclusion of some writers from the 'Third World' in our existing curriculum would surely be a gain, but a relatively less significant one, especially if it is done in an eclectic sort of way and without negotiating the consequences of the fact that 'literature' from other zones of the 'Third World'—African, say, or Arab or Caribbean—comes to us not directly or autonomously but through grids of accumulation, interpretation and relocation which are governed from the metropolitan countries. By the time a Latin American novel arrives in Delhi, it has been selected, translated, published, reviewed, explicated and allotted a place in the burgeoning archive of 'Third World Literature' through a complex set of metropolitan mediations. That is to say, it arrives here with those processes of circulation and classification already inscribed in its very texture. About this contradictory role of imperialism which simultaneously unifies the world, in the form of global channels of circulation, and distributes it into structures of global coercion and domination, I shall say a great deal throughout this book. Suffice it to say here that even as we open ourselves up to the widest possible range of global cultural productions, it is best to keep in view the coercive power of the very channels through which we have access to those productions. Internationalism, in other words, has been one of the constitutive traditions of the Left, but in this age of late capitalism it is best to recognize that certain kinds of internationalism also arise more or less spontaneously out of the circuits of imperialist capital itself, and the lines between the internationalism of the Left and the globalism of capitalist circuits must always be demarcated as rigorously as possible.

It is in the metropolitan country, in any case, that a literary text is first designated a Third World text, levelled into an archive of other such texts, and then globally redistributed with that aura attached to it. It is useful, therefore, to demystify the category of 'Third World Literature' which is emerging in the metropolitan university now as something of a countercanon and which—like any canon, dominant or emer-

gent—does not really exist before its fabrication. What, we may ask, are the conditions within which this new subdiscipline of Literature, namely 'Third World Literature', has been assembled? My summary treatment of these conditions will emphasize a specific grid of four mutually reinforcing elements: (a) the general backgrounds and the contemporary situation of literary theory itself; (b) the new availability and increasing influence in the metropolitan countries of a large number of literary texts composed by non-Western writers; (c) the increasing numbers and therefore far greater social assertion there of immigrant professional strata from non-Western countries; and (d) the arrival, during that same period, of a new political theory—namely, the Three Worlds Theory—which eventually had the widest possible circulation in many variants, including, especially, the one popularized by certain sections of the Parisian avant-garde which saw in it—at a certain stage of its evolution, before settling down into straightforward right-wing positions—a convenient alternative to classical Marxism—convenient, I might add, because one could thus retain, and even enhance, one's radical credentials. Only the first of these elements—the backgrounds and contexts of contemporary literary theory itself—will be addressed in this chapter. . . . This somewhat schematic commentary on the contexts of metropolitan literary Third-Worldism will then make possible fuller discussions of the authors and texts which constitute this ideological tendency, the Three Worlds Theory as such, the constitutive role of nationalism in that theory, and some alternative starting points.

I

As regards the contemporary situation of literary theory, it is as well to recall that even the more advanced sectors of English Studies during the period between the two World Wars were dominated by four main—and in some significant respects overlapping—tendencies: the practical criticism of I.A. Richards;[2] the conservative, monarchist, quasi-Catholic criticism of T.S. Eliot; some elements of avant-gardist modernism which nevertheless remained much less theorized in the English-speaking countries than in continental Europe; and the then newly emergent 'New Criticism' of Ransom, Tate and others in the United States.[3]

The impulse to resist these exclusivist—and, in many areas, technicist—emphases was stronger in England, where there had been a much older tradition of socially conscious literary study. The *Scrutiny* group, led by F.R. Leavis, assimilated the pedagogical value of practical criticism, making its salutary move to define objective criteria for literary analysis to displace the aristocratic notions of literary 'taste', while also insisting on locating the texts of English literature in the larger narrative of English social life. More recent critiques of the Leavisite tendency have documented this group's own deep complicity in the ideologies of the Tory middle class; Leavis's own almost messianic vision of English Studies as the determinate mode of cultural salvation for England has been documented often enough.[4] There was also, however, a populist kind of radicalism in their positions.[5] That populist edge was what Raymond Williams picked up, and then combined with his own Welsh working-class background, as well as with the kind of radicalism that had once brought him into the Communist Party, even as he returned from the war and started working on his magisterial survey in *Culture and Society*. Over the next twenty years or so, he produced a large number of studies—including *The Country and the City*, possibly the most moving book of literary criticism ever written in the English language—which went over the same territory that had been marked earlier by Leavis, remapping it in highly original, radical and persuasive ways. By the time Williams died, in 1988, he had revamped the very terms in which English Studies had conceived of the relation between literature, culture,

society and history. I do not mean that Williams ever came to command the kind of power that, let us say, Eliot had once commanded—and continues to command in some circles, especially in *our* university departments and among the genteel literati. One could safely say, however, that between Leavis's Tory populism and Williams's increasingly Marxist perspectives—and the kinds of thinking these two represented, the influences they exercised—the more advanced sectors of the academic literary intelligentsia in British universities continued to grapple relatively more steadily with the social matrix of literary production, even at the height of the Cold War.

In some ways, this British development was in sharp contrast with the American, which will be discussed below, and this too can be briefly clarified if we take a slightly more extended look at Williams's career. He had started exercising his broad influence in Britain with the publication of *Culture and Society* (1958), at about the same time as Northrop Frye published his *magnum opus, Anatomy of Criticism* (1957), when the careers of the likes of Paul de Man and Harold Bloom also got going. In other words, while the reaction against 'New Criticism' in the United States moved increasingly into the questions of genre, conservatively defined, or towards deconstruction and associated positions, the critique of I.A. Richards and Leavis in England moved leftward. Nor was it a solitary endeavour, even though Williams's later ruminations about how alone he felt at the time deserve our respect.[6] For it was precisely at the time when the intellectual climate in the United States had solidified into the worst kind of Cold War anti-communism that the Communist Party Historians' Group was assembled as a collective enterprise and began changing the British intellectual landscape.[7] Two members, Maurice Dobb and Christopher Hill, had published substantial work before,[8] but their assertion as a group, as well as the best work of each of them, came after the war—the period being inaugurated, so to speak, with the publication of

Dobb's *Studies in the Development of Capitalism* in 1946. That kind of research, of course, provided a sustaining climate for work like Williams's, so far as strictly literary and cultural studies were concerned, but it is worth remarking that much more than simple sustenance from a cognate academic discipline is involved here. There were, of course, personal associations which, judging from available evidence, seem not to have broken down entirely, even though Williams dissociated himself from the party after returning from the war, but then there is also the fact that several of these historians made immeasurable contributions to cultural studies directly. Victor Kiernan is a substantial critic of literature in his own right, and Hill himself is one of the most authoritative scholars of Milton and of seventeenth-century 'culture' generally[9]—not to speak of E.P. Thompson, whose first major work was a study of William Morris[10] and whose *The Making of the English Working Class* (1963) should be one of the fundamental texts for any Cultural Studies Programme, anywhere in the world. That ensemble of intellectual productions was one part—and surely a shaping part—of the milieu in which Williams's own intellectual formation took place, even though he kept his distance from Marxism at that time. But there were other things as well, such as the adult education work in which Williams found partnerships with intellectuals like Hoggart,[11] and direct political activism in such organizations as the Campaign for Nuclear Disarmament (CND), which proved equally sustaining and, for Williams himself, a bridge both towards the 'New Left', when that emerged as a distinct tendency in the 1960s, and into the lived pressure of collective engagements which helped him define for himself, over the years, a much finer Marxism than anything he had known in his youth.

Williams's was a peculiar odyssey, quite the reverse of what happens so very often when the commitments and passions of youth give way to professional incorporation and increasing embourgeoisement. Williams's intellect, always cautious and always reluctant to press too far beyond thresholds of existing convictions, kept moving leftward. What he had gained in the writing of the earlier books he never lost, but the culture of his ideas in, say, *Problems of Materialism and Culture* (1980) is doubtless much wider, more to the Left, more theoretically grounded. But then, as one reads the two posthumous collections of his essays, *The Politics of Modernism and Resources of Hope* (1989), one is struck by the fact that in those closing years of his life his mind had become, if anything, more passionate. *Culture and Society* had doubtless had enormous impact in Britain, though much less in the United States. Even so, right up to and after the publication of *The Country and the City* (1973), Williams was seen only as a very distinctive kind of literary/cultural critic, and his continuing activist affiliation with the Left throughout that period—preserved now in such documents as *Mayday Manifesto* (1968)—was seen as not central to his critical enterprise, partly because of the ambiguous relationship Williams himself had maintained with theoretical Marxism.

The real turn came, in fact, in the mid 1970s and after. In part, of course, Williams's turn towards theoretical Marxism at this juncture was connected with the introduction, mainly via *New Left Review,* of many texts of continental Marxism (Gramsci to Colletti, Althusser to Goldmann) into the British Isles. But, characteristically, it took the form of rethinking the existing categories of his own thought. His recovery and reconsideration of the categorical apparatus that had been in the background of *Culture and Society,* which he now published in *Keywords* (1976; enlarged, revised edition 1984), precisely at the time when he was working on his *Marxism and Literature* (1977), has the status, I think, of a symptomatic caesura, connecting his earlier work with the later but also beginning to form a line of clear demarcation. This task of reconsideration then took the shape of what is to my mind a very moving book in its own right, *Politics and Letters* (1979), in which Williams submitted himself to sustained questioning, at once courteous and firm, by Marxist scholars of a younger generation, responding with reflections on his own work with astonishing—and, in the fullest sense of the word, *enabling*—veracity. The work of his last decade went from strength to strength thereafter, though the breadth of its engagements was hardly to be contained in a given book. In the process, Williams helped to sustain a level of critical discourse not easily dislodged by the kind of new fashions and new orthodoxies that came to dominate literary studies—in sections of the British Left itself but, even more, in the United States.

For the American intellectual formation had been different in significant ways. There was no working-class culture of the kind England had had since at least the Chartists. The chief characteristics of the bourgeois revolution in the United States had been that (a) it was carried out by a section of the settler population against the colonial regime which had constituted that population in the first place; and (b) bourgeois hegemony was established before the full consolidation of the classes of industrial capitalism, and under a leadership ideologically as advanced as in revolutionary France but drawn, in its class composition, substantially from the plantation economy of slaveowners, with the predominantly commercial and petty capitals of New England occupying a subordinate position. The contradictory consequence was that the American Revolution was, simultaneously, in some fundamental ways even more advanced than the French, while it retained some aspects so retrograde that its full elaboration spanned virtually a whole century and was completed only in 1864 with the destruction of the plantation economy and the assimilation of the slave population first into sharecropping and then increasingly into wage-labour circuits.

The origins of English Romanticism are inseparable from the anti-capitalist passions of Blake, and it had the Cromwellian radicalism of Milton in its past; even Wordsworth and Co-leridge had been, before their respective Tory conversions, radical supporters of the Jacobin content in the French Revolution. The main currents of American Romanticism were, by contrast, oracular and transcendentalist, optimistic and confident; this one can see readily if one were to pause and think what 'transcendence' might have meant to, say, Blake and Emerson respectively. In the nineteenth-century American pantheon it is only in people like Frederick Douglass—in the songs and narratives of the slaves; in Sojourner Truth, in John Brown, in radical Abolitionism—that one sees the Cromwellian element, but the racism of the American literary Establishment has been such that even the inclusion of Douglass in this pantheon has been only a recent and is still a very sectoral matter; all the rest is consigned to the obscurity of 'minority literature'. Among the great American poets of that time, Whitman is of course the most 'Jacobin', but it is symptomatic of this oracular tendency in American Romanticism that whenever Whitman errs, he errs into sugariness and mist. The experience which had produced this Romanticism—especially in the dominant, Emersonian current—was not the experience of industrial capitalism, as in England, but that of a society of independent petty commodity producers, which was the predominant mode of existence for the middling classes of the Eastern seaboard until the mid nineteenth century.

The case of Emily Dickinson, the most moving nineteenth-century American poet and one of the most thoroughly nuanced literary intelligences ever to be born in the United States, is indicative in this regard. She wrote some of her greatest poems in the years of the American Civil War, and the pain of them is quite as excruciating as in Blake; yet, except for a handful of oblique references and metaphors, that decisive experience of her generation is entirely absent from her work. Lacking other sorts of traditions and communities, she seems to have been driven to experience her deepest pains in a privacy that had been radically separated, in order to be understood, from the public and the political. I do not mean that either Emerson or Dickinson was even remotely conservative by persuasion, in the way that British Tories always are; nor do I mean that other currents were not there, even within the dominant tradition. There is the overwhelming presence of Mark Twain, for example, in the latter part of the nineteenth century. And if one steps out of the dominant tradition, there is of course a large body of writings by women who tell us a great deal about the stresses of embourgeoisement in a gendered society, not to speak of Black literature, which documents in very straightforward ways much of the pain and cruelty upon which the splendour of America has been built.

What I do mean, however, is that the tradition of letters American modernism inherited from its own elite past had rarely been informed by energies of the working class; was dominated largely by the boundless and somewhat philistine optimism of New England's petty commodity producers; and had made a truce, by and large, with the racism and mercantilism of its own society. Even as this mercantilism and petty commodity production in New England, as well as the slave society of the South, gave way, in the latter half of the nineteenth century, to the social predominance of large-scale industrial capital, the critical issue for masters of American fiction, such as Henry James, was whether the ruling class of this new industrial society would learn the leisured manners of European aristocracy, or descend into the purest forms of commodity fetishism. A particular tension in James's work, of course, is that he is more or less equally attracted and repelled by both the aristocratic arrogances of the European cultural elite and by the forms of self-aggrandizing bourgeois individualisms that were taking shape in the USA more firmly and visibly than in Europe. What the cost of this unprecedented American growth was—for the immigrant, the Black, the poor farmer of the Midwest—James did not, at any rate, care about much.

It is hardly surprising, in this context, that American modernism turned out to be deeply conservative and elitist, often with racist overtones. Of the four poets—Pound, Eliot, Stevens and Williams—who are commonly considered the masters of American modernism, only Williams had even a populist strand.[12] Admittedly, the 1930s also experienced a sudden wave of literary and cultural radicalism, but the two remarkable things about that radicalism are (a) the fact that it left behind no body of radical critical thought, even on the order of, let us say, Christopher Cauldwell in England; and (b) the quickness with which it disappeared as a *literary* phenomenon, leaving little trace upon the subsequent postwar literary culture even though it left behind many undercurrents in the larger society which then fed, more or less silently, into the rise of the New Left during the 1960s. After World War II, as the USA consolidated its position as the leading capitalist power in the world, so immense was the right-wing national consensus, so pathological the anti-communist phobia, that those lonely figures, such as Kenneth Burke, who continued to do serious radical work in literary and cultural theory were thoroughly marginalized.

The cumulative weight of this cultural configuration has been such that when 'New Criticism' appeared on the horizon—with its fetishistic notions of the utter autonomy of each single literary work, and its post-Romantic idea of 'Literature' as a special kind of *language* which yields a special kind of knowledge—its practice of reified reading proved altogether hegemonic in American literary studies for a quarter-century or more, and it proved extremely useful as a pedagogical tool in the American classroom precisely because it required of the student little knowledge of anything not strictly 'literary'— no history which was not predominantly literary history, no science of the social, no philosophy—except the procedures and precepts of literary formalism, which, too, it could not entirely accept in full objectivist rigour thanks to its prior commitment to squeezing a particular ideological meaning out of each literary text. The favourite New Critical text was the short lyric, precisely because the lyric could be detached with comparatively greater ease from the larger body of texts, and indeed from the world itself, to become the ground for analysis of compositional minutiae; the pedagogical advantage was, of course, that such analyses of short lyrics could fit rather neatly into one hour in the undergraduate classroom. This pedagogical advantage, and the attendant detachment of 'Literature' from the crises and combats of real life, served also to conceal the ideology of some of the leading lights of 'New Criticism' who were quaintly called 'Agrarian Populist' but were really bourgeois gentlemen of the New South, the cultural heirs of the old slaveowning class. What is even more significant, however, is that 'New Criticism' reached its greatest power in the late 1940s, as the USA launched the Cold War and entered the period of McCarthyism, and that its definitive decline from hegemony began in the late 1950s as McCarthyism, in the strict sense, also receded and the Eisenhower doctrine began to give way to those more contradictory trends which eventually flowered during the Kennedy era—those golden years of US liberalism which gave us the Vietnam War. The peculiar blend of formalist detachment and deliberate distancing from forms of the prose narrative, with their inescapable locations in social life, into reified readings of short lyrics was, so to speak, the objective correlative of other kinds of distancing and reifications required by the larger culture.

The first dissent against New Criticism came at this transitional time—from critics like Northrop Frye, who retained the conception of Literature as a special language yielding a special kind of knowledge, but insisted also that individual literary texts simply could not be discussed outside some larger narrative. What Frye wanted, of course, was that any given poem or novel should be placed within a wider, formalist narrative of all-encompassing genres and literary

modes. His preferred text was not so much the short lyric as the longer narrative poem, preferably in the genre of romance or comedy, which are as a rule much less tainted by the stresses of lived socialities. Literature's true residence was still, in any case, in the metaphysical, preferably religious, Sublime: the poem, we were told, writes itself through the poet, and the closed, self-reproducing history of genres is the true history of civilization's deep structures in which the individual poet performs only a communicative and incidental function, as the site of more or less linguistic elaboration. This kind of literary-critical training was later to prove helpful in paving the way for structuralism, as well as what came to be known as Discourse Theory: language doing the speaking through human beings, human agency constituted by discourse itself, with each genre now seen either as a distinct discourse or, alternatively, as a specific form in Literature's discursive regularities. The job of the critic came to reside, therefore, in the power of these regularities to generate enunciations, more or less infinitely. The training also facilitated various kinds of Romantic, anti-humanist irrationalisms, through its emphasis both on extra-rational inspiration, thus reiterating the Romantic trope of poet as prophet and oracle, and on writing emanating neither from the pressures of history and society nor from the writer's own choice, but from literature's power to write itself through the medium of the writer. The crucial period of Frye's intellectual formation, from *Fearful Symmetry* (1947) to *Anatomy of Criticism* (1957), encompassed the heyday of McCarthyism, and it was after the appearance of the latter work that his influence became, for a time, decisive.

The figures who came to dominate the US literary scene from the 1960s onwards—figures like Paul de Man and Harold Bloom—had emerged towards the end of this transition from Dulles-style, pathological anti-communism to the Kennedy-style, hard-edged 'liberal' imperialism—the transition, one might say, from Korea to Vietnam. The political origins of de Man's ideas are, of course, far more complex and dis-agreeable, given his own Nazi associations, to which he never confessed or faced up publicly during his lifetime, but certain broad emphases may also be identified. Bloom's early work had the effect, first, of privileging the Romantic Movement as *the* modern movement, thus ex-tending the tendencies which were already there in Frye and Cleanth Brooks but taking them further in Nietzschean directions; and, second, of locating the difference of later texts in the anxieties produced by earlier ones, so that the field of textual production becomes contentious and conflictual, while the history of such pro-ductions and contentions itself remains strictly textual. Even though Bloom was later to be greatly disturbed by the ascendancy of decon-struction, he was entirely incapable of mounting a *theoretical* counter-offensive because of his es-sentially untheoretical, literary-critical bent and his prior complicity in the Romantic, the reli-gious, the prophetic and the oracular—Emer-sonian in one breath, Nietzschean in another, biblical in yet another. That same privileging of Romanticism is there in de Man's early work, even though it was mediated even then by his own preference for reading the Romantics themselves through Heidegger. It is at least ar-guable that his later slide into Derridean posi-tions was facilitated by the specifically Heideg-gerian forms of anti-rationalism. The overall thrust of American deconstruction was in any case highly technicist, shorn of whatever politi-cal radicalism there might have been in the orig-inal French formation; the net effect was to make the text entirely hermetic. If the New Critics had privileged the isolated text in order to contemplate its beauty and principle of co-herence, deconstruction isolated it for identify-ing the principle of dissolution inherent in its very textuality; but the closure of the text, its hermetic distancing, was in either case the pre-condition for its reading. That Frye, Bloom and de Man were all attracted, in their respective ways, by versions of the irrational, the religious and the Romantic contributed to a structure of

feeling in American literary criticism which was implicitly already hostile to rationalism and therefore particularly receptive to sloganeering against the Enlightenment, and so on, when the fashion arrived from Paris.

If New Critical close reading had had the ef-fect of offering a method which took the literary text out of the chitchat of leisured gentlemen, a method that could be taught to undergraduates in repeated fifty-minute doses, deconstructionist close reading became a fully fledged technology requiring specialist training that would span both the undergraduate and the graduate class-rooms for about ten years. It was, in the mo-ment of the emergence of this full-scale technol-ogy—launched, paradoxically enough, in contemptuous dismissal of rationalism for its claims to scientificity—that literary criticism in the English-speaking countries gave way to what came to be known as literary theory. The general political climate which attended its birth and the technological hermeticism of textuality which is deconstruction's main concern have left their mark on the very structure of US literary theory, with the result that the younger critics who came to constitute the left wing of the US literary Establishment in the Carter and Reagan years were themselves hung, excruciatingly, be-tween de Man and lessons of the Vietnam War. The mystique of Left professionalism, which grew alongside literary theory, was a precise ex-pression of this self-division. If the lessons of the Vietnam War took one into politics, the tech-nologism of theory took one deeper and deeper into mastery of the professional field, and radi-cal literary theory, like any professional field, also developed a language and a way of referenc-ing other signposts within it, which were inac-cessible to those located outside its boundaries.[13]

II

It was in the 1960s, in any case, that contentions were really sharpened, in the form of a three-way split. The great majority of teachers and critics have continued to function, in both Britain and North America, as if nothing much has changed since T.S. Eliot and the 'New Criticism'. An entirely new kind of literary avant-garde has also arisen, however, on both sides of the Atlantic, which functions now—alongside and in conflict with the conservative majority—under the insignia not of criticism but of theory. This shift in the governing insignia indicates, for the bulk of this avant-garde, both a continuity of perspective and a sea-change in method: the idea of the *specialness* of literature (special language, special kind of knowledge, answerable only to its own past practices and rules of composition—now invoked as forms of discourse—and not to the world outside the text) is retained and vastly complicated, but the analytic method refers now not to the enclosed world of 'literary criticism' but to a whole host of 'extra-literary' theoretical positions, from psychoanalysis to phenomenology, linguistics to philosophy. (Psychology, of course, was there even as early as Richards, but the resurfacing of Freud, via Lacan, in the new literary theory was of an entirely different kind.) In an accompanying move, 'Literature' undergoes both a deflation and an aggrandizement: it becomes, in one sort of reading, just *one* discourse among other discourses, with its *specialness* residing simply in the *difference* of its language; but in a much more radical and now quite pervasive displacement—which asserts that there is really nothing outside language, outside textuality, outside representation—*everything* becomes, in a sense, 'Literature'.

The *bulk* of this avant-garde is essentially technicist, much more so than poor old 'New Criticism' ever dreamed of being, but alongside this bulk there is also a minoritarian current within the avant-garde. Sometimes overlapping with that dominant current and sometimes resisting some of its technicist stridencies, but almost always—and increasingly so in the 1980s—needing to respond to that dominance in its own terms, this minoritarian current attempts to fashion, with lesser or greater success, politically informed readings. But the question

of what constitutes political reading is itself greatly complicated for this radical current because of the character of its own intellectual formation as it went through graduate schools, solidified its theoretical bearings and affiliations, and began joining the profession during precisely the period about which Lentricchia has written with such elegance. He has described the shaping influences for this period (1957–77):

Northrop Frye, Wallace Stevens, Frank Kermode, Jean-Paul Sartre, Georges Poulet, Martin Heidegger, Ferdinand de Saussure, Claude Lévi-Strauss, Roland Barthes, Jacques Derrida, and Michel Foucault have largely set the terms and themes of recent critical controversies in the country. Theodor Adorno, Walter Benjamin, Georg Lukács, Antonio Gramsci, Louis Althusser, Lucien Goldmann, and others in their tradition have a great deal to say to American critics, but in the period I have chosen to study they have not been shaping influences.[14]

Two clarifications about the inclusion of Sartre in the first list must be made. For if he was one of those who 'set the terms' for American criticism during that period, it was *not* through his growing concern with political engagement or his later turn towards Marxism but through his 'existentialism' and, specifically, his very early work, *The Psychology of Imagination*. Furthermore, the younger critics who came of age at this time read the later Sartre, if at all, not directly but through the disparaging critiques of Lévi-Strauss, Derrida, and others. More generally, Lentricchia's two contrasting lists—of those who 'set the terms', and of the absences—makes it quite clear that what came to be known later as 'Western Marxism'[15] was not a part of the intellectual formation of that generation of American critics, and by the time the more radical among them began to read these other kinds of theorists, their basic critical positions had been formed quite solidly by deconstruction, etc. When any sustained reading began of Gramsci, whose name was to be much abused in later theorizations, his work was as a rule read into a theoretical position already framed by Derrida and Paul de Man, Foucault and Lyotard; the question was how to assimilate Gramsci *into* this preexisting structure. This, then, determined the nature of the 'political' readings which followed.

Politically more engaged in its earlier projects, increasingly more professionalized and confined to the academy since the recooling of America began in the latter 1970s, this minoritarian current of radicals in contemporary literary theory has its origins in those new groupings among students and teachers of the 1960s which had at that time begun to interrogate the very 'literariness' of the literary text, so as to locate it not in the history of genres and styles but in the larger history of the world itself. When Marxism had proposed such a worldly approach to literature, a confident American literary Establishment had dismissed it out of hand, as mere 'sociology'. Now, under mounting pressures, a whole range of people—only a few of them Marxist in any fashion or degree—have had to open up this buried continent of Literature to the scrutinizing gaze of history and politics. How this has come about is a complex tale, and this is not the occasion to tell it, but it is worth emphasizing that the emergence of this current—complex as it was, fragmented as it remained, and regardless of all its later detours and largely successful incorporation into poststructuralism—was connected, in its origins, with the crisis provoked in the Western academy first by the Algerian Revolution and then by the Vietnam War. It was in the crucible of those wars that at least some of the intellectuals of the contemporary West learned to question their own place in the world, and hence also to question the hegemonic closure of the texts upon which their epistemologies were based. One of the side-effects of that overall crisis was that Literature was pressed to disclose the strategic complicities whereby it had traditionally represented races—and genders—and empires.

The first breaks came, predictably, in France. For one thing, the 'Jacobin' element was much older, more deeply rooted, in the French universities, where even the most revered institutions had long been dominated not by an aristocracy, as in England, but by the petty bourgeoisie, thanks to the legacy of the Revolution itself. Then, in sharp contrast to the American variant of modernism, Paris, one of the main sites for the emergence of that modernism (Berlin and Vienna were, arguably, the other two), had become, by the early decades of this century, the home of the more radical, anti-bourgeois positions within modernism, such as the Cubist Movement or the more politically motivated strands in Dada and Surrealism. The inter-war years also witnessed the emergence of the first sizeable Marxist philosophical tradition in France (much later than in Germany or Russia or even Italy, but earlier and more articulated than in the predominantly Anglo-Saxon countries); the emergence also of mass labour and communist movements; the first Popular Front government; and the widely felt radicalizing influence of the Spanish Civil War. On the heels of all that came the Nazi Occupation, which gave numerous French intellectuals, especially those who actually fought in the underground Resistance, some imaginative understanding of the meaning of colonial subjection and the legitimacy of combat for liberation. Finally, it was in the *French* colonies, Indochina and Algeria, that the two great wars of anti-colonial national liberation broke out. For a whole generation of French writers, from Merleau-Ponty to André Malraux, support for the anti-colonial struggles was the natural extension of the anti-fascist struggles at home and the earlier movement of solidarity with the Republic in Spain; for others, the issues of colony and empire served to open up a whole range of other buried areas as well, from ontology to gendering. Thus, for example, Sartre's philosophical and literary radicalism from the late 1940s onwards, as well as Simone de Beauvoir's emergence in the 1950s as the seminal figure in modern feminism, are inseparable from the reshaping of their lives and ideas due to their involvement in the French anti-war movement during the Algerian Revolution; and it is symptomatic of the whole drift of modern French thought that the decisive attack on Sartre, mounted by Claude Lévi-Strauss—and mounted, precisely, in the name of the anthropological pre-modern—came towards the very end of the Algerian War.[16]

The two decades of the greatest radicalism in French thought—roughly from 1945 to 1965—were also the decades in which the colonial question became the principal point of contention within French society, just as the rise and fall of American radicalism in the subsequent decade, from about 1965 to 1975, was also a direct consequence of the Vietnam War. Inside France, however, the years of the Indochinese and Algerian wars had coincided with the installation of a new-style, Fordist regime of capital accumulation, thanks largely to French acceptance of the Marshall Plan. While the labour movement itself had gradually been tamed through the 1950s, facilitated further by the French Communist Party's convergence with its own bourgeoisie on the colonial question, the defeat in Indochina and the bloody combat in *colon*-dominated Algeria served to move large sections of the French population, including substantial sections of the intelligentsia, into the Right's embrace. The settlement of the Algerian War then paved the way for full-scale consolidation of Hugh Gaullism. It was at this point that the ascendancy of structuralism and then of semiotics began—first in fairly radical variants, in keeping with the temper of the times, and then in increasingly formalist, domesticated directions. Both Lévi-Strauss and Roland Barthes, for example, had

initially indicated affinities with Marxism, claiming for linguistics, in earlier phases of their respective careers, not so much an *ontological* primacy as, basically, a *methodological* efficacy. The real trends remained so unclear for so many years that the Events of 1968, when they burst upon the French scene, were widely viewed as the inaugural gesture of a new generation of radical, even revolutionary, intellectuals and militants, and *neither* as the process that propelled the worst kind of anti-communism to an hegemonic position among the Parisian avant-garde *nor* as the last rites for an antiquated form of capitalism which was soon to be replaced by a more efficient, more consumptionist form.[17] In the course of the decade following 1968, Paris was at length normalized. Many of the more strident members of the generation of '68, from Kristeva to Glucksmann, then passed into the ultra-Right of the 'New Philosophers', and the voices that came to dominate French intellectual life—Derrida and Foucault, Lyotard and Baudrillard, Deleuze and Guattari—quite comfortably announced 'the death of the subject', 'the end of the social', and so on.[18]

Developments in the USA were somewhat different. *There* 1968 was not a year of defeat or disorganization for the Left—such as it was. Rather, 1968, from the American point of view, was the year of the spectacular victories of the Vietnamese Tet offensive, the high point of the Black rebellion inside the country, the abdication of Lyndon Johnson, the hot summer of the anti-war movement. The historical underpinnings of the American anti-war movement were no doubt contradictory and ambiguous. On the one hand, the political underdevelopment of the United States was such that the anti-war movement could not even become a properly anti-imperialist movement, let alone a revolutionary one; for most of its participants, it was simply a movement against the direct involvement of the US armed forces in Vietnam, and it fizzled out as soon as Nixon started bringing back the troops. On the other hand, so massive was the mobilization of millions of people—men and women, black and white—that they were able, over a decade or more, to put on the social agenda questions that had been suppressed for far too long.

There were four consequences for the teaching of literature; these can be listed here separately for the sake of clarity, though in actual fact there was considerable overlap among the forces and human agencies which produced them. First, the anti-war radicalism was combined with the preceding and in some ways overlapping Black Civil Rights Movement and what came to be known as Black Cultural Nationalism; colleges and universities were opened up for Black students and faculty as never before; and Black literature, which had never been taught in the US academy with any degree of coherence, now became a serious, albeit still very marginalized, discipline. Second, this confluence (or at least simultaneity) of the predominantly white anti-war movement and the many strands of Black oppositional politics opened up a much wider political space in which a whole range of other social agents, by no means *constituted* by those movements, nevertheless began to articulate their own agendas in new and much larger ways than previously; the movements of Hispanic-Americans and of Mexican agricultural labour within the USA are cases in point. It is significant that some of the more influential figures in that first wave of the contemporary Women's Movement in the USA which began to gather force in the late 1960s—figures as different as Shulamith Firestone and Adrienne Rich, Robin Morgan and Angela Davis—had been radicalized first within those other movements; it was only somewhat later that they began to think consistently of their own positions as women, of the larger history of those positions, and of the many modes of women's resistance, past and present. As a fully fledged women's movement gathered momentum—not centralized but dispersed at many sites, originating as

much in a common history as in diverse local pressures—the impact began to be felt within the academy as well, and Women's Studies programmes were organized throughout the United States as never before; many would argue that it is precisely in the academy that the Women's Movement has made its largest gains. Third, and as a result of an equally diverse 'New Left' which was nevertheless based largely on campuses, Marxism itself made its first serious appearance as a theoretical position within the US academy.[19] The short-lived communist growth of the 1930s had doubtless given rise to many writers, intellectuals and teachers who were on the Left, either sympathetic towards communism or communists themselves. But they had been activists rather than theorists—indeed, many of them had thought of theoretical work and political practice as radical opposites—and as they began to be purged from the universities during the McCarthy era, they left behind a relatively meagre theoretical legacy, beyond the Leftist version of the well-known Reflection Theory of Realism, as regards presuppositions which governed the teaching of literature. What happened *now* was that as the student generation of the 1960s started teaching in the university during the 1970s, at least a few of them became serious Marxist intellectuals, dispersed as they were in several disciplines, including Literature. Given the absence of any real socialist movement outside the university, this was usually a very academic kind of Marxism; and, given the absence of a preceding Marxist cultural tradition, this new Marxism was frequently and fashionably combined with all sorts of other things, in all kinds of eclectic and even esoteric ways. The fact remains, however, that even these inroads were more than the US academy had ever known—unlike the European academy, where Marxism had had a much older presence. Fourth, and finally, there was the issue of colonialism and imperialism, which was addressed now, in any sort of systematic fashion, for the first time in the history of US literary criticism.

This last issue—that of colony and empire, and its relationship with Marxist cultural theory—is obviously central to my argument, but I need to make one further observation about this background before coming to the issue at hand—namely, that this issue of the literary representation of colony and empire in Euro-American literary discourses was posed in the US academy, from the beginning, not from Marxist positions but in response to nationalist pressures, so that the subsequent theorizing of the subject, even when undertaken by Marxists, proceeded from the already-existing nationalist premisses and predispositions. This becomes quite clear as soon as one looks at the actual pressures which opened up the question in the first place.

It is symptomatic, for example, that this issue was first posed in the colleges and universities of the USA *not* in relation to the uses of literature in the building and representing of empires in Asia and Africa, but in relation to the *Black* experience *within* the United States. In so far as African-American intellectuals have no historical or cultural basis for thinking of Greece and Rome, the Cathedrals of St Peter and St Paul, Dante and Shakespeare, as *their* cultural past—at least, not in an exclusive way—significant segments among them, starting most markedly with Martin Delaney and DuBois, have often looked to Africa for their cultural origins. African literature now made its appearance in the American literary syllabi under increased Black nationalist pressure, not so much as an object of critical inquiry as evidence of achievement; the right to teach Senghor and Diop, Soyinka or Ngugi, was won against such odds and so very provisionally that one could not possibly interrogate this emergent counter-canon as one was only too glad to interrogate the existing canonicities.[20] Second, opposition to the Vietnam War brought up, strictly within the field of literary studies, the question of how colony and empire had been represented in Western literatures. There has since been a considerable rereading of at least parts of the estab-lished canon. Gradually, it has dawned upon some that no reading of English and French literatures was possible without taking into account the constitutive presence of the colonial experience in these literatures: Shakespeare and Jane Austen, Samuel Johnson and George Eliot, Shelley and Tennyson, André Gide and St John Perse were all implicated in it, and the vocabulary of colonial racism was there even in texts that were ostensibly not about colonialism at all—*Wuthering Heights,* for example. As African literature was inserted into the American syllabi under Black nationalist pressure, anti-colonial nationalism was the theoretical insignia for rereading the dominant cultural texts of the colonizing West. By the time the theoretical category of 'Colonial Discourse Analysis' arose, however, this perfectly necessary rereading of the Western archive was extended to produce the more or less dubious claim that the whole of it was an archive of bad faith and 'Orientalist' deformation. Third—and more important from the theoretical point of view—was the issue of the exclusive emphasis, in the Western academy, on the experience of Europe and North America—corners of the globe which are relatively small if you look at the whole world. This is the point where the issue of cultural production in the larger, non-Western part of the world—in Asia, Africa, Latin America—came to be posed. In the fullness of time, the literary documents of this other kind of cultural production would be called 'Third World Literature', within a discourse that would speak of a fundamental, generic difference between West and non-West, redefined now as a binary opposition between First and Third Worlds—and an opposition, moreover, which was said to be partly an effect of colonialism but partly a matter also of civilizational, primordial Difference. If the whole history of Western textualities, from Homer to Olivia Manning, was a history of Orientalist ontology, Third World Literature was *prima facie* the site of liberationist practice. The two theoretical categories, 'Colonial Discourse' (or 'Orientalism', in the Saidian sense) and 'Third World Literature', were thus conjoined, even if the actual practitioners of the one or the other were differentially located in the division of academic labours. Inevitably, then, cultural nationalism of one kind or another continues to be the constitutive ideology of the theoretical positions from which these issues are raised.

III

I have presented a very complex history in such telegraphic terms with three purposes in mind. First, I want to emphasize the sheer weight of reactionary positions in the Anglo-American literary formations. Second, I do want to stress the gains which have been made there since the 1960s, despite the havoc caused recently by the more mindless kinds of poststructuralism; for the first time in its history the metropolitan university is being forced, in some of its nooks and niches, to face issues of race and gender and empire in a way it has never done before. One simply has to compare the nature and breadth of today's debates on these issues with the absence of such debates in the 1950s, and even the 1930s, to grasp the degree of change. But, third, I also want to stress that the political vagrancy of much of the radical literary intelligentsia in the USA is such that it has been difficult—so far impossible, in fact—to constitute a properly Marxist political or literary culture, on any appreciable scale. The fundamental and constant danger faced by each radicalism—whether Black, or feminist, or Third-Worldist—is the danger of embourgeoisement. And the triple signs under which radical movements of this kind are at length assimilated into the main currents of bourgeois culture itself are the signs, these days, of Third-Worldist nationalism, essentialism, and the currently fashionable theories of the fragmentation and/or death of the Subject: the politics of discrete exclusivities and localisms on the one hand, or, on the other—as some of the poststructuralisms would have it—the very *end* of the social, the *impossibility* of stable subject positions, hence the *death* of politics as such. In more recent years, of course, we have also witnessed many attempts to reconcile Third-Worldist nationalism with poststructuralism itself.

These possibilities of internal erosion, which exist within the body of the radical discourse as it were, are then greatly augmented, from the outside, by the enormous pressures of the lingering Thatcherite-Reaganite consensus in the metropolitan culture at large. This consensus, especially aggressive now in the moment of imperialism's greatest triumph in its history, is unwilling to grant any considerable space to fundamental dissent of *any* kind, so that demands even for simple decency—that non-Western texts be integrated into the basic syllabi, that women have the right to abortion or equal pay or the writing of their own history, that normative pressures concede ground to individual sexual choice—are construed as mad attacks on Western civilization and 'family values', and as outright degenerations against which 'the American mind', as Alan Bloom tendentiously calls it, needs to defend itself. I cannot analyse the structure of that pressure here, but a particular consequence is that the individual practitioner of academic radicalism comes to occupy so beleaguered a space that any critical engagement with the limitations of one's own intellectual and political formation becomes difficult. The Right's attack tends, rather, to confirm the sense of one's own achievement. This power of the Right more or less to dictate the terms of engagement, not only in the academy but (even more so) in the culture at large, is surely not a *creation* of the university-based Left—it is, rather, evidence of the Right's power, and sets the objective limits for the Left itself. This pressure on the public space available for dialogues and projects of the Left also has the potential, however, of disorientating further theoretical development inside the restricted space that still does exist.

Those younger literary theorists in Britain and North America who had come out of the student movements of the late 1960s and early 1970s, and started their academic careers more or less after the cooling of America began with Nixon's second Presidential term and as Britain started skidding from the Wilsonian variants of Labourism to outright Thatcherite reaction, found their radicalism caught in a series of contradictions. The *international situation* which had framed much of their radicalism had been intensely revolutionary: the Vietnam War, the Chinese Cultural Revolution, the wars of liberation in the Portuguese colonies, the immensely powerful figures of Fidel and Che Guevara, the victory of *Unidad Popular* in Chile, the student uprisings from Mexico City to Paris to Lahore. Their *academic* training, meanwhile, had been an affair mainly of choosing between 'New Criticism' on the one hand, Frye and Bloom and Paul de Man on the other. Few enough had negotiated, by then, their way through Lukács; Gramsci was then almost entirely unknown in the English-speaking world, and much of the best of Raymond Williams was yet to come. The gap between what moved them politically and what they were doing academically was large enough, but then there was the 'movement' of which they had been, unevenly, a part. Those who were politically the most involved rarely found a coherent organizing centre for their activity once the intensity of the mobilization had peaked; those who found such a centre, for good or ill, disappeared into the anonymity of direct political work; few enough finished their PhDs, and those who did rarely gained the academic sophistication to become theorists. Those who became theorists had been, as a rule, only marginally involved in the *political* movement. Most of them had known the 'movement' mostly in its other kinds of social emphases: certainly the music, the alternative readings of Laing and Marcuse, surely the occasional demonstration—

but there had been, through it all, the pressure to write brilliant term papers and equally brilliant dissertations. It was, in other words, mostly the *survivors* of the 'movement' who later became so successful in the profession. Radicalism had been, for most of them, a state of mind, brought about by an intellectual identification with the revolutionary wave that had gripped so much of the world when they were truly young; of the day-to-day drudgeries of, say, a political party or a trade union they had been (and were to remain) largely innocent.

By the time they had secured their teaching positions, the international situation itself had changed. In the metropolises, the Civil Rights Movement had been contained through patronage for segments of the Black petty bourgeoisie, the political content of the anti-war movement frittered away after the retreat of US troops from Vietnam, and Paris itself was normalized soon after the uprising. The cycles of economic recession and stagnation which set in during the early 1970s had the effect, furthermore, of putting the movements for social justice on the defensive. In the imperialized world, meanwhile, Chile was decisively beaten, Cuba contained, China largely incorporated, and the wave of anti-capitalist revolutions was mainly over by the mid 1970s. The revolutionary states which arose at that time were encircled economically and derailed by invasions and insurgencies that were engineered through surrogates; none of them, from Angola to Vietnam, was allowed to become a model of development for postcolonial societies. The revolutionary upheavals which occurred thereafter—in Ethiopia or Afghanistan, for example—had problematic beginnings at best, originating in the radical sectors of the military. Their subsequent development was no better than that of other regimes based on the 'progressive' *coups d'état* elsewhere in Asia and Africa. In other words, for the revolutionary movements and states of the postcolonial world, this was a period of retreat and even outright disorientation.

In a parallel movement, moreover, this was also a period of increasing consolidation of the bourgeois nation-state in much of the rest of the post-colonial world. The international focus shifted accordingly, from revolutionary war ('Two, Three, Many . . . Vietnams') to such strategies for favourable terms of incorporation within the capitalist world as the Non-Aligned Movement, the North–South Dialogue, UNC-TAD, the New Economic Order, the Group 77 at the United Nations, or commodity cartels such as OPEC. If in 1968 the epoch had seemed to belong to the revolutionary vanguard, it seemed to belong now, as the 1980s dawned, to the national bourgeoisie. Radical thought in the universities paid its homage to this new consolidation of the post-colonial national bourgeoisies by shifting its focus, decisively, from socialist revolution to Third-Worldist nationalism—first in political theory, then in its literary reflections.

It was in this moment of retreat for socialism, and resurgence of the nationalism of the national bourgeoisie, that the *theoretical* category of 'Third World Literature' arose, as did the new emphasis on analyses of the 'Colonial Discourse', pushing the focus of thought not into the future but into the past. Since nationalism had been designated during this phase as the determinate source of ideological energy in the Third World by those same critics who had themselves been influenced mainly by poststructuralism, the disillusionment with the (national-bourgeois) state of the said Third World which began to set in towards the later 1980s then led those avant-garde theorists to declare that poststructuralism and deconstruction were the determinate theoretical positions for the critique of nationalism itself. Edward Said is thus quite astute in describing Ranajit Guha, and by extension the Subalternist project as a whole, as 'poststructuralist'.[21] This same tendency can be witnessed in a great many of the more recent literary theorists themselves, as exemplified by

Homi K. Bhabha among others. The positioning of poststructuralism as the alternative to nationalism is thus quite evident in his own definition of the project as he has assembled it in *Nation and Narration:*

> My intention was that we should develop, in a nice collaborative tension, a range of readings that engaged the insights of poststructuralist theories of narrative knowledge. . . . The marginal or 'minority' is not the space of a celebratory, or utopian, self-marginalization. It is a much more substantial intervention into those justifications of modernity—progress, homogeneity, cultural organicism, the deep nation, the long past—that rationalize the authoritarian, 'normalizing' tendencies within cultures in the name of national interest . . . (p. 4)

Bhabha, of course, lives in those material conditions of *post*modernity which presume the benefits of modernity as the very ground from which judgements on that past of this *post-* may be delivered. In other words, it takes a very modern, very affluent, very uprooted kind of intellectual to debunk both the idea of 'progress' and the sense of a 'long past', not to speak of 'modernity' itself, as mere 'rationalizations' of 'authoritarian tendencies within cultures'—in a theoretical *mélange* which randomly invokes Lévi-Strauss in one phrase, Foucault in another, Lacan in yet another. Those who live within the consequences of that 'long past', good and bad, and in places where a majority of the population has been denied access to such benefits of 'modernity' as hospitals or better health insurance or even basic literacy; can hardly afford the terms of such thought. The affinities of class and location then lead Bhabha, logically, to an exorbitant celebration of Salman Rushdie which culminates in pronouncements like the following, itself assembled in the manner of a postmodern pastiche:

America leads to Africa; the nations of Europe and Asia meet in Australia; the margins of the nation displace the centre; the peoples of the periphery return to write the history and fiction of the metropolis. The island story is told from the eye of the aeroplane which becomes that 'ornament that holds the public and the private in suspense'. The bastion of Englishness crumbles at the sight of immigrants and factory workers. The great Whitmanesque sensorium of America is exchanged for a Warhol blowup, a Kruger installation, or Mapplethorpe's naked bodies. 'Magical Realism', after the Latin American boom, becomes the literary language of the emergent post-colonial world. (p. 6)

It is doubtful, of course, that 'magical realism' has become 'the literary language of the emergent post-colonial world', any more than the 'national allegory' is the unitary generic form for all Third World narrativities, as Jameson would contend. Such pronouncements are now routine features of the metropolitan theory's inflationary rhetoric. Not all his collaborators write in accordance with his prescription, but Bhabha's own essay at the end of the volume makes a very considerable effort, albeit in very arcane ways, to pre-empt other kinds of critiques of nationalism by offering such familiar plays on 'poststructuralist theories'.

For these more recent developments in 'theory', especially for those sections of literary theory which surely set the terms for dealing with issues of empire, colony and nation, this general situation had peculiarly disorientating effects. In one kind of pressure, politics as such has undergone remarkable degrees of diminution. Any attempt to *know* the world as a whole, or to hold that it is open to rational comprehension, let alone the desire to change it, was to be dismissed as a contemptible attempt to construct 'grand narratives' and 'totalizing (totalitarian?) knowledges'. The theorist spoke often enough of imperialism and nationalism, sometimes as dialectical opposites but increasingly as twin faces of the same falsity, but the main business of radicalism came to reside in the rejection of rationalism itself (the Enlightenment project, as it came to be called).[22] Only Power was universal and immutable; resistance could only be local; knowledge, even of Power, always partial. Affiliations could only be shifting and multiple; to speak of a stable subject position was to chase the chimera of the 'myth of origins'. In some American dilutions of this theory of the dispersal and fracturing of historical subjects, the idea of 'inquiry', which presumes the possibility of finding some believable truth, was to be replaced with the idea of 'conversation' which is by its nature inconclusive. This idea of theory as 'conversation', may at times pass itself off as Bakhtinian dialogism, but in reality it moves inevitably in one of two possible directions.

The more common one is doubtless that of a peculiarly American kind of pluralism, with no small hint of politeness, accommodation and clubby gentlemanliness, albeit expressed in avant-gardist critical circles in the Barthesian language of 'pleasure of the text', 'free play of the Signifier', etc. The alternative direction, on the other hand, is a more sombre one, for if we accept the more extreme versions of the Foucauldian propositions (a) that whatever claims to be a *fact* is none other than a truth-*effect* produced by the ruse of discourse, and (b) that whatever claims to resist Power is already constituted as Power, then there really is nothing for Theory to *do* except to wander aimlessly through the effects—counting them, consuming them, producing them—and in the process submitting to the interminable whisperings of Discourse, both as Origin and as Fate. This theory-as-conversation also has a remarkably strong levelling effect. One is now free to cite Marxists and anti-Marxists, feminists and anti-feminists, deconstructionists, phenomenologists, or whatever other theorist comes to mind, to validate successive positions within an argument, so long as one has a long list of citations, bibliographies, etc., in the well-behaved academic manner. Theory itself becomes a marketplace of ideas, with massive supplies of theory as usable commodity, guaranteeing consumers' free choice and a rapid rate of obsolescence. If one were to refuse this model of the late-capitalist market economy, and dared instead to *conclude* a conversation or to advocate strict partisanship in the politics of theory, one would then be guilty of rationalism, empiricism, historicism, and all sorts of other ills—the idea of historical agents and/or knowing subjects, for example—perpetrated by the Enlightenment. One major aspect of this particular drift in the theory of the grand masters was summed up succinctly by Lyotard, no small master himself: the age of Marxism is over, 'the age of the enjoyment of goods and services' is here! The world was, in other words, bourgeois.

Much of the avant-garde literary theory of today comes out of such moorings, intellectual and political, with a distinctly consumptionist slant. Quite apart from the remarkable claim that politics resides mainly in radicalizing the practice of one's own academic profession, there has grown, because of equal allegiance to irreconcilable pressures, that same kind of eclecticism among the politically engaged theorists as among the more technicist, conservative ones; it is not uncommon to find, say, Gramsci and Matthew Arnold being cited in favour of the same theoretical position, as if the vastly different political allegiances of these two figures were quite immaterial for the main business of literary criticism. In some of these radicalized versions too, thus, that same market-economy model of theory obtains.

NOTES

1. This chapter substantially reproduces the notes I first made for a Seminar at the School of Languages, Jawaharlal Nehru University, and kept revising for subsequent uses

elsewhere in Delhi. In revising that material for present publication, I am now quite unable to find a voice that presumes no audience.

2. See Raymond Williams's fine essay 'Cambridge English, Past and Present', in his *Writing in Society,* for a judicious summation of the decisive contributions—but also the ultimate failures—of Richards, and of much besides, in Cambridge and beyond.

3. 'New Criticism', with its considerable borrowings from Richards, Eliot and Leavis, turned out to be far more sweepingly hegemonic in the United States than 'Practical Criticism' ever was in Britain, though the American Left (with the single exception of Kenneth Burke) never defined its own terms of contestation against it as the British Left—Williams, Terry Eagleton, Mulhern and others—were to define in relation to Leavis in particular and 'Practical Criticism' and the technicist variants of 'close reading' generally. The most substantial challenge to 'New Criticism' came, rather, from individuals like Krieger (*The New Apologists for Poetry,* 1956), Frye (*Anatomy of Criticism,* 1957), Kermode (*The Romantic Image,* also 1957) and Graff (*Poetic Statement and Critical Dogma,* 1970) or, as a sustained position, from deconstruction, which partly explains the American Left's own symbiosis with these positions, especially the deconstructionist one.

4. By far the most sustained critique of the Leavis tendency has been assembled by Francis Mulhern, though it must be said that his own magnificent essay 'English Reading' in Homi K. Bhabha, ed., *Nation and Narration* (London: Routledge, 1990) is qualitatively superior to his own previous book, *The Moment of 'Scrutiny'* (London: Verso, 1979), which had seemed definitive.

5. Mulhern is especially good in deconstructing the masculinist aspects of this populism, enacted in the personal life and public personae of F.R. and Q.D. Leavis in valorization of the ideologies of the athletic male and the good housewife. This particular variant of masculinism underlies, one need hardly add, Leavis's inordinate admiration of Lawrence and his reading, especially, of *Women in Love.*

6. See, for example, Williams's introductory remarks in *Marxism and Literature* about the isolation he faced at the time, in literary studies specifically.

7. *Monthly Review* also started publication—in New York, in 1949—in the period of the HUAC hearings and the onset of the Cold War. That journal, preoccupied more with political economy than with history, and engaged in defining a Marxism much sharper and broader than that of the official Communist Party, shared with its publishing house an influence that was by no means in-

significant in its own terms. Compared with the British developments of the same time, however, that influence remained confined to a much narrower intellectual stratum in the United States, making hardly a mark on the culture at large—and it was the *literary* Left that remained the least affected.

8. See, for example, Dobbs's *Political Economy and Capitalism* (1937) and Hill's *The English Revolution 1640* (1940).

9. There is, of course, his superb *Milton and the English Revolution* (1977) as well as the lesser-known *Some Intellectual Consequences of the English Revolution* (1980), not to speak of the equally superb *The Experience of Defeat: Milton and Some Contemporaries* (1984). The point, nevertheless, is that Hill's entire *œuvre* is really an engagement, using the tools of a magnificently careful historian, with that particular point of confluence at which culture *becomes* history.

10. See *William Morris: Romantic to Revolutionary* (originally published 1955, revised 1977). A comparative reading of the two texts provides fascinating and essential clues to Thompson's own intellectual trajectory over roughly a quarter-century, from communism to a certain kind of Left Labourism.

11. Richard Hoggart later emerged as a founder of the Centre for Contemporary Cultural Studies. Among his publications, *The Uses of Literacy* (1957) is, of course, something of a classic.

12. Eliot's monarchist and colonialist persuasions are well enough known, and these surface in *The Waste Land,* in the most disagreeable ways, alongside his contempt for the sexuality of poor and working women, which is constrasted in the structure of the poem with the calm splendours of—of all the people—'Queen Elizabeth and Leicester/Beating oars'. See, in particular, the third section of the poem, subtitled 'The Fire Sermon'. In Pound's case, shrill support for Mussolini is a mere tip of the iceberg; the entire structure of *The Cantos* is inseparable from his affiliations with fascism, anti-Semitism, racism of various sorts, and his general preference for authoritarian, aristocratic rule in all epochs and civilizations.

13. It is symptomatic of the whole drift of American Left Criticism that Frank Lentricchia's *After the New Criticism* (Chicago: University of Chicago Press, 1980), surely the central and in some ways a genuinely brilliant summation of the vast changes that have occurred in US literary criticism and theory in the two key decades between 1957 and 1977, makes scant effort to locate the disciplinary developments in any history other than the literary-theoretical. It is only by holding on to one's own memory and by fixing this memory on stray remarks here and there that one re-

calls, while reading the book, that these same twenty years were known in other kinds of narratives for quite other sorts of developments, such as the revolutions in Algeria, Cuba, Indochina and Southern Africa.

14. *After the New Criticism,* p. xii.

15. The sense in which I use the convenient term 'Western Marxism' here was given the widest currency and almost self-evident meaning by a number of writers associated with *New Left Review,* most notably Perry Anderson. For an anthology of some articles which contributed to the construction of the category, see *Western Marxism—A Critical Reader* (London: New Left Books; Verso 1983). For categorical definition and a certain kind of summation, see Anderson's own *Considerations on Western Marxism* (London: New Left Books, 1976; Verso 1979). There is, of course, an earlier history of this term, dating back to the 1920s, but we are not concerned with that here.

16. See *The Savage Mind* (French publication 1962; English translation 1966), especially the concluding chapter, in which Lévi-Strauss mounts a savage attack on historicism in general and on Sartre's construction of it in particular. Sartre had exchanged famous polemics in previous years as well, notably with Camus and Merleau-Ponty, but the attack by Lévi-Strauss proved decisive, in the sense that it inaugurated a shift in intellectual hegemony among the most influential stratum of Parisian intelligentsia as such, in favour of structuralism, with consequences for the English and American avant-gardes as well.

17. See, for this last point about 1968, Regis Debray's 'A Modest Contribution . . .', *New Left Review,* no. 115, May–June 1979. Elsewhere, in his delightful polemic on the vicissitudes of the French intelligentisa, *Teachers, Writers, Celebrities: Intellectuals in Modern France* (French publication 1979; English translation 1981), Debray establishes three periods in the history of this intelligentsia, from 1880 onwards: the first (1880–1930) dominated by schools and universities; the second (from 1930 to the 1960s) dominated by publishing; and the third (inaugurated by the Events of 1968 and still ascendant) dominated by the media. This last one might designate a dark age perpetrated by the silver screen.

18. I know that my polemic here lumps together diverse positions, but lack of space makes it impossible to develop the argument. Among the voluminous writings on the subject, I could confirm my own very considerable agreement with at least two. Perry Anderson's Wellek Library Lectures of 1982, *In the Tracks of Historical Materialism* (Chicago: University of Chicago Press, 1984) would be to

my mind, but for those pages on Habermas, an exemplary introduction. Peter Dews's *Logics of Disintegration* (London: Verso, 1988), deliberately narrower in focus, is written with less verve but is essentially sound and illuminating, especially on Lyotard.

19. 'New Left' means a great many different things in different contexts, but as a distinct political tendency within the plethora of diverse radicalisms which arose in this period, the term has to have, I believe, some claim to an affiliation with Marxism, however the affiliation or the Marxism may be conceived. In Britain, surely, the roots go back to at least the consequences of 1956 (Suez, Hungary, the Khrushchev Report). In the USA, the Cuban Revolution was perhaps more decisive, even though *Monthly Review* had started even earlier to define an alternative kind of Marxism, different from the Stalinist one. It is possible to argue, in any case, that while the *origins* of the 'New Left' may be traced back even to the 'Old Left' of the 1930s, it was in 1967–68 that it first made major interventions in most Western societies, especially the universities.

20. The category of 'Commonwealth Literature' came to play the same function of affirming beleaguered identities—and, in the fullness of time, opening up careers—for immigrant intelligentsias in Britain. It was on the prior basis of 'African Literature' and 'Commonwealth Literature' that the category of 'Third World Literature' first arose, often duplicating those very pedagogical procedures and ideological moorings.

21. See Edward Said's essay "Third World Intellectuals and Metropolitan Culture" in *Raritan* (Winter) 1990.

22. These familiar themes of recent French theory were then applied to matters of colony and empire, in both the literary and the sociological theories, in characteristically subordinate and dependent modes, by a number of the Indian members of this 'post-structuralist' avant-garde, from Homi Bhabha to Partha Chatterjee. For the latter's highly derivative debunkings of 'the Enlightenment', 'myths of progress', etc., see *Nationalist Thought and the Colonial World: A Derivative Discourse* (London: Zed Press, Delhi: Oxford University Press, 1986)

10

Edward W. Said
1935–

Edward Said is Parr Professor of English and comparative literature at Columbia University. An Arab-Palestinian intellectual and activist who has lived much of his adult life in "exile" in the United States, Said is one of the principal twentieth-century theorists and scholars of cultural theory and colonial and postcolonial discourse. Since the early 1970s, he has also been an influential interpreter in the English-speaking world of European poststructuralism, mediating especially between Michel Foucault's discourse, institution-centered cultural critique, and Jacques Derrida's philosophical deconstruction. In addition, he has contributed significantly to the criticism and interpretation of Anglo-American, Continental, colonial, and postcolonial novelistic fiction and nonfictional prose from the eighteenth century to the present. His diverse scholarly, critical, and political engagements have shaped much of the critique of Eurocentrism and of the Western literary and cultural canon that has affected academic studies in the humanities around the world during the last two decades. Among his most frequently cited books are *Beginnings* (1976); *Orientalism* (1978); *The World, the Text, and the Critic* (1983); and *Culture and Imperialism* (1993).

In "The Politics of Knowledge" (1991), Said argues again for a "*worldly* criticism" that can accomplish what Raymond Williams's cultural materialism and Foucault's analyses of discursive and cultural practices, disciplinary formations, and institutional histories were intended to accomplish. From Said's viewpoint, both literature and criticism (where the latter brings together engagements with history, politics, interpretation, and theory) are inescapably "worldly," material practices and constantly need to be understood as such. To analyze their worldliness or materiality adequately, the engaged intellectual and critic needs to focus on concrete historical particulars, as well as on such relatively abstract, global phenomena as culture, imperialism, domination, subjection, racism, native resistance, and nationalism. The critique of such phenomena, however, now runs into several problems arising from, for example, dogmatic contemporary demands for "political correctness," as well as complicitous, postcolonial, non-Western defenses of "the benefits of colonization." Said argues against both types of objections to his work by claiming that "we ought . . . to reconsider the ties between the text and the world in a serious and uncoercive way," and that "it does not finally matter *who* wrote what, but rather *how* a work is written and *how* it is read." In taking this position, Said generates a space for criticism in which "it is not necessary to regard every reading or interpretation of a text as the moral equivalent of a war or a political crisis," even as we remember "to underline the fact that whatever else they are, works of literature are not merely texts."

The Politics of Knowledge

Last fall I was invited to participate in a seminar at a historical studies center of a historically renowned American university. The subject of the seminar for this and the next academic year is imperialism, and the seminar discussions are chaired by the center's director. Outside participants are asked to send a paper before their arrival; it is then distributed to the members of the seminar, who are graduate students, fellows, and faculty. They will have read the paper in advance, precluding any reading of a lecture to them by the visitor, who is instead asked to summarize its main points for about ten minutes. Then for an hour and a half, there is an open discussion of the paper—a fairly rigorous but stimulating exercise. Since I have been working for some years on a sequel to *Orientalism*—it will be a long book that deals with the relationship between modern culture and imperialism—I sent a substantial extract from the introduction, in which I lay out the main lines of the book's argument. I there begin to describe the emergence of a global consciousness in Western knowledge at the end of the nineteenth century, particularly in such apparently unrelated fields as geography and comparative literature. I then go on to argue that the appearance of such cultural disciplines coincides with a fully global imperial perspective, although such a coincidence can only be made to seem significant from the point of view of later history, when nearly everywhere in the colonized world there emerged resistance to certain oppressive aspects of imperial rule like theories of subject races and peripheral regions, and the notions of backward, primitive or undeveloped cultures. *Because* of that native resistance—for instance, the appearance of many nationalist and independence movements in India, the Caribbean, Africa, the Middle East—it is now evident that culture and imperialism in the West could be understood as offering support, each to the other. Here I referred to the extraordinary work of a whole range of non-Western writers and activists, including Tagore, Fanon, C. L. R. James, Yeats, and many others, figures who have given integrity to anti-imperialist cultural resistance.

The first question after my brief resumé was from a professor of history, a black woman of some eminence who had recently come to the university, but whose work was unfamiliar to me. She announced in advance that her question was to be hostile, "a very hostile one in fact." She then said something like the following: for the first thirteen pages of your paper you talked only about white European males. Thereafter, on page fourteen, you mention some names of non-Europeans. "How could you do such a thing?" I remonstrated somewhat, and tried to explain my argument in greater detail—after all, I said, I was discussing European imperialism, which would not have been likely to include in its discourse the work of African-American women. I pointed out that in the book I say quite a bit about the response to imperialism all over the world; that point was a place in my argument where it would be pertinent to focus on the work of such writers as—and here I again mentioned the name of a great Caribbean writer and intellectual whose work has a special importance for my own—C. L. R. James. To this my critic replied with a stupefying confidence that my answer was not satisfactory since C. L. R. James was dead! I must admit that I was nonplussed by the severity of this pronouncement. James indeed *was* dead, a fact that needn't, to a historian, have made further discussion impossible. I waited for her to resume, hoping that she might expatiate on what she meant by having suggested that even in discussions of what dead white European males said on a given topic it was inappropriate to confine oneself to what they said while leaving out the work of living African-American, Arab, and Indian writers.

But she did not proceed, and I was left to suppose that she considered her point sufficiently and conclusively made: I was guilty of not mentioning living non-European non-males, even when it was not obvious to me or, I later gathered, to many members of the seminar, what their pertinence might have been. I noted to myself that my antagonist did not think it necessary to enumerate what specifically in the work of living non-Europeans I should have used, or which books and ideas by them she found important and relevant. All I had been given to work with was the asserted necessity to mention some approved names—which names did not really matter—as if the very act of uttering them was enough. I was also left unmistakably with the impression that as a nonwhite—a category incidentally to which as an Arab I myself belong—she was saying that to affirm the existence of non-European "others" took the place of evidence, argument, discussion.

It would be pointless to deny that the exchange was unsettling. Among other things I was chagrined at the distortions of my position and for having responded to the distortions so clumsily. It did not seem to matter that a great deal of my own work has concerned itself with just the kind of omission with which I was being charged. What apparently mattered now was that having contributed to an early trend, in which Western and European intellectuals were arraigned for having their work constructed out of the suffering and deprivations of so many people of color, I was now allegedly doing what such complicit intellectuals had always done. For if in one place you criticize the exclusion of Orientals, as I did in *Orientalism,* the exclusion of "others" from your work in another place becomes, on one level, difficult to justify or explain. I was disheartened not because I was being attacked, but because the general validity of the point made in *Orientalism* still obtained and yet was now being directed at me. It was *still* true that various Others—the word has acquired a sheen of modishness that has become extremely objectionable—were being represented

unfairly, their reality distorted, their truth either denied or twisted with malice. Yet instead of joining in their behalf, I felt I was being asked to get involved in an inconsequential academic contest. I had wanted to say, but didn't, "Is all that matters about the issue of exclusion and misrepresentation the fact that *names* were left out? Why are you detaining us with such trivialities?"

To make matters worse, a few minutes later in the discussion I was attacked by a retired professor of Middle Eastern studies, himself an Orientalist. Like me, he was an Arab, but he had consistently identified himself with intellectual tendencies of which I had always been critical. He now intervened to defend imperialism, saying in tones of almost comic reverence, that it had accomplished things that natives couldn't have done for themselves. It had taught them, among other things, he said, how to appreciate the cuneiform and hieroglyphics of their own traditions. As he droned on about the imperial schools, railroads, hospitals, and telegraphs in the Third World that stood for examples of British and French largesse, the irony of the whole thing seemed overpowering. It appeared to me that there had to be something to say that surrendered neither to the caricatural reductiveness of the two positions by then arrayed against me, and against each other, nor to that verbal quality in each that was determined to remain ideologically correct and little else.

I was being reminded by such negative flat-minded examples of thinking, that the one thing that intellectuals *cannot* do without is the full intellectual process itself. Into it goes historically informed research as well as the presentation of a coherent and carefully argued line that has taken account of alternatives. In addition, there must be, it seems to me, a theoretical presumption that in matters having to do with human history and society any rigid theoretical ideal, any simple additive or mechanical notion of what is or is not factual, must yield to the central factor of human work, the actual participation of peoples in the making of human life. If that is so then it must also be true that, given the very nature of human work in the construction of human society and history, it is impossible to say of it that its products are so rarified, so limited, so beyond comprehension as to exclude most other people, experiences, and histories. I mean further, that this kind of human work, which is intellectual work, is worldly, that it is situated in the world, and about that world. It is not about things that are so rigidly constricted and so forbiddingly arcane as to exclude all but an audience of like-minded, already fully convinced persons. While it would be stupid to deny the importance of constituencies and audiences in the construction of an intellectual argument, I think it has to be supposed that many arguments can be made to more than one audience and in different situations. Otherwise we would be dealing not with intellectual argument but either with dogma, or with a technological jargon designed specifically to repel all but a small handful of initiates or coteries.

Lest I fall into the danger myself of being too theoretical and specialized, I shall be more specific now and return to the episode I was discussing just a moment ago. At the heart of the imperial cultural enterprise I analyzed in *Orientalism* and also in my new book, was a politics of identity. That politics has needed to assume, indeed needed firmly to believe, that what was true about Orientals or Africans was *not* however true about or for Europeans. When a French or German scholar tried to identify the main characteristics of, for instance, the Chinese mind, the work was only partly intended to do that; it was also intended to show how different the Chinese mind was from the Western mind.

Such constructed things—they have only an elusive reality—as the Chinese mind or the Greek spirit have always been with us; they are at the source of a great deal that goes into the making of individual cultures, nations, traditions, and peoples. But in the modern world considerably greater attention has generally been given to such identities than was ever given in earlier historical periods, when the world was

larger, more amorphous, less globalized. Today a fantastic emphasis is placed upon a politics of national identity, and to a very great degree, this emphasis is the result of the imperial experience. For when the great modern Western imperial expansion took place all across the world, beginning in the late eighteenth century, it accentuated the interaction between the identity of the French or the English and that of the colonized native peoples. And this mostly antagonistic interaction gave rise to a separation between people as members of homogenous races and exclusive nations that was and still is one of the characteristics of what can be called the epistemology of imperialism. At its core is the supremely stubborn thesis that everyone is principally and irreducibly a member of some race or category, and that race or category cannot ever be assimilated to or accepted by others—except as itself. Thus came into being such invented essences as the Oriental or Englishness, as Frenchness, Africanness, or American exceptionalism, as if each of those had a Platonic idea behind it that guaranteed it as pure and unchanging from the beginning to the end of time.

One product of this doctrine is nationalism, a subject so immense that I can treat it only very partially here. What interests me in the politics of identity that informed imperialism in its global phase is that just as natives were considered to belong to a different category—racial or geographical—from that of the Western white man, it also became true that in the great anti-imperialist revolt represented by decolonization this same category was mobilized around, and formed the resisting identity of, the revolutionaries. This was the case everywhere in the Third World. Its most celebrated instance is the concept of *négritude,* as developed intellectually and poetically by Aimé Césaire, Leopold Senghor, and, in English, W. E. B. Du Bois. If blacks had once been stigmatized and given inferior status to whites, then it has since become necessary not to deny blackness, and not to aspire to whiteness, but to accept and celebrate blackness, to give it the dignity of poetic as well as metaphysical status. Thus *négritude* acquired positive Being where before it had been a mark of degradation and inferiority. Much the same revaluation of the native particularity occurred in India, in many parts of the Islamic world, China, Japan, Indonesia, and the Philippines, where the denied or repressed native essence emerged as the focus of, and even the basis for, nationalist recovery.

It is important to note that much of the early cultural resistance to imperialism on which nationalism and independence movements were built was salutary and necessary. I see it essentially as an attempt on the part of oppressed people who had suffered the bondage of slavery, colonialism, and—most important—spiritual dispossession, to reclaim their identity. When that finally occurred in places such as Algeria, the grander nationalist efforts amounted to little short of a reconstructed communal political and cultural program of independence. Where the white man had once only seen lazy natives and exotic customs, the insurrection against imperialism produced, as in Ireland for example, a national revolt, along with political parties dedicated to independence, which, like the Congress party in India, was headed by nationalist figures, poets, and military heroes. There were remarkably impressive results from this vast effort at cultural reclamation, most of which are well known and celebrated.

But while the whole movement toward autonomy and independence produced in effect newly independent and separate states constituting the majority of new nations in the postcolonial world today, the nationalist politics of identity has nonetheless quickly proved itself to be insufficient for the ensuing period.

Inattentive or careless readers of Frantz Fanon, generally considered one of the two or three most eloquent apostles of anti-imperialist resistance, tend to forget his marked suspicions of unchecked nationalism. So while it is appropriate to draw attention to the early chapters on violence in *The Wretched of the Earth,* it should be noticed that in subsequent chapters he is sharply critical of what he called the pitfalls of national consciousness. He clearly meant this to be a paradox. And for the reason that while nationalism is a necessary spur to revolt against the colonizer, national consciousness must be immediately transformed into what he calls "social consciousness," just as soon as the withdrawal of the colonizer has been accomplished.

Fanon is scathing on the abuses of the post-independence nationalist party, on, for instance, the cult of the Grand Panjandrum (or maximum leader), or the centralization of the capital city, which Fanon said flatly needed to be deconsecrated, and most importantly, on the hijacking of common sense and popular participation by bureaucrats, technical experts, and jargon-wielding obfuscators. Well before V. S. Naipaul, Fanon was arguing against the politics of mimicry and separatism which produced the Mobutus, Idi Amins, and Saddams, as well as the grotesqueries and pathologies of power that gave rise to tyrannical states and praetorian guards while obstructing democratic freedoms in so many countries of the Third World. Fanon also prophesied the continuing dependency of numerous postcolonial governments and philosophies, all of which preached the sovereignty of the newly independent people of one or another new Third World state, and, having failed to make the transition from nationalism to true liberation, were in fact condemned to practice the politics, and the economics, of a new oppression as pernicious as the old one.

At bottom, what Fanon offers most compellingly is a critique of the separatism and mock autonomy achieved by a pure politics of identity that has lasted too long and been made to serve in situations where it has become simply inadequate. What invariably happens at the level of knowledge is that signs and symbols of freedom and status are taken for the reality: you want to be named and considered for the sake of being named and considered. In effect this really means that just to be an independent postcolonial Arab, or black, or Indonesian is not a program, nor a process, nor a vision. It is no more than a convenient starting point from which the real work, the hard work, might begin.

As for that work, it is nothing less than the reintegration of all those people and cultures, once confined and reduced to peripheral status, with the rest of the human race. After working through *négritude* in the early sections of *Cahier d'un retour,* Aimé Césaire states this vision of integration in his poem's climatic moment: "no race possesses the monopoly of beauty, of intelligence, of force, and there is a place for all at the rendez-vous of victory."

Without this concept of "place for all at the rendez-vous of victory," one is condemned to an impoverishing politics of knowledge based only upon the assertion and reassertion of identity, an ultimately uninteresting alternation of presence and absence. If you are weak, your affirmation of identity for its own sake amounts to little more than saying that you want a kind of attention easily and superficially granted, like the attention given an individual in a crowded room at a roll call. Once having such recognition, the subject has only to sit there silently as the proceedings unfold as if in his or her absence. And, on the other hand, though the powerful get acknowledged by the sheer force of presence, this commits them to a logic of displacement, as soon as someone else emerges who is as, or more, powerful.

This has proved a disastrous process, whether for postcolonials, forced to exist in a marginal and dependent place totally outside the circuits of world power, or for powerful societies, whose triumphalism and imperious wilfullness have done so much to devastate and destabilize the world. What has been at issue between Iraq and the United States is precisely such a logic of exterminism and displacement, as unedifying as it is unproductive. It is risky, I know, to move from the realm of interpretation to the realm of world politics, but it seems to me true that the relationship between them is a real one, and the light that one realm can shed on the other is quite illuminating. In any case the politics of knowledge that is based principally on the affirmation of identity is very similar, is indeed directly related to, the unreconstructed nationalism that has guided so many postcolonial states today. It asserts a sort of separatism that wishes only to draw attention to itself; consequently it neglects the integration of that earned and achieved consciousness of self within "the rendez-vous of victory." On the national and on the intellectual level the problems are very similar.

Let me return therefore to one of the intellectual debates that has been central to the humanities in the past decade, and which underlies the episode with which I began. The ferment in minority, subaltern, feminist, and postcolonial consciousness has resulted in so many salutary achievements in the curricular and theoretical approach to the study of the humanities as quite literally to have produced a Copernican revolution in all traditional fields of inquiry. Eurocentrism has been challenged definitively; most scholars and students in the contemporary American academy are now aware, as they were never aware before, that society and culture have been the heterogeneous product of heterogeneous people in an enormous variety of cultures, traditions, and situations. No longer does T. S. Eliot's idea of the great Western masterpieces enduring together in a constantly redefining pattern of monuments have its old authority; nor do the sorts of patterns elucidated with such memorable brilliance in formative works like *Mimesis* or *The Anatomy of Criticism* have the same cogency for today's student or theorist as they did even quite recently.

And yet the great contest about the canon continues. The success of Allan Bloom's *The Closing of the American Mind,* the subsequent publication of such works as Alvin Kernan's *The Death of Literature,* and Roger Kimball's *Tenured Radicals* as well as the rather posthumous energies displayed in journals like *The American*

Scholar (now a neo-conservative magazine), *The New Criterion,* and *Commentary*—all this suggests that the work done by those of us who have tried to widen the area of awareness in the study of culture is scarcely finished or secure. But our point, in my opinion, cannot be simply and obdurately to reaffirm the paramount importance of formerly suppressed or silenced forms of knowledge and leave it at that, nor can it be to surround ourselves with the sanctimonious piety of historical or cultural victimhood as a way of making our intellectual presence felt. Such strategies are woefully insufficient. The whole effort to deconsecrate Eurocentrism cannot be interpreted, least of all by those who participate in the enterprise, as an effort to supplant Eurocentrism with, for instance, Afrocentric or Islamocentric approaches. On its own, ethnic particularity does not provide for intellectual process—quite the contrary. At first, you will recall, it was a question, for some, of adding Jane Austen to the canon of male Western writers in humanities courses; then it became a matter of displacing the entire canon of American writers like Hawthorne and Emerson with best-selling writers of the same period like Harriet Beecher Stowe and Susan Warner. But after that the logic of displacement became even more attenuated, and the mere names of politically validated living writers became more important than anything about them or their works.

I submit that these clamorous dismissals and swooping assertions are in fact caricatural reductions of what the great revisionary gestures of feminism, subaltern or black studies, and anti-imperialist resistance originally intended. For such gestures it was never a matter of replacing one set of authorities and dogmas with another, nor of substituting one center for another. It was always a matter of opening and participating in a central strand of intellectual and cultural effort and of showing what had always been, though indiscernibly, a part of it, like the work of women, or of blacks and servants—but which had been either denied or derogated. The power

and interest of—to give two examples particularly dear to me—Tayib Salih's *Season of Migration to the North* is not only how it memorably describes the quandary of a gifted young Sudanese who has lived in London but then returns home to his ancestral village alongside the Nile; the novel is also a rewriting of Conrad's *Heart of Darkness,* seen now as the tale of someone who voyages into the heart of light, which is modern Europe, and discovers there what had been hidden deep within him. To read the Sudanese writer is of course to interpret an Arabic novel written during the late sixties at a time of nationalism and a rejection of the West. The novel is therefore affiliated with other Arabic novels of the postwar period including the works of Mahfouz and Idriss; but given the historical and political meaning of a narrative that quite deliberately recalls and reverses Conrad—something impossible for a black man at the time *Heart of Darkness* was written—Tayib Salih's masterpiece is necessarily to be viewed as, along with other African, Indian, and Caribbean works, enlarging, widening, refining the scope of a narrative form at the center of which had heretofore always been an exclusively European observer or center of consciousness.

There is an equally complex resonance to Ghassan Kanafani's *Men in the Sun,* a compelling novella about the travails of three Palestinian refugees who are trying to get from Basra in Iraq to Kuwait. Their past in Palestine is evoked in order to contrast it with the poverty and dispossession of which they are victims immediately after 1948. When they find a man in Basra whose occupation is in part to smuggle refugees across the border in the belly of his empty watertruck, they strike a deal with him, and he takes them as far as the border post where he is detained in conversation in the hot sun. They die of asphyxiation, unheard and forgotten. Kanafani's novella belongs to the genre of immigrant literature contributed to by an estimable number of postwar writers—Rushdie, Naipaul, Berger, Kundera, and others. But it is also a poignant meditation on the Palestinian fate, and of course eerily prescient about Palestinians in the current Gulf crisis. And yet it would do the subject of the work and its literary merit an extraordinary disservice were we to confine it to the category of national allegory, to see in it only a mirroring of the actual plight of Palestinians in exile. Kanafani's work is literature connected both to its specific historical and cultural situations as well as to a whole world of other literatures and formal articulations, which the attentive reader summons to mind as the interpretation proceeds.

The point I am trying to make can be summed up in the useful notion of worldliness. By linking works to each other we bring them out of the neglect and secondariness to which for all kinds of political and ideological reasons they had previously been condemned. What I am talking about therefore is the opposite of separatism, and also the reverse of exclusivism. It is only through the scrutiny of these works *as* literature, as style, as pleasure and illumination, that they can be brought in, so to speak, and kept in. Otherwise they will be regarded only as informative ethnographic specimens, suitable for the limited attention of experts and area specialists. *Worldliness* is therefore the restoration to such works and interpretations of their place in the global setting, a restoration that can only be accomplished by an appreciation not of some tiny, defensively constituted corner of the world, but of the large, many-windowed house of human culture as a whole.

It seems to me absolutely essential that we engage with cultural works in this unprovincial, interested manner while maintaining a strong sense of the contest for forms and values which any decent cultural work embodies, realizes, and contains. A great deal of recent theoretical speculation has proposed that works of literature are completely determined as such by their situation, and that readers themselves are totally determined in their responses by their respective cultural situations, to a point where no value, no

reading, no interpretation can be anything other than the merest reflection of some immediate interest. All readings and all writing are reduced to an assumed historical emanation. Here the indeterminacy of deconstructive reading, the airy insouciance of postaxiological criticism, the casual reductiveness of some (but by no means all) ideological schools are principally at fault. While it is true to say that because a text is the product of an unrecapturable past, and that contemporary criticism can to some extent afford a neutral disengagement or opposed perspective impossible for the text in its own time, there is no reason to take the further step and exempt the interpreter from *any* moral, political, cultural, or psychological commitments. All of these remain at play. The attempt to read a text in its fullest and most integrative context commits the reader to positions that are educative, humane, and engaged, positions that depend on training and taste and not simply on a technologized professionalism, or on the tiresome playfulness of "postmodern" criticism, with its repeated disclaimers of anything but local games and pastiches. Despite Lyotard and his acolytes, we are still in the era of large narratives, of horrendous cultural clashes, and of appallingly destructive war—as witness the recent conflagration in the Gulf—and to say that we are against theory, or beyond literature, is to be blind and trivial.

I am not arguing that every interpretive act is equivalent to a gesture either for or against life. How could anyone defend or attack so crudely general a position? I am saying that once we grant intellectual work the right to exist in a relatively disengaged atmosphere, and allow it a status that isn't disqualified by partisanship, we ought then to reconsider the ties between the text and the world in a serious and uncoercive way. Far from repudiating the great advances made when Eurocentrism and patriarchy began to be demystified, we should consolidate these advances, using them so as to reach a better understanding of the degree to which literature and artistic genius belong to and are some part of the world where all of us also do other kinds of work.

This wider application of the ideas I've been discussing cannot even be attempted if we simply repeat a few names or refer to a handful of approved texts ritualistically or sanctimoniously. Victimhood, alas, does not guarantee or necessarily enable an enhanced sense of humanity. To testify to a history of oppression is necessary, but it is not sufficient unless that history is redirected into intellectual process and universalized to include all sufferers. Yet too often testimony to oppression becomes only a justification for further cruelty and inhumanity, or for high sounding cant and merely "correct" attitudes. I have in mind, for instance, not only the antagonists mentioned at the beginning of this essay but also the extraordinary behavior of an Elie Wiesel who has refused to translate the lessons of his own past into consistent criticisms of Israel for doing what it has done and is doing right now to Palestinians.

So while it is not necessary to regard every reading or interpretation of a text as the moral equivalent of a war or a political crisis, it does seem to me to be important to underline the fact that whatever else they are, works of literature are not merely texts. They are in fact differently constituted and have different values, they aim to do different things, exist in different genres, and so on. One of the great pleasures for those who read and study literature is the discovery of longstanding norms in which all cultures known to me concur: such things as style and performance, the existence of good as well as lesser writers, and the exercise of preference. What has been most unacceptable during the many harangues on both sides of the so-called Western canon debate is that so many of the combatants have ears of tin, and are unable to distinguish between good writing and politically correct attitudes, as if a fifth-rate pamphlet and a great novel have more or less the same significance. Who benefits from leveling attacks on the canon? Certainly not the disadvantaged person or class whose history, if you bother to read it at all, is full of evidence that popular resistance to injustice has always derived immense benefits from literature and culture in general, and very few from invidious distinctions made between ruling-class and subservient cultures. After all, the crucial lesson of C. L. R. James's *Black Jacobins,* or of E. P. Thompson's *Making of the English Working Class* (with its reminder of how important Shakespeare was to nineteenth-century radical culture), is that great antiauthoritarian uprisings made their earliest advances, not by denying the humanitarian and universalist claims of the general dominant culture, but by attacking the adherents of that culture for failing to uphold their own declared standards, for failing to extend them to all, as opposed to a small fraction, of humanity. Toussaint L'Ouverture is the perfect example of a downtrodden slave whose struggle to free himself and his people was informed by the ideas of Rousseau and Mirabeau.

Although I risk over-simplification, it is probably correct to say that it does not finally matter *who* wrote what, but rather *how* a work is written and *how* it is read. The idea that because Plato and Aristotle are male and the products of a slave society they should be disqualified from receiving contemporary attention is as limited an idea as suggesting that *only* their work, because it was addressed to and about elites, should be read today. Marginality and homelessness are not, in my opinion, to be gloried in; they are to be brought to an end, so that more, and not fewer, people can enjoy the benefits of what has for centuries been denied the victims of race, class, or gender.

PART III

Rhetoric and Reader Response

"As individual speech acts are to the language in which they are spoken, so are many other individual actions to the codes of the cultures in which they occur." Although speaking as a semiotician, Robert Scholes in these opening words from *Textual Power* underlines the contemporary sense of language as a field of action. He also catches the sense of action as an arrangement and effect within the rhetoric of texts and lived lives. This broad view of rhetoric as applicable to a multiplicity of sites in life and letters, as "equipment for living" in Kenneth Burke's conception, or as the "interface between information technology and culture" that Stuart Moulthrop describes in his essay in this section, is indeed a contemporary but also an ancient idea about rhetoric's utility. Tracing the history of rhetoric as equipment for living and as a determining factor for "culture" more generally entails the recognition of rhetoric as the oldest form of textual criticism in Western culture—the oldest rigorous study of verbal texts. In the ancient world and throughout the Middle Ages, rhetoric, the method of teaching the practical uses and effects of language—rhetoric, that is, as the "technologies" of language—was the avenue to reading, speaking, and writing in areas such as politics, law, and even theology. Rhetoric then and now studies the *effects* of language at its various sites of significance in verbal communication as well as in texts of social practice. This includes the effects of certain tropes, strategies, and technologies, how to be persuasive, how to elicit emotional affect, how to achieve clarity, and attempts to understand how language functions to reach these ends and to have an effect on the world.

Rhetoric, in other words, emphasizes the essential function but also the *social* aspect of language and literature, its intersubjective affects, and its impact in particular situations as potential equipment for living. As such, the aims of rhetoric are as far as possible from the formalist approaches to language and literature as we describe them in relation to New Criticism and Russian Formalism (in the introductions to "What Is Literary Studies?" [Part I] and "Structuralism and Semiotics" [Part IV]). Yet, in another sense, rhetoric participates in all of the schools of contemporary criticism examined in this book because all criticism at some point must address the effects of language, however those effects are achieved or defined.

There have always been two distinct conceptions of the nature of rhetoric that correspond to the functions of criticism and critique that we discuss in the General Introduction. In one conception, rhetoric examines how language persuades and uses so-called ornaments to achieve certain ends in the world—to say, in short, what could have been said differently but, instead, was modulated to create a certain effect. Barbara Johnson offers an extreme (and negative) version of this definition at the beginning of "Apostrophe, Animation, and Abortion" when she describes the "deviousness" of language in which "rhetoric is defined as language that says one thing and means another." A special and instructive case of such an "instrumental" conception of language can be found in the way that the philosopher John Searle defines "speech acts." For Searle, speech acts are uses of language that clearly accomplish immediate ends, where language directly is an action in the world, as in saying "I do" in a courtroom or wedding ceremony. This is rhetoric in the utterly pragmatic sense of criticism, as an accounting for the function of and "explaining" certain effects. The debate between Searle and Jacques Derrida over the meaning of speech acts (that Jonathan Culler describes in his article in "Deconstruction and Poststructuralism" [Part V]) hinges on Searle's pragmatic and commonsensical definition of speech acts.

In a second conception of rhetoric, both Stanley Fish and Patrocinio Schweickart contest Searle's commonsense assumptions concerning the nature of linguistic "facts" and the seeming "unsituated" nature of the subject of rhetoric in terms of gender, class, and race. In their work, rhetoric examines how language conditions experience and how it allows members of a (social or linguistic) community to see and apprehend experience in a particular way. Fish makes this argument about "experience" in this section when he argues that "formal units are always a function of the interpretative model one brings to bear," and Schweickart makes this argument about how the "experience" of being a woman in our particular culture is conditioned by "immasculating" strategies of reading. (In "Structuralism and Semiotics" [Part IV] Teresa de Lauretis examines the category of "experience" within the contexts of semiotics and feminism.) In his essay "Semiology and Rhetoric" (in *Allegories of Reading*), Paul de Man emphasizes this understanding of rhetoric as "the study of tropes and of figures (. . . not in the derived sense of comment or of eloquence or persuasion)." This would potentially be rhetoric, as Susan Miller writes in *Textual Carnivals: The Politics of Composition,* conceived as a "radical theory of language as constitutive of a greater reality" than the formal sphere of rhetoric can show. To see language in its social context and as having a social effect is to see language "as a form of power." "Understanding discourse," in this sense of rhetoric, Miller continues, "means understanding its relation to power."

Terry Eagleton develops the global, dual conception of rhetoric in its examination of the "concrete performance" and "people's responses to discourse in terms of linguistic structures and the material situations in which they functioned." He argues,

> Rhetoric, or discourse theory, shares with Formalism, structuralism and semiotics an interest in the formal devices of language, but like reception theory it is also concerned with how these devices are actually effective at the point of "consumption"; its preoccupation with discourse as a form of power and desire can learn much from deconstruction and psychoanalytical theory, and its belief that discourse can be a humanly transformative affair shares a good deal with liberal humanism.

In this description, Eagleton is situating rhetoric as the place where formalism ("the formal devices of language") and history ("the point of 'consumption'") intersect. That is, if rhetoric focuses on the "ornamental" nature of language, it also studies the discontinuous and nonformal spheres in which language operates, the possibilities of figures and tropes that govern rather than ornament meaning—in effect, that govern power in the verbal and nonverbal dimensions of a social context. Johnson clearly focuses on this intersection in her examination of the rhetorics of poetry and law in relation to abortion, and Stuart Moulthrop does so implicitly in his examination of the relationship between technologies of language and discourse and social formations. It follows that all schools of criticism and theory can be understood in their formal interworkings and patterning *and* in terms of the force of their social impact—their worldly effect. It is in this dual sense that rhetoric can be said to run interference for and encompass all contemporary literary criticism.

RHETORIC AND THE TECHNOLOGIES OF DISCOURSE

The two definitions of rhetoric create a useful distinction beyond the narrow conception of rhetoric as the study of the interpersonal and immediate effects of language. In the current section, we see this division in the study of the rhetoric of particular texts and of larger social or cultural formations. This dimension is perhaps most clear in Johnson's essay, which examines the relationship between politics and rhetoric. But the self-conscious study of rhetoric tends toward what Susan Miller helpfully designates as a "cognitive sociology of the text." This position on the "sociological view of rhetoric" shares much with the Marxist approach of Mikhail Bakhtin (see especially his early essay, published under the name V. N. Vološinov, "Discourse in Life and Discourse in Art (Concerning Sociological Poetics)" in "Historical Criticism" [Part VII]). In this "sociological" view, both literature and its rhetorical effects are essentially "functional," not aiming at articulating global or transcendental truths, or human nature or a vision of "reality" or anything else "for its own sake." Literature and rhetorical effects, rather, are a form of social activity and a gesture that accomplishes an end, maybe not always the end that was intended but an end with social consequences nonetheless. In this "functional" understanding, the technologies of discourse are of the utmost importance.

In his early and valuable contributions to contemporary rhetorical studies, the critic and rhetorician Walter Ong pursued a similar rhetorical conception of literature that looks forward to developments in rhetorical studies applied to discursive technologies represented here in Moulthrop's essay. Ong is best known for his work on the relationship between oral and written discourses, an area with strong relevance to the rhetorical analyses of literature. Influenced most strongly by Peter Ramus, Eric Havelock, and Marshall McLuhan—though more conservative than the "sociological" approaches of Kenneth Burke and Bakhtin—he attempts to describe literary history in terms of the different "roles" that the technology of *written* literature creates for its readers throughout literary history. He focuses on the sense in which oral literature always has a *present* audience and examines how the responses of a (usually) absent audience to a written text are fully determined by that written text. This mode of argument is parallel to that of Jay David Bolter, cited by Moulthrop, who makes the global claim that the "emerging writing systems [implicit in computer technologies are] dynamic, spatial, and antihierarchical." The approaches of both Ong and Bolter, as Schweickart says, are fully "text dominant." The "fiction" of the audience's role is determined by textual rhetoric in that the language of the text constructs particular roles for the reader, and Ong studies both those roles and the language creating them in work that also looks forward to Fish's rhetoric of style and postulation of "interpretive communities."

Similarly, Moulthrop surveys theorists of hypertext who share "the conviction that the transition from a mode of production to a 'mode of information' has effects exceeding the traditional boundaries of economics and politics." Both the early work of Ong and contemporary studies of hypertextuality attempt to mark the place where contemporary literary criticism and practical and theoretical discussions of composition and discourse production intersect in the examination of rhetorical practices. In Ong's work, the technologies of print in relation to oral cultures and the dynamics of power between them in both the ancient and modern worlds provide a context for understanding the relays of power and the intricacies of ideology as one cultural sphere acts on another. Moulthrop's argument both articulates and criticizes such claims about the global social effects of technologically determined rhetorics in the context of technologies of computer hypertext in relation to print culture. In this argument, Moulthrop's study of "postmodern" understandings of the rhetorical and social implications of discourse technologies ending this section takes its place in the oldest contexts of literary and cultural studies.

THE RHETORIC OF READER RESPONSE

The school of criticism called "Reader Response" is closely related to the kind of rhetorical criticism that examines the actual production of texts. The rhetoric of Aristotle, Ong, and even Moulthrop examines the relationships of tropes and verbal devices in writing and speech and larger technologies of discourse beyond local verbal devices. By contrast, it is also possible to account for the effects of rhetoric by focusing on the reader's response, as can be seen in the relationship between interpretation and the protocols of reading. It has even been argued that the common denominator of literary studies after the New Criticism—that is, the structuralist, poststructuralist, psychoanalytic, feminist, and New Historicist criticisms of our book—is the way they focus on the reception rather than the production of texts. A. J. Greimas has defined structuralism as based upon "a linguistics of perception and not of expression." And Roland Barthes, in a gesture of "poststructuralism," argues that a text's unity resides "not in its origin but in its destination."

Criticism that focuses on readers has always been a dimension of classical rhetoric, at least since Aristotle. In the *Poetics,* Aristotle speaks of the cathartic, purging effect of tragedy and, in this way, defines a major component of tragedy as a genre in terms of a reader's reaction to rhetorical effects. Coleridge, too, emphasizes the importance of a reader's response in his conception—a major part of romantic poetics—of esemplastic power. By "esemplastic power" he means the reader's sympathetic response to natural forms in nature and in literature, and in important ways romantic sensibility is defined by this human ability to interact with the rhetorical effects of nature. In the 1920s, the modern British critic I. A. Richards proposed to catalog readers' strategies for understanding and interpreting poetry. In a manner quite distinct from the New Critics he influenced so heavily, he discussed the practical steps readers actually go through and the assumptions they make as they read. Kenneth Burke, too, in work only recently finding full appreciation, attempted to chart what readers actually do, the strategies by which they adopt "terministic screens" and "dramatistic" poses in reading literature. In sum, these critics, among others, have found the reading activity itself to be a primary channel for understanding textual experience.

Modern Reader-Response theory, from the late 1960s through the present, concentrates intensely on what readers do and how they do it. This movement draws significant inspiration from psychoanalysis, but a major formulation of Reader-Response theory, found in the work of Wolfgang Iser and Hans Robert Jauss, is phenomenology. As defined by Edmund Husserl and Martin Heidegger, phenomenology is a philosophical view that posits a continuous field of experience between the perceiver (subject) and the object of experience and focuses on bringing to light the relations of subject and object. A phenomenologist believes that objects-in-the-world cannot be the valid focus of a rigorous philosophical investigation. Rather, the contents of consciousness itself—"objects" as constituted by the mechanism of consciousness—should be investigated. As elaborated by Maurice Merleau-Ponty, Ludwig Binswanger, Hans-Georg Gadamer, and Gaston Bachelard, this view defines literary experience as a gestalt, holistically, with a minimal sense of separation between text and its interpretation. Phenomenology posits the inseparability of text and its reception. Fish contrasts the phenomenology of "experience" in reading to apparently preexisting "facts" and argues "that the form of the reader's experience, formal units, and the structure of intention are one, that they come into view simultaneously, and that therefore the questions of priority and independence do not arise."

Georges Poulet's "Phenomenology of Reading," to which Schweickart alludes in her essay included here, is a primary, early document of Reader-Response theory. Poulet sees the dynamics of the reading process as centered on the reader. This focus, because it reveals new and unfamiliar material—always confronting something strange within a familiar context—produces an experience of the unfamiliar, "otherness." The reader begins a text presumably "thinking one's own thought," as Poulet says. This means that readers initially are comfortable with a misrecognition—their early false sense of a familiar encounter as they read an unknown text. Eventually, however, the text offers up unfamiliar encounters and reveals itself as alien to the reader's experience prior to this text and, in its own way, quite odd. These "alien" thoughts then coalesce into a kind of alternative consciousness as a counterperspective separate from and *not* the reader's own. The result of this process is that eventually, he says, "my consciousness [as a reader] behaves as though it were the consciousness of another." This other consciousness, as Poulet reasons, must be held as a thought by someone, by a subject. He then posits that "this *thought* which is alien to me and yet in me, must also have [created] in me a *subject* which is alien to me."

This process of discovering "otherness" in reading culminates in a direct confrontation with a kind of transcendental subjectivity, a "being" or other outside one's own experience. That is, "when reading a literary work," as Poulet goes on, "there is a moment when it seems to me that the subject *present* in this work disengages itself from all that surrounds it, and stands alone." This confrontation with independent "being" is such that "no object can any longer express it, no structure can any longer define it; it is exposed in its ineffability and in its fundamental indeterminacy." The act of reading, in this way, begins with the gradual discovery of "otherness" but eventually opens upon an experience wherein the difference, or gap, separating subjects from objects, and reader from text, is transcended altogether. In reading, subject and object ultimately are shown to be merged—in fact, were never "really" separate—in a continuous field of experience.

On this basis, phenomenological literary criticism explores not just the dynamics of individual texts but the boundaries and operations of each author's "world," a particular staging of the process that opens upon the disengaged subject. The philosopher Ludwig Binswanger, along this line, has explored Henrik Ibsen's dramatic "world," and J. Hillis Miller—in the phenomenological phase of his work—investigated the fictional "world" of Charles Dickens just as he explored the "experience" (the "world") of modernity in *Poets of Reality* (1965) and *The Disappearance of God* (1963). In each case, the emphasis is on a "descriptive" approach that gradually, and painstakingly, isolates the text's presentation of subject/object relations. Out of these connections, usually made for several works or for a writer's whole corpus, emerges the "consciousness" that constitutes the authorial world. The descriptive technique of this phenomenological criticism appears to link it with formalism, but the aim here, by contrast, is precisely to capture "experience," not form, and to disregard and overrun formal limits—particularly a work's chronological development, the functions of language, and the like—in characterizing the essential aspects of any text.

Much contemporary reader-oriented criticism is carried out against the background of this earlier work—as well as the background of the two conceptions of rhetoric we have examined—but tends, as Steven Mailloux notes, to divide into three separate strains: phenomenology, subjectivism, and structuralism. The line of phenomenology moves through Poulet, Hans-Georg Gadamer, Hans Robert Jauss, and Wolfgang Iser. Particularly important theoretically is Gadamer's *Truth and Method* (trans. 1975), which attempts to rethink the confluence of phenomenology and literary criticism by returning to Heidegger's discussion of consciousness as always *situated* culturally, as what Heidegger called *Dasein*—"being there," or "being-in-the-world." *Dasein* as a concept stresses the mediational role of consciousness situated between a sense of an objective world "out there" and one's most intimate thoughts and responses. Gadamer's work brought about a minor revival of interest in phenomenological reading, not least because of his influence on Hans Robert Jauss, also a phenomenologist, who examines a work's reception (what Jauss calls "reception esthetic") within a cultural milieu and attempts to establish a "horizon of expectation," or a "paradigm" accounting for a particular culture's responses to literature at a certain moment. His work, especially in medieval studies, has stimulated a new kind of "historical" criticism and has even been useful to the New Historicism examined in the Introduction to "Historical Criticism" (Part VII).

Wolfgang Iser is responsible for another influential version of Reader-Response criticism, especially in his earlier work—one still in the phenomenological camp but intensely concerned with the pragmatics of reading in actual interpretation. Wolfgang Iser builds a reader-oriented theory around the concept of narrative "gaps." "Gaps" for Iser mean the absent details or connections—the vaguenesses—within a story that a reader must fill in or make up from his or her own experience. No story, no matter how "realistic," can provide the number of details that would obviate such gaps. The structural need to fill these gaps is the text's way of completing itself through the reader's experience and of ensuring the reader's investment in that work. Ambiguous in this thinking, however, is the question of the reader's apparent control of the reading experience. Is the text in charge of reading, or does the reader virtually write the text by filling its gaps without external constraint? The problem of deciding whether the text (author) or the reader is in charge in the act of reading is a recurrent and as yet unanswered question in Reader-Response criticism.

In the related school that Mailloux calls subjectivism, this same problem concerning the authority of interpretation persists and is intensified. Drawing from psychoanalytic theory, David Bleich, for instance, practices a "subjective criticism" that assumes that literary interpretation is never more than an elaboration of a person's most personal motivations and desires, which are projected or "discovered," perhaps even "disavowed," in the literary text. Bleich's method involves establishing the connection between literary interpretation, the aesthetic effect of a text, and the individual search for self-knowledge. By psychologizing the reading process in this way, Bleich resolves the text/reader question in the reader's favor. The reader is in charge, but this strategy, as some believe, leaves the text virtually undefined and without intrinsic meaning— "blank," so to speak.

Initially, Norman N. Holland, also a Freudian and an important literary critic of the mid-twentieth century, seemed to resolve the text/reader question without losing the text, but the result of his criticism (with some differences) is similar to Bleich's. In *5 Readers Reading* and *Poems in Persons*, Holland attempts "to understand the combination of text and personal association," an approach suggesting evenhandedness in the text/reader dispute. For Holland, as Mailloux points out, "the reader makes sense of the text by creating a meaningful unity out of its elements." There is no unity "in the text [itself] but [only] in the mind of the reader." More pointedly, concerning the text's authority, Holland says in *5 Readers Reading* that "the reader is surely responding to *something*. The literary text may be only so many marks on a page—at most a matrix of psychological possibilities for its readers." This minimalist sense of the literary text as "marks on a page," much like Bleich's subjective criticism, again leaves little sense of the text as anything more than a reflection, a mirroring, of the reader's personal concerns. Again, the text/reader question is resolved completely in the reader's favor, leaving the literary text in the role of mere stimulus (again, a virtually "blank" text) for the reader's response.

Stanley Fish and Jonathan Culler try to avoid the ambiguities of Bleich's and Holland's subjectivism through a third approach to reading, one that Mailloux calls structuralism. They begin by imagining, as do Bleich and Holland, that reading and interpretation initially are "free" activities virtually ungoverned by the texts being read.

Fish and Culler then move to place constraints on reading so as to lay the foundation for what may be considered a "valid" interpretation of a particular text. In "Interpreting the *Variorum,*" Fish's major document about Reader-Response criticism, Fish explains how the stylistic economy of a text initially elicits multiple and conflicting responses. Any one text, though, will not finally be read in a multiplicity of ways by a single reader. Readers all have personal limitations and tend to interpret texts in fairly narrow and prescribed ways. Particular interpretive choices are based on the reader's belonging to an "interpretive community" of other readers, and this community will allow certain readings as normative and reject others as untenable. From this communal censoring activity, in other words, will emerge "valid," or normative, readings of a text. Similarly, drawing on Noam Chomsky's distinction between competence and performance, Culler posits a set of reading conventions, or strategies for understanding written texts, that a qualified reader in a culture will learn and employ. A person's measurable ability to implement these conventions constitutes reading "competence," which for Fish and Culler—under different names—becomes nearly the whole substance of the reading activity. Again, in this focus on competence we are witnessing the virtual obliteration of any sense of an objective "text."

Fish and Culler go on to place "common-sense" restrictions on an activity in reading that most readers would tend to agree is, in some way, bounded or constrained. Readers do not generally report reading any text from every conceivable perspective simultaneously. Rather, readers tend to experience the extremes of indeterminacy in interpretation only at the initial stage of reading, before external constraints of an interpretive community come into play. Unlike Bleich and Holland, Fish and Culler—most explicitly in Culler's *Structuralist Poetics*—attempt to articulate a conception of the "facts" in literature in a way that grows out of Saussure's description of the nature of linguistic fact (see Saussure's texts in "Structuralism and Semiotics" [Part IV]). Fish also describes the contextual and conventional nature of literary "facts" when he says that "phonological 'facts' are no more uninterpreted (or less conventional) than the 'facts' of orthography; the distinctive features that make articulation and reception possible are the product of a system of differences that must be *imposed* before it can be recognized." "The patterns the ear hears (like the patterns the eye sees)," Fish goes on, "are the patterns its perceptual habits make available."

Reader-Response criticism, as we can see here, draws on pragmatic notions about the nature of reading and making sense of reading. It does seem eminently reasonable to assume, with Fish and Culler, that constraints on reading do exist and that those constraints are analogous to the lexical and grammatical constraints on language at its elemental level of functioning. However, the hypothesis about an interpretive community's implementation of constraints on reading is supported by most people's intuition but difficult to verify critically. One must grant with Bleich and Holland that meaning, or the authority of any single interpretation, is difficult to locate or prove within a text. Few contemporary theorists or critics would maintain that a text is self-defining or authorizing. Texts do not tell readers how to read them or exercise textual or interpretive judgments to support a particular interpretation. Can an inanimate text even be thought to possess an intention? In the practices of contemporary criticism, there are many different answers to this question. However, the simple relocation of interpretive authority from the text to a community of readers does not necessarily solve the problem. Who can know all of the interpretive communities any one reader belongs to? Who will be sufficiently "competent" within any one community to determine the proper communal interpretation of any one text? How is the authority of an interpretive community established?

A moment's reflection on these and other questions suggests that the "interpretive community" is a rich notion, but it cannot be set up unequivocally as a clear arbitrator of interpretation. "Interpretive community" is no more of a decidable, unambiguous concept in interpretation than is the idea of "textual" authority. Fish and Culler have apparently "solved" the problem of interpretation once again by deferring it. The "interpretive community" and "competence" are themselves indeterminate and problematic concepts, in effect, new difficulties to deal with. The text/reader question remains as open for Fish and Culler as for Bleich and Holland.

THE NEW RHETORIC OF THE TEXT

While current Reader-Response criticism has not actually solved many primary questions about its procedures, it has been and continues to be a creative and vital movement nonetheless. Like many critical schools since World War II, Reader-Response argues against the exclusive use of formalist approaches to literature by emphasizing reading or interpretation as an *activity*, as an ongoing performative rather than as a static or contained event. At the same time, Reader-Response criticism participates in the generalizing practices of formalism that West, Ahmad, and even de Man argue against. Schweickart addresses this issue in the feminist critique of "Reading Ourselves: Toward a Feminist Theory of Reading" and offers a helpful overview of various practices of Reader-Response criticism, exploring the universalizing and "utopian" aim within contemporary criticism. Schweickart notes that much contemporary theory and criticism often overlooks "the issues of race, class, and sex."

After surveying the various schools of Reader-Response criticism, Schweickart discusses the gender-based aspects of reading and describes two different *kinds* of Reader-Response criticism. The first, an important development in feminist criticism, is carried out "under the sign of the 'Resisting Reader,'" wherein the goal is to *resist* the "fiction" intended for a male audience and, in doing so, to expose "the androcentricity of what has customarily passed for the universal." The second kind of Reader-Response criticism creates a new role for the reader, a feminine role for the reader of women's writing, which—eschewing "mainstream reader-response theories [which are] preoccupied with issues of control and partition"—seeks to discover "the dialectic of communication informing the relationship between the feminist reader and the female author/text." In this description, Schweickart is attempting to articulate a rhetoric of reading—functioning "equipment"—that is both textual and reader-oriented. Here is a description of "rhetoric," once again, that attempts to connect reader and text. In her feminist critique, Schweickart is describing ways in which contemporary rhetorical analyses of literature can create new ways of reading and understanding.

Johnson's "Apostrophe, Animation, and Abortion" exemplifies the operation of a rhetorical dialectic—in this case, the relationship between the feminist reader and the female author/text. In Johnson's conception of rhetoric, there are no encompassing interpretive communities of response to texts but, rather, particular practices and tactics. This conception of rhetoric has the obvious strength of being situated complexly in relation to particular rhetorical strategies in the text and the particular strategies of readers in relation to those texts. This is a conception of rhetoric that highlights the social force of certain rhetorical strategies and the potential of an ideological critique that can focus on the relation among texts in a specific and situated sense. In the manner Schweickart calls for, Johnson examines the poetic tropes used to address abortion, showing that "there are striking and suggestive parallels between the 'different voices' involved in the abortion debate and the shifting address-structures of poems like Gwendolyn Brooks's 'The Mother.'" Johnson explores the extent to which abortion and miscarriage as the objects of discourse are "inextricably connected to the figure of apostrophe."

Johnson is at once specific in her use of literary and other texts and critical in her rhetorical exploration of those texts. Johnson deploys rhetorical tropes to represent the positions and investments of gender. In this way, rhetoric focuses on the relations of value and ideology at different sites of the cultural text. In the manner of cultural studies, following what Gilles Deleuze and Félix Guattari call the "rhizomic" logic of cultural determination that Moulthrop uses as a central metaphor for comprehending the implications of new discursive technologies, she finds in the course of this inquiry that "rhetorical, psychoanalytical, and political structures are profoundly implicated in one another." Such "implications" can be fruitfully conceived as hypertextual in the sense that they define, in Moulthrop's terms, "the reader's implicit task . . . to build a network of virtual connections" within the "smooth" but discontinuous phenomena of postmodern culture. Quoting Deleuze and Guattari, Moulthrop describes "a chaotically distributed network (the rhizome) rather than a regular hierarchy of trunk and branches. 'Many people have a tree growing in their heads,' Deleuze and Guattari observe, 'but the brain itself is much more a grass than a tree.'" Rhetorical criticism in America is now moving strongly in the direction of the particularities of grassy plains (such as ours in Oklahoma); it is moving in the direction of situated understandings—the circumstances of history and technology and the specific effects of local institutions.

Focusing on a variety of electronic and other emergent kinds of texts, this movement is concerned with style, including the "difficulties" of criticism we discussed in the General Introduction and the local difficulties of the figurative and jargon-laden language Moulthrop quotes from Deleuze and Guattari. Gerald Graff begins *Beyond the Culture Wars: How Teaching the Conflicts Can Revitalize American Education* by saying, "Writing for a general audience is not an easy thing for the average academic. As writers we academics are spoiled. We are used to writing for other academics, usually those in our particular fields, and this protection from outside perspectives lets us fall into cozy ways of thinking and expressing ourselves." Graff's attempt to contextualize the jargony in-writing typical of most "academic" writers is a way, as Scholes says, of teaching the "cultural text." In light of this contextualization, Graff's plain style of writing his book without the implicit layering of presupposition and guild recognition among specialist academics constitutes a rhetorical stance of its own with evident ideological implications. Even in his essay in "What Is Literary Studies?" (Part I), we can notice a scarcity of quoted lines and an absence of technical reference and convoluted periodic sentence construction. Graff's rhetorical strategy suggests that an academic writer should no longer use as a cover for bad writing the blanket excuse that academic complexity and richness of thought can be housed only in convoluted rhetoric and the most specialized terminology. In this way, Graff's relatively new and accessible prose style (significantly different from that of his earlier published works) is itself a critique of and a challenge to other academic writers. In something as seemingly "ornamental" as style, there is a message and an implicit definition of the nature of efficacious work in a plural, democratic culture.

The study of contemporary rhetorical practice, in short, is currently taking the form of a cognitive sociology of the text in its examination of working subjectivities—or working sets of assumptions about value—evident in the perspectives created by actual written and other kinds of texts. This approach potentially takes in, as Susan Miller writes, "the 'actual' [production of texts] and systems of control, theorized horizontal and vertical planes on which social practices and discursive formations meet." The study of rhetoric and writing in this way becomes a kind of study of cultural production and cultural reception, a view of each text as "deployed" by the culture—situated where it is in class terms to serve a specific and definable end. Even Walter Ong sees and admits, as Miller notes, "that classical rhetoric was itself a combative, disciplined, male pursuit and has accounted for its [own] disappearance with curious . . . arguments."

This current, cultural-studies approach to rhetoric not only assumes the connectedness and cross-indexed relations—"hypertextual" relations—of different rhetorical texts in the culture. It also chooses sites for rhetorical critique that were once thought to be marginal, and this choice in itself becomes, by implication, a focused critique of the customary and accepted sites for rhetorical analysis in canonical literature and well-defined subcultures. By contrast, rhetoricians are now willing and able to look at the previously ignored circumstances of standard writing situations, situations with a largely ignored and hence invisible impact. In *Textual Carnivals,* for example, Miller examines the cultural frame that produces the "required subjectivity [which is "infantilized"] of the composition student." She discusses the "characterizations of the composition course as a transition to college life and its reliance on pedagogies often used at much earlier levels, but also from the persistent objectification/subjection of the student that follows from requirements, from placement and 'diagnostic' exams, and from the absence of choice among the emphases or conduct of sections of one course taught by those described in class schedules as anonymous 'staff.'" Working within this cultural text marked as marginalized and insignificant, the composition teacher and others belonging to culture's deciding group, in this instance, initiate "students into the culture's discourse on language, which is always at one with action, emotion, and regulatory establishments."

Significant here are the theoretical critique of the subject in a writing situation but also the choice of a writing situation in Miller's analysis. The rhetorical situation of a college composition course is merely "factual" and without need of comment or critique according to many previous rhetorical analyses. In Miller's analysis, however, the choice of a previously marginalized set of circumstances for writing (unremarkable and seldom remarked on) is a strategic move that defines rhetorical analysis not simply in the explanatory terms of criticism but also in the transformative potential of critique and the instigation of change. This transformative potential of rhetorical analysis is foregrounded in many current practices as an intentionally probing and somewhat disruptive version of the textual analysis that has always been the strength of rhetorical criticism. Current practices in the rhetorical analysis of literary and non-literary texts appropriate the techniques of classical and contemporary analyses to serve goals that are no longer set exclusively within established institutional models. Evident in current practices is the emergence of a practice as yet unnamed—strong rhetorical critique as a tool of cultural understanding and change.

RELATED READING IN *CONTEMPORARY LITERARY CRITICISM*

Mikhail Bakhtin, "Discourse in Life and Discourse in Art (Concerning Sociological Poetics)"
Jonathan Culler, "Convention and Meaning: Derrida and Austin"
Paul de Man, "The Resistance to Theory"
Shoshana Felman, "Psychoanalysis and Education: Teaching Terminable and Interminable"
J. Hillis Miller, "The Search for Grounds in Literary Study"

REFERENCES AND FURTHER READING

Bakhtin, M. M., *Speech Genres and Other Late Essays,* trans. Vern McGee (Austin: University of Texas Press, 1986).

Benedict, Barbara M., *Making the Modern Reader: Cultural Mediation in Early Modern Literary Anthologies* (Princeton, NJ: Princeton University Press, 1996).

Bleich, David, *Readings and Feelings: An Introduction to Subjective Criticism* (New York: Harper & Row, 1977).

———, *Subjective Criticism* (Baltimore: Johns Hopkins University Press, 1978).

Booth, Wayne C., *The Rhetoric of Fiction* (Chicago: University of Chicago Press, 1961).

Britton, Bruce K., and Glynn M. Shawn, *Computer Writing Environments: Theory, Research, and Design* (Hillsdale, NJ: Erlbaum, 1989).

Chabot, Barry C., ". . . Reading Readers Reading Readers Reading . . . ," in *Diacritics,* 5, No. 3 (1975), 24–38.

Chatman, Seymour, *Narrative Structure in Fiction and Film* (Ithaca, NY: Cornell University Press, 1978).

Culler, Jonathan, "Stanley Fish and the Righting of the Reader," in *Diacritics,* 5, No. 1 (1975), 26–31.

———, *Structuralist Poetics* (Ithaca, NY: Cornell University Press, 1975).

Delany, Paul, and George P. Landow, *Technical Communication* (Cambridge, MA: MIT Press, 1991).

de Man, Paul, "Semiology and Rhetoric," in *Allegories of Reading* (New Haven, CT: Yale University Press, 1979).

Eagleton, Terry, *Literary Theory: An Introduction* (Minneapolis: University of Minnesota Press, 1983).

Finneran, Richard J., *The Literary Text in the Digital Age* (Ann Arbor: University of Michigan Press, 1996).

Fish, Stanley, *Is There a Text in This Class? The Authority of Interpretive Communities* (Cambridge, MA: Harvard University Press, 1980).

———, *Self-Consuming Artifacts: The Experience of Seventeenth-Century Literature* (Berkeley: University of California Press, 1972).

———, *Surprised by Sin: The Reader in* "Paradise Lost" (Berkeley: University of California Press, 1967).

———, "Why No One's Afraid of Wolfgang Iser," in *Diacritics,* 11, No. 1 (1981), 2–13.

Gadamer, Hans-Georg, *Truth and Method* (New York: Seabury Press, 1975).

Graff, Gerald, *Beyond the Culture Wars: How Teaching the Conflicts Can Revitalize American Education* (New York: Norton, 1992).

Havelock, Eric, *Preface to Plato* (Cambridge, MA: Harvard University Press, 1963).

Holland, Norman N., *The Dynamics of Literary Response* (New York: Oxford University Press, 1968).

———, *5 Readers Reading* (New Haven, CT: Yale University Press, 1975).

———, *Poems in Persons* (New York: Norton, 1973).

Horner, Winifred Bryan, and Michael C. Leff, *Rhetoric and Pedagogy: Its History, Philosophy, and Practice: Essays in Honor of James J. Murphy* (Mahwah, NJ: Erlbaum, 1995).

Ingarden, Roman, *The Cognition of the Literary Work of Art* (Evanston, IL: Northwestern University Press, 1973).

Iser, Wolfgang, *The Act of Reading* (Baltimore: Johns Hopkins University Press, 1978).

———, *The Implied Reader: Patterns of Communication in Prose Fiction from Bunyan to Beckett* (Baltimore: Johns Hopkins University Press, 1974).

Jauss, Hans Robert, "Literary History as a Challenge to Literary Theory," in *New Directions in Literary History,* ed. Ralph Cohen (Baltimore: Johns Hopkins University Press, 1974), 11–41.

———, *Toward an Aesthetic of Reception,* trans. Timothy Bahti (Minneapolis: University of Minnesota Press, 1982).

Joyce, Michael, *Of Two Minds: Hypertext Pedagogy and Poetics* (Ann Arbor: University of Michigan Press, 1995).

Landow, George P., *Hyper/Text/Theory* (Baltimore: Johns Hopkins University Press, 1994).

———, *Hypertext: The Convergence of Contemporary Critical Theory and Technology* (Baltimore: Johns Hopkins University Press, 1992).

Mailloux, Steven, *Interpretive Conventions: The Reader in the Study of American Fiction* (Ithaca, NY: Cornell University Press, 1982).

McKnight, Cliff, Andrew Dillon, and John Richardson, *Hypertext in Context* (New York: Cambridge University Press, 1991).

Miller, Susan, *Textual Carnivals: The Politics of Composition* (Carbondale: Southern Illinois University Press, 1991).

Ong, Walter S. J., *Fighting for Literacy: Contest, Sexuality, and Consciousness* (Ithaca, NY: Cornell University Press, 1981).

———, *Orality and Literacy* (New York: Methuen, 1982).

———, *Rhetoric, Romance, and Technology* (Ithaca, NY: Cornell University Press, 1971).

Poulet, Georges, "Phenomenology of Reading," in *New Literary History 1,* 1 (October) 1969, 53–68.

Pratt, Mary Louise, *Toward a Speech Act Theory of Literary Discourse* (Bloomington: Indiana University Press, 1977).

Prince, Gerald, "Introduction a l'étude de narrataire," in *Poetique,* 14 (1973), 178–96.

"Reading, Interpretation, Response," special section of *Genre,* 10 (1977), 363–453.

Roudiez, Leon, "Notes on the Reader as Subject," in *Semiotext(e)*, 1, No. 3 (1975), 69–80.

Scholes, Robert, *Textual Power* (New Haven, CT: Yale University Press, 1985).

Starobinski, Jean, *Word Upon Words* (New Haven, CT: Yale University Press, 1979).

Suleiman, Susan, and Inge Corsman, eds., *The Reader in the Text: Essays on Audience and Interpretation* (Princeton, NJ: Princeton University Press, 1980).

Tompkins, Jane, ed., *Reader-Response Criticism* (Baltimore: Johns Hopkins University Press, 1980).

11

Stanley Fish
1938–

Stanley Fish has taught at the University of California at Berkeley, Johns Hopkins University, and Duke University. His training was in seventeenth-century British literature, but as a critic he has been identified with the development of Reader-Response criticism since the publication of *Surprised by Sin: The Reader in "Paradise Lost"* (1967). His approach to reading is fiercely pragmatic, and he tends to shun philosophical or abstract formulation of his methods: The temperament and tone of his work place it close to that of Ordinary Language philosophers (especially John L. Austin). His method consists largely of anticipating the direction of narrative development and then discussing in detail how closely actual development coincides with or frustrates what was expected. He tends to think of interpretive strategies as guided by a reader's "interpretive community." His work, in addition to many essays, includes *John Skelton's Poetry* (1965), *Self-consuming Artifacts: The Experience of Seventeenth-Century Literature* (1972), *Is There a Text in This Class? The Authority of Interpretive Communities* (1980), *Doing What Comes Naturally: Change, Rhetoric, and the Practice of Theory in Literary and Legal Studies* (1989), *Professional Corrections: Literary Studies and Political Change* (1995), and *There's No Such Thing as Free Speech—And It's a Good Thing, Too* (1994).

Fish's "Interpreting the *Variorum*" (1980) is a critical document remarkable for its insight into reading and for its candor. Fish looks at volumes of the Milton *Variorum Commentary*, noting that again and again the *Variorum* gives evidence for multiple readings of key passages in Milton's work. Fish then does two things. First, he demonstrates how a reader transforms an interpretive dispute by making it "signify, first by regarding it as evidence of an experience and then by specifying for that experience a meaning." This reader-oriented approach, however, is marked by its "inability to say how it is that one ever begins" to read and interpret. Fish's answer is that readers are guided by "interpretive communities" of readers. Second, Fish asks, "How can any one of us know whether or not he is a member of the same interpretive community as any other of us?" His answer is that we can never be sure, but that our commonsense experience tends to confirm the existence of such reading communities.

Interpreting the *Variorum*

I

The first two volumes of the Milton *Variorum Commentary* have now appeared, and I find them endlessly fascinating. My interest, however, is not in the questions they manage to resolve (although these are many) but in the theoretical assumptions which are responsible for their occasional failures. These failures constitute a pattern, one in which a host of commentators—separated by as much as two hundred and seventy years but contemporaries in their shared concerns—are lined up on either side of an interpretive crux. Some of these are famous, even infamous: what is the two-handed engine in *Lycidas?* what is the meaning of Haemony in *Comus?* Others, like the identity of whoever or whatever comes to the window in *L'Allegro,* line 46, are only slightly less notorious. Still others are of interest largely to those who make editions: matters of pronoun referents, lexical ambiguities, punctuation. In each instance, however, the pattern is consistent: every position taken is supported by wholly convincing evidence—in the case of *L'Allegro* and the coming to the window there is a persuasive champion for every proper noun within a radius of ten lines—and the editorial procedure always ends either in the graceful throwing up of hands, or in the recording of a disagreement between the two editors themselves. In short, these are problems that apparently cannot be solved, at least not by the methods traditionally brought to bear on them. What I would like to argue is that they are not *meant* to be solved, but to be experienced (they signify), and that consequently any procedure that attempts to determine which of a number of readings is correct will necessarily fail. What this means is that the commentators and editors have been asking the wrong questions and that a new set of questions based on new assumptions must be formulated. I would like at least to make a beginning in that

direction by examining some of the points in dispute in Milton's sonnets. I choose the sonnets because they are brief and because one can move easily from them to the theoretical issues with which this paper is finally concerned.

Milton's twentieth sonnet—"Lawrence of virtuous father virtuous son"—has been the subject of relatively little commentary. In it the poet invites a friend to join him in some distinctly Horatian pleasures—a neat repast intermixed with conversation, wine, and song; a respite from labor all the more enjoyable because outside the earth is frozen and the day sullen. The only controversy the sonnet has inspired concerns its final two lines:

Lawrence of virtuous father virtuous son,
   Now that the fields are dank, and ways
     are mire,
   Where shall we sometimes meet, and
     by the fire
   Help waste a sullen day; what may be
     won
From the hard season gaining; time will   5
   run
   On smoother, till Favonius reinspire
   The frozen earth; and clothe in fresh
     attire
   The lily and rose, that neither sowed
     nor spun.
What neat repast shall feast us, light and
     choice,
   Of Attic taste, with wine, whence we   10
     may rise
   To hear the lute well touched, or artful
     voice
Warble immortal notes and Tuscan air?
He who of those delights can judge, and
   spare
To interpose them oft, is not unwise.[1]

The focus of the controversy is the word "spare," for which two readings have been proposed: leave time for and refrain from. Obviously the point is crucial if one is to resolve the sense of the lines. In one reading "those delights" are being recommended—he who can leave time for them is not unwise; in the other, they are the subject of a warning—he who knows when to refrain from them is not unwise. The proponents of the two interpretations cite as evidence both English and Latin syntax, various sources and analogues, Milton's "known attitudes" as they are found in his other writings, and the unambiguously expressed sentiments of the following sonnet on the same question. Surveying these arguments, A. S. P. Woodhouse roundly declares: "It is plain that all the honours rest with" the meaning "refrain from" or "forbear to." This declaration is followed immediately by a bracketed paragraph initialled D. B. for Douglas Bush, who, writing presumably after Woodhouse has died, begins "In spite of the array of scholarly names the case for 'forbear to' may be thought much weaker, and the case for 'spare time for' much stronger, than Woodhouse found them."[2] Bush then proceeds to review much of the evidence marshaled by Woodhouse and to draw from it exactly the opposite conclusion. If it does nothing else, this curious performance anticipates a point I shall make in a few moments: evidence brought to bear in the course of formalist analyses—that is, analyses generated by the assumption that meaning is embedded in the artifact—will always point in as many directions as there are interpreters; that is, not only will it prove something, it will prove anything.

It would appear then that we are back at square one, with a controversy that cannot be settled because the evidence is inconclusive. But what if that controversy is *itself* regarded as evidence, not of an ambiguity that must be removed, but of an ambiguity that readers have always experienced? What, in other words, if for the question "what does 'spare' mean?" we substitute the question "what does the fact that the meaning of 'spare' has always been an issue mean"? The advantage of this question is that it can be answered. Indeed it has already been an-

swered by the readers who are cited in the *Variorum Commentary.* What these readers debate is the judgment the poem makes on the delights of recreation; what their debate indicates is that the judgment is blurred by a verb that can be made to participate in contradictory readings. (Thus the important thing about the evidence surveyed in the *Variorum* is not how it is marshaled, but that it could be marshaled at all, because it then becomes evidence of the equal availability of both interpretations.) In other words, the lines first generate a pressure for judgment—"he who of those delights can judge"—and then decline to deliver it; the pressure, however, still exists, and it is transferred from the words on the page to the reader (the reader is "he who"), who comes away from the poem not with a statement, but with a responsibility, the responsibility of deciding when and how often—if at all—to indulge in "those delights" (they remain delights in either case). This transferring of responsibility from the text to its readers is what the lines ask us to do—it is the essence of their experience—and in my terms it is therefore what the lines *mean.* It is a meaning the *Variorum* critics attest to even as they resist it, for what they are laboring so mightily to do by fixing the sense of the lines is to give the responsibility back. The text, however, will not accept it and remains determinedly evasive, even in its last two words, "not unwise." In their position these words confirm the impossibility of extracting from the poem a moral formula, for the assertion (certainly too strong a word) they complete is of the form, "He who does such and such, of him it cannot be said that he is unwise"; but of course neither can it be said that he is wise. Thus what Bush correctly terms the "defensive" "not unwise" operates to prevent us from attaching the label "wise" to any action, including *either* of the actions—leaving time for or refraining from—represented by the ambiguity of "spare." Not only is the pressure of judgment taken off the poem, it is taken off the activity the poem at first pretended to judge. The issue is finally not the moral status of "those delights"—they become in seventeenth-century terms "things indifferent"—but on the good or bad uses to which they can be put by readers who are left, as Milton always leaves them, to choose and manage by themselves.

Let us step back for a moment and see how far we've come. We began with an apparently insoluble problem and proceeded, not to solve it, but to make it signify; first by regarding it as evidence of an experience and then by specifying for that experience a meaning. Moreover, the configurations of that experience, when they are made available by a reader-oriented analysis, serve as a check against the endlessly inconclusive adducing of evidence which characterizes formalist analysis. That is to say, any determination of what "spare" means (in a positivist or literal sense) is liable to be upset by the bringing forward of another analogue, or by a more complete computation of statistical frequencies, or by the discovery of new biographical information, or by anything else; but if we first determine that everything in the line before "spare" creates the expectation of an imminent judgment, then the ambiguity of "spare" can be assigned a significance in the context of that expectation. (It disappoints it and transfers the pressure of judgment to us.) That context is experiential, and it is within its contours and constraints that significances are established (both in the act of reading and in the analysis of that act). In formalist analyses the only constraints are the notoriously open-ended possibilities and combination of possibilities that emerge when one begins to consult dictionaries and grammars and histories; to consult dictionaries, grammars, and histories is to assume that meanings can be specified independently of the activity of reading; what the example of "spare" shows is that it is in and by that activity that meanings—experiential, not positivist—are created.

In other words, it is the structure of the reader's experience rather than any structures available on the page that should be the object of description. In the case of Sonnet XX, that experiential structure was uncovered when an examination of formal structures led to an impasse; and the pressure to remove that impasse led to the substitution of one set of questions for another. It will more often be the case that the pressure of a spectacular failure will be absent. The sins of formalist-positivist analysis are primarily sins of omission, not an inability to explain phenomena, but an inability to see that they are there because its assumptions make it inevitable that they will be overlooked or suppressed. Consider, for example, the concluding lines of another of Milton's sonnets, "Avenge O Lord thy slaughtered saints."

> Avenge O Lord thy slaughtered saints, whose bones
>> Lie scattered on the Alpine mountains cold,
>> Even them who kept thy truth so pure of old
>> When all our fathers worshipped stocks and stones,
> Forget not: in thy book record their   5
>> groans
>> Who were thy sheep and in their ancient fold
>> Slain by the bloody Piedmontese that rolled
>> Mother with infant down the rocks. Their moans
> The vales redoubled to the hills, and they
>> To heaven. Their martyred blood and   10
>> ashes sow
>> O'er all the Italian fields where still doth sway
> The triple Tyrant: that from these may grow
>> A hundredfold, who having learnt thy way
>> Early may fly the Babylonian woe.

In this sonnet, the poet simultaneously petitions God and wonders aloud about the justice of allowing the faithful—"Even them who kept thy truth"—to be so brutally slaughtered. The note struck is alternately one of plea and complaint, and there is more than a hint that God is being called to account for what has happened to the Waldensians. It is generally agreed, however, that the note of complaint is less and less sounded and that the poem ends with an affirmation of faith in the ultimate operation of God's justice. In this reading, the final lines are taken to be saying something like this: From the blood of these martyred, O God, raise up a new and more numerous people, who, by virtue of an early education in thy law, will escape destruction by fleeing the Babylonian woe. Babylonian woe has been variously glossed[3]; but whatever it is taken to mean it is always read as part of a statement that specifies a set of conditions for the escaping of destruction or punishment; it is a warning to the reader as well as a petition to God. As a warning, however, it is oddly situated since the conditions it seems to specify were in fact met by the Waldensians, who of all men most followed God's laws. In other words, the details of their story would seem to undercut the affirmative moral the speaker proposes to draw from it. It is further undercut by a reading that is fleetingly available, although no one has acknowledged it because it is a function, not of the words on the page, but of the experience of the reader. In that experience, line 13 will for a moment be accepted as a complete sense unit and the emphasis of the line will fall on "thy way" (a phrase that has received absolutely no attention in the commentaries). At this point "thy way" can refer only to the way in which God has dealt with the Waldensians. That is, "thy way" seems to pick up the note of outrage with which the poem began, and if we continue to so interpret it, the conclusion of the poem will be a grim one indeed: since by this example it appears that God rains down punishment indiscriminately, it would be best perhaps to withdraw from the arena of his service, and thereby hope at least to be safely out of the line of fire. This is not the conclusion we carry away, because as line 14 un-

folds, another reading of "thy way" becomes available, a reading in which "early" qualifies "learnt" and refers to something the faithful should do (learn thy way at an early age) rather than to something God has failed to do (save the Waldensians). These two readings are answerable to the pulls exerted by the beginning and ending of the poem: the outrage expressed in the opening lines generates a pressure for an explanation, and the grimmer reading is answerable to that pressure (even if it is also disturbing); the ending of the poem, the forward and upward movement of lines 10–14, creates the expectation of an affirmation, and the second reading fulfills that expectation. The criticism shows that in the end we settle on the more optimistic reading—it feels better—but even so the other has been a part of our experience, and because it has been a part of our experience, it *means*. What it means is that while we may be able to extract from the poem a statement affirming God's justice, we are not allowed to forget the evidence (of things seen) that makes the extraction so difficult (both for the speaker and for us). It is a difficulty we experience in the act of reading, even though a criticism which takes no account of that act has, as we have seen, suppressed it.

II

In each of the sonnets we have considered, the significant word or phrase occurs at a line break where a reader is invited to place it first in one and then in another structure of syntax and sense. This moment of hesitation, of semantic or syntactic slide, is crucial to the experience the verse provides, but, in a formalist analysis, that moment will disappear, either because it has been flattened out and made into an (insoluble) interpretive crux, or because it has been eliminated in the course of a procedure that is incapable of finding value in temporal phenomena. In the case of "When I consider how my light is spent," these two failures are combined.

When I consider how my light is spent,
  Ere half my days, in this dark world
    and wide,
  And that one talent which is death to
    hide,
  Lodged with me useless, though my
    soul more bent
To serve therewith my maker, and present   5
  My true account, lest he returning
    chide,
  Doth God exact day-labour, light
    denied,
  I fondly ask; but Patience to prevent
That murmur, soon replies, God doth not
    need
  Either man's work or his own gifts, who 10
    best
  Bear his mild yoke, they serve him best,
    his state
Is kingly. Thousands at his bidding speed
  And post o'er land and ocean without
    rest:
  They also serve who only stand and
    wait.

The interpretive crux once again concerns the final line: "They also serve who only stand and wait." For some this is an unqualified acceptance of God's will, while for others the note of affirmation is muted or even forced. The usual kinds of evidence are marshaled by the opposing parties, and the usual inconclusiveness is the result. There are some areas of agreement. "All the interpretations," Woodhouse remarks, "recognize that the sonnet commences from a mood of depression, frustration [and] impatience."[4] The object of impatience is a God who would first demand service and then take away the means of serving, and the oft noted allusion to the parable of the talents lends scriptural support to the accusation the poet is implicitly making: you have cast the wrong servant into unprofitable darkness. It has also been observed that the syntax and rhythm of these early lines, and especially of lines 6–8, are rough and uncertain; the speaker is struggling with his agitated thoughts and he changes directions abruptly, with no regard for the line as a unit of sense. The poem, says one critic, "seems almost out of control."[5]

The question I would ask is "whose control?"; for what these formal descriptions point to (but do not acknowledge) is the extraordinary number of adjustments required of readers who would negotiate these lines. The first adjustment is the result of the expectations created by the second half of line 6—"lest he returning chide." Since there is no full stop after "chide," it is natural to assume that this will be an introduction to reported speech, and to assume further that what will be reported is the poet's anticipation of the voice of God as it calls him, to an unfair accounting. This assumption does not survive line 7—"Doth God exact day-labour, light denied"—which rather than chiding the poet for his inactivity seems to rebuke him for having expected that chiding. The accents are precisely those heard so often in the Old Testament when God answers a reluctant Gideon, or a disputatious Moses, or a self-justifying Job: do you presume to judge my ways or to appoint my motives? Do you think I would exact day labor, light denied? In other words, the poem seems to turn at this point from a questioning of God to a questioning of that questioning; or, rather, the reader turns from the one to the other in the act of revising his projection of what line 7 will say and do. As it turns out, however, that revision must itself be revised because it had been made within the assumption that what we are hearing is the voice of God. This assumption falls before the very next phrase "I fondly ask," which requires not one, but two adjustments. Since the speaker of line 7 is firmly identified as the poet, the line must be reinterpreted as a continuation of his complaint—Is that the way you operate, God, denying light, but exacting labor?—but even as that interpretation emerges, the poet withdraws from it by inserting the adverb "fondly," and once again the line slips out of the reader's control.

In a matter of seconds, then, line 7 has led four experiential lives, one as we anticipate it, another as that anticipation is revised, a third when we retroactively identify its speaker, and a fourth when that speaker disclaims it. What changes in each of these lives is the status of the poet's murmurings—they are alternately expressed, rejected, reinstated, and qualified—and as the sequence ends, the reader is without a firm perspective on the question of record: does God deal justly with his servants?

A firm perspective appears to be provided by Patience, whose entrance into the poem, the critics tell us, gives it both argumentative and metrical stability. But in fact the presence of Patience in the poem finally assures its continuing instability by making it impossible to specify the degree to which the speaker approves, or even participates in, the affirmation of the final line: "They also serve who only stand and wait." We know that Patience to prevent the poet's murmur soon replies (not soon enough however to prevent the murmur from registering), but we do not know when that reply ends. Does Patience fall silent in line 12, after "kingly"? or at the conclusion of line 13? or not at all? Does the poet appropriate these lines or share them or simply listen to them, as we do? These questions are unanswerable, and it is because they remain unanswerable that the poem ends uncertainly. The uncertainty is not in the statement it makes—in isolation line 14 is unequivocal—but in our inability to assign that statement to either the poet or to Patience. Were the final line marked unambiguously for the poet, then we would receive it as a resolution of his earlier doubts; and were it marked for Patience, it would be a sign that those doubts were still very much in force. It is marked for neither, and therefore we are without the satisfaction that a firmly conclusive ending (in *any* direction) would have provided. In short, we leave the poem unsure, and our unsureness is the realization (in our experience) of the unsureness with which the affirmation of the final line is, or is

not, made. (This unsureness also operates to actualize the two possible readings of "wait": wait in the sense of expecting, that is waiting for an opportunity to serve actively; or wait in the sense of waiting *in* service, a waiting that is itself fully satisfying because the impulse to self-glorifying action has been stilled.)

The question debated in the *Variorum Commentary* is, how far from the mood of frustration and impatience does the poem finally move? The answer given by an experiential analysis is that you can't tell, and the fact that you can't tell is responsible for the uneasiness the poem has always inspired. It is that uneasiness which the critics inadvertently acknowledge when they argue about the force of the last line, but they are unable to make analytical use of what they acknowledge because they have no way of dealing with or even recognizing experiential (that is, temporal) structures. In fact, more than one editor has eliminated those structures by punctuating them out of existence: first by putting a full stop at the end of line 6 and thereby making it unlikely that the reader will assign line 7 to God (there will no longer be an expectation of reported speech), and then by supplying quotation marks for the sestet in order to remove any doubts one might have as to who is speaking. There is of course no warrant for these emendations, and in 1791 Thomas Warton had the grace and honesty to admit as much. "I have," he said, "introduced the turned commas both in the question and answer, not from any authority, but because they seem absolutely necessary to the sense."[6]

III

Editorial practices like these are only the most obvious manifestations of the assumptions to which I stand opposed: the assumption that there *is* a sense, that it is embedded or encoded in the text, and that it can be taken in at a single glance. These assumptions are, in order, positivist, holistic, and spatial, and to have them is to be committed both to a goal and to a procedure. The goal is to settle on a meaning, and the procedure involves first stepping back from the text, and then putting together or otherwise calculating the discrete units of significance it contains. My quarrel with this procedure (and with the assumptions that generate it) is that in the course of following it through the reader's activities are at once ignored and devalued. They are ignored because the text is taken to be self-sufficient—everything is *in* it—and they are devalued because when they are thought of at all, they are thought of as the disposable machinery of extraction. In the procedures I would urge, the reader's activities are at the center of attention, where they are regarded, not as leading to meaning, but as *having* meaning. The meaning they have is a consequence of their not being empty; for they include the making and revising of assumptions, the rendering and regretting of judgments, the coming to and abandoning of conclusions, the giving and withdrawing of approval, the specifying of causes, the asking of questions, the supplying of answers, the solving of puzzles. In a word, these activities are interpretive—rather than being preliminary to questions of value they are at every moment settling and resettling questions of value—and because they are interpretive, a description of them will also be, and without any additional step, an interpretation, not after the fact, but of the fact (of experiencing). It will be a description of a moving field of concerns, at once wholly present (not waiting for meaning, but constituting meaning) and continually in the act of reconstituting itself.

As a project such a description presents enormous difficulties, and there is hardly time to consider them here;[7] but it should be obvious from my brief examples how different it is from the positivist-formalist project. Everything depends on the temporal dimension, and as a consequence the notion of a mistake, at least as something to be avoided, disappears. In a sequence where a reader first structures the field he inhabits and then is asked to restructure it (by changing an assignment of speaker or realigning attitudes and positions) there is no question of priority among his structurings; no one of them, even if it is the last, has privilege; each is equally legitimate, each equally the proper object of analysis, because each is equally an event in his experience.

The firm assertiveness of this paragraph only calls attention to the questions it avoids. Who is this reader? How can I presume to describe his experiences, and what do I say to readers who report that they do not have the experiences I describe? Let me answer these questions or rather make a beginning at answering them in the context of another example, this time from Milton's *Comus*. In line 46 of *Comus* we are introduced to the villain by way of a genealogy:

Bacchus that first from out the purple grape,
Crushed the sweet poison of misused wine.

In almost any edition of this poem, a footnote will tell you that Bacchus is the god of wine. Of course most readers already know that, and because they know it, they will be anticipating the appearance of "wine" long before they come upon it in the final position. Moreover, they will also be anticipating a negative judgment on it, in part because of the association of Bacchus with revelry and excess, and especially because the phrase "sweet poison" suggests that the judgment has already been made. At an early point then, we will have both filled in the form of the assertion and made a decision about its moral content. That decision is upset by the word "misused"; for what "misused" asks us to do is transfer the pressure of judgment from wine (where we have already placed it) to the abusers of wine, and therefore when "wine" finally appears, we must declare it innocent of the charges we have ourselves made.

This, then, is the structure of the reader's experience—the transferring of a moral label from a thing to those who appropriate it. It is an experience that depends on a reader for whom the name Bacchus has precise and immediate associations; another reader, a reader for whom those associations are less precise will not have that experience because he will not have rushed to a conclusion in relation to which the word "misused" will stand as a challenge. Obviously I am discriminating between these two readers and between the two equally real experiences they will have. It is not a discrimination based simply on information, because what is important is not the information itself, but the action of the mind which its possession makes possible for one reader and impossible for the other. One might discriminate further between them by noting that the point at issue—whether value is a function of objects and actions or of intentions—is at the heart of the seventeenth-century debate over "things indifferent." A reader who is aware of that debate will not only *have* the experience I describe; he will recognize at the end of it that he has been asked to take a position on one side of a continuing controversy; and that recognition (also a part of his experience) will be part of the disposition with which he moves into the lines that follow.

It would be possible to continue with this profile of the optimal reader, but I would not get very far before someone would point out that what I am really describing is the intended reader, the reader whose education, opinions, concerns, linguistic competences, etc. make him capable of having the experience the author wished to provide. I would not resist this characterization because it seems obvious that the efforts of readers are always efforts to discern and therefore to realize (in the sense of becoming) an author's intention. I would only object if that realization were conceived narrowly, as the single act of comprehending an author's purpose, rather than (as I would conceive it) as the succession of acts readers perform in the continuing assumption that they are dealing with intentional beings. In this view discerning an

intention is no more or less than understanding, and understanding includes (is constituted by) all the activities which make up what I call the structure of the reader's experience. To describe that experience is therefore to describe the reader's efforts at understanding, and to describe the reader's efforts at understanding is to describe his realization (in two senses) of an author's intention. Or to put it another way, what my analyses amount to are descriptions of a succession of decisions made by readers about an author's intention; decisions that are not limited to the specifying of purpose but include the specifying of every aspect of successively intended worlds; decisions that are precisely the shape, because they are the content, of the reader's activities.

Having said this, however, it would appear that I am open to two objections. The first is that the procedure is a circular one. I describe the experience of a reader who in his strategies is answerable to an author's intention, and I specify the author's intention by pointing to the strategies employed by that same reader. But this objection would have force only if it were possible to specify one independently of the other. What is being specified from either perspective are the conditions of utterance, of what could have been understood to have been meant by what was said. That is, intention and understanding are two ends of a conventional act, each of which necessarily stipulates (includes, defines, specifies) the other. To construct the profile of the informed or at-home reader is at the same time to characterize the author's intention and vice versa, because to do either is to specify the *contemporary* conditions of utterance, to identify, by becoming a member of, a community made up of those who share interpretive strategies.

The second objection is another version of the first: if the content of the reader's experience is the succession of acts he performs in search of an author's intentions, and if he performs those acts at the bidding of the text, does not the text then produce or contain everything—intention *and* experience—and have I not compromised my antiformalist position? This objection will have force only if the formal patterns of the text are assumed to exist independently of the reader's experience, for only then can priority be claimed for them. Indeed, the claims of independence and priority are one and the same; when they are separated it is so that they can give circular and illegitimate support to each other. The question "do formal features exist independently?" is usually answered by pointing to their priority: they are "in" the text before the reader comes to it. The question "are formal features prior?" is usually answered by pointing to their independent status: they are "in" the text before the reader comes to it. What looks like a step in an argument is actually the spectacle of an assertion supporting itself. It follows then that an attack on the independence of formal features will also be an attack on their priority (and vice versa), and I would like to mount such an attack in the context of two short passages from *Lycidas.*

The first passage (actually the second in the poem's sequence) begins at line 42:

The willows and the hazel copses green
Shall now no more be seen,
Fanning their joyous leaves to thy soft lays.
[L1. 42–44]

It is my thesis that the reader is always making sense (I intend "making" to have its literal force), and in the case of these lines the sense he makes will involve the assumption (and therefore the creation) of a completed assertion after the word "seen," to wit, the death of Lycidas has so affected the willows and the hazel copses green that, in sympathy, they will wither and die (will no more be seen by *anyone*). In other words at the end of line 43 the reader will have hazarded an interpretation, or performed an act of perceptual closure, or made a decision as to what is being asserted. I do not mean that he has done four things, but that he has done one thing the description of which might take any

one of four forms—making sense, interpreting, performing perceptual closure, deciding about what is intended. (The importance of this point will become clear later.) Whatever he has done (that is, however we characterize it) he will undo it in the act of reading the next line; for here he discovers that his closure, or making of sense, was premature and that he must make a new one in which the relationship between man and nature is exactly the reverse of what was first assumed. The willows and the hazel copses green will in fact be seen, but they will not be seen by Lycidas. It is he who will be no more, while they go on as before, fanning their joyous leaves to someone else's soft lays (the whole of line 44 is now perceived as modifying and removing the absoluteness of "seen"). Nature is not sympathetic, but indifferent, and the notion of her sympathy is one of those "false surmises" that the poem is continually encouraging and then disallowing.

The previous sentence shows how easy it is to surrender to the bias of our critical language and begin to talk as if poems, not readers or interpreters, did things. Words like "encourage" and "disallow" (and others I have used in this paper) imply agents, and it is only "natural" to assign agency first to an author's intentions and then to the forms that assumedly embody them. What really happens, I think, is something quite different: rather than intention and its formal realization producing interpretation (the "normal" picture), interpretation creates intention and its formal realization by creating the conditions in which it becomes possible to pick them out. In other words, in the analysis of these lines from *Lycidas* I did what critics always do: I "saw" what my interpretive principles permitted or directed me to see, and then I turned around and attributed what I had "seen" to a text and an intention. What my principles direct me to "see" are readers performing acts; the points at which I find (or to be more precise, declare) those acts to have been performed become (by a sleight of hand) demarcations *in* the text; those demarcations are then available for the designation "formal features," and as formal features they can be (illegitimately) assigned the responsibility for producing the interpretation which in fact produced them. In this case, the demarcation my interpretation calls into being is placed at the end of line 42; but of course the end of that (or any other) line is worth noticing or pointing out only because my model *demands* (the word is not too strong) perceptual closures and therefore locations at which they occur; in that model this point will be one of those locations, although (1) it needn't have been (not every line ending occasions a closure) and (2) in another model, one that does not give value to the activities of readers, the possibility of its being one would not have arisen.

What I am suggesting is that formal units are always a function of the interpretative model one brings to bear; they are not "in" the text, and I would make the same argument for intentions. That is, intention is no more embodied "in" the text than are formal units; rather an intention, like a formal unit, is made when perceptual or interpretive closure is hazarded; it is verified by an interpretive act, and I would add, it is not verifiable in any other way. This last assertion is too large to be fully considered here, but I can sketch out the argumentative sequence I would follow were I to consider it: intention is known when and only when it is recognized; it is recognized as soon as you decide about it; you decide about it as soon as you make a sense; and you make a sense (or so my model claims) as soon as you can.

Let me tie up the threads of my argument with a final example from *Lycidas:*

He must not float upon his wat'ry bier
Unwept . . .

                                        [Ll. 13–14]

Here the reader's experience has much the same career as it does in lines 42–44: at the end of line 13 perceptual closure is hazarded, and a sense is made in which the line is taken to be a resolution bordering on a promise: that is, there is now an expectation that something will be

done about this unfortunate situation, and the reader anticipates a call to action, perhaps even a program for the undertaking of a rescue mission. With "Unwept," however, that expectation and anticipation are disappointed, and the realization of that disappointment will be inseparable from the making of a new (and less comforting) sense: nothing will be done; Lycidas will continue to float upon his wat'ry bier, and the only action taken will be the lamenting of the fact that no action will be efficacious, including the actions of speaking and listening to this lament (which in line 15 will receive the meretricious and self-mocking designation "melodious tear"). Three "structures" come into view at precisely the same moment, the moment when the reader having resolved a sense unresolves it and makes a new one; that moment will also be the moment of picking out a formal pattern or unit, end of line/beginning of line, and it will also be the moment at which the reader having decided about the speaker's intention, about what is meant by what has been said, will make the decision again and in so doing will make another intention.

This, then, is my thesis: that the form of the reader's experience, formal units, and the structure of intention are one, that they come into view simultaneously, and that therefore the questions of priority and independence do not arise. What does arise is another question: what produces *them?* That is, if intention, form, and the shape of the reader's experience are simply different ways of referring to (different perspectives on) the same interpretive act, what is that act an interpretation *of?* I cannot answer that question, but neither, I would claim, can anyone else, although formalists try to answer it by pointing to patterns and claiming that they are available independently of (prior to) interpretation. These patterns vary according to the procedures that yield them: they may be statistical (number of two-syllable words per hundred words), grammatical (ratio of passive to active constructions, or of right-branching to left-branching sentences, or of anything else); but whatever they are I would argue that they do not lie innocently in the world but are themselves constituted by an interpretive act, even if, as is often the case, that act is unacknowledged. Of course, this is as true of my analyses as it is of anyone else's. In the examples offered here I appropriate the notion "line ending" and treat it as a fact of nature; and one might conclude that as a fact it is responsible for the reading experience I describe. The truth I think is exactly the reverse: line endings exist by virtue of perceptual strategies rather than the other way around. Historically, the strategy that we know as "reading (or hearing) poetry" has included paying attention to the line as a unit, but it is precisely that attention which has made the line as a unit (either of print or of aural duration) available. A reader so practiced in paying that attention that he regards the line as a brute fact rather than as a convention will have a great deal of difficulty with concrete poetry; if he overcomes that difficulty, it will not be because he has learned to ignore the line as a unit but because he will have acquired a new set of interpretive strategies (the strategies constitutive of "concrete poetry reading") in the context of which the line as a unit no longer exists. In short, what is noticed is what has been *made* noticeable, not by a clear and undistorting glass, but by an interpretive strategy.

This may be hard to see when the strategy has become so habitual that the forms it yields seem part of the world. We find it easy to assume that alliteration as an effect depends on a "fact" that exists independently of any interpretive "use" one might make of it, the fact that words in proximity begin with the same letter. But it takes only a moment's reflection to realize that the sameness, far from being natural, is enforced by an orthographic convention; that is to say, it is the product of an interpretation. Were we to substitute phonetic conventions for orthographic ones (a "reform" traditionally urged by purists), the supposedly "objective" basis for al-

literation would disappear because a phonetic transcription would require that we distinguish between the initial sounds of those very words that enter into alliterative relationships; rather than conforming to those relationships the rules of spelling make them. One might reply that, since alliteration is an aural rather than a visual phenomenon when poetry is heard, we have unmediated access to the physical sounds themselves and hear "real" similarities. But phonological "facts" are no more uninterpreted (or less conventional) than the "facts" of orthography; the distinctive features that make articulation and reception possible are the product of a system of differences that must be *imposed* before it can be recognized; the patterns the ear hears (like the patterns the eye sees) are the patterns its perceptual habits make available.

One can extend this analysis forever, even to the "facts" of grammar. The history of linguistics is the history of competing paradigms each of which offers a different account of the constituents of language. Verbs, nouns, cleft sentences, transformations, deep and surface structures, semes, rhemes, tagmemes—now you see them, now you don't, depending on the descriptive apparatus you employ. The critic who confidently rests his analyses on the bedrock of syntactic descriptions is resting on an interpretation; the facts he points to *are* there, but only as a consequence of the interpretive (man-made) model that has called them into being.

The moral is clear: the choice is never between objectivity and interpretation but between an interpretation that is unacknowledged as such and an interpretation that is at least aware of itself. It is this awareness that I am claiming for myself, although in doing so I must give up the claims implicitly made in the first part of this paper. There I argue that a bad (because spatial) model had suppressed what was really happening, but by my own declared principles the notion "really happening" is just one more interpretation.

IV

It seems then that the price one pays for denying the priority of either forms or intentions is an inability to say how it is that one ever begins. Yet we do begin, and we continue, and because we do there arises an immediate counter-objection to the preceding pages. If interpretive acts are the source of forms rather than the other way around, why isn't it the case that readers are always performing the same acts or a random succession of forms? How, in short, does one explain these two "facts" of reading?: (1) the same reader will perform differently when reading two "different" (the word is in quotation marks because its status is precisely what is at issue) texts; and (2) different readers will perform similarly when reading the "same" (in quotes for the same reason) text. That is to say, both the stability of interpretation among readers and the variety of interpretation in the career of a single reader would seem to argue for the existence of something independent of and prior to interpretive acts, something which produces them. I will answer this challenge by asserting that both the stability and the variety are functions of interpretive strategies rather than of texts.

Let us suppose that I am reading *Lycidas*. What is it that I am doing? First of all, what I am not doing is "simply reading," an activity in which I do not believe because it implies the possibility of pure (that is, disinterested) perception. Rather, I am proceeding on the basis of (at least) two interpretive decisions: (1) that *Lycidas* is a pastoral and (2) that it was written by Milton. (I should add that the notions "pastoral" and "Milton" are also interpretations; that is they do not stand for a set of indisputable, objective facts; if they did, a great many books would not now be getting written.) Once these decisions have been made (and if I had not made these I would have made others, and they would be consequential in the same way), I am immediately predisposed to perform certain acts, to "find," by looking for, themes (the relationship between natural processes and the careers of men, the efficacy of poetry or of any other action), to confer significances (on flowers, streams, shepherds, pagan deities), to mark out "formal" units (the lament, the consolation, the turn, the affirmation of faith, etc.). My disposition to perform these acts (and others; the list is not meant to be exhaustive) constitutes a set of interpretive strategies, which, when they are put into execution, become the large act of reading. That is to say, interpretive strategies are not put into execution after reading (the pure act of perception in which I do not believe); they are the shape of reading, and because they are the shape of reading, they give texts their shape, making them rather than, as it is usually assumed, arising from them. Several important things follow from this account:

1. I did not have to execute this particular set of interpretive strategies because I did not have to make those particular interpretive (prereading) decisions. I could have decided, for example, that *Lycidas* was a text in which a set of fantasies and defenses find expression. These decisions would have entailed the assumption of another set of interpretive strategies (perhaps like that put forward by Norman Holland in *The Dynamics of Literary Response*) and the execution of that set would have made another text.

2. I could execute this same set of strategies when presented with texts that did not bear the title (again a notion which is itself an interpretation) *Lycidas, A Pastoral Monody* . . . . I could decide (it is a decision some have made) that *Adam Bede* is a pastoral written by an author who consciously modeled herself on Milton (still remembering that "pastoral" and "Milton" are interpretations, not facts in the public domain); or I could decide, as Empson did, that a great many things not usually considered pastoral were in fact to be

so read; and either decision would give rise to a set of interpretive strategies, which, when put into action, would *write* the text I write when reading *Lycidas.* (Are you with me?)

3. A reader other than myself who, when presented with *Lycidas,* proceeds to put into execution a set of interpretive strategies similar to mine (how he could do so is a question I will take up later), will perform the same (or at least a similar) succession of interpretive acts. He and I then might be tempted to say that we agree about the poem (thereby assuming that the poem exists independently of the acts either of us performs); but what we really would agree about is the way to write it.

4. A reader other than myself who, when presented with *Lycidas* (please keep in mind that the status of *Lycidas* is what is at issue), puts into execution a different set of interpretive strategies will perform a different succession of interpretive acts. (I am assuming, it is the article of my faith, that a reader will always execute some set of interpretive strategies and therefore perform some succession of interpretive acts.) One of us might then be tempted to complain to the other that we could not possibly be reading the same poem (literary criticism is full of such complaints) and he would be right; for each of us would be reading the poem he had made.

The large conclusion that follows from these four smaller ones is that the notions of the "same" or "different" texts are fictions. If I read *Lycidas* and *The Waste Land* differently (in fact I do not), it will not be because the formal structures of the two poems (to term them such is also an interpretive decision) call forth different interpretive strategies but because my predisposition to execute different interpretive strategies will *produce* different formal structures. That is, the two poems are different because I have decided that they will be. The proof of this is the possibility of doing the reverse (that is why point 2 is so important). That is to say, the an-

swer to the question "why do different texts give rise to different sequences of interpretive acts?" is that *they don't have to,* an answer which implies strongly that "they" don't exist. Indeed it has always been possible to put into action interpretive strategies designed to make all texts one, or to put it more accurately, to be forever making the same text. Augustine urges just such a strategy, for example, in *On Christian Doctrine* where he delivers the "rule of faith" which is of course a rule of interpretation. It is dazzlingly simple: everything in the Scriptures, and indeed in the world when it is properly read, points to (bears the meaning of) God's love for us and our answering responsibility to love our fellow creatures for His sake. If only you should come upon something which does not at first seem to bear this meaning, that "does not literally pertain to virtuous behavior or to the truth of faith," you are then to take it "to be figurative" and proceed to scrutinize it "until an interpretation contributing to the reign of charity is produced." This then is both a stipulation of what meaning there is and a set of directions for finding it, which is of course a set of directions—of interpretive strategies—for making it, that is, for the endless reproduction of the same text. Whatever one may think of this interpretive program, its success and ease of execution are attested to by centuries of Christian exegesis. It is my contention that any interpretive program, any set of interpretive strategies, can have a similar success, although few have been as spectacularly successful as this one. (For some time now, for at least three hundred years, the most successful interpretive program has gone under the name "ordinary language.") In our own discipline programs with the same characteristic of always reproducing one text include psychoanalytic criticism, Robertsonianism (always threatening to extend its sway into later and later periods), numerology (a sameness based on the assumption of innumerable fixed differences).

The other challenging question—"why will different readers execute the same interpretive strategy when faced with the 'same' text?"—can be handled in the same way. The answer is again that *they don't have to,* and my evidence is the entire history of literary criticism. And again this answer implies that the notion "same text" is the product of the possession by two or more readers of similar interpretive strategies.

But why should this ever happen? Why should two or more readers ever agree, and why should regular, that is, habitual, differences in the career of a single reader ever occur? What is the explanation on the one hand of the stability of interpretation (at least among certain groups at certain times) and on the other of the orderly variety of interpretation if it is not the stability and variety of texts? The answer to all of these questions is to be found in a notion that has been implicit in my argument, the notion of *interpretive communities.* Interpretive communities are made up of those who share interpretive strategies not for reading (in the conventional sense) but for writing texts, for constituting their properties and assigning their intentions. In other words these strategies exist prior to the act of reading and therefore determine the shape of what is read rather than, as is usually assumed, the other way around. If it is an article of faith in a particular community that there are a variety of texts, its members will boast a repertoire of strategies for making them. And if a community believes in the existence of only one text, then the single strategy its members employ will be forever writing it. The first community will accuse the members of the second of being reductive, and they in turn will call their accusers superficial. The assumption in each community will be that the other is not correctly perceiving the "true text," but the truth will be that each perceives the text (or texts) its interpretive strategies demand and call into being. This, then, is the explanation both for the stability of interpretation among different readers (they belong to the same community) and for the regularity with which a single reader will employ different interpretive strategies and thus make different texts (he belongs to different communities). It also explains why there are dis-

agreements and why they can be debated in a principled way: not because of a stability in texts, but because of a stability in the makeup of interpretive communities and therefore in the opposing positions they make possible. Of course this stability is always temporary (unlike the longed for and timeless stability of the text). Interpretive communities grow larger and decline, and individuals move from one to another; thus while the alignments are not permanent, they are always there, providing just enough stability for the interpretive battles to go on, and just enough shift and slippage to assure that they will never be settled. The notion of interpretive communities thus stands between an impossible ideal and the fear which leads so many to maintain it. The ideal is of perfect agreement and it would require texts to have a status independent of interpretation. The fear is of interpretive anarchy, but it would only be realized if interpretation (text making) were completely random. It is the fragile but real consolidation of interpretive communities that allows us to talk to one another, but with no hope or fear of ever being able to stop.

In other words interpretive communities are no more stable than texts because interpretive strategies are not natural or universal, but *learned.* This does not mean that there is a point at which an individual has not yet learned any. The ability to interpret is not acquired; it is constitutive of being human. What is acquired are the ways of interpreting and those same ways can also be forgotten or supplanted, or complicated or dropped from favor ("no one reads that way anymore"). When any of these things happens, there is a corresponding change in texts, not because they are being read differently, but because they are being written differently.

The only stability, then, inheres in the fact (at least in my model) that interpretive strategies are always being deployed, and this means that communication is a much more chancy affair than we are accustomed to think it. For if there are no fixed texts, but only interpretive strategies making them; and if interpretive strategies are

not natural, but learned (and are therefore unavailable to a finite description), what is it that
utterers (speakers, authors, critics, me, you) do?
In the old model utterers are in the business of
handing over ready made or prefabricated
meanings. These meanings are said to be encoded, and the code is assumed to be in the
world independently of the individuals who are
obliged to attach themselves to it (if they do not
they run the danger of being declared deviant).
In my model, however, meanings are not extracted but made and made not by encoded
forms but by interpretive strategies that call
forms into being. It follows then that what utterers do is give hearers and readers the opportunity to make meanings (and texts) by inviting
them to put into execution a set of strategies. It
is presumed that the invitation will be recognized, and that presumption rests on a projection on the part of a speaker or author of the
moves *he* would make if confronted by the
sounds or marks he is uttering or setting down.

It would seem at first that this account of
things simply reintroduces the old objection; for
isn't this an admission that there is after all a formal encoding, not perhaps of meanings, but of
the directions for making them, for executing interpretive strategies? The answer is that they will
only *be* directions to those who already have the
interpretive strategies in the first place. Rather
than producing interpretive acts, they are the
product of one. An author hazards his projection, not because of something "in" the marks,
but because of something he assumes to be in his
reader. The very existence of the "marks" is a
function of an interpretive community, for they
will be recognized (that is, made) only by its
members. Those outside that community will be
deploying a different set of interpretive strategies
(interpretation cannot be withheld) and will
therefore be making different marks.

So once again I have made the text disappear,
but unfortunately the problems do not disappear with it. If everyone is continually executing
interpretive strategies and in that act constitut-

ing texts, intentions, speakers, and authors, how
can any one of us know whether or not he is a
member of the same interpretive community as
any other of us? The answer is that he can't,
since any evidence brought forward to support
the claim would itself be an interpretation (especially if the "other" were an author long dead).
The only "proof" of membership is fellowship,
the nod of recognition from someone in the
same community, someone who says to you
what neither of us could ever prove to a third
party: "we know." I say it to you now, knowing
full well that you will agree with me (that is, understand) only if you already agree with me.

NOTES

1. All references are to *The Poems of John Milton,* ed. John
Carey and Alastair Fowler (London, 1968).

2. *A Variorum Commentary on the Poems of John Milton,*
vol. 2, pt. 2. ed. A. S. P. Woodhouse and Douglas Bush
(New York, 1972), p. 475.

3. It is first of all a reference to the city of iniquity from
which the Hebrews are urged to flee in Isaiah and Jere-
miah. In Protestant polemics Babylon is identified with the
Roman Church whose destruction is prophesied in the
book of Revelation. And in some Puritan tracts, Babylon is
the name for Augustine's earthly city, from which the
faithful are to flee inwardly in order to escape the fate
awaiting the unregenerate. See *Variorum Commentary,* pp.
440–41.

4. *Variorum Commentary,* p. 469.

5. Ibid., p. 457.

6. *Poems Upon Several Occasions, English, Italian, And
Latin, With Translations, By John Milton,* ed. Thomas
Warton (London, 1791), p. 352.

7. See my *Surprised by Sin: The Reader in* Paradise Lost
(London and New York, 1967); *Self-consuming Artifacts:
The Experience of Seventeenth-Century Literature* (Berkeley,
1972); "What Is Stylistics and Why Are They Saying Such
Terrible Things About It?" in *Approaches to Poetics,* ed.
Seymour Chatman (New York, 1973), pp. 109–52; "How
Ordinary Is Ordinary Language?" in *New Literary History,*
5 (Autumn 1973): 41–54; "Facts and Fictions: A Reply to
Ralph Rader," *Critical Inquiry,* 1 (June 1975): 883–91.

12

Patrocinio Schweickart
1942–

Patrocinio Schweickart is a leader in the development of new theories of feminist Reader-Response criticism. She has published articles on literary theory and women's literature in *Modern Fiction Studies, Signs,* and the *Canadian Journal of Social and Political Theory.* With Elizabeth A. Flynn she edited *Gender and Reading* (1986), and her essay "Engendering Critical Discourse" is included in *The Currents in Criticism: Essays on the Present and Future of Literary Theory* (1987). Schweickart is an associate professor of English at the University of New Hampshire.

Schweickart's "Reading Ourselves: Toward a Feminist Theory of Reading" won the 1984 Florence Howe Award for Outstanding Feminist Scholarship. In this essay, Schweickart calls for a change in the "utopian" nature of standard forms of Reader-Response criticism (both the text-oriented and reader-oriented varieties) to include considerations of gender. She asserts that it is possible to locate the "difference" in women's writing: then it must be possible to locate the "difference" in women's reading. Feminist critics and Reader-Response theorists must develop "reading strategies consonant with the concerns, experiences, and formal devices" that inform women's reading. Women, especially women in the academy, have been "immasculated" by their training; they have been taught to read as men, thereby denying meaning that a text may have for them as women. Rather than accepting a traditional interpretation, women must learn to read a text as it was "not meant to be read," to read it "against itself." In doing so, Schweickart hopes, women readers may be able to reverse the process of immasculation. Such a reversal may lead not only to a reevaluation of texts by male writers but to a reevaluation of women writers whose works have been devalued by years of misreading.

Reading Ourselves: Toward a Feminist Theory of Reading

THREE STORIES OF READING

A. Wayne Booth begins his Presidential Address to the 1982 MLA Convention by considering and rejecting several plausible myths that might enable us "to dramatize not just our inescapable plurality but the validity of our sense that [as teachers and scholars of literature and composition] we belong together, somehow working on common ground." At last he settles on one story that is "perhaps close enough to our shared experience to justify the telling."[1]

Once upon a time there was a boy who fell in love with books. When he was very young he heard over and over the legend of his great-grandfather, a hard-working weaver who so desired knowledge that he figured out a way of working the loom with one hand, his legs, and his feet, leaving the other hand free to hold a book, and worked so steadily in that crooked position that he became permanently crippled. The boy heard other stories about the importance of reading. Salvation, he came to believe, was to be found in books. When he was six years old, he read *The Wizard of Oz*—his first *real* book—and was rewarded by his Great-Aunt Manda with a dollar.

When the boy grew up, he decided to become a teacher of "litcomp." His initiation into the profession was rigorous, and there were moments when he nearly gave up. But gradually, "there emerged from the trudging a new and surprising love, a love that with all my previous reading I had not dreamed of: the love of skill, of craft, of getting clear in my mind and then in my writing what a great writer had got right in his work" (Booth, p. 315). Eventually, the boy, now grown, got his doctorate, and after teaching for thirteen years in small colleges, he returned to his graduate institution to become one of its eminent professors.

Booth caps his narration by quoting from *The Autobiography of Malcolm X*. It was in prison that Malcolm learned to read:

For the first time I could pick up a book and now begin to understand what the book was saying. Anyone who has read a great deal can imagine the new world that opened. Let me tell you something: from then until I left that prison, in every free moment I had, if I was not reading in the library, I was reading on my bunk. . . . [M]onths passed without my even thinking about being imprisoned. In fact, up to then, I never had been so truly free in my life. (As quoted by Booth, p. 317)

"Perhaps," says Booth, "when you think back now on my family's story about great-grandfather Booth, you will understand why reading about Malcolm X's awakening speaks to the question of where I got my 'insane love' [for books]" (p. 317)

B. When I read the Malcolm X passage quoted in Booth's address, the ellipsis roused my curiosity. What, exactly, I wondered, had been deleted? What in the original exceeded the requirements of a Presidential Address to the MLA? Checking, I found the complete sentence to read: "Between Mr. Muhammad's teachings, my correspondence, my visitors—usually Ella and Reginald—and my reading, months passed without my even thinking about being imprisoned."[2] Clearly, the first phrase is the dissonant one. The reference to the leader of the notorious Black Muslims suggests a story of reading very different from Booth's. Here is how Malcolm X tells it. While serving time in the Norfolk Prison Colony, he hit on the idea of teaching himself to read by copying the dictionary.

In my slow, painstaking, ragged handwriting, I copied into my tablet everything on that first page, down to the punctuation marks. . . . Then, aloud, to myself, I read back everything I'd written on the table. . . . I woke up the next morning thinking about these words—immensely proud to realize that not only had I written so much at one time, but I'd written words that I never knew were in the world. . . . That was the way I started copying what eventually became the entire dictionary. (p. 172)

After copying the dictionary, Malcolm X began reading the books in the prison library. "No university would ask any student to devour literature as I did when this new world opened to me, of being able to read and *understand*" (p. 173). Reading had changed the course of his life. Years later, he would reflect on how "the ability to read awoke inside me some long dormant craving to be mentally alive" (p. 179).

What did he read? What did he understand? He read Gregor Mendel's *Findings in Genetics* and it helped him to understand "that if you started with a black man, a white man could be produced; but starting with a white man, you never could produce a black man—because the white chromosome is recessive. And since no one disputes that there was but one Original Man, the conclusion is clear" (p. 175). He read histories, books by Will Durant and Arnold Toynbee, by W. E. B. du Bois and Carter G. Woodson, and he saw how "the glorious history of the black man" had been "bleached" out of the history books written by white men.

> [His] eyes opened gradually, then wider and wider, to how the world's white men had indeed acted like devils, pillaging and raping and bleeding and draining the whole world's non-white people. . . . I will never forget how shocked I was when I began reading about slavery's total horror. . . . The world's most monstrous crime, the sin and the blood on the white man's hands, are almost impossible to believe. (p. 175)

He read philosophy—the works of Schopenhauer, Kant, Nietzsche, and Spinoza—and he concluded that the "whole stream of Western Philosophy was now wound up in a cul-de-sac" as a result of the white man's "elaborate, neurotic necessity to hide the black man's true role in history" (p. 180). Malcolm X read voraciously, and book after book confirmed the truth of Elijah Muhammad's teachings. "It's a crime, the lie that has been told to generations of black men and white both. . . . Innocent black children growing up, living out their lives, dying of old age—and all of their lives ashamed of being black. But the truth is pouring out of the bag now" (p. 181).

Wayne Booth's story leads to the Crystal Ballroom of the Biltmore Hotel in Los Angeles, where we attend the protagonist as he delivers his Presidential Address to the members of the Modern Language Association. Malcolm X's love of books took him in a different direction, to the stage of the Audubon Ballroom in Harlem, where, as he was about to address a mass meeting of the Organization of Afro-American Unity, he was murdered.

C. As we have seen, an ellipsis links Wayne Booth's story of reading to Malcolm X's. Another ellipsis, this time not graphically marked, signals the existence of a third story. Malcolm X's startling reading of Mendel's genetics overlooks the most rudimentary fact of human reproduction: whether you start with a black man or a white man, without a woman, you get *nothing*. An excerpt from Virginia Woolf's *A Room of One's Own* restores this deleted perspective.[3]

The heroine, call her Mary, says Woolf, goes to the British Museum in search of information about women. There she discovers to her chagrin that woman is, "perhaps, the most discussed animal in the universe?"

> Why does Samuel Butler say, "Wise men never say what they think of women?" Wise men never say anything else apparently. . . . Are they capable of education? Napoleon thought them incapable. Dr. Johnson thought the opposite. Have they souls or have they not souls? Some savages say they have none. Others, on the contrary, say women are half divine and worship them on that account. Some sages hold that they are shallower in the brain; others that they are deeper in consciousness. Goethe honoured them; Mussolini despises them. Wherever one looked men thought about women and thought differently. (pp. 29–30)

Distressed and confused, Mary notices that she has unconsciously drawn a picture in her notebook, the face and figure of Professor von X. engaged in writing his monumental work,

The Mental, Moral, and Physical Inferiority of the Female Sex. "His expression suggested that he was labouring under some emotion that made him jab his pen on the paper as if he were killing some noxious insect as he wrote, but even when he had killed it that did not satisfy him; he must go on killing it. . . . A very elementary exercise in psychology . . . showed me . . . that the sketch had been made in anger" (pp. 31–32).

Nothing remarkable in that, she reflects, given the provocation. But "How explain the anger of the professor? . . . For when it came to analysing the impression left by these books, . . . there was [an] element which was often present and could not be immediately identified. Anger, I called it. . . . To judge from its effects, it was anger disguised and complex, not anger simple and open" (p. 32).

Disappointed with essayists and professors, Mary turns to historians. But apparently women played no significant role in history. What little information Mary finds is disturbing: "Wife-beating, I read, was a recognized right of a man, and was practiced without shame by high as well as low" (p. 44). Oddly enough, literature presents a contradictory picture.

If women had not existence save in fiction written by men, we would imagine her to be a person of utmost importance; very various; heroic and mean; splendid and sordid; infinitely beautiful and hideous in the extreme; as great as a man, some think even greater. But this is women in fiction. In fact, as Professor Trevelyan points out, she was locked up, beaten and flung about the room. (p. 45)

At last, Mary can draw but one conclusion from her reading. Male professors, male historians, and male poets cannot be relied on for the truth about women. Woman herself must undertake the study of woman. Of course, to do so, she must secure enough money to live on and a room of her own.

Booth's story, we recall, is told within the framework of a professional ritual. It is intended to remind us of "the loves and fears that inform our daily work" and of "what we do when we are at our best," to show, if not a unity, then enough of a "center" "to shame us whenever we violate it." The principal motif of the myth is the hero's insane love for books, and the way this develops with education and maturity into "critical understanding," which Booth defines as that synthesis of thought and passion which should replace, "on the one hand, sentimental and uncritical identifications that leave minds undisturbed, and on the other, hypercritical negations that freeze or alienate" (pp. 317–18). Booth is confident that the experience celebrated by the myth is archetypal. "Whatever our terms for it, whatever our theories about how it happens or why it fails to happen more often, can we reasonably doubt the importance of the moment, at any level of study, when any of us—you, me, Malcolm X, my great-grandfather—succeeds in entering other minds, or 'taking them in,' as nourishment for our own?" (p. 318).

Now, while it is certainly true that something one might call "critical understanding" informs the stories told by Malcolm X and Virginia Woolf, these authors fill this term with thoughts and passions that one would never suspect from Booth's definition. From the standpoint of the second and third stories of reading, Booth's story is utopian. The powers and resources of his hero are equal to the challenges he encounters. At each stage he finds suitable mentors. He is assured by the people around him, by the books he reads, by the entire culture, that he is right for the part. His talents and accomplishments are acknowledged and justly rewarded. In short, from the perspective of Malcolm X's and Woolf's stories, Booth's hero is fantastically privileged.

Utopian has a second meaning, one that is by no means pejorative, and Booth's story is utopian in this sense as well. In overlooking the realities highlighted by the stories of Malcolm X

- differs in idea of control

and Virginia Woolf, Booth's story anticipates what might be possible, what "critical understanding" might mean for *everyone,* if only we could overcome the pervasive systemic injustices of our time.

READER-RESPONSE THEORY AND FEMINIST CRITICISM

Reader-response criticism, as currently constituted, is utopian in the same two senses. The different accounts of the reading experience that have been put forth overlook the issues of race, class, and sex, and give no hint of the conflicts, sufferings, and passions that attend these realities. The relative tranquility of the tone of these theories testifies to the privileged position of the theorists. Perhaps, someday, when privileges have withered away or at least become more equitably distributed, some of these theories will ring true. Surely we ought to be able to talk about reading without worrying about injustice. But for now, reader-response criticism must confront the disturbing implications of our historical reality. Paradoxically, utopian theories that elide these realities betray the utopian impulses that inform them.

To put the matter plainly, reader-response criticism needs feminist criticism. The two have yet to engage each other in a sustained and serious way, but if the promise of the former is to be fulfilled, such an encounter must soon occur. Interestingly, the obvious question of the significance of gender has already been explicitly raised, and—this testifies to the increasing impact of feminist criticism as well as to the direct ideological bearing of the issue of gender on reader-response criticism—not by a feminist critic, but by Jonathan Culler, a leading theorist of reading: "If the experience of literature depends upon the qualities of a reading self, one can ask what difference it would make to the experience of literature and thus to the meaning of

literature if this self were, for example, female rather than male. If the meaning of a work is the experience of a reader, what difference does it make if the reader is a woman?"[4]

Until very recently this question has not occurred to reader-response critics. They have been preoccupied with other issues. Culler's survey of the field is instructive here, for it enables us to anticipate the direction reader-response theory might take when it is shaken from its slumber by feminist criticism. According to Culler, the different models (or "stories") of reading that have been proposed are all organized around three problems. The first is the issue of control: Does the text control the reader, or vice versa? For David Bleich, Norman Holland, and Stanley Fish, the reader holds controlling interest. Readers read the poems they have made. Bleich asserts this point most strongly: the constraints imposed by the words on the page are "trivial," since their meaning can always be altered by "subjective action." To claim that the text supports this or that reading is only to "moralistically claim . . . that one's own objectification is more authoritative than someone else's."[5]

At the other pole are Michael Riffaterre, Georges Poulet, and Wolfgang Iser, who acknowledge the creative role of the reader, but ultimately take the text to be the dominant force. To read, from this point of view, is to create the text according to *its* own promptings. As Poulet puts it, a text, when invested with a reader's subjectivity, becomes a "subjectified object," a "second self" that depends on the reader, but is not, strictly speaking, identical with him. Thus, reading "is a way of giving way not only to a host of alien words, images and ideas, but also to the very alien principle which utters and shelters them. . . . I am on loan to another, and this other thinks, feels, suffers and acts within me."[6] Culler argues persuasively that, regardless of their ostensible theoretical commitments, the prevailing stories of reading generally vacillate

Fish, Iser

between these reader-dominant and text-dominant poles. In fact, those who stress the subjectivity of the reader as against the objectivity of the text ultimately portray the text as determining the responses of the reader. "The more active, projective, or creative the reader is, the more she is manipulated by the sentence or by the author" (p. 71).

The second question prominent in theories of reading is closely related to the first. Reading always involves a subject and an object, a reader and a text. But what constitutes the objectivity of the text? What is "in" the text? What is supplied by the reader? Again, the answers have been equivocal. On the face of it, the situation seems to call for a dualistic theory that credits the contributions of both text and reader. However, Culler argues, a dualistic theory eventually gives way to a monistic theory, in which one or the other pole supplies everything. One might say, for instance, that Iser's theory ultimately implies the determinacy of the text and the authority of the author: "The author guarantees the unity of the work, requires the reader's creative participation, and through his text, prestructures the shape of the aesthetic object to be produced by the reader."[7] At the same time, one can also argue that the "gaps" that structure the reader's response are not built into the text, but appear (or not) as a result of the particular interpretive strategy employed by the reader. Thus, "there is no distinction between what the text gives and what the reader supplies; he supplies *everything*."[8] Depending on which aspects of the theory one takes seriously, Iser's theory collapses either into a monism of the text or a monism of the reader.

The third problem identified by Culler concerns the ending of the story. Most of the time stories of reading end happily. "Readers may be manipulated and misled, but when they finish the book their experience turns into knowledge . . . as though finishing the book took them outside the experience of reading and gave them mastery of it" (p. 79). However, some critics—

Harold Bloom, Paul de Man, and Culler himself—find these optimistic endings questionable, and prefer instead stories that stress the impossibility of reading. If, as de Man says, rhetoric puts "an insurmountable obstacle in the way of any reading or understanding," then the reader "may be placed in impossible situations where there is no happy issue, but only the possibility of playing out the roles dramatized in the text" (Culler, p. 81).

Such have been the predominant preoccupations of reader-response criticism during the past decade and a half. Before indicating how feminist critics could affect the conversation, let me consider an objection. A recent and influential essay by Elaine Showalter suggests that we should not enter the conversation at all. She observes that during its early phases, the principal mode of feminist criticism was "feminist critique," which was counter-ideological in intent and concerned with the feminist as *reader*. Happily, we have outgrown this necessary but theoretically unpromising approach. Today, the dominant mode of feminist criticism is "gynocritics," the study of woman as *writer*, of the "history, styles, themes, genres, and structures of writing by women; the psychodynamics of female creativity; the trajectory of the individual or collective female career; and the evolution and laws of a female literary tradition." The shift from "feminist critique" to "gynocritics"—from emphasis on woman as reader to emphasis on woman as writer—has put us in the position of developing a feminist criticism that is "genuinely woman-centered, independent, and intellectually coherent."

> To see women's writing as our primary subject forces us to make the leap to a new conceptual vantage point and to redefine the nature of the theoretical problem before us. It is no longer the ideological dilemma of reconciling revisionary pluralisms but the essential question of difference. How can we constitute women as a distinct literary group? What is the *difference* of women's writing?[9]

But why should the activity of the woman writer be more conducive to theory than the activity of the woman reader is? If it is possible to formulate a basic conceptual framework for disclosing the "difference" of women's writing, surely it is no less possible to do so for women's reading. The same difference, be it linguistic, biological, psychological, or cultural, should apply in either case. In addition, what Showalter calls "gynocritics" is in fact constituted by feminist *criticism*—that is, *readings*—of female texts. Thus, the relevant distinction is not between woman as reader and woman as writer, but between feminist readings of male texts and feminist readings of female texts, and there is no reason why the former could not be as theoretically coherent (or irreducibly pluralistic) as the latter.

On the other hand, there are good reasons for feminist criticism to engage reader-response criticism. Both dispute the fetishized art object, the "Verbal Icon," of New Criticism, and both seek to dispel the objectivist illusion that buttresses the authority of the dominant critical tradition. Feminist criticism can have considerable impact on reader-response criticism, since, as Culler has noticed, it is but a small step from the thesis that the reader is an active producer of meaning to the recognition that there are many different kinds of readers, and that women—because of their numbers if because of nothing else—constitute an essential class. Reader-response critics cannot take refuge in the objectivity of the text, or even in the idea that a gender-neutral criticism is possible. Today they can continue to ignore the implications of feminist criticism only at the cost of incoherence or intellectual dishonesty.

It is equally true that feminist critics need to question their allegiance to text- and author-centered paradigms of criticism. Feminist criticism, we should remember, is a mode of *praxis*. The point is not merely to interpret literature in various ways; the point is to *change the world*. We cannot afford to ignore the activity of read-

ing, for it is here that literature is realized as *praxis*. Literature acts on the world by acting on its readers.

To return to our earlier question: What will happen to reader-response criticism if feminists enter the conversation? It is useful to recall the contrast between Booth's story and those of Malcolm X and Virginia Woolf. Like Booth's story, the "stories of reading" that currently make up reader-response theory are mythically abstract, and appear, from a different vantage point, to be by and about readers who are fantastically privileged. Booth's story had a happy ending; Malcolm's and Mary's did not. For Mary, reading meant encountering a tissue of lies and silences; for Malcolm it meant the verification of Elijah Muhammad's shocking doctrines.

Two factors—gender and politics—which are suppressed in the dominant models of reading gain prominence with the advent of a feminist perspective. The feminist story will have *at least* two chapters: one concerned with feminist readings of male texts, and another with feminist readings of female texts. In addition, in this story, gender will have a prominent role as the locus of political struggle. The story will speak of the difference between men and women, of the way the experience and perspective of women have been systematically and fallaciously assimilated into the generic masculine, and of the need to correct this error. Finally, it will identify literature—the activities of reading and writing—as an important arena of political struggle, a crucial component of the project of interpreting the world in order to change it.

Feminist criticism does not approach reader-response criticism without preconceptions. Actually, feminist criticism has always included substantial reader-centered interests. In the next two sections of this paper, I will review these interests, first with respect to male texts, then with respect to female texts. In the process, I will uncover some of the issues that might be addressed and clarified by a feminist theory of reading.

THE FEMALE READER AND THE LITERARY CANON

Although reader-response critics propose different and often conflicting models, by and large the emphasis is on features of the process of reading that do not vary with the nature of the reading material. The feminist entry into the conversation brings the nature of the text back into the foreground. For feminists, the question of *how* we read is inextricably linked with the question of *what* we read. More specifically, the feminist inquiry into the activity of reading begins with the realization that the literary canon is androcentric, and that this has a profoundly damaging effect on women readers. The documentation of this realization was one of the earliest tasks undertaken by feminist critics. Elaine Showalter's 1971 critique of the literary curriculum is exemplary of this work.

> [In her freshman year a female student] . . . might be assigned an anthology of essays, perhaps such as *The Responsible Man,* . . . or *Conditions of Man,* or *Man in Crisis,* or again, *Representative Man: Cult Heroes of Our Time,* in which thirty-three men represent such categories of heroism as the writer, the poet, the dramatist, the artist, and the guru, and the only two women included are the actress Elizabeth Taylor, and the existential heroine Jacqueline Onassis.
>
> Perhaps the student would read a collection of stories like *The Young Man in American Literature: The Initiation Theme,* or sociological literature like *The Black Man and the Promise of America.* In a more orthodox literary program she might study eternally relevant classics, such as *Oedipus;* as a professor remarked in a recent issue of *College English,* all of us want to kill our fathers and marry our mothers. And whatever else she might read, she would inevitably arrive at the favorite book of all Freshman English courses, the classic of adolescent rebellion, *The Portrait of the Artist as a Young Man.*

> By the end of her freshman year, a woman student would have learned something about intellectual neutrality; she would be learning, in fact, how to think like a man. And so she would go on, increasingly with male professors to guide her.[10]

The more personal accounts of other critics reinforce Showalter's critique.

> The first result of my reading was a feeling that male characters were at the very least more interesting than women to the authors who invented them. Thus if, reading their books as it seemed their authors intended them, I naively identified with a character, I repeatedly chose men; I would rather have been Hamlet than Ophelia, Tom Jones instead of Sophia Western, and, perhaps, despite Dostoevsky's intention, Raskolnikov not Sonia.
>
> More peculiar perhaps, but sadly unsurprising, were the assessments I accepted about fictional women. For example, I quickly learned that power was unfeminine and powerful women were, quite literally, monstrous. . . . Bitches all, they must be eliminated, reformed, or at the very least, condemned. . . . Those rare women who are shown in fiction as both powerful and, in some sense, admirable are such because their power is based, if not on beauty, then at least on sexuality.[11]

For a woman, then, books do not necessarily spell salvation. In fact, a literary education may very well cause her grave psychic damage: schizophrenia "is the bizarre but logical conclusion of our education. Imagining myself male, I attempted to create myself male. Although I knew the case was otherwise, it seemed I could do nothing to make this other critically real."[12]

To put the matter theoretically, androcentric literature structures the reading experience differently depending on the gender of the reader. For the male reader, the text serves as the meeting ground of the personal and the universal. Whether or not the text approximates the particularities of his own experience, he is invited to validate the equation of maleness with humanity. The male reader feels his affinity with the universal, with the paradigmatic human being, precisely because he is male. Consider the famous scene of Stephen's epiphany in *The Portrait of the Artist as a Young Man.*

A girl stood before him in midstream, alone and still, gazing out to sea. She seemed like one whom magic had changed into the likeness of a strange and beautiful seabird. Her long slender bare legs were delicate as a crane's and pure save where an emerald trail of seaweed had fashioned itself as a sign upon the flesh. Her thighs, fuller and softhued as ivory, were bared almost to the hips, where the white fringes of her drawers were like feathering of soft white down. Her slateblue skirts were kilted boldly about her waist and dovetailed behind her. Her bosom was a bird's, soft and slight, slight and soft, as the breast of some dark plummaged dove. But her long fair hair was girlish: and touched with the wonder of mortal beauty, her face.[13]

A man reading this passage is invited to identify with Stephen, to feel "the riot in his blood," and, thus, to ratify the alleged universality of the experience. Whether or not the sight of a girl on the beach has ever provoked similar emotions in him, the male reader is invited to feel his *difference* (concretely, *from the girl*) and to equate that with the universal. Relevant here is Lévi-Strauss's theory that woman functions as currency exchanged between men. The woman in the text converts the text into a woman, and the circulation of this text/woman becomes the central ritual that establishes the bond between the author and his male readers.[14]

The same text affects a woman reader differently. Judith Fetterley gives the most explicit theory to date about the dynamics of the woman reader's encounter with androcentric literature. According to Fetterley, notwithstanding the prevalence of the castrating bitch stereotype, "the cultural reality is not the emasculation of men by women, but the *immasculation* of women by men. As readers and teachers and scholars, women are taught to think as men, to identify with a male point of view, and to accept as normal and legitimate a male system of values, one of whose central principles is misogyny."[15]

The process of immasculation does not impart virile power to the woman reader. On the contrary, it doubles her oppression. She suffers "not simply the powerlessness which derives from not seeing one's experience articulated, clarified, and legitimized in art, but more significantly, the powerlessness which results from the endless division of self against self, the consequence of the invocation to identify as male while being reminded that to be male—to be universal— . . . is to be *not female*."[16]

A woman reading Joyce's novel of artistic awakening, and in particular the passage quoted above, will, like her male counterpart, be invited to identify with Stephen and therefore to ratify the equation of maleness with the universal. Androcentric literature is all the more efficient as an instrument of sexual politics because it does not allow the woman reader to seek refuge in her difference. Instead, it draws her into a process that uses her against herself. It solicits her complicity in the elevation of male difference into universality and, accordingly, the denigration of female difference into otherness without reciprocity. To be sure, misogyny is abundant in the literary canon.[17] It is important, however, that Fetterley's argument can stand on a weaker premise. Androcentricity is a sufficient condition for the process of immasculation.

Feminist critics of male texts, from Kate Millett to Judith Fetterley, have worked under the sign of the "Resisting Reader." Their goal is to disrupt the process of immasculation by exposing it to consciousness, by disclosing the androcentricity of what has customarily passed for the universal. However, feminist criticism written under the aegis of the resisting reader leaves certain questions unanswered, questions that are becoming ripe for feminist analysis: Where does the text get its power to draw us into its designs? Why do some (not all) demonstrably sexist texts remain appealing even after they have been subjected to thorough feminist critique? The usual answer—that the power of male texts is the power of the false consciousness into which women as well as men have been socialized—oversimplifies the problem and prevents us from comprehending both the force of literature and the complexity of our responses to it.

Fredric Jameson advances a thesis that seems to me to be a good starting point for the feminist reconsideration of male texts: "The effectively ideological is also at the same time necessarily utopian."[18] This thesis implies that the male text draws its power over the female reader from authentic desires, which it rouses and then harnesses to the process of immasculation.

A concrete example is in order. Consider Lawrence's *Women in Love,* and for the sake of simplicity, concentrate on Birkin and Ursula. Simone de Beauvoir and Kate Millet have convinced me that this novel is sexist. Why does it remain appealing to me? Jameson's thesis prompts me to answer this question by examining how the text plays not only on my false consciousness but also on my authentic liberatory aspirations—that is to say, on the very impulses that drew me to the feminist movement.

The trick of role reversal comes in handy here. If we reverse the roles of Birkin and Ursula, the ideological components (or at least the most egregious of these, e.g., the analogy between women and horses) stand out as absurdities. Now, if we delete these absurd components while keeping the roles reversed, we have left the story of a woman struggling to combine her passionate desire for autonomous conscious being with an equally passionate desire for love and for other human bonds. This residual story is not far from one we would welcome as expressive of a feminist sensibility. Interestingly enough, it

also intimates a novel Lawrence might have written, namely, the proper sequel to *The Rainbow.*

My affective response to the novel Lawrence did write is bifurcated. On the one hand, because I am a woman, I am implicated in the representation of Ursula and in the destiny Lawrence has prepared for her: man is the son of god, but woman is the daughter of man. Her vocation is to witness his transcendence in rapt silence. On the other hand, Fetterley is correct that I am also induced to identify with Birkin, and in so doing, I am drawn into complicity with the reduction of Ursula, and therefore of myself, to the role of the other.

However, the process of immasculation is more complicated than Fetterley allows. When I identify with Birkin, I unconsciously perform the two-stage rereading described above. I reverse the roles of Birkin and Ursula and I suppress the obviously ideological components that in the process show up as absurdities. The identification with Birkin is emotionally effective because, stripped of its patriarchal trappings, Birkin's struggle and his utopian vision conform to my own. To the extent that I perform this feminist rereading *unconsciously,* I am captivated by the text. The stronger my desire for autonomous selfhood and for love, the stronger my identification with Birkin, and the more intense the experience of bifurcation characteristic of the process of immasculation.

The full argument is beyond the scope of this essay. My point is that *certain* (not all) male texts merit a dual hermeneutic: a negative hermeneutic that discloses their complicity with patriarchal ideology, and a positive hermeneutic that recuperates the utopian moment—the authentic kernel—from which they draw a significant portion of their emotional power.[19]

READING WOMEN'S WRITING

Showalter is correct that feminist criticism has shifted emphasis in recent years from "critique" (primarily) of male texts to "gynocritics," or the study of women's writing. Of course, it is worth remembering that the latter has always been on the feminist agenda. *Sexual Politics,* for example, contains not only the critique of Lawrence, Miller, and Mailer that won Millett such notoriety, but also her memorable rereading of *Villette.*[20] It is equally true that interest in women's writing has not entirely supplanted the critical study of patriarchal texts. In a sense "critique" has provided the bridge from the study of male texts to the study of female texts. As feminist criticism shifted from the first to the second, "feminist critique" turned its attention from androcentric texts per se to the androcentric critical strategies that pushed women's writing to the margins of the literary canon. The earliest examples of this genre (for instance, Showalter's "The Double Critical Standard," and Carol Ohmann's "Emily Brontë in the Hands of Male Critics") were concerned primarily with describing and documenting the prejudice against women writers that clouded the judgment of well-placed readers, that is, reviewers and critics.[21] Today we have more sophisticated and more comprehensive analyses of the androcentric critical tradition.

One of the most cogent of these is Nina Baym's analysis of American literature.[22] Baym observes that, as late as 1977, the American canon of major writers did not include a single woman novelist. And yet, in terms of numbers and commercial success, women novelists have probably dominated American literature since the middle of the nineteenth century. How to explain this anomaly?

One explanation is simple bias of the sort documented by Showalter, Ohmann, and others. A second is that women writers lived and worked under social conditions that were not particularly conducive to the production of "excellent" literature: "There tended to be a sort of immediacy in the ambitions of literary women leading them to professionalism rather than artistry, by choice as well as by social pressure

and opportunity."[23] Baym adduces a third, more subtle, and perhaps more important reason. There are, she argues, "gender-related restrictions that do not arise out of the cultural realities contemporary with the writing woman, but out of later critical theories . . . which impose their concerns anachronistically, after the fact, on an earlier period."[24] If one reads the critics most instrumental in forming the current theories about American literature (Matthiessen, Chase, Feidelson, Trilling, etc.), one finds that the theoretical model for the canonical American novel is the "melodrama of beset manhood." To accept this model is also to accept as a consequence the exclusion from the canon of "melodramas of beset womanhood," as well as virtually all fiction centering on the experience of women.[25]

The deep symbiotic relationship between the androcentric canon and androcentric modes of reading is well summarized by Kolodny.

> *Insofar as we are taught to read, what we engage are not texts, but paradigms . . . .* Insofar as literature is itself a social institution, so, too, reading is a highly socialized—or learned— activity. . . . We read well, and with pleasure, what we already know how to read; and what we know how to read is to a large extent dependent on what we have already read [works from which we have developed our expectations and learned our interpretive strategies]. What we then choose to read—and, by extension, teach and thereby "canonize"—usually follows upon our previous reading.[26]

We are caught, in other words, in a rather vicious circle. An androcentric canon generates androcentric interpretive strategies, which in turn favor the canonization of androcentric texts and the marginalization of gynocentric ones. To break this circle, feminist critics must fight on two fronts: for the revision of the canon to include a significant body of works by women, and for the development of the reading strategies consonant with the concerns, experiences, and formal devices that constitute these texts. Of course, to succeed, we also need a community of women readers who are qualified by experience, commitment, and training, and who will enlist the personal and institutional resources at their disposal in the struggle.[27]

The critique of androcentric reading strategies is essential, for it opens up some ideological space for the recuperation of women's writing. Turning now to this project, we observe, first, that a large volume of work has been done, and, second, that this endeavor is coming to look even more complicated and more diverse than the criticism of male texts. Certainly, it is impossible in the space of a few pages to do justice to the wide range of concerns, strategies, and positions associated with feminist readings of female texts. Nevertheless, certain things can be said. For the remainder of this section, I focus on an exemplary essay: "Vesuvius at Home: The Power of Emily Dickinson," by Adrienne Rich.[28] My commentary anticipates the articulation of a paradigm that illuminates certain features of feminist readings of women's writing.

I am principally interested in the rhetoric of Rich's essay, for it represents an implicit commentary on the process of reading women's writing. Feminist readings of male texts are, as we have seen, primarily resisting. The reader assumes an adversarial or at least a detached attitude toward the material at hand. In the opening pages of her essay, Rich introduces three metaphors that proclaim a very different attitude toward her subject.

> The methods, the exclusions, of Emily Dickinson's existence could not have been my own; yet more and more, as a woman poet finding my own methods, I have come to understand her necessities, could have served as witness in her defense. (p. 158)

> I am traveling at the speed of time, along the Massachusetts Turnpike. . . . "Home is not where the heart is," she wrote in a letter, "but the house and adjacent buildings." . . . I am traveling at the speed of time, in the direction of the house and buildings. . . . For years, I have been not so much envisioning Emily Dickinson as trying to visit, to enter her mind through her poems and letters, and through my own intimations of what it could have meant to be one of the two mid-nineteenth century American geniuses, and a woman, living in Amherst, Massachusetts. (pp. 158–59)

> For months, for most of my life, I have been hovering like an insect against the screens of an existence which inhabited Amherst, Massachusetts between 1830 and 1886. (p. 158) . . . Here [in Dickinson's bedroom] I become again, an insect, vibrating at the frames of windows, clinging to the panes of glass, trying to connect. (p. 161)

A commentary on the process of reading is carried on silently and unobtrusively through the use of these metaphors. The first is a judicial metaphor: the feminist reader speaks as a witness in defense of the woman writer. Here we see clearly that gender is crucial. The feminist reader takes the part of the woman writer against patriarchal misreadings that trivialize or distort her work.[29] The second metaphor refers to a principal tenet of feminist criticism: a literary work cannot be understood apart from the social, historical, and cultural context within which it was written. As if to acquiesce to the condition Dickinson had imposed on her friends, Rich travels through space and time to visit the poet on her own *premises*. She goes to Amherst, to the house where Dickinson lived. She rings the bell, she goes in, then upstairs, then into the bedroom that had been "freedom" for the poet. Her destination, ultimately, is Dickinson's mind. But it is not enough to read the poet's poems and letters. To reach her heart and mind, one must take a detour through "the house and adjacent buildings."

Why did Dickinson go into seclusion? Why did she write poems she would not publish?

What mean these poems about queens, volcanoes, deserts, eternity, passion, suicide, wild beasts, rape, power, madness, the daemon, the grave? For Rich, these are related questions. The revisionary re-reading of Dickinson's work is of a piece with the revisionary re-reading of her life. "I have a notion genius knows itself; that Dickinson chose her seclusion, knowing what she needed. . . . She carefully selected her society and controlled the disposal of her time. . . . Given her vocation, she was neither eccentric nor quaint; she was determined to survive, to use her powers, to practice necessary economies" (p. 160).

> To write [the poetry that she needed to write] she had to enter chambers of the self in which
> Ourself, concealed—
> Should startle most—
> and to relinquish control there, to take those risks, she had to create a relationship to the outer world where she could feel in control. (p. 175)

The metaphor of visiting points to another feature of feminist readings of women's writing, namely, the tendency to construe the text not as an object, but as the manifestation of the subjectivity of the absent author—the "voice" of another woman. Rich is not content to revel in the textuality of Dickinson's poems and letters. For her, these are doorways to the "mind" of a "woman of genius." Rich deploys her imagination and her considerable rhetorical skill to evoke "the figure of powerful will" who lives at the heart of the text. To read Dickinson, then, is to try to visit with her, to hear her voice, to make her live *in* oneself, and to feel her impressive "personal dimensions."[30]

At the same time, Rich is keenly aware that visiting with Dickinson is *only* a metaphor for reading her poetry, and an inaccurate one at that. She signals this awareness with the third metaphor. It is no longer possible to visit with Dickinson; one can only enter her mind

through her poems and letters as one can enter her house—through the backdoor out of which her coffin was carried. In reading, one encounters only a text, the trail of an absent author. Upstairs, at last, in the very room where Dickinson exercised her astonishing craft, Rich finds herself again "an insect, vibrating at the frames of windows, clinging to panes of glass, trying to connect." But though "the scent is very powerful," Dickinson herself is absent.

Perhaps the most obvious rhetorical device employed by Rich in this essay, more obvious even than her striking metaphors, is her use of the personal voice. Her approach to Dickinson is self-consciously and unabashedly subjective. She clearly describes her point of view—what she saw as she drove across the Connecticut Valley toward Amherst (ARCO stations, McDonald's, shopping plazas, as well as "light-green spring softening the hills, dogwood and wild fruit trees blossoming in the hollows"), and what she thought about (the history of the valley, "scene of Indian uprisings, religious revivals, spiritual confrontations, the blazing-up of the lunatic fringe of the Puritan coal," and her memories of college weekends in Amherst). Some elements of her perspective—ARCO and McDonald's—would have been alien to Dickinson; others—the sight of dogwood and wild fruit trees in the spring, and most of all, the experience of being a woman poet in a patriarchal culture—would establish their affinity.

Rich's metaphors together with her use of the personal voice indicate some key issues underlying feminist readings of female texts. On the one hand, reading is necessarily subjective. On the other hand, it must not be wholly so. One must respect the autonomy of the text. The reader is a visitor and, as such, must observe the necessary courtesies. She must avoid unwarranted intrusions—she must be careful not to appropriate what belongs to her host, not to impose herself on the other woman. Furthermore, reading is at once an intersubjective encounter and something less than that. In reading Dickinson, Rich seeks to enter her mind, to feel her presence. But the text is a screen, an inanimate object. Its subjectivity is only a projection of the subjectivity of the reader.

Rich suggests the central motivation, the regulative ideal, that shapes the feminist reader's approach to these issues. If feminist readings of male texts are motivated by the need to disrupt the process of immasculation, feminist readings of female texts are motivated by the need "to connect," to recuperate, or to formulate—they come to the same thing—the context, the tradition, that would link women writers to one another, to women readers and critics, and to the larger community of women. Of course, the recuperation of such a context is a necessary basis for the nonrepressive integration of women's point of view and culture into the study of a Humanities that is worthy of its name.[31]

FEMINIST MODELS OF READING: A SUMMARY

As I noted in the second section, mainstream reader-response theory is preoccupied with two closely related questions: (1) Does the text manipulate the reader, or does the reader manipulate the text to produce the meaning that suits her own interests? and (2) What is "in" the text? How can we distinguish what it supplies from what the reader supplies? Both of these questions refer to the subject-object relation that is established between reader and text during the process of reading. A feminist theory of reading also elaborates this relationship, but for feminists, gender—the gender inscribed in the text as well as the gender of the reader—is crucial. Hence, the feminist story has two chapters, one concerned with male texts and the other with female texts.

The focus of the first chapter is the experience of the woman reader. What do male texts *do* to her? The feminist story takes the subject-object relation of reading through three mo-

ments. The phrasing of the basic question signals the first moment. Control is conferred on the text: the woman reader is immasculated by the text. The feminist story fits well at this point in Iser's framework. Feminists insist that the androcentricity of the text and its damaging effects on women readers are not figments of their imagination. These are implicit in the "schematized aspects" of the text. The second moment, which is similarly consonant with the plot of Iser's story, involves the recognition of the crucial role played by the subjectivity of the woman reader. Without her, the text is *nothing*. The process of immasculation is latent in the text, but it finds its actualization only through the reader's activity. In effect, the woman reader is the agent of her own immasculation.[32]

Here we seem to have a corroboration of Culler's contention that dualistic models of reading inevitably disintegrate into one of two monisms. Either the text (and, by implication, the author) or the woman reader is responsible for the process of immasculation. The third moment of the subject-object relation—ushered in by the transfiguration of the heroine into a feminist—breaks through this dilemma. The woman reader, now a feminist, embarks on a critical analysis of the reading process, and she realizes that the text has power to structure her experience. Without androcentric texts she will not suffer immasculation. However, her recognition of the power of the text is matched by her awareness of her essential role in the process of reading. Without her, the text is nothing—it is inert and harmless. The advent of feminist consciousness and the accompanying commitment to emancipatory *praxis* reconstitutes the subject-object relationship within a dialectical rather than a dualistic framework, thus averting the impasse described by Culler between the "dualism of narrative" and the "monism of theory." In the feminist story, the breakdown of Iser's dualism does not indicate a mistake or an irreducible impasse, but the necessity of *choosing* between two modes of reading. The reader can submit to the power of the text, or she can take control of the reading experience. The recognition of the existence of a choice suddenly makes visible the normative dimension of the feminist story: She *should* choose the second alternative.

But what does it mean for a reader to take control of the reading experience? First of all, she must do so without forgetting the androcentricity of the text or its power to structure her experience. In addition, the reader taking control of the text is not, as in Iser's model, simply a matter of selecting among the concretizations allowed by the text. Recall that a crucial feature of the process of immasculation is the woman reader's bifurcated response. She reads the text both as a man and as a woman. But in either case, the result is the same: she confirms her position as other. Taking control of the reading experience means reading the text as it was *not* meant to be read, in fact, reading it against itself. Specifically, one must identify the nature of the choices proffered by the text and, equally important, what the text precludes—namely, the possibility of reading as a woman *without* putting one's self in the position of the other, of reading so as to affirm womanhood as another, equally valid, paradigm of human existence.

All this is easier said than done. It is important to realize that reading a male text, no matter how virulently misogynous, could do little damage if it were an isolated event. The problem is that within patriarchal culture, the experience of immasculation is paradigmatic of women's encounters with the dominant literary and critical traditions. A feminist cannot simply refuse to read patriarchal texts, for they are everywhere, and they condition her participation in the literary and critical enterprise. In fact, by the time she becomes a feminist critic, a woman has already read numerous male texts—in particular, the most authoritative texts of the literary and critical canons. She has introjected not only androcentric texts, but also androcentric reading strategies and values. By the time she becomes a feminist, the bifurcated response

characteristic of immasculation has become second nature to her. The feminist story stresses that patriarchal constructs have objective as well as subjective reality; they are inside and outside the text, inside and outside the reader.

The pervasiveness of androcentricity drives feminist theory beyond the individualistic models of Iser and of most reader-response critics. The feminist reader agrees with Stanley Fish that the production of the meaning of a text is mediated by the interpretive community in which the activity of reading is situated: the meaning of the text depends on the interpretive strategy one applies to it, and the choice of strategy is regulated (explicitly or implicitly) by the canons of acceptability that govern the interpretive community.[33] However, unlike Fish, the feminist reader is also aware that the ruling interpretive communities are androcentric, and that this androcentricity is deeply etched in the strategies and modes of thought that have been introjected by all readers, women as well as men.

Because patriarchal constructs have psychological correlates, taking control of the reading process means taking control of one's reactions and inclinations. Thus, a feminist reading—actually a re-reading—is a kind of therapeutic analysis. The reader recalls and examines how she would "naturally" read a male text in order to understand and therefore undermine the subjective predispositions that had rendered her vulnerable to its designs. Beyond this, the pervasiveness of immasculation necessitates a collective remedy. The feminist reader hopes that other women will recognize themselves in her story, and join her in her struggle to transform the culture.[34]

"Feminism affirms women's point of view by revealing, criticizing and examining its impossibility."[35] Had we nothing but male texts, this sentence from Catherine MacKinnon's brilliant essay on jurisprudence could serve as the definition of the project of the feminist reader. The significant body of literature written by women presents feminist critics with another, more heartwarming, task: that of recovering, articulating, and elaborating positive expressions of women's point of view, of celebrating the survival of this point of view in spite of the formidable forces that have been ranged against it.

The shift to women's writing brings with it a shift in emphasis from the negative hermeneutic of ideological unmasking to a positive hermeneutic whose aim is the recovery and cultivation of women's culture. As Showalter has noted, feminist criticism of women's writing proposes to articulate woman's difference: What does it mean for a woman to express herself in writing? How does a woman write as a woman? It is a central contention of this essay that feminist criticism should also inquire into the correlative process of *reading:* What does it mean for a woman to read without condemning herself to the position of other? What does it mean for a woman, reading as a woman, to read literature written by a woman writing as a woman?[36]

The Adrienne Rich essay discussed in the preceding section illustrates a contrast between feminist readings of male texts and feminist readings of female texts. In the former, the object of the critique, whether it is regarded as an enemy or as symptom of a malignant condition, is the text itself, *not* the reputation or the character of the author.[37] This impersonal approach contrasts sharply with the strong personal interest in Dickinson exhibited by Rich. Furthermore, it is not merely a question of friendliness toward the text. Rich's reading aims beyond "the unfolding of the text as a living event," the goal of aesthetic reading set by Iser. Much of the rhetorical energy of Rich's essay is directed toward evoking the personality of Dickinson, toward making *her* live as the substantial, palpable presence animating her works.

Unlike the first chapter of the feminist story of reading, which is centered around a single heroine—the woman reader battling her way out of a maze of patriarchal constructs—the second chapter features two protagonists—the woman reader and the woman writer—in the context of two settings. The first setting is judicial: one woman is standing witness in defense of the other; the second is dialogic: the two women are engaged in intimate conversation. The judicial setting points to the larger political and cultural dimension of the project of the feminist reader. Feminist critics may well say with Harold Bloom that reading always involves the "art of defensive warfare."[38] What they mean by this, however, would not be Bloom's individualistic, agonistic encounter between "strong poet" and "strong reader," but something more akin to "class struggle." Whether concerned with male or female texts, feminist criticism is situated in the larger struggle against patriarchy.

The importance of this battle cannot be overestimated. However, feminist reading of women's writing opens up space for another, equally important, critical project, namely, the articulation of a model of reading that is centered on a female paradigm. While it is still too early to present a full-blown theory, the dialogic aspect of the relationship between the feminist reader and the woman writer suggests the direction that such a theory might take. As in all stories of reading, the drama revolves around the subject-object relationship between text and reader. The feminist story—exemplified by the Adrienne Rich essay discussed earlier—features an intersubjective construction of this relationship. The reader encounters not simply a text, but a "subjectified object": the "heart and mind" of another woman. She comes into close contact with an interiority—a power, a creativity, a suffering, a vision—that is *not* identical with her own. The feminist interest in construing reading as an intersubjective encounter suggests an affinity with Poulet's (rather than Iser's) theory, and, as in Poulet's model, the subject of the literary work is its author, *not* the reader: "A book is not only a book; it is a means by which an author actually preserves [her] ideas, [her] feelings, [her] modes of dreaming and living. It is a means of saving [her] identity from death. . . .

To understand a literary work, then, is to let the individual who wrote it reveal [herself] to us *in us*."[39]

For all this initial agreement, however, the dialogic relationship the feminist reader establishes with the female subjectivity brought to life in the process of reading is finally at odds with Poulet's model. For the interiorized author is "alien" to Poulet's reader. When he reads, he delivers himself "bound hand and foot, to the omnipotence of fiction." He becomes the "prey" of what he reads. "There is no escaping this takeover." His consciousness is "invaded," "annexed," "usurped." He is "dispossessed" of his rightful place on the "center stage" of his own mind. In the final analysis, the process of reading leaves room for only one subjectivity. The work becomes "a sort of human being" at "the expense of the reader whose life it suspends."[40] It is significant that the metaphors of mastery and submission, of violation and control, so prominent in Poulet's essay, are entirely absent in Rich's essay on Dickinson. In the paradigm of reading implicit in her essay, the dialectic of control (which shapes feminist readings of male texts) gives way to the dialectic of communication. For Rich, reading is a matter of "trying to connect" with the existence behind the text.

This dialectic also has three moments. The first involves the recognition that genuine intersubjective communication demands the duality of reader and author (the subject of the work). Because reading removes the barrier between subject and object, the division takes place *within* the reader. Reading induces a doubling of the reader's subjectivity, so that one can be placed at the disposal of the text while the other remains with the reader. Now, this doubling presents a problem, for in fact there is only one subject present—the reader. The text—the words on the page—has been written by the writer, but meaning is always a matter of interpretation. The subjectivity roused to life by reading, while it may be attributed to the author, is nevertheless not a separate subjectivity

but a projection of the subjectivity of the reader. How can the duality of subjects be maintained in the absence of the author? In an actual conversation, the presence of another person preserves the duality. Because each party must assimilate and interpret the utterances of the other, we still have the introjection of the subject-object division, as well as the possibility of hearing only what one wants to hear. But in a real conversation, the other person can interrupt, object to an erroneous interpretation, provide further explanations, change her mind, change the topic, or cut off conversation altogether. In reading, there are no comparable safeguards against the appropriation of the text by the reader. This is the second moment of the dialectic—the recognition that reading is necessarily subjective. The need to keep it from being *totally* subjective ushers in the third moment of the dialectic.

In the feminist story, the key to the problem is the awareness of the double context of reading and writing. Rich's essay is wonderfully illustrative. To avoid imposing an alien perspective on Dickinson's poetry, Rich informs her reading with the knowledge of the circumstances in which Dickinson lived and worked. She repeatedly reminds herself and her readers that Dickinson must be read in light of her *own* premises, that the "exclusions" and "necessities" she endured, and, therefore, her choices, were conditioned by her own world. At the same time, Rich's sensitivity to the context of writing is matched by her sensitivity to the context of reading. She makes it clear throughout the essay that her reading of Dickinson is necessarily shaped by her experience and interests as a feminist poet living in the twentieth-century United States. The reader also has her own premises. To forget these is to run the risk of imposing them surreptitiously on the author.

To recapitulate, the first moment of the dialectic of reading is marked by the recognition of the necessary duality of subjects; the second, by the realization that this duality is threatened by the author's absence. In the third moment, the duality of subjects is referred to the duality of contexts. Reading becomes a mediation between author and reader, between the context of writings and the context of reading.

Although feminists have always believed that objectivity is an illusion, Rich's essay is the only one, as far as I know, to exhibit through its rhetoric the necessary subjectivity of reading coupled with the equally necessary commitment to reading the text as it was meant to be read.[41] The third moment of the dialectic is apparent in Rich's weaving—not blending—of the context of writing and the context of reading, the perspective of the author and that of the reader. The central rhetorical device effecting this mediation is her use of the personal voice. As in most critical essays, Rich alternates quotes from the texts in question with her own commentary, but her use of the personal voice makes a difference. In her hands, this rhetorical strategy serves two purposes. First, it serves as a reminder that her interpretation is informed by her own perspective. Second, it signifies her tactful approach to Dickinson; the personal voice serves as a gesture warding off any inclination to appropriate the authority of the text as a warrant for the validity of the interpretation. Because the interpretation is presented as an *interpretation,* its claim to validity rests on the cogency of the supporting arguments, *not* on the authorization of the text.

Rich accomplishes even more than this. She reaches out to Dickinson not by identifying with her, but by establishing their affinity. Both are American, both are women poets in a patriarchal culture. By playing this affinity against the differences, she produces a context that incorporates both reader and writer. In turn, this common ground becomes the basis for drawing the connections that, in her view, constitute the proper goal of reading.

One might ask: Is there something distinctively female (rather than "merely feminist") in this dialogic model? While it is difficult to specify what "distinctively female" might mean,

there are currently very interesting speculations about differences in the way males and females conceive of themselves and of their relations with others. The works of Jean Baker Miller, Nancy Chodorow, and Carol Gilligan suggest that men define themselves through individuation and separation from others, while women have more flexible ego boundaries and define and experience themselves in terms of their affiliations and relationships with others.[42] Men value autonomy, and they think of their interactions with others principally in terms of procedures for arbitrating conflicts between individual rights. Women, on the other hand, value relationships, and they are most concerned in their dealings with others to negotiate between opposing needs so that the relationship can be maintained. This difference is consistent with the difference between mainstream models of reading and the dialogic model I am proposing for feminist readings of women's writing. Mainstream reader-response theories are preoccupied with issues of control and partition—how to distinguish the contribution of the author/text from the contribution of the reader. In the dialectic of communication informing the relationship between the feminist reader and the female author/text, the central issue is not of control or partition, but of managing the contradictory implications of the desire for relationship (one must maintain a minimal distance from the other) and the desire for intimacy, up to and including a symbiotic merger with the other. The problematic is defined by the drive "to connect," rather than that which is implicit in the mainstream preoccupation with partition and control—namely, the drive to get it right. It could also be argued that Poulet's model represents reading as an intimate, intersubjective encounter. However, it is significant that in his model, the prospect of close rapport with another provokes both excitement and anxiety. Intimacy, while desired, is also viewed as a threat to one's integrity. For Rich, on the other hand, the prospect of merging with another is problematical, but not threatening.

Maybe not dialectic tho → but possibility also common female understanding of love + marriage?

Let me end with a word about endings. Dialectical stories look forward to optimistic endings. Mine is no exception. In the first chapter the woman reader becomes a feminist, and in the end she succeeds in extricating herself from the androcentric logic of the literary and critical canons. In the second chapter the feminist reader succeeds in effecting a mediation between her perspective and that of the writer. These "victories" are part of the project of producing women's culture and literary tradition, which in turn is part of the project of overcoming patriarchy. It is in the nature of people working for revolutionary change to be optimistic about the prospect of redirecting the future.

Culler observes that optimistic endings have been challenged (successfully, he thinks) by deconstruction, a method radically at odds with the dialectic. It is worth noting that there is a deconstructive moment in Rich's reading of Dickinson. Recall her third metaphor: the reader is an insect "vibrating the frames of windows, clinging to the panes of glass, trying to connect." The suggestion of futility is unmistakable. At best, Rich's interpretation of Dickinson might be considered as a "strong misreading" whose value is in its capacity to provoke other misreadings.

We might say this—but must we? To answer this question, we must ask another: What is at stake in the proposition that reading is impossible? For one thing, if reading is impossible, then there is no way of deciding the validity of an interpretation—the very notion of validity becomes problematical. Certainly it is useful to be reminded that the validity of an interpretation cannot be decided by appealing to what the author "intended," to what is "in" the text, or to what is "in" the experience of the reader. However, there is another approach to the problem of validation, one that is consonant with the dialogic model of reading described above. We can think of validity not as a property inherent in an interpretation, but rather as a *claim* implicit in the *act* of propounding an interpretation. An interpretation, then, is not valid or invalid in itself. Its validity is contingent on the agreement of others. In this view, Rich's interpretation of

Dickinson, which is frankly acknowledged as conditioned by her own experience as a twentieth-century feminist poet, is not necessarily a misreading. In advancing her interpretation, Rich implicitly claims its validity. That is to say, to read a text and then to write about it is to seek to connect not only with the author of the original text, but also with a community of readers. To the extent that she succeeds and to the extent that the community is potentially all-embracing, her interpretation has that degree of validity.[43]

Feminist reading and writing alike are grounded in the interest of producing a community of feminist readers and writers, and in the hope that ultimately this community will expand to include everyone. Of course, this project may fail. The feminist story may yet end with the recognition of the impossibility of reading. But this remains to be seen. At this stage I think it behooves us to *choose* the dialectical over the deconstructive plot. It is dangerous for feminists to be overly enamored with the theme of impossibility. Instead, we should strive to redeem the claim that it is possible for a woman, reading as a woman, to read literature written by women, for this is essential if we are to make the literary enterprise into a means for building and maintaining connections among women.

NOTES

I would like to acknowledge my debt to David Schweickart for the substantial editorial work he did on this chapter.

1. Wayne Booth, Presidential Address, "Arts and Scandals 1982," *PMLA* 98 (1983): 313. Subsequent references to this essay are cited parenthetically in the text.

2. *The Autobiography of Malcolm X,* written with Alex Haley (New York: Grove Press, 1964), p. 173. Subsequent references are cited parenthetically in the text.

3. Virginia Woolf, *A Room of One's Own* (New York: Harcourt Brace Jovanovich, 1981). Subsequent references are cited parenthetically in the text.

4. Jonathan D. Culler, *On Deconstruction: Theory and Criticism after Structuralism* (Ithaca: Cornell University Press, 1982), p. 42. (Subsequent references are cited parenthetically in the text.) Wayne Booth's essay "Freedom of Interpretation: Bakhtin and the Challenge of Feminist Criticism," *Critical Inquiry* 9 (1982): 45–76, is another good omen of the impact of feminist thought on literary criticism.

5. David Bleich, *Subjective Criticism* (Baltimore: Johns Hopkins University Press, 1978), p. 112.

6. George Poulet, "Criticism and the Experience of Interiority," trans. Catherine and Richard Macksey, in *Reader-Response Criticism: From Formalism to Structuralism,* ed. Jane Tompkins (Baltimore: Johns Hopkins University Press, 1980), p. 43. Poulet's theory is not among those discussed by Culler. However, since he will be useful to us later, I mention him here.

7. This argument was advanced by Samuel Weber in "The Struggle for Control: Wolfgang Iser's Third Dimension," cited by Culler in *On Deconstruction,* p. 75.

8. Stanley E. Fish, "Why No One's Afraid of Wolfgang Iser," *Diacritics* 11 (1981): 7. Quoted by Culler in *On Deconstruction,* p. 75.

9. Elaine Showalter, "Feminist Criticism in the Wilderness," *Critical Inquiry* 8 (1981): 182–85. Showalter argues that if we see feminist critique (focused on the reader) as our primary critical project, we must be content with the "playful pluralism" proposed by Annette Kolodny: first because no single conceptual model can comprehend so eclectic and wide-ranging an enterprise, and second because "in the free play of the interpretive field, feminist critique can only compete with alternative readings, all of which have the built-in obsolescence of Buicks, cast away as newer readings take their place" (p. 182). Although Showalter does not support Wimsatt and Beardsley's proscription of the "affective fallacy," she nevertheless subscribes to the logic of their argument. Kolodny's "playful pluralism" is more benign than Wimsatt and Beardsley's dreaded "relativism," but less fatal, in Showalter's view, to theoretical coherence.

10. Elaine Showalter, "Women and the Literary Curriculum," *College English* 32 (1971): 855. For an excellent example of recent work following in the spirit of Showalter's critique, see Paul Lauter, *Reconstructing American Literature* (Old Westbury, N.Y.: Feminist Press, 1983).

11. Lee Edwards, "Women, Energy, and *Middlemarch,*" *Massachusetts Review* 13 (1972): 226.

12. Ibid.

13. James Joyce, *The Portrait of the Artist as a Young Man* (London: Jonathan Cape, 1916), p. 195.

14. See also Florence Howe's analysis of the same passage, "Feminism and Literature," in *Images of Women in Fiction: Feminist Perspectives,* ed. Susan Koppelman Cornillon (Bowling Green, Ohio: Bowling Green State University Press, 1972), pp. 262–63.

15. Judith Fetterley, *The Resisting Reader: A Feminist Approach to American Fiction* (Bloomington: Indiana University Press, 1978), p. xx. Although Fetterley's remarks refer specifically to American Literature, they apply generally to the entire traditional canon.

16. Fetterley, *Resisting Reader,* p. xiii.

17. See Katharine M. Rogers, *The Troublesome Helpmate: A History of Misogyny in Literature* (Seattle: University of Washington Press, 1966).

18. Fredric Jameson, *The Political Unconscious: Narrative as a Socially Symbolic Act* (Ithaca: Cornell University Press, 1981), p. 286.

19. In *Woman and the Demon: The Life of a Victorian Myth* (Cambridge: Harvard University Press, 1982), Nina Auerbach employs a similar—though not identical—positive hermeneutic. She reviews the myths and images of women (as angels, demons, victims, whores, etc.) that feminist critics have "gleefully" unmasked as reflections and instruments of sexist ideology, and discovers in them an "unexpectedly empowering" mythos. Auerbach argues that the "most powerful, if least acknowledged creation [of the Victorian cultural imagination] is an explosively mobile, magic woman, who breaks the boundaries of family within which her society restricts her. The triumph of this overweening creature is a celebration of the corporate imagination that believed in her" (p. 1). See also, "Magi and Maidens: The Romance of the Victorian Freud," *Critical Inquiry* 8 (1981): 281–300. The tension between the positive and negative feminist hermeneutics is perhaps most apparent when one is dealing with the "classics." See, for example, Carol Thomas Neely, "Feminist Modes of Shakespeare Criticism: Compensatory, Justificatory, Transformational," *Women's Studies* 9 (1981): 3–15.

20. Kate Millett, *Sexual Politics* (New York: Avon Books, 1970).

21. Elaine Showalter, "The Double Critical Standard and the Feminine Novel," chap. 3 in *A Literature of Their Own: British Women Novelists from Brontë to Lessing* (Princeton: Princeton University Press, 1977), pp. 73–99; Carol Ohmann, "Emily Brontë in the Hands of Male Critics," *College English* 32 (1971): 906–13.

22. Nina Baym, "Melodramas of Beset Manhood: How Theories of American Fiction Exclude Women Authors," *American Quarterly* 33 (1981): 123–39.

23. Ibid., p. 125.

24. Ibid., p. 130. One of the founding works of American Literature is "The Legend of Sleepy Hollow," about which Leslie Fiedler writes: "It is fitting that our first successful homegrown legend would memorialize, however playfully, the flight of the dreamer from the shrew" (*Love and Death in the American Novel* [New York: Criterion, 1960], p. xx).

25. Nina Baym's *Women's Fiction: A Guide to Novels by and about Women in America, 1820–1870* (Ithaca: Cornell University Press, 1978) provides a good survey of what has been excluded from the canon.

26. Annette Kolodny, "Dancing through the Minefield: Some Observations on the Theory, Practice, and Politics of a Feminist Literary Criticism," *Feminist Studies* 6 (1980): 10–12. Kolodny elaborates the same theme in "A Map for Rereading: Or, Gender and the Interpretation of Literary Texts," *New Literary History* 11 (1980): 451–67.

27. For an excellent account of the way in which the feminist "interpretive community" has changed literary and critical conventions, see Jean E. Kennard, "Convention Coverage, or How to Read Your Own Life," *New Literary History* 8 (1981): 69–88. The programs of the MLA Convention during the last twenty-five years offer more concrete evidence of the changes in the literary and critical canons, and of the ideological and political struggles effecting these changes.

28. In Adrienne Rich, *On Lies, Secrets, and Silence: Selected Prose, 1966–1978* (New York: W.W. Norton, 1979). Subsequent references are cited parenthetically in the text.

29. Susan Glaspell's story "A Jury of Her Peers" revolves around a variation of this judicial metaphor. The parable of reading implicit in this story has not been lost on feminist critics. Annette Kolodny, for example, discusses how it "explores the necessary gender marking which *must* constitute any definition of 'peers' in the complex process of unraveling truth or meaning." Although the story does not exclude male readers, it alerts us to the fact that "symbolic representations depend on a fund of shared recognitions and potential references," and in general, "female meaning" is inaccessible to "male interpretation." "However inadvertently, [the male reader] is a *different kind* of reader and, . . . where women are concerned, he is often an inadequate reader" ("Map for Rereading," pp. 460–63).

30. There is a strong counter-tendency, inspired by French poststructuralism, which privileges the appreciation of textuality over the imaginative recovery of the woman writer as subject of the work. See, for example, Mary Jacobus, "Is There a Woman in This Text?" *New Literary History* 14 (1982): 117–41, especially the concluding paragraph. The last sentence of the essay underscores the controversy: "Perhaps the question that feminist critics should be asking is not 'Is there a woman in this text?' but rather: 'Is there a text in this woman?'"

31. I must stress that although Rich's essay presents a significant paradigm of feminist readings of women's writing, it is not the only such paradigm. An alternative is proposed by Caren Greenberg, "Reading Reading: Echo's Abduction of Language," in *Women and Language in Literature and Society,* ed. Sally McConnell-Ginet, Ruth Borker, and Nelly Furman (New York: Praeger, 1980), pp. 304–9.

Furthermore, there are many important issues that have been left out of my discussion. For example:

a. The relationship of her career as reader to the artistic development of the woman writer. In *Madwoman in the Attic* (New Haven: Yale University Press, 1980) Sandra Gilbert and Susan Gubar show that women writers had to struggle to overcome the "anxiety of authorship" which they contracted from the "sentences" of their predecessors, male as well as female. They also argue that the relationship women writers form with their female predecessors does not fit the model of oedipal combat proposed by Bloom. Rich's attitude toward Dickinson (as someone who "has been there," as a "foremother" to be recovered) corroborates Gilbert and Gubar's claim.

b. The relationship between women writers and their readers. We need actual reception studies as well as studies of the way women writers conceived of their readers and the way they inscribed them in their texts.

c. The relationship between the positive and the negative hermeneutic in feminist readings of women's writing. Rich's reading of Dickinson emphasizes the positive hermeneutic. One might ask, however, if this approach is applicable to *all* women's writing. Specifically, is this appropriate to the popular fiction written by women, e.g., Harlequin Romances? To what extent is women's writing itself a bearer of patriarchal ideology? Janice Radway addresses these issues in "Utopian Impulse in Popular Literature: Gothic Romances and 'Feminist Protest,'" *American Quarterly* 33 (1981): 140–62, and "Women Read the Romance: The Interaction of Text and Context," *Feminist Studies* 9 (1983): 53–78. See also Tania Modleski, *Loving with a Vengeance: Mass-Produced Fantasies for Women* (New York: Methuen, 1982).

32. Iser writes:

Text and reader no longer confront each other as object and subject, but instead the "division" takes place within

the reader [herself]. . . . As we read, there occurs an artificial division of our personality, because we take as a
theme for ourselves something we are not. Thus, in reading there are two levels—the alien "me" and the real, virtual "me"—which are never completely cut off from
each other. Indeed, we can only make someone else's
thoughts into an absorbing theme for ourselves provided
the virtual background of our personality can adapt to it.
("The Reading Process: A Phenomenological Approach," in Tompkins, *Reader-Response Criticism,* p. 67)
Add the stipulation that the alien "me" is a male who
has appropriated the universal into his maleness, and
we have the process of immasculation described in the
third section.

33. Stanley E. Fish, *Is There a Text in This Class? The Authority of Interpretive Communities* (Cambridge: Harvard
University Press, 1980), especially pt. 2.

34. Although the woman reader is the "star" of the feminist story of reading, this does not mean that men are excluded from the audience. On the contrary, it is hoped
that on hearing the feminist story they will be encouraged
to revise their own stories to reflect the fact that they, too,
are gendered beings, and that, ultimately, they will take
control of their inclination to appropriate the universal at
the expense of women.

35. Catherine A. MacKinnon, "Feminism, Marxism,
Method, and the State: Toward Feminist Jurisprudence,"
Signs 8 (1981): 637.

36. There is lively debate among feminists about whether
it is better to emphasize the essential similarity of women
and men, or their difference. There is much to be said intellectually and politically for both sides. However, in one
sense, the argument centers on a false issue. It assumes that
concern about women's "difference" is incompatible with
concern about the essential humanity shared by the sexes.
Surely, "difference" may be interpreted to refer to what is
distinctive in women's lives and works, *including* what
makes them essentially human; unless, of course, we remain captivated by the notion that the standard model for
humanity is male.

37. Although opponents of feminist criticism often find it
convenient to characterize such works as a personal attack
on authors, for feminist critics themselves, the primary
consideration is the function of the text as a carrier of patriarchal ideology, and its effect as such especially (but not
exclusively) on women readers. The personal culpability of
the author is a relatively minor issue.

38. Harold Bloom, *Kabbalah and Criticism* (New York:
Seabury, 1975), p. 126.

39. Poulet, "Criticism and the Experience of Interiority,"
p. 46.

40. Ibid., p. 47. As Culler has pointed out, the theme of
control is prominent in mainstream reader-response criticism. Poulet's story is no exception. The issue of control is
important in another way. Behind the question of whether
the text controls the reader or vice versa is the question of
how to regulate literary criticism. If the text is controlling,
then there is no problem. The text itself will regulate the
process of reading. But if the text is not necessarily controlling, then, how do we constrain the activities of readers
and critics? How can we rule out "off-the-wall" interpretations? Fish's answer is of interest to feminist critics. The
constraints, he says, are exercised not by the text, but by
the institutions within which literary criticism is situated.
It is but a small step from this idea to the realization of the
necessarily political character of literature and criticism.

41. The use of the personal conversational tone has been
regarded as a hallmark of feminist criticism. However, as
Jean E. Kennard has pointed out ("Personally Speaking:
Feminist Critics and the Community of Readers," *College
English* 43 [1981]: 140–45), this theoretical commitment
is not apparent in the overwhelming majority of feminist
critical essays. Kennard found only five articles in which
the critic "overtly locates herself on the page." (To the five
she found, I would add three works cited in this essay:
"Women, Energy, and *Middlemarch,*" by Lee Edwards;
"Feminism and Literature," by Florence Howe; and "Vesuvius at Home," by Adrienne Rich.) Kennard observes further that, even in the handful of essays she found, the personal tone is confined to a few introductory paragraphs.
She asks: "If feminist criticism has on the whole remained
faithful to familiar methods and tone, why have the few articles with an overt personal voice loomed so large in our
minds?" Kennard suggests that these personal introductions are invitations "to share a critical response which depends upon unstated, shared beliefs and, to a large extent,
experience; that of being a female educated in a male tradition in which she is no longer comfortable." Thus, these
introductory paragraphs do not indicate a "transformed
critical methodology; they are devices for transforming the
reader. I read the later portions of these essays—and by extension other feminist criticism—in a different way because I have been invited to participate in the underground. . . . I am part of a community of feminist readers"
(pp. 143–44).

I would offer another explanation, one that is not necessarily inconsistent with Kennard's. I think the use of a personal and conversational tone represents an overt gesture indicating the dialogic mode of discourse as the "regulative ideal" for all feminist discourse. The few essays—indeed, the few introductory paragraphs—that assert this regulative ideal are memorable because they strike a chord in a significant segment of the community of feminist critics. To the extent that we have been touched or transformed by this idea, it will be implicit in the way we read the works of others, in particular, the works of other women. Although the ideal must be overtly affirmed periodically, it is not necessary to do so in all of our essays. It remains potent as long as it is assumed by a significant portion of the community. I would argue with Kennard's distinction between indicators of a transformed critical methodology and devices for transforming the reader. To the extent that critical methodology is a function of the conventions implicitly or explicitly operating in an interpretive community—that is, of the way members of the community conceive of their work and of the way they read each other—devices for transforming readers are also devices for transforming critical methodology.

42. Jean Baker Miller, *Toward a New Psychology of Women* (Boston: Beacon Press, 1976); and Nancy Chodorow, *The Reproduction of Mothering: Psychoanalysis and the Sociology of Gender* (Berkeley and Los Angeles: University of California Press, 1978); and Carol Gilligan, *In a Different Voice: Psychological Theory and Women's Development* (Cambridge: Harvard University Press, 1982).

43. I am using here Jurgen Habermas's definition of truth or validity as a claim (implicit in the act of making assertions) that is redeemable through discourse—specifically, through the domination-free discourse of an "ideal speech situation." For Habermas, consensus attained through domination-free discourse is the warrant for truth. See "Wahrheitstheorien," in *Wirklichkeit und Reflexion: Walter Schulz zum 60. Geburtstag* (Pfullingen: Nesge, 1973), pp. 211–65. I am indebted to Alan Soble's unpublished translation of this essay.

13

Barbara Johnson
1947–

Barbara Johnson is currently a professor of comparative literature and French at Harvard University. Her work includes "The Frame of Reference" (1977), *Defigurations du langage poetique* (1979), *The Critical Difference* (1980), the translation of Derrida's *Dissemination* (1981), *A World of Difference* (1987), *Freedom and Interpretation* (1993), and *The Wake of Destruction* (1994). She also edited *The Psychological Imperative: Teaching as a Literary Genre* (1982). In her work she consistently shows how language subverts a writer's or speaker's intentions and the authorial position of power.

In "Apostrophe, Animation, and Abortion" (1986), Johnson investigates how the politics encoded in the rhetorical figure *apostrophe* affect the way we deal with issues such as abortion. She asks, "Is there any inherent connection between figurative language and questions of life and death, of who will wield and who will receive violence in a given human society?" Johnson focuses on how apostrophe "manipulates the I/Thou structure" so that an "inanimate entity is . . . made present, animate, and anthropomorphic." In her analysis of Baudelaire's poem "Moesta et Errabunda" (whose Latin title means "sad and vagabond") and Shelley's "Ode to the West Wind," she discusses the use of direct address to give animation and demonstrate the "desire for the other's voice." Accordingly, the absence of direct address is assessed as an acting out of "a loss of animation." Johnson, along with Baudelaire and Shelley, also considers how effective rhetorical strategies are in bridging the gaps between life and death, times, and locations and in healing loss.

The relation between abortion and figurative language is addressed more specifically in her treatment of Gwendolyn Brooks's "The Mother," Lucille Clifton's "the lost baby poem," Anne Sexton's "The Abortion," and Adrienne Rich's "To a Poet," among other poems, and Carol Gilligan's study of gender differences in patterns of ethical thinking and male and female logic in her book *In a Different Voice*. Johnson closes the essay by pointing out "the ways in which legal and moral discussions of abortion tend to employ . . . the figure of apostrophe" and discusses how Lacan's analysis of the verbal development of an infant as originating in a demand addressed to the mother may cause us to see lyric poetry as a "fantastically intricate history of endless elaborations and displacements of the single cry, 'Mama!'"

"What happens when the poet is speaking as a mother—a mother whose cry arises out of—and is addressed to—a dead child?" Whether language alone can "bridge the gaps among birth, life, and death" and heal loss is not only a common theme of all the poems Johnson studies but also the overriding focus of this article. Language "blurs the boundary between life and death" and, consequently, complicates the question of "when life begins." She says that it is no wonder the distinction between addresser and addressee should become so problematic in poems about abortion. It is also no wonder that the debate about abortion should refuse to settle into a single voice.

Apostrophe, Animation, and Abortion

The abortion issue is as alive and controversial in the body politic as it is in the academy and the courtroom.
—Jay L. Garfield,
Abortion: Moral and Legal Perspectives

Although rhetoric can be defined as something politicians often accuse each other of, the political dimensions of the scholarly study of rhetoric have gone largely unexplored by literary critics. What, indeed, could seem more dry and apolitical than a rhetorical treatise? What could seem farther away from budgets and guerrilla warfare than a discussion of anaphora, antithesis, prolepsis, and preterition? Yet the notorious CIA manual[1] on psychological operations in guerrilla warfare ends with just such a rhetorical treatise: an appendix on techniques of oratory which lists definitions and examples for these and many other rhetorical figures. The manual is designed to set up a Machiavellian campaign of propaganda, indoctrination, and infiltration in Nicaragua, underwritten by the visible display and selective use of weapons. Shoot softly, it implies, and carry a big schtick. If rhetoric is defined as language that says one thing and means another, then the manual is in effect attempting to maximize the collusion between deviousness in language and accuracy in violence, again and again implying that targets are most effectively hit when most indirectly aimed at. Rhetoric, clearly, has everything to do with covert operations. But are the politics of violence already encoded in rhetorical figures as such? In other words, can the very essence of a political issue—

an issue like, say, abortion—hinge on the structure of a figure? Is there any *inherent* connection between figurative language and questions of life and death, of who will wield and who will receive violence in a given human society?

As a way of approaching this question, I will begin in a more traditional way by discussing a rhetorical device that has come to seem almost synonymous with the lyric voice: the figure of apostrophe. In an essay in *The Pursuit of Signs,* Jonathan Culler indeed sees apostrophe as an embarrassingly explicit emblem of procedures inherent, but usually better hidden, in lyric poetry as such.[2] Apostrophe in the sense in which I will be using it involves the direct address of an absent, dead, or inanimate being by a first-person speaker: "O wild West Wind, thou breath of Autumn's being . . . ." Apostrophe is thus both direct and indirect: based etymologically on the notion of turning aside, of digressing from straight speech, it manipulates the I/Thou structure of *direct* address in an indirect, fictionalized way. The absent, dead, or inanimate entity addressed is thereby made present, animate, and anthropomorphic. Apostrophe is a form of ventriloquism through which the speaker throws voice, life, and human form into the addressee, turning its silence into mute responsiveness.

Baudelaire's poem "Moesta et Errabunda,"[3] whose Latin title means "sad and vagabond," raises questions of rhetorical animation through several different grades of apostrophe. Inanimate objects like trains and ships or abstract entities like perfumed paradises find themselves called upon to attend to the needs of a plaintive and restless lyric speaker. Even the poem's title poses questions of life and death in linguistic terms: the fact that Baudelaire here temporarily resuscitates a dead language prefigures the poem's attempts to function as a finder of lost loves. But in the opening lines of the poem, the direct-address structure seems straightforwardly *un*figurative: "Tell me, Agatha." This could be called a minimally fictionalized apostrophe, although that is of course its fiction. Nothing at first indicates that Agatha is any more dead, absent, or inanimate than the poet himself.

The poem's opening makes explicit the relation between direct address and the desire for the *other's* voice: "Tell me—*you* talk." But something strange soon happens to the face-to-face humanness of this conversation. What Agatha is supposed to talk about starts a process of dismemberment that might have something to do with a kind of reverse anthropomorphism: "Does your heart sometimes take flight?" Instead of conferring a human shape, this question starts to undo one. Then, too, why the name Agatha? Baudelaire scholars have searched in vain for a biographical referent, never identifying one, but always presuming that one exists. In the Pléiade edition of Baudelaire's complete works, a footnote sends the reader to the only other place in Baudelaire's oeuvre where the name Agathe appears—a page in his *Carnets* where he is listing debts and appointments. This would seem to indicate that Agathe was indeed a real person. What do we know about her? A footnote to the *Carnets* tells us she was probably a prostitute. Why? See the poem "Moesta et Errabunda." This is a particularly stark example of the inevitable circularity of biographical criticism.

If Agathe is finally only a proper name written on two different pages in Baudelaire, then the name itself must have a function as a name. The name is a homonym for the word "agate," a semiprecious stone. Is Agathe really a stone? Does the poem express the Orphic hope of getting a stone to talk?

In a poem about wandering, taking flight, getting away from "here," it is surprising to find that, structurally, each stanza acts out not a departure but a return to its starting point, a repetition of its first line. The poem's structure is at odds with its *apparent* theme. But we soon see that the object of the voyage is precisely to return—to return to a prior state, planted in the first stanza as virginity, in the second as motherhood (through the image of the nurse and the pun on *mer/mère*), and finally as childhood love and furtive pleasure. The voyage outward in space is a figure for the voyage backward in time. The poem's structure of address backs up, too, most explicitly in the third stanza. The cry apostrophizing train and ship to carry the speaker off leads to a seeming reprise of the opening line, but by this point the inanimate has entirely taken over: instead of addressing Agatha directly, the poem asks whether Agatha's heart ever speaks the line the poet himself has spoken four lines earlier. Agatha herself now drops out of the poem, and direct address is temporarily lost, too, in the grammar of the sentence (*"Est-il vrai que . . ."*). The poem seems to empty itself of all its human characters and voices, acting out a *loss* of animation—which is in fact its subject: the loss of childhood aliveness brought about by the passage of time. The poem thus enacts in its own temporality the loss of animation it situates in the temporality of the speaker's life.

At this point it launches into a new apostrophe, a new direct address to an abstract, lost state: "How far away you are, sweet paradise." The poem reanimates, addresses an image of fullness and wholeness, and perfect correspondence ("what we love is worthy of our loves"). This height of liveliness, however, culminates strangely in an image of death. The heart that formerly kept trying to fly away now drowns in the moment of reaching its destination ("Où dans la volupté pure le coeur se noie!"). There may be something to gain, therefore, by deferring arrival, as the poem next seems to do by interrupting itself before grammatically completing the fifth stanza. The poem again ceases to employ direct address and ends by asking two drawn-out, self-interrupting questions. Is that paradise now farther away than India or China? Can one call it back and animate it with a silvery voice? This last question—"Peut-on le rappeler avec des cris plaintifs,/Et l'animer encor d'une voix argentine . . . ?"—is a perfect description of apostrophe itself: a trope which, by means of the silvery voice of rhetoric, calls up and animates the absent, the lost, and the dead. Apostrophe itself, then, has become not just the poem's mode but also the poem's theme. In other words, what the poem ends up wanting to know is not how far away childhood is, but whether its own rhetorical strategies can be effective. The final question becomes: can this gap be bridged; can this loss be healed, through language alone?

Shelley's "Ode to the West Wind," which is perhaps the ultimate apostrophic poem, makes even more explicit the relation between apostrophe and animation. Shelley spends the first three stanzas demonstrating that the west wind is a figure for the power to animate: it is described as the breath of being, moving everywhere, blowing movement and energy through the world, waking it from its summer dream, parting the waters of the Atlantic, uncontrollable. Yet the wind animates by bringing death, winter, destruction. How do the rhetorical strategies of the poem carry out this program of animation through the giving of death?

The apostrophe structure is immediately foregrounded by the interjections, four times spelled "O" and four times spelled "oh." One of the bridges this poem attempts to build is the bridge between the "O" of the pure vocative, Jakobson's conative function, or the pure presencing of the second person, and the "oh" of pure subjectivity, Jakobson's emotive function, or the pure presencing of the first person.

The first three stanzas are grammatical amplifications of the sentence "Oh thou, hear, oh, hear!" All the vivid imagery, all the picture painting, come in clauses subordinate to this ob-

sessive direct address. But the poet addresses, gives animation, gives the capacity of responsiveness, to the wind, not in order to make it speak but in order to make it listen to him—in order to make it listen to him doing nothing but address *it*. It takes him three long stanzas to break out of this intense near-tautology. As the fourth stanza begins, the "I" starts to inscribe itself grammatically (but not thematically) where the "thou" has been. A power struggle starts up for control over the poem's grammar, a struggle which mirrors the rivalry named in such lines as: "If I were now what I was then, I would ne'er have *striven as thus with thee* in prayer in my sore need." This rivalry is expressed as a comparison: "less free than thou," but then: "One *too like* thee." What does it mean to be "too like"? Time has created a loss of similarity, a loss of animation that has made the sense of similarity even more hyperbolic. In other words, the poet, in becoming less than—less like the wind—somehow becomes more like the wind in his rebellion against the loss of likeness.

In the final stanza the speaker both inscribes and reverses the structure of apostrophe. In saying "be thou me," he is attempting to restore metaphorical exchange and equality. If apostrophe is the giving of voice, the throwing of voice, the giving of animation, then a poet using it is always in a sense saying to the addressee, "Be thou me." But this implies that a poet has animation to give. And *that* is what this poem is saying is not, or is no longer, the case. Shelley's speaker's own sense of animation is precisely what is in doubt, so that he is in effect saying to the wind, "I will animate you so that you will animate, or reanimate, me." "Make me thy lyre . . . ."

Yet the wind, which is to give animation, is also a giver of death. The opposition between life and death has to undergo another reversal, another transvaluation. If death could somehow become a positive force for animation, then the poet would thereby create hope for his own "dead thoughts." The animator that will blow his words around the world will also instate the power of their deadness, their deadness as power, the place of maximum potential for renewal. This is the burden of the final rhetorical question. Does death necessarily entail rebirth? If winter comes, can spring be far behind? The poem is attempting to appropriate the authority of natural logic—in which spring always does follow winter—in order to clinch the authority of cyclic reversibility for its own prophetic powers. Yet because this clincher is expressed in the form of a rhetorical question, it expresses natural certainty by means of a linguistic device that mimics *no* natural structure and has no stable one-to-one correspondence with a meaning. The rhetorical question, in a sense, leaves the poem in a state of suspended animation. But that, according to the poem, is the state of maximum potential.

Both the Baudelaire and the Shelley, then, end with a rhetorical question that both raises and begs the question of rhetoric. It is as though the apostrophe is ultimately directed toward the reader, to whom the poem is addressing Mayor Koch's question: "How'm I doing?" What is at stake in both poems is, as we have seen, the fate of a lost child—the speaker's own former self—and the possibility of a new birth or a reanimation. In the poems that I will discuss next, these structures of apostrophe, animation, and lost life will take on a very different cast through the foregrounding of the question of motherhood and the premise that the life that is lost may be someone else's.

In Gwendolyn Brooks's poem "The Mother," the structures of address are shifting and complex. In the first line ("Abortions will not let you forget"), there is a "you" but there is no "I." Instead, the subject of the sentence is the word "abortions," which thus assumes a position of grammatical control over the poem. As entities that disallow forgetting, the abortions are not only controlling but animate and anthropomorphic, capable of treating persons as objects. While Baudelaire and Shelley addressed the anthropomorphized other in order to repossess

their lost selves, Brooks is representing the self as eternally addressed and possessed by the lost, anthropomorphized other. Yet the self that is possessed here is itself already a "you," not an "I." The "you" in the opening lines can be seen as an "I" that has become alienated, distanced from itself, and combined with a generalized other, which includes and feminizes the reader of the poem. The grammatical I/Thou starting point of traditional apostrophe has been replaced by a structure in which the speaker is simultaneously eclipsed, alienated, and confused with the addressee. It is already clear that something has happened to the possibility of establishing a clear-cut distinction in this poem between subject and object, agent and victim.

The second section of the poem opens with a change in the structure of address. "I" takes up the positional place of "abortions," and there is temporarily no second person. The first sentence narrates: "I have heard in the voices of the wind the voices of my dim killed children." What is interesting about this line is that the speaker situates the children's voices firmly in a traditional romantic locus of lyric apostrophe— the voices of the wind, Shelley's "West Wind," say, or Wordsworth's "gentle breeze."[4] Gwendolyn Brooks, in other words, is here explicitly rewriting the male lyric tradition, textually placing aborted children in the spot formerly occupied by all the dead, inanimate, or absent entities previously addressed by the lyric. And the question of animation and anthropomorphism is thereby given a new and disturbing twist. For if apostrophe is said to involve language's capacity to give life and human form to something dead or inanimate, what happens when those questions are literalized? What happens when the lyric speaker assumes responsibility for producing the death in the first place, but without being sure of the precise degree of human animation that existed in the entity killed? What is the debate over abortion about, indeed, if not the question of when, precisely, a being assumes a human form?

It is not until line 14 that Brooks's speaker actually addresses the dim killed children. And she does so not directly, but in the form of a self-quotation: "I have said." This embedding of the apostrophe appears to serve two functions here, just as it did in Baudelaire: a self-distancing function, and a foregrounding of the question of the adequacy of language. But whereas in Baudelaire the distance between the speaker and the lost childhood is what is being lamented, and a restoration of vividness and contact is what is desired, in Brooks the vividness of the contact is precisely the source of the pain. While Baudelaire suffers from the dimming of memory, Brooks suffers from an inability to forget. And while Baudelaire's speaker actively seeks a fusion between present self and lost child, Brooks's speaker is attempting to fight her way out of a state of confusion between self and other. This confusion is indicated by the shifts in the poem's structures of address. It is never clear whether the speaker sees herself as an "I" or a "you," an addressor or an addressee. The voices in the wind are not created *by* the lyric apostrophe; they rather initiate the need for one. The initiative of speech seems always to lie in the other. The poem continues to struggle to clarify the relation between "I" and "you," but in the end it only succeeds in expressing the inability of its language to do so. By not closing the quotation in its final line, the poem, which began by confusing the reader with the aborter, ends by implicitly including the reader among those aborted—and loved. The poem can no more distinguish between "I" and "you" than it can come up with a proper definition of life. For all the Yeatsian tripartite aphorisms about life as what is past or passing or to come, Brooks substitutes the impossible middle ground between "You were born, you had body, you died" and "It is just that you never giggled or planned or cried."

In line 28, the poem explicitly asks, "Oh, what shall I say, how is the truth to be said?" Surrounding this question are attempts to make impossible distinctions: got/did not get, deliberate/not deliberate, dead/never made. The uncertainty of the speaker's control as a subject mirrors the uncertainty of the children's status as an object. It is interesting that the status of the human subject here hinges on the word "deliberate." The association of deliberateness with human agency has a long (and very American) history. It is deliberateness, for instance, that underlies that epic of separation and self-reliant autonomy, Thoreau's *Walden*. "I went to the woods," writes Thoreau, "because I wished to live deliberately, to front only the essential facts of life" (66). Clearly, for Thoreau, pregnancy was not an essential fact of life. Yet for him as well as for every human being that has yet existed, someone else's pregnancy is the very *first* fact of life. How might the plot of human subjectivity be reconceived (so to speak) if pregnancy rather than autonomy is what raises the question of deliberateness?

Much recent feminist work has been devoted to the task of rethinking the relations between subjectivity, autonomy, interconnectedness, responsibility, and gender. Carol Gilligan's book *In a Different Voice* (and this focus on "voice" is not irrelevant here) studies gender differences in patterns of ethical thinking. The central ethical question analyzed by Gilligan is precisely the decision whether to have, or not to have, an abortion. The first time I read the book, this struck me as strange. Why, I wondered, would an investigation of gender differences focus on one of the questions about which an even-handed comparison of the male and the female points of view is impossible? Yet this, clearly, turns out to be the point: there is difference because it is not always possible to make symmetrical oppositions. As long as there is symmetry, one is not dealing with difference but rather with versions of the same. Gilligan's difference arises out of the impossibility of maintaining a rigorously logical binary model for ethical choices. Female logic, as she defines it, is a way of rethinking the logic of choice in a situation in which none of the choices are good. "Believe that even in my deliberateness I was not deliberate": believe that the agent is not entirely autonomous, believe that I can be subject and object of violence at the same time, believe that I have not chosen the conditions under which I must choose. As Gilligan writes of the abortion decision, "the occurrence of the dilemma itself precludes nonviolent resolution" (94). The choice is not between violence and nonviolence, but between simple violence to a fetus and complex, less determinate violence to an involuntary mother and/or an unwanted child.

Readers of Brooks's poem have often read it as an argument against abortion. And it is certainly clear that the poem is not saying that abortion is a good thing. But to see it as making a simple case for the embryo's right to life is to assume that a woman who has chosen abortion does not have the right to mourn. It is to assume that no case *for* abortion can take the woman's feelings of guilt and loss into consideration, that to take those feelings into account is to deny the right to choose the act that produced them. Yet the poem makes no such claim: it attempts the impossible task of humanizing both the mother and the aborted children while presenting the inadequacy of language to resolve the dilemma without violence.

What I would like to emphasize is the way in which the poem suggests that the arguments for and against abortion are structured through and through by the rhetorical limits and possibilities of something akin to apostrophe. The fact that apostrophe allows one to animate the inanimate, the dead, or the absent implies that whenever a being is apostrophized, it is thereby automatically animated, anthropomorphized, "personified." (By the same token, the rhetoric of calling makes it difficult to tell the difference between the animate and the inanimate, as anyone with a telephone answering machine can attest.) Because of the ineradicable tendency of language to animate whatever it addresses, rhetoric itself can always have already answered "yes" to the question of whether a fetus is a human being. It is no accident that the anti-abortion film most often shown in the United States should be entitled "The Silent Scream." By activating the imagination to believe in the anthropomorphized embryo's mute responsiveness in exactly the same way that apostrophe does, the film (which is of course itself a highly rhetorical entity) is playing on rhetorical possibilities that are inherent in all linguistically-based modes of representation.

Yet the function of apostrophe in the Brooks poem is far from simple. If the fact that the speaker addresses the children at all makes them human, then she must pronounce herself guilty of murder—but only if she discontinues her apostrophe. As long as she addresses the children, she can keep them alive, can keep from finishing with the act of killing them. The speaker's attempt to absolve herself of guilt depends on never forgetting, never breaking the ventriloquism of an apostrophe through which she cannot define her identity otherwise than as the mother eaten alive by the children she has never fed. Who, in the final analysis, exists by addressing whom? The children are a rhetorical extension of the mother, but she, as the poem's title indicates, has no existence apart from her relation to them. It begins to be clear that the speaker has written herself into a poem she cannot get out of without violence. The violence she commits in the end is to her own language: as the poem ends, the vocabulary shrinks away, words are repeated, nothing but "all" rhymes with "all." The speaker has written herself into silence. Yet hers is not the only silence in the poem: earlier she had said, "You will never . . . silence or buy with a sweet." If sweets are for silencing, then by beginning her apostrophe, "Sweets, if I sinned . . ." the speaker is already saying that the poem, which exists to memorialize those whose lack of life makes them eternally alive, is also attempting to silence once and for all the voices of the children in the wind. It becomes impossible to tell whether language is what gives life or what kills.

> *Women have said again and again "This body is my body!" and they have reason to feel angry, reason to feel that it has been like shouting into the wind.*
>
> —Judith Jarvis Thomson,
> "A Defense of Abortion"

It is interesting to note the ways in which legal and moral discussions of abortion tend to employ the same terms as those we have been using to describe the figure of apostrophe. "These disciplines [philosophy, theology, and civil and canon law] variously approached the question in terms of the point at which the embryo or fetus became 'formed' or recognizably human, or in terms of when a 'person' came into being, that is, infused with a 'soul' or 'animated'" (Blackmun, *Roe vs. Wade, Abortion: Moral and Legal Perspectives,* Garfield and Hennessey, Eds. 15). The issue of "fetal personhood" (Garfield and Hennessey, 55) is of course a way of bringing to a state of explicit uncertainty the fundamental difficulty of defining personhood in general (cf. Luker 6). Even if the question of defining the nature of "persons" is restricted to the question of understanding what is meant by the word "person" in the United States Constitution (since the Bill of Rights guarantees the rights only of "persons"), there is not at present, and probably will never be, a stable legal definition. Existing discussions of the legality and morality of abortion almost invariably confront, leave unresolved, and detour around the question of the nature and boundaries of human life. As Justice Blackmun puts it in *Roe vs. Wade:* "We need not resolve the difficult question of when life begins. When those trained in the respective disciplines of medicine, philosophy, and theology are unable to arrive at any consensus, the judiciary, at this point in the develop-

ment of man's knowledge, is not in a position to speculate as to the answer" (27). In the case of *Roe vs. Wade,* the legality of abortion is derived from the pregnant couple's right to privacy—an argument which, as Catherine MacKinnon argues in "*Roe vs. Wade:* A Study in Male Ideology" (Garfield and Hennessey 45–54), is itself problematic for women, since by protecting "privacy" the courts also protect the injustices of patriarchal sexual arrangements. When the issue is an unwanted pregnancy, some sort of privacy has already, in a sense, been invaded. In order for the personal to avoid being reduced once again to the non-political, privacy, like deliberateness, needs to be rethought in terms of sexual politics. Yet even the attempt to re-gender the issues surrounding abortion is not simple. As Kristin Luker convincingly demonstrates, the debate turns around the claims not only of woman vs. fetus or of woman vs. patriarchal state, but also of woman vs. woman:

> Pro-choice and pro-life activists live in different worlds, and the scope of their lives, as both adults and children, fortifies them in their belief that their views on abortion are the more correct, more moral, and more reasonable. When added to this is the fact that should "the other side" win, one group of women will see the very real devaluation of their lives and life resources, it is not surprising that the abortion debate has generated so much heat and so little light. (Luker 215)

Are pro-life activists, as they claim, actually reaching their cherished goal of "educating the public to the humanity of the unborn child?" As we begin to seek an answer, we should recall that motherhood is a topic about which people have very complicated feelings, and because abortion has become the battleground for different definitions of motherhood, neither the pro-life nor the pro-choice movement has ever been "representative" of how most Americans feel about abortion. More to the point, all our data suggest that *neither of these groups will ever be able to be representative.* (224, emphasis in original)

It is often said, in literary-theoretical circles, that to focus on undecidability is to be apolitical. Everything I have read about the abortion controversy in its present form in the United States leads me to suspect that, on the contrary, the undecidable *is* the political. There is politics precisely because there is undecidability.

And there is also poetry. There are striking and suggestive parallels between the "different voices" involved in the abortion debate and the shifting address-structures of poems like Gwendolyn Brooks's "The Mother." A glance at several other poems suggests that there tends indeed to be an overdetermined relation between the theme of abortion and the problematization of structures of address. In Anne Sexton's "The Abortion," six 3-line stanzas narrate, in the first person, a trip to Pennsylvania where the "I" has obtained an abortion. Three times the poem is interrupted by the italicized lines:

Somebody who should have been born
is gone.

Like a voice-over narrator taking superegoistic control of the moral bottom line, this refrain (or "burden," to use the archaic term for both "refrain" and "child in the womb") puts the first-person narrator's authority in question without necessarily constituting the voice of a separate entity. Then, in the seventh and final stanza, the poem extends and intensifies this split:

Yes, woman, such logic will lead
to loss without death. Or say what you meant,
you coward . . . this baby that I bleed.

Self-accusing, self-interrupting, the narrating "I" turns on herself (or is it someone else?) as "you," as "woman." The poem's speaker becomes as split as the two senses of the word "bleed." Once again, "saying what one means"

can only be done by ellipsis, violence, illogic, transgression, silence. The question of who is addressing whom is once again unresolved.

As we have seen, the question of "when life begins" is complicated partly because of the way in which language blurs the boundary between life and death. In "Menstruation at Forty," Sexton sees menstruation itself as the loss of a child ("two days gone in blood")—a child that exists because it can be called:

I was thinking of a son. . . .
You! . . .
Will you be the David or the Susan?

. . .
David! Susan! David! David!

. . .
my carrot, my cabbage,
I would have possessed you before all women,
calling your name,
calling you mine.

The political consequences and complexities of addressing—of "calling"—are made even more explicit in a poem by Lucille Clifton entitled "The Lost Baby Poem." By choosing the word "dropped" ("i dropped your almost body down"), Clifton renders it unclear whether the child has been lost through abortion or through miscarriage. What is clear, however, is that that loss is both mourned and rationalized. The rationalization occurs through the description of a life of hardship, flight, and loss: the image of a child born into winter, slipping like ice into the hands of strangers in Canada, conflates the scene of Eliza's escape in *Uncle Tom's Cabin* with the exile of draft resisters during the Vietnam War. The guilt and mourning occur in the form of an imperative in which the notion of "stranger" returns in the following lines:

if I am ever less than a mountain
for your definite brothers and sisters. . . .
. . . let black men call me stranger
always for your never named sake.

The act of "calling" here correlates a lack of name with a loss of membership. For the sake of the one that cannot be called, the speaker invites an apostrophe that would expel *her* into otherness. The consequences of the death of a child ramify beyond the mother-child dyad to encompass the fate of an entire community. The world that has created conditions under which the loss of a baby becomes desirable must be resisted, not joined. For a black woman, the loss of a baby can always be perceived as a complicity with genocide. The black mother sees her own choice as one of being either a stranger or a rock. The humanization of the lost baby addressed by the poem is thus carried out at the cost of dehumanizing, even of rendering inanimate, the calling mother.

Yet each of these poems exists, finally, *because* a child does not.[5] In Adrienne Rich's poem "To a Poet," the rivalry between poems and children is made quite explicit. The "you" in the poem is again aborted, but here it is the mother herself who could be called "dim and killed" by the fact not of abortion but of the institution of motherhood. And again, the structures of address are complex and unstable. The deadness of the "you" cannot be named: not suicide, not murder. The question of the life or death of the addressee is raised in an interesting way through Rich's rewriting of Keats's sonnet on his mortality. While Keats writes, "When I have fears that *I* will cease to be" ("When I Have Fears"), Rich writes "and I have fears that *you* will cease to be." If poetry is at stake in both intimations of mortality, what is the significance of this shift from "I" to "you"? On the one hand, the very existence of the Keats poem indicates that the pen has succeeded in gleaning something before the brain has ceased to be. No such grammatical guarantee exists for the "you." Death in the Keats poem is as much a source as it is a threat to writing. Hence, death, for Keats, could be called the mother of poetry while motherhood, for Rich, is precisely the death of poetry. The Western myth of the conjunction of word and

flesh implied by the word "incarnate" is undone by images of language floating and vanishing in the toilet bowl of real-flesh needs. The word is not made flesh; rather, flesh unmakes the mother-poet's word. The difficulty of retrieving the "you" as poet is enacted by the structures of address in the following lines:

> I write this   not for you
> who fight to write your own
> words   fighting up the falls
> but for another woman   dumb

In saying "I write this not for you," it is almost as though Rich is excluding as addressee anyone who could conceivably be reading this poem. The poem is setting aside both the "I" and the "you"—the pronouns Benveniste associates with personhood—and reaches instead toward a "she," which belongs in the category of "nonperson." The poem is thus attempting the impossible task of directly addressing not a second person but a third person—a person who, if she is reading the poem, cannot be the reader the poem has in mind. The poem is trying to include what is by its own grammar excluded from it—to animate through language the nonperson, the "other woman." Therefore, this poem, too, is bursting the limits of its own language, inscribing a logic that it itself reveals to be impossible—but necessary. Even the divorce between writing and childbearing is less absolute than it appears: in comparing the writing of words to the spawning of fish, Rich's poem reveals itself to be trapped between the inability to combine and the inability to separate the woman's various roles.

In each of these poems, then, a kind of competition is implicitly instated between the bearing of children and the writing of poems. Something unsettling has happened to the analogy often drawn by male poets between artistic creation and procreation. For it is not true that literature contains no examples of male pregnancy. Sir Philip Sidney, in the first sonnet from "Astrophel and Stella," describes himself as "great with child to speak," but the poem is ultimately produced at the expense of no literalized child. Sidney's labor pains are smoothed away by a midwifely apostrophe ("Fool," said my Muse to me, 'look in thy heart, and write!'") (*The Norton Anthology of Poetry,* 1: 12–14), and by a sort of poetic Caesarian section, out springs the poem we have, in fact, already finished reading. Mallarmé, in "Don du poème," describes himself as an enemy father seeking nourishment for his monstrous poetic child from the woman within apostrophe-shot who is busy nursing a literalized daughter. But since the woman presumably has two breasts, there seems to be enough to go around. As Shakespeare assures the fair young man, "But were some child of yours alive that time,/ You should live twice in it and in my rhyme" (*Sonnets,* 17: 13–14). Apollinaire, in his play *Les Mamelles de Tirésias,* depicts woman as a de-maternalized neo-Malthusian leaving the task of childbearing to a surrealistically fertile husband. But again, nothing more disturbing than Tiresian cross-dressing seems to occur. Children are alive and well, and far more numerous than ever. Indeed, in one of the dedicatory poems, Apollinaire indicates that his drama represents a return to health from the literary reign of the *poète maudit:*

> La féconde raison a jailli de ma fable,
> Plus de femme stérile et non plus
>   d'avortons . . .
>
> [Fertile reason springs out of my fable,
> No more sterile women, no aborted children]

This dig at Baudelaire, among others, reminds us that in the opening poem to *Les Fleurs du Mal* ("Bénédiction"), Baudelaire represents the poet himself as an abortion *manqué,* cursed by the poisonous words of a rejecting mother. The question of the unnatural seems more closely allied with the bad mother than with the pregnant father.

Even in the seemingly more obvious parallel provided by poems written to dead children by male poets, it is not really surprising to find that the substitution of poem for child lacks the sinister undertones and disturbed address exhibited by the abortion poems we have been discussing. Ben Jonson, in "On My First Son," calls his dead child "his best piece of poetry," while Mallarmé, in an only semi-guilty *Aufhebung,* transfuses the dead Anatole to the level of an idea. More recently, Jon Silkin has written movingly of the death of a handicapped child ("something like a person") as a change of silence, not a splitting of voice. And Michael Harper, in "Nightmare Begins Responsibility," stresses the powerlessness and distrust of a black father leaving his dying son to the care of a "white-doctor-who-breathed-for-him-all-night." But again, whatever the complexity of the voices in that poem, the speaker does not split self-accusingly or infra-symbiotically in the ways we have noted in the abortion/motherhood poems. While one could undoubtedly find counter-examples on both sides, it is not surprising that the substitution of art for children should not be inherently transgressive for the male poet. Men have in a sense always had no choice but to substitute something for the literal process of birth. That, at least, is the belief that has long been encoded into male poetic conventions. It is as though male writing were by nature procreative, while female writing is somehow by nature infanticidal.

It is, of course, as problematic as it is tempting to draw general conclusions about differences between male and female writing on the basis of these somewhat random examples. Yet it is clear that a great many poetic effects may be colored according to *expectations* articulated through the gender of the poetic speaker. Whether or not men and women would "naturally" write differently about dead children, there is something about the connection between motherhood and death that refuses to remain comfortably and conventionally figurative. When a woman speaks about the death of children in any sense other than that of pure loss, a powerful taboo is being violated. The indistinguishability of miscarriage and abortion in the

Clifton poem indeed points to the notion that *any* death of a child is perceived as a crime committed by the mother, something a mother ought by definition to be able to prevent. That these questions should be so inextricably connected to the figure of apostrophe, however, deserves further comment. For there may be a deeper link between motherhood and apostrophe than we have hitherto suspected.

The verbal development of the infant, according to Lacan, begins as a demand addressed to the mother, out of which the entire verbal universe is spun. Yet the mother addressed is somehow a personification, not a person—a personification of presence or absence, of Otherness itself.

> Demand in itself bears on something other than the satisfactions it calls for. It is demand of a presence or of an absence—which is what is manifested in the primordial relation to the mother, pregnant with that Other to be situated *within* the needs that it can satisfy. Insofar as [man's] needs are subjected to demand, they return to him alienated. This is not the effect of his real dependence . . . , but rather the turning into signifying form as such, from the fact that it is from the locus of the Other that its message is emitted. [*Écrits* 286]

If demand is the originary vocative, which assures life even as it inaugurates alienation, then it is not surprising that questions of animation inhere in the rhetorical figure of apostrophe. The reversal of apostrophe we noted in the Shelley poem ("animate me") would be no reversal at all, but a reinstatement of the primal apostrophe in which, despite Lacan's disclaimer, there is precisely a link between demand and animation, between apostrophe and life-and-death dependency.[6] If apostrophe is structured like demand, and if demand articulates the primal relation to the mother as a relation to the Other, then lyric poetry itself—summed up in the figure of apostrophe—comes to look like the fantastically intricate history of endless elaborations and displacements of the single cry, "Mama!" The

question these poems are asking, then, is what happens when the poet is speaking as a mother—a mother whose cry arises out of—and is addressed to—a dead child?

It is no wonder that the distinction between addressor and addressee should become so problematic in poems about abortion. It is also no wonder that the debate about abortion should refuse to settle into a single voice. Whether or not one has ever been a mother, everyone participating in the debate has once been a child. Rhetorical, psychoanalytical, and political structures are profoundly implicated in one another. The difficulty in all three would seem to reside in the attempt to achieve a full elaboration of any discursive position other than that of child.

WORKS CITED

Allison et al., Eds. *The Norton Anthology of Poetry.* New York: W. W. Norton, 1975.

Apollinaire, Guillaume. "Les Mamelles de Tirésias." *L'Enchanteur pourrissant.* Paris: Gallimard, 1972.

Baudelaire, Charles. *Oeuvres complètes.* Paris: Pleiade, 1976.

Brooks, Gwendolyn. "The Mother." *Selected Poems.* New York: Harper & Row, 1963.

Clifton, Lucille. "The Lost Baby Poem." *Good News About the Earth.* New York: Random House, 1972.

Cohen, Marion Deutsche, Ed. *The Limits of Miracles.* South Hadley, Eng.: Bergin & Garvey, 1985.

Culler, Jonathan. *The Pursuit of Signs.* Ithaca: Cornell UP, 1981.

de Man, Paul. "Lyrical Voice in Contemporary Theory." *Lyric Poetry: Beyond New Criticism.* Ed. Hosek and Parker. Ithaca: Cornell UP, 1985.

Gilligan, Carol. *In a Different Voice.* Cambridge, MA: Harvard UP, 1982.

Harper, Michael. *Nightmare Begins Responsibility.* Urbana: U of Illinois P, 1975.

Jarrell, Randall. "A Sick Child." *The Voice that is Great within Us.* Ed. Hayden Caruth. New York: Bantam, 1970.

Jonson, Ben. "On My First Son." *The Norton Anthology of Poetry.* Ed. Allison et al. New York: W. W. Norton, 1975.

Keats, John. "When I Have Fears." *The Norton Anthology of Poetry.* Ed. Allison et al. New York: W. W. Norton, 1975.

Lacan, Jacques. *Écrits.* Trans. Sheridan. New York: W. W. Norton, 1977.

Luker, Kristin. *Abortion and the Politics of Motherhood.* Berkeley: U of California P, 1984.

Mallarmé, Stéphane. *Oeuvres complète.* Paris: Pléiade, 1961.

———. *Pour un tombeau d'Anatole.* Ed. Richard. Paris: Seuil, 1961.

Rich, Adrienne. "To a Poet." *The Dream of a Common Language.* New York: W. W. Norton, 1978.

Sexton, Anne. "The Abortion." *The Complete Poems.* Boston: Houghton Mifflin, 1981.

Shakespeare, William. *Sonnets.* Ed. Booth. New Haven: Yale UP, 1977.

Shelley, Percy Bysshe. "Ode to the West Wind." *The Norton Anthology of Poetry.* Ed. Allison et al. New York: W. W. Norton, 1975.

Sidney, Sir Philip. "Astrophel and Stella." *The Norton Anthology of Poetry.* Ed. Allison et al. New York: W. W. Norton, 1975.

Thomson, Judith Jarvis. "A Defense of Abortion." *Rights, Restitution, Risk.* Ed. William Parent. Cambridge, MA: Harvard UP, 1986.

Thoreau, Henry David. *Walden.* New York: Signet, 1960.

Wordsworth, William. *The Prelude.* Ed. de Selincourt. London: Oxford UP, 1959.

NOTES

1. I would like to thank Tom Keenan of Yale University for bringing this text to my attention. The present essay has in fact benefited greatly from the suggestions of others, among whom I would like particularly to thank Marge Garber, Rachel Jacoff, Carolyn Williams, Helen Vendler, Steven Melville, Ted Morris, Stamos Metzidakis, Steven Ungar, and Richard Yarborough.

2. Cf. also Paul de Man, in "Lyrical Voice in Contemporary Theory": "Now it is certainly beyond question that the figure of address is recurrent in lyric poetry, to the point of constituting the generic definition of, at the very least, the ode (which can, in turn, be seen as paradigmatic for poetry in general)" [61].

3. For complete texts of the poems under discussion, see the appendix to this article.

4. It is interesting to note that the "gentle breeze," apostrophized as "Messenger" and "Friend" in the 1805–6 Prelude (Book I, line 5), is, significantly, not directly addressed in the 1850 version. One might whether this change stands as a sign of the much-discussed waning of Wordsworth's poetic inspiration, or whether it is, rather, one of a number of strictly rhetorical shifts that give the impression of a wane, just as the shift in Gwendolyn

Brooks's poetry from her early impersonal poetic narratives to her more recent direct-address poems gives the impression of a politicization.

5. For additional poems dealing with the loss of babies, see the anthology *The Limits of Miracles* collected by Marion Deutsche Cohen. Sharon Dunn, editor of the *Agni Review,* told me recently that she has in fact noticed that such poems have begun to form almost a new genre.

6. An interesting example of a poem in which an apostrophe confers upon the total Other the authority to animate the self is Randall Jarrell's "A Sick Child," which ends: "All that I've never thought of—think of me!"

MOESTA ET ERRABUNDA

Dis-moi, ton coeur parfois s'envole-t-il, Agathe,
Loin du noir océan de l'immonde cité,
Vers un autre océan où la splendeur éclate,
Bleu, clair, profond, ainsi que la virginité?
Dis-moi, ton coeur parfois s'envole-t-il, Agathe?

La mer, la vaste mer, console nos labeurs!
Quel démon a doté le mer, rauque chanteuse
Qu'accompagne l'immense orgue des vents grondeurs,
De cette fonction sublime de berceuse?
La mer, la vaste mer, console nos labeurs!

Emporte-moi, wagon! elève-moi, frégate!
Loin, loin! ici la boue est faite de nos pleurs!
—Est-il vrai que parfois le triste coeur d'Agathe
Dise: Loin des remords, des crimes, des douleurs,
Emporte-moi, wagon, enlève-moi, frégate?

Comme vous êtes loin, paradis parfumé,
Où sous un clair azur tour n'est qu'amour et joie,
Où tout ce que l'on aime est digne d'être aimé,
Où dans la volupté pure le coeur se noie!
Comme vous êtes loin, paradis parfumé!

Mais le vert paradis des amours enfantines,
Les courses, les chansons, les baisers, les bouquets,
Les violons vibrant derrière les collines,
Avec les brocs de vin, le soir, dans les bosquets,
—Mais le vert paradis des amours enfantines,

L'innocent paradis, plein de plaisirs furtifs,
Est-il déjà plus loin que l'Inde et que la Chine?
Peut-on le rappeler avec des cris plaintifs,
Et l'animer encor d'une voix argentine,
L'innocent paradis plein de plaisirs furtifs?

—Charles Baudelaire

MOESTA ET ERRABUNDA

Tell me, Agatha, does your heart take flight
Far from the city's black and filthy sea
Off to another sea of splendid light,
Blue, bright, and deep as virginity?
Tell me, Agatha, does your heart take flight?

Seas, unending seas, console our trials!
What demon gave the sea this raucous voice
With organ music from the rumbling skies,
And made it play the role of sublime nurse?
Seas, unending seas, console our trials!

Carry me off, engines! lift me, bark!
Far, far away! our tears here turn to mud!
—Can it be true that sometimes Agatha's heart
Says: far from the crimes, remorse, distress, and dread
Carry me off, engines! lift me, bark!

How far away you are, sweet paradise,
Where what we love is worthy of our loves,
Where all is pleasure under azure skies,
Where hearts are drowned in pure voluptuous floods!
How far away you are, sweet paradise!

That verdant paradise of childhood loves,
The songs and games and kisses and bouquets,
The trembling violins in wooded groves,
The wine behind the hills as evening greys,
—That verdant paradise of childhood loves,

That paradise of blameless, furtive joys—
Does it lie farther off than China lies?
Can it be called back with a silvery voice
And animated again with plaintive cries,
That paradise of blameless, furtive joys?

                        —Trans. B. Johnson

ODE TO THE WEST WIND

1

O wild West Wind, thou breath of Autumn's being,
Thou, from whose unseen presence the leaves dead
Are driven, like ghosts from an enchanter fleeing.

Yellow, and black, and pale, and hectic red,
Pestilence-stricken multitudes: O thou,
Who chariotest to their dark wintry bed

The wingéd seeds, where they lie cold and low,
Each like a corpse within its grave, until
Thine azure sister of the Spring shall blow

Her clarion o'er the dreaming earth, and fill
(Driving sweet buds like flocks to feed in air)
With living hues and odors plain and hill:

Wild Spirit, which art moving everywhere;
Destroyer and preserver; hear, oh, hear!

2

Thou on whose stream, mid the steep sky's
    commotion,
Loose clouds like earth's decaying leaves are shed,
Shook from the tangled boughs of Heaven and
    Ocean,

Angels of rain and lightning: there are spread
On the blue surface of thine aëry surge,
Like the bright hair uplifted from the head

Of some fierce Maenad, even from the dim verge
Of the horizon to the zenith's height,
The locks of the approaching storm. Thou dirge

Of the dying year, to which this closing night
Will be the dome of a vast sepulcher,
Vaulted with all thy congregated might

Of vapors, from whose solid atmosphere
Black rain, and fire, and hail will burst: oh, hear!

3

Thou who didst waken from his summer dreams
The blue Mediterranean, where he lay,
Lulled by the coil of his crystálline streams,

Beside a pumice isle in Baiae's bay,
And say in sleep old palaces and towers
Quivering within the wave's intenser day,

All overgrown with azure moss and flowers
So sweet, the sense faints picturing them! Thou
For whose path the Atlantic's level powers

Cleave themselves into chasms, while far below
The sea-blooms and the oozy woods which wear
The sapless foliage of the ocean, know

Thy voice, and suddenly grow gray with fear,
And tremble and despoil themselves: oh, hear!

4

If I were a dead leaf thou mightest bear;
If I were a swift cloud to fly with thee;
A wave to pant beneath thy power, and share

The impulse of thy strength, only less free
Than thou, O uncontrollable! If even
I were as in my boyhood, and could be

The comrade of thy wanderings over Heaven,
As then, when to outstrip thy skyey speed
Scarce seem a vision; I would ne'er have striven

As thus with thee in prayer in my sore need.
Oh, lift me as a wave, a leaf, a cloud!
I fall upon the thorns of life! I bleed!

A heavy weight of hours has chained and bowed
One too like thee: tameless, and swift, and proud.

5

Make me thy lyre, even as the forest is:
What if my leaves are falling like its own!
The tumult of thy mighty harmonies

Will take from both a deep, autumnal tone,
Sweet though in sadness. Be thou, Spirit fierce,
My spirit! Be thou me, impetuous one!

Drive my dead thoughts over the universe
Like withered leaves to quicken a new birth!
And, by the incantation of this verse,

Scatter, as from an unextinguished hearth
Ashes and sparks, my words among mankind!
Be through my lips to unawakened earth

The trumpet of a prophecy! O Wind,
If Winter comes, can Spring be far behind?
                              —Percy Bysshe Shelley

THE ABORTION

*Somebody who should have been born
is gone.*

Just as the earth puckered its mouth,
each bud puffing out from its knot,
I changed my shoes, and then drove south.

Up past the Blue Mountains, where
Pennsylvania humps on endlessly,
wearing, like a crayoned cat, its green hair,

its roads sunken in like a gray washboard;
where, in truth, the ground cracks evilly,
a dark socket from which the coal has poured,

*Somebody who should have been born
is gone.*

the grass as bristly and stout as chives,
and me wondering when the ground would break,
and me wondering how anything fragile survives;

up in Pennsylvania, I met a little man,
not Rumpelstiltskin, at all, at all . . .
he took the fullness that love began.

Returning north, even the sky grew thin
like a high window looking nowhere.
The road was as flat as a sheet of tin.

*somebody who should have been born
is gone.*

Yes, woman, such logic will lead
to loss without death. Or say what you meant,
you coward . . . this baby that I bleed.
                              —Anne Sexton

THE LOST BABY POEM

the time i dropped your almost body down
down to meet the waters under the city
and run one with the sewage to the sea
what did i know about waters rushing back
what did i know about drowning
or being drowned

you would have been born into winter
in the year of the disconnected gas
and no car   we would have made the thin
walk over Genessee hill into the Canada wind
to watch you slip like ice into strangers' hands
you would have fallen naked as snow into winter
if you were here i could tell you these
and some other things

if i am ever less than a mountain
for your definite brothers and sisters
let the rivers pour over my head
let the sea take me for a spiller
of seas   let black men call me stranger
always   for your never named sake
                              —Lucille Clifton

TO A POET

Ice splits   under the metal
shovel   another day
hazed light off fogged panes
cruelty of winter   landlocked   your life
wrapped round you   in your twenties

an old bathrobe   dragged down
with milkstains   tearstains   dust

Scraping eggcrust from the child's
dried dish   skimming the skin
from cooled milk   wringing diapers
Language floats at the vanishing-point
incarnate   breathes the fluorescent bulb
primary   states the scarred grain of the floor
and on the ceiling in torn plaster
    laughs *imago*

    and I have fears that you will cease to be
    before your pen has glean'd your
    teeming brain

for you are not a suicide
but no-one calls this murder
Small mouths, needy, suck you: *This is love*

I write this   not for you
who fight to write your own
words   fighting up the falls
but for another woman   dumb
with loneliness   dust   seeping plastic bags
with children   in a house
where language floats and spins
abortion   in
the bowl

        —Adrienne Rich

ACKNOWLEDGMENTS

"The Abortion," from *All My Pretty Ones* by Anne Sexton. Copyright © 1962 by Anne Sexton, renewed 1990 by Linda G. Sexton. Reprinted by permission of Houghton Mifflin, Co. All rights reserved.

"The lost baby poem," by Lucille Clifton, copyright © 1987 by Lucille Clifton. Reprinted from *Good Woman: Poems and a Memoir 1969–1980,* by Lucille Clifton, with the permission of BOA Editions, Ltd., 92 Park Avenue, Brockport, NY 14420.

"To a Poet" is reprinted from *The Dream of a Common Language, Poems 1974–1977,* by Adrienne Rich, by permission of the author and W. W. Norton & Company, Inc. Copyright © 1978 by W. W. Norton and Company, Inc.

"A Defense of Abortion," by Judith Jarvis Thomson. Reprinted by permission of the publishers from *Rights, Restitution, and Risk: Essays in Moral Theory* by Judith Jarvis Thomson, edited by William Parent, Cambridge, Mass.: Harvard University Press, Copyright © 1986 by the President and Fellows of Harvard College.

14

Stuart Moulthrop
1952–

Stuart Moulthrop is an associate professor of communications design at the University of Baltimore. He is coeditor of the journal *Postmodern Culture* and has published several articles about the technical, cultural, and literary aspects of electronic texts. Moulthrop is also the author of two works of fiction in hypertext: *Victory Garden* (1991) and *Hegirascope* (1995). As a noted hypertext theorist and practitioner, he is respected by many of those concerned with issues of hypermedia and the effects of emerging technologies.

Stuart Moulthrop's assessment of hypertext marks a moment of critical transition in the nature of discourse and is part of a debate about the emerging nonlinear discourses of electronic texts. The assumption made by the prophets of a new age in discourse is that the nonlinear structure of hypertext, as well as the ambiguous position the author is forced to take in electronic texts, radically changes our book-based literacy into a new form. This change in the nature of discourse is, according to those Moulthrop cites, comparable to the radical changes from oral (preliterate) culture to the literate culture that has prevailed since the printing press. This comparison is considered particularly apt because in both the shift from orality to literacy and the shift from (print-based) literacy to hypertext the advance in technology brought about epistemological changes that resonated throughout the cultures. On the political or social-economic level, this information revolution is compared to the Industrial Revolution in its alteration of power relations inside technologically advanced cultures. However, even these comparisons are denied by those who argue that the language we have for such radical change (e.g., "paradigm shift" or "revolution") is inadequate because it is the language of the old, linear order. In this essay, Moulthrop seizes upon the use of the Greek words *logos* ("word") and *nomos* ("law") in an effort to find language for the distinctions between the rhetorical-philosophical foundations of the print-based text and the electronic text.

The discourses Moulthrop outlines tend to use spatial metaphors to describe electronic texts and electronic literacies. Such metaphors derive from the computer technologies but serve also as a connection with preliterate mnemonic systems. Such systems understood themselves to be working with the natural memory storage and retrieval modes of the human brain, just as some of the theorists Moulthrop cites claim electronic information storage and retrieval systems operate. Some theorists, therefore, conceive of electronic literacies as operating in more nearly organic ways than print-based literacies do. Hence, the spatial metaphors of electronic epistemology mix with organic metaphors in the discourses Moulthrop cites as well as in his own text.

That the new technologies disrupt the established power of publishing institutions, state or institutional censorship, and the closed artifact of the printed text renders them a possible site for political resistance. Or, as theorists, who understand the change to be still more radical, argue, these technologies are themselves political resistance since they are not merely tools but heralds of new epistemologies. The assumption is that interactive media suggest the possibility of interactive culture as an alternative to the capitalist culture of production and consumption. After all, theorists of hypermedia argue, there is no sure distinction between producer and consumer (author and reader) in interactive electronic texts.

Moulthrop's article, however, is a survey of the discourse on electronic media rather than an argument for hypertext's capacity to fulfill or despoil the dreams of poststructuralists or Marxists. He acknowledges the devastating critiques by those theorists who refuse to see in hypertext a means of subversion or the dawn of a new age. Moulthrop concedes that, on its way to new frontiers, hypertext inevitably carries with it the literate baggage that is its heritage.

Rhizome and Resistance:
Hypertext and the Dreams of a New Culture

LONG DREAMS

In his novel *The War Outside of Ireland,* and more recently in his hypertext fiction *Afternoon,* Michael Joyce remarks on a shift in the post-industrial wind. We seem, he suggests, to be undergoing a change of identity, weaving a fresh social fabric. "I have argued elsewhere that Japan is now everywhere. It is the long dream of a new culture."[1] Like Roland Barthes before him (*Empire of Signs*) and William Gibson after (*Neuromancer*), Joyce registers the rising appeal of a dream-state characterized by headlong technological advancement and the groundless play of signifiers. There are many reasons to think of this state as Greater Nippon—not just the recent economic prominence of Japan, but also the example it offers of a hyperadaptive, *bricoleur* society rebuilding itself from its own ruins. As Joyce says, however, "Japan" is now

everywhere, not a state but a state of mind, so the name seems somewhat arbitrary. We could as easily invoke other dreams of cultural revolution: George Bush's megalo-American "new world order"; Jean Baudrillard's nightmare of "total spatio-dynamic theatre"; Donna J. Haraway's vision of cyborg politics played out within "a polymorphous information system" that has become "a deadly game."[2]

All of these long dreams have something in common: the conviction that the transition from a mode of production to a "mode of information" has effects exceeding the traditional boundaries of economics and politics.[3] The transforming effect of rapidly evolving communication and information technologies appears first in the marketplace, but like Joyce's imaginary Japan, the marketplace of semiotic exchange is now everywhere: in our homes, in our bedrooms, in our minds. Changes in technology portend more than, in Mark Poster's phrase, "the end of the proletariat as Marx knew it" (129); they suggest possibilities for a reformulation of the subject, a truly radical revision of identity and social relations (111). The effects will touch us (so we dream) in our languages, our narratives, our domestic objects, our fashion systems, our games and entertainments. The changes will be felt throughout our culture.

"The long dream of a new culture" is in fact less a revolution or overturning of the old order than it is an ecstasy, an attempt to stand outside any stable order, old or new. As Jean-François Lyotard observes, the concept of revolution itself has become invalid (along with such models as evolution, enlightenment, and class struggle). Postmodernism begins for Lyotard with "incredulity toward metanarratives," a rejection of any mythology, explanatory fiction, or paradig-m*atic* story.[4] In place of *paradigm* Lyotard submits *paralogy* (61), or language gaming, a strategy that advances the play of discourse by declaring the rules for commercial or intellectual performance continually negotiable. The dream of a new culture is a fantasy of immanent change, or as Gilles Deleuze and Félix Guattari put it, "smooth voyaging": "Voyaging smoothly is a becoming, and a difficult, uncertain becoming at that. It is not a question of returning to preastronomical navigation, nor to the ancient nomads. The confrontation between the smooth and the striated, the passages, alternations, and superpositions, are underway today, running in the most varied directions."[5] It is precisely this "confrontation between the smooth and the striated," between two fundamentally different cultural registers, on which I want to focus in order to explore the interface between information technology and culture. This interface is in many ways a site of resistance, for the smooth and the striated can at times manifest an almost dialectical opposition; but it is also a place where polemics predicated on this apparent dialectic necessarily break down. In examining the nature of this failure we may come to a better understanding of interactive media and how they are implicated in our neocultural dreams.

HYPERTEXT AND RHIZOME

We begin on the *Thousand Plateaus*—which is appropriate for a commentary on hypertext and culture, since Deleuze and Guattari's rhizome-book may itself be considered an incunabular hypertext. Though the text arrives as a print artifact, it was designed as a matrix of independent but cross-referential discourses which the reader is invited to enter more or less at random (Deleuze and Guattari, xx). Having no defined sequence beyond a stipulation that the conclusion be save for last, the book's sections or "plateaus" may be read in any order. The reader's implicit task is to build a network of virtual connections (which more than one reader of my acquaintance has suggested operationalizing as a web of hypertext links).

But *A Thousand Plateaus* serves in this discussion as more than an example of proto-hypertext. It has also been a major influence on social theories and polemics that have a strong bearing on the cultural integration of new media. In the entire poststructuralist pharmacopeia, Deleuze and Guattari's cultural critique seems the most potent of psychotropics. Their major work, *Capitalism and Schizophrenia,* sets in motion perhaps the most radical reinterpretation of Western culture attempted in the second half of this century. Geopolitics, psychoanalysis, neurobiology, sexuality, mathematics, linguistics, semiotics, and philosophy all fall within the purview of their encyclopedic project. Like other poststructuralist enterprises, its major efforts are directed against the order of the signified in favor of the signifier; but, especially in the second part of *A Thousand Plateaus,* Deleuze and Guattari do not simply uproot the old order, they go on to postulate a vividly conceived alternative.

As Brian Massumi points out in his introduction, Deleuze and Guattari's dreamed-of new culture proceeds not from *logos,* the law of substances, but rather from *nomos,* the designation of places or occasions (xiii). Hence their various co-resonating tropes of nomadism or nomadology, deterritorialization, lines of flight, smooth and striated spaces, double articulation, war machines, refrains, and rhizomes. The generating body for all these tropes (the arch-rhizome) is the concept of a social order defined by active traversal or encounter rather than objectification. Figures for this order include the ocean of the navigator or the desert of the nomad, as opposed to the Cartesian space of the engineer or the urban grid of the policeman. Or, to invoke organic metaphors, what Deleuze and Guattari have in mind is a chaotically distributed network (the rhizome) rather than a regular hierarchy of trunk and branches. "Many people have a tree growing in their heads," Deleuze and Guattari observe, "but the brain itself is much more a grass than a tree" (15). All these metaphors attempt to displace a language founded on logocentric, hierarchically grounded truth and replace it with an unfounded play of anarchistic, contingent paralogies.

Energized by opposition to the rightward political drift of the West and the demise of state socialism in the East, these ideas have spread rhizomatically among poststructuralists and postmodernists, especially those committed to social alternatives. Thomas Pynchon's nod to Deleuze and Guattari in *Vineland* may seem trivial (he credits them with "the indispensable Italian Wedding Fake Book," which saves the day at a gangster wedding), but it suggests deeper connections between their work and his own subversive fictions.[6] In a less oblique homage, the anarcho-theorist Hakim Bey invokes nomadology to justify his "temporary autonomous zone," a site of resistance designed for "an era in which the State is omnipresent and all-powerful and yet simultaneously riddled with cracks and vacancies."[7] The grammatologist Gregory Ulmer

takes this line of thinking further in his introduction to *Teletheory,* acknowledging that "the challenge for us is to think nomadically from within the State apparatus."[8] Even the fundamentally traditional theorist Jay David Bolter, who does not invoke nomadology directly, seems more inclined to *nomos* than *logos* when he describes emerging writing systems as dynamic, spatial, and antihierarchical.[9]

Bolter's description of our historical moment as "the late age of print" (2) suggests that our dreams of a new culture are implicated in a specific *technologique:* the transition from a social order founded on the printing press to one in which discursive practices are redefined for newer technologies like hypertext. Likewise, Ulmer speculates on the cultural complex "TV/AI," the intersection of video and the digital processing of language (which may have less to do with artificial intelligence than it does with interactive media). We need to inquire more closely into the relationship between these conceptions and post-logocentric or nomadic thinking. What might Deleuze and Guattari's radical theories of information and culture mean for people concerned with practical informatics, especially in the areas of hypertext and hypermedia?

SMOOTH AND STRIATED WRITING SPACES

Certainly the idea of a discourse system founded on *nomos* as opposed to *logos* relates strongly to current thinking about hypertext systems, especially those which are not viewed simply as "electronic books," or print by another name. According to Michael Joyce, who has used hypertext extensively in the teaching of writing, the medium offers writers "a structure for what does not yet exist." This is a space for improvisation and discovery where users may pursue multiple lines of association or causation rather than having to fit assertions into an exclusive, singular logic.[10] Martin Rosenberg's RHIZOME writing software . . . represents a similar overture toward multiple and explicitly recursive forms of expression. It is not hard to relate these conceptions of writing space, which Joyce calls "constructive hypertext," to the distinction Deleuze and Guattari draw between smooth and striated cultural spaces.

Striated space is the domain of routine, specification, sequence, and causality. Phenomenologically, it consists of the world of perception as processed by the coordinate grid or some other geometric structure into a set of specified identities. Socially, striated space manifests itself in hierarchical and rule-intensive cultures, like the military, the corporation, and the university. As Marshall McLuhan observed, the dominant medium of communication in such cultures—print—fosters an objectified and particularized view of knowledge.[11] Striated space is defined and supported by books, those totemic objects that Alvin Kernan celebrated as "ordered, controlled, teleological, referential, and autonomously meaningful."[12] The occupants of striated space are the champions of order, purpose, and control—defenders of logos, or the Law.

In smooth space, by contrast, "the points are subordinated to the trajectory" (Deleuze and Guattari, 478). Smooth space is defined dynamically, in terms of transformation instead of essence. Thus, one's momentary location is less important than one's continuing movement or line of flight; this space is by definition a structure for what does not yet exist. Smooth social structures include ad hoc or populist political movements, cooperatives, communes, and some small businesses, subcultures, fandoms, and undergrounds. Smooth societies favor invention and indeed entrepreneurship, consensual decision making as opposed to command, and holistic, parallel awareness over particular and serial analysis.

Interactive media do not represent the first technological expression of this social order. McLuhan's electronically mediated global village

and Ulmer's age of video both operate in smooth space, which is best served not by the linearizing faculties of print but by the parataxis and bricolage of broadcasting. In spite of being a champion striathlete, the media critic Neil Postman reveals a fundamental truth about television when he links its basic grammar to the pseudotransition "Now . . . this."[13] Paradoxically, smooth social space is mediated by discontinuities. It propagates in a matrix of breaks, jumps, and implied or contingent connections which are enacted (Joyce would say, constructed) by the viewer or receiver. The textual model here is not the book, or, as Roland Barthes called it, "the work," but rather "the text," a dynamic network of discursive relations of which any material record can represent only a subset.[14] Smooth space is an occasion; Deleuze and Guattari call it a becoming.

Does hypertext represent a smooth space for discourse and, beyond that, for textually mediated social relations? After all, interactive media exhibit the same phenomenological structure as cinema and video. Hypertexts are composed of nodes and links, local coherences and linearities broken across the gap or synapse of transition, a space which the receiver must somehow fill with meaning.[15] In describing the rhizome as a model of discourse, Deleuze and Guattari invoke the "principle of asignifying rupture" (9), a fundamental tendency toward unpredictability and discontinuity. Perhaps, then, hypertext and hypermedia represent the expression of the rhizome in the social space of writing. If so, they might indeed belong in our dreams of a new culture. It might be attractive, especially if one wanted to make radical social claims, to argue that hypertext provides a laboratory or site of origin for a smoothly structured, nomadic alternative to the discursive space of late capitalism.

HYPERTEXT AND CULTURE

Claims along these lines have been advanced (carefully and with due reservation) by the hypertext theorists Ted Nelson, Jay David Bolter, and George Landow. Nelson suggests that interactive media will encourage "populitism," the dissemination of specialized knowledge within unconventional or unofficial networks.[16] Bolter notes the gradual erosion of absolute social hierarchies in the West and suggests that networks and hypermedia will administer the *coup de grâce*. He notes Elizabeth Eisenstein's thesis that print was an important factor in the consolidation of bourgeois culture. As Bolter sees it, however, "electronic writing has just the opposite effect. It opposes standardization and unification as well as hierarchy. It offers as a paradigm the text that changes to suit the reader rather than expecting the reader to conform to its standards" (233).

Landow is more cautious about such revolutionary claims. He considers the possibility that a decentered culture might overwhelm critical voices, yielding not a rainbow coalition but a majority blasted into silence by the explosion of electronic discourse. But though he raises concerns about the design of large-scale networks, Landow does not ultimately give this objection much credence. What reassures him is the importance of active reception in hypermedia. Landow maintains that the constantly repeated requirement of articulated choice in hypertext will produce an enlightened, self-empowered respondent: "In linking and following links lie responsibility—political responsibility—since each reader establishes his or her own line of reading."[17]

All of these conceptions (Landow's in particular) at least resemble operations in smooth social space. The hypertextual reader traces threads in any direction across the docuverse without regard to textual hierarchies. She is free (and as Landow insists, specifically licensed) to create linkages not sanctioned by the present divisions of culture and discipline—free to construct idiosyncratic networks of knowledge, or "mystories" (84) as Gregory Ulmer calls them. The genre of mystory is a way of thinking about the matrix of ideas that cuts across cultural registers, mixing the disciplinary with the personal

or the ludic. Ulmer offers among his examples the (indeed plausible) linking of Ludwig Wittgenstein's *Philosophical Investigations* to the films of Carmen Miranda (62). Until now, this sort of intertextual play has been the preserve of poststructuralist critics like Hélène Cixous and Jacques Derrida, or postmodern novelists like Kathy Acker and Thomas Pynchon. Yet, this kind of textual promiscuity would be a regular feature of the cultural systems that Nelson, Bolter, and Landow describe and have undertaken to create.

Nor are these visions of smooth information systems limited to humanist concerns like literary criticism and philosophy. Nelson's Xanadu, which is still the grandest scheme for hypertext yet proposed, promises to network *all* the world's textual information. Nelson imagines a genre of information production something like the mystory, consisting almost entirely of connections between divergent texts and disciplines.[18] Presumably such a system would represent as important a resource for scientists as it would for humanists, as K. Eric Drexler has realized in his own forecasts for the future of scientific communication. Drexler proposes a hypertextual network for researchers engaged in nanotechnology, both as a medium for quicker dissemination of intellectual output and as a check on dangerous experimental practices.[19]

More recently, a group of information system designers from the Boeing Corporation have suggested something like smooth discursive space as a medium for large engineering projects: "Certainly hypermedia will continue to be an effective way of presenting static reference information," they note, "but a larger role for hypermedia requires eliminating the distinction between authors and readers. We assume that all members of engineering teams will be able to create and access information in a shared, distributed environment."[20] Though the idea of computer-supported collaborative work is hardly new, the Boeing proposal introduces a fairly radical element into the shared work environment: the notion of "eliminating the distinction between authors and readers." In general, the Boeing proposal seems about as far from Deleuze and Guattari as one could imagine, except for this one striking design specification. If the distinction between author and reader were indeed eliminated, one would also have to discard any sense of textual identity or hierarchy, at least in absolute terms. Since the hyperdocument would always be in flux, it could not be constituted as a series of discursive stabilities but would in actual fact represent a smooth space constantly reconfigured by lines of flight (a phrase which, in the case of Boeing, might be more than figurative).

This scenario calls to mind a somewhat unbelievable prospect. Nomad *engineering?* Surely the intellectual domain of the engineer is the epitome of striated consciousness, dedicated as it is to precision, causality, and method. Wittgenstein meets Carmen Miranda may be one thing, but we have just infiltrated Deleuze and Guattari into Boeing Information Systems—an insurgency that must give us pause. What is really likely to happen when the hierarchically organized, routinized space of the corporation meets the rhizomatic propensities of electronic media? Are such encounters conceivable as anything more than flights of fancy, or might the ostensible "smoothness" of the new writing systems be more delusion than Deleuzean? These questions are bound to disturb our dreams of a new culture.

DESIGN ANYTHING THAT WAY . . .

Dreams, after all, correspond only obliquely to waking experience. Thomas Pynchon, who has a lot of interesting things to say about both dreams and technologies, has given us a parable that may be of use here. It is found in *Gravity's Rainbow*, a fiction that departs from the principles of realist narrative in ways that themselves suggest a smooth or nomadic mode of discourse.

The central mysteries of the novel are never resolved, tailing off into arabesques of impossibility. The protagonist neither dies nor survives at the end but is "broken down . . . and scattered," his identity no longer definable in narrative terms.[21] Ostensibly unconnected characters and events participate in shadowy, irrational schemes of analogy and inversion, patterns that seem closer to intuition or dreamwork than to logical relations, yet the author of this rhizomatic text has his roots in the striated space of the military-industrial complex. Before turning to fiction, Pynchon studied applied physics at Cornell and worked as an engineering assistant for none other than the Boeing Corporation. Moreover, the great obsession of his novel is a weapons system, the German V-2 rocket, one of the direst instruments of striated *technologique*.

Pynchon articulates the convergence of the nomadic and the techno/logical throughout *Gravity's Rainbow*, but it surfaces most vividly in the stories of Leni and Franz Pökler, two of the more ideologically significant characters in the novel. They are a classic misalliance, Cancer and Aquarius, *nomos* and *logos* sharing the same unhappy bed. Franz is a young chemical engineer who is gradually drawn into the Nazi secret weapons program. Leni is a somewhat naive socialist who travels the opposite route, joining street actions against the fascists. The marriage is doomed, but in its final days the conflict crystallizes in a way we may find instructive:

He was the cause-and-effect man: he kept at her astrology without mercy, telling her what she was supposed to believe, then denying it. "Tides, radio interference, damned little else. There is no way for changes out there to produce changes here."

"Not produce," she tried, "not cause. It all goes together. Parallel, not series. Metaphor. Signs and symptoms. Mapping on to different coordinate systems, I don't know . . ." She didn't know, all she was trying to do was reach.

But he said: "Try to design anything that way and have it work." (159)

The domestic troubles of Franz and Leni Pökler illustrate the tension between smooth and striated cultures: the mystic and the engineer, the revolutionary and the obedient servant, the street fighter and the lab worker. In Leni's holistic or metaphoric world view, events relate semiotically, not as intersections of forces but as intertextual references among "different coordinate systems." This scheme itself maps rather neatly onto the idea of smooth space, since it describes the universe as a plenum of evocative possibilities ("signs and symptoms") rather than a hierarchy of necessary connections. We might also note that Leni becomes in the course of the novel a literal nomad. The end of the war finds her a camp survivor and a displaced person, haunted by nightmares of the deportation trains.

Franz, on the other hand, still believes that the striated culture of science will deliver transcendence in the form of interplanetary flight. "Cause-and-effect man," man of the Law, he derides his wife's mysticism in the name of the reality principle. For him the tangible, measurable world is all that can be the case. If information does not have direct physical consequence, if it is not *data* given over to some form of analysis, then he regards it as worthless. By the end of the novel, Franz will learn the horror of his ways—most brutally when he discovers the slave labor camp that adjoins the Nordhausen missile factory. But despite this conversion, his rebuke to Leni hangs over the remainder of the novel, which after all is itself the kind of rhizomatic enterprise that Franz so deeply mistrusts.

As an implicit critique of Deleuze and Guattari's radical vision, Franz's operationalizing challenge must resonate sharply against our dreams of a nomadic hypertextual culture. *Try to design anything that way*—as a parallelistic network of signifiers with no hierarchy of sequence and no

constraint on future expansion—*and have it work.* This would seem an enormous undertaking. Perhaps Boeing will need to rehire Thomas Pynchon. More likely not, though. It seems improbable that any practical communications system can be conceived as a nomad space, a network of signs and symptoms, or perhaps even a structure for what does not yet exist. Novels, maybe; engineering systems, probably not.

For that matter, some critics insist that even hypertextual fiction must retain a degree of striation. Thinking about the application of interactive technologies to narrative, Robert Coover notes that we may be approaching a great reversal. If multilinear forms like hypertext have emerged partly from writers' dissatisfaction with the monology of print, then perhaps, Coover speculates, writers in the age of hypertext will have the opposite complaint: "One will feel the need, even while using these vast networks and principles of randomness and expansive story line, to struggle against them, just as one now struggles against the linear constraints of the printed book" (cited in Landow, 119). Writers of hypertext—even writers of hypertext fiction—may need to carry both the Pöklers in their minds: the anima of parallel consciousness as well as the animus who always insists that things be made to work.

THE PERILS OF GEOMETRY

What does it mean in practical terms to resist the "randomness and expansiveness" of hypertext? Coover suggests that we must reinvent conventions, modifying familiar fictional properties like plot and character to suit the multifarious context of hypermedia.[22] Anyone who actually tries to create a large-scale hyperdocument will recognize the wisdom of this counsel. Vastness and randomness are not particularly valuable per se. Some principles of regulation and constraint are essential. Thus various theorists have represented hypertextual discourse, not as a wholesale embrace of indeterminacy, but rather as the articulation of global variability in tension against local coherence.[23] In other words, hypertext may not be quite the smooth or rhizomatic structure some have made it out to be.

This concession to operational demands raises some distinctly disturbing questions about our dreams of a new culture. Deleuze and Guattari register a significant warning about the misleading possibilities of techniques for multiple discourse:

> To attain the multiple, one must have a method that effectively constructs it; no typographical cleverness, no lexical agility, no blending or creation of words, no syntactical boldness, can substitute for it. In fact, these are more often than not merely mimetic procedures used to disseminate or disperse a unity that is retained in a different dimension for an image-book. Technonarcissism. Typographical, lexical, or syntactic creations are necessary only when they no longer belong to the form of expression of a hidden unity, becoming themselves dimensions of the multiplicity under consideration; we only know of rare successes in this. (22)

Though Deleuze and Guattari have print rather than electronic composition in mind here (most prominently *Finnegans Wake*), the seduction of "technonarcissism" is a very clear danger for hypertext. In designing a discursive practice dedicated to multiplicity and flexible articulation, we must always be aware of "hidden unity." That which purports to be a true multiple—a rhizome, a nomadology, a smooth space—may in fact be only a little world made cunningly, some deterministic system passing itself off as a structure for what does not yet exist. It may even be the case, as Martin Rosenberg argues in this volume, that we are hopelessly bound to determinism as a consequence of our engagement with technologies of writing.

With these possibilities in mind we may need to broaden the terms of Coover's prognosis. As interactive systems come into wider use, we are indeed likely to develop a resistance to their properties; but this resistance will probably involve at least two stages. The strictly operational resistance that Coover foresees is only the beginning. If hypermedia systems do become regular features of working life in organizations like Boeing, then this problem will no doubt find a range of solutions. The struggle against hypertextual vastness will generate rhetorical or generic strategies that limit the most problematic propensities of the medium. Landow's "rhetoric of arrivals and departures"[24] and Ulmer's mystory are both likely prototypes for this response. But these rhetorical compromises will not end the troubles that Coover predicts.

A second wave of critique or resistance is likely to follow once such strategies are in place: a resistance predicated not on practice but on ideology. An early indication of this emerging line of criticism can be found in Martin Rosenberg's skeptical assessment of current hypertext theory, laid out in his contribution to this book, "Physics and Hypertext: Liberation and Complicity in Art and Pedagogy." Rosenberg registers a crucial dissent from the generally celebratory treatment of hypertext and its cultural possibilities. His analysis of hypertext theory's reliance on tropes of reversible time and linear geometry brilliantly reveals the bad faith in which many of us (myself included) have been known to operate. But precisely because Rosenberg's critique is so devastating, it leaves us all (himself included) with very little in the way of an ideological standpoint. As the title of Landow's chapter asks, *What's a critic to do?* The prospects are daunting. Nonetheless, since Rosenberg is most assuredly right in his objections, we must give his attempt at theoretical resistance close attention.

Rosenberg has recognized the hazard of technonarcissism. Developers of interactive media, in his assessment, have been irresistibly seduced by a logocentric world-view. He points out that "*anything* produced out of a systemic relationship between lexias and links, cards, buttons, and fields also participates in the same geometrical episteme that produced Newton's laws and classical stasis theory, Feynman diagrams of subatomic particle interactions, formal logic, computer languages, and the fractal scaling of seacoasts, black holes, and chess."[25] Hypertext systems are entirely routinized, after all: they are contrivances composed of discrete rules and relationships, designed to be regular and reliable even in their "vastness and randomness." But despite this underlying allegiance to system, Rosenberg asserts, hypermedia theorists present their products as alternatives to striated discourse and its culture. He points out that this is pure delusion. Just as the lexical play of *Finnegans Wake* does not really liberate Joyce's text from the constraints of *logos,* so no amount of apparent multiplicity can exonerate hypertext of its complicity in military-entertainment-information culture. Claiming that hypertext effects a transition from reductive hierarchies to polyvalent networks will not do. As Rosenberg observes, linearity and multilinearity are identical from a topological perspective. Why should they be any different in terms of ideology? Lines are still lines, *logos* and not *nomos,* even when they are embedded in a hypertextual matrix. Such matrices are always edifices, never autonomous zones; they are structures that do not allow for deterritorialization. No technologically mediated link can ever constitute a genuine line of flight.

Rosenberg's critique is indeed chastening, and it should provoke theorists of interactive media to serious reconsideration of our more radical claims. But unlike Robert Coover, Rosenberg is unwilling to adopt an overt conservatism—as a result of which, his critique forces us to confront a crucial problem. Where Coover acknowledges that writing systems are indeed systematic, Rosenberg insists on the possibility of a true construction of the multiple, or, as he

puts it, "liberation." "Liberated human consciousness," he argues, "means liberation from a geometric ideological construct that disguises the nature of human awareness in order for it better to plot industrial schedules, the trajectories of cannonballs, the circumnavigation of the globe." This is indeed a noble goal, and one that most hypertext theorists, as well as most liberal intellectuals, would probably espouse. But how are we to arrive at this goal? Freely (and courageously) confessing that he shares the "naivety" of most hypertext theorists, Rosenberg admits that his work on RHIZOME, a constructive hypertext system for writing pedagogy, betrays its own geometrical complicities. "As a teacher," Rosenberg notes, "I recognize that logocentric thought is precisely what my students need to master as a discourse that empowers them in the world." This is honesty. But it does leave us at the mercy of Franz Pökler's challenge: "try to design anything that way and have it work."

If we take Rosenberg's critique seriously, we come swiftly to the limit not just of our terms but of our communications technologies. Rosenberg has demonstrated how the concepts of *techne,* and indeed function itself, are at odds with our rhetoric of liberation. Our dream of a new culture requires us to abandon all operational thinking, so there is no point, really, in discussing implementations. Rosenberg's critique forces us to consider another Pynchonian fable, the fragment called "New Dope": "the minute you take it you are rendered incapable of ever telling anybody what it's like, or worse, where to get any" (*Gravity's Rainbow,* 745).

The allegorical possibilities of "New Dope" are numerous: it might stand for the ultimate *Steigerung* of gnostic enlightenment, or, more simply, for death, or it might represent the state of mind necessary to fully understand *Gravity's Rainbow* (once you do, you can't tell anybody about it). For our purposes, though, an economic or ideological interpretation seems more appropriate. The new dope is a commercial failure because it represents a true alternative to the capitalist order, a product which can never be advertised or effectively organized into a market—it may be significant that in Pynchon's novel "New Dope" is presented as an underground film conceived by the black marketeer and film director Gerhardt von Göll. This could be the arch-capitalist's worst nightmare. "Dealers are as in the dark as anybody," Pynchon explains. Connections can occur only by accident. "It is the dope that finds *you,* apparently" (745).

In acknowledging Rosenberg's critique of hypertextual geometries, we may have to admit that our visions of cultural revolution represent the same old new dope, a pure utopia of pure paralogia, beyond any requirements of design or rational implementation and thus absolutely unrealistic—a very long dream indeed. Though, of course, the reality principle cannot be kept at bay forever. If all we can do is wait for the change to find us, then what are we to do in the meantime? If engagement with hypertext and other technologies can only lead back into the logocentric matrix, then what action should we undertake instead? These questions open onto an even more salient issue: if the operational struggle against hypertext leads to rhetorical compromise, then where does an uncompromising ideological resistance lead?

One answer is, unsurprisingly, right back to the late age of print. Rosenberg alludes briefly to practical experiments in interactive media by figures like Michael Joyce and Donald Byrd, but most of his text is devoted to an admirably erudite commentary on theories of time and geometry, ranging from Bergson and Duchamp to Prigogine and Deleuze and Guattari. I want to criticize this stance, but I cannot do so justly without admitting that the very same objection could be made (with less credit for scholarship) against my own essay. Our various appeals to intellectual heritage are not without their ideological implications. *What's a critic to do?* Having failed to theorize interactive technologies as genuine avenues of change, we retreat into a battle of the books, appealing to the core of our bibliographic tradition. In this instance the strategy is the message, and the message concerns the medium. What do we do while waiting for the new dope to find us? We write yet more literary theory—which is arguably the most self-serving and self-involved form of logocentrism. Absent any truly transformative engagement with the pragmatics of new media, the ideological resistance to hypertext seems to lead Rosenberg and me and a fair number of our colleagues right back to the striated space of the library—where most humanists have always been most comfortable in the first place.

RESISTANCE IS FUTILE

Suppose, however, that one were willing to leave the library and to develop an ideological critique of hypertext through a practical engagement with the medium. To echo Deleuze and Guattari, we know of only rare successes in this, though the ostensible failures may be much more interesting. Bolter raises the possibility of such an implicated critique of hypertext with his electronic version of *Writing Space,* available as a separate title from the publishers of the book. The two texts, print and hypertext, differ significantly. The copyright provisions for the hypertext, for instance, are designed to accommodate the temptations of electronic copying and redistribution. Bolter in effect grants reproduction rights to his readers with only a few conditions and cautions:

> As long as you keep [this] text in the electronic medium, you may also change it as you see fit and hand the changes on to others. You may want to indicate that you have changed the text. On the other hand, you may not, but then your readers will probably falsely assume that the original author was responsible for the text you wrote. All readers should be aware that anything in the text

may have been added by someone other than the original author. But of course, this caveat applies in a Borgesian way to the previous sentence as well.[26]

Bolter's Borgesian copyright notice gestures toward a kind of textual smoothness, a writing space in which individual lines of authority or proprietorship may be blurred or rearranged. The recursive playfulness of the last sentence underscores this point: perhaps even the author-function who warns you about multiple authorship is other than the one countersigned "Jay David Bolter." Welcome to the text-as-rhizome, where every apparently stable or atomic division of expression can break down to reveal a subtext, some less-than-primal scene of writing.

The playfulness of this text is in no way disingenuous. The electronic version of *Writing Space* is published in an open, read-write format: its reader can actually intervene in the text. Suppose a writer were to attempt a critique of hypertext in just such a "constructive" context, within the terms of "a structure which does not yet exist" in any fixed or definitive form. We do know of one very interesting attempt at this. The writing in question was undertaken (and this may be indicative) not by a professional critic but by an undergraduate at Carnegie Mellon University, a school known for its emphasis on science and technology. This response to hypertext came out of a pedagogical experiment inspired by theories of resistant or "strong" interpretation, in which students were asked to use hypertext to interrogate the authority of authors and teachers.[27]

The task given to students in this experiment matched the terms of Coover's prediction: both as readers and writers, they were asked to struggle against the randomness and expansiveness of the hypertextual medium as expressed in a particular electronic text. The object of their attention was a pastiche of Borges's "The Garden of Forking Paths," a story that provides some of the conceptual groundwork for hypertext fic-

tion. In the story, Borges deconstructs the linearity of detective fiction by presenting the reader with an alternative conception of narrative time: "In all fictional works, each time a man is confronted with several alternatives, he chooses one and eliminates the others; in the fiction of Ts'ui Pên, he chooses—simultaneously—all of them. He *creates,* in this way, diverse futures, diverse times which themselves also proliferate and fork. . . . Sometimes, the paths of this labyrinth converge: for example, you arrive at this house, but in one of the possible pasts you are my enemy, in another, my friend."[28] The electronic pastiche attempts to realize the model of narrative discourse outlined in this passage, adding to the original Borges text a number of related and tangential story lines, all of them connected by a series of hypertextual links. Students could explore (and expand if they wished) a fairly dense network of narrative. But the emphasis in the experiment lay on interpretive independence, which was defined as the ability both to recognize a text's basic procedures and to imagine alternatives. The implicit challenge for students, therefore, was to subvert the hypertextual structure of multiplicity and variation, more or less as Coover has specified.

The writer who responded to this challenge most ingeniously, Karl Crary, distanced himself from the hypertextual pastiche by proposing a taxonomy for this heterogeneous writing. He created categories for original, imitated, and added material, attempting to set the text in order by naming its parts and their origins. He would thus give back to Borges what was his and identify his teachers' incursions as something less than original. Crary included with this catalogue a thoughtful discussion of both the legal standing of the pastiche (dubious) and its aesthetic legitimacy (about which he was more generous). But the most crucial aspects of Crary's work lay in its material context. To begin with, he wrote not a conventional, linear essay but a hypertext, a network of places and links which can be traversed according to various sequences. Even more significant, Crary's commentary was attached to the structure of the pastiche as a subnetwork accessible at various points from the older text. Crary's submission was a composite electronic document comprising the text on which he had been asked to comment and his own discourse, both integrated into a single hypertextual network.

Because of this strategy of production, Crary's project represents a particularly clever and illuminating failure. Though his intervention makes a very bold attempt at resistant interpretation, it could not fulfill its subversive designs on the hypertextual pastiche. The reasons are fairly clear. Since Crary built his taxonomy within the hypertext on which it comments, he opened himself to a fatal recursion: his taxonomy includes itself within one of its own categories (material with no direct bearing on the Borgesian story). Because of this, although the taxonomy may comment on the pastiche, it cannot achieve any discursive separation from the original structure. It is, indeed, irresistibly joined to the object of its commentary not by a logical but by a nomadic relationship, a pathway laid out in writing space. The sort of resistance Crary sets out to practice depends upon the striated space of the humanist library, where the words in the books stay between their covers. In the promiscuous or rhizomatic environment of hypertext, this kind of resistance is futile.

The limits on Crary's resistance are easiest to appreciate if we consider his text from the perspective of a subsequent reader, one who knows nothing about its authors or the conditions of its creation. Since Crary merged his contribution into the existing hypertext, it may be perceived by a subsequent reader-constructor not as authoritative critical discourse but rather as another paralogical move in the game of pastiche. That game involves a complicated nesting of fictions within fictions. Borges's main narrative consists of the memoirs of an executed spy, framed by an unnamed editor who reminds us

that the first two pages of the original text are missing. The spy's story mentions an ancestor, Ts'ui Pên, who has written a novel called (of course) "The Garden of Forking Paths." To make matters even more confusing, the pastiche adds several metafictional characters who comment on the narrative structure that contains them. Later readers have no reason to find Crary, author of the taxonomy, any less fictional than these characters, or Ts'ui Pên, or the nameless editor. Perhaps we made him up, or perhaps Borges did, or perhaps Borges invented the whole bunch of us. Or vice versa. As Bolter observes, *caveat lector.*

But in bringing this warning to our attention, Karl Crary's ostensible failure produces a very enlightening demonstration of hypertextual discourse in action. It is, clearly, a failure only by the narrow definition of one pedagogical language game. In fact what Crary has produced is an example of a metalepsis, or jump outside the game, a transforming (perhaps even liberating) move which allows us to perceive the constraints our writing systems impose on us. Having perceived and mapped these limits, we may be able to reconstitute our thinking about hypertext and rhizomatic discourse. Crary's paralogy might not lead us to the threshold of a new culture, but it might help us understand the changes that have come about in our old one.

In outcome at least, Crary's resistance to hypertext contrasts sharply with that of literary theorists. We who write theory tend to suffer from a surfeit of idealism and an antipathy to operational compromise. Confronted with the geometrical complicity of hypertext, some of us fail to acknowledge our naivety and fall back into the discursive space of print and an often unexamined nostalgia for the *logos.* Perhaps Crary fails for the opposite reason, because (at the beginning of his college career, after all) he is so solidly committed to the possibility of rational solutions. He sets out to save the text for the Law because he believes erroneously that he can design something that works, a scheme for sorting out the bewildering tangle of hypertextual relations.

This account gives Crary much less credit than he deserves. In fact, his problematic encounter with hypertext represents not just the complement of our critical errors but a model of erratic progress. For all his understandable logocentrism, Crary does not turn back to the library but instead takes his chances in the new medium. He could have hit the books and written a conventional paper, as many of his classmates did; but Crary chose to work in hypertext, which takes a certain intellectual boldness to begin with. Moreover, he elected to work *within the object text itself,* and this choice was definitive. Crary invades the nomadic space of hypertext in the name of the *logos*—and if he ends up planting his flag in a hall of mirrors, he has nonetheless made a very important discovery, both for himself and for his teachers.

That discovery is the practical proof of a principle expounded by Deleuze and Guattari, namely, that smooth and striated spaces "exist only in mixture: smooth space is constantly being translated, transversed into a striated space; striated space is constantly being reversed, returned to a smooth space" (474). The dyad of smooth/striated represents not a dialectic but a continuum—a conception that has considerable consequences for our understanding of hypertext and its possibilities for cultural change. To begin with, it suggests that Robert Coover is right to characterize the future of interactive media in terms of "struggle" (as Martin Rosenberg says in his article, cultural "war"). Our work in hypertext will involve a constant alternation between *nomos* and *logos*. We will create structures which we will then deconstruct or deterritorialize and which we will replace with new structures, passing again from smooth to striated space and starting the process anew.

Above all, Crary's lesson in the futility of resistance can teach us something about the nature of the new culture of which we dream when we venture into hypertext. It suggests that this culture may not resemble the liberated or autonomous zones which Hakim Bey and Thomas Pynchon have fantasized. Hypertext—and its as yet more distant cousins, virtual reality and cyberspace—will not produce anarchist enclaves or pirate utopias. Rosenberg is right: with apologies to all utopian theorists, hypertext will not liberate us from geometry, rationalist method, or the other routinizing side effects of alphanumeric thinking. Nor does hypertext represent Coover's "end of books," though the foundations of print culture are bound to be shaken a bit by the new media. Hypertext and other emerging technologies mark not a terminus but a transition. As Bolter has written, "the computer is simply the technology by which literacy will be carried into a new age" (237).

There will, of course, be nothing simple about the new age or its technologies. The transition seems likely to be both permanent and perpetual. If our destiny is indeed some version of Greater Japan, then we are in for more complexity, not less, more turbulent transversals of hierarchy into nomad space, more anxious reversals of chaos into new order. Such instability and complexity come with the deterritorialized territory. Think of Tokyo, an urban immensity without street names, where every house and building has its number in the striated grid, but where personal navigation is strictly nomadic, a matter of sketches and narratives. *What's a critic to do?* Head east till you come to the OnoSendai Building, hang a left at the statue of Colonel Sanders, third pachinko parlor on the right, you can't miss it.

If we can say anything at this point about interactive media and their possibilities for cultural change, it must be that any new culture will be as promiscuous as its texts, always seeking new relations, fresh paralogical permutations of order and chaos. This activity may not make us avant-garde, but it should keep us busy. We may discover that we are the children of Leni and Franz Pökler, inheritors of both a mother-right and a patrimony, a capacity for cosmic understanding and a knack for making things work. In Pynchon's novel, Franz and Leni's daughter, Ilse, is taken away by the SS and made into a kind of living movie, returned to her father once a year for brief glimpses. In our relationship to our dream parents we will need to circumvent such dire machinations. Our medium of expression will not be anything so linear and monologic as cinema, but rather the hybrid, smooth-striated domain of hypertext, the new writing space. "Writing is pre-eminently the technology of cyborgs," Donna Haraway reminds us (176), and our encounter with these new media may well be a first step toward cyborganism, which is perhaps the ultimate transversal of rhizome and machine.

We may find ourselves one day arriving as the first nomads of cyberspace, voyaging smoothly across the grids of consensual hallucination. But such excursions are a few years off yet. For the moment, as we wait for century and millennium to play themselves out, we must be satisfied with less grandiose visions and more pragmatic insights. Here is one: in our long dreams of a new culture, we may be better served by an erroneous but venturesome conservation than by the most radical strains of pure theory.

NOTES

1. Michael Joyce, *Afternoon, a story* (Cambridge, Mass.: Eastgate Systems, 1990). In hypertext documents, citations are most conveniently made by the title of the node or lexia from which the quotation comes, in this case, "Japan".

2. Jean Baudrillard, *Simulations,* trans. P. Foss, P. Patton, and P. Beitchmann (New York: Semiotext(e), 1983), 140; Donna Haraway, *Simians, Cyborgs, and Women: The Reinvention of Nature* (New York: Routledge, 1991), 161.

3. Mark Poster, *The Mode of Information: Poststructuralism and Social Context* (Chicago: University of Chicago Press, 1990), 16.

4. Jean-François Lyotard, *The Postmodern Condition: A Report on Knowledge,* trans. Geoff Bennington and Brian Massumi (Minneapolis: University of Minnesota Press, 1984), xxiv.

5. Gilles Deleuze and Félix Guattari, *A Thousand Plateaus: Capitalism and Schizophrenia,* trans. Brian Massumi (Minneapolis: University of Minnesota Press, 1987), 482. For further discussion of Deleuze and Guattari and electronic textuality, see Martin Rosenberg's . . . [x-ref]. "Physics and Hypertext: Liberation and Complicity in Art and Pedagogy"

6. Thomas Pynchon, *Vineland* (New York: Little, Brown, 1990), 97. For more on the Pynchon-Deleuze connection, see Martin Rosenberg's "Invisibility, the War Machine, and Prigogine: Dissipative Structures and Aggregating Processes in the Zone of *Gravity's Rainbow,*" *Pynchon Notes* 29 [forthcoming].

7. Hakim Bey, *T.A.Z.: The Temporary Autonomous Zone, Ontological Anarchy, Poetic Terrorism* (New York: Autonomedia, 1991), 101.

8. Gregory Ulmer, *Teletheory: Grammatology in the Age of Video* (New York: Routledge, 1990), 169.

9. Jay David Bolter, *Writing Space: The Computer, Hypertext, and the History of Writing* (Hillsdale, N.J.: Lawrence Erlbaum, 1991), 159, 231.

10. Michael Joyce, "Siren Shapes: Exploratory and Constructive Hypertext," *Academic Computing* 3 (Nov. 1988): 11 ff.

11. H. Marshall McLuhan, *The Gutenberg Galaxy: The Making of Typographic Man* (New York: Signet, 1969), 155.

12. Alvin Kernan, *The Death of Literature* (New Haven: Yale University Press, 1990), 144.

13. Neil Postman, *Amusing Ourselves to Death: Political Discourse in the Age of Show Business* (New York: Penguin, 1985), 99.

14. Roland Barthes, *The Rustle of Language,* trans. Richard Howard (New York: Hill & Wang, 1986), 61.

15. On the significance of gaps in the semiotics of hypertext, see Terence Harpold, "The Contingencies of the Hypertext Link," *Writing on the Edge* 2 (1991): 126–39; and [x-ref].

16. Theodor Holm Nelson, "How Hypertext (Un)Does the Canon" (address to the Modern Language Association, Chicago, Dec. 28, 1990).

17. George P. Landow, *Hypertext: The Convergence of Contemporary Critical Theory and Technology* (Baltimore: Johns Hopkins University Press, 1992), 184.

18. Theodor Holm Nelson, *Literary Machines* (Sausalito: Mindful Press, 1990), 1/5.

19. K. Eric Drexler, *Engines of Creation: The Coming Era of Nanotechnology* (New York: Anchor, 1987), 230.

20. Kathryn Malcolm, Steven Poltrock, and Douglas Schuler, "Industrial-Strength Hypermedia: Requirements for a Large Engineering Enterprise," P. Stotts and R. Furuta, eds. *Hypertext '91* (New York: Association for Computing Machinery, 1991), 15. For more on the applications of hypertext in industry, see H. Van Dyke Parunak, "Toward Industrial-Strength Hypermedia," in *Hypertext/Hypermedia Handbook,* ed. E. Berk and J. Devlin (New York: McGraw-Hill, 1991), 381–89.

21. Thomas Pynchon, *Gravity's Rainbow* (New York: Viking, 1973), 737.

22. Robert Coover, "The End of Books," *New York Times Book Review,* June 21, 1992, p. 25.

23. See Bolter, Joyce, Harpold, Landow.

24. George P. Landow, "The Rhetoric of Hypermedia: Some Rules for Authors," in *Hypermedia and Literary Studies,* ed. Paul Delany and George P. Landow (Cambridge: MIT Press, 1991), 81–104.

25. Martin Rosenberg, "Physics and Hypertext: Liberation and Complicity in Art and Pedagogy."

26. Jay David Bolter, *Writing Space* (hypertext version), "Copyright III."

27. See Stuart Moulthrop and Nancy Kaplan, "They Became What They Beheld: The Futility of Resistance in the Space of Electronic Writing," in *Literacy and Computers,* ed. C. Selfe and S. Hilligoss (New York: Modern Language Association).

28. Jorge Luis Borges, *Labyrinths,* trans. Donald A. Yates (New York: New Directions, 1962), 26.

In m
of lit
scribe
muni
ine th
seek t
is po
cism?
litera
twent
vance
semic
move
all, th
cial n
Louis
alyze
they i
ues w
This
affect
analy
Stuar

STRU

At the
study
asking
the et
tics—

results or effects they had. In other words, Saussure replaced the "diachronic" study of language through time, the study of the *development* of language, with the "synchronic" study of the particular formation of language *at a particular moment.* In this it is clear that Saussure is related to—and, in fact, influenced—the formalism of Russian Formalism and, indirectly, the New Criticism we mentioned in the Introduction to "What Is Literary Studies?" (Part I). As Saussure himself notes in the *Course in General Linguistics,* the elements of linguistic science—and of language as well—are "*a form not a substance.*" Saussure's description of language in terms of form is at the heart of Barthes's definition of literature as "a very special semantic system, whose goal is to put 'meaning' in the world, but not 'a meaning.'" As Barthes notes earlier in this passage, language itself is "the formal system of logical constraints elaborated by the author according to his own period."

From the assumption of the formal nature of linguistic elements come the crucial, reorienting assumptions of Saussure's linguistic work. (1) Saussure's formal or "structural" linguistics suggests that the nature of linguistic elements is *relational* and that the entities of language are a product of relationship: as Saussure says here, "it is the viewpoint that creates the object" of linguistic science. (2) It further assumes the *arbitrary* nature of the linguistic sign. Since the relationships rather than the "elements" of a system of language are crucial, all the elements of language could be different from what they are. Implicit in this assumption is that language takes whatever material is at hand in order to create its meanings and communication. (3) Its third assumption is that of the *synchronic* method of study that refuses to seek explanations in terms of cause and effect but, rather, seeks understanding in terms of function and activity. Formal relationships are simultaneous rather than sequential; moreover, meaning is more readily apprehended and analyzed through visual models rather than narrative discourse. (In this section Louis Marin makes this explicitly clear in his analysis of the visual representation of Disneyland. Teresa de Lauretis's focus on subjectivity and "experience," moreover, implicitly critiques the static nature of "formal," visual representations.) (4) Finally, Saussurean formalism suggests the *double nature* of language and linguistic elements, including, most significantly here, the double nature of the linguistic sign as the combination of a signified and a signifier, and the double nature of language itself (the French term Saussure uses is *langage*), its particular manifestations in speech (*parole*) and the system (the order or *structure* of its code), language as system (*la langue*). As Saussure says elsewhere, "the absolutely final law of language is, we dare say, that there is nothing which can ever reside in *one* term, as a direct consequence of the fact that linguistic symbols are unrelated to what they should designate."

These assumptions lead Saussure to posit, as he does here, the possibility of a new science for the twentieth century, "*a science that studies the life of signs within society,*" what he calls "semiology." At the same time as Saussure was working, in the United States Charles Sanders Peirce, philosopher and logician, suggested a similar new science, which he called "semiotics." (De Lauretis, unlike Barthes and Marin, is working out of Peirce's analysis of language and discourse; at the end of this Introduction we examine the significant differences between Peirce and Saussure.) As it is practiced today, semiotics examines *meaningful* cultural phenomena from the viewpoint of the conditions that make such meaningful phenomena possible, including the structures that give rise to that meaning—"the codes by which people make reality significant" that Marin describes in his semiotic analysis of Disneyland and the conditions that Barthes describes under which "meaning" in general arises and not particular "meanings." That is, semiotics takes its methods from the *structural linguistics* Saussure initiated (and, sometimes, from the *pragmatics* Peirce initiated) in order to understand the conditions governing meaning in society.

Russian Formalism does much of the same thing in its attempt to isolate the formal "devices" that create the effects it defines as "literary," and this is the reason we think it is necessary to examine Russian Formalism here. But even Northrop Frye calls for a kind of systematic and scientific study of literature in "The Function of Criticism at the Present Time" ("What Is Literary Studies?" [Part I]). Semiotics pursues this kind of analysis more systematically. It does this whether that meaning is found in literary texts or in more cultural and "ideological" objects such as de Lauretis's "experience" and Marin's Disneyland. And semiotics can even take general cultural concepts (such as the concepts of "author" and "subjectivity" that Foucault and Belsey examine in "Deconstruction and Poststructuralism" [Part V]) or gestural communication or the study of the concept of "culture" (such as those of Mulvey, Hebdige, and Hall in "Psychology and Psychoanalysis" [Part VI] and "Cultural Studies" [Part IX]) or even the myths of "primitive" societies in Lévi-Strauss (or in Armstrong and Clifford in "Historical Criticism" [Part VII] and "Cultural Studies" [Part IX]).

The last examples—the semiotic or structural study of myth and culture—has been the lifework of the foremost practitioner of structuralism in Western Europe, the French anthropologist Claude Lévi-Strauss. Lévi-Strauss has studied a wide range of myths, mostly Amerindian myths, and has attempted to discover the structure—or what might be called the grammar—of mythological narrative. In other words, Lévi-Strauss has attempted to apply the methods of structural linguistics to narrative so that, in just the way linguistics analyzes sentences, structural anthropology—as he calls it—can analyze narrative discourse. In this endeavor, he has articulated the highest *scientific* ambition of structuralism and semiotics. In *The Raw and the Cooked,* he says: "I have tried to transcend the contrast between the tangible and the intelligible by operating from the outset at the sign level. The function of signs, is, precisely, to express the one by means of the other." This, then, is the aim of semiotics and structuralism: to attempt to isolate and define the conditions of meaning in culture, to articulate the relationship between the tangible entities of nature and the intelligible meanings of culture.

Structuralism—beginning with Lévi-Strauss's analyses of narrative discourse in the early 1950s in France—has had a huge impact on twentieth-century criticism, much more than the structuralism and semiotics of Eastern Europe that was effectively ended by Stalinism and World War II. Anticipating the many developments of poststructuralism, French structuralism of the 1960s and early 1970s has proved to be a watershed in modern criticism, causing a major reorientation in literary studies. Prior to structuralism, literary studies often seemed insular and isolated even in the humanities. After it, literary criticism seemed more actively engaged in the discourse of the human sciences, a vital participant and in some areas a guide. In fact, by basing its methods on those of linguistics, structuralism helped to transform the traditional "humanities" into what has come to be called the "human sciences."

At first, the rise of structuralism was greeted with considerable hostility by critics in the United States and Europe. It was generally acknowledged that this movement was attempting an ambitious, "scientific" examination of literature in all its dimensions. To some, however, the supposed detachment of such an investigation appeared to be offensively antihumanistic and unrelated to the values of a Western liberal education. Anthropologist Alfred Kroeber argued that "structure" is a redundant concept that needs no articulation, and many literary critics judged this new movement to be an ephemeral fad. Not only was structuralism considered antihumanistic; to the Anglo-American world it was further suspect as a French import, merely an exotic dalliance for a few intellectuals who were arrogantly and blindly worshipping a foreignism. In 1975, however, the Modern Language Association awarded Jonathan Culler's *Structuralist Poetics* the annual James Russell Lowell Prize for a literary study, and the Anglo-American academy (if not critics and readers generally) began to acknowledge that, for good or ill, structuralism was in place as a functioning critical system.

In retrospect, what is equally notable is the ways in which structuralism was transformed, almost immediately in the United States, into simply a step or stage of a host of critical and cultural programs that can be called "poststructural." As we can see in essays throughout this book—Paul de Man, J. Hillis Miller, Catherine Belsey, Slavoj Žižek, Laura Mulvey, Diana Fuss, Donna Haraway, Stuart Hall, even Stuart Moulthrop in his uses of binary oppositions articulated by Deleuze and Guattari—rigorous structural analyses form parts of arguments whose aims are very different from the presumably "disinterested" and "scientific" methods of structuralism. Teresa de Lauretis's article in this section spells out some of the reasons semiotics has widened its purview but still participates in its methods of rigorous analyses of meaning and signification. The growth and influence of structuralism and semiotics—its development in Western Europe since the 1960s, and the rise of various "post" structuralisms in the 1970s—vividly dramatize the extent to which modern criticism has become an interdisciplinary phenomenon. Rigorous structuralism and semiotics continue to constitute a scholarly "field" in themselves, with intellectual methods and scholarly journals and conferences. Yet by taking meaning and the varying conditions of meaning as their "objects" of study, they cut through, without being confined to, traditional "humanities" and "social sciences" such as literary studies, philosophy, history, linguistics, psychology, and anthropology, all of which directly influenced literary theory since the late 1960s. (De Man's essay in "What Is Literary Theory?" [Part II] virtually defines "literary theory" in terms of its appropriation of linguistics and the "object of discussion [of linguistics,] . . . the modalities of production and of reception of meaning and of value.")

LITERARY STRUCTURALISM

Literature, as Julia Kristeva has argued in a manner similar to Barthes's discussion of criticism, has a special relationship to semiotics both as a privileged field in which to examine the semiotic functioning of meaning and as a particular "object" of semiotic study. Literature, she writes, "is a *particular semiotic practice* which has the advantage of making more accessible than others the problematics of the production of meaning." In other words, the semiotic study of literature offers methods to study other cultural discursive formations—fashion, advertisements, even Disneyland. This is what de Lauretis means when she suggests that "in the last decade or so, semiotics has undergone a shift of its theoretical gears: a shift away from the classification of sign systems—their basic units, their levels of structural organization—and toward the exploration of the modes of production of signs and meanings, the ways in which systems and codes are used, transformed or transgressed in social practice. While formerly the emphasis was on studying sign systems (language, literature, cinema, architecture, music, etc.), conceived of as mechanisms that generate messages, what is now being examined is the work performed through them." A good example of the "former" emphasis of semiotics (one that still has strong currency, we should add) is the systematic study of literature and "literariness" of Russian Formalism. Russian Formalism illustrates the aims and methods of structural linguistics applied to literary studies, while French structuralism offers examples of wider semiotic practices focused on literature.

Russian Formalism

In its literary criticism, structuralism is closely related to literary formalism, as represented by both American New Criticism (which we discussed in the Introduction to "What Is Literary Studies?" [Part I]) and Russian Formalism. The principal aim of these movements was to displace "content" in literary analysis and to focus, instead, on literary "form" in a detailed manner analogous to the methods of empirical scientific research. Both movements also sought to organize the generic structures of literature into a system consistent with the inner ordering of works that close reading revealed. In each case, literature is viewed as a complex system of "forms" analyzable with considerable objectivity at different levels of generality—from the specific components of a poetic image or line through the poem's genre to that genre's place in the system of literature. Both New Criticism and Russian Formalism promoted the view of literature as a system and took a general scientific approach to literary analysis. (Northrop Frye called for an analogous systematization of literary studies in "The Function of Criticism at the Present Time" in "What Is Literary Studies?" [Part I].) In the same way as structural linguistics attempts to view language not as something "given" that can be studied only by examining its history but as something that can be analyzed in the way chemistry analyzes molecules and particles, Russian Formalism and literary structuralism—and, to a lesser extent, American New Criticism—attempt to view literature not as constituted by its intrinsic ("natural") meaning, as an imitation of reality, but in terms of relational patterns that are meaningful in a particular work and genre. This systematizing and scientistic impulse, especially as formulated in the linguistically oriented theories of Russian Formalism, is a major link between American New Critical formalism and the structuralism of the 1960s.

Russian Formalism was the work of two groups of critics, the Moscow Linguistic Circle, begun in 1915, and OPOYAZ (Society for the Study of Poetic Language), started in 1916. Both groups were disbanded in 1930 in response to official Soviet condemnation of their willingness to depart from the ideological and aesthetic standards of Soviet socialist realism. Their influence continued strongly in the work of the Prague Linguistic Circle (founded in 1926), of which Roman Jakobson is perhaps the best-known figure, and in a few key works such as Vladimir Propp's *Morphology of the Folktale* (1928). It is an oddity of the modern history of ideas, however, that after 1930 the Russian Formalists had almost no impact on Western criticism and theory but resurfaced thirty years later with the advent of literary structuralism in France and the United States in the 1960s.

Like Eliot and the Modernists in general, the Russian Formalists sought to move away from nineteenth-century romantic attitudes in criticism and to avoid all romantic notions about poetic inspiration, genius, or aesthetic organicism. Instead, the Formalists adopted a deliberately mechanistic view of poetry and other literary art as the products of *craft*. Considered as *fancy*, poetry-as-craft may be investigated according to immediately analyzable literary functions. Thus, while the Formalists believed that no particular deployment of words, images, or other language effects is intrinsically literary (there being no such thing as literary language), they saw that literature, like other usages of language, could have a particular *function*, could "work" to accomplish particular ends, an assumption shared with Mikhail Bakhtin (see "Historical Criticism" [Part VII]), even though Bakhtin was very critical of literary formalism in general and Russian Formalism in particular. This is because even while Bakhtin and the Formalists shared a kind of "functional" understanding of literature, the Formalists are more linguistic rather than "sociological" (as Bakkhtin calls his work); they want to see language deployed as *language* and highlight its linguistic functioning as the object of criticism. Linguistic properties then become the primary concern—instead of "inspiration," "poetic genius," or "poetic organicism"—as a poem's meaning and effect are sought. The Formalists attempted to maintain and extend this view at every step of analysis by identifying formal properties as *effective* properties through detailed dissections of poetic (and narrative) technique.

This impulse in theory toward a literary formalism can be seen most clearly in Viktor Shklovsky's definition of literary "device" aimed at effecting some end (a concept analogous to Saussure's "functional" definition of linguistic entities) in his influential essay "Art as Technique" (1917). Central to Russian Formalism, for example, is Shklovsky's argument against the aesthetic notion of "art as thinking in images" and his promotion, instead, of the importance of literary (and nonimagistic) devices. A concentration on images, Shklovsky maintained, leads one to view a poem as having actual "content," and this assumption inhibits any truly formal or relational analysis. What may appear as "content" needs to be considered as "device," or any operation in language that promotes "defamiliarization." (In "Psychology and Psychoanalysis" [Part VI] Slavoj Žižek offers a fine "structural" analysis of the "quasi-Brechtian effect of estrangement," or "denaturing" in relation to psychoanalysis and detective fiction.) That is, since language is a medium of communication before it is used in art, its expressions and conventions inevitably will be overly familiar to the reader and too feeble to have a fresh or significant impact in a poem. To be made new and poetically useful, such language must be "defamiliarized" and "made strange" through linguistic displacement, which means deploying language in an unusual context or effecting its presentation in a novel way. Rhyme schemes (or lack of rhyme), chiasmus (rhetorical balance and reversal), catachresis (the straining of a word or figure beyond its usual meaning), conceits, mixed metaphors, and so on—all these devices for producing particular effects in literature can be used to defamiliarize language and to awaken readers to the intricacy and texture of verbal structure. Such defamiliarization is, therefore, the manner in which poetry functions to rejuvenate and revivify language. All this is quite different from romantic criticism's view of what happens in a poem as the expressive channel for transcendent (or divine) feelings or poetic (or personal) genius.

French Structuralism

For structuralism the same assumptions hold: its aim is to "account for" literature and other cultural objects as fully and objectively as possible, without recourse to such "mysterious" and unanalyzable concepts such as "genius" or "inexhaustible richness" or "poetic language" unassimilable into general linguistics and semiotics. Thus, as a school of literary criticism, structuralism is dedicated to explaining literature as a system of signs and codes and the conditions which allow that system to function, including relevant cultural frames. Marin follows this discursive and "literary" project here by describing Disneyland "as a text," which "can be viewed as thousands and thousands of narratives uttered by the visitors" and analyzed "according to the codes (vocabulary and syntax) imposed by the makers of Disneyland." In this we can see that with its intense rationalism and sophisticated models, structuralism at its inception seemed without bounds in what it could "understand." A. J. Greimas wrote in 1966, "It may be—it is a philosophic and not linguistic question—that the phenomenon of language as such is mysterious, but there are no mysteries in language." As the most ambitious movement in recent literary studies, structuralism in the 1960s seemed poised to explain literature in every respect.

Structuralism's strength as an analytical technique, however, was connected to what many conceive to be its major weakness. The power of structuralism derived, as Roland Barthes said in "The Structuralist Activity," from its being "essentially an *activity*" that could "reconstruct an 'object' in such a way as to manifest thereby the rules of functioning." Julia Kristeva articulates this more formally when she describes semiotics as the "development of *models,* that is, of formal systems whose structure is isomorphic or analogous to the structure of another system." For Barthes the system or rules are manifested as the "intelligible" *imitation* of a literary object. By this, Barthes meant that structuralism focused on the *synchronic* dimension of a literary text (*langue* as opposed to *parole*), the specific ways in which a text is like other texts. So if the goal of literature is conceived as putting meaning in the world, but not *a* meaning, then the structural comparison of texts is based on similarities of function (character development, plot, theme, ideology, and so on), relationships that Lévi-Strauss called *homologies*. The predominately synchronic analysis of homologies "recreates" the text as a "paradigm," a timeless system of structural possibilities.

Thus, in a structural analysis, changes within and among texts or genres can be accounted for as "transformations" in the synchronic system. However, structuralism, in its scientific project, tends to focus on the fixity of relations within synchronic paradigms at the expense of temporality, or the "diachronic" dimension, which involves history. (Marin offers no discussion of the development of Disneyland, for example; he simply wants to analyze the meanings implicit in its "map.") This tendency to avoid dealing with time and social change concerned many critics of structuralism from its beginning and ultimately became a main target of deconstruction's critique of the prior movement. De Lauretis, in her essay here, is at great pains to demonstrate the compatibility of structuralist semiotics and the political and historical engagements of feminism.

While the critique of structuralism is an important development (that will be discussed in more detail later), structuralism's achievement in practical criticism is undeniable and must be underlined. Roland Barthes's work, for example, charting a course through the early and late stages of structuralism, illuminated semiotic theory, the system of fashion, narrative structure, textuality, and many other topics. These stand as important achievements in modern criticism. The work of Roman Jakobson is important in this regard. Marin's terms—"semantic," "*langue*," "phatic," "mythic," "lexie," etc.—are derived from the work of Saussure, Lévi-Strauss, Jakobson, and Barthes. Jakobson is perhaps the most rigorous critic to use linguistic analyses—he made significant contributions to linguistics in both Prague and Paris—using the terms and methods of linguistics to analyze poems and narratives. Others, such as Tzvetan Todorov, have pursued these methods to create analyses of the "system" of literature altogether. Frye pursues a similar aim in *Anatomy of Criticism,* yet it is not a structuralist analysis because, as Todorov argues, it defines its discussions in terms of literary content rather than the structural relationships that allow that content to be articulated and communicated.

Besides the structural analysis of the "system" of literature which, more or less rigorously, genre theory attempts, structuralism has more broadly attempted to analyze the structures (or grammar) of narrative. As already mentioned, Lévi-Strauss's work has been very important in this regard, leading to such diverse approaches as those of Greimas, Genette, Bremond, and others. A particularly influential example of structuralism's positive achievement is Lévi-Strauss's early essay "The Structural Study of Myth" (1955), an anthropological study that heavily influenced subsequent literary studies. In this essay Lévi-Strauss presents a structural analysis of narrative in which the diachronic dimension (the story line) is eclipsed in favor of a synchronic "reading" of "mythemes" (recurrent narrative structures) in several versions of the Oedipus story. Athough this structural analysis seemed quite bold at the time, similar structural connections are now routinely made and assumed to be literary common sense. Thus, Lévi-Strauss codified, extended, and even created structuralist possibilities for literary analysis. Objections arose about the "hidden" subjectivity or the bias of Lévi-Strauss's selection of mythemes for analysis, and even about the arbitrariness of what could be called a "mytheme." Nevertheless, "The Structural Study of Myth" and Lévi-Strauss's work as a whole had a tremendously stimulating effect on narrative study and induced Anglo-American criticism to reexamine its own formalistic and strongly descriptive tendencies.

THE CRITIQUE OF STRUCTURALISM

Structuralism's self-imposed limitations, especially its lack of concern with diachronic change and its focus on general systems rather than on individual cases, have occasioned several critiques. The French philosopher Jacques Derrida offered a particularly decisive critique, a central example of which is "Structure, Sign, and Play in the Discourse of the Human Sciences." This piece focuses on the structural anthropology of Lévi-Strauss. Derrida connects structuralism with a traditional Western blindness to the "structurality" of structure, or an unwillingness to examine the theoretical and ideological implications of "structure" as a concept. Derrida points out that the attempt to investigate structure implies the ability to stand outside and apart from it—as if one could move outside of cultural understanding in order to take a detached view of culture. In specific terms, Derrida's critique of Lévi-Strauss (not only in "Structure, Sign and Play," but in his *Grammatology* and many other works) is a critique of the privileging of the opposition between "nature" and "culture"—what in *The Raw and the Cooked* Lévi-Strauss calls the tangible and the intelligible. Derrida argues that since one never transcends culture, one can never examine it from the "outside"; there is no standing free of structure, no so-called natural state free of the structural interplay that, in the structuralist analysis, constitutes meaning. There is no objective examination of structure. Therefore, Derrida argues, the attempt to "read" and "interpret" cultural structures cannot be adequately translated into exacting scientific models. If "structure," therefore, cannot be isolated and examined, then structuralism is seriously undermined as a method. Derrida, in fact, argues that in place of structuralism we should recognize the interplay of differences among texts, the activity that he and others call *structuration*.

Julia Kristeva pursues a similar critique, as Teresa de Lauretis notes in her essay, by defining "a 'cross-roads' where the theory of meaning encounters the 'ghost' of the subject." That subject, like the subject of psychoanalysis pursued in "Psychology and Psychoanalysis" (Part VI), is a "divided subject." Kristeva, de Lauretis argues, pursues "a critical semiotics [which] itself finds the way ahead divided, like that subject, split into conscious and unconscious, social constraints and pre-symbolic drives." In her work, which stands strongly within the French tradition of semiotics, Kristeva emphasizes the double nature of the structuralist project. Semiotics, she has argued, is not only a "science." It also is a critique of science in the sense of bringing to light and calling into question the silent (and often unconscious) assumptions that govern scientific "rigor." Chief among these is the assumption that the objects of science and the elements of scientific method can be simple and "pure": Kristeva even notes that "the classical distinction between the natural and the human sciences also considers the former to be more 'pure' than the latter." Similarly, Lévi-Strauss assumes that both "nature" and "culture" are simply and purely themselves and that the difference between them is self-evidently clear. What Kristeva finds, however, is that "semiotic research" always "ultimately uncovers its own ideological gesture." Semiotics, she writes, "begins with a certain knowledge as its goal, and ends up discovering a *theory* which, since it is itself a signifying system, returns semiotic research to its point of departure, to the model of semiotics itself, which it criticizes or overthrows." In part this is due to the *complex* nature of semiotic study, which seeks to know both how meaning is conditioned and how it is communicated—the double project of the "articulation" and "communication" of meaning. But more importantly, it is due to the overwhelmingly *cultural* nature of language and discourse, how it always exists within a context of more than one person, more than one meaning. As the structural linguist Emile Benveniste has argued, "we can never get back to man separate from language and we shall never see him inventing it. We shall never get back to man reduced to himself and exercising his wits to conceive of the existence of another." Human beings, in this conception, *always* exist in societies of human beings, and their language both communicates their thoughts and articulates and structures what can be thought. For this reason, as Kristeva says, semiotics always turns and returns to "ideology" and the cultural formations in which it works. In this, Kristeva, throughout her work, offers a structural/semiotic analysis that both is informed by structuralism and has a tendency toward poststructuralism; she employs both the scientific method of semiotics and the deconstructive critique of that method.

De Lauretis takes a different path from that of Kristeva (and also from that of Umberto Eco, whom she also cites). In her essay in this section she turns to Charles Sanders Peirce rather than Saussure for an understanding of "semiotics." Saussure's semiotic structures are relentlessly binary—Jakobson even argues, following Saussure, that the very structure of the human mind possesses a kind of binarity. For Peirce, however, the functioning of signs is tripartite: sign-interpretant-object. Thus, de Lauretis quotes "Peirce's famous definition" of the sign function in which "context," marked by the "interpretant," remains part of the way signification works. Such a context comes close to what Kristeva means by "ideology"—others in our book, such as Belsey, Fuss, and Bakhtin, deal with ideology as a significant aspect of meaning and discourse—and with it, as de Lauretis notes, "Peirce greatly complicates the picture in which a signifier would immediately correspond to a signified."

That "complication," as she argues, allows "experience" to become an active aspect of signification rather than the kinds of "accidents" of *parole* that Saussure often suggests it is. (The fact that Saussure's *Course in General Linguistics* was compiled by colleagues and students after his death makes definitiveness in his work sometimes elusive.) Such "experience" is an important aspect of de Lauretis's—and feminism's—*political* program of changing social and semiotic institutions that condition our senses of meaning, feeling, subjectivity, and other such things. "The final interpretant," she writes, "is not 'logical' in the sense in which a syllogism is logical, or because it is the result of an 'intellectual' operation like deductive reasoning. It is 'logical' in the sense that it is 'self-analyzing' or, put another way, that it 'makes sense' of the emotion and muscular/mental effort that preceded it, by providing a conceptual representation of that effort." Her "rereading" of Peirce, like Eco's, allows her "to find the 'missing link' between signification and physical reality"—the "referent" that is all but absent in Saussurean linguistics and which, as Paul de Man notes in "What Is Literary Theory?" (Part II), is the central "problem" of theory. That link is "human action," phenomena closely related to the "human work" Edward Said describes in "What Is Literary Theory?" (Part II). For her, as for Said, "action" is worldly and interested, just as semiotics allows the possibility of "experience" that is not quickly avoided for the sake of abstract science, but embraced as the realm in which meaning and value necessarily are enacted. In other words, for de Lauretis "discourse (including 'political' discourse) is not just laden with pitfalls but is itself a pitfall." Or in still other words, semiotics offers the possibility of "theorizing" experience itself. This, she argues, is "the real difficulty, but also the most exciting, original project of feminist theory": namely, "how to theorize that experience, which is at once social and personal, and how to construct the female subject from . . . political and intellectual rage." De Lauretis is seeking to articulate a political semiotics, a worldly semiotics, in which "discursive and representational structures" (she is describing patriarchy) have political and worldly effects that are so important that the modes of analysis that recognizes and "theorizes" them are themselves of the utmost importance. Such structures, like the forms of meaning (the "meaning-effects") that comprise our world and our experience— meaning-effects such as subjectivity, sexuality, aesthetics, self-evidence, work itself, and the very language we speak and dream in—are "most personal and at the same time most socially determined, most defining of the self and most exploited or controlled." That structuralism and semiotics can offer us, in our readings of literature and culture, these kinds of recognitions is, as de Lauretis says, the difficulty and the excitement of their work.

RELATED ESSAYS IN *CONTEMPORARY LITERARY CRITICISM*

Judith Butler, "Variations on Sex and Gender: Beauvoir, Wittig, and Foucault"
Paul de Man, "The Resistance to Theory"
Northrop Frye, "The Function of Criticism at the Present Time"
Diana Fuss, "Reading Like a Feminist"
Stuart Hall, "Cultural Studies: Two Paradigms"
J. Hillis Miller, "The Search for Grounds in Literary Study"
Laura Mulvey, "Visual Pleasure and Narrative Cinema"
Slavoj Žižek, "Two Ways to Avoid the Real of Desire"

REFERENCES AND FURTHER READING

Bannet, Eve Tavor, *Structuralism and the Logic of Dissent: Barthes. Derrida. Foucault. Lacan* (Urbana: University of Illinois Press, 1989).
Barthes, Roland, *Critical Essays,* trans. Richard Howard (Evanston, IL: Northwestern University Press, 1972).
———, *Elements of Semiology,* trans. A. Lavers and C. Smith (New York: Hill and Wang, 1977).
Benveniste, Emile, *Problems in General Linguistics,* trans. Mary Elizabeth Meek (Coral Gables, FL: University of Miami Press, 1971).
Bloom, Harold, *The Anxiety of Influence: A Theory of Poetry* (New York: Oxford University Press, 1973).
Culler, Jonathan, *Ferdinand de Saussure* (Baltimore: Penguin Books, 1976).
———, *Framing the Sign: Criticism and Its Institutions* (Norman: University of Oklahoma Press, 1988).
———, *Structuralist Poetics: Structuralism, Linguistics, and the Study of Literature* (Ithaca, NY: Cornell University Press, 1975).
Derrida, Jacques, *Of Grammatology,* trans. Gayatri Spivak (Baltimore: Johns Hopkins University Press, 1976).

Easterlin, Nancy, and Barbara Riebling, *After Poststructuralism: Interdisciplinarity and Literary Theory* (Evanston, IL: Northwestern University Press, 1993).

Ehrmann, Jacques, ed., *Structuralism* (Garden City, NY: Doubleday, 1970).

Fischer-Lichte, Erika, *The Semiotics of Theater* (Bloomington: Indiana University Press, 1992).

Galan, F. W., *Historical Structures: The Prague School Project, 1928–1946* (Austin: University of Texas Press, 1985).

Genette, Gerard, *Figures of Discourse,* trans. A. Sheridan (New York: Columbia University Press, 1982).

Greimas, A. J., *On Meaning: Selected Writings in Semiotic Theory,* trans. Paul Perron and Frank Collins (Minneapolis: University of Minnesota Press, 1987).

———, *Structural Semantics: An Attempt at a Method,* trans. Daniele McDowell, Ronald Schleifer, and Alan Velie, Intro. Ronald Schleifer (Lincoln: University of Nebraska Press, 1983).

Hawkes, Terence, *Structuralism and Semiotics* (Berkeley: University of California Press, 1977).

Jackson, Leonard, *The Poverty of Structuralism: Literature and Structuralist Theory* (New York: Longman, 1991).

Jakobson, Roman, *Language and Literature,* ed. Krystyna Pomorska and Stephen Rudy (Cambridge, MA: Harvard University Press, 1987).

Jameson, Fredric, *The Prison-House of Language: A Critical Account of Structuralism and Russian Formalism* (Princeton, NJ: Princeton University Press, 1972).

Kristeva, Julia, *Revolution in Poetic Language,* trans. Margaret Waller (New York: Columbia University Press, 1984).

Leitch, Vincent B., *Cultural Criticism, Literary Theory, Poststructuralism* (New York: Columbia University Press, 1992).

Lentricchia, Frank, *After the New Criticism* (Chicago: University of Chicago Press, 1980).

Lévi-Strauss, Claude, *The Raw and the Cooked,* trans. John Weightman and Doreen Weightman (New York: Harper, 1975).

———, *Structural Anthropology,* trans. Claire Jacobson and Brooke Schoepf (New York: Basic Books, 1963).

———, *Structural Anthropology,* Vol. II, trans. Monique Layton (New York: Basic Books, 1976).

Macksey, Richard, and Eugenio Donato, eds., *The Languages of Criticism and the Sciences of Man: The Structuralist Controversy* (Baltimore: Johns Hopkins University Press, 1970).

Meese, Elizabeth A., *(SEM) erotics: Theorizing Lesbian: Writing* (New York: Cutting Edge, 1992).

Peirce, Charles S., *Collected Papers,* ed. Charles Hartshorne and Paul Weiss (Cambridge, MA: Harvard University Press, 1931–58).

Propp, Vladimir, *The Morphology of the Folktale,* trans. Laurence Scott (Austin: University of Texas Press, 1968).

Riffaterre, Michael, *Semiotics of Poetry* (Bloomington: Indiana University Press, 1978).

Saussure, Ferdinand de, *Course in General Linguistics,* trans. Wade Baskin (1916; rpt. New York: McGraw-Hill, 1966).

Schleifer, Ronald, *A. J. Greimas and the Nature of Meaning: Linguistics, Semiotics, and Discourse Theory* (Lincoln: University of Nebraska Press, 1987).

———, "Semiotics and Criticism," in *Literary Criticism and Theory: The Greeks to the Present,* ed. Robert Con Davis and Laurie Finke (New York: Longman, 1989).

Scholes, Robert, *Structuralism in Literature: An Introduction* (New Haven, CT: Yale University Press, 1974).

Steiner, Peter, *Russian Formalism: A Metapoetics* (Ithaca, NY: Cornell University Press, 1984).

Tejera, Victorino, *Literature, Criticism, and the Theory of Signs* (Philadelphia: Benjamins, 1995).

Todorov, Tzvetan, *The Fantastic: A Structural Approach to a Literary Genre,* trans. R. Howard (Ithaca, NY: Cornell University Press, 1975).

———, *Introduction to Poetics,* trans. R. Howard (Minneapolis: University of Minnesota Press, 1981).

15

Ferdinand de Saussure
1857–1913

Ferdinand de Saussure, Swiss linguist, is known as the founder of modern linguistics and structuralism. His intensive theories of language established new ways of studying human behavior and revealed strategies of modernist thought. Speaking French, German, English, and Greek by the age of fifteen, Saussure achieved international fame at twenty-one with *Memoire sur le système primitif des voyelles dans les langues indo-européennes* (Memoir on the Primitive System of Vowels in Indo-European Languages). His value to modern literary theory, however, comes from his work in Paris at École Pratique des Hautes Études and the University of Geneva. This work was available only after his death in 1913 when his students and colleagues published *Course in General Linguistics* (1916) from class notes.

The sections from the *Course* excerpted here present a cross-section of Saussure's thinking that influenced twentieth-century ideas of how language and texts operate. In the first section Saussure distinguishes various levels of words and sounds and determines that what is fundamental to humans is not the ability to speak but the ability to construct a language or sign system. He details the nature of communication in terms of processes: concept and sound production and concept and sound reception. He also addresses the social relationship of mankind and language and asserts that the reality of language is found in an intellectual process (as opposed to a physical one). Most importantly, he predicts the development of semiotics, the study of all sign systems, as a discipline that could shed light on the basic nature of social life. In the second section Saussure explains the arbitrary nature of the linguistic sign and establishes the duality of its nature as signified (concept) and signifier (sound-image). The third section explains Saussure's understanding of the planes on which language operates, especially the synchronic (simultaneous) versus diachronic (chronological). He begins by asserting that language is a system based entirely on the opposition of units. He then states the need to determine the identity of those units that convey conventional meaning yet simultaneously convey new shades of meaning as well. Saussure is especially concerned with the notion of value in a system where the basic unit has meaning only in relation to another unit. Recent theorists see these processes and realms of study as having larger applications. In fact Saussure's notion of relationships as a focus of study is fundamental to twentieth-century literary theory beginning with structuralism and continuing through deconstruction. Essentially, Saussure saw such complexity and chaos in language that he wished to organize and classify universal qualities. The work in discourse is so rich that the basic thoughts of modern theorists such as Derrida, Fish, de Man, Eagleton, and other Poststructuralists are easily traced back to Saussure.

the stamp of collective approval—and which added together constitute language—are realities that have their seat in the brain. Besides, linguistic signs are tangible; it is possible to reduce them to conventional written symbols, whereas it would be impossible to provide detailed photographs of acts of speaking [*actes de parole*]; the pronunciation of even the smallest word represents an infinite number of muscular movements that could be identified and put into graphic form only with great difficulty. In language, on the contrary, there is only the sound-image, and the latter can be translated into a fixed visual image. For if we disregard the vast number of movements necessary for the realization of sound-images in speaking, we see that each sound-image is nothing more than the sum of a limited number of elements or phonemes that can in turn be called up by a corresponding number of written symbols. The very possibility of putting the things that relate to language into graphic form allows dictionaries and grammars to represent it accurately, for language is a storehouse of sound-images, and writing is the tangible form of those images.

3. PLACE OF LANGUAGE IN HUMAN FACTS: SEMIOLOGY

The foregoing characteristics of language reveal an even more important characteristic. Language, once its boundaries have been marked off within the speech data, can be classified among human phenomena, whereas speech cannot.

We have just seen that language is a social institution; but several features set it apart from other political, legal, etc. institutions. We must call in a new type of facts in order to illuminate the special nature of language.

Language is a system of signs that express ideas, and is therefore comparable to a system of writing, the alphabet of deaf-mutes, symbolic rites, polite formulas, military signals, etc. But it is the most important of all these systems.

A science that studies the life of signs within society is conceivable; it would be a part of social psychology and consequently of general psychology; I shall call it *semiology*[1] (from Greek *semeîon* 'sign'). Semiology would show what constitutes signs, what laws govern them. Since the science does not yet exist, no one can say what it would be; but it has a right to existence, a place staked out in advance. Linguistics is only a part of the general science of semiology; the laws discovered by semiology will be applicable to linguistics, and the latter will circumscribe a well-defined area within the mass of anthropological facts.

To determine the exact place of semiology is the task of the psychologist.[2] The task of the linguist is to find out what makes language a special system within the mass of semiological data. This issue will be taken up again later; here I wish merely to call attention to one thing: if I have succeeded in assigning linguistics a place among the sciences, it is because I have related it to semiology.

Why has semiology not yet been recognized as an independent science with its own object like all the other sciences? Linguists have been going around in circles: language, better than anything else, offers a basis for understanding the semiological problem; but language must, to put it correctly, be studied in itself; heretofore language has almost always been studied in connection with something else, from other viewpoints.

There is first of all the superficial notion of the general public: people see nothing more than a name-giving system in language, thereby prohibiting any research into its true nature.

Then there is the viewpoint of the psychologist, who studies the sign-mechanism in the individual; this is the easiest method, but it does not lead beyond individual execution and does not reach the sign, which is social.

Or even when signs are studied from a social viewpoint, only the traits that attach language to the other social institutions—those that are more or less voluntary—are emphasized; as a result, the goal is bypassed and the specific characteristics of semiological systems in general and of language in particular are completely ignored. For the distinguishing characteristic of the sign—but the one that is least apparent at first sight—is that in some way it always eludes the individual or social will.

In short, the characteristic that distinguishes semiological systems from all other institutions shows up clearly only in language where it manifests itself in the things which are studied least, and the necessity or specific value of a semiological science is therefore not clearly recognized. But to me the language problem is mainly semiological, and all developments derive their significance from that important fact. If we are to discover the true nature of language we must learn what it has in common with all other semiological systems; linguistic forces that seem very important at first glance (e.g., the role of the vocal apparatus) will receive only secondary consideration if they serve only to set language apart from the other systems. This procedure will do more than to clarify the linguistic problem. By studying rites, customs, etc. as signs, I believe that we shall throw new light on the facts and point up the need for including them in a science of semiology and explaining them by its laws.

NOTES

1. *Semiology* should not be confused with *semantics*, which studies changes in meaning, and which de Saussure did not treat methodically.

2. Cf. A. Naville, *Classification des Sciences* (2nd. ed.), p. 104. [Ed.] The scope of semiology (or semiotics) is treated at length in Charles Morris' *Signs, Language and Behavior* (New York: Prentice-Hall, 1946). [Tr.]

Nature of the Linguistic Sign

1. SIGN, SIGNIFIED, SIGNIFIER

Some people regard language, when reduced to its elements, as a naming-process only—a list of words, each corresponding to the thing that it names. For example:

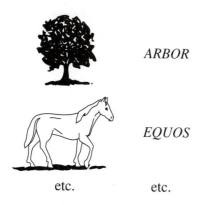

ARBOR

EQUOS

etc.   etc.

This conception is open to criticism at several points. It assumes that ready-made ideas exist before words (on this point, see below); it does not tell us whether a name is vocal or psychological in nature (*arbor*, for instance, can be considered from either viewpoint); finally, it lets us assume that the linking of a name and a thing is a very simple operation—an assumption that is anything but true. But this rather naive approach can bring us near the truth by showing us that the linguistic unit is a double entity, one formed by the associating of two terms.

We have seen in considering the speaking-circuit that both terms involved in the linguistic sign are psychological and are united in the brain by an associative bond. This point must be emphasized.

The linguistic sign unites, not a thing and a name, but a concept and a sound-image.[1] The latter is not the material sound, a purely physical thing, but the psychological imprint of the sound, the impression that it makes on our senses. The sound-image is sensory, and if I happen to call it "material," it is only in that sense, and by way of opposing it to the other term of the association, the concept, which is generally more abstract.

The psychological character of our sound-images becomes apparent when we observe our own speech. Without moving our lips or tongue, we can talk to ourselves or recite mentally a selection of verse. Because we regard the words of our language as sound-images, we must avoid speaking of the "phonemes" that make up the words. This term, which suggests vocal activity, is applicable to the spoken word only, to the realization of the inner image in discourse. We can avoid that misunderstanding by speaking of the *sounds* and *syllables* of a word provided we remember that the names refer to the sound-image.

The linguistic sign is then a two-sided psychological entity that can be represented by the drawing:

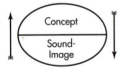

The two elements are intimately united, and each recalls the other. Whether we try to find the meaning of the Latin word *arbor* or the word that Latin uses to designate the concept "tree," it is clear that only the associations sanctioned by that language appear to us to conform to reality, and we disregard whatever others might be imagined.

Our definition of the linguistic sign poses an important question of terminology. I call the combination of a concept and a sound-image a *sign,* but in current usage the term generally designates only a sound-image, a word, for example (*arbor,* etc.). One tends to forget that *arbor* is called a sign only because it carries the concept "tree," with the result that the idea of the sensory part implies the idea of the whole.

Ambiguity would disappear if the three notions involved here were designated by three names, each suggesting and opposing the others. I propose to retain the word *sign* [*signe*] to designate the whole and to replace *concept* and *sound-image* respectively by *signified* [*signifié*] and *signifier* [*signifiant*]; the last two terms have the advantage of indicating the opposition that separates them from each other and from the whole of which they are parts. As regards *sign,* if I am satisfied with it, this is simply because I do not know of any word to replace it, the ordinary language suggesting no other.

The linguistic sign, as defined, has two primordial characteristics. In enunciating them I am also positing the basic principles of any study of this type.

2. PRINCIPLE I: THE ARBITRARY NATURE OF THE SIGN

The bond between the signifier and the signified is arbitrary. Since I mean by sign the whole that results from the associating of the signifier with the signified, I can simply say: *the linguistic sign is arbitrary.*

The idea of "sister" is not linked by any inner relationship to the succession of sounds *s-ö-r* which serves as its signifier in French; that it could be represented equally by just any other sequence is proved by differences among languages and by the very existence of different languages: the signified "ox" has as its signifier *b-ö-f* on one side of the border and *o-k-s (Ochs)* on the other.

No one disputes the principle of the arbitrary nature of the sign, but it is often easier to discover a truth than to assign to it its proper place. Principle I dominates all the linguistics of language; its consequences are numberless. It is true that not all of them are equally obvious at first glance; only after many detours does one discover them, and with them the primordial importance of the principle.

One remark in passing: when semiology becomes organized as a science, the question will arise whether or not it properly includes modes of expression based on completely natural signs, such as pantomime. Supposing that the new science welcomes them, its main concern will still be the whole group of systems grounded on the arbitrariness of the sign. In fact, every means of expression used in society is based, in principle, on collective behavior or—what amounts to the same thing—on convention. Polite formulas, for instance, though often imbued with a certain natural expressiveness (as in the case of a Chinese who greets his emperor by bowing down to the ground nine times), are nonetheless fixed by rule; it is this rule and not the intrinsic value of the gestures that obliges one to use them. Signs that are wholly arbitrary realize better than the others the ideal of the semiological process; that is why language, the most complex and universal of all systems of expression, is also the most characteristic; in this sense linguistics can become the master-pattern for all branches of semiology although language is only one particular semiological system.

The word *symbol* has been used to designate the linguistic sign, or more specifically, what is here called the signifier. Principle I in particular weighs against the use of this term. One characteristic of the symbol is that it is never wholly arbitrary; it is not empty, for there is the rudiment of a natural bond between the signifier and the signified. The symbol of justice, a pair of scales, could not be replaced by just any other symbol, such as a chariot.

The word *arbitrary* also calls for comment. The term should not imply that the choice of the signifier is left entirely to the speaker (we shall see below that the individual does not have the power to change a sign in any way once it has become established in the linguistic community); I mean that it is unmotivated, i.e. arbitrary in that it actually has no natural connection with the signified.

In concluding let us consider two objections that might be raised to the establishment of Principle I:

1. *Onomatopoeia* might be used to prove that the choice of the signifier is not always arbitrary. But onomatopoeic formations are never organic elements of a linguistic system. Besides, their number is much smaller than is generally supposed. Words like French *fouet* 'whip' or *glas* 'knell' may strike certain ears with suggestive sonority, but to see that they have not always had this property we need only examine their Latin forms (*fouet* is derived from *fagus* 'beech-tree,' *glas* from *classicum* 'sound of a trumpet'). The quality of their present sounds, or rather the quality that is attributed to them, is a fortuitous result of phonetic evolution.

As for authentic onomatopoeic words (e.g. *glug-glug, tick-tock*, etc.), not only are they limited in number, but also they are chosen somewhat arbitrarily, for they are only approximate and more or less conventional imitations of certain sounds (cf. English *bow-bow* and French *ouaoua*). In addition, once these words have been introduced into the language, they are to a certain extent subjected to the same evolution—phonetic, morphological, etc—that other words undergo (cf. *pigeon*, ultimately from Vulgar Latin *pipio*, derived in turn from an onomatopoeic formation): obvious proof that they lose something of their original character in order to assume that of the linguistic sign in general, which is unmotivated.

2. *Interjections,* closely related to onomatopoeia, can be attacked on the same grounds and come no closer to refuting our thesis. One is tempted to see in them spontaneous expressions of reality dictated, so to speak, by natural forces. But for most interjections we can show that there is no fixed bond between their signified and their signifier. We need only compare two languages on this point to

see how much such expressions differ from one language to the next (e.g. the English equivalent of French *aïe!* is *ouch!*). We know, moreover, that many interjections were once words with specific meanings (cf. French *diable!* 'darn!' *mordieu!* 'golly!' from *mort Dieu* 'God's death,' etc.).[2]

Onomatopoeic formations and interjections are of secondary importance, and their symbolic origin is in part open to dispute.

3. PRINCIPLE II: THE LINEAR NATURE OF THE SIGNIFIER

The signifier, being auditory, is unfolded solely in time from which it gets the following characteristics: (a) it represents a span, and (b) the span is measurable in a single dimension; it is a line.

While Principle II is obvious, apparently linguists have always neglected to state it, doubtless because they found it too simple; nevertheless, it is fundamental, and its consequences are incalculable. Its importance equals that of Principle I; the whole mechanism of language depends upon it. In contrast to visual signifiers (nautical signals, etc.) which can offer simultaneous groupings in several dimensions, auditory signifiers have at their command only the dimension of time. Their elements are presented in succession; they form a chain. This feature becomes readily apparent when they are represented in writing and the spatial line of graphic marks is substituted for succession in time.

Sometimes the linear nature of the signifier is not obvious. When I accent a syllable, for instance, it seems that I am concentrating more than one significant element on the same point. But this is an illusion; the syllable and its accent constitute only one phonational act. There is no duality within the act but only different oppositions to what precedes and what follows.

NOTES

1. The term sound-image may seem to be too restricted inasmuch as besides the representation of the sounds of a word there is also that of its articulation, the muscular image of the phonational act. But for F. de Saussure language is essentially a depository, a thing received from without. The sound-image is par excellence the natural representation of the word as a fact of potential language, outside any actual use of it in speaking. The motor side is thus implied or, in any event, occupies only a subordinate role with respect to the sound-image. [Ed.]

2. Cf. English *goodness!* and *zounds!* (from *God's wounds*). [Tr.]

The Concrete Entities of Language

1. DEFINITION: ENTITY AND UNIT

The signs that make up language are not abstractions but real objects; signs and their relations are what linguistics studies; they are the *concrete entities* of our science.

Let us first recall two principles that dominate the whole issue:

1. The linguistic entity exists only through the associating of the signifier with the signified. Whenever only one element is retained, the entity vanishes; instead of a concrete object we are faced with a mere abstraction. We constantly risk grasping only a part of the entity and thinking that we are embracing it in its totality; this would happen, for example, if we divided the spoken chain into syllables, for the syllable has no value except in phonology. A succession of sounds is linguistic only if it supports an idea. Considered independently, it is material for a physiological study, and nothing more than that.

The same is true of the signified as soon as it is separated from its signifier. Considered independently, concepts like "house," "white," "see," etc. belong to psychology. They become linguistic entities only when associated with sound-images; in language, a concept is a quality of its phonic substance just as a particular slice of sound is a quality of the concept.

The two-sided linguistic unit has often been compared with the human person, made up of the body and the soul. The comparison is hardly satisfactory. A better choice would be a chemical compound like water, a combination of hydrogen and oxygen; taken separately, neither element has any of the properties of water.

2. The linguistic entity is not accurately defined until it is *delimited*, i.e. separated from everything that surrounds it on the phonic chain. These delimited entities or units stand in opposition to each other in the mechanism of language.

One is at first tempted to liken linguistic signs to visual signs, which can exist in space without becoming confused, and to assume that separation of the significant elements can be accomplished in the same way, without recourse to any mental process. The word "form," which is often used to indicate them (cf. the expression "verbal form," "noun form") gives support to the mistake. But we know that the main characteristic of the sound-chain is that it is linear. Considered by itself, it is only a line, a continuous ribbon along which the ear perceives no self-sufficient and clear-cut division; to divide the chain, we must call in meanings. When we hear an unfamiliar language, we are at a loss to say how the succession of sounds should be analyzed, for analysis is impossible if only the phonic side of the linguistic phenomenon is considered. But when we know the meaning and function that must be attributed to each part of the chain, we see the parts detach themselves from each other and the shapeless ribbon break into segments. Yet there is nothing material in the analysis.

To summarize: language does not offer itself as a set of predelimited signs that need

only be studied according to their meaning and arrangement; it is a confused mass, and only attentiveness and familiarization will reveal its particular elements. The unit has no special phonic character, and the only definition that we can give it is this: it is *a slice of sound which to the exclusion of everything that precedes and follows it in the spoken chain is the signifier of a certain concept.*

2. METHOD OF DELIMITATION

One who knows a language singles out its units by a very simple method—in theory, at any rate. His method consists of using speaking as the source material of language and picturing it as two parallel chains, one of concepts *(A)* and the other of sound-images *(B).*

In an accurate delimitation, the division along the chain of sound-images *(a, b, c)* will correspond to the division along the chain of concepts *(a', b', c')*:

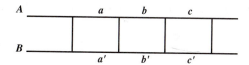

Take French *sizlaprā*. Can we cut the chain after *l* and make *sizl* a unit? No, we need only consider the concepts to see that the division is wrong. Neither is the syllabic division *siz-la-prā* to be taken for granted as having linguistic value. The only possible divisions are these: (1) *si-ž-la-prā (si je la prends* 'if I take it') and (2) *si-ž-l-aprā (si je l'apprends* 'if I learn it'), and they are determined by the meaning that is attached to the words.[1]

To verify the result of the procedure and be assured that we are really dealing with a unit, we must be able in comparing a series of sentences in which the same unit occurs to separate the unit from the rest of the context and find in each instance that meaning justifies the delimitation. Take the two French phrases *aforsdüvā* (la *force du*

vent 'the *force* of the wind'), and *abudfors* (a bout
de *force* 'exhausted'; *literally:* 'at the end of one's
force'). In each phrase the same concept coincides
with the same phonic slice, *fors;* thus it is certainly
a linguistic unit. But in *ilmeforsaparle* (il me *force*
a parler 'he *forces* me to talk') *fors* has an entirely
different meaning: it is therefore another unit.

3. PRACTICAL DIFFICULTIES OF DELIMITATION

The method outlined above is very simple in theory, but is it easy to apply? We are tempted to
think so if we start from the notion that the units
to be isolated are words. For what is a sentence
except a combination of words? And what can be
grasped more readily than words? Going back to
the example given above, we may say that the
analysis of the spoken chain *sižlaprã* resulted in
the delimiting of four units, and that the units are
words: *si-je-l-apprends*. But we are immediately
put on the defensive on noting that there has
been much disagreement about the nature of the
word, and a little reflection shows that the usual
meaning of the term is incompatible with the notion of concrete unit.

To be convinced, we need only think of French
cheval 'horse' and its plural form *chevaux*. People
readily say that they are two forms of the same
word; but considered as wholes, they are certainly
two distinct things with respect to both meaning
and sound. In *mwa* (mois, as in le *mois* de Septem-
bre 'the *month* of September') and *mwaz* (mois, in
un *mois* après 'a *month* later') there are also two
forms of the same word, and there is no question
of a concrete unit. The meaning is the same, but
the slices of sound are different. As soon as we try
to liken concrete units to words, we face a
dilemma: we must either ignore the relation—
which is nonetheless evident—that binds *cheval*
and *chevaux,* the two sounds of *mwa* and *mwaz,*
etc. and say that they are different words, or instead of concrete units be satisfied with the abstraction that links the different forms of the same

word. The concrete unit must be sought, not in
the word, but elsewhere. Besides, many words are
complex units, and we can easily single out their
subunits (suffixes, prefixes, radicals). Derivatives
like *pain-ful* and *delight-ful* can be divided into
distinct parts, each having an obvious meaning
and function. Conversely, some units are larger
than words: compounds (French *porte-plume*
'penholder'), locutions (*s'il vous plait* 'please'), inflected forms (*il a été* 'he has been'), etc. But these
units resist delimitation as strongly as do words
proper, making it extremely difficult to disentangle the interplay of units that are found in a
sound-chain and to specify the concrete elements
on which a language functions.

Doubtless speakers are unaware of the practical difficulties of delimiting units. Anything that
is of even the slightest significance seems like a
concrete element to them and they never fail to
single it out in discourse. But it is one thing to
feel the quick, delicate interplay of units and
quite another to account for them through methodical analysis.

A rather widely held theory makes sentences
the concrete units of language: we speak only in
sentences and subsequently single out the
words. But to what extent does the sentence belong to language? If it belongs to speaking, the
sentence cannot pass for the linguistic unit. But
let us suppose that this difficulty is set aside. If
we picture to ourselves in their totality the sentences that could be uttered, their most striking
characteristic is that in no way do they resemble
each other. We are at first tempted to liken the
immense diversity of sentences to the equal diversity of the individuals that make up a zoolog-
ical species. But this is an illusion: the characteristics that animals of the same species have in
common are much more significant than the
differences that separate them. In sentences, on
the contrary, diversity is dominant, and when
we look for the link that bridges their diversity,
again we find, without having looked for it, the
word with its grammatical characteristics and
thus fall back into the same difficulties as before.

4. CONCLUSION

In most sciences the question of units never even arises: the units are delimited from the outset. In zoology, the animal immediately presents itself. Astronomy works with units that are separated in space, the stars. The chemist can study the nature and composition of potassium bichromate without doubting for an instant that this is a well-defined object.

When a science has no concrete units that are immediately recognizable, it is because they are not necessary. In history, for example, is the unit the individual, the era, or the nation? We do not know. But what does it matter? We can study history without knowing the answer.

But just as the game of chess is entirely in the combination of the different chesspieces, language is characterized as a system based entirely on the opposition of its concrete units. We can neither dispense with becoming acquainted with them nor take a single step without coming back to them; and still, delimiting them is such a delicate problem that we may wonder at first whether they really exist.

Language then has the strange, striking characteristic of not having entities that are perceptible at the outset and yet of not permitting us to doubt that they exist and that their functioning constitutes it. Doubtless we have here a trait that distinguishes language from all other semiological institutions.

NOTE

1. Cf. the sounds [*jurmain*] in English: "your mine" or "you're mine." [Tr.]

Identities, Realities, Values

The statement just made brings us squarely up against a problem that is all the more important because any basic notion in static linguistics depends directly on our conception of the unit and even blends with it. This is what I should like successively to demonstrate with respect to the notions of synchronic identity, reality, and value.

A. What is a synchronic *identity?* Here it is not a question of the identity that links the French negation *pas* 'not' to Latin *passum,* a diachronic identity that will be dealt with elsewhere, but rather of the equally interesting identity by virtue of which we state that two sentences like je ne sais *pas* 'I *don't* know' and ne dîtes *pas* cela '*don't* say that' contain the same element. An idle question, one might say; there is identity because the same slice of sound carries the same meaning in the two sentences. But that explanation is unsatisfactory, for if the correspondence of slices of sound and concepts is proof of iden-tity, the reverse is not true. There can be identity without this correspondence. When *Gentlemen!* is repeated several times during a lecture, the listener has the feeling that the same expression is being used each time, and yet variations in utterance and intonation make for appreciable phonic differences in diverse contexts—differences just as appreciable as those that elsewhere separate different words (cf. French *pomme* 'apple' and *paume* 'palm,' *goutte* 'drop' and *je goute* 'I taste,' *fuir* 'flee,' and *fouir* 'stuff,' etc.);[1] besides, the feeling of identity persists even though there is no absolute identity between one *Gentlemen!* and the next from a semantic viewpoint either. In the same vein, a word can express quite different ideas without compromising its identity (cf. French *adopter* une mode '*adopt* a fashion' and *adopter* un enfant '*adopt* a child,' la *fleur* du pommier 'the *flower* of the apple tree' and la *fleur* de la noblesse 'the *flower* of nobility,' etc.).

The linguistic mechanism is geared to differences and identities, the former being only the counterpart of the latter. Everywhere then, the problem of identities appears; moreover, it blends partially with the problem of entities and units and is only a complication—illuminating at some points—of the larger problem. This characteristic stands out if we draw some comparisons with facts taken from outside speech. For instance, we speak of the identity of two "8:25 p.m. Geneva-to-Paris" trains that leave at twenty-four hour intervals. We feel that it is the same train each day, yet everything—the locomotive, coaches, personnel—is probably different. Or if a street is demolished, then rebuilt, we say that it is the same street even though in a material sense, perhaps nothing of the old one remains. Why can a street be completely rebuilt and still be the same? Because it does not constitute a purely material entity; it is based on certain conditions that are distinct from the materials that fit the conditions, e.g. its location with respect to other streets. Similarly, what makes the express is its hour of departure, its route, and in general every circumstance that sets it apart from other trains. Whenever the same conditions are fulfilled, the same entities are obtained. Still, the entities are not abstract since we cannot conceive of a street or train outside its material realization.

Let us contrast the preceding examples with the completely different case of a suit which has been stolen from me and which I find in the window of a second-hand store. Here we have a material entity that consists solely of the inert substance—the cloth, its lining, its trimmings, etc. Another suit would not be mine regardless of its similarity to it. But linguistic identity is not that of the garment; it is that of the train and the street. Each time I say the word *Gentlemen!* I renew its substance; each utterance is a new phonic act and a new psychological act. The bond between the two uses of the same word depends neither on material identity nor on sameness in meaning but on elements which must be sought after and which will point up the true nature of linguistic units.

B. What is a synchronic *reality?* To what concrete or abstract elements of language can the name be applied?

Take as an example the distinction between the parts of speech. What supports the classing of words as substantives, adjectives, etc.? Is it done in the name of a purely logical, extra-linguistic principle that is applied to grammar from without like the degrees of longitude and latitude on the globe? Or does it correspond to something that has its place in the system of language and is conditioned by it? In a word, is it a synchronic reality? The second supposition seems probable, but the first could also be defended. In the French sentence *ces gants sont bon marché* 'these gloves are cheap,' is *bon marché* an adjective? It is apparently an adjective from a logical viewpoint but not from the viewpoint of grammar, for *bon marché* fails to behave as an adjective (it is invariable, it never precedes its noun, etc.); in addition, it is composed of two words. Now the distinction between parts of speech is exactly what should serve to classify the words of language. How can a group of words be attributed to one of the "parts"? But to say that *bon* 'good' is an adjective and *marché* 'market' a substantive explains nothing. We are then dealing with a defective or incomplete classification; the division of words into substantives, verbs, adjectives, etc. is not an undeniable linguistic reality.[2]

Linguistics accordingly works continuously with concepts forged by grammarians without knowing whether or not the concepts actually correspond to the constituents of the system of language. But how can we find out? And if they are phantoms, what realities can we place in opposition to them?

To be rid of illusions we must first be convinced that the concrete entities of language are not directly accessible. If we try to grasp them, we come into contact with the true facts. Starting from there, we can set up all the classifications that linguistics needs for arranging all the facts at its disposal. On the other hand, to base the classifications on anything except concrete entities—

to say, for example, that the parts of speech are the constituents of language simply because they correspond to categories of logic—is to forget that there are no linguistic facts apart from the phonic substance cut into significant elements. **C.** Finally, not every idea touched upon in this chapter differs basically from what we have elsewhere called *values*. A new comparison with the set of chessmen will bring out this point. Take a knight, for instance. By itself is it an element in the game? Certainly not, for by its material make-up—outside its square and the other conditions of the game—it means nothing to the player; it becomes a real, concrete element only when endowed with value and wedded to it. Suppose that the piece happens to be destroyed or lost during a game. Can it be replaced by an equivalent piece? Certainly. Not only another knight but even a figure shorn of any resemblance to a knight can be declared identical provided the same value is attributed to it. We see then that in semiological systems like language, where elements hold each other in equilibrium in accordance with fixed rules, the notion of identity blends with that of value and *vice versa*.

In a word, that is why the notion of value envelops the notions of unit, concrete entity, and reality. But if there is no fundamental difference between these diverse notions, it follows that the problem can be stated successively in several ways. Whether we try to define the unit, reality, concrete entity, or value, we always come back to the central question that dominates all of static linguistics.

It would be interesting from a practical viewpoint to begin with units, to determine what they are and to account for their diversity by classifying them. It would be necessary to search for the reason for dividing language into words—for in spite of the difficulty of defining it, the word is a unit that strikes the mind, something central in the mechanism of language—but that is a subject which by itself would fill a volume. Next we would have to classify the subunits, then the larger units, etc. By determining in this way the elements that it manipulates, synchronic linguistics would completely fulfill its task, for it would relate all synchronic phenomena to their fundamental principle. It cannot be said that this basic problem has ever been faced squarely or that its scope and difficulty have been understood; in the matter of language, people have always been satisfied with ill-defined units.

Still, in spite of their capital importance, it is better to approach the problem of units through the study of value, for in my opinion value is of prime importance.

Translated by Wade Baskin

NOTES

1. Cf. English *bought: boat, naught: note, far: for: four* (for many speakers). [Tr.]

2. Form, function, and meaning combine to make the classing of the parts of speech even more difficult in English than in French. Cf. *ten-foot: ten feet in a ten-foot pole: the pole is ten feet long.* [Tr.]

16

Roland Barthes
1915–1980

At the time of his death, Roland Barthes was a professor at the Collége de France, the highest position in the French academic system. Throughout his academic career, he held chairs in lexicology, the social and economic sciences, and, finally, semiology. The variety of his study indicates the breadth of his published writing. No one essay or book is representative of the complete scope of Barthes's interests, intellectual ability, or influence. His work of the early 1960s articulated the concerns of and objectives for structuralism, as *S/Z* did for poststructuralism in the 1970s. His major works include *Writing Degree Zero* (1953; translated into English 1968), *Michelet par lui-meme* (1954), *Mythologies* (1957; trans. 1972), *On Racine* (1963, trans. 1964), *Elements of Semiology* (1964; trans. 1967), *Critique et vérité* (1966), *Système de la mode* (1967), *S/Z* (1970; trans. 1975), *Empire of Signs* (1970; trans. 1982), *Sade/Fourier/Loyola* (1971; trans. 1976), *The Pleasure of the Text* (1973; trans. 1976), *Roland Barthes by Roland Barthes* (1975; trans. 1977), *A Lover's Discourse: Fragments* (1977; trans. 1978), and *The Grain of the Voice: Interviews 1962–1980* (1981; trans. 1985).

"What Is Criticism?" first appeared in *Critical Essays* (1964), a collection that marks the beginning of Barthes's work in structuralism along with a range of other critical interests. As he states in "The Structuralist Activity," another essay in the collection, structuralism is an *activity*—not a school or movement—that reconstructs an "'object' in such a way as to manifest thereby the rules of functioning . . . of this object." The reconstruction of the object, what Barthes calls a "simulacrum," an "imitation," produces its intelligibility because now its function, invisible in its "natural" state, is realized.

The critical activity that Barthes describes in "What Is Criticism?" follows the structuralist criteria he sets out in "The Structuralist Activity." He answers not only the question in the title of the essay along structuralist lines, but the other questions the essay raises as well. What is the object of criticism? What is the critic's responsibility? What is the critic's task? The answers lie in Barthes's definition of "metalanguage," which is a "second language" or "discourse upon discourse." In a sense, the object of criticism—the metalanguage—is similar to the reconstruction of the object, for both produce the text's intelligibility. Thus, the critic's responsibility and task are to reconstruct not a work's meaning, but the "rules and constraints of that meaning's elaboration"; in other words, the critic reconstructs the *system* of a text because literature is a "language . . . a system of signs."

What Is Criticism?

It is always possible to prescribe major critical principles in accord with one's ideological situation, especially in France, where theoretical models have a great prestige, doubtless because they give the practitioner an assurance that he is participating at once in a combat, a history, and a totality; French criticism has developed in this way for some fifteen years, with various fortunes, within four major "philosophies." First of all, what is commonly—and questionably— called existentialism, which has produced Sartre's critical works, his *Baudelaire,* his *Flaubert,* the shorter articles on Proust, Mauriac, Giraudoux, and Ponge, and above all his splendid *Genet.* Then Marxism: we know (the argument is already an old one) how sterile orthodox Marxism has proved to be in criticism, proposing a purely mechanical explanation of works or promulgating slogans rather than criteria of values; hence it is on the "frontiers" of Marxism (and not at its avowed center) that we find the most fruitful criticism: Lucien Goldmann's work explicitly owes a great deal to Lukacs; it is among the most flexible and the most ingenious criticism which takes social and political history as its point of departure. And then psychoanalysis; in France today, the best representative of Freudian criticism is Charles Mauron, but here too it is the "marginal" psychoanalysis which has been most fruitful; taking its departure from an analysis of substances (and not of works), following the dynamic distortions of the image in a great number of poets, Bachelard has established something of a critical school, so influential that one might call French criticism today, in its most developed form, a criticism of Bachelardian inspiration (Poulet, Starobinski, Richard). Finally structuralism (or to simplify to an extreme and doubtless abusive degree: formalism): we know the importance, even the vogue of this movement in France since Lévi-Strauss has opened to it the methods of the social sciences and a certain philosophical reflection; few critical works have as yet resulted from it, but they are in preparation, and among them we shall doubtless find, in particular, the influence of linguistic models constructed by Saussure and extended by Jakobson (who himself, early in his career, participated in a movement of literary criticism, the Russian formalist school): it appears possible, for example, to develop an entire literary criticism starting from the two rhetorical categories established by Jakobson: metaphor and metonymy.

As we see, this French criticism is at once "national" (it owes little or nothing to Anglo-American criticism, to Spitzer and his followers, to the Croceans) and contemporary (one might even say "faithless"): entirely absorbed in a certain ideological present, it is reluctant to acknowledge any participation in the critical tradition of Sainte-Beuve, Taine, or Lanson. This last model nonetheless raises a special problem for our contemporary criticism. The work, method, and spirit of Lanson, himself a prototype of the French professor, has controlled, through countless epigones, the whole of academic criticism for fifty years. Since the (avowed) principles of this criticism are rigor and objectivity in the establishment of facts, one might suppose that there is no incompatibility between Lansonism and the ideological criticisms, which are all criticisms of interpretation. However, though the majority of French critics today are themselves professors, there is a certain tension between interpretive criticism and positivist (academic) criticism. This is because Lansonism is itself an ideology; not content to demand the application of the objective rules of all scientific investigation, it implies certain general convictions about man, history, literature, and the relations between author and work; for example, the psychology of Lansonism is utterly dated, consisting essentially of a kind of analogical determinism, according to which the details of a work must *resemble* the details of a life, the soul of a character must *resemble* the soul of the author, etc.—a very special ideology, since it is precisely in the years following its formulation that psychoanalysis, for example, has posited contrary relations, relations of denial, between a work and its author. Indeed, philosophical postulates are inevitable; Lansonism is not to be blamed for its prejudices but for the fact that it conceals them, masks them under the moral alibi of rigor and objectivity: ideology is smuggled into the baggage of scientism like contraband merchandise.

If these various ideological principles are possible at the same time (and for my part, in a certain sense I subscribe to each of them at the same time), it is doubtless because an ideological choice does not constitute the Being of criticism and because "truth" is not its sanction. Criticism is more than discourse in the name of "true" principles. It follows that the capital sin in criticism is not ideology but the silence by which it is masked: this guilty silence has a name: *good conscience,* or again, *bad faith.* How could we believe, in fact, that the work is an object exterior to the psyche and history of the man who interrogates it, an object over which the critic would exercise a kind of extraterritorial right? By what miracle would the profound communication which most critics postulate between the work and its author cease in relation to their own enterprise and their own epoch? Are there laws of creation valid for the writer but not for the critic? All criticism must include in its discourse (even if it is in the most indirect and modest manner imaginable) an implicit reflection on itself; every criticism is a criticism of the work *and* a criticism of itself. In other words, criticism is not at all a table of results or a body of judgments, it is essentially an activity, i.e., a series of intellectual acts profoundly committed to the historical and subjective existence (they are the same thing) of the man who performs them. Can an activity be "true"? It answers quite different requirements.

Every novelist, every poet, whatever the detours literary theory may take, is presumed to speak of objects and phenomena, even if they are imaginary, exterior and anterior to language: the world exists and the writer speaks: that is literature. The object of criticism is very different; the object of criticism is not "the world" but a discourse, the discourse of someone else: criticism is discourse upon a discourse; it is a second language, or a *metalanguage* (as the logicians would say), which operates on a first language (or *language object*). It follows that the critical language must deal with two kinds of relations: the relation of the critical language to the language of the author studied, and the relation of this language object to the world. It is the "friction" of these two languages which defines criticism and perhaps gives it a great resemblance to another mental activity, logic, which is also based on the distinction between language object and metalanguage.

For if criticism is only a metalanguage, this means that its task is not at all to discover "truths," but only "validities." In itself, a language is not true or false, it is or is not valid: valid, i.e., constitutes a coherent system of signs. The rules of literary language do not concern the conformity of this language to reality (whatever the claims of the realistic schools), but only its submission to the system of signs the author has established (and we must, of course, give the word *system* a very strong sense here). Criticism has no responsibility to say whether Proust has spoken "the truth," whether the Baron de Charlus was indeed the Count de Montesquiou, whether Françoise was Céleste, or even, more generally, whether the society Proust described reproduces accurately the historical conditions of the nobility's disappearance at the end of the nineteenth century; its role is solely to elaborate a language whose coherence, logic, in short whose *systematics* can collect or better still can "integrate" (in the mathematical sense of the word) the greatest possible quantity of Proustian language, exactly as a logical equation tests the validity of reasoning without taking sides as to the "truth" of the arguments it mobilizes. One can say that the critical task (and this is the sole guarantee of its universality) is purely formal: not to "discover" in the work or the author something "hidden," "profound," "secret" which hitherto passed unnoticed (by what miracle? Are we more perspicacious than our predecessors?), but only to adjust the language his period affords him (existentialism, Marxism, psychoanalysis) to the language, i.e., the formal system of logical constraints elaborated by the author according to his own period. The "proof" of a criticism is not of an "alethic" order (it does not proceed from truth), for critical discourse—like logical discourse, moreover—is never anything but tautological: it consists in saying ultimately, though placing its whole being within that delay, what thereby is not insignificant: Racine is Racine, Proust is Proust; critical "proof," if it exists, depends on an aptitude not to *discover* the work in question but on the contrary to *cover* it as completely as possible by its own language.

Thus we are concerned, once again, with an essentially formal activity, not in the esthetic but in the logical sense of the term. We might say that for criticism, the only way of avoiding "good conscience" or "bad faith" is to take as a moral goal not the decipherment of the work's meaning but the reconstruction of the rules and constraints of that meaning's elaboration; provided we admit at once that a literary work is a very special semantic system, whose goal is to put "meaning" in the world, but not "a meaning"; the work, at least the work which ordinarily accedes to critical scrutiny—and this is perhaps a definition of "good" literature—the work is never entirely nonsignifying (mysterious or "inspired"), and never entirely clear; it is, one may say, a *suspended* meaning: it offers itself to the reader as an avowed signifying system yet withholds itself from him as a signified object. This disappointment of meaning explains on the one hand why the literary work has so much power to ask the world questions (undermining the assured meanings which ideologies, beliefs, and common sense seem to possess), yet without ever answering them (there is no great work which is "dogmatic"), and on the other hand why it offers itself to endless decipherment, since there is no reason for us ever to stop speaking of Racine or Shakespeare (unless by a disaffection which will itself be a language): simultaneously an insistent proposition of meaning and a stubbornly fugitive meaning, literature is indeed only a *language,* i.e., a system of signs; its being is not in its message but in this "system." And thereby the critic is not responsible for reconstructing the work's message but only its system, just as the linguist is not responsible for deciphering the sentence's meaning but for establishing the formal structure which permits this meaning to be transmitted.

It is by acknowledging itself as no more than a language (or more precisely, a metalanguage) that criticism can be—paradoxically but authentically—both objective and subjective, historical and existential, totalitarian and liberal. For on the one hand, the language each critic chooses to speak does not come down to him from Heaven; it is one of the various languages his age affords him, it is objectively the end product of a certain historical ripening of knowledge, ideas, intellectual passions—it is a *necessity;* and on the other hand, this necessary language is chosen by each critic as a consequence of a certain existential organization, as the exercise of an intellectual function which belongs to him in his own right, an exercise in which he puts all his "profundity," i.e., his choices, his pleasures, his resistances, his obsessions. Thus begins, at the heart of the critical work, the dialogue of two histories and two subjectivities, the author's and the critic's. But this dialogue is egoistically shifted toward the present: criticism is not an "homage" to the truth of the past or to the truth of "others"—it is a construction of the intelligibility of our own time.

Translated by Richard Howard

17

Louis Marin
1931–1992

Louis Marin, author of a wide range of studies on Christianity, the French monarchy, Italian Renaissance painting, semiotics, and the human body in art and literature, posed questions throughout his career about the critical activity of reading and the ways we make meaning of human experience, be it an afternoon at an amusement park or our understanding of a particular work of art or literature. Marin taught at the École des Hautes Études en Sciences Sociales in Paris. Currently, four of his books have been translated into English: *Semiotics of the Passion Narrative* (1971; trans. 1980), *Utopics: Spatial Play* (1973; trans. 1984), *Portrait of the King* (1981; trans. 1988), and *Food for Thought* (1986; trans. 1989).

"Disneyland: A Degenerate Utopia" (1977) is based upon the study of utopias that he conducted in *Utopics: Spatial Play*. In his book, Marin looked at utopia from the meaning suggested by its etymology: Greek *ou,* "no" + Greek *topos,* "place." In contemporary usage, utopia is something in which we find (or construct) an unlikely state of perfection. But this involves a contradiction between utopia as a place and its self-proclaimed "no-place" neutrality, a contradiction that Marin seizes by asking, "Is it possible to dispel the contradiction in utopia without destroying utopia as well?" In the essay here, Marin focuses his attention on popular culture and examines a utopian prototype of American cultural life: the amusement park. Taking Disneyland as his model, Marin shows that such modern-day theme parks have a function that runs much deeper than mere amusement: such utopian playgrounds negate historical and social reality through the representation of opposites. In this case, the opposite of contemporary history is transcendental fantasy, or Disneyland.

The first objective of the essay is to illustrate the function and the permanence of utopian spaces through the "critical power" that they possess—the ability to represent "*differences* between social reality" and the ideal. In other words, what Disneyland does for us, says Marin, is reverse the content of a perception, show us how *unlike* utopia our world really is. This function, the ability to call attention to something by representing its opposite, is what Marin calls "metadiscourse," a form of critique that substitutes a practical activity (reading a map of Disneyland) for an ideological one (indulging the Disney fantasy). The second objective of the essay is to show how utopias undermine historical awareness, how they relegate meaning to the sphere of "entertainment," myth or fantasy. The dominant culture, says Marin, prevents our experience of Disneyland from having any meaningful relation to the culture on which it is based and instead dissolves knowledge into "fantasmic projections." These "fantasmic projections" are meant to amuse us; they are not to be taken seriously. In order to see beyond the fantasyland shrouded in the euphoria of the fantastic, we must become "liberated from [utopia's] fascinating grasp." To fail to do this is to be alienated from one's own history, transported to a "no-place" where we become the actors of a mythic drama on the stage of Fantasyland.

Disneyland: A Degenerate Utopia

My reflection on utopia was provoked by fascination with the signifier Ou-topia in which "something" was inscribed by Thomas More on a geographical chart: a name given by him at the beginning of the sixteenth century to a blessed island *between* England and America, *between* the Old and the New World.

The name Utopia is obviously written, through its Greek etymology, as a geographical referent; simultaneously in this writing, in this name, a play on words is also evident: Ou-topia is also Eu-topia, a play on words written by More in the margins of his book entitled *Utopia.* Sometimes, if not always, edges and borders have the precise and concealed function of indicating the center. Outopia can be written Eutopia by substitution of the first letters of the two words. I shall analyze such a play on words, through the play on spaces, as the core of the matrix of utopia. This play on words is also a play on letters which may be read as an indication of the utopian question: Nowhere, or the place of happiness.

Let me say, and this is my first step in another path toward utopia—a path leading my reading astray, a perverted path—that the topographical, political, social spaces articulated by the utopian text *play,* they shrink and swell, they warp, they do not fit exactly together: there are empty places between these spaces. The discourse held on utopia attempts, through the constructed reading of the text, to make the

spaces signified by the utopian text coherent and consistent by filling them up with its own signifying substance. When the discourse on utopia dismantles the parts of the utopian totality in order to explain how utopia is functioning, it prohibits the utopian text to play. The quasisystem of the utopian construction becomes, by this metadiscourse, a real system, a structured whole where space no longer plays. This is the essential critique I make of my former study of utopia.[1] It did not leave the text playing and the only way to restore the utopian text is to displace its inconsistencies, its deficiencies, and its excesses, its quasisystem toward mere fantasy, mere ludicity, to take our pleasure without speculative or practical interest in order to inquire ultimately into the nature of the instantaneous manifestation of this pleasure.

I might say that, in my first attempts on utopia, I tried to formalize what its name indicates—*ou-topia,* no-where—with the notion of "neutrality" which was also approached by Blanchot and Derrida. Such a notion does not concern origin and *telos;* the question is not that of the neutrality of the institutionalized power, be this power that of the dominant truth. What is in question is not this imaginary representation where utopia unfolds its architectural perfection by fulfilling its wish of escaping the historical determinations. Neutral is the name given to limits, to contradiction itself. It seems that the fate of all theoretical knowledge and of the practice which derives from it is to dissolve contradiction, to solve it in a change that neutralizes it by overtaking it, a change by which the whole reconstitutes itself, in its identity, on every synthetic level it reaches. So the traces of contradiction, of differentiation are nothing else than the determinations of the totality which capitalizes them as its properties. All forms of dialectical thinking and knowledge are apparent in this description.

Is it possible to think of and to formulate the contradiction signified by that notion of neutral? And to keep it working? I try to discern in the utopian texts the traces of contradiction as its *fiction,* opposed to concept or image. Being such a fiction, utopia transforms contradiction into a representation and, in its turn, my own discourse about utopia transformed it into theory. A reading authority, an interpretive power settled down in the nowhere of the limits, occupied this no-place, possessed it in the name of truth, repeating the gesture already accomplished by utopia itself which endlessly recuperates the unbearable neutral with a logic joining together the contradictory terms. To take a paradigmatic example in More's *Utopia* at the very moment when wealth and poverty are negated—utopia is neither rich nor poor— More creates the harmonious image or representation of a society which is at the same time rich and poor, rich to corrupt and dominate its imaginary outside, poor to maintain virtue and to build with its citizens the ethico-religious monument of the State.

Moreover, a discourse on utopia can formulate the critical analysis of More's *Utopia* and discern, in the synoptic and totalizing image derived from the esthetic *affabulation,* the power of a scheme of pure imagination, to use Kantian language, and in the matrix of that scheme, the communication between concept and history. Without any doubt, a discourse on utopia can attempt to display the "vertical" relationships, formulated in terms of misreading and recognition, which allow the levels of the utopian text to generate each other and to sketch what Lyotard has called a figure in the discourse.[2] A figurative mode of discourse, utopia as the textual product of utopian practice or fiction is produced, in its turn, by the critical discourse as a possible synthesis of an historical contradiction. The critical-theoretical discourse will show, but always *post festum,* how a representation can have been produced from the negation of contemporary history; history that is the absent referent of the utopian representation. The utopian representation denotes a reality which is not signified by the utopian figure, but whose true signified is the critical discourse given at the end of the representation's own historical time.

To be effective, such a critical discourse on utopia has to lean back against the wall, (the thesis) of a final truth of history, a place from which it is formulated. But what would happen to its authority if the wall cracks and splits?

In other words and to conclude this introduction, I might say that in describing the utopian space in a critical way, my theoretical discourse was formulated in terms of a topic and its fabricated utopian figure consisted in making coherent the spatial inconsistencies which the utopian image structured as a whole. I would not emphasize the topic of the utopian fantasy, which is also a fantasmatic topic since the theoretical discourse about utopia operates (like in dreams, the screen memory) by filling up the gaps and the blanks of the utopian text, of the utopian space, by producing the systematic elements which are necessary to make the text intelligible. This production was possible only *après coup,* in a site supposed to be the true knowledge of the end of history that is the end of utopia as well. The topic of utopian fantasy as well as the fantasmatic topic of the critical-theoretical discourse on utopia rest on that basis.

In trying to analyse Disneyland as a utopian space, I aim at two targets. [A more detailed version of this analysis originally appeared in *Utopiques, jeux d'espaces.*—Eds.] First, I mean to show the permanence of some patterns of spatial organization which the history of ideas and myths allows us to call utopian. We find these patterns in the architectural schemes and the texts which can roughly be viewed as utopian, but which also fill a specific function with regard to reality, history, and social relationships. This function is a critical one: it shows, through the picture drawn by the utopian writer or designer, the *differences* between social reality and a projected model of social existence. But the utopian representation possesses this critical power without being aware of it; that is, unconsciously. In a sense, I apply to utopian texts (or spaces) what has been suggested by Lévi-Strauss' methodology of distinguishing models—the conscious representation built by societies to explain and legitimate their specific existences—and structures—the "unconscious" set of transformations that the anthropologist's analysis displays in the models themselves. The critical impact of utopia is not the fact of the model itself, but the differences between the model and reality; these differences being exhibited by the utopian picture. But this critical discourse, which is a latent characteristic of all utopias, is not separated from dominant systems of ideas and values: it expresses itself through the structures, the vocabulary of those systems by which individuals, a social class, decision-making groups represent the real conditions of their existence. It is this latent critique which is unfolded, *post-festum,* by a theory of society, a metadiscourse which, generally speaking, substitutes a rational understanding of the social reality for what it considers to be an ideological system of representation. Utopia is a social theory, the discourse of which has not yet attained theoretical status. In other words, utopia expresses a "possible" intervention of reason in the social field, but a "possible" which remains possible. Utopia is the real, iconic, or textual picture of this "possible." Therefore, utopia has a two-sided nature. On the one hand, it expresses what is absolutely new, the "possible as such," what is unthinkable in the common categories of thought used by the peoples of a given time in its history. So it employs fiction, fable to say what it has to say. On the other hand, utopia

cannot transcend the common and ordinary language of a period and of a place. It cannot transgress completely the codes by which people make reality significant, by which they interpret reality, that is, the systems of representation of signs, symbols, and values which recreate, as significant for them, the real conditions of their existence. So Disneyland shows us the structure and the functions of utopia in its real topography and through its use by the visitor. From this vantage point, the possible tour which the visitor commences when he comes to Disneyland can be viewed as the narrative which characterizes utopia. The map of Disneyland he buys in order to know how to go from one place to another can play the role of the description; it performs the part of the representational picture which also characterizes utopia.

But Disneyland is more interesting from another point of view which is the second aim of our analysis: to show how a utopian structure and utopian functions degenerate, how the utopian representation can be entirely caught in a dominant system of ideas and values and, thus, be changed into a myth or a collective fantasy. Disneyland is the representation realized in a geographical space of the imaginary relationship which the dominant groups of American society maintain with their real conditions of existence or, more precisely, with the real history of the United States and with the space outside of its borders. Disneyland is a fantasmatic projection of the history of the American nation, of the way in which this history was conceived with regard to other peoples and to the natural world. Disneyland is an immense and displaced metaphor of the system of representations and values unique to American society.[3]

This projection has the precise function of alienating the visitor by a distorted and fantasmatic representation of daily life, by a fascinating picture of the past and the future, of what is estranged and what is familiar: comfort, welfare, consumption, scientific and technological progress, superpower, and morality. But this projection no longer has its critical impact: yes, to be sure, all the forms of alienation are represented in Disneyland, and we could believe Disneyland is the stage of these representations thanks to which they are known as such and called into critical question. But, in fact, this critical process is not possible in Disneyland in so far as the visitor to Disneyland is not a spectator estranged from the show, distanced from the myth, and liberated from its fascinating grasp. The visitor is on the stage; he performs the play; he is alienated by his part without being aware of performing a part. In "performing" Disney's utopia, the visitor realizes the models and the paradigms of his society in the mythical story by which he imagines his social community has been constructed.

THE LIMIT

One of the most notable features of the utopian picture is its limit: the utopian discourse inscribes the utopian representation in the imaginary space of a map, but at the same time, it makes this inscription in a geographical map impossible. We can make the survey of the blessed island described by Thomas More, but we cannot draw the geographical map in which this survey could take place. The utopian land belongs to "our world," but there is an insuperable gap between our world and utopia. More has given the paradigmatic example of this distance; he explains that when someone asked Raphael: "Where is the island of Utopia?" Raphael gave the precise information, but his words were hidden by a servant's cough. This mark in the discourse ironically designates the figurative process by signifying one of the conditions of the possibility of representation: it is a semiotic transposition of the frame of a painting.

This gap is a neutral space, the place of the limit between reality and utopia: by this distance which is a zero-point, utopia appears to be not a world beyond, but the reverse side of this world.

In Disneyland, the neutral space of the limit is displayed by three places, each of these having

a precise function. (1) The outer limit is the parking area, an open, unlimited space, weakly structured by the geometrical net of the parking lot. The parking area, where the visitor leaves his car, is the limit of the space of his daily life of which the car is one of the most powerful markers. The fact of leaving his car is an overdetermined sign of a codical change; for pragmatic utility, for his adjustment to a certain system of signs and behavior, the visitor substitutes another system of signs and behaviors, the system of playful symbols, the free field of consumption for nothing, the *passeist* and aleatory tour in the show. (2) The intermediary limit is lineal and discontinuous: the row of booths where a monetary substitution takes place. With his money, the visitor buys the Disneyland money, the tickets which allow him to participate in the Disneyland life. Thus, the Disneyland money is less a money than a language; with his real money the visitor buys the signs of the Disneyland vocabulary thanks to which he can perform his part, utter his "speech" or his individual narrative, take his tour in Disneyland. The amount of the exchange of real money for utopian signs determines the importance of his visit, the semantic volume of his tour, the number and the nature of its entertainments, in other words, it indirectly determines the number of syntactic rules which can be set working to coordinate the different signifying units. For example, with six dollars (four years ago), I received ten utopian signs—one A, one B, two C, three D, three E—and I was able to give utterance to a series of alternative narratives. (3) The inner limit is circular, linear, continuous, and articulated. It is the embankment of the Sante Fe and Disneyland Railway with its stations. This last limit is not a border line for the visitor or the "performer," since he does not necessarily use the train to go into Disneyland, but it is a limit for the utopian space which is encircled and closed by it. This limit belongs to the picture, to the representation, or to the map more than it appears as a limit to the traveller and to the tour he takes in the land. When he passes beyond the embankment, he is definitely in Disneyland. What I mean is that this element, the Railway, is a limit *in the map* for a dominant, all-seeing eye; it is not a limit for the visitor, the consumer, or performer of Disneyland; it is the first of the entertainments which he can consume. But, in fact, without being aware of it, the visitor is forced to spell the vocabulary in the right order. In other words, this structure which belongs to the map is a concealed *rule* of behavior for the visitor.

THE ACCESS TO THE CENTER

Disneyland is a centered space. Main Street USA leads the visitor to the center. But this route toward the central plaza is also the way toward Fantasyland, one of the four districts of Disneyland. So the most obvious axis of Disney's utopia leads the visitor not only from the circular limit or perimeter to the core of the closed space, but also from reality to fantasy. This fantasy is the trademark, the sign, the symbolic image of Disney's utopia. Fantasyland is made up of images, characters, animals of the tales illustrated by Disney in his animated films, magazines, books, and so on. This district is constituted by images; of particular significance is the fact that these images are realized, are made living by their transformation into real materials, wood, stone, plaster . . . and through their animation by men and women disguised as movie or storybook characters. Image is duplicated by reality in two opposite senses: on the one hand, it becomes real, but on the other, reality is changed into image, is grasped by the "imaginary." Thus, the visitor who has left reality outside finds it again, but as a real "*imaginaire*"; a fixed, stereotyped, powerful fantasy. The utopian place to which Main Street USA leads is the fantasmatic return of reality, its hallucinatory presence. This coming back of reality as a fantasy, as an hallucinatory wish-fulfillment, is in fact mediated by a complete system of representations elaborated by Walt Disney which constitutes a rhetorical and iconic code and vo-

cabulary that have been perfectly mastered by the visitor-performer. So this coming back appears to be brought about through a secondary process which is not only the stuff of images and representations molded by wish, but which constitutes the very actuality of the fantasy where wish is caught in its snare. That snare is the collective, totalitarian form taken by the "*imaginaire*" of a society, blocked by its specular self-image. One of the essential functions of the utopian image is to make apparent a wish in a *free* image of itself, in an image which can play in opposition to the fantasy which is an inert, blocked, and recurrent image. Disneyland is on the side of the fantasy and not on that of a free or utopian representation.

Main Street USA is the way of access to the center, to begin the visitor's tour, to narrate his story, to perform his speech. From the center, he can articulate the successive sequences of his narrative by means of the signs he has received in exchange for his money at the entrance. If we consider Disneyland as a text, Main Street USA is the channel of transmission of the story narrated by the visitor in making his tour. It allows him to communicate. Its function is phatic: it is the most primitive function of the communication since it only permits communication to take place without communicating anything. Thus, Disneyland can be viewed as thousands and thousands of narratives uttered by the visitors. Its text is constituted by this plurality of "lexies," to speak like Barthes, which are exchanged endlessly by the visitors according to the codes (vocabulary and syntax) imposed by the makers of Disneyland.

Now this semiotic function, the condition of possibility of all the messages, all the tours, all the stories told by the visitors, is taken into account structurally in a "lexie" belonging to a superior level, in the diagrammatic scheme of all the possible tours, an open and yet finite totality, the Disneyland map. When we look at this map (figure 17.1), we acknowledge a feature which we do not perceive when we recite the story in passing from the entrance to the center:

the fact that Main Street USA is not only a street, but a "district," a land which separates and links Frontierland and Adventureland on the one hand, and Tomorrowland on the other. For the visitor-performer, Main Street USA is an axis which allows him to begin to tell his story. For the spectator, it is a place in the map which articulates two worlds; this place makes him look at the relations and at the differences between these worlds. But as a route to Fantasyland, it is the axis of the founding principle of Disneyland.

We can sum up this analysis in the following terms: Main Street USA is a universal operator which articulates and builds up the text of Disneyland on all of its levels. We have discovered three functions of this operator, (1) *phatic:* it allows all the possible stories to be narrated; (2) *referential:* through it, reality becomes a fantasy and an image, a reality; (3) *integrative:* it is the space which divides Disneyland into two parts, left and right, and which relates these two parts to each other. It is at the same time a condition by which the space takes on meaning for the viewer and a condition by which the space can be narrated by the visitor (the actor). These three functions are filled up by a semantic content. Main Street USA is the place where the visitor can buy, in a nineteenth-century American decor, actual and real commodities with his real, actual money. Locus of exchange of meanings and symbols in the imaginary land of Disney, Main Street USA is also the real place of exchange of money and commodity. It is the locus of the societal truth—consumption—which is the truth for all of Disneyland. With Main Street USA, we have a part of the whole which is as good as the whole, which is equivalent to the whole. The fact that this place is also an evocation of the past is an attempt to reconcile or to exchange, in the space occupied by Main Street USA, the past and the present, that is, an ideal past and a real present. *USA Today* appears to be the *term referred to and represented;* it is the term through which all the contrary poles of the structure are exchanged, in the semantic and

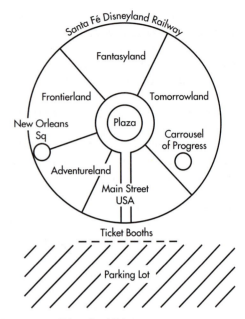

FIGURE 17.1 Disneyland Diagram.

economic meanings of the term, or, in other words, through which they are fictively reconciled. And by his narrative, the visitor performs, enacts reconciliation. This is the mythical aspect of Disneyland.

DISNEYLAND'S WORLDS: FROM THE NARRATIVE TO THE SYSTEM OF READINGS

Let us now leave the narrator-visitor and his *énonciation* to the hazards of his possible tours. As we have seen, the syntax of his "discourse-tour" is defined first by his passing through the limits and by his journey to the center. The visitor has learned the codes of the language of Disneyland and has thus been given the possibilities to tell his individual story. Yet, his freedom, the freedom of his *parole* (his tour) is constrained not only by these codes but also by the representation of an imaginary history. This imaginary history is contained in a stereotyped system of representations. In order to utter his own story, the visitor is forced to borrow these representations. He is manipulated by the system, even when he seems to freely choose his tour. Now these remarks allow us to substitute the analysis of the map for a possible narrative and for its performative narration; the analysis of the map or the description not of a *parcours* in time (which is always a narrative) but of a picture, the parts of which coexist in the space of the analogue-model. Methodologically, we assume that the narrative tours constitute a total system and that the map is the structure of this total system. But we have had to justify this substitution by ascertaining that the possible tours in Disneyland are absolutely constrained by the codes which the visitors are given. The interplay of the codes is reduced to nothing. In a real town, in an actual house, there are some codes constraining the freedom or the randomness of the individual routes or passageways, but these codes do not inform the totality of the messages emitted by the inhabitants of the town or the house. By *realizing* a pure model, that is, by making an "abstract" model a reality, the makers of Disneyland have excluded any possibility of code interference, of code interplay. Not only are the different possible tours strictly determined, but the map of Disneyland can be substituted for a visit. In other words, Disneyland is an example of a *langue* reduced to a univocal code, without *parole,* even though its visitors have the feeling of living a personal and unique adventure on their tour. And since this *langue* is a stereotyped fantasy, the visitor is caught in it, without any opportunity to escape. This can be a definition of an ideological conditioning, or of a collective neurosis. But Disneyland provides us with a valuable lesson. If the substitution of the map for the narrative is somehow a necessary condition of the analysis of a town, a house, etc., we must remember not to jumble together the narrative processes by which people live, thus consuming their town or their house and the textual system which gives them the signs, the symbols, and the syntactic rules through which they display and perform these narrative processes. An

architectural set is at the same time a set of places, routes, and pathways and a visible, "spectacular" totality. From this point of view, a progressive architecture seems to me to be defined as an attempt to build up a totality in which different codes are competing, are in conflict, are not coherent, in order to give to people living in this totality, and consuming it, an opportunity to perform their specific *parole,* to use the town as a multicoded or overcoded totality, codes subverting each other to the benefit of a poetic *parole.* I mean a totality allowing for behaviors characterized by a factor of unpredictability. Viewed from this perspective, Disneyland is an extra-ordinary dystopia. It displaces the spatial habitability, what we have called its narrativity, into its spectacular representation; it reduces the dynamic organization of the places, the aleatory unity of a possible tour to a univocal scheme allowing only the same redundant behavior. So we are justified in viewing the map of Disneyland as an analogue-model which assimilates the possible narratives of its space.

On the left of the map, two districts: Adventureland and Frontierland. The first is the representation of scenes of wildlife in exotic countries which are viewed during a boat trip on a tropical river. The second is the representation of scenes of the final conquest of the West. The latter district signifies the temporal distance of the past history of the American nation, the former, the spatial distance of the outside geographical world, the world of natural savagery. The two left districts represent the two distances of history and geography, and distance represented inside America in the first, and the distance represented outside in the second.

The right of the map is occupied by a single district: Tomorrowland, which consists principally of representations of the Future-as-Space, Einsteinian Time-Space which realizes the harmonious synthesis of the two-dimensional world represented on the left part as time and space, time as historical, national past and space as strange, exotic primitivism. Tomorrowland is space as time, the universe captured by science

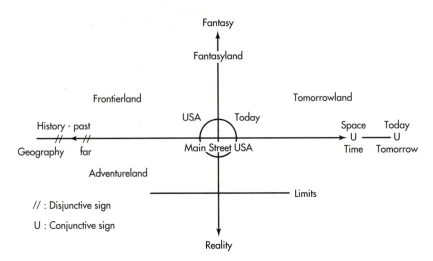

FIGURE 17.2 Semantic Structure of the Map.

and technology. In each of the two parts of Disneyland, we find an eccentric center, New Orleans Square on the left and the Carrousel of Progress, a gift of the General Electric Corporation, on the right. We can construct two models which are secondary representations of the map. The first is a purely analogous diagram, the second, a semantic structure (see figures 17.1 and 17.2).

Consideration of the center of these two models elicits the following remarks: (1) The center in the map is not the center in the semantic structure; in other words, the structure is not a simplified map. In the structure, the center is the sign of the numerous semiotic functions of Main Street USA as a route to the mapped center, an axis converting reality into fantasy, and vice versa, and an axis exchanging a scientific and technological conjunction of space and time for the historico-geographical distance.

(2) In the semantic structure, Main Street USA appears to be on different levels, formal and material, semiotic and semantic, a place of *exchange:* exchange of commodities and objects of consumption, but also of significations and symbols. The center of the structure functions

at once inside and outside the structure. Inside, it is determined rigorously by the two main correlations of which it is made up—reality and fantasy: historic-geographical distance and space-time. But it is not only an intersecting point of these two semantic axes; somehow it produces them as well. Through it, the contrary poles of the correlations exchange their meaning: reality becomes fantasmatic and fantasy, actual. The remoteness of exotic places and of the American national past becomes the universal space-time of science and technology and this universality becomes American. In the semiotic theory of the narrative, the center is the representation of the dialectical mediation from which springs the narrative solution: it is the image of the inventions determined by the story on its different levels.

(3) It is not without significance that in this case, this image, this representation is named USA and is declined in the present tense. The ultimate meaning of the center is the conversion of history into representation, a conversion by which the utopian space itself is caught in the representation. This representational mediation makes it clear that in the utopian place, com-

modities are significations and significations are commodities. By the selling of up-to-date consumer goods in the setting of a nineteenth-century street, between the adult reality and the childish fantasy, Walt Disney's utopia converts the commodities into significations. Reciprocally, what is bought there are signs, but these signs are *commodities.*

(4) *The Eccentric Centers:* I shall just describe the Pirates of the Caribbean attraction at the New Orleans Square center, in the left part of the map. This place reveals all of its semantic content only in its narration. So the visitor must begin to speak again in order to recite the underground tour, for the syntagmatic organization of his ride displays a primary and essential level of meaning. The first sequence of the narrative discourse is a place where skulls and skeletons are lying on heaps of gold and silver, diamonds and pearls. Next, the visitor goes through a naval battle in his little boat; then he sees offshore the attack of a town launched by the pirates. In the last sequence, the spoils are piled up in the pirate ships, the visitor is cheered by pirates feasting and revelling; and his tour is concluded. The narrative unfolds its moments in a reverse chronological order; the first scene in the tour-narrative is the last scene in the "real" story. And this inversion has an ethical meaning: crime does not pay. The morality of the fable is presented before the reading of the story in order to constrain the comprehension of the fable by a preexisting moral code. The potential force of the narrative, its unpredictability, is neutralized by the moral code which makes up all of the representation. But if we introduce the story into the structural scheme of the map and especially if we do so by relating it to the structural center, another meaning appears beneath the moral signification. The center, you remember, is a place of exchange of actual products and commodities of *today:* it is a marketplace and a place of consumption. Correlated to the eccentric center of the left part, Main Street USA signifies to the visitor that life is an endless

exchange and a constant consumption and, reciprocally, that the feudal accumulation of riches, the Spanish hoarding of treasure, the Old World conception of gold and money are not only morally criminal, but they are, economically, signs and symptoms of death. The treasure buried in the ground is a dead thing, a corpse. The commodity produced and sold is a living good because it can be consumed.

I do not want to overemphasize this point; but in Tomorrowland, on the right side of the map, the same meaning is made obvious by another eccentric center, the Carrousel of Progress. Here, the visitor becomes a spectator, immobilized and passive, seated in front of a circular and moving stage which shows him successive scenes taken from family life in the nineteenth century, the beginning of the twentieth century, today, and tomorrow. It is the *same* family that is presented in these different historical periods; the story of this "permanent" family is told to visitors who no longer narrate their own story. History is neutralized; the scenes only change in relation to the increasing quantity of electric implements, the increasing sophistication of the utensil-dominated human environment. The individual is shown to be progressively mastered, dominated by utensility. The scenic symbols of wealth are constructed by the number and variety of the means and tools of consumption, that is, by the quantity and variation of the technical and scientific mediations of consumption. The circular motion of the stage expresses this endless technological progress, as well as its necessity, its fate. And the specific organization of the space of representation symbolizes the passive satisfaction of endlessly increasing needs.

So the eccentric centers have powerful meaning-effects on Disneyland as a totality and on its districts.

We shall conclude our analysis with the following brief remarks. The left side of the map illustrates both the culture supplied by Americans to nineteenth-century America, and the one produced, at the same time, by adult, civilized, male, white people in exotic and remote countries. The living beings of Adventureland and Frontierland are only reproductions of reality. All that is living is an artifact; Nature is a simulacrum. Nature is a wild, primitive, savage world, but this world is only the appearance taken on by the machine in the utopian play. In other words, what is signified by the left part of the map is this assumption that the Machine is the truth, the actuality of the living. Mechanism and a mechanistic conception of the world, which are basic tenets of the utopian mode of thinking from the sixteenth century until today, are at work in Disneyland, no longer as a form of knowledge but as a disguised apparatus which can be taken for its contrary, the natural life.

On the right side of the map, the underlying truth of the left side becomes obvious. In Tomorrowland, machines are everywhere: from the atomic submarine to the moon rocket. The concealed meaning of the left side is now revealed thanks to the mediating center, Main Street USA. But these machines are neither true nor false; they are not, as in the left part, false reproductions. Instead, they are scaled-down models of the actual machines. We have false duplicates of living beings and concealed mechanistic springs on the left, obvious machines and true models on the right. Real nature is an appearance and the reduced model of the machine is reality. The ideology of representation and machine is all-pervading, and man is twice removed from Nature and science. Nature, which he sees, is a representation, the reverse side of which is a machine. Machines that he uses and with which he sometimes plays are the reduced models of a machinery which seizes him and which plays with him.

We find the same function of the reduced models, but on a different plane, in Fantasyland. This district is constituted by the real-realized images of the tales animated by Walt Disney. Fantasyland is the return of reality in a regressive and hallucinatory form. This imaginary *real* is a reproduction of the scenes the visitor has seen in the pirates' cave; but it is a regressive reproduction on a tiny and childish scale. We find the same fantasies of death, superpower, violence, destruction, and annihilation, but as reduced models of the attractions of the left side. Reduced models like those of Tomorrowland, but reduced models of death, strangeness, exoticism in the imaginary; they are the opposite of the reduced models of the right side, which show life, consumption, and techniques in their images. The realm of the Living in life-size is the realm of natural appearance in its historical past or geographical, anthropological remoteness. The realm of the Machine as a reduced model is the cultural truth of the American way of life, here and now, looking at itself as a universal way of living.

The function of Disney's utopia is to represent the exchange of the first and second realms of Natural Life and Scientific Technique and to express the ideology of this exchange on the stage and in the decor of utopia. Disneyland's ideological exchange can be illustrated by an elaboration of the semantic structure of the map (see Figure 17.3).

Five years ago, I concluded my first visit to Disneyland by making the following statements:

Axioms:

1. An ideology is a system of representations of the imaginary relationships which individuals have with their real living conditions.
2. Utopia is an ideological locus: it belongs to the ideological discourse.
3. Utopia is an ideological locus where ideology is put into play and called into question. Utopia is the stage where an ideology is performed or represented.
4. A myth is a narration which fantastically "resolves" a fundamental contradiction in a given society.

Theorem: A degenerate utopia is a fragment of the ideological discourse realized in the form of a myth or a collective fantasy.

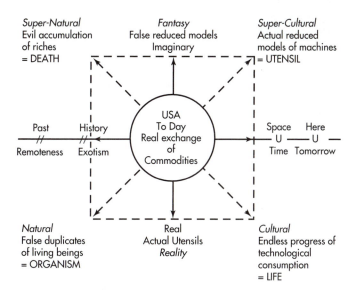

FIGURE 17.3 Semantic Structure of the Ideological Representation in Disneyland Utopia.

It seems to me, today, that these statements articulate only one side of the utopian problem, a side that relies on some questionable philosophical presuppositions, as I attempted to show at the beginning of this essay. Perhaps I was not aware five years ago that my own discourse in the past and, in a sense, the paper I publish today are also degenerate utopias, critical myths, theoretical fantasies. Perhaps I was not fully aware that science, theory have to get out of their Disneylands to discover their utopias.

NOTES

1. *Utopiques, jeux d'espaces* (Paris: Editions de Minuit, Collection Critique, 1973).

2. See Jean-François Lyotard, *Discours, Figure* (Paris: Klincksieck, 1971).

3. However, today I would be more careful: these statements are perhaps like the statements of an anthropologist visiting his research field for the first time. They may be characteristic of a foreigner reading the "Other" by superimposing upon it his own set of values and notions.

18

Teresa de Lauretis

1938–

Teresa de Lauretis is a professor of the history of consciousness at the University of California, Santa Cruz. She is the editor of *Feminist Studies/Critical Studies* (1986) and *Queer Theory: Lesbian and Gay Sexualities* (a special issue of the journal *differences*). She is also the author of several books, including *The Cinematic Apparatus* (1980), *The Technological Imagination: Theories and Fictions* (1980), *Technologies of Gender: Essays on Theory, Film, and Fiction* (1987), *Feminist Studies/Critical Studies* (1986), *The Practice of Love: Lesbian Sexuality and Perverse Desire* (1994), and *Alice Doesn't: Feminism, Semiotics, Cinema* (1984), from which the following chapter was taken. In this, and in her other work, de Lauretis works critically to explore personal/political issues relating to the theoretical notion of "subjectivity" by analyzing culture using methodologies from film theory, semiotics, marxism, feminism, and psychoanalysis.

In "Semiotics and Experience," de Lauretis uses Charles Sanders Peirce's semiotics to inform her discussion of subjectivity. She begins by noting that subjectivity is a process, an ongoing construction produced "not by external ideal, values, or material causes, but by one's own personal, subjective, engagement in the practices, discourses, and institutions that lend significance (value, meaning, and affect) to the events of the world." She analyzes Lévi-Strauss's theory of subjectivity and uncovers that his theory accounts only for male subjectivity. She compares this to the argument implicit in grammatical usage of "man" to refer to humankind, which, in turn, relates to her finding that the "subject," like "man," is a generic term, "and as such can designate equally and at once the female and the male subjects, with the result of erasing sexuality and sexual difference from subjectivity." She makes the point that many feminists fall into the same kind of trap that they are criticizing in their attempt to "collapse distinct orders of discourse into a single discourse that will account for contradictions and resolve them." However, de Lauretis believes that discussions of political issues of sexuality do not necessarily have to fall into the trap of sexism. De Lauretis tells us that Marx and Freud must be retained and worked through in the effort to figure out what she sees as the fundamental project of feminist theory—"how to theorize that experience, which is at once social and personal, and how to construct the female subject from that political and intellectual rage."

In order to do this, de Lauretis looks to semiotics. She criticizes Umberto Eco because his semiotics exclude the area in which human physicality is signified—an area she sees as being delineated in the work of Freud and of utmost importance to a study of how subjectivity works. She sees Eco's exclusion of this area in his semiotics as a political gesture declaring the body a "demilitarized zone." De Lauretis looks to Peirce to work through the problem of the body and its relation to subjectivity. She explains Peirce's three general classes of signs, defined by their effects, or interpretants: the emotional interpretant (or the feeling produced by the sign); the energetic interpretant (or the physical or mental effort required by the sign); and the logical interpretant (or the habit change the sign requires). De Lauretis is particularly interested in the final interpretant and discusses its role as forming habit, or experience, or subjectivity. In this way, she sees Peircian semiotics equipped to deal with the notion of female subjectivity and feminist theory.

De Lauretis argues that Peirce's definition of the "sign" shifts the emphasis from the sign, or the signifier, to the subject. In this way, she finds Peirce more helpful than Lacan, whose "formula is intended to stress the 'causation' of the subject in language (the 'discourse of the Other') and the subject's inadequacy, its 'lack-in-being.'" Whereas in "Peirce's formula, the subject's division from itself occurs in a temporal dimension ('in the flow of time'), . . . it also occurs by means of its relations to the chain of interpretants." It is the process of the habit-change that stops the process, provisionally, allowing the signification to attach itself to a subject.

By borrowing Peirce's notion of "habit," de Lauretis defines "experience more accurately as a complex of habits resulting from the semiotic interaction of 'outer world' and 'inner world,' the continuous engagement of a self or subject in social reality." Her reading of Peirce alongside Eco and Lacan allows her to restore the body to the subject. She argues that the subject "is the place in which, the body in whom, the significate effect of the sign takes hold and is real-ized."

Semiotics and Experience

There is a famous passage toward the beginning of *A Room of One's Own,* in which Woolf's fictional "I," sitting on the banks of the Oxbridge river to meditate on the topic of women and fiction, is suddenly seized by a great excitement, a tumult of ideas. No longer able to sit still, though lost in thought, "I" starts walking rapidly across the campus lawn.

> Instantly a man's figure rose to intercept me. Nor did I at first understand that the gesticulations of a curious-looking object, in a cutaway coat and evening shirt, were aimed at me. His face expressed horror, and indigna-

tion. *Instant rather than reason came to my help; he was a Beadle; I was a woman.* This was the turf; there was the path. Only the Fellows and Scholars are allowed here; the gravel is the place for me.[1]

The irony of the passage, with its exaggerated contrast and the emphatic disproportion of the two figures, "I" and the enforcer of academic patriarchy, comes into sharp focus in the sentences I underline. For what Woolf calls "instinct rather than reason" is in fact not instinct but inference, that is, the very process on which reasoning is based; reasoning which (this is the point of the passage) is neither admitted of, nor allowed to, women. And yet, to call it "instinct" is not quite so inaccurate, for what is instinct but a kind of knowledge internalized from daily, secular repetition of actions, impressions, and meanings, whose cause-and-effect or otherwise binding relation has been accepted as certain and even necessary? But since "instinct" carries too strong a connotation of automatic, brute, mindless response, it may be best to find a term more suggestive of the particular manner of knowledge or apprehension of self which leads Woolf's "I" to the gravel, to know that such is her place, and that she is not just *not* a Fellow or *not* a Scholar, but positively a woman. What term, other than "instinct" or "reason," can best designate that process of "understanding," of which the walk across the campus (rapid, excited, though "lost in thought") is the fictional analogue, the objective correlative; that process of self-representation which defines "I" as a woman or, in other words, en-genders the subject as female? Peirce might have called it "habit," as we shall see. But I will propose, at least provisionally, the term "experience."

"Experience" is a word widely recurrent in the feminist discourse, as in many others ranging from philosophy to common conversational speech. My concern here is only with the former. Though very much in need of clarification and elaboration, the notion of experience seems to me to be crucially important to feminist theory in that it bears directly on the major issues that have emerged from the women's movement—subjectivity, sexuality, the body, and feminist political practice. I should say from the outset that, by experience, I do not mean the mere registering of sensory data, or a purely mental (psychological) relation to objects and events, or the acquisition of skills and competences by accumulation or repeated exposure. I use the term not in the individualistic, idiosyncratic sense of something belonging to one and exclusively her own even though others might have "similar" experiences; but rather in the general

sense of a *process* by which, for all social beings, subjectivity is constructed. Through that process one places oneself or is placed in social reality, and so perceives and comprehends as subjective (referring to, even originating in, oneself) those relations—material, economic, and interpersonal—which are in fact social and, in a larger perspective, historical.[2] The process is continuous, its achievement unending or daily renewed. For each person, therefore, subjectivity is an ongoing construction, not a fixed point of departure or arrival from which one then interacts with the world. On the contrary, it is the effect of that interaction—which I call experience; and thus it is produced not by external ideas, values, or material causes, but by one's personal, subjective, engagement in the practices, discourses, and institutions that lend significance (value, meaning, and affect) to the events of the world.

But if it is to further our critical understanding of how the female subject is en-gendered, which is also to say, how the relation of women to woman is set up and variously reproduced (endlessly, it would seem), the notion of experience must be elaborated theoretically. It must be confronted, for one thing, with relevant theories of meaning or signification and, for another, with relevant conceptions of the subject. The following pages discuss the most urgent questions brought up by such a confrontation, and sketch out something of a direction for feminist theory.

In recent years the problem of the subject has come to be seen as fundamental for any inquiry, be it humanistic or social scientific, aimed at what may be broadly called a theory of culture. The terms in which the question of the subject was to be cast and recast in various disciplines, especially semiotics and film theory, had been set since the fifties and the well-known debate between Sartre and Lévi-Strauss, when the former accused the nascent structuralist method in the human sciences of doing away with the concrete, existential, historical subject in favor of ahistorical structures immanent in the mind. The reply of Lévi-Strauss, whose position on the matter was to weigh heavily not only on semiotics but on Lacanian psychoanalysis and Althusser's theory of ideology, was stated in the last volume of his *Mythologiques.* Its title was *L'homme nu, Naked Man.*[3] Thus whether one accepted the structuralist or the existential definition, the human subject was theoretically inscribed—hence solely conceivable—in the terms of a patriarchal symbolic order; and of that subject, women represented the sexual component or counterpart. The unstated assumption became explicit in Lévi-Strauss's paradoxical thesis that women are both like men and unlike men: they are human beings (like men), but their special function in culture and society is to be exchanged and circulated among men (unlike men). His theory stands on the premise that, because of their "value" as means of sexual reproduction, women are the means, objects, and signs, of social communication (among human beings).[4] Nevertheless, as he is unwilling to renounce humanism altogether, he cannot exclude women from humanity or "mankind." He therefore compromises by saying that women are also human beings, although in the symbolic order of culture they do not speak, desire, or produce meaning *for themselves,* as men do, by means of the exchange of women. One can only conclude that, insofar as women are human beings, they are (like) men. In short, be he naked or clothed by culture and history, this human subject is male.

A similar paradox was found to be concealed in the "grammatical" argument that "man" was the generic term for humankind. As studies in language-usage demonstrate, if "man" includes women (while the obverse is not true, for the term "woman" is always gendered, i.e., sexually connoted) it is only to the extent that, in the given context, women are (to be) perceived as non-gendered "human beings," and therefore, again, as man.[5] The feminist efforts to displace this assumption have been more often than not caught in the logical trap set up by the paradox. Either they have assumed that "the subject," like "man," is a generic term, and as such can designate equally and at once the female and the male subjects, with the result of erasing sexuality and sexual difference from subjectivity.[6] Or else they have been obliged to resort to an oppositional notion of "feminine" subject defined by silence, negativity, a natural sexuality, or a closeness to nature not compromised by patriarchal culture.[7] But such a notion—which simply reverts woman to the body and to sexuality as an immediacy of the biological, as nature—has no autonomous theoretical grounding and is moreover quite compatible with the conceptual framework of the sciences of man, as Lévi-Strauss makes clear. This feminine subject is not a different subject, one engendered or semiotically constituted as female by a specific kind of experience, but instead can easily continue to be seen as merely the sexual component or counterpart of the generic (masculine or male) subject. And indeed the maleness of that human subject and of his discourse is not only affirmed but universalized by theorizing woman as its repressed, its "negative semantic space," or its imaginary fantasy of coherence.

Another debate, not less important to our ends than the more illustrious one already mentioned, may serve to bring home the difficulty of constructing a notion of female subject from current discourses, as well as its vital theoretical necessity. The debate took place around the work of the British film journal *Screen,* whose special issue on Brecht (15 [Summer 1974]) marked the beginning of a project the journal was to develop over the next several years: a critique of the ideological structures of representational, classical narrative cinema. The debate was prompted by an American marxist-feminist film critic's response to *Screen's* introduction of psychoanalytic concepts such as fetishism and (symbolic) castration into film theory. Despite the journal's usefulness in making available "Continental Marxist-oriented studies" to

American film students, Julia Lesage charged, *Screen* writers "use certain premises from orthodox Freudianism as the basis for their political arguments about narrative form: premises . . . which are not only false but overtly sexist and as such demand political refutation."[8] Lesage's argument develops along two lines. First, she takes issue with the employ of what she calls "orthodox Freudianism" in a critical project that would otherwise be politically sound; and second, she objects to the textual interpretations offered by the *Screen* contributors, which she considers misreadings or distortions of the texts in question, one of them being Barthes's *S/Z*. In the latter case, too, the misreading is attributed to "a strictly Freudian interpretation of Barthes's use of the term 'fetishism' [which] finally undermines Heath's whole political argument in his reading of Brecht" (pp. 80–81).

While the two lines of the argument proceed from a single objection, the critic's aversion to "Freudian orthodoxy," they do not intersect again to produce the expected "refutation." I shall discuss them separately, beginning with the second.

> The major theoretical point made in the Brecht issue of *Screen* is that representational art—either a fictional narrative where there is an omniscient point of view or a feature film where we are given a superior viewpoint from which to judge the characters—makes us into 'subjects'. We consume the knowledge offered by the narrative, and as spectators, we get a sense of ourselves as unified, not as living in contradiction. [p. 81]

The alternative proposed by *Screen*, and supported by Lesage as politically correct, is "a Brechtian cinema," such as Godard's, in which "the spectator's very position is no longer one of pseudo-dominance; rather, it is given as critical and contradictory" (pp. 81–82). So far so good. But for the feminist critic the difficulties begin when the theoretical premises of this analysis

(and of Godard's cinema, I would insinuate) are made explicit. For the conception of the subject underlying this critique of classical representation and *its* unified subject comes not from orthodox Freudianism, as Lesage thinks, but from Lacan's rereading of Freud, and *there* the notion of castration (and consequently fetishism) is not only central but absolutely determining of subject processes."[9] In other words, the split, noncoherent subject that may be engaged or produced by a "Brechtian" cinema, as understood by the *Screen* contributors, is a subject constituted by the symbolic function of castration. And only with respect to this (Lacanian) subject, can it be said that representation is a structure of fetishism, serving to guarantee the subject's imaginary self-coherence, the delusion of one's stable identity. This, Lesage cannot accept: "Fetishism is described solely in phallic terms. . . . For Heath spectators are all the same—all male" (p. 83). Thus, she concludes, the "profound political implications" of the *Screen* critique of classical narrative cinema are severely undermined by positing the subject "as a monolith without contradictions: that is as male" (p. 82).

The problem here is that, for better or for worse, fetishism can only be "described" in phallic terms, at least by psychoanalysis. Any nonphallic description—assuming one were possible—would simply hide the term's discursive ground, the semantic network in which it takes its meaning, its conceptual basis in a certain epistemology; and at best we would be back with the humanistic subject, male but pretending to be "the human being." As the *Screen* contributors point out in their response, "if 'phallic' is *simply* made to mean 'masculine' and hence 'repressive', and then pushed back onto psychoanalysis as a monolithic orthodoxy, it will be easy to dismiss Freud, but what gets dismissed along with this is, again, the whole question of the process of the subject" (p. 89). The exchange is an excellent example of how discourse (including "political" discourse) is not just laden with pitfalls but is itself a pitfall. Lesage's argument falls into the very "trap" she accuses Heath of falling into; that is to say, the trap of representational coherence (Woolf's "reason"?), the pressure to collapse distinct orders of discourse into a single discourse that will account for contradictions and resolve them. "Phallic terms" and "male spectators," for example, cannot sit side by side; the political as practice (e.g., consciousness-raising groups) cannot be reduced to the adjective "political" used to mean a marxist or materialist textual interpretation; nor can the term "psychoanalysis," referring to the elaboration of a theory of the unconscious, be immediately compared and contrasted with "Freudianism," designating several popular and heterogeneous discourses on sexuality, from Karen Horney to Kate Millett to Masters and Johnson, which Lesage cites against "Freudian orthodoxy." Finally, if her argument fails to produce a refutation of the *Screen* critique or of its premises, it is because Lesage is unwilling to throw away the "political" baby (the "Brechtian" cinema and its divided subject) with the "sexist" bath water (the phallic order of the Lacanian symbolic) in which it is immersed.

The bind of theoretical feminism in its effort to work through the discourses of psychoanalysis and marxism is sharply focused in the writers' reply to Lesage's criticism of their use of the pronoun "he" in reference to the subject. Her point is well taken, they admit, but what pronoun should be used?

> What is probably needed in English is a movement between 'it', the subject in psychoanalysis, male and female (remember the importance of the thesis of bisexuality), and '/she', the subject defined as exchange value in the ideological assignation of discourse in so far as this is the positioning of a 'masculinity' in which 'femininity' is placed and displaced. [p. 86]

As noted in previous chapters, while psychoanalysis recognizes the inherent bisexuality of the subject, for whom femininity and masculinity are not qualities or attributes but positions in the symbolic processes of (self)-representation, psychoanalysis is itself caught up in "the ideological assignation of discourse," the structures of representation, narrative, vision, and meaning it seeks to analyze, reveal, or bring to light. Whence the tendency toward "he" in psychoanalytic writings, or indeed "/she," with femininity *sous rature* (as Derrida would have it).[10] Lacan's statement "The woman does not exist," Jacqueline Rose explains, "means, not that women do not exist, but that her status as an absolute category and guarantor of fantasy (exactly *The* woman) is false (The)." In his theory of psychoanalysis, therefore, "the question then becomes not so much the 'difficulty' of feminine sexuality consequent on phallic division, as what it means, given that division, to speak of the 'woman' at all."[11] However, although it is often stressed that "femininity" is not the same as "femaleness," just as "woman" is not the same as "women" (or the phallus is not the same as the penis), the two sets of terms continually overlap and slide onto each other, even in the writings of those who would insist that the distinction, tenuous as it is, is absolute. I think they should be taken at their word.[12]

That femininity *is* but the underside of masculinity—that is what taking them at their word implies—is no less evident in the practice of Freud's research than in the theory it has since produced: his work with Breuer on hysteria and the evidence collected from female patients were cast aside until the full elaboration of the Oedipus theory would require, toward the end of his life's work, a direct inquiry into female sexuality. This is well known. Why are we still surprised or unwilling to accept that, like the *Screen* discourse on the subject, psychoanalytic theory can only speak of women as woman, "/she," or "the woman"? Quite correctly Rose points out: "The description of feminine sexuality is, therefore, an exposure of the terms of its definition, the very opposite of a demand as to what that sexuality should be."[13] This definition is obviously inadequate to the current task of feminist theory, which, I believe, must address women, not woman, and question precisely that specific relation to sexuality which constitutes femaleness as the experience of a female subject. But this inadequacy, this inability of psychoanalytic theory to provide a satisfactory answer (which no other theory, by the way, provides), is not sufficient cause for dismissing Freud, who, unlike Jung or Horney, to say nothing of Masters and Johnson, does account for the continued existence and the functioning of patriarchy as a structure of subjectivity; in the same way as Marx accounts for the socioeconomic relations of capital that inform patriarchy in our times. Unless we too want to toss the baby along with the bath water, both Marx and Freud must be retained and worked through at once. And this has been the insistent emphasis of *Screen,* and its extraordinarily important contribution to film theory and, beyond it, to feminism.

That patriarchy exists concretely, in social relations, and that it works precisely through the very discursive and representational structures that allow us to recognize it, is the problem and the struggle of feminist theory. It is also, and more so, a problem of women's life. Thus, the relevance of this debate on the subject extends beyond its immediate context—the introduction of psychoanalytic terms into film studies in the early seventies—to the present impasse in the theoretical and political struggle. For the feminist critique of ideology, it is still the first line of Lesage's argument that carries its critical weight: her reaction of "political and intellectual rage." It is most appropriately a rage, an intensely personal response, grounded in the historical experience of both psychoanalytic and feminist practices in the United States. As she tells it.

As child of the 50's in the US, I lived in a milieu where I interpreted all personal relations and most literature I read in Freudian terms, where psychoanalysis promised the middle class solutions to their identity problems and angst, and where vulgarised Freudian concepts were part of daily life in the childbearing advice of Spock and Gessell, the advice columns of Dear Abby, and the sentimental filmic melodramas of Douglas Sirk. . . . In the 60's one of the first victories of the women's movement in the US was to liberate ourselves both academically and personally from the Freud trap. On the personal level, we stopped seeing ourselves as sick people who needed to be *cured* of masochism or of not having vaginal orgasms. We saw that the definition of an arrival at womanhood could not come through orthodox psychotherapy but rather through an understanding of the mechanisms of socialisation, which are inherently oppressive to women. [pp. 77–78]

If her argument fails to refute, and in fact corroborates, her opponents' contention that theory must be argued against in theoretical terms and at its own level of conceptual abstraction, the fundamental political (this time without quotation marks) validity of her intervention is summed up in the statement: "We not only have to recognize differences of class but *entirely different social experiences* based on the fact of sex, the fact of the oppression of one sex" (p. 83, my emphasis). The real difficulty, but also the most exciting, original project of feminist theory remains precisely this—how to theorize that experience, which is at once social and personal, and how to construct the female subject from that political and intellectual rage.

Women, writes Catharine MacKinnon, acquire gender identification "not so much through physical maturation or inculcation into appropriate role behavior as through the experience of sexuality."[14] Sex means both sexuality and gender, and the two are usually defined in terms of each other, in a vicious circle. But it is sexuality that determines gender, not vice versa; and sexuality, she says, is "a complex unity of physicality, emotionality, identity, and status affirmation." This is her description of how one "becomes a woman":

> Socially, femaleness means femininity, which means attractiveness to men, which means sexual attractiveness, which means sexual availability on male terms. What defines woman as such is what turns men on. Good girls are "attractive," bad girls "provocative." Gender socialization is the process through which women come to identify themselves as sexual beings, as beings that exist for men. It is that process through which women internalize (make their own) a male image of their sexuality *as* their identity as women. It is not just an illusion. [pp. 530–31]

Brilliant as this insight is in its dazzling concision, we still need to be more precise as to the ways in which the process works and how the experience of sexuality, in en-gendering one as female, does effect or construct what we may call a female subject. In order to begin to articulate, however tentatively, the relation of experience to subjectivity, we must make a detour through semiotics, where the question of the subject, as it happens, has become more prominent and more urgent.

In the last decade or so, semiotics has undergone a shift of its theoretical gears: a shift away from the classification of sign systems—their basic units, their levels of structural organization—and toward the exploration of the modes of production of signs and meanings, the ways in which systems and codes are used, transformed or transgressed in social practice. While formerly the emphasis was on studying sign systems (language, literature, cinema, architecture, music, etc.), conceived of as mechanisms that generate messages, what is now being examined is the work performed through them. It is this work or activity which constitutes and/or transforms the codes, at the same time as it consti-

tutes and transforms the individuals using the codes, performing the work; the individuals who are, therefore, the subjects of semiosis.

"Semiosis," a term borrowed from Charles Sanders Peirce, is expanded by Eco to designate the process by which a culture produces signs and/or attributes meanings to signs. Although for Eco meaning production or semiosis is a social activity, he allows that subjective factors are involved in each individual act of semiosis. The notion then might be pertinent to the two main emphases of current, or poststructuralist, semiotic theory. One is a semiotics focused on the subjective aspects of signification and strongly influenced by Lacanian psychoanalysis, where meaning is construed as a subject-effect (the subject being an effect of the signifier). The other is a semiotics concerned to stress the social aspect of signification, its practical, aesthetic, or ideological use in interpersonal communication; there, meaning is construed as semantic value produced through culturally shared codes. I am referring in particular, for the first emphasis, to the work of Julia Kristeva and Christian Metz (the Metz of *The Imaginary Signifier*), who maintain an affiliation with semiotics, though strongly influenced by psychoanalytic theory and, in Kristeva's case, intent on redefining in that perspective the very field and theoretical object of semiotics. The second emphasis is that of the work of Umberto Eco, whose attitude toward psychoanalysis has been consistently one of non-collaboration.

I will contend that there is, between these two emphases of semiotics, an area of theoretical overlap, a common ground; and there one ought to pose the question of the subject, locating subjectivity in the space contoured by the discourses of semiotics and psychoanalysis, neither in the former nor in the latter, but rather in their discursive intersection. Whether, or to what extent, the notion of semiosis may be stretched to reach into that common ground and to account for the subjective and the social aspects of meaning production, or whether indeed it can be said to mediate between them, will determine its usefulness in mapping the relations of meaning to what I have proposed to call experience.

At the end of *A Theory of Semiotics,* in a short, hasty chapter entitled "The Subject of Semiotics," Eco asks:

> Since it has been said that the labor of sign production also represents a form of social criticism and of social practice, a sort of ghostly presence, until now somewhat removed from the present discourse, finally makes an unavoidable appearance. What is, in the semiotic framework, the place of the *acting subject* of every semiosic act?[15]

From the answer given, it is clear that by "acting subject" he means the sender of the message, the subject of enunciation or of a speech act, not its addressee or receiver; not the reader but the speaker/writer. Moreover such a subject, insofar as it is presupposed by its statements, must be "'read' as an element of the conveyed content" (*TS,* p. 315). And although he grants that "a theory of the relationship of sender-addressee should also take into account the role of the 'speaking' subject not only as a communicational figment but as a concrete historical, biological, psychic subject, as it is approached by psychoanalysis and related disciplines," nevertheless, for Eco, semiotics can approach the subject only by semiotic categories—and these exclude all presymbolic or unconscious processes. He professes awareness, however, that some attempts have been made, within semiotics, to specify the subjective determinants of a text, or the "creative activity of a semiosis-making subject"; and in a footnote we find the reference to, and a long quotation from, Julia Kristeva. As the quotation sets out the other term of Eco's argument and identifies his interlocutor (Kristeva's "speaking subject" is ostensibly the only notion of the subject against which he debates), it is necessary to cite it in its entirety here. Kristeva writes:

One phase of semiology is now over: that which runs from Saussure and Peirce to the Prague School and structuralism, and has made possible the systematic description of the social and/or symbolic constraint within each significant practice. . . . A critique of this "semiology of systems" and of its phenomenological foundations is possible only if it starts from a theory of meaning which must necessarily be a theory of the speaking subject. . . . The theory of meaning now stands at a cross-roads: either it will remain an attempt at formalizing meaning-systems by increasing sophistication of the logico-mathematical tools which enable it to formulate models on the basis of a conception (already rather dated) of meaning as the act of a *transcendental ego,* cut off from its body, its unconscious, and also its history; or else it will attune itself to the theory of the speaking subject as a divided subject (conscious/unconscious) and go on to attempt to specify the types of operations characteristic of the two sides of this split: thereby exposing them . . . on the one hand, to bio-physiological processes (themselves already an inescapable part of signifying processes; what Freud labelled "drives"), and, on the other hand, to social constraints (family structures, modes of production, etc.).[16]

With these words, Kristeva defines (and Eco implicitly accepts her definition) a fork in the path of semiotic research, a "cross-roads" where the theory of meaning encounters the "ghost" of the subject. After abandoning the path of the transcendental ego to follow the divided subject, a critical semiotics itself finds the way ahead divided, like that subject, split into conscious and unconscious, social constraints and pre-symbolic drives. And while Kristeva's work will increasingly inscribe itself on the "side of the split" investigated by the science of the unconscious, Eco's situates itself squarely on the other side. Thus, in his response, he concedes that the subjective determinants and the "individual material subjects" of a text are part of the signifying process, but at the same time excludes them from the semiotic field of inquiry: "either [the subjects] can be defined in terms of semiotic structures or—from this point of view—they do not exist at all" (*TS*, p. 316). For just as the subjective determinants can only be studied semiotically "as contents of the text itself," so can the subject be affirmed or known only as a textual element. "Any other attempt to introduce a consideration of the subject into the semiotic discourse would make semiotics trespass on one of its 'natural' boundaries" (*TS*, p. 315).[17] And it is not by chance, he adds slyly, that Kristeva calls her work not "semiotics" but "*sémanalyse.*"

Something of a territorial struggle transpires from these remarks of Eco's, and I will return to it later on; however, he is not alone in maintaining the "split," if not the disciplinary distinction, between discourses which take as their theoretical objects, respectively, the conscious and the unconscious. . . . Kristeva herself, who pinpointed the problem exactly, in the essay just cited, seems to be exclusively concerned with the operations of the unconscious insofar as they exceed or escape the symbolic; this was already clear in her strategy of shifting the ground of the term "semiotic" (*le sémiotique*) to the domain of bio-physiological or pre-symbolic processes, a strategy that does not appear to have been successful. For my present purposes, the advantage of Eco's stance with regard to what comprises the object, field, and method of semiotics is that his position is unambiguously spelled out, and thus offers us the possibility not only of assessing its limits, but also of engaging it constructively, of working through it, and displacing its "boundaries."

Unlike Kristeva's, the boundaries which Eco imposes on the field and on the theoretical object of semiotics are postulated methodologically and are not to be ascribed to an ontology. His boundaries are posed as terms of a cultural process and a perspective from which to understand it, with no claim whatsoever as to their being substantive (hence the quotation marks he

puts around the word "natural"). Yet one cannot help observing that they do coincide almost too neatly with a pre-Freudian perspective that reproposes a dichotomous idea of body and mind, matter and intellect, physis and reason. On one side is the area of stimuli and what Eco calls "physical information," thus suggesting its nonsignificant, mechanical nature—for example, the salivation of the dog in Pavlov's famous experiment. These constitute "the lower threshold" of the semiotic domain, before which there is no semiosis, signification, or culture. On the other side, at the "upper threshold," are those phenomena which, universally shared by all societies, must therefore be taken as the very foundation of culture, its institutive moment: kinship, tool production, and the economic exchange of goods. But these latter too are communicative exchanges, says Eco after Marx and Lévi-Strauss, no less productive of meanings and social relations than is language itself. Thus all of culture and its laws can be studied semiotically, as a system of systems of signification. In other words, the semiotic perspective would subsume the fields of cultural anthropology and political economy—the upper threshold extending all the way to the vanishing point—but exclude the entire area of human physicality, the body, instincts, drives, and their representations (it is no coincidence that the single example of "stimulus" to be found in *A Theory of Semiotics*, Pavlov's dog, is derived from the non-human world). Eco's semiotics excludes, that is, the very area in which human physicality comes to be represented, signi-fied, assumed in the relations of meaning, and thus productive of subjectivity—the area delineated and sketched out by the work of Freud.

The "methodological" decision to exclude this no man's land between nature and culture (a no man's land, exactly, where Lévi-Strauss had stumbled and found himself bogged down) amounts to a political gesture: to declare it a demilitarized zone, a theoretical Berlin Wall. This gesture has many advantages for a theory of meaning production that wants to be scientific and uncompromisingly historical-materialist, as Eco's does.

> By accepting this limit, semiotics fully avoids any risk of idealism. On the contrary semiotics recognizes as the only testable subject matter of its discourse the social existence of the universe of signification, as it is revealed by the physical testability of interpretants—which are, to reinforce this point for the last time, *material expressions*. [*TS,* p. 317]

To escape the idealist danger is doubtless of the utmost importance, given the historical context of Eco's work and the philosophical tradition to which he may be the last innovative contributor—the Italian tradition of secular, progressive, democratic rationalism, that in our century has included Croce as well as Gramsci. It remains to be seen, however, whether another, equally serious danger can be avoided, a risk against which no methodological disclaimer can insure: that of elaborating a historical-materialist theory of culture which must deny the materiality and the historicity of the subject itself, or rather the *subjects* of culture. For it is not just the "speaking subject" of Kristeva's narrowly linguistic, or language-determined, perspective that is at issue, but subjects who speak and listen, write and read, make and watch films, work and play, and so forth; who are, in short, concurrently and often contradictorily engaged in a plurality of heterogeneous experiences, practices, and discourses, where subjectivity and gender are constructed, anchored, or reproduced.

Eco's project is the outline of a materialist, nondeterministic theory of culture, one in which aesthetics can be founded in social communication, and creativity integrated in human work; semiosis being a work by and through signs, and signs being—he unequivocally asserts—social forces. This is the sense of his rereading of Peirce, of what he calls Peirce's "not ontological but pragmatic realism": Peirce was not only interested in "objects as ontological sets of properties," but more importantly he conceived of objects as "occasions and results of active experience. To discover an object means to discover the way by which we operate upon the world, producing objects or producing practical uses of them."[18] Eco's debt to Peirce is extensive. The latter's concepts of interpretant and unlimited semiosis are pivotal to *A Theory of Semiotics,* which turns on the notion of a dialectic interaction between codes and modes of sign production. They serve to bridge the gap between discourse and reality, between the sign and its referent (the empirical object to which the sign refers); and so they usher in a theory of meaning as a continual cultural production that is not only susceptible of ideological transformation, but materially based in historical change.

When Eco redefines the classical notion of sign as a sign-function, and proposes it to be the complex, but temporary and even unstable correlation between a sign-vehicle and a sign content, rather than a fixed, though arbitrary, relationship between a signifier and a signified; and when he further allows that the correlation is dependent on the context, including the conditions of enunciation and reception in actual communicative situations, he is following a trail marked out in Peirce's famous definition:

> A sign, or representamen, is something which stands to somebody for something in some respect or capacity. It addresses somebody, that is, it creates in the mind of that person an equivalent sign, or perhaps a more developed sign. That sign which it creates I call the *interpretant* of the first sign. The sign stands for something, its *object.* It stands for that object, not in all respects, but in reference to a sort of idea, which I have sometimes called the *ground* of the representation.[19]

Peirce greatly complicates the picture in which a signifier would immediately correspond to a signified. As Eco notes, the notions of meaning, ground, and interpretant all pertain in some degree to the area of the signified, while interpretant and ground also pertain in some degree to the area of the referent (Object). Moreover, Peirce distinguishes a Dynamic Object and an Immediate Object, and it is the notion of ground that sustains the distinction. The Dynamic Object is external to the sign: it is that which "by some means contrives to determine the sign to its representation" (4.536). On the contrary, the Immediate Object ("the object as the sign itself represents it") is internal; it is an "Idea" or a "mental representation." From the analysis of the notion of "ground" (a sort of context of the sign, which makes pertinent certain attributes or aspects of the object and thus is already a component of meaning), Eco argues that not only does the sign in Peirce appear as a textual matrix; the object too, "is not necessarily a thing or a state of the world but a rule, a law, a prescription: it appears as the operational description of a set of possible experiences" (*RR*, p. 181).

> Signs have a direct connection with Dynamic Objects only insofar as objects determine the formation of a sign; on the other hand, signs only "know" Immediate Objects, that is, meanings. There is a difference between *the object of which a sign is a sign* and the *object of a sign:* the former is the Dynamic Object, a state of the outer world; the latter is a semiotic construction. [*RR*, p. 193]

But the Immediate Object's relation to the representamen is established by the interpretant, which is itself another sign, "perhaps a more developed sign." Thus, in the process of unlimited semiosis the nexus object-sign-meaning is a series of ongoing mediations between "outer world" and "inner" or mental representations. The key term, the principle that supports the series of mediations, is the interpretant. However, cautions Eco, the potentially endless succession of interpretants is not to be construed as infinite semiotic regression, a free circulation of meaning: for the pragmatist, reality is a construction, "more a Result than a mere Datum" and "the idea of *meaning* is such as to involve some reference to a *purpose*" (5.175). Hence the crucial notion, for both Eco and Peirce, is that of a final or "ultimate" interpretant.

As Peirce puts it, "the problem of what the 'meaning' of an intellectual concept is can only be solved by the study of the interpretants, or proper significate effects, of signs" (5.475). He then describes three general classes. 1. "The first proper significate effect of a sign is a *feeling* produced by it." This is the *emotional* interpretant. Although its "foundation of truth" may be slight at times, often this remains the only effect produced by a sign such as, for example, the performance of a piece of music. 2. When a further significate effect is produced, however, is it "through the mediation of the emotional interpretant"; and this second type of meaning effect he calls the *energetic* interpretant, for it involves an "effort," which may be a muscular exertion but is more usually a mental effort, "an exertion upon the Inner World." 3. The third and final type of meaning effect that may be produced by the sign, through the mediation of the former two, is "a *habit-change*": "a modification of a person's tendencies toward action, resulting from previous experiences or from previous exertions." This is the "ultimate" interpretant of the sign, the effect of meaning on which the process of semiosis, in the instance considered, comes to rest. "The real and living logical conclusion *is* that habit," Peirce states, and designates the third type of significate effect, the *logical* interpretant. But immediately he adds a qualification, distinguishing this logical interpretant from the concept or "intellectual" sign:

> The concept which is a logical interpretant is only imperfectly so. It somewhat partakes of the nature of a verbal definition, and is as inferior to the habit, and much in the same way, as a verbal definition is inferior to the real definition. The deliberately formed, self-analyzing habit—self-analyzing because

formed by the aid of analysis of the exercises that nourished it—is the living definition, the veritable and final logical interpretant. [5.491]

The final interpretant, then, is not "logical" in the sense in which a syllogism is logical, or because it is the result of an "intellectual" operation like deductive reasoning. It is "logical" in the sense that it is "self-analyzing" or, put another way, that it "makes sense" of the emotion and muscular/mental effort that preceded it, by providing a conceptual representation of that effort. Such a representation is implicit in the notion of habit as a "tendency toward action" and in the solidarity of habit and belief.[20]

This logical interpretant is precisely illustrated, I submit, in the passage cited from Woolf's text. What she calls "instinct rather than reason" is semiosis as Peirce describes it: the process by which the "I" interprets the sign (the "curious-looking object, in cut-away coat and evening shirt") to mean a Beadle, and his gesticulations to convey the patriarchal prohibition well known to her as a result of habit, of previous emotional and muscular/mental effort; their ultimate "significate effect" being the "logical" representation, "I was a woman." Having so understood the sign, the "I" acts accordingly—she moves over to the gravel path. ("The real and living logical conclusion *is* that habit," as Peirce said.) This notion of semiosis, therefore, need not be stretched to reach into the two semiotic territories marked out, by their respective proponents, as the biophysiological and the social operations of signification. It is already so stretched to span them both and to connect them, though obviously, in Peirce, it has no purchase on the unconscious, no hold on unconscious processes. And whether it may even venture, so to speak, into that side of the "split" must remain in question for the time being. But with regard to the more immediate problem of articulating the relation of meaning production to experience, and hence to the construction of

subjectivity, Peirce's semiosis appears to have a usefulness that Eco vehemently denies and that I, on the contrary, will attempt to demonstrate further.

The importance of Peirce's formulation of the ultimate interpretant for Eco's own theory is that it provides him with the link between semiosis and reality, between signification and concrete action. The final interpretant is not a Platonic essence or a transcendental law of signification but a result, as well as a rule: "to have understood the sign as a rule through the series of its interpretants means to have acquired the habit to act according to the prescription given by the sign. . . . The action is the place in which the *haecceitas* ends the game of semiosis" (*RR,* pp. 194–95). This theory of meaning does not incur the risk of idealism because the system of systems of signs which makes human communication possible is translatable into habits, concrete action upon the world; and this action then rejoins the universe of signification by converting itself into new signs and new semiotic systems. At this point in his theory, however, Eco again needs to distance or to ward off the possibility that something of a subjective order might enter the semiotic field, specifically through the energetic interpretant.

In order to make the interpretant a fruitful notion, one must first of all free it from any psychological misunderstanding. . . . According to [Peirce] even ideas are signs, in various passages the interpretants appear also as mental events. I am only suggesting that from the point of view of the theory of signification, *we should perform a sort of surgical operation* and retain only a precise aspect of this category. Interpretants are the testable and describable correspondents associated *by public agreement* to another sign. In this way the analysis of content becomes a cultural operation which works only on physically testable cultural products, that is, other signs and their reciprocal correlations. [*RR,* p. 198; my emphasis]

On the one hand, then, the rereading of Peirce allows Eco to find the "missing link" between signification and physical reality, that link being human action. On the other, that human action must be excised (by a "surgical operation") of its psychological, psychic, and subjective component. This paradoxical situation is most evident in Eco's subsequent work, in particular the title essay of the volume *The Role of the Reader* (1979), where the essay on Peirce I have been discussing is also published, though it was written in 1976, at the time of *A Theory of Semiotics,* and thus constitutes a bridge between the two works. Published in Italy in a book-length version, with the Latin title *Lector in fabula* ("The Reader in the Fable")—but that title is a pun on the proverb "*lupus in fabula,*" speak of the devil—the later book is logcally, all too logically, devoted to the Reader. It provides a painstakingly detailed account of the "role" of the reader in interpreting the text; interpretation being the manner in which the reader cooperates with the text's own construction of meaning, its "generative structure."

More pointedly than "the subject of semiotics," Eco's Model Reader is presented as a *locus* of logical moves, impervious to the heterogeneity of historical process, to difference or contradiction. For the Reader is already contemplated by the text, is in fact an element of its interpretation. Like the Author, the Reader is a textual strategy, a set of specific competences and felicitous conditions established by the text, which must be met if the text is to be "fully actualized" in its potential content (*RR,* p. 11). Such a theory of textuality, in short, at one and the same time invokes a reader who is already "competent," a subject fully constituted prior to the text and to reading, *and* poses the reader as the term of the text's production of certain meanings, as an effect of its structure.[21] The circularity of the argumentation and the reappearance of terms and concerns recurrent in structuralist writers like Lévi-Strauss and Greimas suggest a kind of retrenchment on Eco's part to the positions which he himself was among the very first to criticize in *La struttura assente* (1968), and which his *Theory of Semiotics* subsequently argued to be untenable.[22] Why, then, such retrenchment? I will offer two reasons, not unrelated to one another and to the purpose that has led me to consider Eco's rereading of Peirce.

Firstly, it seems to me that the problem, and the limit, of Eco's theory of reading is once again the subject, much more pressing now behind the reader, not merely *in* the text or simply *outside* the text, but as an instance of textuality. As the earlier book ended by posing the question of the subject, almost off-handedly and with reference to Kristeva, so does *Lector in fabula* begin. Both the English and the Italian introductions allude more or less explicitly to Kristeva and Barthes, two writers for whom the centrality of the subject, or the process of the subject, in language goes hand in hand with the exploration of textuality, and whose theories and practices of reading necessitate an attention to the discourse of psychoanalysis. It is Eco's defensiveness toward the latter, I suspect, and his determination to keep semiotics "free" of it, that forces him to perform on the reader a surgical operation analogous to the one auspicated for the interpretant, and so deprive him of a body as well as subjectivity. I said "deprive *him* of a body," because there is no doubt that Eco's reader is masculine in gender. And is not gender in fact usually construed as the addition of feminine markers to the morphological form of the masculine, and the concomitant attribution of the body to the feminine?

Secondly and less speculatively, even perhaps in greater fairness to Eco, we may be reminded that his productivist emphasis has its roots in the philosophical tradition of historical materialism. The priority of the sphere of production, of the work or text as artifact over the conditions of its enunciation and reception, and the priority given to artistic creativity ("invention") over other modes of sign production derive, as I suggest elsewhere in this volume, from his theoretical grounding in classical aesthetics and marxism.[23] Whence, too, the confident image of *homo faber* which emerges as the protagonist of his *Theory:* the subject of semiotics is the materialist subject of history. Thus, while no one could deny Eco's awareness of the social and dialogic nature of all communicative intercourse, and the active participation in it of both "producers" and "users" of signs, one cannot but recognize in his work an emphasis, a sharper focus, a special attention paid to one of the two poles of the communicative exchange, the moment of enunciation, of production: "the moment of production"—so-called with all the ideological connotations that the words "production" and "productivity" carry. Among them, first and foremost, is the implication of a creative and enriching "activity" (one makes art and history, one makes oneself or another, one has made it, etc.) as opposed to the "passivity" of reception, consumption, entertainment and enjoyment, whether hedonistic or economic. For example, Eco does not rule out the possibility that other forms of social practice may effect a transformation of the codes, and hence of the universe of meaning, as much as or more than artistic practice. Nevertheless his definition of "invention" as a "creative" use of the codes that produces new meanings and percepts seems to exclude all practices which do not result in actual texts, or "physically testable cultural products." And yet there are such practices—political or more often micropolitical: consciousness-raising groups, alternative forms of labor organization, familial or interpersonal relations, and so on—which produce no texts as such, but by shifting the "ground" of a given sign (the conditions of pertinence of the representamen in relation to the object), effectively intervene upon the codes, codes of perception as well as ideological codes. What these practices do produce, in Peirce's terms, is a habit-change; consequently, for their "users" or practitioners—their subjects—they are rather interpretants than texts or signs, and as interpretants they result in "a modification of consciousness" (5.485).

Let us go back to Peirce, then, whose view of semiotics as the study of the varieties of possible semiosis appears to be less restrictive than Eco's.[24] When Peirce speaks of habit as the result of a process involving emotion, muscular and mental exertion, and some kind of conceptual representation (for which he finds a peculiar term: self-analysis), he is thinking of individual persons as the subjects of such process. If the modification of consciousness, the habit or habit-change, is indeed the meaning effect, the "real and living" conclusion of each single process of semiosis, then where "the game of semiosis" ends, time and time again, is not exactly in "concrete action," as Eco sees it, but in a disposition, a readiness (for action), a set of expectations. Moreover, if the chain of meaning comes to a halt, however temporarily, it is by anchoring itself to somebody, some body, an individual subject.[25] As we use or receive signs, we produce interpretants. Their significate effects must pass through each of us, each body and each consciousness, before they may produce an effect or an action upon the world. *The individual's habit as a semiotic production is both the result and the condition of the social production of meaning.*

With regard to Eco's view of the dialectic of codes and modes of sign production, this puts into question the corollary opposition, between producers and users of signs, that seems integral to it. But to question the theoretical validity of that opposition is not to counter it with the identity of writer and reader, to say that filmmaker and spectator, or speaker and listener are interchangeable positions. For this would abolish the important distinction between enunciation and reception, and thus preempt any critical analysis of their context and of the political nature of address: the relations of power involved in enunciation and reception, which sustain the hierarchies of communication; the control of the means of production; the ideological construction of authorship and mastery; or more plainly, who speaks to whom, why, and for whom. If I question the necessity of a theoretical opposition, albeit dialectical, between producers and users, it is with another objective: to shift its ground and its focus, to say that the interpreter, the "user" of the sign(s), is also the producer of the meaning (interpretant) because that interpreter is the place in which, the body in whom, the significate effect of the sign takes hold. That is the subject in and for whom semiosis takes effect.

It might be interesting here to reconsider Peirce's definition (1897),

A sign, or representamen, is something which stands to somebody for something in some respect or capacity. It addresses somebody, that is, it creates in the mind of that person an equivalent sign, or perhaps a more developed sign [the interpretant].

and bring it face to face with Lacan's equally famous, and ostensibly antithetical, formula: "a signifier represents a subject for another signifier."[26] In light of Peirce's later elaboration of the notion of interpretant (dated ca. 1905), as I have discussed it, the doubt crops up whether the two formulations of the relation of subject and sign are so antithetical, worlds apart, irreconcilable, or whether, after all, they may be more compatible than they are made out to be. We may keep in mind that the essay in which Lacan's statement appears, "Position de l'inconscient" (1964), makes a direct if nameless reference to Peirce's, with the clear intent to oppose it.[27]

The second sentence in Peirce's statement, which is more often than not omitted when the definition is quoted, shifts the emphasis from the sign or representamen (the signifier) to the subject, the person for whom the interpretant represents "perhaps *a more developed sign.*" Peirce's subject is thus actually placed between the two signs, as Lacan's is between two signifiers. The difference is in the orientation of the movement, the sense of the representation as expressed by the word "for": Peirce's signs represent *for* a subject, Lacan's subject represents *for* the signifiers. Lacan's formula is intended to stress the "causation" of the subject in language (the "discourse of the Other") and the subject's inadequacy, its "lack-in-being" vis-à-vis the Other; for in the very moment and by the very fact of its utterance, the subject of the enunciation is split from itself as subject of the enounced. Consequently, the speaking subject and the subject of its, or rather *the,* statement are never one; the subject does not own its statement, the signifier, which is in the domain of the Other. In the process of signification conceived of as a chain of signifiers, then, the relation of the subject to the chain of its discourse is always of the order of a near-miss. As Lacan puts it, the signifier plays and wins (*joue et gagne*) before the subject is aware of it. For Lacan, the division or alienation of the subject in language is constitutive ("*originaire*") and structural, a-temporal.

In Peirce's formula, the subject's division from itself occurs in a temporal dimension ("in the flow of time" [5.421]), but it also occurs by means of its relation to the chain of interpretants. As each interpretant results in habit or habit-change, the process of semiosis comes to a stop, provisionally, by fixing itself to a subject who is but *temporarily* there.[28] In Lacanian terms, this fixing might be designated by the term "suture," which carries the implication of delusion, "pseudo-identification," imaginary closure, even false consciousness, as the product of the operations of ideology. And in the general critical discourse based on Lacanian psychoanalysis and Althusser's theory of ideology, "suture" is bad.[29] Peirce, on the other hand, does not say whether the habit that provisionally joins the subject to social and ideological formations is good or bad. But this, there should be no need to point out, is hardly the same as claiming a transcendental reality for the subject or for the world. It seems to me, in short, that in opposing the truth of the unconscious to the illusion of an always already-false consciousness, the general critical discourse based on Lacanian psychoanalysis subscribes too easily, as Eco does, to the territorial distinction between subjective and social modes of signification and the cold war that is its issue.

If one looks up the word "desire" in the index of subjects of Peirce's *Collected Papers,* one finds it in volume 5, cross-referenced with "Effort." In 5.486, it is mentioned as one of the four categories of mental facts that are of general reference: desires, expectations, conceptions, and habits. Unlike habit, which is the effect of effort (or more exactly of the combined action of semiosis through the three types of interpretants), desire for Peirce "is cause, not effect, of effort." That is to say, desires—the plural is significant—are something of a conceptual nature, like expectations and conceptions. In Laplanche and Pontalis's *Vocabulaire de la psychanalyse,* published in English as *The Language of Psycho-Analysis,* the word "Desire" appears in parentheses behind the title of the entry "Wish." The authors explain that Freud's term, *Wunsch,* corresponds rather to "wish" than to "desire," and that although *Wunsch* refers primarily to unconscious wishes, Freud did not always use the word strictly in that sense. At any rate, Freud did not use the word "desire." Lacan did, as he "attempted to re-orientate Freud's doctrine around the notion of desire," distinguishing it from the adjacent concepts of need (directed toward specific objects and satisfied by them) and demand (addressed to others and, regardless of its object, essentially a demand for love or recognition by the other). "Desire appears in the rift which separates need and demand." Like the subject, whose division it signifies, desire is an alienation in language.

The caption definition of "Wish (Desire)," however, states:

[In Freud] unconscious wishes tend to be fulfilled through the restoration of signs which are bound to the earliest experiences of satisfaction; this restoration operates according to the laws of primary processes. . . . Wishes, in the form of compromises, may be identified in symptoms.[30]

I do not think it preposterous to read the definition as bearing the possible meaning that (unconscious) wishes are the effect of unconscious effort and indeed habit; thereby to speculate that, if such a thing as unconscious habit (unconscious in Freud's sense, habit in Peirce's) can be theoretically conceivable, wishes—whether conscious or unconscious—may be thought of as both the effect and the cause of effort and habit; and then finally to suggest that a cautious, very cautious journey into the terrain of subjectivity as conscious *and* unconscious might begin here for someone not willing to accept Eco's or Kristeva's boundaries, heedless of the territorial claims of either discourse, semiotics or psychoanalysis, someone refusing to choose between instinct and reason.[31]

I started out, in this chapter, from a question only implicit in the irony of Woolf's "instinct rather than reason" quip, but explicitly posed as the very project of her book, *A Room of One's Own*—a book and a question, furthermore, explicitly addressed to women: how does "I" come to know herself as "a woman," how is the speaking/writing self en-gendered as a female subject? The answer rendered in the passage is only a partial answer. By certain signs, Woolf says; not only language (no words are exchanged between "I" and the Beadle) but gestures, visual signs, and something else which establishes their relation to the self and thus their meaning, "I was a woman." That something, she calls "instinct" for lack of a better word. In order to pursue the question, I have proposed instead the term "experience" and used it to designate an ongoing process by which subjectivity is constructed semiotically and historically. Borrowing Peirce's notion of "habit" as the issue of a series of "significate effects," or meaning effects, produced in semiosis, I have then sought to define experience more accurately as a complex of habits resulting from the semiotic interaction of "outer world" and "inner world," the continuous engagement of a self or subject in social reality. And since both the subject and social reality are understood as entities of a semiotic nature, as "signs," semiosis names the process of their reciprocally constitutive effects.

The question can now be rephrased in this way: is the female subject one constituted in a particular kind of relation to social reality? by a particular kind of experience, specifically a particular experience of sexuality? And if we answer that, yes, a certain experience of sexuality does effect a social being which we may call the female subject; if it is that experience, that complex of habits, dispositions, associations and perceptions, which en-genders one as female, then *that* is what remains to be analyzed, understood, articulated by feminist theory. The point of my return to Peirce, rereading him through Eco, was to restore the body to the interpreter, the subject of semiosis. That subject, I have argued, is the place in which, the body in whom, the significate effect of the sign takes hold and is real-ized. It should not be inferred, however, that Peirce ever so much as suggests what kind of body it is, or how the body is itself produced as a sign *for* the subject and variously represented in the mutually constitutive interaction of inner and outer worlds. In this question, Peirce is no help at all. Nevertheless, the notion of habit as "energetic" attitude, a somatic disposition at once abstract and concrete, the crystallized form of past muscular/mental effort, is powerfully suggestive of a subject touched by the practice of signs, a subject physically implicated or bodily engaged in the production of meaning, representation and self-representation.

We may recall, in this context, the observations made . . . on the basis of Kaja Silverman's assertion that the female body "is charted, zoned and made to bear . . . a meaning which proceeds entirely from external relationships, but which is always subsequently apprehended as an internal condition or essence."[32] In her textual example, the heroine's recollection of a picture of a woman about to be beaten by a man, is prompted by an identical actual event, the whipping of the heroine by her master. The cultural meaning of the image, woman's subjugation, acquires its subjective meaning (guilt and pleasure) for the heroine through her identification with the image, an identification resulting from the identical behavior of the two men. As Silverman notes, the representation structures and gives meaning to the present event (her whipping by her master), and yet the "memory" of the picture occurs as a consequence of that very event. The nexus sign-meaning, in other words, is not only significant *for* a subject, the heroine in whose body the muscular/mental effort produces the "logical" significate effect (her identification with the "guilty woman"), the memory and the habit (woman's subjection and masochistic pleasure). But the significance of the sign could not take effect, that is to say, the sign would not be a sign, without the existence or the subject's experience of a *social practice* in which the subject is physically involved; in this case, the employ of corporal punishment to chastise and educate, or rather, chastise and educate to give pleasure.

The intimate relationship of subjectivity to practices is recognized by psychoanalysis and semiotics in the expression "signifying practice(s)," but seldom analyzed outside of verbal or literary textual practices, cinema being the notable exception. The dominance of linguistic determination in theories of the subject, and the objectivist or logico-mathematical bias of most semiotic research have made the notion of signifying practice restrictive and over-specialized, forcing it into what amounts to theoretical obsolescence. This could have severe consequences for feminism, a critical discourse that begins as a reflection on practice and only exists as such in conjunction with it. Feminist theory constitutes itself as a reflection on practice and experience: an experience to which sexuality must be seen as central in that it determines, through gender identification, the social dimension of female subjectivity, one's personal experience of femaleness; and a practice aimed at confronting that experience and changing women's lives concretely, materially, and through consciousness.

The relevance to theoretical feminism of the notion of semiosis, such as I have outlined it, seems undeniable. In the first place, semiosis specifies the mutual overdetermination of meaning, perception, and experience, a complex nexus of reciprocally constitutive effects between the subject and social reality, which, in the subject, entail a continual modification of consciousness; that consciousness in turn being the condition of social change. In the second place, the notion of semiosis is *theoretically* dependent on the intimate relationship of subjectivity and practices; and the place of sexuality in that relationship, feminism has shown, is what defines sexual difference *for women,* and gives femaleness its meaning as the experience of a female subject.

If, as Catharine MacKinnon states in the essay cited earlier on, "sexuality is to feminism what work is to marxism: that which is most one's own, yet most taken away" (p. 515), that which is most personal and at the same time most socially determined, most defining of the self and most exploited or controlled, then to ask the question of what constitutes female sexuality, for women and for feminism (the emphasis is important), is to come to know things in a different way, and to come to know them as political. Since one "becomes a woman" through the experience of sexuality, issues such as lesbianism, contraception, abortion, incest, sexual harassment, rape, prostitution, and pornography are not merely social (a problem for society as a whole) or merely sexual (a private affair between "consenting adults" or within the privacy of the family); for women, they are political and epistemological. "To feminism, the personal is epistemologically the political, and its epistemology *is* its politics" (p. 535). This is the sense

in which it is possible to argue, as MacKinnon does, that consciousness raising is a "critical method," a specific mode of apprehension or "appropriation" of reality. The fact that today the expression "consciousness raising" has become dated and more than slightly unpleasant, as any word will that has been appropriated, diluted, digested and spewed out by the media, does not diminish the social and subjective impact of a practice—the collective articulation of one's experience of sexuality and gender—which has produced, and continues to elaborate, a radically new mode of understanding the subject's relation to social-historical reality. Consciousness raising is the original critical instrument that women have developed toward such understanding, the analysis of social reality, and its critical revision. The Italian feminists call it "*autocoscienza*," selfconsciousness, and better still, self consciousness. For example, Manuela Fraire: "the practice of self consciousness is the way in which women reflect politically on their own condition."[33]

I have been struck by the resonance of this word, self consciousness (which in the re-translation seems to lose its popular sense of uneasiness or excessive preoccupation with one's manner or looks, and to revert to the more literal sense of "consciousness of self"), with the curious adjective, "self-analyzing," that Peirce saw fit to use as modifier of "habit" in his description of the ultimate meaning-effect of signs: "The deliberately formed self-analyzing habit—self-analyzing because formed by the aid of analysis of the exercises that nourished it—is the living definition, the veritable and final logical interpretant" (5.491). This statement occurs in the context of an example Peirce gives to illustrate the process of semiosis. The point of the example is to show how one acquires a demonstrative knowledge of the solution of a certain problem of reasoning. A few lines above those just quoted we read: "the activity takes the form of experimentation in the inner world; and the conclusion (if it comes to a definite conclusion), is that under given conditions, the interpreter will have formed the habit of acting in a given way whenever he may desire a given kind of result. The real and living logical conclusion *is* that habit; the verbal formulation merely expresses it." I am again struck by the coincidence, for the feminist mode of analyzing self and reality has also been a mode of acting politically, in the public as well as in the private sphere. As a form of political critique or critical politics. feminism has not only "invented" new strategies, new semiotic contents and new signs, but more importantly it has effected a habit-change in readers, spectators, speakers, etc. And with that habit-change it has produced a new social subject, women. The practice of self consciousness, in short, has a constitutiveness as well as a constituency.

This is where the specificity of a feminist theory may be sought: not in femininity as a privileged nearness to nature, the body, or the unconscious, an essence which inheres in women but to which males too now lay a claim; not in a female tradition simply understood as private, marginal and yet intact, outside of history but fully there to be discovered or recovered; not, finally, in the chinks and cracks of masculinity, the fissures of male identity or the repressed of phallic discourse; but rather in that political, theoretical, self-analyzing practice by which the relations of the subject in social reality can be rearticulated from the historical experience of women. Much, very much, is still to be done, therefore. "Post-feminism," the *dernier cri* making its way across the Atlantic into feminist studies and the critical establishment, "is not an idea whose time has come," Mary Russo remarks, and then goes on to show how indeed "it is not an idea at all."[34]

From a city built to represent woman, but where no women live, we have come to the gravel path of the academic campus. We have learned that one becomes a woman in the very practice of signs by which we live, write, speak,

see. . . . This is neither an illusion nor a paradox. It is a real contradiction—women continue to become woman. The essays collected here have attempted to work through and with the subtle, shifting, duplicitous terms of that contradiction, but not to reconcile them. For it seems to me that only by knowingly enacting and re-presenting them, by knowing us to be both woman and women, does a woman today become a subject. In this 1984, it is the signifier who plays and wins before Alice does, even when she's aware of it. But to what end, if Alice doesn't?

NOTES

1. Virginia Woolf, *A Room of One's Own* (New York and London: Harcourt Brace Jovanovich, 1929), p. 6. My emphasis.

2. The process I here call experience might have been called ideology by others. The reasons for my choice of word, if not already apparent, must become clearer later on.

3. Claude Lévi-Strauss, *Mythologiques, IV: L'homme nu* (Paris: Plon, 1971); *The Naked Man,* trans. John and Doreen Weightman (New York: Harper and Row, 1981), in particular, "Finale," pp. 625–95.

4. See chapter 1 in Teresa de Lauretis, *Alice Doesn't: Feminism, Semiotics, Cinema* (Bloomington: Indiana University Press, 1984).

5. See Dale Spender, *Man Made Language* (London: Routledge & Kegan Paul, 1980). In explaining the asymmetrical position of women and men in the semantic space of the English language ("the meanings available within the language"), Spender argues that the assumption of (male) grammarians that English is a language based on natural, rather than grammatical, gender has gone hand in hand with another, unstated, assumption: that the male is the norm of what is natural. Thus gender distinctions in language are constructed by the semantic markers "plus male" or "minus male" (i.e., female), with the result that the "positive" space is reserved for males. After surveying an impressive amount of sociolinguistic research conducted from the premise that both language and language research are slanted against women, Spender convincingly makes the point that all mixed-group linguistic interaction

tends, not just to devalue women's speech, but to "construct women's silence"; and this tendency is further enforced by the institutionalized inaccessibility of women to one another's speech, since the places and occasions for "women's talk" have been severely restricted. Hence, she contends, the vital importance to women of consciousness raising groups and the feminist intervention in language, spoken and written, as a "politics of naming."

6. This is a rather marginal position within American feminism, but see, for example, Ursula K. Le Guin, "Is Gender Necessary?" in *The Language of the Night* (New York, 1979).

7. For example, Susan Griffin, *Woman and Nature: The Roaring Inside Her* (New York: Harper and Row, 1978). This is the dominant position, not only within American feminism, and is too extensive to be documented here.

8. Julia Lesage, "The Human Subject—You, He, or Me? (Or, The Case of the Missing Penis)," *Jump Cut*, no. 4 (November–December 1974), reprinted in *Screen* 16, no. 2 (Summer 1975): 73. A "Comment" by the writers in question, Ben Brewster. Stephen Heath, Colin MacCabe, follows on pp. 83–90. All further references to this work will be cited in the text.

9. One should actually be more precise and say that the conception of the subject defended by Brewster, Heath and MacCabe in their reply to Lesage actually comes from *their reading* of Lacan's rereading of Freud and from their historical materialist perspective, which brings them to claim for Lacan something that may not be his due: "Lacan's restitution of Freudian analysis as 'materialist theory of language'" (p. 86). At any rate, the "attempt to articulate the process of the subject within historical materialism" for film theory is not Lacan's or Althusser's but, admittedly, their own.

10. On Derrida's views of femininity, see Gayatri Chakravorty Spivak, "Displacement and the Discourse of Woman," in *Displacement: Derrida and After,* ed. Mark Krupnick (Bloomington and London: Indiana University Press, 1983).

11. Jacqueline Rose, "Introduction—II," in Jacques Lacan and the *école freudienne, Feminine Sexuality,* trans. Jacqueline Rose, ed. Juliet Mitchell and Jacqueline Rose (New York and London: W. W. Norton, 1982), p. 48.

12. So, for example, I believe Rose's other explanation, offered a couple of pages later in defense of Lacan against the "demands" of feminist analysts: "When Lacan says that women do not know, while, at one level, he relegates women outside, and against, the very mastery of his own

statement, he was [*sic*] also recognising the binding, or restricting, of the parameters of knowledge itself ('masculine knowledge irredeemably an erring')" (p. 51). Woman is indeed nothing more and nothing less than "a 'symptom' for the man," his aching rib.

13. Rose, p. 44. Kaja Silverman, *The Subject of Semiotics* (New York: Oxford University Press, 1983), the most recent and systematic effort to argue for the centrality of the subject in theories of meaning, proposes that psychoanalysis be seen as, in effect, a branch of semiotics: and further, that if "semiotics as a self-conscious theory emerged only at the beginning of this century, in the writings of Charles Sanders Peirce and Ferdinand de Saussure . . . it achieved maturity only when it was consolidated with psychoanalysis" by the work of Lacan (p. 3). The subject which assumes priority in this "history" of semiotics is the subject as psychoanalysis defines it. And in such perspective Silverman is obliged to say: "We will endeavor to create a space for the female subject within these pages, even if that space is only a negative one" (p. 131).

14. Catharine A. MacKinnon, "Feminism, Marxism, Method, and the State: An Agenda for Theory," *Signs* 7. no. 3 (Spring 1982): 531. All further references to this work will be cited in the text.

15. Umberto Eco, *A Theory of Semiotics* (Bloomington and London: Indiana University Press, 1976), p. 314. All further references to this work will be cited in the text, preceded by the abbreviation *TS.*

16. Julia Kristeva, "The System and the Speaking Subject," *The Times Literary Supplement.* October 12, 1973, p. 1249, quoted by Eco, *A Theory of Semiotics,* p. 317. Kristeva's works most recently translated into English are *Desire in Language: A Semiotic Approach to Literature and Art.* Thomas Gora, Alice Jardine, and Leon S. Roudiez, ed. Leon S. Roudiez (New York: Columbia University Press, 1980), containing essays from *Semeivtiké: Recherches pour une sémanalyse* (Paris: Seuil, 1969) and *Polylogue* (Paris: Seuil, 1977); and *Powers of Horror: An Essay on Abjection,* trans. Leon S. Roudiez (New York: Columbia University Press, 1982).

17. In the last footnote of Eco's *Theory,* the possibility is admitted that semiotics will overcome this "natural" boundary and, from a theory of codes and sign production, semiotics will develop (as he puts it) "a theory of the 'deep' individual origins of any 'wish to produce signs.'" In this sense "a threshold-trespassing semiotics could be conceived, which the present book does not dare to take into account" (p. 318). In his subsequent book, however, the concession will be effectively withdrawn.

18. "Peirce and the Semiotic Foundations of Openness," in Umberto Eco, *The Role of the Reader: Explorations in the Semiotics of Texts* (Bloomington and London: Indiana University Press, 1979), pp. 193–94. All further references to this work will be cited in the text, preceded by the abbreviation *RR.* The essay was first published, with minor variations, as "Peirce and Contemporary Semantics," *Versus,* no. 15 (1976).

19. Charles Sanders Peirce, *Collected Papers,* vols. 1–8 (Cambridge, Mass.: Harvard University Press, 1931–1958). All further references to this work will be cited in the text by the volume number followed by the paragraph number. This passage is in 2.228 (cited by Eco, *RR,* p. 180).

20. "A practical belief may, therefore, be described as a habit of deliberate behavior. The word 'deliberate' is hardly completely defined by saying that it implies attention to memories of past experience and to one's present purpose, together with self-control" (5.538). As for the term *habit,* Peirce uses it in a much wider sense than natural disposition or acquired habit, to include "associations" and even "dissociations." "Let us use the word 'habit', throughout this book . . . in its wider and perhaps still more usual sense, in which it denotes such a specialization, original or acquired, of the nature of a man, or an animal, or a vine, or a crystallizable chemical substance, or anything else, that he or it will behave, or always tend to behave, in a way describable in general terms upon every occasion (or upon a considerable proportion of the occasions) that may present itself of a generally describable character" (5.538).

21. The formulation is apparently very close to Althusser's view of the relation of the subject to ideology: the "concrete individual" (which we understand to mean an already constituted individual) is interpellated or "recruited" by ideology—which exists and works through the material practices of the ideological state apparatuses—and is thus "transformed" into a subject. At the same time, because ideology "is eternal" (a-temporal, or structural, like the Lacanian symbolic), individuals are "always-already interpellated by ideology as subjects." See Louis Althusser, *Lenin and Philosophy,* trans. Ben Brewster (New York and London: Monthly Review Press, 1971), p. 176. For a well-argued comparison of Eco's and Althusser's theories and their congruence with regard to, especially, aesthetic production, see Thomas E. Lewis, "Notes toward a Theory of the Referent." *PMLA* 94 (May 1979): 459–75. In defending Althusser from the accusation of theoreticism often leveled against him, Lewis states: "Although Althusser unfortunately does not make this point clearly enough, *his notion of open-ended scientific knowledge implies precisely the*

intervention of practice and the presence of cultural determination in the production of scientific knowledge" (p. 474; my emphasis). The same objection, and the same defense could be raised for Eco's theory of textuality as put forth in *Lector in fabula* (Milan: Bompiani, 1979), but the defense is rather weak. Merely to *imply* a relation of the subject to practices is not enough when the weight of the argument is otherwise on the structures.

22. I cannot do justice to Eco by developing my critique of *Lector in fabula* in this context, and must therefore refer the reader to my *Umberto Eco* (Firenze: La Nuova Italia, 1981).

23. See chapter 1, p. 35 and chapter 2, p. 55 in Teresa de Lauretis, *Alice Doesn't.*

24. Peirce takes full credit for establishing pragmatism as a theory of meaning (or better, "a method of determining the meaning of intellectual concepts, that is, of those upon which reasoning may turn," [5.8]), and even resorts to changing its name to "pragmaticism" ("which is ugly enough to be safe from kidnappers," [5.414]) after William James and F. C. S. Schiller have appropriated "pragmatism" for their own respective interests. But as far as semiotics is concerned, he declares himself to be "a pioneer, or rather a backwoodsman, in the work of clearing and opening up what I call *semiotic,* that is the doctrine of the essential nature and fundamental varieties of possible semiosis; and I find the field too vast, the labor too great, for a first-comer" (5.488). In Peirce's view, then, the semiotic domain is not coextensive with pragmaticism, a theory of meaning which addresses "intellectual concepts," but much broader; it encompasses all *possible* varieties of semiosis.

25. On Peirce's understanding of the self as a product of inference rather than intuition, and hence as a sign, see Walter Benn Michaels, "The Interpreter's Self: Peirce on the Cartesian 'Subject'," in *Reader-Response Criticism,* ed. Jane P. Tompkins (Baltimore and London: The Johns Hopkins University Press, 1980), pp. 185–200. Briefly, Michaels argues that Peirce's view develops out of his critique of the Cartesian *cogito* and the primacy, autonomy or transcendence which it confers upon the ego. "For Descartes, the self is primary—it can be known directly, and its existence is the single privileged certainty; for Peirce the self is derived—it can only be known by inference from the existence of ignorance and error" (p. 194). As a sign, the self is embedded in the larger system of signs Peirce calls "reality," and therefore subject to its "constitutive effects."

26. "Le registre du signifiant s'institue de ce qu'un signifiant représente un sujet pour un autre signifiant. C'est la

structure, rêve, lapsus et mot d'esprit, de toutes les formations de l'inconscient. Et c'est aussi celle qui explique la division originaire du sujet." Jacques Lacan, *Écrits* (Paris: Seuil, 1966), p. 840. This essay, not selected for the English translation of *Écrits* (New York: W. W. Norton, 1977), is discussed in Anika Lamaire, *Jacques Lacan,* trans. David Macey (London: Routledge & Kegan Paul, 1977), pp. 72–77.

27. "Les signes sont plurivalents: *ils représentent sans doute quelque chose pour quelqu'un;* mais ce quelqu'un, son statut est incertain . . ." Lacan (*Écrits,* p. 840; my emphasis).

28. While he does not conceive of the subject quite as Lacan does, still Peirce's subject is a subject in language and, in its fashion, divided: "Two things here are all-important to assure oneself of and to remember. The first is that a person is not absolutely an individual. His thoughts are what he is 'saying to himself,' that is, is saying to that other self that is just coming into life in the flow of time. When one reasons, it is that critical self that one is trying to persuade; and all thought whatsoever is a sign, and is mostly of the nature of language. The second thing to remember is that the man's circle of society (however widely or narrowly this phrase may be understood), is a sort of loosely compacted person, in some respects of higher rank than the person of an individual organism" (5.421).

29. A more balanced and critically useful elaboration of the notion of suture is given by Stephen Heath, "Notes on Suture" in *Questions of Cinema* (Bloomington: Indiana University Press, 1981), pp. 106–107: "Suture names the relation of the subject in the symbolic which is its join in the chain, its representation from signifier to signifier ('a signifier represents a subject for another signifier') and its identification as one in the fiction of the sign ('a sign represents something for someone'). The division-separation causation of the subject describes this process, the subject always returning in its implication in the desire of the Other . . . in which the subject always fails . . . and is always found again . . . taken up immediately in meanings and their production in discursive formations. A theory of ideology must then begin not from the subject but as an account of suturing effects, the effecting of the join of the subject in structures of meaning; which account would thus involve an attention to the whole history of the sub-

ject, the interminable movement of that history, and not its simple equation with ideology." It is this attention to the "whole history" of the subject—marking an important departure from the received definition of the relation (the "simple equation") of subject and ideology—that I wish to convey by the term "experience" (see note 2 above). But "experience" in its turn lends itself, because of its popular usage, to a "simple equation" of subject with individual, without social or semiotic mediation. Hence the necessity for a theoretical elaboration of the notion of experience, particularly within the feminist discourse.

30. J. Laplanche and J.-B. Pontalis, *The Language of Psycho-Analysis,* trans. Donald Nicholson-Smith (New York: W. W. Norton, 1973), pp. 481–82.

31. Though Peirce was well aware that his notion of habit extended far beyond consciousness and thus exceeded the boundaries of positivistic psychology (see, for example, his remarks about his contemporaries' "delusion that Mind is just Consciousness" and Von Hartmann's studies of the unconscious mind, in 7.364 ff.), he did not have the advantage of a developed theory of the unconscious with which his theory of habit might be confronted. We, however, do. That Peirce and Freud are even stranger bedfellows than Marx and Freud, and certainly no less reluctant to mutual "integration," need not discourage a rereading aimed at, not the integration but the possible articulation of one theory of meaning to the other.

32. See chapter 5, note 65 in Teresa de Lauretis, *Alice Doesn't.*

33. Manuela Fraire. "La politica del femminismo," *Quaderni piacentini,* no. 62–63 (1977), p. 195. Fraire is reviewing a volume of materials and documents—articles, position papers, editorials, manifestos, press releases and other statements issued by various feminist groups and women's collectives in Italy between 1973 and 1976—edited by Biancamaria Frabotta, *La politica del femminismo* (Rome: Savelli, 1976).

34. Mary Russo, "Notes on 'Post-Feminism'," in *The Politics of Theory,* ed. Francis Barker et al. (Colchester: University of Essex, 1983), p. 27. Russo is discussing the recent work of Julia Kristeva and Maria Antonietta Macciocchi, the two intellectual figures principally associated with this latest "ism," and their attempts to bring feminism in line with antihumanist philosophy.

PART V

Deconstruction and Poststructuralism

The Introduction to "Structuralism and Semiotics" (Part IV) ended with a discussion of Jacques Derrida's "deconstructive" critique of structuralism and a brief look at the Derrida essay "Structure, Sign, and Play in the Discourse of the Human Sciences." It also discussed how Teresa de Lauretis examined the critique implicit in the structuralist project in her linking of "semiotics" with "experience." Structuralism and semiotics, as Derrida explicitly suggests not only in "Structure, Sign, and Play" but also in "The Principle of Reason," and as de Lauretis suggests in her exposition and use of Peirce's work, are firmly embedded in the tradition of Western thought and science; their aim, typical of most Western thought, is to find ways of "understanding" phenomena through models of explanation that offer *coherent* pictures of the order of things, pictures that embody what Michel Foucault calls a "principle of unity," the *self-consistency* we mentioned in the Introduction to "What Is Literary Theory?" (Part I). As Jonathan Culler says in his discussion of the relation between Derrida and the English philosopher J. L. Austin at the beginning of this section, the aim of understanding is to find a way to present and master the context of whatever is to be understood. "Meaning," Culler writes, "is context-bound." At the end of this section Catherine Belsey concludes her essay "Constructing the Subject: Deconstructing the Text" with a discussion of "understanding" in relation to Sherlock Holmes and classic realism. In "Structuralism and Semiotics" (Part IV), de Lauretis examines an alternative to the "logical" that treads closely to the limits of self-consistency and coherence in the concept and analysis of "experience," and much of the criticism that John Searle directs at Derrida in the controversy that Culler recounts can be understood as a criticism of Derrida's questioning of the assumptions of "common-sense" limits and *definitions* (i.e., "delimitations") that allow understanding (the "obviousness" with which Belsey, following Louis Althusser, characterizes ideology).

The overall aim of *post*structuralism and deconstructive "critique" is different from the rigorous and "scientific" analyses of structuralism. Instead of attempting to account for how things are, their order, deconstruction and poststructuralism aim at describing the limits of understanding in terms of such various factors as the intellectual assumptions that allow limits and definitions to be assumed, the social relationships of power that are served by these definitions, and individual and "subjective" ends that are served. As J. Hillis Miller says in "The Search for Grounds in Literary Study"

319

in "What Is Literary Theory?" (Part II), "the fundamental sense of [deconstructive] 'critique' [is] discriminating [and] testing out." That is, deconstructive critique examines and tests the assumptions supporting intellectual insight in order to interrogate the "self-evident" truths they are based on. It tests the legitimacy of the contextual "bounds" (or "definitions") that understanding both presents and requires. Rather than seeking a way of "understanding"—that is, a way of incorporating new phenomena into coherent (i.e., "bounded") existing or modified models—a deconstructive critique seeks to uncover the unexamined axioms that give rise to those models and their boundaries.

DECONSTRUCTION

"Deconstruction" is a mode of the kind of "critique" we described in the General Introduction. It was named in the 1960s by Jacques Derrida, who in 1967 began to describe certain events he saw taking place in the history of philosophy, that is, events in Western modes of conceiving and articulating knowledge. In sweeping analyses, Derrida noted that traditional embodiments of legitimate authority have traditionally been taken to be self-evident in their absolute "rightness," as is the case with concepts such as "goodness," "naturalness," "reason," and "truth." The same is true of more abstract versions of authority such as (in Derrida's examples) "*aletheia,* transcendentality, consciousness, or conscience, God, man, and so forth"—all assumed in the West to be self-evident givens of understanding and "correct." He also noted that such concepts are necessarily defined in relation to their opposites. Further, Derrida explained in "Structure, Sign, and Play," authority in the West is generally conceived as existing in a structure and thought to be the precise *center* "at which the substitution of contents, elements, or terms is no longer possible." "It has always been thought," Derrida wrote, "that [this] center, which is by definition unique, constituted that very thing within a structure which governs the structure, while escaping structurality." Certain aspects of understanding, in other words, are themselves taken to be self-evidently "true." Thus, the concept of "center," or foundation of knowledge, is an epistemologically immovable mover, on which structures and hierarchies of belief or understanding have been thought to be based or securely "centered."

One version of this "center," Derrida argues in "The Principle of Reason," is the Enlightenment conception of reason as the *ground* of understanding. But Derrida has focused on many other "central" concepts as well: the self-evidence of speech, the simple humanity of "man" (as opposed to gendered individuals), the solidity of "seriousness" (as opposed to playfulness), the profundity of "philosophy" (as opposed to literature), the basic category of "nature" (as opposed to culture). Throughout his career Derrida has attempted to "deconstruct" the self-evidence of such concepts, to subject the very basic assumptions governing the apprehension of knowledge to critical analysis. That attempt involves demonstrating the local and historical nature of seemingly universal concepts. The word "deconstruction" itself is Derrida's coinage in response to the philosopher Martin Heidegger's idea of "destructive" analysis, the attempt to introduce time as a decisive element of the way we understand the world. In the same way that time inevitably upsets and reshapes any human scheme of understanding, so—as Derrida shows—meanings and values, by their very nature, are so mutually interdependent in *local* systems of thought that they continually destabilize each other and even themselves. This is why Derrida is at such pains to demonstrate that even "reason" itself has a history, and that history also involves its seeming opposite, irrationality: "the theme of extravagance as an irrationalism," he writes, ". . . dates from the period when the principle of reason was being formulated," the Enlightenment period of Leibniz and Kant.

Deconstruction is a "concept"—though Derrida would say, as he does of his neologism *différance,* it is "neither a word nor a concept"—that focuses on this instability of meaning. However, by "unstable" deconstruction does not suggest that there are *no* meanings (as many of its critics argue), but rather that meaning is historical, local, and subject to change: the principle of reason, for instance, is a powerful local concept defined, as it was by Kant, as the opposite of "applied" reason (or technology) that, as Derrida says, "we can no longer dissociate . . . from the very idea of technology." Thus, deconstruction rises out of Derrida's recognition that in modern conceptions of knowledge there is a temporal "decentering" or a "rupture" in the conventional order—the secular, liberal-humanist Enlightenment order that began in the West in the seventeenth and eighteenth centuries (which Michel Foucault mentions as decisive moments in the history of the concept of "author"). That order is based (or "grounded") on reason, which is why "The Principle of Reason," as Christopher Norris suggests, is so important. Derrida records or enacts a dramatic and decisive shift in this traditional, "rational," humane relation to authority, what might be termed a radical challenge to all authority. That is, the Western mind has learned to accept authority only by positing its underlying basis—what both Derrida and Miller ("What Is Literary Theory?" [Part II]) describe as its "ground"—around or upon which that "authority" is founded and beyond which one cannot go.

This Enlightenment tradition, as Belsey notes, is one of "liberal humanism." "The ideology of liberal humanism," she writes, "assumes a world of non-contradictory (and therefore fundamentally unalterable) individuals whose unfettered consciousness is the origin of meaning, knowledge and action. It is in the interest of this ideology above all to suppress the role of language in the construction of the subject, and its own role in the interpellation of the subject, and to present the individual as a free, unifed, autonomous subjectivity." In this tradition, as Belsey also notes, the disinterested use of reason (as in Sherlock Holmes) is the paramount "method." The opposite of reason, as it is found in René Descartes at the beginning of the Enlightenment, Ernest Gellner has argued, is "culture": for Descartes, he argues, "liberation from error requires liberation from culture, from 'example and custom' as he calls it." Enlightenment reason—and the "liberal humanism" Belsey describes to which it gives rise—aims at *universalizing* understanding by detaching it from the particular and local historical contexts in which it arises, the very "custom" and "tradition" to which Descartes opposes reason. Similarly, Enlightenment understanding is *individualized.* As Gellner says, Enlightenment rationalism is "profoundly individualist": whatever is "collective" as well as whatever is "customary" is "non-rational, and the overcoming of unreason and of collective custom are one and the same process." Thus, Enlightenment rationalism posits a unitary *subject* of reason who participates in *universal* and *transhistorical* truths. Such a rational subject is, in fact, universal: as Samuel Johnson says, reason itself is always the same so that even the Creator is subject to its power. "It is no limitation on omnipotence," he wrote in *Rasselas* in 1759, "to suppose that one thing is not consistent with another, that the same proposition cannot be at once true and false, that the same number cannot be even and odd, that cogitation cannot be conferred on that which is created incapable of cogitation." Moreover, even feeling comes within the compass of Enlightenment reason: as Terry Eagleton has argued, the same forces in the Enlightenment that gave rise to rationality and liberal humanism also gave rise to philosophical aesthetics in the eighteenth century. (See the discussion of aesthetics in the introduction to "What Is Literary Theory?" [Part II].) In fact, when Paul de Man suggests in "The Resistance to Theory" that persuasion by proof—that is, by *rational* argument—is a form of rhetoric, he is "deconstructing" the opposition between reason and feeling, showing them to "rise" out of the same local conditions.

The opposite to the Enlightenment "order" of reason is the order of culture, which is historical and collective. (Another "opposite" to this order is the irrationalism Derrida mentions that arose with rationalism in the seventeenth and eighteenth centuries, or the philosophy of feeling Eagleton traces in aesthetics.) This is why the deconstructive critique of Enlightenment reason—and Derrida, among others, has important discussions of Leibniz, Kant, Rousseau, and other figures of the eighteenth century—focuses so often on the local nature of seemingly universal ideas. In this way, the investigation or "interrogation" of deconstructive critique reveals an underlying "authority" (or "center" or "ground") beneath or temporally prior to the present authority, and so on.

In Derrida's critique, the "ground" beneath Kant's attempt to demonstrate the priority of "pure" over "applied" science is the valorization of the "objectivity" of reason and the self-evidence of its "representations." In this regress of certainty and absolute reference points, modern thought—especially in the nineteenth and twentieth centuries—brings about a depreciation, or displacement, of conventional cultural references, of notions such as "truth," "objectivity," and so on. This "decentering," in other words, deeply undercuts or destroys all notions of self-evident and absolute grounds in knowledge. In short, as Nietzsche said, God, or any absolute reference point, really does "die" (does become "decentered") for the modern world. Accordingly, there is the recognition in modern thought of what Derrida calls in "Structure, Sign, and Play" the "structurality of structure" and what he calls in "The Principle of Reason" the special status of sight, the fact that "theory" is closely linked to visual contemplation. Such contemplation presents as self-evident the equation of knowledge and *spatial structures,* knowledge conceived as ideal "form" beginning with Plato and Aristotle. Among other things, Derrida wants to suggest that this is ultimately problematic and "undecidable," that we can also think about knowledge, as Heidegger does, in terms of apostrophe and hearing.

Deconstruction does not altogether abandon the "formalism" of structuralism—its reliance on synchronic structures, relationality, and seeming timelessness. Rather, it *complicates* it with temporality and, as we mentioned in the Introduction to "What Is Literary Studies?" (Part I), with "history." The major critique of deconstruction, as we shall see, focuses on its tendency to avoid explicitly political concerns in its apparent push toward more or less "formal" analyses, what Aijaz Ahmad calls in "What Is Literary Theory?" (Part II) its "technicism." (De Man's concern for the "logic" of referentiality in "The Resistance to Theory," for instance, has been taken to be a covert means of avoiding questions of history, politics, and responsibility.) Yet deconstruction *complicates* formalism with temporality (if not history proper): it makes, as Culler argues about Derrida's thinking, "context" a constituent aspect of meaning. This is why Derrida describes the work of deconstruction as "irreducibly nonsimple," where even his term *nonsimple* is a complicated articulation of the "simpler" concept *complex.* In a sense, deconstruction is formalism without reductions, without the reconciliations of conflicting forms—which is to say, it is formalism at odds with itself. At the same time, as Culler also demonstrates, deconstruction makes "experience" itself a problem. (This is one of the reasons for the antagonism that Diana Fuss describes [in "Feminism and Gender Studies" (Part VIII)] between deconstruction and feminism. That de Lauretis attempts to bring together semiotics and experience marks her project as "poststructuralist" in a particular way.) As Derrida said in comments related to "Structure, Sign, and Play," "Now I don't know what perception is and I don't believe that anything like perception exists. Perception is precisely a concept, a concept of an intuition or of a given originating from the thing itself, present itself in its meaning, independently from language, from the system of reference." For Derrida, the *immediacy* of "perception" and "experience," their working without systems or "structures" that *mediate* and allow them to be apprehended as perception and experience, is a problem. This is why he began his career—and the career of deconstruction—with a critique of structuralism in *Of Grammatology* and a critique of phenomenology in *Speech and Phenomena.*

DECONSTRUCTIVE CRITICISM

As it bears on literary criticism, as our allusion to de Man suggests, deconstruction is a *strategy* of reading. Derrida describes deconstructive reading as starting from a philosophical hierarchy in which two opposed terms are presented as the "superior" general case and the "inferior" special case. These oppositions are Western culture's most important categories of thought, such as truth/error, health/disease, male/female, nature/culture, philosophy/literature, speech/writing, seriousness/play, reason/practice. De Man adds to this list the certainties of grammar/the uncertainties of rhetoric; and Jonathan Culler gives the example of language conceived as "constative" (i.e., as essentially a system of true or false meanings) versus language conceived as "performative" (i.e., the actual *activity* of using language). Another example, as much feminist criticism suggests, is the generally accepted use of "man" to mean "human" and "woman" to mean only the special case of a female human being. And, as Belsey argues, we can see yet another example in the opposition between the project of "total explicitness, total verisimilitude in the interests of a plea for scientificity" embodied not only in the methods of Sherlock Holmes, but in literary "realism" more generally, as opposed to the "shadowy, mysterious and often silent women" that "haunt" the Holmes detective stories.

Deconstruction isolates such oppositions and points out that they are indeed *hierarchically* opposed, general to special case. It then reverses such crucial hierarchies so as to elevate the "inferior" over the "superior"—making, as Culler says, "the constative a special case of the performative," or reason a "case" of technology, or, as in de Man, "proof" a kind of "persuasion." The purpose of these reversals, however, is not merely to invert value systems; doing such, Derrida says elsewhere, would only "confirm" the old system of opposition that is the object of analysis. Rather, deconstruction attempts to "explode" (in Derrida's metaphor) the original relationship of "superior" and "inferior" that gives rise to the semantic horizon—the possibility of any particular meaning, the possibility of particular "definitions"—in a discourse. Deconstruction attempts, as Derrida says in "Structure, Sign, and Play," to confront one interpretation "of interpretation, of structure, of sign, of freeplay"—one that seeks "a truth or an origin which is free from freeplay and from the order of the sign"—with another interpretation of interpretation "which is no longer turned toward the origin, [but] affirms freeplay and tries to pass beyond man and humanism." In de Man's terms, this second interpretation refuses the specific meanings of grammar for the "suspended" logic and meanings of rhetoric, the "tropological dimension" of language that de Man chooses to call "literature." It refuses the propositional logic of language conceived as constative, information or knowledge as exclusively "true or false," for the open-ended "promises" of performative language. Such a confrontation, though, should not constitute itself into a new hierarchy. Rather, it presents an "undecidability," an inability to choose, an "aporia" in rhetorical terms—the inability to decide how to proceed.

While in de Man such a confrontation remains more or less "rhetorical," it can also create the basis of critique that goes beyond the "institutional" critique of linguistic analysis to "transformative" forms of critique. As Belsey says, "the object of deconstructing the text is to examine the *process of its production*—not the private experience of individual author, but the mode of production, the materials and their arrangement in the work. The aim is to locate the point of contradiction within the text, the point at which it transgresses the limits within which it is constructed, breaks free of the constraints imposed by its own realist form. Composed of contradictions," she concludes, "the text is no longer restricted to a single, harmonious and authoritative reading." Neither, as she argues, is the psychological "subject," the social "experience" (of ideology), or even the canons of positive "science." Each of these things can be shown to be inhabited by "the contrary meanings which are the inevitable condition of its existence as a signifying practice" so that they "are unable to explain an area which none the less they cannot ignore." Such moments of contradiction allow for the possibilities of transformation as well as analysis that inhabit critique.

Before we turn to these possibilities—the "possibilities" of poststructuralism—we can take three issues from Derrida's general theories and specific commentaries that have a direct bearing on literary theory and criticism: textuality, undecidability, and strategy. By "textuality," Derrida means largely what the Structuralists mean by that term: anything that can be known will be articulated *as a text* within a system of differences, in Saussure's description, *without positive terms.* Consequently, because it is a system without positive terms (i.e., without a "center"), textuality is subject to a certain instability, or undecidability. That is, texts of any sort (social or literary phenomena, for example) will produce meanings, but since the production of meaning cannot be arrested through a relationship with absolute referents (positive terms) or absolutely closed contexts (centers or grounds), textuality will always be in progress and unfinished—thus, undecidable. The notion of deconstructive textuality, as de Man, Hillis Miller, Barbara Johnson, Shoshana Felman, Diana Fuss, and others have shown, is easily applicable in practical criticism. Indeed, in practical criticism, the dimension of undecidability separates the structuralist from the deconstructionist version of the text.

Most decisive for deconstructive literary criticism, though, is the issue of deconstructive strategy we have described above, its two strategic "moves." A deconstructive analysis of literature involves reversing and reinscribing the terms of a hierarchy. Such reversals and reinscriptions are of course playful, but with a playfulness intended to be radically disruptive—in a way, as if to institute a kind of nonsense. But however innocuous such a strategy of "nonsense" may seem, Derrida is playful with the "seriousness" of the "new responsibilities" he speaks of in "The Principle of Reason": responsibilities toward a "future" created by "new modes of questioning that are also a new relation to language and tradition, a new *affirmation,* and new ways of taking responsibility." This new mode of responsibility includes "play" that is intended to subvert the most fundamental strictures of seriousness and, thus, to displace and "contaminate" the very basis of (Western) authority. (The issue of seriousness is central to Culler's discussion in this section and Felman's in "Psychology and Psychoanalysis" [Part VI].) It is play, in other words, aimed at producing revolutionary changes in thought. In fact, deconstructive play offers a virtual model of the continual revolution (political and intellectual) of critique in its drive to overturn the status quo and then to institute a new order. In this way, as Derrida and other deconstructionists have become more playful, rhetorically and conceptually, they have also become more intent about instituting new practices in writing and thinking.

Such readings of literature can be seen in Belsey's reading of Doyle or Barbara Johnson's reading of poetry. Similarly, Stanley Fish presents a deconstructive reading of "reading" in "Interpreting the *Variorum,*" which is even more playful than de Man's discussion, and both Shoshana Felman and Slajov Žižek offer "deconstructive" readings of Freud and Lacan. What these readings all do, to different extents, is confront the performances of authors/narrators/texts with their "constative" meanings in order to examine texts in a broad, performative dimension. These critics make us confront the two senses of rhetoric discussed in the Introduction to "Rhetoric and Reader Response" (Part III).

Along with this confrontation, deconstruction, as Derrida himself suggests, involves a reversal and reinscription of the usual patterns of interpretation—that is, it examines criticism as well as literature. In fact, one hierarchical opposition that it has brought into question is the opposition between literature/criticism, "primary" and "secondary" texts, and in this, perhaps more than anywhere else, deconstructive criticism has encountered resistance. Among others, critics who taught and wrote at Yale

University during the 1970s (J. Hillis Miller and Geoffrey Hartman along with de Man) attempted to challenge the "superiority" of literature over criticism. De Man, in particular, claims a "literary" status for critique itself—"the key to this critique of metaphysics," he writes in *Allegories of Reading,*" is the rhetorical model of the trope or, if one prefers to call it that, literature"—and claims the essentially "critical" nature of literature. By conceiving of literature or rhetoric as the site of critique, the literary studies following from Derrida's work take in a large area of literary criticism. Current psychoanalytic criticism, influenced by Lacan, decenters the traditional Freudian version of the "subject" and is distinctly deconstructive in its practice. Feminism, too, especially in the work of Hélène Cixous, Barbara Johnson, Jane Gallop, Patrocinio Schweickart, and Diana Fuss, uses deconstructive strategies for displacing maleness and "male" readings of literary texts. Marxist critics, especially Louis Althusser, Fredric Jameson, John Ellis and Rosalind Coward, and Michael Ryan have found deep affinities between the Marxist and deconstructive critiques of cultural production. All these critics have adopted a deconstructive approach to literary texts and have attempted from different angles to understand the forces that shape and "rupture" those texts. In one sense, deconstructive poststructuralism can be said to cover all post-Derridean developments in criticism, including the contemporary rhetoric examined earlier in this book (though it could be plausibly argued—Newton Garver and Richard Rorty have made this argument—that Derrida is the latest example of a long tradition in philosophy that is quintessentially *rhetorical*). It is, in any event, difficult to find the limits of deconstruction's influence. More conservatively, these approaches to literary texts arise from definitions of literature and criticism that have followed from Derrida's ideas about textuality, undecidability, and strategy.

POSTSTRUCTURALISM

Still, the deconstructive critique of reading can be extended, as "The Principle of Reason" suggests, to Western epistemology as a whole, and this has led to the deconstruction of many institutions of Western culture—that is, it has led to the extension of linguistic and epistemological analyses into areas of actual practice and, thus, to investigate at first hand the cultural changes first described in general terms. As we see in Belsey, this has been done extensively with psychoanalysis and literary criticism (especially theories of representation, or mimesis). These studies have proceeded to offer another sense of "poststructuralism" that is equally important, namely the articulation of a *critique* of deconstruction itself. For, as we have already suggested, the constant danger of deconstruction is that it falls into the same kinds of hierarchies it attempts to expose. Derrida himself is quite aware of this danger, and his response—really a *rhetorical* response—is recurrently to present "deconstruction" in relation to particular textual practices, those of Lévi-Strauss or Saussure or Austin, and recurrently to articulate that practice in terminology specific to those contexts ("writing" in discussing Saussure, "structure" in relation to Lévi-Strauss, "iteration" in relation to Austin, "render" in relation to reason, etc.). Nevertheless, if, like rhetoric, deconstruction aims at situating the concepts that are assumed in any particular discourse, then deconstruction can have its own focus on discourse also subject to examination.

In "What Is an Author?" Michel Foucault performs this very "poststructuralist" critique. In that essay Foucault examines the *function* of the author-role as a social function, a "position" (like the positions that structural analysis describes). It is not enough "to repeat the empty affirmation that the author has disappeared," Foucault writes. "Instead, we must locate the space left empty by the author's disappearance, follow the distribution of gaps and breaches, and watch for the openings that this disappearance uncovers." In this way, Foucault attempts to describe the social and political "role" of the author, the ends it serves as a principle of unity, its links with juridical and institutional systems, its function within different classes, and, finally, its changing nature.

Foucault's essay can be profitably contrasted with Roland Barthes's essay "The Death of the Author" (1968), which is more conventionally a "deconstructive," poststructuralist work. There Barthes argues that in discourse "it is language which speaks, not the author; to write is, through a prerequisite impersonality . . . , to reach that point where only language acts, 'performs,' and not 'me.'" In this discussion, Barthes hypothesizes "language" rather than situating it; instead of examining the "death" of the author in situated terms, regarding what Foucault calls the "author function," he reverses the opposition between author and reader and claims, in a deconstructive gesture of reversal, that it is in "the place of the reader, not . . . the author" that writing exists: "a text's unity lies not in its origin but in its destination." And in the second move of deconstruction, Barthes explodes this opposition altogether by making the reader and the author equally unrecoverable; "this destination," he adds, "cannot any longer be personal: the reader is without history, biography, or psychology. He is simply that *someone* who holds together in a single field all the traces by which the written text is constituted." But what Barthes fails to do is precisely what constitutes Foucault's implicit critique: he fails to show what situated function the role of author—or even Barthes's role of reader—serves: how it *works* within the confines of particular discursive practices which are, also, practices of power.

Here Foucault is offering an implicit critique of deconstruction analogous to the critique of scientific structuralism Derrida offers or the critique of Reader-Response criticism Schweickart presents. Like deconstruction itself, Foucault's critique uses the categories of the object of critique to demonstrate its shortcomings. Yet Foucault—unlike Derrida or Schweickart—never makes that critique explicit. Instead, he offers a reading of a cultural and socially defined category, the "author," which Barthes "deconstructs" and both modernist formalism and structuralism erase in their different ways (Eliot in his talk of the "impersonality" of poetry and Lévi-Strauss in his description of structuralism as "Kantianism without a transcendental subject") in order to show the relationship between discursive social "categories" and practices and strategies of power within culture itself. Such an analysis, as we shall see, offers the possibility, articulated by Stephen Greenblatt in "Historical Criticism" (Part VII), of a "new historicism" in literary criticism.

Finally, poststructuralism offers the possibility of studying "culture"—the "example and custom" that Gellner cites from Descartes—in the practices of cultural studies. When Mark Conroy asks, as we noted in the Introduction to "What Is Literary

Theory?" (Part II), how Paul de Man can be practicing the same craft as the critics who have come after him in the last fifteen years, "our present day stars of gender studies, culture critique and socio- and psychocriticism," he is pointing out the *temporalization* of what seems, from the local view of the present, to be a kind of once-and-for-all vision of the world. "Like the return of the repressed," Conroy goes on, "the panoply of anthropological interests scorned by de Man now have possession of the debate." "The return of the repressed" is Freud's description of neurotic symptom, how what is excluded returns, calls attention to itself, in some other form. In a way, "the return of the repressed" might well characterize the "moves" of deconstruction we have described, where hierarchical binary oppositions are teased out of seemingly self-evident and simple "experience" in order to demonstrate the "mediated" or constructed nature of what we tend to feel is unmediated and natural. Thus, Derrida and Foucault trace the "history" of things that, as Foucault says elsewhere, "we tend to feel [are] without history"; they articulate the "repressed" history of "reason" and "author," which we tend to think are universal categories that never had to arise at a particular moment.

But return of the repressed haunts the essays of this section in another way, a "formal" unconsciousness that is linked, in deconstruction, with "historical" unconsciousness. Culler quotes Vincent Descombes's redefinition of the unconscious "not as a phenomenon of the will but as a phenomenon of enunciation"; and Belsey quotes Althusser's definition of ideology as the "obvious" and then goes on to describe ideology as "partial truths," a "set of omissions, gaps rather than lies." Both of these critics are doing formally and structurally what Derrida and Foucault do in their historical study of concepts: they answer the Enlightenment dream of reason and, indeed, "enlightened" clarity and self-conscious comprehension with its structural underside of unreason, obscure forces, unknown "formations" that mediate what seemed unmediated, the return of what was repressed and suppressed. What is "unconscious"—not necessarily in a formal Freudian sense, but perhaps more fully in Barthes's sense of an unknown "destination," a future and historical stopping point—governs much of the force and performance of these essays. In this sense, the "ethics" of theory we spoke of in the Introduction to "What Is Literary Theory?" (Part II), the future-oriented response and responsibility that Derrida describes here, might well be an integral element of "deconstruction," only now perceptible after the "panoply of anthropological interests" have arisen that seem, on first glance, a far cry from the formalisms of deconstruction. If so, deconstruction may well have led to the psychological, historicist, gendered, and more generally cultural criticisms that follow in this book—even if that direction moves, in Belsey's words, toward the "condition of action" rather than toward a clear and distinct program.

RELATED ESSAYS IN *CONTEMPORARY LITERARY CRITICISM*

Judith Butler, "Variations on Sex and Gender: Beauvoir, Wittig, and Foucault"
Paul de Man, "The Resistance to Theory"
Ferdinand de Saussure, Selections from *Course in General Linguistics*

Shoshana Felman, "Psychoanalysis and Education: Teaching, Terminable and Interminable"
Stanley Fish, "Interpreting the *Variorum*"
Diana Fuss, "Reading Like a Feminist"
Donna Haraway, "A Cyborg Manifesto: Science, Technology, and Socialist-Feminism in the Late Twentieth Century"
Barbara Johnson, "Apostrophe, Animation, and Abortion"
J. Hillis Miller, "The Search for Grounds in Literary Study"

REFERENCES AND FURTHER READING

Arac, Jonathan, et al., *The Yale Critics: Deconstruction in America* (Minneapolis: University of Minnesota Press, 1983).

Baker, Peter, *Deconstruction and the Ethical Turn* (Gainesville: University Press of Florida, 1995).

Barthes, Roland, "The Death of the Author," in *Image-Music-Text,* trans. Stephen Heath (New York: Hill and Wang, 1977).

———, *S/Z,* trans. Richard Miller (New York: Hill and Wang, 1974).

Bloom, Harold, et al., *Deconstruction and Criticism* (New York: Continuum, 1979).

Brunnette, Peter, and David Wills, *Deconstruction and the Visual Arts: Art, Media, Architecture* (New York: Cambridge University Press, 1994).

Chang, Briankle G., *Deconstructing Communication: Representation, Subject, and Economies of Exchange* (Minneapolis: University of Minnesota Press, 1996).

Culler, Jonathan, *On Deconstruction: Theory and Criticism After Structuralism* (Ithaca, NY: Cornell University Press, 1982).

———, *The Pursuit of Signs: Semiotics, Literature, Deconstruction* (Ithaca, NY: Cornell University Press, 1981).

Davis, Robert Con, and Ronald Schleifer, eds., *Rhetoric and Form: Deconstruction at Yale* (Norman: University of Oklahoma Press, 1985).

de Man, Paul, *Allegories of Reading: Figural Language in Rousseau, Nietzsche, Rilke, and Proust* (New Haven: Yale University Press, 1979).

———, *Blindness and Insight: Essays in the Rhetoric of Contemporary Criticism* (Minneapolis: University of Minnesota Press, 1983).

Derrida, Jacques, *Acts of Literature* (New York: Routledge, 1992).

———, "Difference," in *Speech and Phenomena, and Other Essays on Husserl's Theory of Signs,* trans. David B. Allison (Evanston, IL: Northwestern University Press, 1973).

———, *Dissemination,* trans. Barbara Johnson (Chicago: University of Chicago Press, 1981).

———, *Of Grammatology,* trans. Gayatri Spivak (Baltimore: Johns Hopkins University Press, 1976).

———, "Structure, Sign, and Play in the Discourse of the Human Sciences," in *The Structuralist Controversy,* eds. Richard Macksey and Eugenio Donato (Baltimore: Johns Hopkins University Press, 1972), 247–72.

———, *Writing and Difference,* trans. Alan Bass (Chicago: University of Chicago Press, 1978).

Eagleton, Terry, *The Ideology of the Aesthetic* (Cambridge, MA: Blackwell, 1990).

Easterlin, Nancy, and Barbara Riebling, *After Poststructuralism: Interdisciplinarity and Literary Theory* (Evanston, IL: Northwestern University Press, 1993).

Eco, Umberto, *A Theory of Semiotics* (Bloomington: Indiana University Press, 1976).

Elam, Diane, *Feminism and Deconstruction: Ms. en Abyme* (New York: Routledge, 1994).

Felman, Shoshana, *The Literary Speech Act: Don Juan with J. L. Austin, or Seduction in Two Languages,* trans. Catherine Porter (Ithaca, NY: Cornell University Press, 1983)

Felperin, Howard, *Beyond Deconstruction: The Uses and Abuses of Literary Theory* (Oxford: Clarendon Press, 1985).

Ferris, David, *Theory and the Evasion of History* (Baltimore: Johns Hopkins University Press, 1993).

Garver, Newton, "Preface," in Jacques Derrida, *Speech and Phenomena, and Other Essays on Husserl's Theory of Signs,* trans. David B. Allison (Evanston, IL: Northwestern University Press, 1973).

Gasché, Rodolphe, "Deconstruction as Criticism," in *Glyph* 6 (1979), 177–215.

Harari, Josué, ed., *Textual Strategies: Perspectives in Post-Structuralist Criticism* (Ithaca, NY: Cornell University Press, 1979).

Hartman, Geoffrey H., *Criticism in the Wilderness* (New Haven, CT: Yale University Press, 1980).

Johnson, Barbara, *The Critical Difference: Essays in the Contemporary Rhetoric of Reading* (Baltimore: Johns Hopkins University Press, 1980).

———, *The Wake of Deconstruction* (Cambridge, MA: Blackwell, 1994).

Leitch, Vincent B., *Deconstructive Criticism: An Advanced Introduction and Survey* (New York: Columbia University Press, 1982).

Loesberg, Jonathan, *Aestheticism and Deconstruction: Pater, Derrida, and de Man* (Princeton, NJ: Princeton University Press, 1991).

May, Todd, *The Moral Theory of Poststructuralism* (University Park: Pennsylvania State University Press, 1995).

Norris, Christopher, *The Contest of Faculties: Philosophy and Theory After Deconstruction* (New York: Methuen, 1985).

———, *Derrida* (Cambridge, Mass.: Harvard UniversityPress, 1987).

Royle, Nicholas, *After Derrida* (New York: St. Martin's Press, 1995).

Ryan, Michael, *Marxism and Deconstruction* (Baltimore: Johns Hopkins University Press, 1982).

Sim, Stuart, *Beyond Aesthetics: Confrontations with Poststructuralism and Postmodernism* (Toronto: University of Toronto Press, 1992).

Wheeler, Kathleen M., *Romanticism, Pragmatism, and Deconstruction* (Cambridge, MA: Blackwell, 1993).

19

Jonathan Culler

1944–

Born in Ohio in 1944, Jonathan Culler completed his undergraduate degree at Harvard in 1966 and was a Rhodes scholar from 1966 until 1969. He completed his D.Phil. (the British equivalent of the Ph.D.) at Oxford in 1972, and until 1977, when he became professor of English and comparative literature at Cornell University, he was a lecturer at Cambridge and Oxford. In 1975, while a visiting professor in French and comparative literature at Yale, Culler received the prestigious James Russell Lowell Prize for his second book, *Structuralist Poetics* (1975). This book is a revised and expanded version of his doctoral dissertation, which was an investigation of contemporary French criticism's theoretical foundations and a discussion of the usefulness of the model of structural linguistics for literary criticism. Culler has also written *Flaubert: The Uses of Uncertainty* (1974), *Saussure* (1976), *Roland Barthes* (1983), *On Deconstruction* (1982), and *Framing the Sign: Criticism and Its Institutions* (1988). He also served as translator for Derrida's *Memoires for Paul de Man* (1986, 1989).

The following article, "Convention and Meaning: Derrida and Austin" (1981), is an excerpt from *On Deconstruction,* where it appears in expanded form as the chapter "Meaning and Iterability." The article provides an account of the debate between the American philosopher and speech-act theorist John Searle and the French philosopher Jacques Derrida concerning their different readings of J. L. Austin's *How to Do Things with Words,* a seminal British work in Ordinary Language philosophy. Culler takes Derrida's part in the debate, discussing to what extent Searle's responses to Derrida miss the thrust of Derrida's approach. The article is a significant contribution to literary criticism because it summarizes and clarifies a debate of much importance to both literary critics and philosophers studying the philosophy of language. Moreover, Culler's article makes an understanding of Derrida's deconstruction of texts accessible to a wide audience that might sometimes be overwhelmed by the rhetoric of Derrida's work in deconstruction.

Very briefly, Culler begins with Austin's attempt to address the meaning of utterances in terms of a system of speech acts, a system to provide conventional rules of meaning involving the contextual features of utterances. Austin's attempt purportedly provides an account of utterance and meaning that is independent of a speaker's intention—what the speaker has in mind to say when speaking. However, in providing his account in *How to Do Things with Words,* Austin introduces a distinction between serious and nonserious speech acts. Derrida contends that this introduction provides the wedge by which the speaker's intention is reintroduced into the account of meaning, thus defeating Austin's project—a project with which Derrida is somewhat sympathetic. Searle's countercontention, in defense of Austin, is that Derrida misunderstands Austin's methodological use of "serious" and makes more of this use than is warranted. In the article, Culler discusses Searle's failure to address the issues Derrida raises in his criticism of Austin, as well as Searle's possible oversight on the scope of Austin's project: "The project of clarifying all possible ways and varieties of *not exactly doing things*," Culler quotes Austin, ". . . has to be carried through if we are to understand properly what doing this is."

In reading Culler, one should pay particular attention to the account of supplementarity and iterability, key concepts to understanding the fundamentals of the Searle-Derrida debate. Supplementarity is a Derridean term that (in French) means both a supplement—an addition—to something and a substitution—a supplanting—of something. Iterability, the possibility of repeating discourse, is the notion of an infinite number of contexts for an utterance that make for the undecidability of meaning without reference to a code for the conventions of context. But it is Derrida's point, ultimately, that the possibility of an infinite number of conventions defeats the project of providing a systematic code for them.

Convention and Meaning: Derrida and Austin[1]

In the Saussurian perspective, meaning is the product of linguistic conventions, the effect of a system of differences. To account for meaning is to set forth the relations of contrast and the possibilities of combination that constitute a language. However, as many have observed, a theory that derives meaning from linguistic conventions does not account for it completely. If one conceives of meaning as the effect of linguistic relations manifested in an utterance, then one must contend with the fact that, as we say, a speaker can mean different things by the same linguistic sequence on different occasions. "Could you move that box?" may be a request, or a question about one's interlocutor's strength, or even, as rhetorical question, the resigned indication of an impossibility.

Such examples seem to reinstate a model in which the subject—the consciousness of the speaker—is made the source of meaning: despite the contribution of linguistic structure, the meaning of the utterance varies from case to case; its meaning is what the speaker means by it. Confronted with such a model, the partisan of structural explanation will ask what makes it possible for the speaker to mean these several things by the one utterance. Just as we account for the meaning of sentences by analyzing the linguistic system, so we should account for the meaning of utterances (or as Austin calls it, their illocutionary force) by analyzing another system: the system of speech acts. As the founder of speech act theory, Austin is, in fact, repeating at another level (though less explicitly) the crucial move made by Saussure: to account for signifying events (*parole*) one attempts to describe the system that makes them possible.

Thus Austin argues, for example, that to mean something by an utterance is not to perform an inner act of meaning that accompanies the utterance. The notion that I may mean different things by "Can you move this box?" seems to urge that we explain meaning by inquiring what the speaker has in mind, as though this were the determining factor, but this is what Austin denies. What makes an utterance a command or a promise or a request is not the speaker's state of mind at the moment of utterance but conventional rules involving features of the context. If in appropriate circumstances I say "I promise to return this to you," I have made a promise, whatever was running through my mind at the time; and conversely, when earlier in this sentence I wrote the words "I promise to return this to you," I did not succeed in making a promise, even if the thoughts in my mind were similar to those that occurred on an occasion when I did make a promise. Promising is an act governed by certain conventions which the theorist of speech acts attempts to make explicit.

Austin's project is thus an attempt at structural explanation which offers a pertinent critique of logocentric premises, but in his discussion he reintroduces precisely those assumptions that his project puts in question. Derrida outlines this self-deconstructive movement in a section of "Signature événement contexte" in *Marges de la philosophie,* but John Searle's egregious misunderstanding in his "Reiterating the Differences: A Reply to Derrida" indicates that it may be important to proceed more slowly than Derrida does, with fuller discussion of Austin's project and Derrida's observations.

Austin begins *How to Do Things with Words* with the observation that "it was for too long the assumption of philosophers that the business of a 'statement' can only be to 'describe' some state of affairs, or to 'state some fact,' which it must do either truly or falsely."[2] The normal sentence was conceived as a true or false representation of a state of affairs, and numerous sentences which failed to correspond to this model were treated either as unimportant exceptions or as deviant "pseudo-statements." "Yet we, that is, even philosophers, set some limits to the amount of nonsense that we are prepared to admit we talk; so that it was natural to go on to ask, as a second stage, whether many apparent pseudo-statements really set out to be 'statements' at all."

Austin thus proposes to attend to cases previously ignored as marginal and problematic and to treat them not as failed statements but as an independent type. He proposes a distinction between statements, or *constative* utterances, which describe a state of affairs and are true or false, and another class of utterances which are not true or false and which actually perform the action to which they refer (e.g., "I promise to pay you tomorrow" accomplishes the act of promising). These he calls *performatives.*

This distinction between *performative* and *constative* has proved very fruitful in the analysis of language, but as Austin presses further in his description of the distinctive features of the performative and the various forms it can take, he reaches a surprising conclusion. An utterance such as "I hereby affirm that the cat is on the mat" seems also to possess the crucial feature of accomplishing the act (of affirming) to which it refers. *I affirm X,* like *I promise X,* is neither true nor false but performs the act it denotes. It would thus seem to count as a performative. But another important feature of the performative, Austin has shown, is the possibility of deleting the explicit performative verb. Instead of saying "I promise to pay you tomorrow," one can in appropriate circumstances perform the act of promising by saying "I will pay you tomorrow"—a statement whose illocutionary force remains performative. Similarly, one can perform the act of affirming or stating while omitting "I hereby affirm that." "The cat is on the mat" may be seen as a shortened version of "I hereby state that the cat is on the mat" and thus a performative. But, of course, "The cat is on the mat" is the classic example of a constative utterance.

Austin's analysis provides a splendid instance of the logic of supplementarity at work. Starting from the philosophical hierarchy that makes true or false statements the norm of language and treats other utterances as flawed statements or as extra—supplementary—forms, Austin's investigation of the qualities of the marginal case leads to a deconstruction and inversion of the hierarchy: the performative is not a flawed constative; rather, the constative is a special case of the performative. The conclusion that a constative is a performative from which one of various performative verbs has been deleted has since been adopted by numerous linguists. John Lyons notes, "It is natural to consider the possibility of deriving all sentences from underlying structures with an optionally deletable main clause containing a first-person subject, a performative verb of saying and optionally an indirect-object expression referring to the addressee."[3]

This would be a way of extending grammar to account for part of the force of utterances. Instead of saying that speakers can mean different things by the sentence "This chair is broken," linguists can extend the linguistic system to account for certain variations in meaning. "This chair is broken" can have different meanings because it can be derived from any of several underlying strings—strings which could be expressed as "I warn you that this chair is broken," "I inform you that this chair is broken," "I concede to you that this chair is broken," "I proclaim to you that this chair is broken," "I complain to you that this chair is broken."

Austin does not cast his theory in this form and would be skeptical of such attempts to extend grammar. He cites relationships between such pairs as "I warn you that this chair is broken" and "This chair is broken" to show that illocutionary force does not necessarily follow from grammatical structure. Indeed, he proposes a distinction between locutionary and illocutionary acts. When I say "This chair is broken," I perform the locutionary act of uttering a particular English sentence and the illocutionary act of stating, warning, proclaiming, or complaining. (There is also what Austin calls a perlocutionary act, the act I may accomplish by my performance of the locutionary and illocutionary acts: by arguing I may persuade you, by proclaiming something I may bring you to know it.) The rules of the linguistic system account for the meaning of the locutionary act; the goal of speech act theory is to account for the meaning of the illocutionary act or, as Austin calls it, the illocutionary force of an utterance.

To explain illocutionary force is to set forth the conventions that make it possible to perform various illocutionary acts: what one has to do in order to promise, to warn, to complain, to command. "Besides the uttering of the words of the so-called performative," Austin writes, "a good many other things have as a general rule to be right and to go right if we are to be said to have happily brought off our action. What these are we may hope to discover by looking at and classifying types of case in which something goes wrong and the act—marrying, betting, bequeathing, christening, or what not—is therefore at least to some extent a failure" (*How to . . .*, p. 14). Austin thus does not treat failure as an external accident that befalls performatives and has no bearing on their nature. The possibility of failure is internal to the performative and a point of departure for investigating it. Something cannot be a performative unless it can go wrong.

This approach may seem unusual, but in fact it accords with the basic axioms of semiotics. "A sign," writes Umberto Eco in *A Theory of Semiotics,* "is everything which can be taken as significantly substituting for something else. . . . *Semiotics is in principle the discipline studying everything which can be used in order to lie.* If something cannot be used to tell a lie, conversely it cannot be used to tell the truth."[4] "The bat is on my hat" would not be a signifying sequence if it were not possible to utter it falsely. Similarly, "I now pronounce you man and wife" is not a performative unless it is possible for it to misfire, to be used in inappropriate circumstances and without the effect of performing a marriage.

For the smooth functioning of a performative, Austin says, "(A.1) There must exist an accepted conventional procedure having a certain conventional effect, that procedure to include the uttering of certain words by certain persons in certain circumstances, and further, (A.2) the particular persons and circumstances in a given case must be appropriate for the invocation of the particular procedure invoked. (B.1) The procedure must be executed by all participants both correctly and (B.2) completely" (*How to . . .* , pp. 14–15). As these formulations suggest, to promise is to utter one of the conventional formulae in appropriate circumstances. It would be wrong, Austin argues, to think of the utterance "as (merely) the outward and visible sign, for convenience or other record or for information, of an inward and spiritual act" (*How to . . .* , p. 9). For example, "the act of marrying, like, say, the act of betting, is at least *preferably* . . . to be described as *saying certain words,* rather than as performing a different, inward and spiritual, action of which these words are merely the outward and audible sign. That this is so can perhaps hardly be proved, but it is, I should claim, a fact" (*How to . . .* , p. 13).

Austin refuses to explain meaning in terms of a state of mind and proposes, rather, an analysis of the conventions of discourse. Can such an account be developed? Can Austin proceed without reinstating the notion of meaning as a signifying intention present to consciousness at the moment of utterance and thus treating the meaning of a speech act as ultimately determined by or grounded in a consciousness whose intention is fully present to itself? Derrida's reading focuses on the way in which this reintroduction occurs. An especially interesting moment in which the argument can be shown to involve such an appeal occurs in the opening pages of *How to Do Things with Words,* as Austin is staking out the ground for his enterprise. After chastizing philosophers for treating as marginal any utterances that are not true or false statements and thus leading us to suppose that he himself will be concerned with such things as fictional utterances which are neither true nor false, Austin proposes an objection to the notion of performative utterance: "Surely the words must

be spoken 'seriously' and so as to be taken 'seriously'? This is, though vague, true enough in general—it is an important commonplace in discussing the purport of any utterance whatsoever. I must not be joking, for example, nor writing a poem" (*How to . . .* , p. 9).

The rhetorical structure of this passage is itself quite revealing. Although he proposes to exclude the nonserious, Austin offers no characterization of it, presumably because he is particularly anxious at this point to avoid the reference to an inner intention that such description would doubtless involve. Instead his text posits an anonymous objection which introduces "seriously" in quotation marks, as if it were itself not altogether serious. Doubling itself to produce this objection whose key term remains unanchored, the text can then grant the objection as something to be taken for granted.

Once, Austin has already told us, it was customary for philosophers to exclude—unjustifiably—utterances that were not true or false statements. Now his own text makes it appear customary to exclude utterances that are not serious. We have here, as the remark about the vagueness of the "serious" indicates, not a rigorous move within philosophy but a customary exclusion on which philosophy relies.

This exclusion is repeated in a longer passage which helps to indicate what is at stake. After listing various failures that may prevent the accomplishment of a performative, Austin notes that performatives are subject

to certain other kinds of ill which infect all utterances. And these likewise, though again they might be brought into a more general account, we are deliberately at present excluding. I mean, for example, the following: a performative utterance will, for example, be in a peculiar way hollow or void if said by an actor on the stage, or if introduced in a poem, or spoken in soliloquy. This applies in a similar manner to any and every utterance—a sea-change in special circumstances. Language in such circumstances is in special ways—intelligibly—used not seriously, but in ways parasitic upon its normal use—ways which fall under the doctrine of the etiolations of language. All this we are excluding from consideration. Our performative utterances, felicitous or not, are to be understood as issued in ordinary circumstances. [*How to . . .*, pp. 21–22]

As the image of the parasite suggests, we have here a familiar relationship of supplementarity: the nonserious use of language is something extra, added to ordinary language and wholly dependent upon it. It need not be taken into consideration in discussing ordinary language use since it is only a parasite.

John Searle argues in his reply to Derrida that this exclusion is of no importance but purely provisional.

> Austin's idea is simply this: if we want to know what it is to make a promise or make a statement we had better not start our investigation with promises made by actors on stage in the course of a play or statements made in a novel by novelists about characters in the novel, because in a fairly obvious way such utterances are not standard cases of promises and statements. . . . Austin correctly saw that it was necessary to hold in abeyance one set of questions, about parasitic discourse, until one has answered a logically prior set of questions about "serious" discourse.[5]

This may well have been "Austin's idea," but the appropriateness of such an idea is precisely what is in question. "What is at stake," Derrida writes, "is above all the structural impossibility and illegitimacy of such an 'idealization,' even one which is methodological and provisional."[6] Indeed, Austin himself, who begins his investigation of performatives by looking at ways in

which they can go wrong, contests Searle's notion of simple logical priority: "The project of clarifying all possible ways and varieties of *not exactly doing things . . .* has to be carried through if we are to understand properly what doing things is" (Austin's italics).[7] To set aside as parasitic certain uses of language in order to base one's theory on other, "ordinary" uses of language is to beg precisely those questions about the essential nature of language that a theory of language ought to answer. Austin objected to such an exclusion by his predecessors: in assuming that the ordinary use of language was to make true or false statements, they excluded precisely those cases that enable him to conclude that statements are a particular case of performative. When Austin then performs a similar exclusion, his own example prompts us to ask whether it is not equally illicit, especially since both he and Searle, by putting "serious" in quotation marks, suggest the dubiousness of the hierarchical opposition serious/nonserious. The fact that Austin's own writing is often highly playful and seductive, or that he does not hesitate to undermine distinctions that he proposes, only emphasizes the inappropriateness of excluding nonserious discourse from consideration.[8]

Searle uses his "Reply to Derrida" not to explore this problem but dogmatically to reaffirm the structure in question. "The existence of the pretended form of the speech act is logically dependent on the possibility of the nonpretended speech act in the same way that any pretended form of behavior is dependent on nonpretended forms of behavior, and in that sense the pretended forms are *parasitical* on the nonpretended forms."[9]

In what sense is the pretended dependent upon the nonpretended? Searle gives an example: "There could not, for example, be promises made by actors in a play if there were not the possibility of promises made in real life." We are certainly accustomed to thinking in this way: a promise I make is real; a promise in a play is a fictional imitation of a real promise, an empty iteration of a formula used to make real promises. But in fact one can argue that the relation of dependency works the other way. If it were not possible for a character in a play to make a promise, there could be no promises in real life, for what makes it possible to promise, as Austin tells us, is the existence of a conventional procedure, of formulae one can repeat. For me to be able to make a promise in "real life," there must be iterable procedures or formulae, such as are used on stage.

"Could a performative utterance succeed," Derrida asks or pretends to ask, "if its formulation did not repeat a 'coded' or iterable utterance, or in other words, if the formula I pronounce in order to open a meeting, to launch a ship or a marriage were not identifiable as *conforming* with an iterable model, if it were not thus identifiable in some way as 'citation'?"[10] For the "standard case" of promising to occur, it must be recognizable as the repetition of conventional procedure, and the actor's performance on the stage is an excellent model of such repetition. The possibility of "serious" performatives depends upon the possibility of performances, because performatives depend upon the iterability that is most explicitly manifested in performances.[11] Just as Austin reversed his predecessors' hierarchical opposition by showing that constatives were a special case of performatives, so we can reverse Austin's opposition between the serious and the parasitic by showing that his so-called serious performatives are only a special case of performances.

Indeed, this is a principle of considerable breadth. Something can be a signifying sequence only if it is iterable, only if it can be repeated in various serious and nonserious contexts, cited, and parodied. Imitation is not an accident that befalls an original but its condition of possibility. There is such a thing as an original Hemingway style only if it can be cited, imitated, and parodied. For there to be such a style, there must be recognizable features that characterize it and produce its distinctive effects;

for features to be recognizable, one must be able to isolate them as elements that could be repeated, and thus the iterability manifested in the inauthentic, the derivative, the imitative, the parodic is what makes possible the authentic or original.

A deconstructive reading of Austin focuses on the way he repeats the move that he identifies and criticizes in others and on the way in which the distinction between the serious and the parasitic, which makes it possible for him to undertake an analysis of speech acts, is undone by the implications of that analysis. Since any serious performative can be reproduced in various ways and is itself a repetition of a conventional procedure, the possibility of repetition is not something external that may afflict the serious performative. On the contrary, Derrida insists, the performative is from the outset structured by this possibility. "This *possibility* is part of the so-called 'standard case.' It is an essential, internal, and permanent part, and to exclude what Austin himself admits is a constant possibility from one's description is to describe something other than the so-called standard case."[12]

Nevertheless, Austin's exclusion of the parasitic is not simply an error, an error he might have avoided. It is a strategic part of his enterprise. As we saw above, for Austin an utterance can function as a performative and thus have a certain meaning or illocutionary force when there exists a conventional procedure involving "the utterance of certain words by certain persons in certain circumstances" and when these specified conditions are actually fulfilled. Illocutionary force is thus held to depend upon context, and the theorist must, in order to account for meaning, specify the necessary features of the context—the nature of the words, persons, and circumstances required. What happens when one attempts such specification? Marriage is an example Austin cites. When the minister says "I now pronounce you man and wife," his utterance successfully performs the act of uniting a couple in marriage if the context meets certain conditions. The speaker must be one authorized to perform weddings; the persons he addresses must be a man and a woman who are not married, who have obtained a license to marry, and who have uttered the required phrases in the preceding ceremony. But when one formulates such conditions regarding the words, persons, and circumstances that are necessary for an utterance to have a particular meaning or force, a listener or critic can usually without great difficulty imagine circumstances that fit these conditions but in which the utterance would not have the illocutionary force that is supposed to follow from them. Suppose that the requirements for a marriage ceremony were met but that one of the parties were under hypnosis, or again that the ceremony were impeccable in all respects but had been called a "rehearsal," or finally, that while the speaker was a minister licensed to perform weddings and the couple had obtained a license, the three of them were on this occasion acting in a play that, coincidentally, included a wedding ceremony.

When anyone proposes an example of a meaningless sentence, listeners can usually imagine a context in which it would in fact have meaning; by placing a frame around it, they can make it signify. This aspect of the functioning of language, the possibility of grafting a sequence onto a context that alters its functioning, is also at work in the case of performatives. For any specification of the circumstances under which an utterance counts as a promise, we can either imagine further details that would make a difference or else place a further frame around the circumstances. (We imagine that the conditions are fulfilled on a stage or in an example.)

In order to arrest or control this process, which threatens the possibility of a successful theory of speech acts, Austin is led to reintroduce the notion, previously rejected, that the meaning of an utterance depends on the presence of a signifying intention in the consciousness of the speaker. First, he sets aside the nonserious—a notion not explicitly defined but which clearly would involve reference to intention: a "serious" speech act is one in which the speaker consciously assents to the act he appears to be performing. Second, he introduces intention as one feature of the circumstances by setting aside speech acts performed unintentionally—"done under duress, or by accident, or owing to this or that variety of mistake, say, or otherwise unintentionally" (*How to . . .* , p. 21).

However, this reintroduction does not solve the problem; intention cannot serve as the decisive determinant or the ultimate foundation of a theory of speech acts. To see this, one need only consider what would happen if, after apparently completing a marriage ceremony, one of the parties said that he had been joking when he uttered his lines—only pretending, just rehearsing, or acting under duress. Assuming that the others believe his report of his intention, it will not in itself be decisive. What he had in mind at the moment of utterance does not determine what speech act his utterance performed. On the contrary, the question of whether a marriage did indeed take place will depend upon further discussion of the circumstances. If the minister had said that there would be a full dress rehearsal immediately before the real ceremony, or if the groom can sustain his claim that throughout the ceremony the bride's father was threatening him with a pistol, then one might reach a different conclusion about the illocutionary force of their utterances. What counts is the plausibility of the description of the circumstances: whether the features of the context adduced create a frame that alters the illocutionary force of the utterances.

Thus the possibility of grafting an utterance upon a new context, of repeating a formula in different circumstances, does not discredit the principle that illocutionary force is determined by context rather than by intention. On the contrary, it confirms this principle: in citation, iteration, or framing, it is new contextual features that alter illocutionary force. We are here approaching a general principle of considerable importance. What the indissociability of performative and performance puts in question is not the determination of illocutionary force by context but the possibility of mastering the domain of speech acts by exhaustively specifying the contextual determinants of illocutionary force. A theory of speech acts must in principle be able to specify every feature of context that might affect the success or failure of a given speech act or that might affect what particular speech act an utterance effectively performed. This would require, as Austin recognizes, a mastery of the total context: "The total speech act in the total speech situation is the only actual phenomenon which, in the last resort, we are engaged in elucidating" (*How to . . .* , p. 148). But total context is unmasterable, both in principle and in practice. Meaning is context-bound, but context is boundless.[13]

This is true in two senses. First, any given context is always open to further description. There is no limit in principle to what might be included in a given context, to what might be shown relevant to the interpretation of a particular speech act. This structural openness of context is essential to all disciplines: the scientist discovers that factors previously disregarded are relevant to the behavior of particular objects; the historian brings new or reinterpreted data to bear on a particular event; the critic relates a particular passage or text to contexts that make it appear in a new light. A striking instance of the possibilities of further specification of context, Derrida notes, is the question of the unconscious. In his *Speech Acts* Searle proposes, as one of the conditions of promising, that "if a purported promise is to be non-defective, the thing promised must be something the hearer wants done, or considers to be in his interest."[14] An utterance that promised to do what the listener apparently wants but unconsciously dreads might thus cease to be a promise and become instead a threat; conversely, an utterance that seemed a defective promise—a threat to do what the listener claims not to want—may be-

come a well-formed promise, should unconscious desire be specified as part of the total context.[15] This example illustrates very well how meaning is determined by context and for that very reason open to further possibilities.

Context is also unmasterable in a second sense: any attempt to codify context can always be grafted onto the context it sought to describe, yielding a new context which escapes the previous formulation. Attempts to describe limits always make possible a displacement of those limits, so that Wittgenstein's suggestion that one cannot say "bububu" and mean "if it does not rain I shall go out for a walk" has, paradoxically, made it possible to do just that. Its denial establishes a connection that can be exploited. Adepts of speech act theory, interested in excluding nonserious utterances from the corpus they are attempting to master, might admire the principle at work in a sign displayed in certain American airports at the spot where passengers and hand luggage are searched: "All remarks concerning bombs and weapons will be taken seriously." Designed to master signification by specifying the illocutionary force of certain statements in this context, it attempts to preclude the possibility of saying in jest "I have a bomb in my shoe" by identifying such utterances as serious statements. But this codification fails to arrest the play of meaning, nor is its failure an accident. The structure of language grafts this codification onto the context it attempts to master, and the new context creates new opportunities for obnoxious behavior. "If I were to remark that I had a bomb in my shoe, you would have to take it seriously, wouldn't you?" is only one of numerous remarks whose force is a function of context but which escape the prior attempt to codify contextual force. A metasign, "All remarks about bombs and weapons, including remarks about remarks about bombs and weapons, will be taken seriously," would escalate the struggle without arresting it, engendering the possibility of obnoxious remarks about this sign about remarks.

But if this seems a nonserious example, let us consider a more serious instance. What speech act is more serious than the act of signing a document, a performance whose legal, financial, and political implications may be enormous? Austin cites the act of signature as the equivalent in writing of explicit performative utterances with the form "I hereby . . . ," and indeed it is in appending a signature that one can in our culture most authoritatively take responsibility for an utterance. By signing a document, one intends its meaning and seriously performs the signifying act it accomplishes.

Derrida concludes "Signature événement contexte" with what he calls an "improbable signature," the "reproduction" of a "J. Derrida" in script above a printed "J. Derrida," accompanied by the following "Remark": "(Remark: the—written—text of this—oral—communication should have been sent to the Association des sociétés de philosophie de langue française before the meeting. That dispatch should thus have been signed. Which I do, and counterfeit, here. Where? There. J.D.)."[16] Is the cursive "J. Derrida" a signature even if it is a citation of the signature appended to the copy of this text sent through the mails? Is it still a signature when the supposed signatory calls it counterfeit? Can one counterfeit one's own signature? What, in sum, is a signature?

Traditionally, as Austin's remarks suggest, a signature is supposed to attest to the presence to consciousness of a signifying intention at a particular moment. Whatever my thoughts before or after, there was a moment when I fully intended a particular meaning. The notion of signature thus seems to imply a moment of presence to consciousness which is the origin of subsequent obligations or other effects. But if we ask what enables a signature to function in this way, we find that effects of signature depend on iterability. As Derrida writes, "The condition of possibility of those effects is simultaneously, once again, the condition of their impossibility, of the impossibility of their rigorous purity. In order to function, that is, to be readable, a signature must have a repeatable, iterable, imitable form; it must be able to be detached from the present and singular intention of its production. It is its sameness which, by corrupting its identity and its singularity, divides its seal."[17]

A proper signature, one that will validate a check or some other document, is one that conforms to a model and can be recognized as a repetition. This iterability, an essential feature of the structure of the signature, introduces as part of its structure an independence from any signifying intention. If the signature on a check corresponds to the model, the check can be cashed whatever my intentions at the moment of signature. So true is this that the empirical presence of the signatory is not even an essential feature of the signature. It is part of the structure of the signature that it can be produced by a stamp or by a machine. We can, fortunately, cash checks signed by a machine and receive a salary even though the signatory never saw the check nor entertained a specific intention to pay us the sum in question.

It is tempting to think of checks signed by a machine as a perverse exception irrelevant to the fundamental nature of signatures. Logocentric idealization sets aside such cases as accidents, "supplements," or "parasites" in its attempt to preserve a model predicated upon the presence of a full intention to consciousness at the moment of signature. But such cases could not occur if they did not belong to the structure of the phenomenon in question, and far from being a perverse exception, the check signed by machine is a logical and explicit example of the fundamental iterability of signatures. The requirement that a signature be recognizable as a repetition introduces the possibility of a machine as part of the structure of the signature at the same time as it eliminates the need for any particular intention at the point of signature.

Signatures thus ought to be included in what Derrida calls "a typology of forms of iteration":

In such a typology the category of intention will not disappear: it will have its place, but from that place it will no longer be able to govern the entire scene and system of utterance. Above all, we will then be dealing with different kinds of marks or chains of iterable marks and not with an opposition between citational utterances on the one hand and singular and original event-utterances on the other. The first consequence of this will be the following: given that structure of iteration, the intention animating the utterance will never be through and through present to itself and to its content. The iteration structuring it introduces into it a priori an essential dehiscence and cleft [*brisure*].[18]

It is not a matter of denying that signatories have intentions but of situating those intentions. One way of doing this would be to take the unconscious, as Vincent Descombes has argued, "not as a phenomenon of the will but as a phenomenon of enunciation."[19] The thesis of the unconscious "makes sense only in relation to the subject of enunciation: he does not know what he says."[20] The unconscious is the excess of what one says over what one knows, or of what one says over what one wants to say. Either the speaker's intention is whatever content is present to consciousness at the moment of utterance, in which case it is variable and incomplete, unable to account for the illocutionary force of utterances, or else it is comprehensive and divided—conscious and unconscious—a structural intentionality which is never anywhere present and which includes implications that never, as we say, entered my mind. This latter notion of intention, marked by what Derrida calls an essential cleft or division, is indeed quite common. When questioned about the implications of an utterance, I may quite routinely include in my intention implications that had never occurred to me before I was questioned.

Either way, intention is perhaps best thought of as a product. To the extent one can ever "fully intend" what one's signature accomplishes, it is because one has read the document and one's signature as an iterable act, an act with certain consequences on any occasion when it is performed, and thus anticipates further explanations one might give if questioned on any point. Intentions are not a delimited content but open sets of discursive possibilities—what one will say in response to questions about an act.

The example of the signature thus presents us with the same structure we encountered in the case of other speech acts: (1) the dependence of meaning on conventional and contextual factors, but (2) the impossibility of exhausting contextual possibilities so as to specify the limits of illocutionary force, and thus (3) the impossibility of controlling effects of signification or the force of discourse by a theory, whether it appeal to intentions of subjects or to codes and contexts.

The view of meaning to which this leads is not simple: it entails, on the one hand, the contextual, conventional determination of meaning and, on the other hand, the impossibility of ever saturating or limiting context so as to control or rigorously determine the "true" meaning. It is thus possible, and even appropriate, to proclaim the indeterminacy of meaning—though the smug iconoclasm apparent in many such proclamations is irritating. On the other hand, it is necessary and appropriate to continue to interpret texts, classify speech acts, and generally elucidate as far as possible the conditions of signification. Though Austin demonstrates the collapse of his distinction between performative and constative, he does not for that reason abandon his attempt to discriminate various classes of performative. Even though one may have reason to believe, as Derrida says, that "the language of theory always leaves a residue that is neither formalizable nor idealizable in terms of that theory of language," this is no reason to stop work on theory.[21] In mathematics, for example, Gödel's demonstration of the incompleteness of metamathematics (the impossibility of constructing a theoretical system within which all true statements of number theory are theorems) does not lead mathematicians to abandon their work. The humanities, however, often seem touched with the belief that a theory which asserts the ultimate indeterminacy of meaning renders all effort pointless. The fact that such assertions emerge from essays that propose numerous particular determinations of meaning, specific interpretations of passages and texts, should indicate that we are dealing with a double, not a simple, view of meaning: if language always evades its conventions, it also depends on them.

NOTES

1. This is an excerpt from my book *On Deconstruction: Literary Theory in the 1970s,* published in 1982 by the Cornell University Press.

2. J. L. Austin, *How to Do Things with Words* (Cambridge, Mass., 1975), p. 1; hereafter cited in text as "*How to. . . .*"

3. John Lyons, *Semantics* II (Cambridge, 1977), p. 778.

4. Umberto Eco, *A Theory of Semiotics* (Bloomington, 1976), p. 7.

5. John Searle, "Reiterating the Differences: A Reply to Derrida," *Glyph* 1 (1977), pp. 204–5.

6. Jacques Derrida, *Limited Inc* (Bakimore, 1977) [supplement to *Glyph* 2], 39. English translation: "Limited Inc a b c . . . ," *Glyph* 2 (1977), p. 206.

7. Austin, *Philosophical Papers* (London, 1970), p. 27.

8. Shoshana Felman, in a fascinating discussion, casts Austin in the role of a Don Juan who seduces readers and disrupts all norms. She attempts to set aside Austin's exclusion of nonserious discourse by arguing that when Austin writes "I must not be joking, for example, or writing a poem" (in the example cited above), "cette phrase ne pourrait-elle pas être considérée elle-même comme une dénégation—comme une plaisanterie?" ["Could not this sentence itself be considered as a denial—as a joke?"]. *Le Scandale du corps parlant: Don Juan avec Austin, ou la séduction en deux langues* (Paris, 1980), p. 188. This is a clever suggestion, part of a sustained attempt to attribute to Austin everything she has learned from Derrida—in order then to accuse Derrida of misreading Austin. But to treat the ex-

clusion of jokes as a joke prevents one from explaining the logical economy of Austin's project, which can admit infelicities and exploit them so profitably only by excluding the fictional and the nonserious This logic is what is at stake, not Austin's attitude or his liking for what Felman calls "le fun." Felman does argue convincingly, however, that by comparison with his successors, who see misfires and infelicities as events to be eliminated by a more rigorous idealization. Austin is a powerful defender of the irreducibility of the negative.

9. Searle, "Reiterating the Differences," p. 205.

10. Jacques Derrida, "Signature événement contexte," *Marges de la philosophie* (Paris. 1972), 389. English translation: "Signature Event Context," *Glyph* 1 (1977), pp. 191–92.

11. Searle accuses Derrida of confusing "no less than three separate and distinct phenomena: iterability, citationality, and parasitism." "There is a basic difference in that in parasitic discourse the expressions are being *used* and not *mentioned*"—a difference Derrida is said not to understand ("Reiterating the Differences," p. 206). But the distinction between use and mention is precisely one of the hierarchizations that Derrida's argument contests. The distinction seems clear and important in the classic examples: "Boston is populous" uses the word or expression *Boston,* while "*Boston* is disyllabic" does not use the expression but mentions it—mentions the word *Boston* by using an expression which is a metaname. Here the distinction seems important because it points to the difference between using a word to talk about a city and talking about a word. But when we turn to other examples of citation the problem becomes more complicated. If I write of a scholar, "Some of my colleagues think his work 'boring and incompetent' or 'pointless,' " what have I done? Have I used the expressions *boring* and *incompetent* and *pointless* as well as mentioned them? If we wish to preserve the distinction between use and mention here, we shall fall back on those notions of seriousness and of intention which Derrida claims are involved. I use the expressions insofar as I seriously intend the meanings of the sign sequences I utter; I mention them when I reiterate some of these signs (within quotation marks, for example) without committing myself to the meaning they convey. Mentioning, for Searle, would thus be parasitic upon use, and the distinction would separate the proper use of language, where I seriously intend the meaning of the signs I use, from a derivative reiteration that only mentions. We thus have a distinction—am I "seriously" applying the expressions boring, incompetent, and pointless or only men-

tioning them?—between two sorts of iteration, apparently based on intention. and Derrida is quite right to claim that use/mention is ultimately a hierarchy of the same sort as serious/nonserious and speech/writing. Each attempts to control language by characterizing distinctive aspects of its iterability as parasitic, derivative. A deconstructive reading would demonstrate that the hierarchy should be inverted and that use is but a special case of mentioning.

The distinction is still useful: among other things it helps us to describe how language subverts it. However much I may wish only to mention to a friend what others say about him, I effectively use these expressions, giving them meaning and force in my discourse. And no matter how wholeheartedly I may wish to "use" certain expressions, I find myself mentioning them: "I love you" is always something of a quotation, as many lovers have attested.

12. Derrida, *Limited Inc,* p. 61; "Limited Inc a b c . . . ," p. 231.

13. For discussion of this perspective, see Stanley Fish, *Is There a Text in This Class?* (Cambridge, 1980), 268–92 and 305–21; and esp. Susan Horton, *Interpreting Interpreting: Interpreting Dickens's "Dombey"* (Baltimore, 1979). In an excellent analysis of how interpretations are produced and justified, Horton argues that "each situation permits of innumerable acts of contextualizing" (p. 128) and that "what is responsible for those apparently infinite and infinitely variable interpretations of our texts, including *Dombey and Son,* is that everything else in that hermeneutical circle and not just the reader is in motion at the same time" (p. 17). Horton helped me to see that "interpretive conventions," on which Fish and I had tended to focus, should be seen as part of this boundless context. For another argument that breaks down the distinction between convention and context—but then draws the wrong conclusions—see Jay Schleusener, "Convention and the Context of Reading," *Critical Inquiry* 6, No. 4 (Summer 1980), 669–80.

14. Searle, *Speech Acts: An Essay on the Philosophy of Language* (Cambridge, 1969), 59.

15. Derrida, *Limited Inc,* p. 47: "Limited Inc a b c . . . ," p. 215.

16. Derrida, "Signature événement contexte." p. 393: "Signature Event Context." p. 196.

17. "Signature événement contexte." pp. 391–92: "Signature Event Context." p. 194.

18. "Signature événement contexte." p. 389: "Signature Event Context." p. 192.

19. Vincent Descombes, *L'Inconscient malgré lui* (Paris, 1977), p. 85.

20. Descombes, p. 15.

21. Derrida, *Limited Inc,* p. 41: "Limited Inc a b c . . . ," p. 209. The first part of this sentence is missing from the French text of *Limited Inc.* A line of typescript has apparently been omitted from line 35 of p. 41 following "toujours."

20

Jacques Derrida
1930–

Born in Algiers and educated in France, Jacques Derrida has become one of the most prominent thinkers of the poststructuralist movement. He teaches the history of philosophy at the École Normale Supérieure in Paris and teaches regularly at universities in the United States. Although he is not primarily a literary critic, Derrida's work, particularly his articulation and development of "deconstruction," has had great influence on literary studies. Since the 1960s, the force of his ideas has affected other areas, including theology, sociology, and the interdisciplinary practice of discourse theory. Although some might call his ideas subversive and others might argue that they are visionary, few doubt Derrida's impact on literary criticism and classroom practice. He is a prolific writer in many areas of study (including literature, art, psychology, linguistics, theater, theology, and philosophy). His books include *Speech and Phenomena* (1967; translated into English 1973), *Writing and Difference* (1967; trans. 1978), *Of Grammatology* (1967; trans. 1976), *Margins of Philosophy* (1972; trans. 1983), *Dissemination* (1972; trans. 1981), *Glas* (1974; trans. 1987), *The Postcard* (1980; trans. 1987), and *The Other Heading: Reflections on Today's Europe* (1991; trans. 1992). (For a useful bibliography see Peggy Kamufs *A Derrida Reader: Between the Blinds* [New York: Columbia University Press, 1991.]) More recent works include *Acts of Literature* (1992) and *Specters of Marx* (1994).

Originally given as an inaugural address when Derrida was Cornell University's Andrew Dickson White Professor-at-Large, "The Principle of Reason: The University in the Eyes of Its Pupils" (1983) is an important articulation of the relationship between academic understanding, philosophy, and discourse. Significant in part because Derrida moves his critique of Western metaphysics to the university and its modes of inquiry, but perhaps also because of its ongoing connections to the literature of crisis surrounding the humanities in the academy, Derrida's comments here remain crisp and relevant. His "deconstruction" of the binary opposition between reason and unreason in the cultural context of institutions of learning is a notable refocusing of his philosophical work.

This essay probes the nature of the university by considering its point of view and how it responds to sight. Derrida is trying to "view viewing," as he calls it. He asks questions: "What can the University's body see or not see of its own destination, of that in view of which it stands its ground? Is the University the master of its own diaphragm?" This question frames his inquiry as an issue of opening the eyes or closing them to privilege other senses and other ways of knowing—a trope Derrida juxtaposes with the idea of the university's role in Enlightenment. By contrasting the relationships of the university to that which surrounds it and by considering its *raison d'etre*—both the functions of reason and the nature of being—Derrida probes Leibniz's concept of the moral imperative behind rendering reason. This sense of obligation, Derrida argues, leads to the important issue of the university's "responsibility." He asks, "But is answering *to* the principle of reason the same act as answering *for* the principle of reason?" The question leads to the dilemmas related to grounding the university in reason—what Derrida calls grounding it in the principle of grounding.

The implications of these issues for the modern university, and indeed for inquiry itself (including the reasoned discourse of literary criticism), are sharply focused in the last half of the essay, where Derrida brings the abstractions of Aristotle, Kant, Heidegger, and Nietzsche into the realm of the modern university in the larger questions concerning the nature of "normative" knowledge—of "objectivity"—and concerning who or what is served by the disciplinary "knowledge" of the university, what he calls the "politics of knowledge." Even those, he writes, who work "on structures of the simulacrum or of literary fiction, on a poetic rather than an informative value of language, on the effects of undecidability, and so on, by that very token . . . are interested in possibilities that arise at the outer limits of the authority and the power of the principle of reason."

The Principle of Reason: The University in the Eyes of Its Pupils

Today, how can we not speak of the university?

I put my question in the negative, for two reasons. On the one hand, as we all know, it is impossible, now more than ever, to dissociate the work we do, within one discipline or several, from a reflection on the political and institutional conditions of that work. Such a reflection is unavoidable. It is no longer an external complement to teaching and research; it must make its way through the very objects we work with, shaping them as it goes, along with our norms, procedures, and aims. We cannot not speak of such things. On the other hand, the question "how can we not" gives notice of the *negative,* or perhaps we should say *preventive,* complexion of the preliminary reflections I should like to put to you. Indeed, since I am seeking to initiate

discussion, I shall content myself with saying how one should not speak of the university. Some of the typical risks to be avoided, it seems to me, take the form of a bottomless pit, while others take the form of a protectionist barrier.

Does the university, today, have what is called a *raison d'être?* I have chosen to put my question in a phrase—*raison d'être,* literally, "reason to be"—which is quite idiomatically French. In two or three words, that phrase names everything I shall be talking about: reason and being, of course, and the essence of the University in its connections to reason and being; but also the cause, purpose, direction, necessity, justification, meaning and mission of the University; in a word, its destination. To have a *raison d'être,* a reason for being, is to have a justification for existence, to have a meaning, an intended purpose, a destination; but also, to have a cause, to be explainable according to the "principle of reason" or the "law of sufficient reason," as it is sometimes called—in terms of a reason which is also a cause (a ground, *ein Grund*), that is to say also a footing and a foundation, ground to stand on. In the phrase *raison d'être,* that idea of causality takes on above all the sense of final cause, in the wake of Leibniz, the author of the formulation—and it was much more than a formulation—"the Principle of Reason." To ask whether the University has a reason for being is to wonder why there is a University, but the question "why" verges on "with a view to what?" The University with a view to what? What is the University's view? What are its views? Or again: what do we see from the University, whether for instance, we are simply in it, on board; or whether, puzzling over destinations, we look out from it while in port or, as French has it, "*au large,*" on the open sea, "at large"? As you may have noticed, in asking "what is the view from the University?" I was echoing the title of the impeccable parable James Siegel published in *Diacritics* two years ago: "Academic Work: The View from Cornell" [Spring, 1981]. Today, indeed, I shall do no more than decipher that parable in my own way. More precisely, I shall be transcribing in a different code what I read in that article—the dramatic, exemplary nature of the topology and politics of this university, in terms of its views and its site: the topolitics of the Cornellian point of view.

Starting with its first words, Metaphysics associates sight with knowledge, and knowledge with knowing how to learn and knowing how to teach. I am referring of course to Aristotle's *Metaphysics.* I shall return presently to the political import of its opening lines: for the moment, let us look at the very first sentence: "All men, by nature, have the desire to know." Aristotle thinks he sees a sign of this in the fact that sensations give pleasure, "even apart from their usefulness." The pleasure of useless sensations explains the desire to know for the sake of knowing, the desire for knowledge with no practical purpose. And this is more true of sight than of the other senses. We give preference to sensing "through the eyes" not only for taking action, but even when we have no praxis in view. This one sense, naturally theoretical and contemplative, goes beyond practical usefulness and provides us with more to know than any other, indeed, it unveils countless differences. We give preference to sight just as we give preference to the uncovering of difference.

But is sight enough? For learning and teaching, does it suffice to know how to unveil differences? In certain animals, sensation engenders memory, and that makes them more intelligent and more capable of learning. But for knowing how to learn, and learning how to know, sight, intelligence and memory are not enough. We must also know how to hear, and to listen. I might suggest somewhat playfully that we have to know how to shut our eyes in order to be better listeners. Bees know many things, since they can see; but they cannot learn, since they are among the animals that lack the faculty of hearing. Thus, despite appearances to the contrary, the University, the place where people know how to learn and learn how to know, can never be a kind of hive. Aristotle, let us note in passing, has ushered in a long tradition of frivolous remarks on the philosophical commonplace of the bee, the sense and senses of the bee, and the bee's reason for being. Marx was doubtless not the last to have overworked that topos, when he insisted on distinguishing human industry from animal industry, as exemplified in bee society. Seeking such nectar as may be gathered from the vast anthology of philosophical bees, I find a remark of Schelling's, in his *Lessons on the Method of Academic Studies,*[1] more to my taste. An allusion to the sex of bees often comes to the aid of the rhetoric of naturalism, organicism, or vitalism as it plays upon the theme of the complete and interdisciplinary unity of knowledge, the theme of the university as an organic social system. This is in the most classic tradition of interdisciplinary studies. I quote Schelling:

> The aptitude for doing thoughtful work in the specialized sciences, the capacity to work in conformity with that higher inspiration which is called scientific genius, depends upon the ability to see each thing, including specialized knowledge, in its cohesion with what is originary and unified. Any thought which has not been formed in this spirit of unity and totality [*der Ein- und Allheit*] is empty in itself, and must be challenged; whatever is incapable of fitting harmoniously within that budding, living totality is a dead shoot which sooner or later will be eliminated by organic laws; doubtless there also exist, within the realm of science, numerous sexless bees [*geschlechtlose Bienen*] who, since they have not been granted the capacity to create, multiply in inorganic shoots the outward signs of their own witlessness [*ihre eigne Geistlosigkeit*]. [*Philosophies de l'université*, p. 49]

(I don't know what bees, not only deaf but sexless, Schelling had in mind at the time. But I am sure that even today such rhetorical weapons would find many an eager buyer. One professor has recently written that a certain theoretical movement was mostly supported, within the university, by homosexuals and feminists—a fact which seemed very significant to him, and doubtless a sign of asexuality.)

Opening the eyes to know, closing them—or at least listening—in order to know how to learn and to learn how to know; here we have a first sketch of the rational animal. If the University is an institution for science and teaching, does it have to go beyond memory and sight? In what rhythm? To hear better and learn better, must it close its eyes or narrow its outlook? In cadence? What cadence? Shutting off sight in order to learn is of course only a figurative man-

ner of speaking. No one will take it literally, and I am not proposing to cultivate an art of blinking. And I am resolutely in favor of a new university Enlightenment [*Aufklärung*]. Still, I shall run the risk of extending my figuration a little farther, in Aristotle's company. In his *De anima* (421b) he distinguishes between man and those animals that have hard, dry eyes [*tôn sklerophtalmôn*], the animals lacking eyelids, that sort of sheath or tegumental membrane [*phragma*] which serves to protect the eye and permits it, at regular intervals, to close itself off in the darkness of inward thought or sleep. What is terrifying about an animal with hard eyes and a dry glance is that it always sees. Man can lower the sheath, adjust the diaphragm, narrow his sight, the better to listen, remember, and learn. What might the University's diaphragm be? The University must not be a sclerophthalmic animal, a hard-eyed animal; when I asked, a moment ago, how it should set its sights and adjust its views, that was another way of asking about its reasons for being and its essence. What American English calls "the faculty," those who teach, is in French *le corps enseignant*, the teaching corps (just as we say "the diplomatic corps") or teaching body. What can the University's body see or not see of its own destination, of that in view of which it stands its ground? Is the University the master of its own diaphragm?

Now that I have opened up this perspective, allow me to close it off quick as a wink and, in the twinkling of an eye, let me confide in you, to make what in French I could call a *confidence* but in English must call a confession.

Before preparing the text of a lecture, I find I must prepare myself for the scene I shall encounter as I speak. That is always a painful experience, an occasion for silent, paralytic deliberation. I feel like a hunted animal, looking in darkness for a way out where none is to be found. Every exit is blocked. In the present case, the task seemed triply impossible.

In the first place, this was not to be just a lecture like any other, rather, it had to be something like an inaugural address. Of course, Cornell University has welcomed me generously many times since I first came to speak here in 1975. I have many friends here, and Cornell is in fact the first American university I ever taught for. That was in Paris, in 1967–68, as David Grossvogel will undoubtedly remember: he was in charge of a program that had also been directed by Paul de Man. But today, for the first time, I am taking the floor to speak as an Andrew Dickson White Professor-at-Large. In French, "Au large" is the expression a great ship uses to hail a small craft about to cross her course: "Wear off. Give way." In this case, the title with which your university has honored me at once brings me closer to you and adds to the anguish of the cornered animal. Was this inaugural lecture a well-chosen moment to ask whether the University has a reason for being? Wasn't I about to act with all the unseemliness of a stranger who in return for noble hospitality plays prophet of doom with his hosts, or at best eschatological harbinger, like Elijah denouncing the power of kings or announcing the end of the realm?

A second cause for worry is that I find myself involved already, quite imprudently, that is, blindly and without foresight, in an act of dramaturgy, writing out the play of that view in which Cornell, from its beginnings, has felt so much to be at stake. The question of the view has informed the writing-out of the institutional scene, the landscape of your university, the alternatives of expansion and enclosure, life and death. From the first it was considered vital not to close off the view. This was recognized by Andrew Dickson White, Cornell's first president: may I pay him this homage? At a moment when the trustees wanted to locate the university closer to town, Ezra Cornell took them to the top of East Hill to show them the sights, and the site, he had in mind. "We viewed the landscape," writes Andrew Dickson White. "It was a beautiful day and the panorama was magnificent. Mr. Cornell urged reasons on behalf of the upper site, the main one being that there was so

much more room for expansion."[2] Ezra Cornell gave good reasons, and since the Board of Trustees, reasonably enough, concurred with them, reason won out. But in this case was reason quite simply on the side of life? Drawing on K. C. Parsons' account of the planning of the Cornell campus, James Siegel observes (and I quote) that

> for Ezra Cornell the association of the view with the university had something to do with death. Indeed Cornell's plan seems to have been shaped by the thematics of the Romantic sublime, which practically guaranteed that a cultivated man in the presence of certain landscapes would find his thoughts drifting metonymically through a series of topics—solitude, ambition, melancholy, death, spirituality, "classical inspiration"—which could lead, by an easy extension, to questions of culture and pedagogy. [p. 69]

A matter of life and death. The question arose once again in 1977, when the university administration proposed to erect protective railings on the Collegetown bridge and the Fall Creek suspension bridge to check thoughts of suicide inspired by the view of the gorge. "Barriers" was the term used; we could say "diaphragm," borrowing a word which in Greek literally means "partitioning fence." Beneath the bridges linking the university to its surroundings, connecting its inside to its outside, lies the abyss. In testimony before the Campus Council, one member of the faculty did not hesitate to express his opposition to the barriers, those diaphragmatic eyelids, on the grounds that blocking the view would mean, to use his words, "destroying the essence of the university." What did he mean? What is the essence of the university?

Perhaps now you can better imagine with what shudders of awe I prepared myself to speak to you on the subject—quite properly sublime—of the essence of the University. Sublime in the Kantian sense of the term: in the *Conflict of the Faculties,* Kant averred that the University should be governed by "an idea of reason," the idea of the whole field of what is presently teachable [*das ganze gegenwärtige Feld der Gelehrsamkeit*]. As it happens, no experience in the present allows for an adequate grasp of that present, presentable totality of doctrine, of teachable theory. But the crushing sense of that inadequacy is the exalting, desperate sense of the sublime, suspended between life and death.

Kant says, too, that the approach of the sublime is first heralded by an inhibition. There was a third reason for the inhibition I myself felt as I thought about speaking to you today. I was resolved of course to limit myself to preliminary, preventive remarks—propedeutical remarks, to use the word German took over from Greek to designate the teaching that comes before teaching. I would speak only of the risks to be avoided, the abyss, and bridges, and boundaries as one struggles with such fearful questions. But that would still be too much, because I wouldn't know how to pick and choose. In my teaching in Paris I have devoted a year-long seminar to the question of the University. Furthermore, I was recently asked by the French government to write a proposal for the establishment of an International College of Philosophy, a proposal which for literally hundreds of pages considers all of the difficulties involved. To speak of such things in an hour would be more than just a challenge. As I sought to encourage myself, daydreaming a bit, it occurred to me that I didn't know how many meanings were conveyed by the phrase "at large," as in "professor at large." I wondered whether a professor at large, not belonging to any department, nor even to the university, wasn't rather like the person who in the old days was called *un ubiquiste,* a "ubiquitist," if you will, in the University of Paris. A ubiquitist was a doctor of theology not attached to any particular college. Outside that context, in French, an *ubiquiste* is someone who travels a lot and travels fast, giving the illusion of being everywhere at once. Perhaps a professor at large, while

not exactly a ubiquitist, is also someone who, having spent a long time on the high seas, "*au large,*" occasionally comes ashore, after an absence which has cut him off from everything. He is unaware of the context, the proper rituals, and the changed environment. He is given leave to consider matters loftily, from afar. People indulgently close their eyes to the schematic, drastically selective views he has to express in the rhetoric proper to an academic lecture about the academy. But they may be sorry that he spends so much time in a prolonged and awkward attempt to capture the benevolence of his listeners.

As far as I know, nobody has ever founded a university against reason. So we may reasonably suppose that the University's reason for being has always been reason itself, and some essential connection of reason to being. But what is called the principle of reason is not simply reason. We cannot for now plunge into the history of reason, its words and concepts, into the puzzling scene of translation which has shifted *logos* to *ratio* to *raison, reason, Grund,* ground, *Vernunft,* and so on. What for three centuries now has been called the principle of reason was thought out and formulated, several times, by Leibniz. His most often quoted statement holds that "Nothing is without reason, no effect is without cause." According to Heidegger, though, the only formulation Leibniz himself considered authentic, authoritative, and rigorous is found in a late essay, *Specimen inventorum:* "There are two first principles in all reasoning, the principle of non-contradiction, of course . . . and the principle of rendering reason." The second principle says that for any truth—for any true proposition, that is—a reasoned account is possible. "*Omnis veritatis reddi ratio potest.*" Or, to translate more literally, for any true proposition, reason can be rendered.[3]

Beyond all those big philosophical words—reason, truth, principle—that generally command attention, the principle of reason also holds that reason must be rendered. (In French the expression corresponding to Leibniz's *reddere rationem* is *rendre raison de quelque chose;* it means to explain or account for something.) But what does "render" mean with respect to reason? Could reason be something that gives rise to exchange, circulation, borrowing, debt, donation, restitution? But in that case, who would be responsible for that debt or duty, and to whom? In the phrase *reddere rationem, "ratio"* is not the name of a faculty or power (*Logos, Ratio, Reason, Vernunft*) that is generally attributed by metaphysics to man, *zoon logon ekon,* the rational animal. If we had more time, we could follow out Leibniz's interpretation of the semantic shift which leads from the *ratio* of the *principium reddendae rationis,* the principle of rendering reason, to reason as the rational faculty—and in the end, to Kant's definition of reason as the faculty of principles. In any case, if "reason" in the principle of reason is not the rational faculty or power, that does not mean it is a thing, encountered somewhere among the beings and the objects in the world, which must be rendered up, given back. The question of this reason cannot be separated from a question about the modal verb "must" and the phrase "must be rendered." The "must" seems to cover the essence of our relationship to principle, it seems to mark out for us requirement, debt, duty, request, command, obligation, law, the imperative. Whenever reason can be rendered (*reddi potest*), it must. Can we, without further precautions, call this a moral imperative, in the Kantian sense of pure practical reason? It is not clear that the sense of "practical," as it is determined by a critique of pure practical reason, gets to the bottom of the "must," or reveals its origin, although such a critique has to presuppose such a "must." It could be shown, I think, that the critique of practical reason continually calls on the principle of reason, on its "must" which, although it is certainly not of a theoretical order, is nonetheless not simply "practical" or "ethical" in the Kantian sense.

A responsibility is involved here, however. We have to respond to the call of the principle of reason. In *Der Satz vom Grund [The Principle of Reason]*, Heidegger names that call *Anspruch*: requirement, claim, request, demand, command, convocation; it always entails a certain addressing of speech. The word is not seen, it has to be heard and listened to, this apostrophe that enjoins us to respond to the principle of reason.

A question of responsibility, to be sure. But is answering *to* the principle of reason the same act as answering *for* the principle of reason? Is the scene the same? Is the landscape the same? And where is the university located within this space?

To respond to the call of the principle of reason is to "render reason," to explain effects through their causes, rationally; it is also to ground, to justify, to account for on the basis of principles or roots. Keeping in mind that Leibnizian moment whose originality should not be underestimated, the response to the call of the principle of reason is thus a response to the Aristotelian requirements, those of metaphysics, of primary philosophy, of the search for "roots," "principles," and "causes." At this point, scientific and technoscientific requirements lead back to a common origin. And one of the most insistent questions in Heidegger's meditation is indeed that of the long "incubation" time that separated this origin from the emergence of the principle of reason in the seventeenth century. Not only does that principle constitute the verbal formulation of a requirement present since the dawn of Western science and philosophy, it provides the impetus for a new era of purportedly "modern" reason, metaphysics and technoscience. And one cannot *think* the possibility of the modern university, the one that is re-structured in the nineteenth century in all the Western countries, without inquiring into that event, that institution of the principle of reason.

But to answer for the principle of reason (and thus for the university), to answer for this call, to raise questions about the origin or ground of this principle of foundation (*Der Satz vom Grund*), is not simply to obey it or to respond in the face of this principle. We do not listen in the same way when we are responding to a summons as when we are questioning its meaning, its origin, its possibility, its goal, its limits. Are we obeying the principle of reason when we ask what grounds this principle which is itself a principle of grounding? We are not—which does not mean that we are disobeying it, either. Are we dealing here with a circle or with an abyss? The circle would consist in seeking to account for reason by reason, to render reason to the principle of reason, in appealing to the principle in order to make it speak of itself at the very point where, according to Heidegger, the principle of reason says nothing about reason itself. The abyss, the hole, the *Abgrund,* the empty "gorge" would be the impossibility for a principle of grounding to ground itself. This very grounding, then, like the university, would have to hold itself suspended above a most peculiar void. Are we to use reason to account for the principle of reason? Is the reason for reason rational? Is it rational to worry about reason and its principle? Not *simply;* but it would be overhasty to seek to disqualify this concern and to refer those who experience it back to their own irrationalism, their obscurantism, their nihilism. Who is more faithful to reason's call, who hears it with a keener ear, who better sees the difference, the one who offers questions in return and tries to think through the possibility of that summons, or the one who does not want to hear any question about the reason of reason? This is all played out, along the path of the Heideggerian question, in a subtle difference of tone or stress, according to the particular words emphasized in the formula *nihil est sine ratione.* This statement has two different implications according to whether "*nihil*" and "*sine*" are stressed, or "*est*" and "*ratione.*" I shall not attempt here, given the limits of this talk, to pursue all of the reckonings involved in this shift of emphasis. Nor shall I attempt—among other things, and for the same reasons—to reconstitute a dialogue between Heidegger and for example Charles

Sanders Peirce. A strange and necessary dialogue on the compound theme, indeed, of the university and the principle of reason. In a remarkable essay on "The limits of Professionalism," Samuel Weber quotes Peirce who, in 1900, "in the context of a discussion on the role of higher education" in the United States, concludes as follows:

> Only recently have we seen an American man of science and of weight discuss the purpose of education, without once alluding to the only motive that animates the genuine scientific investigator. I am not guiltless in this matter myself, for in my youth I wrote some articles to uphold a doctrine called pragmatism, namely, that the meaning and essence of every conception lies in the application that is to be made of it. That is all very well, when properly understood. I do not intend to recant it. But the question arises, *what* is the ultimate application; and at that time I seem to have been inclined to subordinate the *conception* to the *act,* knowing to doing. Subsequent experience of life has taught me that the only thing that is really *desirable* without a reason for being so, is to render ideas and things reasonable. *One cannot well demand a reason for reasonableness itself.*[4]

To bring about such a dialogue between Peirce and Heidegger, we would have to go beyond the conceptual opposition between "conception" and "act," between "conception" and "application," theoretical view and praxis, theory and technique. This passage *beyond* is sketched out briefly by Peirce in the very movement of his dissatisfaction: what might the ultimate application be? What Peirce only outlines is the path where Heidegger feels the most to be at stake, especially in *Der Satz vom Grund.* Being unable to follow this path myself here in the way I have attempted to follow it elsewhere, I shall merely draw from it two assertions, at the risk of oversimplifying.

1. The modern dominance of the principle of reason had to go hand in hand with the interpretation of the essence of beings as objects, an object present as representation [*Vortstellung*], an object placed and positioned *before a subject.* This latter, a man who says "I," an ego certain of itself, thus ensures his own technical mastery over the totality of what is. The "re-" of *repraesentatio* also expresses the movement that accounts for—"renders reason to"—a thing whose presence is encountered by rendering it present, by bringing it to the subject of representation, to the knowing self. This would be the place, if we only had the time, to consider the way Heidegger makes the language do its work (the interaction between *begegnen, entgegen, Gegenstand, Gegenwart* on the one hand. *Stellen, Vorstellen, Zustellen* on the other hand).[5] This relation of representation—which in its whole extension is not merely a relation of knowing—has to be grounded, ensured, protected: that is what we are told by the principle of reason, the *Satz vom Grund.* A dominance is thus assured for representation, for *Vorstellen,* for the relation to the object, that is, to the being that is located *before* a subject that says "I" and assures itself of its own present existence. But this dominance of the "being-before" does not reduce to that of sight or of *theoria,* nor even to that of a metaphor of the optical (or indeed sklerophthalmic) dimension. It is in *Der Satz vom Grund* that Heidegger states all his reservations on the very presuppositions of such rhetoricizing interpretations. It is not a matter of distinguishing here between sight and non-sight, but rather between two ways of thinking of sight and of light, as well as between two conceptions of listening and voice. But it is true that a caricature of representational man, in the Heideggerian sense, would readily endow him with hard eyes permanently open to a nature that he is to dominate, to rape if necessary, by fixing it in front of himself, or by swooping down on it like a bird of prey. The principle of reason installs its em-

pire only to the extent that the abyssal question of the being that is hiding within it remains hidden, and with it the question of the grounding of the ground itself, of grounding as gruden (to ground, to give or take ground: *Boden-nehmen*), as *begrunden* (to motivate, justify, authorize) or especially as *stitten* (to erect or institute, a meaning to which Heidegger accords a certain pre-eminence).[6]

2. Now that institution of modern technoscience that is the university *Stiftung* is built both on the principle of reason and on what remains hidden in that principle. As if in passing, but in two passages that are important to us, Heidegger asserts that the modern university is "grounded" [*gegrundet*], "built" [*gebaut*] on the principle of reason, it "rests" [*ruht*] on this principle.[7] But if today's university, locus of modern science, "is grounded on the principle of grounding," that is, on reason [*grundet auf dem Satz vom Grund*], nowhere do we encounter within it the principle of reason itself, nowhere is this principle thought through, scrutinized, interrogated as to its origin. Nowhere, within the university as such, is anyone wondering from where that call [*Anspruch*] of reason is voiced, nowhere is anyone inquiring into the origin of that demand for grounds, for reason that is to be provided, rendered, delivered: "*Woher spricht dieser Anspruch des Grundes aus seine Zustellung?*" And this dissimulation of its origin within what remains unthought is not harmful, quite the contrary, to the development of the modern university; indeed, Heidegger in passing makes certain laudatory remarks about that university: progress in the sciences, its militant interdisciplinarity, its discursive zeal, and so on. But all this is elaborated above an abyss, suspended over a "gorge"—by which we mean on grounds whose own grounding remains invisible and unthought.

Having reached this point in my reading, instead of involving you in a micrological study of Heidegger's *Der Satz vom Grund* or of his earlier texts on the University (in particular his inaugural lesson of 1929, *Was ist Metaphysik,* or the Rector's Speech of 1933, *Die Selbstbehauptung der deutschen Universitat*)—a study which I am attempting elsewhere, in Paris, and to which we shall doubtless refer in the discussions that come after this talk—instead of meditating at the edge of the abyss—even if on a bridge protected by "barriers"—I prefer to return to a certain concrete actuality in the problems that assail us in the university.

The framework of grounding, or foundation, and the dimension of the fundamental impose themselves on several counts in the space of the university, whether we are considering the question of its reason for being in general, or its specific missions, or the politics of teaching and research. Each time, what is at stake is the principle of reason as principle of grounding, foundation or institution. A major debate is under way today on the subject of the politics of research and teaching, and on the role that the university may play in this arena: whether this role is central or marginal, progressive or decadent, collaborative with or independent of that of other research institutions sometimes considered better suited to certain ends. The terms of this debate tend to be analogous—I am not saying they are identical—in all the highly industrialized countries, whatever their political regime, whatever role the State traditionally plays in this arena (and, as we all know, even the Western democracies vary considerably in this respect). In the so-called "developing countries," the problem takes shape according to models that are certainly different but in all events inseparable from the preceding ones.

Such a problematics cannot always—cannot any longer—be reduced to a problematics centered on the nation-state; it is now centered instead on multinational military-industrial complexes or techno-economic networks, or rather international technomilitary networks that are apparently multi- or trans-national in form. In France, for some time, this debate has been organized around what is called the "orientation" [*finalisation*] of research. "Oriented" research is research that is programmed, focused, organized in an authoritarian fashion *in view* of its utilization (in view of "*ta khreia,*" Aristotle would say), whether we are talking about technology, economy, medicine, psychosociology, or military power—and in fact we are talking about all of these at once. There is doubtless greater sensitivity to this problem in countries where the politics of research depend closely upon state-managed or "nationalized" structures, but I believe that conditions are becoming more and more homogeneous among all the technologically advanced industrialized societies. We speak of "oriented" research where, not so long ago, we spoke—as Peirce did—of "application." For it is growing more and more obvious that, without being immediately applied or applicable, research may "pay off," be usable, "end-oriented," in more or less deferred ways. And what is at stake is not merely what sometimes used to be called the techno-economic, medical, or military "by-products" of pure research. The detours, delays and relays of "orientation," its random aspects as well, are more disconcerting than ever. Hence the attempt, by every possible means, to take them into account, to integrate them to the rational calculus of programmed research. A term like "orient" is preferred to "apply," in addition, because the word is less "utilitarian," it leaves open the possibility that noble aims may be written into the program.

You may wonder what is being advocated, in France, in opposition to this concept of oriented research. The answer is basic, "fundamental" research, disinterested research with aims that would not be pledged in advance to some utilitarian purpose. Once upon a time it was possible to believe that pure mathematics, theoretical physics, philosophy (and, within philosophy, especially metaphysics and ontology) were basic disciplines shielded from power, inaccessible to programming by the pressures of the State or, under cover of the State, by civil society or capital interests. The sole concern of such basic research would be knowledge, truth, the disinterested exercise of reason, under the sole authority of the principle of reason.

And yet we know better than ever before what must have been true for all time, that this opposition between the basic and the end-oriented is of real but limited relevance. It is difficult to maintain this opposition with thoroughgoing conceptual as well as practical rigor, especially in the modern fields of the formal sciences, theoretical physics, astrophysics (consider the remarkable example of the science of astronomy, which is becoming useful after having been for so long the paradigm of disinterested contemplation), chemistry, molecular biology, and so forth. Within each of these fields—and they are more interrelated than ever—the so-called basic philosophical questions no longer simply take the form of abstract, sometimes epistemological questions raised after the fact; they arise at the very heart of scientific research in the widest variety of ways. One can no longer distinguish between technology on the one hand and theory, science and rationality on the other. The term techno-science has to be accepted, and its acceptance confirms the fact that an essential affinity ties together objective knowledge, the principle of reason, and a certain metaphysical determination of the relation to truth. We can no longer—and this is finally what Heidegger recalls and calls on us to think through—we can no longer dissociate the principle of reason from the very idea of technology in the realm of their modernity. One can no longer maintain the boundary that Kant, for example, sought to establish between the schema that he called "technical" and the one he called "architectonic" in the systematic organization of knowledge—which was also to ground a systematic organization of the university. The architectonic is the art of systems. "Under the government of reason, our knowledge in general," Kant says, "should not form a rhapsody, but it must form a system in which alone it can support and favor the essential aims of reason." To that pure rational unity of the architectonic,

Kant opposes the scheme of the merely technical unity that is empirically oriented, according to views and ends that are incidental, not essential. It is thus a limit between two aims that Kant seeks to define, the essential and noble ends of reason that give rise to a fundamental science versus the incidental and empirical ends which can be systematized only in terms of technical schemas and necessities.

Today, in the orientation or "finalization" of research—forgive me for presuming to recall such obvious points—it is impossible to distinguish between these two sets of aims. It is impossible, for example, to distinguish programs that one would like to consider "worthy," or even technically profitable for humanity, from other programs that would be destructive. This is not new; but never before has so-called basic scientific research been so deeply committed to aims that are at the same time military aims. The very essence of the military, the limits of military technology and even the limits of its accountability are no longer definable. When we hear that two million dollars a minute are being spent in the world today for armaments, we may assume that this figure represents simply the cost of weapons manufacture. But military investments do not stop at that. For military power, even police power, and more generally speaking the entire defensive and offensive security establishment benefits from more than just the "by-products" of basic research. In the advanced technological societies, this establishment programs, orients, orders, and finances, directly or indirectly, through the State or otherwise, the front-line research that is apparently the least "end-oriented" of all. This is all too obvious in such areas as physics, biology, medicine, biotechnology, bioprogramming, data processing and telecommunications. We have only to mention telecommunications and data processing to assess the extent of the phenomenon: the "orientation" of research is limitless, everything in these areas proceeds "in view" of technical and instrumental security. At the service of war, of national and international security, research programs have to encompass the entire field of information, the stockpiling of knowledge, the workings and thus also the essence of language and of all semiotic systems, translation, coding and decoding, the play of presence and absence, hermeneutics, semantics, structural and generative linguistics, pragmatics, rhetoric. I am accumulating all these disciplines in a haphazard way, on purpose, but I shall end with literature, poetry, the arts and fiction in general: the theory that has these disciplines as its object may be just as useful in ideological warfare as it is in experimentation with variables in all-too-familiar perversions of the referential function. Such a theory may always be put to work in communications strategy, the theory of commands, the most refined military pragmatics of jussive utterances (by what token, for example, will it be clear that an utterance is to be taken as a command in the new technology of telecommunications? How are the new resources of simulation and simulacrum to be controlled? And so on . . .). One can just as easily seek to use the theoretical formulations of sociology, psychology, even psychoanalysis in order to refine what was called in France during the Indochinese or Algerian wars the powers of "psychological action"—alternating with torture. From now on, so long as it has the means, a military budget can invest in anything at all, in view of deferred profits: "basic" scientific theory, the humanities, literary theory and philosophy. The compartment of philosophy which covered all this, and which Kant thought ought to be kept unavailable to any utilitarian purpose and to the orders of any power whatsoever in its search for truth, can no longer lay claim to such autonomy. What is produced in this field can always be used. And even if it should remain useless in its results, in its productions, it can always serve to keep the masters of discourse busy: the experts, professionals of rhetoric, logic or philosophy who might otherwise be applying their energy elsewhere. Or again, it may in certain situations se-

cure an ideological bonus of luxury and gratuitousness for a society that can afford it, within certain limits. Furthermore, when certain random consequences of research are taken into account, it is always possible to have in view some eventual benefit that may ensue from an apparently useless research project (in philosophy or the humanities, for example). The history of the sciences encourages researchers to integrate that margin of randomness into their centralized calculation. They then proceed to adjust the means at their disposal, the available financial support, and the distribution of credits. A State power or the forces that it represents no longer need to prohibit research or to censor discourse, especially in the West. It is enough that they can limit the means, can regulate support for production, transmission, and diffusion. The machinery for this new "censorship" in the broad sense is much more complex and omnipresent than in Kant's day, for example, when the entire problematics and the entire topology of the university were organized around the exercise of royal censorship. Today, in the Western democracies, that form of censorship has almost entirely disappeared. The prohibiting limitations function through multiple channels that are decentralized, difficult to bring together into a system. The unacceptability of a discourse, the noncertification of a research project, the illegitimacy of a course offering are declared by evaluative actions: studying such evaluations is, it seems to me, one of the tasks most indispensable to the exercise of academic responsibility, most urgent for the maintenance of its dignity. Within the university itself, forces that are apparently external to it (presses, foundations, the mass media) are intervening in an ever more decisive way. University presses play a mediating role that entails the most serious responsibilities, since scientific criteria, in principle represented by the members of the university corporation, have to come to terms with many other aims. When the margin of randomness has to be narrowed, restrictions on support affect the disciplines that are the least profitable in the short run. And that provokes, within the professions, all kinds of effects, certain ones of which seem to have lost any direct relation to that causality—which is itself still largely overdetermined. The shifting determination of the margin of randomness always depends upon the techno-economic situation of a society in its relation to the entire world arena. In the United States, for example (and it is not just one example among others), without even mentioning the economic regulation that allows certain surplus values—through the channel of private foundations among others—to sustain research or creative projects that are not immediately or apparently profitable, we also know that military programs, especially those of the Navy, can very rationally subsidize linguistic, semiotic or anthropological investigations. These in turn are related to history, literature, hermeneutics, law, political science, psychoanalysis, and so forth.

The concept of information or informatization is the most general operator here. It integrates the basic to the oriented, the purely rational to the technical, thus bearing witness to that original intermingling of the metaphysical and the technical. The value of "form" is not foreign to it; but let us drop this difficult point for now. In *Der Satz vom Grund,* Heidegger locates this concept of "information" (understood and pronounced as in English, he says at the time when he is putting America and Russia side by side like two symmetrical and homogeneous continents of metaphysics as technique) in a dependence upon the principle of reason, as a principle of integral calculability. Even the principle of uncertainty (and he would have said the same thing of a certain interpretation of undecidability) continues to operate within the problematics of representation and of the subject-object relation. Thus he calls this the atomic era and quotes a book of popularization entitled "We shall live thanks to atoms" with prefaces both by Otto Hahn, Nobel prize-winner and "funda-

mentalist" physicist, and Franz Joseph Strauss, then minister of national defense. Information ensures the insurance of calculation and the calculation of insurance. In this we recognize the period of the principle of reason. Leibniz, as Heidegger recalls, is considered to have been the inventor of life insurance. In the form of information [in *der Gestalt der Information*], Heidegger says, the principle of reason dominates our entire representation [*Vorstellen*] and delineates a period for which everything depends upon the delivery of atomic energy. Delivery in German is *Zustellung,* a word that also applies, as Heidegger points out, to the delivery of mail. It belongs to the chain of *Gestell,* from the *Stellen* group [*Vorstellen, Nachstellen, Zustellen, Sicherstellen*] that characterizes technological modernity. "Information" in this sense is the most economic, the most rapid and the clearest (univocal, *eindeutig*) stockpiling, recording and communication of news. It must instruct men about the safeguarding [*Sicherstellung*] of what will meet their needs, *ta khreia.* Computer technology, data banks, artificial intelligences, translating machines, and so forth, all these are constructed on the basis of that instrumental determination of a calculable language. Information does not inform merely by delivering an information content, it gives form, *"in-formiert," "formiert zugleich."* It installs man in a form that permits him to ensure his mastery on earth and beyond. All this has to be pondered as the effect of the principle of reason, or, put more rigorously, has to be analyzed as the effect of a dominant interpretation of that principle, of a certain emphasis in the way we heed its summons. But I have said that I cannot deal with the question of such stress here; it lies outside the scope of my topic.

What, then, is my topic? What do I have in view that has led me to present things as I have done so far? I have been thinking especially of the necessity to awaken or to resituate a responsibility, in the university or in face of the university, whether one belongs to it or not.

Those analysts who study the informative and instrumental value of language today are necessarily led to the very confines of the principle of reason thus interpreted. This can happen in any number of disciplines. But if the analysts end up for example working on the structures of the simulacrum or of literary fiction, on a poetic rather than an informative value of language, on the effects of undecidability, and so on, by that very token they are interested in possibilities that arise at the outer limits of the authority and the power of the principle of reason. On that basis, they may attempt to define new responsibilities in the face of the university's total subjection to the technologies of informatization. Not so as to refuse them; not so as to counter with some obscurantist irrationalism (and irrationalism, like nihilism, is a posture that is completely symmetrical to, thus dependent upon, the principle of reason). The theme of extravagance as an irrationalism—there is very clear evidence for this—dates from the period when the principle of reason was being formulated. Leibniz denounced it in his *New Essays on Human Understanding*. To raise these new questions may sometimes protect an aspect of philosophy and the humanities that has always resisted the influx of knowledge; it may also preserve the memory of what is much more deeply buried and ancient than the principle of reason. But the approach I am advocating here is often felt by certain guardians of the "humanities" or of the positive sciences as a threat. It is interpreted as such by those who most often have never sought to understand the history and the system of norms specific to their own institution, the deontology of their own profession. They do not wish to know how their discipline has been constituted, particularly in its modern professional form, since the beginning of the nineteenth century and under the watchful vigilance of the principle of reason. For the principle of

reason may have obscurantist and nihilist effects. They can be seen more or less everywhere, in Europe and in America among those who believe they are defending philosophy, literature and the humanities against these new modes of questioning that are also a new relation to language and tradition, a new *affirmation,* and new ways of taking responsibility. We can easily see on which side obscurantism and nihilism are lurking when on occasion great professors or representatives of prestigious institutions lose all sense of proportion and control; on such occasions they forget the principles that they claim to defend in their work and suddenly begin to heap insults, to say whatever comes into their heads on the subject of texts that they obviously have never opened or that they have encountered through a mediocre journalism that in other circumstances they would pretend to scorn.[8]

It is possible to speak of this new responsibility that I have invoked only by sounding a call to practice it. It would be the responsibility of a community of thought for which the frontier between basic and oriented research would no longer be secured, or in any event not under the same conditions as before. I call it a community of thought in the broad sense—"at large"—rather than a community of research, of science or philosophy, since these values are most often subjected to the unquestioned authority of a principle of reason. Now reason is only one species of thought—which does not mean that thought is "irrational." Such a community would interrogate the essence of reason and of the principle of reason, the values of the basic, of the principial, of radicality, of the *arkhe* in general, and it would attempt to draw out all the possible consequences of this questioning. It is not certain that such thinking can bring together a community or found an institution in the traditional sense of these words. What is meant by community and institution must be rethought. This thinking must also unmask—

an infinite task—all the ruses of end-orienting reason, the paths by which apparently disinterested research can find itself indirectly reappropriated, reinvested by programs of all sorts. That does not mean that "orientation" is bad in itself and that it must be combatted, far from it. Rather, I am defining the necessity for a new way of educating students that will prepare them to undertake new analyses in order to evaluate these ends and to choose, when possible, among them all.

As I mentioned earlier, along with some colleagues I was asked last year by the French government to prepare a report in view of the creation of an International College of Philosophy. I insisted, in that report, on stressing the dimension that in this context I am calling "thought"—a dimension that is not reducible to technique, nor to science, nor to philosophy. This International College would not only be a College of Philosophy but also a place where philosophy itself would be questioned. It would be open to types of research that are not perceived as legitimate today, or that are insufficiently developed in French or foreign institutions, including some research that could be called "basic"; but it would not stop there. We would go one step further, providing a place to work on the *value and meaning* of the basic, the fundamental, on its opposition to goal-orientation, on the ruses of orientation in all its domains. As in the seminar that I mentioned earlier, the report confronts the political, ethical, and juridical consequences of such an undertaking. I cannot go into more detail here without keeping you much too long.

These new responsibilities cannot be purely academic. If they remain extremely difficult to assume, extremely precarious and threatened, it is because they must at once keep alive the memory of a tradition and make an opening beyond any program, that is, toward what is called the future. And the discourse, the works, or the position-taking that these responsibilities inspire, as to the institution of science and research, no longer stem solely from the sociology of knowledge, from sociology or politology.

These disciplines are doubtless more necessary than ever; I would be the last to want to disqualify them. But whatever conceptual apparatus they may have, whatever axiomatics, whatever methodology (Marxist or neo-Marxist, Weberian or neo-Weberian, Mannheimian, some combination of these or something else entirely), they never touch upon that which, in themselves, continues to be based on the principle of reason and thus on the essential foundation of the modern university. They never question scientific normativity, beginning with the value of objectivity or of objectivation, which governs and authorizes their discourse. Whatever may be their scientific value—and it may be considerable—these sociologies of the institution remain in this sense internal to the university, intra-institutional, controlled by the deep-seated standards, even the programs, of the space that they claim to analyze. This can be observed, among other things, in the rhetoric, the rites, the modes of presentation and demonstration that they continue to respect. Thus I shall go so far as to say that the discourse of Marxism and psychoanalysis, including those of Marx and Freud, inasmuch as they are standardized by a project of scientific practice and by the principle of reason, are intra-institutional, in any event homogeneous with the discourse that dominates the university in the last analysis. And the fact that this discourse is occasionally proffered by people who are not professional academics changes nothing essential. It simply explains, to a certain extent, the fact that even when it claims to be revolutionary, this discourse does not always trouble the most conservative forces of the university. Whether it is understood or not, it is enough that it does not threaten the fundamental axiomatics and deontology of the institution, its rhetoric, its rites and procedures. The academic landscape easily accommodates such types of discourse more easily within its economy and its ecology; however, when it does not simply exclude those who raise questions at the level of the foundation or non-foundation of the foundation of the university, it reacts much more fearfully to those that address sometimes the same questions to Marxism, to psychoanalysis, to the sciences, to philosophy and the humanities. It is not a matter simply of questions that one formulates while submitting oneself, as I am doing here, to the principle of reason, but also of preparing oneself thereby to transform the modes of writing, approaches to pedagogy, the procedures of academic exchange, the relation to languages, to other disciplines, to the institution in general, to its inside and its outside. Those who venture forth along this path, it seems to me, need not set themselves up in opposition to the principle of reason, nor need they give way to "irrationalism." They may continue to assume within the university, along with its memory and tradition, the imperative of professional rigor and competence. There is a double gesture here, a double postulation: to ensure professional competence and the most serious tradition of the university even while going as far as possible, theoretically and practically, in the most directly underground thinking about the abyss beneath the university, to think at one and the same time the entire "Cornellian" landscape—the campus on the heights, the bridges, and if necessary the barriers above the abyss—and the abyss itself. It is this double gesture that appears unsituatable and thus unbearable to certain university professionals in every country who join ranks to foreclose or to censure it by all available means, simultaneously denouncing the "professionalism" and the "antiprofessionalism" of those who are calling others to these new responsibilities.

I shall not venture here to deal with the debate on "professionalism" that is developing in your country. Its features are, to a certain extent at least, specific to the history of the American university. But I shall conclude on this general theme of "professions." At the risk of contradicting what I have been urging here, I should like to caution against another kind of precipitous reaction. For the responsibility that I am trying to situate cannot be simple. It implies

multiple sites, a stratified terrain, postulations that are undergoing continual displacement, a sort of strategic rhythm. I said earlier that I would be speaking only of a certain rhythm, for example that of the blinking of an eye, and that I would only be playing one risk off against another, the barrier against the abyss, the abyss against the barrier, the one with the other and the one under the other.

Beyond technical goal-orientation, even beyond the opposition between technical goal-orientation and the principle of sufficient reason, beyond the affinity between technology and metaphysics, what I have here called "thought" risks in its turn (but I believe this risk is unavoidable—it is the risk of the future itself) being reappropriated by socio-political forces that could find it in their own interest in certain situations. Such a "thought" indeed cannot be produced outside of certain historical, techno-economic, politico-institutional and linguistic conditions. A strategic analysis that is to be as vigilant as possible must thus with its eyes wide open attempt to ward off such reappropriations. (I should have liked to situate at this point certain questions about the "politics" of Heideggerian thought, especially as elaborated prior to *Der Satz vom Grund,* for example in the two inaugural discourses of 1929 and 1933.)

I shall limit myself, however, to the double question of "professions." First: does the university have as its essential mission that of producing professional competencies, which may sometimes be external to the university? Second: is the task of the university to ensure within itself—and under what conditions—the reproduction of professional competence by preparing professors for pedagogy and for research who have respect for a certain code? One may answer the second question in the affirmative without having done so for the first, and seek to keep professional forms and values internal to the university outside the marketplace while keeping the goal-orientation of social work outside of the university. The new responsibility of the "thought" of which we are speaking cannot fail to be accompanied at least by a movement of suspicion, even of rejection with respect to the professionalization of the university in these two senses, and especially in the first, which regulates university life according to the supply and demand of the marketplace and according to a purely technical ideal of competence. To this extent at least, such "thought" may, at a minimum, result in reproducing a highly traditional politics of knowledge. And the effects may be those that belong to a social hierarchy in the exercise of technopolitical power. I am not saying that this "thought" is identical with that politics, and that it is therefore necessary to abstain from it; I am saying that under certain conditions it can serve that politics, and that everything thus comes down to the analysis of those conditions. In modern times, Kant, Nietzsche, Heidegger and numerous others have all said as much, quite unmistakably: the essential feature of academic responsibility must not be professional education (and the pure core of academic autonomy, the essence of the university, is located in the philosophy department, according to Kant). Does this affirmation not repeat the profound and hierarchizing political evaluation of Metaphysics, I mean of Aristotle's *Metaphysics*? Shortly after the passage that I read at the beginning (981b and following), one sees a theoretico-political hierarchy being put into place. At the top, there is theoretical knowledge. It is not sought after in view of its utility; and the holder of this knowledge, which is always a knowledge of causes and of principles, is the leader or *arkhitekton* of a society at work, is positioned above the manual laborer [*kheiroteknes*] who acts without knowing, just as a fire burns. Now this theoretician leader, this knower of causes who has no need of "practical" skill, is in essence a *teacher*. Beyond the fact of knowing causes and of possessing reason [*to logon ekhein*], he bears another mark [*semeion*] of recognition: the "capacity to teach" [*to dunasthai didaskein*]. To

teach, then, and at the same time to direct, steer, organize the empirical work of the laborers. The theoretician-teacher or "architect" is a leader because he is on the side of the *arkhe*, of beginning and commanding. He commands—he is the premier or the prince—because he knows causes and principles, the "whys" and thus also the "wherefores" of things. Before the fact, and before anyone else, he answers to the principle of reason which is the first principle, the principle of principles. And that is why he takes orders from no one; it is he, on the contrary, who orders, prescribes, lays down the law (982a 18). And it is normal that this superior science, with the power that it confers by virtue of its very lack of utility, is developed in places [*topoi*], in regions where leisure is possible. Thus Aristotle points out that the mathematical arts were developed in Egypt owing to the leisure time enjoyed by the priestly caste [*to ton iereon ethnos*], the priestly folk.

Kant, Nietzsche and Heidegger, speaking of the university, premodern or modern, do not say exactly what Aristotle said, nor do all three of them say exactly the same thing. But they also do say the same thing. Even though he admits the industrial model of the division of labor into the university, Kant places the so-called "lower" faculty, the faculty of philosophy—a place of pure rational knowledge, a place where truth has to be spoken without controls and without concern for "utility," a place where the very meaning and the autonomy of the university meet—Kant places this faculty above and outside professional education: the architectonic schema of pure reason is above and outside the technical schema. In his *Lectures on the Future of our Educational Establishments,* Nietzsche condemns the division of labor in the sciences, condemns utilitarian and journalistic culture in the service of the State, condemns the professional ends of the University. The more one does [*tut*] in the area of training, the more one has to think [*denken*]. And, still in the first Lecture: *"Man muss nicht nur Standpunkte, sondern auch*

Gedanken haben!"; one must not have view-points alone, but also thoughts! As for Heidegger, in 1929, in his inaugural lesson entitled "What Is Metaphysics?" he deplores the henceforth technical organization of the university and its compartmentalizing specialization. And even in his Rector's Speech, at the very point where he makes an appeal on behalf of the three services (*Arbeitsdienst, Wehrdienst, Wissensdienst,* the service of work, the military, and knowledge), at the very point where he is recalling that these services are of equal rank and equally original (he had recalled earlier that for the Greeks *theoria* was only the highest form of *praxis* and the mode, par excellence, of *energeia*), Heidegger nevertheless violently condemns disciplinary compartmentalization and "exterior training in view of a profession," as "an idle and inauthentic thing" [*Das Mussige und Unechte ausserlicher Berufsabrichtung . . .*].

Desiring to remove the university from "useful" programs and from professional ends, one may always, willingly or not, find oneself serving unrecognized ends, reconstituting powers of caste, class, or corporation. We are in an implacable political topography: one step further in view of greater profundity or radicalization, even going beyond the "profound" and the "radical," the principal, the *arkhe,* one step further toward a sort of original an-archy risks producing or reproducing the hierarchy. "Thought" requires *both* the principle of reason *and* what is beyond the principle of reason, the *arkhe* and an-archy. Between the two, the difference of a breath or an accent, only the *enactment* of this "thought" can decide. That decision is always risky, it always risks the worst. To claim to eliminate that risk by an institutional program is quite simply to erect a barricade against a future. The decision of thought cannot be an intra-institutional event, an academic moment.

All this does not define a politics, nor even a responsibility. Only, at best, some negative conditions, a "negative wisdom," as the Kant of *The Conflict of the Faculties* would say: preliminary

cautions, protocols of vigilance for a new *Aufklärung,* what must be seen and kept in sight in a modern re-elaboration of that old problematics. Beware of the abysses and the gorges, but also of the bridges and the barriers. Beware of what opens the university to the outside and the bottomless, but also of what, closing it in on itself, would create only an illusion of closure, would make the university available to any sort of interest, or else render it perfectly useless. Beware of ends; but what would a university be without ends?

Neither in its medieval nor in its modern form has the university disposed freely of its own absolute autonomy and of the rigorous conditions of its own unity. During more than eight centuries, "university" has been the name given by a society to a sort of supplementary body that at one and the same time it wanted to project outside itself and to keep jealously to itself, to emancipate and to control. On this double basis, the university was supposed to *represent* society. And in a certain way it has done so: it has reproduced society's scenography, its views, conflicts, contradictions, its play and its differences, and also its desire for organic union in a total body. Organicist language is always associated with "techno-industrial" language in "modern" discourse on the university. But with the relative autonomy of a technical apparatus, indeed that of a machine and of a prosthetic body, this artifact that is the university has *reflected society* only in giving it the chance for reflection, that is, also, for *dissociation.* The time for reflection, here, signifies not only that the internal rhythm of the university apparatus is relatively independent of social time and relaxes the urgency of command, ensures for it a great and precious freedom of play. An empty place for chance: the invagination of an inside pocket. The time for reflection is also the chance for turning back on the very conditions of reflection, in all the senses of that word, as if with the help of a new optical device one could finally see sight, could not only view the natural landscape, the city, the bridge and the abyss, but could view viewing. As if through an acoustical device one could hear hearing, in other words, seize the inaudible in a sort of poetic telephony. Then the time of reflection is also an other time, it is heterogeneous with what it reflects and perhaps gives time for what calls for and is called thought. It is the chance for an event about which one does not know whether or not, presenting itself *within* the university, it belongs to the history of the university. It may also be brief and paradoxical, it may tear up time, like the instant invoked by Kierkegaard, one of those thinkers who are foreign, even hostile to the university, who give us more to think about, with respect to the essence of the university, than academic reflections themselves. The chance for this event is the chance of an instant, an *Augenblick,* a "wink" or a "blink," it takes place "in the twinkling of an eye." I would say, rather, "in the twilight of an eye," for it is in the most crepuscular, the most westerly situations of the Western university that the chances of this "twinkling" of thought are multiplied. In a period of "crisis," as we say, a period of decadence and renewal, when the institution is "on the blink," provocation to think brings together in the *same* instant the desire for memory and exposure to the future, the fidelity of a guardian faithful enough to want to keep even the chance of a future, in other words the singular responsibility of what he does not have and of what is not yet. Neither in his keeping nor in his purview. Keep the memory and keep the chance—is this possible? And chance—can it be kept? Is it not, as its name indicates, the risk or the advent of the fall, even of decadence, the falling-due that befalls you at the bottom of the "gorge"? I don't know. I don't know if it is possible to keep both memory and chance. I am tempted to think, rather, that the one cannot be kept without the other, without keeping the other and being kept from the other. Differently. That double guard will be assigned, as its responsibility, to the strange destiny of the university. To its law, to its reason for being and to

its truth. Let us risk one more etymological wink: truth is what keeps, that is, both preserves and is preserved. I am thinking here of *Wahrheit,* of the *Wahren* of *Wahrheit* and of *veritas*—whose name figures on the coat of arms of so many American universities. It institutes guardians and calls upon them to watch faithfully—truthfully—over itself.

Let me recall my *incipit* and the single question that I raised at the outset: how can we not speak, today, of the university? Have I said it, or done it? Have I said how one must not speak, today, of the university? Or have I rather spoken as one should not do today, within the University? Only others can answer. Beginning with you.

Translated by Catherine Porter
and Edward P. Morris

NOTES

1. In regard to this "naturalism" (a frequent, but not general phenomenon that Kant, for example, eludes at the beginning of the *Conflict of the Faculties*), and also to the classic motif of interdisciplinarity as an effect of the architectonic totality; see, for example, Schleiermacher's 1808 essay "Geregenther Gedanken über Universitaten in deutschem Sinn, nepst einem Annang über ein neu zu errontence." French translation of this text appears in a noteworthy collection, *Philosophies de l'université l'idéalism allemand et la question de l'Université,* ed. Ferry, Pesron, Renault [Paris: Pavon, 1979].

2. James Siegel, "Academic Work: The View from Cornell," *Diacritics* 11:1 [Spring 1981], 68–83; the quotation, on page 69, is taken from Kermit Parsons, *The Cornell Campus: A History of Its Planning and Development* [Ithaca: Cornell University Press, 1968].

3. Translator's Note. About national idioms and idioms which, like Latin, aspire to greater catholicity: Leibniz's *rationem reddere*—a phrase by no means his exclusive property, but common to philosophy at large—is easily carried over into ordinary French as *rendre raison, rendre raison de quelque chose;* but in English, today, "render reason" sounds outlandish. The Oxford dictionary shows that English had the idiom at one time; setting aside a willfully archaic and dialectical sentence from Walter Scott, the most recent example adduced is from *An Exposition of the Creed,* by John Pearson, bishop of Chester, published in London

in 1659, and it is an example not without interest for our purposes. "Thus," says Pearson as he expounds Article IX. "the Church of Christ in it's [sic] primary institution was made to be of a diffusive nature, to spread and extend itself from the City of *Jerusalem,* where it first began, to all the parts and corners of the earth. This reason did the ancient fathers render why the Church was called Catholick." [*An Exposition* . . . (Ann Arbor, Michigan: University Microfilms, 1968), p. 697.] He then goes on to say that for a second reason the church is called catholic because it teaches everything, or at least everything necessary to Christian faith. Apparently, there was a whole teaching of diffusion and dissemination well before our own time. To judge from the quotations given by OED, *to render reason* (to give it back, as it were) worked in exchange and concert with *to yield reason* and *to give reason:* any one of the three could mean to give grounds for one's thoughts and assertions, but also, to give an account of one's acts or conduct, when summoned to do so: to be held accountable and to speak accordingly. In 1690, writing not of reason but only of understanding, Locke argued that we rank things under distinct names "according to complex ideas in us," as he says, "and not according to precise, distinct, real essences in them." We cannot denominate things by their real essences, as Locke puts the matter, for the good reason that "we know them not." Even the familiar objects of our everyday world are composed we know not how; they must have their reason, but we cannot give it back to them. Thus, for all his practical bent, Locke is drawn to say, and I quote him once again, "When we come to examine the stones we tread on, or the iron we daily handle, we presently find that we know not their make, and can give no reason of the different qualities we find in them" [*An Essay concerning Human Understanding,* III, vi, 8–9]. In English, as in French or Latin, at one time people could give reason, or render it, or not be able to render it.—E.P.M.

4.   In this quotation from Peirce's *Values in a Universe of Chance* [(Stanford, Ca.: Stanford University Press, 1958), p. 332], in addition to the last sentence, I have italicized the allusion to *desire* in order to echo the opening words of Aristotle's *Metaphysics.* Weber's article appeared in a double issue of *The Oxford Literary Review* 5: 1–2 (1982), pp. 59–79.

5.   Here is but one example: "Rationem reddere heisst: den Grund zurückgeben. Weshal zurück und wohin zurück? Weil es sich in den Bewisgängen, allgemein gesprochen im Erkennen um das *Vor*-stellen der Gegenstände handelt, kommt dieses zurück ins Spiel. Die

lateinische, Sprache der Philosophie sagt es deutlicher: das Vorstellen is re-praesentatio. Das Begegnende wird auf das vorstellende Ich zu, auf es zurück und ihm entgegen praesentiert, in eine Gegenwart gestellt. Gemäss dem principium reddendae rationis muss das Vorstellen, wenn es ein erkennendes sein soll, den Grund des Gegegnenden auf das Vorstellen zu un d.h. ihm zurückgeben (reddere). Im erkennenden Vorstellen wird dem erkennenden Ich der Grund zu-gestellt. Dies Verlangt das principium rationis. Des Satz vom Grund is darum für Leibniz der Grundsatz des zuzustellenden Grundes" [*Der Satz vom Grund* (Pfullingen: G. Neske, 1957), p. 45].

6.   In "Vom Wesen des Grundes," *Wegmarken* [Frankfurt am Main: Klostermann, 1976], pp. 60–61.

7.   "And yet, without this all powerful principle there would be no modern science, and without such a science there would be no university today. The latter rests upon the princple of reason [*Diese gründet auf dem Satz vom Grund*]. How should we represent that to ourselves [*Wie sollen wir uns dies vorstellen*], the university founded *gegründet* on a sentence (a primary proposition: *auf einen Satz*)? Can we risk such an assertion [*Dürfen wir eine solche Behauptung wagen*]" [*Der Satz vom Grund, Dritte Stunde,* p. 49].

8.   Among many possible examples, I shall mention only two recent articles. They have at least one trait in common: their authors are highly placed representatives of two institutions whose power and influence hardly need to be recalled. I refer to "The Crisis in English Studies" by Walter Jackson Bate, Kingsley Porter University Professor at Harvard [*Harvard Magazine,* Sept./Oct. 1982], and to "The Shattered Humanities" by William J. Bennett, Chairman of the National Endowment for the Humanities [*Wall Street Journal,* Dec. 31, 1982]. The latter of these articles carries ignorance and irrationality so far as to write the following: "A popular movement in literary criticism called "Deconstruction" denies that there are any texts at all. If there are no texts, there are no great texts, and no argument for reading." The former makes remarks about deconstruction—and this is not by chance—that are, we might say, just as unnerved. As Paul de Man notes in an admirable short essay ["The Return to Philogy," *Times Literary Supplement,* December 10, 1982], Professor Bate "has this time confined his sources of information to *Newsweek* magazine. . . . What is left is a matter of law-enforcement rather than a critical debate. One must be feeling very threatened indeed to become so aggressively defensive."

21

Michel Foucault
1926–1984

Along with Jacques Derrida, Michel Foucault has become one of the most prominent European influences directing the pursuit of theory in recent American literary studies. Foucault's thought, however, has not been as readily integrated into literary criticism as have the ideas of Derrida and the "poststructuralist" work of Roland Barthes, Jacques Lacan, and Julia Kristeva (even though he has written on Gustave Flaubert, Maurice Blanchot, and Raymond Roussel). This difficulty of integration results from the specific concerns of his work. Unlike most "Poststructuralists," Foucault is less concerned with language at the level of the sign and much more concerned with the relationship of language and social institutions, a relationship that he calls "discourse." To examine language at the level of discourse is to identify the institutional rules that make possible particular signification and, consequently, make possible particular forms of knowledge.

This concern with underlying rules that govern the production of knowledge is found in Foucault's early major work, in which he identifies the conditions that made possible the emergence and development of modern areas of knowledge and their corresponding institutions: the diagnosis of madness and the emergence of asylums (*Madness and Civilization,* 1961; translated into English 1965), scientific medicine and the emergence of clinics (*Birth of the Clinic,* 1963; trans. 1973), and the emergence of the human sciences in eighteenth-century Europe (*The Order of Things,* 1966; trans. 1970). Though Foucault, in his later work, remained interested in the social conditions of knowledge, his focus shifted following the failed leftist uprising in Paris during May 1968. The failure of this uprising led Foucault to an analysis of the exercise of power through social practices, including uses of language, or "discursive practices." This shift of interest coincided with a prestigious appointment to the College de France in 1970.

His inaugural lecture in this position, *The Discourse on Language* (1971; trans. 1972), presents the agenda for future work by outlining the ways in which "in every society the production of discourse is at once controlled, selected, organized and redistributed according to a certain number of procedures. . . ." In *Discipline and Punish* (1975; trans. 1977) Foucault combined his interest in the emergence of social institutions (in this case, the rise of prisons in the early nineteenth century) and the exercise of power through discipline, especially discipline of the body. This interest in the application of discipline through discursive and other practices continues in the last of Foucault's major works, the three volumes of *History of Sexuality* (1976, 1984;

trans. 1978, 1986). Foucault's thought, therefore, does not lend itself to commentaries on individual literary works as much as it directs us to view literature as a socially determined discursive practice. Also, Foucault's work has influenced several American critics to examine literary criticism (and its history) as a discursive practice.

"What Is an Author?" was first published in 1969, and, while it continues to probe the institutional forces that affect writing and knowledge (a project that he theorized in *The Archeology of Knowledge,* 1969; trans. 1972), it was the first work to reflect his new concern with the exercise of power. Foucault frames the essay by observing a contradiction in modern culture: in many ways our culture regards the author as unimportant (for example, formalist literary criticism and the structuralist approach to the human sciences), yet in our criticism we do not hesitate to use the names of authors. On the basis of this contradiction, Foucault sets the direction of his inquiry: "I am not certain that consequences derived from the disappearance, or deathbed, of the author have been fully explored or that the importance of this event has been appreciated." Foucault, therefore, in posing the question "What is an author?" is asking, "In what ways do we use the notion of author?" Foucault observes that we use the name of an author to do more than to refer to a person. Instead, the notion of author, unlike the notion of writer, is used to authorize certain writings, to privilege those writings. Thus, by focusing on the notion of author, Foucault is able to raise the more general questions of what conditions and interests allow one writer to be regarded an "author" and another writer not. Also Foucault uses this insight into the social-political nature of the notion of author to problematize the subjectivity of the writer, that is, to assert that a text is never the product of a unified consciousness (the author) but consists of several socially determined roles, or "author-functions."

What Is an Author?

The coming into being of the notion of "author" constitutes the privileged moment of *individualization* in the history of ideas, knowledge, literature, philosophy, and the sciences. Even today, when we reconstruct the history of a concept, literary genre, or school of philosophy, such categories seem relatively weak, secondary, and superimposed scansions in comparison with the solid and fundamental unit of the author and the work.

I shall not offer here a sociohistorical analysis of the author's persona. Certainly it would be worth examining how the author became individualized in a culture like ours, what status he has been given, at what moment studies of authenticity and attribution began, in what kind of system of valorization the author was involved, at what point we began to recount the lives of authors rather than of heroes, and how this fundamental category of "the-man-and-his-work criticism" began. For the moment, however, I want to deal solely with the relationship between text and author and with the manner in which the text points to this "figure" that, at least in appearance, is outside it and antecedes it.

Beckett nicely formulates the theme with which I would like to begin: "'What does it matter who is speaking,' someone said, 'what does it matter who is speaking.'" In this indifference appears one of the fundamental ethical principles of contemporary writing *(écriture)*. I say "ethical" because this indifference is not really a trait characterizing the manner in which one speaks and writes, but rather a kind of immanent rule, taken up over and over again, never fully applied, not designating writing as something completed, but dominating it as a practice. Since it is too familiar to require a lengthy analysis, this immanent rule can be adequately illustrated here by tracing two of its major themes.

First of all, we can say that today's writing has freed itself from the dimension of expression. Referring only to itself, but without being restricted to the confines of its interiority, writing is identified with its own unfolded exteriority. This means that it is an interplay of signs arranged less according to its signified content than according to the very nature of the signifier. Writing unfolds like a game *(jeu)* that invariably goes beyond its own rules and transgresses its limits. In writing, the point is not to manifest or exalt the act of writing, nor is it to pin a subject within language; it is rather a question of creating a space into which the writing subject constantly disappears.

The second theme, writing's relationship with death, is even more familiar. This link subverts an old tradition exemplified by the Greek epic, which was intended to perpetuate the immortality of the hero: if he was willing to die young, it was so that his life, consecrated and magnified by death, might pass into immortality; the narrative then redeemed this accepted death. In another way, the motivation, as well as the theme and the pretext of Arabian narratives—such as *The Thousand and One Nights*—was also the eluding of death: one spoke, telling stories into the early morning, in order to forestall death, to postpone the day of reckoning that would silence the narrator. Scheherazade's narrative is an effort, renewed each night, to keep death outside the circle of life.

Our culture has metamorphosed this idea of narrative, or writing, as something designed to ward off death. Writing has become linked to sacrifice, even to the sacrifice of life: it is now a voluntary effacement which does not need to be represented in books, since it is brought about in the writer's very existence. The work, which once had the duty of providing immortality, now possesses the right to kill, to be its author's murderer, as in the cases of Flaubert, Proust, and Kafka. That is not all, however, this relationship between writing and death is also manifested in the effacement of the writing subject's individual characteristics. Using all the contrivances that he sets up between himself and what he writes, the writing subject cancels out the signs of his particular individuality. As a result, the mark of the writer is reduced to nothing more than the singularity of his absence; he must assume the role of the dead man in the game of writing.

None of this is recent; criticism and philosophy took note of the disappearance—or death—of the author some time ago. But the consequences of their discovery of it have not been sufficiently examined, nor has its import been accurately measured. A certain number of notions that are intended to replace the privileged position of the author actually seem to preserve that privilege and suppress the real meaning of his disappearance. I shall examine two of these notions, both of great importance today.

The first is the idea of the work. It is a very familiar thesis that the task of criticism is not to bring out the work's relationships with the author, nor to reconstruct through the text a thought or experience, but rather, to analyze the work through its structure, its architecture, its intrinsic form, and the play of its internal relationships. At this point, however, a problem arises: "What is a work? What is this curious unity which we designate as a work? Of what elements is it composed? Is it not what an author has written?" Difficulties appear immediately. If an individual were not an author, could we say that what he wrote, said, left behind in his papers, or what has been collected of his remarks, could be called a "work"? When Sade was not considered an author, what was the status of his papers? Were they simply rolls of paper onto which he ceaselessly uncoiled his fantasies during his imprisonment?

Even when an individual has been accepted as an author, we must still ask whether everything that he wrote, said, or left behind is part of his work. The problem is both theoretical and technical. When undertaking the publication of Nietzsche's works, for example, where should one stop? Surely everything must be published, but what is "everything"? Everything that Nietzsche himself published, certainly. And what about the rough drafts for his works? Obviously. The plans for his aphorisms? Yes. The deleted passages and the notes at the bottom of the page? Yes. What if, within a workbook filled with aphorisms, one finds a reference, the notation of a meeting or of an address, or a laundry list: is it a work, or not? Why not? And so on, ad infinitum. How can one define a work amid the millions of traces left by someone after his death? A theory of the work does not exist, and the empirical task of those who naively undertake the editing of works often suffers in the absence of such a theory.

We could go even further: does *The Thousand and One Nights* constitute a work? What about Clement of Alexandria's *Miscellanies* or Diogenes Laertius' *Lives?* A multitude of questions arises with regard to this notion of the work. Consequently, it is not enough to declare that we should do without the writer (the author) and study the work in itself. The word "work" and the unity that it designates are probably as problematic as the status of the author's individuality.

Another notion which has hindered us from taking full measure of the author's disappearance, blurring and concealing the moment of this effacement and subtly preserving the author's existence, is the notion of writing [*écriture*]. When rigorously applied, this notion should allow us not only to circumvent references to the author, but also to situate his recent

absence. The notion of writing, as currently employed, is concerned with neither the act of writing nor the indication—be it symptom or sign—of a meaning which someone might have wanted to express. We try, with great effort, to imagine the general condition of each text, the condition of both the space in which it is dispersed and the time in which it unfolds.

In current usage, however, the notion of writing seems to transpose the empirical characteristics of the author into a transcendental anonymity. We are content to efface the more visible marks of the author's empiricity by playing off, one against the other, two ways of characterizing writing, namely, the critical and the religious approaches. Giving writing a primal status seems to be a way of retranslating, in transcendental terms, both the theological affirmation of its sacred character and the critical affirmation of its creative character. To admit that writing is, because of the very history that it made possible, subject to the test of oblivion and repression, seems to represent, in transcendental terms, the religious principle of the hidden meaning (which requires interpretation) and the critical principle of implicit significations, silent determinations, and obscured contents (which gives rise to commentary). To imagine writing as absence seems to be a simple repetition, in transcendental terms, of both the religious principle of inalterable and yet never fulfilled tradition, and the aesthetic principle of the work's survival, its perpetuation beyond the author's death, and its enigmatic *excess* in relation to him.

This usage of the notion of writing runs the risk of maintaining the author's privileges under the protection of writing's a priori status: it keeps alive, in the grey light of neutralization, the interplay of those representations that formed a particular image of the author. The author's disappearance, which, since Mallarmé, has been a constantly recurring event, is subject to a series of transcendental barriers. There seems to be an important dividing line between those who believe that they can still locate today's discontinuities *(ruptures)* in the historicotranscendental tradition of the nineteenth century, and those who try to free themselves once and for all from that tradition.[1]

It is not enough, however, to repeat the empty affirmation that the author has disappeared. For the same reason, it is not enough to keep repeating (after Nietzsche) that God and man have died a common death. Instead, we must locate the space left empty by the author's disappearance, follow the distribution of gaps and breaches, and watch for the openings that this disappearance uncovers.

First, we need to clarify briefly the problems arising from the use of the author's name. What is an author's name? How does it function? Far from offering a solution, I shall only indicate some of the difficulties that it presents.

The author's name is a proper name, and therefore it raises the problems common to all proper names. (Here I refer to Searle's analyses, among others.[2]) Obviously, one cannot turn a proper name into a pure and simple reference. It has other than indicative functions: more than an indication, a gesture, a finger pointed at someone, it is the equivalent of a description. When one says "Aristotle," one employs a word that is the equivalent of one, or a series of, definite descriptions, such as "the author of the *Analytics*," "the founder of ontology," and so forth. One cannot stop there, however, because a proper name does not have just one signification. When we discover that Rimbaud did not write *La Chasse spirituelle*, we cannot pretend that the meaning of this proper name, or that of the author, has been altered. The proper name and the author's name are situated between the two poles of description and designation: they must have a certain link with what they name, but one that is neither entirely in the mode of designation nor in that of description; it must be a *specific* link. However—and it is here that the particular difficulties of the author's name arise—the links between the proper name and the individual named and between the author's name and what it names are not isomorphic and do not function in the same way. There are several differences.

If, for example, Pierre Dupont does not have blue eyes, or was not born in Paris, or is not a doctor, the name Pierre Dupont will still always refer to the same person; such things do not modify the link of designation. The problems raised by the author's name are much more complex, however. If I discover that Shakespeare was not born in the house that we visit today, this is a modification which, obviously, will not alter the functioning of the author's name. But if we proved that Shakespeare did not write those sonnets which pass for his, that would constitute a significant change and affect the manner in which the author's name functions. If we proved that Shakespeare wrote Bacon's *Organon* by showing that the same author wrote both the works of Bacon and those of Shakespeare, that would be a third type of change which would entirely modify the functioning of the author's name. The author's name is not, therefore, just a proper name like the rest.

Many other facts point out the paradoxical singularity of the author's name. To say that Pierre Dupont does not exist is not at all the same as saying that Homer or Hermes Trismegistus did not exist. In the first case, it means that no one has the name Pierre Dupont; in the second, it means that several people were mixed together under one name, or that the true author had none of the traits traditionally ascribed to the personae of Homer or Hermes. To say that X's real name is actually Jacques Durand instead of Pierre Dupont is not the same as saying that Stendhal's name was Henri Beyle. One could also question the meaning and functioning of propositions like "Bourbaki is so-and-so, so-and-so, etc." and "Victor Eremita, Climacus, Anticlimacus, Frater Taciturnus, Constantine Constantius, all of these are Kierkegaard."

These differences may result from the fact that an author's name is not simply an element in a discourse (capable of being either subject or object, of being replaced by a pronoun, and the like); it performs a certain role with regard to narrative discourse, assuring a classificatory function. Such a name permits one to group together a certain number of texts, define them, differentiate them from and contrast them to others. In addition, it establishes a relationship among the texts. Hermes Trismegistus did not exist, nor did Hippocrates—in the sense that Balzac existed—but the fact that several texts have been placed under the same name indicates that there has been established among them a relationship of homogeneity, filiation, authentification of some texts by the use of others, reciprocal explication, or concomitant utilization. The author's name serves to characterize a certain mode of being of discourse: the fact that the discourse has an author's name, that one can say "this was written by so-and-so" or "so-and-so is its author," shows that this discourse is not ordinary everyday speech that merely comes and goes, not something that is immediately consumable. On the contrary, it is a speech that must be received in a certain mode and that, in a given culture, must receive a certain status.

It would seem that the author's name, unlike other proper names, does not pass from the interior of a discourse to the real and exterior individual who produced it; instead, the name seems always to be present, marking off the edges of the text, revealing, or at least characterizing, its mode of being. The author's name manifests the appearance of a certain discursive set and indicates the status of this discourse within a society and a culture. It has no legal status, nor is it located in the fiction of the work; rather, it is located in the break that founds a certain discursive construct and its very particular mode of being. As a result, we could say that in a civilization like our own there are a certain number of discourses that are endowed with the "author-function," while others are deprived of it. A private letter may well have a signer—it does not have an author; a contract may well have a guarantor—it does not have an author. An anonymous text posted on a wall probably has a writer—but not an author. The author-function is therefore characteristic of the mode of existence, circulation, and functioning of certain discourses within a society.

Let us analyze this "author-function" as we have just described it. In our culture, how does one characterize a discourse containing the author-function? In what way is this discourse different from other discourses? If we limit our remarks to the author of a book or a text, we can isolate four different characteristics.

First of all, discourses are objects of appropriation. The form of ownership from which they spring is of a rather particular type, one that has been codified for many years. We should note that, historically, this type of ownership has always been subsequent to what one might call penal appropriation. Texts, books, and discourses really began to have authors (other than mythical, "sacralized" and "sacralizing" figures) to the extent that authors became subject to punishment, that is, to the extent that discourses could be transgressive. In our culture (and doubtless in many others), discourse was not originally a product, a thing, a kind of goods; it was essentially an act—an act placed in the bipolar field of the sacred and the profane, the licit and the illicit, the religious and the blasphemous. Historically, it was a gesture fraught with risks before becoming goods caught up in a circuit of ownership. Once a system of ownership for texts came into being, once strict rules concerning author's rights, author-publisher relations, rights of reproduction, and related matters were enacted—at the end of the eighteenth and the beginning of the nineteenth century— the possibility of transgression attached to the act of writing took on, more and more, the form of an imperative peculiar to literature. It is as if the author, beginning with the moment at which he was placed in the system of property that characterizes our society, compensated for the status that he thus acquired by rediscovering the old bipolar field of discourse, systematically practicing transgression and thereby restoring danger to a writing which was now guaranteed the benefits of ownership.

The author-function does not affect all discourses in a universal and constant way, however. This is its second characteristic. In our civilization, it has not always been the same types of texts which have required attribution to an author. There was a time when the texts that we today call "literary" (narratives, stories, epics, tragedies, comedies) were accepted, put into circulation, and valorized without any question about the identity of their author; their anonymity caused no difficulties since their ancientness, whether real or imagined, was regarded as a sufficient guarantee of their status. On the other hand, those texts that we now would call scientific—those dealing with cosmology and the heavens, medicine and illnesses, natural sciences and geography—were accepted in the Middle Ages, and accepted as "true," only when marked with the name of their author. "Hippocrates said," "Pliny recounts," were not really formulas of an argument based on authority; they were the markers inserted in discourses that were supposed to be received as statements of demonstrated truth.

A reversal occurred in the seventeenth or eighteenth century. Scientific discourses began to be received for themselves, in the anonymity of an established or always redemonstrable truth; their membership in a systematic ensemble, and not the reference to the individual who produced them, stood as their guarantee. The author-function faded away, and the inventor's name served only to christen a theorem, proposition, particular effect, property, body, group of elements, or pathological syndrome. By the same token, literary discourses came to be accepted only when endowed with the author-function. We now ask of each poetic or fictional text: from where does it come, who wrote it, when, under what circumstances, or beginning with what design? The meaning ascribed to it and the status or value accorded it depend upon the manner in which we answer these questions. And if a text should be discovered in a state of anonymity—whether as a consequence of an accident or the author's explicit wish—the game becomes one of rediscovering the author. Since literary anonymity is not tolerable, we can accept it only in the guise of an enigma. As a result, the author-function today plays an important role in our view of literary works. (These are obviously generalizations that would have to be refined insofar as recent critical practice is concerned.)

The third characteristic of this author-function is that it does not develop spontaneously as the attribution of a discourse to an individual. It is, rather, the result of a complex operation which constructs a certain rational being that we call "author." Critics doubtless try to give this intelligible being a realistic status, by discerning, in the individual, a "deep" motive, a "creative" power, or a "design," the milieu in which writing originates. Nevertheless, these aspects of an individual which we designate as making him an author are only a projection, in more or less psychologizing terms, of the operations that we force texts to undergo, the connections that we make, the traits that we establish as pertinent, the continuities that we recognize, or the exclusions that we practice. All these operations vary according to periods and types of discourse. We do not construct a "philosophical author" as we do a "poet," just as, in the eighteenth century, one did not construct a novelist as we do today. Still, we can find through the ages certain constants in the rules of author-construction.

It seems, for example, that the manner in which literary criticism once defined the author—or rather constructed the figure of the author beginning with existing texts and discourses—is directly derived from the manner in which Christian tradition authenticated (or rejected) the texts at its disposal. In order to "rediscover" an author in a work, modern criticism uses methods similar to those that Christian exegesis employed when trying to prove the value of a text by its author's saintliness. In *De viris illustribus,* Saint Jerome explains that homonymy is not sufficient to identify legitimately authors of more than one work: different individuals could have had the same name, or one man could have, illegitimately, borrowed another's patronymic. The name as an individual trademark is not enough when one works within a textual tradition.

How then can one attribute several discourses to one and the same author? How can one use the author-function to determine if one is dealing with one or several individuals? Saint Jerome proposes four criteria: (1) if among several books attributed to an author one is inferior to the others, it must be withdrawn from the list of the author's works (the author is therefore defined as a constant level of value); (2) the same should be done if certain texts contradict the doctrine expounded in the author's other works (the author is thus defined as a field of conceptual or theoretical coherence); (3) one must also exclude works that are written in a different style, containing words and expressions not ordinarily found in the writer's production (the author is here conceived as a stylistic unity); (4) finally, passages quoting statements that were made, or mentioning events that occurred after the author's death must be regarded as interpolated texts (the author is here seen as a historical figure at the crossroads of a certain number of events).

Modern literary criticism, even when—as is now customary—it is not concerned with questions of authentication, still defines the author the same way: the author provides the basis for explaining not only the presence of certain events in a work, but also their transformations, distortions, and diverse modifications (through his biography, the determination of his individual perspective, the analysis of his social posi-

tion, and the revelation of his basic design). The author is also the principle of a certain unity of writing—all differences having to be resolved, at least in part, by the principles of evolution, maturation, or influence. The author also serves to neutralize the contradictions that may emerge in a series of texts: there must be—at a certain level of his thought or desire, of his consciousness or unconscious—a point where contradictions are resolved, where incompatible elements are at last tied together or organized around a fundamental or originating contradiction. Finally, the author is a particular source of expression that, in more or less completed forms, is manifested equally well, and with similar validity, in works, sketches, letters, fragments, and so on. Clearly, Saint Jerome's four criteria of authenticity (criteria which seem totally insufficient for today's exegetes) do define the four modalities according to which modern criticism brings the author-function into play.

But the author-function is not a pure and simple reconstruction made secondhand from a text given as passive material. The text always contains a certain number of signs referring to the author. These signs, well known to grammarians, are personal pronouns, adverbs of time and place, and verb conjugation. Such elements do not play the same role in discourses provided with the author-function as in those lacking it. In the latter, such "shifters" refer to the real speaker and to the spatio-temporal coordinates of his discourse (although certain modifications can occur, as in the operation of relating discourses in the first person). In the former, however, their role is more complex and variable. Everyone knows that, in a novel narrated in the first person, neither the first person pronoun, nor the present indicative refer exactly either to the writer or to the moment in which he writes, but rather to an alter ego whose distance from the author varies, often changing in the course of the work. It would be just as wrong to equate the author with the real writer as to equate him with the fictitious speaker; the author-function is carried out and operates in the scission itself, in this division and this distance.

One might object that this is a characteristic peculiar to novelistic or poetic discourse, a "game" in which only "quasi-discourses" participate. In fact, however, all discourses endowed with the author-function do possess this plurality of self. The self that speaks in the preface to a treatise on mathematics—and that indicates the circumstances of the treatise's composition—is identical neither in its position nor in its functioning to the self that speaks in the course of a demonstration, and that appears in the form of "I conclude" or "I suppose." In the first case, the "I" refers to an individual without an equivalent who, in a determined place and time, completed a certain task; in the second, the "I" indicates an instance and a level of demonstration which any individual could perform provided that he accept the same system of symbols, play of axioms, and set of previous demonstrations. We could also, in the same treatise, locate a third self, one that speaks to tell the work's meaning, the obstacles encountered, the results obtained, and the remaining problems; this self is situated in the field of already existing or yet-to-appear mathematical discourses. The author-function is not assumed by the first of these selves at the expense of the other two, which would then be nothing more than a fictitious splitting in two of the first one. On the contrary, in these discourses the author-function operates so as to effect the dispersion of these three simultaneous selves.

No doubt analysis could discover still more characteristic traits of the author-function. I will limit myself to these four, however, because they seem both the most visible and the most important. They can be summarized as follows: (1) the author-function is linked to the juridical and institutional system that encompasses, determines, and articulates the universe of discourses; (2) it does not affect all discourses in the same way at all times and in all types of civilization; (3) it is not defined by the spontaneous attribution of a discourse to its producer, but rather by a series of specific and complex operations; (4) it does not refer purely and simply to a real individual, since it can give rise simultaneously to several selves, to several subjects—positions that can be occupied by different classes of individuals.

Up to this point I have unjustifiably limited my subject. Certainly the author-function in painting, music, and other arts should have been discussed, but even supposing that we remain within the world of discourse, as I want to do, I seem to have given the term "author" much too narrow a meaning. I have discussed the author only in the limited sense of a person to whom the production of a text, a book, or work can be legitimately attributed. It is easy to see that in the sphere of discourse one can be the author of much more than a book—one can be the author of a theory, tradition, or discipline in which other books and authors will in their turn find a place. These authors are in a position which we shall call "transdiscursive." This is a recurring phenomenon—certainly as old as our civilization. Homer, Aristotle, and the Church Fathers, as well as the first mathematicians and the originators of the Hippocratic tradition, all played this role.

Furthermore, in the course of the nineteenth century, there appeared in Europe another, more uncommon, kind of author, whom one should confuse with neither the "great" literary authors, nor the authors of religious texts, nor the founders of science. In a somewhat arbitrary way we shall call those who belong in this last group "founders of discursivity." They are unique in that they are not just the authors of their own works. They have produced something else: the possibilities and the rules for the formation of other texts. In this sense, they are very different, for example, from a novelist, who is, in fact, nothing more than the author of his own text. Freud is not just the author of *The Interpretation of Dreams* or *Jokes and their Relation to the Unconscious;* Marx is not just the author of the

Communist Manifesto or *Capital:* they both have established an endless possibility of discourse.

Obviously, it is easy to object. One might say that it is not true that the author of a novel is only the author of his own text; in a sense, he also, provided that he acquires some "importance," governs and commands more than that. To take a very simple example, one could say that Ann Radcliffe not only wrote *The Castles of Athlin and Dunbayne* and several other novels, but also made possible the appearance of the Gothic horror novel at the beginning of the nineteenth century; in that respect, her author-function exceeds her own work. But I think there is an answer to this objection. These founders of discursivity (I use Marx and Freud as examples, because I believe them to be both the first and the most important cases) make possible something altogether different from what a novelist makes possible. Ann Radcliffe's texts opened the way for a certain number of resemblances and analogies which have their model or principle in her work. The latter contains characteristic signs, figures, relationships, and structures which could be reused by others. In other words, to say that Ann Radcliffe founded the Gothic horror novel means that in the nineteenth-century Gothic novel one will find, as in Ann Radcliffe's works, the theme of the heroine caught in the trap of her own innocence, the hidden castle, the character of the black, cursed hero devoted to making the world expiate the evil done to him, and all the rest of it.

On the other hand, when I speak of Marx or Freud as founders of discursivity, I mean that they made possible not only a certain number of analogies, but also (and equally important) a certain number of differences. They have created a possibility for something other than their discourse, yet something belonging to what they founded. To say that Freud founded psychoanalysis does not (simply) mean that we find the concept of the libido or the technique of dream analysis in the works of Karl Abraham or Melanie Klein; it means that Freud made possi-

ble a certain number of divergences—with respect to his own texts, concepts, and hypotheses—that all arise from the psychoanalytical discourse itself.

This would seem to present a new difficulty, however: is the above not true, after all, of any founder of a science, or of any author who has introduced some important transformation into a science? After all, Galileo made possible not only those discourses that repeated the laws that he had formulated, but also statements very different from what he himself had said. If Cuvier is the founder of biology or Saussure the founder of linguistics, it is not because they were imitated, nor because people have since taken up again the concept of organism or sign; it is because Cuvier made possible, to a certain extent, a theory of evolution diametrically opposed to his own fixism; it is because Saussure made possible a generative grammar radically different from his structural analyses. Superficially, then, the initiation of discursive practices appears similar to the founding of any scientific endeavor.

Still, there is a difference, and a notable one. In the case of a science, the act that founds it is on an equal footing with its future transformations; this act becomes in some respects part of the set of modifications that it makes possible. Of course, this belonging can take several forms. In the future development of a science, the founding act may appear as little more than a particular instance of a more general phenomenon which unveils itself in the process. It can also turn out to be marred by intuition and empirical bias; one must then reformulate it, making it the object of a certain number of supplementary theoretical operations which establish it more rigorously, etc. Finally, it can seem to be a hasty generalization which must be limited, and whose restricted domain of validity must be retraced. In other words, the founding act of a science can always be reintroduced within the machinery of those transformations that derive from it.

In contrast, the initiation of a discursive practice is heterogeneous to its subsequent transformations. To expand a type of discursivity, such as psychoanalysis as founded by Freud, is not to give it a formal generality that it would not have permitted at the outset, but rather to open it up to a certain number of possible applications. To limit psychoanalysis as a type of discursivity is, in reality, to try to isolate in the founding act an eventually restricted number of propositions or statements to which, alone, one grants a founding value, and in relation to which certain concepts or theories accepted by Freud might be considered as derived, secondary, and accessory. In addition, one does not declare certain propositions in the work of these founders to be false: instead, when trying to seize the act of founding, one sets aside those statements that are not pertinent, either because they are deemed inessential, or because they are considered "prehistoric" and derived from another type of discursivity. In other words, unlike the founding of a science, the initiation of a discursive practice does not participate in its later transformations.

As a result, one defines a proposition's theoretical validity in relation to the work of the founders—while, in the case of Galileo and Newton, it is in relation to what physics or cosmology *is* (in its intrinsic structure and "normativity") that one affirms the validity of any proposition that those men may have put forth. To phrase it very schematically: the work of initiators of discursivity is not situated in the space that science defines; rather, it is the science or the discursivity which refers back to their work as primary coordinates.

In this way we can understand the inevitable necessity, within these fields of discursivity, for a "return to the origin." This return, which is part of the discursive field itself, never stops modifying it. The return is not a historical supplement which would be added to the discursivity, or merely an ornament; on the contrary, it constitutes an effective and necessary task of transforming the discursive practice itself. Re-exami-

nation of Galileo's text may well change our knowledge of the history of mechanics, but it will never be able to change mechanics itself. On the other hand, re-examining Freud's texts modifies psychoanalysis itself just as a re-examination of Marx's would modify Marxism.[3]

What I have just outlined regarding the initiation of discursive practices is, of course, very schematic; this is true, in particular, of the opposition that I have tried to draw between discursive initiation and scientific founding. It is not always easy to distinguish between the two; moreover, nothing proves that they are two mutually exclusive procedures. I have attempted the distinction for only one reason: to show that the author-function, which is complex enough when one tries to situate it at the level of a book or a series of texts that carry a given signature, involves still more determining factors when one tries to analyze it in larger units, such as groups of works or entire disciplines.

To conclude, I would like to review the reasons why I attach a certain importance to what I have said.

First, there are theoretical reasons. On the one hand, an analysis in the direction that I have outlined might provide for an approach to a typology of discourse. It seems to me, at least at first glance, that such a typology cannot be constructed solely from the grammatical features, formal structures, and objects of discourse: more likely there exist properties or relationships peculiar to discourse (not reducible to the rules of grammar and logic), and one must use these to distinguish the major categories of discourse. The relationship (or nonrelationship) with an author, and the different forms this relationship takes, constitute—in a quite visible manner—one of these discursive properties.

On the other hand, I believe that one could find here an introduction to the historical analysis of discourse. Perhaps it is time to study discourses not only in terms of their expressive value or formal transformations, but according to their modes of existence. The modes of circulation, valorization, attribution, and appropriation of discourses vary with each culture and are modified within each. The manner in which they are articulated according to social relationships can be more readily understood, I believe, in the activity of the author-function and in its modifications, than in the themes or concepts that discourses set in motion.

It would seem that one could also, beginning with analyses of this type, re-examine the privileges of the subject. I realize that in undertaking the internal and architectonic analysis of a work (be it a literary text, philosophical system, or scientific work), in setting aside biographical and psychological references, one has already called back into question the absolute character and founding role of the subject. Still, perhaps one must return to this question, not in order to re-establish the theme of an originating subject, but to grasp the subject's points of insertion, modes of functioning, and system of dependencies. Doing so means overturning the traditional problem, no longer raising the questions "How can a free subject penetrate the substance of things and give it meaning? How can it activate the rules of a language from within and thus give rise to the designs which are properly its own?" Instead, these questions will be raised: "How, under what conditions and in what forms can something like a subject appear in the order of discourse? What place can it occupy in each type of discourse, what functions can it assume, and by obeying what rules?" In short, it is a matter of depriving the subject (or its substitute) of its role as originator, and of analyzing the subject as a variable and complex function of discourse.

Second, there are reasons dealing with the "ideological" status of the author. The question then becomes: How can one reduce the great peril, the great danger with which fiction threatens our world? The answer is: One can reduce it with the author. The author allows a limitation of the cancerous and dangerous proliferation of significations within a world where one is thrifty not only with one's resources and riches, but also with one's discourses and their significations. The author is the principle of thrift in the proliferation of meaning. As a result, we must entirely reverse the traditional idea of the author. We are accustomed, as we have seen earlier, to saying that the author is the genial creator of a work in which he deposits, with infinite wealth and generosity, an inexhaustible world of significations. We are used to thinking that the author is so different from all other men, and so transcendent with regard to all languages that, as soon as he speaks, meaning begins to proliferate, to proliferate indefinitely.

The truth is quite the contrary: the author is not an indefinite source of significations which fill a work; the author does not precede the works, he is a certain functional principle by which, in our culture, one limits, excludes, and chooses; in short, by which one impedes the free circulation, the free manipulation, the free composition, decomposition, and recomposition of fiction. In fact, if we are accustomed to presenting the author as a genius, as a perpetual surging of invention, it is because, in reality, we make him function in exactly the opposite fashion. One can say that the author is an ideological product, since we represent him as the opposite of his historically real function. (When a historically given function is represented in a figure that inverts it, one has an ideological production.) The author is therefore the ideological figure by which one marks the manner in which we fear the proliferation of meaning.

In saying this, I seem to call for a form of culture in which fiction would not be limited by the figure of the author. It would be pure romanticism, however, to imagine a culture in which the fictive would operate in an absolutely free state, in which fiction would be put at the disposal of everyone and would develop without passing through something like a necessary or constraining figure. Although, since the eighteenth century, the author has played the role of the regulator of the fictive, a role quite characteristic of our era of industrial and bourgeois society, of individualism and private property, still, given the historical modifications that are taking place, it does not seem necessary that the author-function remain constant in form, complexity, and even in existence. I think that, as our society changes, at the very moment when it is in the process of changing, the author-function will disappear, and in such a manner that fiction and its polysemic texts will once again function according to another mode, but still with a system of constraint—one which will no longer be the author, but which will have to be determined or, perhaps, experienced.

All discourses, whatever their status, form, value, and whatever the treatment to which they will be subjected, would then develop in the anonymity of a murmur. We would no longer hear the questions that have been rehashed for so long: "Who really spoke? Is it really he and not someone else? With what authenticity or originality? And what part of his deepest self did he express in his discourse?" Instead, there would be other questions, like these: "What are the modes of existence of this discourse? Where has it been used, how can it circulate, and who can appropriate it for himself? What are the places in it where there is room for possible subjects? Who can assume these various subject-functions?" And behind all these questions, we would hear hardly anything but the stirring of an indifference: "What difference does it make who is speaking?"

Translated by Josué V. Harart

NOTES

1. For a discussion of the notions of discontinuity and historical tradition see Foucault's *Les Mots et les choses* (Paris: Gallimard, 1966), translated as *The Order of Things* (New York: Pantheon, 1971).—Trans.

2. John Searle, *Speech Acts: An Essay in the Philosophy of Language* (Cambridge: Cambridge University Press, 1969), pp. 162–174.—Trans.

3. To define these returns more clearly, one must also emphasize that they tend to reinforce the enigmatic link between an author and his works. A text has an inaugurative value precisely because it is the work of a particular author, and our returns are conditioned by this knowledge. As in the case of Galileo, there is no possibility that the rediscovery of an unknown text by Newton or Cantor will modify classical cosmology or set theory as we know them (at best, such an exhumation might modify our historical knowledge of their genesis). On the other hand, the discovery of a text like Freud's "Project for a Scientific Psychology"—insofar as it is a text by Freud—always threatens to modify not the historical knowledge of psychoanalysis, but its theoretical field, even if only by shifting the accentuation or the center of gravity. Through such returns, which are part of their make-up, these discursive practices maintain a relationship with regard to their "fundamental" and indirect author unlike that which an ordinary text entertains with its immediate author.—Trans.

22

Catherine Belsey
1940–

Catherine Belsey lectures in English at the University of Wales, College of Cardiff. She is the author of *Critical Practice* (1980), *The Subject of Tragedy: Identity and Difference in Renaissance Drama* (1985), *John Milton: Language, Gender, Power* (1988), and *Desire: Love Stories in Western Cultures* (1994). She is also editor, with Jane Moore, of *The Feminist Reader: Essays in Gender and the Politics of Literary Criticism* (1989). Belsey's *Critical Practice* was one of the most important and influential books in introducing contemporary French Marxist, feminist, psychoanalytical, and post-structuralist theory to the English-speaking world. Along with Terry Eagleton, she argued for the materialist and historical view of literature and culture championed in France by Louis Althusser and Pierre Macherey and in the early work of Roland Barthes. Her work has drawn the ire of defenders of traditional liberal humanism, who see her ideas on the cultural constitution of the subject or self and the systemic shaping effects of discourse as threats to the ethical basis of Western civilization. Belsey, however, uses theory to support a broad cultural and intellectual critique of endemic class- and gender-based oppression under the surface of parliamentary democracy and humanist "freedoms."

At the heart of Belsey's account of critical practice is the critique of the "normal," "self-evident" view of the human self or subject and its relation to language and to power relations in society. In "Constructing the Subject: Deconstructing the Text" (1985), she again concentrates on the constitution of the self in and through discourse, and on the particular functions of literature, "as one of the more persuasive uses of language," in affecting the ways in which people understand themselves and their relations with each other and the world. Belsey reiterates here, as in *Critical Practice,* the implications of Saussure's theory of language: "there is no unmediated experience," and "the subject is constructed in language and in discourse and, since the symbolic order in its discursive use is closely related to ideology, in ideology." She continues, "Ideology suppresses the role of language in the construction of the subject," and "as a result, people 'recognize' (misrecognize) themselves" according to the ways in which society "'interpellates'" them. In this way the role of constituted "subjects" is twofold, Belsey argues. Within bourgeois ideology, which relies on the idea of individual fixed identities, lies the "subjected being" who believes she is choosing freely to accept what is, in fact, a constructed identity.

These basic assumptions, of course, have implications for the authors of literature, as well as for the texts themselves. Relying on Lacan and Macherey, Belsey looks carefully in this article at classic realism and the gap "between the ideological project and

terms, "I" designates only the subject of a specific utterance. "And so it is literally true that the basis of subjectivity is in the exercise of language. If one really thinks about it, one will see that there is no other objective testimony to the identity of the subject except that which he himself thus gives about himself" (ibid., p. 226).

Within ideology, of course, it seems "obvious" that the individual speaker is the origin of the meaning of his or her utterance. Post-Saussurean linguistics, however, implies a more complex relationship between the individual and meaning, since it is language itself which, by differentiating between concepts, offers the possibility of meaning. In reality, it is only by adopting the position of the subject within language that the individual is able to produce meaning. As Derrida puts it,

> what was it that Saussure in particular reminded us of? That "language [which consists only of differences] is not a function of the speaking subject." This implies that the subject (self-identical or even conscious of self-identity, self-conscious) is inscribed in the language, that he is a "function" of the language. He becomes a *speaking* subject only by conforming his speech . . . to the system of linguistic prescriptions taken as the system of differences. (Derrida 1973, pp. 145–6)

Derrida goes on to raise the question whether, even if we accept that it is only the signifying system which makes possible the speaking subject, the signifying subject, we cannot none the less conceive of a non-speaking, non-signifying subjectivity, "a silent and intuitive consciousness" (ibid., p. 146). The problem here, he concludes, is to define consciousness-in-itself as distinct from consciousness of something, and ultimately as distinct from consciousness of self. If consciousness is finally consciousness of self, this in turn implies that consciousness depends on differentiation, and specifically on Benveniste's differentiation between "I" and "you," a process made possible by language.

The implications of this concept of the primacy of language over subjectivity have been developed by Jacques Lacan's reading of Freud. Lacan's theory of the subject as constructed in language confirms the *decentring* of the individual consciousness so that it can no longer be seen as the origin of meaning, knowledge and action. Instead, Lacan proposes that the infant is initially an "hommelette"—"a little man and also like a broken egg spreading without hindrance in all directions" (Coward and Ellis 1977, p. 101). The child has no sense of identity, no way of conceiving of itself as a unity, distinct from what is "other," exterior to it. During the "mirror-phase" of its development, however, it "recognizes" itself in the mirror as a unit distinct from the outside world. This "recognition" is an identification with an "imaginary" (because imaged) unitary and autonomous self. But it is only with its entry into language that the child becomes a full subject. If it is to participate in the society into which it is born, to be able to act deliberately within the social formation, the child must enter into the symbolic order, the set of signifying systems of culture of which the supreme example is language. The child who refuses to learn the language is "sick," unable to become a full member of the family and of society.

In order to speak the child is compelled to differentiate; to speak of itself it has to distinguish "I" from "you." In order to formulate its needs the child learns to identify with the first person singular pronoun, and this identification constitutes the basis of subjectivity. Subsequently it learns to recognize itself in a series of subject-positions ("he" or "she," "boy" or "girl," and so on) which are the positions from which discourse is intelligible to itself and others. "Identity," subjectivity, is thus a matrix of subject-positions, which may be inconsistent or even in contradiction with one another.

Subjectivity, then, is linguistically and discursively constructed and displaced across the range of discourses in which the concrete individual participates. It follows from Saussure's theory of language as a system of differences that the world is intelligible only in discourse: there is no unmediated experience, no access to the raw reality of self and others. Thus:

> As well as being a system of signs related among themselves, language incarnates meaning in the form of the series of positions it offers for the subject from which to grasp itself and its relations with the real. (Nowell-Smith 1976, p. 26)

The subject is constructed in language and in discourse and, since the symbolic order in its discursive use is closely related to ideology, in ideology. It is in this sense that ideology has the effect, as Althusser argues, of constituting individuals as subjects, and it is also in this sense that their subjectivity appears "obvious." Ideology suppresses the role of language in the construction of the subject. As a result, people "recognize" (misrecognize) themselves in the ways in which ideology "interpellates" them, or in other words, addresses them as subjects, calls them by their names and in turn "recognizes" their autonomy. As a result, they "work by themselves" (Althusser 1971, p. 169), they "willingly" adopt the subject-positions necessary to their participation in the social formation. In capitalism they "freely" exchange their labour-power for wages, and they "voluntarily" purchase the commodities produced. In patriarchal society women "choose" to do the housework, to make sacrifices for their children, not to become engineers. And it is here that we see the full force of Althusser's use of the term "subject," originally borrowed, as he says, from law. The subject is not only a grammatical subject, "a centre of initiatives, author of and responsible for its actions," but also a *subjected being* who submits to the authority of the social formation represented in ideology as the Absolute Subject (God, the king, the boss, Man, conscience): "the individual *is interpellated as a (free) subject in order that he shall submit freely to the commandments of the Subject, i.e. in order that he shall (freely) accept his subjection*" (ibid., p. 169).

Ideology interpellates concrete individuals as subjects, and bourgeois ideology in particular emphasizes the fixed identity of the individual. "I'm just *like* that"—cowardly, perhaps, or aggressive, generous or impulsive. Astrology is only an extreme form of the determinism which attributes to us given essences which cannot change. Popular psychology and popular sociology make individual behaviour a product of these essences. And underlying them all, ultimately unalterable, is "human nature." In these circumstances, how is it possible to suppose that, even if we could break in theoretical terms with the concepts of the ruling ideology, we are ourselves capable of change, and therefore capable both of acting to change the social formation and of transforming ourselves to constitute a new kind of society? A possible answer can be found in Lacan's theory of the precariousness of conscious subjectivity, which in turn depends on the Lacanian conception of the unconscious.

In Lacan's theory the individual is not in reality the harmonious and coherent totality of ideological misrecognition. The mirror-phase, in which the infant perceives itself as other, an image, exterior to is own perceiving self, necessitates a splitting between the *I* which is perceived and the *I* which does the perceiving. The entry into language necessitates a secondary division which reinforces the first, a split between the *I* of discourse, the subject of the utterance, and the *I* who speaks, the subject of the enunciation. There is thus a contradiction between the conscious self, the self which appears in its own discourse, and the self which is only partly represented there, the self which speaks. The unconscious comes into being in the gap which is formed by this division. The unconscious is constructed in the moment of entry into the symbolic order, simultaneously with the construction of the subject. The repository of repressed and prelinguistic signifiers, the unconscious is a constant source of potential disruption of the symbolic order. To summarize very briefly what in Lacan is a complex and elusive theory, entry into the symbolic order liberates the child into the possibility of social relationship; it also reduces its helplessness to the extent that it is now able to articulate its needs in the form of demands. But at the same time a division within the self is constructed. In offering the child the possibility of formulating its desires the symbolic order also betrays them, since it cannot by definition formulate those elements of desire which remain unconscious. Demand is always only a metonymy of desire (Lemaire 1977, p. 64). The subject is thus the site of contradiction, and is consequently perpetually in the process of construction, thrown into crisis by alterations in language and in the social formation, capable of change. And in the fact that the subject is a *process* lies the possibility of transformation.

In addition, the displacement of subjectivity across a range of discourses implies a range of positions from which the subject grasps itself and its relations with the real, and these positions may be incompatible or contradictory. It is these incompatibilities and contradictions within what is taken for granted which exert a pressure on concrete individuals to seek new, non-contradictory subject-positions. Women as a group in our society are both produced and inhibited by contradictory discourses. Very broadly, we participate both in the liberal-humanist discourse of freedom, self-determination and rationality and at the same time in the specifically feminine discourse offered by society of submission, relative inadequacy and irrational intuition. The attempt to locate a single and coherent subject-position within these contradictory discourses, and in consequence to find a non-contradictory pattern of behaviour, can create intolerable pressures. One way of responding

to this situation is to retreat from the contradictions and from discourse itself, to become "sick"—more women than men are treated for mental illness. Another is to seek a resolution of the contradictions in the discourses of feminism. That the position of women in society has changed so slowly, in spite of such a radical instability in it, may be partly explained in terms of the relative exclusion of women from the discourse of liberal humanism. This relative exclusion, supported in the predominantly masculine institutions of our society, is implicit, for example, in the use of masculine terms as generic ("rational man," etc.).

Women are not an isolated case. The class structure also produces contradictory subject-positions which precipitate changes in social relations not only between whole classes but between concrete individuals within those classes. Even at the conscious level, although this fact may itself be unconscious, the individual subject is not a unity, and in this lies the possibility of deliberate change.

This does not imply the reinstatement of individual subjects as the agents of change and changing knowledge. On the contrary, it insists on the concept of a dialectical relationship between concrete individuals and the language in which their subjectivity is constructed. In consequence, it also supports the concept of subjectivity as in process.

It is because subjectivity is perpetually in process that literary texts can have an important function. No one, I think, would suggest that literature alone could precipitate a crisis in the social formation. None the less, if we accept Lacan's analysis of the importance of language in the construction of the subject it becomes apparent that literature as one of the most persuasive uses of language may have an important influence on the ways in which people grasp themselves and their relation to the real relations in which they live. The interpellation of the reader in the literary text could be argued to have a role in reinforcing the concepts of the world and of subjectivity which ensure that people "work by themselves" in the social formation. On the other hand, certain critical modes could be seen to challenge these concepts, and to call in question the particular complex of imaginary relations between individuals and the real conditions of their existence which helps to reproduce the present relations of class, race and gender.

THE SUBJECT AND THE TEXT

Althusser analyses the interpellation of the subject in the context of ideology in general; Benveniste in discussing the relationship between language and subjectivity is concerned with language in general. None the less, it readily becomes apparent that capitalism in particular needs subjects who work by themselves, who freely exchange their labour-power for wages. It is in the epoch of capitalism that ideology emphasizes the value of individual freedom, freedom of conscience and, of course, consumer choice in all the multiplicity of its forms. The ideology of liberal humanism assumes a world of non-contradictory (and therefore fundamentally unalterable) individuals whose unfettered consciousness is the origin of meaning, knowledge and action. It is in the interest of this ideology above all to suppress the role of language in the construction of the subject, and its own role in the interpellation of the subject, and to present the individual as a free, unified, autonomous subjectivity. Classic realism, still the dominant popular mode in literature, film and television drama, roughly coincides chronologically with the epoch of industrial capitalism. It performs, I wish to suggest, the work of ideology, not only in its representation of a world of consistent subjects who are the origin of meaning, knowledge and action, but also in offering the reader, as the position from which the text is most readily intelligible, the position of subject

as the origin both of understanding and of action in accordance with that understanding.

It is readily apparent that Romantic and post-Romantic poetry, from Wordsworth through the Victorian period at least to Eliot and Yeats, takes subjectivity as its central theme. The developing self of the poet, his consciousness of himself as poet, his struggle against the constraints of an outer reality, constitute the preoccupations of *The Prelude, In Memoriam* or *Meditations in Time of Civil War.* The "I" of these poems is a kind of super-subject, experiencing life at a higher level of intensity than ordinary people and absorbed in a world of selfhood which the phenomenal world, perceived as external and antithetical, either nourishes or constrains. This transcendence of the subject in poetry is not presented as unproblematic, but it is entirely overt in the poetry of this period. The "I" of the poem directly addresses an individual reader who is invited to respond equally directly to this interpellation.

Fiction, however, in this same period, frequently appears to deal rather in social relationships, the interaction between the individual and society, to the increasing exclusion of the subjectivity of the author. Direct intrusion by the author comes to seem an impropriety; impersonal narration, "showing" (the truth) rather than "telling" it, is a requirement of prose fiction by the end of the nineteenth century. In drama too the author is apparently absent from the self-contained fictional world on the stage. Even the text effaces its own existence as text: unlike poetry, which clearly announces itself as formal, if only in terms of the shape of the text on the page, the novel seems merely to transcribe a series of events, to report on a palpable world, however fictional. Classic realist drama displays transparently and from the outside how people speak and behave.

Nevertheless, as we know while we read or watch, the author is present as a shadowy authority and as source of the fiction, and the author's presence is substantiated by the name on the cover of the programme: "a novel by Thomas Hardy," "a new play by Ibsen." And at the same time, as I shall suggest in this section, the *form* of the classic realist text acts in conjunction with the expressive theory and with ideology by interpellating the reader as subject. The reader is invited to perceive and judge the "truth" of the text, the coherent, non-contradictory interpretation of the world as it is perceived by an author whose autonomy is the source and evidence of the truth of the interpretation. This model of intersubjective communication, of shared understanding of a text which re-presents the world, is the guarantee not only of the truth of the text but of the reader's existence as an autonomous and knowing subject in a world of knowing subjects. In this way classic realism constitutes an ideological practice in addressing itself to readers as subjects, interpellating them in order that they freely accept their subjectivity and their subjection.

It is important to reiterate, of course, that this process is not inevitable, in the sense that texts do not determine like fate the ways in which they *must* be read. I am concerned at this stage primarily with ways in which they are conventionally read: conventionally, since language is conventional, and since modes of writing as well as ways of reading are conventional, but conventionally also in that new conventions of reading are available. In this sense meaning is never a fixed essence inherent in the text but is always constructed by the reader, the result of a "circulation" between social formation, reader and text (Heath 1977–8, p. 74). In the same way, "inscribed subject positions are never hermetically sealed into a text, but are always positions in ideologies" (Willemen 1978, p. 63). To argue that classic realism interpellates subjects in certain ways is not to propose that this process is ineluctable; on the contrary it is a matter of choice. But the choice is ideological: certain ranges of meaning (there is always room for debate) are "obvious" within the currently domi-

nant ideology, and certain subject-positions are equally "obviously" the positions from which these meanings are apparent.

Classic realism is characterized by "illusionism," narrative which leads to "closure," and a "hierarchy of discourses" which establishes the "truth" of the story. "Illusionism" is, I hope, self-explanatory. The other two defining characteristics of classic realism need some discussion. Narrative tends to follow certain recurrent patterns. Classic realist narrative, as Barthes demonstrates in *S/Z*, turns on the creation of enigma through the precipitation of disorder which throws into disarray the conventional cultural and signifying systems. Among the commonest sources of disorder at the level of plot in classic realism are murder, war, a journey or love. But the story moves inevitably towards closure which is also disclosure, the dissolution of enigma through the re-establishment of order, recognizable as a reinstatement or a development of the order which is understood to have preceded the events of the story itself.

The moment of closure is the point at which the events of the story become fully intelligible to the reader. The most obvious instance is the detective story where, in the final pages, the murderer is revealed and the motive made plain. But a high degree of intelligibility is sustained throughout the narrative as a result of the hierarchy of discourses in the text. The hierarchy works above all by means of a privileged discourse which places as subordinate all the discourses that are literally or figuratively between inverted commas.

By these means classic realism offers the reader a position of knowingness which is also a position of identification with the narrative voice. To the extent that the story first constructs, and then depends for its intelligibility, on a set of assumptions shared between narrator and reader, it confirms both the transcendent knowingness of the reader-as-subject and the "obviousness" of the shared truths in question.

DECONSTRUCTING THE TEXT

Ideology, masquerading as coherence and pleni-tude, is in reality inconsistent, limited, contra-dictory, and the realist text as a crystallization of ideology participates in this incompleteness even while it diverts attention from the fact in the ap-parent plenitude of narrative closure. The object of deconstructing the text is to examine the *process of its production*—not the private experi-ence of the individual author, but the mode of production, the materials and their arrangement in the work. The aim is to locate the point of contradiction within the text, the point at which it transgresses the limits within which it is con-structed, breaks free of the constraints imposed by its own realist form. Composed of contradic-tions, the text is no longer restricted to a single, harmonious and authoritative reading. Instead it becomes *plural,* open to rereading, no longer an object for passive consumption but an object of work by the reader to produce meaning.

It is the work of Derrida which has been most influential in promoting deconstruction as a critical strategy. Refusing to identify meaning with authorial intention or with the theme of the work, deconstruction tends to locate mean-ing in areas which traditional criticism has seen as marginal—in the metaphors, the set of oppo-sitions or the hierarchies of terms which provide the framework of the text. The procedure, very broadly, is to identify in the text the contrary meanings which are the inevitable condition of its existence as a signifying practice, locating the trace of otherness which undermines the overt project.

Derrida, however, says little specifically about literary criticism or about the question of mean-ing in fiction. Nor is his work directly political. In order to produce a politics of reading we need to draw in addition on the work of Roland Barthes and Pierre Macherey. In *S/Z,* first pub-lished in 1970 (English translation 1975), Barthes deconstructs (without using the word) a

short story by Balzac. *Sarrasine* is a classic realist text concerning a castrato singer and a fortune. The narrative turns on a series of enigmas (What is the source of the fortune? Who is the little old man? Who is La Zambinella? What is the connection between all three?). Even in summarizing the story in this way it is necessary to "lie": there are not "three" but two, since the little old "man" is "La" Zambinella. Barthes breaks the text into fragments of varying lengths for analysis, and adds a number of "divaga-tions," pieces of more generalized commentary and exploration, to show *Sarrasine* as a "limit-text," a text which uses the modes of classic real-ism in ways which constitute a series of "trans-gressions" of classic realism itself. The sense of plenitude, of a full understanding of a coherent text which is the normal result of reading the re-alist narrative, cannot here be achieved. It is not only that castration cannot be named in a text of this period. The text is compelled to trans-gress the conventional antithesis between the genders whenever it uses a pronoun to speak of the castrato. The story concerns the scandal of castration and the death of desire which follows its revelation; it concerns the scandalous origin of wealth; and it demonstrates the collapse of language, of antithesis (difference) as a source of meaning, which is involved in the disclosure of these scandals.

Each of these elements of the text provides a point of entry into it, none privileged, and these approaches constitute the degree of polyphony, the "parsimonious plural" of the readable *(lisi-ble)* text. The classic realist text moves inevitably and irreversibly to an end, to the conclusion of an ordered series of events, to the disclosure of what has been concealed. But even in the realist text certain modes of signification within the discourse—the symbolic, the codes of reference and the *semes*—evade the constraints of the nar-rative sequence. To the extent that these are "re-versible," free-floating and of indeterminate au-thority, the text is plural. In the writable *(scriptible),* wholly plural text all statements are of indeterminate origin, no single discourse is privileged, and no consistent and coherent plot constrains the free play of the discourses. The totally writable, plural text does not exist. At the opposite extreme, the readable text is barely plural. The readable text is merchandise to be consumed, while the plural text requires the production of meanings through the identification of its polyphony. Deconstruction in order to reconstruct the text as a newly intelligible, plural object is the work of criticism.

Barthes's own mode of writing demonstrates his contempt for the readable: *S/Z* is itself a polyphonic critical text. It is impossible to summarize adequately, to reduce to systematic accessibility, and it is noticeable that the book contains no summarizing conclusion. Like *Sarrasine, S/Z* offers a number of points of entry, critical discourses which generate trains of thought in the reader, but it would be contrary to Barthes's own (anarchist) argument to order all these into a single, coherent methodology, to constitute a new unitary way of reading, however comprehensive, and so to become the (authoritative) author of a new critical orthodoxy. As a result, the experience of reading *S/Z* is at once frustrating and exhilarating. Though it offers a model in one sense—it implies a new kind of critical practice—it would almost certainly not be possible (or useful) to attempt a wholesale imitation of its critical method(s).

It seems clear that one of the most influential precursors of *S/Z,* though Barthes does not allude to it, was Pierre Macherey's (Marxist) *A Theory of Literary Production,* first published in 1966 (English translation 1978). Despite real and important differences between them, there are similarities worth noting. For instance, Macherey anticipates Barthes in demonstrating that contradiction is a condition of narrative. The classic realist text is constructed on the basis of enigma. Information is initially withheld on condition of a "promise" to the reader that it will finally be revealed. The disclosure of this "truth" brings the story to an end. The movement of narrative is thus both towards disclosure—the end of the story—and towards concealment—prolonging itself by delaying the end of the story through a series of "reticences," as Barthes calls them, snares for the reader, partial answers to the questions raised, equivocations (Macherey 1978, pp. 28–9; Barthes 1975, pp. 75–6). Further, narrative involves the reader in an experience of the inevitable in the form of the unforeseen (Macherey 1978, p. 43). The hero encounters an obstacle: will he attempt to overcome it or abandon the quest? The answer is already determined, though the reader, who has only to turn the page to discover it, experiences the moment as one of choice for the hero. In fact, of course, if the narrative is to continue the hero must go on (Barthes 1975, p. 135). Thus the author's autonomy is to some degree illusory. In one sense the author determines the nature of the story: he or she decides what happens. In another sense, however, this decision is itself determined by the constraints of the narrative (Macherey 1978, p. 48), or by what Barthes calls the "interest" (in both the psychological and the economic senses) of the story (Barthes 1975, p. 135).

The formal constraints imposed by literary form on the project of the work in the process of literary production constitute the structural principle of Macherey's analysis. It is a mistake to reduce the text to the product of a single cause, authorial determination *or* the mechanics of the narrative. On the contrary, the literary work "is composed from a real diversity of elements which give it substance" (Macherey 1978, p. 49). There may be a direct contradiction between the project and the formal constraints, and in the transgression thus created it is possible to locate an important object of the critical quest.

Fiction for Macherey (he deals mainly with classic realist narrative) is intimately related to ideology, but the two are not identical. Literature is a specific and irreducible form of discourse, but the language which constitutes the raw material of the text is the language of ideology. It is thus an inadequate language, incomplete, partial, incapable of concealing the real contradictions it is its purpose to efface. This language, normally in flux, is arrested, "congealed" by the literary text.

The realist text is a determinate representation, an intelligible structure which claims to convey intelligible relationships between its elements. In its attempt to create a coherent and internally consistent fictive world the text, in spite of itself, exposes incoherences, omissions, absences and transgressions which in turn reveal the inability of the language of ideology to create coherence. This becomes apparent because the contradiction between the diverse elements drawn from different discourses, the ideological project and the literary form, creates an absence at the centre of the work. The text is divided, split as the Lacanian subject is split, and Macherey compares the "lack" in the consciousness of the work, its silence, what it cannot say, with the unconscious which Freud explored (ibid., p. 85).

The unconscious of the work (*not,* it must be insisted, of the author) is constructed in the moment of its entry into literary form, in the gap between the ideological project and the specifically literary form. Thus the text is no more a transcendent unity than the human subject. The texts of Jules Verne, for instance, whose work Macherey analyses in some detail, indicate that "if Jules Verne chose to be the spokesman of a certain ideological condition, he could not choose to be what he in fact became" (ibid., p. 94). What Macherey reveals in Verne's *The Secret of the Island* is an unpredicted and contradictory element, disrupting the colonialist ideology which informs the conscious project of the work. Within the narrative, which concerns the willing surrender of nature to improvement by a team of civilized and civilizing colonizers, there *insists* an older and contrary myth which the consciousness of the text rejects. Unexplained events imply another mysterious presence on what is apparently a desert island. Captain

Nemo's secret presence, and his influence on the fate of the castaways from a subterranean cave, is the source of the series of enigmas and the final disclosure which constitute the narrative. But his existence in the text has no part in the overt ideological project. On the contrary, it represents the return of the repressed in the form of a re-enacting of the myth of Robinson Crusoe. This myth evokes both a literary ancestor—Defoe's story—on which all subsequent castaway stories are to some degree conditional, and an ancestral relationship to nature—the creation of an economy by Crusoe's solitary struggle to appropriate and transform the island—on which subsequent bourgeois society is also conditional. The Robinson Crusoe story, the antithesis of the conscious project of the narrative, is also the condition of its existence. It returns, as the repressed experience returns to the consciousness of the patient in dreams and slips of the tongue and in doing so it unconsciously draws attention to an origin and a history from which both desert island stories and triumphant bourgeois ideology are unable to cut themselves off, and with which they must settle their account. *The Secret of the Island* thus reveals, through the discord within it between the conscious project and the insistence of the disruptive unconscious, the *limits* of the coherence of nineteenth-century ideology.

The object of the critic, then, is to seek not the unity of the work, but the multiplicity and diversity of its possible meanings, its incompleteness, the omissions which it displays but cannot describe, and above all its contradictions. In its absences, and in the collisions between its divergent meanings, the text implicitly criticizes its own ideology; it contains within itself the critique of its own values, in the sense that it is available for a new process of production of meaning by the reader, and in this process it can provide a knowledge of the limits of ideological representation.

Macherey's way of reading is precisely contrary to traditional Anglo-American critical practice, where the quest is for the unity of the work, its coherence, a way of repairing any deficiencies in consistency by reference to the author's philosophy or the contemporary world picture. In thus smoothing out contradiction, closing the text, criticism becomes the accomplice of ideology. Having created a canon of acceptable texts, criticism then provides them with acceptable interpretations, thus effectively censoring any elements in them which come into collusion with the dominant ideology. To deconstruct the text, on the other hand, is to open it, to release the possible positions of its intelligibility, including those which reveal the partiality (in both senses) of the ideology inscribed in the text.

THE CASE OF SHERLOCK HOLMES

In locating the transitions and uncertainties of the text it is important to remember, Macherey insists, sustaining the parallel with psychoanalysis, that the problem of the work is not the same as its *consciousness* of a problem (Macherey 1978, p. 93). In "Charles Augustus Milverton," one of the short stories from *The Return of Sherlock Holmes,* Conan Doyle presents the reader with an ethical problem. Milverton is a black-mailer, blackmail is a crime not easily brought to justice since the victims are inevitably unwilling to make the matter public; the text therefore proposes for the reader's consideration that in such a case illegal action may be ethical. Holmes plans to burgle Milverton's house to recover the letters which are at stake, and both Watson and the text appear to conclude, after due consideration, that the action is morally justifiable. The structure of the narrative is symmetrical: one victim initiates the plot, another concludes it. While Holmes and Watson hide in Milverton's study a woman shoots him, protesting that he has ruined her life. Inspector Lestrade asks Holmes to help catch the murderer. Holmes replies that certain crimes justify private revenge, that his sympathies are with the criminal and that he will not handle the case. The reader

is left to ponder the ethical implications of his position.

Meanwhile, on the fringes of the text, another narrative is sketched. It too contains problems but these are not foregrounded. Holmes's client is the Lady Eva Blackwell, a beautiful debutante who is to be married to the Earl of Dovercourt. Milverton has secured letters she has written "to an impecunious young squire in the country." Lady Eva does not appear in the narrative in person. The content of the letters is not specified, but they are "imprudent, Watson, nothing worse." Milverton describes them as "sprightly." Holmes's sympathies, and ours, are with the Lady Eva. None the less we, and Holmes, accept without question on the one hand that the marriage with the Earl of Dovercourt is a desirable one and on the other that were he to see the letters he would certainly break off the match. The text's elusiveness on the content of the letters, and the absence of the Lady Eva herself, deflects the reader's attention from the potentially contradictory ideology of marriage which the narrative takes for granted.

This second narrative is also symmetrical. The murderer too is a woman with a past. She is not identified. Milverton has sent her letters to her husband who in consequence "broke his gallant heart and died." Again the text is unable to be precise about the content of the letters since to do so would be to risk losing the sympathy of the reader for either the woman or her husband.

In the mean time Holmes has become engaged. By offering to marry Milverton's housemaid he has secured information about the layout of the house he is to burgle. Watson remonstrates about the subsequent fate of the girl, but Holmes replies:

> "You can't help it, my dear Watson. You must play your cards as best you can when such a stake is on the table. However, I rejoice to say that I have a hated rival who will certainly cut me out the instant that my back is turned. What a splendid night it is."

The housemaid is not further discussed in the story.

The sexuality of these three shadowy women motivates the narrative and yet is barely present in it. The disclosure which ends the story is thus scarcely a disclosure at all. Symbolically Holmes has burnt the letters, records of women's sexuality. Watson's opening paragraph constitutes an apology for the "reticence" of the narrative: "with *due suppression* the story may be told"; "The reader will excuse me if I conceal the date *or any other fact*" (my italics).

The project of the Sherlock Holmes stories is to dispel magic and mystery, to make everything explicit, accountable, subject to scientific analysis. The phrase most familiar to all readers—"Elementary, my dear Watson"—is in fact a misquotation, but its familiarity is no accident since it precisely captures the central concern of the stories. Holmes and Watson are both men of science. Holmes, the "genius," is a scientific conjuror who insists on disclosing how the trick is done. The stories begin in enigma, mystery, the impossible, and conclude with an explanation which makes it clear that logical deduction and scientific method render all mysteries accountable to reason:

> I am afraid that my explanation may disillusionize you, but it has always been my habit to hide none of my methods, either from my friend Watson or from anyone who might take an intelligent interest in them. ("The Reigate Squires," *The Memoirs of Sherlock Holmes*)

The stories are a plea for science not only in the spheres conventionally associated with detection (footprints, traces of hair or cloth, cigarette ends), where they have been deservedly influential on forensic practice, but in all areas. They reflect the widespread optimism characteristic of their period concerning the comprehensive power of positivist science. Holmes's ability to deduce Watson's train of thought, for in-

stance, is repeatedly displayed, and it owes nothing to the supernatural. Once explained, the reasoning process always appears "absurdly simple," open to the commonest of common sense.

The project of the stories themselves, enigma followed by disclosure, echoes precisely the structure of the classic realist text. The narrator himself draws attention to the parallel between them:

> "Excellent!" I cried.
> "Elementary," said he. "It is one of those instances where the reasoner can produce an effect which seems remarkable to his neighbour because the latter has missed the one little point which is the basis of the deduction. The same may be said, my dear fellow, for the effect of some of these little sketches of yours, which is entirely meretricious, depending as it does upon your retaining in your own hands some factors in the problem which are never imparted to the reader. Now, at present I am in the position of these same readers, for I hold in this hand several threads of one of the strangest cases which ever perplexed a man's brain, and yet I lack the one or two which are needful to complete my theory. But I'll have them, Watson, I'll have them!" ("The Crooked Man," *Memoirs*)

(The passage is quoted by Macherey [1978, p. 35] in his discussion of the characteristic structure of narrative.)

The project also requires the maximum degree of "realism"—verisimilitude, plausibility. In the interest of science no hint of the fantastic or the implausible is permitted to remain once the disclosure is complete. This is why even their own existence as writing is so frequently discussed within the texts. The stories are alluded to as Watson's "little sketches," his "memoirs." They resemble fictions because of Watson's unscientific weakness for story-telling:

> "I must admit, Watson, that you have some power of selection which atones for much

which I deplore in your narratives. Your fatal habit of looking at everything from the point of view of a story instead of as a scientific exercise has ruined what might have been an instructive and even classical series of demonstrations." ("The Abbey Grange," *The Return of Sherlock Holmes*)

In other words, the fiction itself accounts even for its own fictionality, and the text thus appears wholly transparent. The success with which the Sherlock Holmes stories achieve an illusion of reality is repeatedly demonstrated. In their Foreword to *The Sherlock Holmes Companion* (1962) Michael and Mollie Hardwick comment on their own recurrent illusion "that we were dealing with a figure of real life rather than of fiction. How vital Holmes appears, compared with many people of one's own acquaintance."

De Waal's bibliography of Sherlock Holmes lists twenty-five "Sherlockian" periodicals apparently largely devoted to conjectures, based on the "evidence" of the stories, concerning matters only hinted at in the texts—Holmes's education, his income and his romantic and sexual adventures. According to *The Times* in December 1967, letters to Sherlock Holmes were then still commonly addressed to 221B Baker Street, many of them asking for the detective's help.

None the less these stories, whose overt project is total explicitness, total verisimilitude in the interests of a plea for scientificity, are haunted by shadowy, mysterious and often silent women. Their silence repeatedly conceals their sexuality, investing it with a dark and magical quality which is beyond the reach of scientific knowledge. In "The Greek Interpreter" (*Memoirs*) Sophie Kratides has run away with a man. Though she is the pivot of the plot she appears only briefly: "I could not see her clearly enough to know more than that she was tall and graceful, with black hair, and clad in some sort of loose white gown." Connotatively the white gown marks her as still virginal and her flight as the result of romance rather than desire. At the

same time the dim light surrounds her with shadow, the unknown. "The Crooked Man" concerns Mrs Barclay, whose husband is found dead on the day of her meeting with her lover of many years before. Mrs Barclay is now insensible, "temporarily insane" since the night of the murder and therefore unable to speak. In "The Dancing Men" (*Return*) Mrs Elsie Cubitt, once engaged to a criminal, longs to speak but cannot bring herself to break her silence. By the time Holmes arrives she is unconscious, and she remains so for the rest of the story. Ironically the narrative concerns the breaking of the code which enables her former lover to communicate with her. Elsie's only contribution to the correspondence is the word, "Never." The precise nature of their relationship is left mysterious, constructed of contrary suggestions. Holmes says she feared and hated him; the lover claims, "She had been engaged to me, and she would have married me, I believe, if I had taken over another profession." When her husband moves to shoot the man whose coded messages are the source of a "terror" which is "wearing her away," Elsie restrains him with compulsive strength. On the question of her motives the text is characteristically elusive. Her husband recounts the story:

> "I was angry with my wife that night for having held me back when I might have caught the skulking rascal. She said that she feared that I might come to harm. For an instant it had crossed my mind that what she really feared was that *he* might come to harm, for I could not doubt that she knew who this man was and what he meant by those strange signals. But there is a tone in my wife's voice, Mr Holmes, and a look in her eyes which forbid doubt, and I am sure that it was indeed my own safety that was in her mind."

After her husband's death Elsie remains a widow, faithful to his memory and devoting her life to the care of the poor, apparently expiating something unspecified, perhaps an act or a state of feeling, remote or recent.

"The Dancing Men" is "about" Holmes's method of breaking the cipher. Its project is to dispel any magic from the deciphering process. Elsie's silence is in the interest of the story since she knows the code. But she also "knows" her feelings towards her former lover. Contained in the completed and fully disclosed story of the decipherment is another uncompleted and undisclosed narrative which is more than merely peripheral to the text as a whole. Elsie's past is central and causal. As a result, the text with its project of dispelling mystery is haunted by the mysterious state of mind of a woman who is unable to speak.

The classic realist text had not yet developed a way of signifying women's sexuality except in a metaphoric or symbolic mode whose presence disrupts the realist surface. Joyce and Lawrence were beginning to experiment at this time with modes of sexual signification but in order to do so they largely abandoned the codes of realism. So much is readily apparent. What is more significant, however, is that the presentation of so many women in the Sherlock Holmes stories as shadowy, mysterious and magical figures precisely contradicts the project of explicitness, transgresses the values of the texts, and in doing so throws into relief the poverty of the contemporary concept of science. These stories, pleas for a total explicitness about the world, are unable to explain an area which none the less they cannot ignore. The version of science which the texts present would constitute a clear challenge to ideology: the interpretation of all areas of life, physical, social and psychological, is to be subject to rational scrutiny and the requirements of coherent theorization. Confronted, however, by an area in which ideology itself is uncertain, the Sherlock Holmes stories display the limits of their own project and are compelled to manifest the inadequacy of a bourgeois scientificity which, working within the constraints of ideology, is thus unable to challenge it.

Perhaps the most interesting case, since it introduces an additional area of shadow, is "The Second Stain" (*Return*), which concerns two letters. Lady Hilda Trelawney Hope does speak. She has written before her marriage "an indiscreet letter . . . a foolish letter, a letter of an impulsive, loving girl." Had her husband read the letter his confidence in her would have been forever destroyed. Her husband is none the less presented as entirely sympathetic, and here again we encounter the familiar contradiction between a husband's supposed reaction, accepted as just, and the reaction offered to the reader by the text. In return for her original letter Lady Hilda gives her blackmailer a letter from "a certain foreign potentate" stolen from the dispatch box of her husband, the European Secretary of State. This political letter is symbolically parallel to the first sexual one. Its contents are equally elusive but it too is "indiscreet," "hot-headed"; certain phrases in it are "provocative." Its publication would produce "a most dangerous state of feeling" in the nation. Lady Hilda's innocent folly is the cause of the theft: she knows nothing of politics and was not in a position to understand the consequences of her action. Holmes ensures the restoration of the political letter and both secrets are preserved.

Here the text is symmetrically elusive concerning both sexuality and politics. Watson, as is so often the case where these areas are concerned, begins the story by apologizing for his own reticence and vagueness. In the political instance what becomes clear as a result of the uncertainty of the text is the contradictory nature of the requirements of verisimilitude in fiction. The potentate's identity and the nature of his indiscretion cannot be named without involving on the part of the reader either disbelief (the introduction of a patently fictional country would be dangerous to the project of verisimilitude) or belief (dangerous to the text's status as fiction, entertainment; also quite possibly politically dangerous). The scientific project of the texts require that they deal in "facts," but their nature as fiction forbids the introduction of facts.

The classic realist text instills itself in the space between fact and illusion through the presentation of a simulated reality which is plausible but *not real*. In this lies its power as myth. It is because fiction does not normally deal with "politics" directly, except in the form of history or satire, that it is ostensibly innocent and therefore ideologically effective. But in its evasion of the real also lies its weakness as "realism." Through their transgression of their own values of explicitness and verisimilitude, the Sherlock Holmes stories contain within themselves an implicit critique of their limited nature as characteristic examples of classic realism. They thus offer the reader through the process of deconstruction a form of knowledge, not about "life" or "the world," but about the nature of fiction itself.

Thus, in adopting the form of classic realism, the only appropriate literary mode, positivism is compelled to display its own limitations. Offered as science, it reveals itself to a deconstructive reading as ideology at the very moment that classic realism, offered as verisimilitude, reveals itself as fiction. In claiming to make explicit and *understandable* what appears mysterious, these texts offer evidence of the tendency of positivism to push to the margins of experience whatever it cannot explain or understand. In the Sherlock Holmes stories classic realism ironically tells a truth, though not the truth about the world which is the project of classic realism. The truth the stories tell is the truth about ideology, the truth which ideology represses, its own existence as ideology itself.

REFERENCES

Althusser, Louis (1971) *Lenin and Philosophy and Other Essays,* tr. Ben Brewster (London: New Left Books).

Barthes, Roland (1975) *S/Z,* tr. Richard Miller (London: Cape).

Benveniste, Emile (1971) *Problems in General Linguistics* (Miami: University of Miami Press).

Conan Doyle, Arthur (1950) *The Memoirs of Sherlock Holmes* (Harmondsworth: Penguin).

Conan Doyle, Arthur (1976) *The Return of Sherlock Holmes* (London: Pan).

Coward, Rosalind and John Ellis (1977) *Language and Materialism* (London: Routledge & Kegan Paul).

Derrida, Jacques (1973) *Speech and Phenomena,* tr. David B. Allison (Evanston: Northwestern University Press).

De Waal, Ronald (1972) *The World Bibliography of Sherlock Holmes* (Greenwich, Conn.: New York Graphic Society).

Hardwick, Michael and Mollie (1962) *The Sherlock Holmes Companion* (London: John Murray).

Heath, Stephen (1977–8) "Notes on Suture" *Screen* 18:4, pp. 48–76.

Lemaire, Anika (1977) *Jacques Lacan,* tr. David Macey (London: Routledge & Kegan Paul).

Macherey, Pierre (1978) *A Theory of Literary Production,* tr. Geoffrey Wall (London: Routledge & Kegan Paul).

Nowell-Smith, Geoffrey (1976) "A note on history discourse," *Edinburgh 76 Magazine* 1, pp. 26–32.

Saussure, Ferdinand de (1974) *Course in General Linguistics,* tr. Wade Baskin (London: Fontana).

Willemen, Paul (1978) "Notes on subjectivity—on reading 'Subjectivity Under Siege'" *Screen* 19:1, pp. 41–69.

PART VI

Psychology and Psychoanalysis

Psychoanalysis has inspired much of the literary and cultural criticism in the twentieth century. This influence ranges from early attempts at criticism by Ernest Jones, Marie Bonaparte, and Freud himself to more recent work by Jacques Lacan and a whole generation of feminists to reimagine Freudian thought in relation to literary texts, language, female sexuality, and political power. (For the latter, see Teresa de Lauretis in "Structuralism and Semiotics" [Part IV], Cathernie Belsey in "Deconstruction and Poststructuralism" [Part V], and Diana Fuss in "Feminism and Gender Studies" [Part VIII], as well as Shoshana Felman and Laura Mulvey in this section.) The use of psychoanalysis has taken many forms in literary and cultural studies and continues to undergo radical and frequent revision. It is as if psychoanalysis is less a fully determined body of doctrine and procedures than, as W. H. Auden wrote in his elegy for Freud, a "climate of opinion" so that, as Michel Foucault argues in "What Is an Author?" ("Deconstruction and Poststructuralism" [Part V]), Freud himself has become a "founder of discursivity" who is not just the "author" of his books but has "established an endless possibility of discourse."

The incorporation of depth psychology—whether Jungian or Freudian—in literary studies is characteristic of modernist culture in the twentieth century for at least two reasons. The more important is the possibility of interpreting disconnected or fragmented aspects of modern culture within the revealing schemes of psychoanalysis. In this regard Freud's conception of "overdetermination"—the phenomenon of multiple causes or origins for what seems to be the "singular" effect of a dream image or a neurotic symptom—offers an alternative to the Enlightenment criteria of simplicity and coherence for making sense out of experience. This concept is congruent with the overwhelming sense of complexity that is part of twentieth-century experience; it is a concept that calls simple formalism into question. The second, closely connected reason is that psychoanalysis can show a literary or cultural text to have multiple meanings of various kinds on several levels simultaneously. Thus, elements of an oedipal complex could be discerned in *Hamlet*'s overall dramatic structure, and this kind of analysis depends little on a discussion of character makeup. This second implication of psychoanalysis is an example of what Slavoj Žižek describes in "Two Ways to Avoid the Real of Desire" as psychoanalytic formalism, the "formal level" of analysis. The attention given to the interpretation of fragments and to coordinating a

393

multiplicity of meanings strongly connects psychoanalysis and modernism generally. Together, they suggest the rethinking of formalism.

As a basis for much cultural theory, psychoanalysis provides the frame for relating many aspects of culture, the events and texts of everyday life, the history of religion, art, sexuality, and so on. This potential to connect various sectors of culture and society, to underwrite interpretive change in productive ways, does much to explain the strong continuing interest in the psychoanalytic understanding of literature and culture throughout this century. At the end of the century, in the work of Jacques Lacan and others on the Continent and in the United States, the extension of psychoanalysis into the discourse on language, cultural critique, female sexuality, and forms of power has made Freudian thought vital in contemporary criticism.

ARCHETYPAL CRITICISM

But before moving to the contemporary scene, let us think first about the once influential but now much diminished offshoot of Freudian criticism called *archetypal criticism*. At midcentury there were two dominant formalist movements in American and European criticism: the New Criticism and *explication du texte*. Each approach prescribed a method of close reading and attempted to account for a variety of textual information, including imagery and image patterns, rhythm, sound, tone, and overall structure. Each method presented itself as potentially exhaustive, able to discover and catalogue *all* pertinent textual details in a manner approximating empirical observation in thoroughness and supposed objectivity. In the Anglo-American academy, however, the active development of the New Criticism came to an end in the late 1950s with the rise of archetypal criticism associated with the psychologist Carl Jung, which rapidly supplanted the New Criticism in practical influence and prestige. Archetypal criticism exploited certain aspects of the New Criticism (mainly, the deployment of paradox and irony) and then moved directly into areas that the New Criticism refused or failed to develop, particularly the relationship between literature and objects of study that exist "outside" the narrow formalist conception of literature. These areas included "mind," or personal psychology, history, and culture, and also included attempts to systemize the understanding of literature and culture in what Northrop Frye specifically called the "conceptual framework" of literature conceived as a "properly organized" intellectual discipline, the system of literature, that is, taken as more than "a huge aggregate or miscellaneous pile of creative efforts." (See "The Function of Criticism at the Present Time" in "What Is Literary Studies?" [Part I.]) On this issue, Frye thought that the extreme formalism of New Critics such as Cleanth Brooks, Wimsatt and Beardsley, John Crowe Ransom, Mark Schorer, and Joseph Frank had taken literary criticism outside of history and could no longer account for the changes that take place in culture.

Approaches to archetypal criticism are varied, but the central paradigm for it comes from the work of Carl Jung. Jung was Freud's close friend and protégé through the 1920s. Freud had already described a psychoanalytic theory of archetypes in his book *Totem and Taboo* (1918). Jung went on to develop an explicit theory, through which he separated himself from Freud, of the "collective unconscious," a realm of transpersonal imagery preserved and repeated throughout human experience. Belonging to the human race and also to individual people (at levels "below" consciousness), the collective unconscious contains "archetypes," or fundamental patterns and forms of human experience, such as "mother," "rebirth," "spirit," and "trickster." Such archetypes are based on the "commonsense" assumption that all human beings across different times and places have shared certain situations and experiences (i.e., birth, death, life stages, sexuality) and that these shared situations, like other shared human characteristics (i.e., hands, brains, speech), resulted in psychic as well as physical traits common to all people. Apprehendable only as fragments, or incomplete representations, the archetypes are like the light flickering on the walls of Plato's cave. Archetypal images, that is—never the totality of an archetype—are cast upon the screen of conscious thought, constituting informative patterns that are never quite unambiguous or completely unified.

In literary interpretation, archetypes show up in character, plot, and setting. Apparently unrelated textual elements as well as realistic, representational details form patterns suggestive of one or more of the archetypes. These patterns establish an archetypal orientation in the work and reflect what lies "beneath" the work's narrative and imagistic surface. Archetypal interpretation organizes each literary text into a narrative surface composed of images and a textual "depth" where the connection with archetypes takes place. A full archetypal interpretation seeks to make explicit what is only implicit in the text's fragmented evocation of archetypes. An archetypal understanding of a text, in short, necessitates seeing how the appearance of merely suggestive details in a minimal sequence is, in reality, a disguised archetypal pattern.

The possibility of narrative progression in archetypal criticism is crucial for understanding archetypalism's ascendancy over the New Criticism. After all, the New Critical emphasis on imagery as the object of analysis depends on evidence drawn from poetry, particularly modernism's highly figurative, non-narrative poetry (such as that of Eliot). And as is often noted, the New Critics foundered on the difficulty of applying imagery and paradox/irony (essentially static and even pictorial in their avoidance of history) to fiction and its profoundly temporal dimension. Only late in the movement's development, during the late 1940s and 1950s, did Joseph Frank and Mark Schorer seek to recast the poetic image as "spatial form" and suggest "technique as [as a form of] discovery" in prose fiction. By contrast, archetypalism from its start attempted to define itself precisely in relation to a temporal order, that of the "monomyth" or "quest." As Erich Neumann and others have shown, the coherence of the archetypes rests precisely on their placement within a narrative development that moves from total narcissism toward the hero's individuation and relative autonomy, each stage in the quest being a further step toward independence from the Great Mother. This pattern is *monomythic* because it encompasses all possible human change and growth within a single story. The quest-narrative unites the repeatable form of each archetype with the principle of change dictated by the ongoing temporal development of a story itself. The potential circularity of merely locating self-defining archetypes in literature—in which discoveries are dictated by foreknown patterns—is avoided through the necessity of accounting for the dynamic operation of narrative ("mythic") progression in particular cases.

The definitive archetypal approach to literature is presented in Frye's *Anatomy of Criticism* (1957) (for which "The Function of Criticism at the Present Time," included in "What Is Literary Studies?" [Part I], became the "Polemical Introduction"). Frye was the most formidable archetypal critic to announce a decisive break, as he said, with the "ironic provincialism" and "delicate learning" of the New Criticism. Uncharacteristically disdainful in his appraisal of this literary school, Frye rejected what he considered the New Criticism's limited range and lack of sophistication. Also, the implicit religious—and "typological"—perspective of Frye's criticism conflicted with the implicit skepticism of the New Criticism. His harshest slap at the New Criticism was his choice of a title for the *Anatomy*'s first essay, "Historical Criticism: Theory of Modes," where with polemical bravado Frye attempted to situate the archetypal project on the very historical terrain abandoned by the New Critical formalism. Frye proclaimed, in effect, that archetypal criticism's success would be precisely where the prior movement had failed. He then went on in "four essays" to erect the monomyth's structure over the whole of culture in a "proto-structuralist" reading of Western literature's archetypal development—from prehistoric and sacred "myth" to present-day "irony." In a remarkable elaboration of literary archetypes, Frye laid out a comprehensive catalog of literary forms (genre, sound, rhythm, tone, and so on) as part of his complex presentation of the archetypal paradigm. Implicit in his discussion is, in fact, a sense of the "development" of Western literature—his "Historical Criticism"—as Frye simultaneously suggested both an archetypal "conceptual framework" for criticism and an examination of the "history" of literature.

Throughout the 1960s, Frye's version of archetypalism influenced much theory and practical criticism, especially in medieval-Renaissance studies. Gradually, however, Frye's approach came under attack from three directions: historical critics, Structuralists, and feminists. Historicists like A. S. P. Woodhouse, Roy Harvey Pearce, and Lionel Trilling began to point out the failure of both the New Criticism and archetypalism in dealing with history except within narrow bounds. They argued that archetypalism developed a "historical" theory of modes (myth, romance, high mimetic, low mimetic, and irony) in order merely to turn Western literature itself into a huge, static structure—an all-inclusive closed system. Whereas historical criticism should be able to analyze change, account for the as yet unmet and unthought, archetypalism apparently did nothing more than impose a static grid over literature and culture as a substitute for historical understanding.

The structuralists of the 1960s and 1970s argued with Frye's complicated but, in their view, often naive and overly rigid schema. In the first chapter of *The Fantastic,* for example, Tzvetan Todorov criticized Frye's tendency to analyze literature for "content," actual images (like a "tree" and "shore") in literature, when his professed aim was to examine literary structure as positioned beyond concrete examples. Todorov also noted the formal rigidity of Frye's schema and simultaneous logical lapses in it—for example, the seasonal four-part structure of the "mythoi" as opposed to the five-part structure of his historical "modes." Most devastating, though, was the feminist critique of Frye, focused on the Jungian paradigm and the notion of the monomyth standing behind Frye's work. As Catherine Belsey charged in *Critical Practice,* "underlying Frye's formalism, therefore, [was] a concept of human nature and of culture

which sees literature as imitating not the world but rather 'the total dream of *man*' "
(emphasis added to Frye's quote by Belsey). Many feminists pointed out that the archetypal hero is at base a male figure attempting to bring reconciliation with an "original" female (the Great Mother) and with a potential "anima" figure who is both the
hero's ideal mate and his reward for success on the quest. This exclusively male paradigm assumes a male subject, and nowhere in Jung's thought, or Frye's, is there a serious attempt to conceive a woman's experience outside of support for a man. Whereas
some teachers and practical critics have continued to employ archetypalism for specific ends, especially to create contexts for genre distinctions, the influence of archetypalism has declined markedly. Our sense is that this decline is directly related to the
weaknesses of its conception of history, its willingness, as in Frye, to attend to change
in literary forms and modes while failing to attend to larger historical forces outside
the "conceptual universe" of literature. Still, archetypalism itself had a particular historical and critical value as a major critique of the New Criticism and contributed to
the revaluation of formalism that is still very much in evidence today.

FREUDIAN CRITICISM

Psychoanalysis is the intellectual parent of archetypalism, but, as it happens, psychoanalytic criticism both precedes archtypalism in the first-generation Freudians beginning in the 1920s and 1930s and succeeds it in the more recent movement, the semiotic "return to Freud." Archetypal criticism, for all its virtues and power, and in spite
of its criticism of the New Criticism, finally participates in a version of the positivist
assumptions that govern New Critical formalism and the earlier criticism of Freudian
ego psychologists (even if the positive "objects" of study are not independent texts but
rather particular, transcendental archetypes). This can be seen, in fact, in Frye's attempt to develop a discipline of criticism as a social science in "The Function of Criticism at the Present Time." By contrast, the great strength of contemporary psychoanalytic criticism—contemporary Freudian criticism—is that it goes beyond some of
the positivist assumptions of its master to use Freud's work to critique those assumptions and develop discursive modes of interpretations not only of individuals, but of
larger cultural and social formations.

Critical movements tend to develop through a life cycle and then eventually fade
away even as they stimulate and then make way for new movements to follow. With
psychoanalysis, the pattern has been a persistant cycle of rebirths. A first generation of
Freudian criticism continued until the 1940s and included such names as Ernest
Jones, Marie Bonaparte, and Edmund Wilson. After World War II a group of university critics came into prominence, such as Lionel Trilling, Frederick Crews, Frederick
Hoffman, Norman Holland, and others. Then a new literary Freudianism, based initially on the suggestions made in Jacques Lacan's seminars, was reborn in France in
the 1960s. Since the mid-1970s, the "French Freud" approach to understanding literature and culture has been extremely successful in the United States and Europe and
around the world.

This new Freudian criticism came out of the intellectual joining of Ferdinand de Saussure (see "Structuralism and Semiotics" [Part IV]) with Sigmund Freud: semiotics and psychoanalysis. This combining of intellectual paradigms took place in Jacques Lacan's work first, but it is Lacan's claim that Freud developed semiotic insights and semiotic methods of analysis all through the development of psychoanalysis. In the late-nineteenth- and early-twentieth-century work of Charles Sanders Peirce and Ferdinand de Saussure emerged the idea of *signifiers* as the smallest constituent units of meaning. In turn, those units (such as words) are elaborated according to the invariant mechanisms of meaning production—how texts work—that govern the operation of signifiers in all cultures. (This "scientific" approach to semiotics was prevalent, though now much challenged by poststructuralism, early in the twentieth century.) Signifiers are combined by particular cultures as meaningful ("significant") units according to the signifying practices already established as that society's system of culture. It was Lacan's insight to see that Freud had made the same basic claim about the workings of signification in his formulation of psychoanalysis. Freud's theories were simply a formulation of the workings of the invariant cultural scheme for understanding the semiotic practices of neurotic and psychotic patients—as well as whole cultures. This is why in "Structuralism and Semiotics" (Part IV) de Lauretis cites "Lacan's . . . formula: 'a signifier represents a subject for another signifier'" in her essay. Lacan, in this formulation, is describing the psychological subject as a function of a structural "position" that makes it meaningful and significant. Similarly, in this section Žižek offers a Saussurean reading of Lacan's other famous assertion: "the unconscious is structured like a language." "The basic feature of the signifier," Žižek writes, "is its differential character: since the identity of a signifier consists in the bundle of differences from other signifiers, the absence of a trait itself can have a positive value. Which is why the detective's artifice lies not simply in his capacity to grasp the possible meaning of 'insignificant details,' but perhaps even more in his capacity to apprehend absense itself (the nonoccurrence of some detail) as meaningful." (Note here that if archetypalism focuses on "positive" similarities and identities across experience, semiotics focuses on differences.)

Lacan argues, in effect, that both semiotics and psychoanalysis have the potential to dislodge and reorient traditional ways of understanding human experience. Lacan advances this notion in his critique of the Western, generally Cartesian, notion of human understanding as grounded in a substantial self (or "subject") who does *all* of the understanding. That is, the Cartesian view that Lacan critiques argues that a generally independent observer exists within each one of us. We then have the potential, if disciplined and trained, to collect data and information through distinterested observation. This nonparticipant observer can examine a world that stays forever separate from the activity of observing that world. In this model, knowledge as the product of inquiry matches the conscious formulation of intentions and aims, both in the generation and understanding of texts. For example, according to this model, a literary text would tend to "make sense" when the author's "actual" aims can be retrieved and accurately understood, that is, as a message intended by the author and actually received by the reader. The textual "form" conveying this message takes shape around the manifest representational figures (characters, settings, images deployed in both, etc.) that appear more or less empirically in and form the substance of the text.

(Jacques Derrida critiques another aspect of the Cartesian framework of understanding in "The Principle of Reason" in "Deconstruction and Poststructuralism" [Part V].)

Compared to this view of the text, Lacan's idea of reading and interpretation (of a person's experience or of an event in culture) may at first seem counterintuitive and indeed odd. The Lacanian idea of the text (much like Saussure's definition) opposes—as Lacan says in "The Mirror Stage"—"any philosophy directly issuing from the *Cogito* [substantial ego]." For Lacan, rather, interpretation begins with the idea of a text as an unending interplay of signifiers—not a substantial, fixed message, an absolute given to be investigated empirically in the process of reading—but differential and semiotic. The text is not a continuous, fixed form at all, or a "substance," but a network of signifiers. Thus constituted semiotically as a network of signs, texts are also composed of gaps and inconsistencies. There can be no inherently meaningful sign or entity, not part of a semiotic network, for the letter, as Lacan says in one of his seminars, is "a pure signifier" determined by its position within discourse. Barbara Johnson makes the same point in her essay on the relationship between Derrida and Lacan, "The Frame of Reference," when she says that "the letter, then, acts as a signifier not because its contents are lacking, but because its function is not dependent on the knowledge or nonknowledge of those contents. . . . It is not something with 'an identity to itself inaccessible to dismemberment' as Derrida interprets it; it is a difference."

In this sense, as Lacan explains in *Écrits,* the signifier has "priority in relation to the signified" and is an activity of making meaning more than a fixable meaning in and of itself. Signifying (semiosis)—in short—precedes and creates the matrix of meaning, and not vice versa. In fact, Lacan says, "we teach that the unconscious means that man is inhabited by [constituted by] the signifier." To be thus inhabited by the signifier, in Johnson's words, is to be "knotted up, entangled in semiotic relations." Signifiers create "texts," and "knot" captures the etymological sense of the figural weaving that constitutes them. This weaving can be seen in the complex strands that constitute Žižek's reading of detective fiction. In "Two Ways to Avoid the Real of Desire" Žižek locates a series of misplaced signifiers of desire that comprises repeated "attempt[s] at disception" in the complicated "dialectic of truth and deception" that not only constitutes fictions of detection, but constitutes the (semiotic) structure of the unconscious. "The very deceit the murderer invents to save himself is the cause of his downfall," Žižek writes. "Such a paradoxical conjunction in which it is the very attempt at deception that betrays us is of course possible only in the domain of 'meaning,' of signifying structure; it is on this account that the detective's 'omniscience' is strictly homologous to that of the psychoanalyst, who is taken by the patient as the 'subject supposed to know' (*le sujet supposé savoir*)." The interweaving of these signifiers, the "knot" of deception and truth, can be read and interpreted by untying and sorting out the various signifying strands. Žižek's reading of fiction, including his reading of Freud and Lacan into these texts, proceeds in precisely this semiotic/psychoanalytic manner of identifying and relating the situating of certain codes within a psychoanlytic framework. That is, he shows this text to be made up of signifiers of desire linked together and deployed according to the analytic codes that Freud identified in the workings of the unconscious. Žižek's interpretations, moreover, are played out against the background of Lacan's idea that "the unconscious . . . is structured like a language." That is, in the case of both the unconscious and language, meaning and significance are always textual effects produced by semiotic processes.

The language of contemporary psychoanalysis may be the most difficult of all the contemporary discourses in that it consistently attempts, as in Barbara Johnson's description, to create effects of "power" in itself—effects "on" and "within" the reader—as much as descriptions of meaning. Shoshana Felman highlights this dimension of psychoanalysis in "Psychoanalysis and Education: Teaching Terminable and Interminable" when she discusses the nature and role of teaching. "Teaching," she says, "like analysis, does not deal so much with lack of knowledge as with resistances to knowledge." Felman analyzes the relationships of knowledge and ignorance—between teacher and student—in a way suggestive of structuralism's reconsideration of the actual phenomena of language—what it calls "language-effects"—as opposed to the unconscious structures that allow language to function. In this way, Felman attempts to situate the practice of pedagogy, that is, to "reorient" it in relation to the interpersonal relationships of power that discourse conveys along with its "knowledge."

Felman traces the relationship between knowledge and ignorance in teaching and psychoanalysis in ways that shed light on the rethinking of criticism and the discipline of English studies more generally. Teaching, psychoanalysis teaches us, must learn to learn from ignorance, since ignorance is not simply the absence of knowledge, but a resistance to knowledge that "itself can teach us something." (This is similar to Žižek's point that the absence of evidence itself is a form of evidence.) The aim of teaching "is not the transmission of ready-made knowledge; it is rather the creation of a new condition of knowledge." According to Lacan, the analyst—and implicitly the teacher—does not possess what the patient, or the student, wants to know. The analyst's "competence, insists Lacan, lies in 'what I would call textual knowledge,'" which is, Felman says, "the very stuff the literature teacher is supposed to deal in— . . . knowledge of the functioning of language, of symbolic structures, of the signifier, knowledge at once derived from—and directed towards—interpretation."

In this reorienting of what the teacher does, knowledge "cannot be exchanged[;] it has to be used." This is also the reorientation in English studies from a model of the transmission of great, independent works of art to the study of the conditions and realization of discourse in its myriad forms—psychological, social, linguistic, and inflected by social forces such as gender, race, and class. Teaching uncovers the conditions of knowledge, and it functions as much by performative "utterances" as it does by constative statements. (For a discussion of these terms, see Jonathan Culler, "Convention and Meaning," in "Deconstruction and Poststructuralism" [Part V].) "Misinterpretations of the psychoanalytical critique of pedagogy," Felman argues, "refer exclusively to Lacan's or Freud's explicit *statements* about pedagogy, and thus fail to see the illocutionary force, the didactic function of the *utterance* as opposed to the mere content of the statement."

One of the most influential understandings of this performative dimension of culture in psychoanalytic terms is Laura Mulvey's "Visual Pleasure and Narrative Cinema." In this often-cited article, Mulvey isolates the scenario of viewing the "classic Hollywood" film and reads it as a performance text. Key here, and this is a dimension to note carefully in her work, is the situating of a semiotic text (the genre of the Hollywood film) within a broad historical and social situation. In this case, a genre is understood as a cultural institution intended for a mass audience. In other words, in what has been a groundbreaking study for film and cultural criticism, Mulvey relates the material conditions of film viewing to the ideological implications of the gender relations that dominate in Hollywood film. She then situates these generic concerns in relation to the capitalistic production mode of the American film industry. In working this way across signifying codes, Mulvey brings to realization a certain potential of psychoanalysis to function synthetically and quite effectively as cultural critique on several levels. (In many ways, this would also describe Žižek's and Felman's goals.)

This manner of positing a semiotic "subject" within a cultural institution, of projecting meaning *and* interpretation as semiotic operations, has made Freud (via Lacan) newly useful for feminists, Marxists, and others working in cultural theory. Feminist critics such as Luce Irigaray, Hélène Cixous, Laura Mulvey, Teresa de Lauretis, Diana Fuss, and Shoshana Felman have found in the "French Freud" a potential for interpreting literary texts from other than a male (or "phallogocentric") perspective. Starting with Lacan's work, but often revising his critique of the subject of interpretation, feminists have profitably read literary and other cultural texts psychoanalytically. Likewise, Michael Warner's critique of heterosexuality (in "Feminism and Gender Studies" [Part VIII]) itself can be seen as a "neo-Freudian" critique of received notions of gender—including Freud's own assumptions—that nevertheless participates in many of Freud's and Lacan's insights about the economy of psychological life. In addition, Marxist critics such as Fredric Jameson, Louis Althusser, and Anthony Wilden have worked from Lacan's figure of the split subject to integrate the political and the psychological critiques of literary texts. An important result of this project is the idea of a "political unconscious," an approach to power relations that uses Freud's model to analyze manifest and unconscious discourses. For scholars working in both gender studies and Marxist analyses of culture, Lacanian thought can be deployed in a strategy for overturning the traditional Western subject and reinscribing (reimagining) the workings of subjectivity in a largely unconscious discourse that is not "personal" or "individualist" in any usual sense.

The importance of psychoanalysis is everywhere evident in contemporary literary criticism. In "Constructing the Subject: Deconstructing the Text" (in "Deconstruction and Poststructuralism" [Part V]), Catherine Belsey uses a Lacanian mode of analysis to bring together the work of feminism and of Marxist and ideological analyses of culture. Similarly, Fuss expands Lacanian psychoanalysis to a wider cultural use in "Feminism and Critical Theory" (in "Feminism and Gender Studies" [Part VIII]). And, finally, in the General Introduction we try to show the central place of the critique of the subject (initiated in psychoanalysis) in contemporary literary and cultural studies. Lacan's is a difficult view of the text, but it is precisely the radicality—the semiotic and deconstructive dimension—in the "new" psychoanalysis that has once more given Freud importance in contemporary literary and cultural criticism.

RELATED ESSAYS IN *CONTEMPORARY LITERARY CRITICISM*

Catherine Belsey, "Constructing the Subject: Deconstructing the Text"
Teresa de Lauretis, "Semiotics and Experience"
Ferdinand de Saussure, Selections from *Course in General Linguistics*
Diana Fuss, "Reading Like a Feminist"
Barbara Johnson, "Apostrophe, Animation, and Abortion"
Michael Warner, "Homo-Narcissism; or, Heterosexuality"

REFERENCES AND FURTHER READING

Abraham, Nicolas, and Maria Torok, *Cryptonymie: Le verbier de l'homme aux loups* (Paris: Aubier-Flammarion, 1976).

Alcorn, Marshall W., *Narcissism and the Literary Libido: Rhetoric, Text, and Subjectivity* (New York: New York University Press, 1994).

Barr, Marleen S., *Discontented Discourses: Feminism/Textual/Intervention/Psychoanalysis* (Urbana: University of Illinois Press, 1989).

Bellemin-Noel, Jean, *Vers l'inconscient du texte* (Paris: Presses Universitaires de France, 1979).

Belsey, Catherine, *Critical Practice* (New York: Methuen, 1980).

Berman, Emanuel, *Essential Papers on Literature and Psychoanalysis* (New York: New York University Press, 1993).

Bodkin, Maud, *Archetypal Patterns in Poetry* (New York: Vintage, 1958).

Bowie, Malcolm, *Psychoanalysis and the Future of Theory* (Cambridge, MA: Blackwell, 1994).

Brooks, Peter, "Fictions of the Wolfman: Freud and Narrative Understanding," in *Diacritics* 9, No. 1 (1979), 72–83.

————, *Psychoanalysis and Storytelling* (Cambridge, MA: Blackwell, 1994).

Campbell, Joseph, *The Hero with a Thousand Faces* (New York: Pantheon, 1949).

Caroll, David, "Freud and the Myth of Origins," in *New Literary History* 6 (1975), 511–28.

Crews, Frederick C., *Out of My System* (New York: Oxford University Press, 1975).

————, ed., *Psychoanalysis and Literary Process* (Cambridge, MA: Winthrop, 1970).

————, *The Sins of the Fathers* (New York: Oxford University Press, 1966).

Davis, Robert Con, ed., *The Fictional Father: Lacanian Readings of the Text* (Amherst: University of Massachusetts Press, 1981).

————, ed., *Lacan and Narration: The Psychoanalytic Difference in Narrative Theory* (Baltimore: Johns Hopkins University Press, 1984).

Derrida, Jacques, *The Postcard,* trans. Alan Bass (Chicago: University of Chicago Press, 1987).

————, "Freud and the Scene of Writing," in his *Writing and Difference,* trans. Alan Bass (Chicago: University of Chicago Press, 1978), 196–231.

Felman, Shoshana, "Beyond Oedipus: The Specimen Story of Psychoanalysis," in Robert Con Davis, ed., *Lacan and Narration: The Psychoanalytic Difference in Narrative Theory* (Baltimore: Johns Hopkins University Press, 1984), 1021–53.

————, *Jacques Lacan and the Adventure of Insight: Psychoanalysis in Contemporary Culture* (Cambridge, MA: Harvard University Press, 1987).

————, *The Literary Speech Act: Don Juan with J. L. Austin, or Seduction in Two Languages,* trans. Catherine Porter (Ithaca, NY: Cornell University Press, 1983).

————, ed., *Literature and Psychoanalysis: The Question of Reading—Otherwise* (Baltimore: Johns Hopkins University Press, 1982).

————, *What Does a Woman Want? Reading and Sexual Difference* (Baltimore: Johns Hopkins University Press, 1993).

Freud, Sigmund, *Totem and Taboo,* trans A. A. Brill (New York: Moffat, Yard, 1918).

Frye, Northrop, *Anatomy of Criticism: Four Essays* (Princeton, NJ: Princeton University Press, 1957).

Gallop, Jane, *The Daughter's Seduction: Feminism and Psychoanalysis* (Ithaca, NY: Cornell University Press, 1982).

Gliserman, Martin J., *Psychoanalysis, Language, and the Body of the Text* (Gainesville: University of Press of Florida, 1996).

Goux, Jean-Joseph, *Freud, Marx: Economie et symbolique* (Paris: Seuil, 1973).

Hartman, Geoffrey H., "Psychoanalysis: The French Connection," in *Psychoanalysis and the Question of the Text,* ed. Geoffrey H. Hartman (Baltimore: Johns Hopkins University Press, 1978), 86–113.

Hert, Neil, "Freud and the Sandman," in *Textual Strategies,* ed. Josué Harari (Ithaca, NY: Cornell University Press, 1979), 296–321.

Hoffman, Frederick J., *Freudianism and the Literary Mind,* 2nd ed. (Baton Rouge: Louisiana State University Press, 1957).

Holland, Norman N., *The Dynamics of Literary Response* (New York: Oxford University Press, 1968).

————, *5 Readers Reading* (New Haven, CT: Yale University Press, 1975).

————, *Poems in Persons* (New York: Norton, 1973).

Johnson, Barbara, "The Frame of Reference," *Yale French Studies* 55/56 (1977), 457–505.

Lacan, Jacques, *Écrits: A Selection,* trans. Alan Sheridan (New York: Norton, 1977).

————, *Speech and Language in Psychoanalysis,* trans., notes, and commentary by Anthony G. Wilden (Baltimore: Johns Hopkins University Press, 1982).

————, and the École Freudienne, *Feminine Sexuality,* ed. Juliet Mitchell and Jacqueline Rose, trans. J. Rose (New York: Norton, 1982).

Lesser, Simon O., *Fiction and the Unconscious* (Boston: Beacon Press, 1957).

Leupin, Alexandre, *Lacan and the Human Sciences* (Lincoln: University of Nebraska Press, 1991).

MacCabe, Colin, ed., *The Talking Cure: Essays in Psychoanalysis and Language* (London: Macmillan, 1981).

Masse, Michelle A., *In the Name of Love: Women, Masochism, and the Gothic* (Ithaca, NY: Cornell University Press, 1992).

Mulvey, Laura, *Visual and Other Pleasures* (London: Macmillan, 1989).

Penley, Constance, ed., *Feminism and Film Theory* (New York: Routledge, 1989).

Phillips, Adam, *On Flirtation* (Cambridge, MA: Harvard University Press, 1994).

Rimmon-Kenan, Shlomith, *Discourse in Psychoanalysis and Literature* (New York: Methuen, 1987).

Rose, Jacqueline, *State of Fantasy* (New York: Oxford University Press, 1996).

Siegel, Carol, *Male Masochism: Modern Revisions of the Story of Love* (Bloomington: Indiana University Press, 1995).

Spivak, Gayatri Chakravorty, "The Letter as Cutting Edge," in *Yale French Studies* 55/56 (1977), 208–26.

Stoltzfus, Ben, *Lacan and Literature: Purloined Pretexts* (Albany: State University of New York Press, 1996),

Trilling, Lionel, *Freud and the Crisis of Our Culture* (Boston: Beacon Press, 1995).

————, *The Liberal Imagination* (New York: Viking, 1951).

Wilson, Edmund, *The Triple Thinkers* (New York: Harcourt, Brace, 1938).

————, *The Wound and the Bow* (Boston: Houghton Mifflin, 1941).

Wright, Elizabeth, *Psychoanalytic Criticism: Theory in Practice* (London: Methuen, 1984).

23

Jacques Lacan
1901–1981

From his earliest writings, including his doctoral thesis (1932), Jacques Lacan expressed discontent with the limits of traditional psychoanalysis as practiced by rigid Freudians. After parting ways first with the French and then the international psychoanalytic establishment, in 1953 Lacan began weekly seminars attended by students, philosophers, and linguists. Along with his essays, most of which appear in his *Écrits* (1966; trans. 1977), these seminars provided Lacan with a field for his most important work. Lacan's intent was to reinterpret Freud, with special attention to Freud's treatment of the unconscious, which communicates its formal structure through a specialized language. For Lacan, the true subject—of psychoanalysis and discourse—is the unconscious rather than the ego; at the same time, Lacan refused to reify the unconscious, given that a unified subject, he argued, is illusory.

Like that of Lévi-Strauss, Foucault, Barthes, and Derrida, Lacan's work was deeply affected by structural linguistics, and in it he particularly concentrated on the functions of signs. From this study, Lacan determined that the unconscious is "structured like language" and reveals meaning only in the connections among signifiers. This linguistic model surfaced in Lacan's *Rome Discourse* (1953; trans. 1968) entitled "The Function and Field of Speech and Language in Psychoanalysis." Lacan's seminar on Poe's "The Purloined Letter" (1956; trans. 1972) best illustrates his nexus of discourse and the psychoanalytic process; in tracing the path of the displaced signifier, Poe's story became, for Lacan, a parable of the linguistic sign in its creation of the speaking subject. His 1957 essay in *Écrits,* "The Instance of the Letter, or Reason Since Freud," a Saussurean reading of the unconscious, took this attention to the signifier one step further by making the signifier the primary component of the signifier/signified schema, thereby reversing the traditional Western notion of the primacy of the concept.

Lacan's essay reprinted here, "The Mirror Stage as Formative of the Function of the I as Revealed in Psychoanalytic Experience" (1949), identifies the point at which the *I* begins to formulate itself as a socially constructed agent, or a subject fabricated by virtue of the preexisting social order of language. In the infant's recognition of the mirror image as its own, Lacan identifies the first stage of development toward an eventual sense of both "permanence of the *I*"—its fundamentally spatial reality—and alienation of the *I* from a unified sense of self. The mirror image's reduplication begins the process of mediating the *I* through the desire of and identification with others, a stage entailing the profit of recognizing the self as an agent among others in history and the loss of perceived unified sufficiency. In one move, then, Lacan joins the phenomena of doubling and narcissism to tease out a source, psychoanalytically speaking, for what literary critics will see as two ubiquitous literary tropes, metaphor and metonymy.

The Mirror Stage as Formative of the Function of the I as Revealed in Psychoanalytic Experience

Delivered at the 16th International Congress of Psychoanalysis, Zürich, July 17, 1949

The conception of the mirror stage that I introduced at our last congress, thirteen years ago, has since become more or less established in the practice of the French group. However, I think it worthwhile to bring it again to your attention, especially today, for the light it sheds on the formation of the *I* as we experience it in psychoanalysis. It is an experience that leads us to oppose any philosophy directly issuing from the *Cogito*.

Some of you may recall that this conception originated in a feature of human behaviour illuminated by a fact of comparative psychology. The child, at an age when he is for a time, however short, outdone by the chimpanzee in instrumental intelligence, can nevertheless already recognize as such his own image in a mirror. This recognition is indicated in the illuminative mimicry of the *AhaErlebnis,* which Köhler sees as the expression of situational apperception, an essential stage of the act of intelligence.

This act, far from exhausting itself, as in the case of the monkey, once the image has been mastered and found empty, immediately rebounds in the case of the child in a series of gestures in which he experiences in play the rela-

tion between the movements assumed in the image and the reflected environment, and between this virtual complex and the reality it reduplicates—the child's own body, and the persons and things, around him.

This event can take place, as we have known since Baldwin, from the age of six months, and its repetition has often made me reflect upon the startling spectacle of the infant in front of the mirror. Unable as yet to walk, or even to stand up, and held tightly as he is by some support, human or artificial (what, in France, we call a "trotte-bébé"), he nevertheless overcomes, in a flutter of jubilant activity, the obstructions of his support and, fixing his attitude in a slightly leaning-forward position, in order to hold it in his gaze, brings back an instantaneous aspect of the image.

For me, this activity retains the meaning I have given it up to the age of eighteen months. This meaning discloses a libidinal dynamism, which has hitherto remained problematic, as well as an ontological structure of the human world that accords with my reflections on paranoiac knowledge.

We have only to understand the mirror stage *as an identification,* in the full sense that analysis *identification*

gives to the term: namely, the transformation that takes place in the subject when he assumes an image—whose predestination to this phase-effect is sufficiently indicated by the use, in analytic theory, of the ancient term *imago*.

This jubilant assumption of his specular image by the child at the *infans* stage, still sunk in his motor incapacity and nursling dependence, would seem to exhibit in an exemplary situation the symbolic matrix in which the *I* is precipitated in a primordial form, before it is objectified in the dialectic of identification with the other, and before language restores to it, in the universal, its function as subject.

This form would have to be called the Ideal-I,[1] if we wished to incorporate it into our usual register, in the sense that it will also be the source of secondary identifications, under which term I would place the functions of libidinal normalization. But the important point is that this form situates the agency of the ego, before its social determination, in a fictional direction, which will always remain irreducible for the individual alone, or rather, which will only rejoin the coming-into-being *(le devenir)* of the subject asymptotically, whatever the success of the dialectical syntheses by which he must resolve as *I* his discordance with his own reality.

The fact is that the total form of the body by which the subject anticipates in a mirage the maturation of his power is given to him only as *Gestalt,* that is to say, in an exteriority in which this form is certainly more constituent than constituted, but in which it appears to him above all in a contrasting size *(un relief de stature)* that fixes it and in a symmetry that inverts it, in contrast with the turbulent movements that the subject feels are animating him. Thus, this *Gestalt*—whose pregnancy should be regarded as bound up with the species, though its motor style remains scarcely recognizable—by these two aspects of its appearance, symbolizes the mental permanence of the *I,* at the same time as it prefigures its alienating destination; it

is still pregnant with the correspondences that unite the *I* with the statue in which man projects himself, with the phantoms that dominate him, or with the automation in which, in an ambiguous relation, the world of his own making tends to find completion.

Indeed, for the *imagos*—whose veiled faces it is our privilege to see in outline in our daily experience and in the penumbra of symbolic efficacity[2]—the mirror-image would seem to be the threshold of the visible world, if we go by the mirror disposition that the *imago of one's own body* presents in hallucinations or dreams, whether it concerns its individual features, or even its infirmities, or its object-projections; or if we observe the role of the mirror apparatus in the appearances of the *double,* in which psychical realities, however heterogeneous, are manifested.

That a *Gestalt* should be capable of formative effects in the organism is attested by a piece of biological experimentation that is itself so alien to the idea of psychical causality that it cannot bring itself to formulate its results in these terms. It nevertheless recognizes that it is a necessary condition for the maturation of the gonad of the female pigeon that it should see another member of its species, of either sex; so sufficient in itself is this condition that the desired effect may be obtained merely by placing the individual within reach of the field of reflection of a mirror. Similarly, in the case of the migratory locust, the transition within a generation from the solitary to the gregarious form can be obtained by exposing the individual, at a certain stage, to the exclusively visual action of a similar image, provided it is animated by movements of a style sufficiently close to that characteristic of the species. Such facts are inscribed in an order of homeomorphic identification that would itself fall within the larger question of the meaning of beauty as both formative and erogenic.

But the facts of mimicry are no less instructive when conceived as cases of heteromorphic identification, in as much as they raise the problem of the signification of space for the living organism—psychological concepts hardly seem less appropriate for shedding light on these matters than ridiculous attempts to reduce them to the supposedly supreme law of adaptation. We have only to recall how Roger Caillois (who was then very young, and still fresh from his breach with the sociological school in which he was trained) illuminated the subject by using the term "*legendary psychasthenia*" to classify morphological mimicry as an obsession with space in its derealizing effect.

I have myself shown in the social dialectic that structures human knowledge as paranoiac[3] why human knowledge has greater autonomy than animal knowledge in relation to the field of force of desire, but also why human knowledge is determined in that "little reality" *(ce peu de réalité),* which the Surrealists, in their restless way, saw as its limitation. These reflections lead me to recognize in the spatial captation manifested in the mirror stage, even before the social dialectic, the effect in man of an organic insufficiency in his natural reality—in so far as any meaning can be given to the word "nature."

I am led, therefore, to regard the function of the mirror stage as a particular case of the function of the *imago,* which is to establish a relation between the organism and its reality—or, as they say, between the *Innenwelt* and the *Umwelt.*

In man, however, this relation to nature is altered by a certain dehiscence at the heart of the organism, a primordial Discord betrayed by the signs of uneasiness and motor uncoordination of the neo-natal months. The objective notion of the anatomical incompleteness of the pyramidal system and likewise the presence of certain humoral residues of the maternal organism confirm the view I have formulated as the fact of a real *specific prematurity of birth* in man.

It is worth noting, incidentally, that this is a fact recognized as such by embryologists, by the term *foetalization,* which determines the preva-

lence of the so-called superior apparatus of the neurax, and especially of the cortex, which psycho-surgical operations lead us to regard as the intra-organic mirror.

This development is experienced as a temporal dialectic that decisively projects the formation of the individual into history. The *mirror stage* is a drama whose internal thrust is precipitated from insufficiency to anticipation—and which manufactures for the subject, caught up in the lure of spatial identification, the succession of phantasies that extends from a fragmented body-image to a form of its totality that I shall call orthopaedic—and, lastly, to the assumption of the armour of an alienating identity, which will mark with its rigid structure the subject's entire mental development. Thus, to break out of the circle of the *Innenwelt* into the *Umwelt* generates the inexhaustible quadrature of the ego's verifications.

This fragmented body—which term I have also introduced into our system of theoretical references—usually manifests itself in dreams when the movement of the analysis encounters a certain level of aggressive disintegration in the individual. It then appears in the form of disjointed limbs, or of those organs represented in exoscopy, growing wings and taking up arms for intestinal persecutions—the very same that the visionary Hieronymus Bosch has fixed, for all time, in painting, in their ascent from the fifteenth century to the imaginary zenith of modern man. But this form is even tangibly revealed at the organic level, in the lines of "fragilization" that define the anatomy of phantasy, as exhibited in the schizoid and spasmodic symptoms of hysteria.

Correlatively, the formation of the *I* is symbolized in dreams by a fortress, or a stadium—its inner arena and enclosure, surrounded by marshes and rubbish-tips, dividing it into two opposed fields of contest where the subject flounders in quest of the lofty, remote inner castle whose form (sometimes juxtaposed in the same scenario) symbolizes the id in a quite startling way. Similarly, on the mental plane, we find realized the structures of fortified works, the metaphor of which arises spontaneously, as if issuing from the symptoms themselves, to designate the mechanisms of obsessional neurosis—inversion, isolation, reduplication, cancellation and displacement.

But if we were to build on these subjective givens alone—however little we free them from the condition of experience that makes us see them as partaking of the nature of a linguistic technique—our theoretical attempts would remain exposed to the charge of projecting themselves into the unthinkable of an absolute subject. This is why I have sought in the present hypothesis, grounded in a conjunction of objective data, the guiding grid for a *method of symbolic reduction.*

It establishes in the *defences of the ego* a genetic order, in accordance with the wish formulated by Miss Anna Freud, in the first part of her great work, and situates (as against a frequently expressed prejudice) hysterical repression and its returns at a more archaic stage than obsessional inversion and its isolating processes, and the latter in turn as preliminary to paranoic alienation, which dates from the deflection of the specular *I* into the social *I.*

This moment in which the mirror stage comes to an end inaugurates, by the identification with the *imago* of the counterpart and the drama of primordial jealousy (so well brought out by the school of Charlotte Bühler in the phenomenon of infantile *transitivism*), the dialectic that will henceforth link the *I* to socially elaborated situations.

It is this moment that decisively tips the whole of human knowledge into mediatization through the desire of the other, constitutes its objects in an abstract equivalence by the co-operation of others, and turns the *I* into that apparatus for which every instinctual thrust constitutes a danger, even though it should correspond to a natural maturation—the very

normalization of this maturation being henceforth dependent, in man, on a cultural mediation as exemplified, in the case of the sexual object, by the Oedipus complex.

In the light of this conception, the term primary narcissism, by which analytic doctrine designates the libidinal investment characteristic of that moment, reveals in those who invented it the most profound awareness of semantic latencies. But it also throws light on the dynamic opposition between this libido and the sexual libido, which the first analysts tried to define when they invoked destructive and, indeed, death instincts, in order to explain the evident connection between the narcissistic libido and the alienating function of the *I,* the aggressivity it releases in any relation to the other, even in a relation involving the most Samaritan of aid.

In fact, they were encountering that existential negativity whose reality is so vigorously proclaimed by the contemporary philosophy of being and nothingness.

But unfortunately that philosophy grasps negativity only within the limits of a self-sufficiency of consciousness, which, as one of its premises, links to the *méconnaissances* that constitute the ego, the illusion of autonomy to which it entrusts itself. This flight of fancy, for all that it draws, to an unusual extent, on borrowings from psychoanalytic experience, culminates in the pretention of providing an existential psychoanalysis.

At the culmination of the historical effort of a society to refuse to recognize that it has any function other than the utilitarian one, and in the anxiety of the individual confronting the "concentrational"[4] form of the social bond that seems to arise to crown this effort, existentialism must be judged by the explanations it gives of the subjective impasses that have indeed resulted from it; a freedom that is never more authentic than when it is within the walls of a prison; a demand for commitment, expressing the impotence of a pure consciousness to master any situation; a voyeuristic-sadistic idealization of the sexual relation; a personality that realizes itself

We i essentially fragmented

only in suicide; a consciousness of the other that can be satisfied only by Hegelian murder.

These propositions are opposed by all our experience, in so far as it teaches us not to regard the ego as centered on the *perception-consciousness system,* or as organized by the "reality principle"—a principle that is the expression of a scientific prejudice most hostile to the dialectic of knowledge. Our experience shows that we should start instead from the *function of méconnaissance* that characterizes the ego in all its structures, so markedly articulated by Miss Anna Freud. For, if the *Verneinung* represents the patent form of that function, its effects will, for the most part, remain latent, so long as they are not illuminated by some light reflected on to the level of fatality, which is where the id manifests itself.

We can thus understand the inertia characteristic of the formations of the *I,* and find there the most extensive definition of neurosis—just as the captation of the subject by the situation gives us the most general formula for madness, not only the madness that lies behind the walls of asylums, but also the madness that deafens the world with its sound and fury.

The sufferings of neurosis and psychosis are for us a schooling in the passions of the soul, just as the beam of the psychoanalytic scales, when we calculate the tilt of its threat to entire communities, provides us with an indication of the deadening of the passions in society.

At this junction of nature and culture, so persistently examined by modern anthropology, psychoanalysis alone recognizes this knot of imaginary servitude that love must always undo again, or sever.

For such a task, we place no trust in altruistic feeling, we who lay bare the aggressivity that underlies the activity of the philanthropist, the idealist, the pedagogue, and even the reformer.

In the recourse of subject to subject that we preserve, psychoanalysis may accompany the patient to the ecstatic limit of the "*Thou art that,*" in which is revealed to him the cipher of his mortal destiny, but it is not in our mere power as practitioners to bring him to that point where the real journey begins.

Translated by Alan Sheridan

NOTES

1. Throughout this article I leave in its peculiarity the translation I have adopted for Freud's *Ideal-Ich* [i.e., "je-idéal"], without further comment, other than to say that I have not maintained it since.

2. Cf. Claude Lévi-Strauss, *Structural Anthropology,* Chapter X.

3. Cf. "Aggressivity in Psychoanalysis," p. 8 and *Écrits,* p. 180.

4. "*Concentrationnaire,*" an adjective coined after World War II (this article was written in 1949) to describe the life of the concentration-camp. In the hands of certain writers it became, by extension, applicable to many aspects of "modern" life [Tr.].

24

Shoshana Felman

1942–

Shoshana Felman is the Thomas E. Donnelley Professor of French and Comparative Literature at Yale University. She is a leading exponent of psychoanalytic literary criticism. Her lucid explications of the theories of Jacques Lacan and, through Lacan, of Freud, and her practical applications of those theories to the study of literature, have helped make the practice of psychoanalytic literary criticism accessible to a wide audience. Felman's work includes *La "Folie" dans l'oeuvre romanesquede Stendhal* (1971), *The Literary Speech Act: Don Juan with J. L. Austin, Or Seduction in Two Languages* (1980; trans. 1983), *Writing and Madness* (1978; trans. 1985), *Jacques Lacan and the Adventure of Insight* (1987), *Testimony: Crises of Witnessing in Literature, Psychoanalysis, and History* (1991), and *What Does a Woman Want? Reading and Sexual Difference* (1993). She also edited *Literature and Psychoanalysis* (1982).

In "Psychoanalysis and Education: Teaching Terminable and Interminable" (1982), Felman discusses what she calls the "radical impossibility of teaching." With close attention to the writings of Freud and Lacan, she demonstrates the similarities between the relationships of teacher and student and analyst and analysand, indicating the ways in which psychoanalytic methodology can be used as a tool to facilitate the learning process. That is, she argues that there is a parallel between the analysand's "repression" or "resistance" in psychotherapy and students' "ignorance." Teaching, like psychoanalysis, must "deal not so much with *lack* of knowledge as with *resistances* to knowledge"; the teacher, like the analyst, must learn not to "*exchange*" knowledge with students but to "*use*" his or her knowledge to help students discover (or rediscover) their own. Psychoanalytic methods are, in Felman's view, especially applicable to the teaching of literature; literature, like the recovering analysand and the brighter student, "*knows it knows, but does not know the meaning of its knowledge*—it does not know *what* it knows."

Psychoanalysis and Education: Teaching Terminable and Interminable

In memory of Jacques Lacan

MENO: Can you tell me, Socrates, if virtue can be taught? Or is it not teachable but the result of practice, or is it neither of these, but men possess it by nature?

SOCRATES: . . . You must think me happy indeed if you think I know whether virtue can be taught . . . I am so far from knowing whether virtue can be taught or not that I do not even have any knowledge of what virtue itself is.

. . .

MENO: Yes, Socrates, but how do you mean that we do not learn, but that what we call learning is recollection? Can you teach me how this is so?

SOCRATES: . . . Meno, you are a rascal. Here you are asking me to give you my "teaching," I who claim that there is no such thing as teaching, only recollection.

—Plato, *Meno*[1]

THE MEASURE OF A TASK

Socrates, that extraordinary teacher who taught humanity what pedagogy is, and whose name personifies the birth of pedagogics as a science, inaugurates his teaching practice, paradoxically enough, by asserting not just his own ignorance, but the radical impossibility of teaching.

Another extraordinarily effective pedagogue, another one of humanity's great teachers, Freud, repeats, in his own way, the same conviction that teaching is a fundamentally impossible profession. "None of the applications of psychoanalysis," he writes, "has excited so much interest and aroused so many hopes . . . as its use in the theory and practice of education . . .":

My personal share in this application of psychoanalysis has been very slight. At an early stage I had accepted the *bon mot* which lays it down that there are three impossible professions—educating, healing, governing—and I was already fully occupied with the second of them.[2]

In a later text—indeed the very last one that he wrote—Freud recapitulates this paradoxical conviction which time and experience seem to have only reinforced, confirmed:

It almost looks as if analysis were the third of those 'impossible' professions in which one can be sure beforehand of achieving unsatisfying results. The other two, which have been known much longer, are education and government. [Standard, XXIII, 248]

If teaching is impossible—as Freud and Socrates both point out—what are we teachers doing? How should we understand—and carry out—our task? And why is it precisely two of the most effective teachers ever to appear in the intellectual history of mankind, who regard the task of teaching as impossible? Indeed, is not their radical enunciation of the impossibility of teaching itself actively engaged in teaching, itself part of the lesson they bequeath us? And if so, what can be learnt from the fact that it is impossible to teach? What can the impossibility of teaching teach us?

As much as Socrates, Freud has instituted, among other things, a revolutionary pedagogy. It is my contention—which I will here attempt to elucidate and demonstrate—that it is precisely in giving us unprecedented insight into the impossibility of teaching, that psychoanalysis has opened up unprecedented teaching possibilities, renewing both the questions and the practice of education.

This pedagogical renewal was not, however, systematically thought out by Freud himself, or systematically articulated by any of his followers; nor have its thrust and scope been to date fully assimilated or fully grasped, let alone utilized, exploited in the classroom. The only truly different pedagogy to have practically emerged from what might be called the psychoanalytic lesson is the thoroughly original teaching-style of Jacques Lacan, Freud's French disciple and interpreter. If Lacan is, as I would argue, Freud's best student—that is, the most radical effect of the insights of Freud's teaching—perhaps his teaching practice might give us a clue to the newness of the psychoanalytic lesson about lessons, and help us thus define both the actual and, more importantly, the potential contribution of psychoanalysis to pedagogy.

WHAT IS A CRITIQUE OF PEDAGOGY?

Lacan's relationship with pedagogy has, however, been itself—like that of Freud—mostly oversimplified, misunderstood, reduced. The reason for the usual misinterpretations of both Lacan's and Freud's pedagogical contribution lies in a misunderstanding of the critical position taken by psychoanalysis with respect to traditional methods and assumptions of education. Lacan's well-known critique of what he has pejoratively termed "academic discourse" (*le discours universitaire)* situates "the radical vice" in "the transmission of knowledge." "A Master of Arts," writes Lacan ironically, "as well as other titles, protect the secret of a substantialized knowledge,"[3] Lacan thus blames "the narrow-minded horizon of pedagogues" for having "reduced" the "strong notion" of "teaching"[4] to a "functional apprenticeship" (E 445).

Whereas Lacan's pedagogical critique is focused on grown-up training—on academic education and the ways it handles and structures knowledge, Freud's pedagogical critique is mainly concerned with children's education and the ways it handles and structures repression. "Let us make ourselves clear," writes Freud, "as to what the first task of education is":

The child must learn to control his instincts. It is impossible to give him liberty to carry out all his impulses without restriction . . . Accordingly, *education must inhibit, forbid and suppress*[5] and this is abundantly seen in all periods of history. But we have learnt from analysis that precisely this suppression of instincts involves the risk of neurotic illness. . . . Thus education has to find its way between the Scylla of non-interference and the Charybdis of frustration. . . . An optimum must be discovered which will enable education to achieve the most and damage the least. . . . A moment's reflection tells us that hitherto education has fulfilled its task very badly and has done children great damage. [Standard, XXII, 149]

Thus, in its most massive statements and in its polemical pronouncements, psychoanalysis, in Freud as well as in Lacan—although with different emphases—is first and foremost *a critique of pedagogy.* The legacy of this critique has been, however, misconstrued and greatly oversimplified, in that the critical stance has been understood—in both Lacan's and Freud's case—as a desire to escape the pedagogical imperative: a desire—whether possible or impossible—to do away with pedagogy altogether. "Psychoanalysis," writes Anna Freud, "whenever it has come into contact with pedagogy, has always expressed the wish to *limit education.* Psychoanalysis has brought before us the quite definite danger arising from education."[6]

The illocutionary force of the psychoanalytical (pedagogical) critique of pedagogy has thus been reduced, either to a simple negativity, or to a simple positivity, of that critique. Those who, in an oversimplification of the Freudian lesson, equate the psychoanalytic critical stance with a simple positivity, give consequently positive advice to educators, in an attempt to conceive of more liberal methods for raising children— methods allowing "to each stage in the child's life the right proportion of instinct-gratification and instinct-restriction."[7] Those who, on the other hand, in an oversimplification of the Lacanian lesson, equate the psychoanalytical critical stance with a simple negativity, see in psychoanalysis "literally an inverse pedagogy": "the analytic process is in effect a kind of reverse pedagogy, which aims at undoing what has been established by education."[8] In the title of a recent book on the relationship of Freud to pedagogy, Freud is thus defined as "The Anti-Pedagogue."[9] This one-sidedly negative interpretation of the relation of psychoanalysis to pedagogy fails to see that every true pedagogue is in effect an anti-pedagogue, not just because every pedagogy has historically emerged as a critique of pedagogy (Socrates: "There's a chance, Meno, that we, you as well as me . . . have been inadequately educated, you by Gorgias, I by Prodicus"[10]), but because, in one way or another, every pedagogy stems from its confrontation with the impossibility of teaching (Socrates: "You see, Meno, that I am not teaching . . . anything, but all I do is question . . ."[11]). The reductive conception of "Freud: The Anti-Pedagogue" thus fails to see that there is no such thing as an anti-pedagogue: an anti-pedagogue is *the* pedagogue par excellence. Such a conception overlooks, indeed, and fails to reckon with, Freud's own stupendous pedagogical performance, and its relevance to his declarations about pedagogy.

The trouble, both with the positivistic and with the negativistic misinterpretations of the psychoanalytical critique of pedagogy, is that they refer exclusively to Lacan's or Freud's explicit *statements* about pedagogy, and thus fail to see the illocutionary force, the didactic function of the *utterance* as opposed to the mere content of the statement. They fail to see, in other words, the pedagogical situation—the pedagogical dynamic in which statements function not as simple truths but as performative speech-*acts*. Invariably, all existing psychoanalytically-inspired theories of pedagogy fail to address the question of the pedagogical speech-act of Freud himself, or of Lacan himself: what can be learnt about pedagogy not just from their theories (which only fragmentarily and indirectly deal with the issue of education) but from their way of *teaching* it, from their own practice as teachers, from their own pedagogical performance.

Lacan refers explicitly to what he calls the psychoanalyst's "mission of teaching" (E 241, N 34 TM),[12] and speaks of his own teaching—the bi-monthly seminar he gave for forty years—as a vocation, "a function . . . to which I have truly devoted my entire life" (S-XI, 7, N 1).[13] Unlike Lacan, Freud addresses the issue of teaching more indirectly, rather by refusing to associate his person with it:

> But there is one topic which I cannot pass over so easily—*not, however, because I understand particularly much about it* or have contributed very much to it. Quite the contrary: *I have scarcely concerned myself with it at all.* I must mention it because it is so exceedingly important, so rich in hopes for the future, perhaps the most important of all the activities of analysis. What I am thinking of is the application of psychoanalysis to education. [Standard, XXII, 146]

This statement thus promotes pedagogy to the rank of "perhaps the most important of all the activities of analysis" only on the basis of Freud's denial of his own personal involvement with it. However, this very statement, this very denial is itself engaged in a dramatic pedagogical performance; it itself is part of an imaginary "lecture," significantly written in the form of an academic public address and of a dialogue with students—a pedagogic dialogue imaginarily conducted by a Freud who, in reality terminally ill and having undergone an operation for mouth-cancer, is no longer capable of speech:

> My *Introductory Lectures on Psychoanalysis* were delivered . . . in a lecture room of the Vienna Psychiatric Clinic before an audience gathered from all the Faculties of the University. . . .
>
> These new lectures, unlike the former ones, have never been delivered. My age had in the meantime absolved me from the obligation of giving expression to my membership in the University (which was in any case a peripheral one) by delivering lectures; and a surgical operation had made speaking in public impossible for me. If, therefore, I once more take my place in the lecture room during the remarks that follow, it is only by an artifice of the imagination; it may help me not to forget to bear the reader in mind as I enter more deeply into my subject. . . . Like their predecessors, [these lectures] are addressed to the multitude of educated people to whom we may perhaps attribute a benevolent, even though cautious, interest in the characteristics and discoveries of the young science. This time once again it has been my chief aim to make no sacrifice to an appearance of being simple, complete or rounded-off, not to disguise problems and not to deny the existence of gaps and uncertainties. [Standard, XXII, 5–6]

No other such coincidence of fiction and reality, biography and theory, could better dramatize Freud's absolutely fundamental pedagogic gesture. What better image could there be for the pedagogue in spite of himself, the pedagogue in spite of everything—the dying teacher whose imminent death, like that of Socrates, only confirms that he is a born teacher—than this pathetic figure, this living allegory of the speechless speaker, of the teacher's teaching out of—through—the very radical impossibility of teaching?

Pedagogy in psychoanalysis is thus not just a theme: it is a rhetoric. It is not just a statement: it is an utterance. It is not just a meaning: it is action; an action which itself may very well, at times, belie the stated meaning, the didactic *thesis,* the theoretical assertion. It is essential to become aware of this complexity of the relationship of pedagogy and psychoanalysis, in order to begin to think out what the psychoanalytic teaching about teaching might well be.

Discussing "The Teaching of Psychoanalysis in Universities," Freud writes: "it will be enough if [the student] learns something *about* psychoanalysis and something *from* it" (Standard, XVII, 173). To learn "something *from* psychoanalysis" is a very different thing than to learn "something *about* it: "it means that psychoanalysis is not a simple *object* of the teaching, but its *subject.* In his essay, "Psychoanalysis and Its Teaching," Lacan underlines the same ambiguity, the same dynamic complexity, indicating that the true object of psychoanalysis, the object of his teaching, can only be that mode of learning which institutes psychoanalysis itself as subject—as the purveyor of the act of teaching. "How can what psychoanalysis teaches us be taught?," he asks (E 439).

As myself both a student of psychoanalysis and a teacher, I would here like to suggest that the lesson to be learnt about pedagogy from psychoanalysis is less that of "the *application* of psychoanalysis to pedagogy" than that of the *implication* of psychoanalysis in pedagogy and of pedagogy in psychoanalysis. Attentive, thus, both to the pedagogical speech act of Freud and to the teaching-practice of Lacan, I would like to address the question of teaching as itself a psychoanalytic question. Reckoning not just with the pedagogical thematics *in* psychoanalysis, but with the pedagogical rhetoric *of* psychoanalysis, not just with what psychoanalysis says *about* teachers but with psychoanalysis *itself as teacher,* I will attempt to analyze the ways in which—modifying the conception of what *learning* is and of what *teaching* is—psychoanalysis has shifted pedagogy by radically displacing our very modes of intelligibility.

ANALYTICAL APPRENTICESHIP

Freud conceives of the process of a psychoanalytic therapy as a learning process—an apprenticeship whose epistemological validity far exceeds the contingent singularity of the therapeutic situation:

Psychoanalysis sets out to explain . . . uncanny disorders; it engages in careful and laborious investigations . . . until at length it can speak thus to the ego:

". . . A part of the activity of your own mind has been withdrawn from your knowledge and from the command of your will . . . you are using one part of your force to fight the other part. . . . A great deal more must constantly be going on in your mind than can be known to your consciousness. Come, *let yourself be taught . . .* ! What is in your mind does not coincide with what you are conscious of; whether something is going on in your mind and whether you hear of it, are two different things. In the ordinary way, I will admit, the intelligence which reaches your consciousness is enough for your needs; and *you may cherish the illusion that you learn of all the more important things.* But in some cases, as in that of an instinctual conflict . . . your intelligence service breaks down. . . . In every case, the news that reaches your consciousness is incomplete and often not to be relied on. . . . Turn your eyes inward . . . *learn first to know yourself!* . . .

It is thus that *psychoanalysis has sought to educate the ego.* [Standard, XVII, 142–143]

Psychoanalysis is thus a pedagogical experience: as a process which gives access to new knowledge hitherto denied to consciousness, it affords what might be called a lesson in cognition (and in miscognition), an epistemological instruction.

Psychoanalysis institutes, in this way, a unique and radically original mode of learning: original not just in its procedures, but in the fact that it gives access to information unavailable through any other mode of learning—unprecedented information, hitherto *unlearnable.* "We learnt," writes Freud, "a quantity of things which could not have been learnt except through analysis" (Standard, XXII, 147).

This new mode of investigation and of learning has, however, a very different temporality than the conventional linear—cumulative and progressive—temporality of learning, as it has traditionally been conceived by pedagogical theory and practice. Proceeding not through linear progression, but through breakthroughs, leaps, discontinuities, regressions, and deferred action, the analytic learning-process puts indeed in question the traditional pedagogical belief in intellectual perfectibility, the progressistic view of learning as a simple one-way road from ignorance to knowledge.

It is in effect the very concept of both ignorance and knowledge—the understanding of what "to know" and "not to know" may really mean—that psychoanalysis has modified, renewed. And it is precisely the originality of this renewal which is central to Lacan's thought, to Lacan's specific way of understanding the cultural, pedagogical and epistemological revolution implied by the discovery of the unconscious.

KNOWLEDGE

Western pedagogy can be said to culminate in Hegel's philosophical didacticism: the Hegelian concept of "absolute knowledge"—which for Hegel defines at once the potential aim and the actual end of dialectics, of philosophy—is in effect what pedagogy has always aimed at as its ideal: the exhaustion—through methodical investigation—of all there is to know; the absolute completion—termination—of apprenticeship. Complete and totally appropriated knowledge will become—in all senses of the word—a *mastery*. "In the Hegelian perspective," writes Lacan, "the complete discourse" is "an instrument of power, the scepter and the property of those who know" (S-II, 91). "What is at stake in absolute knowledge is the fact that discourse closes back upon itself, that it is entirely in agreement with itself" (S-II, 91).

But the unconscious, in Lacan's conception, is precisely the discovery that human discourse can by definition never be entirely in agreement with itself, entirely identical to its knowledge of itself, since, as the vehicle of unconscious knowledge, it is constitutively the material locus of a signifying difference from itself.

What, indeed, is the unconscious, if not a kind of *unmeant knowledge* which escapes intentionality and meaning, a knowledge which is spoken by the language of the subject (spoken, for instance, by his "slips" or by his dreams), but which the subject cannot recognize, assume as *his,* appropriate; a speaking knowledge which is nonetheless denied to the speaker's knowledge. In Lacan's own terms, the unconscious is "knowledge which can't tolerate one's knowing that one knows" (Seminar, Feb. 19, 1974; unpublished). "Analysis appears on the scene to announce that there is *knowledge which does not know itself,* knowledge which is supported by the signifier as such" (S-XX, 88). "It is from a place which differs from any capture by a subject that a knowledge is surrendered, since that knowledge offers itself only to the subject's slips—to his misprision" (*Scilicet* I, 38).[14] "The discovery of the unconscious . . . is that the implications of meaning infinitely exceed the signs manipulated by the individual" (S-II, 150). "As far as signs are concerned, man is always mobilizing many more of them than he knows" (S-II, 150).

If this is so, there can constitutively be no such thing as absolute knowledge: absolute knowledge is knowledge that has exhausted its

own articulation; but articulated knowledge is by definition what cannot exhaust its own self-knowledge. For knowledge to be spoken, linguistically articulated, it would constitutively have to be supported by the ignorance carried by language, the ignorance of the *excess of signs* that of necessity its language—its articulation—"mobilizes." Thus, human knowledge is, by definition, that which is *untotalizable,* that which rules out any possibility of totalizing what it knows or of eradicating its own ignorance.

The epistemological principle of the irreducibility of ignorance which stems from the unconscious, receives an unexpected confirmation from modern science, to which Lacan is equally attentive in his attempt to give the theory of the unconscious its contemporary scientific measure. The scientific a-totality of knowledge is acknowledged by modern mathematics, in set theory (Cantor: "the set of all sets in a universe does not constitute a set"); in contemporary physics, it is the crux of what is known as "the uncertainty principle" of Heisenberg:

> This is what the Heisenberg principle amounts to. When it is possible to locate, to define precisely one of the points of the system, it is impossible to formulate the others. When the place of electrons is discussed . . . it is no longer possible to know anything about . . . their speed. And inversely . . . [S-II, 281]

From the striking and instructive coincidence between the revolutionary findings of psychoanalysis and the new theoretical orientation of modern physics, Lacan derives the following epistemological insight—the following pathbreaking pedagogical principle:

> Until further notice, we can say that *the elements do not answer in the place where they are interrogated.* Or more exactly, as soon as they are interrogated somewhere, it is impossible to grasp them in their totality. [S-II, 281]

IGNORANCE

Ignorance is thus no longer simply *opposed* to knowledge: it is itself a radical condition, an integral part of the very *structure* of knowledge. But what does ignorance consist of, in this new epistemological and pedagogical conception?

If ignorance is to be equated with the a-totality of the unconscious, it can be said to be a kind of forgetting—of forgetfulness: while learning is obviously, among other things, remembering and memorizing ("all learning is recollection," says Socrates), ignorance is linked to what is *not remembered,* what will not be memorized. But what will not be memorized is tied up with repression, with the imperative to forget—the imperative to exclude from consciousness, to not admit to knowledge. Ignorance, in other words, is not a passive state of absence—a simple lack of information: it is an active dynamic of negation, an active refusal of information. Freud writes:

> It is a long superseded idea . . . that the patient suffers from a sort of ignorance, and that if one removes this ignorance by giving him information (about the causal connection of his illness with his life, about his experiences in childhood, and so on) he is bound to recover. The pathological factor is not his ignorance in itself, but the root of this ignorance in his *inner resistances;* it was they who first called this ignorance into being, and they still maintain it now. The task of the treatment lies in combating these resistances. [Standard, XI, 225]

Teaching, like analysis, has to deal not so much with *lack* of knowledge as with *resistances* to knowledge. Ignorance, suggests Lacan, is a "passion." Inasmuch as traditional pedagogy postulated a desire for knowledge, an analytically informed pedagogy has to reckon with "the passion for ignorance" (S-XX, 110). Ignorance, in other words is nothing other than a *desire to ignore:* its nature is less cognitive than performative; as in the case of Sophocles' nuanced representation of the ignorance of Oedipus, it is not a simple lack of information but the incapacity—or the refusal—to acknowledge *one's own implication* in the information.

The new pedagogical lesson of psychoanalysis is not subsumed, however, by the revelation of the dynamic nature—and of the irreducibility—of ignorance. The truly revolutionary insight—the truly revolutionary *pedagogy* discovered by Freud—consists in showing the ways in which, however irreducible, *ignorance itself can teach us something*—become itself *instructive.* This is, indeed, the crucial lesson that Lacan has learnt from Freud:

> It is necessary, says Freud, to interpret the phenomenon of doubt as an integral part of the message. [S-II, 155]

> The forgetting of the dream is . . . itself part of the dream. [S-II, 154]

> The message is not forgotten in any manner. . . . A censorship is an intention. Freud's argumentation properly reverses the burden of the proof—"In these elements that you cite in objection to me, the memory lapses and the various degradations of the dream, I continue to see a meaning, and even an additional meaning. When the phenomenon of forgetting intervenes, it interests me all the more . . . *These negative phenomena. I add them to the interpretation of the meaning. I recognize that they too have the function of a message.* Freud discovers this dimension. . . . What interests Freud . . . [is] *the message as an interrupted discourse,* and which insists. [S-II, 153]

The pedagogical question crucial to Lacan's own teaching will thus be: *Where does it resist?* Where does a text (or a signifier in a patient's conduct) precisely make no sense, that is, *resist interpretation?* Where does what I see—and what I read—resist my understanding? Where is the *ignorance*—the resistance to knowledge—located? And what can I thus *learn* from the locus of that ignorance? How can I interpret *out of* the dynamic ignorance I analytically encounter, both in others and in myself? How can I turn ignorance into an instrument of teaching?

> . . . Teaching—says Lacan—is something rather problematic. . . . As an American poet has pointed out, no one has ever seen a professor who has fallen short of the task because of ignorance . . .
>
> One always knows enough in order to occupy the minutes during which one exposes oneself in the position of the one who knows. . . .
>
> This makes me think that there is no true teaching other than the teaching which succeeds in provoking in those who listen an insistence—this desire to know which can only emerge when they themselves have *taken the measure of ignorance as such*—of ignorance inasmuch as it is, as such, fertile—in the one who teaches as well. [S-II, 242]

THE USE OF THAT WHICH CANNOT BE EXCHANGED

Teaching, thus, is not the transmission of ready-made knowledge, it is rather the creation of a new *condition* of knowledge—the creation of an original learning-disposition. "What I teach you," says Lacan, "does nothing other than express the *condition* thanks to which what Freud says is possible" (S-II, 368). The lesson, then, does not "teach" Freud: it teaches the "condition" which makes it *possible to learn* Freud—the condition which makes possible Freud's teaching. What is this condition?

In analysis, what sets in motion the psychoanalytical apprenticeship is the peculiar pedagogical structure of the analytic situation. The analysand speaks to the analyst, whom he en-

dows with the authority of the one who possesses knowledge—knowledge of what is precisely lacking in the analysand's own knowledge. The analyst, however, knows nothing of the sort. His only competence, insists Lacan, lies in "what I would call *textual knowledge,* so as to oppose it to the referential notion which only masks it" (*Scilicet* I, 21). Textual knowledge—the very stuff the literature teacher is supposed to deal in—is knowledge of the functioning of language, of symbolic structures, of the signifier, knowledge at once derived from—and directed towards—interpretation.

But such knowledge cannot be acquired (or possessed) once and for all: each case, each text, has its own specific, singular symbolic functioning, and requires thus a different—an original—interpretation. The analysts, says Lacan, are "those who share this knowledge only at the price, on the condition of their *not being able to exchange it*" (*Scilicet* I, 59). Analytic (textual) knowledge cannot be *exchanged,* it has to be *used*—and used in each case differently, according to the singularity of the case, according to the specificity of the text. Textual (or analytic) knowledge is, in other words, that peculiarly specific knowledge which, unlike any commodity, is subsumed by its *use* value, having no exchange value whatsoever.[15] Analysis has thus no use for ready-made interpretations, for knowledge given in advance. Lacan insists on "the insistence with which Freud recommends to us to approach each new case as if we had never learnt anything from his first interpretations" (*Scilicet,* I, 20). "What the analyst must know," concludes Lacan, "is how to ignore what he knows."

DIALOGIC LEARNING, OR THE ANALYTICAL STRUCTURE OF INSIGHT

Each case is thus, for the analyst as well as for the patient, a new apprenticeship. "If it's true that our knowledge comes to the rescue of the patient's ignorance, it is not less true that, for our part, we, too, are plunged in ignorance"

(S-I, 78). While the analysand is obviously ignorant of his own unconscious, the analyst is doubly ignorant: pedagogically ignorant of his suspended (given) knowledge; actually ignorant of the very knowledge the analysand presumes him to possess of his own (the analysand's) unconscious: knowledge of the very knowledge he—the patient—lacks. In what way does knowledge, then, emerge in and from the analytic situation?

Through the analytic dialogue the analyst, indeed, has first to learn where to situate the ignorance: where his own textual knowledge is *resisted.* It is, however, out of this resistance, out of the patient's active ignorance, out of the patient's speech which says much more than it itself knows, that the analyst will come to *learn* the *patient's own* unconscious *knowledge,* that knowledge which is inaccessible to itself because it cannot tolerate knowing that it knows; and it is the signifiers of this constitutively a-reflexive knowledge coming from the patient that the analyst *returns* to the patient from his different vantage point, from his non-reflexive, asymmetrical position as an Other. Contrary to the traditional pedagogical dynamic, in which the teacher's question is addressed to an answer from the other—from the student—which is totally reflexive, and expected, "the true Other" says Lacan, "is the Other who gives the answer one does not expect" (S-II, 288). Coming from the Other, knowledge is, by definition, that which comes as a surprise, that which is constitutively the return of a difference:

TEIRESIAS: . . . You are the land's pollution.
OEDIPUS: How shamelessly you started up this taunt! How do you think you will escape?
TEIRESIAS: . . . I have escaped; the truth is what I cherish and that's my strength.
OEDIPUS: And *who has taught you* truth? Not your profession surely!
TEIRESIAS: *You have taught me,* for you have made me speak against my will.

OEDIPUS: Speak what? Tell me again that I may *learn* it better.
TEIRESIAS: Did you not understand before or would you provoke me into speaking?
OEDIPUS: *I did not grasp it, not so to call it known.* Say it again.
TEIRESIAS: I say you are the murderer of the king whose murderer you seek.[16]

As Teiresias—so as to be able to articulate the truth—must have been "*taught*" not by "his profession" but *by Oedipus,* so the analyst precisely must be *taught* by the analysand's unconscious. It is by structurally occupying the position of the analysand's unconscious, and by thus making himself a *student of the patient's knowledge,* that the analyst becomes the patient's teacher—makes the patient learn what would otherwise remain forever inaccessible to him.

For teaching to be realized, for knowledge to be learnt, the position of alterity is therefore indispensable: knowledge is what is already there, but always in the Other. Knowledge, in other words, is not a *substance* but a structural dynamic: it is not *contained* by any individual but comes about out of the mutual apprenticeship between two partially unconscious speeches which both say more than they know. Dialogue is thus the radical condition of learning and of knowledge, the analytically constitutive condition through which ignorance becomes structurally informative; knowledge is essentially, irreducibly dialogic. "No knowledge," writes Lacan, "can be supported or transported by one alone" [*Scilicet* I, 59].

Like the analyst, the teacher, in Lacan's eyes, cannot in turn be, alone, a *master* of the knowledge which he teaches. Lacan transposes the radicality of analytic dialogue—as a newly understood structure of insight—into the pedagogical situation. This is not simply to say that he encourages "exchange" and calls for students' interventions—as many other teachers do.

Much more profoundly and radically, he attempts to *learn from the students his own knowledge*. It is the following original pedagogical appeal that he can thus address to the audience of his seminar:

> It seems to me I should quite naturally be the point of convergence of the questions that may occur to you.

> Let everybody tell me, in his own way, *his idea of what I am driving at*. How, for him, is opened up—or closed—or how already he resists, the question as I pose it. [S-II, 242]

THE SUBJECT PRESUMED TO KNOW

This pedagogical approach, which makes no claim to total knowledge, which does not even claim to be in possession of its own knowledge, is, of course, quite different from the usual pedagogical pose of mastery, different from the image of the self-sufficient, self-possessed proprietor of knowledge, in which pedagogy has traditionally featured the authoritative figure of the teacher. This figure of infallible human authority implicitly likened to a God, that is, both modeled on and guaranteed by divine *omniscience,* is based on an illusion: the illusion of a consciousness transparent to itself. "It is the case of the unconscious," writes Lacan, "that it abolishes the postulate of the subject presumed to know" (*Scilicet* I, 46).

Abolishing a postulate, however, doesn't mean abolishing an illusion: while psychoanalysis uncovers the mirage inherent in the function of the subject presumed to know, it also shows the prestige and the affective charge of that mirage to be constitutively irreducible, to be indeed most crucial to, determinant of, the emotional dynamic of all discursive human interactions, of all human relationships founded on sustained interlocution. The psychoanalytical account of the functioning of this dynamic is the most directly palpable, the most explicit lesson psychoanalysis has taught us about teaching.

In a brief and peculiarly introspective essay called "Some Reflections on Schoolboy Psychology," the already aging Freud nostalgically probes into his own "schoolboy psychology," the affect of which even time and intellectual achievements have not entirely extinguished. "As little as ten years ago," writes Freud, "you may have had moments at which you suddenly felt quite young again":

> As you walked through the streets of Vienna—already a grey-beard and weighed down by all the cares of family life—you might come unexpectedly on some well-preserved, elderly gentleman, and would greet him humbly almost, because you had recognized him as one of your former schoolmasters. But afterwards, you would stop and reflect: "Was that really he? or only someone deceptively like him? How youthful he looks! And how old you yourself have grown! . . . *Can it be possible that the men who used to stand for us as types of adulthood were so little older than we were?*" [Standard, XIII, 241]

Commenting on "my emotion at meeting my old schoolmaster," Freud goes on to give an analytical account of the emotional dynamic of the pedagogical situation:

> It is hard to decide whether what affected us more . . . was our concern with the sciences that we were taught or with . . . our teachers . . . In many of us *the path to the sciences led only through our teachers. . . .*

> We courted them and turned our backs on them, we imagined sympathies and antipathies which probably had no existence . . .

> . . . *psychoanalysis has taught us* that the individual's emotional attitudes to other people . . . are . . . established at an unexpectedly early age. . . . The people to whom [the

child] is in this way fixed are his parents. . . . His later acquaintances are . . . obliged to *take over a kind of emotional heritage,* they encounter sympathies and antipathies to the production of which they themselves have contributed little . . .

These men [the teachers] became our *substitute fathers.* That was why, even though they were still quite young, *they struck us as so mature and so unattainably adult.* We transferred to them *the respect and expectations attaching to the omniscient father of our childhood,* and then we began to treat them as we treated our own fathers at home. We confronted them with the *ambivalence* that we had acquired in our own families and with its help we struggled with them as we had been in the habit of struggling with our fathers . . . [Standard, XI, 242–44]

This phenomenon of the compulsive unconscious reproduction of an archaic emotional pattern, which Freud called "transference" and which he saw both as the energetic spring and as the interpretive key to the psychoanalytic situation, further thought out by Lacan as what accounts for the functioning of authority in general: as essential, thus, not just to any pedagogic situation but to the problematics of knowledge as such. "As soon as there is somewhere a subject presumed to know, there is transference," writes Lacan (S-XI, 210).

Since "transference is the acting out of the reality of the unconscious" (S-XI, 150, 240, N 174, 267), teaching is not a purely cognitive, informative experience, it is also an emotional, erotical experience. "I deemed it necessary," insists Lacan, "to support the idea of transference, as indistinguishable from love, with the formula of the subject presumed to know. I cannot fail to underline the new resonance with which this notion of knowledge is endowed. The person in whom I presume knowledge to exist, thereby acquires my love" (S-XX, 64). "The question of love is thus linked to the question of knowl-

edge" (S-XX, 84). "Transference *is* love . . . I insist: it is love directed toward, addressed to, knowledge" (*Scilicet* V, 16).

"Of this subject presumed to know, who," asks Lacan, "can believe himself to be entirely invested?—That is not the question. The question, first and foremost, for each subject, is how to situate *the place from which he himself addresses* the subject presumed to know?" (S-XX, 211). Insofar as knowledge is itself *a structure of address,* cognition is always both motivated and obscured by love; theory, both guided and misguided by an implicit transferential structure.

ANALYTIC PEDAGOGY, OR DIDACTIC PSYCHOANALYSIS: THE INTERMINABLE TASK

In human relationships, sympathies and antipathies usually provoke—and call for—a similar emotional response in the person they are addressed to. Transference on "the subject presumed to know"—the analyst or the teacher—may provoke a counter-transference on the latter's part. The analytic or the pedagogical situation may thus degenerate into an imaginary mirror-game of love and hate, where each of the participants would unconsciously enact past conflicts and emotions, unwarranted by the current situation and disruptive with respect to the real issues, unsettling the topical stakes of analysis or education.

In order to avoid this typical degeneration, Freud conceived of the necessity of a preliminary psychoanalytic training of "the subjects presumed to know," a practical didactic training through their own analysis which, giving them insight into their own transferential structure, would later help them understand the students' or the patients' transferential mechanisms and, more importantly, keep under control their own—avoid being entrapped in counter-transference. "The only appropriate preparation for the profession of educator," suggests Freud, "is a thorough psycho-analytic training . . . The analysis of teachers and educators seems to be a more efficacious prophylactic measure than the analysis of children themselves" (Standard, XXII, 150).

While this preliminary training (which has come to be known as "didactic psychoanalysis") is, however, only a recommendation on Freud's part as far as teachers are concerned, it is an absolute requirement and precondition for the habilitation—and qualification—of the psychoanalyst. In his last and therefore, in a sense, testamentary essay, "Analysis Terminable and Interminable," Freud writes:

Among the factors which influence the prospects of analytic treatment and add to its difficulties in the same manner as the resistances, must be reckoned not only the nature of the patient's ego but the individuality of the analyst.

It cannot be disputed that *analysts . . . have not invariably come up to the standard* of psychical normality *to which they wish to educate their patients.* Opponents of analysis often point to this fact with scorn and use it as an argument to show the uselessness of analytic exertions. We might reject this criticism as making unjustifiable demands. *Analysts are people who have learnt to practice a particular art;* alongside of this, they may be allowed to be *human beings like anyone else.* After all, nobody maintains that a physician is incapable of treating internal diseases if his own internal organs are not sound; on the contrary, it may be argued that there are certain advantages in a man who is himself threatened with tuberculosis specializing in the treatment of persons suffering from that disease. . . .

It is reasonable, [however,] . . . to expect of an analyst, as part of his qualifications, a considerable degree of mental normality and correctness. In addition, he must possess some kind of superiority, so that in certain analytic situations he can *act as a model for his patient*

and in others *as a teacher.* And finally, we must not forget that the analytic relationship is based on a love of truth—that is, on a recognition of reality—and that it precludes any kind of sham or deceit. . . .

It almost looks as if analysis were the third of those 'impossible' professions . . . *Where is the poor wretch to acquire the ideal qualifications* which he will need in his profession? *The answer is, in an analysis of himself,* with which his preparation for his future activity begins. For practical reasons this analysis can only be short and incomplete. . . . It has accomplished its purpose if it gives *the learner* a firm conviction of the existence of the unconscious, if it enables him . . . to perceive in himself things which would otherwise be incredible to him, and if it shows him a first example of the technique . . . in analytic work. *This alone would not suffice for his instruction; but we reckon on the stimuli he has received in his own analysis not ceasing when it ends* and *on the process of remodelling the ego continuing* spontaneously in the analysed subject and making use of all subsequent experiences in this newly-acquired sense. This does in fact happen, and *in so far as it happens, it makes the analysed subject qualified to be an analyst.* [Standard, XXIII, 247–49]

Nowhere else does Freud describe as keenly *the revolutionary radicality of the very nature of the teaching* to be (practically and theoretically) derived from the originality of the psychoanalytical experience. The analysand is qualified to be an analyst as of the point at which he understands his own analysis to be inherently unfinished, incomplete, as of the point, that is, at which he settles into his own didactic analysis—or his own analytical apprenticeship—as fundamentally interminable. It is, in other words, as of the moment the student recognizes that *learning has no term,* that he can himself become a teacher, assume the position of the teacher. But the position of the teacher is itself the position of *the one who learns,* of the one who *teaches* nothing other than *the way he learns.* The subject of teaching is interminably—a student; the subject of teaching is interminably—a learning. This is the most radical, perhaps the most far-reaching insight psychoanalysis can give us into pedagogy.

Freud pushes this original understanding of what pedagogy is to its logical limit. Speaking of the "defensive" tendency of psychoanalysts "to divert the implications and demands of analysis from themselves (probably by directing them on to other people)"—of the analysts' tendency, that is, "to *withdraw from the critical and corrective influence of analysis,*" as well as of the temptation of power threatening them in the very exercise of their profession, Freud enjoins:

> Every analyst should periodically—at intervals of five years or so—submit himself to analysis once more, without feeling ashamed of taking this step. This would mean, then, that not only the therapeutic analysis of patients[17] but *his own analysis would change from a terminable into an interminable task.* [Standard, XXIII, 249]

Of all Freud's followers, Lacan alone has picked up on the radicality of Freud's pedagogical concern with didactic psychoanalysis, not just as a subsidiary technical, pragmatic question (how should analysts be trained?), but as a major theoretical concern, as a major pedagogical investigation crucial to the very innovation, to the very revolutionary core of psychoanalytic insight. The highly peculiar and surprising style of Lacan's own teaching-practice is, indeed, an answer to, a follow-up on, Freud's ultimate suggestion—in Lacan's words—"to make psychoanalysis and education (training) collapse into each other" (E 459).

This is the thrust of Lacan's original endeavor both as psychoanalyst and as teacher: "in the field of psychoanalysis," he writes, "what is necessary is the restoration of the identical status of didactic psychoanalysis and of the teaching of psychoanalysis, in their common scientific opening" (E 236).

As a result of this conception, Lacan considers not just the practical analyses which he—as analyst—directs, but his own public teaching, his own seminar—primarily directed towards the (psychoanalytical) training of analysts—as partaking of didactic psychoanalysis, as itself, thus, analytically didactic and didactically analytical, in a new and radical way.

"How can what psychoanalysis teaches us be taught?" (E 439)—Only by continuing, in one's own teaching, one's own interminable didactic analysis. Lacan has willingly transformed himself into the *analysand* of his Seminar[18] so as to teach, precisely, psychoanalysis *as* teaching, and teaching *as* psychoanalysis.

Psychoanalysis as teaching, and teaching as psychoanalysis, radically subvert the demarcation-line, the clear-cut opposition between the analyst and the analysand, between the teacher and the student (or the learner)—showing that what counts, in both cases, is precisely the transition, the struggle-filled *passage* from one position to the other. But the passage is itself interminable; it can never be crossed once and for all: "The psychoanalytic act has but to falter slightly, and it is the analyst who becomes the analysand" (*Scilicet* I, 47). Lacan denounces, thus, "the reactionary principle" of the professional belief in "the duality of the one who suffers and the one who cures," in "the opposition between the one who knows and the one who does not know. . . . The most corrupting of comforts is intellectual comfort, just as one's *worst* corruption is the belief that one is *better*" (E 403).

Lacan's well-known polemical and controversial stance—his *critique of psychoanalysis*—itself partakes, then, of his understanding of the pedagogical imperative of didactic psychoanalysis. Lacan's original endeavor is to submit *the whole discipline of psychoanalysis* to what Freud called "the critical and corrective influence of analysis"

(Standard, XXIII, 249). Lacan, in other words, is the first to understand that the psychoanalytic discipline is an unprecedented one in that its *teaching* does not just reflect upon itself, but turns back upon itself so as to *subvert itself,* and truly *teaches* only insofar as it subverts itself. Psychoanalytic teaching is pedagogically unique in that it is inherently, interminably, self-critical. Lacan's amazing pedagogical performance thus sets forth the unparalleled example of a teaching whose fecundity is tied up, paradoxically enough, with the inexhaustibility—the interminability—of its *self-critical potential.*

From didactic analysis, Lacan derives, indeed, a whole new theoretical (didactic) mode of *self-subversive self-reflection.*

> A question suddenly arises . . . : in the case of the knowledge yielded solely to the subject's mistake, what kind of subject could ever be in a position to know it in advance? [*Scilicet* I, 38]

> Retain at least what this text, which I have tossed out in your direction, bears witness to: my enterprise does not go beyond the act in which it is caught, and, therefore, its only chance lies in its being mistaken. [*Scilicet* I, 41]

> This lesson seems to be one that should not have been forgotten, had not psychoanalysis precisely taught us that it is, as such, forgettable. [E 232]

Always submitting analysis itself to the instruction of an unexpected analytic turn of the screw, to the surprise of an additional reflexive turn, of an additional self-subversive ironic twist, didactic analysis becomes for Lacan what might be called a *style*: a teaching style which has become at once a life-style and a writing style: "the ironic style of calling into question the very foundations of the discipline" (E 238).

Any return to Freud founding a teaching worthy of the name will occur only on that pathway where truth . . . becomes manifest in the revolutions of culture. That pathway is the only training we can claim to transmit to those who follow us. It is called—a style. [E 458]

Didactic analysis is thus invested by Lacan not simply with the practical, pragmatic value, but with the theoretical significance—the allegorical instruction—of a paradigm: a paradigm, precisely, of the interminability, not just of teaching (learning) and of analyzing (being analyzed), but of the very act of thinking, theorizing: of teaching, analyzing, thinking, theorizing, in such a way as to make of psychoanalysis "what it has never ceased to be: an act that is yet to come" (*Scilicet* I, 9).

TEACHING AS A LITERARY GENRE

Among so many other things, Lacan and Freud thus teach us teaching, teach us—in a radically new way—what it might mean to teach. Their lesson, and their pedagogical performance, profoundly renew at once the meaning and the status of the very act of teaching.

If they are both such extraordinary teachers, it is—I would suggest—because they both are, above all, quite extraordinary learners. In Freud's case, I would argue, the extraordinary teaching stems from Freud's original—unique—position as a student; in Lacan's case, the extraordinary teaching stems from Lacan's original—unique—position as disciple.

"One might feel tempted," writes Freud, "to agree with the philosophers and the psychiatrists and like them, rule out the problem of dream-interpretation as a purely fanciful task. *But I have been taught better*" (Standard, IV, 100).

By whom has Freud been taught—taught better than by "the judgement of the prevalent science of today," better than by the established scholarly authorities of philosophy and psychiatry? Freud has been taught *by dreams* themselves: his own, and those of others; Freud has been taught by his own patients: "*My patients . . . told me their dreams and so taught me . . .*—" (Standard, VI, 100–101).

Having thus been taught by dreams, as well as by his patients, that—contrary to the established scholarly opinion—dreams do have meaning, Freud is further taught by a literary text:

> This discovery is confirmed by a legend that has come down to us from antiquity. . . .
>
> While the poet . . . brings to light the guilt of Oedipus, he is at the same time compelling us to recognize our own inner minds . . .
>
> Like Oedipus, we live in ignorance of these wishes . . . and after their revelation, we may all of us well seek to close our eyes to the scenes of our childhood. [Standard, VI, 261–263]

"But I have been taught better." What is unique about Freud's position as a student—as a learner—is that he learns from, or puts in the position of his teacher, the least authoritative sources of information that can be imagined: that he knows how to derive a teaching, or a lesson, from the very unreliability—the very *non-authority*—of literature, of dreams, of patients. For the first time in the history of learning, Freud, in other words, has recourse—scientific recourse—to a knowledge which is not authoritative, which is not that of a master, a knowledge which does not know what it knows, and is thus *not in possession of itself.*

Such, precisely, is the very essence of literary knowledge. "I went to the poets," says Socrates; ". . . I took them some of the most elaborate passages in their own writings, and asked them what was the meaning of them—thinking that they would teach me something. Will you believe me? I am almost ashamed to confess the truth, but I must say that there is hardly a person present who would not have talked better about their poetry than they did themselves. Then I knew that *not by wisdom do poets write poetry, but by a sort of genius or inspiration;* they

are like diviners or soothsayers who also *say many fine things, but do not understand the meaning of them*. The poets appeared to me to be much in the same case."[19] From a philosophical perspective, knowledge is mastery—that which is in mastery of its own meaning. Unlike Hegelian philosophy, which *believes it knows all that there is to know;* unlike Socratic (or contemporary post-Nietzschean) philosophy, which *believes it knows it does not know*—literature, for its part, *knows it knows, but does not know the meaning of its knowledge*—does not know *what* it knows.

For the first time then, Freud gives authority to the instruction—to the teaching—of a knowledge which does not know its own meaning, to a knowledge (that of dreams, of patients, of Greek tragedy) which we might define as literary: knowledge that is not in mastery of itself.

Of all Freud's students and disciples, Lacan alone has understood and emphasized the *radical* significance of Freud's indebtedness to literature: the role played by *literary knowledge* not just in the historical constitution of psychoanalysis, but in the very actuality of the psychoanalytic act, of the psychoanalytic (ongoing) *work* of learning and of teaching. Lacan alone has understood and pointed out the ways in which Freud's teaching—in all senses of the word—is not accidentally, but radically and fundamentally, a *literary* teaching. Speaking of "the training of the analysts of the future," Lacan thus writes:

> One has only to turn the pages of his works for it to become abundantly clear that Freud regarded a study . . . of the resonances . . . of literature and of the significations involved in works of art as necessary to an understanding of the text of our experience. Indeed, Freud himself is a striking instance of his own belief: he derived his inspiration, his ways of thinking and his technical weapons, from just such a study. But he also regarded it as a necessary condition in any teaching of psychoanalysis. [E 435, N 144]

This [new] technique [of interpretation] would require for its teaching as well as for its learning a profound assimilation of the resources of a language, and especially of those that are concretely realized in its poetic texts. It is well known that Freud was in this position in relation to German literature, which, by virtue of an incomparable translation, can be said to include Shakespeare's plays. Every one of his works bears witness to this, and to the continual recourse he had to it, no less in his technique than in his discovery. [E 295, N 83]

The psychoanalytic experience has rediscovered in man the imperative of the Word as the law that has formed him in its image. It manipulates the poetic function of language to give to his desire its symbolic mediation. [E 322, N 106]

Freud had, eminently, this feel for meaning, which accounts for the fact that any of his works, *The Three Caskets,* for instance, gives the reader the impression that it is written by a soothsayer, that it is guided by that kind of meaning which is of the order of poetic inspiration. [S-II, 353]

It is in this sense, among others, that Lacan can be regarded as Freud's best student: Lacan is the sole Freudian who has sought to learn from Freud how to learn Freud: Lacan is "taught" by Freud in much the same way Freud is "taught" by dreams; Lacan reads Freud in much the same way Freud reads *Oedipus the King,* specifically seeking in the text its *literary knowledge*. From Freud as teacher, suggests Lacan, we should learn to derive that kind of *literary teaching* he himself derived in an unprecedented way from literary texts. Freud's text should thus itself be read as a poetic text:

. . . the notion of the death instinct involves a basic irony, since its meaning has to be sought in the conjunction of two contrary terms: instinct . . . being the law that governs . . . a cycle of behavior whose goal is the accomplishment of a vital function; and death appearing first of all as the destruction of life . . . .

This notion must be approached through its resonances in what I shall call *the poetics of the Freudian corpus,* the first way of access to the penetration of its meaning, and the essential dimension, from the origins of the work to the apogee marked in it by this notion, for an understanding of its dialectical repercussions. [E 316–17, N 101–02]

It is here, in conjunction with Lacan's way of relating to Freud's literary teaching and of learning from Freud's literary knowledge, that we touch upon the historical uniqueness of Lacan's position as disciple, and can thus attempt to understand the way in which this pedagogically unique discipleship accounts for Lacan's astounding originality as a teacher.

"As Plato pointed out long ago," says Lacan, "it is not at all necessary that the poet know what he is doing, in fact, it is preferable that he not know. That is what gives a primordial value to what he does. We can only bow our heads before it" (Seminar, April 9, 1974, unpublished). Although apparently Lacan seems to espouse Plato's position, his real pedagogical stance is, in more than one way, at the antipodes of that of Plato; and not just because he bows his head to poets, whereas Plato casts them out of the Republic. If Freud himself, indeed, bears witness, in h text, to some poetic—literary—knowledge, it is to the extent that, like the poets, he, too, cannot exhaust the meaning of his text—he too partakes of the poetic ignorance of his own knowledge. Unlike Plato who, from his position as an admiring disciple, reports Socrates' assertion of his ignorance without—it might be assumed—really believing in the *nonironic truth* of that assertion ("For the hearers," says Socrates, "always imagine that I myself possess the wisdom I find wanting in others"[20]), Lacan can be said to be the first disciple in the whole history of pedagogy and of culture who *does indeed believe in the ignorance of his teacher—of his master.* Paradoxically enough, this is why he can be said to be, precisely, Freud's best student: a student of Freud's own revolutionary way of learning, of Freud's own unique position as the unprecedented student of unauthorized, unmastered knowledge. "The truth of the subject," says Lacan, "even when he is the position of a master, is not in himself" (S-XI, 10).

[Freud's] texts, to which for the past . . . years I have devoted a two-hour seminar every Wednesday . . . without having covered a quarter of the total, . . . , have given me, and those who have attended my seminars, the surprise of genuine discoveries. These discoveries, which range from concepts that have remained unused to clinical details uncovered by our exploration, demonstrate *how far the field investigated by Freud extended beyond the avenues that he left us to tend,* and how little his observation, which sometimes gives an impression of exhaustiveness, was the slave of what he had to demonstrate. Who . . . has not been moved by this research in action, whether in 'The Interpretation of Dreams,' 'The Wolf Man,' or 'Beyond the Pleasure Principle?' [E 404, N 117, TM]

Commenting on *The Interpretation of Dreams,* Lacan situates in Freud's text the discoverer's own transferential structure—Freud's own unconscious structure of address:

What polarizes at the moment Freud's discourse; what organizes the whole of Freud's existence, is the conversation with Fliess. . . . It is in this dialogue that Freud's self-analysis is realized. . . . This vast speech addressed to Fliess will later become the whole written work of Freud.

The conversation of Freud with Fliess, this fundamental discourse, which at that moment is unconscious, is the essential dynamic element [of *The Interpretation of Dreams*]. Why is it unconscious at that moment? Because its significance goes far beyond what both of them, as individuals, can consciously apprehend or understand of it at the moment. As individuals, they are nothing other, after all, than two little erudites who are in the process of exchanging rather weird ideas.

The discovery of the unconscious, in the full dimension with which it is revealed at the very moment of its historical emergence, is that the scope, the implications of meaning go far beyond the signs manipulated by the individual. As far as signs are concerned, man is always mobilizing many more of them than he knows. [S-II, 150]

It is to the extent that Lacan precisely teaches us to read in Freud's text (in its textual excess) the signifiers of Freud's ignorance—his ignorance of his own knowedge—that Lacan can be considered Freud's best reader, as well as the most compelling teacher of the Freudian pedagogical imperative: the imperative to learn from and through the insight which does not know its own meaning, from and through the knowledge which is not entirely in mastery—in possession—of itself.

This unprecedented *literary* lesson, which Lacan derives from Freud's revolutionary way of learning and in the light of which he learns Freud, is transformed, in Lacan's own work, into a deliberately literary style of teaching. While—as a subject of praise or controversy—the originality of Lacan's eminently literary, eminently "poetic" style has become a stylistic *cause célèbre* often commented upon, what has not been understood is the extent to which this style—this poetic theory or theoretical poetry—is *pedagogically* poetic: poetic in such a way as to raise, through every answer that it gives, the literary question of its non-mastery of itself. In pushing its own thought beyond the limit of its self-possession, beyond the limitations of its own capacity for mastery, in passing on understanding which does not fully understand what it understands; in *teaching,* thus, *with blindness*—with and through the very blindness of its literary knowledge, of insights not entirely transparent to themselves—Lacan's unprecedented theoretically *poetic pedagogy* always implicitly opens up onto the infinitely literary, infinitely *teaching* question: What is the "navel"[21] of my own theoretical dream of understanding? What is the specificity of my incomprehension? What is the riddle which I in effect here pose under the guise of knowledge?

"But what was it that Zarathustra once said to you? That poets lie too much? But Zarathustra too is a poet. Do you believe that in saying this he spoke the truth? Why do you believe that?"

The disciple answered, "I believe in Zarathustra."[22] But Zarathustra shook his head and smiled.

Any return to Freud founding a teaching worthy of the name will occur only on that pathway where truth . . . becomes manifest in the revolutions of culture. That pathway is the only training we can claim to transmit to those who follow us. It is called—a style. [E 458][23]

NOTES

1. Plato, *Meno,* 70a, 71a, 82a. Translated by G.M.A. Grube (Indianapolis: Hackett Publishing Company, 1980), pp. 3, 14 (translation modified).

2. *The Complete Psychological Works of Sigmund Freud,* translated from the German under the general editorship of James Strachey (London: The Hogarth Press and the Institute of Psychoanalysis). volume XIX, p. 273. Hereafter, this edition will be referred to as "Standard," followed by volume number (in roman numerals) and page number (in arabic numerals).

3. Jacques Lacan. *Écrits* (Paris: Seuil, 1966), p. 233, my translation. Henceforth I will be using the abbreviations: "E" (followed by page number)—for this original French edition of the *Écrits,* and "N" (followed by page number) for the corresponding Norton edition of the English translation (*Écrits: A Selection.* translated by Alan Sheridan, New York: Norton, 1977). When the reference to the French edition of the *Écrits* (E) is not followed by a reference to the Norton English edition (N), the passage quoted (as in this case) is in my translation and has not been included in the "Selection" of the Norton edition.

4. Which for Lacan involves "the relationship of the individual to language": E445.

5. Italics mine. As a rule, in the quoted passages, italics are mine unless otherwise indicated.

6. Anna Freud, *Psychoanalysis for Teachers and Parents.* translated by Barbara Low (Boston: Beacon Press, 1960), pp. 95–6.

7. Ibid., p. 105.

8. Catherine Millot, interview in *l'Ane, le magasine freudien,* No. 1, April–May 1981, p. 19.

9. Catherine Millot, *Freud Anti-Pedagogue* (Paris: Bibliothèque d'Ornicar, 1979).

10. Plato, *Meno,* 96 d, op. cit., p. 28 (translation modified).

11. Ibid., 82 e, p. 15.

12. The abbreviation "TM"—"translation modified"—will signal my alterations of the official English translation of the work in question.

13. The abbreviation S-XI (followed by page number) refers to Jacques Lacan, *Le Séminaire, livre XI, Les Quatre concepts fondamentaux de la psychoanalyse* (Paris: Seuil, 1973). The following abbreviation "N" (followed by page number) refers to the corresponding English edition: *The Four Fundamental Concepts of Psychoanalysis,* edited by Jacques-Alain Miller, translated by Alan Sheridan (New York: Norton, 1978).

As for the rest of Lacan's Seminars which have appeared in book form, the following abbreviations will be used:

S-I (followed by page number), for. J. Lacan, *Le Séminaire, livre I: Les Écrits techniques de Freud* (Paris: Seuil, 1975);

S-II (followed by page number), for. J. Lacan, *Le Séminaire, livre II: le Moi dans la théorie de Freud et dans la techniquè de la psychoanalyse* (Paris: Seuil, 1978);

S-XX (followed by page number), for. J. Lacan, *Le Séminaire, livre XX: Encore* (Paris: Seuil, 1975).

All quoted passages from these (as yet untranslated) Seminars are here in my translation.

14. Abbreviated for Lacan's texts published in *Scilicet: Tu peux savoir ce qu'en pensé l'école freudienne de Paris* (Paris: Seuil). The roman numeral stands for the issue number (followed by page number). Number 1 appeared in 1968.

15. As soon as analytic knowledge *is* exchanged, it ceases to be knowledge and becomes opinion, prejudice, presumption: "the sum of prejudices that every knowledge contains, and that each of us transports. . . . Knowledge is always, somewhere, only one's belief that one knows" (S-II, 56).

16. Sophocles, *Oedipus the King,* translated by David Grene, in *Sophocles I* (Chicago & London: The University of Chicago Press, 1954), pp. 25–6.

17. The therapeutic analysis of patients is "interminable" to the extent that repression can never be totally lifted, only displaced. Cf. Freud's letter to Fliess, dated April 16, 1900. "E's career as a patient has at last come to an end. . . . His riddle is *almost* completely solved, his condition is excellent. . . . At that moment a residue of his symptoms remains. I am beginning to understand that the apparently interminable nature of the treatment is something determined by law and is dependent on the transference." Hence, Freud speaks of "the asymptotic termination of treatment" (Standard, XXIII, 215) Freud's italics.

18. The occasional master's pose—however mystifying to the audience—invariably exhibits itself as a parodic symptom of the analysand.

19. Plato, *Apology,* 22 a–c, in *Dialogues of Plato.* Jowett translation, edited by J. D. Kaplan (New York: Washington Square Press, Pocket Books, 1973), p. 12.

20. Plato, *Apology,* 22 a–c, op. cit., p. 12.

21. "There is," writes Freud, "at least one spot in every dream at which it is unplumbable—a navel, as it were, that is its point of contact with the unknown" (Standard IV, III).

22. Nietzsche, *Thus Spoke Zarathustra,* translated by Walter Kaufmann, (T.M.) in *The Portable Nietzsche* (New York: The Viking Press, 1971), p. 239, "On Poets."

23. The present essay is a chapter from *Jacques Lacan and the Adventure of Insight: Psychoanalysis in Contemporary Culture* (Cambridge, Mass.: Harvard University Press, 1987).

The news of Lacan's death (on September 9, 1981) reached me as I was writing the section here entitled "The Interminable Task." The sadness caused by the cessation of a life as rich in insight and as generous in instruction, was thus accompanied by an ironic twist which itself felt like a typical Lacanian turn, one of the ironies of his teaching, teaching terminable and interminable. . . . Few deaths, indeed, have been as deeply inscribed as a lesson in a teaching, as Lacan's, who always taught the implications of the Master's death. "Were I to go away," he said some time ago, "tell yourselves that it is in order to at last be truly Other."

I have deliberately chosen not to change, and to pursue, the grammatical present tense which I was using to describe Lacan's teaching; since his life has ceased to be, his teaching is, indeed, all the more present, all the more alive, all the more interminably "what it has never ceased to be: an act that is yet to come."

25

Slavoj Žižek
1949–

Slavoj Žižek, widely recognized by American academics for his Lacanian psychoanalytic approach to cinema, is an eminent European intellectual and philosopher specializing in the works of Western philosophers such as Kant, Hegel, and Althusser and using their work to examine the changing political ideologies of contemporary social movements in Eastern and Central Europe. A senior researcher at the Institute for Social Sciences at the University of Ljubljana in Slovenia, Žižek was the pro-reform candidate in 1990 for the presidency of the Republic of Slovenia. In addition to editing works on Lacan, Žižek has published several books, such as *The Sublime Object of Ideology* (1989), *Enjoy Your Symptom! Jacques Lacan in Hollywood and Out* (1992), *Tarrying with the Negative: Kant, Hegel, and the Critique of Ideology* (1993), and *The Indivisible Remainder: An Essay on Schelling and Related Matters* (1996).

In "Two Ways to Avoid the Real of Desire," which appears as chapter 3 in *Looking Awry: An Introduction to Jacques Lacan Through Popular Culture*, Žižek illustrates Lacanian thoughts on subjectivity by comparing the analyst's role to that of the "classic" detective in the Conan Doyle novels. Žižek contends that analysts and detectives discover clues in much the same manner. An analyst working in the psychoanalytic process employs Freudian dream interpretation to explain that the signifier-signified relationship is literal. Rather than looking for the "hidden meaning" of "things," the analyst identifies the "ingredient that functions as a stopgap, as a filler holding the place of what is necessarily lacking in it." The detective must look at the "false image" presented by the murderer and expose the "small detail . . . that renders the whole picture strange and uncanny."

Analyst and detective are both placed in the position as the "subject supposed to know." However, Žižek notes that the analyst and the detective hold conflicting positions. The first "avoidance of the real of desire" is when the detective solves the murder by singling out the murderer from a group of suspects. This action employs only the "'external' reality" without considering the "domain of the 'inner' libininal economy." The detective "discharges us of all guilt for the realization of our desire," whereas the analyst "confronts us precisely with the price we have to pay for the access to our desire."

Within this chapter, he traces the shift from the "exteriority" of the "classic" detective as the "subject supposed to know" to the "involved" presence of the "hard-boiled" detective in the novels of Philip Marlowe and the film noir genre of cinema. The "hard-boiled" detective solves mysteries because he feels "he has a certain debt to honor." In this instance, the detective rather than the group of suspects "undergoes a loss of reality," and the "deceitful character of the universe" is the femme fatale who "does not cede her desire," thereby becoming the scapegoat and relieving the detective of guilt.

Žižek's popular culture examples not only clarify Lacan's often difficult and challenging language for the reader; they also convey the pleasure Žižek derives from testing the possibilities of psychoanalytic theory in the contemporary cultural studies arena.

Two Ways to Avoid the Real of Desire
The Sherlock Holmes Way

THE DETECTIVE AND THE ANALYST

there's been a change, study its form

The easiest way to detect changes in the so-called *Zeitgeist* is to pay careful attention to the moment when a certain artistic (literary, etc.) form becomes "impossible," as the traditional psychological-realist novel did in the 1920s. The '20s mark the final victory of the "modern" over the traditional "realist" novel. Afterward, it was, of course, actually still possible to write "realist" novels, but the norm was set by the modern novel, the traditional form was—to use the Hegelian term—already "mediated" by it. After this break, the common "literary taste" perceived newly written realist novels as ironic pastiches, as nostalgic attempts to recapture a lost unity, as outward inauthentic "regression," or simply as no longer pertaining to the domain of art. What is of interest here, however, is a fact that usually goes unnoticed: the breakdown of the traditional "realist" novel in the '20s coincides with the shift of accent from the detective *story* (Conan Doyle, Chesterton, etc.) to the detective *novel* (Christie, Sayers, etc.) in the domain of popular culture. The novel form is not yet possible with Conan Doyle, as is clear from his novels themselves: they are really just ex-

tended short stories with a long flashback written in the form of an adventure story (*The Valley of Fear*) or they incorporate elements of another genre, the Gothic novel (*The Hound of the Baskervilles*). In the '20s, however, the detective story quickly disappears as a genre and is replaced by the classic form of the "logic and deduction" detective novel. Is this coincidence between the final breakdown of the "realist" novel and the rise of the detective novel purely contingent, or is there significance in it? Do the modern novel and the detective novel have something in common, in spite of the gulf separating them?

The answer usually escapes us because of its very obviousness: both the modern novel and the detective novel are centered around the same formal problem—the *impossibility of telling a story in a linear, consistent way,* of rendering the "realistic" continuity of events. It is of course a commonplace to affirm that the modern novel replaces realistic narration with a diversity of new literary techniques (stream of consciousness, pseudodocumentary style, etc.) bearing witness to the impossibility of locating the individual's fate in a meaningful, "organic" historical totality; but on another level, the problem of the detective story is the same: the traumatic act (murder) cannot be located in the meaningful totality of a life story. There is a certain self-reflexive strain in the detective novel: it is a story of the detective's effort to tell the story, i.e., to reconstitute what "really happened" around and before the murder, and the novel is finished not when we get the answer to "Whodunit?" but when the detective is finally able to tell "the real story" in the form of a linear narrative.

An obvious reaction to this would be: yes, but the fact remains that the modern novel is a form of art, while the detective novel is sheer entertainment governed by firm conventions, principal among them the fact that we can be absolutely sure that at the end, the detective will succeed in explaining the entire mystery and in reconstructing "what really happened." It is, however, precisely this "infallibility" and "omniscience" of the detective that constitutes the stumbling block of the standard deprecatory theories of the detective novel: their aggressive dismissal of the detective's power betrays a perplexity, a fundamental incapacity to explain how it works and why it appears so "convincing" to the reader in spite of its indisputable "improbability." Attempts to explain it usually follow two opposing directions. On the one hand, the figure of the detective is interpreted as "bourgeois" scientific rationalism personified; on the other, he is conceived as successor to the romantic clairvoyant, the man possessing an irrational, quasisupernatural power to penetrate the mystery of another person's mind. The inadequacy of both these approaches is evident to any admirer of a good logic and deduction story. We are immensely disappointed if the denouement is brought about by a pure scientific procedure (if, for example, the assassin is identified simply by means of a chemical analysis of the stains on the corpse). We feel that "there is something missing here," that "this is not deduction proper." But it is even more disappointing if, at the end, after naming the assassin, the detective claims that "he was guided from the very beginning by some unmistakable instinct"—here we

are clearly deceived, the detective must arrive at the solution on the basis of *reasoning,* not by mere "intuition."[1]

Instead of striving for an immediate solution to this riddle, let us turn our attention to another subjective position that arouses the same perplexity, that of the analyst in the psychoanalytic process. Attempts to locate this position parallel those made in relation to the detective: on the one hand, the analyst is conceived as somebody who tries to reduce to their rational foundation phenomena that, at first sight, belong to the most obscure and irrational strata of the human psyche; on the other hand, he again appears as successor to the romantic clairvoyant, as a reader of dark signs, producing "hidden meanings" not susceptible to scientific verification. There is a whole series of circumstantial evidence pointing to the fact that this parallel is not without foundation: psychoanalysis and the logic and deduction story made their appearance in the same epoch (Europe at the turn of the century). The "Wolf Man," Freud's most famous patient, reports in his memoirs that Freud was a regular and careful reader of the Sherlock Holmes stories, not for distraction but precisely on account of the parallel between the respective procedures of the detective and the analyst. One of the Sherlock Holmes pastiches, Nicholas Meyer's *Seven Per-Cent Solution,* has as its theme an encounter between Freud and Sherlock Holmes, and it should be remembered that Lacan's *Écrits* begins with a detailed analysis of Edgar Allan Poe's "The Purloined Letter," one of the archetypes of the detective story, in which Lacan's accent is on the parallel between the subjective position of Auguste Dupin—Poe's amateur detective—and that of the analyst.

THE CLUE

The analogy between the detective and the analyst has been drawn often enough. There are a wide range of studies that set out to reveal the psychoanalytic undertones of the detective story: the primordial crime to be explained is parricide, the prototype of the detective is Oedipus, striving to attain the terrifying truth about himself. What we would prefer to do here, however, is to tackle the task on a different, "formal" level. Following Freud's casual remarks to the "Wolf Man," we will focus on the respective *formal procedures* of the detective and the psychoanalyst. What distinguishes, then, the psychoanalytic interpretation of the formations of the unconscious—of dreams, for example? The following passage from Freud's *Interpretation of Dreams* provides a preliminary answer:

The dream-thoughts are immediately comprehensible, as soon as we have learnt them. The dream-content, on the other hand, is expressed as it were in a pictographic script, the characters of which have to be transposed individually into the language of the dream-thoughts. If we attempted to read these characters according to their pictorial value instead of according to their symbolic relation, we should clearly be led into error. Suppose I have a picture-puzzle, a rebus, in front of me. It depicts a house with a boat on its roof, a single letter of the alphabet, the figure of a running man whose head has been conjured away, and so on. Now I might be misled into raising objections and declaring that the picture as a whole and its component parts are nonsensical. A boat has no business to be on the roof of a house, and a headless man cannot run. Moreover, the man is bigger than the house; and if the whole picture is intended to represent a landscape, letters of the alphabet are out of place in it since such objects do not occur in nature. But obviously we can only form a proper judgement of the rebus if we put aside criticisms such as these of the whole composition and its parts and if, instead, we try to replace each separate element by a syllable or word that can be presented by that element in some way or other. The words which are put together in this way are no longer nonsensical but may form a po-

etical phrase of the greatest beauty and significance. A dream is a picture-puzzle of this sort and our predecessors in the field of dream-interpretation have made the mistake of treating the rebus as a pictorial composition: and as such it has seemed to them nonsensical and worthless.[2]

Freud is quite clear when faced with a dream, we must absolutely avoid the search for the so-called "symbolic meaning" of its totality or of its constituent parts: we must *not* ask the question "what does the house mean? what is the meaning of the boat on the house? what could the figure of a running man symbolize?" What we must do is translate the objects back into words, replace things by words designating them. In a rebus, things literally *stand for their names,* for their signifiers. We can see, now, why it is absolutely misleading to characterize the passage from word presentations (*Wort-Vorstellungen*) to thing presentations (*Sach-Vorstellungen*)—so-called "considerations of representability" at work in a dream—as a kind of "regression" from language to prelanguage representations. In a dream, "things" themselves are already "structured like a language," their disposition is regulated by the signifying chain for which they stand. The signified of this signifying chain, obtained by means of a retranslation of "things" into "words," is the "dream-thought." On the level of meaning, this "dream-thought" is in no way connected in its content with objects depicted in the dream (as in the case of a rebus, whose solution is in no way connected with the meaning of the objects depicted in it). If we look for the "deeper, hidden meaning" of the figures appearing in a dream, we *blind* ourselves to the latent "dream-thought" articulated in it. The link between immediate "dream-contents" and the latent "dream-thought" exists only on the level of wordplay, i.e., of nonsensical signifying material. Remember Aristander's famous interpretation of the dream of Alexander of Macedon, reported by Artemidorus? Alexander "had surrounded Tyre and was besieging it but was feeling uneasy and disturbed because of the length of time the siege was taking. Alexander dreamt he saw a satyr dancing on his shield. Aristander happened to be in the neighborhood of Tyre. . . . By dividing the word for satyr into *sa* and *tyros* he encouraged the king to press home the siege so that he became master of the city." As we can see, Aristander was quite uninterested in the possible "symbolic meaning" of the figure of a dancing satyr (ardent desire? joviality?): instead, he focused on the *word* and divided it, thus obtaining the message of the dream: *sa Tyros* = Tyre is thine.

There is, however, a certain difference between a rebus and a dream, which makes a rebus much easier to interpret. In a way, a rebus is like a dream that has not undergone "secondary revision," whose purpose is to satisfy the "necessity for unification." For that reason, a rebus is immediately perceived as something "nonsensical," a bric-a-brac of unconnected, heterogeneous elements, while a dream conceals its absurdity through "secondary revision," which lends the dream at least a superficial unity and consistency. The image of a dancing satyr is thus perceived as an organic whole, there is nothing in it that would indicate that the sole reason for its existence is to lend an imaginary figuration to the signifying chain *sa Tyros*. Herein lies the role of the imaginary "totality of meaning," the final result of the "dream-work": to blind us—by means of the appearance of organic unity—to the effective reason for its existence.

The basic presupposition of psychoanalytic interpretation, its methodologic a priori, is, however, that every final product of the dream work, every manifest dream content, contains *at least one* ingredient that functions as a stopgap, as a filler holding the place of what is necessarily *lacking* in it. This is an element that at first sight fits perfectly into the organic whole of the manifest imaginary scene, but which effectively holds within it the place of what this imaginary scene must "repress," exclude, force out, in order to constitute itself. It is a kind of umbilical cord tying the imaginary structure to the "repressed" process of its structuration. In short, secondary revision never fully succeeds, not for empirical reasons, but on account of an a priori structural necessity. In the final analysis, an element always "sticks out," marking the dream's constitutive lack, i.e., representing within it its exterior. This element is caught in a paradoxical dialectic of simultaneous lack and surplus: but for it, the final result (the manifest dream text) would not hold together, something would be missing. Its presence is absolutely indispensable to create the sense that the dream is an organic whole: once this element is in place, however, it is in a way "in excess," it functions as an embarrassing plethora:

> We are of the opinion that in every structure there is a lure, a place-holder of the lack, comprised by what is perceived, but at the same time the weakest link in a given series, the point which vacillates and only seems to belong to the actual level: in it is *compressed* the whole virtual level [of the structuring space]. This element is *irrational* in reality, and by being included in it, it indicates the place of lack in it.[3]

And it is almost superfluous to add that the interpretation of dreams must begin precisely by isolating this paradoxical element, the "place-holder of the lack," the point of the signifier's non-sense. Starting from this point, dream interpretation must proceed to "denature," to dissipate the false appearance of the manifest dream-content's totality of meaning, i.e., to penetrate through to the "dream-work," to render visible the montage of heterogeneous ingredients effaced by its own final result. With this we have arrived at the similarity between the procedure of the analyst and that of the detective: the scene of the crime with which the detective is confronted is also, as a rule, a false image put together by the murderer in order to efface the traces of his act. The scene's organic, natural quality is a lure, and the detective's task is to denature it by first discovering the inconspicuous details that stick out, that do not fit into the frame of the surface image. The vocabulary of detective narration contains a precise *terminus technicus* for such a detail: *clue,* indicated by a whole series of adjectives: "'odd'—'queer'— 'wrong'—'strange'—'fishy'—rummy'—'doesn't make sense,' not to mention stronger expressions like 'eerie.' 'unreal,' 'unbelievable,' up to the categorical 'impossible.'"[4] What we have here is a detail that *in itself* is usually quite insignificant (the broken handle of a cup, the changed position of a chair, some transitory remark of a witness, or even a nonevent, i.e., the fact that something *did not* happen), but which nonetheless *with regard to its structural position* denatures the scene of the crime and produces a quasi-Brechtian effect of estrangement—like the alteration of a small detail in a well-known picture that all of a sudden renders the whole picture strange and uncanny. Such clues can of course be detected only if we put in parentheses the scene's totality of meaning and focus our attention on details. Holmes's advice to Watson not to mind the basic impressions but to take into consideration details echoes Freud's assertion that psychoanalysis employs interpretation *en détail* and not *en masse:* "It regards dreams from the very first as being of a composite character, as being conglomerates of psychical formations."[5]

Starting from clues, the detective thus unmasks the imaginary unity of the scene of the crime as it was staged by the assassin. The detective grasps the scene as a *bricolage* of heterogeneous elements, in which the connection between the murderer's mise-en-scène and the "real events" corresponds exactly to that between the manifest dream contents and the latent dream thought, or between the immediate figuration of the rebus and its solution. It consists solely in the "doubly inscribed" signifying material, like the "satyr" that means first the dancing figure of the satyr and then "Tyre is thine." The relevance of this "double inscription" for the detective story was already noticed by Victor Shklovsky: "The writer looks for cases in which two things which do not correspond, coincide nonetheless in some specific feature."[6] Shklovsky also pointed out that the privileged case of such a coincidence is a word-play: he refers to Conan Doyle's "The Adventure of the Speckled Band" where the key to the solution is hidden in the statement of the dying woman: "It was the speckled band. . . ." The wrong solution is based on the reading of *band* as *gang,* and is suggested by the fact that a band of gypsies was camped near the site of the murder, thus evoking the "convincing" image of the exotic gypsy murderer, while the real solution is arrived at only when Sherlock Holmes reads *band* as *ribbon.* In the majority of cases, this "doubly inscribed" element consists of course of nonlinguistic material, but even here it is already structured like a language (Shklovsky himself mentions one of Chesterton's stories that concerns the similarity between a gentleman's evening wear and a valet's dress).

WHY IS THE "FALSE SOLUTION" NECESSARY?

The crucial thing about the distance separating the false scene staged by the murderer and the true course of events is *the structural necessity of the false solution* toward which we are enticed because of the "convincing" character of the staged scene, which is—at least in the classic logic and deduction story—usually sustained by representatives of "official" knowledge (the police). The status of the false solution is epistemologically internal to the detective's final, true solution. The key to the detective's procedure is that the relation to the first, false solutions is not simply an external one: the detective does not apprehend them as simple obstacles to be cast away in order to obtain the truth, rather it is only *through* them that he can arrive at the truth, for there is no path leading immediately to the truth.[7]

In Conan Doyle's "The Red-Headed League," a redheaded client calls on Sherlock Holmes, telling him his strange adventure. He read an advertisement in a newspaper, offering redheaded men a well-paid temporary job. After presenting himself at the appointed place, he was chosen from among a great number of men, although the hair of many of the others was much redder. The job was indeed well paid, but utterly senseless: every day, from nine to five, he copies parts of the Bible. Holmes quickly solves the enigma: next to the house in which the client lives (and where he usually stayed during the day when he was unemployed), there is a large bank. The criminals put the advertisement in the newspaper so that he would respond to it. Their purpose was to ensure his absence from his home during the day so that they could dig a tunnel from his cellar into the bank. The only significance of their specification of hair color was to lure him. In Agatha Christie's *The ABC Murders,* a series of murders take place in which the names of the victims follow a complicated alphabetical pattern: this inevitably produces the impression that there is a pathological motivation. But the solution reveals quite a different motivation: the assassin really intended to kill just one person, not for "pathological" reasons but for very "intelligible" material gain. In order to lead the police astray, however, he murdered a few extra people, chosen so that their names form an alphabetical pattern and thus guaranteeing that the murders will be perceived as the work of some lunatic. What do these two stories have in common? In both cases, the deceitful first impression offers an image of pathological excess, a "loony" formula covering a multitude of people (red hair, alphabet), while the operation, in fact, is aimed at a single person. The solution is not arrived at by scrutinizing the possible hidden meaning of the surface impression

(What could the pathological fixation on red hair mean? What is the meaning of the alphabetical pattern?): it is precisely by indulging in this kind of deliberation that we fall into a trap. The only proper procedure is to put in parentheses the field of meaning imposed upon us by the deceitful first impression and to devote all our attention to the details *abstracted from their inclusion in the imposed field of meaning.* Why was this person hired for a senseless job *regardless of the fact that he is a redhead?* Who derives profit from the death of a certain person *regardless of the first letter of this person's name?* In other words, we must continually bear in mind that the fields of meaning imposing the "loony" frame of interpretation on us *"exist only in order to conceal the reason of their existence"*:[8] their meaning consists solely in the fact that "others" (*doxa,* common opinion) will think they have meaning. The sole "meaning" of red hair is that the person chosen for the job should believe his red hair played a role in the choice: the sole "meaning" of the ABC pattern is to lure the police into thinking this pattern has meaning.

This intersubjective dimension of the meaning that pertains to the false image is most clearly articulated in "The Adventure of the Highgate Miracle," a Sherlock Holmes pastiche written by John Dickson Carr and Adrian Conan Doyle, son of Arthur. Mister Cabpleasure, a merchant married to a wealthy heiress, suddenly develops a "pathological" attachment to his walking stick: he never parts from it, carrying it day and night. What does this sudden "fetishistic" attachment mean? Does the stick serve as a hiding place for the diamonds that recently vanished from Mrs. Cabpleasure's drawer? A detailed examination of the stick excludes this possibility: it is just an ordinary stick. Finally, Sherlock Holmes discovers that the whole attachment to the stick was staged in order to confer credibility on the scene of Cabpleasure's "magic" disappearance. During the night prior to his planned escape, he slips out of his home unobserved, goes to the milkman, and bribes him into lending him his outfit and letting him take his place. Dressed as a milkman, he appears next morning in front of his house with the milkman's handcart, takes out a bottle, and enters the house as usual to leave the bottle in the kitchen. Once inside the house, he quickly puts on his own overcoat and hat and steps out *without his stick;* halfway through the garden, he grimaces, as if suddenly remembering that he forgot his beloved stick, turns around, and runs quickly into the house. Behind the entrance door, he again changes into the milkman's outfit, walks calmly to the handcart and moves off. Cabpleasure, it turns out, stole his wife's diamonds; he knew that his wife suspected him and that she had hired detectives to watch the house during the day. He counted on his "loony" attachment to the stick being observed so that when, on his way through the garden, after noticing the lack of his stick, he shrinks and runs back, his actions appear natural to the detectives observing the house. In short, the sole "meaning" of his attachment to the stick was to make others think it has meaning.

It should be clear, now, why it is totally misleading to conceive of the detective's procedure as a version of the procedure proper to "precise" natural sciences: it is true that the "objective" scientist also "penetrates through false appearance into the hidden reality," but this false appearance with which he has to deal *lacks the dimension of deception.* Unless we accept the hypothesis of an evil, deceitful God, we can in no way maintain that the scientist is "deceived" by his object, i.e., that the false appearance confronting him "exists only to conceal the reason of its existence." In contrast to the "objective" scientist, however, the detective does not attain the truth by simply canceling the false appearance: he takes it into consideration. When confronted with the mystery of Cabpleasure's stick, Holmes does not say to himself "Let us leave out its meaning, it is just a lure," he asks himself a quite different question: "The stick has no meaning, the special meaning supposedly at-

tached to it is of course just a lure; but what precisely did the criminal achieve by luring us into believing that the stick has special meaning for him?" The truth lies not "beyond" the domain of deception, it lies in the "intention," in the intersubjective function of the very deception. The detective does not simply disregard the meaning of the false scene: he pushes it to the point of self-reference, i.e., to the point at which it becomes obvious that its sole meaning consists in the fact that (others think) it possesses some meaning. At the point at which the murderer's position of enunciation is that of a certain *I am deceiving you,* the detective is finally capable of sending back to him the true significance of his message:

> The *I am deceiving you* arises from the point at which the detective awaits the murderer and sends back to him, according to the formula, his own message in its true significance, that is to say, in an inverted form. He says to him—*in this* I am deceiving you, *what you are sending as message is what I express to you, and in doing so you are telling the truth.*[9]

THE DETECTIVE AS THE "SUBJECT SUPPOSED TO KNOW"

Now we are finally in a position to locate properly the detective's ill-famed "omniscience" and "infallibility." The certainty on the part of the reader that, at the end, the detective will solve the case does not include the supposition that he will arrive at the truth notwithstanding all deceitful appearances. The point is rather that he will literally *catch the murderer in his deception,* i.e., that he will trap him by taking into account his cunning. The very deceit the murderer invents to save himself is the cause of his downfall. Such a paradoxical conjunction in which it is the very attempt at deception that betrays us is of course possible only in the domain of "meaning," of a signifying structure; it is on this account that the detective's "omniscience" is strictly homologous to that of the psychoanalyst, who is taken by the patient as the "subject supposed to know" (*le sujet supposé savoir*)—supposed to know what? The true meaning of our act, the meaning visible in the very falseness of the appearance. The detective's domain, as well as that of the psychoanalyst, is thus thoroughly the domain of *meaning*, not of "facts": as we have already noted, the scene of the crime analyzed by the detective is by definition "structured like a language." The basic feature of the signifier is its differential character: since the identity of a signifier consists in the bundle of differences from other signifiers, the absence of a trait itself can have a positive value. Which is why the detective's artifice lies not simply in his capacity to grasp the possible meaning of "insignificant details," but perhaps even more in his capacity to apprehend absence itself (the nonoccurrence of some detail) as meaningful—it is perhaps not by chance that the most famous of all Sherlock Holmes's dialogues is the following from "Silver Blaze":

> "Is there any point to which you wish to draw my attention?"
> "To the curious incident of the dog in the night."
> "The dog did nothing in the night."
> "That was the curious incident," remarked Holmes.

This is how the detective traps the murderer: not simply by perceiving the traces of the deed the murderer failed to efface, but by perceiving the very absence of a trace as itself a trace.[10] We could then specify the function of the detective *qua* "subject supposed to know" in the following way: the scene of the crime contains a diversity of clues, of meaningless, scattered details with no obvious pattern (like "free associations" of the analysand in the psychoanalytic process),

and *the detective, solely by means of his presence, guarantees that all these details will retroactively acquire meaning.* In other words, his "omniscience" is an effect of *transference* (the person in a relation of transference toward the detective is above all his Watsonian companion, who provides him with information the meaning of which escapes the companion completely).[11] And it is precisely on the basis of this specific position of the detective as "guarantor of meaning" that we can elucidate the circular structure of the detective story. What we have at the beginning is a void, a blank of the unexplained, more properly, of the *unnarrated* ("How did it happen? What happened on the night of the murder?"). The story encircles this blank, it is set in motion by the detective's attempt to reconstruct the missing narrative by interpreting the clues. In this way, we reach the proper beginning only at the very end, when the detective is finally able to narrate the whole story in its "normal," linear form, to reconstruct "what really happened," by filling in all the blanks. At the beginning, there is thus the murder—a traumatic shock, an event that cannot be integrated into symbolic reality because it appears to interrupt the "normal" causal chain. From the moment of this eruption, even the most ordinary events of life seem loaded with threatening possibilities; everyday reality becomes a nightmarish dream as the "normal" link between cause and effect is suspended. This radical opening, this dissolution of symbolic reality, entails the transformation of the lawlike succession of events into a kind of "lawless sequence" and therefore bears witness to an encounter with the "impossible" real, resisting symbolization. Suddenly, "everything is possible," including the impossible. The detective's role is precisely to demonstrate how "the impossible is possible" (Ellery Queen), that is, to resymbolize the traumatic shock, to integrate it into symbolic reality. The very presence of the detective guarantees in advance the transformation of the lawless sequence into a lawful sequence; in other words, the reestablishment of "normality."

What is of crucial importance here is the *intersubjective* dimension of the murder, more properly, of the *corpse*. The corpse as object works to bind a group of individuals together: the corpse constitutes them as a group (a group of suspects), it brings and keeps them together through their shared feeling of guilt—any one of them *could have been* the murderer, each had motive and opportunity. The role of the detective is, again, precisely to dissolve the impasse of this universalized, free-floating guilt by localizing it in a single subject and thus exculpating all others.[12] Here, however, the homology between the procedure of the analyst and that of the detective reveals its limits. That is to say, it is not enough to draw a parallel and affirm that the psychoanalyst analyzes "inner," psychic reality, while the detective is confined to "external," material reality. The thing to do is to define the space where the two of them overlap, by asking the crucial question: how does this transposition of the analytic procedure onto "external" reality bear on the very domain of the "inner" libidinal economy? We have already indicated the answer: the detective's act consists in annihilating the libidinal possibility, the "inner" truth that each one in the group might have been the murderer (i.e., that we *are* murderers in the unconscious of our desire, insofar as the actual murderer realizes the desire of the group constituted by the corpse) on the level of "reality" (where the culprit singled out *is* the murderer and thus

the guarantee of *our* innocence). Herein lies the fundamental untruth, the existential falsity of the detective's "solution": the detective plays upon the difference between the factual truth (the accuracy of facts) and the "inner" truth concerning our desire. On behalf of the accuracy of facts, he compromises the "inner," libidinal truth and discharges us of all guilt for the realization of our desire, insofar as this realization is imputed to the culprit alone. In regard to the libidinal economy, the detective's "solution" is therefore nothing but a kind of realized hallucination. The detective "proves by facts" what would otherwise remain a hallucinatory projection of guilt onto a scapegoat, i.e., he proves that the scapegoat is effectively guilty. The immense pleasure brought about by the detective's solution results from this libidinal gain, from a kind of surplus profit obtained from it: our desire is realized and we do not even have to pay the price for it. The contrast between the psychoanalyst and the detective is thus clear: psychoanalysis confronts us precisely with the price we have to pay for the access to our desire, with an irredeemable loss (the "symbolic castration"). The way in which the detective functions as a "subject supposed to know" also changes accordingly: what does he guarantee by his mere presence? He guarantees precisely that we will be discharged of any guilt, that the guilt for the realization of our desire will be "externalized" in the scapegoat and that, consequently, we will be able to desire without paying the price for it.

The Philip Marlowe Way

THE CLASSICAL VERSUS THE HARD-BOILED DETECTIVE

Perhaps the greatest charm of the classical detective narrative lies in the fascinating, uncanny, dreamlike quality of the story the client tells the detective at the very beginning. A young maid tells Sherlock Holmes how, every morning on her way from the train station to work, a shy man with a masked face follows her at a distance on a bicycle and draws back as soon as she tries to approach him. Another woman tells Holmes of strange things her employer demands of her: she is handsomely paid to sit by the window for a couple of hours every evening, dressed in an old-fashioned gown, and braid. These scenes exert such a powerful libidinal force that one is almost tempted to hypothesize that the main function of the detective's "rational explanation" is to break the spell they have upon us, i.e., to spare us the encounter with the real of our desire that these scenes stage. The hard-boiled detective novel presents in this regard a totally different situation. In it, the detective loses the distance that would enable him to analyze the false scene and to dispel its charm; he becomes an active hero confronted with a chaotic, corrupt world, the more he intervenes in it, the more involved in its wicked ways he becomes.

It is therefore totally misleading to locate the difference between the classical and the hard-boiled detective as one of "intellectual" versus "physical" activity, to say that the classical detective of logic and deduction is engaged in reasoning while the hard-boiled detective is mainly engaged in chase and fight. The real break consists in the fact that, existentially, the classical detective is not "engaged" at all: he maintains an eccentric position throughout; he is excluded from the exchanges that take place among the group of suspects constituted by the corpse. It is precisely on the basis of this exteriority of his position (which is of course not to be confused with the position of the "objective" scientist: the latter's distance toward the object of his research is of quite another nature) that the homology between the detective and the analyst is founded. One of the clues indicating the difference between the two types of detective is their respective attitudes toward financial reward. After solving the case, the classical detective accepts with accentuated pleasure payment for the services he has rendered, whereas the hard-boiled detective as a rule disdains money and solves his cases with the personal commitment of somebody fulfilling an ethical mission, although this commitment is often hidden under a mask of cynicism. What is at stake here is not the classical detective's simple greed or his callousness toward human suffering and injustice—the point is much finer: the payment enables him to avoid getting mixed up in the libidinal circuit of (symbolic) debt and its restitution. The symbolic value of payment is the same in psychoanalysis: the fees of the analyst allow him to stay out of the "sacred" domain of exchange and sacrifice, i.e., to avoid getting involved in the analysand's libidinal circuit, Lacan articulates this dimension of payment precisely apropos of Dupin who, at the end of "The Purloined Letter," makes the prefect of police understand that he already has the letter, but is prepared to deliver it only for an appropriate fee:

> Does this mean that this Dupin, who up until then was an admirable, almost excessively lucid character, has all of a sudden become a small time wheeler and dealer? I don't hesitate to see in this action the re-purchasing of what one could call the bad *mana* attached to the letter. And indeed, from the moment he receives his fee, he has pulled out of the game. It isn't only because he has handed the letter over to another, but because his mo-

tives are clear to everyone—he got his money, it's no longer of any concern to him. The sacred value of remuneration, of the fee, is clearly indicated by the context. . . . We, who spend our time being the bearers of all the purloined letters of the patient, also get paid somewhat dearly. Think about this with some care—were we not to be paid, we would get involved in the drama of Atreus and Thyestes, the drama in which all the subjects who come to confide their truth in us are involved. . . . Everyone knows that money doesn't just buy things, but that the prices which, in our culture, are calculated at rock-bottom, have the function of neutralizing something infinitely more dangerous than paying in money, namely owing somebody something.[13]

In short, by demanding a fee, Dupin forestalls the "curse"—the place in the symbolic network—that befalls those who come into possession of the letter. The hard-boiled detective is, on the contrary, "involved" from the very beginning, caught up in the circuit: this involvement defines his very subjective position. What causes him to solve the mystery is first of all the fact that he has a certain debt to honor. We can locate this "settlement of (symbolic) accounts" on a wide scale ranging from Mike Hammer's primitive vendetta ethos in Mickey Spillane's novels to the refined sense of wounded subjectivity that characterizes Chandler's Philip Marlowe. Let us take, as an exemplary case of the latter, "Red Wind," one of Chandler's early short stories. Lola Barsley once had a lover who died unexpectedly. As a memento of her great love, she keeps an expensive pearl necklace, a gift from him, but in order to avoid her husband's suspicion she invents the story that the necklace is an imitation. Her ex-chauffeur steals the necklace and blackmails her, guessing that the necklace is real and what it means to her. He wants money for the necklace and for not telling her husband that it is not a fake. After the black-

mailer is murdered, Lola asks John Dalmas (a precursor of Marlowe) to find the missing necklace, but when he obtains it and shows it to a professional jeweller, the necklace turns out to be a fake. Lola's great love was also an impostor, it seems, and her memory an illusion. Dalmas, however, does not want to hurt her, so he hires a cheap forger to manufacture a deliberately raw imitation of the imitation. Lola, of course, immediately sees that the necklace Dalmas gives her is not her own and Dalmas explains that the blackmailer probably intended to return her this imitation and to keep the original for himself so that he might resell it later on. The memory of Lola's great love, which gives meaning to her life, is thus left unspoiled. Such an act of goodness is, of course, not without a kind of moral beauty, but it nonetheless runs contrary to the psychoanalytic ethic: it intends to spare the other the confrontation with a truth that would hurt him/her by demolishing his/her ego-ideal.

Such an involvement entails the loss of the "excentric" position by means of which the classical detective plays a role homologous to the "subject supposed to know." That is to say, the detective is never, as a rule, the narrator of the classical detective novel, which has either an "omniscient" narrator or one who is a sympathetic member of the social milieu, preferably the detective's Watsonian companion—in short, the person *for whom* the detective is a "subject supposed to know." The "subject supposed to know" is an effect of transference and is as such *structurally impossible in the first person:* he is by definition "supposed to know" by another subject. For that reason, it is strictly prohibited to divulge the detective's "inner thoughts." His reasoning must be concealed till the final triumphal denouement, except for occasional mysterious questions and remarks whose function is to emphasize even further the inaccessible character of what goes on in the detective's head. Agatha Christie is a great master of such remarks, although she seems sometimes to push them to a mannerist extreme: in the midst of an intricate investigation, Poirot usually asks a question such as "Do you know by any chance what was the color of the stockings worn by the lady's maid?"; after obtaining the answer, he mumbles into his moustache: "Then the case is completely clear!"

The hard-boiled novels are in contrast generally narrated in the first person, with the detective himself as narrator (a notable exception, which would require exhaustive interpretation, is the majority of Dashiell Hammett's novels). This change in narrative perspective has of course profound consequences for the dialectic of truth and deception. By means of his initial decision to accept a case, the hard-boiled detective gets mixed up in a course of events that he is unable to dominate; all of a sudden it becomes evident that he has been "played for a sucker." What looked at first like an easy job turns into an intricate game of criss-cross, and all his effort is directed toward clarifying the contours of the trap into which he has fallen. The "truth" at which he attempts to arrive is not just a challenge to his reason but concerns him ethically and often painfully. The deceitful game of which he has become a part poses a threat to his very identity as a subject. In short, the dialectic of deception in the hard-boiled novel is the dialectic of an active hero caught in a nightmarish game whose real stakes escape him. His acts acquire an unforeseen dimension, he can hurt somebody unknowingly—the guilt he thus contracts involuntarily propels him to "honor his debt."[14]

In this case, then, it is the detective himself—not the terrified members of the "group of suspects"—who undergoes a kind of "loss of reality," who finds himself in a dreamlike world where it is never quite clear who is playing what game. And the person who embodies this deceitful character of the universe, its fundamental corruption, the person who lures the detective and "plays him for a sucker," is as a rule the femme fatale, which is why the final "settlement of accounts" usually consists in the detective's

confrontation with her. This confrontation results in a range of reactions, from desperate resignation or escape into cynicism in Hammett and Chandler to loose slaughter in Mickey Spillane (in the final page of *I, the Jury*, Mike Hammer answers "It was easy" when his dying, treacherous lover asks him how he could kill her in the middle of making love). Why is this ambiguity, this deceitfulness and corruption of the universe embodied in a woman whose promise of surplus enjoyment conceals mortal danger? What is the precise dimension of this danger? Our answer is that, contrary to appearance, the femme fatale embodies a radical *ethical* attitude, that of "not ceding one's desire," of persisting in it to the very end when its true nature as the death drive is revealed. It is the hero who, by rejecting the femme fatale, breaks with his ethical stance.

THE WOMAN WHO "DOES NOT CEDE HER DESIRE"

What precisely is meant here by "ethics" can be elucidated by reference to the famous Peter Brooks version of Bizet's *Carmen*. That is to say, our thesis is that, by means of the changes he introduced into the original plot, Brooks made Carmen not only a tragic figure but, more radically, an *ethical* figure of the lineage of Antigone. Again, at first it seems that there could be no greater contrast than that between Antigone's dignified sacrifice and the debauchery that leads to Carmen's destruction. Yet the two are connected by the same ethical attitude that we could describe (according to the Lacanian reading of *Antigone*) as an unreserved acceptance of the death drive, as a striving for radical self-annihilation, for what Lacan calls the "second death" going beyond mere physical destruction, i.e., entailing the effacement of the very symbolic texture of generation and corruption. Brooks was quite justified in making the aria about the "merciless card" the central musical motif of the entire work: the aria about the card that "always shows death" (in the third act) designates the precise moment at which Carmen assumes an ethical status, accepting without reserve the imminence of her own death. The cards that, in their chance fall, always predict death, are the "little piece of the real" to which Carmen's death drive clings. And it is precisely at the moment when Carmen not only becomes aware that she—as a woman marking the fate of the men she encounters—is herself the victim of fate, a plaything in the hands of forces she cannot dominate, but also fully accepts her fate by not ceding her desire that she becomes a "subject" in the strict Lacanian meaning of this term. For Lacan, a subject is in the last resort the name for this "empty gesture" by means of which we freely assume what is imposed on us, the real of the death drive. In other words, up until the aria about the "merciless card," Carmen was an object for men, her power of fascination depended on the role she played in their fantasy space, she was nothing but their symptom, although she lived under the illusion that she was effectively "pulling the strings." When she finally becomes an object *for herself also,* i.e., when she realizes that she is just a passive element in the interplay of libidinal forces, she "subjectifies" herself, she becomes a "subject." From the Lacanian perspective, "subjectification" is thus strictly correlative to experiencing oneself as an object, a "helpless victim", it is the name for the gaze by means of which we confront the utter nullity of our narcissistic pretentions.

To prove that Brooks was fully aware of this, it suffices to mention his most ingenious intervention: the radical change of the denouement of the opera. Bizet's original version is well known. In front of the arena in which the toreador Escamillo pursues his victorious fight. Carmen is approached by the desperate Jose who begs her to live with him again. His demand is met with rebuff, and while the song in the background announces another triumph for Es-

camillo, Jose stabs Carmen to death—the usual drama of a rejected lover who cannot bear his loss. With Brooks, however, things turn out quite differently. Jose resignedly *accepts* Carmen's final rebuff, but as Carmen is walking away from him, the servants bring her the dead Escamillo—he lost the fight, the bull has killed him. It is Carmen who is now broken. She leads Jose to a lonely place near the arena, kneels down and offers herself to him to be stabbed. Is there a denouement more desperate than this? Of course there is: Carmen might have left with Jose, this weakling, and continued to live her miserable everyday life. The "happy ending," in other words, would be the most desperate of all.

And it is the same with the figure of the femme fatale in hard-boiled novels and in *film noir:* she who ruins the lives of men and is at the same time victim of her own lust for enjoyment, obsessed by a desire for power, who endlessly manipulates her partners and is at the same time slave to some third, ambiguous person, sometimes even an impotent or sexually ambivalent man. What bestows on her an aura of mystery is precisely the way she cannot be clearly located in the opposition between master and slave. At the moment she seems permeated with intense pleasure, it suddenly becomes apparent that she suffers immensely; when she seems to be the victim of some horrible and unspeakable violence, it suddenly becomes clear that she enjoys it. We can never be quite sure if she enjoys or suffers, if she manipulates or is herself the victim of manipulation. It is this that produces the deeply ambiguous character of those moments in the *film noir* (or in the hard-boiled detective novel) when the femme fatale breaks down, loses her powers of manipulation, and becomes the victim of her own game. Let us just mention the first model of such a breakdown, the final confrontation between Sam Spade and Brigid O'Shaughnessy in *The Maltese Falcon.* As she begins to lose her grasp of the situation, Brigid suffers a hysterical breakdown; she passes immediately from one strategy to another. She first threatens, then she cries and maintains that she did not know what was really happening to her, then suddenly she assumes again an attitude of cold distance and disdain, and so on. In short, she unfolds a whole fan of inconsistent hysterical masks. This moment of the final breakdown of the femme fatale—who now appears as an entity without substance, a series of inconsistent masks without a coherent ethical attitude—this moment when her power of fascination evaporates and leaves us with feelings of nausea and disgust, this moment when we see "nought but shadows of what is not" where previously we saw clear and distinct form exerting tremendous powers of seduction, this moment of reversal is at the same time the moment of triumph for the hard-boiled detective. Now, when the fascinating figure of the femme fatale disintegrates into an inconsistent bric-a-brac of hysterical masks, he is finally capable of gaining a kind of distance toward her and of rejecting her.

The destiny of the femme fatale in *film noir*, her final hysterical breakdown, exemplifies perfectly the Lacanian proposition that "Woman does not exist": she is nothing but "the symptom of man," her power of fascination masks the void of her nonexistence, so that when she is finally rejected, her whole ontological consistency is dissolved. But precisely as nonexisting, i.e., at the moment at which, through hysterical breakdown, she *assumes* her nonexistence, she constitutes herself as "subject": what is waiting for her *beyond* hysterization is the death drive in its purest. In feminist writings on *film noir* we often encounter the thesis that the femme fatale presents a mortal threat to man (the hard-boiled detective), i.e., that her boundless enjoyment menaces his very identity as subject: by rejecting her at the end, he regains his sense of personal integrity and identity. This thesis is true, but in a sense that is the exact opposite of the way it is usually understood. What is so menacing about the femme fatale is not the boundless enjoyment that overwhelms the man and makes him woman's plaything or slave. It is not Woman as

object of fascination that causes us to lose our sense of judgment and moral attitude but, on the contrary, that which remains hidden beneath this fascinating mask and which appears once the masks fall off: the dimension of the pure subject fully assuming the death drive. To use Kantian terminology, woman is not a threat to man insofar as she embodies pathological enjoyment, insofar as she enters the frame of a particular fantasy. The real dimension of the threat is revealed when we "traverse" the fantasy, when the coordinates of the fantasy space are lost via hysterical breakdown. In other words, what is really menacing about the femme fatale is not that she is fatal for *men* but that she presents a case of a "pure," nonpathological subject fully assuming *her own* fate. When the woman reaches this point, there are only two attitudes left to the man: either he "cedes his desire," rejects her and regains his imaginary, narcissistic identity (Sam Spade at the end of *The Maltese Falcon*), or he *identifies* with the woman as symptom and meets his fate in a suicidal gesture (the act of Robert Mitchum in what is perhaps the crucial *film noir*, Jacques Tourneur's *Out of the Past*).[15]

NOTES

1. It is needless to add that attempts at a pseudo: "dialectical" synthesis conceiving the figure of the detective as the contradictory fusion of bourgeois rationality and its reverse, irrational intuition, fare no better: both sides together fail to procure what each of them lacks.

2. Freud, *The Interpretation of Dreams,* pp. 277–278.

3. Jacques-Alain Miller, "Action de la structure," in *Cahiers pour l'Analyse* 9, Paris, Graphe, 1968, pp. 96–97.

4. Richard Alewyn, "Anatomie des Detektivromans," in Jochen Vogt, ed., *Der Kriminalroman,* Munich, UTB-Verlag, 1971, vol. 2, p 35.

5. Freud, *The Interpretation of Dreams,* p. 104.

6. Victor Shklovsky, "Die Kriminalerzaehlung bei Conan Doyle," in Jochen Vogt, ed., *Der Kriminalroman,* Munich, UTB-Verlag, 1971, vol. 1, p 84.

7. It is on the basis of this structural necessity of the false solution that we can explain the role of one of the standard figures of the classical detective story: the detective's naive, everyday companion who is usually also the narrator (Holmes's Watson, Poirot's Hastings, etc.). In one of Agatha Christie's novels, Hastings asks Poirot of what use he is to him in his work of detection, insofar as he is just an ordinary, average person, full of everyday prejudices. Poirot answers that he needs Hastings *precisely on that account,* i.e., precisely because he is an ordinary man who embodies what we could call the field of *doxa,* spontaneous common opinion. That is to say, after accomplishing his crime, the murderer must efface its traces by composing an image that conceals its true motive and points toward a false culprit (a classical topos: the murder is accomplished by a victim's close relative who arranges things to give the impression that the act was performed by a burglar surprised by the unexpected arrival of the victim). *Whom,* precisely, does the murderer want to deceive by means of this false scene? What is the "reasoning" of the murderer when he stages the false scene? It is of course the very field of *doxa,* of "common opinion" embodied in the detective's faithful companion. Consequently, the detective does not need his Watson in order to point out the contrast between his dazzling perspicacity and the companion's ordinary humanity; instead Watson, with his commonsense reactions, is necessary in order to exhibit in the clearest possible way the effect that the murderer intended to produce by his staging of a false scene.

8. Miller, "Action de la structure," p. 96.

9. Lacan, *The Four Fundamental Concepts of Psycho-Analysis,* pp. 139–140 (the quotation is, of course, slightly changed to suit our purposes).

10. Which is why the "retired colourman" in one of the late Sherlock Holmes stories, although ingenious enough, does not really take advantage of all the ruses of deception proper to the order of the signifier. This old official, whose wife was missing and presumed to have escaped with a young lover, suddenly started to repaint his house—why? In order that the strong smell of fresh paint would prevent the visitors from detecting another smell, that of the decaying bodies of his wife and her lover whom he killed and hid in the house. An even more ingenious deception would have been to paint the walls in order to provoke the impression that the smell of paint is meant to cover up another smell, i.e., to provoke the impression that we are hiding something, while in reality there is nothing to hide.

11. Apropos of the "subject supposed to know," it is absolutely crucial to grasp this link between knowledge and the stupid, senseless *presence* of the subject embodying it. The "subject supposed to know" is someone who, *by his mere presence,* guarantees that the chaos will acquire meaning, i.e., that "there is a method in this madness." Which is why the title of Hal Ashby's film about the effects of transference, *Being There,* is thoroughly adequate: it is enough for the poor gardener Chance, played by Peter Sellers, to find himself—by means of a purely contingent misapprehension—at a certain place, to occupy the place of transference for the others, and already he operates as the wise "Chauncey Gardener." His stupid phrases, scraps of his gardening experience and of what he remembers from watching TV incessantly, are all of a sudden supposed to contain another, metaphorical, "deeper" meaning. His childish utterances about how to take care of a garden in winter and spring, for example, are read as profound allusions to the thawing of relations between the superpowers. Those critics who saw in the film a eulogy of the simple man's commonsense, its triumph over the artificiality of experts, were totally wrong. In this respect, the film is definitely not spoiled by any compromise. Chance is depicted as completely and painfully idiotic, the whole effect of his "wisdom" results from his "being there," at the place of transference. Even though the American psychoanalytical establishment has been unable to swallow Lacan, Hollywood, happily, has been more accommodating.

12. Agatha Christie's *Murder on the Orient-Express* confirms this by way of an ingenious exception: here, the murder is accomplished by the entire group of suspects, and it is precisely for this reason that they cannot be guilty, so the paradoxical although necessary outcome is that *the culprit coincides with the victim,* i.e., the murder proves to be a well-deserved punishment.

13. Jacques Lacan *The Ego in Freud's Theory and in the Technique of Psychoanalysts,* New York, Norton, 1988, p. 204.

14. We have of course left out of consideration the extremely interesting rise of the postwar "crime novel" which shifts the attention from the detective (either as the "subject supposed to know" or as the first-person narrator) to the victim (Boileau-Narcejac) or the culprit (Patricia Highsmith, Ruth Rendell). The necessary consequence of this shift is that the entire temporal structure of the narrative is changed. The story is presented in the "usual" linear way, with the accent placed on what goes on *before* the crime, i.e., we are no longer concerned with the *aftermath* of

crime and with attempts to reconstruct the course of events leading up to it. In Boileau-Narcejac's novels (*Les Diaboliques,* for example), the story is usually told from the perspective of the future victim, a woman to whom strange things seem to happen, foreboding a horrible crime, though we are not sure until the final denouement if all this is true or just her hallucination. On the other hand, Patricia Highsmith depicts the whole diversity of contingencies and psychological impasses that could induce an apparently "normal" person to commit a murder. Even in her first novel, *Strangers on a Train,* she established her elementary matrix: that of a transferential relationship between a psychotic murderer capable of performing the act and a hysteric who organizes his desire by means of a reference to the psychotic, i.e., who literally *desires by proxy* (no wonder Hitchcock recognized immediately the affinity between this matrix and his motif of the "transference of guilt"). Incidentally, an interesting case in respect to this opposition between the "victim" novel and the "culprit" novel is Margaret Millar's masterpiece *Beast in View,* in which the two coincide: the culprit turns out to be the victim of the crime itself, a pathologically split personality.

15. The fact that this is a matter of a postfantasy "purification" of desire is attested by an ingenious detail: in the final scene, the wardrobe of Jane Greer unmistakably resembles that of a nun.

26

Laura Mulvey
1941–

Laura Mulvey is a British film theorist and filmmaker, currently teaching film at the University of East Anglia. Her semiotic analysis of film seeks to deconstruct the classical tropes of traditional narrative cinema with a discourse employing feminist, Marxist, and Freudian concepts. Mulvey's text "Visual Pleasure and Narrative Cinema" (1975) was first published in *Screen* magazine. Since its publication in the mid-1970s, this article has helped initiate a new vocabulary through which visual analysis can simultaneously articulate a feminist critique. Mulvey has published on the broad spectrum of issues of spectatorship involving not only film but also photography, art, and myth. In addition to the films entitled *Penthesilea* (1974), *Riddles of the Sphinx* (1978), *Amyl* (1980), *Crystal Gazing* (1981), and *The Bad Sister* (1983), Mulvey has published two books, *Visual and Other Pleasures* in 1989 and *Citizen Kane* in 1992. As Mulvey states in *Visual and Other Pleasures*, her 1975 article "has seemed, over the last decade, to take on a life of its own." Noting the response its publication generated, Mulvey wrote "Afterthoughts on Visual Pleasure and Narrative Cinema" inspired by King Vidor's *Duel in the Sun*, which appeared in *Framework* in 1981.

Mulvey's article "Visual Pleasure and Narrative Cinema" seeks to shatter the patriarchal "pleasure" of classical narrative cinema in which, as Mulvey states, "the meaning of woman is sexual difference." Unacknowledged systems of film convention construct male identity in association with activity, subjectivity, voyeurism, and scopophilia, while female identity is rendered as a passive (disempowered) icon of sexuality, utterly fetishized as "other," and as object of the male gaze. Mulvey describes this male gaze as projecting "its fantasy" onto the female body, "which is styled accordingly." "In their traditional exhibitionist role," she argues, "women are simultaneously looked at and displayed, with their appearancce coded for strong visual and erotic impact so that they can be said to connote *to-be-looked-at-ness*" in what Mulvey terms "a heterosexual division of labor" that controls narrative structure. In her argument, Mulvey describes an indissoluble link between heterosexism and patriarchal capitalism. In the language of psychoanalysis, she also identifies the male desire in film as a drive to fetishize and contain—to "demystify" woman, as a drive to destroy what it cannot understand in its quest for self-reflection. Mulvey asserts that for Freud the tension between scopophilia and narcissism was crucial in ego construction and that this binary tension applies fundamentally to the ways in which cinema coerces the audience's looking as voyeurism and scopophilia (just as the characters in classical narrative cinema are conditioned by the same processes of looking and of "being looked at"). Through a textual analysis of film form, and by defining the three looks of cinema, Mulvey provides a new discourse to the analysis of media and of gender representation.

Visual Pleasure and Narrative Cinema[1]

I INTRODUCTION

(a) A Political Use of Psychoanalysis

This paper intends to use psychoanalysis to discover where and how the fascination of film is reinforced by pre-existing patterns of fascination already at work within the individual subject and the social formations that have moulded him. It takes as its starting-point the way film reflects, reveals and even plays on the straight, socially established interpretation of sexual difference which controls images, erotic ways of looking and spectacle. It is helpful to understand what the cinema has been, how its magic has worked in the past, while attempting a theory and a practice which will challenge this cinema of the past. Psychoanalytic theory is thus appropriated here as a political weapon, demonstrating the way the unconscious of patriarchal society has structured film form.

The paradox of phallocentrism in all its manifestations is that it depends on the image of the castrated woman to give order and meaning to its world. An idea of woman stands as linchpin to the system: it is her lack that produces the phallus as a symbolic presence, it is her desire to make good the lack that the phallus signifies. Recent writing in *Screen* about psychoanalysis and the cinema has not sufficiently brought out the importance of the representation of the female form in a symbolic order in which, in the last resort, it speaks castration and nothing else. To summarise briefly: the function of woman in forming the patriarchal unconscious is two-fold:

she firstly symbolises the castration threat by her real lack of a penis and secondly thereby raises her child into the symbolic. Once this has been achieved, her meaning in the process is at an end. It does not last into the world of law and language except as a memory, which oscillates between memory of maternal plenitude and memory of lack. Both are posited on nature (or on anatomy in Freud's famous phrase). Woman's desire is subjugated to her image as bearer of the bleeding wound; she can exist only in relation to castration and cannot transcend it. She turns her child into the signifier of her own desire to possess a penis (the condition, she imagines, of entry into the symbolic). Either she must gracefully give way to the word, the name of the father and the law, or else struggle to keep her child down with her in the half-light of the imaginary. Woman then stands in patriarchal culture as a signifier for the male other, bound by a symbolic order in which man can live out his fantasies and obsessions through linguistic command by imposing them on the silent image of woman still tied to her place as bearer, not maker, of meaning.

There is an obvious interest in this analysis for feminists, a beauty in its exact rendering of the frustration experienced under the phallocentric order. It gets us nearer to the roots of our oppression, it brings closer an articulation of the problem, it faces us with the ultimate challenge: how to fight the unconscious structured like a language (formed critically at the moment of arrival of language) while still caught within the language of the patriarchy? There is no way in which we can produce an alternative out of the blue, but we can begin to make a break by examining patriarchy with the tools it provides, of which psychoanalysis is not the only but an important one. We are still separated by a great gap from important issues for the female unconscious which are scarcely relevant to phallocentric theory: the sexing of the female infant and her relationship to the symbolic, the sexually mature woman as non-mother, maternity outside the signification of the phallus, the vagina. But, at this point, psychoanalytic theory as it now stands can at least advance our understanding of the *status quo*, of the patriarchal order in which we are caught.

(b) Destruction of Pleasure as a Radical Weapon

As an advanced representation system, the cinema poses questions about the ways the unconscious (formed by the dominant order) structures ways of seeing and pleasure in looking. Cinema has changed over the last few decades. It is no longer the monolithic system based on large capital investment exemplified at its best by Hollywood in the 1930s, 1940s and 1950s. Technological advances (16mm and so on) have changed the economic conditions of cinematic production, which can now be artisanal as well as capitalist. Thus it has been possible for an alternative cinema to develop. However self-conscious and ironic Hollywood managed to be, it always restricted itself to a formal *mise en scène* reflecting the dominant ideological concept of the cinema. The alternative cinema provides a space for the birth of a cinema which is radical in both a political and an aesthetic sense and challenges the basic assumptions of the mainstream film. This is not to reject the latter moralistically, but to highlight the ways in which its formal preoccupations reflect the psychical obsessions of the society which produced it and, further, to stress that the alternative cinema must start specifically by reacting against

these obsessions and assumptions. A politically and aesthetically avant-garde cinema is now possible, but it can still only exist as a counterpoint.

The magic of the Hollywood style at its best (and of all the cinema which fell within its sphere of influence) arose, not exclusively, but in one important aspect, from its skilled and satisfying manipulation of visual pleasure. Unchallenged, mainstream film coded the erotic into the language of the dominant patriarchal order. In the highly developed Hollywood cinema it was only through these codes that the alienated subject, torn in his imaginary memory by a sense of loss, by the terror of potential lack in fantasy, came near to finding a glimpse of satisfaction: through its formal beauty and its play on his own formative obsessions. This article will discuss the interweaving of that erotic pleasure in film, its meaning and, in particular, the central place of the image of woman. It is said that analysing pleasure, or beauty, destroys it. That is the intention of this article. The satisfaction and reinforcement of the ego that represent the high point of film history hitherto must be attacked. Not in favour of a reconstructed new pleasure, which cannot exist in the abstract, nor of intellectualised unpleasure, but to make way for a total negation of the ease and plenitude of the narrative fiction film. The alternative is the thrill that comes from leaving the past behind without simply rejecting it, transcending outworn or oppressive forms, and daring to break with normal pleasurable expectations in order to conceive a new language of desire.

II PLEASURE IN LOOKING/ FASCINATION WITH THE HUMAN FORM

A. The cinema offers a number of possible pleasures. One is scopophilia (pleasure in looking). There are circumstances in which looking itself is a source of pleasure, just as, in the reverse formation, there is pleasure in being looked at.

Originally, in his *Three Essays on Sexuality,* Freud isolated scopophilia as one of the component instincts of sexuality which exist as drives quite independently of the erotogenic zones. At this point he associated scopophilia with taking other people as objects, subjecting them to a controlling and curious gaze. His particular examples centre on the voyeuristic activities of children, their desire to see and make sure of the private and forbidden (curiosity about other people's genital and bodily functions, about the presence or absence of the penis and, retrospectively, about the primal scene). In this analysis scopophilia is essentially active. (Later, in "Instincts and Their Vicissitudes," Freud developed his theory of scopophilia further, attaching it initially to pre-genital auto-eroticism, after which, by analogy, the pleasure of the look is transferred to others. There is a close working here of the relationship between the active instinct and its further development in a narcissistic form.) Although the instinct is modified by other factors, in particular the constitution of the ego, it continues to exist as the erotic basis for pleasure in looking at another person as object. At the extreme, it can become fixated into a perversion, producing obsessive voyeurs and Peeping Toms whose only sexual satisfaction can come from watching, in an active controlling sense, an objectified other.

At first glance, the cinema would seem to be remote from the undercover world of the surreptitious observation of an unknowing and unwilling victim. What is seen on the screen is so manifestly shown. But the mass of mainstream film, and the conventions within which it has consciously evolved, portray a hermetically sealed world which unwinds magically, indifferent to the presence of the audience, producing for them a sense of separation and playing on their voyeuristic fantasy. Moreover the extreme contrast between the darkness in the auditorium (which also isolates the spectators from one another) and the brilliance of the shifting patterns of light and shade on the screen helps to promote the illusion of voyeuristic separation. Although the film is really being shown, is there to be seen, conditions of screening and narrative conventions give the spectator an illusion of looking in on a private world. Among other things, the position of the spectators in the cinema is blatantly one of repression of their exhibitionism and projection of the repressed desire onto the performer.

B. The cinema satisfies a primordial wish for pleasurable looking, but it also goes further, developing scopophilia in its narcissistic aspect. The conventions of mainstream film focus attention on the human form. Scale, space, stories are all anthropomorphic. Here, curiosity and the wish to look intermingle with a fascination with likeness and recognition: the human face, the human body, the relationship between the human form and its surroundings, the visible presence of the person in the world. Jacques Lacan has described how the moment when a child recognises its own image in the mirror is crucial for the constitution of the ego. Several aspects of this analysis are relevant here. The mirror phase occurs at a time when children's physical ambitions outstrip their motor capacity, with the result that their recognition of themselves is joyous in that they imagine their mirror image to be more complete, more perfect than they experience in their own body. Recognition is thus overlaid with misrecognition: the image recognised is conceived as the reflected body of the self, but its misrecognition as superior projects this body outside itself as an ideal ego, the alienated subject which, reintrojected as an ego ideal, prepares the way for identification with others in the future. This mirror moment predates language for the child.

Important for this article is the fact that it is an image that constitutes the matrix of the imaginary, of recognition/misrecognition and identification, and hence of the first articulation of the I, of subjectivity. This is a moment when an older fascination with looking (at the mother's face, for an obvious example) collides with the initial inklings of self-awareness. Hence it is the birth of the long love affair/despair between image and self-image which has found such intensity of expression in film and such joyous recognition in the cinema audience. Quite apart from the extraneous similarities between screen and mirror (the framing of the human form in its surroundings, for instance), the cinema has structures of fascination strong enough to allow temporary loss of ego while simultaneously reinforcing it. The sense of forgetting the world as the ego has come to perceive it (I forgot who I am and where I was) is nostalgically reminiscent of that pre-subjective moment of image recognition. While at the same time, the cinema has distinguished itself in the production of ego ideals, through the star system for instance. Stars provide a focus or centre both to screen space and screen story where they act out a complex process of likeness and difference (the glamorous impersonates the ordinary).

C. Sections A and B have set out two contradictory aspects of the pleasurable structures of looking in the conventional cinematic situation. The first, scopophilic, arises from pleasure in using another person as an object of sexual stimulation through sight. The second, developed through narcissism and the constitution of the ego, comes from identification with the image seen. Thus, in film terms, one implies a separation of the erotic identity of the subject from the object on the screen (active scopophilia), the other demands identification of the ego with the object on the screen through the spectator's fascination with and recognition of his like. The first is a function of the sexual instincts, the second of ego libido. This dichotomy was crucial for Freud. Although he saw the two as interacting and overlaying each other, the tension between instinctual drives and self-preservation polarises in terms of pleasure. But both are formative structures, mechanisms without intrinsic meaning. In themselves they have no significa-

tion, unless attached to an idealisation. Both pursue aims in indifference to perceptual reality, and motivate eroticised phantasmagoria that affect the subject's perception of the world to make a mockery of empirical objectivity.

During its history, the cinema seems to have evolved a particular illusion of reality in which this contradiction between libido and ego has found a beautifully complementary fantasy world. In *reality* the fantasy world of the screen is subject to the law which produces it. Sexual instincts and identification processes have a meaning within the symbolic order which articulates desire. Desire, born with language, allows the possibility of transcending the instinctual and the imaginary, but its point of reference continually returns to the traumatic moment of its birth: the castration complex. Hence the look, pleasurable in form, can be threatening in content, and it is woman as representation/image that crystallises this paradox.

III WOMAN AS IMAGE, MAN AS BEARER OF THE LOOK

A. In a world ordered by sexual imbalance, pleasure in looking has been split between active/male and passive/female. The determining male gaze projects its fantasy onto the female figure, which is styled accordingly. In their traditional exhibitionist role women are simultaneously looked at and displayed, with their appearance coded for strong visual and erotic impact so that they can be said to connote *to-be-looked-at-ness.* Woman displayed as sexual object is the *leitmotif* of erotic spectacle: from pin-ups to strip-tease, from Ziegfeld to Busby Berkeley, she holds the look, and plays to and signifies male desire. Mainstream film neatly combines spectacle and narrative. (Note, however, how in the musical song-and-dance numbers interrupt the flow of the diegesis.) The presence of woman is an indispensable element of spectacle in normal narrative film, yet her visual presence tends to work against the development of a story-line, to freeze the flow of action in moments of erotic contemplation. This alien presence then has to be integrated into cohesion with the narrative. As Budd Boetticher has put it:

> What counts is what the heroine provokes, or rather what she represents. She is the one, or rather the love or fear she inspires in the hero, or else the concern he feels for her, who makes him act the way he does. In herself the woman has not the slightest importance.

(A recent tendency in narrative film has been to dispense with this problem altogether; hence the development of what Molly Haskell has called the "buddy movie," in which the active homosexual eroticism of the central male figures can carry the story without distraction.) Traditionally, the woman displayed has functioned on two levels: as erotic object for the characters within the screen story, and as erotic object for the spectator within the auditorium, with a shifting tension between the looks on either side of the screen. For instance, the device of the showgirl allows the two looks to be unified technically without any apparent break in the diegesis. A woman performs within the narrative; the gaze of the spectator and that of the male characters in the film are neatly combined without breaking narrative verisimilitude. For a moment the sexual impact of the performing woman takes the film into a no man's land outside its own time and space. Thus Marilyn Monroe's first appearance in *The River of No Return* and Lauren Bacall's songs in *To Have and Have Not*. Similarly, conventional close-ups of legs (Dietrich, for instance) or a face (Garbo) integrate into the narrative a different mode of eroticism. One part of a fragmented body destroys the Renaissance space, the illusion of depth demanded by the narrative; it gives flatness, the quality of a cut-out or icon, rather than verisimilitude, to the screen.

B. An active/passive heterosexual division of labour has similarly controlled narrative structure. According to the principles of the ruling ideology and the psychical structures that back it up, the male figure cannot bear the burden of sexual objectification. Man is reluctant to gaze at his exhibitionist like. Hence the split between spectacle and narrative supports the man's role as the active one of advancing the story, making things happen. The man controls the film fantasy and also emerges as the representative of power in a further sense: as the bearer of the look of the spectator, transferring it behind the screen to neutralise the extra-diegetic tendencies represented by woman as spectacle. This is made possible through the processes set in motion by structuring the film around a main controlling figure with whom the spectator can identify. As the spectator identifies with the main male protagonist, he projects his look onto that of his like, his screen surrogate, so that the power of the male protagonist as he controls events coincides with the active power of the erotic look, both giving a satisfying sense of omnipotence. A male movie star's glamorous characteristics are thus not those of the erotic object of the gaze, but those of the more perfect, more complete, more powerful ideal ego conceived in the original moment of recognition in front of the mirror. The character in the story can make things happen and control events better than the subject/spectator, just as the image in the mirror was more in control of motor co-ordination.

In contrast to woman as icon, the active male figure (the ego ideal of the identification process) demands a three-dimensional space corresponding to that of the mirror recognition, in which the alienated subject internalised his own representation of his imaginary existence. He is a figure in a landscape. Here the function of film is to reproduce as accurately as possible the so-called natural conditions of human perception. Camera technology (as exemplified by deep focus in particular) and camera movements (determined by the action of the protagonist), combined with invisible editing (demanded by realism), all tend to blur the limits of screen space. The male protagonist is free to command the stage, a stage of spatial illusion in which he articulates the look and creates the action. (There are films with a woman as main protagonist, of course. To analyse this phenomenon seriously here would take me too far afield. Pam Cook and Claire Johnston's study of *The Revolt of Mamie Stover* in Phil Hardy (ed.), *Raoul Walsh* (Edinburgh, 1974), shows in a striking case how the strength of this female protagonist is more apparent than real.)

C1. Sections III A and B have set out a tension between a mode of representation of woman in film and conventions surrounding the diegesis. Each is associated with a look: that of the spectator in direct scopophilic contact with the female form displayed for his enjoyment (connoting male fantasy) and that of the spectator fascinated with the image of his like set in an illusion of natural space, and through him gaining control and possession of the woman within the diegesis. (This tension and the shift from one pole to the other can structure a single text. Thus both in *Only Angels Have Wings* and in *To Have and Have Not*, the film opens with the woman as object of the combined gaze of spectator and all the male protagonists in the film. She is isolated, glamorous, on display, sexualized. But as the narrative progresses she falls in love with the main male protagonist and becomes his property, losing her outward glamorous characteristics, her generalised sexuality, her show-girl connotations; her eroticism is subjected to the male star alone. By means of identification with him, through participation in his power, the spectator can indirectly possess her too.)

But in psychoanalytic terms, the female figure poses a deeper problem. She also connotes something that the look continually circles around but disavows: her lack of a penis, implying a threat of castration and hence unpleasure. Ultimately, the meaning of woman is sexual difference, the visually ascertainable absence of the penis, the material evidence on which is based the castration complex essential for the organisation of entrance to the symbolic order and the law of the father. Thus the woman as icon, displayed for the gaze and enjoyment of men, the active controllers of the look, always threatens to evoke the anxiety it originally signified. The male unconscious has two avenues of escape from this castration anxiety: preoccupation with the re-enactment of the original trauma (investigating the woman, demystifying her mystery), counterbalanced by the devaluation, punishment or saving of the guilty object (an avenue typified by the concerns of the *film noir*); or else complete disavowal of castration by the substitution of a fetish object or turning the represented figure itself into a fetish so that it becomes reassuring rather than dangerous (hence overvaluation, the cult of the female star).

This second avenue, fetishistic scopophilia, builds up the physical beauty of the object, transforming it into something satisfying in itself. The first avenue, voyeurism, on the contrary, has associations with sadism: pleasure lies in ascertaining guilt (immediately associated with castration), asserting control and subjugating the guilty person through punishment or forgiveness. This sadistic side fits in well with narrative. Sadism demands a story, depends on making something happen, forcing a change in another person, a battle of will and strength, victory/defeat, all occurring in a linear time with a beginning and an end. Fetishistic scopophilia, on the other hand, can exist outside linear time as the erotic instinct is focused on the look alone. These contradictions and ambiguities can be illustrated more simply by using works by Hitchcock and Sternberg, both of whom take the look almost as the content or subject matter of many of their films. Hitchcock is the more complex, as he uses both mechanisms. Sternberg's work, on the other hand, provides many pure examples of fetishistic scopophilia.

C2. Sternberg once said he would welcome his films being projected upside-down so that story and character involvement would not interfere with the spectator's undiluted appreciation of the screen image. This statement is revealing but ingenuous: ingenuous in that his films do demand that the figure of the woman (Dietrich, in the cycle of films with her, as the ultimate example) should be identifiable; but revealing in that it emphasises the fact that for him the pictorial space enclosed by the frame is paramount, rather than narrative or identification processes. While Hitchcock goes into the investigative side of voyeurism, Sternberg produces the ultimate fetish, taking it to the point where the powerful look of the male protagonist (characteristic of traditional narrative film) is broken in favour of the image in direct erotic rapport with the spectator. The beauty of the woman as object and the screen space coalesce; she is no longer the bearer of guilt but a perfect product, whose body, stylised and fragmented by close-ups, is the content of the film and the direct recipient of the spectator's look.

Sternberg plays down the illusion of screen depth; his screen tends to be one-dimensional, as light and shade, lace, steam, foliage, net, streamers and so on reduce the visual field. There is little or no mediation of the look through the eyes of the main male protagonist. On the contrary, shadowy presences like La Bessière in *Morocco* act as surrogates for the director, detached as they are from audience identification. Despite Sternberg's insistence that his stories are irrelevant, it is significant that they are concerned with situation, not suspense, and cyclical rather than linear time, while plot complications revolve around misunderstanding rather than conflict. The most important absence is that of the controlling male gaze within the screen scene. The high point of emotional drama in the most typical Dietrich films, her supreme moments of erotic meaning, take place in the absence of the man she loves in the fiction. There are other witnesses, other spectators watching her on the screen, their gaze is one with, not standing in for, that of the audience. At the end of *Morocco*, Tom Brown has already

disappeared into the desert when Amy Jolly kicks off her gold sandals and walks after him. At the end of *Dishonoured*, Kranau is indifferent to the fate of Magda. In both cases, the erotic impact, sanctified by death, is displayed as a spectacle for the audience. The male hero misunderstands and, above all, does not see.

In Hitchcock, by contrast, the male hero does see precisely what the audience sees. However, although fascination with an image through scopophilic eroticism can be the subject of the film, it is the role of the hero to portray the contradictions and tensions experienced by the spectator. In *Vertigo* in particular, but also in *Marnie* and *Rear Window*, the look is central to the plot, oscillating between voyeurism and fetishistic fascination. Hitchcock has never concealed his interest in voyeurism, cinematic and non-cinematic. His heroes are exemplary of the symbolic order and the law—a policeman (*Vertigo*), a dominant male possessing money and power (*Marnie*)—but their erotic drives lead them into compromised situations. The power to subject another person to the will sadistically or to the gaze voyeuristically is turned onto the woman as the object of both. Power is backed by a certainty of legal right and the established guilt of the woman (evoking castration, psychoanalytically speaking). True perversion is barely concealed under a shallow mask of ideological correctness—the man is on the right side of the law, the woman on the wrong. Hitchcock's skilful use of identification processes and liberal use of subjective camera from the point of view of the male protagonist draw the spectators deeply into his position, making them share his uneasy gaze. The spectator is absorbed into a voyeuristic situation within the screen scene and diegesis, which parodies his own in the cinema.

In an analysis of *Rear Window*, Douchet takes the film as a metaphor for the cinema. Jeffries is the audience, the events in the apartment block opposite correspond to the screen. As he watches, an erotic dimension is added to his look, a central image to the drama. His girlfriend Lisa had been of little sexual interest to him, more or less a drag, so long as she remained on the spectator side. When she crosses the barrier between his room and the block opposite, their relationship is reborn erotically. He does not merely watch her through his lens, as a distant meaningful image, he also sees her as a guilty intruder exposed by a dangerous man threatening her with punishment, and thus finally giving him the opportunity to save her. Lisa's exhibitionism has already been established by her obsessive interest in dress and style, in being a passive image of visual perfection; Jeffries's voyeurism and activity have also been established through his work as a photo-journalist, a maker of stories and captor of images. However, his enforced inactivity, binding him to his seat as a spectator, puts him squarely in the fantasy position of the cinema audience.

In *Vertigo*, subjective camera predominates. Apart from one flashback from Judy's point of view, the narrative is woven around what Scottie sees or fails to see. The audience follows the growth of his erotic obsession and subsequent despair precisely from his point of view. Scottie's voyeurism is blatant: he falls in love with a woman he follows and spies on without speaking to. Its sadistic side is equally blatant: he has chosen (and freely chosen, for he had been a successful lawyer) to be a policeman, with all the attendant possibilities of pursuit and investigation. As a result, he follows, watches and falls in love with a perfect image of female beauty and mystery. Once he actually confronts her, his erotic drive is to break her down and force her *to tell* by persistent cross-questioning.

In the second part of the film, he reenacts his obsessive involvement with the image he loved to watch secretly. He reconstructs Judy as Madeleine, forces her to conform in every detail to the actual physical appearance of his fetish. Her exhibitionism, her masochism, make her an ideal passive counterpart to Scottie's active sadistic voyeurism. She knows her part is to perform, and only by playing it through and then replaying it can she keep Scottie's erotic interest. But in the repetition he does break her down and

succeeds in exposing her guilt. His curiosity wins through; she is punished.

Thus, in *Vertigo*, erotic involvement with the look boomerangs: the spectator's own fascination is revealed as illicit voyeurism as the narrative content enacts the processes and pleasures that he is himself exercising and enjoying. The Hitchcock hero here is firmly placed within the symbolic order, in narrative terms. He has all the attributes of the patriarchal superego. Hence the spectator, lulled into a false sense of security by the apparent legality of his surrogate, sees through his look and finds himself exposed as complicit, caught in the moral ambiguity of looking. Far from being simply an aside on the perversion of the police, *Vertigo* focuses on the implications of the active/looking, passive/looked-at split in terms of sexual difference and the power of the male symbolic encapsulated in the hero. Marnie, too, performs for Mark Rutland's gaze and masquerades as the perfect to-be-looked-at image. He, too, is on the side of the law until, drawn in by obsession with her guilt, her secret, he longs to see her in the act of committing a crime, make her confess and thus save her. So he, too, becomes complicit as he acts out the implications of his power. He controls money and words; he can have his cake and eat it.

IV SUMMARY

The psychoanalytic background that has been discussed in this article is relevant to the pleasure and unpleasure offered by traditional narrative film. The scopophilic instinct (pleasure in looking at another person as an erotic object) and, in contradistinction, ego libido (forming identification processes) act as formations, mechanisms, which mould this cinema's formal attributes. The actual image of woman as (passive) raw material for the (active) gaze of man takes the argument a step further into the content and structure of representation, adding a further layer of ideological significance demanded by the patriarchal order in its favourite cinematic form—illusionistic narrative film. The argument must return again to the psychoanalytic background: women in representation can signify castration, and activate voyeuristic or fetishistic mechanisms to circumvent this threat. Although none of these interacting layers is intrinsic to film, it is only in the film form that they can reach a perfect and beautiful contradiction, thanks to the possibility in the cinema of shifting the emphasis of the look. The place of the look defines cinema, the possibility of varying it and exposing it. This is what makes cinema quite different in its voyeuristic potential from, say, strip-tease, theatre, shows and so on. Going far beyond highlighting a woman's to-be-looked-at-ness, cinema builds the way she is to be looked at into the spectacle itself. Playing on the tension between film as controlling the dimension of time (editing, narrative) and film as controlling the dimension of space (changes in distance, editing), cinematic codes create a gaze, a world and an object, thereby producing an illusion cut to the measure of desire. It is these cinematic codes and their relationship to formative external structures that must be broken down before mainstream film and the pleasure it provides can be challenged.

To begin with (as an ending), the voyeuristic-scopophilic look that is a crucial point of traditional filmic pleasure can itself be broken down. There are three different looks associated with cinema: that of the camera as it records the pro-filmic event, that of the audience as it watches the final product, and that of the characters at each other within the screen illusion. The conventions of narrative film deny the first two and subordinate them to the third, the conscious aim being always to eliminate intrusive camera presence and prevent a distancing awareness in the audience. Without these two absences (the material existence of the recording process, the critical reading of the spectator), fictional drama cannot achieve reality, obviousness and truth. Nevertheless, as this article has argued, the structure of looking in narrative fiction film contains a contradiction in its own premises: the female image as a castration threat constantly endangers the unity of the diegesis and bursts through the world of illusion as an intrusive, static, one-dimentional fetish. Thus the two looks materially present in time and space are obsessively subordinated to the neurotic needs of the male ego. The camera becomes the mechanism for producing an illusion of Renaissance space, flowing movements compatible with the human eye, an ideology of representation that revolves around the perception of the subject; the camera's look is disavowed in order to create a convincing world in which the spectator's surrogate can perform with verisimilitude. Simultaneously, the look of the audience is denied an intrinsic force: as soon as fetishistic representation of the female image threatens to break the spell of illusion, and the erotic image on the screen appears directly (without mediation) to the spectator, the fact of fetishisation, concealing as it does castration fear, freezes the look, fixates the spectator and prevents him from achieving any distance from the image in front of him.

This complex interaction of looks is specific to film. The first blow against the monolithic accumulation of traditional film conventions (already undertaken by radical film-makers) is to free the look of the camera into its materiality in time and space and the look of the audience into dialectics and passionate detachment. There is no doubt that this destroys the satisfaction, pleasure and privilege of the "invisible guest," and highlights the way film has depended on voyeuristic active/passive mechanisms. Women, whose image has continually been stolen and used for this end, cannot view the decline of the traditional film form with anything much more than sentimental regret.

NOTE

1. Written in 1973 and published in 1975 in *Screen.*

PART VII

Historical Criticism

Since the 1980s, literary critics have focused with renewed intensity on the possibilities of historical understanding in literary and cultural studies. This interest has prompted much productive debate about what constitutes effective historical criticism and how historical criticism can be articulated along with other critical approaches. This movement has been in reaction to more traditional historical criticism that tends to confine itself to inquiry moving strictly along three lines of historical understanding. The first is to cast light on and clarify the text as a document or a kind of material cultural artifact. This may mean fixing the date of composition and also establishing the authoritative version of a text (addressing such questions as "Does it correspond with known manuscripts?" and "Are there spurious editions of this text?"). The text can also be clarified by identifying references to history—allusions to actual people, political events, civic upheavals, economic trends, and so on. This effort locates the text as a historical phenomenon—and it includes the "source study" that Stephen Greenblatt describes in "Shakespeare and the Exorcists" as "the elephants' graveyard of literary history."

The second goal is to describe the author/artist as having a past made up of certain significant events and, in light of that past, to see a predisposition to write in a certain manner and style. The goal of most literary biography, this approach tends to cover a broad area of intellectual, cultural, and aesthetic concerns, including the "symptomatic" (highly person-oriented) reading of literature that dominated the work of Freudian ego-psychology, which analyzes literature in the same way the psychoanalyst analyzes the discourse of the patient in the "talking cure" of therapy. This last is "history" in the sense of being a single author's "life" or "life and work": just as Freud analyzes the language of his patients in psychoanlysis in order to discover the coherent narrative—the case *history*—in studies of "Dora" and "the Wolf Man," so the literary critic analyzes the author's language to discover the coherent underlying psychoanalytic narrative.

The third goal is to grasp a literary work as it reflects the historical forces that shaped it initially. This approach assumes that a historical moment—enormously complex in its diverse representations—produces the factors that shape a particular work of literary art. This approach projects the historical process itself as the instigator and actual shaper of all dimensions of culture, a kind of ultimate author, both the origin and real composer of specific works, too. J. Hillis Miller in "The Search for

Grounds in Literary Study" (in "What Is Literary Theory?" [Part II]) offers an abstract version of this approach in what Mikhail Bakhtin calls in this section "sociological poetics." Bakhtin can be contrasted with the psychoanalytic technique of someone like Žižek precisely in the fact that while Freudian psychology analyzes discourse attached to an explicitly named author, Bakhtin is interested in more anonymous social discourse (though the sophistication of Žižek and Mulvey lies in their ability to focus on works like Doyle's almost "mythic" Sherlock Holmes or socially produced film, both of which approach the subtle sense of the more or less anonymous "ideology" that Bakhtin pursues and Raymond Williams describes).

Successful historical criticism in the traditional mold we are describing—criticism that accomplishes all three goals—endeavors, as Hippolyte Taine advanced in the nineteenth century, to recover "from the monuments of literature, a knowledge of the manner in which men thought and felt centuries ago." Taine's approach to historical criticism, known today as the "traditional" approach, thus defines literary interpretation on a *genetic* model, as an explanation of how a work's genesis in a historical situation (where specific causes are manifested) brings the work into being as a distinct aesthetic object. From this standpoint, the literary critic necessarily studies history as an end in itself, since the literary text is an object produced by history's operation. Indeed, because history produces or determines the shape and content of literature, the study of literature must first be a study of history, the virtual master text. From this perspective at least, contrary to Aristotle's opinion, history is superior to literature in that it shapes literature and determines its nature.

Such traditional historical study, in the analysis of Walter Benjamin, an important German cultural critic of the 1930s, is the opposite of the politically oriented sense of history in Marxist historical materialism. More recently, Stephen Greenblatt defined traditional historical study as "old" historicism as against a "New Historicism," the "old" being "the dominant historical scholarship of the past." In the Introduction to *The Forms of Power and the Power of Forms in the Renaissance,* he says that the "old" kind "tends to be monological; that is, it is concerned with discovering a single political vision, usually identical to that said to be held by the entire literate class or indeed the entire population." As such, he argues, "this vision can serve as a stable point of reference, beyond contingency, to which literary interpetation can securely refer. Literature is conceived to mirror the period's beliefs, but to mirror them, as it were, from a safe distance." Greenblatt refers specifically to traditional literary scholarship, but he is also describing, in this critique, the traditional Marxist distinction between the historical economic "base" of social relationships—the modes of production at a given historical moment—and the "superstructure" of ideology, beliefs, and assumptions embodied in art, intellectual worldviews, and other consciously or unconsciously held ideas.

MARXIST CRITICISM

Much modern historical criticism has tended to veer away from the "old" historicism and has disrupted the hierarchy of history as superior to literature, closing the distance between the two. Instead of viewing history as the determining context for literature, many critics throughout the twentieth century—Georg Lukács and Raymond Williams, for example—have reconceived history as a field of discourse in which literature and criticism make their own impact as political forces and, in effect, participate in a historical dialectic. In the Marxist view of literary criticism, the critic is a member of an intellectual class that promotes cultural revolution through a political commitment expressed in literary studies; the critic is positioned to participate in what Aijaz Ahmad calls (in "What Is Literary Theory?" [Part II]) "politically informed readings." Lukács fulfilled this social commitment by attempting to "lay bare" the "devices" of literature that can show the ideological orientation of a work. In the case of modernist literature, particularly James Joyce's *Ulysses*, Lukács demonstrated the dehumanizing and fragmenting effect of capitalist culture and, further, showed how a modernist novel can silently promote the acceptance of underlying social principles and values. As Lukács says of Franz Kafka, the "mood of total impotence, of paralysis in the face of the unintelligible power of circumstances, informs" the Modernists' worldview and exposes bourgeois ideology. Fredric Jameson, in *The Political Unconscious,* attempts to modify this extreme view of modernism by isolating the "utopian vocation" in modernist discourse, its "mission . . . to restore at least a symbolic experience of libidinal gratification."

Patrocinio Schweickart uses Jameson's concept and offers a helpful example of the dialectical relationship between the negative and positive elements of modernism in "Reading Ourselves" (in "Rhetoric and Reader Response" [Part III]), while Cora Kaplan (in "Feminism and Gender Studies" [Part VIII]) and Ahmad (in "What Is Literary Theory?" [Part II]) offer Marxist readings of literary history and the history of literary theory, and those readings are little informed by psychoanalytic categories.

Raymond Williams has influenced many doing historical and cultural criticism. Both Ahmad and Stuart Hall (in "Cultural Studies" [Part IX]) offer discussions of Williams's important work. He investigates crucial areas of modern culture in the attempt to understand subtle coercion in the promotion of capitalist ideology. At the same time, he broke with an older Marxism by positing the potential productive effect of cultural developments on dimensions of the economic "base" that were previously thought to dictate all aspects of culture. Typical of Williams is his groundbreaking analysis of the "country and city" in English literature. He shows the way in which certain values have been projected in the ideal pastoral setting of "country" communities. Other values are depicted as primarily urban and even antipastoral. Such an "opposition" is governed, above all, by the contradictions (dialectical contradictions) that drive social life and reveal the "real" relations of the "base" (economic) and "superstructure" (social and cultural) relationship. As Williams notes in "Base and Superstructure in Marxist Cultural Theory" in this section, "it is indeed one of the central propositions of Marx's sense of history that there are deep contradictions in the relationships of production and in the consequent social relationships." The economic "base" of a society, as manifested in the "relations of production," he goes on, determines that society's "superstructure"—its arts and ideology—as a "consequence" of the underlying "mode" of production, such as feudalism or capitalism.

On this point, Williams articulates a somewhat modified version of the central tenet of Marxist literary criticism in that he also recognizes the effect of the super-structure on the base, though he does not go as far as Nancy Armstrong does in this section when she asserts that her analysis "will be inverting the usual priorities of cause and effect maintained by mainstream modern historiography." Still, Williams argues that literature, art, and culture are social practices inseparable "from other kinds of social practice, in such a way as to make them subject to quite special and distinct laws. They may have quite specific features as practices, but they cannot be separated from the general social process." In the words of Étienne Balibar and Pierre Macherey, literature "does not 'fall from the heavens,' the product of a mysterious 'creation,' but is the product of social practice (rather a particular social practice); nei-ther is it an 'imaginary' activity, albeit it produces imaginary effects, but inescapably part of a material process." The term "imaginary" they use is taken from Lacanian psychoanalysis and applied to social contexts. Catherine Belsey, in "Constructing the Subject: Deconstructing the Text" (in "Deconstruction and Poststructuralism" [Part V]), explicates this "transference" of psychoanalytic categories to social situations in explaining "ideology." She, like Balibar and Macherey, is following the French Marx-ist theoretician Louis Althusser.

Other Marxist critics also assume that literature and discourse are best analyzed as the product of particular social practices. For instance, the large corpus of work asso-ciated with the Russian scholar Mikhail Bakhtin, represented here in an essay signed by V. N. Vološinov, "Discourse in Life and Discourse in Art (Concerning Sociological Poetics)," aims at exploring the interpersonal and social contexts of art and discourse. Under the term "dialogism"—the study of language in the processes of the social in-teractions of dialogue and contest—Bakhtin has, in recent years, been greatly influen-tial. (The work associated with him that sometimes was published under the names of friends and associates during Stalin's repressive regime in the Soviet Union demon-strates in the very ambiguity surrounding its "authorship" precisely the "dialogism" that it propounds. Moreover, in an "inverse" historiography we are discussing him here *after* Williams because, though he wrote earlier than Williams, Bakhtin's work has only recently become influential in the West.) In his studies of particular authors and genres, Bakhtin attempts to analyze the play of different voices, articulating dif-fering ideological positions, within the discourse of the novel and other literary forms. "Discourse in Life and Discourse in Art" maintains that there is a "social essence of art." "Verbal discourse," this essay asserts, "is a social event; it is not self-contained in the sense of some abstract linguistic quantity, nor can it be derived psy-chologically from the speaker's subjective consciousness taken in isolation." Rather, the extraverbal—the "historical"—situation enters into verbal discourse including lit-erary discourse "as an essential constitutive part of the structure of its import." Bakhtin is particularly interested in the relationship between history and "so-called *theoretical poetics*"—that is, working at a historical moment at which Russian Formal-ism was a vital contemporary force, he is profoundly interested in the relationship be-tween history and formalism—and his work, like that of Williams, attempts to un-derstand *forms* of intelligibility in relation to historical forces.

Thus, for either Bakhtin or Williams the audience—the "listener"—is not, as rhetoricians like Walter Ong suggest, simply a "formal" category, a function of a text; rather, the listener, as Bakhtin says, "has his own independent place in the event of artistic creation." In this way, a Marxist rhetoric is quite different from that of Ong or Peter Ramus. Rather than stabilizing the position of the reader, creating a normative or fictional reader, as Ong advances that literature does in "The Writer's Audience Is Always a Fiction," "literature" itself is the product of—or completely wound up and "imbricated" in—the social contexts out of which it grows. Another Marxist critic, Terry Eagleton, goes so far as to argue that the rhetorical function of literature is precisely to *destabilize* the reader, to create what the Marxist playwright Bertold Brecht called an "alienation effect." Destabilization is related to the "defamiliarization" of Russian Formalism. In fact, "defamiliarization" is another translation of the "quasi-Brechtian effect of estrangement" Slavoj Žižek mentions in "Psychology and Psychoanalysis" (Part VI). Destabilization, however, functions politically or ethically (as opposed to aesthetically) in allowing the reader or audience to reconceive of his or her position as situated within a particular social structure. Alienation, Eagleton argues, "hollows out the imaginary plenitude of everyday actions, deconstructing them into their social determinants and inscribing within them the conditions of their making." Art, at least as Brecht conceived it, can reveal the artificial in the seemingly "natural," to ask the "crude" question of what ends particular discursive practices serve rather than "refined" questions that assume the stability and permanence of those practices. This is the effect, as Eagleton argues, of Brecht's slogan *"plumpes Denken"*—think crudely.

In this way, contemporary Marxism situates criticism as it does literature. In *Literary Theory* Terry Eagleton argues "that the history of modern literary theory is part of the political and ideological history of our epoch," and many contemporary critics—including Jameson, Williams, Eagleton, Cornel West, bell hooks, Gayatri Chakravorty Spivak, Ahmad, Edward Said, Catherine Belsey, and most of the feminist critics represented in this book—share a strong sense of criticism as a historically situated activity that deeply involves the critic, so that the critic cannot stand apart from the text being read and interpreted but can only choose to recognize his or her own effect on the text at a particular historical moment. Any literary theory in use, as Eagleton says, is "indissociably bound up with political beliefs and ideological values"—that is, has taken some stand in relation to such beliefs. In denoting performance and power rather than meaning and knowledge, Brecht's "crude" thinking reminds the reader that the "superstructure" of knowledge and meaning has a material base that has not been produced by the refinements of a superstructure developing from that base. Crude thinking reminds the critic that even the most "disinterested" contemplation of meaning and art—even the most esoteric criticism—is situated in a social and political world and, for that reason, is a more or less "crude" activity with social and political consequences that can never achieve the purity of "disinterestedness."

A good example of this perspective is the work of Walter Benjamin we mentioned earlier. Benjamin, who was both a Marxist and a Jew fleeing Nazi Germany, offers profound meditations on the very idea of "history" in the modern world that are very important to contemporary Marxist literary criticism. Traditional historians (such as Taine), according to Benjamin, aim at "disinterestedness" in their attempt to "blot out everything they know about the later course of history"; they conceive of history as taking place in "homogeneous, empty time" and culminating in "universal history," in which it is possible to distinguish "between major and minor" events. Such distinctions are always made from the point of view of of history's "victors," the ruling class that defines the "cultural treasures" of history. From Benjamin's Marxist point of view, history must be read in relation to the activities of the present to allow a dialectic mode of apprehension. (Bakhtin's dialogism makes a similar assumption.) Such a mode allows history itself—and its cultural treasures, including literature—to be inhabited by more than one historical narrative, more than one historical significance: cultural treasures, Benjamin writes, "owe their existence not only to the efforts of great minds and talents who have created them, but also to the anonymous toil of their contemporaries. There is no document of civilization which is not at the same time a document of barbarism." Moreover, such a dialectic allows the past and the present to interpenetrate one another, not only so that the activities of the past inform the present, but more profoundly so that our activities now, in the present, can change or "redeem" the past. In language that is at once religious and political, Benjamin argues that the historical materialist can recognize "a sign of a Messianic cessation of happening, or, put differently, a revolutionary chance in the fight for the oppressed past." Earlier he writes that "there is a secret agreement between past generations and the present one. Our coming was expected on earth," and the "agreement" he speaks of would allow the past itself to be changed and revalued by making what it *resulted in*—namely, the present—different.

In Benjamin we can see a second way in which contemporary criticism "situates" itself in history. Not only do Marxist critics want criticism to be constantly aware of history—both present and past history—in reading literature, they also demand that criticism become more overtly political or, in Ahmad's terms, "polically informed," so that it attempts, as Marx said, not simply to interpret but to change the world. This sense of the need for commitment and the political responsibility of the literary critic pervades the work of these critics and much of contemporary literary criticism carried out from a historical viewpoint. (Such commitment can be heard in West's, bell hooks's, and Said's essays in "What Is Literary Studies?" [Part I] and "What Is Literary Theory?" [Part II] as well as in Kaplan's piece in "Feminism and Gender Studies" [Part VIII] and Haraway's in "Cultural Studies" [Part IX].) This stance is clear in Williams's (implicitly "utopian") assertion that human practices are "inexhaustible" and, consequently, one can always imagine and work for a world better than the present world. "No mode of production," he writes, "and therefore no dominant society or order of society, and therefore no dominant culture, in reality exhausts the full range of human practice, human energy, human intention." This stance is evident, too, in Eagleton's description of the function of Brecht's "alienation effect" and in Frank Lentricchia's definition of criticism in *Criticism and Social Change* as "the production of knowledge to the ends of power and, maybe, of social change." "The activity that a Marxist literary intellectual preeminently engages in—should engage in—" Lentricchia goes on, "is the activity of interpretation . . . which does not passively 'see,' as [Kenneth] Burke put it, but constructs a point of view in its engagement with textual events, and in so constructing produces an image of history as social struggle, of, say, class struggle." "This sort of interpretation," he concludes, "will above all else attempt to displace traditional interpretations which cover up the political work of culture."

Fredric Jameson, the most prominent Marxist critic in America today, has consistently pursued such politically oriented cultural work in his literary criticism—what he calls in *Postmodernism, or, The Cultural Logic of Late Capitalism* the disengagment of the "seeds of the future" from the present "both through analysis and through political praxis." This extensive range of vision distinguishes Jameson's work, as it does Williams's. Jameson has consistently attempted to discover the usefulness in a Marxist sense of contemporary literary theory. *The Political Unconscious,* for instance, uses Freudian, structuralist, and poststructuralist concepts in its "political work of culture." In *Postmodernism* Jameson brings the same range of methods and interests to bear in a Marxist analysis. He attempts to present a sophisticated analysis of the relationship between the base and superstructure regarding the specific cultural phenomenon of "postmodernism." Rather than seeing it as an isolated cultural phenomenon or a mere symptom of the so-called "postindustrial" society, Jameson tries to show how postmodernism is related to and serves the economic order, how what is most often conducted as an aesthetic debate about the nature of "postmodernism" actually defines "political positions." The seemingly disinterested aesthetic discussions of such artistic or cultural phenomena as postmodernism, he argues, "can always be shown to articulate visions of history" and can, in fact, be related to "moments of the capitalism from which it emerged." Jameson analyzes the cultural artifacts of contemporary culture ranging from architecture to pop art, from literature to television, in relation to the ideology of late capitalism not simply to interpret culture, but to situate it in relation to its historical "base." His aim is to present an analysis of the social forces that govern consciousness and, consequently, govern action. The aim here, as is was for Marx, is to create a situation from which to imagine the world different from the existing social and political institutions—to change the world.

THE NEW HISTORICISM

The New Historicism in America, as a movement since the early 1980s, brings the tools of contemporary critical discourse to the understanding of history and historical texts. The two highly influential figures here are Raymond Williams and Michel Foucault. For Williams, especially, with his wide-ranging interest in culture and critical methodology, we can see midcentury historical criticism moving away from the traditional hierarchy of history over literature. It does so, at least in part, under the sway of Continental philosopher-critics—particularly the French—who have redrawn the boundaries of history as a discipline. Foucault, in particular, has influenced cultural critics with his view of history as "discursive practice," what it is possible to say in one era as opposed to another. In "What Is an Author?" (in "Deconstruction and Post-structuralism" [Part V]), Foucault says that "the author's name manifests the appearance of a certain discursive set and indicates the status of this discourse within a society and a culture." Such discursive practices are, as Williams says, "hegemonic" in their effect, both creating and created by "a whole body of practices and expectations." ("Hegemony," a term developed by the Marxist writer Antonio Gramsci in the 1920s, describes the more or less "unconscious" assumptions about experience that people hold and that, in fact, are not disinterested or "objective" but serve the dominant classes in society. Hegemony is discussed by Williams in this section and by Dick Hebdige in "Cultural Studies" [Part IX].) Hans Robert Jauss, Hans-Georg Gadamer, and Eugene Vance, likewise, have suggested new ways of understanding history not only as a language but also as a horizon for both narration and social activity in relation to which textual effects are constructed.

Stephen Greenblatt, who coined the term "New Historicism," has asserted, for example, that "history cannot be divorced from textuality." The union of history and textuality has led to a rebirth of historical studies in contemporary criticism; it has led to a host of questions about the relationship Hunter Cadzow describes "between texts and the cultural system in which they were produced," between textual practice and historical events. In "Invisible Bullets: Renaissance Authority and Its Subversion," Greenblatt examines the construction of a version of social authority and the way a textual economy works within that construction. In this essay, his aim is to recover the *power* of ideas in cultural artifacts not in order "to expose [them] as mere illusion or anachronism" but in order to trace their functioning within the social world in which they appeared. He traces the power and struggle attendant to the use of the idea of "atheism" in seventeenth-century England in order to show, among other things, that the relationship between political and "cultural" events—between Thomas Harriot's *A Brief and True Report on the New Found Land of Virginia* and Shakespeare's *1 Henry IV*—is not a simple hierarchy (of base and superstructure, say) but a complicated interweaving of modes of apprehension. Even the critical term "subversion," Greenblatt argues—a term that he uses throughout his essay—is "historicized": "we locate as 'subversive' in the past precisely those things that are *not* subversion to ourselves, that pose no threat to the order by which we live and allocate resources." More generally, the mode of critical-historical analysis Greenblatt (among others) pursues abandons any notion of history as direct mimesis, any belief in history as a mere imitation of events in the world—history as a reflection of an activity happening "out there." Hayden White, especially, tends to view history as fundamentally a narrative, a narrated sequence always positioned within a genre of historical inquiry.

The sequence of history itself elaborates relationships that belong to an "episteme," not a mode of thought that characterizes an age (as in the "old" historicism) but the discursive limits in culture on what can be thought (i.e., "discursivized") at any particular moment, so that history as a discipline necessarily traces ruptures rather than continuities, empty spaces of thought within and between epistemes. This is an intentionally problematic view of history, nearly a contradiction in historical terms, in which historicity, as Foucault says in *The Order of Things*, "in its very fabric, makes possible the necessity of an origin which must be both internal and foreign to it." Rather than proposing an integrated story about the world, this model suggests that history is fundamentally comprehensible as a way, or as ways, of knowing the world, as successive forms of discourse or, in Greenblatt's term, "textuality." In Nancy Armstrong's essay "The Occidental Alice," such "textuality" manifests itself in the ways that historical "events" are comprehended in terms of "discourses": the discourses of law, "the new and flourishing social sciences" of the late nineteenth century, the analytic languages surrounding English and European imperialism, and the representations of consumption and appetite in a book like *Alice in Wonderland*. Such discourses, especially when they are juxtaposed, present "history" as a way of "thinking the Other," a sequential elaboration of the lacunae in experience. Foucault is quick to caution that these gaps in history are not lacunae "that must be filled." They are "nothing more," he explains, "and nothing less, than the unfolding of a space in which it is once more possible to think."

Fundamentally, the writing of history in this new view is a continual renewal of the cultural grids for thinking and constitutes an epistemological posture (a way of knowing—an "episteme") in and "about" the world. For this reason Armstrong can talk about *Alice in Wonderland* as an initiation of "a new moment in the history of desire" and assert that "my reading of *Alice's Adventures in Wonderland* attempts to show . . . that during the second half of the nineteenth century something happened to [the] relationship between subjects and objects." That is, Armstrong is attempting to demonstrate the historical nature of how we study history; "what we tend to feel," in Foucault's words, "is without history." Armstrong's examples are consumption and race—seemingly "objective" representations (such as photographs and scientific descriptions), sexual differences, and, above all, "fetishized" commodities. In Armstrong's analysis of Marx's notion of "fetish" can be seen the interplay of this term that exists in both the discourses of (personal) psychology and of (social) history. (Here we can understand more fully the connections between the discussions of "fetishized" literature in Cornel West and Mikhail Bakhtin and of Freudian "fetishization" in Slovoj Žižek. One good definition of "fetish" is an object that seems to exist without history.) Foucault's examples of such "objects" that need to acquire a history are "sentiments, love, conscience, [and] instinct." Another example, implicit in Armstrong and Greenblatt, and more or less explicit in Foucault's "What Is an Author?" is "literature" as a disinterested, aesthetic object.

It would be misleading to think of this definition of history as solely a contemporary phenomenon. Both Benjamin and Bakhtin, for example, give historical-materialist versions of this interactive sense of history, discourse, and the common perception of everyday life (and both are influential among New Historicists). In sum, this sense of history holds true for the histories we write as well as for the immediate sense we have of history as "reality," even in its personal impact. This is why Armstrong can end her study of Victorian culture with a discussion of those aspects of *our* culture that allowed her to pursue such a "historical" study. In its feminist enterprise, her essay erases the absolute distinction between present and past and discusses what much contemporary literary criticism has taught us about the ethics of reading, the positionality of comprehension, and the imbrication of history and the discourses that constitute historical epochs. The new "textual" sense of history—what Stanley Fish calls "wall-to-wall textuality"—difficult and sometimes forbidding in its terminology, has done much to encourage literary critics both to view history as a species of language and to look beyond formalist aesthetics in order to read literature in the context of power relations and ever wider contexts of culture.

The current view of history as a "discourse" indeed reverses the hierarchy of history over literature. Now history, like literature, is projected as a product of language, and both represent themselves as formed in a sequence of gaps, as a narrative discourse. If fundamentally a breached narrative, history in its constitution is virtually indistinguishable from literature. This comparison should not suggest that history is "made up"—"fictitious" or "mythical" in the derogatory sense—and trivial as a cultural and social pattern of interpretation. On the contrary, the reality of history in this new view (as what "hurts") is as "real" and intractible and even as potentially "hurtful" as it ever was. The new awareness is that history, like a fictional narrative, exists in a dialogue with something "foreign" or "other" to it that can never be contained or controlled by a historian who stands "outside" it, in some "disinterested" future. In this view, instead of being a more or less accurate story about what already exists, history is a knowing that is also a making, although it is a making that never quite makes what was intended.

Alternatively—looking back at traditional views of history—we can try to make of history a process of repetition, as T. S. Eliot imagined, so that what was valuable in the past is continually regained in cultural terms through poetry ("made new") in a kind of cultural retrieval mechanism. Or we can make of history an apocalyptic promise to be fulfilled in time, as Northrop Frye in *Anatomy of Criticism*—and, indeed, the Bible—envisioned it. And we can project history as a series of irrational ruptures, as Friedrich Nietzsche and Foucault imagined it. But whether as repetition, apocalypse, or rupture, history for the New Historicists is not an order in the world that simply is copied in our written histories but an order of encounter with the world like that which Heidegger called *Dasein*—"being-in-the-world," a conception of making and participating with the world.

As one result of this reconception of history and the historicity of literature, New Historicism attempts to situate literary works, as Marxist criticism does, within a historical matrix. Following Williams, New Historicism does not define that matrix as a one-way relationship between base and superstructure. Rather, following Foucault as well as Williams, New Historicism describes both history and literature in terms that eschew universalizing and transcendental descriptions and draws on the "discursive" presuppositions we have been describing. As Greenblatt says in "Shakespeare and the Exorcists," "for me the study of literature is the study of contingent, particular, intended, and historically embedded works." Armstrong, as well as Greenblatt, demonstrates such "embeddedness" of literary works in the culture that literature represents and reflects. This is a conception of literature as not being "autonomous, separable from its cultural context and hence divorced from the social, ideological, and material matrix in which all art is produced and consumed." Joined by the work of Jonathan Goldberg, Louis Marin, Louis Montrose, Leonard Tennenhouse, and others, Greenblatt has produced a significant rereading of Renaissance literature in terms of a sense that, in Tennenhouse's words, "the history of a culture is a history of all its products, literature being just one such product, social organization another, the legal apparatus yet another, and so on."

Tennenhouse argues, further, that "one is forced to make an artificial distinction among cultural texts between those which are literary and those which are political in the effort to demonstrate how, in sharing common themes and a common teleology, they actually comprised a seamless discourse." This project of articulating what Greenblatt calls "cultural poetics" has not been limited to Renaissance studies. Armstrong "historicizes" (in the sense we are discussing) feminist readings of nineteenth-century culture in "The Occidental Alice" and elsewhere; and Walter Ben Michaels has reread American naturalism in this way. Similar work for other periods in literary history is going on, and what they all attempt to do (as does Marxist criticism) is to read in literature what Greenblatt calls "a deeper and unexpressed institutional exchange," and what Armstrong describes as the forms of representation that constitute culture. "In trying to link Victorian sexuality to British imperialism," she writes, "I will be inverting the usual priorities of cause and effect maintained by mainstream modern historiography. By so doing, however, I will simply be taking up the logic England used to describe other cultures—and using that logic to describe English culture itself." That "logic" is the logic of representation, which is part and parcel of history itself.

In this project, the New Historicism shares a good deal with Marxist literary criticism—in fact, some critics have argued that it is a part of Marxist criticism. Whether or not this is so—and certainly self-consciously Marxist readers like Jameson have offered strong critiques of the New Historicism—nevertheless, both Marxism and New Historicism recognize in literary texts, as Catherine Belsey says, "not 'knowledge' but ideology itself in all its inconsistency and partiality." In doing so, they situate literary criticism in a larger framework of cultural criticism, what Eagleton calls "rhetoric" and "discourse theory." Such theory above all attempts to understand literature as historically situated practices that encompass power as much as knowledge.

RELATED TEXTS IN *CONTEMPORARY LITERARY CRITICISM*

Aijaz Ahmad, "Literary Theory and 'Third World Literature': Some Contexts"
Catherine Belsey, "Constructing the Subject: Deconstructing the Text"
Michel Foucault, "What Is an Author?"
Donna Haraway, "A Cyborg Manifesto: Science, Technology, and Socialist-Feminism in the Late Twentieth Century"
Cora Kaplan, "Pandora's Box: Subjectivity, Class and Sexuality in Socialist Feminist Criticism"
Edward Said, "The Politics of Knowledge"
Cornel West, "Black Critics and the Pitfalls of Canon Formation"

REFERENCES AND FURTHER READING

Adorno, Theodor W., *Prisms,* trans. Samuel Weber and Shierry Weber (Cambridge, MA: MIT Press, 1983).

Althusser, Louis, *For Marx* (New York: Pantheon Books, 1969).

————, *Lenin and Philosophy and Other Essays,* trans. B. Brewster (New York: Monthly Review, 1971).

Auerbach, Erich, *Mimesis: The Representation of Reality in Western Literature,* trans. Willard Trask (Princeton, NJ: Princeton University Press, 1953).

Bakhtin, M. M., *The Dialogic Imagination: Four Essays* (Austin: University of Texas Press, 1981).

Balibar, Étienne, and Pierre Macherey, "On Literature as an Ideological Form," trans. Ian McLeod, John Whitehead, and Ann Wordsworth, in *Untying the Text,* ed. Robert Young (London: Routledge, 1981).

Belsey, Catherine, *Critical Practice* (London: Methuen, 1980).

Benjamin, Walter, *Illuminations* (New York: Schocken, 1970).

Bowers, Fredson, *Textual and Literary Criticism* (New York: Cambridge University Press, 1959).

Brown, Marshall, *The Uses of Literary History* (Durham, NC: Duke University Press, 1995).

Cadzow, Hunter, "The New Historicism," in *The Johns Hopkins Guide to Literary Theory,* ed. Martin Kreisworth and Michael Gordon (Baltimore: Johns Hopkins University Press, 1993).

Cottom, Daniel, *Ravishing Tradition: Cultural Forces and Literary History* (Ithaca, NY: Cornell University Press, 1996).

Cox, Jeffrey N., and Larry J. Reynolds, *New Historical Literary Study: Essays on Reproducing Texts, Representing History* (Princeton, NJ: Princeton University Press, 1993).

Coward, Rosalind, and John Ellis, *Language and Materialism: Developments in Semiology and the Theory of the Subject* (London: Routledge, 1977).

Eagleton, Terry, *Criticism and Ideology* (New York: Schocken, 1978).

————, *Literary Theory: An Introduction* (Minneapolis: University of Minnesota Press, 1983).

————, *Marxism and Literary Criticism* (Berkeley: University of California Press, 1976).

Ferris, David, *Theory and the Evasion of History* (Baltimore: Johns Hopkins University Press, 1993).

Foucault, Michel, *Language, Counter-Memory, Practice,* trans. Donald F. Bouchard (Ithaca, NY: Cornell University Press, 1977).

————, *Madness and Civilization,* trans. Richard Howard (New York: Pantheon, 1965).

————, *The Order of Things* (New York: Pantheon, 1972).

Goldmann, Lucien, *The Hidden God,* trans. Philip Thody (New York: Humanities Press, 1976).

Greenblatt, Stephen Jay, *The Power of Forms in the English Renaissance* (Norman, OK: Pilgrim Books, 1982).

————, *Redrawing the Boundaries: The Transformation of English and American Literary Studies* (New York: MLA, 1992).

————, *Renaissance Self-Fashioning: From More to Shakespeare* (Chicago: University of Chicago Press, 1980).

Grumley, John E., *History and Totality: Radical Historicism from Hegel to Foucault* (New York: Routledge, 1989).

Hamilton, Paul, *Historicism* (New York: Routledge, 1996).

Hawthorn, Jeremy, *Cunning Passages: New Historicism, Cultural Materialism, and Marxism in the Contemporary Literary Debate* (New York: St. Martin's Press, 1996).

Hicks, Granville, *The Great Tradition* (New York: Macmillan, 1933; rev. 1935).

Holquist, Michel, *Dialogism: Bakhtin and His World* (New York: Routledge, 1990).

Jackson, J. R. de J., *Historical Criticism and the Meaning of Texts* (New York: Routledge, 1989).

James, C. Vaughan, *Soviet Socialist Realism: Origins and Theory* (New York: Macmillan, 1973).

Jameson, Fredric, *Marxism and Form: Twentieth-Century Dialectical Theories of Literature* (Princeton, NJ: Princeton University Press, 1971).

———, *The Political Unconscious: Narrative as a Socially Symbolic Act* (Ithaca, NY: Cornell University Press, 1981).

———, *Postmodernism, or, The Cultural Logic of Late Capitalism* (Durham, NC: Duke University Press, 1991).

———, *The Prison-House of Language: A Critical Account of Structuralism and Russian Formalism* (Princeton, NJ: Princeton University Press, 1972).

Jay, Martin, *The Dialectical Imagination: A History of the Frankfurt School* (Boston: Little, Brown, 1973).

Kenshur, Oscar, *Dilemmas of Enlightenment: Studies in the Rhetoric and Logic of Ideology* (Berkeley: University of California Press, 1993).

Lentricchia, Frank, *Criticism and Social Change* (Chicago: University of Chicago Press, 1983).

Levin, David, *Forms of Uncertainty: Essays in Historical Criticism* (Charlottesville: University Press of Virginia, 1992).

Lukács, Georg, *The Historical Novel* (London: Merlin Press, 1962).

———, *Realism in Our Time* (New York: Harper Torchbooks, 1971).

Macherey, Pierre, *A Theory of Literary Production,* trans. G. Wall (London: Routledge, 1978).

Ong, Walter, S.J., "The Writer's Audience Is Always a Fiction," *PMLA* 90 (1975): 9–21.

Robertson, D. W., Jr., "Historical Criticism," in *English Institute Essays: 1950,* ed. Alan S. Downer (New York: Columbia University Press, 1951), 3–31.

Royle, Nicholas, *After Derrida* (New York: St. Martin's Press, 1995).

Sartre, Jean Paul, *What Is Literature?* (New York: Philosophical Library, 1949).

Schleifer, Ronald, "Walter Benjamin and the Crisis of Representation: Multiplicity, Meaning, and Athematic Death," in *Death and Representation,* ed. Sara Goodwin and Elisabeth Bronfen (Baltimore: Johns Hopkins University Press, 1993).

Strier, Richard, *Resistant Structures: Particularity, Radicalism, and Renaissance Texts* (Berkeley: University of California Press, 1995).

Thomas, Brook, *The New Historicism: And Other Old-Fashioned Topics* (Princeton, NJ: Princeton University Press, 1991).

H. Aram Vesser, ed., *The New Historicism* (New York: Routledge, 1989).

———, *The New Historicism Reader* (New York: Routledge, 1994).

Wellek, René, "Literary Theory, Criticism, and History," in *Sewanee Review* 68 (1960), 1–19.

White, Hayden, *Metahistory: The Historical Imagination in Nineteenth-Century Europe* (Baltimore: John Hopkins University Press, 1973).

———, *Tropics of Discourse: Essays in Cultural Criticism* (Baltimore: Johns Hopkins University Press, 1978).

Willett, John, ed., *Brecht on Theatre* (London: Methuen, 1964).

Williams, Raymond, *Marxism and Literature* (New York: Oxford University Press, 1977).

———, *Problems in Materialism and Culture* (New York: Schocken, 1981).

Wimsatt, W. K., Jr., "History and Criticism: A Problematic Relationship," in *PMLA* 66 (1951), 21–31.

27

Mikhail Bakhtin

1875–1975

Mikhail Bakhtin's greatest periods of productivity—the 1920s and 1930s—were troubled first by the effects of the Russian civil war and revolution and then by the repressive Stalin regime. During the 1920s, three books and several articles were published under the names of his friends; these include *The Formal Method in Literary Scholarship; Freudianism: A Critical Sketch; Marxism and the Philosophy of Language;* "Beyond the Social"; "Contemporary Vitalism"; and "Discourse in Life and Discourse in Art." In 1946 and 1949, the State Accrediting Bureau rejected his 1940 dissertation, "Rabelais and Folk Culture of the Middle Ages and Renaissance," and it remained unpublished until 1965. Since that time it has gone through several editions in Japanese, German, and English.

Bakhtin's early work was devoted to developing a philosophy of language grounded in the interplay of communication. Bakhtin first defended the utterance as a dialogic process, involving both the speaker or writer and the implied or actual listener or reader, in his "Problems of Dostoevsky's Art" (1929). In the dialogic process, the importance of context becomes crucial to understanding the meaning of an utterance. Language, like all art, Bakhtin defined as an "exchange" or clash of values between a work and its audience. This definition of language, a "sociological poetics," views language as both determining and determined by historical components of particular utterances. Consequently, it rejects both the formalism that treats texts as static, purely linguistic objects and the "vulgar" Marxism that would define texts as determined entirely by their creator and reader.

Bakhtin's first attempts to define a theory of utterance appeared in "Discourse in Life and Discourse in Art" (1926), published under V. N. Vološinov's name but attributed by most scholars to Bakhtin. Bakhtin asserts here that context, including nonverbal elements, is an integral component rather than external to utterance. Artistic form, he concludes, is largely influenced by "extra-artistic" reality. In the course of his discussion, Bakhtin attacks the traditional sociological method of studying art. The Marxist terminology is used to enter into dialogue with the Marxist sociologies of literature; but Bakhtin uses this terminology to propose a brand of analysis more radical than that of the Marxists in its definition of language as an "event" in which both linguistic and social elements predetermine one another in a struggle toward textual meaning.

Discourse in Life and Discourse in Art
(Concerning Sociological Poetics)

I

In the study of literature, the sociological method has been applied almost exclusively for treating historical questions while remaining virtually untouched with regard to the problems of so-called *theoretical poetics*—that whole area of issues involving artistic form and its various factors, style, and so forth.

A fallacious view, but one adhered to even by certain Marxists, has it that the sociological method becomes legitimate only at that point where poetic form acquires added complexity through the ideological factor (the content) and begins to develop historically in conditions of external social reality. Form in and of itself, according to this view, possesses its own special, not sociological but specifically artistic, nature and system of governance.

Such a view fundamentally contradicts the very basis of the Marxist method—its monism and its historicity. The consequence of this and similar views is that form and content, theory and history, are rent asunder.

But we cannot dismiss these fallacious views without further, more detailed inquiry; they are too characteristic for the whole of the modern study of the arts.

The most patent and consistent development of the point of view in question appeared recently in a work by Professor P. N. Sakulin.[1] Sakulin distinguishes two dimensions in literature and its history: the immanent and the causal. The immanent "artistic core" of literature possesses special structure and governance peculiar to itself alone: so endowed, it is capable of autonomous evolutionary development "by nature." But in the process of this development, literature becomes subject to the "causal" influence of the extra-artistic social milieu. With the "immanent core" of literature, its structure and autonomous evolution, the sociologist can have nothing to do—those topics fall within the exclusive competence of theoretical and historical poetics and their special methods.[2] The sociological method can successfully study only the causal interaction between literature and its surrounding extra-artistic social milieu. Moreover, immanent (nonsociological) analysis of the essence of literature, including its intrinsic, autonomous governance, must precede sociological analysis.[3]

Of course, no Marxist sociologist could agree with such an assertion. Nevertheless, it has to be admitted that sociology, up to the present moment, has dealt almost exclusively with concrete issues in history of literature and has not made a single serious attempt to utilize its methods in the study of the so-called "immanent" structure of a work of art. That structure has, in plain fact, been relegated to the province of aesthetic or psychological or other methods that have nothing in common with sociology.

To verify this fact we need only examine any modern work on poetics or even on the theory of art study in general. We will not find a trace of any application of sociological categories. Art is treated as if it were nonsociological "by nature" just exactly as is the physical or chemical structure of a body. Most West European and Russian scholars of the arts make precisely this claim regarding literature and art as a whole, and on this basis persistently defend the study of art as a special discipline against sociological approaches of any kind.

They motivate this claim of theirs in approximately the following way. Every item that becomes the object of supply and demand, that is, that becomes a commodity, is subject, as concerns its value and its circulation within human society, to the governing socioeconomic laws.

Let us suppose that we know those laws very well: still, despite that fact, we shall understand exactly nothing about the physical and chemical structure of the item in question. On the contrary, the study of commodities is itself in need of preliminary physical and chemical analysis of the given commodity. And the only persons competent to perform such analysis are physicists and chemists with the help of the specific methods of their fields. In the opinion of these art scholars, art stands in an analogous position. Art, too, once it becomes a social factor and becomes subject to the influence of other, likewise social, factors, takes its place, of course, within the overall system of sociological governance—but from that governance we shall never be able to derive art's *aesthetic essence,* just as we cannot derive the chemical formula for this or that commodity from the governing economic laws of commodity circulation. What art study and theoretical poetics are supposed to do is to seek such a formula for a work of art—one that is *specific* to art and independent of sociology.

This conception of the essence of art is, as we have said, fundamentally in contradiction with the bases of Marxism. To be sure, you will never find a chemical formula by the sociological method, but a scientific "formula" for any domain of *ideology* can be found, and can only be found, by the methods of sociology. All the other—"immanent"—methods are heavily involved in subjectivism and have been unable, to the present day, to break free of the fruitless controversy of opinions and points of view and, therefore, are least of all capable of finding anything even remotely resembling the rigorous and exact formulas of chemistry. Neither, of course, can the Marxist method claim to provide such a "formula"; the rigor and exactness of the natural sciences are impossible within the domain of ideological study due to the very nature of what it studies. But the closest approximation to genuine scientificness in the study of ideological creativity has become possible for the first time thanks to the sociological method in its Marxist

conception. Physical and chemical bodies or substances exist outside human society as well as within it, but all products of ideological creativity arise in and for human society. Social definitions are not applicable from outside, as is the case with bodies and substances in nature—*ideological formations are intrinsically, immanently sociological.* No one is likely to dispute that point with respect to political and juridical forms—what possible nonsociological, immanent property could be found in them? The most subtle formal nuances of a law or of a political system are all equally amenable to the sociological method and only to it. But exactly the same thing is true for other ideological forms. They are all *sociological through and through,* even though their structure, mutable and complex as it is, lends itself to exact analysis only with enormous difficulty.

Art, too, is just as immanently social; the extra-artistic social milieu, affecting art from outside, finds direct, intrinsic response within it. This is not a case of one foreign element affecting another but of one social formation affecting another social formation. The *aesthetic,* just as the juridical or the cognitive, is *only a variety of the social.* Theory of art, consequently, can only be a *sociology of art.*[4] No "immanent" tasks are left in its province.

II

If sociological analysis is to be properly and productively applied to the theory of art (poetics in particular), then two fallacious views that severely narrow the scope of art by operating exclusively with certain isolated factors must be rejected.

The first view can be defined as the *fetishization of the artistic work artifact.* This fetishism is the prevailing attitude in the study of art at the present time. The field of investigation is restricted to the work of art itself, which is analyzed in such a way as if everything in art were exhausted by it alone. The creator of the work and the work's contemplators remain outside the field of investigation.

The second point of view, conversely, restricts itself to the study of the psyche of the creator or of the contemplator (more often than not, it simply equates the two). For it, all art is exhausted by the experiences of the person doing the contemplating or doing the creating.

Thus, for the one point of view the object of study is only the structure of the work artifact, while for the other it is only the individual psyche of the creator or contemplator.

The first point of view advances the material to the forefront of aesthetic investigation. Form, understood very narrowly as the form of the material—that which organizes it into a single unified and complete artifact—becomes the main and very nearly exclusive object of study.

A variety of the first point of view is the so-called formal method. For the formal method, a poetic work is verbal material organized by form in some particular way. Moreover, it takes the *verbal* not as a sociological phenomenon but from an abstract linguistic point of view. That it should adopt just such a point of view is quite understandable: Verbal discourse, taken in the broader sense as a phenomenon of cultural communication, ceases to be something self-contained and can no longer be understood independently of the social situation that engenders it.

The first point of view cannot be consistently followed out to the end. The problem is that if one remains within the confines of the artifact aspect of art, there is no way of indicating even such things as the boundaries of the material or which of its features have artistic significance. The material in and of itself directly merges with the extra-artistic milieu surrounding it and has an infinite number of aspects and definitions—in terms of mathematics, physics, chemistry, and so forth as well as of linguistics. However far we go in analyzing all the properties of the material and all the possible combinations of those properties, we shall never be able to find their aesthetic significance unless we slip in

the contraband of another point of view that does not belong within the framework of analysis of the material. Similarly, however far we go in analyzing the chemical structure of a body or substance, we shall never understand its value and significance as a commodity unless we draw economics into the picture.

The attempt of the second view to find the aesthetic in the individual psyche of the creator or contemplator is equally vain. To continue our economic analogy, we might say that such a thing is similar to the attempt to analyze the individual psyche of a proletarian in order thereby to disclose the objective production relations that determine his position in society.

In the final analysis, both points of view are guilty of the same fault: *They attempt to discover the whole in the part,* that is, they take the structure of a part, abstractly divorced from the whole, and claim it as the structure of the whole. Meanwhile, "the artistic" in its total integrity is not located in the artifact and not located in the separately considered psyches of creator and contemplator; it encompasses all three of these factors. It is a *special form of interrelationship between creator and contemplator fixed in a work of art.*

This *artistic communication* stems from the basis common to it and other social forms, but, at the same time, it retains, as do all other forms, its own uniqueness; it is a special type of communication, possessing a form of its own peculiar to itself. *To understand this special form of social communication realized and fixed in the material of a work of art—that precisely is the task of sociological poetics.*

A work of art, viewed outside this communication and independently of it, is simply a physical artifact or an exercise in linguistics. It becomes art only in the process of the interaction between creator and contemplator, as the essential factor in this interaction. Everything in the material of a work of art that cannot be drawn into the communication between creator and contemplator, that cannot become the "medium," the means of their communication, cannot be the recipient of artistic value, either.

Those methods that ignore the social essence of art and attempt to find its nature and distinguishing features only in the organization of the work artifact are in actuality obliged to project the social interrelationship of creator and contemplator into various aspects of the material and into various devices for structuring the material. In exactly the same way, psychological aesthetics projects the same social relations into the individual psyche of the perceiver. This projection distorts the integrity of these interrelationships and gives a false picture of both the material and the psyche.

Aesthetic communication, fixed in a work of art, is, as we have already said, entirely unique and irreducible to other types of ideological communication such as the political, the juridical, the moral, and so on. If political communication establishes corresponding institutions and, at the same time, juridical forms, aesthetic communication organizes only a work of art. If the latter rejects this task and begins to aim at creating even the most transitory of political organizations or any other ideological form, then by that very fact it ceases to be aesthetic communication and relinquishes its unique character. *What characterizes aesthetic communication is the fact that it is wholly absorbed in the creation of a work of art and in its continuous recreations in the co-creation of contemplators, and it does not require any other kind of objectification.* But, needless to say, this unique form of communciation does not exist *in isolation;* it participates in the unitary flow of social life, it reflects the common economic basis, and it engages in interaction and exchange with other forms of communication.

The purpose of the present study is to try to reach an understanding of the poetic utterance as a form of this special, verbally implemented aesthetic communication. But in order to do so, we must first analyze in detail certain aspects of verbal utterances outside the realm of art—

utterances in the *speech of everyday life and behavior,* for in such speech are already embedded the bases, the potentialities of artistic form. Moreover, the social essence of verbal discourse stands out here in sharper relief and the connection between an utterance and the surrounding social milieu lends itself more easily to analysis.

III

In life, verbal discourse is clearly not self-sufficient. It arises out of an extraverbal pragmatic situation and maintains the closest possible connection with that situation. Moreover, such discourse is directly informed by life itself and cannot be divorced from life without losing its import.

The kind of characterizations and evaluations of pragmatic, behavioral utterances we are likely to make are such things as: "that's a lie," "that's the truth," "that's a daring thing to say," "you can't say that," and so on and so forth.

All these and similar evaluations, whatever the criteria that govern them (ethical, cognitive, political, or other), take in a good deal more than what is enclosed within the strictly verbal (linguistic) factors of the utterance. *Together with the verbal factors, they also take in the extraverbal situation of the utterance.* These judgments and evaluations refer to a certain whole wherein the verbal discourse directly engages an event in life and merges with that event, forming an indissoluble unity. The verbal discourse itself, taken in isolation as a purely linguistic phenomenon, cannot, of course, be true or false, daring or diffident.

How does verbal discourse in life relate to the extraverbal situation that has engendered it? Let us analyze this matter, using an intentionally simplified example for the purpose.

Two people are sitting in a room. They are both silent. Then one of them says, "Well!" The other does not respond.

For us, as outsiders, this entire "conversation" is utterly incomprehensible. Taken in isolation, the utterance "Well!" is empty and unintelligible. Nevertheless, this peculiar colloquy of two persons, consisting of only one—although, to be sure, one expressively intoned—word, does make perfect sense, is fully meaningful and complete.

In order to disclose the sense and meaning of this colloquy, we must analyze it. But what is it exactly that we can subject to analysis? Whatever pains we take with the purely verbal part of the utterance, however subtly we define the phonetic, morphological, and semantic factors of the word *well,* we shall still not come a single step closer to an understanding of the whole sense of the colloquy.

Let us suppose that the intonation with which this word was pronounced is known to us: indignation and reproach moderated by a certain amount of humor. This intonation somewhat fills in the semantic void of the adverb *well* but still does not reveal the meaning of the whole.

What is it we lack, then? We lack the "extraverbal context" that made the word *well* a meaningful locution for the listener. This *extraverbal context* of the utterance is comprised of three factors: (1) the *common spatial purview* of the interlocutors (the unity of the visible—in this case, the room, the window, and so on), (2) the interlocutors' *common knowledge and understanding of the situation,* and (3) their *common evaluation* of that situation.

At the time the colloquy took place, both interlocutors *looked up* at the window and *saw* that it had begun to snow; *both knew* that it was already May and that is was high time for spring to come; finally, *both* were *sick and tired* of the protracted winter—*they both were looking forward* to spring and *both were bitterly disappointed* by the late snowfall. On this "jointly seen" (snowflakes outside the window), "jointly known" (the time of year—May), and "unanimously evaluated" (winter wearied of, spring

looked forward to)—on all this the utterance *directly depends,* all this is seized in its actual, living import—is its very sustenance. And yet all this remains without verbal specification or articulation. The snowflakes remain outside the window: the date, on the page of a calendar; the evaluation, in the psyche of the speaker; and nevertheless, all this is *assumed* in the word *well.*

Now that we have been let in on the "assumed," that is, now that we know the *shared spatial and ideational purview,* the whole sense of the utterance "Well!" is perfectly clear to us and we also understand its intonation.

How does the extraverbal purview relate to the verbal discourse, how does the said relate to the unsaid?

First of all, it is perfectly obvious that, in the given case, the discourse does not at all reflect the extraverbal situation in the way a mirror reflects an object. Rather, the discourse here *resolves the situation,* bringing it to an *evaluative conclusion,* as it were. Far more often, behavioral utterances actively continue and develop a situation, adumbrate a plan for future action, and organize that action. But for us it is another aspect of the behavioral utterance that is of special importance: Whatever kind it be, the behavioral utterance always joins the participants in the situation together as *co-participants* who know, understand, and evaluate the situation in like manner. *The utterance,* consequently, *depends on their real, material appurtenance to one and the same segment of being and gives this material commonness ideological expression and further ideological development.*

Thus, the extraverbal situation is far from being merely the external cause of an utterance—it does not operate on the utterance from outside, as if it were a mechanical force. Rather, *the situation enters into the utterance as an essential constitutive part of the structure of its import.* Consequently, a behavioral utterance as a meaningful whole is comprised of two parts: (1) the part realized or actualized in words and (2) the assumed part. On this basis, the behavioral utterance can be likened to the enthymeme.[5]

However, it is an enthymeme of a special order. The very term enthymeme (literally translated from the Greek, something located in the heart or mind) sounds a bit too psychological. One might be led to think of the situation as something in the mind of the speaker on the order of a subjective-psychical act (a thought, idea, feeling). But that is not the case. The individual and subjective are backgrounded here by *the social and objective*. What *I* know, see, want, love, and so on cannot be assumed. Only what all of us speakers know, see, love, recognize—only those points on which we are all united can become the assumed part of an utterance. Furthermore, this fundamentally social phenomenon is completely objective: it consists, above all, of *the material unity of world that enters the speakers' purview* (in our example, the room, the snow outside the window, and so on) and of *the unity of the real conditions of life* that generate a *community of value judgments*—the speakers' belonging to the same family, profession, class, or other social group, and their belonging to the same time period (the speakers are, after all, contemporaries). Assumed value judgments are, therefore, not individual emotions but regular and essential social acts. *Individual* emotions can come into play only as *overtones* accompanying the *basic tone of social evaluation.* "I" can realize itself verbally only on the basis of "we."

Thus, every utterance in the business of life is an objective social enthymeme. It is something like a "password" known only to those who belong to the same social purview. The distinguishing characteristic of behavioral utterances consists precisely in the fact that they make myriad connections with the extraverbal context of life and, once severed from that context, lose almost all their import—a person ignorant of the immediate pragmatic context will not understand these utterances.

This immediate context may be of varying scope. In our example, the context is extremely narrow: it is *circumscribed by the room and the moment of occurrence,* and the utterance makes an intelligible statement only for the two persons involved. However, the unified purview on which an utterance depends can expand in both space and time: *The "assumed" may be that of the family, clan, nation, class and may encompass days or years or whole epochs.* The wider the overall purview and its corresponding social group, the more constant the assumed factors in an utterance become.

When the assumed real purview of an utterance is narrow, when, as in our example, it coincides with the actual purview of two people sitting in the same room and seeing the same thing, then even the most momentary change within that purview can become the assumed. Where the purview is wider, the utterance can operate only on the basis of constant, stable factors in life and substantive, fundamental social evaluations.

Especially great importance, in this case, belongs to assumed evaluations. The fact is that all the basic social evaluations that stem directly from the distinctive characteristics of the given social group's economic being are usually not articulated: They have entered the flesh and blood of all representatives of the group; they organize behavior and actions; they have merged, as it were, with the objects and phenomena to which they correspond, and for that reason they are in no need of special verbal formulation. We seem to perceive the value of a thing together with its being as one of its qualities; we seem, for instance, to sense, along with its warmth and light, the sun's value for us, as well. All the phenomena that surround us are similarly merged with value judgments. If a value judgment is in actual fact conditioned by the being of a given community, it becomes a matter of dogmatic belief, something taken for granted and not subject to discussion. On the contrary, whenever some basic value judgment is verbalized and justified, we may be certain that it has already become dubious, has separated from its referent, has ceased to organize life, and, consequently, has lost its connection with the existential conditions of the given group.

A healthy social value judgment remains within life and from that position organizes the very form of an utterance and its intonation, but it does not at all aim to find suitable expression in the content side of discourse. Once a value judgment shifts from formal factors to content, we may be sure that a reevaluation is in the offing. Thus, a viable value judgment exists wholly without incorporation into the content of discourse and is not derivable therefrom; instead, it determines the *very selection of the verbal material and the form of the verbal whole.* It finds its purest expression in *intonation.* Intonation establishes a firm link between verbal discourse and the extraverbal context—genuine, living intonation moves verbal discourse beyond the border of the verbal, so to speak.

Let us stop to consider in somewhat greater detail the connection between intonation and the pragmatic context of life in the example utterance we have been using. This will allow us to make a number of important observations about the social nature of intonation.

IV

First of all, we must emphasize that the word *well*—a word virtually empty semantically—cannot to any extent predetermine intonation through its own content. Any intonation—joyful, sorrowful, contemptuous, and so on—can freely and easily operate in this word; it all depends on the context in which the word appears. In our example, the context determining the intonation used (indignant-reproachful but moderated by humor) is provided entirely by the extraverbal situation that we have already analyzed, since, in this instance, there is no immediate verbal context. We might say in advance that even were such an immediate verbal context present and even, moreover, if that context were entirely sufficient from all other points of view, the intonation would still take us beyond its confines. Intonation can be thoroughly

understood only when one is in touch with the assumed value judgments of the given social group, whatever the scope of that group might be. *Intonation always lies on the border of the verbal and the nonverbal, the said and the unsaid.* In intonation, discourse comes directly into contact with life. And it is in intonation above all that the speaker comes into contact with the listener or listeners—intonation is social par excellence. It is especially sensitive to all the vibrations in the social atmosphere surrounding the speaker.

The intonation in our example stemmed from the interlocutors' shared yearning for spring and shared disgruntlement over the protracted winter. This commonness of evaluations assumed between them supplied the basis for the intonation, the basis for the distinctness and certitude of its major tonality. Given an atmosphere of sympathy, the intonation could freely undergo deployment and differentiation within the range of the major tone. But if there were no such firmly dependable "choral support," the intonation would have gone in a different direction and taken on different tones—perhaps those of provocation or annoyance with the listener, or perhaps the intonation would simply have contracted and been reduced to the minimum. When a person anticipates the disagreement of his interlocutor or, at any rate, is uncertain or doubtful of his agreement, he intones his words differently. We shall see later that not only intonation but the whole formal structure of speech depends to a significant degree on what the relation of the utterance is to the assumed community of values belonging to the social milieu wherein the discourse figures. A creatively productive, assured, and rich intonation is possible only on the basis of presupposed "choral support." Where such support is lacking, the voice falters and its intonational richness is reduced, as happens, for instance, when a person laughing suddenly realizes that he is laughing alone—his laughter either ceases or degenerates, becomes forced, loses its assurance and clarity and its ability to generate joking and amusing talk. *The commonness of assumed basic value judgments constitutes the canvas upon which living human speech embroiders the designs of intonation.*

Intonation's set toward possible sympathy, toward "choral support," does not exhaust its social nature. It is only one side of intonation—the side turned toward the listener. But intonation contains yet another extremely important factor for the sociology of discourse.

If we scrutinize the intonation of our example, we will notice that it has one "mysterious" feature requiring special explanation.

In point of fact, the intonation of the word *well* voiced not only passive dissatisfaction with an occurring event (the snowfall) but also active indignation and reproach. To whom is this reproach addressed? Clearly not to the listener but to somebody else. This tack of the intonational movement patently makes an opening in the situation for a *third participant*. Who is this third participant? Who is the recipient of the reproach? The snow? Nature? Fate, perhaps?

Of course, in our simplified example of a behavioral utterance the third participant—the "hero" of this verbal production—has not yet assumed full and definitive shape; the intonation has demarcated a definite place for the hero but his semantic equivalent has not been supplied and he remains nameless. Intonation has established an active attitude toward the referent, toward the object of the utterance, an attitude of a kind verging on *apostrophe* to that object as the incarnate, living culprit, while the listener—the second participant—is, as it were, called in *as witness and ally.*

Almost any example of live intonation in emotionally charged behavioral speech proceeds as if it addressed, behind inanimate objects and phenomena, animate participants and agents in life; in other words, it has an inherent *tendency toward personification.* If the intonation is not held in check, as in our example, by a certain amount of irony, then it becomes the source of

the mythological image, the incantation, the prayer, as was the case in the earliest stages of culture. In our case, however, we have to do with an extremely important phenomenon of language creativity—*the intonational metaphor:* The intonation of the utterance "Well!" makes the word sound as if it were reproaching the living culprit of the late snowfall—winter. We have in our example an instance of *pure* intonational metaphor wholly confined within the intonation; but latent within it, in cradle, so to speak, there exists the possibility of the usual *semantic metaphor.* Were this possibility to be realized, the word *well* would expand into some such metaphorical expression as: "What a *stubborn winter! It just won't give up,* though goodness knows it's time!" But this possibility, inherent in the intonation, remained unrealized and the utterance made do with the almost semantically inert adverb *well.*

It should be noted that the intonation in behavioral speech, on the whole, is a great deal more metaphorical than the words used: The aboriginal myth-making spirit seems to have remained alive in it. Intonation makes it sound as if the world surrounding the speaker were still full of animate forces—it threatens and rails against or adores and cherishes inanimate objects and phenomena, whereas the usual metaphors of colloquial speech for the most part have been effaced and the words become semantically spare and prosaic.

Close kinship unites the intonational metaphor with the *gesticulatory metaphor* (indeed, words were themselves originally lingual gestures constituting one component of a complex, omnicorporeal gesture)—the term "gesture" being understood here in a broad sense including miming as facial gesticulation. Gesture, just as intonation, requires the choral support of surrounding persons; only in an atmosphere of sympathy is free and assured gesture possible. Furthermore, and again just as intonation, gesture makes an opening in the situation and introduces a third participant—the hero. Gesture always has latent within itself the germ of attack or defence, of threat or caress, with the contemplator and listener relegated to the role of ally or witness. Often, the "hero" is merely some inanimate thing, some occurrence or circumstance in life. How often we shake our fist at "someone" in a fit of temper or simply scowl at empty space, and there is literally nothing we cannot smile at—the sun, trees, thoughts.

A point that must constantly be kept in mind (something that psychological aesthetics often forgets to do) is this: *Intonation and gesture are active and objective by tendency.* They not only express the passive mental state of the speaker but also always have embedded in them a living, forceful relation with the external world and with the social milieu—enemies, friends, allies. When a person intones and gesticulates, he assumes an active social position with respect to certain specific values, and this position is conditioned by the very bases of his social being. It is precisely this objective and sociological, and not subjective and psychological, aspect of intonation and gesture that should interest theorists of the various relevant arts, inasmuch as it is here that reside forces in the arts that are responsible for aesthetic creativity and that devise and organize artistic form.

As we see then, every instance of intonation is oriented *in two directions:* with respect to the listener as ally or witness and with respect to the object of the utterance as the third, living participant whom the intonation scolds or caresses, denigrates or magnifies. *This double social orientation is what determines all aspects of intonation and makes it intelligible.* And this very same thing is true for all the other factors of verbal utterances: They are all organized and in every way given shape in the same process of the speaker's *double orientation;* this social origin is only most easily detectable in intonation since it is the verbal factor of greatest sensitivity, elasticity, and freedom.

Thus, as we now have a right to claim, *any locution actually said aloud or written down for intelligible communication* (i.e., anything but words merely reposing in a dictionary) *is the expression and product of the social interaction of three participants: the speaker* (author), *the listener* (reader), and the *topic* (the who or what) *of speech* (the hero). Verbal discourse is a social event; it is not self-contained in the sense of some abstract linguistic quantity, nor can it be derived psychologically from the speaker's subjective consciousness taken in isolation. Therefore, both the formal linguistic approach and the psychological approach equally miss the mark: The concrete, sociological essence of verbal discourse, that which alone can make it true or false, banal or distinguished, necessary or unnecessary, remains beyond the ken and reach of both these points of view. Needless to say, it is also this very same "social soul" of verbal discourse that makes it beautiful or ugly, that is, that makes it artistically meaningful, as well. To be sure, once subordinated to the basic and more concrete sociological approach, both abstract points of view—the formal linguistic and the psychological—retain their value. Their collaboration is even absolutely indispensable; but separately, each by itself in isolation, they are inert.

The concrete utterance (and not the linguistic abstraction) is born, lives, and dies in the process of social interaction between the participants of the utterance. Its form and meaning are determined basically by the form and character of this interaction. When we cut the utterance off from the real grounds that nurture it, we lose the key to its form as well as to its import—all we have left is an abstract linguistic shell or an equally abstract semantic scheme (the banal "idea of the work" with which earlier theorists and historians of literature dealt)—two abstractions that are not mutually joinable because there are no concrete grounds for their organic synthesis.

It remains for us now only to sum up our short analysis of utterance in life and of those *artistic potentials, those rudiments of future form and content,* that we have detected in it.

The meaning and import of an utterance in life (of whatever particular kind that utterance may be) do not coincide with the purely verbal composition of the utterance. Articulated words are impregnated with assumed and unarticulated qualities. What are called the "understanding" and "evaluation" of an utterance (agreement or disagreement) always encompass the extraverbal pragmatic situation together with the verbal discourse proper. Life, therefore, does not affect an utterance from without; it penetrates and exerts an influence on an utterance from within, as that unity and commonness of being surrounding the speakers and that unity and commonness of essential social value judgments issuing from that being without all of which no intelligible utterance is possible. Intonation lies on the border between life and the verbal aspect of the utterance: it, as it were, pumps energy from a life situation into the verbal discourse, it endows everything linguistically stable with living historical momentum and uniqueness. Finally, the utterance reflects the social interaction of the speaker, listener, and hero as the product and fixation in verbal material of the act of living communication among them.

Verbal discourse is like a *"scenario"* of a certain event. A viable understanding of the whole import of discourse must *reproduce* this event of the mutual relationship between speakers, must, as it were, "reenact" it, with the person wishing to understand taking upon himself the role of the listener. But in order to carry out that role, he must distinctly understand the positions of the other two participants, as well.

For the linguistic point of view, neither this event nor its living participants exist, of course; the linguistic point of view deals with abstract, bare words and their equally abstract components (phonetic, morphological, and so on). Therefore, the *total import of discourse* and *its ideological value*—the cognitive, political, aesthetic, or other—are inaccessible to it. Just as

there cannot be a linguistic logic or a linguistic politics, so there cannot be a linguistic poetics.

V

In what way does an artistic verbal utterance—a complete work of poetic art—differ from an utterance in the business of life?

It is immediately obvious that discourse in art neither is nor can be so closely dependent on all the factors of the extraverbal context, on all that is seen and known, as in life. A poetic work cannot rely on objects and events in the immediate milieu as things "understood," without making even the slightest allusion to them in the verbal part of the utterance. In this regard, a great deal more is demanded of discourse in literature: Much that could remain outside the utterance in life must find verbal representation. Nothing must be left unsaid in a poetic work from the pragmatic-referential point of view.

Does it follow from this that in literature the speaker, listener, and hero come in contact for the first time, knowing nothing about one another, having no purview in common, and are, therefore, bereft of anything on which they can jointly rely or hold assumptions about? Certain writers on these topics are inclined to think so.

But in actuality a poetic work, too, is closely enmeshed in the unarticulated context of life. If it were true that author, listener, and hero, as abstract persons, come into contact for the first time devoid of any unifying purview and that the words used are taken as from a dictionary, then it is hardly likely that even a nonpoetic work would result, and certainly not a poetic one. Science does to some degree approach this extreme—a scientific definition has a minimum of the "assumed"; but it would be possible to prove that even science cannot do entirely without the assumed.

In literature, assumed value judgments play a role of particular importance. We might say that *a poetic work is a powerful condenser of unarticu-*

lated social evaluations—each word is saturated with them. *It is these social evaluations that organize form as their direct expression.*

Value judgments, first of all, determine the author's *selection of words* and the reception of that selection (the coselection) by the listener. The poet, after all, selects words not from the dictionary but from the context of life where words have been steeped in and become permeated with value judgments. Thus, he selects the value judgments associated with the words and does so, moreover, from the standpoint of the incarnated bearers of those value judgments. It can be said that the poet constantly works in conjunction with his listener's sympathy or antipathy, agreement or disagreement. Furthermore, evaluation is operative also with regard to the object of the utterance—the hero. The simple selection of an epithet or a metaphor is already an active evaluative act with orientation in both directions—toward the listener and toward the hero. *Listener and hero are constant participants in the creative event,* which does not for a single instant cease to be an event of living communication involving all three.

The problem of sociological poetics would be resolved if each factor of form could be explained as the active expression of evaluation in these two directions—toward the listener and toward the object of utterance, the hero.[6] But at the present time the data are too insufficient for such a task to be carried out. All that can be done is to map out at least the preliminary steps leading toward that goal.

The formalistic aesthetics of the present day defines artistic forms as *the form of the material.* If this point of view be carried out consistently, content must necessarily be ignored, since no room is left for it in the poetic work; at best, it may be regarded as a factor of the material and in that way, indirectly, be organized by artistic form in its direct bearing on the material.[7]

So understood, form loses its active evaluative character and becomes merely a stimulus of passive feelings of pleasure in the perceiver.

It goes without saying that form is realized with the help of the material—it is fixed in material; but by virtue of *its significance* it exceeds the material. *The meaning, the import of form has to do not with the material but with the content.* So, for instance, the form of a statue may be said to be not the form of the marble but the form of the human body, with the added qualification that the form "heroicizes" the human depicted or "dotes upon" him or, perhaps, denigrates him (the caricature style in the plastic arts); that is, the form expresses some specific evaluation of the object depicted.

The evaluative significance of form is especially obvious in verse. Rhythm and other formal elements of verse overtly express a certain active attitude toward the object depicted: The form celebrates or laments or ridicules that object.

Psychological aesthetics calls this the "emotional factor" of form. But it is not the psychological side of the matter that is important for us, not the identity of the psychical forces that take part in the creation of form and the cocreative perception of form. What is important is the significance of these experiences, their active role, their bearing on content. Through the agency of artistic form the creator takes up *an active position with respect to content.* The form in and of itself need not necessarily be pleasurable (the hedonistic explanation of form is absurd); what it must be is a *convincing evaluation* of the content. So, for instance, while the form of "the enemy" might even be repulsive, the positive state, the pleasure that the contemplator derives in the end, is a consequence of the fact that the form is *appropriate to the enemy* and that it is *technically perfect* in its realization through the agency of the material. It is in these two aspects that form should be studied: with respect to content, as its ideological evaluation, and with respect to the material, as the technical realization of that evaluation.

The ideological evaluation expressed through form is not at all supposed to transpose into content as a maxim or a proposition of a moral, political, or other kind. The evaluation should remain in the rhythm, *in the very evaluative impetus* of the epithet or metaphor, *in the manner of the unfolding* of the depicted event; it is supposed to be realized by the formal means of the material only. But, at the same time, while not transposing into content, the form must not lose its connection with content, its correlation with it, otherwise it becomes a technical experiment devoid of any real artistic import.

The general definition of style that classical and neoclassical poetics had advanced, together with the basic division of style into "high" and "low," aptly brings out precisely this active evaluative nature of artistic form. The structure of form is indeed *hierarchical,* and in this respect it comes close to political and juridical gradations. Form similarly creates, in an artistically configured content, a complex system of hierarchical interrelations: Each of its elements—an epithet or a metaphor, for instance—either raises the designatum to a higher degree or lowers it or equalizes it. The selection of a hero or an event determines from the very outset the general level of the form and the admissibility of this or that particular set of configuring devices. And this basic requirement of *stylistic suitability* has in view *the evaluative-hierarchical suitability of form and content:* They must be *equally adequate* for one another. The selection of content and the selection of form constitute one and the same act establishing the creator's basic position; and in that act one and the same social evaluation finds expression.

VI

Sociological analysis can take its starting point only, of course, from the purely verbal, linguistic makeup of a work, but it must not and cannot confine itself within those limits, as linguistic poetics does. Artistic contemplation via the reading of a poetic work does, to be sure, start from the grapheme (the visual image of written

or printed words), but at the very instant of perception this visual image gives way to and is very nearly obliterated by other verbal factors—articulation, sound image, intonation, meaning—and these factors eventually take us beyond the border of the verbal altogether. And so it can be said that *the purely linguistic factor of a work is to the artistic whole as the grapheme is to the verbal whole.* In poetry, as in life, verbal discourse is a *"scenario" of an event.* Competent artistic perception reenacts it, sensitively surmising from the words and the forms of their organization the specific, living interrelations of the author with the world he depicts and entering into those interrelations as a third participant (the listener's role). Where linguistic analysis sees only words and the interrelations of their abstract factors (phonetic, morphological, syntactic, and so on), there, for living artistic perception and for concrete sociological analysis, relations among *people* stand revealed, relations merely reflected and fixed in verbal material. Verbal discourse is the skeleton that takes on living flesh only in the process of creative perception—consequently, only in the process of living social communication.

In what follows here we shall attempt to provide a brief and preliminary sketch of the essential factors in the interrelationships of the participants in an artistic event—those factors that determine the broad and basic lines of poetic style as a social phenomenon. Any further detailing of these factors would, of course, go beyond the scope of the present essay.

The author, hero, and listener that we have been talking about all this time are to be understood not as entities outside the artistic event but only as entities of the very perception of an artistic work, entities that are essential constitutive factors of the work. They are the living forces that determine form and style and are distinctly detectable by any competent contemplator. This means that all those definitions that a historian of literature and society might apply to the author and his heroes—the author's biography, the precise qualifications of heroes in chronological and sociological terms and so on—are excluded here: They do not enter directly into the structure of the work but remain outside it. The listener, too, is taken here as the listener whom the author himself takes into account, the one toward whom the work is oriented and who, consequently, intrinsically determines the work's structure. Therefore, we do not at all mean the actual people who in fact made up the reading public of the author in question.

The first form-determining factor of content is the *evaluative rank* of the depicted event and its agent—the hero (whether named or not), taken in strict correlation with the rank of the creator and contemplator. Here we have to do, just as in legal or political life, with a *two-sided relationship:* master-slave, ruler-subject, comrade-comrade, and the like.

The basic stylistic tone of an utterance is therefore determined above all by who is talked about and what his relation is to the speaker—whether he is higher or lower than or equal to him on the scale of the social hierarchy. King, father, brother, slave, comrade, and so on, as heroes of an utterance, also determine its formal structure. And this *specific hierarchical weight* of the hero is determined, in its turn, by that unarticulated context of basic evaluations in which a poetic work, too, participates. Just as the "intonational metaphor" in our example utterance from life established an organic relationship with the object of the utterance, so also all elements of the style of a poetic work are permeated with the author's evaluative attitude toward content and express his basic social position. Let us stress once again that we have in mind here not those ideological evaluations that are incorporated into the content of a work in the form of judgments or conclusions but that deeper, more ingrained kind of *evaluation via form* that finds expression in the very manner in which the artistic material is viewed and deployed.

Certain languages, Japanese in particular, possess a rich and varied store of special lexical and grammatical forms to be used in strict accordance with the rank of the hero of the utterance (language etiquette).[8]

We might say that what is still a *matter of grammar* for the Japanese has already become for us a *matter of style.* The most important stylistic components of the heroic epic, the tragedy, the ode, and so forth are determined precisely by the hierarchical status of the object of the utterance with respect to the speaker.

It should not be supposed that this hierarchical interdefinition of creator and hero has been eliminated from modern literature. It has been made more complex and does not reflect the contemporary sociopolitical hierarchy with the same degree of distinctness as, say, classicism did in its time—but *the very principle of change of style in accordance with change in the social value of the hero of the utterance* certainly remains in force as before. After all, it is not his personal enemy that the poet hates, not his personal friend that his form treats with love and tenderness, not the events from his private life that he rejoices or sorrows over. Even if a poet has in fact borrowed his passion in good measure from the circumstances of his own private life, still, he must *socialize* that passion and, consequently, elaborate the event with which it corresponds to the level of *social significance.*

The second style-determining factor in the interrelationship between hero and creator is *the degree of their proximity to one another.* All languages possess direct grammatical means of expression for this aspect: first, second, and third persons and variable sentence structure in accordance with the person of the subject ("I" or "you" or "he"). The form of a proposition about a third person, the form of an address to a second person, the form of an utterance about oneself (and their modifications) are already different in terms of grammar. Thus, here *the very structure of the language reflects the event of the speakers' interrelationship.*

Certain languages have purely grammatical forms capable of conveying with even greater flexibility the nuances of the speakers' social interrelationship and the various deGrees of their proximity. From this angle, the so-called "inclusive" and "exclusive" forms of the plural in certain languages present a case of special interest. For example, if a speaker using the form *we* has the listener in mind and includes him in the subject of the proposition, then he uses one form, whereas if he means himself and some other person (*we* in the sense of *I* and *he*), he uses a different form. Such is the use of the dual in certain Australian languages, for instance. There, too, are found two special forms of the triad: one meaning *I and you and he;* the other, *I and he and he* (with *you*—the listener—excluded).⁹

In European languages these and similar interrelationships between speakers have no special grammatical expression. The character of these languages is more abstract and not so capable of reflecting the situation of utterance via grammatical structure. However, interrelationships between speakers do find expression in these languages—and expression of far greater subtlety and diversity—*in the style and intonation of utterances.* Here the social situation of creativity finds thoroughgoing reflection in a work by means of purely artistic devices.

The form of a poetic work is determined, therefore, in many of its factors by *how the author perceives his hero*—the hero who serves as the organizing center of the utterance. The form of *objective narration,* the form of *address or apostrophe* (prayer, hymn, certain lyric forms), the form of *self-expression* (confession, autobiography, lyric avowal—an important form of the love lyric) are determined precisely by the *degree of proximity between author and hero.*

Both the factors we have indicated—the hierarchical value of the hero and the degree of his proximity to the author—are as yet insufficient, taken independently and in isolation, for the determination of artistic form. The fact is that a third participant is constantly in play as well—the listener, whose presence affects the interrelationship of the other two (creator and hero).

The interrelationship of author and hero never, after all, actually is an intimate relationship of two; all the while form makes provision for the third participant—the listener—who exerts crucial influence on all the other factors of the work.

In what way can the listener determine the style of a poetic utterance? Here, too, we must distinguish two basic factors: first, the listener's proximity to the author and, second, his relation to the hero. Nothing is more perilous for aesthetics than to ignore the autonomous role of the listener. A very commonly held opinion has it that the listener is to be regarded as equal to the author, excepting the latter's technical performance, and that the position of a competent listener is supposed to be a simple reproduction of the author's position. In actual fact this is not so. Indeed, the opposite may sooner be said to be true: The listener never equals the author. The listener has *his own independent place* in the event of artistic creation; he must occupy a special, and, what is more, a *two-sided* position in it—with respect to the author and with respect to the hero—and it is this position that has determinative effect on the style of an utterance.

How does the author sense his listener? In our example of an utterance in the business of life, we have seen to what degree the presumed agreement or disagreement of the listener shaped an utterance. Exactly the same is true regarding all factors of form. To put it figuratively, the listener normally stands *side by side* with the author as his ally, but this classical positioning of the listener is by no means always the case.

Sometimes the listener begins to lean toward the hero of the utterance. The most unmistakable and typical expression of this is the polemical style that aligns the hero and the listener together. Satire, too, can involve the listener as someone calculated to be close to the hero ridiculed and not to the ridiculing author. This constitutes a sort of *inclusive form of ridicule* distinctly different from the exclusive form where the listener is in solidarity with the jeering author. In romanticism, an interesting phenomenon can be observed where the author *concludes an alliance,* as it were, *with his hero against the listener* (Friedrich Schlegel's *Lucinda* and, in Russian literature, *Hero of Our Time* to some extent).

Of very special character and interest for analysis is the author's sense of his listener in the forms of the confession and the autobiography. All shades of feeling from humble reverence before the listener, as before a veritable judge, to contemptuous distrust and hostility can have determinative effect on the style of a confession or an autobiography. Extremely interesting material for the illustration of this contention can be found in the works of Dostoyevsky. The confessional style of Ippolit's "article" (*The Idiot*) is determined by an almost extreme degree of contemptuous distrust and hostility directed toward all who are to hear this dying confession. Similar tones, but somewhat softened, determine the style of *Notes from Underground*. The style of "Stavrogin's Confession" (*The Possessed*) displays far greater trust in the listener and acknowledgments of his rights, although here too, from time to time, a feeling almost of hatred for the listener erupts, which is what is responsible for the jaggedness of its style. Playing the fool, as a special form of utterance, one, to be sure, lying on the periphery of the artistic, is determined above all by an extremely complex and tangled conflict of the speaker with the listener.

A form especially sensitive to the position of the listener is the lyric. The underlying condition for lyric intonation is *the absolute certainty of the listener's sympathy.* Should any doubt on this score creep into the lyric situation, the style of the lyric changes drastically. This conflict with the listener finds its most egregious expression in so-called lyric irony (Heine, and in modern poetry, Laforgue, Annenskij, and others). The form of irony in general is conditioned by a social conflict: It is the encounter in one voice of two incarnate value judgments and their interference with one another.

In modern aesthetics a special, so-called juridical theory of tragedy was proposed, a theory amounting essentially to the attempt to conceive of *the structure of a tragedy as the structure of a trial in court.*[10]

The interrelationshp of hero and chorus, on the one side, and the overall position of the listener, on the other, do indeed, to a degree, lend themselves to juridical interpretation. But of course this can only be meant as *an analogy.* The important common feature of tragedy—indeed of any work of art—and judicial process comes down merely to the existence of "sides," that is, the occupying by the several participants of *different positions.* The terms, so widespread in literary terminology, that define the poet as "judge," "exposer," "witness," "defender," and even "executioner" (the phraseology for "scourging satire"—Juvenal, Barbier, Nekrasov, and others), and associated definitions for heroes and listeners, reveal by way of analogy, the same social base of poetry. At all events, author, hero, and listener nowhere merge together into one indifferent mass—they occupy *autonomous positions,* they are indeed "sides," the sides not of a judicial process but of an artistic event with specific social structure the "protocol" of which is the work of art.

It would not be amiss at this point to stress once again that we have in mind, and have had in mind all this time, the listener as an immanent participant in the artistic event who has determinative effect on the form of the work from within. This listener, on a par with the author and the hero, is an essential, intrinsic factor of the work and does not at all coincide with the so-called reading public, located outside the work, whose artistic tastes and demands can be consciously taken into account. Such a conscious account is incapable of direct and profound effect on artistic form in the process of its living creation. What is more, if this conscious account of the reading public does come to occupy a position of any importance in a poet's creativity, that creativity inevitably loses its artistic purity and degrades to a lower social level.

This external account bespeaks the poet's loss of *his immanent listener,* his divorce from the *social whole* that *intrinsically,* aside from all abstract considerations, has the capability of determining *his value judgments* and the artistic form of his poetic utterances, which form is the expression of those crucial social value judgments. The more a poet is cut off from the social unity of his group, the more likely he is to take into account the *external* demands of a *particular reading public.* Only a social group alien to the poet can determine his creative work from outside. One's *own* group needs no such external definition: It exists in the poet's voice, in the basic tone and intonations of that voice—whether the poet himself intends this or not.

The poet acquires his words and learns to intone them *over the course of his entire life* in the process of his every-sided contact with his environment. The poet begins to use those words and intonations already in the *inner speech* with the help of which he thinks and becomes conscious of himself, even when he does not produce utterances. It is naive to suppose that one can assimilate as one's own *an external speech that runs counter to one's inner speech,* that is, runs counter to one's whole inner verbal manner of being aware of oneself and the world. Even if it is possible to create such a thing for some pragmatic occasion, still, as something cut off from all sources of sustenance, it will be devoid of any artistic productiveness. A poet's style is engendered from *the style of his inner speech,* which does not lend itself to control, and his inner speech is itself the product of his entire social life. "Style is the man," they say; but we might say: Style is at least two persons or, more accurately, one person plus his social group in the form of its authoritative representative, the listener—the constant participant in a person's inner and outward speech.

The fact of the matter is that no conscious act of any degree of distinctness can do without inner speech, without words and intonations—without evaluations—and, consequently, every conscious act is already a social act, an act of communication. Even the most intimate self-awareness is an attempt to translate oneself into the common code, to take stock of another's point of view, and, consequently, entails orientation toward a possible listener. This listener may be only the bearer of the value judgments of the social group to which the "conscious" person belongs. In this regard, consciousness, provided that we do not lose sight of its content, is *not just a psychological phenomenon* but also, and above all, an *ideological phenomenon, a product of social intercourse.* This constant *coparticipant* in all our conscious acts determines not only the content of consciousness but also—and this is the main point for us—the very *selection* of the content, the selection of what precisely we become conscious of, and thus determines also those *evaluations* which permeate consciousness and which psychology usually calls the "emotional tone" of consciousness. It is precisely from this constant participant in all our conscious acts that the listener who determines artistic form is engendered.

There is nothing more perilous than to conceive of this subtle social structure of verbal creativity as analogous with the conscious and cynical speculations of the bourgeois publisher who "calculates the prospects of the book market." and to apply to the characterization of the immanent structure of a work categories of the "supply-demand" type. Alas, all too many "sociologists" are likely to identify the creative writer's service to society with the vocation of the enterprising publisher.

Under the conditions of the bourgeois economy, the book market does, of course, "regulate" writers, but this is not in any way to be identified with the regulative role of the listener as a constant structural element in artistic creativity. For a historian of the literature of the capitalist era, the market is a very important factor, but for theoretical poetics, which studies the basic ideological structure of art, that external factor is irrelevant. However, even in the historical study of literature the history of the book market must not be confused with the history of literature.

VII

All the form-determining factors of an artistic utterance that we have analyzed—(1) the hierarchical value of the hero or event serving as the content of the utterance, (2) the degree of the latter's proximity to the author, and (3) the listener and his interrelationship with the author, on the one side, and the hero, on the other—all those factors are *the contact points between the social forces of extra-artistic reality and verbal art.* Thanks precisely to that kind of *intrinsically social structure* which artistic creation possesses, it is *open on all sides to the influence of other domains of life.* Other ideological spheres, prominently including the sociopolitical order and the economy, have determinative effect on verbal art not merely from outside but with direct bearing upon its intrinsic structural elements. And, conversely, the artistic interaction of author, listener, and hero may exert its influence on other domains of social intercourse.

Full and thoroughgoing elucidation of questions as to who the typical heroes of literature at some particular period are, what the typical formal orientation of the author toward them is, what the interrelationships of the author and hero with the listener are in the whole of an artistic creation—elucidation of such questions presupposes thoroughgoing analysis of the economic and ideological conditions of the time.

But these concrete historical issues exceed the scope of theoretical poetics which, however, still does include one other important task. Up to now we have been concerned only with those factors which determine form in its relation to content, that is, form as the embodied social evaluation of precisely that content, and we have ascertained that every factor of form is a product of social interaction. But we also pointed out that form must be understood from another angle, as well—as form realized with the help of *specific material.* This opens up a whole long series of questions connected with *the technical aspect of form.*

Of course, *these technical questions can be separated out from questions of the sociology of form only*

in abstract terms: *in actuality* it is impossible to divorce the *artistic import* of some device, say, a metaphor that relates to content and expresses the formal evaluation of it (i.e., the metaphor degrades the object or raises it to a higher rank), from *the purely linguistic* specification of that device.

The extraverbal import of a metaphor—a regrouping of values—and its *linguistic covering*—a semantic shift—are merely different points of view on one and the same real phenomenon. But the second point of view is subordinate to the first: a poet uses a metaphor in order to regroup values and not for the sake of a linguistic exercise.

All questions of form can be taken in relation with material—in the given case, in relation with language in its linguistic conception. Technical analysis will then amount to the question as to *which linguistic means are used for the realization of the socioartistic purpose of the form.* But if that purpose is not known, if its import is not elucidated in advance, technical analysis will be absurd.

Technical questions of form, of course, go beyond the scope of the task we have set ourself here. Moreover, their treatment would require an incomparably more diversified and elaborated analysis of the socioartistic aspect of verbal art. Here we have been able to provide only a brief sketch of the basic directions such an analysis must take.

If we have succeeded in demonstrating even the mere possibility of a sociological approach to the immanent structure of poetic form, we may consider our task to have been fulfilled.

NOTES

1. P. N. Sakulin, *Sociologičeskij metod v literaturovedenii [The Sociological Method in the Study of Literature]* (1925).

2. "Elements of poetic form (sound, word, image, rhythm, composition, genre), poetic thematics, artistic style in totality—all these things are studied, as preliminary matters, with the help of methods that have been worked out by theoretical poetics, grounded in psychology, aes-

and the oppositional. This schema has been widely taken up by other Marxist critics (see, for example, Fredric Jameson's various essays on postmodernism) and provides an extremely useful analytical tool. Williams's work in the sociology of culture has laid the groundwork for much of the most important contemporary work in the area of cultural studies.

Base and Superstructure in Marxist Cultural Theory

Any modern approach to a Marxist theory of culture must begin by considering the proposition of a determining base and a determined superstructure. From a strictly theoretical point of view this is not, in fact, where we might choose to begin. It would be in many ways preferable if we could begin from a proposition which originally was equally central, equally authentic: namely the proposition that social being determines consciousness. It is not that the two propositions necessarily deny each other or are in contradiction. But the proposition of base and superstructure, with its figurative element, with its suggestion of a fixed and definite spatial relationship, constitutes, at least in certain hands, a very specialized and at times unacceptable version of the other proposition. Yet in the transition from Marx to Marxism, and in the development of mainstream Marxism itself, the proposition of the determining base and the determined superstructure has been commonly held to be the key to Marxist cultural analysis.

It is important, as we try to analyse this proposition, to be aware that the term of relationship which is involved, that is to say "determines," is of great linguistic and theoretical complexity. The language of determination and even more of determinism was inherited from idealist and especially theological accounts of the world and man. It is significant that it is in one of his familiar inversions, his contradictions of received propositions, that Marx uses the word which becomes, in English translation, "determines" (the usual but not invariable German word is *bestimmen*). He is opposing an ideology that had been insistent on the power of certain forces outside man, or, in its secular version, on an abstract determining consciousness. Marx's own proposition explicitly denies this, and puts the origin of determination in men's own activities. Nevertheless, the particular history and continuity of the term serves to remind us that there are, within ordinary use—and this is true of most of the major European languages—quite different possible meanings and implications of the word "determine." There is, on the one hand, from its theological inheritance, the notion of an external cause which totally predicts or prefigures, indeed totally controls a subsequent activity. But there is also, from the experience of social practice, a notion of determination as setting limits, exerting pressures.[1]

Now there is clearly a difference between a process of setting limits and exerting pressures, whether by some external force or by the internal laws of a particular development, and that other process in which a subsequent content is essentially prefigured, predicted and controlled by a preexisting external force. Yet it is fair to say, looking at many applications of Marxist cultural analysis, that it is the second sense, the notion of prefiguration, prediction or control, which has often explicitly or implicitly been used.

SUPERSTRUCTURE: QUALIFICATIONS AND AMENDMENTS

The term of relationship is then the first thing that we have to examine in this proposition, but we have to do this by going on to look at the related terms themselves. "Superstructure" (*Überbau*) has had most attention. In common usage, after Marx, it acquired a main sense of a unitary "area" within which all cultural and ideological activities could be placed. But already in Marx himself, in the later correspondence of Engels, and at many points in the subsequent Marxist tradition, qualifications were made about the determined character of certain superstructural activities. The first kind of qualification had to do with delays in time, with complications, and with certain indirect or relatively distant relationships. The simplest notion of a superstructure, which is still by no means entirely abandoned, had been the reflection, the imitation or the reproduction of the reality of the base in the superstructure in a more or less direct way. Positivist notions of reflection and reproduction of course directly supported this. But since in many real cultural activities this relationship cannot be found, or cannot be found without effort or even violence to the material or practice being studied, the notion was introduced of delays in time, the famous lags; of various technical complications; and of indirectness, in which certain kinds of activity in the cultural sphere—philosophy, for example—were situated at a greater distance from the primary economic activities. That was the first stage of qualification of the notion of superstructure: in effect, an operational qualification. The second stage was related but more fundamental, in that the process of the relationship itself was more substantially looked at. This was the kind of reconsideration which gave rise to the modern notion of "mediation," in which something more than simple reflection or reproduction—indeed something radically different from either reflection or reproduction—actively occurs. In the later twentieth century there is the notion of "homologous structures," where there may be no direct or easily apparent similarity, and certainly nothing like reflection or reproduction, between the superstructural process and the re-

ality of the base, but in which there is an essential homology or correspondence of structures, which can be discovered by analysis. This is not the same notion as "mediation," but it is the same kind of amendment in that the relationship between the base and the superstructure is not supposed to be direct, nor simply operationally subject to lags and complications and indirectnesses, but that of its nature it is not direct reproduction.

These qualifications and amendments are important. But it seems to me that what has not been looked at with equal care is the received notion of the "base" (*Basis, Grundlage*). And indeed I would argue that the base is the more important concept to look at if we are to understand the realities of cultural process. In many uses of the proposition of base and superstructure, as a matter of verbal habit, "the base" has come to be considered virtually as an object, or in less crude cases, it has been considered in essentially uniform and usually static ways. "The base" is the real social existence of man. "The base" is the real relations of production corresponding to a stage of development of the material productive forces. "The base" is a mode of production at a particular stage of its development. We make and repeat propositions of this kind, but the usage is then very different from Marx's emphasis on productive activities, in particular structural relations, constituting the foundation of all other activities. For while a particular stage of the development of production can be discovered and made precise by analysis, it is never in practice either uniform or static. It is indeed one of the central propositions of Marx's sense of history that there are deep contradictions in the relationships of production and in the consequent social relationships. There is therefore the continual possibility of the dynamic variation of these forces. Moreover, when these forces are considered, as Marx always considers them, as the specific activities and relationships of real men, they mean something very much more active, more complicated and more contradictory than the developed metaphorical notion of "the base" could possibly allow us to realize.

THE BASE AND THE PRODUCTIVE FORCES

So we have to say that when we talk of "the base," we are talking of a process and not a state. And we cannot ascribe to that process certain fixed properties for subsequent translation to the variable processes of the superstructure. Most people who have wanted to make the ordinary proposition more reasonable have concentrated on refining the notion of superstructure. But I would say that each term of the proposition has to be revalued in a particular direction. We have to revalue "determination" towards the setting of limits and the exertion of pressure, and away from a predicted, prefigured and controlled content. We have to revalue "superstructure" towards a related range of cultural practices, and away from a reflected, reproduced or specifically dependent content. And, crucially, we have to revalue "the base" away from the notion of a fixed economic or technological abstraction, and towards the specific activities of men in real social and economic relationships, containing fundamental contradictions and variations and therefore always in a state of dynamic process.

It is worth observing one further implication behind the customary definitions. "The base" has come to include, especially in certain twentieth-century developments, a strong and limiting sense of basic industry. The emphasis on heavy industry, even, has played a certain cultural role. And this raises a more general problem, for we find ourselves forced to look again at the ordinary notion of "productive forces." Clearly what we are examining in the base is primary productive forces. Yet some very crucial distinctions have to be made here. It is true that in his analysis of capitalist production Marx considered

"productive work" in a very particular and specialized sense corresponding to that mode of production. There is a difficult passage in the *Grundrisse* in which he argues that while the man who makes a piano is a productive worker, there is a real question whether the man who distributes the piano is also a productive worker, but he probably is, since he contributes to the realization of surplus value. Yet when it comes to the man who plays the piano, whether to himself or to others, there is no question: he is not a productive worker at all. So piano-maker is base, but pianist superstructure. As a way of considering cultural activity, and incidentally the economics of modern cultural activity, this is very clearly a dead-end. But for any theoretical clarification it is crucial to recognize that Marx was there engaged in an analysis of a particular kind of production, that is capitalist commodity production. Within his analysis of this mode, he had to give to the notion of "productive labour" and "productive forces" a specialized sense of primary work on materials in a form which produced commodities. But this has narrowed remarkably, and in a cultural context very damagingly, from his more central notion of *productive forces,* in which, to give just brief reminders, the most important thing a worker ever produces is himself, himself in the fact of that kind of labour, or the broader historical emphasis of men producing themselves, themselves and their history. Now when we talk of the base, and of primary productive forces, it matters very much whether we are referring, as in one degenerate form of this proposition became habitual, to primary production within the terms of capitalist economic relationships, or to the primary production of society itself, and of men themselves, the material production and reproduction of real life. If we have the broad sense of productive forces, we look at the whole question of the base differently, and we are then less tempted to dismiss as superstructural, and in that sense as merely secondary, certain vital productive social forces, which are in the broad sense, from the beginning, basic.

USES OF TOTALITY

Yet, because of the difficulties of the ordinary proposition of base and superstructure, there was an alternative and very important development, an emphasis primarily associated with Lukács, on a social "totality." The totality of social practices was opposed to this layered notion of base and a consequent superstructure. This concept of a totality of practices is compatible with the notion of social being determining consciousness, but it does not necessarily interpret this process in terms of a base and a superstructure. Now the language of totality has become common, and it is indeed in many ways more acceptable than the notion of base and superstructure. But with one very important reservation. It is very easy for the notion of totality to empty of its essential content the original Marxist proposition. For if we come to say that society is composed of a large number of social practices which form a concrete social whole, and if we give to each practice a certain specific recognition, adding only that they interact, relate and combine in very complicated ways, we are at one level much more obviously talking about reality, but we are at another level withdrawing from the claim that there is any process of determination. And this I, for one, would be very unwilling to do. Indeed, the key question to ask about any notion of totality in cultural theory is this: whether the notion of totality includes the notion of intention.

If totality is simply concrete, if it is simply the recognition of a large variety of miscellaneous and contemporaneous practices, then it is essentially empty of any content that could be called Marxist. Intention, the notion of intention, restores the key question, or rather the key emphasis. For while it is true that any society is

a complex whole of such practices, it is also true that any society has a specific organization, a specific structure, and that the principles of this organization and structure can be seen as directly related to certain social intentions, intentions by which we define the society, intentions which in all our experience have been the rule of a particular class. One of the unexpected consequences of the crudeness of the base/superstructure model has been the too easy acceptance of models which appear less crude—models of totality or of a complex whole—but which exclude the facts of social intention, the class character of a particular society and so on. And this reminds us of how much we lose if we abandon the superstructural emphasis altogether. Thus I have great difficulty in seeing processes of art and thought as superstructural in the sense of the formula as it is commonly used. But in many areas of social and political thought—certain kinds of ratifying theory, certain kinds of law, certain kinds of institution, which after all in Marx's original formulations were very much part of the superstructure—in all that kind of social apparatus, and in a decisive area of political and ideological activity and construction, if we fail to see a superstructural element we fail to recognize reality at all. These laws, constitutions, theories, ideologies, which are so often claimed as natural, or as having universal validity or significance, simply have to be seen as expressing and ratifying the domination of a particular class. Indeed the difficulty of revising the formula of base and superstructure has had much to do with the perception of many militants—who have to fight such institutions and notions as well as fighting economic battles—that if these institutions and their ideologies are not perceived as having that kind of dependent and ratifying relationship, if their claims to universal validity or legitimacy are not denied and fought, then the class character of the society can no longer be seen. And this has been the effect of some versions of totality as the description of cultural process. Indeed I think we can properly use the notion of totality only when we combine it with that other crucial Marxist concept of "hegemony."

THE COMPLEXITY OF HEGEMONY

It is Gramsci's great contribution to have emphasized hegemony, and also to have understood it at a depth which is, I think, rare. For hegemony supposes the existence of something which is truly total, which is not merely secondary or superstructural, like the weak sense of ideology, but which is lived at such a depth, which saturates the society to such an extent, and which, as Gramsci put it, even constitutes the substance and limit of common sense for most people under its sway, that it corresponds to the reality of social experience very much more clearly than any notions derived from the formula of base and superstructure. For if ideology were merely some abstract, imposed set of notions, if our social and political and cultural ideas and assumptions and habits were merely the result of specific manipulation, of a kind of overt training which might be simply ended or withdrawn, then the society would be very much easier to move and to change than in practice it has ever been or is. This notion of hegemony as deeply saturating the consciousness of a society seems to me to be fundamental. And hegemony has the advantage over general notions of totality, that it at the same time emphasizes the facts of domination.

Yet there are times when I hear discussions of hegemony and feel that it too, as a concept, is being dragged back to the relatively simple, uniform and static notion which "superstructure" in ordinary use had become. Indeed I think that we have to give a very complex account of hegemony if we are talking about any real social formation. Above all we have to give an account which allows for its elements of real and constant change. We have to emphasize that hege-

mony is not singular; indeed that its own internal structures are highly complex, and have continually to be renewed, recreated and defended; and by the same token, that they can be continually challenged and in certain respects modified. That is why instead of speaking simply of "the hegemony," "a hegemony," I would propose a model which allows for this kind of variation and contradiction, its sets of alternatives and its processes of change.

For one thing that is evident in some of the best Marxist cultural analysis is that it is very much more at home in what one might call *epochal* questions than in what one has to call *historical* questions. That is to say, it is usually very much better at distinguishing the large features of different epochs of society, as commonly between feudal and bourgeois, than at distinguishing between different phases of bourgeois society, and different moments within these phases: that true historical process which demands a much greater precision and delicacy of analysis than the always striking epochal analysis which is concerned with main lineaments and features.

The theoretical model which I have been trying to work with is this. I would say first that in any society, in any particular period, there is a central system of practices, meanings and values, which we can properly call dominant and effective. This implies no presumption about its value. All I am saying is that it is central. Indeed I would call it a corporate system, but this might be confusing, since Gramsci uses "corporate" to mean the subordinate as opposed to the general and dominant elements of hegemony. In any case what I have in mind is the central, effective and dominant system of meanings and values, which are not merely abstract but which are organized and lived. That is why hegemony is not to be understood at the level of mere opinion or mere manipulation. It is a whole body of practices and expectations; our assignments of energy, our ordinary understanding of the nature of man and of his world. It is a set of meanings and values which as they are experienced as practices appear as reciprocally confirming. It thus constitutes a sense of reality for most people in the society, a sense of absolute because experienced reality beyond which it is very difficult for most members of the society to move, in most areas of their lives. But this is not, except in the operation of a moment of abstract analysis, in any sense a static system. On the contrary we can only understand an effective and dominant culture if we understand the real social process on which it depends: I mean the process of incorporation. The modes of incorporation are of great social significance. The educational institutions are usually the main agencies of the transmission of an effective dominant culture, and this is now a major economic as well as a cultural activity; indeed it is both in the same moment. Moreover, at a philosophical level, at the true level of theory and at the level of the history of various practices, there is a process which I call the *selective tradition:* that which, within the terms of an effective dominant culture, is always passed off as "*the* tradition," "*the* significant past." But always the selectivity is the point; the way in which from a whole possible area of past and present, certain meanings and practices are chosen for emphasis, certain other meanings and practices are neglected and excluded. Even more crucially, some of these meanings and practices are reinterpreted, diluted, or put into forms which support or at least do not contradict other elements within the effective dominant culture. The processes of education; the processes of a much wider social training within institutions like the family; the practical definitions and organization of work; the selective tradition at an intellectual and theoretical level: all these forces are involved in a continual making and remaking of an effective dominant culture, and on them, as experienced, as built into our living, its reality depends. If what we learn there were merely an imposed ideology, or if it were only the isolable meanings and practices of the ruling class, or of a section

of the ruling class, which gets imposed on others, occupying merely the top of our minds, it would be—and one would be glad—a very much easier thing to overthrow.

It is not only the depths to which this process reaches, selecting and organizing and interpreting our experience. It is also that it is continually active and adjusting; it isn't just the past, the dry husks of ideology which we can more easily discard. And this can only be so, in a complex society, if it is something more substantial and more flexible than any abstract imposed ideology. Thus we have to recognize the alternative meanings and values, the alternative opinions and attitudes, even some alternative senses of the world, which can be accommodated and tolerated within a particular effective and dominant culture. This has been much under-emphasized in our notions of a superstructure, and even in some notions of hegemony. And the under-emphasis opens the way for retreat to an indifferent complexity. In the practice of politics, for example, there are certain truly incorporated modes of what are nevertheless, within those terms, real oppositions, that are felt and fought out. Their existence within the incorporation is recognizable by the fact that, whatever the degree of internal conflict or internal variation, they do not in practice go beyond the limits of the central effective and dominant definitions. This is true, for example, of the practice of parliamentary politics, though its internal oppositions are real. It is true about a whole range of practices and arguments, in any real society, which can by no means be reduced to an ideological cover, but which can nevertheless be properly analysed as in my sense corporate, if we find that, whatever the degree of internal controversy and variation, they do not in the end exceed the limits of the central corporate definitions.

But if we are to say this, we have to think again about the sources of that which is not corporate; of those practices, experiences, meanings, values which are not part of the effective dominant culture. We can express this in two ways. There is clearly something that we can call alternative to the effective dominant culture, and there is something else that we can call oppositional, in a true sense. The degree of existence of these alternative and oppositional forms is itself a matter of constant historical variation in real circumstances. In certain societies it is possible to find areas of social life in which quite real alternatives are at least left alone. (If they are made available, of course, they are part of the corporate organization.) The existence of the possibility of opposition, and of its articulation, its degree of openness, and so on, again depends on very precise social and political forces. The facts of alternative and oppositional forms of social life and culture, in relation to the effective and dominant culture, have then to be recognized as subject to historical variation, and as having sources which are very significant as a fact about the dominant culture itself.

RESIDUAL AND EMERGENT CULTURES

I have next to introduce a further distinction, between *residual* and *emergent* forms, both of alternative and of oppositional culture. By "residual" I mean that some experiences, meanings and values, which cannot be verified or cannot be expressed in terms of the dominant culture, are nevertheless lived and practised on the basis of the residue—cultural as well as social—of some previous social formation. There is a real case of this in certain religious values, by contrast with the very evident incorporation of most religious meanings and values into the dominant system. The same is true, in a culture like Britain, of certain notions derived from a rural past, which have a very significant popularity. A residual culture is usually at some distance from the effective dominant culture, but one has to recognize that, in real cultural activities, it may get incorporated into it. This is because some part of it, some version of it—and especially if the residue is from some major area of the past—will in many cases have had to be incorporated if the effective dominant culture is to

make sense in those areas. It is also because at certain points a dominant culture cannot allow too much of this kind of practice and experience outside itself, at least without risk. Thus the pressures are real, but certain genuinely residual meanings and practices in some important cases survive.

By "emergent" I mean, first, that new meanings and values, new practices, new significances and experiences, are continually being created. But there is then a much earlier attempt to incorporate them, just because they are part—and yet not a defined part—of effective contemporary practice. Indeed it is significant in our own period how very early this attempt is, how alert the dominant culture now is to anything that can be seen as emergent. We have then to see, first, as it were a temporal relation between a dominant culture and on the one hand a residual and on the other hand an emergent culture. But we can only understand this if we can make distinctions, that usually require very precise analysis, between residual-incorporated and residual not incorporated, and between emergent-incorporated and emergent not incorporated. It is an important fact about any particular society, how far it reaches into the whole range of human practices and experiences in an attempt at incorporation. It may be true of some earlier phases of bourgeois society, for example, that there were some areas of experience which it was willing to dispense with, which it was prepared to assign as the sphere of private or artistic life, and as being no particular business of society or the state. This went along with certain kinds of political tolerance, even if the reality of that tolerance was malign neglect. But I am sure it is true of the society that has come into existence since the last war, that progressively, because of developments in the social character of labour, in the social character of communications, and in the social character of decision, it extends much further than ever before in capitalist society into certain hitherto resigned areas of experience and practice and meaning. Thus the effective decision, as to whether a practice is alternative or oppositional, is often now made within a very much narrower scope. There is a simple theoretical distinction between alternative and oppositional, that is to say between someone who simply finds a different way to live and wishes to be left alone with it, and someone who finds a different way to live and wants to change the society in its light. This is usually the difference between individual and small-group solutions to social crisis and those solutions which properly belong to political and ultimately revolutionary practice. But it is often a very narrow line, in reality, between alternative and oppositional. A meaning or a practice may be tolerated as a deviation, and yet still be seen only as another particular way to live. But as the necessary area of effective dominance extends, the same meanings and practices can be seen by the dominant culture, not merely as disregarding or despising it, but as challenging it.

Now it is crucial to any Marxist theory of culture that it can give an adequate explanation of the sources of these practices and meanings. We can understand, from an ordinary historical approach, at least some of the sources of residual meanings and practices. These are the results of earlier social formations, in which certain real meanings and values were generated. In the subsequent default of a particular phase of a dominant culture, there is then a reaching back to those meanings and values which were created in real societies in the past, and which still seem to have some significance because they represent areas of human experience, aspiration and achievement, which the dominant culture under-values or opposes, or even cannot recognize. But our hardest task, theoretically, is to find a non-metaphysical and non-subjectivist explanation of emergent cultural practice. Moreover, part of our answer to this question bears on the process of persistence of residual practices.

CLASS AND HUMAN PRACTICE

We have indeed one source to hand from the central body of Marxist theory. We have the for-

mation of a new class, the coming to consciousness of a new class. This remains, without doubt, quite centrally important. Of course, in itself, this process of formation complicates any simple model of base and superstructure. It also complicates some of the ordinary versions of hegemony, although it was Gramsci's whole purpose to see and to create by organization that hegemony of a proletarian kind which would be capable of challenging the bourgeois hegemony. We have then one central source of new practice, in the emergence of a new class. But we have also to recognize certain other kinds of source, and in cultural practice some of these are very important. I would say that we can recognize them on the basis of this proposition: that no mode of production, and therefore no dominant society or order of society, and therefore no dominant culture, in reality exhausts the full range of human practice, human energy, human intention (this range is not the inventory of some original "human nature" but, on the contrary, is that extraordinary range of variations, both practised and imagined, of which human beings are and have shown themselves to be capable). Indeed it seems to me that this emphasis is not merely a negative proposition, allowing us to account for certain things which happen outside the dominant mode. On the contrary, it is a fact about the modes of domination that they select from and consequently exclude the full range of actual and possible human practice. The difficulties of human practice outside or against the dominant mode are, of course, real. It depends very much whether it is in an area in which the dominant class and the dominant culture have an interest and a stake. If the interest and the stake are explicit, many new practices will be reached for, and if possible incorporated, or else extirpated with extraordinary vigour. But in certain areas, there will be in certain periods practices and meanings which are not reached for. There will be areas of practice and meaning which, almost by definition from its own limited character, or in its profound deformation, the dominant culture is unable in any real terms to recognize. This gives us a bearing on the observable difference between, for example, the practices of a capitalist state and a state like the contemporary Soviet Union in relation to writers. Since from the whole Marxist tradition literature was seen as an important activity, indeed a crucial activity, the Soviet state is very much sharper in investigating areas where different versions of practice, different meanings and values, are being attempted and expressed. In capitalist practice, if the thing is not making a profit, or if it is not being widely circulated, then it can for some time be overlooked, at least while it remains alternative. When it becomes oppositional in an explicit way, it does, of course, get approached or attacked.

I am saying then that in relation to the full range of human practice at any one time, the dominant mode is a conscious selection and organization. At least in its fully formed state it is conscious. But there are always sources of actual human practice which it neglects or excludes. And these can be different in quality from the developing and articulate interests of a rising class. They can include, for example, alternative perceptions of others, in immediate personal relationships, or new perceptions of material and media, in art and science, and within certain limits these new perceptions can be practised. The relations between the two kinds of source—the emerging class and either the dominatively excluded or the more generally new practices—are by no means necessarily contradictory. At times they can be very close, and on the relations between them much in political practice depends. But culturally and as a matter of theory the areas can be seen as distinct.

Now if we go back to the cultural question in its most usual form—what are the relations between art and society, or literature and society?—in the light of the preceding discussion, we have to say first that there are no relations between literature and society in that abstracted way. The literature is there from the beginning as a practice in the society. Indeed until it and all other practices are present, the society cannot

be seen as fully formed. A society is not fully available for analysis until each of its practices is included. But if we make that emphasis we must make a corresponding emphasis: that we cannot separate literature and art from other kinds of social practice, in such a way as to make them subject to quite special and distinct laws. They may have quite specific features as practices, but they cannot be separated from the general social process. Indeed one way of emphasizing this is to say, to insist, that literature is not restricted to operating in any one of the sectors I have been seeking to describe in this model. It would be easy to say, it is a familiar rhetoric, that literature operates in the emergent cultural sector, that it represents the new feelings, the new meanings, the new values. We might persuade ourselves of this theoretically, by abstract argument, but when we read much literature, over the whole range, without the sleight-of-hand of calling literature only that which we have already selected as embodying certain meanings and values at a certain scale of intensity, we are bound to recognize that the act of writing, the practices of discourse in writing and speech, the making of novels and poems and plays and theories, all this activity takes place in all areas of the culture.

Literature appears by no means only in the emergent sector, which is always, in fact, quite rare. A great deal of writing is of a residual kind, and this has been deeply true of much English literature in the last half-century. Some of its fundamental meanings and values have belonged to the cultural achievements of long-past stages of society. So widespread is this fact, and the habits of mind it supports, that in many minds "literature" and "the past" acquire a certain identity, and it is then said that there is now no literature: all that glory is over. Yet most writing, in any period, including our own, is a form of contribution to the effective dominant culture. Indeed many of the specific qualities of literature—its capacity to embody and enact and perform certain meanings and values, or to create in single particular ways what would be otherwise merely general truths—enable it to fulfill this effective function with great power. To literature, of course, we must add the visual arts and music, and in our own society the powerful arts of film and of broadcasting. But the general theoretical point should be clear. If we are looking for the relations between literature and society, we cannot either separate out this one practice from a formed body of other practices, nor when we have identified a particular practice can we give it a uniform, static and ahistorical relation to some abstract social formation. The arts of writing and the arts of creation and performance, over their whole range, are parts of the cultural process in all the different ways, the different sectors, that I have been seeking to describe. They contribute to the effective dominant culture and are a central articulation of it. They embody residual meanings and values, not all of which are incorporated, though many are. They express also and significantly some emergent practices and meanings, yet some of these may eventually be incorporated, as they reach people and begin to move them. Thus it was very evident in the sixties, in some of the emergent arts of performance, that the dominant culture reached out to transform, or seek to transform, them. In this process, of course, the dominant culture itself changes, not in its central formation, but in many of its articulated features. But then in a modern society it must always change in this way, if it is to remain dominant, if it is still to be felt as in real ways central in all our many activities and interests.

CRITICAL THEORY AS CONSUMPTION

What then are the implications of this general analysis for the analysis of particular works of art? This is the question towards which most discussion of cultural theory seems to be directed: the discovery of a method, perhaps even a methodology, through which particular works

of art can be understood and described. I would not myself agree that this is the central use of cultural theory, but let us for a moment consider it. What seems to me very striking is that nearly all forms of contemporary critical theory are theories of *consumption*. That is to say, they are concerned with understanding an object in such a way that it can profitably or correctly be consumed. The earliest stage of consumption theory was the theory of "taste," where the link between the practice and the theory was direct in the metaphor. From taste there came the more elevated notion of "sensibility," in which it was the consumption by sensibility of elevated or insightful works that was held to be the essential practice of reading, and critical activity was then a function of this sensibility. There were then more developed theories, in the 1920s with I. A. Richards, and later in New Criticism, in which the effects of consumption were studied directly. The language of the work of art as object then became more overt. "What effect does this work ('the poem' as it was ordinarily described) have on me?" Or, "what impact does it have on me?" as it was later to be put in a much wider area of communication studies. Naturally enough, the notion of the work of art as *object,* as *text,* as an isolated artifact, became central in all these later consumption theories. It was not only that the practices of *production* were then overlooked, though this fused with the notion that most important literature anyway was from the past. The real social conditions of production were in any case neglected because they were believed to be at best secondary. The true relationship was seen always as between the taste, the sensibility or the training of the reader and this isolated work, this object "as in itself it really is," as most people came to put it. But the notion of the work of art as object had a further large theoretical effect. If you ask questions about the work of art seen as object, they may include questions about the components of its production. Now, as it happened, there was a use of the formula of base and superstructure which was precisely in line with this. The components of a work of art were the real activities of the base, and you could study the object to discover these components. Sometimes you even studied the components and then projected the object. But in any case the relationship that was looked for was one between an object and its components. But this was not only true of Marxist suppositions of a base and a superstructure. It was true also of various kinds of psychological theory, whether in the form of archetypes, or the images of the collective unconscious, or the myths and symbols which were seen as the *components* of particular works of art. Or again there was biography, or psychobiography and its like, where the components were in the man's life and the work of art was an object in which components of this kind were discovered. Even in some of the more rigorous forms of New Criticism and of structuralist criticism, this essential procedure of regarding the work as an object which has to be reduced to its components, even if later it may be reconstituted, came to persist.

OBJECTS AND PRACTICES

look at wk of art like a practice not an object

Now I think the true crisis in cultural theory, in our own time, is between this view of the work of art as object and the alternative view of art as a practice. Of course it is at once argued that the work of art *is* an object: that various works have survived from the past, particular sculptures, particular paintings, particular buildings, and these are objects. This is of course true, but the same way of thinking is applied to works which have no such singular existence. There is no *Hamlet,* no *Brothers Karamazov,* no *Wuthering Heights,* in the sense that there is a particular great painting. There is no *Fifth Symphony,* there is no work in the whole area of music and dance and performance, which is an object in any way comparable to those works in the visual arts which have survived. And yet the habit of treating all such works as objects has persisted because this is a basic theoretical and practical pre-

supposition. But in literature (especially in drama), in music and in a very wide area of the performing arts, what we permanently have are not objects but *notations.* These notations have then to be interpreted in an active way, according to the particular conventions. But indeed this is true over an even wider field. The relationship between the making of a work of art and its reception is always active, and subject to conventions, which in themselves are forms of (changing) social organization and relationship, and this is radically different from the production and consumption of an object. It is indeed an activity and a practice, and in its accessible forms, although it may in some arts have the character of a singular object, it is still only accessible through active perception and interpretation. This makes the case of notation, in arts like drama and literature and music, only a special case of a much wider truth. What this can show us here about the practice of analysis is that we have to break from the common procedure of isolating the object and then discovering its components. On the contrary we have to discover the nature of a practice and then its conditions.

Often these two procedures may in part resemble each other, but in many other cases they are of radically different kinds, and I would conclude with an observation on the way this distinction bears on the Marxist tradition of the relation between primary economic and social practices, and cultural practices. If we suppose that what is produced in cultural practice is a series of objects, we shall, as in most current forms of sociological-critical procedure, set about discovering their components. Within a Marxist emphasis these components will be from what we have been in the habit of calling the base. We then isolate certain features which we can so to say recognize in component form, or we ask what processes of transformation or mediation these components have gone through before they arrived in this accessible state.

But I am saying that we should look not for the components of a product but for the conditions of a practice. When we find ourselves looking at a particular work, or group of works, often realizing, as we do so, their essential community as well as their irreducible individuality, we should find ourselves attending first to the reality of their practice and the conditions of the practice as it was then executed. And from this I think we ask essentially different questions. Take for example the way in which an object—"a text"—is related to a genre, in orthodox criticism. We identify it by certain leading features, we then assign it to a larger category, the genre, and then we may find the components of the genre in a particular social history (although in some variants of criticism not even that is done, and the genre is supposed to be some permanent category of the mind).

It is not that way of proceeding that is now required. The recognition of the relation of a collective mode and an individual project—and these are the only categories that we can initially presume—is a recognition of related practices. That is to say, the irreducibly individual projects that particular works are, may come in experience and in analysis to show resemblances which allow us to group them into collective modes. These are by no means always genres. They may exist as resemblances within and across genres. They may be the practice of a group in a period, rather than the practice of a phase in a genre. But as we discover the nature of a particular practice, and the nature of the relation between an individual project and a collective mode, we find that we are analysing, as two forms of the same process, both its active composition and its conditions of composition, and in either direction this is a complex of extending active relationships. This means, of course, that we have no built-in procedures of the kind which is indicated by the fixed character of an object. We have the principles of the relations of practices, within a discoverably intentional organization, and we have the available hypotheses of dominant, residual and emergent. But what we are actively seeking is the true practice which has been alienated to an object, and the true conditions of practice—whether as literary conventions or as social relationships—which have been alienated to components or to mere background.

As a general proposition this is only an emphasis, but it seems to me to suggest at once the point of break and the point of departure, in practical and theoretical work, within an active and self-renewing Marxist cultural tradition.

NOTE

1. For a further discussion of the range of meanings in "determine" see *Keywords,* London 1976, pp. 87–91.

29

Stephen Jay Greenblatt
1943–

For more than a decade now, Stephen Greenblatt, the Class of 1932 Professor of English Literature at the University of California, Berkeley, has been a leading contributor to the critical movement called the New Historicism. Greenblatt himself invented this title in the early 1980s to distinguish the reading practices that he and a number of like-minded colleagues, including Louis Montrose and Richard Helgerson, had developed from two interpretive approaches that had shaped much of the research that had been conducted by a previous generation of Renaissance scholars. Rejecting both the New Critical assumption that Renaissance works belong to an autonomous aesthetic realm and the older historicist premise that Renaissance literature mirrored, from a distant point of observation, a coherent worldview, Greenblatt argued that critics who wish to understand Tudor and Stuart writing must situate specific texts within the irreducibly complex network of authorities that constituted Renaissance culture in its entirety.

To spell out the implications of Greenblatt's position, we can briefly summarize the thesis of his highly influential *Renaissance Self-Fashioning* (1980). In this work, Greenblatt demonstrates that sixteenth- and seventeenth-century English society was regulated by an array of institutions—for instance, the court, the church, and the colonial administration—that sponsored a varied, occasionally contradictory, assortment of beliefs, customs, and activities. These codes and practices were actually cultural conventions, social constructions of reality, but the authorities that disseminated these systems of comportment invested their positions with the aura of naturalness and thus sought to stigmatize those who sponsored alternative paradigms for understanding behavior—including members of other nations and proponents of other faiths—by describing these rivals as aliens. Since Renaissance writers were endowed with subjectivity or selfhood at the point when they allied themselves with or rose in opposition to one of these formidable institutions, their views were shaped by the cultural authority they identified with or resisted, and they used their texts either to depict the strategies that their allies might deploy to overcome figures of otherness, or to denounce the tactics that a power mobilized to expand its sphere of influence. Given that Renaissance authors were fully engaged with the social problems of their time, the critic's job is to reconstruct the political terrain in which their writers performed their ideological labors, and to chart, in dialectical fashion, the ways that texts both represented a community's behavior patterns and endorsed, perpetuated, or critiqued that culture's dominant codes.

To produce the sophisticated interpretations that his polemical statements invite, Greenblatt forges a powerful interdisciplinary approach to the study of Renaissance writing. Following cultural anthropologists, especially Clifford Geertz, he speaks of public actions as elements in a discursive or signifying system, and this assumption allows him to disclose the ways that apparently minor events, such as casual encounters between colonists and native Americans, encoded the beliefs, tactics, and values that gave an entire community its coherence. In addition, Greenblatt is indebted to Michel Foucault, for the prominent French theorist provides him with models of coercive and corrective power relations that shape his analysis of Renaissance institutions. Marx and his followers also provide Greenblatt with paradigms that he invokes to discuss the political function of literature. Indeed, Althusser's notion that art makes us perceive, by a process of internal distancing, the ideology in which it is held informs many of Greenblatt's comments on the question of whether Renaissance texts could subvert the social order that was dominant at the time they were written. Having developed this complicated theoretical orientation while authoring *Renaissance Self-Fashioning,* Greenblatt applied it with some modification in his subsequent book-length studies of culture, and as a result he has offered his readers telling analyses of strategies of social reproduction and tactics of colonial domination in *Shakespearian Negotiations* (1988) and *Marvelous Possessions* (1991), respectively.

In the essay that follows, "Invisible Bullets: Renaissance Authority and Its Subversion" (1981), Greenblatt explores an issue that has become one of the leading concerns of the New Historicists, namely, how orthodox and defiant impulses are related within the specific cultural formations they study. Contrary to scholars who have posited the existence of radical Renaissance intellectual traditions and scientific communities, Greenblatt argues that the texts of authors who ostensibly seek to celebrate political authority actually register some of Elizabethan society's most subtly subversive insights about power. To prove his point, he examines the practices of testing, recording, and explaining as they appear in *A Brief and True Report of the New Found Land of Virginia,* and he demonstrates that Thomas Harriot can provide a skeptical representation of religion—one which confirms the Machiavellian view that theology is a collection of tricks that allows the civilized to control the savage—precisely because this author is a vigilant defender of a colonial administration that defines itself in opposition to native American voices it projects as Other. In pursuing such an analysis, Greenblatt does not mean to imply that Harriot was fully conscious of the subversive potential implicit in his depiction of power. In fact, he takes the unintentionally radical character of the *Report* as a sign that this text replicates mechanisms that shape the apprehensions of an entire community. This maneuver allows Greenblatt to trace in some of Shakespeare's plays the same tactics of testing and recording that he found in Harriot's work, and in doing so he fulfills the New Historicist's obligation to delineate the ways that texts were linked to the network of institutions, practices, and beliefs that constituted a particular culture.

Invisible Bullets: Renaissance Authority and Its Subversion

I

In his notorious police report of 1593 on Christopher Marlowe, the Elizabethan spy Richard Baines informed his superiors that Marlowe had declared, among other monstrous opinions, that "Moses was but a Juggler, and that one Heriots being Sir W Raleighs man Can do more than he."[1] The "Heriots" cast for a moment in this lurid light is Thomas Harriot, the most profound Elizabethan mathematician, an expert in cartography, optics, and navigational science, an adherent of atomism, the first Englishman to make a telescope and turn it on the heavens, the author of the first original book about the first English colony in America, and the possessor throughout his career of a dangerous reputation for atheism.[2] In all of his extant writings, private correspondence as well as public discourse, Harriot professes the most reassuringly orthodox religious faith, but the suspicion persisted. When he died of cancer in 1621, one of his contemporaries, persuaded that Harriot had challenged the doctrinal account of creation *ex nihilo,* remarked gleefully that "a *nihilum* killed him at last: for in the top of his nose came a little red speck (exceeding small), which grew bigger and bigger, and at last killed him."[3]

Charges of atheism leveled at Harriot or anyone else in this period are difficult to assess, for such accusations were smear tactics, used with reckless abandon against anyone whom the accuser happened to dislike. At a dinner party one summer evening in 1593, Sir Walter Ralegh teased an irascible country parson named Ralph Ironside and found himself the subject of a state investigation; at the other end of the social scale, in the same Dorsetshire parish, a drunken servant named Oliver complained that in the Sunday sermon the preacher had praised Moses ex-

cessively but had neglected to mention his fifty-two concubines, and Oliver too found himself under official scrutiny.[4] Few, if any, of these investigations turned up what we would call atheists, even muddled or shallow ones; the stance that seemed to come naturally to me as a green college freshman in mid–twentieth-century America seems to have been almost unthinkable to the most daring philosophical minds of late sixteenth-century England.

The historical evidence is unreliable; even in the absence of social pressure, people lie readily about their most intimate beliefs. How much more must they have lied in an atmosphere of unembarrassed repression. Still, there is probably more than politic concealment involved here. After all, treason was punished as harshly as atheism, yet while the period abounds in documented instances of treason in word and deed, there are virtually no professed atheists.[5] If ever there were a place to confirm that in a given social construction of reality certain interpretations of experience are sanctioned and others excluded, it is here, in the boundaries that contained sixteenth-century skepticism. Like Machiavelli and Montaigne, Thomas Harriot professed belief in God, and there is no justification in any of these cases for dismissing the profession of faith as mere hypocrisy.

I am arguing not that atheism was literally unthinkable in the late sixteenth century but rather that it was almost always thinkable only as the thought of another. This is one of its attractions as a smear; atheism is a characteristic mark of otherness—hence the ease with which Catholics can call Protestant martyrs atheists and Protestants routinely make similar charges against the pope.[6] The pervasiveness and frequency of these charges, then, does not signal the existence of a secret society of freethinkers, a

School of Night, but rather registers the operation of a religious authority, whether Catholic or Protestant, that confirms its power by disclosing the threat of atheism. The authority is secular as well as religious, since atheism is frequently adduced as a motive for heinous crimes, as if all men and women would inevitably conclude that if God does not exist, everything is permitted. At Ralegh's 1603 treason trial, for example, Justice Popham solemnly warned the accused not to let "Harriot, nor any such Doctor, persuade you there is no eternity in Heaven, lest you find an eternity of hell-torments."[7] Nothing in Harriot's writings suggests that he held the position attributed to him here, but the charge does not depend upon evidence: Harriot is invoked as the archetypal corrupter, Achitophel seducing the glittering Absalom. If the atheist did not exist, he would have to be invented.

Yet atheism is not the only mode of subversive religious doubt, and we cannot discount the persistent rumors of Harriot's heterodoxy by pointing to either his conventional professions of faith or the conventionality of the attacks upon him. Indeed I want to suggest that if we look closely at *A Brief and True Report of the New Found Land of Virginia* (1588), the only work Harriot published in his lifetime and hence the work in which he was presumably the most cautious, we can find traces of material that could lead to the remark attributed to Marlowe, that "Moses was but a Juggler, and that one Heriots being Sir W Raleighs man Can do more than he." And I want to suggest further that understanding the relation between orthodoxy and subversion in Harriot's text will enable us to construct an interpretive model that may be used to understand the far more complex problem posed by Shakespeare's history plays.

Those plays have been described with impeccable intelligence as deeply conservative and with equally impeccable intelligence as deeply radical. Shakespeare, in Northrop Frye's words, is "a born courtier," the dramatist who organizes his representation of English history around the hegemonic mysticism of the Tudor myth; Shakespeare is also a relentless demystifier, an interrogator of ideology, "the only dramatist," as Franco Moretti puts it, "who rises to the level of Machiavelli in elaborating all the consequences of the separation of political praxis from moral evaluation."[8] The conflict glimpsed here could be investigated, on a performance-by-performance basis, in a history of reception, but that history is shaped, I would argue, by circumstances of production as well as consumption. The ideological strategies that fashion Shakespeare's history plays help in turn to fashion the conflicting readings of the plays' politics. And these strategies are no more Shakespeare's invention than the historical narratives on which he based his plots. As we shall see from Harriot's *Brief and True Report,* in the discourse of authority a powerful logic governs the relation between orthodoxy and subversion.

I should first explain that the apparently feeble wisecrack about Moses and Harriot finds its way into a police file on Marlowe because it seems to bear out one of the Machiavellian arguments about religion that most excited the wrath of sixteenth-century authorities: Old Testament religion, the argument goes, and by extension the whole Judeo-Christian tradition, originated in a series of clever tricks, fraudulent illusions perpetrated by Moses, who had been trained in Egyptian magic, upon the "rude and gross" (and hence credulous) Hebrews.[9] This argument is not actually to be found in Machiavelli, nor does it originate in the sixteenth century; it is already fully formulated in early pagan polemics against Christianity. But it seems to acquire a special force and currency in the Renaissance as an aspect of a heightened consciousness, fueled by the period's prolonged crises of doctrine and church governance, of the social function of religious belief.

Here Machiavelli's writings are important. *The Prince* observes in its bland way that if Moses' particular actions and methods are examined closely, they appear to differ little from those employed by the great pagan princes; the *Discourses* treats religion as if its primary function were not salvation but the achievement of civic discipline, as if its primary justification were not truth but expediency.[10] Thus Romulus's successor Numa Pompilius, "finding a very savage people, and wishing to reduce them to civil obedience by the arts of peace, had recourse to religion as the most necessary and assured support of any civil society" (*Discourses,* 146). For although "Romulus could organize the Senate and establish other civil and military institutions without the aid of divine authority, yet it was very necessary for Numa, who feigned that he held converse with a nymph, who dictated to him all that he wished to persuade the people to." In truth, continues Machiavelli, "there never was any remarkable lawgiver amongst any people who did not resort to divine authority, as otherwise his laws would not have been accepted by the people" (147).

From here it was only a short step, in the minds of Renaissance authorities, to the monstrous opinions attributed to the likes of Marlowe and Harriot. Kyd, under torture, testified that Marlowe had affirmed that "things esteemed to be done by divine power might have as well been done by observation of men," and the Jesuit Robert Parsons claimed that in Ralegh's "school of Atheism," "both Moses and our Savior, the old and the New Testament, are jested at."[11] On the eve of Ralegh's treason trial, some "hellish verses" were lifted from an anonymous tragedy written ten years earlier and circulated as Ralegh's own confession of atheism. At first the earth was held in common, the verses declare, but this golden age gave way to war, kingship, and property:

> Then some sage man, above the vulgar wise,
> Knowing that laws could not in quiet dwell,
> Unless they were observed, did first devise
> The names of Gods, religion, heaven, and hell
> . . . Only bug-bears to keep the world in
>   fear.[12]

The attribution of these lines to Ralegh is instructive: the fictional text returns to circulation as the missing confessional language of real life. That fiction is unlikely to represent an observable attitude in the "real" world, though we can never altogether exclude that possibility; rather it stages a cultural conceit, the recurrent fantasy of the archcriminal as atheist. Ralegh already had a reputation as both a poet and a freethinker; perhaps one of his numerous enemies actually plotted to heighten the violent popular hostility toward him by floating under his name a forgotten piece of stage villainy.[13] But quite apart from a possible conspiracy, the circulation fulfills a strong cultural expectation. When a hated favorite like Ralegh was accused of treason, what was looked for was not evidence but a performance, a theatrical revelation of motive and an enactment of despair. If the motives for treason revealed in this performance could be various—ambition, jealousy, greed, spite, and so forth—what permitted the release of these motives into action would always be the same: atheism. No one who actually loved and feared God would allow himself to rebel against an anointed ruler, and atheism, conversely, would lead inevitably to treason. Since atheism was virtually always, as I have argued, the thought of the other, it would be difficult to find a first-person confession—except, of course, in fiction and above all in the theater. The soliloquy is lifted from its theatrical context and transformed into "verses" that the three surviving manuscripts declare were "devised by that Atheist and Traitor Ralegh as it is said." The last phrase may signal skepticism about the attribution, but such reservations do not count for much: the "hellish verses" are what men like Marlowe, Harriot, or Ralegh would have to think in their hearts.

Harriot does not voice any speculations remotely resembling the hypotheses that a punitive religion was invented to keep men in awe and that belief originated in a fraudulent imposition by cunning "jugglers" on the ignorant, but his recurrent association with the forbidden thoughts of the demonized other may be linked to something beyond malicious slander. If we look attentively at his account of the first Virginia colony, we find a mind that seems interested in the same set of problems, a mind, indeed, that seems to be virtually testing the Machiavellian hypotheses. Sent by Ralegh to keep a record of the colony and to compile a description of the resources and inhabitants of the area, Harriot took care to learn the North Carolina Algonquian dialect and to achieve what he calls a "special familiarity with some of the priests."[14] The Virginian Indians believe, Harriot writes, in the immortality of the soul and in otherworldly punishments and rewards for behavior in this world: "What subtlety soever be in the *Wiroances* and Priests, this opinion worketh so much in many of the common and simple sort of people that it maketh them have great respect to the Governors, and also great care what they do, to avoid torment after death and to enjoy bliss" (374).[15] The split between the priests and people implied here is glimpsed as well in the description of the votive images: "They think that all the gods are of human shape, and therefore they represent them by images in the forms of men, which they call Kewasowak. . . . The common sort think them to be also gods" (373). And the social function of popular belief is underscored in Harriot's note to an illustration showing the priests carefully tending the embalmed bodies of the former chiefs: "These poor souls are thus instructed by nature to reverence their princes even after their death" (De Bry, p. 72).

We have then, as in Machiavelli, a sense of religion as a set of beliefs manipulated by the subtlety of priests to help instill obedience and respect for authority. The terms of Harriot's analysis—"the common and simple sort of people," "the Governors," and so forth—are obviously drawn from the language of comparable social analyses of England; as Karen Kupperman has most recently demonstrated, sixteenth- and seventeenth-century Englishmen characteristically describe the Indians in terms that closely replicate their own self-conception, above all in matters of *status*.[16] The great mass of Indians are seen as a version of "the common sort" at home, just as Harriot translates the Algonquian *weroan* as "great Lord" and speaks of "the chief Ladies," "virgins of good parentage," "a young gentlewoman," and so forth. There is an easy, indeed almost irresistible, analogy in the period between accounts of Indian and European social structure, so that Harriot's description of the inward mechanisms of Algonquian society implies a description of comparable mechanisms in his own culture.[17]

To this we may add a still more telling observation not of the internal function of native religion but of the impact of European culture on the Indians: "Most things they saw with us," Harriot writes, "as mathematical instruments, sea compasses, the virtue of the loadstone in drawing iron, a perspective glass whereby was showed many strange sights, burning glasses, wildlife works, guns, books, writing and reading, spring clocks that seem to go of themselves, and many other things that we had, were so strange unto them, and so far exceeded their capacities to comprehend the reason and means how they should be made and done, that they thought they were rather the works of gods than of men, or at the leastwise they had been given and taught us of the gods" (375–76). This delusion, born of what Harriot supposes to be the vast technological superiority of the European, caused the savages to doubt that they possessed the truth of God and religion and to suspect that such truth "was rather to be had from us, whom God so specially loved than from a people that were so simple, as they found themselves to be in comparison of us" (376).

Here, I suggest, is the very core of the Machiavellian anthropology that posited the origin of religion in an imposition of socially coercive doctrines by an educated and sophisticated lawgiver on a simple people. And in Harriot's list of the marvels—from wildfire to reading—with which he undermined the Indians' confidence in their native understanding of the universe, we have the core of the claim attributed to Marlowe: that Moses was but a juggler and that Ralegh's man Harriot could do more than he. The testing of this hypothesis in the encounter of the Old World and the New was appropriate, we may add, for though vulgar Machiavellianism implied that all religion was a sophisticated confidence trick, Machiavelli himself saw that trick as possible only at a radical point of origin: "If any one wanted to establish a republic at the present time," he writes, "he would find it much easier with the simple mountaineers, who are almost without any civilization, than with such as are accustomed to live in cities, where civilization is already corrupt; as a sculptor finds it easier to make a fine statue out of a crude block of marble than out of a statue badly begun by another."[18] It was only with a people, as Harriot says, "so simple, as they found themselves to be in comparison of us," that the imposition of a coercive set of religious beliefs could be attempted.

In Harriot, then, we have one of the earliest instances of a significant phenomenon: the testing upon the bodies and minds of non-Europeans or, more generally, the noncivilized, of a hypothesis about the origin and nature of European culture and belief. In encountering the Algonquian Indians, Harriot not only thought he was encountering a simplified version of his own culture but also evidently believed that he was encountering his own civilization's past.[19] This past could best be investigated in the privileged anthropological moment of the initial encounter, for the comparable situations in Europe itself tended to be already contaminated by prior contact. Only in the forest, with a people ignorant of Christianity and startled by its bearers' technological potency, could one hope to reproduce accurately, with live subjects, the relation imagined between Numa and the primitive Romans, Moses and the Hebrews. The actual testing could happen only once, for it entails

not detached observation but radical change, the change Harriot begins to observe in the priests who "were not so sure grounded, nor gave such credit to their traditions and stories, but through conversing with us they were brought into great doubts of their own" (375).[20] I should emphasize that I am speaking here of events as reported by Harriot. The history of subsequent English-Algonquian relations casts doubt on the depth, extent, and irreversibility of the supposed Indian crisis of belief. In the *Brief and True Report,* however, the tribe's stories begin to *collapse* in the minds of their traditional guardians, and the coercive power of the European beliefs begins to show itself almost at once in the Indians' behavior: "On a time also when their corn began to wither by reason of a drought which happened extraordinarily, fearing that it had come to pass by reason that in some thing they had displeased us, many would come to us and desire us to pray to our God of England, that he would preserve their corn, promising that when it was ripe we also should be partakers of their fruit" (377). If we remember that the English, like virtually all sixteenth-century Europeans in the New World, resisted or were incapable of provisioning themselves and in consequence depended upon the Indians for food, we may grasp the central importance for the colonists of this dawning Indian fear of the Christian God.

As early as 1504, during Columbus's fourth voyage, the natives, distressed that the Spanish seemed inclined to settle in for a long visit, refused to continue to supply food. Knowing from his almanac that a total eclipse of the moon was imminent, Columbus warned the Indians that God would show them a sign of his displeasure; after the eclipse, the terrified Indians resumed the supply. But an eclipse would not always be so conveniently at hand. John Sparke, who sailed with Sir John Hawkins in 1564–65, noted that the French colonists in Florida "would not take the pains so much as to fish in the river before their doors, but would have all things put in their mouths."[21] When the Indians wearied of this arrangement, the French turned to extortion and robbery, and before long there were bloody wars. A similar situation seems to have arisen in the Virginia colony: despite land rich in game and ample fishing grounds, the English nearly starved to death when the exasperated Algonquians refused to build fishing weirs and plant corn.[22]

It is difficult to understand why men so aggressive and energetic in other regards should have been so passive in the crucial matter of feeding themselves. No doubt there were serious logistic problems in transporting food and equally serious difficulties adapting European farming methods and materials to the different climate and soil of the New World, yet these explanations seem insufficient, as they did even to the early explorers themselves. John Sparke wrote that "notwithstanding the great want that the Frenchmen had, the ground doth yield victuals sufficient, if they would have taken pains to get the same; but they were being soldiers, desired to live by the sweat of other mens brows" (Hakluyt 10:56). This remark bears close attention: it points not to laziness or negligence but to an occupational identity, a determination to be nourished by the labor of others weaker, more vulnerable, than oneself. This self-conception was not, we might add, exclusively military: the hallmark of power and wealth in the sixteenth century was to be waited on by others. "To live by the sweat of other men's brows" was the enviable lot of the gentleman; indeed in England it virtually defined a gentleman. The New World held out the prospect of such status for all but the poorest cabin boy.[23]

But the prospect could not be realized through violence alone, even if the Europeans had possessed a monopoly of it, because the relentless exercise of violence could actually reduce the food supply. As Machiavelli understood, physical compulsion is essential but never sufficient; the survival of the rulers depends upon a supplement of coercive belief. The Indi-

ans must be persuaded that the Christian God is all-powerful and committed to the survival of his chosen people, that he will wither the corn and destroy the lives of savages who displease him by disobeying or plotting against the English. Here is a strange paradox: Harriot tests and seems to confirm the most radically subversive hypothesis in his culture about the origin and function of religion by imposing his religion—with its intense claims to transcendence, unique truth, inescapable coercive force—on others. Not only the official purpose but the survival of the English colony depends upon this imposition. This crucial circumstance licensed the testing in the first place; only as an agent of the English colony, dependent upon its purposes and committed to its survival, is Harriot in a position to disclose the power of human achievements—reading, writing, perspective glasses, gunpowder, and the like—to appear to the ignorant as divine and hence to promote belief and compel obedience.

Thus the subversiveness that is genuine and radical—sufficiently disturbing so that to be suspected of it could lead to imprisonment and torture—is at the same time contained by the power it would appear to threaten. Indeed the subversiveness is the very product of that power and furthers its ends. One may go still further and suggest that the power Harriot both serves and embodies not only produces its own subversion but is actively built upon it: the project of evangelical colonialism is not set over against the skeptical critique of religious coercion but battens on the very confirmation of that critique. In the Virginia colony, the radical undermining of Christian order is not the negative limit but the positive condition for the establishment of that order. And this paradox extends to the production of Harriot's text: *A Brief and True Report,* with its latent heterodoxy, is not a reflection upon the Virginia colony or even a simple record of it—it is not, in other words, a privileged withdrawal into a critical zone set apart from power—but a continuation of the colonial enterprise.

By October 1586, rumors were spreading in England that Virginia offered little prospect of profit, that the colony had been close to starvation, and that the Indians had turned hostile. Harriot accordingly begins his report with a descriptive catalog in which the natural goods of the land are turned into social goods, that is, into "merchantable commodities": "Cedar, a very sweet wood and fine timber; whereof if nests of chests be there made, or timber thereof fitted for sweet and fine bedsteads, tables, desks, lutes, virginals, and many things else, . . . [it] will yield profit" (329–30).[24] The inventory of these commodities is followed by an inventory of edible plants and animals, to prove to readers that the colony need not starve, and then by the account of the Indians, to prove that the colony could impose its will on them. The key to this imposition, as we have seen, is the coercive power of religious belief, and the source of the power is the impression made by advanced technology upon a "backward" people.

Hence Harriot's text is committed to record what I have called his confirmation of the Machiavellian hypothesis, and hence too the potential subversiveness of this confirmation is invisible not only to those on whom the religion is supposedly imposed but also to most readers and quite possibly to Harriot himself. It may be that Harriot was demonically conscious of what he was doing—that he found himself situated exactly where he could test one of his culture's darkest fears about its own origins, that he used the Algonquians to do so, and that he wrote a report on his own findings, a coded report, since as he wrote to Kepler years later, "our situation is such that I still may not philosophize freely."[25] But this is not the only Harriot we can conjure up. A scientist of the late sixteenth century, we might suppose, would have regarded the natives' opinion that English technology was god-given—indeed divine—with something like corroboratory complacency. It would, as a colleague from whom I borrow this conjecture remarked, "be just like an establishment intellec-

tual, or simply a well-placed Elizabethan bourgeois, to accept that his superior 'powers'—moral, technological, cultural—were indeed signs of divine favor and that therefore the superstitious natives were quite right in their perception of the need to submit to their benevolent conquerors."[26]

Now Harriot does not in fact express such a view of the ultimate origin of his trunk of marvels—and I doubt that he held the view in this form—but it is significant that in the next generation Bacon, perhaps recalling Harriot's text or others like it, claims in *The New Organon* that scientific discoveries "are as it were new creations, and imitations of God's works" that may be justly regarded *as if* they were manifestations not of human skill but of divine power: "Let a man only consider what a difference there is between the life of men in the most civilized province of Europe, and in the wildest and most barbarous districts of New India; he will feel it to be great enough to justify the saying that 'man is a god to man,' not only in regard to aid and benefit, but also by a comparison of condition. And this difference comes not from soil, not from climate, not from race, but from the arts."[27] From this perspective the Algonquian misconception of the origin and nature of English technology would be evidence not of the power of Christianity to impose itself fraudulently on a backward people but of the dazzling power of science and of the naive literalism of the ignorant, who can conceive of this power only as the achievement of actual gods.[28]

Thus, for all his subtlety and his sensitivity to heterodoxy, Harriot might not have grasped fully the disturbing implications of his own text. The plausibility of a picture of Harriot culturally insulated from the subversive energies of his own activity would seem to be enhanced elsewhere in *A Brief and True Report* by his account of his missionary efforts:

Many times and in every town where I came, according as I was able, I made declaration of the contents of the Bible; that therein was set forth the true and only God, and his mighty works, that therein was contained the true doctrine of salvation through Christ, with many particularities of Miracles and chief points of religion, as I was able then to utter, and thought fit for the time. And although I told them the book materially and of itself was not of any such virtue, as I thought they did conceive, but only the doctrine therein contained; yet would many be glad to touch it, to embrace it, to kiss it, to hold it to their breasts and heads, and stroke over all their body with it; to show their hungry desire of that knowledge which was spoken of. (376–77)

Here the heathens' confusion of material object and religious doctrine does not seem to cast doubts upon the truth of the Holy Book; rather it signals precisely the naive literalism of the Algonquians and hence their susceptibility to idolatry. They are viewed with a touch of amusement, as Spenser in the *Faerie Queene* views the "salvage nation" who seek to worship Una herself rather than the truth for which she stands:

> During which time her gentle wit she plyes,
> To teach them truth, which worshipt her in
>   vaine,
> And made her th'Image of Idolatryes;
> But when their bootlesse zeale she did
>   restraine
> From her own worship, they her Asse would
>   worship fayn.
>
>   (1.6.19)[29]

Harriot, for his part, is willing to temper the view of the savage as idolater by reading the Algonquian fetishism of the book as a promising sign, an allegory of "their hungry desire of that knowledge which was spoken of." Such a reading, we might add, conveniently supports the claim that the English would easily dominate and civilize the Indians and hence advances the general purpose of *A Brief and True Report.*

The apparent religious certainty, cultural confidence, and national self-interest here by no means rule out the possibility of what I have called demonic consciousness—we can always postulate that Harriot found ever more subtle ways of simultaneously recording and disguising his dangerous speculations—but the essential point is that we need no such biographical romance to account for the apparent testing and confirmation of the Machiavellian hypothesis: the colonial power produced the subversiveness in its own interest, as I have argued, and *A Brief and True Report,* appropriately, was published by the great Elizabethan exponent of missionary colonialism, the Reverend Richard Hakluyt.

The thought that Christianity served to shore up the authority of the colonists would not have struck Hakluyt or the great majority of his readers as subversive. On the contrary, the role of religion in preserving the social order was a commonplace that all parties vied with each other in proclaiming. The suggestion that religions should be ranked according to their demonstrated ability to control their adherents would have been unacceptable, however, and the suggestion that reinforcing civil discipline must be the real origin and ultimate purpose of Christianity would have been still worse. These were possible explanations of the religion of another—skeptical arguments about ideological causality always work against beliefs one does not hold—but as we might expect from the earlier discussion of atheism, the application of this explanation to Christianity itself could be aired, and sternly refuted, only as the thought of another. Indeed a strictly functionalist explanation even of false religions was rejected by Christian theologians of the period. "It is utterly vain," writes Calvin, "for some men to say that religion was invented by the subtlety and craft of a few to hold the simple folk in thrall by this device and that those very persons who originated the worship of God for others did not in the least believe that any God existed." He goes on to concede "that in order to hold men's minds in greater subjection, clever men have devised very many things in religion by which to inspire the common folk with reverence and strike them with terror. But they would never have achieved this if men's minds had not already been imbued with a firm conviction about God, from which the inclination toward religion springs as from a seed."[30] Similarly, Hooker argues, "lest any man should here conceive, that it greatly skilleth not of what sort our religion be, inasmuch as heathens, Turks, and infidels, impute to religion a great part of the same effects which ourselves ascribe thereunto," that the good moral effects of false religions result from their having religious—that is, Christian—truths "entwined" in them.[31]

This argument, which derives from the early chapters of the Epistle to the Romans, is so integral to what John Coolidge has called the Pauline Renaissance in England that Harriot's account of the Algonquians would have seemed, even for readers who sensed something odd about it, closer to confirmation than to subversion of religious orthodoxy. Yet it is misleading, I think, to conclude without qualification that the radical doubt implicit in Harriot's account is *entirely* contained. After all, Harriot was hounded through his whole life by charges of atheism, and, more tellingly, the remark attributed to Marlowe suggests that a contemporary could draw the most dangerous conclusions from the Virginia report. Both of these signs of slippage are compromised by their links to the society's well-developed repressive apparatus: rumors, accusations, police reports. But if we should be wary of naively accepting a version of reality proffered by the secret police, we cannot at the same time dismiss that version altogether. There is a perversely attractive, if bleak, clarity in such a dismissal—in deciding that subversive doubt was totally produced and totally contained by the ruling elite—but the actual evidence is tenebrous. We simply do not know what was thought in silence, what was written and then carefully burned, what was whispered

by Harriot to Ralegh. Moreover, the "Atlantic Republican tradition," as Pocock has argued, does grow out of the "Machiavellian moment" of the sixteenth century, and that tradition, with its transformation of subjects into citizens, its subordination of transcendent values to capital values, does ultimately undermine, in the interests of a new power, the religious and secular authorities that had licensed the American enterprise in the first place.[32] In Harriot's text the relation between orthodoxy and subversion seems, at the same interpretive moment, to be both perfectly stable and dangerously volatile.

We can deepen our understanding of this apparent paradox if we consider a second mode of subversion and its containment in Harriot's account. Alongside the *testing* of a subversive interpretation of the dominant culture, we find the *recording* of alien voices or, more precisely, of alien interpretations. The occasion for this recording is another consequence of the English presence in the New World, not in this case the threatened extinction of the tribal religion but the threatened extinction of the tribe: "There was no town where we had any subtle device practiced against us," Harriot writes, "but that within a few days after our departure from every such town, the people began to die very fast, and many in short space; in some towns about twenty, in some forty, in some sixty and in one six score, which in truth was very many in respect of their numbers. The disease was so strange, that they neither knew what it was, nor how to cure it; the like by report of the oldest man in the country never happened before, time out of mind" (378).[33] Harriot is writing, of course, about the effects of measles, smallpox, or perhaps simply influenza on people with no resistance to them, but a conception of the biological basis of epidemic disease lies far, far in the future. For the English the deaths must be a moral phenomenon—this notion for them is as irresistible as the notion of germs for ourselves—and hence the "facts" as they are observed are already moralized: the deaths occurred only "where they used some practice against us," that is, where the Indians conspired secretly against the English. And with the wonderful self-validating circularity that characterizes virtually all powerful constructions of reality, the evidence for these secret conspiracies is precisely the deaths of the Indians.[34]

It is not surprising that Harriot seems to endorse the idea that God protects his chosen people by killing off untrustworthy Indians; what is surprising is to find him interested in the Indians' own anxious speculations about the unintended biological warfare that was destroying them. Drawing upon his special familiarity with the priests, he records a remarkable series of conjectures, almost all of which assume—correctly, as we now know—a link between the Indians' misfortune and the presence of the strangers. "Some people," observing that the English remained healthy while the Indians died, "could not tell," Harriot writes, "whether to think us gods or men"; others, seeing that the members of the first colony were all male, concluded that they were not born of women and therefore must be spirits of the dead returned to mortal form. Some medicine men learned in astrology blamed the disease on a recent eclipse of the sun and on a comet—a theory Harriot considers seriously and rejects— while others shared the prevailing English view and said "that it was the special work of God" on behalf of the colonists. And some who seem in historical hindsight eerily prescient prophesied "that there were more of [the English] generation yet to come, to kill theirs and take their places." The supporters of this theory even worked out a conception of the disease that in some features resembles our own: "Those that were immediately to come after us [the first English colonists], they imagined to be in the air, yet invisible and without bodies, and that they by our entreaty and for the love of us did make the people to die . . . by shooting invisible bullets into them" (380).

For a moment, as Harriot records these competing theories, it may seem to us as if there were no absolute assurance of God's national interest,

as if the drive to displace and absorb the other had given way to conversation among equals, as if all meanings were provisional, as if the signification of events stood apart from power. Our impression is intensified because we know that the theory that would ultimately triumph over the moral conception of epidemic disease was already present, at least metaphorically, in the conversation.[35] In the very moment that the moral conception is busily authorizing itself, it registers the possibility (indeed from our vantage point, the inevitability) of its own destruction.

But why, we must ask ourselves, should power record other voices, permit subversive inquiries, register at its very center the transgressions that will ultimately violate it? The answer may be in part that power, even in a colonial situation, is not monolithic and hence may encounter and record in one of its functions materials that can threaten another of its functions; in part that power thrives on vigilance, and human beings are vigilant if they sense a threat; in part that power defines itself in relation to such threats or simply to that which is not identical with it. Harriot's text suggests an intensification of these observations: English power in the first Virginia colony *depends* upon the registering and even the production of potentially unsettling perspectives. "These their opinions I have set down the more at large," Harriot tells the "Adventurers, Favorers, and Wellwishers" of the colony to whom his report is addressed, "that it may appear unto you that there is good hope that they may be brought through discreet dealing and government to the embracing of the truth, and consequently to honor, obey, fear, and love us" (381). The recording of alien voices, their preservation in Harriot's text, is part of the process whereby Indian culture is constituted as a culture and thus brought into the light for study, discipline, correction, transformation. The momentary sense of instability or plenitude—the existence of other voices—is produced by the monological power that ultimately denies the possibility of plenitude, just as the subversive hypothesis about European religion is tested and confirmed only by the imposition of that religion.

We may add that the power of which we are speaking is in effect an allocation method—a way of distributing to some and denying to others critical resources (here primarily corn and game) that prolong life. In a remarkable study of the "tragic choices" societies make in allocating scarce resources (for example, kidney machines) or in determining high risks (for example, the military draft), Guido Calabresi and Philip Bobbitt observe that by complex mixtures of approaches, societies attempt to avert "tragic results, that is, results which imply the rejection of values which are proclaimed to be fundamental." Although these approaches may succeed for a time, it will eventually become apparent that some sacrifice of fundamental values has taken place, whereupon "fresh mixtures of methods will be tried, structured . . . by the shortcomings of the approaches they replace." These too will in time give way to others in a "strategy of successive moves," an "intricate game" that reflects the simultaneous perception of an inherent flaw and the determination to "forget" that perception in an illusory resolution.[36] Hence the simple operation of any systematic order, any allocation method, inevitably risks exposing its own limitations, even (or perhaps especially) as it asserts its underlying moral principle.

This exposure is most intense at moments when a comfortably established ideology confronts unusual circumstances, when the moral value of a particular form of power is not merely assumed but explained. We may glimpse such a moment in Harriot's account of a visit from the colonists' principal Indian ally, the chief Wingina. Wingina, persuaded that the disease ravaging his people was indeed the work of the Christian God, had come to request that the English ask their God to direct his lethal magic against an enemy tribe. The colonists tried to explain that such a prayer would be "ungodly," that their God was indeed responsible for the

disease but that in this as in all things, he would act only "according to his good pleasure as he had ordained" (379). Indeed, if men asked God to make an epidemic, he probably would not do it; the English could expect such providential help only if they made sincere "petition for the contrary," that is, for harmony and good fellowship in the service of truth and righteousness.

The problem with these assertions is not that they are self-consciously wicked (in the manner of Richard III or Iago) but that they are dismayingly moral and logically coherent; or rather, what is unsettling is one's experience of them, the nasty sense that they are at once irrefutable ethical propositions and pious humbug with which the English conceal from themselves the rapacity and aggression, or simply the horrible responsibility, implicit in their very presence. The explanatory moment manifests the self-validating, totalizing character of Renaissance political theology—its ability to account for almost every occurrence, even (or above all) apparently perverse or contrary occurrences—and at the same time confirms for us the drastic disillusionment that extends from Machiavelli to its definitive expression in Hume and Voltaire. In his own way, Wingina himself clearly thought his lesson in Christian ethics was polite nonsense. When the disease spread to his enemies, as it did shortly thereafter, he returned to the English to thank them—I presume with the Algonquian equivalent of a sly wink—for their friendly help, for "although we satisfied them not in promise, yet in deeds and effect we had fulfilled their desires" (379). For Harriot, this "marvellous accident," as he calls it, is another sign of the colony's great expectations.

Once again a disturbing vista—a skeptical critique of the function of Christian morality in the New World—is glimpsed only to be immediately closed off. Indeed we may feel at this point that subversion scarcely exists and may legitimately ask ourselves how our perception of the subversive and orthodox is generated. The answer, I think, is that the term *subversive* for us designates those elements in Renaissance culture that contemporary audiences tried to contain or, when containment seemed impossible, to destroy and that now conform to our own sense of truth and reality. That is, we find "subversive" in the past precisely those things that are *not* subversive to ourselves, that pose no threat to the order by which we live and allocate resources: in Harriot's *Brief and True Report,* the function of illusion in the establishment of religion, the displacement of a providential conception of disease by one focused on "invisible bullets," the exposure of the psychological and material interests served by a certain conception of divine power. Conversely, we identify as principles of order and authority in Renaissance texts what we would, if we took them seriously, find subversive for ourselves: religious and political absolutism, aristocracy of birth, demonology, humoral psychology, and the like. That we do not find such notions subversive, that we complacently identify them as principles of aesthetic or political order, replicates the process of containment that licensed the elements we call subversive in Renaissance texts: that is, our own values are sufficiently strong for us to contain alien forces almost effortlessly. What we find in Harriot's *Brief and True Report* can best be described by adapting a remark about the possibility of hope that Kafka once made to Max Brod: There is subversion, no end of subversion, only not for us.

II

Shakespeare's plays are centrally, repeatedly concerned with the production and containment of subversion and disorder, and the three practices that I have identified in Harriot's text—testing, recording, and explaining—all have their recurrent theatrical equivalents, above all in the plays that meditate on the consolidation of state power.

These equivalents are not unique to Shakespeare; they are the signs of a broad institutional appropriation that is one of the root sources of the theater's vitality. Elizabethan playing companies contrived to absorb, refashion, and exploit some of the fundamental energies of a political authority that was itself already committed to histrionic display and hence was ripe for appropriation. But if he was not alone, Shakespeare nonetheless contrived to absorb more of these energies into his plays than any of his fellow playwrights. He succeeded in doing so because he seems to have understood very early in his career that power consisted not only in dazzling display—the pageants, processions, entries, and progresses of Elizabethan statecraft—but also in a systematic structure of relations, those linked strategies I have tried to isolate and identify in colonial discourse at the margins of Tudor society. Shakespeare evidently grasped such strategies not by brooding on the impact of English culture on far-off Virginia but by looking intently at the world immediately around him, by contemplating the queen and her powerful friends and enemies, and by reading imaginatively the great English chroniclers. And the crucial point is less that he *represented* the paradoxical practices of an authority deeply complicit in undermining its own legitimacy than that he *appropriated* for the theater the compelling energies at once released and organized by these practices.

The representation of a self-undermining authority is the principal concern of *Richard II,* which marks a brilliant advance over the comparable representation in the *Henry VI* trilogy, but the full appropriation for the stage of that authority and its power is not achieved until *1 Henry IV.* We may argue, of course, that in this play there is little or no "self-undermining" at all: emergent authority in *1 Henry IV*—that is, the authority that begins to solidify around the figure of Hal—is strikingly different from the enfeebled command of Henry VI or the fatally self-wounded royal name of Richard II. "Who does not all along see," wrote Upton in the mid–eighteenth century, "that when prince

Henry comes to be king he will assume a character suitable to his dignity?" My point is not to dispute this interpretation of the prince as, in Maynard Mack's words, "an ideal image of the potentialities of the English character,"[37] but to observe that such an ideal image involves as its positive condition the constant production of its own radical subversion and the powerful containment of that subversion.

We are continually reminded that Hal is a "juggler," a conniving hypocrite, and that the power he both serves and comes to embody is glorified usurpation and theft.[38] Moreover, the disenchantment makes itself felt in the very moments when Hal's moral authority is affirmed. Thus, for example, the scheme of Hal's redemption is carefully laid out in his soliloquy at the close of the first tavern scene, but as in the act of *explaining* that we have examined in Harriot, Hal's justification of himself threatens to fall away at every moment into its antithesis. "By how much better than my word I am," Hal declares, "By so much shall I falsify men's hopes" (1.2.210–11). To falsify men's hopes is to exceed their expectations, and it is also to disappoint their expectations, to deceive men, to turn hopes into fictions, to betray.

At issue are not only the contradictory desires and expectations centered on Hal in the play— the competing hopes of his royal father and his tavern friends—but our own hopes, the fantasies continually aroused by the play of innate grace, limitless playfulness, absolute friendship, generosity, and trust. Those fantasies are symbolized by certain echoing, talismanic phrases ("when thou art king," "shall we be merry?" "a thousand pound"), and they are bound up with the overall vividness, intensity, and richness of the theatrical practice itself. Yeats's phrase for the quintessential Shakespearean effect, "the emotion of multitude," seems particularly applicable to *1 Henry IV* with its multiplicity of brilliant characters, its intensely differentiated settings, its dazzling verbal wit, its mingling of high comedy, farce, epic heroism, and tragedy. The play

awakens a dream of superabundance, which is given its irresistible embodiment in Falstaff.

But that dream is precisely what Hal betrays or rather, to use his own more accurate term, "falsifies." He does so in this play not by a decisive act of rejection, as at the close of *2 Henry IV,* but by a more subtle and continuous draining of the plentitude. "This chair shall be my state," proclaims Falstaff, improvising the king's part, "this dagger my sceptre, and this cushion my crown." Hal's cool rejoinder cuts deftly at both his real and his surrogate father: "Thy state is taken for a join'd-stool, thy golden sceptre for a leaden dagger, and thy precious rich crown for a pitiful bald crown" (2.4.378–82). Hal is the prince and principle of falsification—he is himself a counterfeit companion, and he reveals the emptiness in the world around him. "Dost thou hear, Hal?" Falstaff implores, with the sheriff at the door. "Never call a true piece of gold a counterfeit. Thou art essentially made, without seeming so" (2.4.491–93). The words, so oddly the reverse of the ordinary advice to beware of accepting the counterfeit for reality, attach themselves to both Falstaff and Hal: do not denounce me to the law for I, Falstaff, am genuinely your adoring friend and not merely a parasite; and also, do not think of yourself, Hal, as a mere pretender, do not imagine that your value depends upon falsification.

The "true piece of gold" is alluring because of the widespread faith that it has an intrinsic value, that it does not depend upon the stamp of authority and hence cannot be arbitrarily duplicated or devalued, that it is indifferent to its circumstances, that it cannot be robbed of its worth. This is the fantasy of identity that Falstaff holds out to Hal and that Hal empties out, as he empties out Falstaff's pockets. "What hast thou found?" "Nothing but papers, my lord" (2.4.532–33).[39] Hal is an anti-Midas: everything he touches turns to dross. And this devaluation is the source of his own sense of value, a value not intrinsic but contingent, dependent upon the circulation of counterfeit coin and the subtle manipulation of appearances:

And like bright metal on a sullen ground,
My reformation, glitt'ring o'er my fault,
Shall show more goodly and attract more eyes
Than that which hath no foil to set it off.
I'll so offend, to make offense a skill,
Redeeming time when men think least I will.

(1.2.212–17)

Such lines, as Empson remarks, "cannot have been written without bitterness against the prince," yet the bitterness is not incompatible with an "ironical acceptance" of his authority.[40] The dreams of plenitude are not abandoned altogether—Falstaff in particular has an imaginative life that overflows the confines of the play itself—but the daylight world of *1 Henry IV* comes to seem increasingly one of counterfeit, and hence one governed by Bolingbroke's cunning (he sends "counterfeits" of himself out onto the battlefield) and by Hal's calculations. A "starveling"—fat Falstaff's word for Hal—triumphs in a world of scarcity. Though we can perceive at every point, through our own constantly shifting allegiances, the potential instability of the structure of power that has Henry IV and his son at the pinnacle and Robin Ostler, who "never joy'd since the price of oats rose" (2.1.12–13), near the bottom, Hal's "redemption" is as inescapable and inevitable as the outcome of those practical jokes the madcap prince is so fond of playing. Indeed, the play insists, this redemption is not something toward which the action moves but something that is happening at every moment of the theatrical representation.

The same yoking of the unstable and the inevitable may be seen in the play's acts of *recording*, that is, the moments in which we hear voices that seem to dwell outside the realms ruled by the potentates of the land. These voices exist and have their apotheosis in Falstaff, but their existence proves to be utterly bound up with Hal, contained politically by his purposes as they are justified aesthetically by his involvement. The perfect emblem of this containment is Falstaff's company, marching off to Shrews-

bury: "discarded unjust servingmen, younger sons to younger brothers, revolted tapsters, and ostlers trade-fall'n, the cankers of a calm world and a long peace" (4.2.27–30). As many a homily would tell us, these are the very types of Elizabethan subversion—the masterless men who rose up periodically in desperate protests against their social superiors. A half century later they would swell the ranks of the New Model Army and be disciplined into a revolutionary force. But here they are pressed into service as defenders of the established order, "good enough to toss," as Falstaff tells Hal, "food for powder, food for powder" (4.2.65–66). For power as well as powder, and we may add that this food is produced as well as consumed by the great.

Shakespeare gives us a glimpse of this production in the odd little scene in which Hal, with the connivance of Poins, reduces the puny tapster Francis to the mechanical repetition of the word "Anon":

PRINCE: Nay, but hark you, Francis: for the sugar thou gavest me, 'twas a pennyworth, was't not?
FRANCIS: O Lord, I would it had been two!
PRINCE: I will give thee for it a thousand pound. Ask me when thou wilt, and thou shalt have it.
POINS (*within*): Francis!
FRANCIS: Anon, anon.
PRINCE: Anon, Francis? No, Francis; but tomorrow, Francis; or, Francis, a' Thursday; or indeed, Francis, when thou wilt.

(2.4.58–67)

The Bergsonian comedy in such a moment resides in Hal's exposing a drastic reduction of human possibility: "That ever this fellow should have fewer words than a parrot," he says at the scene's end, "and yet the son of a woman!" (2.4.98–99). But the chief interest for us resides in Hal's producing the very reduction he exposes. The fact of this production, its theatrical demonstration, implicates Hal not only in the linguistic poverty upon which he plays but in the poverty of the five years of apprenticeship Francis has yet to serve: "Five year!" Hal exclaims, "by'r lady, a long lease for the clinking of pewter" (2.4.45–46). And as the prince is implicated in the production of this oppressive order, so is he implicated in the impulse to abrogate it: "But, Francis, darest thou be so valiant as to play the coward with thy indenture, and show it a fair pair of heels and run from it?" (2.4.46–48).

It is tempting to think of this particular moment—the prince awakening the apprentice's discontent—as linked darkly with some supposed uneasiness in Hal about his own apprenticeship.[41] The momentary glimpse of a revolt against authority is closed off at once, however, with a few obscure words calculated to return Francis to his trade without enabling him to understand why he must return to it:

> PRINCE: Why then your brown bastard is your
>   only drink! for look you, Francis, your white
>   canvas doublet will sully. In Barbary, sir, it
>   cannot come to so much.
> FRANCIS: What, sir?
> POINS (*within*): Francis!
> PRINCE: Away, you rogue, dost thou not hear
>   them call?
>
>   (2.4.73–79)

If Francis takes the earlier suggestion, robs his master and runs away, he will find a place for himself, the play implies, only as one of the "revolted tapsters" in Falstaff's company, men as good as dead long before they march to their deaths as upholders of the crown. Better that he should follow the drift of Hal's deliberately mystifying words and continue to clink pewter. As for the prince, his interest in the brief exchange, beyond what we have already sketched, is suggested by his boast to Poins moments before Francis enters: "I have sounded the very basestring of humility. Sirrah, I am sworn brother to a leash of drawers, and can call them all by their christen names, as Tom, Dick, and Francis" (2.4.5–8). The prince must sound the basestring of humility if he is to play all of the chords and hence be the master of the instrument, and his ability to conceal his motives and render opaque his language offers assurance that he himself will not be played on by another.

I have spoken of such scenes in *1 Henry IV* as resembling what in Harriot's text I have called *recording*, a mode that culminates for Harriot in a glossary, the beginnings of an Algonquian-English dictionary, designed to facilitate further acts of recording and hence to consolidate English power in Virginia. The resemblance may be seen most clearly perhaps in Hal's own glossary of tavern slang: "They call drinking deep, dyeing scarlet, and when you breathe in your watering, they cry 'hem!' and bid you play it off. To conclude, I am so good a proficient in one quarter of an hour, that I can drink with any tinker in his own language during my life" (2.4.15–20). The potential value of these lessons, the functional interest to power of recording the speech of an "under-skinker" and his mates, may be glimpsed in the expressions of loyalty that Hal laughingly recalls: "They take it already upon their salvation, that . . . when I am King of England I shall command all the good lads in Eastcheap" (2.4.9–15).

It may be objected that there is something slightly absurd in likening such moments to aspects of Harriot's text; *1 Henry IV* is a play, not a tract for potential investors in a colonial scheme, and the only values we may be sure Shakespeare had in mind, the argument would go, are theatrical values. But theatrical values do not exist in a realm of privileged literariness, of textual or even institutional self-referentiality. Shakespeare's theater was not isolated by its wooden walls, nor did it merely reflect social and ideological logical forces that lay entirely outside it: rather the Elizabethan and Jacobean theater was itself a *social event* in reciprocal contact with other social events.

One might add that *1 Henry IV* itself insists upon the impossibility of sealing off the interests of the theater from the interests of power. Hal's characteristic activity is playing or, more precisely, theatrical improvisation—his parts include his father, Hotspur, Hotspur's wife, a thief in buckram, himself as prodigal, and himself as penitent—and he fully understands his own behavior through most of the play as a role that he is performing. We might expect that this role playing gives way at the end of his true identity: "I shall hereafter," Hal has promised his father, "Be more myself" (3.2.92–93). With the killing of Hotspur, however, Hal clearly does not reject all theatrical masks but rather replaces one with another. "The time will come," Hal declares midway through the play, "That I shall make this northern youth exchange/His glorious deeds for my indignities" (3.2.144–46); when that time *has* come, at the play's close, Hal hides with his "favors" (that is, a scarf or other emblem, but the word *favor* also has in the sixteenth century the sense of "face") the dead Hotspur's "mangled face" (5.4.96), as if to mark the completion of the exchange.

Theatricality, then, is not set over against power but is one of power's essential modes. In lines that anticipate Hal's promise, the angry Henry IV tells Worcester, "I will from henceforth rather be myself,/Mighty and to be fear'd, than my condition" (1.3.5–6). "To be oneself" here means to perform one's part in the scheme of power rather than to manifest one's natural disposition, or what we would normally designate as the very core of the self. Indeed it is by no means clear that such a thing as a natural disposition exists in the play except as a theatrical fiction: we recall that in Falstaff's hands the word *instinct* becomes histrionic rhetoric, an improvised excuse for his flight from the masked prince. "Beware instinct—the lion will not touch the true prince. Instinct is a great matter; I was now a coward on instinct. I shall think the better of myself, and thee, during my life; I for a valiant lion, and thou for a true prince" (2.4.271–75). Both claims—Falstaff's to natural valor, Hal's to legitimate royalty—are, the lines darkly imply, of equal merit.

Again and again in *1 Henry IV* we are tantalized by the possibility of an escape from theatricality and hence from the constant pressure of improvisational power, but we are, after all, in the theater, and our pleasure depends upon there being no escape, and our applause ratifies the triumph of our confinement. The play operates in the manner of its central character, charming us with its visions of breadth and solidarity, "redeeming" itself in the end by betraying our hopes, and earning with this betrayal our slightly anxious admiration. Hence the odd balance in this play of spaciousness—the constant multiplication of separate, vividly realized realms—and militant claustrophobia: the absorption of all of these realms by a power at once vital and impoverished. The balance is almost perfect, as if Shakespeare had somehow reached through in *1 Henry IV* to the very center of the system of opposed and interlocking forces that held Tudor society together.

III

When we turn, however, to the plays that continue the chronicle of Hal's career, *2 Henry IV* and *Henry V*, we find not only that the forces balanced in the earlier play have pulled apart—the claustrophobia triumphant in *2 Henry IV*, the spaciousness triumphant in *Henry V*[42]—but that from this new perspective the familiar view of *1 Henry IV* as a perfectly poised play must be revised. What appeared as "balance" may on closer inspection seem like radical instability tricked out as moral or aesthetic order; what appeared as clarity may seem now like a conjurer's trick concealing confusion in order to buy time and stave off the collapse of an illusion.[43] Not waving but drowning.

In *2 Henry IV* the characteristic operations of power are less equivocal than they had been in the preceding play: there is no longer even the lingering illusion of distinct realms, each with its own system of values, its soaring visions of plenitude, and its bad dreams. There is manifestly a single system now, one based on predation and betrayal. Hotspur's intoxicating dreams of honor are dead, replaced by the cold rebellion of cunning but impotent schemers. The warm, roistering noise overheard in the tavern—noise that seemed to signal a subversive alternative to rebellion—turns out to be the sound of a whore and a bully beating a customer to death. And Falstaff, whose earlier larcenies were gilded by fantasies of innate grace, now talks of turning diseases to commodity (1.2.248).

Only Prince Hal seems in this play less meanly calculating, subject now to fits of weariness and confusion, though this change serves less to humanize him (as Auerbach argued in a famous essay) than to make it clear that the betrayals are systematic. They happen to him and for him. He need no longer soliloquize his intention to "falsify men's hopes" by selling his wastrel friends: the sale will be brought about by the structure of things, a structure grasped in this play under the twinned names of time and necessity. So too there is no longer any need for heroic combat with a dangerous, glittering enemy like Hotspur (the only reminder of whose voice in this play is Pistol's parody of Marlovian swaggering); the rebels are deftly, if ingloriously, dispatched by the false promises of Hal's younger brother, the primly virtuous John of Lancaster. To seal his lies, Lancaster swears fittingly "by the honor of my blood" (4.2.55)—the cold blood, as Falstaff observes of Hal, that he inherited from his father.

The recording of alien voices—the voices of those who have no power to leave literate traces of their existence—continues in this play, but without even the theatrical illusion of princely complicity. The king is still convinced that his son is a prodigal and that the kingdom will fall to ruin after his death—perhaps he finds a peculiar consolation in the thought—but it is no longer Hal alone who declares (against all appearances) his secret commitment to disciplinary authority. Warwick assures the king that the prince's interests in the good lads of Eastcheap are entirely what they should be:

> The Prince but studies his companions
> Like a strange tongue, wherein, to gain the
>   language,
> 'Tis needful that the most immodest word
> Be look'd upon and learnt, which once
>   attain'd,
> Your Highness knows, comes to no further use
> But to be known and hated. So, like gross
>   terms,
> The Prince will in the perfectness of time
> Cast off his followers, and their memory
> Shall as a pattern or a measure live,
> By which his Grace must mete the lives of
>   other,
> Turning past evils to advantages.
>
>   (4.4.68–78)

At first the language analogy likens the prince's low-life excursions to the search for proficiency: perfect linguistic competence, the "mastery" of a language, requires the fullest possible vocabulary. But the darkness of Warwick's words—"to be known and hated"—immediately pushes the goal of Hal's linguistic researches beyond proficiency. When in *1 Henry IV* Hal boasts of his mastery of tavern slang, we are allowed for a moment at least to imagine that we are witnessing a social bond, the human fellowship of the extremest top and bottom of society in a homely ritual act of drinking together. The play may make it clear, as I have argued, that well-defined political interests are involved, but these interests may be bracketed, if only briefly, for the pleasure of imagining what Victor Turner calls "communitas"—a union based on the momentary breaking of the hierarchical order that normally governs a community.[44] And even when we pull back from this spacious sense of union, we are permitted for much of the play to take pleasure at least in Hal's surprising skill, the proficiency he rightly celebrates in himself.

To learn another language is to acknowledge the existence of another people and to acquire the ability to function, however crudely, in another social world. Hal's remark about drinking with any tinker in his own language suggests, if only jocularly, that for him the lower classes are virtually another people, an alien tribe—immensely more populous than his own—within the kingdom. That this perception extended beyond the confines of Shakespeare's play is suggested by the evidence that middle- and upper-class English settlers in the New World regarded the American Indians less as another race than as a version of their own lower classes; one man's tinker is another man's Indian.[45]

If Hal's glossary initially seems to resemble Harriot's practical word list in the *Brief and True Report,* with its Algonquian equivalents for *fire, food, shelter,* Warwick's account of Hal's intentions suggests a deeper resemblance to a different kind of glossary, one more specifically linked to the attempt to understand and control the lower classes. I refer to the sinister glossaries appended to sixteenth-century accounts of criminals and vagabonds. "Here I set before the good reader the lewd, lousy language of these loitering lusks and lazy lorels," announces Thomas Harman as he introduces (with a comical flourish designed to display his own rhetorical gifts) what he claims is an authentic list, compiled at great personal cost.[46] His pamphlet, *A Caveat for Common Cursitors,* is the fruit, he declares, of personal research, difficult because his informants are "marvellous subtle and crafty." But "with fair flattering words, money, and good cheer," he has learned much about their ways, "not without faithful promise made unto them never to discover their names or anything they showed me" (82). Harman cheerfully goes on to publish what they showed him, and he ends his work not only with a glossary of "peddler's French" but with an alphabetical list of names, so that the laws made for "the extreme punishment" of these wicked idlers may be enforced.

It is not clear that Harman's subjects—upright men, doxies, Abraham men, and the like—bear any more relation to social reality than either Doll Tearsheet or Mistress Quickly.[47] Much of the *Caveat,* like the other cony-catching pamphlets of the period, has the air of a jest book: time-honored tales of tricksters and rogues, dished out as realistic observation. (It is not encouraging that the rogues' term for the stocks in which they were punished, according to Harman, is "the harmans.") But Harman is concerned to convey at least the impression of accurate observation and recording—clearly, this was among the book's selling points—and one of the principal rhetorical devices he uses to do so is the spice of betrayal: he repeatedly calls attention to his solemn promises never to reveal anything he has been told, for his breaking of his word assures the accuracy and importance of what he reveals.

A middle-class Prince Hal, Harman claims that through dissembling he has gained access to a world normally hidden from his kind, and he will turn that access to the advantage of the kingdom by helping his readers to identify and eradicate the dissemblers in their midst. Harman's own personal interventions—the acts of detection and apprehension he proudly reports (or invents)—are not enough; only his book can fully expose the cunning sleights of the rogues and thereby induce the justices and shrieves to be more vigilant and punitive. Just as theatricality is thematized in the *Henry IV* plays as one of the crucial agents of royal power, so in *A Caveat for Common Cursitors* (and in much of the cony-catching literature of the period in England and France) printing is represented in the text itself as a force for social order and the detection of criminal fraud. The printed book can be widely disseminated and easily revised, so that the vagabonds' names and tricks may be known before they themselves arrive at an honest citizen's door; as if this mobility were not tangible enough, Harman claims that when his pamphlet was only halfway printed, his printer helped him apprehend a particularly sly "counterfeit crank"—a pretended epileptic. In Harman's account the printer turns detective, first running down the street to apprehend the dissembler, then on a subsequent occasion luring him "with fair allusions" (116) and a show of charity into the hands of the constable. With such lurid tales Harman literalizes the power of the book to hunt down vagabonds and bring them to justice.

The danger of such accounts is that the ethical charge will reverse itself, with the forces of order—the people, as it were, of the book—revealed as themselves dependent on dissembling and betrayal and the vagabonds revealed either as less fortunate and well-protected imitators of their betters or, alternatively, as primitive rebels against the hypocrisy of a cruel society. Exactly such a reversal seems to occur again and again in the rogue literature of the period, from the doxies and morts who answer Harman's rebukes with unfailing, if spare, dignity to the more articulate defenders of vice elsewhere who insist that their lives are at worst imitations of the lives of the great:

> Though your experience in the world be not so great as mine [says a cheater at dice], yet am I sure ye see that no man is able to live an honest man unless he have some privy way to help himself withal, more than the world is witness of. Think you the noblemen could do as they do, if in this hard world they should maintain so great a port only upon their rent? Think you the lawyers could be such purchasers if their pleas were short, and all their judgments, justice and conscience? Suppose ye that offices would be so dearly bought, and the buyers so soon enriched, if they counted not pillage an honest point of purchase? Could merchants, without lies, false making their wares, and selling them by a crooked light, to deceive the chapman in the thread or colour, grow so soon rich and to a baron's possessions, and make all their posterity gentlemen?[48]

Though these reversals are at the very heart of the rogue literature, it would be as much of a mistake to regard their intended effect as subversive as to regard in a similar light the comparable passages—most often articulated by Falstaff—in Shakespeare's histories. The subversive voices are produced by and within the affirmations of order; they are powerfully registered, but they do not undermine that order. Indeed, as the example of Harman—so much cruder than Shakespeare—suggests, the order is neither possible nor fully convincing without both the presence and perception of betrayal.

This dependence on betrayal does not prevent Harman from leveling charges of hypocrisy and deep dissembling at the rogues and from urging his readers to despise and prosecute them. On the contrary, Harman's moral indignation seems paradoxically heightened by his own implication in the deceitfulness that he condemns, as if the rhetorical violence of the condemnation cleansed him of any guilt. His broken promises are acts of civility, necessary strategies for securing social well-being. The "rowsy, ragged rabblement of rakeshells" has put itself outside the bounds of civil conversation; justice consists precisely in taking whatever measures are necessary to eradicate them. Harman's false oaths are the means of identifying and ridding the community of the purveyors of false oaths. The pestilent few will "fret, fume, swear, and stare at this my book," in which their practices, disclosed after they had received fair promises of confidentiality, are laid open, but the majority will band together in righteous reproach: "The honourable will abhor them, the worshipful will reject them, the yeomen will sharply taunt them, the husbandmen utterly defy them, the labouring men bluntly chide them, the women with clapping hands cry out at them" (84). To like reading about vagabonds is to hate them and to approve of their ruthless betrayal.

"The right people of the play," a gifted critic of *2 Henry IV* observes, "merge into a larger order; the wrong people resist or misuse that larger order."[49] True enough, but like Harman's community of vagabond-haters, the "larger order" of the Lancastrian state in this play seems to batten on the breaking of oaths. Shakespeare does not shrink from any of the felt nastiness implicit in this sorting out of the right people and the wrong people; he takes the discursive mode that he could have found in Harman and a hundred other texts and intensifies it, so that the founding of the modern state, like the self-fashioning of the modern prince, is shown to be based upon acts of calculation, intimidation, and deceit. And these acts are performed in an entertainment for which audiences, the subjects of this very state, pay money and applaud.

There is, throughout *2 Henry IV*, a sense of constriction that is only intensified by the obsessive enumeration of details: "Thou didst swear to me upon a parcel-gilt goblet, sitting in my Dolphin chamber, at the round table by a sea-coal fire, upon Wednesday in Wheeson week . . ." (2.1.86–89). We may find, in Justice Shallow's garden, a few twilight moments of release from this oppressive circumstantial and strategic constriction, but Falstaff mercilessly deflates them—and the puncturing is so wonderfully adroit, so amusing, that we welcome it: "I do remember him at Clement's Inn, like a man made after supper of a cheese-paring. When 'a was naked, he was for all the world like a fork'd redish, with a head fantastically carv'd upon it with a knife" (3.2.308–12).

What remains is the law of nature: the strong eat the weak. Yet this is not quite what Shakespeare invites the audience to affirm through its applause. Like Harman, Shakespeare refuses to endorse so badly cynical a conception of the social order; instead actions that should have the effect of radically undermining authority turn out to be the props of that authority. In this play, even more cruelly than in *1 Henry IV*, moral values—justice, order, civility—are secured through the apparent generation of their subversive contraries. Out of the squalid betray-

als that preserve the state emerges the "formal majesty" into which Hal at the close, through a final, definitive betrayal—the rejection of Falstaff—merges himself.

There are moments in *Richard II* when the collapse of kingship seems to be confirmed in the discovery of the physical body of the ruler, the pathos of his creatural existence:

> throw away respect,
> Tradition, form, and ceremonious duty,
> For you have but mistook me all this while.
> I live with bread like you, feel want,
> Taste grief, need friends: subjected thus,
> How can you say to me I am a king?
> (3.2.172–77)

By the close of *2 Henry IV* such physical limitations have been absorbed into the ideological structure, and hence justification, of kingship. It is precisely because Prince Hal lives with bread that we can understand the sacrifice that he and, for that matter, his father have made. Unlike Richard II, Henry IV articulates this sacrifice not as a piece of histrionic rhetoric but as a private meditation, the innermost thoughts of a troubled, weary man:

> Why rather, sleep, liest thou in smoky cribs,
> Upon uneasy pallets stretching thee,
> And hush'd with buzzing night-flies to thy
>   slumber,
> Than in the perfum'd chambers of the great,
> Under the canopies of costly state,
> And lull'd with sound of sweetest melody?
> (3.1.9–14)

Who knows? Perhaps it is even true; perhaps in a society in which the overwhelming majority of men and women had next to nothing, the few who were rich and powerful did lie awake at night. But we should understand that this sleeplessness was not a well-kept secret: the sufferings of the great are one of the familiar themes in the literature of the governing classes in the sixteenth century.[50] Henry IV speaks in soliloquy, but as is so often the case in Shakespeare, his isolation only intensifies the sense that he is addressing a large audience: the audience of the theater. We are invited to take measure of his suffering, to understand—here and elsewhere in the play—the costs of power. And we are invited to understand these costs in order to ratify the power, to accept the grotesque and cruelly unequal distribution of possessions: everything to the few, nothing to the many. The rulers earn, or at least pay for, their exalted position through suffering, and this suffering ennobles, if it does not exactly cleanse, the lies and betrayals upon which this position depends.

As so often, Falstaff parodies this ideology, or rather—and more significantly—presents it as humbug *before* it makes its appearance as official truth. Called away from the tavern to the court, Falstaff turns to Doll and Mistress Quickly and proclaims sententiously: "You see, my good wenches, how men of merit are sought after. The undeserver may sleep when the man of action is call'd on" (2.4.374–77). Seconds later this rhetoric—marked out as something with which to impress whores and innkeepers to whom one owes money one does not intend to pay—recurs in the speech and, by convention of the soliloquy, the innermost thoughts of the king.

This staging of what we may term anticipatory, or proleptic, parody is a major structural principle of Shakespeare's play. Its effect is not (as with straightforward parodies) to ridicule the claims of high seriousness but rather to mark them as slightly suspect and to encourage guarded skepticism. Thus in the wake of Falstaff's burlesque of the weariness of the virtuous, the king's insomniac pathos reverberates hollowness as well as poignancy. At such moments *2 Henry IV* seems to be testing and confirming a dark and disturbing hypothesis about the nature of monarchical power in England: that its moral authority rests upon a hypocrisy so deep that the hypocrites themselves believe it. "Then (happy) low, lie down!/Uneasy lies the head that wears a crown" (3.1.30–31): so the old pike tells the young dace. But the old pike actually seems to believe in his own speeches, just as he may believe that he never really sought the crown, "But that necessity so bow'd the state/That I and greatness were compell'd to kiss" (3.1.73–74). Our privileged knowledge of the network of state betrayals and privileged access to Falstaff's cynical wisdom can make this opaque hypocrisy transparent. Yet even with *2 Henry IV,* where the lies and the self-serving sentiments are utterly inescapable, where the illegitimacy of legitimate authority is repeatedly demonstrated, where the whole state seems—to adapt More's phrase—a conspiracy of the great to enrich and protect their interests under the name of commonwealth, even here the state, watchful for signs of sedition on the stage, was not prodded to intervene. We may choose to attribute this apparent somnolence to incompetence or corruption, but the linkages I have sketched between the history plays and the discursive practices represented by Harriot and Harman suggest another explanation. Once again, though in a still more iron-age spirit than at the close of *1 Henry IV,* the play appears to ratify the established order, with the new-crowned Henry V merging his body into "the great body of our state," with Falstaff despised and rejected, and with Lancaster—the coldhearted betrayer of the rebels—left to admire his still more coldhearted brother: "I like this fair proceeding of the King's" (5.5.97).[51]

The mood at the close remains, to be sure, an unpleasant one—the rejection of Falstaff has been one of the nagging "problems" of Shakespeare criticism—but the discomfort only serves to verify Hal's claim that he has turned away his former self. If there is frustration at the harshness of the play's end, the frustration confirms a carefully plotted official strategy whereby subversive perceptions are at once produced and contained:

My father is gone wild into his grave;
For in his tomb lie my affections,
And with his spirits sadly I survive,

To mock the expectation of the world,
To frustrate prophecies, and to rase out
Rotten opinion. . . .

                                        (5.2.123–28)

IV

The first part of *Henry IV* enables us to feel at moments that we are like Harriot, surveying a complex new world, testing upon it dark thoughts without damaging the order that those thoughts would seem to threaten. The second part of *Henry IV* suggests that we are still more like the Indians, compelled to pay homage to a system of beliefs whose fraudulence only confirms their power, authenticity, and truth. The concluding play in the series, *Henry V,* insists that we have all along been both colonizer and colonized, king and subject. The play deftly registers every nuance of royal hypocrisy, ruthlessness, and bad faith—testing, in effect, the proposition that successful rule depends not upon sacredness but upon demonic violence—but it does so in the context of a celebration, a collective panegyric to "This star of England," the charismatic leader who purges the commonwealth of its incorrigibles and forges the martial national state.

By yoking together diverse peoples—represented in the play by the Welshman Fluellen, the Irishman Macmorris, and the Scotsman Jamy, who fight at Agincourt alongside the loyal Englishmen—Hal symbolically tames the last wild areas in the British Isles, areas that in the sixteenth century represented, far more powerfully than any New World people, the doomed outposts of a vanishing tribalism.[52] We might expect then that in *Henry V* the mode that I have called recording would reach its fullest flowering, and in a sense it does. The English allies are each given a distinct accentual notation—"'a utt'red as prave words at the pridge as you shall see in a summer's day"; "By Chrish law, 'tish ill done! The work ish give over"; "It

sall be vary gud, gud feith, gud captens bath, and I sall quit you with gud leve"—a notation that helped determine literary representations of the stock Welshman, Irishman, and Scotsman for centuries to come. But their distinctness is curiously formal, a collection of mechanistic attributes recalling the heightened but static individuality of Jonson's humorous grotesques.

The verbal tics of such characters interest us because they represent not what is alien but what is predictable and automatic. They give pleasure because they persuade an audience of its own mobility and complexity; even a spectator gaping passively at the play's sights and manipulated by its rhetoric is freer than these puppets jerked on the strings of their own absurd accents. Only Fluellen (much of the time an exuberant, bullying prince-pleaser) seems at one moment to articulate perceptions that lie outside the official line, and he arrives at these perceptions not through his foreignness but through his relentless pursuit of classical analogies. Teasing out a Plutarch-like parallel between Hal and "Alexander the Pig"—"There is a river in Macedon, and there is also moreover a river at Monmouth," and so forth—Fluellen reaches the observation that Alexander "did, in his ales and his angers, look you, kill his best friend, Clytus." Gower quickly intervenes: "Our King is not like him in that; he never kill'd any of his friends." But Fluellen persists: "as Alexander kill'd his friend Clytus, being in his ales and his cups; so also Harry Monmouth, being in his right wits and his good judgments, turn'd away the fat knight with the great belly doubled. He was full of jests, and gipes, and knaveries, and mocks—I have forgot his name." Gower provides it: "Sir John Falstaff" (4.7.26–51).

The moment is potentially devastating. The comparison with drunken Alexander focuses all our perceptions of Hal's sober cold-bloodedness, from his rejection of Falstaff—"The King has kill'd his heart" (2.1.88)—to his responsibility for the execution of his erstwhile boon companion Bardolph. The low-life characters in the earlier plays had been the focus of Hal's language lessons, but as Warwick had predicted, the prince studied them as "gross terms," no sooner learned than discarded.

The discarding in *Henry V* is not an attractive sight but is perfectly consistent with the practice we have analyzed in Harman's *Caveat*. Indeed in a direct recollection of the cony-catching literature, Fluellen learns that Pistol, whom he had thought "as valiant a man as Mark Antony" (3.6.13–14), is "a rogue, that now and then goes to the wars, to grace himself at his return into London under the form of a soldier" (3.6.67–69). "You must learn to know such slanders of the age," remarks Gower in a line that could serve as Harman's epigraph, "or else you may be marvellously mistook" (3.6.79–81). And how does Fluellen learn that Pistol is one of the slanders of the age? What does Pistol do to give himself away? He passionately pleads that Fluellen intervene to save Bardolph, who has been sentenced to die for stealing a "pax of little price." "Let gallows gape for dog, let man go free," rages Pistol, "and let not hemp his windpipe suffocate" (3.6.42–43). Fluellen refuses; Bardolph hangs; and this attempt to save his friend's life marks Pistol as a "rascally, scald, beggarly, lousy, pragging knave" (5.1.5–6). By contrast, Hal's symbolic killing of Falstaff—which might have been recorded as a bitter charge against him—is advanced by Fluellen as the climactic manifestation of his virtues. No sooner is it mentioned than the king himself enters in triumph, leading his French prisoners. This entrance, with its military "Alarum" followed by a royal "Flourish," is the perfect emblematic instance of a potential dissonance being absorbed into a charismatic celebration. The betrayal of friends does not subvert but rather sustains the moral authority and the compelling glamour of power. That authority, as the play defines it, is precisely the ability to betray one's friends without stain.

If neither the English allies nor the low-life characters seem to fulfill adequately the role of aliens whose voices are "recorded," *Henry V* ap-

parently gives us a sustained, even extreme, version of this practice in the dialogue of the French characters, dialogue that is in part presented untranslated in the performance. This dialogue includes even a language lesson, the very emblem of "recording" in the earlier plays. Yet like the English allies, the French enemies say remarkably little that is alien or disturbing in relation to the central voice of authority in the play. To be sure, several of the French nobles contemptuously dismiss Hal as "a vain, giddy, shallow, humorous youth" (2.4.28), but these terms of abuse are outmoded; it is as if news of the end of *1 Henry IV* or of its sequel had not yet crossed the Channel. Likewise, the easy French assumption of cultural and social superiority to the English—"The emptying of our fathers' luxury,/Our scions, put in wild and savage stock" (3.5.6–7)—is voiced only to be deflated by the almost miraculous English victory. The glamour of French aristocratic culture is not denied (see, for example, the litany of noble names beginning at 3.5.40), but it issues in overweening self-confidence and a military impotence that is explicitly thematized as sexual impotence. The French warriors "hang like roping icicles/Upon our houses' thatch," while the English "Sweat drops of gallant youth in our rich fields!" (3.5.23–25). In consequence, complains the Dauphin,

> Our madams mock at us, and plainly say
>> Our mettle is bred out, and they will give
>> Their bodies to the lust of English youth.
>> (3.5.28–30)

Thus the affirmation of French superiority is immediately reprocessed as an enhancement of English potency. By the play's close, with a self-conscious gesture toward the conventional ending of a comedy, the sexualized violence of the invasion is transfigured and tamed in Hal's wooing of Princess Katherine: "I love France so well that I will not part with a village of it; I will have it all mine. And, Kate, when France is mine and

I am yours, then yours is France and you are mine" (5.2.173–76). Acknowledgment of the other has now issued in the complete absorption of the other.

As for the language lesson, it is no longer Hal but the French princess who is the student. There is always a slight amusement in hearing one's own language spoken badly, a gratifying sense of possessing effortlessly what for others is a painful achievement. This sense is mingled at times with a condescending encouragement of the childish efforts of the inept learner, at times with delight at the inadvertent absurdities or indecencies into which the learner stumbles. (I spent several minutes in Bergamo once convulsing passersby with requests for directions to the Colleone Chapel. It was not until much later that I realized that I was pronouncing it the "Coglioni"—"Balls"—Chapel.) In *Henry V* the pleasure is intensified because the French princess is by implication learning English as a consequence of the successful English invasion, an invasion graphically figured as a rape. And the pleasing sense of national and specifically male superiority is crowned by the comic spectacle of the obscenities into which the princess is inadvertently led.[53]

If the subversive force of "recording" is substantially reduced in *Henry V,* the mode I have called explaining is by contrast intensified in its power to disturb. The war of conquest that Henry V launches against the French is depicted as carefully founded on acts of "explaining." The play opens with a notoriously elaborate account of the king's genealogical claim to the French throne, and, as in the comparable instances in Harriot, this ideological justification of English policy is an unsettling mixture of "impeccable" reasoning (once its initial premises are accepted) and gross self-interest.[54] In the ideological apologies for absolutism, the self-interest of the monarch and the interest of the nation are identical, and both in turn are secured by God's overarching design. Hence Hal's personal triumph at Agincourt is represented as the nation's

triumph, which in turn is represented as God's triumph. When the deliciously favorable kill ratio—ten thousand French dead compared to twenty-nine English[55]—is reported to the king, he immediately gives "full trophy, signal, and ostent," as the Chorus later puts it, to God: "Take it, God,/For it is none but thine!" (4.8.11–12).

Hal evidently thinks this explanation of the English victory—this translation of its cause and significance from human to divine agency—needs some reinforcement:

> And be it death proclaimed through our host
> To boast of this, or take that praise from God
> Which is his only.
>
> (4.8.114–116)

By such an edict God's responsibility for the slaughter of the French is enforced, and with it is assured at least the glow of divine approval over the entire enterprise, from the complex genealogical claims to the execution of traitors, the invasion of France, the threats leveled against civilians, the massacre of the prisoners. Yet there is something disconcerting as well as reinforcing about this draconian mode of ensuring that God receive credit: with a strategic circularity at once compelling and suspect, God's credit for the killing can be guaranteed only by the threat of more killing. The element of compulsion would no doubt predominate if the audience's own survival were at stake—the few Elizabethans who openly challenged the theological pretensions of the great found themselves in deep trouble—but were the stakes this high in the theater? Was it not possible inside the playhouse walls to question certain claims elsewhere unquestionable?

A few years earlier, at the close of *The Jew of Malta,* Marlowe had cast a witheringly ironic glance, worthy of Machiavelli, at the piety of the triumphant: Ferneze's gift to God of the "trophy, signal, and ostent" of the successful betrayal of Barabas is the final bitter joke of a bitter play. Shakespeare does not go so far. But he does take pains to call attention to the problem of invoking a God of battles, let alone enforcing the invocation by means of the death penalty. On the eve of Agincourt, the soldier Williams had responded unenthusiastically to the disguised king's claim that his cause was good:

> But if the cause be not good, the King himself hath a heavy reckoning to make, when all those legs, and arms, and heads, chopp'd off in a battle, shall join together at the latter day and cry all, "We died at such a place"—some swearing, some crying for a surgeon, some upon their wives left poor behind them, some upon the debts they owe, some upon their children rawly left. I am afeard there are few die well that die in a battle; for how can they charitably dispose of any thing, when blood is their argument? 4.1.134–43)

To this the king replies with a string of awkward "explanations" designed to show that "the King is not bound to answer the particular endings of his soldiers" (4.1.155–56)—as if death in battle were a completely unforeseen accident or, alternatively, as if each soldier killed were being punished by God for a hidden crime or, again, as if war were a religious blessing, an "advantage" to a soldier able to "wash every mote out of his conscience" (4.1.179–80). Not only are these explanations mutually contradictory, but they cast long shadows on the king himself. For in the wake of this scene, as the dawn is breaking, Hal pleads nervously with God not to think—at least "not to-day"—upon the crime from which he has benefited: his father's deposition and killing of Richard II. The king calls attention to all the expensive and ingratiating ritual acts that he has instituted to compensate for the murder of the divinely anointed ruler—reinterment of the corpse, five hundred poor "in yearly pay" to plead twice daily for pardon, two chantries where priests say mass for Richard's soul—and he promises to do more. Yet in a moment that anticipates Claudius's inadequate repentance of old Hamlet's murder, inadequate since he is "still possess'd/Of those effects" for which the crime was committed (*Hamlet* 3.3.53–54), Hal acknowledges that these expiatory rituals and even "contrite tears" are worthless:

> Though all that I can do is nothing worth,
> Since that my penitence comes after all,
> Imploring pardon.
>
> (4.1.303–5)[56]

If by nightfall Hal is threatening to execute anyone who denies God full credit for the astonishing English victory, the preceding scenes would seem to have fully exposed the ideological and psychological mechanisms behind such compulsion, its roots in violence, magical propitiation and bad conscience. The pattern disclosed here is one we have glimpsed in *2 Henry IV:* we witness an anticipatory subversion of each of the play's central claims. The archbishop of Canterbury spins out an endless public justification for an invasion he has privately confessed would relieve financial pressure on the church; Hal repeatedly warns his victims that they are bringing pillage and rape upon themselves, but he speaks as the head of the invading army that is about to pillage and rape them; Gower claims that the king has ordered the killing of the prisoners in retaliation for the attack on the baggage train, but we have just been shown that the king's order preceded that attack.[57] Similarly, Hal's meditation on the sufferings of the great—"What infinite heart's ease/Must kings neglect, that private men enjoy!" (4.1.236–37)—suffers from his being almost single-handedly responsible for a war that by his own earlier account and that of the enemy is causing immense civilian misery. And after watching a scene in which anxious, frightened troops sleeplessly await the dawn, it is difficult to be fully persuaded by Hal's climactic vision of the "slave" and "peasant" sleeping comfortably, little knowing "What watch the King keeps to maintain the peace" (4.1.283).

This apparent subversion of the monarch's glorification has led some critics since Hazlitt to view the panegyric as bitterly ironic or to argue, more plausibly, that Shakespeare's depiction of Henry V is radically ambiguous.[58] But in the light of Harriot's *Brief and True Report,* we may suggest that the subversive doubts the play continually awakens originate paradoxically in an effort to intensify the power of the king and his war. The effect is bound up with the reversal that we have noted several times—the great events and speeches all occur twice: the first time as fraud, the second as truth. The intimations of bad faith are real enough, but they are deferred—deferred until after Essex's campaign in Ireland, after Elizabeth's reign, after the monarchy itself as a significant political institution. Deferred indeed even today, for in the wake of full-scale ironic readings and at a time when it no longer seems to matter very much, it is not at all clear that *Henry V* can be successfully performed as subversive.

The problem with any attempt to do so is that the play's central figure seems to feed on the doubts he provokes. For the enhancement of royal power is not only a matter of the deferral of doubt: the very doubts that Shakespeare raises serve not to rob the king of his charisma but to heighten it, precisely as they heighten the theatrical interest of the play; the unequivocal, unambiguous celebrations of royal power with which the period abounds have no theatrical force and have long since fallen into oblivion. The charismatic authority of the king, like that of the stage, depends upon falsification.

The audience's tension, then, enhances its attention; prodded by constant reminders of a gap between real and ideal, the spectators are induced to make up the difference, to invest in the illusion of magnificence, to be dazzled by their own imaginary identification with the conqueror. The ideal king must be in large part the invention of the audience, the product of a will to conquer that is revealed to be identical to a need to submit. *Henry V* is remarkably self-con-

scious about this dependence upon the audience's powers of invention. The prologue's opening lines invoke a form of theater radically unlike the one that is about to unfold: "A kingdom for a stage, princes to act,/And monarchs to behold the swelling scene!" (3–4). In such a theater-state there would be no social distinction between the king and the spectator, the performer and the audience; all would be royal, and the role of the performance would be to transform not an actor into a king but a king into a god: "Then should the warlike Harry, like himself,/Assume the port of Mars" (5–6). This is in effect the fantasy acted out in royal masques, but Shakespeare is intensely aware that his play is not a courtly entertainment, that his actors are "flat unraised spirits," and that his spectators are hardly monarchs—"gentles all," he calls them, with fine flattery.[59] "Let us," the prologue begs the audience, "On your imaginary forces work. . . . For 'tis your thoughts that now must deck our kings" (17–18, 28). This "must" is cast in the form of an appeal and an apology—the consequence of the miserable limitations of "this unworthy scaffold"—but the necessity extends, I suggest, beyond the stage: all kings are "decked" out by the imaginary forces of the spectators, and a sense of the limitations of king or theater only excites a more compelling exercise of those forces.

Power belongs to whoever can command and profit from this exercise of the imagination, hence the celebration of the charismatic ruler whose imperfections we are invited at once to register and to "piece out" (Prologue, 23). Hence too the underlying complicity throughout these plays between the prince and the playwright, a complicity complicated but never effaced by a strong counter-current of identification with Falstaff. In Hal, Shakespeare fashions a compelling emblem of the playwright as sovereign "juggler," the minter of counterfeit coins, the genial master of illusory subversion and redemptive betrayal. To understand Shakespeare's conception of Hal, from rakehell to monarch, we need in effect a poetics of Elizabethan power, and this in turn will prove inseparable, in crucial respects, from a poetics of the theater. Testing, recording, and explaining are elements in this poetics, which is inseparably bound up with the figure of Queen Elizabeth, a ruler without a standing army, without a highly developed bureaucracy, without an extensive police force, a ruler whose power is constituted in theatrical celebrations of royal glory and theatrical violence visited upon the enemies of that glory. Power that relies on a massive police apparatus, a strong middle-class nuclear family, an elaborate school system, power that dreams of a panopticon in which the most intimate secrets are open to the view of an invisible authority— such power will have as its appropriate aesthetic form the realist novel;[60] Elizabethan power, by contrast, depends upon its privileged visibility. As in a theater, the audience must be powerfully engaged by this visible presence and at the same time held at a respectful distance from it. "We princes," Elizabeth told a deputation of Lords and Commons in 1586, "are set on stages in the sight and view of all the world."[61]

Royal power is manifested to its subjects as in a theater, and the subjects are at once absorbed by the instructive, delightful, or terrible spectacles and forbidden intervention or deep intimacy. The play of authority depends upon spectators—"For 'tis your thoughts that now must deck our kings"—but the performance is made to seem entirely beyond the control of those whose "imaginary forces" actually confer upon it its significance and force. These matters, Thomas More imagines the common people saying of one such spectacle, "be king's games, as it were stage plays, and for the more part played upon scaffolds. In which poor men be but the lookers-on. And they that wise be will meddle no farther."[62] Within this theatrical setting, there is a notable insistence upon the paradoxes, ambiguities, and tensions of authority, but this apparent production of subversion is, as we have already seen, the very condition of

power. I should add that this condition is not a theoretical necessity of theatrical power in general but a historical phenomenon, the particular mode of this particular culture. "In sixteenth century England," writes Clifford Geertz, comparing Elizabethan and Majapahit royal progresses, "the political center of society was the point at which the tension between the passions that power excited and the ideals it was supposed to serve was screwed to its highest pitch. . . . In fourteenth century Java, the center was the point at which such tension disappeared in a blaze of cosmic symmetry."[63]

It is precisely because of the English form of absolutist theatricality that Shakespeare's drama, written for a theater subject to state censorship, can be so relentlessly subversive: the form itself, as a primary expression of Renaissance power, helps to contain the radical doubts it continually provokes. Of course, what is for the state a mode of subversion contained can be for the theater a mode of containment subverted: there are moments in Shakespeare's career—*King Lear* is the greatest example[64]—when the process of containment is strained to the breaking point. But the histories consistently pull back from such extreme pressure. Like Harriot in the New World, the Henry plays confirm the Machiavellian hypothesis that princely power originates in force and fraud even as they draw their audience toward an acceptance of that power. And we are free to locate and pay homage to the plays' doubts only because they no longer threaten us.[65] There is subversion, no end of subversion, only not for us.

NOTES

1. John Bakeless, *The Tragicall History of Christopher Marloue,* 2 vols. (Cambridge, Mass.: Harvard University Press, 1942), 1:111. *Juggler* is a richly complex word, including in its range of associations con man, cheap entertainer, magician, trickster, storyteller, conjurer, actor, and dramatist.

2.   On Harriot, see especially *Thomas Harriot, Renaissance Scientist,* ed. John W. Shirley (Oxford: Clarendon Press, 1974); Muriel Rukeyser, *The Traces of Thomas Harriot* (New York: Random House, 1970); and Jean Jacquot, "Thomas Harriot's Reputation for Impiety," *Notes and Records of the Royal Society* 9 (1952): 164–87. Harriot himself appears to have paid close attention to his reputation; see David B. Quinn and John W. Shirley, "A Contemporary List of Harriot References," *Renaissance Quarterly* 22 (1969): 9–26.

3.   John Aubrey, *Brief Lives,* 2 vols., ed. Andrew Clark (Oxford: Clarendon Press, 1898), 1:286.

4.   For the investigation of Ralegh, see *Willobie His Avisa* (1594), ed. G. B. Harrison (London: John Lane, 1926), app. 3, pp. 255–71; for Oliver's story, see Ernest A. Strathmann, *Sir Walter Ralegh: A Study in Elizabethan Skepticism* (New York: Columbia University Press, 1951), p. 50.

5.   There are, to be sure, some evangelical professions of having been *saved* from atheism. On treason see Lacey Baldwin Smith, "English Treason Trials and Confessions in the Sixteenth Century," *Journal of the History of Ideas* 15 (1954): 471–98.

6.   See, for example, the story William Strachey borrows from Henri Estienne's commentary on Herodotus: "Pope Leo the 10. answered Cardinall Bembo that alleadged some parte of the Ghospell into him: 'Lord Cardinall, what a wealth this fable of Jesus Christ hath gotten vs?'" (William Strachey, *The Historie of Travell into Virginia Britania* [1612], ed. Louis B. Wright and Virginia Freund, Hakluyt Society 2d ser., no. 103 [London, 1953], p. 101).

7.   Jacquot, "Thomas Harriot's Reputation for Impiety," p. 167. In another official record, Popham is reported to have said ominously, "You know what men say of *Hereiat*" (John W. Shirley, "Sir Walter Ralegh and Thomas Harriot," in *Thomas Harriot, Renaissance Scientist,* p. 27). The logic (if that is the word for it) would seem to be this: since God clearly supports the established order of things and punishes offenders with eternal torments, a criminal must be someone who has been foolishly persuaded that God does not exist. The alternative theory posits wickedness, a corruption of the will so severe as to lead people against their own better knowledge into the ways of crime. The two arguments are often conflated, since atheism is the heart of the greatest wickedness, as well as the greatest folly.

8.   Northrop Frye, *On Shakespeare* (New Haven: Yale University Press, 1986), p. 10 (see also p. 60: "Shakespeare's social vision is a deeply conservative one"); Franco Moretti, "'Huge Eclipse': Tragic Form and the Deconsecration of Sovereignty," in *The Power of Forms in the English Renaissance,* ed. Stephen Greenblatt (Norman, Okla.: Pilgrim Books, 1982), p. 31. On the histories as occasioning an interrogation of ideology, see Jonathan Dollimore and Alan Sinfield, "History and Ideology: The Instance of *Henry V,*" in John Drakakis, *Alternative Shakespeares* (London: Methuen, 1985), pp. 205–27.

9.   Here is how Richard Baines construes Marlowe's version of this argument: "He affirmeth . . . That the first beginning of Religion was only to keep men in awe. That it was an easy matter for Moyses being brought vp in all the artes of the Egiptians to abuse the Jewes being a rude & grosse people" (C. F. Tucker Brooke, *The Life of Marlowe* [London: Methuen, 1930], app. 9, p. 98). For other versions, see Strathmann, *Sir Walter Ralegh,* pp. 70–72, 87.

10.   "To come to those who have become princes through their own merits and not by fortune, I regard as the greatest, Moses, Cyrus, Romulus, Theseus, and their like. And although one should not speak of Moses, he having merely carried out what was ordered him by God, still he deserves admiration, if only for that grace which made him worthy to speak with God. But regarding Cyrus and others who have acquired or founded kingdoms, they will all be found worthy of admiration; and if their particular actions and methods are examined they will not appear very different from those of Moses, although he had so great a Master [che ebbe si gran precettore]" (Niccolò Machiavelli, *The Prince,* trans. Luigi Ricci, revised E. R. P. Vincent [New York: Random House, 1950], p. 20). Christian Detmold translated the *Discourses,* in the same volume.

The delicate ironies here are intensified in the remarks on ecclesiastical principalities:

> They are acquired either by ability or by fortune; but are maintained without either, for they are sustained by ancient religious customs, which are so powerful and of such quality, that they keep their princes in power in whatever manner they proceed and live. These princes alone have states without defending them, have subjects without governing them, and their states, not being defended are not taken from them; their subjects not being governed do not resent it, and neither think nor are capable of alienating themselves from them. Only those principalities, therefore, are secure and happy. But as they are upheld by higher causes, which the human mind cannot attain to, I will abstain from speaking of them; for being exalted and maintained by

indeed since the formation of the whole ideological myth of Prince Hal.

39. In the battle of Shrewsbury, when Falstaff is pretending he is dead, Hal, seeing the body of his friend, thinks with an eerie symbolic appropriateness of having the corpse literally emptied. As Hal exits, Falstaff rises up and protests. If Falstaff is an enormous mountain of flesh, Hal is the quintessential thin man: "you starveling," Falstaff calls him (2.4.244). From Hal's point of view, Falstaff's fat prevents him from having any value at all: "there's no room for faith, truth, nor honesty in this bosom of thine; it is all fill'd up with guts and midriff" (3.3.153–55).

Here and throughout the discussion of *1 Henry IV*, I am indebted to Edward Snow.

40. William Empson, *Some Versions of Pastoral* (London: Chatto and Windus, 1968), p. 103.

41. See S. P. Zitner, "Anon, Anon; or, a Mirror for a Magistrate," *Shakespeare Quarterly* 19 (1968): 63–70.

42. More accurately, the ratios are redistributed. For example, *Henry V* insists that the world represented in the play is extraordinarily spacious, varied, and mobile, while the stage itself is cramped and confining:

> Can this cockpit hold
> The vasty fields of France? Or may we cram
> Within this wooden O the very casques
> That did affright the air at Agincourt?
>
> (Prologue, 11–14)

The Chorus calls attention to this contradiction to exhort the audience to transcend it "In the quick forge and working-house of thought" (5.0.23). We have to do not with a balance of forces but with an imbalance that must be rectified by the labor of the imagination:

> Piece out our imperfections with your thoughts;
> Into a thousand parts divide one man,
> And make imaginary puissance.
>
> (Prologue, 23–25)

43. What we took to be the "center" may be part of the remotest periphery. More unsettling still, topographic accounts of both theater and power may be illusions: there may be no way to locate oneself securely in relation to either.

44. See, for example, Victor Turner, *Drama, Fields, and Metaphors: Symbolic Action in Human Society* (Ithaca: Cornell University Press, 1974).

45. The evidence is amply documented by Karen Kupperman, *Settling with the Indians.*

46. Thomas Harman, *A Caueat or Warening, for Commen Cursetors Vulgarely Called Vagabones* (1566), in *Cony-Catchers and Bawdy Baskets,* ed. Gamini Salgado (Middlesex: Penguin, 1972), p. 146.

47. On the problems of Elizabethan representations of the underworld, see A. L. Beier, *Masterless Men: The Vagrancy Problem in England, 1560–1640* (London: Methuen, 1985).

48. [Gilbert Walker?] *A manifest detection of the moste vyle and detestable use of Diceplay* (c. 1552), in Salgado, *Cony-Catchers and Bawdy Baskets,* pp. 42–43.

49. Norman N. Holland, in the Signet Classic edition of *2 Henry IV* (New York: New American Library, 1965), p. xxxvi.

50. See Frank Whigham, *Ambition and Privilege: The Social Tropes of Elizabethan Courtesy Theory* (Berkeley: University of California Press, 1984).

51. The public response to betrayal is extremely difficult to measure. Lawrence Stone suggests that there is a transition in the early years of the seventeenth century: "Up to the end of the sixteenth century men saw nothing dishonorable in attacking by surprise with superior forces, and nothing in hitting a man when he was down. By the second decade of the seventeenth century, however, such behaviour was becoming discreditable and is much less frequently met with" (Lawrence Stone, *The Crisis of the Aristocracy, 1558–1641,* abridged edition [New York: Oxford University Press, 1967], p. 109).

52. The presence of the Irishman among the English forces is especially significant since as the Chorus points out, an English expeditionary army was attempting at the moment of the play to subjugate the Irish. It is not the least of the play's bitter historical ironies that in four hundred years this attempt has not become an anachronism.

53. It would not have escaped at least some members of an Elizabethan audience that an English gentleman or woman would have been far more likely to learn French than a Frenchman English. The language lesson, Steven Mullaney suggests, is Shakespeare's "rearward glance at the improprieties that occupied the ambivalent center of Hal's prodigality." Whereas in the first and second parts of *Henry IV,* the recording of the language of the other has an element of tragedy, its equivalent in *Henry V* has only the spirit of French farce (Steven Mullaney, "Strange Things, Gross Terms, Curious Customs: The Rehearsal of Cultures in the Late Renaissance," *Representations* 3 [1983]: 63–64).

54. "This does not sound like hypocrisy or cynicism. The Archbishop discharges his duty faithfully, as it stands his

reasoning is impeccable. . . . Henry is not initiating aggression" (J. H. Walter, in the Arden edition of *King Henry V* [London: Methuen, 1954], p. xxv).

55. The kill ratio is highly in the English favor in all accounts, but Shakespeare adopts from Holinshed the most extreme figure. Holinshed himself adds that "other writers of greater credit affirm that there were slain above five or six hundred" Englishmen (Holinshed, in the Oxford Shakespeare edition of *Henry V*, ed. Gary Taylor [Oxford: Oxford University Press, 1984], p. 308). Similarly, Shakespeare makes no mention of the tactical means by which the English army achieved its victory. The victory is presented as virtually miraculous.

56. In a long appendix to his edition of *Henry V*, Gary Taylor attempts to defend his emendation of "all" to "ill" in these lines, on the grounds that an interpretation along the lines of Claudius's failed repentance would be difficult for an actor to communicate and, if communicated, would make "the victory of Agincourt morally and dramatically incomprehensible" (Taylor, p. 298). The interpretive framework that I am sketching in this chapter should make the Folio's reading fully comprehensible; the effect of the victory is, by my account, intensified by the play's moral problems.

57. Taylor makes a subtle and, I think, implausible attempt to reduce the unintended irony of Gower's line, "wherefore the King, most worthily, hath caus'd every soldier to cut his prisoner's throat" (4.7.8–10): "Gower is not saying (as all editors and critics seem to have understood him) 'the king *caused* the prisoners to be executed because of the attack on the baggage train' but 'given the barbarity of the subsequent French conduct, the king *has* quite justifiably *caused* the death of his prisoners'" (Taylor, p. 243). Even were we to understand the line in Taylor's sense, it would open a moral problem still worse than the political problem that has been resolved.

58. See the illuminating discussion in Norman Rabkin, *Shakespeare and the Problem of Meaning* (Chicago: University of Chicago Press, 1981), pp. 33–62.

59. This is flattery carefully echoed in Hal's promise to his troops on the eve of Agincourt that "be he ne'er so vile,/This day shall gentle his condition" (4.3.62–63). The promise is silently forgotten after the battle.

60. For a brilliant exploration of this hypothesis, see D. A. Miller, "The Novel and the Police," in *Glyph* 8 (1981): 127–47.

61. Quoted in J. E. Neale, *Elizabeth I and Her Parliaments, 1584–1601,* 2 vols. (London: Cape, 1965), 2:119. For the complex relation between theater and absolutism, see Stephen Orgel, *The Illusion of Power: Political Theater in the English Renaissance* (Berkeley: University of California Press, 1975); Jonathan Goldberg, *James I and the Politics of Literature: Jonson, Shakespeare, Donne, and Their Contemporaries* (Baltimore: Johns Hopkins University Press, 1983); Jonathan Dollimore, *Radical Tragedy: Religion, Ideology, and Power in the Drama of Shakespeare and His Contemporaries* (Brighton: Harvester, 1983); Greenblatt, *The Power of Forms in the English Renaissance;* Steven Mullaney, "Lying like Truth: Riddle, Representation, and Treason in Renaissance England," *ELH* 47 (1980): 32–47; Paola Colaiacomo, "Il teatro del principe," *Calibano* 4 (1979): 53–98; Christopher Pye, "The Sovereign, the Theater, and the Kingdome of Darknesse: Hobbes and the Spectacle of Power," *Representations* 8 (1984): 85–106.

62. *The History of King Richard III,* ed. R. S. Sylvester, in *The Complete Works of St. Thomas More,* vol. 3 (New Haven: Yale University Press, 1963), p. 80.

63. Clifford Geertz, "Centers, Kings, and Charisma: Reflections on the Symbolics of Power," in *Culture and Its Creators: Essays in Honor of Edward Shils,* ed. Joseph Ben David and Terry Nichols Clark (Chicago: University of Chicago Press, 1977), p. 160.

64. The nameless servant in *Lear* who can no longer endure what he is witnessing and who heroically stabs his master Cornwall, the legitimate ruler of half of England, inhabits a different political world from the one sketched here, a world marked out by Shakespeare as tragic.

65. Perhaps we should imagine Shakespeare writing at a moment when none of the alternatives for a resounding political commitment seemed satisfactory; when the pressure to declare himself unequivocally an adherent of one or another faction seemed narrow, ethically coarse, politically stupid; when the most attractive political solution seemed to be to keep options open and the situation fluid.

30

Nancy Armstrong
1938–

Nancy Armstrong is a professor of comparative literature at Brown University. Her criticism of eighteenth- and nineteenth-century British literature examines power relations and the interplay between discourse and historical events. She also posits women's sexual history as the primary site of cultural contestation. In *Desire and Domestic Fiction: A Political History of the Novel* (1987), she argues that through the eighteenth-century novel a particular model for middle-class women—psychologically interior, domestic, self-monitoring, free from sexual desire—not only became standard for women but later provided a model for *male* behavior as well. For Armstrong, then, women are much more "subjects" than "objects" (terms she criticizes in the essay given here) and should be so considered in literary histories. She does so in *The Imaginary Puritan: Literature, Intellectual Labor, and the Origins of Personal Life* (written with Leonard Tennenhouse, 1992), *The Ideology of Conduct: Essays on Literature and the History of Sexuality* (edited with Tennenhouse, 1987), "Some Call It Fiction: On the Politics of Domesticity" (1990), and "History in the House of Culture: Social Disorder and Domestic Fiction in Early Victorian England" (1986).

"The Occidental Alice" (1990), like Armstrong's other work, places the history of British female sexuality at the center of cultural history. She describes how a spate of British legislation in the 1860s, most importantly the Contagious Diseases Acts, defined and institutionalized proper middle-class English motherhood in large part by defining its opposite—sexual desire, disease, and contagion among working-class women. The female body was increasingly understood to be a kind of text "whereon those deviant qualities of mind became especially legible"; "one could determine the nature and behavior of one end of a woman by looking at the other." The same logic was applied to Asian and African women (and soon after to the men, as well), who, according to the male scientists examining them, "bore the very features of face and genitals that characterized only prostitutes and madwomen in Europe." Victorian scientific photography and popular art made familiar the "double-bodied woman," two sides of one cultural coin: the fair, lithe "salon body" (for example, that of Alice Liddell, Lewis Carroll's inspiration for the *Alice* books), and its concomitant and opposite, the dark-skinned, rough body. Both the colonial Other and the unideal woman were viewed as deviant, dark, disease-bearing, desiring, lacking in self-control, and eminently readable. Both provided negative standards in opposition to which middle-class British society—male and female—could define itself; they constituted the "Oriental" in distinction to which the "Occidental" could exist.

And *that* is what the *Alice* books, which were published in 1864 and 1871, have to do with British colonialism. In them John Tenniel's illustrations and Lewis Carroll's text "make it very clear that there only two kinds of women in Wonderland—pretty little girls who control themselves and hideous women who do not." Alice exemplifies the proper self-regulation of female desires; in doing so, she also demonstrates the proper acquisition of "the very kind of knowledge-power characterizing modern institutional cultures," namely, "the power that subjects exercise over objects, the power to classify, to evaluate, to consume." She learns to control the notoriously evasive objects and words of Wonderland by learning to control herself. Thus, given the immense popularity of Alice's story, "an entire class of people . . . eventually understood who they were as Europeans in relation to an imaginary woman."

The Occidental Alice

Alice's Adventures in Wonderland offers special access to that moment in the history of sexuality when, as Foucault tells it, the normal couple retired from public view, and Western culture began its century-long preoccupation with the sexual behavior of women, children, the mentally disturbed, masturbators, homosexuals, paupers, natives, regional types, and ethnics. I will use this extraordinarily successful work of children's literature to show how the image of a bad and ugly woman reshaped the late Victorian readership's understanding of what children were and thus what adults were supposed to be.

But before reading *Alice* I must provide some sense of the extensive set of cultural references this woman brought with her into Lewis Carroll's fanciful representation of childhood. In doing so, I will be using the "other" woman to establish a link between what Foucault calls the turn to deviance and the European manner of dealing with the Asian and African populations newly taken over by the great imperial nations. My brief history of this figure will suggest how the same culture that authorized certain Englishmen to oversee other Englishmen in the manner so eloquently chronicled by E. P. Thompson turned abruptly and yet imperceptibly toward a project of an entirely different order and magnitude.[1] Less concerned with class

difference than they had been during the early nineteenth century, the Victorian ruling classes refocused much of their cultural energy on the colonies. Adopting many descriptive procedures of the sort that Edward Said identifies with Orientalism, they developed a dense and pervasive set of differences between themselves as English men and women and people of non-European origins. In explaining how the image of a bad and ugly woman shaped the middle-class idea of childhood, then, I will also be suggesting how this shift of focus from normalcy onto deviance changed England's sense of itself as a nation.

Said's study of Orientalism implies that some of the most effective methods of imperialism may seem quite removed from matters of political policy. Orientalism was a scholarly project, as he explains, that "kept intact the separateness of the Orient, its eccentricity, its backwardness, its silent indifference, its feminine penetrability, its supine malleability" (206). Though a scholarly project, this way of representing the non-European helped to divide the world into what we now call First and Third Worlds. Through such writing, Said continues, "The Orient existed as a place isolated from the mainstream of European progress in the sciences, arts, and commerce" (206). He thus allows us to imagine how this way of representing the non-European could create a bond among members of the First World as they were extending themselves into Asia and Africa, a bond that transcended their national differences.[2] However, even the best accounts of cultural imperialism assume that power flows only one way—from the European ruling classes to the lower classes and out into the colonies. In giving us an intricate description of a characteristic means by which the European middle classes situated other ethnic groups in a negative relation to themselves, Said never asks how this image in turn changed the people who used it—the sense they had of themselves as a nation of men and women, the uses to which they put their own bodies, the form and content of their desires and fears, and therefore the basis for an identification among Europeans. I use the term Occidentalism to refer to these effects of the practices of Orientalism.

By restricting political power to those forms of power originating in real men, their labor and institutions, even cultural histories so helpful as Said's remain unconscious of the degree to which gender collaborated with race to produce modern Occidentalism. To historians politically far less self-conscious than himself, he concedes the point that imperialism was economically motivated and propelled.[3] In accepting this assumption, furthermore, historians of many different stripes also accept the nineteenth-century belief that business not only determined the quality of one's personal life but also testified to the stability of the nation as a whole. And like their nineteenth-century counterparts in another respect as well, these scholars tend to use an alternative set of assumptions when describing the organization of non-industrial societies. It can be argued that in fact they accept the basic premises of theories designed to prove other cultures are less developed than Western Europe's (Bolt). Extensive studies in comparative anthropology conducted during the nineteenth century showed that different sexual practices gave rise to less effective forms of government

and systems of economic exchange (Stocking, Levy, Gilman). Regarding such practices as inherently deviant, these studies reached the conclusion that the desires of primitive people were somehow like those desires that moral reformers, medical doctors, social scientists, and politicians had attributed to European prostitutes.[4] From these assumptions, it was an easy step for them to see the people ruled by such desires as both childish and criminoid, primitive and degenerate versions of the European.[5] The same logic that said a man's family was healthy because his business was good could also be used to insist that other cultures were poor because their women were bad. Cultures that failed to domesticate their women consequently existed in the Occidental imaginary as places, in the words of Said, "requiring Western attention, reconstruction, even redemption" (206).

In trying to link Victorian sexuality to British imperialism, then, I will be inverting the usual priorities of cause and effect maintained by mainstream modern historiography. By so doing, however, I will simply be taking up the logic England used to describe other cultures— and using that logic to describe English culture itself. I will try to show how the image of a woman disfigured by the expression of sexual desire not only came to define certain women as non-European but also redefined the European body, in turn, as one significantly lacking such desires. In this way, I will suggest, the image of a double-bodied woman provided both the theory necessary for imagining modern imperialism and the psychological equipment for carrying it out. Europe's image of the other woman did not simply denigrate her as well as the desire she might inspire in others. The image did so in such a way as to infuse this desire with a threat of emasculation. For, as I will show, colonial Englishmen evidently found desire for the other woman incompatible with another kind of desire that bound them to one another in mutual devotion to the women back home.

I. PROSTITUTES AND NATIVES

My account of this event begins with a highly contested bit of legislation passed in 1864 and amended in 1866 and again in 1869. As Judith Walkowitz has made unforgettably clear in her study of Victorian prostitution, the Contagious Diseases Acts named prostitutes as the source of venereal disease and attempted to combat the problem of infection quite simply by confining it to their bodies. The new law required all women who were considered prostitutes to register and submit to regular pelvic examinations. It appointed surgeons to carry out these examinations and empowered them to incarcerate infected women for as long as six months. Though space does not allow a full account of the medical procedures, I want to note the zealous efficiency with which such professional men as William Acton carried out this work. Stalwart liberal, esteemed surgeon, and author of numerous medical books and treatises, Acton proudly claimed to have "assisted in the thorough examination of 58 women with the speculum . . . in the course of one hour and three-quarters" (85). One cannot read much of his extended account without understanding it as a record of how one class humiliated another by subjecting its women to involuntary pelvic exams.

It becomes very clear that purification rites of exactly this nature were carried on in the name of national health when we consider what metaphors were used to describe infected women. With the exception of a few dissenting voices (that, for example, of John Stuart Mill), the cast of experts mobilized in defence of the Contagious Diseases Acts used the language of class to think of the women whom they had forced to register as prostitutes. These women were, in the words of one man of medicine,

> dirty, clad in unwomanly rags, some appearing half-starved, covered with vermin, causing those near them to shun them with aver-

sion; careless in matters of common decency, their conversation having mingled with it such words as made one shudder to listen to; wofully ignorant, they appeared, in their utter filth and depravity, lost to all the better qualities of human beings. (Great Britain 727)

Metaphors of pollution encouraged the most technical medical discussions to conclude that these women were in fact the cause of infection, or "poison," as it was more often called. Certain of their assumptions about the female body made it possible for the specialists in the disease to argue that a man contracted the disease from a woman even in cases where his symptoms were far more advanced than hers because her body gave off poisonous fluids even under ordinary conditions. Thus one expert concluded that "uterine discharges are one of its constitutional manifestations, and I think that these discharges, at any rate, may be a vehicle of the virus" (Great Britain 120). Working-class women were still more likely to be infectious because, according to other testimony,

> at those particular times when a woman should retire from all sexual communication, in consequence of her natural monthly disturbance, it is well known that except in rare instances they do not so withdraw, on the contrary they afford intercourse to soldiers as usual, and the menstrual discharge in this class of women being exceedingly irritating, the production of urethritis, orchitis &c., is frequently the consequence. (Great Britain 730)

Though the effects of mercury were known to be extraordinarily toxic, especially when people were worn and undernourished, the medical profession frequently classified it as "an antidote to a poison" (Great Britain 119). The official summary of reports on the effectiveness of the

Contagious Diseases Act passed in 1864 acknowledged that it neither decreased the number of prostitutes nor curtailed the spread of disease. It is particularly revealing, then, that the same report is generally positive about the Act because it inadvertently produced two positive results. First, it produced massive amounts of information about venereal disease that testified "to its prevalence among all classes of society, its insidious nature, the frequent failure of all but men of great experience to recognize it, and, moreover, to the most important fact, that the poisoned *foetus in utero* is no infrequent cause of miscarriage" (44). In other words, according to the summary, women of the lower classes had spread a poison throughout English society that directly assaulted motherhood. Not only were middle-class men removed as the pernicious mediators between the poison inside the bodies of the one class of women and the babies inside the bodies of the other, but those men who had specialized knowledge of the disease, again, middle-class men, were also the only thing that stood between unborn children and a disease that seemed to threaten them directly.

Although they describe their patients in anything but feminine terms, it is important (indeed crucial for purposes of understanding contemporary fetal politics) to note how the same group of experts attributed maternal qualities to the institutions where these women were incarcerated. It is on this basis, for example, that the official summary of reports managed to snatch victory from the jaws of defeat: "The evidence shows that in one most important point the Act has proved successful . . . that which relates to the feelings of the unfortunate women with whom it has to deal; so far from opposing its operation, they appear to appreciate its value to themselves" (Great Britain 44). A doctor offered this evidence to show "that a residence in the hospital, in some cases, has an extraordinary effect":

There was one house into which I went with the inspector of police lately. I heard a

woman reading with a loud voice, when we got to the passage, I stopped to listen, and I found, to my astonishment, that she was reading from "Bunyan's Pilgrim's Progress." I went into the room and found no less than seven women sitting round a good looking woman of 25 who was reading from "Pilgrim's Progress," all paying the greatest attention. (729)

To conclude a string of such observations that contrast strikingly with the image of the venomous woman I described in the preceding paragraph, however, the same man recommended that "fully one-half the class" of prostitutes—presumably not so eager to continue their confinement—be forcibly sent to a reformatory after their illness was cured. "It would," he claimed, "be a charity, as well as a mere precaution, to hide them from gratification of their sin for a year or two" (733).

Let me turn briefly to another cluster of legal measures, also aimed at forcibly regulating working-class sexuality. Beginning in 1859, a whole set of mutually reinforcing practices developed around motherhood to secure institutionally for infants what human nature had evidently failed to supply. The first infant protection societies appeared; safer adoption procedures were put in place; laws were passed to restrict baby farming, register midwives, and prosecute those who dropped newborns down public latrines. By 1874 the English Registration Act was passed as part of a concerted effort on the part of the state to register the birth and death of each child whether bastard or stillborn.[6] But despite all this legislation and the introduction of both the rubber nipple and the first manufactured baby food, it was not until our century—not until the 1920s—that the infant mortality rate decreased substantially in England (Rose 182–86). The very fact that these measures failed as dismally as the Contagious Diseases Acts is, I think, significant. It implies that the public insisted so religiously on regulating working-class women because such insistence itself solved a problem. The symbolic activity around motherhood translated an insurmountable problem in the domain of production into an equally insurmountable problem in the domain of reproduction. In this way, the cause for the deplorable physical condition of the working class could be relocated in the moral condition of their women.

In turning from legal discourse to the new and flourishing social sciences, we can see how the female body developed into a text enabling literate people to establish moral differences between themselves and other social and ethnic groups. During the second half of the nineteenth century, the madhouse population provided subjects for studies that identified women prone to mental illness. In his well-known study *Body and Mind,* for example, Henry Maudsley claimed that women prone to inherited mental defects could be identified by such "'bodily and mental marks' as 'an irregular and unsymmetrical conformation of the head, a want of regularity and harmony of the features . . . malformations of the external ear . . . tics, grimaces . . . stammering and defects of pronunciation . . . peculiarities of the eyes,' and a predilection for puns" (Showalter 106). And men of the literate classes were accordingly advised to inspect a prospective wife for "visible signs of inward and invisible faults which will have their influence in breeding" (Showalter 107).

As Victorian intellectuals became increasingly absorbed in classifying, knowing, and controlling deviance, the female anatomy offered itself as a text whereon those deviant qualities of mind became especially legible. Social scientists discovered, for example, that a woman's moral condition could be read in certain details of her face and genitals. Some found that the genitals of prostitutes were typically enlarged by abscesses and tumors.[7] Others demonstrated that the faces of these women characteristically bore protruding jaws, flat noses, misshapen foreheads, and attached earlobes. On the basis of

such homologies, science developed a set of analytical procedures by which one could determine the nature and behavior of one end of a woman by looking at the other. The same logic of the body drove pioneers in anthropology to perform dissections on women of groups recently brought under European rule. These men discovered that Asian and African women normally bore the very features of face and genitals that characterized only prostitutes and madwomen in Europe.[8]

To grow familiar with these legal and scientific definitions of the body is to recognize a fearful symmetry that organized the visual media as well. During the 1860s, photographers broke away from aestheticized portrayals of madness that celebrated the individuality of human consciousness. Instead, they began to capture the faces of madwomen, whores, and aborigines in a manner resembling the modern mugshot (Figures 30.1, 30.2). In settling upon the new style, science was clearly out to cut a difference between imperial Europe and its others (see Marable, Sekula). For the point of this photography was not to capture the individuality of the deviant person but to classify deviance in a way that included very different cultural attitudes and behaviors within a single classification system in which gender made the difference. Indeed, it can be argued that simply by focusing on prostitutes, madwomen, and native women, this classification system identified forms of cultural difference with promiscuity and mental disease. Another example of scientific photography may help to explain why this style was so effective (Figure 30.3). It reveals the quasi-pornographic quality that comes from subjecting the other's body to the gaze. Taken from a collection of Désiré Charnay's expeditionary photography, these shots give the viewer a sense of surrounding the body and even, in the case of numerous women, penetrating into the body itself (Davis). At the same time, the camera uses this power to strip the other body of all national or ethnic specificity. The photograph of

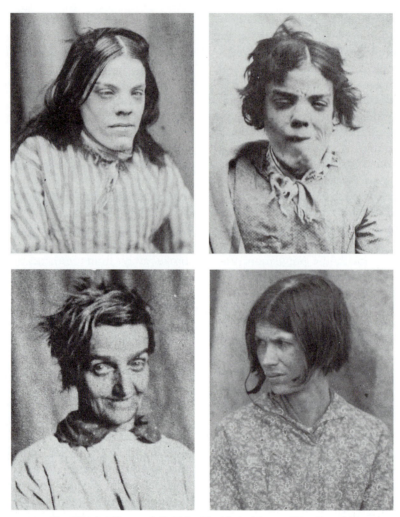

FIGURE 30.1 Dr. Hugh Diamond (1852). Untitled. (*Source:* The Royal Photographic Society, Bath, England.)

native men bears the label "a Macoua, Arab Indian, and black Creole from Reunion," but the photograph itself arranges their bodies so that they seem to present different views of a single person. The other portrait is simply entitled "Group of Negresses" to make native women appear still more generic than native men.

Contemporaneous with the production of this scientific body, one can observe the devel-

opment of an equally stereotypical "salon" body. This is best illustrated by the work of the Julia Margaret Cameron circle, whose subjects were often prominent figures of Victorian society. Members of the circle used the camera to deify emotion in the manner of Pre-Raphaelite painting. Like the painters they admired, these photographers were attracted to women in the act of languishing or even leaving this world (the

FIGURE 30.2 Anomalies of the face and ear in prostitutes. (*Source:* Pauline Tarnowsky, Étude anthropométrique sur les prostituées et les voleuses, Paris: Lecrosnier, 1889.)

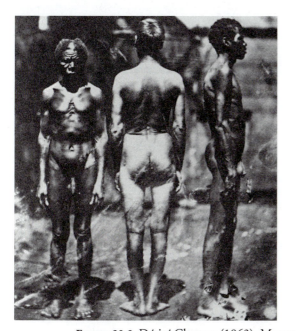 

FIGURE 30.3 Désiré Charnay (1863). Macuoa, Arab Indian, black Creole from Reunion (left) and Group of Negresses (right). (*Source:* Collection of the Musée de l'homme, Place de Trocadero, Paris.)

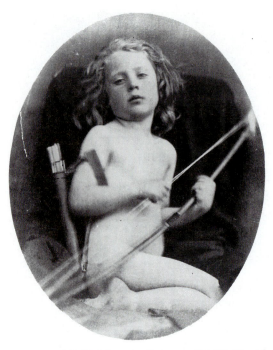

FIGURE 30.4 Julia Margaret Cameron (1866). Cupid. (*Source:* Graham Ovenden, *A Victorian Album: Julia Margaret Cameron and Her Circle,* New York: Da Capo, 1975.)

FIGURE 30.5 Lord Somers (attr.) (1863–65). The Butcher's Visit. (*Source:* Graham Ovenden, *A Victorian Album: Julia Margaret Cameron and Her Circle,* New York: Da Capo, 1975.)

drowning Ophelia and the mad Lady of Shallott were favorite subjects of both). But their work is especially remembered for photographs of pre-pubescent girls (Figure 30.4). Although the highly aestheticized female was the trademark of the group, they occasionally photographed common people. And when they did, they adopted the documentary style. The bodies composing a portrait such as "The Butcher's Visit" present a striking contrast with the thin, white, unworldly art body (Figure 30.5). Coupled with the title, the stockiness of the figures composing this photograph establishes subtle associations between the female servant and the masculine character of her flesh and labor. Nor can we overlook the racism implicit in the duskiness that colors common flesh in contrast with the near translucent blue-white body of an elite fe-

male. Nineteenth-century photography thus established the difference between the two as a difference of the body itself. A case in point is one of Lewis Carroll's photographs of the girl for whom he wrote the *Alice* books. In this photograph, entitled "Alice Liddell as a Beggar Girl," there is no mistaking Alice for a girl of the underclasses. She displays an elite body against a pastoral backdrop as she meets the observer eye to eye (Figure 30.6).

I have stressed the contrast between these two modes of representation in order to establish the collusion between them. Though mutually exclusive, the two were born together and behaved as a single cultural phenomenon, one always calling the other to mind.[9] Before the 1870s were well under way, this image of a double-bodied woman had saturated polite Victorian culture. I have already suggested how she filled the pages of scientific studies and lined the walls of art galleries. But she was also on display on a regular basis in daily newspapers, weekly magazines, as well as monthly and quarterly journals and reviews. She hung for years on tastefully decorated walls in sentimental line drawings and oil paintings; she lay on tea tables in open photo albums; she arrived in vestibules on postcards; she animated advertisements for household products; and she illustrated some of the most popular novels, travel narratives, and missionary accounts of the day.[10]

In many respects, this was the same image that had, earlier on, identified womanhood itself with the women of the new ruling class (Armstrong). But something happened to the image as it began to operate on an international scale, authorizing Englishmen to supervise members of less developed nations on grounds that non-European women were not really women although they were definitely female. It was one thing to define working-class Englishmen in a negative relation to Englishmen who possessed the means of production. It was another thing to "reform" non-industrialized cultures that organized production and reproduction in an entirely different way. It may well have been that cultural differences made the newly subordinated peoples less able to understand themselves as defective versions of middle-class Europe or less willing to feel dependent on their superiors. On their part, however, European intellectuals had to revise the logic and technologies of otherness in order to see such peoples as childlike and feminine versions of themselves. It was through this revision of the categories of self and other at the popular level, I believe, that the colonial venture had the greatest impact on people back home and thus on who as middle-class people we still think we are today.

FIGURE 30.6 Lewis Carroll (1859). Alice Liddell as a Beggar Girl. (*Source:* Helmut Gernsheim, Julia Margaret Cameron: Her Life and Photographic Work. New York: Apertune, 1975.)

II. THE AFRICANIZATION OF ENGLISH GIRLHOOD

Having indicated something of the proportions it had assumed in the culture, I would now like to consider the impact of the double-bodied woman on the class producing it. As promised, I will use Lewis Carroll's *Alice's Adventures in Wonderland* to explain how middle-class women came to understand themselves in relation to their deviant counterparts. Written and published during the 1860s along with the Contagious Diseases Acts and legislation to reduce infant mortality, Carroll's story carried many of the same textualizing procedures into a whole new area of human experience. The link between children's literature and this obsession with the bodies of madwomen and whores can be observed at the very beginning of the story, in the following description of Alice's fall down the rabbit hole:

> First, she tried to look down and make out what she was coming to, but it was too dark to see anything: then she looked at the sides of the well, and noticed that they were filled with cupboards and bookshelves: here and there she saw maps and pictures hung upon pegs. She took down a jar from one of the shelves as she passed: it was labelled "ORANGE MARMELADE," but to her great disappointment it was empty: she did not like to drop the jar, for fear of killing somebody underneath, so she managed to put it into one of the cupboards as she fell past it. (18)

In this passage, I believe, we witness an event of no little historical significance. At the beginning of her fall (always a symbolic tip-off when women are concerned) the source of fear is located in the world outside her body.[11] Even so, Alice is strangely unconcerned about "what she was coming to," and for good reason. Halfway down the rabbit hole, she finds herself in a thoroughly domesticated interior.

Then, as appetites will, Alice's suddenly takes over her body. She grabs a jar marked "marmelade," and this empty sign of gratification mysteriously reverses the trajectory of her desire. Alice temporarily loses her interest in food. She grows anxious. Having disturbed domestic order, she wants nothing so much as to return the jar to its place. Appetite gives way to an equally compulsive desire for self-control, as Alice comes to understand herself as someone who endangers others. Or so Carroll writes: "she did not like to drop the jar, for fear of killing somebody underneath." Nowhere in the earlier fic-

tion I have read—and there was a great deal published telling girls how to be girls—can I recall anything like this: a girl in the act of falling, but a girl only vaguely curious about what would befall her. Then, within the space of very few lines, an almost imperceptible danger outside her body gives way to a danger within, one capable of erupting at any moment. Alice consequently loses her fear of falling and becomes afraid of letting go.

Like those of working-class and foreign women, then, Alice's body is potentially out of control and, by its very nature, in need of regulation. But where the problem with those other female bodies had a genital origin, all the problems with Alice's body begin and end with her mouth. With every mouthful of food comes certain loss of physical control. One such episode sends her shooting up in height through the branches of a tree exactly where an anxious pigeon has sought safety for her eggs beyond the reach of serpents. The following bit of their dialogue explains how eating destabilizes Alice's identity:

> "But I'm *not* a serpent, I tell you!" said Alice. "I'm a—I'm a—"
>
> "Well! What are you?" said the Pigeon. "I can see you're trying to invent something!"
>
> "I—I'm a little girl," said Alice, rather doubtfully, as she remembered the number of changes she had gone through that day.
>
> "A likely story indeed!" said the Pigeon, in a tone of the deepest contempt. "I've seen a good many little girls in my time, but never *one* with such a neck as that! No, no! You're a serpent; and there's no use denying it. I suppose you'll be telling me next that you never tasted an egg!" (54)

Carroll saw to it that Alice would have a problem controlling her mouth when he gave her a prodigious appetite and put her in a world made of food. Wonderland contains such creatures as the mock turtle, the lobster, and the little whitings who manage to swim with their backs well-coated with bread crumbs. Alice's situation, so defined, invites us to consider why Carroll animated a world by bringing the well-to-do dinner table back to life, and why he constructed a girl's identity in relation to objects so strangely revitalized. In view of the immediate and lasting popularity of his book, we must, I feel, seek an answer in the new consumer culture. Its logic alone can link the colonial venture to the appetite of a little girl.

Jennifer Wicke demonstrates convincingly that fiction carried on a long-term intimate relationship with advertising. During the eighteenth century, she argues, fiction borrowed from advertising as a means of self-promotion. During the Victorian period, however, certain novels sought to distinguish themselves from the crass mass culture by criticizing authors and readers who were captivated by the values of the literary marketplace. Novels, in other words, assumed an ambivalent relationship toward their own commercial success and toward the class of people whose moral values provided the basis of literary authority. Rachel Bowlby has further specified the 1860s as the moment when consumerism became part of mothering. Suddenly shopping was something that women, rather than men, were supposed to do.[12] Moreover, department stores appeared in England and France to display the goods of empire in a setting that uniquely combined shopping with dining out and entertainment. In this way, the new mode of shopping associated the acquisition of objects with the pleasure of surveying and literally consuming, or eating, them. The place where all this happened was often described in terms of a wonderland. Thomas Richards shows us how the enchantments of the Crystal Palace in 1851 and the solemnities of the Queen's Jubilee of 1887 carried over into the department store. In what appeared to be vast and illuminated museum-like displays of objects from many corners of the world, he explains, "the consumer was queen and the queen was a consumer, and festivals like the Jubilees served to dramatize that monarch and commoner alike were equals in the eyes of the market" (163). But democracy was dangerous. Elaborating the ways in which art collaborated with commercialism to woo the female shopper, Rémy Saisselin (1984) claims that "the entire machine of the store—the architecture, special displays, special sales and events—was directed to one end: the seduction of woman. It was the modern devil tempting the modern Eve" (39). Indeed, such were the inducements to shop that kleptomania, a compulsion afflicting women of the respectable classes, became a problem for the first time in history (Abelson).

When one brings these insights to a reading of *Alice,* it becomes apparent that her tumble down the rabbit hole initiated a new moment in the history of desire. It is difficult to imagine one of Jane Austen's heroines so endangered by shopping. Overconcern for the goods sold in town could indeed represent a minor flaw in such an otherwise good-hearted woman as Catherine Moreland's chaperone in *Northanger Abbey,* or even betray the malformed sensibility of an Augusta Elton in *Emma,* but neither a woman's eligibility for marriage nor the class status of her family hung in the balance whenever she shopped. Her relation to objects did not determine so much as reveal what kind of woman she was, and the man who finally attracted such a woman revealed substantially more. Her sexual object choice ultimately determined what position that woman would occupy within English society.

Alice's problems with appetite tell us how desire changed as women became consumers in the world of the department store. She feels anxious about a desire that earlier generations simply could not have felt. She is always concerned with fitting in. This anxiety produces a form of taste specifically formed to regulate the desire for food. She consequently stops bolting down every consumable object she encounters and takes to nibbling one side of the mushroom or another, and this behavior stabilizes the body that appetite has disfigured. Such control of consumption allows Alice to grow without ruining her figure. For even though her size increases at the story's end, she retains the prepubescent shape distinguishing her from the other women in that story. As appetite assumes the central role within the child's body, then, we can see how it redefines sexual desire. The girl's ability to master appetite tells us whether or not she contains those desires characterizing men as well as unruly women and if she is destined not to fit in.[13]

As he made sexual desire contingent on the vicissitudes of a form of appetite present in childhood, Carroll also revised the role taste had to play in a world of beckoning objects. It is important to note how carefully he links the problem of appetite with another form of oral aggression. His wonderland is made of both literature and food, and beast fable as well as dinner table supply its characters. Thus from the moment she reaches for the empty jar marked "Marmelade," words and food exist in a curiously interchangeable relationship for Alice. For one thing, she is always in danger of letting it slip that she would not mind eating the very creatures with whom she converses. Along with a persistent hunger, her body contains dissident voices that infiltrate and overturn the content of her speech performances. When requested to stand up and repeat "*'Tis the voice of the sluggard*," Carroll tells us, "her head was so full of the Lobster-Quadrille, that she hardly knew what she was saying; and the words came very queer indeed." When words do come, they are disfigured by appetite: "Tis the voice of the lobster [she says, substituting "lobster" for "sluggard"]: I heard him declare,/'You have baked me too brown, I must sugar my hair'" (98). When she substitutes a lobster for a sluggard, Alice replaces the vice of laziness with an overconcern for food, a specifically female failure. As such, the substitution demonstrates that appetite disfigures female speech as surely as it does the fe-

male body. Indeed, all the elements of the story conspire to convince us that appetite disfigures speech because speech, like appetite, originates within the female body. Writing, on the other hand, comes from the adult world of classrooms and books outside the body. Each flaw in her speech performances therefore intensifies our sense that Alice *could* control her appetite if her speech would only stick to writing.

In the English society Carroll offers up to girls' imaginations, objects behave much like transitional objects in British object relations theory. Both self and non-self, they represent the self as an object in the world. Thus when Alice suddenly grows farther than usual away from her feet, those feet behave as synecdoches of the body itself: "Oh, my poor little feet, I wonder who will put on your shoes and stockings for you now, dears? I'm sure I shan't be able! I shall be a great deal too far off to trouble myself about you" (14). The fracturing effect of this self-objectification actually destroys Alice's self-control in order to produce it: "'But I must be kind to them,' thought Alice, 'or perhaps they won't walk the way I want to go!'" (14–15). In feigning mastery over the rules of her culture, then, she gains new mastery over herself. For it is in this manner that Alice comes to terms with her feet: "'Let me see. I'll give them a new pair of boots every Christmas.' And she went on planning to herself how she would manage it. 'They must go by carrier,' she thought; 'and how funny it'll seem, sending presents to one's own feet.'" (15). Thus Carroll represents childhood as a lack of the very kind of knowledge-power characterizing modern institutional cultures. This is the power that subjects exercise over objects, the power to classify, to evaluate, to consume. And the acquisition of literacy is what empowers subjects to keep objects in their place.

In bringing us to this conclusion, however, Alice's misadventures bring us to the very heart of a contradiction. We must recall that objects tend to come engraved with the invitation to consume them. "Eat me" or "drink me," they say. Her compulsive response to a "marmelade" label indicates that writing in fact creates the appetite that Alice must control through reading and recitation. How, then, can appetite originate inside her body if it originates in writing? *Alice's Adventures in Wonderland* defines the heroine's development as the acquisition of a peculiar kind of literacy that embraces this self-contradiction. Put another way, Alice herself embodies the phantasmagorical spiral of desire and restraint that women would soon experience in relation to a world made of beckoning objects. Alice's tumble down the rabbit hole reveals an appetite for marmelade. Because she has the literacy of the ruling class, however, Alice has acquired an appetite for rules well before her adventures begin. And even though something that seems more like an aversion to books prompts her adventures in wonderland, Alice's story is ultimately a struggle to possess the kind of taste that comes with literacy. Like her wish to enter the rose garden, her appetite for marmelade and whitings is ultimately the expression of that taste.

In order for a woman to grow up within the spiral of desire that constitutes taste, objects must be inherently attractive. They must present themselves to the consumer as things she must resist. There is neither a single form of appetite that does not require control in Carroll's fantasy for little girls, nor any gesture of control that does not imply the presence of some appetite. Whether he knew it or not, it made sense for him to place his heroine in constant danger from her appetite because this relationship to objects was essential to the formation of the new female consumer. Indeed, I have been arguing that his story shows how fear of appetite became necessary to the production of the taste identifying women of the privileged classes. We can, I think, observe precisely this subtle but profound change coming over Alice during the course of her adventures; as she wanders back and forth between the poles of desire and self-restraint, *all possibility for pleasure splits off from appetite and attaches itself to self-control.*

FIGURE 30.7 Quinten Massys. *A Grotesque Old Woman.* (*Source:* The National Gallery, London.)

In reading this account of childhood as a story about a struggle between words and appetite for the power to define the female body, I have tried to suggest how and why a work of children's literature came to reproduce the double-bodied woman that shaped very different territories of Victorian culture and linked them to one another. But nothing makes the point quite so well as the illustrations for the novel that appeared in the 1866 edition published by Macmillan. Studies of these illustrations have turned up several prototypes for the duchess and probably for the queen as well. One possible source from the National Gallery is a portrait entitled "A Grotesque Old Woman" by the late fifteenth-century painter Quinten Massys (Figure 30.7).[14] I must quickly add that this is *not at all* how Carroll himself envisioned these two powerful women when he sketched the designs for his illustrator John

FIGURE **30.8** Lewis Carroll. Royal procession to the garden. (*Source: Alice's Adventures Underground,* New York: American, 1960.)

Tenniel (Figure 30.8). In the original designs, they inhabit normal bodies. It is likely that Tenniel, being more familiar with the iconography of illustration, chose a body that would identify them with the women Victorian science was portraying as sexually defective (Figure 30.9). One of the most curious things about the memorable scene in which the Duchess peppers her baby is the fact she has the same face as her cook, though one figure displays the profile and the other the frontal view (Figure 30.10). In this way, the scene where they nightmarishly confuse cooking food with feeding babies recalls the scientific positioning of natives in the photograph described above. It suggests that the cook and the Duchess offer two views of a single body—a disfigured body housing desires that overturn the maternal norm. In contrast with the other women in the novel, Tenniel drew Alice with the contours of a "salon" body, which he distorted whenever appetite seized control of her. Thus she passed out of the original designs where Carroll sketched her in a pose reminiscent of Ophe-

FIGURE **30.9** John Tenniel. Alice and the Queen of Hearts. (*Source: Alice's Adventures in Wonderland,* New York: American, 1960.)

FIGURE 30.10 John Tenniel. The Duchess. (*Source: Alice's Adventures in Wonderland,* New York: American, 1960.)

lia and into the Tenniel illustration without undergoing any such grotesque transformation (Figures 30.11a, b). The Tenniel illustrations make it very clear that there are only two kinds of women in Wonderland—pretty little girls who control themselves and hideous women who do not. In a particularly telling illustration, Tenniel suggests that, though two sides of a single cultural coin, these women have grown so different they can occupy the same space in fantasy alone (Figure 30.12). In arriving at this conclusion, I am simply suggesting that this celebrated work of children's literature required children of the literate classes to fantasize the body as something already out of control, something always in need of regulation. And so it collaborated with many other kinds of writing to change the fear of being other by which a culture indelibly brands subjects as its own.

III. CONSUMING OBJECTS

In Alice's farewell to Wonderland, "'You're nothing but a pack of cards!,'" Carroll's enchanting tale of childhood could be said to echo Marx's sentiments about the status of objects under conditions of late capitalism in "The Fetishism of the Commodity and its Secret." In this chapter of *Capital,* Marx imagines a moment in the history of industrial cultures when relations among things determine relations among people. The natural relation between people and things consequently undergoes an inversion whereby people are dominated

FIGURE **30.11a** Lewis Carroll. Alice in the Pool of Tears. (*Source: Alice's Adventures Underground,* New York: American, 1960.)

FIGURE **30.11b** John Tenniel. Alice in the Pool of Tears. (*Source: Alice's Adventures in Wonderland,* New York: American, 1960.)

by the things they produce. Human desire ceases to determine what things are under these circumstances, and things determine what people desire. In this respect, the way Marx says objects behave under conditions of late capitalism resembles their behavior in the fantasy Carroll attributes to a child. While this resemblance may pinpoint a historical relationship between the British obsession with childhood sexuality, especially that of little girls, and the new commodity culture, it does not link this peculiar turn in the history of sexuality with imperialism, at least not in an explicit way.

Arjun Appadurai's introduction to *The Social Life of Things* sheds some light on this question. He explains the relationship between Western insistence that words can dominate things and our equally tenacious assumption that subjects have to dominate objects:

Contemporary Western common sense, building on various historical traditions in philosophy, law, and natural science, has a strong tendency to oppose "words" and "things." Though this was not always the case even in the West . . . the powerful contempo-

rary tendency is to regard the world of things as inert and mute, set in motion and animated, indeed knowable, only by persons and their words. (4)

From his perspective, however, most things are *not* meaningful for the reasons people say: "even though from a *theoretical* point of view human actors encode things with significance, from a *methodological* point of view it is the things-in-motion that illuminate their human and social context" (5). In saying this, Appadurai defines a need for better ways of charting a social history of things to include the cultural transformations they undergo in travelling from place to place and the position they come to occupy in relationship with human beings as a result. We already know that any exchange of commodities of course entails an exchange of knowledge. Commodities circulate messages that turn the criteria for their own selection into a complicated game of prestige involving experts from the art world, scholars, dealers, as well as producers and consumers. According to Appadurai, most explanations of commodity culture are conceptual gap and close it. This comparison proceeds on the principle that "as the institutional and spatial journeys of commodities grow more complex, and the alienation of producers, traders, and consumers from one another increases, culturally formed mythologies about commodity flow are likely to emerge" (48). With a significant increase of cognitive and spatial distance between production, distribution, and consumption, furthermore, these accounts take on striking new features. The cargo cults that multiplied in the stateless societies of the Pacific during this century provide an instructive example of this explanatory magic:

> Though often ordered in indigenous patterns, the ritual practice of cargo cults was in many cases no less than a massive effort to mime those European social forms that seemed most conducive to the production of European goods. In a kind of reverse fetishism, what was replicated was what was seen as the most potent of European social and linguistic forms in an effort to increase the likelihood of European commodities. But . . . the cults were, however distorted, pursuits not of *all* European commodities, but only of those commodities that were seen as particularly conducive to the maintenance of status discontinuities in local societies. (52)

This description of cargo cults comes rather close to Roland Barthes's definition of a mythology as a complex image, object, or sign that has been cut off from the history of its production and therefore seems to exist free of any known form of human control. Indeed, there can be no historical explanation for this kind of object since it is its own best explanation or magical narrative.

In one way or another, most literary scholars and historians would concede Foucault's point that the subject's domination over objects was essential to middle-class hegemony from the beginning. That is to say, it gave authority to a

FIGURE 30.12 John Tenniel. Alice and the Duchess. (*Source: Alice's Adventures in Wonderland,* New York: American, 1960.)

content with this understanding—what "Baudrillard sees as the emergence of the 'object,' that is, a thing that is no longer just a product or a commodity, but essentially a sign in a system of signs of status" (45). Just as he is forced to move beyond our own postindustrial culture for a more complete understanding of the way objects behave there, we require something more in order to establish a relationship between British imperialism and the object relations characterizing modern women.

Appadurai's ingenious comparison between consumers in a commodity culture and the members of a cargo cult can help define this class of moral reformers, sanitation experts, professional people, intellectuals, and managers of all sorts over a heterogeneous field of regional and ethnic practices.[15] My reading of *Alice's Adventures in Wonderland* attempts to show, however, that during the second half of the nineteenth century something happened to this relationship between subjects and objects. One could even say they have exchanged properties and positions in relation to one another, were it not for the fact that we always know when things in Wonderland are upside down. Whenever such an exchange occurs, it does not represent the general condition of things but things as they supposedly exist within a child's dream. Things resemble writing in that they often seem to possess some knowledge of their properties that Alice lacks. Like writing, then, they appear to have power over her. Like the objects that are taken up in the intricate ceremonies of the cargo cult, however, the objects composing childish fantasies are distorted messages; rather than reproduce the status distinctions of another culture, things are simply selected and arranged to maintain status distinctions peculiar to domestic England. Alice herself is one of those things. It is worth noting in this regard that Alice's most upsetting moment comes early on in her adventures when she fails, for the first of many times, to recite a poem correctly. "I'm sure those are not the right words," she laments. "I must be Mable after all, and I shall have to go and live in that poky little house after all, and have next to no toys to play with, and, oh, ever so many lessons to learn!" (27).

Pursuing Appadurai's analogy further, then, one is forced to conclude that these distortions of adult Victorian culture are only secondarily a critique or parody of middle-class culture. First of all, let us suppose a culture in which objects have to be kept under control. Let us suppose further that only the legibility of objects makes authority possible, along with one's ability to read them. What would happen, then, if occult objects began to flood into that culture from all

over the Empire—if not strange objects, then part objects and new materials out of which any object might be made, made perhaps by strange hands and in remote places. These objects would no doubt appear to arrive at the household by way of the department store after a long, discontinuous, and apparently arbitrary process that succeeds in destabilizing all sense of the material value of things and of the labor it took to make them. Under these particular circumstances, objects could suddenly acquire mysterious value which one nevertheless had to translate into the status distinctions of polite society or else disrupt that status quo, much as Alice does in imagining she has traded places with the unfortunate Mable and must settle for her meager house and education. Objects would become dangerous, in other words, as their value became increasingly legible as social currency. Alice's dream replicates this transformation of objects in the imperial marketplace. Being a child, however, she works the same distortions on the world of utterly familiar domestic objects. At the simplest level, we may conclude, Carroll's story offered an intricate language of objects for making class distinctions. Not only did it tell adults that such a language was the stuff of fantasy life requiring interventions on the part of official culture; the story also made that language available to successive generations of children.

If the story was indeed produced under the circumstances I have imagined, what, then, does it say about the relationship between such a little girl and British imperialism? For one thing, it tells us that the female body is in some sense the object of objects—the one objectifying the code that regulates them all. For it is Alice's relation to her body that determines the relation of subjects to objects prevailing not only in Wonderland but presumably in the household that will someday quite literally mirror her taste as well. Though contained within a framework marking it as make-believe, the story nevertheless implies that sense itself—the ability of words to dominate things—depends entirely on Alice's ability to dominate an appetite that seems to be only the most direct expression of the body itself. As I have argued, the jar of marmalade is as much the sign of dangerous appetite as of the taste that controls it. Indeed, for taste to exist, appetite must already be present, not in contradiction with taste but as another position along a single continuum of desire.

For it appears that a whole range of cultural practices from nursery to department store worked in concert to produce a desire for objects that appeared irrational to the degree those objects were illegible. As objects were cut off from the history of their production and exchange, taste became less tangible. And as taste became less apparent in things themselves, the quality of objects was apparently transferred onto the consumer. Advertisers consequently began to market their products in terms of such qualities as the female consumer's "belonging, sex appeal, power, distinction, health, togetherness, camaraderie" (Appadurai 56). By a certain point in our own century, "she" had clearly become the object they were selling. Alice brings us in at the beginning of this process. She shows us that no desire for the goods of the Empire was ever free of danger because that desire was located in women. There it took the form of an appetite capable of effacing gender, race, and class; it defined her body as one that could at any time undergo the loss of these distinctions; and it was thus destined to produce fear, not only fear *in* the woman who aspired to middle-class taste, but fear *of* other women who did not bear her distinctive signs of self-control.

IV. EROTICIZING AFRICA

It might be possible to overlook the importance of this image were my argument to remain within the domain of women and children—though that is certainly where I want to locate the center of hegemonic culture. In order to see

how both masculinity and political policy depended on these developments in the feminine and psychological domain, we might turn briefly to H. Rider Haggard's *King Solomon's Mines.* "This novel came off the press in London in September 1885," William Minter tells us, "only six months after the European powers met in Berlin to set the rules for dividing up Africa. An instant success, it sold 31,000 copies in Britain and went through thirteen U.S. editions in the first year alone" (3). Dedicated "to all the big and little boys who read it," Haggard's novel helps to explain where men fit into the psychosexual formation I have been describing; it demonstrates exactly what kind of male is defined in relation to the double-bodied woman who shaped so much of Victorian culture.

To eat in Rider Haggard's Africa is to depend on a nonnurturant woman. Even when the land yields the necessities of life, that food contains possibilities of pollution for Englishmen. It is in such terms that the narrator describes discovering a spring named the "pan of bad water" after days of parched existence in the desert:

> How it came to be in such a strange place we did not stop to inquire, nor did we hesitate at its black and uninviting appearance. It was water, or a good imitation of it, and that was enough for us. We gave a bound and a rush, and in another second were all down on our stomachs sucking up the uninviting fluid as if it were nectar fit for the gods. (287–88)

Even water is black in Africa. Consuming it strangely revitalizes and endangers the white adventurers who grow simultaneously more masculine and less European. As the narrator explains to his English readership, "You, my reader, who have only to turn on a couple of taps and summon 'hot' and 'cold' from an unseen vasty boiler, can have little idea of the luxury of that muddy wallow in brackish, tepid water" (288). Self-restraint makes all the difference, as Conrad would argue within fifteen years or so, in determining whether such moments of the (quite literal) incorporation of Africa will invigorate or corrupt the European.

This becomes particularly apparent when the heroes arrive at another moment of crisis while crossing the frozen mountain peaks that stand between them and the ancient road to Solomon's mines. With what strength remains to them before death by starvation, the Englishmen manage to kill "a great buck." Lacking the fuel with which to cook it, they have to eat raw meat or die. It is with some embarrassment that the narrator recalls this scene for the reader: "It sounds horrible enough, but, honestly, I never tasted anything so good as that raw meat" (296). He offers the fact of their renewal as proof that it was right for the Englishmen to consume this flesh: "In a quarter of an hour we were changed men. Our life and our vigor came back to us, our feeble pulses grew strong again, and the blood went coursing through our veins" (296). The scarcity of Africa may strike us as an antithetical condition to the surplus of consumable items that greets Alice in Wonderland. As one Englishman tells the others, "starving men must not be fanciful" (296). Nevertheless, unregulated eating can be fatal to the bodies of Englishmen in Africa as well. "Mindful of the results of over-feeding on starving stomachs," the narrator invokes the first principle of good taste that is also essential to self-preservation in Alice's world: "we were careful not to eat too much, stopping while we were still hungry" (296). To remain an English girl, Alice must master her own appetite. To remain English men, however, first these Englishmen must squeeze a living from the barren landscape of Africa, and then they have to conquer a bloodthirsty woman.

Although the narrator Quatermain promises, "there is not a *petticoat* in the whole history" (245), this lack of petticoats does not mean an absence of women. For Haggard, the absence of petticoats simply means a lack of women who are properly clothed—a lack, that is, of proper Englishwomen. Indeed, the presence of another

kind of woman permeates the entire story, and the villains of the tale bear the same female defects first discovered by the earliest social scientists and captured by nineteenth-century photographers. These are the terms in which the narrator recalls his initial impression of the witch, Gagoola, terms that elsewhere in the culture distinguished whores and madwomen from decent people. In a scene resembling Jane Eyre's first glimpse of Rochester's "mad, bad and embruted" wife, Quatermain

> observed the wizened, monkey-like figure creeping up from the shadow of the hut. It crept on all fours, but when it reached the place where the king sat it rose upon its feet, and, throwing the furry covering off its face, revealed a most extraordinary and weird countenance. It was (apparently) that of a woman of great age, so shrunken that in size it was no larger than that of a year-old child, and was made up of a collection of deep, yellow wrinkles. Set in the wrinkles was a sunken slit, that represented the mouth, beneath which the chin curved outward to a point. There was no nose to speak of; indeed, the whole countenance might have been taken for that of a sun-dried corpse had it not been for a pair of large black eyes, still full of fire and intelligence, which gleamed and played . . . like jewels in a charnel-house. (Haggard 320–21)

Where the African male is black and often admirable by virtue of his maleness, Gagoola is yellow, a degenerate shade of black that codes her body within Orientalism. There both gender and generational differences disappear into the paradox of the ancient fetus. Like the ugly women in Carroll's narrative, her body provides a space within which the difference between male and female as well as adult and child disintegrates. As women do in *Alice's Adventures,* she enjoys exercising a form of power over her subjects that is murderously antithetical to the maternal role. Men who share her power take on ("cruel and sensuous") feminine features, indicating they share her degeneracy as well (317).

To arrive at the point where they actually confront and overcome this woman, three English adventurers have to travel across a landscape mapped out in much the same sexual terms as Gagoola's body. "I am rendered impotent even before its memory," the narrator confesses. "There straight before us, were two enormous mountains . . . shaped exactly like a woman's breasts" (286). According to the map left to them by a Portuguese adventurer who perished centuries before in search of the mines, the Englishmen must cross a scorching desert and then scale pinnacles that resemble "a woman's breasts" but are in fact a pair of "extinct volcanos" (287). Those who manage to surmount these treacherous peaks descend into territory dominated by homicidal witches before reaching the cave that guards the entrance to the fabled diamond mines.

Lest his readers fail to grasp the heavy-handed symbolism, Haggard provided a map to help them visualize the terrain across which his heroes were travelling—his version of the unconquered territory to the north of the Transvaal in South Africa (Figure 30.13). The map represents this territory as a female figure. According to the logic of the original figure, the incredible wealth within the belly of Africa draws men across a supine female body, enticing them into an opening which could be either the mouth or the genitals—and being either is implicitly both at once. One cannot help but note the resemblance between the map and the body of Gagoola, whose eyes "gleamed and played . . . like jewels in a charnel-house." Both point to the enticing secrets contained within the female body of Africa, knowledge of which could prove lethal for the Europeans to obtain. Given the fact he saw fit to give Africa itself the same body that Europe had given to madwomen and whores, we can well imagine why Haggard brought his story to a close by killing off most of its women along with the men who had fallen

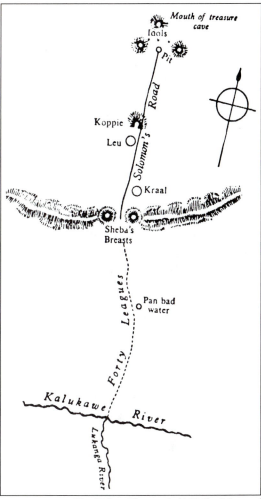

FIGURE 30.13 H. Rider Haggard (1885). Map of Route to King Solomon's Mines. (*Source: King Solomon's Mines.* New York: Dover, 1951.)

under their spell. For the story asks its readers to imagine bringing order to another people by domesticating a dangerous woman.

In describing the poetics of this body of cultural material, I am, as I have suggested, arguing for the causality of an image—a property that only certain images, and often those of the most banal sort, acquired at specific moments in time. This is the power to produce common sense and to make public policy. Modern historiography makes it much easier to understand how Europeans represented Africans and Asians than how bits and pieces of those representations circulated back and forth between fact and fiction to redefine the white middle-class person. Nevertheless, from what we have seen of the exchange between England and its others, it seems altogether possible that an entire class of people—not only authors and intellectuals, but all manner of readers as well as writers—eventually understood who they were as Europeans in relation to an imaginary woman. And thinking of other cultures in terms of her dark and powerful body, these people deemed themselves peculiarly fit to govern Asia and Africa. A paper published in the *Proceedings of the Royal Colonial Institute* for 1869 attributes the unrivaled success of English colonies to the fact that its men were so capable of self-regulation. The report allows that in the "French love of family kind, their cherishing of home ties, their somewhat patriarchal simplicity of life, there is much to admire, much for Englishmen to imitate." But, the author continues, "in the utter absence amongst the French of the vital self governing principle, there is, I apprehend, the fatal source of national stagnation" (Robinson 139). Just as the French lack of self-regulation makes them inferior to the English, their reverence for the family places the French well above those they colonize. While the logic contained in popular images of the female body exalted the national character of each imperial nation, it actually extended beyond nationalism, as the quotation implies, to produce a similar form of male bonding throughout middle-class Europe. This bonding was necessary for empire.

King Solomon's Mines locates England's superiority over Africa not only in the masculine capacity for self-regulation but also in the bond between men. There is never any question in the novel that the homosocial bond is a more important and exalted one than heterosexual love.[16] Cultures where women mix into politics are primitive cultures whose women are markedly unfeminine. The domesticity of European women in turn testifies in turn to the advanced state of its culture. Such a basis for national superiority certainly subordinated women.[17] In making them politically dependent on men, however, the same logic made masculinity symbolically and psychologically dependent on women. Thus each of Haggard's heroes must have a woman in his past. By telling us that marriageable women existed long ago and far away, he also assures the reader that no petticoat will deflect the emotion fusing the three highly individuated men into a single heroic character. At every turn, the perpetuity of the state and the health of the culture depend entirely on maintaining homosocial devotion. But as the ubiquity of bad and ugly women in the tale suggests, such devotion in turn requires her presence along with the absence of English women. Eve Kosofsky Sedgwick has helped us to understand this triangulated configuration as one in which the woman is absolutely necessary.[18] The degraded double of the ideal English woman ensures that the bond among men remains a bond among family-minded men even when they are far away from home. Women of dusky flesh at once embody erotic desire and reduce it to the sordid thrill of gazing. The tales of imperial conquest resemble the photography of whores, madwomen, and natives in that their characteristic maps, pictorial landscapes, and richly detailed description of other peoples inscribed another culture with messages that made it intelligible to Europeans.[19] With seeing, furthermore, came knowing, and with knowing, a sense of themselves as subjects over and above the objects of such a gaze. The eroticism adhering to the disfigured surface of other bodies produced the desire to look and know those bodies, a desire that only reinforced the homosocial bond. Even though the economic machinery of the British empire has been dismantled, something like this psycho-sexual formation remained, I believe, to people postindustrial bureaucracies.

In the last two decades, however, women have begun to cross over into traditionally masculine areas of knowledge. We have gone a long way in articulating a history of ourselves both as women of the dominant class and as the symbolic means by which a class of professional men and managers asserted their authority as subjects over whatever groups they made objects of their analysis. Better understanding of how sexualizing metaphors and domesticating procedures contributed to European domination of Africa and Asia will certainly produce new understanding of the cultural means by which the United States transformed itself from a colony into a "First-World" nation between the end of the eighteenth century and 1916 when Lenin wrote his essay on imperialism. In recent attempts to come to terms with our relationship to people of other classes and cultures, however, a larger stone remains unturned. The new wave of culture criticism still assumes that we must either be a subject who partakes in the power of gazing or else be an object that is by implication the object of a pornographic gaze. The strategy of identifying people according to "subject positions" in a vast and intricate differential system of interests and needs is perhaps the most effective way we now have of avoiding the problem incurred whenever we classify political interests by means of bodies inscribed with signs of race, class, and gender. But even the "subject" of the critical term "subject position" tends to dissolve too readily back into a popular and sentimental version of the bourgeois self. By definition, this self grants priority to an embodied subject over the body as an object. To insist on being "subjects" as opposed to "objects" is to assume that we must have certain powers of observation, classification, and definition in order to exist; these powers make "us" human. According to the logic governing such thinking as it was formulated in the nineteenth century, only certain kinds of subjects are really subjects; to be human, anyone must be one of "us."

If *Alice's Adventures in Wonderland* has a moral to offer contemporary readers, then, it is simply to remind us that objects are neither inert nor speechless. With age, the story suggests, we may have grown unconscious of the heterogeneity of behaviors that are there to be witnessed in objects and of the cacophony of messages that are there to hear. If we feel that objects have gained unprecedented power over our selves, it is perhaps because they do, as Carroll suggests, have the power to classify us as fit for certain social spaces rather than the other way around. And if in fact the message they convey no longer makes objects desirable to us so much as it offers us a self we desire to be, then we have to question the difference between the subjects we believe we are and the images that make it possible for us to see ourselves that way. Without "them," it would seem, there would be none of "us." For *Alice* makes it impossible to imagine middle-class culture either without a dazzling array of unrelated things or without men and women convinced that their status as subjects has something to do with their ability to classify and control that world of objects. The late Victorian construction of gender becomes especially meaningful here.

If there is any truth in my reading of *Alice,* taste is an important means of controlling objects. At the moment in the nineteenth century when things went haywire, taste became the privilege and obligation of women. It identified a specific relationship with objects as the distinguishing features of the female subject; she was what she bought, wore, and put in her house. Upon her self-restraint rested the well-being of British husbands and children, the well-being, in a word, of the nation itself. Upon the presence in her of a dangerous appetite for things, however, rested the whole premise that such taste was necessary, for what else if not her appetite made those objects so desirable? In this respect, it was less important to the national interest if men remained men in the sense defined by Haggard than if women remained women in the sense defined by Carroll. Englishmen may have been peculiarly suited to the imperial venture of domesticating Africa and Asia. But English-women were responsible for putting the objects that flooded in from the colonies in place. To do so, women had to want such objects, and once they did, women became dangerous. With the desire that began to inhabit their bodies some-time during the last decades of the nineteenth century came the possibility that women would someday overthrow the empire of middle-class consciousness and succumb entirely to the allure of the new object world.

This idea began as a paper when I was a Rockefeller Fellow at the Center for the Humanities at Wesleyan University in 1987–88 and grew into its present form during 1989–90 when I had the good fortune to return to the Center. My gratitude goes out to my colleagues at the Center during those years, as well as to former director Richard Vann and present director Richard Ohmann, for providing a genial and challenging intellectual environment in which to work. Special thanks also go to Andrew Szegedy-Maszak, who was the inspiration behind my discussion of photography, the group at the Foundary Café, Evan Watkins, Laura Wexler, and Michael Trask.

NOTES

1. In *Family Fortunes*, Leonore Davidoff and Catherine Hall show how the separation of English home from work-place gave new economic meaning to the home, and the demonstrable well-being of a man's domestic circum-stances began testifying to the prosperity of his business. According to Robert Fishman, elites continued to live in the center of the city during most of the eighteenth century while the lower classes occupied its outer margins. During the early nineteenth century, however, these positions shifted. London merchants began to convert their com-bined home and offices into office and to relocate their families in the agricultural environment immediately sur-rounding the city (Fishman 18–38). This was the same pe-riod when the English economy was particularly prone to

sudden waves of inflation and the banking system tem-porarily abandoned the gold standard (Ashton). According to Davidoff and Hall, those men blessed by a substantial home in the suburbs not only solidified their economic hold over England at this time but also established their peculiar manner of domestic life as the standard of one's capacity for self management. Simply by translating their argument from national into international terms, we can imagine how men who lived this way of life might have ex-tended credit to those with whom they did business abroad, credit for having a house, garden, wife, children, and domestic help similar to their own.

2. Lenin, for example, could look at the Europe of 1916 as one dominated by an international bourgeoisie, a class whose members were quarrelling among themselves for control of what is now called "the Third World." Despite internal tension, it was a class united by a common culture, while the working classes remained sadly divided by race, region, and ethnicity. Lenin ended his famous essay *Impe-rialism* in bewilderment. He could not understand what went wrong with Marx's earlier prediction that the workers of the world would unite to form an international class while the ruling class would contract and divide under the pressure of intensifying competition (123–28).

3. In *Mammon and the Pursuit of Empire*, Lance E. Davis and Robert A. Huttenback acknowledge, "Of all the expla-nations of Empire, none is more compelling than the one concerned with economic gain" (6). However, viewing the economics of empire with the eye of some nineteenth-cen-tury skeptics, Davis and Huttenback explore the degree to which "Britain's prosperity in the late nineteenth century [was] dependent on its economic and political relations with its Empire" (7). They find that while maintaining an empire definitely profited some, it cost England as a whole.

4. Henry Mayhew's *London Labour and the London Poor*, Vol. IV, provides an excellent demonstration of how socio-logical interest in urban crime interlocked conceptually with anthropological focus on primitive cultures. Less than ten pages into their study of the criminal types comprising the category of "those who will not work," Mayhew felt compelled to define prostitution and describe its varieties from ancient times to the present day in all the known countries of the world: "The general design of this inquiry will be to draw a view of the position occupied by the fe-male sex in different ages and countries, to measure the es-timation in which it was held, to fix the accepted standard of morality, to ascertain the recognised significance of the marriage contract, the laws relating to polygamy and con-cubinage, the value at which feminine virtue and modesty

were held, and thus to consider the prostitute in relation to the system of which she formed a part" (37). In this way, Mayhew's research extended the use of a particular brand of heterosexual monogamy from criminalizing the English underclasses to primitivizing other cultures. Thus he converted the particular way in which his class of people regarded women into a universal system of evaluating human beings.

5. Of particular importance in this regard was the rise of physical anthropology championed in England by The Anthropological Society of London. For an account of their attempt to formulate an all-encompassing paradigm linking biological superiority to European features, see Rainger.

6. This Act allowed a grace period of 42 days before the baby had to be registered, and it did not require stillbirths to be registered. Thus there was still considerable opportunity to conceal a baby's existence. For a discussion of this problem, see Rose 121.

7. It should be noted that the procedures for examining prostitutes under the Contagious Diseases Acts were already working, however unconsciously, within a model that detected symmetrical disfigurations at both ends of the female body. William Acton proposes the following list of symptoms gathered from twenty-four female patients admitted to St. Bartholemew's Hospital (26 November, 1840): "1. Bubo, sore at the entrance to vagina. 2. Sores. 3. Condylomata, excoriation. 4. Itch, gonorrhoea, excoriation. 5. Suppurating bubo, gonorrhea. 6. Warts, gonorrhea. 7. Very large sores on thighs. 8. Two large sores on vulva, two buboes. 9. Gonorrhoea, excoriated tongue. 10. Excoriations around the anus. 11. Condylamata of the vulva (very red), two bulboes. 12. Very large condylamata, excoriation of the throat. 13. Condylamata, itch, and a curious eruption. 14. A small sore on vulva, eruption on body, sore throat. 15. Discharge from vagina, raised condylomata. 16. Sores on the labium, perhaps primary. 17. Condylomata. 18. Eczema, itch, phagedaenic sores. 19. Condylomata, excoriation very extensive. 20. Very large condylomata, white excoriation between toes, and on throat. 21. Condylomata, very extensive affectation of the tongue. 22. Condylomata. 23. Discharge from vagina, superficial ulceration. 24. Two buboes, condylomata." I simply want to note that when Acton names an afflicted body part, it is either in the mouth or genital area. He not only zones and links these two areas in examining infected prostitutes but also turns this list into a system for gathering future data. "As each patient is inspected," he suggests, "make a cross upon the proper line, and when the consul-

tation is over, you will have a tabulated view of the forms of disease it has presented to your notice" (52).

8. This practice is closely related to the claims of a reverse Darwinism. See, for example, Pick and Gilman 191–216. It is not surprising to find the attack on the women's movement in the nineteenth century representing such activists as physiologically unlike the "normal" European woman. Cynthia Eagle Russet quotes a Victorian anthropologist who "denounced the 'superficial, flat-chested, thin-voiced Amazons, who are pouring forth sickening prate about the tyranny of men and the slavery of women'" (27).

9. Interestingly, the European prostitute in the colonies threatened to break down the categorical distinction between the two kinds of bodies. Margaret MacMillan writes: "Although a speaker at a meeting on 'Social Evil' in Bombay in 1891 congratulated himself that there was not a single English girl among them, it was feared that Indians might not be able to see the distinction. Not surprisingly, there was also concern in official and unofficial circles over pornography that involved European women" (53).

10. It is important to realize that from early on the nascent art of advertising used the colonial body to ply its wares. See, for example, Richards 119–67.

11. Nina Auerbach has described this fall as "a loving parody of Genesis" and linked it to Alice's appetite.

12. Rémy G. Saisselin offers a useful encapsulation of the historical forces that made possible this regendering—and thus the restaging—of consumption:

> For the first time in history the women of the bourgeoisie found themselves free and with leisure time, whereas formerly they had tended to stay at home and participate in the economic life of the household. The capital accumulation of the nineteenth century made it possible for women of this class to enjoy a certain leisure, leave their interiors, and lead a form of aristocratic life modeled on that of the old nobility. The men worked to assure the women the possibility of conspicuous consumption. This contrast of occupations between men and women was manifest even in their dress: the masculine fashions remained sober, economic, puritan even, while the feminine costume or dress was allowed to be courtly, that is, colorful, luxurious, flowing, impractical, expensive, decorative. Women set the fashion rather than men, as had been the case in the old courtly society. (42)

13. As Frank Mort has argued, a double standard in sexual conduct for men and women shaped the new sexology

whereby male continence was desirable but could not be guaranteed because of the strength of the male urge (79). What could be guaranteed was female purity and therefore their impurity as well. Around midcentury, he explains, this

> had a profound effect on class-specific forms of male sexuality. . . . Both written and visual pornography represented women for the male gaze across the virtue/vice, innocence/depravity oppositions. The clearest examples were in the early photographic studies of child prostitutes dating from the 1860s and 1870s, where childhood innocence was erotically framed against visible signs of immoral sexuality, such as exposed genitalia or the depraved stare. (84)

These and other examples, he continues, "reveal a link between the growing polarization of official definitions of female sexuality and the sexualization of those representations in the fantasies of certain groups of men" (86). Particularly germane to my argument, first, is Mort's description of child porn as a genre that transplants the features of the other woman (exposed genitalia and a depraved stare) onto its very antithesis, the English girl. Second is his use of the double figure of the woman to explain how male desire was historically deflected away from marriageable English women and onto women with whom it was culturally impossible to mate.

14. For a discussion of possible sources for the Duchess illustrations, see Hancher 41–47. Many of my observations on the Alice illustrations, esp. the contrast between Carroll's sketches for *Alice's Adventures under Ground* and Tenniel's illustrations for *Alice's Adventures in Wonderland,* are informed by his research.

15. See Raymond Williams, *Long,* esp. his discussion of the growth of the reading public and popular press, 156–213.

16. Wayne Koestenbaum has discussed the homosocial erotics of Haggard's writing for the "boy-reader" who was "often a grown man" (151–61). Koestenbaum suggests that the rise of pure romance by male authors in the latter half of the nineteenth century offered "a refuge not only from women's fiction, but from an England that they imagined Queen Victoria had feminized" (153). Such writing obviously served the interests of empire as it asserted the manliness of men who were attached to each other by representing the bond between men as that which held the empire together.

17. In her critique of Gareth Stedman Jones's *Languages of Class,* Joan Scott demonstrates that Chartism was in part defeated by the unconscious sexism of its rhetoric. Scott writes, "The 'language' of class, as Chartists spoke it, placed women (and children) in auxiliary and dependent positions. If women mounted speakers' platforms, organized consumer boycotts, and founded special societies of their own, they did so under the Chartist aegis to demand male suffrage and thus assert property rights that came to them through their husbands' and fathers' labor" (64–65). Thus the Chartists acceded to the dominant concept of gender when they made a deal to remove women from the labor pool and base their political rights on the fact that ownership of one's labor entitles one to political rights because it defines one as male. Economic dependency is automatically feminizing within such a frame of reference, feminizing and politically disenfranchising at once.

18. Sedgwick represents the kind of anxiety animating late eighteenth-century fiction as one of the preconditions necessary for the kind of bonding that could maintain an empire. For such anxiety, she says, the "term is 'homophobia.' In the English Gothic novel, the possibility—the attraction, the danger—of simply dropping the female middle term becomes an explicit, indeed an obsessional literary subject. With it comes a much more tightly organized, openly proscriptive approach to sexuality and homosocial bonding" (82).

19. Thomas Richards describes a picture of a group of nomadic Arabs gaping at the slogan "Pear's soap is the best" chalked on a cliff in the middle of the desert. Above this picture appears the claim that the product is "the formula of British conquest." According to Richards, "the real significance of this claim—perhaps the largest promise made by an advertisement in the nineteenth century—lies less in its practical application than in the fact that it was used by English imperialist of the 1890s to represent commodities as a magic medium through which English power and influence could be enforced and enlarged in the colonial world" (122–23). This observation could, I think, apply as well to the map that Haggard includes in his story and the prosthetic gadgets that Good carries into the desert, giving him supernatural powers in the eyes of the natives.

WORKS CITED

Abelson, Elaine S. *When Ladies Go A-Thieving: Middle-Class Shoplifters in the Victorian Department Store.* New York: Oxford UP, 1989.

Acton, William. *Prostitution Considered in its Moral, Social, and Sanitary Aspects.* London: Cass, 1972.

Appadurai, Arjun, ed. *The Social Life of Things: Commodities in Cultural Perspective.* Cambridge: Cambridge UP, 1986.

Armstrong, Nancy. *Desire and Domestic Fiction: a Political History of the Novel.* New York: Oxford UP, 1987.

Ashton, T. S. "The Bill of Exchange and Private Banks in Lancashire, 1790–1830." *Papers in English Monetary History.* Ed. T. S. Ashton and R. S. Sayers. London: Clarendon, 1953. 37–108.

Auerbach, Nina. "Falling Alice, Fallen Women, and Victorian Dream Children." *Soaring with the Dodo: Essays on Lewis Carroll's Life and Art.* Ed. Edward Guiliano and James R. Kincaid. *Carroll Studies* 6 (1982): 46–64.

Barthes, Roland. *Mythologies.* Trans. Annette Lavers. New York: Farrar, 1972.

Bolt, Christine. "Race and the Victorians." *British Imperialism in the Nineteenth Century.* Ed. C. C. Eldridge. New York: St. Martin's, 1984. 126–47.

Bowlby, Rachel. *Just Looking: Consumer Culture in Dreiser, Gissing and Zola.* New York: Methuen, 1985.

Brontë, Charlotte. *Jane Eyre.* Ed. Richard I. Dunn. New York: Norton, 1971.

Carroll, Lewis. *Alice's Adventures in Wonderland and Through the Looking Glass.* New York: New American, 1960.

Conrad, Joseph. *Heart of Darkness: an Authoritative Text, Backgrounds, Sources, and Essays in Criticism.* Ed. Robert Kimbrough. New York: Norton, 1963.

Davidoff, Leonore, and Catherine Hall. *Family Fortunes: Men and Women of the English Middle Class, 1780–1850.* Chicago: U of Chicago P, 1987.

Davis, Keith F. *Désiré Charnay, Expeditionary Photographer.* Albuquerque: U of New Mexico P, 1981.

Davis, Lance E., and Robert A. Huttenback. *Mammon and the Pursuit of Empire: The Economics of British Imperialism.* Abridged Edition. Cambridge: Cambridge UP, 1988.

Fishman, Robert. *Bourgeois Utopias: The Rise and Fall of Suburbia.* New York: Basic, 1987.

Foucault, Michel. *The History of Sexuality, An Introduction.* Trans. Robert Hurley. New York: Pantheon. 1978. Vol. 1 of *The History of Sexuality.* 3 vols, 1978–86.

Gernsheim, Helmut. *Julia Margaret Cameron, her Life and Photographic Work.* New York: Aperture, 1975.

Gilman, Sandor L. *Difference and Pathology: Stereotypes of Sexuality, Race and Madness.* Ithaca: Cornell UP, 1985.

Great Britain. *Reports from the Select Committees on the Contagious Diseases Bill and Act* (1866). British Parliamentary Papers: Health. Infectious Disease Vol. 4. Shannon: Irish UP, 1970.

Haggard, H. Rider. *Three Adventure Novels: She, King Solomon's Mines, Allan Quatermain.* New York: Dover, 1951.

Hancher, Michael. *The Tenniel Illustrations to the "Alice" Books.* Columbus: Ohio State UP, 1985.

Koestenbaum, Wayne. *Double Talk: The Erotics of Male Literary Collaboration.* New York: Routledge, 1989.

Lenin, V. I. *Imperialism, The Highest Stage of Capitalism.* New York: International, 1985.

Levy, Anita. "Blood, Kinship, and Gender." *Genders* 5 (1989): 70–85.

MacMillan, Margaret. *Women of the Raj.* London: Thames and Hudson, 1988.

Marable, Darwin. "Photography and Human Behaviour in the Nineteenth Century." *History of Photography* 9 (1985): 141–47.

Marx, Karl. "The Fetishism of the Commodity and its Secret." *Capital: A Critique of Political Economy.* Vol. 1. Trans. Ben Fowkes. New York: Vintage, 1977. 163–77. 3 vols.

Mayhew, Henry. *London Labour and the London Poor.* Vol. 4. New York: Dover, 1968. 4 vols.

Minter, William. *King Solomon's Mines Revisited: Western Interests and the Burdened History of Southern Africa.* New York: Basic, 1986.

Mort, Frank. *Dangerous Sexualities: Medico-Moral Politics in England since 1830.* London: Routledge, 1987.

Ovenden, Graham. *A Victorian Album: Juliet Margaret Cameron and her Circle.* New York: Da Capo, 1975.

Pick, Daniel. *Faces of Degeneration: A European Disorder, c. 1848–1918.* Cambridge: Cambridge UP, 1989.

Rainger, Ronald. "Race, Politics, and Science: The Anthropological Society in the 1860s." *Victorian Studies* 22 (1978): 51–70.

Richards, Thomas. *The Commodity Culture of Victorian England: Advertising and Spectacle, 1851–1914.* Palo Alto: Stanford UP, 1990.

Robinson, J. "The Social Aspects of Colonisation." *Proceedings of the Royal Colonial Institute* 1 (1870): 135–61.

Rose, Lionel. *Massacre of the Innocents: Infanticide in Great Britain 1800–1939.* London: Routledge, 1986.

Russett, Cynthia Eagle. *Sexual Science: The Victorian Construction of Womanhood.* Cambridge: Harvard UP, 1989.

Said, Edward W. *Orientalism.* New York: Vintage, 1979.

Saisselin, Rémy G. *The Bourgois and the Bibelot.* New Brunswick: Rutgers UP, 1984.

Scott, Joan Wallach. *Gender and the Politics of History.* New York: Columbia UP, 1988.

Sedgwick, Eve Kosofsky. *Between Men: English Literature and Male Homosocial Desire.* New York: Columbia UP, 1985.

Sekula, Allan. "The Body and the Archive." *October* 59 (1986): 3–64.

Showalter, Elaine. *The Female Malady: Women, Madness, and English Culture 1830–1980.* New York: Pantheon, 1985.

Stocking, George. *Victorian Anthropology.* New York: Macmillan, 1987.

Tarnowsky, Pauline. *Etude anthropométrique sur les prostituées et les voleuses.* Paris: Lecroisnier, 1889.

Thompson, E. P. *The Making of the English Working Class.* New York: Random, 1966.

Walkowitz, Judith. *Prostitution and Victorian Society: Women, Class, and the State.* Cambridge: Cambridge UP, 1980.

Wicke, Jennifer. *Advertising Fictions: Literature, Advertisement, and Social Reading.* New York: Columbia UP, 1988.

Williams, Raymond. *The Long Revolution.* Westport: Greenwood, 1975.

PART VIII

Feminism and Gender Studies

Many instances of work being done in contemporary feminist criticism, Susan Sheridan writes in *Grafts: Feminist Cultural Criticism,* "advocate and enact heterogeneity, not as a politically naive pluralism but as an insistence on the complexity of cultural discourses and practices and on the diversity of positions from which feminists engage with them." Her comment can be expanded to say that the current scene, encompassing feminism and gender studies, is so broad that an actual survey of directions and interests would be quickly outdated and impractical. Vastly complicating the picture are the many strong alliances of thought and practice that feminism and gender studies have with cultural studies, Marxist criticism, science studies, and psychoanalysis. It would not even be possible to draw the boundaries with any accuracy between these alliances and what Diana Fuss calls in this section "hybrid positions" ("cyborgs," in Donna Haraway's word [see "Cultural Studies" (Part IX)]). Evident in this activity and cultural reorientation is the urgency to understand literature and culture from a variety of viewpoints—some of which are traditionally defined as "feminine" and homosocial but have only recently been liberated into active cultural expression. In "The Story So Far" (in *The Feminist Reader*) Catherine Belsey and Jane Moore give a sense of how great the effect of feminist studies has been in recent years. In 1970, they write, "three revolutionary books appeared within a few months of each other . . . Germaine Greer's *The Female Eunuch,* Kate Millett's *Sexual Politics* and *Patriarchal Attitudes* by Eva Figes." "It comes as something of a shock," they continue, "to encounter 'he' as the generalized pronoun in these books published in 1970."

At the time of publication of these books, there was little engagement with the areas of psychoanalytic and philosophical discourse that since have become a part of the feminist and gender critique of culture. This limited engagement was apparent in *Sexual Politics* in Millett's dismissal of psychoanalysis as focused exclusively on a theory of "penis-envy." The subsequent, quite different tendency actually to appropriate "theory" of all kinds (especially psychoanalysis) in feminist and gender criticism has empowered feminist and gender critics not only to "identify representations of sexuality and female desire" but to "demonstrate how meanings work and how they can be challenged." "This is done," Belsey and Moore go on, "by seeking out uncertainties—the problems, ambiguities and, above all, contradictions, which the representations reveal." That search for ambiguities has opened gender studies beyond merely traditional representations of women, whether hetero- or homosocial, and has enabled feminists and gender critics to explore the social constructions of gender, even those not explicitly configured as male/female, straight/gay, and so on.

The idea of cultural reorientation, of course, has always been a part of feminist and gender studies. In the last chapter of *Criticism and Culture* ("Notes Towards a Definition of Cultural Studies"), we survey a version of this reorientation, noting Elaine Showalter's 1979 description in "Toward a Feminist Poetics" of a new mode of reading occasioned by feminism and the kind of "androcentric" reading Patrocinio Schweickart cites in "Reading Ourselves: Toward a Feminist Theory of Reading" (in "Rhetoric and Reader Response" [Part III]) that had obscured this mode of reading. But the reorientations occasioned by feminism and gender studies have gone further than the opposition between male and female that governed feminist literary and cultural criticism of the 1970s to encompass viewpoints that were never known before (or were never recognized), including those in gay/lesbian culture. The "most urgent [contemporary] articulation" of these problems of reading, as Diana Fuss comments in this section, are the posttechnological and avant-garde prose experiments of Donna Haraway's work. Such viewpoints are emerging in the texts of current technoculture as subjectivities "in a post-gender world" that, as Haraway says, has "no truck with bisexuality, pre-oedipal symbiosis, unalienated labour, or other seductions to organic wholeness through a final appropriation of all the power of the parts into a higher unity." In the recent avant-gardist developments of feminist and gender studies is the assumption of a diversity of genders and even gender possibilities, according to Haraway and Kathy Acker, that can be conceived only in relation to cybernetic culture, computer interface, and virtual space.

This complex situation is somewhat clarified in terms of the survey of feminist literary criticism that Fuss presents in "Reading Like a Feminist." Fuss foregrounds the issue of "essentialism," or what is taken for granted, assumed, or presented as "natural" in discourse. In her essay, she focuses on a range of attitudes in contemporary criticism in order to ask the question, "What is it exactly that underwrites and subtends the notion of a class of women or a class of men reading?" She repeatedly returns to the issue of essentialism—that which is assumed and not analyzed—and discusses the "essential" foundations that tend to "ground," or provide the enabling assumptions for, current critiques of patriarchal culture advanced in the name of feminism. Her discussion surveys positions that assume biological (or "natural"), linguistic, psychoanalytic, and cultural "grounds" (in J. Hillis Miller's term in "What Is Literary Theory?" [Part II]) of particular ways of reading. Feminist approaches also draw from similar areas of contemporary critical thought (as well as others), and we have included examples of each of these four starting points in this collection. In "Cultural Studies" (Part IX), Donna Haraway's "A Cyborg Manifesto" draws on science, technological studies, and psychoanalysis in her exploration of the figure of the cyborg (and its artificial "biology") in contemporary technoculture. In the same way, Schweickart's essay in "Rhetoric and Reader Response" (Part III) examines the linguistic strategies of literature from a feminist viewpoint, and again that orientation encompasses biological, psychological, and cultural concerns within its rhetorical approach. In "Reading Like a Feminist," Fuss considers Jacques Lacan's "poststructuralist psychoanalysis" as a way of focusing on the "destabilizing and decentering" examination of the idea of the "subject" from psychoanalysis—both the "I" who speaks and the context and mechanism that enables that "I" to speak. (Teresa de Lauretis, in "Structuralism and Semiotics" [Part IV], and Laura Mulvey, in "Psychology and Psychoanalysis" [Part VI], also examine the relationship between psychoanalysis and feminism.) A feminist consideration of psychoanalysis also tends to highlight the question of sexual difference, linguistic strategies, and cultural understanding within that framework. A good example of the cultural interweaving of approaches is the essay by Catherine Belsey in "Deconstruction and Poststructuralism" (Part V). Belsey weaves together the discourses of psychoanalysis, deconstruction, and Marxism to articulate the multifaceted analysis of the representations of women in "realistic" fiction—in Sherlock Holmes stories—to situate those representations within the cultural formations of subjectivity, literature, and ideology. Similarly, Nancy Armstrong (in "Historical Criticism" [Part VII]) offers a "cultural" reading of *Alice in Wonderland* that is conditioned by feminism.

The essays of this section on feminism and gender studies similarly focus on the large cultural questions of politics, literary history, the psychoanalytics of (gendered) subjectivity, and even the relationship of science and "knowledge" in relation to gender. Gender studies as a broad category, in short, comprises the set of issues in various disciplines pertinent to cultural experience that is understood to be always in some relation to gender categories. Just as we suggested in the introduction to "What Is Literary Theory?" (Part II) that ethics is not a simple "object" of study, but rather a set of questions and concerns that are implicated in all areas of study, so in a like way gender is not simply an "object" of study but a way of critiquing and understanding an array of traditional and conventional ideas. That is, feminism and gender studies challenge literary and culture theory to confront the difficult task of assimilating the findings of an expanding sphere of inquiry, including—as we see here—forms of *interdisciplinary* inquiry.

FEMINIST LITERARY AND CULTURAL CRITICISM

As Catherine Belsey and Jane Moore point out, modern feminist criticism continues to be deeply indebted to the work of two writers, Virginia Woolf and Simone de Beauvoir. Their criticism exemplifies the strength as well as the challenge of literary feminism as social critique and as an aesthetic of women's texts or an explanation of how writing by women manifests a *distinctively* female discourse. Woolf displays this dual awareness in *A Room of One's Own* (1924) when she describes women's writing as shaped primarily by its focus and less by the "shadow across the page" (the imposition of ego) characteristic of male discourse. Woolf suggests a model for understanding literary texts. This model contains textual alinearity and plasticity, which Woolf designates as "female," and in contrast to alinearity she places the tendency toward hegemony and rigidity, which she associates with being male. This two-part model guides her understanding of women in a patriarchal culture: they are displaced socially in relation to the "shadow" that the ego of the privileged male casts starkly across Western culture. Woolf's "room of one's own," a domain that allows women both privacy and economic freedom, simultaneously incorporates the interiority of female discourse and the social sanctuary within which a woman may develop strength.

Simone de Beauvoir in *The Second Sex* (1949) most pointedly criticizes patriarchal culture and analyzes the marginal position of women in society and the arts. She describes a male-dominated social discourse within which particular misogynist practices occur. Tending toward a Marxist analysis—and anticipating Shulamith Firestone—de Beauvoir posits a capitalist base of political and economic oppression with a kind of "superstructure" of sexist literature and art. De Beauvoir finds reflections of socioeconomic injustices in what she sees as fundamentally imitative modes of literature (literature conceived as "reflecting" a social reality). While her work illustrates a double focus also evident in Woolf's criticism, it tends to dismiss literary production per se as a strict reflection (mimesis) of social and ideological schemes.

De Beauvoir and Woolf mark out the terrain of feminist literary criticism from social critique to feminist aesthetic and discourse. Elaine Showalter projects the same picture for women's culture with her idea (most fully articulated in "Toward a Feminist Poetics" but also discussed in "Feminist Criticism in the Wilderness") of two "distinct varieties" of feminist criticism as directed toward either *the woman as reader* or *the woman as writer.* "Woman as reader" focuses on the significance of sexual codes ("woman-as-sign") in a historical and political context. This is socially oriented criticism with strong connections to de Beauvoir's critique. "Woman as writer" focuses on the four categories of gender difference we have already discussed. This second focus is close to Woolf's concern and is the area of feminism that Showalter christens *gynocritics* (in "Toward a Feminist Poetics")—"a female framework for the analysis of women's literature" beginning "at the point when we free ourselves from the linear absolutes of male literary history"—the "malestream," as Sheridan says. From the work of "gynocriticism," as Showalter writes, "the lost continent of the female tradition has risen like Atlantis from the sea of English literature."

Extraordinarily influential and still in the process of having an impact in the United States (we included her work in earlier editions of this book) is Hélène Cixous. Through her fiction, criticism, and drama, she has attempted to free readers, female and male, from patriarchal linear absolutes. In essays such as "Castration or Decapitation?" and "Laugh of the Medusa" she enacts a performative critique of patriarchal textual practices. Cixous combines the categories of woman as reader and woman as writer in a wide-ranging literary practice that, as Annette Kuhn has noted, is what Cixous herself calls a "woman-text," "a return of the repressed feminine that with its energetic, joyful, and transgressive 'flying in language and making it fly' dislocates the repressive structures of phallologocentrism." "Cixous's own work," Kuhn continues, offers a practice of writing "that aims to do this by positing plurality against unity; multitudes of meanings against single, fixed meanings; diffuseness against instrumentality; openness against closure." Such performative discourse is what Rachel Blau DuPlessis calls "situational," "a both/and vision born of shifts, contraries, negations, contradictions; linked to personal vulnerability and need." In *The Newly-Born Woman,* Cixous and Catherine Clement write a manifesto of such "shifts" away from "single, fixed meanings." They identify strategies of understanding—"exits," "escapes," and "opportunities" (*sorties*)—outside of the traditional understandings of the "malestream" culture dominated by men.

The difficulty of generating and then sustaining such discourse is formidable. Gayatri Chakravorty Spivak in "Feminism and Critical Theory," for example, discusses the "discourse of the clitoris." In this discourse, she describes a feminine dimension of culture as "women's excess in all areas of production and practice, an excess which must be brought under control [according to patriarchal culture] to keep business going as usual." In women's culture, where we find the discourse of excess, writing is not unified but scattered and "lost" along discontinuous and irregular channels. This version of writing under female authority, distinct from the "phallic" continuity and linearity of male writing, is unavoidably difficult (from a patriarchal perspective) precisely because as we attempt to reconceive writing in such different economies, we are inevitably trying to reconceive humans in relation to the world; even the world itself is being reconceived. (Shoshana Felman addresses the issue of reformulating the nature of human experience in her essay in "Psychology and Psychoanalysis" [Part VI].) Such difficulty is not merely what George Steiner calls a "tactical" problem, or language deployed strategically to jar us from old perceptual patterns. Rather, the difficulty of such feminist discourse goes deeper, to what Steiner calls the "ontological" level (some feminists would say "biological")—the raising of "questions," as Steiner says, "about the nature of human speech [and] about the status of significance." Such discourse forces us to reconceive the very concepts and relations of "self" and "world." The final conclusion of these developments in feminist criticism would be a grand enterprise, indeed—a "field theory," an explanation of the whole range of gender's impact on literature, virtually an ultimate correction of all the world's errors and mysteries, what Nietzsche calls in a very different context a "healing" of the "eternal wound of existence." Like other great inquiries of the twentieth century, to the extent that feminist literary and cultural theory attempt to encompass the entire gender dialectic, the dimensions of Woolf's "room of one's own" and all that lies within its walls, feminism (as de Lauretis, Belsey, Armstrong, Haraway, and others in this book all note) presses on the very questions about private and public life, culture and power, female and male authority that demand attention in the modern and postmodern world.

Cora Kaplan's "Pandora's Box: Subjectivity, Class and Sexuality in Socialist Feminist Criticism," included in this section, maps out this broad terrain. She particularly explores what has happened in contemporary criticism to combine the perspectives of feminist theory and Marxist-socialist theory. How well do these approaches work together, and what has come of attempts to unite in one approach the strengths of each? Kaplan's answer is that the "reports of feminist nuptials with . . . mustachioed Marxism have been greatly exaggerated." The most evident potential incompatibility with Marxism and other forms of "androcentric . . . criticism" is the prospect of feminism's being assimilated and neutralized. In other words, "an unequal[,] dependent alliance with any of the varieties of male-centered criticism" could result in a kind of annexation of feminism and a blunting beyond recognition of its critique of gender in patriarchal culture.

While the danger of assimilation for feminism was perhaps great at one time, the present difficulty of feminist criticism derives more from its evident success. Feminist

criticism has succeeded very well in producing an "autonomous analysis" and critique
of gender and an explanation of gendered mechanisms that produce ill effects for
women in local areas of culture. But the power of that "autonomous analysis" to address and explain the local *effects* of gender has left feminist criticism underdeveloped
in other areas, some of them crucial to the fortunes of women. Kaplan argues that
while feminist criticism has at times been "radical in its discussion of gender," in the
broader expanse where we can view the effect of its work, feminist criticism has remained "implicitly conservative in its assumptions about social hierarchy and female
subjectivity." That is, Kaplan projects a scenario in which feminist analysis should
move further toward understanding the social determinations of its condition, toward an understanding of its social positioning in terms of social class to "other forms
of social determination." Without a radical social critique, she argues, feminist criticism would be isolated from the very social processes it needs to be addressing in order to further its work—or, rather, to have any real work to do. Accordingly, she
writes that if feminist criticism is to do more than serve "as a conservative refuge from
[gender difference's] more disturbing social and psychic implications, the inclusion of
class and race must transform its terms and objectives."

Kaplan argues that there is a veritable "Pandora's box" of feminist criticism in the
question of "female subjectivity," a concept that touches on all issues of women's lives
and culture—issues that range from the psychic life of actual women and the "construction" of women's social roles in relation to men and to each other, to the way
women as a group intersect with lines of power in social and political struggle, including the broadest sweep of women as a disempowered class in history. The "problem for feminism" in dealing with such a vast but unavoidable area has prompted,
historically, the rise of "three main strategies to deal with it." The first involves positing "women's psychic life" as "essentially identical to men's." In this strategy, any contrary evidence suggesting distinctiveness in women's culture or a significant difference
between men and women is attributed to the "vicious" colorings of the patriarchal
world. The second strategy, by contrast, says that women in their nature are wholly
and inherently different from men. Kaplan comments that this assumption about the
nature of being female and of being male is cited frequently by radical feminists as a
defense for the establishment and maintenance of a separate cultural sphere for
women, as in the positing of "female sexuality as independent and virtuous between
women, but degrading in a heterosexual context" (this is the strong suggestion raised
in Adrienne Rich's "Compulsory Heterosexuality and Lesbian Existence," an essay we
considered for inclusion in this section). The third strategy refuses the question of
gender construction as such and, instead, focuses exclusively on ideology.

For Kaplan, the power of "female subjectivity" as an area of inquiry derives from
the fact that "subjectivity," in whatever strategy it is defined, is the grounding of all
the elaborations appearing in culture under the heading of "female," "women's lives,"
"women's culture," "feminist," and so on. In this way, "female subjectivity" is both the
inevitable site for making social change and the site of greatest vexation, the site most
difficult to access for analysis because it runs through all of culture and is manifested
in everything and everywhere under the categories of identity, difference, and historical (ideological) determination. Kaplan's strategy for dealing with such complexity is

to move away from universal representations of women's experience as substantial fact. Instead of seeking support and evidence for apparently universal and "objective" generalizations about women (the ideological motivation of which is hidden under the "objective" status), Kaplan proposes to reinsert all such representations for critique and analysis within historical contexts. "It is that [specific] history" of the female subject, she writes, "which we must uncover and consider." Only "through that analysis [of the historicized female subject] we can work towards change."

Judith Butler is one of three critics included in this section who specifically take up the challenge of understanding the female subject. Butler's particular task is to walk her readers through work by Simone de Beauvoir, Jean Paul Sartre, Monique Wittig, and Michel Foucault to show the difficulty of understanding and defining subjectivity in relation to the materiality of the body. One sign of the difficulty encountered here is that any one definition of subjectivity, or "female subjectivity," must work in three areas—in relation to what actual women experience in their personal lives, in relation to how "woman" functions as a social signifier in patriarchal discourse, and in relation to how the category of "woman" can be used to critique that discourse. Gender categories such as "woman" are at once the starting point of the investigation of gendered subjectivities and the effect that patriarchal societies work toward constructing. Butler highlights this doubleness surrounding gendered subjectivity—"woman" as the category that allows one to think about and also to critique the notion of a female subject in patriarchal culture—when she quotes Simone de Beauvoir in saying that "one is not born [a woman]." Rather, in socialization one "becomes a woman"—"woman" as preexistent category and also as the personal achievement of actual female subjects.

In "Variations on Sex and Gender: Beauvoir, Wittig and Foucault," Butler explores the social construction of gender sufficiently to show the ways in which, as a concept, it is at once both liberating and confining. Butler draws on Simone de Beauvoir's *The Second Sex* to posit that while one is confined by having a physical body, the body necessarily enables a liberation from mere physicality. De Beauvoir, working out of a chapter on the body in Sartre's *Being and Nothingness,* argues that in one sense "the body is coextensive with personal identity," suggesting a symmetry of subject and body. At the same time, consciousness as a feature of being human is housed and made possible by the body, allowing for a "disembodied or transcendent feature of personal identity," consciousness itself. The body creates the conditions for consciousness and for an asymmetry of consciousness and body. To the extent that someone becomes a "woman"—by becoming, owning, and innovating through the consciousness made possible by the body—one chooses the condition of having a particular body. Ironically, one then has the freedom, as Butler describes, of "an active style of living one's body in the world"—the freedom of being able to choose among destinies. Yet to the extent that forces in the culture prohibit or inhibit the expression of female consciousness through culture, "women [are forced to] occupy their bodies," as Butler argues, "as their essential and enslaving identities," as if choice were not a feature of experience.

It is the achievement of patriarchal culture, Butler argues finally, to project certain patterns of being a "woman" or a "man" as inevitable and natural developments.

Much cultural capital, as de Beauvoir argued forcefully before Butler, has been deployed to perpetuate the naturalness of a gender system that imprisons women in their bodies and denies them access to the diversity of spheres and power in culture. Butler then turns to Monique Wittig and Michel Foucault as effective strategists who have devised schemes for unmasking the apparent naturalness of what are demonstrably constructed subjectivities.

Two other feminist theorists known for their detailed treatment of the historical contexts of female subjectivity are Gayatri Chakravorty Spivak and Diana Fuss. Spivak (whose articles have been in the last three editions of *Contemporary Literary Criticism,* and who is cited widely in this edition) has sought consistently in her work to situate the practice of feminist criticism within the context of middle-class academic life, all within the international division of labor in the Western world. As she writes in "Imperialism and Sexual Difference," "even as we feminist critics discover the troping error of the masculist truth-claim to universality or academic objectivity, we perform the lie of constituting a truth of global sisterhood where the model remains . . . European." She notes, in particular, the "post-romantic concept of irony" articulated by one of her students, which springs "from the imposition of her own historical and voluntarist" position within "U.S. academic feminism as a 'universal' model of the 'natural' reactions of the female psyche." Such a practice, Spivak says, carries with it a "*structural* effect" of colonialism and imperialism as marked that of colonialist enterprises such as the East India Company in the nineteenth century. In this way, Spivak articulates a critique of imperialism in the West informed by the advances that structuralism, poststructuralism, Marxism, and feminism have brought to the examination of literature and discourse in general.

In "Reading Like a Feminist," Fuss discusses Spivak's "Subaltern Studies: Deconstructing Historiography," along with Robert Scholes's "Reading Like a Man" and Tania Modleski's "Feminism and the Power of Interpretation," to approach the question of female subjectivity from a different side. "What does it mean," Fuss asks, "to read as a woman or as a man?" The issue of reading from the vantage of one gender or the other, as Fuss shows, necessarily raises the question of subjectivity explored by Kaplan. In Fuss's analysis, Scholes, Modleski, and Spivak all explicitly reject the "essentialist" stance of an autonomous definition of being female that Kaplan describes. "Essentialism" here should be read as the attribution of inherent meaning to something, a situation that usually entails seeing the thing examined as autonomous—that is, as a thing in itself not in relation to other things and not in any constitutive relationship to its historical context. So in place of any such assumed and unproblematic "femaleness," an "essential" femaleness, Kaplan, Butler, Spivak, and Fuss define "female" and reading like a woman (or as a "feminist") as *constructions* to be understood in cultural and semiotic contexts of representation.

As Fuss demonstrates, however, the question of essentialism has a hidden intractability and cannot be dismissed so easily. "In the background of all these [sophisticated] investigations," she writes, we still find "the question of essentialism and the problem of the vexed relation between feminism and deconstruction." Fuss contends, as other feminists argue as well, that any attempt to address questions of gender will be grounded ultimately on a hidden point of essentialism. The choice of what stand to take, being a feminist as opposed to the other choices, will always be to a degree an "essential" choice, a choice revealing the ground of commitment as much as critique. Even theorists guided by the insights of deconstruction, Fuss notes, which "is commonly understood as the very displacement of essence," will at some point deviate from the nonessentialist strategy with a direct reliance on a grounding that is assumed and not accounted for analytically. In critical analysis, to speak at all must assume the choice of an essential ground from which a nonessentialist strategy can be launched. Regardless of claims to the contrary, essentialism is impossible to avoid unless one avoids speech and analytical critique altogether.

The mechanisms of change and the obstacles to it that Spivak and Fuss discuss, particularly the manner in which they chart the emergence and the dialectic movements of new thinking and the continual revision of rethinking, foreground a persistent and profound strength in feminist discourse. Feminist critics and theorists such as Butler, Spivak, Fuss, Nancy Hartsock, Cixous, Luce Irigaray, Monique Wittig, bell hooks, Donna Haraway, Laura Mulvey, Barbara Christian, Laurie Finke, Annette Kuhn, Trinh T. Minh-Ha, Meaghan Morris, and many others, consistently demonstrate both the diversity and strength of contemporary feminisms. We mean that these theorists as a group tend to construct critical discourse according to a model that incorporates and builds on the productive potential of conflict itself, of change. By this we mean that they have a strong tendency to view discourse as open and dynamic, and they generally attempt to respond to their own cultural situatedness and to new developments in the culture itself. Moreover, they tend to capitalize on the opportunities of conflict instead of viewing conflict and change as alien forces.

In "The Body and Cinema: Some Problems for Feminism," an article that we take to be an important statement of gender criticism and cultural studies, and which we wish there were room to include here, Annette Kuhn dramatically demonstrates the productivity of such open discourse. The style of much feminist discourse is exemplified in Kuhn's work, and in what follows we want to highlight Kuhn's style of analysis and the signature moves of a feminist critique as shown in her work. Throughout Kuhn's work the tendency in her manner of presentation and argument is to acknowledge conflicts but not to debate them. Rather, her message is that conflicts are valuable in themselves and are not to be resolved prematurely or too readily. So she refrains strategically from giving even the appearance of wishing to resolve all conflicts. Note, also, Kuhn's foregrounding of the provisional nature of her conclusions, the sense at the end of her discussion that loose ends of consideration still exist for all to see. Along the same line, she dramatizes her own *evolving* subjectivity, the changing perspective that emerges piecemeal in her discussion. She wants to give the impression that her current perspective at any moment is a phase or a stopover and not a final destination, simply part of a progression of thought and experience. In sum, her style in this article is intended to demonstrate the strategic coexistence of analytical rigor and discursive openness to emergent insights and formations.

In "The Body and Cinema: Some Problems for Feminism," Kuhn uses the film *Pumping Iron II—The Women* as a staging for an analysis of contemporary attempts to construct (or reconstruct) the category of the feminine, what it means to be a woman. In the manner of a structuralist, at least initially, she brings forward from the film about female bodybuilders a spectrum of possibility for conceiving of femininity in relation to the absence or presence of muscle and body fat. In this semiotic binarity, she opposes Beverly Francis, the extraordinarily muscled newcomer to bodybuilding competition, against Rachel McLish, the traditional female bodybuilder who has strong muscles but also a body of soft, fluid lines suggestive of traditional images of femininity. In this structuralist analysis of gender construction, the unmarked signifier of a strong but feminine woman is Rachel McLish. In the muscle competition depicted in this film, however, the extraordinary possibility of marking the female body as feminine, but simultaneously as a challenge in musculature to a male body, emerges in the person of Beverly Francis. The subordinate (or "subaltern") status of the female to the master (unmarked) text of the male body is then in danger. That hierarchy would not be served at all if the super-strong Beverly Francis succeeded in establishing validity for something like female parity in relation to a strong male body.

The semiotic/structuralist dimension of Kuhn's analysis, however, is only a portion of her cultural critique. In addition to analyzing women bodybuilders as cultural signifiers for current developments in the rethinking of gender categories, Kuhn constructs a particular subjectivity for undertaking this analysis. She relates the details of her viewing of *Pumping Iron II—The Women* with an "all-female audience" in a "packed auditorium." She describes how this female audience talked back to "characters on the screen, cheering on the 'goodies,' booing the 'baddies.'" "All the viewers," she goes on, "were having a wonderful time, enjoying both the film and the circumstances in which they were watching it." She then narrates the "apparently inconsistent responses of this audience" to the film. They enjoyed the film while watching it, indulging in ironic responses to "good" and "bad" characters, and then advanced a sustained critique in group discussions after the film. In this narration, Kuhn is fully cognizant of the feminist critique of "male/masculine and female/feminine" positions as established "within the cinematic apparatus" of Hollywood films (owing greatly to the work of Laura Mulvey, Stephen Heath, Christian Metz, and a number of critics connected with *Screen* magazine). "Spectators in cinema," Kuhn goes on, "are basically either to take up a masculine subject position . . . or to submit to a masochism of over-identification . . . or to adopt the narcissistic position of taking the screen as mirror and becoming one's own object of desire."

Kuhn never tries to resolve the cultural contradictions that her analysis of *Pumping Iron II—The Women* pushes forward. "The instability of femininity as a subject position [one "potentially monstrous"], and the discomfort involved in identification with it," she writes, "are liable to become evident in looking at this film in ways they are not when such relations are more embedded, more submerged in the text." This assessment of a certain set of relations between gender construction and the medium of film leads Kuhn to explore briefly "representation . . . as a form of regulation" in culture. But for all of Kuhn's incisive analysis, she never tries to explain away or somehow dismiss the contradictory responses of the "all-female audience" with which she watched the film. She also never tries to distance herself analytically from the particular pleasures associated with the Hollywood cinematic apparatus. In fact, it is a strong feature of Kuhn's discourse that she attempts to highlight these "contradictions" of response as markers of the cultural frame from which her critique emanates. In this way, and in the many loose ends that Kuhn narrates but does not attempt to deny, she is positioning herself situationally and discursively in relation to the discourse that is the object of her analysis.

In short, Kuhn—but also all of these theorists we have mentioned—actively works against formalist clarification and final precision (and, thus, a closing down) of cultural discourses. In gestures that constitute a signature of much feminist discourse and inquiry, much that is productive and influential about contemporary feminisms is self-consciously open-ended and dialectical in its operation. In the parlance of our General Introduction, we see a strong tendency toward critique (as opposed to criticism) in the diversity of practices in such contemporary feminist discourse.

GENDER STUDIES

The emergence of gender studies in the last decade overlaps with feminism but also extends well outside it. In the broadest interpretation (one employed by the theorist Laurie Finke), "gender studies" can be taken as an umbrella term encompassing all manner of studying gender—women's studies, feminist theory, and gay/lesbian and sexuality studies. In a narrower designation, "gender studies" sometimes is used to mean a more pluralized focus on the construction of female and male gender roles, including "male" studies as evidenced by the work of Andrew Ross and Michael Warner, but also including specifically gay/lesbian studies. However, those working in gay/lesbian studies—Michael Warner, Eve Kosofsky Sedgwick, Michael Moon, Judith Butler, Marjorie Garber, Jonathan Goldberg, Simon Watney, Audre Lorde, Adrienne Rich, and Monique Wittig, among many others—tend to want more specialized designations than "gender studies" for their projects, often for political effect. And many new modes of inquiry into questions of gender are newly emergent in the academy, articulating extremely important new areas of literary and cultural theory.

A strong example of the relations of gay studies to gender studies generally is Michael Warner's "Homo-Narcissism; or, Heterosexuality." Here Warner makes an argument for seeing homosexuality not as a category subordinate to the hegemony of heterosexuality but as its own discourse in both personal and cultural dimensions. "This utopian self-relation," he writes, "far from being the pathology of the homosexual, could instead be seen as a historical condition and, in the perverse and unrecuperated mode of homosexual subjectivity, the source of a critical potential." Warner works to this conclusion by beginning, as do so many theorists of gender, with Freud's economy of the inevitable "poles of hetero- and homosexuality." Warner critiques the Freudian version of the process of sexual maturation and especially Freud's idea that the "interest in 'an object'" of sexual investment is "normally" a woman. Warner explains:

> Nothing guarantees such an outcome other than the boy's discovery that women are defined as objects to him in a way that other men are not. And since the girl

discovers at the same time that her destiny is to be an object of desire, her encounter with alterity is very different from the boy's. She is not offered the same simple distinction between her own subjectivity and the other's objectivity. The discovery of otherness in the other gender, therefore, is neither neutral nor symmetrical. In de Beauvoir's argument, as in the work of other feminists who continue her Hegelian tradition, this construction of gendered otherness is seen as the structure of domination.

Warner's critique here focuses on what he calls "the phenomenology of difference"—the reduction of one sort of distinction between people to a defining difference. But his ultimate critique focuses on changes under way in contemporary technoculture. Like Haraway, Warner sees reformulations of the lines of power that structure not only markets and communities but gendered identity constructions in contemporary culture. The changing "forms of exchange in capitalism, the role-detachment that comes with a system-differentiated society, the mass imaginary of video capitalism, rituals and markets of adolescence" open up new choices for postmodern subjectivity to express "the utopian erotics of modern subjectivity." "The work of analyzing the subjectivity of these interarticulated contexts," Warner concludes, "has only begun." In quite different styles of gender criticism, Warner and Haraway both project a horizon of technoculture and electronic erotics, an amalgam of gender studies, cultural studies, and future shock. Both focus on the revisions of gender categories in contemporary culture and refuse to endorse, in Haraway's words, "anti-science metaphysics, a demonology of technology," and embrace instead the "task of reconstructing the boundaries of daily life." The resulting critique and interpretation may well be, as Haraway says, "an infidel heteroglossia," and that strange designation, in fact, may be fitting for the "cyborg" constructions of subjectivity and gender that she describes as emerging in contemporary technoculture.

In such alliances with cultural studies, gender, gay/lesbian, and sexuality studies often wager their critique on the revelatory developments of the contemporary scene—on developments in popular culture and technology. Yet as the essays here show, this commitment to the "truth" of the hypernew and the post-postmodern often has less to do with faith in the future and the outcome of current developments of culture and technology than with a strategy for the practice of critique. In much gender criticism (Haraway's article is a good example) the construction and placement of a vantage point is "located" in the future or in the hyperpresent of cultural change. Such a viewpoint functions primarily to enfranchise a certain kind of critique. From that vantage, "in" the culture but by definition a view from "outside," it is possible to direct an oppositional critique of dominant Western practices, particularly in relation to gender construction and social class. This critique is often of the repressions and constraints of those erotic, technological, and economic practices now being threatened and possibly eroded in Western culture.

We have been trying to show that feminist theory and gender studies are, on a number of fronts, principal theoretical sites and venues of critique in current critical studies. This is so, in part, because feminism and gender studies—like rhetorical studies—has the potential to articulate relations among all the other schools of criticism we are discussing in this book. It is this broad articulation of the big picture and possible changes in it that gives much work in this area a liberatory demeanor. "It will require a courageous grasp of the politics and economics . . . of heterosexuality," Rich writes in "Compulsory Heterosexuality and Lesbian Existence," "to carry us beyond individual cases or diversified group situations into the complex kind of overview needed to undo the power men everywhere wield over women." Whereas other sites of critical work have made important contributions in the past, feminism and gender studies are currently engaged in helping to shape the future of literary and cultural studies—in teaching, research, and social life.

RELATED ESSAYS IN *CONTEMPORARY LITERARY CRITICISM*

Nancy Armstrong, "The Occidental Alice"
Catherine Belsey, "Constructing the Subject: Deconstructing the Text"
Donna Haraway, "A Cyborg Manifesto: Science, Technology, and Socialist-Feminism in the Late Twentieth Century"
bell hooks, "Postmodern Blackness"
Barbara Johnson, "Apostrophe, Animation, and Abortion"
Teresa de Lauretis, "Semiotics and Experience"
Laura Mulvey, "Visual Pleasure and Narrative Cinema"
Patrocinio Schweickart, "Reading Ourselves: Toward a Feminist Theory of Reading"

REFERENCES AND FURTHER READING

Bauer, Dale M., *Feminist Dialogics* (New York: State University of New York Press, 1988).

Belsey, Catherine, and Jane Moore, eds., "Introduction: The Story So Far," in *The Feminist Reader: Essays in Gender and the Politics of Literary Criticism* (New York: Blackwell, 1989).

Boone, Joseph Allen, ed., *Engendering Men: The Question of Male Feminist Criticism* (New York: Routledge, 1990).

Brod, Harry, and Michael Kaufman, *Theorizing Masculinities* (Thousand Oaks, CA: Sage, 1994).

Brown, Anne E., and Marjanne Elaine Gooze, *International Women's Writing: New Landscapes of Identity* (Westport, CT: Greenwood Press, 1995).

Cain, William E., *Making Feminist History: The Literary Scholarship of Sandra M. Gilbert and Susan Gubar* (New York: Garland, 1994).

Cixous, Hélène, and Catherine Clement, *The Newly-Born Woman* (Minneapolis: University of Minnesota Press, 1986).

Daly, Mary, *Beyond God the Father: Towards a Philosophy of Women's Liberation* (Boston: Beacon Press, 1973).

———, *Gyn/Ecology: The Metaethics of Radical Feminism* (Boston: Beacon Press, 1978).

———, "The Transformation of Silence into Language and Action," in *Sinister Wisdom*, 6 (1978).

Davis, Robert Con, and Thaïs Morgan, "Two Conversations on Literature, Theory, and the Question of Genders," in *Men Writing the Feminine: Literature, Theory, and the Question of Genders,* ed. Thaïs Morgan (Albany: State University of New York Press, 1994), 189–200.

de Beauvoir, Simone, *The Second Sex,* trans. H. M. Parshley (New York: Knopf, 1953).

Dinnerstein, Dorothy, *The Mermaid and the Minotaur: Sexual Arrangements and Human Malaise* (New York: Harper & Row, 1976).

Donaldson, Laura E., *Decolonizing Feminisms: Race, Gender, and Empire-Building* (Chapel Hill: University of North Carolina Press, 1992).

Donovan, Josephine, ed., *Feminist Literary Criticism* (Lexington: University of Kentucky Press, 1975).

Eagleton, Mary, *Feminist Literary Theory: A Reader* (Cambridge, MA: Blackwell, 1996).

———, *Working with Feminist Criticism* (Cambridge, MA: Blackwell, 1996).

Edwards, Lee, and Arlyn Diamond, eds., *The Authority of Experience: Essays in Feminist Criticism* (Amherst: University of Massachusetts Press, 1977).

Eisenstein, Hester, and Alice Jardine, eds., *The Future of Difference* (Boston: Hall, 1980).

Elam, Diane, *Feminism and Deconstruction: Ms. EN ABYME* (New York: Routledge, 1994).

Ellmann, Mary, *Thinking About Women* (New York: Harcourt, Brace, 1968).

Felman, Shoshana, "Rereading Femininity," in *Yale French Studies,* 62 (1981): 19–44.

———, "*Women and Madness:* The Critical Phallacy," in *Diacritics,* 5, No. 4 (1975), 2–10.

Finke, Laurie, *Feminist Theory, Women's Writing* (Ithaca, NY: Cornell University Press, 1992).

Freedman, Diane P., *An Alchemy of Genres: Cross-genre Writing by American Feminist Poet-Critics* (Charlottesville: University Press of Virginia, 1992).

Fuss, Diana, *Essentially Speaking: Feminism, Nature, and Difference* (New York: Routledge, 1989).

Gallop, Jane, *Around 1981: Academic Feminist Theory* (New York: Routledge, 1992).

Gilbert, Sandra M., and Susan Gubar, *The Madwoman in the Attic* (New Haven, CT: Yale University Press, 1979).

Greene, Gayle, and Coppelia Kahn, *Changing Subjects: The Making of Feminist Literary Criticism* (New York: Routledge, 1993).

Hohne, Karen Ann, and Helen Wussow, *A Dialogue of Voices: Feminist Literary Theory and Bakhtin* (Minneapolis: University of Minnesota Press, 1994).

Humm, Maggie, *Modern Feminisms: Political, Literary, Cultural* (New York: Columbia University Press, 1992).

Irigaray, Luce, *This Sex Which Is Not One,* trans. Caroline Porter (Ithaca, NY: Cornell University Press, 1985).

———, *Speculum of the Other Woman,* trans. Gillian C. Gill (Ithaca, NY: Cornell University Press, 1985).

Jacobus, Mary, ed., *Women Writing and Writing About Women* (London: Croom Helm, 1979).

Jardine, Alice, "Pre-texts for the Transatlantic Feminist," in *Yale French Studies,* 62 (1981): 220–36.

Joeres, Ruth-Ellen B., and Elizabeth Mittman, *The Politics of the Essay: Feminist Perspectives* (Bloomington: Indiana University Press, 1993).

Kamuf, Peggy, "Writing Like a Woman," in *Woman and Language in Literature and Society,* ed. Sally McConnell-Ginet et al. (New York: Praeger, 1980), pp. 284–99.

Kinnahan, Linda A., *Poetics of the Feminine* (New York: Cambridge University Press, 1994).

Kofman, Sarah, "Freud's Suspension of the Mother," in *Enclitic,* 4, 2 (1980), 17–28.

———, "The Narcissistic Woman: Freud and Girard," in *Diacritics,* 10, 3 (1980), 36–45.

Kolodny, Annette, "Some Notes on Defining a 'Feminist Literary Criticism,'" in *Critical Inquiry,* 2 (1975), 75–92.

Kroker, Arthur, and Marilouise Kroker, eds., *The Hysterical Male: New Feminist Theory* (New York: St. Martin's Press, 1991).

Kuhn, Annette, "The Body and Cinema: Some Problems for Feminism," in *Grafts: Feminist Cultural Criticism,* ed. Susan Sheridan (London: Verso, 1988), 11–23.

Landry, Donna, and Gerald M. MacLean, *Materialist Feminisms* (Cambridge, MA: Blackwell, 1993).

Laqueur, Thomas, *Making Sex: Body and Gender from the Greeks to Freud* (Cambridge, MA: Harvard University Press, 1990).

Lovell, Terry, *Feminist Cultural Studies* (Brookfield, VT: Elgar, 1995).

McConnell-Ginet, Sally, et al., eds. *Women and Language in Literature and Society* (New York: Praeger, 1980).

Marks, Elaine, "Women and Literature in France," in *Signs,* 3 (1978), 832–42.

———, and Isabelle Courtivron, eds., *New French Feminisms: An Anthology* (Amherst: University of Massachusetts Press, 1980).

Meese, Elizabeth A., *(SEM) erotics: Theorizing Lesbian: Writing* (New York: New York University Press, 1992).

Miller, Nancy K., *Getting Personal: Feminist Occasions and Other Autobiographical Acts* (New York: Routledge, 1991).

Millett, Kate, *Sexual Politics* (Garden City, NY: Doubleday, 1970)

Mills, Sara, *Feminist Stylistics* (New York: Routledge, 1995).

Montrelay, Michele, "Inquiry into Feminity," trans. Parveen Adams, in *m/f,* 1 (1978), 83–101.

Newton, Judith, and Deborah Rosenfelt, eds., *Feminist Criticism and Social Change* (New York: Methuen, 1985).

Parker, Alice, and Elizabeth A. Meese, *Feminist Critical Negotiations* (Philadelphia: Benjamins, 1992).

Pratt, Annis, *Archetypal Patterns in Women's Fiction* (Bloomington: Indiana University Press, 1981).

Sheridan, Susan, ed., *Grafts: Feminist Cultural Criticism* (London: Verso, 1988).

Showalter, Elaine, *A Literature of Their Own: British Women Novelists from Brontë to Lessing* (Princeton, NJ: Princeton University Press, 1977).

———, "Notes Toward a Feminist Poetics," in *Feminist Criticism,* ed. Elaine Showalter (New York: Pantheon, 1981), 243–70.

Spivak, Gayatri Chakravorty, "French Feminism in an International Frame," in *Yale French Studies,* 62 (1981), 154–84.

———, "Imperialism and Sexual Difference," in *Oxford Literary Review* 8 (1986): 225–40.

———, *In Other Worlds: Essays in Cultural Politics* (New York: Methuen, 1987).

———, *Outside in the Teaching Machine* (New York: Routledge, 1993).

Wittig, Monique, "The Category of Sex," in *Feminist Issues* 2, 1 (Fall 1982): 63–68.

———, "Homo Sum," *Feminist Issues* 10, 1 (Spring 1990): 3–11.

———, "On the Social Contract," in *Feminist Issues* 9, 1 (Spring 1989): 3–12.

———, "One Is Not Born a Woman," in *Feminist Issues* 1, 2 (Winter 1981): 47–54.

Woolf, Virginia, *A Room of One's Own* (New York: Harcourt Brace Jovanovich, 1981).

———, *Collected Essays* (London: Hogarth, 1966).

31

Diana Fuss
1960–

Diana Fuss is a professor of English at Princeton University, where she specializes in feminist theory. Her works include *Essentially Speaking* (1989), *Inside/Out: Lesbian Theories, Gay Theories* (1991), *Identification Papers* (1995), and *Human, All Too Human* (1996). "Reading Like a Feminist," the second chapter of *Essentially Speaking,* situates itself in response to Robert Scholes's "Reading Like a Man" (1987), Tania Modleski's "Feminism and the Power of Interpretation" (1986), Gayatri Chakravorty Spivak's "Subaltern Studies: Deconstructing Historiography" (1987), Peggy Kamuf's "Writing Like a Woman" (1980), and Jonathan Culler's "Reading as a Woman" (1982), among others. Asking the subsidiary questions surrounding the relationships between gender and reading, deconstruction and feminism, essentialism and constructionism, this chapter presents politics as "feminism's essence." *Essentially Speaking* investigates the roles essentialism plays in contemporary literary and cultural theory, without assuming that essentialism is necessarily oppressive. Fuss's writings make clear that the political stakes of feminist debate on essentialism are not simply reducible to the status of oppressed women in a patriarchical society. Instead, she insists upon including such issues as the different status positions of women and men as they are constituted in a racist and heterosexist economy by other axes of difference, namely, class, sexuality, culture, nationality, and ethnicity.

The textual and political effects of essentializing notions such as a "class" of women, of "a shared women's experience," and of a "male reader" or "female reader," among others, remain under critique in "Reading Like a Feminist." Fuss speaks specifically about such terms' lack of epistemological usefulness and their inability to account for real, material differences between women. Collapsing such terms as "woman," "women," "female," and "feminist" and reifying the binarism between feminism and deconstruction, Fuss argues, gloss over not only the hybrid positions of deconstructive feminism and feminist deconstruction, but also the hybrid positions within and of individual lives. Comparing Lacan's move "to reclaim the place of subjectivity as a destabilizing and decentering force," Foucault's "notion of subject-positions as one of the four fundamental components of discursive formations," and Spivak's critique of "Subaltern Studies [because of its] failure to address adequately questions of subjectivity," Fuss discusses the strategic use of essentialist deployment, insisting that the permissibility of engaging in essentialism is framed and determined by the position from which one speaks and acts.

The views of Luce Irigary, Teresa de Lauretis, and Donna Haraway also comprise the framework of Fuss's attempt to come to terms with the essentialism in "anti-essentialism" and the grounds upon which we base notions of "class," "women," "experience," and "politics." Because we cannot identify a group or class "until various social, historical, political coalitions construct the conditions and possibilities of membership," Fuss suggests retaining the idea of women as a "class" because it "might help remind us that the sexual categories we work with are no more and no less than social constructions, subject-positions subject to change and to historical evolution."

Certainly not the first feminist to suggest the political significance of the notion of women as a class, Fuss nevertheless emphasizes this conviction's furthest conclusion by suggesting that politics is "essential to feminism's many self-definitions." After all, "constructionists are willing to displace 'identity,' 'self,' 'experience,' and virtually every other self-evident category, *except* politics." Throughout her work Fuss maintains that arguments for identity politics often fail to address the complicated processes by which identity is formed. Foregrounding politics, she asserts, alongside an understanding of the fundamentally unstable identities produced by psychological and social processes, will allow for "readings" that do not depoliticize or dehistoricize the very subjects they are attempting to address *specifically*—"essentially" and contextually.

Reading Like a Feminist

In light of the pervasive reluctance amongst poststructuralists to acknowledge any possible productive role for essentialism, the issue of constructionism's complicity with essentialism demands more careful and precise demonstration. Let me pose the central problematic in a slightly different way: can social constructionism entirely dispense with the idea of essence? In this chapter I propose not to confront the stronghold of constructionism head-on, . . . but to take a more oblique approach by engaging with the subsidiary debates on gender and reading. What does it mean to read as a woman or as a man? When social constructionist theories of reading posit groups of gendered readers, what is it exactly that underwrites and subtends the notion of a class of women or a class of men reading? Precisely *where,* in other words, does the essentialism inhere in anti-essentialism? Although the present analysis focuses predominantly upon three recent pieces, Robert Scholes's "Reading Like a Man" (1987), Tania Modleski's "Feminism and the Power of Interpretation" (1986), and Gayatri Spivak's "Subaltern Studies: Deconstructing Historiography" (1987), the dispute over "reading as woman" has a much longer history which includes Peggy Kamuf's "Writing Like a Woman" (1980), Jonathan Culler's "Reading as a Woman" (1982), and, most recently, the many contributions to the controversial volume *Men in Feminism* (Jardine and Smith 1987). In the background of all these investigations lies the question of essentialism and the problem of the vexed relation between feminism and deconstruction. How and why have the current tensions between feminism and deconstruction mobilized around the issue of essentialism?

Why indeed is essentialism such a powerful and seemingly intransigent category for both deconstructionists and feminists? Is it possible to be an essentialist deconstructionist, when deconstruction is commonly understood as the very displacement of essence? By the same token, is it legitimate to call oneself an anti-essentialist feminist, when feminism seems to take for granted among its members a shared identity, some essential point of commonality?

ESSENCE, EXPERIENCE, AND EMPOWERMENT

According to one well-known American critic, feminism and deconstruction are fundamentally incompatible discourses since deconstruction displaces the essence of the class "women" which feminism needs to articulate its very politics. The polarization of feminism and deconstruction around the contested sign of essence is perhaps nowhere so clear as in Robert Scholes's "Reading Like a Man," a piece which seeks to disclose the often subtle and frequently suspect strategies which, in this instance, (male?) deconstructors employ to master feminism and to put it in its place. I find Scholes's careful critique of Jonathan Culler's "Reading as a Woman" both incisive and enormously suggestive, but not entirely devoid of certain mastering strategies of its own. It is these strategies that I wish to discuss here, while declaring all the same my fundamental agreement with Scholes's basic premise that the relation between deconstruction and feminism is by no means unproblematic or uncomplicated. The most serious (but also the most intriguing) problem with this essay is that it leaves the feminism/deconstruction binarism firmly in place—it reinforces and solidifies their antithesis in order to claim that deconstruction is bad for feminism. To secure this moral judgment, the hybrid positions of deconstructive feminism and feminist deconstruction are glossed over, rejected from the start as untenable

possibilities—untenable because feminism and deconstruction are "founded upon antithetical principles: feminism upon a class concept and deconstruction upon the deconstructing of all such concepts" (208).

Everything hinges here, as Scholes himself is quick to point out, on the notion of "class." What he objects to, specifically, is deconstruction's rejection of what W. K. Wimsatt, following Locke, calls "nominal universality" (208), that is, nominal essence. Nominal essence, as we recall, refers to the ranking and labeling of things not according to the real essence in them but the complex ideas in us. Scholes believes that feminism needs at least to hold onto the logico-linguistic idea of a class of women in order to be effective. I would not disagree. I would, however, wish to point out that nominal essences are often treated by post-Lockeans *as if* they were real essences, and this is what I perceive to be the main point of vulnerability in "Reading Like a Man." While still subscribing to the "linguistic/logical dimension" of class, Scholes later goes on to endorse "the ability of women to be conscious of themselves as a class . . . bound by a certain shared experience" (212–13). What, then, does the category "experience" signify for Scholes? "Whatever experience is," he concludes, "it is not just a *construct* but something that *constructs*" (215). This definition sounds remarkably similar to Locke's description of "real essence" as the "something I know not what" which nonetheless determines the "what" of who we are. And what is it, exactly, that constitutes that "certain shared experience" which allows women "to be conscious of themselves as a class"? Could it be that which Scholes reprimands Culler for eliding, precisely that which Culler (in Scholes's opinion) rashly jettisons from consideration in his deconstructive third moment: namely, "the bodily experience of menstrual flow" (211)? Of course, not all females, in fact, menstruate. It may well be that Scholes wishes us to think of "experience" in the way Teresa de Lauretis suggests: "an ongoing process by which subjectivity is constructed semiotically and historically" (1984, 182).

But what distinguishes Scholes's understanding of experience from de Lauretis's is the former's hidden appeal to referentiality, to (in this case) the female body, which though constructed is nonetheless constructed *by its own processes,* processes which are seen to be real, immediate, and directly knowable.[1] Bodily experiences may seem self-evident and immediately perceptible but they are always socially mediated. Even if we were to agree that experience is not merely constructed but also itself constructing, we would still have to acknowledge that there is little agreement amongst women on exactly what constitutes "a woman's experience." Therefore, we need to be extremely wary of the temptation to make substantive claims on the basis of the so-called "authority" of our experiences. "No man should seek in any way to diminish the authority which the experience of women gives them in speaking about that experience" (217–18), Scholes insists, and yet, as feminist philosopher Jean Grimshaw rightly reminds us, "experience does not come neatly in segments, such that it is always possible to abstract what in one's experience is due to 'being a woman' from that which is due to 'being married,' 'being middle class' and so forth" (1986, 85). In sum, "experience" is rather shaky ground on which to base the notion of a class of women. But if we can't base the idea of a class of women on "essence" or "experience," then what can we base it on? Before tendering a possible answer to what is admittedly a vexing and frustrating question, much more needs to be said by way of rounding out my critique of Scholes's "Reading Like a Man."

By taking as his model of feminism a humanist or essentialist version, and by reading deconstruction as fundamentally anti-essentialist, Scholes forecloses the possibility of both an anti-essentialist feminism and an essentialist deconstruction. But recent work in feminist theory suggests that not only are these positions possible, they can be powerfully displacing positions from which feminists can speak. To take the first instance, an anti-essentialist feminism, Monique Witting rejects unequivocally the idea of a "class of women" based on shared (biological) experience and bases her feminism on the deconstructive premise that, in Derrida's words, "woman has no essence of her very own" (1985b, 31). To take the second instance, an essentialist deconstruction, Luce Irigaray bases her feminism on the bodily metaphor of "the two lips" in order to construct and *deconstruct* "woman" at the same time. . . . What I wish to emphasize here is that Scholes's feminism/deconstruction binarism is ultimately more harmful than helpful. It leads, for example, to such baffling statements as "feminism is right and deconstruction is wrong" (205). Mastery, in Scholes's work, operates along an ethical axis: feminism is disappropriated from deconstruction so that its alleged moral superiority might be protected from the ill repute and questionable designs of its powerful (male?) suitor, deconstruction. What we see in this piece is a curious form of critical chivalry; feminism, I would submit, has become the angel in the house of critical theory.

But who is this errant knight dedicated to saving feminism, and from what country does he heed? what language does he speak? Does Scholes speak, read, or write as a woman or as a man? The final lines provide the answer we have all eagerly been waiting for:

We are subjects constructed by our experience and truly carry traces of that experience in our minds and on our bodies. Those of us who are male cannot deny this either. With the best will in the world we shall never read as women and perhaps not even like women. For me, born when I was born and living where I have lived, the very best I can do is to be conscious of the ground upon which I stand: to read not as but like a man. (218)

The distinction between the similes "as" and "like" is nothing short of brilliant, but it does not answer a far more interesting question, a question which, through a series of rather nimble acrobatic maneuvers of his own, Scholes manages to sidestep: namely, does he read as or like a *feminist?* It is the very slippages between "woman," "women," "female," and "feminist" throughout the text that permits the writer to defer the question of reading as or like a feminist—the question, in other words, of *political identification.* I read this piece *like* a feminist; what it means to read as or even like a woman I still don't know.

Scholes is not alone in his repudiation of Jonathan Culler's alleged deconstructionist appropriation of feminism; Tania Modleski, in her "Feminism and the Power of Interpretation: Some Critical Readings" also takes Culler to task for "being patriarchal just at the point when he seems to be most feminist," that is, at the point "when he arrogates to himself and to other male critics the ability to read as women by 'hypothesizing' women readers" (133). What allows a male subject to read as a woman is the displacing series of repetitions which Culler adapts from Peggy Kamuf's "Writing Like a Woman": "a woman writing as a woman writing as a woman . . . ." But, to Modleski, the deconstructionist definition of a woman reading (as a woman reading as a woman . . .) simply opens a space for male feminism while simultaneously foreclosing the question of real, material female readers: "a genuinely feminist literary criticism might wish to repudiate the *hypothesis* of a woman reader and instead promote the 'sensible,' visible, actual female reader" (133). While I am not contesting that there are certainly "real," material, gendered readers engaged in the act of reading, I nonetheless stumble over the qualifier "genuinely": what is it, exactly, that might constitute for Modleski a "genuinely feminist literary criticism"?

Read alongside Scholes's "Reading Like a Man," Modleski's "Feminism and the Power of Interpretation" proposes an answer that should perhaps not surprise us: "the experience of real

women" (134) operates as the privileged signifier of the authentic and the real. Experience emerges to fend off the entry of men into feminism and, further, to naturalize and to authorize the relation between biological woman and social women: "to read as a woman in a patriarchal culture necessitates that the *hypothesis* of a woman reader be advanced by an *actual* woman reader: the female feminist critic" (133–134). Like Scholes, Modleski can appeal to experience as the measure of the "genuinely feminist" only by totally collapsing woman, female, and feminist and by prefacing this tricky conflation with the empirical tag "actual." Modleski objects to Kamuf's and Culler's ostensible position that "a 'ground' (like experience) from which to make critical judgments is anathema" (134). If this were an accurate assessment of Kamuf's and Culler's positions I might be inclined to agree, but the poststructuralist objection to experience is not a repudiation of grounds of knowing *per se* but rather a refusal of the hypostatization of experience as *the* ground (and the most stable ground) of knowledge production. The problem with categories like "the female experience" or "the male experience" is that, given their generality and seamlessness, they are of limited epistemological usefulness. When Modleski does some hypothesizing of her own and presents us with her fictional "case of a man and a woman reading Freud's text," and when she informs us (without a hint of irony) that "the woman, accustomed to the experience of being thought more sensual than intellectual, must certainly respond to it differently from the man . . ." (133), what "woman" and what "man" is she talking about? Can we ever speak so simply of "the female reader" or "the male reader" (133), "the woman" and "the man," as if these categories were not transgressed, not already constituted by other axes of difference (class, culture, ethnicity, nationality . . .)? Moreover, are our reading responses really so easily predictable, so readily interpretable?

Both Modleski and Scholes are right to insist that critical interpretation has everything to do with power. Why, then, do I find Modleski's concluding invocation of "female empowerment" so distinctly *disempowering?* Her words are strong, emphatic, a political call to arms: "the ultimate goal of feminist criticism and theory is female empowerment. My particular concern here has been to empower female readers of texts, in part by rescuing them from the oblivion to which some critics would consign them" (136). Perhaps what is discomforting is the singular, declarative, and prescriptive tone of this guideline for political action. But it is more than a question of tone. Exactly which readers is Modleski speaking for, to, and about? Does she propose to rescue *all* female readers, including "third world" readers, lesbian readers, and working-class readers? Are not some female readers *materially* more empowered than others, by virtue of class, race, national, or other criteria? For that matter, are not *some* female readers more empowered than *some* male readers? Do these more privileged readers need to be "rescued"? Modleski seems to be as committed as her male counterpart, Robert Scholes, to saving feminism from the appropriative gestures of men (even well-intentioned ones): "feminist criticism performs an escape act dedicated to freeing women from *all* male captivity narratives, whether these be found in literature, criticism, or theory" (136). Though "Feminism and the Power of Interpretation" presents itself as a materialist investigation of "reading as woman," no allowance is made for the real, material differences between women. In the end, this materialist piece is curiously amaterialist in that the differences between women which would de-essentialize the category of Woman are treated, by their very omission, as *immaterial.*

THE ESSENTIALISM IN ANTI-ESSENTIALISM

All of this brings me to a possible way to negotiate the essentialist dilemma at the heart of these theories of "reading like a man" (Scholes), "reading as a woman" (Culler), or reading like a "female feminist critic" (Modleski). It is by no means insignificant that nearly every piece in the volume *Men in Feminism,* of which Scholes's "Reading Like a Man" is one of the more noteworthy contributions, manifests a preoccupation with the question of place, specifically with the problem of where men stand in relation to feminism. Paul Smith wishes to claim for men the privileged space of displacement, usually reserved in deconstruction for Woman, in order to mark the difference of feminism, the subversive presence within. Stephen Heath speculates that the obsession with place is a male obsession with decidedly phallic overtones: are men "in" or "out" of feminism? Still others, Cary Nelson and Rosi Braidotti, suggest that men have no place (or at least no *secure* place) in feminism; according to this line of thinking, men may need feminism but feminism does not need men.[2] While place emerges as the recurrent theme that pulls together the twenty-four disparate essays which comprise *Men in Feminism,* I am also struck by how many of these articles inevitably come round to the question of essence, eventually invoke essentialism as the real impediment to theorizing men "in" feminism. An unarticulated relation between essence and place seems to motivate each piece. Certainly this book can be described as an investigation of the place of essence in contemporary critical discourse, but perhaps we should be interrogating not only the place of essentialism but the essentialism of place; one question might provide us with a gloss on the other. [I] will demonstrate that the essentialism in "anti-essentialism" inheres in the notion of place or positionality. What is *essential* to social constructionism is precisely this notion of "where I stand," of what has come to be called, appropriately enough, "subject-positions."

To understand the importance of place for social constructionist theory, we must look to Jacques Lacan's poststructuralist psychoanalysis. Lacan's return to Freud is, above all, a project which seeks to reclaim the place of subjectivity as a destabilizing and decentering force from the work of ego psychologists who, through their unquestioned allegiance to Western humanism, seek to re-encapsulate the subject within a stationary, traditional Cartesian framework. It is during the "pre-subject's" passage from the Imaginary into the Symbolic that the child, under the threat of castration, recognizes the different sexed subject-positions ("he," "she") and finally assumes one.[3] It is especially significant that throughout his work Lacan always speaks in terms of the *place* of the subject. His subversive rewriting of Descartes's "I think, therefore I am" (*cogito ergo sum*) as "I think where I am not, therefore I am where I do not think" provides a good case in point ("The Agency of the Letter in the Unconscious or Reason Since Freud" 1977, 166). The emphasis in Lacan's anti-cogito falls on the "where"; the question "who is speaking" can only be answered by shifting the grounds of the question to "where am I speaking from?" But it is important to remember that the place of the subject is nonetheless, ultimately, unlocalizable; were we able to fix the whereabouts of the subject in a static field of determinants, then we would be back in the realm of ego psychology. What is important about Lacan's emphasis on *place* is that thinking in terms of positionality works against the tendency of concepts such as "subject" and "ego," or "I" and "you," to solidify. The "I" in Lacanian psychoanalysis is always a precarious and unstable place to be—"intolerable," in fact, in one critic's estimation (Gallop 1985, 145).

Another recurrent emphasis in Lacan's work, useful for our purposes here, is his insistence on the *construction* of the subject's sexuality rather than the *de facto* assignation of a sex at birth. Lacan teaches us in "The Meaning of the Phallus" that we assume our sex, "take up its attributes only by means of a threat"—the threat of castration (Mitchell and Rose 1982, 75). It is because the birth of the subject does not coincide with the biological birth of the human person (Freud's fundamental insight into the problem

of sexuality) that Lacan can speak in "The Mirror Stage" of "a real *specific prematurity of birth in man*" (1977, 4). Jane Gallop describes our delayed entry into subjectivity this way: "the child, although already born, does not become a self until the mirror stage. Both cases are two-part birth processes: once born into 'nature,' the second time into 'history'" (1985, 85). The "I," then, is not a given at birth but rather is constructed, assumed, taken on during the subject's problematic entry into the Symbolic. Lacan's focus on the complex psychoanalytic processes which participate in the constitution of the subject is, of course, a pre-eminently anti-essentialist position and, as we shall see, it has profound implications for the way in which we think about the subject who reads and the subject who is read.

I turn now to the theory of subject-positions most recently deployed, to brilliant effect, by Gayatri Spivak in her work on the subaltern. Spivak borrows and adapts her theoretical terminology not from Lacan but from Michel Foucault, although Lacan's theory of subjectivity is everywhere in the background here. It is in *The Archaeology of Knowledge* that Foucault elaborates his own notion of subject-positions as one of the four fundamental components of discursive formations. But before discussing the way in which "subject-positions" can help us to read texts and to textualize readers, it is important to situate Spivak's turn to subjectivity in the context of her interest in the Subaltern Studies group, a Marxist historical collective devoted to the project of exposing and undermining the elitism which characterizes traditional approaches to South Asian culture.[4] Spivak's main critique of Subaltern Studies is, in fact, the classic critique generally leveled against materialists—namely, a failure to address adequately questions of subjectivity. Although deconstructivist in their goal to displace traditional historiography, the members of Subaltern Studies nevertheless rely on certain humanist notions such as agency, totality, and presence. Spivak's "Subaltern Studies: Deconstructing Historiography" (1987, 197–221) is a sharp and discerning reading of the way in which the collective's entire attempt to "let the subaltern speak" falls prey to a positivistic search for a subaltern or peasant consciousness, which, in Spivak's opinion, can never be ultimately recovered.[5]

What is strikingly different about Spivak's reading of Subaltern Studies is that she does not dismiss their essentialism out of hand. In fact, she reads the collective's humanist ambitions to locate a subaltern consciousness as "a *strategic* use of positivist essentialism in a scrupulously visible political interest" (205). Wittingly or unwittingly, Subaltern Studies *deploys* essentialism as a provisional gesture in order to align themselves with the very subjects who have been written out of conventional historiography:

> Although the group does not wittingly engage with the post-structuralist understanding of "consciousness," our own transactional reading of them is enhanced if we see them as *strategically* adhering to the essentialist notion of consciousness, that would fall prey to an anti-humanist critique, within a historiographic practice that draws many of its strengths from that very critique. . . . If in translating bits and pieces of discourse theory and the critique of humanism back into an essentialist historiography the historian of subalternity aligns himself to the pattern of conduct of the subaltern himself, it is only a progressivist view, that diagnoses the subaltern as necessarily inferior, that will see such an alignment to be without interventionist value. Indeed it is in their very insistence upon the subaltern as the subject of history that the group acts out such a translating back, an interventionist strategy that is only partially unwitting. (206–207)

Spivak's simultaneous critique and *endorsement* of Subaltern Studies' essentialism suggests that humanism can be activated in the service of the subaltern; in other words, when put into practice by the dispossessed themselves, essentialism can be powerfully displacing and disruptive. This, to me, signals an exciting new way to rethink the problem of essentialism; it represents an approach which evaluates the motivations *behind* the deployment of essentialism rather than prematurely dismissing it as an unfortunate vestige of patriarchy (itself an essentialist category).

I do, however, have some serious reservations about treating essentialism as "a strategy for our times" (207). While I would agree with Spivak that a provisional return to essentialism can successfully operate, in particular contexts, as an interventionary strategy, I am also compelled to wonder at what point does this move cease to be provisional and become permanent? There is always a danger that the long-term effect of such a "temporary" intervention may, in fact, lead once again to a re-entrenchment of a more reactionary form of essentialism. Could it be that the recent calls, such as Spivak's, for a strategic essentialism might be humanism's way of keeping its fundamental tenets in circulation at any cost and under any guise? Could this be "phallocentrism's latest ruse"?[6] It may well be a ruse, but in the end I would agree that the "risk" is worth taking. I cannot help but think that the determining factor in deciding essentialism's political or strategic value is dependent upon who practices it: in the hands of a hegemonic group, essentialism can be employed as a powerful tool of ideological domination; in the hands of the subaltern, the use of humanism to mime (in the Irigarian sense of to undo by overdoing) humanism can represent a powerful displacing repetition. The question of the permissibility, if you will, of engaging in essentialism is therefore framed and determined by the subject-position from which one speaks.

We return, then, to Foucault's poststructuralist definition of "a subject" as "not the speaking consciousness, not the author of the formulation, but a position that may be filled in certain conditions by various individuals" (1972, 115).

It is not difficult to translate Foucault's approach to subjectivity into a general theory of reading. For example, we might ask: what are the various positions a reading subject may occupy? How are these positions constructed? Are there possible distributions of subject-positions located in the text itself? Can a reader refuse to take up a subject-position the text constructs for him/her? Does the text construct the reading subject or does the reading subject construct the text? In "Imperialism and Sexual Difference," Spivak concludes that "the clearing of a subject-position in order to speak or write is unavoidable" (1986, 229). Now it is not clear exactly what Spivak means by this claim; is she referring to a clearing *away* of a previously held subject-position or a clearing the way *for* a particular subject-position? The ambiguity is instructive here, for when reading, speaking, or writing, we are always doing both at once. In reading, for instance, we bring (old) subject-positions to the text at the same time the actual process of reading constructs (new) subject-positions for us. Consequently, we are always engaged in a "double reading"—not in Naomi Schor's sense of the term,[7] but in the sense that we are continually caught within and between *at least* two constantly shifting subject-positions (old and new, constructed and constructing) and these positions may often stand in complete contradiction to each other.

Nothing intrinsic to the notion of subject-positions suggests that it may constitute a specifically *feminist* approach to reading; it is, however, especially compatible with recent feminist reconceptualizations of the subject as a site of multiple and heterogeneous differences. This work seeks to move beyond the self/other, "I"/"not-I" binarism central to Lacan's understanding of subject constitution and instead substitutes a notion of the "I" as a complicated field of multiple subjectivities and competing identities. There is some disagreement over whether or not this new view of the subject as heteronomous and heterogeneous marks a break

with Lacan or represents the logical outcome of his theory. Teresa de Lauretis persuasively argues the former case:

> It seems to me that this notion of identity points to a more useful conception of the subject than the one proposed by neo-Freudian psychoanalysis and poststructuralist theories. For it is not the fragmented, or intermittent, identity of a subject constructed in division by language alone, an "I" continuously prefigured and preempted in an unchangeable symbolic order. It is neither, in short, the imaginary identity of the individualist, bourgeois subject, which is male and white; nor the "flickering" of the posthumanist Lacanian subject, which is too nearly white and at best (fe)male. What is emerging in feminist writings is, instead, . . . a subject that is not divided in, but rather at odds with, language. (1986, 9)

Mary Gentile, another feminist film critic, agrees, arguing that it is precisely women's "tentative" subjectivity (a result of their ambivalent representation as both object of desire and desire unfulfilled) which allows us to see subjectivity as a nexus of possibilities "where there is no clear split between 'I' and 'not-I,' but rather a range or continuum of existence" (1985, 19). My own position on the question is more closely aligned with Constance Penley's reasoning that the seeds of a theory of the subject as dispersed, as multiple, can already be found in Lacan's notion of the subject as a place of contradiction, continually in a state of construction. This view holds that without Lacan's concept of the "split subject," divided against itself, these new feminist theories of identity would not be possible (1986, 145). In any case, what we can take away from this specific debate on Lacan's theory of subjectivity is, first, the strategy of positing the reader as a site of differences and, second, the notion of the reading process as a negotiation amongst discursive subject-positions which the reader, as social subject, may or may not choose to fill.

For Foucault, which subject-positions one is likely to read from is less a matter of "choice" than "assignation." Spivak's work clarifies for us that these "I-slots" are, in fact, institutional subject-positions—"social vacancies that are of course not filled in the same way by different individuals" ("A Literary Representation of the Subaltern" 1987, 304). Though it is always dangerous to speak in terms of "choice" within a poststructuralism which deconstructs such notions as agency and free will, Spivak still provides us with a modicum of movement between institutional subject-positions. Her own reading of Mahasweta Devi's "Breast-Giver" moves carefully and deliberately among the "I-slots" of author, reader, teacher, subaltern, and historian. I see two major difficulties in applying Foucault's notion of subject-positions to either a strategy or a theory of reading.[8] First, it leads to an inclination to taxonomize, to list one's various categorical positions in linear fashion as if they could be easily extracted and unproblematically distinguished from each other. Second, such a reading can easily lend itself to stereotyping, that is, to labeling "kinds" of readers and predicting their institutional responses as Tania Modleski does with her hypothetical male and female reader in "Feminism and the Power of Interpretation." Spivak seems to anticipate this objection when she rightly insists that "all generalizations made from subject-positions are untotalizable" (304); yet her discussions of "the Indian reader," "the Marxist-feminist reader," and especially "the non-Marxist anti-racist feminist readers in the Anglo-U.S." who, "for terminological convenience," she categorizes under the label "liberal feminism" (254) all seem to point to a totalizing picture supporting and upholding each "I-slot." Perhaps it is inevitable that we turn to such labels "for terminological convenience" (after all, how else are we to make any distinctions at all between readers?), yet the phone book compiling of "I-slot" listings can be unsettling if what we wish to emphasize is not the fixed differences between subject-positions but the fluid boundaries and continual commerce between them.

Still, there are a number of benefits to such a theory of reading based on the shifting grounds of subjectivity. First, the notion of subject-positions reintroduces the author into literary criticism without reactivating the intentional fallacy; the author's interpretation of his or her own text is recognized as a legitimate position among a set of possible positions a subject might occupy in relation to the text produced. Second, because subject-positions are multiple, shifting, and changeable, readers can occupy several "I-slots" *at the same time.* This dispersal suggests both that no reader is identical to him or herself and that no reading is without internal contradiction. Third, there is no "natural" way to read a text: ways of reading are historically specific and culturally variable, and reading positions are always constructed, assigned, or mapped. Fourth, basing a theory of reading on subjectivity undermines any notion of "essential readers." Readers, like texts, are constructed; they inhabit reading practices rather than create them *ex nihilo.* Finally, all of these points suggest that if we read from multiple subject-positions, the very act of reading becomes a force for dislocating our belief in stable subjects and essential meanings.

What is particularly surprising to me about the recent men in feminism debates is not the preoccupation with essence and place but the immobility, the intractableness of the privileged terms "men" and "feminism." Robert Scholes and Tania Modleski both work to *reinforce* the bar between men/feminism, each in effect erecting a defense against the incursions of the other. For although the goals of their critical projects are much the same, if not identical (to rescue feminism from the mastering impulses of deconstruction), these critics who are more allies than combatants nonetheless position themselves on opposite sides of the asymmetrical binarism: Scholes electing to read "like a man," and Modleski choosing to read like a "female feminist." Stephen Heath, on the other hand, has argued that "female feminism" can only be viewed as a contradiction in terms. Building on Elaine Showalter's influential "Critical Cross-Dressing: Male Feminists and the Woman of the Year," Heath concludes that a man reading as a feminist always involves a strategy of female impersonation ("Male Feminism," Jardine and Smith, 28). But is there not also a mode of impersonation involved when a woman reads as a feminist, or, indeed, when a woman reads as a woman? Heath tentatively suggests that "maybe the task of male critics is just to read (forget the 'as') . . ." (29), but Scholes is right to insist that we never "just" read, that we always read *from somewhere*. The anti-essentialist "where" is essential to the poststructuralist project of theorizing reading as a negotiation of socially constructed subject-positions. As its linguistic containment within the very term "displacement" might suggest, place can never be entirely displaced, as it were, from deconstruction.

Let me return, in conclusion, to the question I deferred at the beginning of this chapter: upon what grounds can we base the notion of a class of women reading? Both "class" and "women" are political constructs (a point I shall return to in the next chapter on Monique Wittig) but what, we might ask, is "politics"? Politics is precisely the self-evident category in feminist discourse—that which is most irreducible and most indispensable. As feminism's *essential* component, it tenaciously resists definition; it is both the most transparent and the most elusive of terms. The persistent problem for feminist theorists of locating a suitable grounds for a feminist politics finds perhaps its most urgent articulation in Donna Haraway's impressive work on "cyborg politics": "What kind of politics could embrace partial, contradictory, permanently unclosed constructions of personal and collective selves and still be faithful, effective?" (1985, 75). Her answer: a class of women linked together "through coalition—affinity, not

identity"—affinity based on "choice" rather than on "nature" (73). My own inclination is to tackle these same questions of identity, politics, coalition, and feminism, but from the opposite direction. Whereas Haraway posits a coalition of women as the basis of a possible feminist socialist politics, I see politics as the basis of a possible coalition of women. For Haraway, it is affinity which grounds politics; for me, it is politics which grounds affinity. Politics marks the site where Haraway's project begins and where mine ends. In both cases, politics operates as the privileged, self-evident category.

The slippage in the above paragraph from "class" to "coalition" is not merely accidental. I intend to suggest by this shift an anti-essentialist reading of "class" as a *product* of coalition. Coalition precedes class and determines its limits and boundaries; we cannot identify a group of women until various social, historical, political coalitions construct the conditions and possibilities for membership. Many anti-essentialists fear that positing a political coalition of *women* risks presuming that there must first be a natural class of women; but this belief only masks the fact that it is coalition politics which constructs the category of women (and men) in the first place. Retaining the idea of women as a class, if anything, might help remind us that the sexual categories we work with are no more and no less than social constructions, subject-positions subject to change and to historical evolution. I am certainly not the first feminist to suggest that we need to retain the notion of women as a class for political purposes. I would, however, wish to take this conviction to its furthest conclusion and suggest that it is politics which feminism cannot do without, politics that is essential to feminism's many self-definitions. It is telling, I think, that constructionists are willing to displace "identity," "self," "experience," and virtually every other self-evident category *except* politics. To the extent that it is difficult to imagine a *non-political* feminism, politics emerges as feminism's essence.

NOTES

1. For Scholes's project to "save the referent," see "Reference and Difference" in *Textual Power: Literary Theory and the Teaching of English* (86–110).

2. See Paul Smith, "Men in Feminism: Men and Feminist Theory" (33–40); Stephen Heath, "Men in Feminism: Men and Feminist Theory" (41–46); Cary Nelson, "Men, Feminism: The Materiality of Discourse" (153–72); and Rosi Braidotti, "Envy: or With My Brains and Your Looks" (233–41), all in Jardine and Smith (1987).

3. For a more detailed reading of the constitution of the sexed subject, see Lacan's "The Mirror Stage" in *Écrits* (1–7).

4. For a summary statement of the collective's theoretical positions, see Guha (1984, vii–viii).

5. For this critique of essentialism in the Subaltern Studies group, see especially pp. 202–207.

6. The phrase is Naomi Schor's: "what is it to say that the discourse of sexual indifference/pure difference is not the last or (less triumphantly) the latest ruse of phallocentrism?" (1987, 109). This is implicitly a critique of Foucault's *anti*-essentialism, suggesting that both essentialism and anti-essentialism can have reactionary effects.

7. Schor's helpful definition of "reading double" as reading both for and beyond difference can be found in "Reading Double: Sand's Difference," in *The Poetics of Gender,* ed. Nancy K. Miller (New York: Columbia University Press, 1986).

8. Spivak insists hers is merely a reading strategy and not a comprehensive theory. The distinction she makes between these two notions is not entirely clear: is it possible to employ a reading strategy *outside* a larger theoretical framework?

32

Cora Kaplan
1940–

Concerned not only with establishing but also with historicizing the relationships between gender, race, and class, Cora Kaplan is a socialist-feminist critic who incorporates in her work the methods of psychoanalysis, semiotics, and cultural studies, particularly its Marxist varieties. Kaplan has edited anthologies of women's literature, such as *Salt and Bitter and Good: Three Centuries of English and American Women Poets* (1975), as well as collections of cultural criticism, such as *Formations of Fantasy* (1986) and *Conservative Modernity* (1996), but her most significant contribution to contemporary debates in feminism, cultural studies, and Marxist circles is a collection of her own essays, *Sea Changes: Essays on Culture and Feminism* (1986).

Published originally in the *New Accents* anthology *Making a Difference: Feminist Literary Criticism* (1985), "Pandora's Box: Subjectivity, Class and Sexuality in Socialist Feminist Criticism" is an often-anthologized essay, having appeared also in *Feminisms: An Anthology of Literary Theory and Criticism* (1991) and *Contemporary Marxist Literary Criticism* (1992), not to mention Cora Kaplan's own important collection of essays, *Sea Changes: Essays on Culture and Feminism.* In this essay Kaplan criticizes a conservative, reactionary development in recent feminist criticism, the liberal feminist critics' emphasis on the unified female subject. Excluding the class and race perspectives that socialist feminist critics bring to the analysis of both literary texts and their conditions of production, the liberal feminist critic treats feminine subjectivity, and identity in general, in itself, as if it were universal, natural, or essential—as if it were, in other words, transhistorical. Such an approach to subjectivity, which duplicates the structures of "mass-market romance," fails to realize, Kaplan argues, that subjectivity is always articulated in social and cultural terms within systems of difference and structuring hierarchies, so that gender cannot be discussed apart from class and race. Novels, poetry, and drama, in fact, afford ample evidence of this impossibility, for in literature the languages of class, race, and gender are fused.

In order to criticize the position of the liberal or humanist feminist critic, Kaplan provides a genealogy, beginning with Mary Wollstonecraft's *A Vindication of the Rights of Woman* (1792) and concluding with Virginia Woolf's *Women and Fiction* (1929), in which she traces the development of the concept of the independent, autonomous subject, demonstrating not only that it has a history and thus that it is not natural or self-evident but also that it is always articulated within a system of relationships, that it is, in fact, predicated upon exclusions of gender, race, and class. Kaplan's

most impressive evidence for these claims are provided in her discussions of Charlotte
Brontë's *Jane Eyre* and Virginia Woolf's *Women and Fiction*.

In conclusion, after having brought her genealogy to a close, Kaplan reiterates her
main claim, which has profound ramifications for feminism, cultural studies, and
Marxism, that we must redefine the psyche as a structure, not as a content, so that we
can move toward a fuller understanding of how social divisions and the inscription of
gender are mutually secured and given meaning.

Pandora's Box
Subjectivity, Class, and Sexuality in Socialist Feminist Criticism

*Feminist criticism, as its name implies, is criticism
with a Cause, engaged criticism. But the critical model
presented to us so far is merely engaged to be married. It is
about to contract what can only be a* mésalliance *with
bourgeois modes of thought and the critical categories they
inform. To be effective, feminist criticism cannot become
simply bourgeois criticism in drag. It must be ideological
and moral criticism: it must be revolutionary.*

—Lillian Robinson, "Dwelling in
Decencies" (1978)

*The "Marriage" of marxism and feminism has been
like the marriage of husband and wife depicted in English
common law: marxism and feminism are one, and that is
marxism . . . we need a healthier marriage or we need a
divorce.*

—Heidi Hartmann, "The Unhappy Marriage of
Marxism and Feminism" (1981)

I

In spite of the attraction of matrimonial
metaphor, reports of feminist nuptials with either mild-mannered bourgeois criticism or ma-
cho mustachioed Marxism have been greatly exaggerated. Neither liberal feminist criticism
decorously draped in traditional humanism, nor
her red-ragged rebellious sister, socialist feminist
criticism, has yet found a place within androcentric literary criticism, which wishes to embrace feminism through a legitimate public alliance. Nor can feminist criticism today be plausibly evoked as a young deb looking for
protection or, even more problematically, as a
male 'mole' in transvestite masquerade. Feminist
criticism now marks out a broad area of literary
studies, eclectic, original and provocative. Independent still, through a combination of choice
and default, it has come of age without giving
up its name. Yet Lillian Robinson's astute pes-
simistic prediction is worth remembering. With
maturity, the most visible, well-defined and extensive tendency within feminist criticism has
undoubtedly bought into the white, middle-
class, heterosexist values of traditional literary
criticism, and threatens to settle down on her
own in its cultural suburbs. For, as I see it, the
present danger is not that feminist criticism will
enter an unequal dependent alliance with any of
the varieties of male-centered criticism. It does
not need to, for it has produced an all too persuasive autonomous analysis which is in many
ways radical in its discussion of gender, but implicitly conservative in its assumptions about social hierarchy and female subjectivity, the Pandora's box for all feminist theory.

This reactionary effect must be interrogated
and resisted from within feminism and in relation to the wider socialist feminist project. For,

without the class and race perspectives which socialist feminist critics bring to the analysis both of the literary texts and of their conditions of production, liberal feminist criticism, with its emphasis on the unified female subject, will unintentionally reproduce the ideological values of mass-market romance. In that fictional landscape the other structuring relations of society fade and disappear, leaving us with the naked drama of sexual difference as the only scenario that matters. Mass-market romance tends to represent sexual difference as natural and fixed—a constant, transhistorical femininity in libidinized struggle with an equally 'given' universal masculinity. Even where class difference divides lovers, it is there as narrative backdrop or minor stumbling-block to the inevitable heterosexual resolution. Without overstraining the comparison, a feminist literary criticism which privileges gender in isolation from other forms of social determination offers us a similarly partial reading of the role played by sexual difference in literary discourse, a reading bled dry of its most troubling and contradictory meanings.

The appropriation of modern critical theory—semiotic with an emphasis on the psychoanalytic—can be of great use in arguing against concepts of natural, essential and unified identity: against a static femininity and masculinity. But these theories about the production of meaning in culture must engage fully with the effects of other systems of difference than the sexual, or they too will produce no more than an anti-humanist avant-garde version of romance. Masculinity and femininity do not appear in cultural discourse, any more than they do in mental life, as pure binary forms at play. They are always, already, ordered and broken up through other social and cultural terms, other categories of difference. Our fantasies of sexual transgression as much as our obedience to sexual regulation are expressed through these structuring hierarchies. Class and race ideologies are, conversely, steeped in and spoken through the language of sexual differentiation. Class and race meanings are not metaphors for the sexual, or vice versa. It is better though not exact, to see them as reciprocally constituting each other through a kind of narrative invocation, a set of associative terms in a chain of meaning. To understand how gender and class—to take two categories only—are articulated together transforms our analysis of each of them.

The literary text too often figures in feminist criticism as a gripping spectacle in which sexual difference appears somewhat abstracted from the muddy social world in which it is elsewhere embedded. Yet novels, poetry and drama are, on the contrary, peculiarly rich discourses in which the fused languages of class, race and gender are both produced and re-represented through the incorporation of other discourses. The focus of feminist analysis ought to be on that heterogeneity within the literary, on the intimate relation there expressed between all the categories that order social and psychic meaning. This does not imply an attention to content only or primarily, but also entails a consideration of the linguistic processes of the text as they construct and position subjectivity within these terms.

For without doubt literary texts do centre the individual as object and subject of their discourse. Literature has been a traditional space for the exploration of gender relations and sexual difference, and one in which women themselves have been formidably present. The problem for socialist feminists is not the focus on the individual that is special to the literary, but rather the romantic theory of the subject so firmly entrenched within the discourse. Humanist feminist criticism does not object to the idea of an immanent, transcendent subject but only to the exclusion of women from these definitions which it takes as an accurate account of subjectivity rather than as a historically constructed ideology. The repair and reconstitution of female subjectivity through a rereading of literature becomes, therefore, a major part, often unacknowledged, of its critical project. Psychoanalytic and semiotically oriented feminist criticism has argued well against this aspect of feminist humanism, emphasizing the important structural relation between writing and sexuality in the construction of the subject. But both tendencies have been correctly criticized from a socialist feminist position for the neglect of class and race as factors in their analysis. If feminist criticism is to make a central contribution to the understanding of sexual difference, instead of serving as a conservative refuge from its more disturbing social and psychic implications, the inclusion of class and race must transform its terms and objectives.

II

The critique of feminist humanism needs more historical explication than it has so far received. Its sources are complex, and are rooted in that moment almost 200 years ago when modern feminism and Romantic cultural theory emerged as separate but linked responses to the transforming events of the French Revolution. In the heat and light of the revolutionary decade 1790–1800, social, political and aesthetic ideas already maturing underwent a kind of forced ripening. As the progressive British intelligentsia contemplated the immediate possibility of social change, their thoughts turned urgently to the present capacity of subjects to exercise republican freedoms—to rule themselves as well as each other if the corrupt structures of aristocratic privilege were to be suddenly razed. Both feminism as set out in its most influential text, Mary Wollstonecraft's *A Vindication of the Rights of Woman* (1792), and Romanticism as argued most forcefully in Wordsworth's introduction to *Lyrical Ballads* (1800) stood in intimate, dynamic and contradictory relationship to democratic politics. In all three discourses the social and psychic character of the individual was centred and elaborated. The public and private implications of sexual difference as well as of the imagination and its products were both strongly linked to the optimistic, speculative construction of a virtuous citizen subject for a brave new egalitarian world. Theories of reading and writing—Wollstonecraft's and Jane Austen's as well as those of male Romantic authors—were explicitly related to contemporary politics as expressed in debate by such figures as Tom Paine, Edmund Burke and William Godwin.

The new categories of independent subjectivity, however, were marked from the beginning by exclusions of gender, race and class. Jean-Jacques Rousseau, writing in the 1750s, specifically exempted women for his definition: Thomas Jefferson, some twenty years later, excluded blacks. Far from being invisible ideological aspects of the new subject, these exclusions occasioned debate and polemic on both sides of the Atlantic. The autonomy of inner life, the dynamic psyche whose moral triumph was to be the foundation of republican government, was considered absolutely essential as an element of progressive political thought.

However, as the concept of the inner self and the moral psyche was used to denigrate whole classes, races and genders, late-nineteenth-century socialism began to de-emphasize the political importance of the psychic self, and redefine political morality and the adequate citizen subject in primarily social terms. Because of this shift in emphasis, a collective moralism has developed in socialist thought which, instead of criticizing the reactionary interpretation of psychic life, stigmatizes sensibility itself, interpreting the excess of feeling as regressive, bourgeois and non-political.

Needless to say, this strand of socialist thought poses a problem for feminism, which has favoured three main strategies to deal with it. In the first, women's psychic life is seen as being essentially identical to men's, but distorted through vicious and systematic patriarchal inscription. In this view, which is effectively Wollstonecraft's, social reform would prevent women from becoming regressively obsessed with sexuality and feeling. The second strategy wholly of representation go even further in rejecting the possibility of authentic mimetic art. They see the literary text as a system of signs that constructs meaning rather than reflecting it, inscribing simultaneously the subjectivity of speaker and reader. Fiction by bourgeois women writers is spoken from the position of a class-specific femininity. It constructs us as readers in relation to that subjectivity through the linguistic strategies and processes of the text. It also takes us on a tour, so to speak, of a waxworks of other subjects-in-process—the characters of the text. These fictional characters are there as figures in a dream, as constituent structures of the narrative of the dreamer, not as correct reflections of the socially real.

It is hard for feminism to accept the implications of this virtual refusal of textual realism, if only because literature was one of the few public discourses in which women were allowed to speak themselves, where they were not the imaginary representations of men. None the less, the subjectivity of women of other classes and races and with different sexual orientations can never be 'objectively' or 'authentically' represented in literary texts by the white, heterosexual, middle-class woman writer, however sympathetically she invents or describes such women in her narrative. The nature of fiction and the eccentric relation of female subjectivity itself both to culture and to psychic identity, as understood from a psychoanalytic perspective, defeats that aim. We can, however, learn a great deal from women's writing about the cultural meanings produced from the splitting of women's subjectivity, especially her sexuality, into class and race categories. But before we say more about this way of reading women's writing we need a more precise working definition of 'class.'

Unlike subjectivity, 'class' has been a central category for socialist feminist criticism, but remains somewhat inert within it, if not within socialist feminist theory as a whole. Socialist critics hesitate to identify their own object of

study, the literary text, as a central productive site of class meaning, because it seems too far away from 'real' economic and political determinations. The same worry, conversely, can induce a compensatory claim that *all* the material relations of class can be discovered within the discourse; indeed, that they are most fully represented there, because language is itself material. These positions, which I confess I have parodied a little, remain unresolved in current debate, although efforts at *détente* have been made. They indicate the uneasy relationship between the political and the literary in the Marxist critical project, an unease shared by socialist feminists too.

Among socialist historians in the last few years the understanding of the history of class has undergone vigorous reappraisal in response to debates about the changing composition and politics of the working class in modern capitalist societies. In a recent collection of essays, *The Languages of Class,* the British historian of the nineteenth century, Gareth Stedman Jones, proposes some radical approaches to that history which have an immediate relevance for the analysis of representation. First of all, Stedman Jones asks for a more informed and theoretical attention by historians to the linguistic construction of class. '"Class" is a word embedded in language and should be analysed in terms of its linguistic content,' he states. In the second place, 'class' as a concept needs to be unpacked, and its differential construction in discourse recognized and given a certain autonomy:

> because there are different languages of class, one should not proceed upon the assumption that 'class' as an elementary counter of official social description, 'class' as an effect of theoretical discourse about distribution or productive relations, 'class' as the summary of a cluster of culturally signifying practices or 'class' as a species of political or ideological self-definition, share a single reference point in anterior social reality. (Stedman Jones 1983, pp. 7–8)

While 'anterior social reality' hangs slightly loose in this formulation, the oppressively unitary character of class as a concept is usefully broken down. Class can be seen as defined in different terms at different levels of analysis, as well as being 'made' and 'lived' through a variety of languages at any given point in history.

How can this pulling apart of the languages of class help socialist feminist critics to put class and gender, social and psychic together in a non-reductive way? First of all, these distinctions put a useful space between the economic overview of class—the Marxist or socialist analysis—and the actual rhetoric of class as it appears in a novel. The class language of a nineteenth-century novel is not only or even primarily characterized by reference to the material circumstances of the protagonists, though that may be part of its representation there. The language of class in the novel foregrounds the language of the self, the inner discourse of the subject *as* class language, framing that discourse through the dissonant chorus of class voices that it appropriates and invents. In the novel, class discourse *is* gendered discourse; the positions of 'Emile' and 'Sophie' are given dramatic form. Class is embodied in fiction in a way that it never is either in bourgeois economic discourse or in Marxist economic analysis. In those discourses of class, gender is mystified, presented in ideological form. In fiction, though difference may be presented through sexual ideologies, its immanent, crucial presence in the social relations of class, as well as its psychic effects, is strongly asserted. Fiction refuses the notion of a genderless class subjectivity, and resists any simple reduction of class meaning and class identity to productive forces. This refusal and resistance cannot be written off, or reduced to the humanist ideologies of transcendence which those fictions may also enunciate, for the presence of gendered subjectivity in nineteenth-century fiction is always 'in struggle' with the Romantic ideologies of unified identity.

Within socialist feminist cultural analysis it has been easier to describe the visual or linguistic fusion of class and gender meanings in representation than it has been to assess the role such fusion plays in the construction of either category. Let us assume that in these signifying practices class is powerfully defined through sexual difference, and vice versa, and that these representations are constitutive of certain class meanings, not merely a distorted or mendacious reflection of other languages. 'Class' needs to be read through an ensemble of these languages, often contradictory, as well as in terms of an economic overview. The overpowering presence of gender in some languages of class and its virtual absence in others needs to be related not to a single anterior definition of class reality, but to the heterogeneous and contradictory nature of that reality.

Literature is itself a heterogeneous discourse, which appropriates, contextualizes and comments on other 'languages' of class and gender. This process of intertextuality—the dialogic, as the Russian critic Bakhtin called it (Bakhtin 1981)—undermines the aspirations of the text towards a unifying definition. The language of class in the nineteenth-century novel obsessively inscribes a class system whose divisions and boundaries are at once absolute and impregnable and in constant danger of dissolution. Often in these narratives it is a woman whose class identity is at risk or problematic; the woman and her sexuality are a condensed and displaced representation of the dangerous instabilities of class and gender identity for both sexes. The loss and recuperation of female identity within the story—a favourite lost-and-found theme from *Mansfield Park* to *Tess*—provides an imaginary though temporary solution to the crisis of both femininity and class. Neither category—class or gender—was ever as stable as the ideologies that support them must continually insist. The many-layered, compacted representations of class and gender found in imaginative literature flees from the sinister importunities of her titled foreign host. The scene is rural Italy, as far away as possible from genteel British society. Emily's flight from the castle is precipitous, and in her terror and haste she forgets her hat. Within the world of the text, Emily's bare head threatens her identity as pure woman, as surely as do the violent, lascivious attentions of her pursuer. Both the narrative and her flight are interrupted while Emily restores her identity by purchasing 'a little straw hat' from a peasant girl. A woman without a hat was, in specular terms, a whore; the contemporary readership understood the necessary pause in the story. They understood too that the hat, passed from peasant to lady, securing the class and sexual status of the latter, was not only a fragment of domestic realism set against gothic fantasy. Hat and flight are part of a perfectly coherent psychic narrative in which aristocratic seducer, innocent bourgeois victim, peasant girl and straw hat play out the linked meanings of class and sexuality.

Stories of seduction and betrayal, of orphaned, impoverished heroines of uncertain class origin, provided a narrative structure through which the instabilities of class and gender categories were both stabilized and undermined. Across the body and mind of 'woman' as sign, through her multiple representations, bourgeois anxiety about identity is traced and retraced. A favourite plot, of which *Jane Eyre* is now the best-known example, sets the genteel heroine at sexual risk as semi-servant in a grand patriarchal household. This narrative theme allowed the crisis of middle-class femininity to be mapped on to the structural sexual vulnerability of all working-class servants in bourgeois employment. Such dramas were full of condensed meanings in excess of the representation of sexuality and sexual difference. A doubled scenario, in which the ideological and material difference between working-class and bourgeois women is blurred through condensation, it was popular as a plot for melodrama with both 'genteel' and 'vulgar' audiences.

We do not know very much so far about how that fictional narrative of threatened femininity was understood by working-class women, although it appeared in the cheap fiction written for servant girls as well as in popular theatre. Nineteenth-century bourgeois novels like *Jane Eyre* tell us almost nothing about the self-defined subjectivity of the poor, male or female. For, although they are both rich sources for the construction of dominant definitions *of* the inner lives of the working classes, they cannot tell us anything about how even these ideological inscriptions were lived *by* them. For an analysis of the subjectivity of working-class women we need to turn to non-literary sources, to the discourses in which they themselves spoke. That analysis lies outside the project of this paper but is, of course, related to it.

I want to end . . . with an example of the kind of interpretative integration that I have been demanding of feminist critics. No text has proved more productive of meaning from the critic's point of view than Charlotte Bronte's *Jane Eyre*. I have referred to the condensation of class meanings through the characterization and narrative of its heroine, but now I want to turn to that disturbing didactic moment in volume 1, chapter 12, which immediately precedes the entry of Rochester into the text. It is a passage marked out by Virginia Woolf in *A Room of One's Own,* where it is used to illustrate the negative effect of anger and inequality on the female literary imagination. Prefaced defensively—'Anybody may blame me who likes'—it is a passage about need, demand and desire that exceed social possibility and challenge social prejudice. In Jane's soliloquy, inspired by a view reached through raising the 'trap-door of the attic,' the Romantic aesthetic is reasserted for women, together with a passionate refusal of the terms of feminine difference. Moved by a 'restlessness' in her 'nature' that 'agitated me to pain sometimes,' Jane paces the top floor of Thornfield and allows her 'mind's eye to dwell on whatever bright visions rose before it':

to let my heart be heaved by the exultant movement which, while it swelled it in trouble, expanded it with life; and, best of all, to open my inward ear to a tale that was never ended—a tale my imagination created, and narrated continuously; quickened with all of incident, life, fire, feeling, that I desired and had not in my actual existence. (Bronte 1976, p. 110)

This reverie is only partly quoted by Woolf, who omits the 'visionary' section, moving straight from 'pain . . .' to the paragraph most familiar to us through her citation of it:

It is in vain to say that human beings ought to be satisfied with tranquillity; they must have action; and they will make it if they cannot find it. Millions are condemned to a stiller doom than mine, and millions are in silent revolt against their lot. Nobody knows how many rebellions besides political rebellions ferment in the masses of life which people earth. Women are supposed to be very calm generally: but women feel just as men feel: they need exercise for their faculties, and a field for their efforts as much as their brothers do; they suffer from too rigid a restraint, too absolute a stagnation, precisely as men would suffer; and it is narrow-minded in their more privileged fellow-creatures to say that they ought to confine themselves to making puddings and knitting stockings, to playing on the piano and embroidering bags. It is thoughtless to condemn them, or laugh at them, if they seek to do more or learn more than custom has pronounced necessary for their sex.

When thus alone I not unfrequently heard Grace Poole's laugh . . . .

This shift from feminist polemic to the laugh of Grace Poole is the 'jerk,' the 'awkward break' of 'continuity' that Woolf criticizes. The writer of such a flawed passage

will never get her genius expressed whole and entire. Her books will be deformed and twisted. She will write in a rage where she should write calmly. She will write foolishly where she should write wisely. She will write of herself when she should write of her characters. She is at war with her lot. How could she help but die young, cramped and thwarted? (Woolf 1973, p. 70)

It is a devastating, controlled, yet somehow uncontrolled indictment. What elements in this digression, hardly a formal innovation in nineteenth-century fiction, can have prompted Woolf to such excess? Elaine Showalter analyses this passage and others as part of Woolf's 'flight into androgyny,' that aesthetic chamber where masculine and feminine minds meet and marry. Showalter's analysis focuses on Woolf's aesthetic as an effect of her inability to come to terms with her sexuality, with sexual difference itself. Showalter's analysis is persuasive in individual terms, but it does not deal with all of the questions thrown up by Bronte's challenge and Woolf's violent response to it. In the sentences that Woolf omits in her own citation, Bronte insists that even the confined and restless state could produce 'many and glowing' visions. Art, the passage maintains, can be produced through the endless narration of the self, through the mixed incoherence of subjectivity spoken from subordinate and rebellious positions within culture. It was this aesthetic that Woolf as critic explicitly rejected.

However, the passage deals with more than sexual difference. In the references to 'human beings' and to unspecified 'millions' Bronte deliberately and defiantly associates political and sexual rebellion even as she distinguishes between them. In the passage the generic status of 'men' is made truly trans-class and transcultural when linked to 'masses,' 'millions' and 'human beings,' those larger inclusive terms. In 1847, on the eve of the second great wave of modern revolution, it was a dangerous rhetoric to use.

Its meaningful associations were quickly recognized by contemporary reviewers, who deplored the contiguous relationship between revolution and feminism. Lady Eastlake's
comments in the *Quarterly Review* of 1849 are
those most often quoted:

> We do not hesitate to say, that the tone of
> mind and thought which has overthrown au-
> thority and violated every code human and
> divine abroad, and fostered chartism and re-
> bellion at home is the same which has also
> written *Jane Eyre.*

Yet Charlotte Bronte was no political radical.
She is pulled towards the positive linking of
class rebellion and women's revolt in this passage
through her anger at the misrepresentation and
suppression of women's identity, not via an already held sympathy with the other masses and
millions. It is a tentative, partial movement in
spite of its defiant rhetoric, and it is checked in a
moment by the mad, mocking female laughter,
and turned from its course a few pages later by
the introduction of Rochester into the narrative.
For Woolf, Jane's soliloquy spoils the continuity
of the narrative with its 'anger and rebellion.'
Woolf turns away, refuses to comprehend the
logical sequence of the narration at the symbolic
level of the novel.

Jane's revolutionary manifesto of the subject,
which has its own slightly manic register, invokes that sliding negative signification of
women that we have described. At this point in
the story the 'low, slow ha'ha!' and the 'eccentric
murmurs' which 'thrilled' Jane are ascribed to
Grace Poole, the hard-featured servant. But
Grace is only the laugh's reminder, and the
laugh later becomes 'correctly' ascribed to
Rochester's insane wife, Bertha Mason. The uncertain source of the laughter, the narrator's inability to predict its recurrence—'There were
days when she was quite silent; but there were
others when I could not account for the sounds

she made'—both mark out the 'sounds' as the
dark side of Romantic female subjectivity.

Retroactively, in the narratives the laughter
becomes a threat to all that Jane had desired and
demanded in her roof-top reverie. Mad servant,
mad mistress, foreigner, nymphomaniac,
syphilitic, half-breed, aristocrat, Bertha turns violently on keeper, brother, husband and, finally,
rival. She and her noises become the condensed
and displaced site of unreason and anarchy as it
is metonymically figured through dangerous
femininity in all its class, race and cultural projections. Bertha must be killed off, narratively
speaking, so that a moral, Protestant femininity,
licensed sexuality and a qualified, socialized
feminism may survive. Yet the text cannot close
off or recuperate that moment of radical association between political rebellion and gender rebellion, cannot shut down the possibility of a
positive alliance between reason, passion and
feminism. Nor can it disperse the terror that
speaking those connections immediately stirs
up—for Woolf in any case.

Woolf was at her most vehement and most
contradictory about these issues, which brought
together for her, as for many other feminists before and after, a number of deeply connected
anxieties about subjectivity, class, sexuality and
culture. Over and over again in her critical writing, Woolf tries to find ways of placing the questions inside an aesthetic that disallows anger,
unreason and passion as productive emotions.
Like Wollstonecraft before her, she cannot quite
shake off the moral and libidinal economies of
the Enlightenment. In 'Women and Fiction'
(1929) she frames the question another way:

> In *Middlemarch* and in *Jane Eyre* we are con-
> scious not merely of the writer's character, as
> we are conscious of the character of Charles
> Dickens, but we are conscious of a woman's
> presence—of someone resenting the treat-
> ment of her sex and pleading for its rights.
> This brings into women's writing an element

which is entirely absent from a man's, unless, indeed, he happens to be a working man, a Negro, or one who for some other reason is conscious of disability. It introduces a distortion and is frequently the cause of weakness. The desire to plead some personal cause or to make a character the mouthpiece of personal discontent or grievance always has a distressing effect, as if the spot at which the reader's attention is directed were suddenly two-fold instead of single. (Woolf 1979, p. 47)

Note how the plea for a sex, a class, a race becomes reduced to individual, personal grievance, how subordinate position in a group becomes immediately pathologized as private disability, weakness. Note too how 'man' in this passage loses its universal connotation, so that it only refers normatively to men of the ruling class. In this passage, as in *Jane Eyre*, the metonymic evocation of degraded subjectivities is expressed as an effect of subordination, not its rationale nor its cause. But the result is still a negative one. For the power to resist through fictional language, the language of sociality and self; the power to move and enlighten, rather than blur and distress through the double focus, is denied. Instead, Woolf announces the death of the feminist text, by proclaiming, somewhat prematurely, the triumph of feminism.

> The woman writer is no longer bitter. She is no longer angry. She is no longer pleading and protesting as she writes. . . . She will be able to concentrate upon her vision without distraction from outside. (Woolf 1979, p. 48)

This too is a cry from the roof-tops of a desire still unmet by social and psychic experience.

Although the meanings attached to race, class and sexuality have undergone fundamental shifts from Wollstonecraft's (and Woolf's) time to our own, we do not live in a post-class society any more than a post-feminist one. Our identities are still constructed through social hierarchy and cultural differentiation, as well as through those processes of division and fragmentation described in psychoanalytic theory. The identities arrived at through these structures will always be precarious and unstable, though *how* they will be so in the future we do not know. For the moment, women still have a problematic place in both social and psychic representation. The problem for women of woman-as-sign has made the self-definition of women a resonant issue within feminism. It has also determined the restless inability of feminism to settle for humanist definitions of the subject, or for materialism's relegation of the problem to determinations of class only. I have emphasized . . . some of the more negative ways in which the Enlightenment and Romantic paradigms of subjectivity gave hostage to the making of subordinate identities, of which femininity is the structuring instance. Although psychoanalytic theories of the construction of gendered subjectivity stress difficulty, antagonism and contradiction as necessary parts of the production of identity, the concept of the unconscious and the psychoanalytic view of sexuality dissolve in great part the binary divide between reason and passion that dominates earlier concepts of subjectivity. They break down as well the moralism attached to those libidinal and psychic economies. Seen from this perspective, 'individualism' has a different and more contentious history within feminism than it does in androcentric debates.

It is that history which we must uncover and consider, in both its positive and its negative effects, so that we can argue convincingly for a feminist rehabilitation of the female psyche in non-moralized terms. Perhaps we can come to see it as neither sexual outlaw, social bigot nor dark hiding-place for treasonable regressive femininity waiting to stab progressive feminism in the back. *We must redefine* the psyche as a structure, not as a content. To do so is not to move away from a feminist politics which takes race

nomenon, but a mode of intentionality, a directional force and mode of desire. As a condition of access to the world, the body is a being comported beyond itself, referring to the world and thereby revealing its own ontological status as a referential reality. For Sartre, the body is lived and experienced as the context and medium for all human strivings.[3] Because for Sartre all human beings strive after possibilities not yet realized, human beings are to that extent 'beyond' themselves. This *ek-static* condition is itself a corporeal experience; the body is thus experienced as a mode of becoming. Indeed, for Sartre the natural body only exists in the mode of being surpassed: 'We can never apprehend this contingency as such in so far as our body is *for us;* for we are a choice, and for us to be is to choose ourselves . . . this inapprehensible body is precisely the necessity that *there be a choice,* that I do not exist *all at once.*'[4]

Beauvoir does not so much refute Sartre as take him at his non-Cartesian best.[5] Sartre writes in *Being and Nothingness* that 'it would be best to say, using 'exist' as a transitive verb, that consciousness *exists* its body.'[6] The transitive form of 'exist' is not far removed from Beauvoir's disarming use of 'become', and Beauvoir's concept of becoming a gender seems both a radicalization and concretization of the Sartrian formulation. In transposing the identification of corporeal existence and 'becoming' onto the scene of sex and gender, Beauvoir appropriates the ontological necessity of the paradox, but the tension in her theory does not reside between being 'in' and 'beyond' the body, but in the move from the natural to the acculturated body. That one is not born, but rather becomes, a woman does not imply that this 'becoming' traverses a path from disembodied freedom to cultural embodiment. Indeed, one is one's body from the start, and only thereafter becomes one's gender. The movement from sex to gender is internal to embodied life, a sculpting of the original body into a cultural form. To mix Sartrian phraseology with Beauvoir's, we might say

that to 'exist' one's body in culturally concrete terms means, at least partially, to become one's gender.

Although we 'become' our genders in Beauvoir's view, the temporal movement of this becoming does not follow a linear progression. The origin of gender is not temporally discrete precisely because gender is not suddenly originated at some point in time after which it is fixed in form. In an important sense, gender is not traceable to a definable origin because it itself is an originating activity incessantly taking place. No longer understood as a product of cultural and psychic relations long past, gender is a contemporary way of organizing past and future cultural norms, a way of situating oneself in and through those norms, an active style of living one's body in the world.

GENDER AS CHOICE

One chooses one's gender, but one does not choose it from a distance, which signals an ontological juncture between the choosing agent and the chosen gender. The Cartesian space of the deliberate 'chooser' is fictional, but if the distanced deliberations of the spectator are not the choices whereof Beauvoir speaks, then how are we to understand the choice at the origin of gender? Beauvoir's view of gender as an incessant project, a daily act of reconstruction and interpretation, draws upon Sartre's doctrine of prereflective choice and gives that abstract epistemological structure a concrete cultural meaning. Prereflective choice is a tacit and spontaneous act which Sartre terms 'quasi-knowledge'. Not wholly conscious, but nevertheless accessible to consciousness, it is the kind of choice we make and only later realize that we have made. Beauvoir seems to rely on this notion of choice in referring to the kind of volitional act through which gender is assumed. Taking on a gender is not possible at a moment's notice, but is a subtle and strategic project, laborious and for the most part covert. Becoming a gender is an impulsive yet mindful process of interpreting a cultural reality laden with sanctions, taboos and prescriptions. The choice to assume a certain kind of body, to live or wear one's body a certain way, implies a world of already established corporeal styles. To choose a gender is to interpret received gender norms in a way that reproduces and organizes them anew. Less a radical act of creation, gender is a tacit project to renew a cultural history in one's own corporeal terms. This is not a prescriptive task we must endeavor to do, but one in which we have been endeavoring all along.

By scrutinizing the mechanism of agency and appropriation, Beauvoir is attempting, in my mind, to infuse the analysis of women's oppression with emancipatory potential. Oppression is not a self-contained system that either confronts individuals as a theoretical object or generates them as its cultural pawns. It is a dialectical force that requires individual participation on a large scale in order to maintain its malignant life.

Beauvoir does not address directly the burden of freedom that gender presents, but we can extrapolate from her position how constraining gender norms work to subdue the exercise of gender freedom. The social constraints upon gender compliance and deviation are so great that most people feel deeply wounded if they are told that they exercise their manhood or womanhood improperly. In so far as social existence requires an unambiguous gender affinity, it is not possible to exist in a socially meaningful sense outside of established gender norms. The fall from established gender boundaries initiates a sense of radical dislocation which can assume a metaphysical significance. If human existence is always gendered existence, then to stray outside of established gender is in some sense to put one's very existence into question. In these moments of gender dislocation in which we realize that it is hardly necessary that we be the genders we have become, we confront the burden of choice intrinsic to living as a man or a woman or some other gender identity, a freedom made burdensome through social constraint.

The anguish and terror of leaving a prescribed gender or of trespassing upon another gender territory testifies to the social constraints upon gender interpretation as well as to the necessity *that there be* an interpretation, i.e., to the essential freedom at the origin of gender. Similarly, the widespread difficulty in accepting motherhood, for example, as an institutional rather than an instinctual reality expresses this same interplay of constraint and freedom. The effort to interpret maternal feelings as organic necessities discloses a desire to disguise motherhood as an optional practice. If motherhood becomes a choice, then what else is possible? This kind of questioning often engenders vertigo and terror over the possibility of losing social sanctions, of leaving a solid social station and place. That this terror is so well known gives the most credence to the notion that gender identity rests on the unstable bedrock of human invention.

EMBODIMENT AND AUTONOMY

Beauvoir's analysis of the body takes its bearings within the cultural situation in which men have traditionally been associated with the disembodied or transcendent feature of human existence and women with the bodily and immanent feature of human existence. Her own view of an embodied identity that 'incorporates' transcendence subscribes to neither position. Although she occasionally seems to embrace a view of authority modeled on the disembodied transcendence of consciousness, her criticism of this disembodied perspective suggests that another version of autonomy is implicitly at work in her theory.

Women are 'Other' according to Beauvoir in so far as they are defined by a masculine perspective that seeks to safeguard its own disembodied status through identifying women generally with the bodily sphere. Masculine disembodiment is only possible on the condition that women occupy their bodies as their essential and enslaving identities. If women *are* their bodies (to be distinguished from 'existing' their bodies, which implies living their bodies as projects or bearers of created meanings), if women are only their bodies, if their consciousness and freedom are only so many disguised permutations of bodily need and necessity, then women have, in effect, exclusively monopolized the bodily sphere of life. By defining women as 'Other', men are able through the shortcut of definition to dispose of their bodies, to make themselves other than their bodies—a symbol potentially of human decay and transience, of limitation generally—and to make their bodies other than themselves. From this belief that the body is Other, it is not a far leap to the conclusion that others *are* their bodies, while the masculine 'I' is a noncorporeal soul. The body rendered as Other—the body repressed or denied and, then, projected—reemerges for this 'I' as the view of others as essentially body. Hence, women become the Other; they come to embody corporeality itself. This redundancy becomes their essence, and existence as a woman becomes what Hegel termed 'a motionless tautology'.

Beauvoir's dialectic of self and Other argues the limits of a Cartesian version of disembodied freedom, and criticizes implicitly the model of autonomy upheld by these masculine gender norms. The pursuit of disembodiment is necessarily deceived because the body can never really be denied; its denial becomes the condition of its emergence in alien form. Disembodiment becomes a way of existing one's body in the mode of denial. And the denial of the body—as in Hegel's dialectic of master and slave—reveals itself as nothing other than the embodiment of denial.

THE BODY AS SITUATION

Beauvoir suggests an alternative to the gender polarity of masculine disembodiment and feminine enslavement to the body in her notion of the body as a 'situation'. The body as situation has at least a twofold meaning. As a locus of cultural interpretations, the body is a material reality that has already been located and defined within a social context. The body is also the situation of having to take up and interpret that set of received interpretations. As a field of interpretive possibilities, the body is a locus of the dialectical process of interpreting anew a historical set of interpretations which have already informed corporeal style. The body becomes a peculiar nexus of culture and choice, and 'existing' one's body becomes a personal way of taking up and reinterpreting received gender norms. To the extent that gender norms function under the aegis of social constraints, the reinterpretation of those norms through the proliferation and variation of corporeal styles becomes a very concrete and accessible way of politicizing personal life.

If we accept the body as a cultural situation, then the notion of a natural body and, indeed, a natural 'sex' seem increasingly suspect. The limits to gender, the range of possibilities for a lived interpretation of a sexually differentiated anatomy, seem less restricted by anatomy than by the weight of the cultural institutions that have conventionally interpreted anatomy. Indeed, it becomes unclear when we take Beauvoir's formulation to its unstated consequences, whether gender need to be in any way linked with sex, or whether this linkage is itself cultural convention. If gender is a way of existing one's body, and one's body is a situation, a field of cultural possibilities both received and reinterpreted, then both gender and sex seem to be thoroughly cultural affairs. Gender seems less a function of anatomy than one of its possible uses: 'the body of woman is one of the essential elements in her situation in the world. But that body is not enough to define her as woman; there is no true living reality except as manifested by the conscious individual through activities and in the bosom of society.'[7]

THE BODY POLITIC

If the natural body—and natural 'sex'—is a fiction, Beauvoir's theory seems implicitly to ask whether sex was not gender all along. Monique Wittig formulates this challenge to natural 'sex' explicitly. Although Wittig and Beauvoir occupy very different sides of the feminist political spectrum in contemporary France, they are nevertheless joined theoretically in their refusal of essentialist doctrines of femininity. Wittig's article, 'One Is Not Born a Woman', takes its title from Beauvoir's stated formulation, and was initially presented at the Simone de Beauvoir conference in New York City in 1979. Although that piece does not mention Beauvoir after the first few paragraphs, we can nevertheless read it as an effort to make explicit Beauvoir's tacit theory of gender acquisition.

For Wittig, the very discrimination of 'sex' takes place within a political and linguistic network that presupposes, and hence requires, that sex remain dyadic. The demarcation of sexual difference does not *precede* the interpretation of that difference, but this demarcation is itself an interpretive act laden with normative assumptions about a binary gender system. Discrimination is always 'discrimination', binary opposition always serves the purposes of hierarchy. Wittig realizes that her position is counterintuitive, but it is precisely the political education of intuition that she wants to expose. For Wittig, when we name sexual difference, we create it; we restrict our understanding of relevant sexual parts to those that aid in the process of reproduction, and thereby render heterosexuality an ontological necessity. What distinguishes the sexes are those anatomical features, which either bear on reproduction directly, or are construed to aid in its eventual success. Hence, Wittig argues that erogeneity, the body's sexual responsiveness, is restricted through the institutionalization of binary sexual difference; her question: why don't we name as sexual features our mouths, hands, and backs? Her answer: we only name sexual—read, feel sexual—those features functional in reproductive activity.

Her claim is counterintuitive because we see sexual difference constantly, and it seems to us an immediate given of experience. She argues:

Sex . . . is taken as an 'immediate given', a sensible given, 'physical features', belonging to a natural order. But what we believe to be a physical and direct perception is only a sophisticated and mythic construction, an 'imaginary formation', which reinterprets physical features (in themselves as neutral as others but marked by a social system) through the network of relationships in which they are perceived.[8]

Like Beauvoir, Wittig understands gender as a proscription and a task; in effect, gender is a norm that we struggle to embody. In Wittig's words, 'We have been compelled in our bodies and our minds to correspond, feature by feature, with the *idea* of nature that has been established for us.'[9] That we experience ourselves or others as 'men' and 'women' are political categories and not natural facts.[10]

Wittig's theory is alarming for a number of reasons, foremost among them the intimation that discourse about sex creates the misnomer of anatomy. If this were Wittig's point, it would seem that sexual difference has no necessary material foundation, and that seeing differences among bodies, which turn out to be binary, is a deep delusion indulged in by cultures in an almost universal fashion. Luckily, I do not think this is Wittig's claim. Surely, differences do exist which are binary, material and distinct, and we are not in the grips of political ideology when we assent to that fact. Wittig contests the social practice of valorizing certain anatomical features as being definitive not only of anatomical sex but of sexual identity. She points out that there are other kinds of differences among people, differences in shape and size, in earlobe formation and the lengths of noses, but we do not ask when a child enters the world what species of earlobe it has. We immediately ask about certain sexually differentiated anatomical traits because we assume that those traits will in some sense determine that child's social destiny, and that destiny, whatever else it is, is structured by a gender system predicated upon the alleged naturalness of binary oppositions and, consequently, heterosexuality. Hence, in differentiating infants in the ways that we do, we recapitulate heterosexuality as a precondition for human identity, and posit this constraining norm in the guise of a natural fact.

Wittig thus does not dispute the existence or facticity of sexual distinction, but questions the isolation and valorization of certain kinds of distinctions over others. Wittig's *Lesbian Body* is the literary portrayal of an erotic struggle to rewrite the relevant distinctions constitutive of sexual identity. Different features of the female body are detached from their usual places, and remembered, quite literally. The reclamation of diverse bodily parts as sources of erotic pleasure is, for Wittig, the undoing or rewriting of binary restriction imposed at birth. Erogeneity is restored to the entire body through a process of sometimes violent struggle. The female body is no longer recognizable as such; it no longer appears as an 'immediate given of experience'; it is disfigured, reconstructed and reconceived. The emancipation of this consists in the dissolution of the binary framework, in the emergence of essential chaos, polymorphousness, the precultural innocence of 'sex'.

It might well seem that Wittig has entered into a utopian ground that leaves the rest of us situated souls waiting impatiently this side of her liberating imaginary space. After all, the *Lesbian Body* is a fantasy, and it is not clear whether we readers are supposed to recognize a potential course of action in that text, or simply be dislocated from our usual assumptions about bodies

and pleasure. Has Wittig decided that heterosexual norms are cultural norms while lesbian norms are somehow natural? Is the lesbian body that she posits as somehow being prior to and exceeding binary restrictions really a body at all? Has the lesbian preempted the place of the psychoanalytic polymorph in Wittig's particular sexual cosmogony?

Rather than argue for the superiority of a nonheterosexual culture, Wittig envisions a sexless society, and argues that sex, like class, is a construct that must inevitably be deposed. Indeed, Wittig's program seems profoundly humanistic in its call for an eradication of sex. She argues that

> a new personal and subjective definition for all humankind can be found beyond the categories of sex (man and woman) and that the advent of individual subjects demands first destroying the category of sex, ending the use of them, and rejecting all sciences which still use these categories as their fundamentals (practically all social sciences).[11]

On the one hand, Wittig calls for a transcendence of sex altogether, but her theory might equally well lead to an inverse conclusion, to the dissolution of binary restrictions through the *proliferation* of genders.

Because the category of 'sex' only makes sense in terms of a binary discourse on sex in which 'men' and 'women' exhaust the possibilities of sex, and relate to each other as complementary opposites, the category of 'sex' is always subsumed under the discourse of heterosexuality. Hence, Wittig argues that a lesbian is not a woman, because to be a woman means to be set in a binary relation with a man. Wittig does not argue that the lesbian is another sex or gender, but claims that the lesbian 'is the only concept I know which is beyond the category of sex'.[12] But even as Wittig describes the lesbian in relation to this binary opposition of 'man' and 'woman', she underscores the fact that this being beyond opposition is still a way of being related to that opposition, indeed a binary relation at that. In order that the lesbian avoid being caught up in another binary opposition, i.e., the opposition to heterosexuality itself, 'being lesbian' must itself become a multiple cultural phenomenon, a gender with no univocal essence. If binary oppositions imply hierarchies, then postulating a sexual identity 'beyond' culture promises to set up yet another pair of oppositions that, in turn, suggest another hierarchical arrangement; hegemonic heterosexual culture will stand as the 'Other' to that postcultural subject, and a new hierarchy may well replace the old—at least on a theoretical level. Moreover, to define culture as necessarily preoccupied with the reproduction of binary oppositions is to support a structuralist assumption that seems neither valid nor politically beneficial. After all, if binary restrictions are to be overcome in experience, they must meet their dissolution in the creation of new cultural forms. As Beauvoir says, and Wittig should know, there is no meaningful reference to a 'human reality' outside the terms of culture. The political program for overcoming binary restrictions ought to be concerned, then, with cultural innovation rather than myths of transcendence.

Wittig's theory finds support in Foucault's first volume of *The History of Sexuality* which holds improbable but significant consequences for feminist theory. In that Foucault seeks to subvert the binary configuration of power, the juridical model of oppressor and oppressed, he offers some strategies for the subversion of gender hierarchy. For Foucault, the binary organization of power, including that based on strict gender polarities, is effected through a multiplication of productive and strategic forms of power. Hence, Foucault is interested no longer in the Marcusean dream of a sexuality without power, but is concerned with subverting and dissipating the existing terms of juridical power. In this sense, Wittig is paradoxically closer to

Marcuse's theory of sexual emancipation as she does imagine a sexual identity and a sexuality freed of relations of domination. In effect, Foucault writes in the disillusioned aftermath of Marcuse's *Eros and Civilization,* rejecting a progressive model of history based on the gradual release of an intrinsically liberating *eros.* For Foucault, the *eros* which is liberated is always already structured culturally, saturated with power dynamics, thus implicitly raising the same political dilemmas as the repressive culture it was meant to liberate. Like Wittig, however, Foucault does reject 'natural sex' as a primary given, and attempts to understand how 'the deployment of sexuality . . . was what established this notion of "sex".' The category of sex belongs to a juridical model of power that assumes a binary opposition between the 'sexes'.[13] The subversion of binary opposites does not result in their transcendence for Foucault, but in their proliferation to a point where binary oppositions become meaningless in a context where multiple differences, not restricted to binary differences, abound. Foucault seems to suggest 'proliferation' and 'assimilation' as strategies to diffuse the age-old power game of oppressor and oppressed. His tactic, if that it can be called, is not to transcend power relations, but to multiply their various configurations, so that the juridical model of power as oppression and regulation is no longer hegemonic. When oppressors themselves are oppressed, and the oppressed develop alternative forms of power, we are in the presence of postmodern relations of power. For Foucault, this interaction results in yet new and more complicated valences of power, and the power of binary opposition is diffused through the force of internal ambiguity.

For Foucault, the notion of natural sex is neither primary nor univocal. One's 'sex', i.e., one's anatomically differentiated sexual self, is intimately linked to 'sex' as an activity and a drive. The word compromises a variety of meanings that have been clustered under a single name to further certain strategic ends of hegemonic culture:

The notion of 'sex' made it possible to group together, in an artificial unity, anatomic elements, biological functions, conducts, sensations, and pleasures, and it enabled one to make use of this fictitious unity as a causal principle, an omnipresent meaning, a secret to be discovered everywhere: sex was thus able to function as a unique signifier and as a universal signified.[14]

Foucault no more wants to dispute the material reality of anatomically discrete bodies than does Wittig, but asks instead how the materiality of the body comes to signify culturally specific ideas. Hence, he imagines at the close of vol. I of *The History of Sexuality* 'a history of bodies [which shows] the manner in which what is most material and most vital in them has been invested'.[15]

Foucault conducts a phenomenology of such an 'investment' in publishing the journals of Herculine Barbin, a nineteenth-century hermaphrodite whose anatomical ambiguity culminates in an eventual 'confession' and suicide.[16] In his introduction Foucault insists upon the irrelevance of established gender categories for Alexina's (Herculine's) sexual life:

One has the impression, at least if one gives credence to Alexina's story, that everything took place in a world of feelings—enthusiasm, pleasure, sorrow, warmth, sweetness, bitterness—where the identity of the partners and above all the enigmatic character around whom everything centered, had no importance. It was a world in which grins hung about without the cat.[17]

Herculine seems to have escaped univocal sex, and hence the binary system governing sex, and represents for Foucault the literalization of an ambiguity in sex and sexual identity which is the suppressed potential of every proper and univocal sex or gender. Herculine Barbin, our hermaphrodite, is neither here nor there, but neither is she in

some discrete third place. She is an amalgamation of binary opposites, a particular configuration and conflation of male and female. Because of her uncanny intrusion into the male domain, she is punished and banished by the Church authorities, designed univocally as a male. Herculine does not transcend sex as much as she confuses it, and while we can see her fate as to a certain extent anatomical, it is clear that the legal and medical documents that address her anatomical transgression reveal an urgent social need to keep sex down to just the usual two. Hence, it is not her anatomy, but the ways in which that anatomy is 'invested', that causes problems. Her plight reveals in graphic terms the societal urge and strategy to discover and define anatomy within binary terms. Exploding the binary assumption is one of the ways of depriving male hegemony and compulsory heterosexuality of their most treasured of primary premises. When, on the other hand, binary sexual difference is made a function of ontology, then the options for sexual identity are restricted to traditional heterosexual terms; indeed, heterosexuality is itself reduced to a mythical version of itself, disguising its own potential multiplicity beneath a univocal presentation of itself.

CONCLUSION: EMBODYING DISSONANCE

In conclusion, it seems important to note that the challenge to a dyadic gender system that Beauvoir's theory permits and that Wittig and Foucault help to formulate, is also implicitly a challenge to those feminist positions that maintain sexual difference as irreducible, and which seek to give expression to the distinctively feminine side of that binary opposition. If natural sex is a fiction, then the distinctively feminine is a purely historical moment in the development of the category of sex, what Foucault calls, 'the most speculative, most ideal, and most internal element in a deployment of sexuality organized by power in its grip on bodies and their materiality'.[18]

The schematic outline of a theory of gender invention that I have been sketching here does not overcome the existential pitfalls of Sartrianism by the mere fact of its cultural application. Indeed, with Foucauldian proliferation at hand, we seem to have moved full circle back to a notion of radical invention, albeit one that employs and deploys culturally existent and culturally imaginable conventions. The problem with this theory seems twofold, and in many senses the objections that will surely be raised against these visions are ones that have, in altered form, been raised against the existential thesis from both Marxist and psychoanalytic perspectives. The Marxist problem may be understood as that of the social constitution of personal identity and, by implication, gender identity. I not only choose my gender, and not only choose it within culturally available terms, but on the street and in the world I am always constantly constituted by others, so that my self-styled gender may well find itself in comic or even tragic opposition to the gender that others see me through or with. Hence, even the Foucauldian prescription of radical invention presupposes an agency which, *à la Descartes,* definitionally eludes the gaze of the Other.

The psychoanalytic objection is perhaps the most trenchant, for psychoanalytic theories of gender identity and gender acquisition tend to insist that what we become is always in some sense what we have always been, although the process of becoming is of oedipal necessity a process of restricting our sexual ambiguity in accord with identity-founding incest taboos. Ambiguity, whether described in the discourse of bisexuality or polymorphousness, is always to be presupposed, and established gender identity both contains and conceals this repressed ambiguity. The proliferation of gender beyond binary oppositions would thus always constitute a return to a pre-oedipal ambiguity which, I suppose, would take us outside of culture as we know it. According to the psychoanalytic per-

spective, the normative ideal of multiplicitous genders would always be a peculiar mix of memory and fantasy to be understood in the context of an oedipally conditioned subject in an affective quarrel with the incest taboo. This is the stuff of great literature, perhaps, but not necessarily practicable in the cultural struggle to renovate gender relations as we know them. In effect, speaking within this point of view, what I have provided here is a pre-oedipal fantasy that only makes sense in terms of a subject who can never realize this fantasy. In this sense, both the hypothetical Marxist and the psychoanalytic objection would charge that the theory I have presented lacks a reality principle. But, of course, such a charge is tricky, because it is unclear whether the principle governing this reality is a necessary one, or whether other principles of reality might well be 'invented', as it were, and whether such counterintuitive principles as these are part of the cultural fantasies that ultimately do come to constitute new organizations of reality. It is not clear to me that reality is something settled once and for all, and we might do well to urge speculation on the dynamic relation between fantasy and the realization of new social realities.

A good deal of French feminist scholarship has been concerned with specifying the nature of the feminine to settle the question of what women want, how that specific pleasure makes itself known, or represents itself obliquely in the rupture of logocentric language. This principle of femininity is sought in the female body, sometimes understood as the pre-oedipal mother and other times understood naturalistically as a pantheistic principle that requires its own kind of language for expression. In these cases, gender is not constituted, but is considered an essential aspect of bodily life, and we come very near the equation of biology and destiny, that conflation of fact and value, which Beauvoir spent her life trying to refute. In an article entitled 'Women can never be defined', Julia Kristeva remarks that 'the belief that "one is a woman" is almost as absurd and obscurantist as the belief that "one is a man".'[19] Kristeva says 'almost as absurd' because there are practical, strategical reasons for maintaining the notion of women as a class regardless of its descriptive emptiness as a term. Indeed, accepting Wittig's argument that 'women' is a political category, Kristeva goes on to consider whether it might not be a *useful* political category at that. This brings us back to the Marxist objection proffered above, and yet Kristeva is prepared to forfeit the term altogether when its political efficacy is exhausted. Hence, she concludes, 'we must use "we are women" as an advertisement or slogan for our demands. On a deeper level, however, a woman cannot "be"; it is something which does not even belong in the order of *being*.'[20] Women is thus a false substantive and univocal signifier that disguises and precludes a gender experience internally varied and contradictory. And if women are, to return to Beauvoir, such a mode of becoming that is arrested prematurely, as it were, through the reductive imposition of a substantializing nomenclature, then the release of women's internally experience, an experience that would make of the very name 'women's experience', an empty signification, might well become released and or precipitated. And here the task is not simply to change language, but to examine language for its ontological assumptions, and to criticize those assumptions for their political consequences. In effect, to understand woman to exist on the metaphysical order of *being* is to understand her as that which is already accomplished, self-identical, static, but to conceive her on the metaphysical order of *becoming,* is to invent possibility into her experience, including the possibility of never becoming a substantive, self-identical 'woman'. Indeed, such substantives will remain empty descriptions, and other forms of active descriptions may well become desirable.

It is not surprising that Beauvoir derives her philosophical framework from existential philosophy, and that Wittig seems more indebted to Beauvoir than to those French feminists who write either for or against Lacan. Nor is it surprising that Foucault's theory of sexuality and his history of bodies is written against the background of Nietzsche's *Will to Power* and the *Genealogy of Morals* whose method of existential critique regularly revealed how values that appear natural can be reduced to their contingent cultural origins.

The psychoanalytic challenge does well to remind us of the deep-rootedness of sexual and gender identity and the Marxist qualification reinforces the notion that how we are constituted is not always our own affair. It may well be that Wittig and Foucault offer (a) new identity/ies which, despite all their qualification, remain utopian. But it is useful to remember Gayle Rubin's reading of psychoanalysis as the reconstruction of kinship structures in the form of modern gender identities.[21] If she is right to understand gender identity as the 'trace' of kinship, and to point out that gender has become increasingly free of the vestiges of kinship, then we seem justified in concluding that the history of gender may well reveal the gradual release of gender from its binary restrictions. Moreover, any theoretical effort to discover, maintain, or articulate an essential femininity must confront the following moral and empirical problem: What happens when individual women do not recognize themselves in the theories that explain their unsurpassable essences to them? When the essential feminine is finally articulated, and what we have been calling 'women' cannot see themselves in its terms, what then are we to conclude? We can argue that women have a more inclusive essence, or we can return to that promising suggestion of Simone de Beauvoir, namely, that women have no essence at all, and hence, no natural necessity, and that, indeed, what we call an essence or a material fact is simply an enforced cultural option which has disguised itself as natural truth.

NOTES

1.   Simone de Beauvoir, *The Second Sex* (New York, Vintage Press, 1973), p. 301. Parts of the discussion of Simone de Beauvoir's *The Second Sex* are taken from the author's article 'Sex and Gender in Beauvoir's *Second Sex*'. *Yale French Studies.*

2.   Monique Wittig, 'One Is Not Born a Woman', *Feminist Issues,* 1, 2 see also 'The Category of Sex', *Feminist Issues,* 2, 2.

3.   See Thomas W. Busch, 'Beyond the Cogito: The Question of the Continuity of Sartre's Thought', *The Modern Schoolman,* LX (March 1983).

4.   Jean-Paul Sartre, *Being and Nothingness: An Essay in Phenomenological Ontology,* tr. Hazel E. Barnes (New York, Philosophical Library, 1947), p. 329.

5.   Beauvoir's defense of the non-Cartesian character of Sartre's account of the body can be found in 'Merleau-Ponty et le Pseudo-Sartrisme.' *Les Temps Modernes,* 10, (1955).

6.   Sartre, *Being and Nothingness,* p. 329.

7.   Beauvoir, *The Second Sex,* p. 41.

8.   Wittig, 'One Is Not Born a Woman', p. 48.

9.   Ibid., p. 47.

10. Ibid.

11. Wittig, 'The Category of Sex', p. 22.

12. Wittig, 'One Is Not Born a Woman', p. 53.

13. Michel Foucault, *The History of Sexuality* (New York, Random House, 1980), vol. I: *An Introduction,* tr. Robert Hurley, p. 154.

14. Ibid.

15. Ibid., p 152.

16. Michel Foucault, ed., *Herculine Barbin, Being the Recently Discovered Memoirs of a Nineteenth Century Hermaphrodite,* tr. Richard McDougall (New York, Pantheon, 1980).

17. Foucault, *Herculine Barbin,* p. xiii.

18. Foucault, *The History of Sexuality,* vol. I, p. 155.

19. Julia Kristeva, 'Women Can Never be Defined', in Elaine Marks and Isabel de Courtivron, eds. *New French Feminisms* (Brighton, Harvester, 1980), p. 137.

20. Ibid.

21. See Gayle Rubin, 'The Traffic in Women: The Political Economy of Sex', in Rayna R. Reiter, *Toward an Anthropology of Women* (New York, Monthly Review Press, 1975), pp. 178–92.

34

Michael Warner
1958–

Michael Warner, an associate professor of English at Rutgers University, New Brunswick, is a Ph.D. graduate from Johns Hopkins University. Warner's earliest work has been in early modern American literature and culture, an interest that produced his first book, *The Letters of the Republic: Publication and the Public Sphere in Eighteenth-Century America* (1990). From that base in American studies, he has pursued a broad range of critical and theoretical interests, including the history of the profession, American pragmatism, cultural studies, and, perhaps most prominently, the field now called "queer theory." Warner has been not only one of the leading voices in the United States advocating gay and lesbian studies but also one of the most lucid writers tackling theoretical problems in the field. He has edited, with Gerald Graff, *The Origins of Literary Studies in America: A Documentary Anthology* (1988). His essays have appeared in places such as *Representations, Boundary 2, Criticism, Nineteenth-Century Literature,* and *The Village Voice Literary Supplement.* He has written more recently *The Fear of a Queer Planet: Queer Politics and Social Theory* (1993).

"Homo-Narcissism; Or, Heterosexuality" first appeared in a landmark anthology entitled *Engendering Men: The Question of Male Feminist Criticism* (1990), and it represents Warner's attempt to cut through the Gordian knot that in the West has traditionally linked gender and sexuality in the twentieth century. Studying Freud's work on narcissism in detail, Warner explains that psychoanalysis has characterized homo-eroticism as a pathological abnormality in which an individual, especially a man, desires "himself in the guise of another," thereby collapsing the distinction between self and Other in hermetically sealed narcissism. However, Freud also recognizes, argues Warner, that erotic relationships of all kinds involve such a psychological—and clearly narcissistic—transaction of projecting one's own ego ideals onto a love object. Why have Freud, Lacan, and other intellectuals nonetheless persisted in portraying homosexuality as a pathology producing unitary sameness? Warner answers that these writers have proceeded on a fundamental Western assumption that the difference between self and Other is founded on the difference between genders—that "gender is the phenomenology of difference itself." That assumption, he says, undergirds a general cultural system in which heterosexual ego-identity, despite its own narcissistic dynamic, can be naturalized and therefore can attempt to transcend the basic "role of the imaginary in the formation of the erotic."

Warner moves then to urge a large-scale historical investigation of how and why "modern" heterosexuality has relied on and simultaneously displaced its narcissistic component onto a pathologized homosexual. Drawing on Jürgen Habermas's claim that modern human identity is based on the tentative formation of the ego rather than on more definable identity roles, Warner suggests the outline of such a history by proposing that homosexuality takes the "multiple sites of ego-reflection in modern liberal capitalism as multiple sites of erotic play and interaction." It therefore has provided an articulation of modern subjectivity's fluid construction while also serving as denial of the dynamic dimension in "normal" human development.

Homo-Narcissism; or, Heterosexuality

The modern system of sex and gender would not be possible without a disposition to interpret the difference between genders as the difference between self and Other. This elementary structure has been a subject for feminist theory at least since 1949, when Simone de Beauvoir posed it as the central problem of *The Second Sex:* how does it happen that man is constituted as the subject, and woman is constituted as the Other? For de Beauvoir, this is not just what men would like to believe, but the psychic structure of gender. Femininity is learned as a way of constructing oneself as object, a way of attributing full subjectivity only to the masculine. This identification of the male as subject and the female as Other, she argues, underwrites all the asymmetries of gender throughout history.

But the same insidious identification also has a more specially modern variant.[1] In the modern West, having a sexual object of the opposite gender is taken to be the normal and paradigmatic form of an interest either in the Other or, more generally, in others. That is why in our own century it has acquired the name *heterosexuality*—a sexuality of otherness. In this organization of sexuality, heteroerotics can be understood as the opposite *either* of homoerotics *or,* in the more general extension, of autoerotics. Indeed, according to this logic homoerotics is an unrecognized version of autoerotics, or more precisely of narcissism; both are seen as essentially an interest in self rather than in the other. The perverse options are therefore the exceptions that prove the rule, since both are overcome in the otherness of heterosexuality. The very categories of hetero-, homo-, and autoerotics are jointly defined by the same understanding of gender as simple alterity.

In *The Second Sex,* for instance, de Beauvoir herself writes a sentence that is both bland and startling: "When the boy reaches the genital phase, his evolution is completed, though he must pass from the autoerotic inclination, in which pleasure is subjective, to the heteroerotic inclination, in which pleasure is bound up with an object, normally woman."[2] As a summary of Freud, this is quite bland. But in the context of de Beauvoir's argument, this way of opposing interest in others simultaneously to autoerotics and to homoerotics is startling. As she shows so eloquently, there is nothing innocent about the slippage from interest in "an object" to the assumption that such an interest is "normally" in woman. Nothing guarantees such an outcome other than the boy's discovery that women are defined as objects to him in a way that other men are not. And since the girl discovers at the same time that her destiny is to be an object of desire, her encounter with alterity is very different from the boy's. She is not offered the same simple distinction between her own subjectivity and the other's objectivity. The discovery of otherness in the other gender, therefore, is neither neutral nor symmetrical. In de Beauvoir's argument, as in the work of other feminists who continue her Hegelian tradition, this construction of gendered otherness is seen as the structure of domination.[3]

If the scenario of gender difference is difficult to imagine without the asymmetries of domination, it is also true that all of our accounts of this scenario bear the stamp of the modern organization of sexuality. Every description of the subject's access to gender and alterity, beginning with Freud's account of the Oedipus complex, seems already to be oriented by the poles of hetero- and homosexuality. Could the modern system of hetero- and homosexualities be imagined without this ideological core, or vice versa? By shifting the question in this way, I mean to indicate how difficult it is to analyze a discourse of sexuality, when our own tools of analysis already *are* that discourse. But I also mean to indicate ways in which gender domination presents problems besides the obvious one that it poses for women.

Where women are "normally" defined by otherness, the transition from autoerotics to heteroerotics entails a peculiar problem for men. To cite de Beauvoir once more, a key feature of male subjectivity comes about as a corollary of the subjugation of women: "For the male it is always another male who is the fellow being, the other who is also the same, with whom reciprocal relations are established."[4] The point of this for feminism is clear: insofar as woman is Other, she stands outside of reciprocity. But an important question for the male subject is less clear. Since sexual desire is directed toward an object, male desire will be directed only toward women, rather than toward the men who are fellow beings, subjects, the same. But what if this does

not take place? And well it might not: for the man values other men as fellow beings and will accordingly seek their recognition and desire. At the same time, no matter how much he wants to think of the Other as woman, it remains true that men are others to him as well, just as women are fellow beings. When another man, this "other who is also the same," becomes the object of desire, has the male subject failed to distinguish self and other?

It may sound absurd, but that is just what psychoanalysis classically concludes. Psychoanalytic theory has from the beginning described homosexuality—especially among men—as a version of narcissism. Freud, for example, declares that the homosexual chooses "not another of the same sex, but himself in the guise of another."[5] This is not a simple judgment. And it would certainly not hold much intuitive force outside of the modern West, where erotic relations either among men or among women are imagined by most cultures as something other than relations of mere sameness.[6] But there has never been a sustained critique of the premises behind Freud's judgment, on this issue so widely taken as common sense. The gay movement has either ignored it or tried to reject it out of hand, no doubt because its invidious consequences are so easy to apprehend. Yet we need not wave away this powerful tradition, nor even deny that one kind of homoerotics in the modern West has the logic of a relation to self. It is imperative, though immensely difficult, for us to retheorize that relation.

The first difficulty lies in appropriating psychoanalysis. Although it is uniquely equipped to analyze the slippage in our culture between understandings of gender and understandings of self and other, traditionally psychoanalysis has been the principal site of that slippage. "Psychoanalysis," de Beauvoir concludes, "fails to explain why woman is the *Other*."[7] Of course, different directions have been taken by psychoanalytic theory since 1949, and one would not offer so simple a conclusion today. But the related problems of heterosexuality remain as unclear—indeed, ideologically clouded—as they were then. What guarantees that a transition from autoerotics will or should lead to heteroerotics? How does it come to be taken as self-evident that homoerotics is really an arrested form of interest in oneself? Why do we find it so difficult to think about sex and gender without these ideological categories and their teleological narratives? And why do these questions seem linked to the structure of modern liberal society? Only modern liberal society, after all, understands sexuality as a choice between hetero- and homosexualities, conceiving them as sexualities of difference and sameness. The only way to pose such large questions is by examining the theory of narcissism, where the issue of gender and alterity arises with peculiar insistence.

Freud postulated a connection between homosexuality and narcissism before the notion of narcissism was even fully developed. He went so far as to argue that the existence of the link between the two is "the strongest of the reasons which have led us to adopt the hypothesis of narcissism."[8] In the same essay, "On Narcissism," Freud argues that homosexuals express something different from what he calls primary narcissism. In primary narcissism, a child cathects itself in a unity with its parent, without differentiation, without a developed ego. This narcissistic love of the parent-child dyad is what the later love of the parent as a separate person will be propped on. Homosexuality, by contrast, is described by Freud as coming about in the later stage, when the subject's original narcissism encounters "the admonitions of others" and "the awakening of his [sic] own critical judgement."[9] The subject's primary attachment to itself, suddenly broken and troubled by criticism, is recuperated in the development of the ego ideals. It then happens, says Freud, that the individual seeks in another some ideal excellence missing

from his own ego. And this is the type of narcissistic choice made by the homosexual, by which Freud generally means the male homosexual: the choice of what he himself would like to be.

Without reconstructing any more of the difficulties raised by Freud's problematic essay, I would like to make two observations about his argument. The first is that the two kinds of narcissism are very different. One is residual, an effect of infancy that lingers into later life. The other is proleptic and utopian. The homosexual (male), according to Freud, develops his narcissism not simply because of the residual attachment to the parent-child dyad, but because of a developmentally advanced ego ideal that is difficult to realize. I will return to this point later; it is important because Freud's thinking here leads him close to breaking his usual frame of reference. Indeed, by foregrounding the development of critical judgment and the admonitions of others, Freud places the subject in a context much larger than that of the restricted family. And by indicating the relation between narcissism and ideals, Freud works no longer in the realm of simple pathology. What is puzzling, then, is that Freud continues to treat homosexuality as regressive. Although one important criticism of Freud's account is that his narrative is rather arbitrarily committed to a hypotactic logic of linear development, an equally important one is that his own analysis, in this essay, does not necessarily show the homosexual's narcissism as a developmental regression.

A second observation then follows: Freud cannot account for the normative implications of his analysis. It is not a neutral analysis. He speaks with an unmistakable tone of condescension toward the homosexuals who are really seeking themselves. He does not imagine that one might speak of narcissism other than pejoratively in this context, though he does in others.[10] Nor does he acknowledge that to describe homosexuality as *merely* a version of narcissism is counterintuitive. The homosexual, after all, is by definition interested in others in a way that is not true of the narcissist in general. Ovid tells us that Narcissus rejects not just the girls who love him, but also the boys. Those boys, then, have an interest in other persons, if not in the other gender, and the myth of Narcissus does not collapse the two. What warrants the forgetting of this difference, which becomes a nondifference, sameness? Why should gender amount to alterity *tout court?*

Freud's secondary narcissism does not preclude a recognition of alterity. Everyone undergoes—and indeed requires—the kind of narcissism Freud describes. Everyone makes identifications with others on the basis of ego ideals. But we call them ideals only insofar as identification is accompanied by alienation and longing. The act of taking up ego ideals therefore does not foreclose a sense of the other's otherness, no matter how much we might like to eliminate that otherness. Indeed, in the last section of "On Narcissism" Freud suggests that this double movement of identification and desire is what makes the subject truly social. In the very action of taking an ideal, the subject apprehends a difference between the ideal and the actual ego. And that difference is just what produces our sense of longing and our search for the recognition of others. Because the ideals remain alien, insofar as they are ideals at all, they drive the subject to the pursuit of the other.

Identification in this sense is not a satisfactory unity; Freud shows that the ideals of identification have a critical relation to the self that the ego will continue to feel as dissonance, especially in the form of guilt.[11] It follows—though this does not always remain clear in Freud—that they are both identifications and objects of longing. And that can be true even of the ideals that are most critical and guilt-inducing. As Kaja Silverman points out, the most normally Oedipal boy in the world is placed in a relation of longing with the image of the father; insofar as the father's image is taken as an ideal, or superego, it remains "susceptible to sexualization."[12] Identi-

fication, in short, does not result in a relation of identity, and this is especially the case where another subject is involved. The difference that is therefore inevitably involved in taking the other as a sexual object, an other, cannot entirely be elided—even where the desire is founded on an identification. But that is what Freud does when he claims that homosexuals "are plainly seeking *themselves* as a love object."

Freud here imagines, in effect, that the dialectic of desire could not continue beyond the first moment of alienated identification. The figure of Narcissus represents that blockage: in Jacqueline Rose's phrase, Narcissus shows how "an apparent reciprocity reveals itself as *no more than* the return of an image to itself."[13] But it is not so easy to explain any erotic attachment as merely the reflexive attachment of a self to itself. Even the apparent return of an image reveals also some forms of reciprocity. When the subject chooses another on the basis of a desired ego ideal, he or she is already engaged in dialogue with others and in multiple perspectives on self. In Freud's account, the individual is encountering the admonitions of others and the development of his or her own critical judgment. As a result, the subject adopts the position of the other toward him- or herself. This kind of narcissism, therefore, already involves the subject in the negativity of speech.[14] If desire arises in these alienated identifications, it by the same token must always reactivate the potential for mutual recognition. Freud does not imagine this possibility long enough to argue against it. He concludes that homosexual desire *reduces* to narcissism without significant remainder and hence is a developmental misdirection.

Freud's conclusion here has hardly proven to be idiosyncratic. It remains the most powerful way of treating homoerotics as a symptomology, and some version of it still dominates every major branch of psychoanalytic theory.[15] Though the DSM III no longer lists homosexuality as a disease, the theoretical tradition continues to reveal it in the light of pathology. Professional psychology and psychoanalysis continue to understand themselves as explaining homosexuality, as giving its causes. But the entire discourse is possible at all only if the pathological status of the homosexual is assumed from the outset. If homosexuality is taken to be a symptom, then etiology provides a logic for saying that it reduces to narcissism. But if the symptomatic character of homosexuality is not simply taken for granted, then it would be necessary to theorize its dialectical and interactive character—precisely that which would prevent a reductive etiology. It is not surprising to find such ideological effects in the medical and scientific institutions that have, after all, generated the modern discourse of hetero- and homosexualities. It is more surprising to find the normalizing conclusion in Freud, since his own account demonstrates the dialectical and interactive movement that leads from the ego to homoerotics. (And back: one more reason Freud might have avoided his normalizing conclusion is that he was intermittently conscious of his own investment in homoerotics, particularly with Josef Breuer and Wilhelm Fliess. After his break with Fliess, Freud wrote to Sandor Ferenczi about his "overcoming" the trauma of the break: "A part of homosexual cathexis has been withdrawn and made use of to enlarge my own ego.")[16]

My point, however, is not simply that we should depathologize the homosexual. There is also a further, equally unremarked problem in the argument. If normal development leads from autoerotics to narcissism to heterosexuality, how would heterosexuality transcend its sources in narcissism more than homosexuality does? Freud assumes, as does psychoanalytic discourse generally, that the heterosexual (male) is a better realist than the homosexual (male). The heterosexual male chooses the Other—woman—but the homosexual male only *thinks* he chooses another. Yet it is not difficult to read Freud's essay as showing that all erotic life—not just the pathology of homosexuals—takes its form from the search for the ego ideal in the po-

sition of the other. (This of course is the direction in which Jacques Lacan will push the inquiry.) When Freud initially describes how the investment of the ego ideal can be transferred into a sexual desire for another, he is describing the pathology of homosexuals. By the end of the essay, he is using the same language to interpret a form of heterosexual romance. The lover, says Freud, overvalues the other in whose eyes he sees *himself* ideally desired. Yet Freud does not draw the obvious inference that it might not be so easy as first appeared to construct a normative hierarchy of hetero- and homosexuality by showing the function of the ego ideal in generating desire.

What, then, is developmental in the development from narcissism to heterosexuality? Or at least, what is developmental here that is not equally characteristic of homosexuality? Freud's various solutions to this problem come to grief because they are in the last analysis based on an *a priori* opposition of the genders as subject and Other. Nowhere are the difficulties of the project more clear than in *The Ego and the Id,* a text in which Freud returns to the unstable problems of the narcissism essay. In the earlier essay, identification and the ego ideals stemmed from the admonitions of others and the development of the subject's critical judgment. Now, in the later work, Freud writes that the "origin of the ego-ideal" lies in "an individual's first and most important identification, his [sic] identification with the father in his own personal prehistory."[17] The difference is that Freud has now introduced the Oedipus complex in an attempt to explain the developmental path that leads to heterosexuality. But why have the male subject and the male parent been singled out as the primary axis of identification?

In an astonishing footnote to this sentence, Freud acknowledges that there is no good reason at all: "Perhaps it would be safer to say 'with the parents'; for before a child has arrived at definite knowledge of the difference between the sexes, the lack of a penis, it does not distinguish in value between its father and its mother. . . . In order to simplify my presentation I shall discuss only identification with the father." According to the footnote, identification with the father has been emphasized only arbitrarily, for convenience. But the text that it glosses shows that the father must not be just any identification, but "the first and most important" one. That is what guarantees the Oedipalized heterosexual outcome. If nothing naturally makes this axis of identification the primary one, then the heterosexual resolution will be no more of a development than a homosexual one. Without this ideological support, Freud's derivation of heterosexual norms is subject to narrative incoherence.

The footnote admits, in effect, that the father has primacy only in his symbolic cultural value, which is learned later; he has no primacy in the simple development of the child's identification. Both parents are subjects of identification, and both are objects of attachment. This leads Freud to postulate both "positive" and "negative" forms of the Oedipal situation. Again, however, he presupposes the chiastic axes of heterosexuality that the model is designed to derive. Freud assumes that an identification with the mother will retain an attachment to the father and vice versa. He does not imagine that one might identify with the mother and yet have an attachment to other women or identify with the father and yet have an attachment to other men. Nor can he justify the primacy of one axis over another. In an especially striking moment of circularity, Freud writes that only the child's "sexual disposition"—i.e., its "masculine" or "feminine" bent—will determine the relative weight of these identification axes.[18] At this point, nothing establishes which axis—if indeed we can assume their constitution as axes—will be primary, or "positive" rather than "negative."

Freud maintains the normative character of Oedipal resolution only by ignoring these qualifications in a rather blunt declaration that the male child identifies with the father and takes the mother as object. In *Group Psychology and the Analysis of the Ego,* published two years before *The Ego and the Id,* Freud presents this declaration in its most normalized form:

> A little boy will exhibit a special interest in his father; he would like to grow like him and be like him, and take his place everywhere. We may say simply that he takes his father as his ideal. This behaviour has nothing to do with a passive or feminine attitude toward his father (and towards males in general); it is on the contrary typically masculine. It fits very well with the Oedipus complex, for which it helps to prepare the way.
>
> At the same time as this identification with his father, or a little later, the boy has begun to develop a true object cathexis towards his mother according to the attachment [anaclitic] type.[19]

As we know from Freud's qualifications in *The Ego and the Id,* nothing in this narrative can be assumed. The child takes both parents as ideals and has object attachments to both parents. Why does Freud so insist, despite his own observations, on the primacy of this "positive" form of what has already been assumed as a chiastic structure? Both the supremacy of the father and the goal of heterosexuality seem to derive from the Oedipal scene as it is summarized here. If this is the moment when de Beauvoir's mastery relation has been established, it is also the moment when the available object choices have been resolved into hetero- and homosexualities. The father's supremacy is assured since, for children of both sexes, he will be identified with as subject, while the mother's nurturing role will result in an object attachment to her.

But what is easier to miss is that Freud has presupposed that the child's identification and its object attachment will be assigned to different genders. Hence Freud's anxious haste to deny that identification with the father results in a "passive or feminine" attitude toward him. Freud consistently supposes that identification desexualizes the parental image, that the positive Oedipus complex cancels out the object choice of the negative complex and vice versa.[20] This is partly because he presupposes that the parents' heterosexual choices will be internalized along with their images, so that identification with the father will simply transfer the father's gendered desire to the boy. (To explain himself in this way, however, would amount to an admission that heterosexual desire is only a status quo.) But it is also partly because Freud's entire account is based on the exclusiveness of identification and attachment.

Identification and attachment are the structuring moments in psychoanalysis that correspond to subject and object. Identification constructs a feature of the world as a feature of the subject; attachment constructs its features as objects. But the opposition is unstable. As Mikkel Borch-Jacobsen shows, the two operations can be read as mutual forms of denial. If identification denies the radical alterity of the other, attachment-desire "is organized as a vehement rejection of all resemblance, all mimesis."[21] Freud's deepest commitment, throughout the changes in his position on the subject, is that these two operations will be exclusive, and one will be reserved for each gender. An admission that it would be possible both to identify with *and* to desire a gendered image would be the most troubling of all. If Freud implies in "On Narcissism" that the homosexual narcissist does just that, he has a very different account in the later works.

Here it is striking that Freud has two entirely different pathologies for homosexuality, and they accompany entirely different accounts of the ego ideal. Both *Group Psychology* and *The Ego and the Id* attempt to explain the homosexual by means of the chiasmus of gender identification and desire. The ego ideal with which the child identifies is a gendered parental image, and the child's sexual object will accordingly be the parental image of the opposite sex. In both of these later texts, the homosexual is said simply to choose the "negative" axis—for the male child, identifying with the mother and taking on her desire for the father. But in the earliest essay, the sources of the ego ideals had been much more general. They had not necessarily entailed the gendered parental images, with the chiastic Oedipal teleology of those images.

What if it is possible, as Freud implied in the earlier essay, that the boy might both identify with the father and yet desire his image? This possibility is implied insofar as the boy's identification would still not close the gap between himself and the gendered ideal. Indeed, identification could result in a longing because of that gap between actual and ideal. But subject and object would not be distributed to different genders. Freud is therefore obliged in this essay to regard the relation as one of mere sameness. Freud explains homosexuality alternately as sameness (in the earlier essay) or as inverted difference (in the later works). No matter which route of explanation Freud takes, he does not infer from his own insights that difference and sameness might coexist, in both desire and identification, without being reducible to the difference or sameness of gender.

It is only the more striking that Lacan never makes this inference either, since it is he who radicalizes the function of the ego ideal in a way only suggested by Freud. Lacan's analysis of the *imago* of the ego shows it to be *both* the site of identification *and* the source of desire. "We call libidinal investment," he says, "that which makes an object desirable, that is to say, the way it becomes confused with the image we carry within us."[22] Where Freud initially argued that an intricate confusion of the desired object with the image of what one would like to be is just the pathological derivation of homosexuality, Lacan shows that such an investment always structures the erotic. Lacan cites Goethe's Werther as an example of the way heterosexual investment is based not only on anaclitic parental cathexis but also on the reflective function of the ego ideal. When Werther first sees Lotte, he writes,

No, I do not deceive myself! In her dark eyes I have read a genuine sympathy for me and my destiny. Yes, I feel . . . that she loves me! Loves me!—And how precious I become in my own eyes, how I—to you as an understanding person I may say it—how I admire myself since she loves me.

With this passage in mind, Lacan says, "That's what love is. It's one's own ego that one loves in love, one's own ego made real on the imaginary level."[23] Of course, there are other things that one could say about Werther; his is not the only form of "what love is." My point is simply that Lacan made it one of the central projects of his career to critique our elementary assumptions about the difference between identification and desire, subject and object. In so doing, he definitively removed any possibility of making narcissism a basis for a normative hierarchy between hetero- and homosexuality. Homosexuality may indeed be a way of loving one's own ego, but so is heterosexual romance.

Yet however radical and subtle Lacan's analysis of the imaginary might be, it seems never to have occurred to him that it might now be unnecessary to pathologize the homosexual's relation to narcissism. Quite the contrary. In a passage from the seminars of the very same year (1954), Lacan takes it on himself to describe homosexuality as a perversion, not because of the contingency of morals, nor because of the supposed needs of biology, but because of the narcissistic structure of homosexual desire. "It is himself," Lacan says of the homosexual, "whom he pursues." What I find especially incomprehensible about this classical assertion is that it appears as a gloss on one of Lacan's most Hegelian formulations: "the [homosexual] subject exhausts himself in pursuing the desire of the other, which he will never be able to grasp as his own desire, because his own desire is the desire of the other."[24] This, as Lacan notes, is the form of "the imaginary intersubjective relation." Nothing about it is peculiar to homosexuality.

Moreover, when he is pursuing the Hegelian logic of his analysis, Lacan is capable of treating this same imaginary intersubjectivity as opening onto a dialectic of recognition.[25] In this case, he does not do so.

Compare the tone of his account with the tone of the equally Hegelian description that de Beauvoir had given five years earlier of the logic of lesbianism:

> To be willing to be changed into a passive object is not to renounce all claim to subjectivity: woman hopes in this way to find self-realization under the aspect of herself as a thing; but then she will be trying to find herself in her otherness, her alterity. When alone she does not succeed in really creating her double; if she caresses her own bosom, she still does not know how her breasts seem to a strange hand, nor how they are felt to react under a strange hand; a man can reveal to her the existence of her flesh *for herself*—that is to say, as she herself perceives it, but not what it is *to others*. It is only when her fingers trace the body of a woman whose fingers in turn trace her body that the miracle of the mirror is accomplished.

But de Beauvoir does not mean, by "the miracle of the mirror," an entrapment in a circuit of sameness. Far from it. Because she understands the problem of alterity sketched here as one taking place in a setting of domination, the dialectic of lesbianism is a model of how the imaginary transcends its limitations: "in exact reciprocity each is at once subject and object, sovereign and slave; duality becomes mutuality."[26] This is exactly what Lacan denies. Though he offers no reason for this belief, he asserts that the homosexual is perverse because the recognition of the other's desire remains closed to him. Lacan goes so far as to say that it is "not without reason" that homosexuality is called "a desire which dare not speak its name." (Of course, however, Lacan like Freud assumes that only male homosexuality is in question. If the lesbian dialectic allows women access to their subjectivity in addition to their normal objectivity, we might say the reverse for male homosexuals: they seek access to their objectivity in addition to their normal subjectivity. And because that means that would imply a compromise of privilege, a feminization, it is more unthinkable.)

Lacan's position in this respect is not as different as one would like to think from that of the reactionary Christopher Lasch. Lasch's writings on the subject have infinitely less subtlety and intelligence than Lacan's. But partly for that reason they lay bare the politics of the analytic tradition from which Lacan, less understandably, could not free himself. In a complimentary preface to a book by Chasseguet-Smirgel, Lasch claims that by eradicating differences of gender, the homosexual pervert "erases the more fundamental distinction between the self and the not-self, the source of every other distinction."[27] One hardly knows where to begin with this kind of comment. In the first place, it would simply be absurd to think that homosexuals eradicate gender, the very logic of homosexuality as a category is impossible without gender and its utopian identifications. Equally foolish is the rather crude form of heterosexist ideology in which it is supposed that people who have homosexual relations do not also have other kinds.

More deceptive, however, is the assumption that gender is the phenomenology of difference itself. This is the core of the psychoanalytic tradition I am trying to map. It is a staggeringly primitive confusion. Can it actually be imagined that people in homosexual relations have no other way of distinguishing between self and not-self? That no other marker of difference, such as race, could intervene; or that the pragmatics of dialogue would not render alterity meaningful, even in the minimal imaginary intersubjectivity of cruising? Why is gender assumed to be our only access to alterity? It is not even the only line of sameness and difference that structures erotic images. Race, age, and

class are capable of doing that as well. Sexuality has any number of forms of the dialectic between identification and desire. But we do not say of people whose erotic objects are chosen partly on the basis of racial identity or of generation or of class that they have eradicated the distinction between self and not-self. We say that only of gender. The difference between hetero- and homosexualities is not, in fact, a difference between sexualities of otherness and sameness. It is an allegory about gender.

We have only to consider the breathtaking simplicity of the premises for the whole argument to dissolve. But let me emphasize that I am not making a point about Lasch's blindness. He merely reproduces an ideological confusion that is axiomatic for the modern sex/gender system. Even Lacan ascribes to what he calls "the cosmic polarity of male and female"[28] nothing less than the transition from ego-identification to dialogue:

> For it is a truth of experience for analysis that the subject is presented with the question of his [sic] existence, not in terms of the anxiety that it arouses at the level of the ego, and which is only one element in the series, but as an articulated question: 'What am I there?', concerning his sex and his contingency in being, namely, that, on the one hand, he is a man or a woman, and, on the other, that he might not be, the two conjugating their mystery, and binding it in the symbols of procreation and death.[29]

This passage appears exactly as an explanation of how alterity can be grasped within the narcissistic structure of subjectivity. Lacan is explaining the so-called "schema L," which describes the mediations between the subject and the Other, by which Lacan means "the locus from which the question of his existence may be presented to him." He here proposes that it is the otherness of gender that allows the subject to apprehend his or her own ego as an other. If we are to read Lacan generously here, we will emphasize the qualifier "it is a truth *of experience for analysis*" as meaning that the situation he depicts is only a nonnormative description of how gender operates in the present culture. We could then make these assumptions the subject of critique, as does de Beauvoir. But Lacan does not take that step, and it is just as possible to read the emphasis differently: "it is a *truth* of experience for analysis."

The passage is not without a sentimental and mystifying element. Lacan implies that the realization "I am this individual and not that one" not only does but *should* come in the form "I am this gender and not that one." He further assumes that a recognition of gender implicitly contains the particular form of mortality-transcendence found in the myths and rituals of heterosexual conjugality. But the dialectic of identification does not lead without mediation to procreative, genital sexuality. Indeed, Lacan often paints a very different picture himself:

> What is my desire? What is my position in the imaginary structuration? This position is only conceivable in so far as one finds a guide beyond the imaginary, on the level of the symbolic plane, of the legal exchange which can only be embodied in the verbal exchange between human beings. This guide governing the subject is the ego-ideal.[30]

Here, as elsewhere, Lacan argues that the narcissism of desire is transcended only by the rule-governed multiple perspectives of symbolic interaction. Language in general brings about forms of difference and norms of reciprocity and thus allows the subject the negativity with which to consider his or her identity in the role of another. Yet no absolute break with narcissistic identification has occurred, since the subject's ability to do this continues to be regulated by the ego ideals. As a picture of the development of subjectivity, Lacan's scene here resembles the "admonitions" and "critical judgment"

referred to by Freud as the origin of the ego ideals in "On Narcissism." The subject has encountered the Other, "the locus from which the question of his existence may be presented to him." But significantly, that locus and its questioning do not imply the gender of an object choice.

Lacan moves between this account, in which the decisive factor is symbolic interaction, and another account, closer to the so-called second topography of Freud's later work, in which the ego ideal is specifically the paternal image. Again, the generous reading is that Lacan's analysis is descriptive of the way the father's authority stands for the subjective function he describes in our culture. But again, Lacan is not critical of that cultural equation, and he does not analyze the ways in which it is possible for subjects to interact without the prescribed relation to the paternal image. Instead, as we have seen, he adheres to models of pathology that incorporate and presuppose the normative role of gender defined as the simple apprehension of alterity. Because of this elision, the fundamental phenomenology of gender in Lacan's account often has an ideological character, though his most radical (and most Hegelian) arguments work in another direction. Indeed, if the equation between homosexuality and narcissism in psychoanalysis tells us anything, it is that the central premises and vocabulary of psychoanalysis have been designed for a heterosexist self-understanding. They have totalized gender as an allegory of difference, leaving little analytic space between the development of subjectivity and the production of heterosexual norms.

How does this mystification get sustained? When Lasch declares homosexuality perverse because it eradicates the distinction between self and not-self, does he not realize that many of his readers will come to the passage with the experience that must inevitably disclose its falseness? In fact, I think he does not. The entire psychoanalytic heritage on this subject does not imagine itself in dialogue with those it describes.[31] If

I have taken some pains to show this, it is because I consider it a *tactical* necessity to have a better understanding of what the sources of this discourse's power are. If the tradition I have described simply reflects the illiberal intolerance of a few homophobic theorists, then we need not sweat it any more. If it is structural to the premises of psychoanalysis, then we need more of an attack on modern psychoanalysis. If it lies in the heart of modern social organization, then we should consider how, and in what institutions, and where a more organized resistance should begin.

That is not to say that we need a theory of homosexuality in the usual sense. There may be any number of logics lumped together under this heading, from the "lesbian continuum" theorized by Adrienne Rich to the more recent phenomenon of gay communities organized through a discourse of rights. Both for women and for men in our culture there are probably as many ways of cathecting other women or men as there are ways in other cultures, where the discourse of homosexuality remains so foreign. Indeed, part of the oppressiveness of the modern formation is that all forms of erotics among men or among women get classified by the same logic. We might begin to clarify the question by saying that the theorization of homosexuality as narcissism is itself a form of narcissism peculiar to modern heterosexuality. The central imperative of heterosexist ideology is that the homosexual be supposed to be out of dialogue on the subject of his being. Imagining that the homosexual is narcissistically contained in an unbreakable fixation on himself serves two functions at once: it allows a self-confirming pathology by declaring homosexuals' speech, their interrelations, to be an illusion; *and more fundamentally it allows the constitution of heterosexuality as such.*

If that sounds like a strong claim, let me repeat that by heterosexuality I mean the modern discursive organization of sex that treats gender difference as difference in general. It is a sexuality organized by its self-understanding as *heterosexuality* and therefore also includes the categories of homo- and autoerotics against which it defines itself. What I would like to suggest is that it is possible to read this historically recent discourse as, in part, a reaction formation. The allegory of gender protects against a recognition of the role of the imaginary in the formation of the erotic. It provides reassurance that imaginary intersubjectivity has been transcended. To the extent that our culture relies on the allegorization of gender to disguise from itself its own ego erotics, it will recognize those ego erotics only in the person of the homosexual, apparently bereft of the master trope of difference. If it were possible to admit that any relevant forms of otherness operate in homosexuality, then the main feature of heterosexual self-understanding would be lost. The heterosexual would no longer be able to interpret the gendered, binary form of his or her own captation in desire as already being the transcendence of that captation.

But there is a broader issue at stake here, and one that could be raised as an objection. What if we are to return to the more generous reading of Lacan, seeing the psychoanalytic account not only as an ideological rationalization, but as an essentially accurate description of the *cultural* mechanisms whereby gender and alterity are equated? For surely Lacan is correct to point out that the equation takes place not just in psychoanalytic theory, but on very elementary levels of subjective experience. It *is* a truth of experience for analysis, in our society, that the subject is presented with the question of his or her existence through the problematic alterity of gender. That is why the *psychoanalytic* tradition of linking narcissism and homosexuality has been so easy to confirm. And although the categories and norms of that tradition can be shown to be ideological and incoherent, they are the categories and norms of subjective experience in our culture, rather than simply the prejudices of a few theorists. The argument that I have made here therefore raises a whole new problem: what is the social and historical character of this organization of sexuality and gender?

This issue challenges us to separate the two problematics that I have brought together in this essay: on the one hand the problem of women's construction as the Other, with its prehistoric sources in phallocentrism; on the other hand, a sex/gender system in which object choice is posed as an apprehension of alterity *tout court*. These two structures of power are currently coarticulated as a unity of experience, but they have different histories. The system of hetero- and homosexualities is a much more recent phenomenon, codified in discourse only for the past century. Through most of Western history erotics among men in particular have been understood precisely along axes of difference: the active/passive difference in the discourse of sodomy, for instance, or the pedagogic difference of generations in the classical discourse of pederasty. If suddenly it has become necessary and common-sensical to imagine erotics among men or among women as homosexuality, a sexuality of sameness, we might ask how that has come about. We might also ask what relation there might be between this recent organization of sexuality and the longer history of phallocentrism that constructs woman as Other. Indeed, one reason it is so hard for us to imagine hetero- and homosexualities as recent developments is that they have been articulated so closely with that phallocentric construction of Otherness.

Unfortunately, if the organization of sexuality around the axis of the hetero and the homo is the result of historical change, we have virtually no social theory of why its organization in this form should have been so recent or what kind of historical narrative it would call for. The account typically given in the wake of Michel Foucault has been to attribute the system of heterosexuality to its discourse, beginning roughly with the naming of *homosexuality* in the late nineteenth century.[32] The Foucauldian account has an undeniable force in showing that the discourse of sexuality is a form of biotechnical power, not a superstructural effect. Nevertheless, I think my argument suggests, in effect, a different strategy of historicizing the whole organization of sexuality. If I am correct that the ideology of gender as alterity is a special way of not recognizing the imaginary sources of desire, then why should Western society have developed that need for misrecognition so recently? Why should there have been an imperative for such a massive displacement of ego erotics?

To pose the question in this way is to link the problem of heterosexuality not simply to modern society in the sense of recent society, but to the force of modernity. A full critique of heterosexism would involve questions about the role of the ego in post-Enlightenment capitalist society. That debate is a complex one, but I can at least indicate its relevance here. On one side Christopher Lasch, in *The Culture of Narcissism*, laments the ego orientation of consumer society as producing debased forms of individualism and symptomatic perversions such as the gay rights movement.[33] On the other side, Jürgen Habermas can argue that the self-reflection of the autonomous ego is the source of a still progressive modernity. And he can show in a fairly nuanced way that ego-identity becomes both necessary and problematic in a whole new range of social contexts.[34] Both sides agree that a tension between the ego and its ideals has become newly important in post-Enlightenment Western capitalism. In response to that debate, could we speculate that the ego erotics coded in homosexuality is a special feature of this social history?

Obviously, that subject is too large to be treated here. But I should note that the possibility of such an account is already implicit in the way Freud imagines an erotics of the ego ideal. In the essay on narcissism, Freud takes a broad social view. Having once stated that secondary narcissism is possible only after the development of critical judgment and the encountering of the admonitions of others, he returns with an even more general description:

For what prompted the subject to form an ego ideal, on whose behalf his conscience acts as watchman, arose from the critical influence of his parents (conveyed to him by the medium of the voice), to whom were added, as time went on, those who trained and taught him and the innumerable and indefinable host of all the other people in his environment—his fellow men—and public opinion.

In this way large amounts of libido of an essentially homosexual kind are drawn into the formation of the narcissistic ego ideal and find outlet and satisfaction in maintaining it.

Here Freud advances a notion to which he returned often, especially in the *Group Psychology*—the notion that sociality itself is in some essential way a desexualized homosexuality. But when Freud describes the environment to which the subject must relate in such a homosexual way, he depicts an essentially modern society. It is defined by the critical force of training and teaching. It is made up of an "innumerable and indefinable host" of people. And at its limits it finds expression in a highly generalized perspective of criticism: public opinion. This set of social pressures on the ego may also be what Freud has in mind when he links his developmental narrative with the historical transition from traditional to modern. He claims, for instance, that "primitive peoples," like children, orient themselves to the world through primary narcissism rather than secondary.[35] One doesn't have to be uncritical of Freud's ethnocentrism here to imagine that a special role for critical judgment in modern Western societies might also mean that the subject of those societies might be structured by a correspondingly special ego erotics.

Lacan's account also suggests as much, and Lacan in fact often asserts that social modernity has brought about a general pathology of ego erotics.[36] His example of Werther's narcissistic love, we might note, is already articulated within the normative subjectivity of modernity.

We can see how that articulated relation works by taking a strikingly similar example from an American admirer and contemporary of Goethe, Charles Brockden Brown, also writing in the context of the late Enlightenment:

> Good God! You say she loves; loves *me!* me, a boy in age; bred in clownish ignorance; scarcely ushered into the world; more than childishly unlearned and raw; a barn-door simpleton; a plow-tail, kitchen-hearth, turnip-hoeing novice![37]

Arthur Mervyn here encounters his heterosexual love as a relation between his ego ideals and his actual ego. Several things follow. First, it is a moment of narcissistic ego erotics ("loves *me!* me . . ."), but the affective charge is attached to what seems like an unbridgable gulf of difference ("Good God!"). The extravagant otherness of his beloved—she is, in fact, older, foreign, and Jewish—allows her to be the fulcrum of Mervyn's desire-laden self-relation. The passage therefore marks the mutual involvement of a conspicuous *hetero*sexuality with a potentially homoerotic fixation on a reflexive ego erotics. And in fact, its usual charge, both in this novel and in Brown's work generally, is decisively, even sensationally homoerotic. Mervyn's awakening here might be constructed as the origin of heterosexuality, but that only shows how closely linked heterosexuality and homosexuality are in the erotics of the ego.

Mervyn's desirous self-relation, however, is also a moment of critical self-consciousness. In the very act of focusing on himself as a possible object of desire, he confronts the difference between his ideals and his actual ego. He occupies the vantage of a critical public opinion, defining an image of himself there: "a boy in age; bred in clownish ignorance; scarcely ushered into the world; more than childishly unlearned and raw; a barn-door simpleton; a plow-tail, kitchen-hearth, turnip-hoeing novice!" This is exactly the sort of role-detached, posttraditional self-consciousness that Habermas identifies with the normative content of modernity. If this sort of ego erotics seems to bear the stamp of the special social contexts of modernity, with its norm of critical self-consciousness in an environment of equals, then both hetero- and homosexuality share its essential structure.

But I do not wish to emphasize only the normative, critical content of modernity. It should also be possible to specify a whole range of social and historical institutions in which the subject is called on to take an evaluative/desirous posture toward his or her ego ideal. The imaginary register will be important, albeit in different ways, for the discourse of rights, the forms of exchange in capitalism, the role-detachment that comes with a system-differentiated society, the mass imaginary of video capitalism, rituals and markets of adolescence, and the like. The work of analyzing the subjectivity of these interarticulated contexts has only begun.

The possibility I'm trying to indicate is that homosexuality, encoded as such, takes these multiple sites of ego-reflection in modern liberal capitalism as multiple sites of erotic play and interaction. Heterosexuality deploys an understanding of gender as alterity in order to mobilize, but also to obscure, a self-reflexive erotics of the actual ego measured against its ideals. In a modernity constituted by multiple sites of ego erotics, sex ceases to be complacently patriarchal and becomes heterosexual, mystifying its own imaginary register with its liberal logic of difference. Homosexuality, however, engages the same self-reflexive erotics, without the mechanism of obscuring it. The homosexual who makes the choice of "what he himself would like to be" expresses the utopian erotics of modern subjectivity. This utopian self-relation, far from being the pathology of the homosexual, could instead be seen as a historical condition and, in the perverse and unrecuperated mode of homosexual subjectivity, the source of a critical potential.

This is why modern heterosexuality needs a discourse about homosexuality as a displacement of its own narcissistic sources. The psychoanalytic tradition enacts and justifies that displacement.

NOTES

1. The question of what is "modern" can here get a bit tricky. At this point, I mean only the broadest extension of the term: heterosexuality as a cultural system does not date from prehistory, nor is it universally the same. Later on, however, I shall be speaking of links between the sex/gender system of heterosexuality and "modern society." The task then will be to describe the relation of that sex/gender system not simply to a recent period of history, but to the set of social forms and normative principles that are programmatically linked together as "modernity." Included under this heading are the imperatives of universal law and morality, rationalized social life, autonomous disciplines of art, and objective science. And although this development in social organization has sources in the Renaissance, its full and classic expression comes with the height of the Enlightenment and its liberal aftermath. The key descriptions of this term and its history are by Jürgen Habermas; although his defense of modernity is highly controversial, his exposition of its meaning remains unmatched. See, for a brief version, "Modernity—An Incomplete Project," in Hal Foster, ed., *The Anti-Aesthetic* (Seattle: The Bay Press, 1983), 3–15. The much more developed version is in Jürgen Habermas, *The Philosophical Discourse of Modernity*, trans. Frederick Lawrence (Cambridge: MIT Press, 1987), esp. chapters 1 and 2. For the debate about the ongoing value of modernity and Habermas' use of the notion, see the essays in Richard Bernstein, ed., *Habermas and Modernity* (Cambridge: MIT Press, 1985).

2. Simone de Beauvoir, *The Second Sex,* trans. H. M. Parshley (1952; rpt. New York: Vintage, 1974), 44.

3. The best recent example of this tradition is Jessica Benjamin's *The Bonds of Love: Psychoanalysis, Feminism, and the Problem of Domination* (New York: Pantheon, 1988).

4. De Beauvoir, *The Second Sex,* 79.

5. Juliet Mitchell, *Psychoanalysis and Feminism* (New York: Random House, 1974), 34 (summarizing Freud).

6. This appears in a voluminous literature on sexuality in other cultures. For a general survey of the problem of "homo" and "hetero" sexualities, along with the projection of these categories onto cultures that order sexuality differ-

ently, see David Greenberg, *The Construction of Homosexuality* (Chicago: University of Chicago Press, 1988).

7. De Beauvoir, *The Second Sex,* 55 (italics in original). In *Psychoanalysis and Feminism,* Juliet Mitchell offers a critical but, in my reading, not entirely fair account of de Beauvoir's rejection of Freud. See pp. 305–18.

8. Sigmund Freud, "On Narcissism," in James Strachey, ed., *The Standard Edition of the Complete Psychological Works of Sigmund Freud,* 24 vols. (London: Hogarth, 1953–1974), 14:88.

9. "As always where the libido is concerned, man has here again shown himself incapable of giving up a satisfaction he had once enjoyed. He is not willing to forgo the narcissistic perfection of his childhood; and when, as he grows up, he is disturbed by the admonitions of others and by the awakening of his own critical judgement, so that he can no longer retain that perfection, he seeks to recover it in the new form of an ego ideal" ("On Narcissism," 94).

10. Several commentators have noted the evaluative instability of the term, usefully surveyed by Arnold Cooper, "Narcissism," in an excellent collection edited by Andrew Morrison: *Essential Papers on Narcissism* (New York: New York University Press, 1986), 112–43.

11. In *The Ego and the Id,* trans. Joan Riviere (New York: Norton, 1962), by which time Freud has begun to treat the ego ideals as the superego, he writes that "the superego manifests itself essentially as a sense of guilt (or rather, as criticism—for the sense of guilt is the perception in the ego answering to this criticism)" (43). This narrowing of the dissonance of the ego ideals is, in my view, too simple and indicates a symbolic valence that has since eroded. For describing the dissonance between ego and its ideals in modernity, "criticism" is probably more accurate.

12. Kaja Silverman, "Masochism and Male Subjectivity," *Camera Obscura* 17 (1988):41.

13. Jacqueline Rose, *Sexuality in the Field of Vision* (London: Verso, 1986), 170 (emphasis added).

14. For a much fuller version of this argument, see John Brenkman, *Culture and Domination* (Ithaca: Cornell University Press, 1987), especially chapter 5, "The Social Constitution of Subjectivity." Explicating the *fort-da* game, Brenkman writes: "It is essential not to collapse the distinctive moments of the dialectic of desire and interaction; the child's mirror play is already marked with the liberating negativity of speech" (165).

15. There are a number of general surveys on this subject. None, as far as I know, is really satisfactory. The most re-cent is Kenneth Lewes. *The Psychoanalytic Theory of Male Homosexuality* (New York: Simon and Schuster, 1988).

16. Freud to Sandor Ferenczi, 6 October 1910, quoted in Ernest Jones, *The Life and Work of Sigmund Freud,* 3 vols. (New York: Basic Books, 1953), 2:83. On the erotics of Freud's collaborative friendships, see Wayne Koestenbaum, *Double Talk: The Erotics of Male Literary Collaboration* (New York: Routledge, 1989), 17–42.

17. Freud, *The Ego and the Id,* 21.

18. Ibid., 23–24.

19. Sigmund Freud, *Group Psychology and the Analysis of the Ego,* trans. James Strachey (New York: Norton, 1959), 37.

20. See Silverman, "Masochism and Male Subjectivity," 39ff., for a discussion of the implications of this scenario.

21. Mikkel Borch-Jacobsen, *The Freudian Subject,* trans. Catherine Porter (Stanford: Stanford University Press, 1988), 93. The passage continues: "To recognize that I resemble the other, that I resemble myself in him even in my own desire, would be tantamount to admitting the inadmissible: that I am not myself and that my most proper being is over there, in that double who enrages me."

22. Jacques Lacan, *Seminaire* 1 (Paris: Seuil, 1975), 162. Translation modified from the English version: *The Seminar of Jacques Lacan: Book I,* trans. John Forrester (New York: Norton, 1988), 141.

23. Lacan, *Seminar,* 1:142.

24. Ibid., 1:221.

25. There is an excellent article by Wilfried Ver Eecke on this subject: "Hegel as Lacan's Source for Necessity in Psychoanalytic Theory," in Joseph Smith and William Kerrigan, eds., *Interpreting Lacan* (New Haven: Yale University Press, 1983), 113–38.

26. De Beauvoir, *Second Sex,* 464–65.

27. Christopher Lasch, Introduction to Janine Chasseguet-Smirgel, *The Ego Ideal,* trans. Paul Barrows (New York: Norton, 1984), xiii–xiv.

28. Jacques Lacan, "Aggressivity in Psychoanalysis," *Écrits,* trans. Alan Sheridan (New York: Norton, 1977), 27.

29. Jacques Lacan, "On a Question Preliminary to Any Possible Treatment of Psychosis," *Écrits,* 194.

30. Lacan, *Seminar,* 1:141.

31. In this way the discourse on narcissism and homosexuality bears an important resemblance to the psychoanalytic discourse on femininity. See Shoshana Felman, "Rereading Femininity," *Yale French Studies* 62 (1981):19–44.

32. Michel Foucault, *The History of Sexuality, Vol. 1: An Introduction* (New York: Pantheon, 1978). I have no interest in minimizing the value of work that has followed in the same general direction, especially in its value as a critique of the liberal-essentialist discourse of sexuality. For versions that specifically treat the question of homosexuality, see especially Jeffrey Weeks, *Sexuality and Its Discontents: Meanings, Myths, and Modern Sexualities* (London: Routledge, Kegan Paul, 1985); or the work of Eve Sedgwick, most recently exemplified in "Across Gender, Across Sexuality: Willa Cather and Others," *South Atlantic Quarterly* 88 (Winter 1989): 53–72; or David M. Halperin, *One Hundred Years of Homosexuality and Other Essays on Greek Love* (New York: Routledge, 1990).

33. Christopher Lasch, *The Culture of Narcissism* (New York: Norton, 1979).

34. See especially Jürgen Habermas, "Moral Development and Ego Identity," in *Communication and the Evolution of Society,* trans. Thomas McCarthy (Boston: Beacon Press, 1979), 69–94. Habermas argues, for instance, that the subject of modernity "takes into account that traditionally settled forms of life can prove to be mere conventions, to be irrational. Thus he has to retract his ego behind the line of all particular roles and norms and stabilize it only through the abstract ability to present himself credibly in any situation as someone who can satisfy the requirements of consistency even in the face of incompatible role expectations and in the passage through a sequence of contradictory periods of life. Role identity is replaced by ego identity; actors meet as individuals across, so to speak, the objective contexts of their lives" (85–86).

35. Freud, "On Narcissism," 75.

36. See, for instance, Lacan, "Aggressivity," 27.

37. Charles Brockden Brown, *Arthur Mervyn* (1799–1800), ed. Sydney Krause et al. (Kent, Ohio: Kent State University Press, 1980), p. 434.

PART IX
Cultural Studies

Someone new to cultural studies, an advanced undergraduate or graduate student reading this book for the first time, could well describe cultural studies as an interdisciplinary movement with a lot of theory in it, a theory-oriented version of American or Victorian studies but with much broader interests. The many readings in cultural studies in this book—not only the synthesis pieces in this section, "Cultural Studies," but writing by Cornel West, Gauri Viswanathan, Edward Said, Barbara Johnson, Stuart Moulthrop, Laura Mulvey, Nancy Armstrong, Cora Kaplan, for example—will show that cultural studies, indeed both interdisciplinary and theoretical, remains an active area of inquiry that has scarcely solidified into a program of well-defined interests and methods. Cultural studies is shaped by postcolonial inquiries into colonial strategies of cultural oppression and also by *tactics* (to use Michel de Certeau's term) for resisting those practices. It is shaped by gender study, feminist as well as gay/lesbian, and by psychoanalysis and Marxist social theory. It is shaped in relation to, and often as a critique of, traditional practices of anthropology—and also in relation to, and as a critique of, traditional practices of literary studies and aesthetics. Comprised variously by what Henry Louis Gates, Jr., calls "that uneasy, shifting set of alliances formed by feminist critics, critics of so-called minority culture and Marxist and poststructuralist critics generally—in short, the rainbow coalition of contemporary critical theory," cultural studies consistently, since the early 1960s, has asked what it means to know about and be in culture(s) and also what can be done to change and improve culture(s). These are the twin tasks of analyzing existing institutions and transforming those institutions we describe in the General Introduction as "the institutional and transformative concerns of cultural study." Challenging the adequacy of previous formal, "academic" critiques of culture and social practices, this work has shifted cultural and political priorities in what is taught and *how* teaching happens as well as in the kind of inquiries and critiques that get published. In many manifestations, cultural studies is a form of academic rebellion against status quo assumptions about academic work so that it sometimes seems to be a kind of academic "protest" movement seeking to change the nature of what is studied in the academy and even the relations between scholarship and the society that bounds it.

"CULTURE" AS A CONCEPT

The term "cultural studies" is often associated with the work of Raymond Williams. The essays by Dick Hebdige and Stuart Hall in this section make this association

641

abundantly clear, as does Aijaz Ahmad's short history of literary theory in "Literary Theory and 'Third World Literature'" in "What Is Literary Theory?" (Part II). In 1958 Williams published a very influential book, *Culture and Society: 1780–1950,* which pursued the thesis that "the idea of culture, and the word itself in its general modern uses, came into English thinking in the period which we commonly describe as that of the Industrial Revolution." Following the different uses of the term "culture" in different historical settings, Williams examined the social need for this "idea" among English writers and intellectuals. Later, in his book *Keywords,* Williams examined "the issues and problems" that could be traced in particular words, whose "uses bound together certain ways of seeing culture and society." This procedure, as we mention in *Criticism and Culture,* is remarkably parallel to Michel Foucault's description (and pursuit) of Nietzsche's procedure of "genealogy." Hall offers a comparison between Williams and Claude Lévi-Strauss in "Cultural Studies: Two Paradigms" in this section, and Hebdige outlines a more general comparison between "two basic trajectories" of the idea of culture in "From Culture to Hegemony." Hebdige describes culture in terms of the hierarchical past and also in relation to a utopian (and less hierarchical) future. He also shows the convergence of a set of issues within the two very different intellectual traditions of Anglo-American pragmatism and Continental rationalism.

In *Marxism and Literature,* Williams specifically describes the two senses of culture, engendering the "complexity of the concept," in relation to the humanities and the social sciences. The term "culture," he writes, "became a noun of 'inner' process, specialized to its presumed agencies in 'intellectual life' and 'the arts.' It became also a noun of general process, specialized to its presumed configurations in 'whole ways of life.' It played a crucial role in definitions of 'the arts' and 'the humanities,' from the first sense. It played an equally crucial role in definitions of the 'human sciences' and the 'social sciences,' in the second sense. Each tendency is ready to deny any proper use of the concept to the other, in spite of many attempts at reconciliation." Many scholars in cultural studies, along with Williams, want to erase or at least question the absolute opposition between the humanities and the social sciences—what we have called the opposition between aesthetics and ethics in the Introduction to "What Is Literary Theory?" (Part II). This desire is clear not only in Cornel West's discussion of the aesthetic "canon" in relation to the social situation of black people in America but even in Northrop Frye's call for literary studies to take its place among the social sciences (both in "What Is Literary Studies?" [Part I]). Saussure, in "Structuralism and Semiotics" (Part IV), situates the new science of "semiology" among the social sciences, and a significant aspect of the program of the "New Historicism," especially as exampled by the essays by Stephen Greenblatt and Nancy Armstrong in "Historical Criticism" (Part VII), follows Williams's assertion, quoted by Hall, that "we cannot separate literature and art from other kinds of social practice." In his analysis in *Marxism and Literature,* Williams argues that "culture" encompasses the world of art, "imagination," and ideas, and that it also encompasses the social grouping of people in which, in some sense, the whole is greater than the sum of its parts. It describes the ways in which societies make sense of the common experience of its members, situating "culture" within the domain of "ideas," and, in Williams's repeated phrase, it describes "a whole way of living of a people" (cited by both Hebdige and Hall).

These two "tendencies" indicate two different intellectual disciplines for which the term "culture" has been crucial: literary/intellectual studies and anthropology. In other words, we argued in the General Introduction that the concept of "literature" has a history that has been affected by the institutions that define and preserve it. In a like manner, "culture" carries with it the history of the ways it has been put to use. (In his article included here, Hebdige pursues some aspects of this "history.") An early use of the term was that of Matthew Arnold in *Culture and Anarchy* (1869), where he attempted to find a system of values in a world in which traditional religious and social values were crumbling, a world in which the aristocracy no longer commanded the coherence of society and the middle-class ideology of laissez-faire capitalism did not address the needs of social and "cultural" coherence. Another early use was that of E. B. Tylor in *Primitive Culture* (1871), a book often described as a founding document in the establishment of anthropology as an intellectual discipline. Unlike Arnold's description of culture as an agency of intellectual life and the arts, Tylor describes culture as whole ways of life. Instead of Arnold's normative and singular term, Tylor offers the possibility of understanding many different "cultures." That is, the opposition between Arnold and Tylor, as George Stocking has argued, is (paradoxically) the opposition between Arnold's view of culture as a transindividual tradition and Tylor's view of cultures as a plurality of unrelated instances. This opposition, Stocking also argues, can itself be historicized: it is related to the political differences of Arnold's Tory politics and Tylor's Liberal politics in Victorian England.

For these reasons, it is necessary, we think, for cultural studies to acknowledge its relation to the social sciences as well as the humanities: the translation of the "humanities" into the "human sciences" we mentioned in the General Introduction gestures in this direction. The inclusion in this section of James Clifford's essay "The Translation of Cultures" aims at suggesting these links, as does Donna Haraway's "A Cyborg Manifesto." Clifford, an anthropologist, brings together Arnold's "traditional" view of culture in the religious culture of Maurice Leenhardt, an evangelical missionary in New Caledonia at the turn of the twentieth century, and, at the same time, the scientific anthropological study of different cultures in the examination of the confrontation of different languages. The crucial problem for both views of culture—the problem of what Clifford calls "deep translation"—is that of "otherness" or "difference." Haraway resituates this problem within a "postmodern" idiom of irony, fragmentation, and the blurring of "self-evident" distinctions between the sciences and the humanities, the natural and the artificial, and disinterested knowledge and interested politics. The terms "otherness" and "difference" (or implications of them) have reappeared throughout this book—in Viswanathan, Said, Schweickart, Derrida, Greenblatt, Rich, and Warner, and even in Haraway's concept of the "cyborg"—and they are always implicated in any discussion of culture. (Even Arnold, in defining the cultural work of criticism in "The Function of Criticism at the Present Time" in 1865, felt it necessary to discuss the differences of class.) That is, the *problem* of cultural studies is the difficult task of *both* acknowledging cultural and human differences and discovering a means of creating culture and community where whatever people share with one another is not lost in acknowledged difference. In relation to literary criticism, the problem of cultural studies, as Said says, is the difficulty of linking literary and cultural works to each other in order to bring particular works "out of the neglect and secondariness to which for all kinds of political and ideological reasons they had previously been condemned." Williams describes such "otherness" in historical and temporal terms (as opposed to the spatial terms of Clifford's anthropology) when he notes in *The Long Revolution* that different generations "never quite talk 'the same language,'" and Clifford describes it in his narration of Leenhardt's "intercultural translation." And, finally, Haraway focuses on such "otherness" when she examines the fragments, irony, and seeming "non-natural" nature of the postmodern.

THE COMPLEXITY OF CULTURAL STUDIES

The large body of writing and thought that comprises "cultural studies" within literary studies at present blends vocabularies drawn from classical Marxist and current political theory, psychoanalysis, feminism, philosophy, and semiotics. Haraway, trained as a biologist, even appropriates the language of science fiction in her work. In view of this complex blending, cultural studies discourse at times may be formidable in its technical terminology and diversity. Haraway even speaks the strange discourse of what she calls "cyborg semiologies." The reading of a few formative essays, however, can assist immensely to open up for inspection the significant debates about "culture" centered on cultural studies. Dick Hebdige's "From Culture to Hegemony," the introductory chapter of his sociological study *Subculture: The Meaning of Style,* is one such article, especially in its appropriation of Antonio Gramsci's important concept of "hegemony" as a kind of "unconscious" dimension of social value. (See Raymond Williams's essay in "Historical Criticism" [Part VII] for another discussion of this concept.) Stuart Hall's "Cultural Studies: Two Paradigms," which also examines hegemony, divides the expanse of work in cultural studies into the "culturalist" and the "structuralist" initiatives. Hall defines culturalism as moving in a line from Matthew Arnold and F. R. Leavis and down through Raymond Williams. Those who speak of culture in this setting generally assume, in Williams's words, the existence of a "common culture" through which occurs "the sharing of common meanings." Here "culture" means "a whole way of life" that springs from a ground of shared natural experience. This version of "culture," relying on the priority of "experience" conceived as a substance giving form to culture, is essentialist in orientation. The theme of "experience" and its relation to "essentialism" recurs throughout this book. Diana Fuss's essay "Reading Like a Feminist" in "Feminism and Gender Studies" (Part VIII), which is excerpted from her book *Essentially Speaking,* focuses on the issue of "essentialism," the opposition between nature and culture that Haraway takes such pains to dissolve. Both these two essays and Teresa de Lauretis's essay "Semiotics and Experience" in "Structuralism and Semiotics" (Part IV) make clear the importance of the seeming "accidents" of experience (and "homework," as Haraway calls it) to the cultural and political themes of feminism and of the close relationship between feminism and cultural studies. Indeed, it can be argued that cultural studies as an "area" of study in the United States is centrally conditioned by the work of feminism.

The other principal mode for understanding cultural studies in Hall's discussion is a "structuralist" view of culture. Largely semiotic in orientation, "experience" in this view is culturally—and socially—constructed, never "natural" or universal in its range but always specific to a particular culture. De Lauretis's and Fuss's use of Lacanian psychoanalysis—like that use by Belsey and Mulvey—draws upon this second understanding of "experience." In this section, Clifford discusses the "translation" of one culture to another as the "nuanced understanding" of what he calls "reciprocal translation," the attempt of cultures to recognize each other's otherness, without reverting to a psychoanlytic framework. All through Clifford's discussion is the constant reminder that "reciprocal translation," whatever its relative success, also means untranslatability, the suggestion that in a fundamental way cultures may speak to but not *for* each other. In this structuralist line, drawing on modern linguistics and semiotics, are Claude Lévi-Strauss, Michel Foucault, Julia Kristeva, Jacques Lacan, and Jacques Derrida. In their thinking, the languages and codes of culture produce the experiential effects that, as part of their power as instituted practices, give the appearance of being inevitable and unalterably "natural." Many of the critics working currently in cultural studies are aligned on this structuralist side. Hall, however, wisely resists the theoretical closure of choosing one paradigm over the other. He writes in "Cultural Studies: Two Paradigms" that by themselves "neither structuralism nor culturalism will do[;] as self-sufficient paradigms of study, they [together] have a centrality to the field which all the other contenders lack . . . ." The "essential" move of taking a particular position to speak from and the representational function of language that one uses when speaking from that position are not two different assumptions that we can choose between. They are themselves constituent dimensions of what culture can be. As the abstract markers for other possibilities, he goes on, together "they address what must be the *core problem* of cultural studies," the relations of essentialism and representation, saying and doing, as represented in the coupling "culture/ideology."

A number of disciplines have been influenced by cultural studies since 1960s, among them pedagogy, communication, literary criticism, women's studies, legal studies, and the emerging work in the social study of science. (Haraway is a key figure here, along with Bruno Latour, Katherine Hayles, and Robert Markley.) In each case, traditional conceptions of inquiry are recast in light of the social use of knowledge. Much influenced by Raymond Williams's idea of the "politics of intellectual work," these diverse practices all move in the direction of framing "knowing" within the social context of inquiry at a particular historical moment. Knowledge, from this view, can never be disinterested in the manner Arnold took it to be. For as an actual *act* in the world, not something simply that *is,* knowledge is simultaneously an enablement to some who can perform it in a particular way and an impediment to others. Always taking the form of an actual *act,* knowledge is and can always be conceived as part of a discourse, as having a sender and receiver—in other words, as having agency. Cultural studies and this definition of knowledge as an act are currently shaping English and literary studies as a discipline. English and rhetoric, in their *performative* dimension as activities of analysis and interpretation, also help to establish in cultural studies this sense of knowledge as a kind of action taken. (For related discussions, see the examinations of rhetoric in "Rhetoric and Reader Response" (Part III); Jonathan Culler's discussion of the opposition between performative and constative aspects of language in examination of Derrida and Austin in "Deconstruction and Poststructuralism" (Part V); and Shoshana Felman's and Slavoj Žižek's discussions of knowledge in "Psychology and Psychoanalysis" [Part VI].)

In sum, in the "performative" conception of knowledge in cultural studies is a general rejection of knowledge taken as an abstract reference separate from the realm of human activity. Rather, knowledge is something that happens within a scenario of material conditions, within and in relation to the *local* conditions from which it arose. As we noted in the Introduction to "Deconstruction and Poststructuralism" (Part V), the aim of Enlightenment "reason" was to *universalize* and *individualize* understanding by detaching it from the particular and local historical contexts in which it arises, the very "custom" and "tradition" to which Descartes objected. Custom and tradition are the sources and locus of "culture," and cultural studies—whatever discipline or disciplines it is working out of—attempts to make knowledge more complex by returning it to the customs and traditions from which it arises. It attempts to understand knowledge as a phenomenon that is conditioned not by an individual subject, but by a social world. It is against this background of knowledge seen in its performative dimension that the performing of cultural work, the "struggle" over "whole ways of life," to use Williams's words, can be seen as actually creating the dimensions of culture that, when fully instituted, will appear to be inevitable and "natural."

THE POLITICS OF CULTURAL STUDIES

But cultural studies, in its complexity, its interdisciplinarity—even as informed by semiotics—aims at creating new practices, new "cultural" life, as well as objects and forms of knowledge. Practitioners of cultural studies argue that cultural studies fully achieves complete detachment and disinterestedness, and, thus, that cultural studies needs to be measured by its performance and impact as a practice as well as a form of understanding. Other interdisciplinary inquiries in American studies, comparative literature, and African-American studies have not in every instance been highly effective in actual practice. In "Black Critics and the Pitfalls of Canon Formation" (in "What Is Literary Studies?" [Part I]), Cornel West warns against the ways African-American studies can become another version of academic business as usual. Similarly, Henry Giroux, David Shumway, Paul Smith, and James Sosnoski, in "The Need for Cultural Studies: Resisting Intellectual and Oppositional Public Spheres," advance a withering discussion of the prior era of interdisciplinary studies in the 1960s. They argue that interdisciplinary programs such as American studies, Victorian studies, and black studies joined and harmonized too well with the institutions they were a part of. (Patrick Brantlinger also offers a good history of these programs in relation to cultural studies.) In effect, these programs ceased to be *critical* practices in the sense of "transformative critique" common to and useful in cultural studies. Those who advance critiques positioned from outside the academy are more consistently successful, cultural critics such as Gayatri Chakravorty Spivak, Edward Said, and Cornel West. Also, the Birmingham Centre for the Study of Popular Culture in England succeeded for a time in advancing cultural critiques little bounded by the usual institutional constraints. The impetus of such movements, as Spivak argues in *Other Worlds: Essays in Cultural Politics* (1987) and *The Post-Colonial Critic* (1990), is owing to the work of those positioned on the periphery of culture, those who represent discourses that have been excluded from cultural and intellectual power. Such figures speak in a voice closely linked to their status as cultural agents for particular ideological positions, voices "marked" by the signifiers (skin color, accent, place of origin, etc.) of past economic and social marginalization.

The situation of American cultural studies critics is unusual. American academics, with some exceptions historically, have very often gone about their work estranged from other sites of social struggle and commitment and, in the process, have frequently taken up the role of being a legitimating agency ratifying the values and directions of the reigning ideologies; they have seemed, at best, to be "merely" analyzing the phenomena of the human sciences and the *institutions* of social life. In this scenario, an intellectual becomes "in some undismissible sense," as Jim Merod says in *The Political Responsibility of the Critic,* simply "an agent of that power" that supposedly was being analyzed and critiqued. Those working in cultural studies, many of whom work in state-supported colleges and universities around the country, are faced with the dilemma concerning how to maintain the effectiveness of a critique that seeks to *transform* institutions of knowledge and power when working within such institutions. One solution to this dilemma would be "to find an institutional practice in cultural studies that might produce an organic intellectual," that is, one who is aligned, as Hall says in "Cultural Studies and Its Theoretical Legacies," "with an emerging historic movement." If such a practice could be found, such an intellectual would be "organic" in the sense of finding his or her own genesis *as* an intellectual within specific communal needs at a specific moment. The question of whether such a figure as an organic intellectual (Antonio Gramsci's term) can exist in any form is a key question of cultural studies. (When bell hooks points out that she is a member of the local black community in "What Is Literary Theory?" (Part II), or when Haraway notes here the "odd perspective provided by [her] historical position," they are each attempting to engage this question.)

THE SUBJECTS OF CULTURE: KNOWLEDGE AND POWER

The concept and potential of an "organic" intellectual emphasizes the *local* nature of cultural studies: cultural studies addresses situations that occur at a particular place and a particular time, so the "interests" of cultural studies and knowledge can be self-consciously formed in relation to local conditions—in the classroom, in discussions of curricula, in the creation of the possibilities of intellectual and other cultural activities. This definition may help to formulate the "problem" of cultural studies in contemporary culture. For insofar as the academic intellectual (both student and teacher) has a primary investment in the status quo, academic discourse cannot advance a transformative critique. In other words, to what extent can approaches to cultural studies, potentially or at present, produce practices with salutary effects socially and culturally? And how are such "effects" to be identified and measured—by what standard? Dinesh D'Souza's idea in *Illiberal Education*—in some ways the only idea of his book—is that contemporary cultural inquiry is defined and practiced subjectively. In this critique, in a certain sense, he is correct. A primary tenet of the cultural-studies agenda, as advanced by the Birmingham Centre and in much actual practice in Australia and the United States, is for cultural studies to be fundamentally "subjective" in nature—a form of the *local* nature of knowledge. In *Illiberal Education*, D'Souza mistakenly parodies the "subjective" critique of cultural studies as a practice malleable and frivolous, what he identifies as a set of largely Lilliputian abstractions about texts and theoretical approaches to multiculturalism. He advances that a few liberals with left-leaning politics are attempting to fix the world by projecting their own values onto education. But in a sense that D'Souza misses, cultural studies traditionally is, in fact, *subjective*. This is not to say that it is non-"objective" or nonrigorous but, rather, "subjective" in the sense of paying attention to the situation and the context within which we find any inquiring subject. It is such "subjectivity" that makes the immediate setting and history of such importance to many of the essays with vastly different "approaches" in this book.

Hall argues that it became necessary to theorize the "subject" after the rise of structuralism in the 1950s and 1960s. Given the constructionist view in many of the social sciences and cultural studies that says "experience," even when taken to be natural or naturally occurring, is the effect of a certain subjectivity and cultural practice, a critical examination of culture must also define and understand the cultural viewpoint, or "subject"—the set of assumptions on which a particular cultural construction is built. Here the "subject" means, as Hall writes in this section, "a set of positions in language and knowledge, from which culture can appear to be enunciated." So even what we might call observable experience would have to be investigated within the context of the subjectivity that produced it. For these reasons, cultural studies is indeed "subjective" in that insofar as it is "critical" it can never escape examining the perspective and the assumptions that make a critical investigation possible.

Given the working assumption that investigation must include examination of the perspective from which we are doing the investigating, cultural studies necessarily will be an activity defined by specific cultural subjects with specific *interests*. In the absence of a universal or neutral way of studying culture, in the absence of a ground outside of the positions of discourse and interests, there is also no such thing as an innocent observer of culture. As Williams notes, no one can possibly be unaligned and unpositioned culturally. In "The Principle of Reason: The University in the Eyes of Its Pupils" (in "Deconstruction and Poststructuralism" [Part V]), Derrida makes the same argument about the structure and alignment of institutional knowledge. As we discuss in *Criticism and Culture,* the Western university as a site for producing knowledge is a product of the eighteenth-century separation of pure knowledge from ethics, disinterested inquiry from the world of practicality. Aesthetics and art occupy a kind of middle ground between disinterestedness and practicality. They are not categorizable purely as knowledge or practical activity (ethics and/or power). They function, though, as the mediators between knowledge and power and provide an important bridge between them. The objects of cultural studies as forms of knowledge or the activities of knowing—the difficulty of precisely formulating this is the double task of cultural studies—are the texts of social and cultural experience. The linking of knowledge and power engenders a new organization of academic "disciplines" and can create a precise sense of what it means for an inquiry to be *interested*. "Knowing" anything, in this engaged sense that characterizes cultural studies, necessarily involves the specific relation of ethical responsibility in relation to the discourse of inquiry itself.

To speak of "interests" in this way—as Hall notes in "Cultural Studies and Its Theoretical Legacies"—is to admit that inquiry has "some stake in the choices it makes." To have a stake in the choices, in the sense of preferring one social outcome over another in a particular set of conditions, as Hall says, is "the 'political' aspect of cultural studies," the way in which it is situated in power relations. This connection with the issue of power does not hold just for the large, institutional dimensions of inquiry but includes "the question of the personal as political." This is a "radical expansion of the notion of power" in that it does include the personal and private realms of cultural manifestation. By "personal" is meant particularly the areas of gender and sexuality as part of the understanding of power itself. So if cultural studies is professedly "subjective" and "interested" in this manner, then it is ideologically oriented as well. This is why Hebdige takes such pains to understand the concept of culture in relation to the concept of ideology. Part of knowing itself as a subject necessarily involves cultural studies' acknowledgment of its interests in the contest of competing interests, "the contest for forms and values" Said describes. Cultural studies, of course, has an agenda and an aim, "some will to connect," as Hall says, such as (but not limited to) the very "socialist-feminism" Haraway announces in the title of her "manifesto." Whereas rational and traditional scientific inquiry stipulates empirical and detached observation as instrumental to the testing of a hypothesis, in cultural studies there must instead be an acknowledgment of the participants' interests within a historical frame.

In this formulation of the cultural-studies agenda, there is the acknowledgment of the constructed subject within a cultural and historical context—cultural studies as always "subjective." That acknowledgment of subjectivity then facilitates an awareness of the social and economic ties that define an interested participant. Cultural critique is maintained as an actual possibility through a continual resituating of the inquiring subject as a particular organization of power within discourse—cultural studies inquiry, in other words, as an interested and purposeful activity, always ideologically oriented. Indeed, the power to speak about oppression comes from the recognition of economic and ideological interests within history, one's commitment, finally, to the choice of how we want our lives to be and the responsibility defined by that commitment.

CULTURE AS LOCAL

Thus far we have outlined an abstract and rather broad critical agenda for cultural studies. The actual work in this field is often controversial and can present formidable difficulties. Meaghan Morris, for instance, in an essay entitled "Banality in Cultural Studies," investigates the manner in which "theory" can function as "an objectified and objectifying . . . force strategically engaged in an ever more intense process of commodification." She discusses the influential work of Jean Baudrillard and finds that the "banality" of contemporary culture "is associated, quite clearly and conventionally, with negative aspects of media . . . a gross platitudinousness of the all-pervasive present." In an argument nicely parallel to the discussion of the elitist and political functioning of "theory" in Aijaz Ahmad's analysis in "What Is Literary Theory?" (Part II), she examines the way the banality of culture is judged negatively according to the "'aristocratic' ideal of maintaining an elite, arbitrary, and avowedly artificial order." Her concern—one she shares with Cornel West, bell hooks, Adrienne Rich, and others—is that cultural studies could succeed as a coherent practice but fail as actual cultural critique. This could happen because the elitism of its theory could have the effect "of discrediting" the "voices of grumpy feminists and cranky leftists." "To discredit such voices is, as I understand it," she goes on, "one of the immediate political functions of the current boom in cultural studies (as distinct from the intentionality of projects invested by it)."

Most people continue to be cautious about making claims for the achievements of cultural studies. Cultural studies is not a "school" in any formal sense, and it can be called a "movement" in the loosest configuration only dating back to the late 1950s and early 1960s. Along with the critiques of gender studies and the "New Historicism," though, cultural-studies critics have succeeded in foregrounding pressing issues arising out of the articulation of culture and politics. They have elaborated strategies for viewing culture ideologically and dynamically without the reductionism of an old-fashioned and oversimplified base/superstructure relationship. They have helped those in the academy, in fact, to rethink the very nature of culture and its institutions, to understand cultural and political choices and how the culture makes them, and generally, to render problematic prior assumptions about the separation of culture and politics. Finally, "like the cultural critics of old," as West says, they have reminded us that "we must simply know much more than a professional literary critical training provides." In the new cultural-studies criticism, there is the prospect (and not necessarily the full "realization") of a profoundly historical and critical understanding of the relationships of power and culture, and it is for this reason, above all, that cultural studies has attracted such interest.

Still, the reasons for this interest are not always the "same." In this book the local arguments and critiques of received ideas (which are often encountered under the form of disinterested, "aesthetic" ideas) by Graff, Viswanathan, bell hooks, Said, Rich, Žižek, Haraway, Clifford, Derrida, Warner, and many others often have greatly varied goals and agendas. These differences, we think, have allowed cultural studies to revitalize the reading and writing of literary criticism in a variety of ways. Most importantly, cultural studies underlines the various *stakes* in reading and interpreting texts: how these activities, like the "knowledge" they discover and define, make a difference in the world. These stakes are not always congruent or compatible: J. Hillis Miller's attempt to acknowledge the "uncanny" in reading can seem (and has seemed to some) to be a form of quietism in a world of great social injustice. Schweickart's attempt to delineate a "feminist" mode of reading can seem (and has seemed to some) to be an activity for privileged (white) middle-class women. Derrida's critique of reason can seem (and has seemed to some) to be simple, irresponsible wordplay. Haraway's focus on what she calls "situated knowledges" can seem (and has seemed to some) to be a betrayal of the liberal and liberatory ideals of the Enlightenment. Even our raising so many of these issues associated with cultural studies in this book can seem (and has seemed to some) to be a way of participating in the ways "the current boom in cultural studies" blunts, as Meaghan Morris says, other kinds of political action. For others, new contexts create new ways of understanding. In the case of Paul de Man, for instance, the revelation of wartime writings sympathetic with the Nazi occupation of Belgium and his subsequent silence about this collaboration has reshaped the reception of his work and the reception of poststructuralism generally. Most people have felt that the facts of de Man's life connect with and color his work.

The analytical focus on local circumstances is a part of what the anthropologist Clifford Geertz means by "thick description." (Hall alludes to this term when he points out "the experiential 'thickness' of" Williams's concepts in *The Long Revolution*.) But, as we have said, "description" itself—especially if it presents itself as objective and disinterested—is an area that cultural studies has sought to reexamine in light of the question of the social and cultural function it serves. Such a reexamination is what we have called ethics, and ethics calls for procedures—this is part of our point about cultural studies more generally—that do not necessarily have to participate in the simple "wholeness" of what we have described as Enlightenment aesthetics. The parts of cultural studies do not have to hold together "for all time." Rather, like any genuine *ethical* activity, these studies need only engage the *local* investigation and mediate the relationship between local considerations and larger "cultural" concerns, the "postmodern" hybridizations that Haraway pursues under the term "cyborg." The different activities of cultural studies have to be judged individually, in terms of the contest for form and value that each one participates in. That is, rather than compatibility and congruence, cultural studies seeks local activity that can *always* be subject to critique because some particular form or value is always being weighed and is at stake. The stake of "knowledge" as an *act* in the world—*its* reexamination—is simultaneously an enablement to some who can perform it in a particular way and an impediment to others.

George Steiner once asked, "How can there be a general and generalizing treatment of artistic-literary objects which are, by definition, unique?" The answer, as Said and others suggest in this book—we saw it also, in a very different way, in the definition of the humanities by the linguist Louis Hjelmslev in the General Introduction—is that for the "humanities," as for "culture," we do not have to choose, once and for all, between disinterested knowledge and interested action, between "thick" local description and generalizing "human" relevance. Literature is particularly a place—there are many others—in which the forms and values of human life can be known in diverse ways. In the sphere of literature and literary studies, the relationships of knowledge and action can be explored and known at different levels of interest and in various modes of inter-human relationships. Literary studies is a site of aesthetics as well as ideology. We can return to the site of that experience repeatedly—in this case, "literature"—as interests change, as sympathy for other cultures grow, as the understanding of such terms as "knowledge" and "reading" change, and as the need for work in the world, locally and on larger scales, demands attention. These issues and others are at stake in literary and cultural criticism, as they are, we believe, in all of the sections of this book.

RELATED ESSAYS IN *CONTEMPORARY LITERARY CRITICISM*

Aijaz Ahmad, "Literary Theory and 'Third World Literature'"
Judith Butler, "Variations on Sex and Gender: Beauvoir, Wittig, and Foucalt"
Teresa de Lauretis, "Semiotics and Experience"
Jacques Derrida, "The Principle of Reason: The University in the Eyes of Its Pupils"
bell hooks, "Postmodern Blackness"
Barbara Johnson, "Apostrophe, Animation, and Abortion"
Edward Said, "The Politics of Knowledge"
Michael Warner, "Homo-Narcissism; or, Heterosexuality"
Cornel West, "Black Critics and the Pitfalls of Canon Formation"

REFERENCES AND FURTHER READING

Baumann, Gerd, *Contesting Culture: Discourses of Identity in Multi-ethnic London* (New York: Cambridge University Press, 1996).

Bogard, William, *The Simulation of Surveillance: Hypercontrol in Telematic Societies* (New York: Cambridge University Press, 1996).

Boscagli, Maurizia, *Eye on the Flesh: Fashions of Masculinity in the Early Twentieth Century* (Boulder, CO: Westview Press, 1996).

Brantlinger, Patrick, *Crusoe's Footprint: Cultural Studies in Britain and America* (New York: Routledge, 1990).

Cohen, Colleen Ballerino, *Beauty Queens on the Global Stage: Gender, Contests, and Power* (New York: Routledge, 1996).

Curran, James, David Morley, and Valerie Walkerdine, *Cultural Studies and Communications* (New York: St. Martin's Press, 1996).

Davies, Ioan, *Cultural Studies and Beyond: Fragments of Empire* (New York: Routledge, 1995).

Davis, Robert Con, "Cixous, Spivak, and Oppositional Theory," in *Lit*, 4, 1 (1992): 29–42.

———, "Freud, Lacan, and the Subject of Cultural Studies," in *College Literature* 18, 2 (1991): 22–37.

———, *The Paternal Romance: Reading God-the-Father in Early Western Culture* (Urbana: University of Illinois Press, 1993).

Delgado, Richard, ed, *Critical Race Theory: The Cutting Edge* (Philadelphia: Temple University Press, 1995).

Dow, Bonnie J., *Prime-Time Feminism: Television, Media Culture, and the Women's Movement Since 1970* (Philadelphia: University of Pennsylvania Press, 1996).

D'Souza, Dinesh, *Illiberal Education: The Politics of Race and Sex on Campus* (New York: Free Press, 1991).

During, Simon, *The Cultural Studies Reader* (New York: Routledge, 1993).

Erkkila, Betsy, and Jay Grossman, *Breaking Bounds: Whitman and American Cultural Studies* (New York: Oxford University Press, 1996).

Fish, Stanley, "Being Interdisciplinary Is So Very Hard to Do," in *Profession,* 89 (1989): 15–22.

Garber, Marjorie B., Paul Franklin, and Rebecca Walkowitz, *Field Work: Sites in Literary and Cultural Studies* (New York: Routledge, 1996).

Gates, Henry Louis, Jr., "Whose Canon Is It, Anyway?" in *New York Times* (26 February 1989), 7, 1: 1.

Giroux, Henry, David Shumway, Paul Smith, and James Sosnoski, "The Need for Cultural Studies: Resisting Intellectual and Oppositional Public Spheres," *Dalhousie Review* 64, 2 (Summer 1984): 472–86.

Grossberg, Lawrence, Cary Nelson, and Paula Treichler, eds., *Cultural Studies* (New York: Routledge, 1992).

Guillory, John, *Cultural Capital: The Problem of Literary Canon Formation* (Chicago: University of Chicago Press, 1993).

Hall, Stuart, "Cultural Studies and Its Theoretical Legacies," in *Cultural Studies,* ed. Lawrence Grossberg, Cary Nelson, and Paula A. Treichler (New York: Routledge, 1992), 277–94.

Hatfield, Elaine, and Richard L. Rapson, *Love and Sex: Cross-Cultural Perspectives* (Boston: Allyn and Bacon, 1996).

Hay, James, Lawrence Grossberg, and Ellen Wartella, *The Audience and Its Landscape* (Boulder, CO: Westview Press, 1996).

Heath, Stephen, *The Sexual Fix* (London: Macmillan, 1982).

Hebdige, Dick, *Subculture: The Meaning of Style* (New York: Routlege, 1979).

Heide, Margaret J., *Television Culture and Women's Lives:* Thirtysomething *and the Contradictions of Gender* (Philadelphia: University of Pennsylvania Press, 1995).

Henderson, Mae, *Borders, Boundaries, and Frames: Essays in Cultural Criticism and Cultural Studies* (New York: Routledge, 1995).

Herr, Cheryl, *Critical Regionalism and Cultural Studies: From Ireland to the American Midwest* (Gainesville: University Press of Florida, 1996).

Inglis, Fred, *Cultural Studies* (Cambridge, MA: Blackwell, 1993).

"Instituting Cultural Studies: A Dialogue with Gerald Graff, Janice Radway, Gita Rajan, and Robert Con Davis," in *Instituting Cultural Studies,* ed. Isaiah Smithson and Nancy Ruff (Champaign: University of Illinois Press, 1993).

Jackson, Sandra, and José Solis, *Beyond Comfort Zones in Multiculturalism: Confronting the Politics of Privilege* (Westport, CT: Bergin and Garvey, 1995).

Kamuf, Peggy, and Nancy K. Miller, "Parisian Letters: Between Feminism and Deconstruction," in *Conflicts in Feminism,* ed. Marianne Hirsch and Evelyn Fox Keller (New York: Routledge, 1990), 121–33.

Lovell, Terry, *Feminist Cultural Studies* (Brookfield, VT: Elgar, 1995).

Mercer, Kobena, *Welcome to the Jungle: New Positions in Black Cultural Studies* (New York: Routledge, 1994).

Merod, Jim, *The Political Responsibility of the Critic* (Ithaca, NY: Cornell University Press, 1987).

Modleski, Tania, ed., *Studies in Entertainment: Critical Approaches to Mass Culture* (Bloomington: Indiana University Press, 1986).

Morris, Meaghan, "Banality in Cultural Studies," in *Logics of Television: Essays in Cultural Criticism.* ed. Patricia Mellencamp (Madison: University of Wisconsin Press, 1990).

Radway, Janice, *Reading the Romance: Women, Patriarchy, and Popular Literature* (Chapel Hill: University of North Carolina Press, 1984).

Rajchman, John, *The Identity in Question* (New York: Routledge, 1995).

Richardson, Laurel, Verta A. Taylor, and Nancy Whittier, *Feminist Frontiers IV* (New York: McGraw-Hill, 1997).

Schleifer, Ronald, "The Institutions of Cultural Studies," in *Surfaces* 2, 14 (1992), 3–22.

———, Robert Con Davis, and Nancy Mergler, *Culture and Cognition: The Boundaries of Literary and Scientific Inquiry* (Ithaca: Cornell University Press, 1992).

Schwarz, Henry, and Richard Dienst, *Reading the Shape of the World: Toward an International Cultural Studies* (Boulder, CO: Westview Press, 1996).

Sheridan, Susan, *Grafts: Feminist Cultural Criticism* (New York: Verso, 1988).

Sloop, John M., *The Cultural Prison: Discourse, Prisoners, and Punishment* (Tuscaloosa: University of Alabama Press, 1996).

Smith, Paul, *Boys: Masculinities in Contemporary Culture* (Boulder, CO: Westview Press, 1996).

Sosnoski, James J., *Modern Skeletons in Postmodern Closets: A Cultural Studies Alternative* (Charlottesville: University Press of Virginia, 1995).

Spivak, Gayatri Chakravorty, *In Other Worlds: Essays in Cultural Politics* (New York: Methuen, 1987).

———, *The Postcolonial Critic: Interviews, Strategies, Dialogues,* ed. Sarah Harasym (New York: Routledge, 1990).

Steiner, George, "Introduction" to Walter Benjamin, in *The Origin of German Tragic Drama* (London: Verso, 1977).

Stocking, George, *Race, Culture, and Evolution* (New York: Free Press, 1968).

Willemen, Paul, *Looks and Frictions: Essays in Cultural Studies and Film Theory* (Bloomington: Indiana University Press, 1994).

Williams, Raymond, *Culture and Society* (New York: Columbia University Press, 1958).

———, *Keywords,* rev. ed. (New York: Oxford University Press, 1983).

———, *The Long Revolution* (New York: Columbia University Press, 1961).

———, *Marxism and Literature* (New York: Oxford University Press, 1977).

35

Dick Hebdige
1951–

Formerly affiliated with the Centre for Contemporary Cultural Studies (CCCS) at the University of Birmingham, now at the California Institute of the Arts, Dick Hebdige is a cultural critic working within a Marxist, but distinctly British, empirical tradition of cultural analysis that includes the groundbreaking contributions of Raymond Williams and Richard Hoggart. In addition to his numerous empirical studies on English working-class culture, which have appeared individually in various well-received CCCS anthologies such as *Resistance through Rituals: Youth Subcultures in Post-War Britain* (1976), Hebdige also has published three book-length works of cultural analysis, *Subculture: The Meaning of Style* (1979), *Hiding in the Light: On Images and Things* (1988), and *Cut 'n' Mix: Culture, Identity and Caribbean Music (1990).*

Originally an introduction to *Subculture: The Meaning of Style,* "From Culture to Hegemony" is a programmatic statement of Hebdige's Marxist-semiotic approach to cultural analysis. Embedding his statement within a brief history of cultural studies, Hebdige notes that initially cultural studies vacillated uneasily between two competing definitions of culture: the aesthetic definition of "culture as a standard of excellence" and the anthropological definition of "culture as a 'whole way of life.'" The uneasy coexistence of these two definitions within cultural studies, Hebdige argues, manifests itself in the early work of Hoggart and Williams, where a defense of traditional working-class culture is joined surprisingly with a defense of cultural literacy. Condemning the commodification of an authentic working-class culture, Williams and Hoggart ultimately dismiss the anthropological study of contemporary cultural developments, preferring instead to privilege the study of literature, to such an extent that they even establish aesthetic criteria to distinguish good literature from "trash."

Roland Barthes's *Mythologies,* however, reorients the field of cultural studies. Abandoning the aesthetic definition of culture, Barthes exchanges literary for semiotic analysis, applying it without discrimination, Hebdige notes approvingly, to the whole of everyday life, including the commodified culture decried by Hoggart and Williams. Having expanded cultural studies' field of inquiry, Barthes treats the objects and practices of culture as a system of signs, codes, and myths that attempt to naturalize ideology. Culture therefore is not only a system of signs but also a site of political conflict, all signs having an ideological dimension.

Antonio Gramsci's theory of hegemony, Hebdige concludes, provides the most subtle model of the ideological dimension of cultural signification. According to

Gramsci, social groups achieve and maintain power by seeking the consensus of a heterogeneous citizenry through rhetorically persuasive representations emanating from particular institutions in various mediums. The consensus, however, is precarious and can be challenged, just as mythology can be debunked. Gramsci asserts that theorists should consider the importance of agency for a Marxist tradition that has focused too often on the priority of economic determination. Hebdige concurs, saying that social groups—youth subcultures in particular—can adopt an oppositional stance to the mass-produced products of institutions as they can appropriate them, reinvest them with new meaning or style, and thus contradict the myth of consensus. To dismiss contemporary cultural developments, therefore, as Williams and Hoggart had, is to ignore the political, revolutionary contesting of hegemonic discourses that is the focus of Hebdige's Marxist-semiotic approach to cultural analysis.

From Culture to Hegemony

CULTURE

> Culture: cultivation, tending, in Christian authors, worship; the action or practice of cultivating the soil; tillage, husbandry; the cultivation or rearing of certain animals (e.g. fish); the artificial development of microscopic organisms, organisms so produced; the cultivating or development (of the mind, faculties, manners), improvement or refinement by education and training; the condition of being trained or refined; the intellectual side of civilization; the prosecution or special attention or study of any subject or pursuit.
> (*Oxford English Dictionary*)

Culture is a notoriously ambiguous concept as the above definition demonstrates. Refracted through centuries of usage, the word has acquired a number of quite different, often contradictory, meanings. Even as a scientific term, it refers both to a process (artificial development of microscopic organisms) and a product (organisms so produced). More specifically, since the end of the eighteenth century, it has been used by English intellectuals and literary figures to focus critical attention on a whole range of controversial issues. The 'quality of life', the effects in human terms of mechanization, the division of labour and the creation of a mass society have all been discussed within the larger confines of what Raymond Williams has called the 'Culture and Society' debate. It was through this tradition of dissent and criticism that the dream of the 'organic society'—of society as an integrated, meaningful whole—was largely kept alive. The dream had two basic trajectories. One led back to the past and to the feudal ideal of a hierarchically ordered community. Here, culture assumed an almost sacred function. Its 'harmonious perfection' was posited against the Wasteland of contemporary life.

The other trajectory, less heavily supported, led towards the future, to a socialist Utopia where the distinction between labour and leisure was to be annulled. Two basic definitions of culture emerged from this tradition, though these were by no means necessarily congruent with the two trajectories outlined above. The first—the one which is probably most familiar to the reader—was essentially classical and conservative. It represented culture as a standard of aesthetic excellence: 'the best that has been thought and said in the world', and it derived from an appreciation of 'classic' aesthetic form (opera, ballet, drama, literature, art). The second, traced back by Williams to Herder and the eighteenth century, was rooted in anthropology. Here the term 'culture' referred to a

> . . . particular way of life which expresses certain meanings and values not only in art and learning, but also in institutions and ordinary behaviour. The analysis of culture, from such a definition, is the clarification of the meanings and values implicit and explicit in a particular way of life, a particular culture. (Williams 1958)

This definition obviously had a much broader range. It encompassed, in T. S. Eliot's words,

> . . . all the characteristic activities and interests of a people. Derby Day, Henley Regatta, Cowes, the 12th of August, a cup final, the dog races, the pin table, the dartboard, Wensleydale cheese, boiled cabbage cut into sections, beetroot in vinegar, 19th Century Gothic churches, the music of Elgar . . . .

As Williams noted, such a definition could only be supported if a new theoretical initiative was taken. The theory of culture now involved the 'study of relationships between elements in a whole way of life' (Williams 1958). The emphasis shifted from immutable to historical criteria, from fixity to transformation:

> . . . an emphasis [which] from studying particular meanings and values seeks not so much to compare these, as a way of establishing a scale, but by studying their modes of change to discover certain general causes or 'trends' by which social and cultural developments as a whole can be better understood. (Williams 1958)

Williams was, then, proposing an altogether broader formulation of the relationships between culture and society, one which through the analysis of 'particular meanings and values' sought to uncover the conceived fundamentals of history; the 'general causes' and broad social 'trends' which lie behind the manifest appearances of an 'everyday life'.

In the early years, when it was being established in the Universities, Cultural Studies sat rather uncomfortably on the fence between these two conflicting definitions—culture as a standard of excellence, culture as a 'whole way of life'—unable to determine which represented the most fruitful line of enquiry. Richard Hoggart and Raymond Williams portrayed working-class culture sympathetically in wistful accounts of pre-scholarship boyhoods (Leeds for Hoggart [1957], a Welsh mining village for Williams [1958]) but their work displayed a strong bias towards literature and literacy and an equally strong moral tone. Hoggart deplored the way in which the traditional working-class community—a community of tried and tested values despite the dour landscape in which it had been set—was being undermined and replaced by a 'Candy Floss World' of thrills and cheap fiction which was somehow bland *and* sleazy. Williams tentatively endorsed the new mass communications but was concerned to establish aesthetic and moral criteria for distinguishing the worthwhile products from the 'trash'; the jazz—'a real musical form'—and the football—a wonderful game—from the 'rape novel, the Sunday strip paper and the latest Tin Pan drool' (Williams 1961). In 1966 Hoggart laid down the basic premises upon which Cultural Studies were based:

> First, without appreciating good literature, no one will really understand the nature of society, second, literary critical analysis can be applied to certain social phenomena other than 'academically respectable' literature (for example, the popular arts, mass communications) so as to illuminate their meanings for individuals and their societies. (Hoggart 1966)

The implicit assumption that it still required a literary sensibility to 'read' society with the requisite subtlety, and that the two ideas of culture could be ultimately reconciled was also, paradoxically, to inform the early work of the French writer, Roland Barthes, though here it found validation in a method—semiotics—a way of reading signs (Hawkes 1977).

BARTHES: MYTHS AND SIGNS

Using models derived from the work of the Swiss linguist Ferdinand de Saussure Barthes sought to expose the *arbitrary* nature of cultural phenomena, to uncover the latent meanings of an everyday life which, to all intents and purposes, was 'perfectly natural'. Unlike Hoggart, Barthes was not concerned with distinguishing the good from the bad in modern mass culture, but rather with showing how *all* the apparently spontaneous forms and rituals of contemporary bourgeois societies are subject to a systematic distortion, liable at any moment to be dehistoricized, 'naturalized', converted into myth:

> The whole of France is steeped in this anonymous ideology: our press, our films, our theatre, our pulp literature, our rituals, our Justice, our diplomacy, our conversations, our remarks about the weather, a murder trial, a touching wedding, the cooking we dream of, the garments we wear, everything in everyday life is dependent on the representation which the bourgeoisie *has and makes us have* of the relations between men and the world. (Barthes 1972)

Like Eliot, Barthes's notion of culture extends beyond the library, the opera-house and the theatre to encompass the whole of everyday life. But this everyday life is for Barthes overlaid with a significance which is at once more insidious and more systematically organized. Starting from the premise that 'myth is a type of speech', Barthes set out in *Mythologies* to examine the normally hidden set of rules, codes and conventions through which meanings particular to spe-

cific social groups (i.e. those in power) are rendered universal and 'given' for the whole of society. He found in phenomena as disparate as a wrestling match, a writer on holiday, a tourist guide-book, the same artificial nature, the same ideological core. Each had been exposed to the same prevailing rhetoric (the rhetoric of common sense) and turned into myth, into a mere element in a 'second-order semiological system' (Barthes 1972). (Barthes uses the example of a photograph in *Paris-Match* of a Negro soldier saluting the French flag, which has a first and second order connotation: (1) a gesture of loyalty, but also (2) 'France is a great empire, and all her sons, without colour discrimination, faithfully serve under her flag'.)

Barthes's application of a method rooted in linguistics to other systems of discourse outside language (fashion, film, food, etc.) opened up completely new possibilities for contemporary cultural studies. It was hoped that the invisible seam between language, experience and reality could be located and prised open through a semiotic analysis of this kind: that the gulf between the alienated intellectual and the 'real' world could be rendered meaningful and, miraculously, at the same time, be made to disappear. Moreover, under Barthes's direction, semiotics promised nothing less than the reconciliation of the two conflicting definitions of culture upon which Cultural Studies was so ambiguously posited—a marriage of moral conviction (in this case, Barthes's Marxist beliefs) and popular themes: the study of a society's total way of life.

This is not to say that semiotics was easily assimilable within the Cultural Studies project. Though Barthes shared the literary preoccupations of Hoggart and Williams, his work introduced a new Marxist 'problematic' which was alien to the British tradition of concerned and largely untheorized 'social commentary'. As a result, the old debate seemed suddenly limited. In E. P. Thompson's words it appeared to reflect the parochial concerns of a group of 'gentlemen amateurs'. Thompson sought to replace Williams's definition of the theory of culture as 'a theory of relations between elements in a whole way of life' with his own more rigorously Marxist formulation: 'the study of relationships in a whole way of *conflict*'. A more analytical framework was required; a new vocabulary had to be learned. As part of this process of theorization, the word 'ideology' came to acquire a much wider range of meanings than had previously been the case. We have seen how Barthes found an 'anonymous ideology' penetrating every possible level of social life, inscribed in the most mundane of rituals, framing the most casual social encounters. But how can ideology be 'anonymous', and how can it assume such a broad significance? Before we attempt any reading of subcultural style, we must first define the term 'ideology' more precisely.

IDEOLOGY: A *LIVED* RELATION

In the *German Ideology*, Marx shows how the basis of the capitalist economic structure (surplus value, neatly defined by Godelier as 'Profit . . . is unpaid work' [Godelier 1970]) is hidden from the consciousness of the agents of production. The failure to see through appearances to the real relations which underlie them does not occur as the direct result of some kind of masking operation consciously carried out by individuals, social groups or institutions. On the contrary, ideology by definition thrives *beneath* consciousness. It is here, at the level of 'normal common sense', that ideological frames of reference are most firmly sedimented and most effective, because it is here that their ideological nature is most effectively concealed. As Stuart Hall puts it:

It is precisely its 'spontaneous' quality, its transparency, its 'naturalness', its refusal to be made to examine the premises on which it is founded, its resistance to change or to correc-

tion, its effect of instant recognition, and the closed circle in which it moves which makes common sense, at one and the same time, 'spontaneous', ideological and *unconscious*. You cannot learn, through common sense, *how things are*: you can only discover *where they fit* into the existing scheme of things. In this way, its very taken-for-grantedness is what establishes it as a medium in which its own premises and presuppositions are being rendered *invisible* by its apparent transparency. (Hall 1977)

Since ideology saturates everyday discourse in the form of common sense, it cannot be bracketed off from everyday life as a self-contained set of 'political opinions' or 'biased views'. Neither can it be reduced to the abstract dimensions of a 'world view' or used in the crude Marxist sense to designate 'false consciousness'. Instead, as Louis Althusser has pointed out:

. . . ideology has very little to do with 'consciousness'. . . . It is profoundly *unconscious*. . . . Ideology is indeed a system of representation, but in the majority of cases these representations have nothing to do with 'consciousness': they are usually images and occasionally concepts, but it is above all as *structures* that they impose on the vast majority of men, not via their 'consciousness'. They are perceived—accepted—suffered cultural objects and they act functionally on men via a process that escapes them. (Althusser 1969)

Although Althusser is here referring to structures like the family, cultural and political institutions, etc., we can illustrate the point quite simply by taking as our example a physical structure. Most modern institutes of education, despite the apparent neutrality of the materials from which they are constructed (red brick, white tile, etc.) carry within themselves implicit ideological assumptions which are literally structured into the architecture itself. The categorization of knowledge into arts and sciences is reproduced in the faculty system which houses different disciplines in different buildings, and most colleges maintain the traditional divisions by devoting a separate floor to each subject. Moreover, the hierarchical relationship between teacher and taught is inscribed in the very layout of the lecture theatre where the seating arrangements—benches rising in tiers before a raised lectern—dictate the flow of information and serve to 'naturalize' professional authority. Thus, a whole range of decisions about what is and what is not possible within education have been made, however unconsciously, before the content of individual courses is even decided.

These decisions help to set the limits not only on what is taught but on *how* it is taught. Here the buildings literally *reproduce* in concrete terms prevailing (ideological) notions about what education *is* and it is through this process that the educational structure, which can, of course, be altered, is placed beyond question and appears to us as a 'given' (i.e. as immutable). In this case, the frames of our thinking have been translated into actual bricks and mortar.

Social relations and processes are then appropriated by individuals only through the forms in which they are represented to those individuals. These forms are, as we have seen, by no means transparent. They are shrouded in a 'common sense' which simultaneously validates and mystifies them. It is precisely these 'perceived—accepted—suffered cultural objects' which semiotics sets out to 'interrogate' and decipher. All aspects of culture possess a semiotic value, and the most taken-for-granted phenomena can function as signs: as elements in communication systems governed by semantic rules and codes which are not themselves directly apprehended in experience. These signs are, then, as opaque as the social relations which produce them and which they represent. In other words, there is an ideological dimension to every signification.

To uncover the ideological dimension of signs we must first try to disentangle the codes through which meaning is organized. 'Connotative' codes are particularly important. As Stuart Hall has argued, they '. . . cover the face of social life and render it classifiable, intelligible, meaningful' (Hall 1977). He goes on to describe these codes as 'maps of meaning' which are of necessity the product of selection. They cut across a range of potential meanings, making certain meanings available and ruling others out of court. We tend to live inside these maps as surely as we live in the 'real' world: they 'think' us as much as we 'think' them, and this in itself is quite 'natural'. All human societies *reproduce* themselves in this way through a process of 'naturalization'. It is through this process—a kind of inevitable reflex of all social life—that *particular* sets of social relations, *particular* ways of organizing the world appear to us as if they were universal and timeless. This is what Althusser means when he says that 'ideology has no history' and that ideology in this general sense will always be an 'essential element of every social formation' (Althusser and Balibar 1968).

However, in highly complex societies like ours, which function through a finely graded system of divided (i.e. specialized) labour, the crucial question has to do with which specific ideologies, representing the interests of which specific groups and classes will prevail at any given moment, in any given situation. To deal with this question, we must first consider how power is distributed in our society. That is, we must ask which groups and classes have how much say in defining, ordering and classifying out the social world. For instance, if we pause to reflect for a moment, it should be obvious that access to the means by which ideas are disseminated in our society (i.e. principally the mass media) is *not* the same for all classes. Some groups have more say, more opportunity to make the rules, to organize meaning, while others are less favourably placed, have less power to produce and impose their definitions of the world on the world.

Thus, when we come to look beneath the level of 'ideology-in-general' at the way in which specific ideologies work, how some gain dominance and others remain marginal, we can see that in advanced Western democracies the ideological field is by no means neutral. To return to the 'connotative' codes to which Stuart Hall refers we can see that these 'maps of meaning' are charged with a potentially explosive significance because they are traced and re-traced along the lines laid down by the *dominant* discourses about reality, the *dominant* ideologies. They thus tend to represent, in however obscure and contradictory a fashion, the interests of the *dominant* groups in society.

To understand this point we should refer to Marx:

> The ideas of the ruling class are in every epoch the ruling ideas, i.e. the class which is the ruling *material* force of society is at the same time its ruling *intellectual* force. The class which has the means of material production at its disposal, has control at the same time over the means of mental production, so that generally speaking, the ideas of those who lack the means of mental production are subject to it. The ruling ideas are nothing more than the ideal expression of the dominant material relationships grasped as ideas; hence of the relationships which make the one class the ruling class, therefore the ideas of its dominance. (Marx and Engels 1970)

This is the basis of Antonio Gramsci's theory of *hegemony* which provides the most adequate account of how dominance is sustained in advanced capitalist societies.

HEGEMONY: THE MOVING EQUILIBRIUM

> Society cannot share a common communication system so long as it is split into warring classes. (Brecht, *A Short Organum for the Theatre*)

The term hegemony refers to a situation in which a provisional alliance of certain social groups can exert 'total social authority' over other subordinate groups, not simply by coercion or by the direct imposition of ruling ideas, but by 'winning and shaping consent so that the power of the dominant classes appears both legitimate and natural' (Hall 1977). Hegemony can only be maintained so long as the dominant classes 'succeed in framing all competing definitions within their range' (Hall 1977), so that subordinate groups are, if not controlled, then at least contained within an ideological space which does not seem at all 'ideological': which appears instead to be permanent and 'natural', to lie outside history, to be beyond particular interests.

This is how, according to Barthes, 'mythology' performs its vital function of naturalization and normalization and it is in his book *Mythologies* that Barthes demonstrates most forcefully the full extension of these normalized forms and meanings. However, Gramsci adds the important proviso that hegemonic power, precisely *because* it requires the consent of the dominated majority, can never be permanently exercised by the same alliance of 'class fractions'. As has been pointed out, 'Hegemony . . . is not universal and "given" to the continuing rule of a particular class. It has to be won, reproduced, sustained. Hegemony is, as Gramsci said, a "moving equilibrium" containing relations of forces favourable or unfavourable to this or that tendency' (Hall and Jefferson 1976).

In the same way, forms cannot be permanently normalized. They can always be deconstructed, demystified, by a 'mythologist' like Barthes. Moreover commodities can be symbolically 'repossessed' in everyday life, and endowed with implicitly oppositional meanings, by the very groups who originally produced them. The symbiosis in which ideology and social order, production and reproduction, are linked is then neither fixed nor guaranteed. It can be prised open. The consensus can be fractured, challenged, overruled, and resistance to the groups in dominance cannot always be lightly dismissed or automatically incorporated. Although, as Lefebvre has written, we live in a society where '. . . objects in practice become signs and signs objects and a second nature takes the place of the first—the initial layer of perceptible reality' (Lefebvre 1971), there are, as he goes on to affirm, always 'objections and contradictions which hinder the closing of the circuit' between sign and object, production and reproduction.

We can now return to the meaning of youth subcultures, for the emergence of such groups has signalled in a spectacular fashion the breakdown of consensus in the post-war period. It is precisely objections and contradictions of the kind which Lefebvre has described that find expression in subculture. However, the challenge to hegemony which subcultures represent is not issued directly by them. Rather it is expressed obliquely, in style. The objections are lodged, the contradictions displayed (and 'magically resolved') at the profoundly superficial level of appearances: that is, at the level of signs. For the sign-community, the community of myth-consumers, is not a uniform body. As Volosinov has written, it is cut through by class:

> Class does not coincide with the sign community, i.e. with the totality of users of the same set of signs of ideological communication. Thus various different classes will use one and the same language. As a result, differently oriented accents intersect in every ideological sign. Sign becomes the arena of the class struggle. (Volosinov 1973)

The struggle between different discourses, different definitions and meanings within ideology is therefore always, at the same time, a struggle within signification: a struggle for possession of the sign which extends to even the most mundane areas of everyday life. 'Humble objects' can be magically appropriated; 'stolen' by subordinate groups and made to carry 'secret' meanings: meanings which express, in code, a form of resistance to the order which guarantees their continued subordination.

Style in subculture is, then, pregnant with significance. Its transformations go 'against nature', interrupting the process of 'normalization'. As such, they are gestures, movements towards a speech which offends the 'silent majority', which challenges the principle of unity and cohesion, which contradicts the myth of consensus. Our task becomes, like Barthes's, to discern the hidden messages inscribed in code on the glossy surfaces of style, to trace them out as 'maps of meaning' which obscurely re-present the very contradictions they are designed to resolve or conceal.

WORKS CITED

Althusser, Louis, *For Marx* (London: Allen Lane, 1969).

———, and Etienne Balibar, *Reading Capital* (London: New Left Books, 1968).

Barthes, Roland, *Mythologies* (London: Jonathan Cape, 1972).

Godelier, Maurice, "Structure and Contradiction in 'Capital,'" in *Structuralism: A Reader,* ed. Michael Lane (London: Jonathan Cape, 1970), 112–23.

Hall, Stuart, "Culture, the Media and the 'Ideological Effect,'" in *Mass Communication and Society,* ed. J. Curran, M. Gurevitch, and J. Woolacott (London: Edward Arnold, 1977), 315–48.

———, and Tony Jefferson, eds., *Resistance Through Rituals: Youth Subcultures in Post-War Britain* (London: Hutchinson, 1976).

Hawkes, Terence, *Semiotics and Structuralism* (London: Methuen, 1977).

Hoggarth, Richard, "Literature and Society," *The American Scholar* 35:277–89.

———, *The Uses of Literacy* (Harmondsworth: Penguin, 1957).

Lefebvre, Henri, *Everyday Life in the Modern World* (London: Allen Lane, 1971).

Marx, Karl, and Frederick Engels, *The German Ideology* (London: Lawrence and Wishart, 1970).

Volosinov, Valentin Nikolaevic, *Marxism and the Philosophy of Language* (London: Seminar Press, 1973).

Williams, Raymond, *Culture and Society: 1780–1950* (Harmondsworth: Penguin, 1958).

———, *The Long Revolution* (Harmondsworth: Penguin, 1961).

36

Stuart Hall
1932–

Stuart Hall, who is currently a professor of sociology at the Open University, was for a decade the director of the Centre for Contemporary Cultural Studies in Birmingham. Much of Hall's work is done in the style of an interventionist who continually maneuvers himself into conflicts with cultural practices in order to manipulate understandings of "culture" as a phenomenon and as a field of study. He wrote *The Hard Road to Renewal: Thatcherism and the Crisis of the Left* (1988) and *Questions of Cultural Identity* (1996), and he coauthored *Policing the Crisis: Mugging, the State, and Law and Order* (1978) and *Culture, Media, Language: Working Papers in Cultural Studies, 1972–1979* (1980). *Resistance Through Rituals: Youth Subcultures in Post-war Britain* (1976) and *New Times: The Changing Face of Politics in the 1990s* (1990) are two of the numerous volumes he has coedited.

In "Cultural Studies: Two Paradigms" (1980), Hall identifies the "refounding" of cultural studies as "a distinct problematic" and emphasizes "significant *breaks*" of thought worth noting because of the "complex articulation between thinking and historical reality, reflected in the social categories of thought, and the continuous dialectic between 'knowledge' and 'power.'" He begins and ends this essay with the idea that there is "no single, unproblematic definition of 'culture'" and that "the concept remains a complex one—a site of convergent interest, rather than a logically or conceptually clarified idea." By analyzing the perspectives of Raymond Williams, E. P. Thompson, Lucien Goldmann, and Claude Lévi-Strauss, he overlaps and counterposes the precepts of culturalism and structuralism. Whether "experience" is seen as the ground or the effect of consciousness and social conditions, how to "think [about] *both* the specificity of different practices and the forms of the articulated unity they constitute," and how to deal with the "terrain marked out by those strongly coupled but not mutually exclusive concepts culture/ideology" are three primary questions Hall addresses here. In the course of this questioning, Hall calls upon Lacanian psychoanalytic vocabularies, figures from Marxism (such as the "political economy" of culture and the metaphor of "base" and "superstructure"), as well pursuing the "concrete analysis of particular ideological and discursive formations" that is often associated with Gramsci and Foucault. Hall does not describe either culturalism or structuralism as self-sufficient paradigms for the study of culture; instead, he believes that between them, they begin to define the "space . . . and limits within which such a synthesis might be constituted." As "mutually reinforcing antagonisms," they ensure "no promise of an easy synthesis," but instead a recognition that questions and differing views of dialectics are fundamental in constructing the domain of cultural studies.

Cultural Studies: Two Paradigms

In serious, critical intellectual work, there are no "absolute beginnings" and few unbroken continuities. Neither the endless unwinding of "tradition," so beloved in the History of Ideas, nor the absolutism of the "epistemological rupture," punctuating Thought into its "false" and "correct" parts, once favoured by the Althussereans, will do. What we find, instead, is an untidy but characteristic unevenness of development. What is important are the significant *breaks*—where old lines of thought are disrupted, older constellations displaced, and elements, old and new, are regrouped around a different set of premises and themes. Changes in a problematic do significantly transform the nature of the questions asked, the forms in which they are proposed, and the manner in which they can be adequately answered. Such shifts in perspective reflect, not only the results of an internal intellectual labour, but the manner in which real historical developments and transformations are appropriated in thought, and provide thought, not with its guarantee of "correctness" but with its fundamental orientations, its conditions of existence. It is because of this complex articulation between thinking and historical reality, reflected in the social categories of thought, and the continuous dialectic between "knowledge" and "power," that the breaks are worth recording.

Cultural Studies, as a distinctive problematic, emerges from one such moment, in the mid-1950s. It was certainly not the first time that its characteristic questions had been put on the table. Quite the contrary. The two books which helped to stake out the new terrain—Hoggart's *Uses of Literacy* and Williams's *Culture and Society*—were both, in different ways, works (in part) of recovery. Hoggart's book took its reference from the "cultural debate," long sustained in the arguments around "mass society" and in the tradition of work identified with Leavis and *Scrutiny. Culture and Society* reconstructed a long tradition which Williams defined as consisting, in sum, of "a record of a number of important and continuing reactions to . . . changes in our social, economic and political life" and offering "a special kind of map by means of which the nature of the changes can be explored" (p. 16). The books looked, at first, simply like updating of these earlier concerns, with reference to the post-war world. Retrospectively, their "breaks" with the traditions of thinking in which they were situated seem as important, if not more so, than their continuity with them. The *Uses of Literacy* did set out—much in the spirit of "practical criticism"—to "read" working class culture for the values and meanings embodied in its patterns and arrangements: as if they were certain kinds of "texts." But the application of this method to a living culture, and the rejection of the terms of the "cultural debate" (polarized around the high/low culture distinction) was a thorough-going departure. *Culture and Society*—in one and the same movement—constituted a tradition (*the* "culture-and-society" tradition), defined its "unity" (not in terms of common positions but in its characteristic concerns and the idiom of its inquiry), itself made a distinctive modern contribution to it—*and* wrote its epitaph. The Williams book which succeeded it—*The Long Revolution*—clearly indicated that the "culture-and-society" mode of reflection could only be completed and developed by moving somewhere else—to a significantly different kind of analysis. The very difficulty of some of the writing in *The Long Revolution*—with its attempt to "theorize" on the back of a tradition resolutely empirical and particularist in its idiom of thought, the experiential "thickness" of its concepts, and the generalizing movement of argument in it—stems, in part, from this determination to *move on* (Williams's work, right through to the most recent *Politics and Letters,* is exemplary precisely in its sustained developmentalism). The "good" and the "bad" parts of *The Long Revolution* both arise from its status as a work "of the break." The same could be said of E. P. Thompson's *Making of the English Working Class,* which belongs decisively to this "moment," even though, chronologically, it appeared somewhat later. It, too, had been "thought" within certain distinctive historical traditions: English marxist historiography, Economic and "Labour" History. But in its foregrounding of the questions of culture, consciousness and experience, and its accent on agency, it also made a decisive break: with a certain kind of technological evolutionism, with a reductive economism and an organizational determinism. Between them, these three books constituted the *caesura* out of which—among other things—"Cultural Studies" emerged.

They were, of course, seminal and formative texts. They were not, in any sense, "textbooks" for the founding of a new academic sub-discipline: nothing could have been farther from their intrinsic impulse. Whether historical or contemporary in focus, they were, themselves, focused *by,* organized through and constituted responses to, the immediate pressures of the time and society in which they were written. They not only took "culture" seriously—as a dimension without which historical transformations, past and present, simply could not adequately be thought. They were, themselves, "cultural" in the *Culture and Society* sense. They forced on their readers' attention the proposition that "concentrated in the word *culture* are questions directly raised by the great historical changes which the changes in industry, democracy and class, in their own way, represent, and to which the changes in art are a closely related response" (p. 16). This was a question for the 1960s and 70s, as well as the 1860s and 70s. And this is perhaps the point to note that this line of thinking was roughly coterminous with what has been called the "agenda" of the early New Left, to which these writers, in one sense or another, belonged, and whose texts these were.

This connection placed the "politics of intellectual work" squarely at the centre of Cultural Studies from the beginning—a concern from which, fortunately, it has never been, and can never be, freed. In a deep sense, the "settling of accounts" in *Culture and Society,* the first part of *The Long Revolution,* Hoggart's densely particular, concrete study of some aspects of working-class culture and Thompson's historical reconstruction of the formation of a class culture and popular traditions in the 1790–1830 period formed, between them, the break, and defined the space from which a new area of study and practice opened. In terms of intellectual bearings and emphases, this was—if ever such a thing can be found—Cultural Studies moment of "refounding." The institutionalization of Cultural Studies—first, in the Centre at Birmingham, and then in courses and publications from a variety of sources and places—with its characteristic gains and losses, belongs to the 1960s and later.

"Culture" was the site of the convergence. But what definitions of this core concept emerged from this body of work? And, since this line of thinking has decisively shaped Cultural Studies, and represents the most formative *indigenous* or "native" tradition, around what space was its concerns and concepts unified? The fact is that no single, unproblematic definition of "culture" is to be found here. The concept remains a complex one—a site of convergent interests, rather than a logically or conceptually clarified idea. This "richness" is an area of continuing tension and difficulty in the field. It might be useful, therefore, briefly to resume the characteristic stresses and emphases through which the concept has arrived at its present state of (in)-determinacy. (The characterizations which follow are necessarily crude and over-simplified, synthesizing rather than carefully analytic.) Two main problematics only are discussed.

Two rather different ways of conceptualizing "culture" can be drawn out of the many suggestive formulations in Raymond Williams's *Long*

Revolution. The first relates "culture" to the sum of the available descriptions through which societies make sense of and reflect their common experiences. This definition takes up the earlier stress on "ideas", but subjects it to a thorough reworking. The conception of "culture" is itself democratized and socialized. It no longer consists of the sum of the "best that has been thought and said," regarded as the summits of an achieved civilization—that ideal of perfection to which, in earlier usage, all aspired. Even "art"—assigned in the earlier framework a privileged position, as touchstone of the highest values of civilization—is now redefined as only one, special, form of a general social process: the giving and taking of meanings, and the slow development of "common" meanings—a common culture: "culture," in this special sense, "is ordinary" (to borrow the title of one of Williams's earliest attempts to make his general position more widely accessible). If even the highest, most refined of descriptions offered in works of literature are also "part of the general process which creates conventions and institutions, through which the meanings that are valued by the community are shared and made active" (p. 55), then there is no way in which this process can be hived off or distinguished or set apart from the other practices of the historical process: "Since our way of seeing things is literally our way of living, the process of communication is in fact the process of community: the sharing of common meanings, and thence common activities and purposes; the offering, reception and comparison of new meanings, leading to tensions and achievements of growth and change" (p. 55). Accordingly, there is no way in which the communication of descriptions, understood in this way, can be set aside and compared externally with other things. "If the art is part of society, there is no solid whole, outside it, to which, by the form of our question, we concede priority. The art is there, as an activity, with the production, the trading, the politics, the raising of families. To study the relations adequately we must study them actively, seeing all activities as particular and contemporary forms of human energy."

If this first emphasis takes up and re-works the connotation of the term "culture" with the domain of "ideas," the second emphasis is more deliberately anthropological, and emphasizes that aspect of "culture" which refers to social *practices.* It is from this second emphasis that the somewhat simplified definition—"culture is a whole way of life"—has been rather too neatly abstracted. Williams did relate this aspect of the concept to the more "documentary"—that is, descriptive, even ethnographic—usage of the term. But the earlier definition seems to me the more central one, into which "way of life" is integrated. The important point in the argument rests on the active and indissoluble relationships between elements or social practices normally separated out. It is in *this* context that the "theory of culture" is defined as "the study of relationships between elements in a whole way of life." "Culture" is not *a* practice; nor is it simply the descriptive sum of the "mores and folkways" of societies—as it tended to become in certain kinds of anthropology. It is threaded through *all* social practices, and is the sum of their inter-relationship. The question of what, then, is studied, and how, resolves itself. The "culture" is those patterns of organization, those characteristic forms of human energy which can be discovered as revealing themselves—in "unexpected identities and correspondences" as well as in "discontinuities of an unexpected kind" (p. 63)—within or underlying *all* social practices. The analysis of culture is, then, "the attempt to discover the nature of the organization which is the complex of these relationships." It begins with "the discovery of patterns of a characteristic kind." One will discover them, not in the art, production, trading, politics, the raising of families, treated as separate activities, but through "studying a general organization in a particular example" (p. 61). Analytically, one must study "the relationships between these patterns." The purpose of the analysis is to grasp how the interactions between all these practices and patterns are lived and experienced as a whole, in any particular period. This is its "structure of feeling."

It is easier to see what Williams was getting at, and why he was pushed along this path, if we understand what were the problems he addressed, and what pitfalls he was trying to avoid. This is particularly necessary because *The Long Revolution* (like many of Williams's work[s]) carries on a submerged, almost "silent" dialogue with alternative positions, which are not always as clearly identified as one would wish. There is a clear engagement with the "idealist" and "civilizing" definitions of culture—both the equation of "culture" with *ideas,* in the idealist tradition; and the assimilation of culture to an *ideal,* prevalent in the elitist terms of the "cultural debate." But there is also a more extended engagement with certain kinds of Marxism, against which Williams's definitions are consciously pitched. He is arguing against the literal operations of the base/superstructure metaphor, which in classical Marxism ascribed the domain of ideas and of meanings to the "superstructures," themselves conceived as merely reflective of and determined in some simple fashion by "the base"; without a social effectivity of their own. That is to say, his argument is constructed against a vulgar materialism and an economic determinism. He offers, instead, a radical interactionism: in effect, the interaction of all practices in and with one another, skirting the problem of determinacy. The distinctions between practices is overcome by seeing them all as variant forms of *praxis*—of a general human activity and energy. The underlying patterns which distinguish the complex of practices in any specific society at any specific time are the characteristic "forms of its organization" which underlie them all, and which can therefore be traced in each.

There have been several, radical revisions of this early position: and each has contributed much to the redefinition of what Cultural Studies is and should be. We have acknowledged already the exemplary nature of Williams's project, in constantly rethinking and revising older arguments—in going on thinking. Nevertheless, one is struck by a marked line of continuity through these seminal revisions. One such moment is the occasion of his recognition of Lucien Goldmann's work, and through him, of the array of marxist thinkers who had given particular attention to superstructural forms and whose work began, for the first time, to appear in English translation in the mid-1960s. The contrast between the alternative marxist traditions which sustained writers like Goldman and Lukacs, as compared with Williams's isolated position and the impoverished Marxist tradition he had to draw on, is sharply delineated. But the points of convergence—both what they are against, and what they are about—are identified in ways which are not altogether out of line with his earlier arguments. Here is the negative, which he sees as linking his work to Goldmann's: "I came to believe that I had to give up, or at least to leave aside, what I knew as the Marxist tradition: to attempt to develop a theory of social totality; to see the study of culture as the study of relations between elements in a whole way of life; to find ways of studying structure . . . which could stay in touch with and illuminate particular art works and forms, but also forms and relations of more general social life; to replace the formula of base and superstructure with the more active idea of a field of mutually if also unevenly determining forces" (*NLR 67,* May–June 1971). And here is the positive—the point where the convergence is marked between Williams's "structure of feeling" and Goldmann's "genetic structuralism": "I found in my own work that I had to develop the idea of a structure of feeling. . . . But then I found Goldmann beginning . . . from a concept of structure which contained, in itself, a relation between social and literary facts. This relation, he insisted, was not a matter of content, but of mental structures: "categories which simultaneously organize the empirical consciousness of a particular social group, and the imaginative world created by the writer." By definition, these structures are not individually but collectively created. The stress there on the interactivity of practices and on the underlying totalities, and the homologies between them, is characteristic and significant. "A correspondence of content between a writer and his world is less significant than this correspondence of organization, of structure."

A second such "moment" is the point where Williams really takes on board E. P. Thompson's critique of *The Long Revolution* (cf. the review in *NLR* 9 and 10)—that no "whole way of life" is without its dimension of struggle and confrontation between opposed *ways* of life—and attempts to rethink the key issues of determination and domination via Gramsci's concept of "hegemony." This essay ("Base and Superstructure," *NLR* 82, 1973) is a seminal one, especially in its elaboration of dominant, residual and emergent cultural practices, and its return to the problematic of determinacy as "limits and pressures." None the less, the earlier emphases recur, with force: "we cannot separate literature and art from other kinds of social practice, in such a way as to make them subject to quite special and distinct laws." And, "no mode of production, and therefore no dominant society or order of society, and therefore no dominant culture, in reality exhausts human practice, human energy, human intention." And this note is carried forward—indeed, it is radically accented—in Williams's most sustained and succinct recent statement of his position: the masterly condensations of *Marxism and Literature.* Against the structuralist emphasis on the specificity and "autonomy" of practices, and their analytic separation of societies into their discrete instances, Williams's stress is on "constitutive activity" in general, on "sensuous human activity, as practice," from Marx's first "thesis" on Feuerbach; on different practices conceived as a "whole indissoluble practice"; on "totality". "Thus, contrary to one development in Marxism, it is not 'the base' and 'the superstructure' that need to be studied, but specific and indissoluble real processes, within which the decisive relationship, from a Marxist point of view, is that ex-

pressed by the complex idea of 'determination'" (*M & L*, pp. 30–31, 82).

At one level, Williams's and Thompson's work can only be said to converge around the terms of the same problematic through the operation of a violent and schematically dichotomous theorization. The organizing terrain of Thompson's work—classes as relations, popular struggle, and historical forms of consciousness, class cultures in their historical particularity—is foreign to the more reflective and "generalizing" mode in which Williams typically works. And the dialogue between them begins with a very sharp encounter. The review of *The Long Revolution,* which Thompson undertook, took Williams sharply to task for the evolutionary way in which culture as a "whole way of life" had been conceptualized; for his tendency to absorb conflicts between class cultures into the terms of an extended "conversation"; for his impersonal tone—above the contending classes, as it were; and for the imperializing sweep of his concept of "culture" (which, heterogeneously, swept everything into its orbit because it was the study of the interrelationships between the forms of energy and organization underlying *all* practices. But wasn't this—Thompson asked—where History came in?) Progressively, we can see how Williams has persistently rethought the terms of his original paradigm to take these criticisms into account—though this is accomplished (as it so frequently is in Williams) obliquely: via a particular appropriation of Gramsci, rather than in a more direct modification.

Thompson also operates with a more "classical" distinction than Williams, between "social being" and "social consciousness" (the terms he infinitely prefers, from Marx, to the more fashionable "base and superstructure"). Thus, where Williams insists on the absorption of all practices into the totality of "real, indissoluble practice," Thompson does deploy an older distinction between what is "culture" and what is "not culture." "Any theory of culture must include the concept of the dialectical interaction between culture and something that is *not* culture." Yet the definition of culture is not, after all, so far removed from Williams's: "We must suppose the raw material of life experience to be at one pole, and all the infinitely complex human disciplines and systems, articulate and inarticulate, formalised in institutions or dispersed in the least formal ways, which 'handle,' transmit or distort this raw material to be at the other." Similarly, with respect to the commonality of "practice" which underlies all the distinct practices: "It is the active process—which is at the same time the process through which men make their history—that I am insisting upon" (*NLR* 9, p. 33, 1961). And the two positions come closer together around—again—certain distinctive negatives and positives. Negatively, against the "base/superstructure" metaphor, and a reductionist or "economistic" definition of determinacy. On the first: "The dialectical intercourse between social being and social consciousness—or between 'culture' and '*not* culture'—is at the heart of any comprehension of the historical process within the Marxist tradition. . . . The tradition inherits a dialectic that is right, but the particular mechanical metaphor through which it is expressed is wrong. This metaphor from constructional engineering . . . must in any case be inadequate to describe the flux of conflict, the dialectic of a changing social process. . . . All the metaphors which are commonly offered have a tendency to lead the mind into schematic modes and away from the interaction of being-consciousness." And on "reductionism": "Reductionism is a lapse in historical logic by which political or cultural events are 'explained' in terms of the class affiliations of the actors. . . . But the mediation between 'interest' and 'belief' was not through Nairn's 'complex of superstructures' but through the people themselves" ("Peculiarities of the English," *Socialist Register,* 1965, pp. 351–352). And, more positively—a simple statement which may be taken as defining virtually the whole of Thompson's historical work, from *The Making* to *Whigs and*

Hunters, The Poverty of Theory and beyond— "capitalist society was founded upon forms of exploitation which are simultaneously economic, moral and cultural. Take up the essential defining productive relationship . . . and turn it round, and it reveals itself now in one aspect (wage-labour), now in another (an acquisitive ethos), and now in another (the alienation of such intellectual faculties as are not required by the worker in his productive role)" (ibid., p. 356).

Here, then, despite the many significant differences, is the outline of one significant line of thinking in Cultural Studies—some would say, *the* dominant paradigm. It stands opposed to the residual and merely-reflective rôle assigned to "the cultural." In its different ways, it conceptualizes culture as interwoven with all social practices; and those practices, in turn, as a common form of human activity: sensuous human praxis, the activity through which men and women make history. It is opposed to the base-superstructure way of formulating the relationship between ideal and material forces, especially where the "base" is defined as the determination by "the economic" in any simple sense. It prefers the wider formulation—the dialectic between social being and social consciousness: neither separable into its distinct poles (in some alternative formulations, the dialectic between "culture" and "non-culture"). It defines "culture" as *both* the meanings and values which arise amongst distinctive social groups and classes, on the basis of their given historical conditions and relationships, through which they "handle" and respond to the conditions of existence; *and* as the lived traditions and practices through which those "understandings" are expressed and in which they are embodied. Williams brings together these two aspects—definitions and ways of life—around the concept of "culture" itself. Thompson brings the two elements—consciousness and conditions—around the concept of "experience." Both positions entail certain difficult fluctuations around these key terms. Williams so totally absorbs "definitions of experience" into our "ways of living," and both into an indissoluble real material practice-in-general, as to obviate any distinction between "culture" and "not-culture." Thompson sometimes uses "experience" in the more usual sense of consciousness, as the collective ways in which men "handle, transmit or distort" their given conditions, the raw materials of life; sometimes as the domain of the "lived," the mid-term *between* "conditions" and "culture"; and sometimes as the objective conditions themselves—against which particular modes of consciousness are counterposed. But, whatever the terms, both positions tend to read structures of relations in terms of how they are "lived" and "experienced." Williams's "structure of feeling"—with its deliberate condensation of apparently incompatible elements—is characteristic. But the same is true of Thompson, despite his far fuller historical grasp of the "givenness" or structuredness of the relations and conditions into which men and women necessarily and involuntarily enter, and his clearer attention to the determinacy of productive and exploitative relations under capitalism. This is a consequence of giving culture-consciousness and experience so pivotal a place in the analysis. The *experiential pull* in this paradigm, and the emphasis on the creative and on historical agency, constitutes the two key elements in the *humanism* of the position outlined. Each, consequently accords "experience" an authenticating position in any cultural analysis. It is, ultimately, where and how people experience their conditions of life, define them and respond to them, which, for Thompson defines why every mode of production is also a culture, and every struggle between classes is always also a struggle between cultural modalities; and which, for Williams, is what a "cultural analysis," in the final instance, should deliver. In "experience," all the different practices intersect; within "culture" the different practices interact—even if on an uneven and mutually determining basis. This

sense of cultural totality—of *the whole* historical process—over-rides any effort to keep the instances and elements distinct. Their real interconnection, under given historical conditions, must be matched by a totalizing movement "in thought," in the analysis. It establishes for both the strongest protocols against any form of analytic abstraction which distinguishes practices, or which sets out to test the "actual historical movement" in all its intertwined complexity and particularity by any more sustained logical or analytical operation. These positions, especially in their more concrete historical rendering (*The Making, The Country and the City*) are the very opposite of a Hegelian search for underlying Essences. Yet, in their tendency to reduce practices to *praxis* and to find common and homologous "forms" underlying the most apparently differentiated areas, their movement is "essentialising." They have a particular way of understanding the totality—though it is with a small "t," concrete and historically determinate, uneven in its correspondences. They understand it "expressively." And since they constantly inflect the more traditional analysis towards the experiential level, or read the other structures and relations downwards from the vantage point of how they are "lived," they are properly (even if not adequately or fully) characterized as "culturalist" in their emphasis: even when all the caveats and qualifications against a too rapid "dichotomous theorizing" have been entered. (Cf. for "culturalism," Richard Johnson's two seminal articles on the operation of the paradigm: in "Histories of Culture/Theories of Ideology," *Ideology and Cultural Production,* eds. M. Barrett, P. Corrigan *et al.,* Croom Helm, 1979; and "Three Problematics" in *Working Class Culture:* Clarke, Critcher and Johnson, Hutchinsons and CCCS, 1979. For the dangers in "dichotomous theorizing," cf. the Introduction, "Representation and Cultural Production," to Barrett, Corrigan *et al.*)

The "culturalist" strand in Cultural Studies was interrupted by the arrival on the intellectual scene of the "structuralisms." These, possibly more varied than the "culturalisms," nevertheless shared certain positions and orientations in common which makes their designation under a single title not altogether misleading. It has been remarked that whereas the "culturalist" paradigm can be defined without requiring a conceptual reference to the term "ideology" (the *word*, of course, does appear: but it is not a key concept), the "structuralist" interventions have been largely articulated around the concept of "ideology": in keeping with its more impeccably Marxist lineage, "culture" does not figure so prominently. Whilst this may be true of the Marxist structuralists, it is at best less than half the truth about the structuralist enterprise as such. But it is now a common error to condense the latter exclusively around the impact of Althusser and all that has followed in the wake of his interventions—where "ideology" has played a seminal, but modulated rôle: and to omit the significance of Lévi-Strauss. Yet, in strict historical terms, it was Lévi-Strauss, and the early semiotics, which made the first break. And though the Marxist structuralisms have superseded the latter, they owed, and continue to owe, an immense theoretical debt (often fended off or down-graded into footnotes, in the search for a retrospective orthodoxy) to his work. It was Lévi-Strauss's structuralism which, in its appropriation of the linguistic paradigm, after Saussure, offered the promise to the "human sciences of culture" of a paradigm capable of rendering them scientific and rigorous in a thoroughly new way. And when, in Althusser's work, the more classical Marxist themes were recovered, it remained the case that Marx was "read"—and reconstituted—through the terms of the linguistic paradigm. In *Reading Capital,* for example, the case is made that the mode of production—to coin a phrase—could best be understood as if "structured like a language" (through the selective combination of invariant elements). The a-historical and synchronic stress, against the historical emphases of "cultur-

alism," derived from a similar source. So did a preoccupation with "the social, *sui generis*"— used not adjectivally but substantively: a usage Lévi-Strauss derived, not from Marx, but from Durkheim (the Durkheim who analysed the social categories of thought—e.g. in *Primitive Classification*—rather than the Durkheim of *The Division of Labour,* who became the founding father of American structural-functionalism).

Lévi-Strauss did, on occasion, toy with certain Marxist formulations. Thus, "Marxism, if not Marx himself, has too commonly reasoned as though practices followed directly from praxis. Without questioning the undoubted primacy of infrastructures, I believe that there is always a mediator between praxis and practices, namely, the conceptual scheme by the operation of which matter and form, neither with any independent existence, are realized as structures, that is as entities which are both empirical and intelligible." But this—to coin another phrase—was largely "gestural." This structuralism shared with culturalism a radical break with the terms of the base/superstructure metaphor, as derived from the simpler parts of the *German Ideology.* And, though "It is to this theory of the superstructures, scarcely touched on by Marx" to which Lévi-Strauss aspired to contribute, his contribution was such as to break in a radical way with its whole terms of reference, as finally and irrevocably as the "culturalists" did. Here—and we must include Althusser in this characterization—culturalists and structuralists alike ascribed to the domains hitherto defined as "superstructural" a specificity and effectivity, a constitutive primacy, which pushed them beyond the terms of reference of "base" and "superstructure." Lévi-Strauss and Althusser, too, were anti-reductionist and anti-economist in their very cast of thought, and critically attacked that transitive causality which, for so long, had passed itself off as "classical Marxism."

Lévi-Strauss worked consistently with the term "culture." He regarded "ideologies" as of much lesser importance: mere "secondary rationalizations." Like Williams and Goldmann, he worked, not at the level of correspondences between the *content* of a practice, but at the level of their forms and structures. But the manner in which these were conceptualized were altogether at variance with either the "culturalism" of Williams or Goldmann's "genetic structuralism." This divergence can be identified in three distinct ways. First, he conceptualized "culture" as the categories and frameworks in thought and language through which different societies classified out their conditions of existence—above all (since Lévi-Strauss was an anthropologist), the relations between the human and the natural worlds. Second, he thought of the manner and practice through which these categories and mental frameworks were produced and transformed, largely on an analogy with the ways in which language itself—the principal medium of "culture"—operated. He identified what was specific to them and their operation as the "production of meaning": they were, above all, *signifying* practices. Third, after some early flirtations with Durkheim and Mauss's social categories of thought, he largely gave up the question of the relation *between* signifying and non-signifying practices—between "culture" and "not-culture," to use other terms—for the sake of concentrating on the *internal* relations within signifying practices by means of which the categories of meaning were produced. This left the question of determinacy, of totality, largely in abeyance. The causal logic of determinacy was abandoned in favour of a structuralist causality—a logic of *arrangement,* of internal relations, of articulation of parts within a structure. Each of these aspects is also positively present in Althusser's work and that of the Marxist structuralists, even when the terms of reference had been regrounded in Marx's "immense theoretical revolution." In one of Althusser's seminal formulations about ideology—defined as the themes, concepts and representations through which men and women "live," in an imaginary relation, their relation to their real conditions of existence—we can see the skeleton outline of Lévi-Strauss's "conceptual schemes between praxis and practices." "Ideologies" are here being conceptualized, not as the contents and surface forms of ideas, but as the unconscious categories through which conditions are represented and lived. We have already commented on the active presence in Althusser's thinking of the linguistic paradigm—the second element identified above. And though, in the concept of "over-determination"—one of his most seminal and fruitful contributions—Althusser did return to the problems of the relations *between* practices and the question of determinacy (proposing, incidentally, a thoroughly novel and highly suggestive reformulation, which has received far too little subsequent attention), he did tend to reinforce the "relative autonomy" of different practices, and their internal specificities, conditions and effects at the expense of an "expressive" conception of the totality, with its typical homologies and correspondences.

Aside from the wholly distinct intellectual and conceptual universes within which these alternative paradigms developed, there were certain points where, despite their apparent overlaps, culturalism and structuralism were starkly counterposed. We can identify this counterposition at one of its sharpest points precisely around the concept of "experience," and the rôle the term played in each perspective. Whereas, in "culturalism," experience was the ground—the terrain of "the lived"—where consciousness and conditions intersected, structuralism insisted that "experience" could not, by definition, be the ground of anything, since one could only "live" and experience one's conditions *in and through* the categories, classifications and frameworks of the culture. These categories, however, did not arise from or in experience: rather, experience was their "effect." The culturalists had defined the forms of consciousness and culture as collective. But they had stopped far short of the radical proposition that, in culture and in language, the subject was "spoken by" the categories of culture in which he/she thought, rather than "speaking them." These categories were, however, not merely collective rather than individual productions: they were *unconscious* structures. That is why, though Lévi-Strauss spoke only of "Culture," his concept provided the basis for an easy translation, by Althusser, into the conceptual framework of ideology: "Ideology is indeed a system of 'representations,' but in the majority of cases these representations have nothing to do with 'consciousness': . . . it is above all as structures that they impose on the vast majority of men, not via their 'consciousness' . . . it is within this ideological unconsciousness that men succeed in altering the 'lived' relation between them and the world and acquiring that new form of specific unconsciousness called 'consciousness'" (*For Marx*, p. 233). It was, in this sense, that "experience" was conceived, not as an authenticating source but as an effect: not as a reflection of the real but as an "imaginary relation." It was only a short step—the one which separates *For Marx* from the "Ideological State Apparatuses" essay—to the development of an account of how this "imaginary relation" served, not simply the dominance of a ruling class over a dominated one, but (through the reproduction of the relations of production, and the constitution of labour-power in a form fit for capitalist exploitation) the expanded reproduction of the mode of production itself. Many of the other lines of divergence between the two paradigms flow from this point: the conception of "men" as bearers of the structures that speak and place them, rather than as active agents in the making of their own history; the emphasis on a structural rather than a historical "logic"; the preoccupation with the constitution—in "theory"—of a non-ideological, scientific discourse; and hence the privileging of conceptual work and of Theory as guaranteed; the recasting of history as a march of the structures (cf. passim, *The Poverty of Theory*): the structuralist "machine". . . .

There is no space in which to follow through the many ramifications which have followed from the development of one or other of these "master paradigms" in Cultural Studies. Though they by no means account for all, or even nearly all, of the many strategies adopted, it is fair to say that, between them, they have defined the principal lines of development in the field. The seminal debates have been polarized around their thematics; some of the best concrete work has flowed from the efforts to set one or other of these paradigms to work on particular problems and materials. Characteristically—the sectarian and self-righteous climate of critical intellectual work in England being what it is, and its dependency being so marked—the arguments and debates have most frequently been over-polarized into their extremes. At these extremities, they frequently appear only as mirror-reflections or inversions of one another. Here, the broad typologies we have been working with—for the sake of convenient exposition—become the prison-house of thought.

Without suggesting that there can be any easy synthesis between them, it might usefully be said at this point that neither "culturalism" nor "structuralism" is, in its present manifestation, adequate to the task of constructing the study of culture as a conceptually clarified and theoretically informed domain of study. Nevertheless, something fundamental to it emerges from a rough comparison of their respective strengths and limitations.

The great strength of the structuralisms is their stress on "determinate conditions." They remind us that unless the dialectic really can be held, in any particular analysis, between both halves of the proposition—that "men make history . . . on the basis of conditions which are not of their making"—the result will inevitably be a naïve humanism, with its necessary consequence: a voluntarist and populist political practice. The fact that "men" can become conscious of their conditions, organize to struggle against them and in fact transform them—without which no active politics can even be conceived, let alone practised—must not be allowed to override the awareness of the fact that, in capitalist relations, men and women are placed and positioned in relations which constitute them as agents. "Pessimism of the intellect, optimism of the will" is a better starting point than a simple heroic affirmation. Structuralism does enable us to begin to think—as Marx insisted—of the *relations* of a structure on the basis of something other than their reduction to relationships between "people." This was Marx's privileged level of abstraction: that which enabled him to break with the obvious but incorrect starting point of "political economy"—bare individuals.

But this connects with a second strength: the recognition by structuralism not only of the necessity of abstraction as the instrument of thought through which "real relations" are appropriated, but also of the presence, in Marx's work, of a continuous and complex movement *between different levels of abstraction*. It is, of course, the case—as "culturalism" argues—that, in historical reality, practices do not appear neatly distinguished out into their respective instances. However, to think about or to analyse the complexity of the real, the act of practice of thinking is required; and this necessitates the use of the power of abstraction and analysis, the formation of concepts with which to cut into the complexity of the real, in order precisely to reveal and bring to light relationships and structures which cannot be visible to the naïve naked eye, and which can neither present nor authenticate themselves: "In the analysis of economic forms, neither microscopes nor chemical reagents are of assistance. The power of abstraction must replace both." Of course, structuralism has frequently taken this proposition to its extreme. Because thought is impossible without "the power of abstraction," it has confused this with giving an absolute primacy to the level of the formation of concepts—and at the highest, most abstract level of abstraction only: Theory with a capital "T" then becomes judge and jury. But this is precisely to lose the insight just won from Marx's own practice. For it is clear in, for

example, *Capital,* that the *method*—whilst, of course, taking place "in thought" (as Marx asked in the 1857 Introduction, where else?)—rests, not on the simple exercise of abstraction but on the movement and relations which the argument is constantly establishing between *different levels* of abstraction: at each, the premises in play must be distinguished from those which—for the sake of the argument—have to be held constant. The movement to another level of magnification (to deploy the microscope metaphor) requires the specifying of further conditions of existence not supplied at a previous, more abstract level: in this way, by successive abstractions of different magnitudes, to *move towards* the constitution, the *reproduction,* of "the concrete in thought" as an effect of a certain kind of thinking. This method is adequately represented in *neither* the absolutism of Theoretical Practice, in structuralism, nor in the anti-abstraction "Poverty of Theory" position into which, in reaction, culturalism appears to have been driven or driven itself. Nevertheless it is intrinsically *theoretical,* and must be. Here, structuralism's insistence that thought does not reflect reality, but is articulated on and appropriates it, is a necessary starting point. An adequate *working through* of the consequences of this argument might begin to produce a method which takes us outside the permanent oscillations between abstraction–anti-abstraction and the false dichotomies of Theoreticism *vs.* Empiricism which have both marked and disfigured the structuralism-culturalism encounter to date.

Structuralism has another strength in its conception of "the whole." There is a sense in which, though culturalism constantly insists on the radical particularity of its practices, its mode of conceptualizing the "totality" has something of the complex simplicity of an expressive totality behind it. Its complexity is constituted by the fluidity with which practices move into and out of one another: but this complexity is reducible, conceptually, to the "simplicity" of praxis—human activity, as such—in which the same contradictions constantly appear, homologously reflected in each. Structuralism goes too far in erecting the machine of a "Structure," with its self-generating propensities (a "Spinozean eternity," whose function is only the sum of its effects: a truly structural*ist* deviation), equipped with its distinctive instances. Yet it represents an advance over culturalism in the conception it has of the necessary *complexity* of the unity of a structure (over-determination being a more successful way of thinking this complexity than the combinatory invariance of structuralist causality). Moreover, it has the conceptual ability to think of a unity which is constructed through the *differences* between, rather than the homology of, practices. Here, again, it has won a critical insight about Marx's method: one thinks of the complex passages of the 1857 Introduction to the *Grundrisse* where Marx demonstrates how it is possible to think of the "unity" of a social formation as constructed, not out of identity but out of *difference.* Of course, the stress on difference can—and has—led the structuralisms into a fundamental conceptual heterogeneity, in which all sense of structure and totality is lost. Foucault and other post-Althusellereans have taken this devious path into the absolute, not the relative, autonomy of practices, via their necessary heterogeneity and "necessary non-correspondence." But the emphasis on unity-in-difference, on complex unity—Marx's concrete as the "unity of many determinations"—can be worked in another, and ultimately more fruitful direction: towards the problematic of relative autonomy and "over-determination," and the study of *articulation.* Again, articulation contains the danger of a high formalism. But it also has the considerable advantage of enabling us to think of how specific practices (articulated around contradictions which do not all arise in the same way, at the same point, in the same moment), can nevertheless be thought *together.* The structuralist paradigm thus does—if properly developed—enable us to begin really to *conceptualize* the specificity of different practices (analytically distinguished, abstracted out), without losing its grip on the ensemble which they constitute. Culturalism constantly affirms the specificity of different practices—"culture" must not be absorbed into "the economic": but it lacks an adequate way of establishing this specificity theoretically.

The third strength which structuralism exhibits lies in its decentering of "experience" and its seminal work in elaborating the neglected category of "ideology." It is difficult to conceive of a Cultural Studies thought within a Marxist paradigm which is innocent of the category of "ideology." Of course, culturalism constantly make[s] reference to this concept: but it does not in fact lie at the centre of its conceptual universe. The authenticating power and reference of "experience" imposes a barrier between culturalism and a proper conception of "ideology." Yet, without it, the effectivity of "culture" for the reproduction of a particular mode of production cannot be grasped. It is true that there is a marked tendency in the more recent structuralist conceptualisations of "ideology" to give it a functionalist reading—as the necessary cement of the social formation. From this position, it is indeed impossible—as culturalism would correctly argue—to conceive either of ideologies which are not, by definition, "dominant": or of the concept of struggle (the latter's appearance in Althusser's famous ISA's article being—to coin yet another phrase—largely "gestural"). Nevertheless, work is already being done which suggests ways in which the field of ideology may be adequately conceptualized as a terrain of struggle (through the work of Gramsci, and more recently, of Laclau), and these have structuralist rather than culturalist bearings.

Culturalism's strengths can almost be derived from the weaknesses of the structuralist position already noted, and from the latter's strategic absences and silences. It has insisted, correctly, on the affirmative moment of the development of conscious struggle and organization as a necessary element in the analysis of history, ideology and consciousness: against its persistent down-grading in the structuralist paradigm. Here, again, it is largely Gramsci who has provided us with a set of more refined terms through which to link the largely "unconscious" and given cultural categories of "common sense" with the formation of more active and organic ideologies, which have the capacity to intervene in the ground of common sense and popular traditions and, through such interventions, to organize masses of men and women. In this sense, culturalism *properly* restores the dialectic between the unconsciousness of cultural categories and the moment of conscious organization: even if, in its characteristic movement, it has tended to match structuralism's over-emphasis on "conditions" with an altogether too-inclusive emphasis on "consciousness." It therefore not only recovers—as the necessary moment of any analysis—the process by means of which classes-in-themselves, defined primarily by the way in which economic relations position "men" as agents—become active historical and political forces—for-themselves: it also—against its own anti-theoretical good sense—*requires* that, when properly developed, each moment must be understood in terms of the level of abstraction at which the analysis is operating. Again, Gramsci has begun to point a way through this false polarization in his discussion of "the passage between the structure and the sphere of the complex superstructures," and its distinct forms and moments.

We have concentrated in this argument largely on a characterization of what seem to us to be the two seminal paradigms at work in Cultural Studies. Of course, they are by no means the only active ones. New developments and lines of thinking are by no means adequately netted with reference to them. Nevertheless, these paradigms can, in a sense, be deployed to measure what appear to us to be the radical weaknesses or inadequacies of those which offer themselves as alternative rallying-points. Here, briefly, we identify three.

The first is that which follows on from Lévi-Strauss, early semiotics and the terms of the linguistic paradigm, and the centering on "signifying practices," moving by way of psychoanalytic concepts and Lacan to a radical recentering of virtually the whole terrain of Cultural Studies around the terms "discourse" and "the subject." One way of understanding this line of thinking is to see it as an attempt to fill that empty space in early structuralism (of both the Marxist and non-Marxist varieties) where, in earlier discourses, "the subject" and subjectivity might have been expected to appear but did not. This is, of course, precisely one of the key points where culturalism brings its pointed criticisms to bear on structuralism's "process without a subject." The difference is that, whereas culturalism would correct for the hyper-structuralism of earlier models by restoring the unified subject (collective or individual) of consciousness at the centre of "the Structure," discourse theory, by way of the Freudian concepts of the unconscious and the Lacanian concepts of how subjects are constituted in language (through the entry into the Symbolic and the Law of Culture), restores the *decentered* subject, the contradictory subject, as a set of positions in language and knowledge, from which culture can appear to be enunciated. This approach clearly identifies a gap, not only in structuralism but in Marxism itself. The problem is that the manner in which this "subject" of culture is conceptualized is of a trans-historical and "universal" character: it addresses the subject-in-general, not historically-determinate social subjects, or socially determinate particular languages. Thus it is incapable, so far, of moving its ingeneral propositions to the level of concrete historical analysis. The second difficulty is that the processes of contradiction and struggle—lodged by early structuralism wholly at the level of "the structure"—are now, by one of those persistent mirror-inversions, lodged exclusively at the level of the unconscious processes of the subject. It may be, as culturalism often argues, that the "subjective" is a necessary moment of any such analysis. But this is a very different proposition from dismantling the whole of the social processes of particular modes of production and social formations, and reconstituting them exclusively at the level of unconscious psychoanalytic processes. Though important work has been done, both within this paradigm and to define and develop it, its claims to have replaced *all* the terms of the earlier paradigms with a more adequate set of concepts seem wildly over-ambitious. Its claims to have integrated Marxism into a more adequate materialism are, largely, a semantic rather than a conceptual claim.

A second development is the attempt to return to the terms of a more classical "political economy" of culture. This position argues that the concentration on the cultural and ideological aspects has been wildly over-done. It would restore the older terms of "base/superstructure," finding, in the last-instance determination of the cultural-ideological by the economic, that hierarchy of determinations which both alternatives appear to lack. This position insists that the economic processes and structures of cultural production are more significant than their cultural-ideological aspect: and that these are quite adequately caught in the more classical terminology of profit, exploitation, surplus-value and the analysis of culture as commodity. It retains a notion of ideology as "false consciousness."

There is, of course, some strength to the claim that both structuralism and culturalism, in their different ways, have neglected the economic analysis of cultural and ideological production. All the same, with the return to this more "classical" terrain, many of the problems which originally beset it also reappear. The specificity of the effect of the cultural and ideological dimension once more tends to disappear. It tends to conceive the economic level as not only a "necessary" but a "sufficient" explanation of cultural and ideological effects. Its focus on the analysis of the commodity form, similarly, blurs all the carefully established distinctions between different practices, since it is the most *generic* aspects of the commodity-form which attract attention. Its deductions are therefore, largely, confined to an epochal level of abstraction: the generalizations about the commodity-form hold true throughout the capitalist epoch as a whole. Very little by way of concrete and conjunctural analysis can be derived at this high-level "logic of capital" form of abstraction. It also tends to its own kind of functionalism—a functionalism of "logic" rather than of "structure" or history. This approach, too, has insights which are well worth following through. But it sacrifices too much of what has been painfully secured, without a compensating gain in explanatory power.

The third position is closely related to the structuralist enterprise, but has followed the path of "difference" through into a radical heterogeneity. Foucault's work—currently enjoying another of those uncritical periods of discipleship through which British intellectuals reproduce today their dependency on yesterday's French ideas—has had an exceedingly positive effect: above all because—in suspending the nearly-insoluble problems of determination—Foucault has made possible a welcome return to the concrete analysis of particular ideological and discursive formations and the sites of their elaboration. Foucault and Gramsci between them account for much of the most productive work on *concrete analysis* now being undertaken in the field: thereby reinforcing and—paradoxically—supporting the sense of the concrete historical instance which has always been one of culturalism's principal strengths. But, again, Foucault's example is positive only if his general epistemological position is not swallowed whole. For in fact Foucault so resolutely suspends judgment, and adopts so thoroughgoing a scepticism about any determinacy or relationship between practices, other than the largely contingent, that we are entitled to see him, not as an agnostic on these questions, but as deeply committed to the necessary non-correspondence of all practices to one another. From such a position neither a social formation, nor the State, can be adequately thought. And indeed Foucault is constantly falling into the pit which he has dug for himself. For when—against his well-defended epistemological positions—he stumbles across certain "correspondences" (for example, the simple fact that all the major moments of transition he has traced in each of his studies—on the prison, sexuality, medicine, the asylum, language and political economy—all appear to converge around exactly that point where industrial capitalism and the bourgeoisie make their fateful, historical rendezvous), he lapses into a vulgar reductionism, which thoroughly belies the sophisticated positions he has elsewhere advanced.[1]

I have said enough to indicate that, in my view, the line in Cultural Studies which has attempted to *think forwards* from the best elements in the structuralist and culturalist enterprises, by way of some of the concepts elaborated in Gramsci's work, comes closest to meeting the requirements of the field of study. And the reason for that should by now also be obvious. Though neither structuralism nor culturalism will do, as self-sufficient paradigms of study, they have a centrality to the field which all the other contenders lack because, between them (in their divergences as well as their convergences) they address what must be the *core problem* of Cultural Studies. They constantly return us to the terrain marked out by those strongly coupled but not mutually exclusive concepts culture/ideology. They pose, together, the problems consequent on trying to think *both* the specificity of different practices and the forms of the articulated unity they constitute. They make a constant, if flawed, return to the base/superstructure metaphor. They are correct in insisting that this question—which resumes all the problems of a non-reductive determinacy—is the heart of the matter: and that, on the solution of this problem will turn the capacity of Cultural Studies to supercede the endless oscillations between idealism and reductionism. They confront—even if in radically opposed ways—the dialectic between conditions and consciousness. At another level, they pose the question of the relation between the logic of thinking and the "logic" of historical process. They continue to hold out the promise of a properly materialist theory of culture. In their sustained and mutually reinforcing antagonisms they hold out no promise of an easy synthesis. But, between them, they define where, if at all, is the space, and what are the limits, within which such a synthesis might be constituted. In Cultural Studies, theirs are the "names of the game".

NOTE

1. He is quite capable of wheeling in through the back door the classes he recently expelled from the front.

37

James Clifford
1945–

James Clifford has written extensively on anthropology and ethnography in such books as *The Predicament of Culture: Twentieth-Century Ethnography, Literature, and Art* (1988), *Writing Culture: The Poetics and Politics of Ethnography* (1986), *Person and Myth: Maurice Leenhardt in the Melanesian World* (1988), and most recently *Formal Semantics and Pragmatics for Natural Language Querying* (1990). His work is of increasing importance to the field of cultural studies in its focus on the aesthetic, social, and political issues central to an understanding of non-Western cultures.

"The Translation of Cultures" (1982) describes a twenty-five year fragment in the life of the early-twentieth-century Protestant missionary Maurice Leenhardt. Through Leenhardt, Clifford explores the boundaries of person and culture, focusing on the question of how cultures are mediated by traditional structures of power. Leenhardt is an interesting subject for Clifford for several reasons. First, Leenhardt's letters to his family reveal that conventional theory on the religious "conversion" process had virtually no application value in the field. Second, Leenhardt discloses a strong *personal* involvement in his missionary work (as opposed to strictly professional involvement), which was often at odds with the doctrine of the Société des Missions, his sponsoring church in Paris. Third, Leenhardt confessed to his father that parts of the Christian message itself had to be modified for the native culture to be understood. This led, Clifford shows, to the reconfiguration of Leenhardt's political beliefs regarding missionary work. Translation took on new meaning for Leenhardt.

The application of Clifford's sense of translation reaches well beyond religion. He points out not only the problems Leenhardt encountered in finding synonyms for Christian terminology in a pagan dialect, but also the more slippery problem of interpretation. Clifford shows us the extraordinary flexibility that must accompany any attempt to mediate between foreign cultures. For example, Leenhardt found that in Houailou (the Melanesian language), the word for "God" translated as "*Bao,*" which had multiple meaning as "spiritual deity," "human corpse," "old person," and "a dead ancestor." Such latitude in meaning is unthinkable for the translator, but Leenhardt turned the situation to his advantage by letting these multiple connotations in meaning stand. In doing so, however, he faced one of the most important decisions in his work in New Caledonia: torn between the necessity to ensure that the Christian sense of *Bao* became fully integrated into the Melanesian belief system, he struggled to preserve Christianity's taboo of immanent and graven images of God. This crisis of accommodation led to a revolution in cultural translation. What Leenhardt called "inverse acculturation" was the result of his reconciliation of two apparent opposites: pagan heterodoxy and Christian theology. The possibility—even the task—of a reconciliation of this order challenged both the frontiers of language and the core of *both* Christian and Melanesian belief systems. For conversion, as Leenhardt learned, is not merely a matter of transferring one belief system intact into another language, but rather involves reciprocity between cultures—a two-way street of sorts—in which the ethnographer's cultural norms, practices, and dogmas are challenged to the limits of their ability to accommodate difference.

The Translation of Cultures
Maurice Leenhardt's Evangelism, New Caledonia 1902–1926

It is becoming increasingly difficult to speak without second thoughts of "the missionary type" or of a "missionary attitude." The range of "missionary occasions," to appropriate the title of Burridge's thoughtful essay,[1] is broad, so broad that it is no easy matter to decide what essential set of orientations to culture change and to the religious life may be said to unite the intentions and experiences of a list like the following: fire and brimstone fundamentalists, contributors to *Missiology,* intrepid young Mormons, medical technicians, aiders and abettors of national liberation movements, back-country hermits, Billy Graham-style revivalists, and so on. In a post-colonial world the all too familiar sharp silhouette of the evangelist has blurred. But was it in fact ever sharp? Alongside the "man of God"—unbending extirpator of the devil in the bush, in Colin Turnbull's unforgettable and venomous portrait—has always stood the romantic "Father Lobo," also painted by Turnbull, whose church in the jungle is built by Christians, Moslems, and Pagans, and whose joyous service of dedication is attended by dancing pygmies trailing vines.[2]

Between these poles, historians investigating "typical" missionary discourse may, in fact, discover in common words like "god," "adultery," "holy spirit," "devil," "the Word," "conversion," and so on, a spectrum of local renderings, inventions, and heterodox interpretations. The historian of missions must be prepared to discover intransigence coexisting in unexpected ways with what Burridge calls "mutual metanoia," an unpublicized other conversion process that Maurice Leenhardt some time ago termed "acculturation in two directions" and recommended to all participants in colonial situations.[3] The present case is a contribution to a more nuanced understanding of these processes and to a more adequate portrait of the liberal evangelist. It is an example of how a missionary can, perhaps must, be personally involved, and changed, in the complex productive work of reciprocal translation inadequately glossed by the term "conversion."

Maurice Leenhardt's exemplary career is becoming somewhat better known thanks to the recent English edition of his best known work, *Do Kamo: Person and Myth in the Melanesian*

World, and thanks to a special issue of the *Journal de la Société des Océanistes.*[4] The present essay is a portion of a longer study[5] and is devoted solely to Leenhardt's translation work, seen as the core of his evangelical practice and as a personal quest for religious authenticity—a work that would become, also, the primary basis of his ethnological production. It is unfortunately not possible here to discuss Leenhardt's extensive ethnographic *oeuvre* and his second career during the 1930s and 40s as a Paris-based ethnologist. He was founder and first president of the Société des Océanistes and the Institute Français d'Océanie, Professor at the École Pratique des Hautes Études and the Musée de l'Homme, and an enthusiastic ethnographer on renewed field trips in French Melanesia. Here I can only present a part of Leenhardt's total missionary effort in New Caledonia, from 1902 until 1926, ignoring, along with his scientific work, his important "pro-native" political activities on the island.[6] I am not primarily concerned with the history of New Caledonian Protestantism and I do not discuss the actual outcome of Leenhardt's religious work, its dilution by his missionary successors in the 1930s and 1940s, and the history of schism and internal conflict which followed his departure.[7] I am offering merely a description of his interrelated evangelical and personal quests, an account based largely on unpublished family papers (journals and an extensive correspondence with his pastor-naturalist father in France) as well as on materials in the Archives of the Société des Missions Évangeliques in Paris, the missionary society to which Leenhardt belonged.[8]

Maurice Leenhardt was born in 1878 at Montauban where his father, an eminent geologist, taught natural science to pastoral students of France's principal Protestant theological seminary. As a secondary student in the 1890s Leenhardt was won for missions by the vogue for African exploration and evangelism, particularly by the French examples of Casalis in Lessoto and the Livingstone-like Coillard in the upper Zambeze. An independent-minded student of an idealistic and aesthetic temperament, he was unhappy within the lock-step of the French Classical Baccalaureate. He saw in missions an *ouverture,* a constructive escape from a cultural and religious life that had become rigid, hierarchical and abstract. As Bachelor of Theology he wrote a sympathetic study of South African Ethiopianism which openly attacked colonial abuses and evangelical hypocrisy.[9] At his consecration service, just prior to leaving for New Caledonia with his wife Jeanne, he revealed his hopes for mission work in a discourse from which the rhetoric of conquest was notably absent:

> The Christian church seems nowhere so pure as in missions, where it finds itself liberated from the dogmatic political debris with which history has burdened it. Those who have just laid on me their hands will understand what I mean when I speak of the privilege of sowing in a virgin land rather than incessantly pruning sprouts from sick roots. And perhaps, God only knows, it is the young churches in pagan lands who will provide us with the fresh blood needed for the vitalization of our tired milieux.[10]

This, very briefly, was the 24-year-old who in 1902 established himself at Houailou on the east coast of the Grande Terre, or New Caledonian mainland. He remained, to all intents and purposes, the sole European Protestant evangelist on the large island until the early 20s. Communications were slow with colleagues on the Loyalty Islands; the missionary society in Paris was distant; thus Leenhardt enjoyed considerable leeway in deciding mission policy. He was seconded, and in important respects instructed, by about 40 Melanesian pastors called *natas,* "messengers," originating from the Loyalty Islands—and increasingly, as his pastoral school took hold, from New Caledonia. After two decades of sometimes bitter conflict—with the Noumea administration, with farmers and cattlemen, with Catholic evangelical competitors—the Protestant mission radiating from Leenhardt's station, Do Neva, finally established itself securely on the island and was able to claim the stable allegiance of about a third of the Melanesian population. This was accomplished against far superior Marxist resources. The "Melanesian" evangelical style of the Protestant pastoral corps, accepted and systematized by Leenhardt, seems to have been a significant advantage.[11]

The first years at Do Neva were difficult. Beyond the practical and political struggles (Protestantism, "the English religion," was perceived as subversive in the colony), Leenhardt was confronted with the intellectual problem of understanding his pastors, men of experience and, to the young evangelist, often inscrutable—"pagano-protestants," he called them, inelegantly but accurately. Leenhardt was being forced to accept the fact that the land on which he had hoped to sow his faith was anything but virgin. At the end of his first three years, after a series of misunderstandings with the *natas,* resistances, rules imposed by authority, etc., the wiser and considerably bruised evangelist wrote to his father that his work urgently required him to study what he called the "complete psychology" of his Melanesian Christians. "I'm astounded at all the pathways different from ours that I've discovered in their hearts. But it's not enough to discover a country, you've got to know how to map it." Melanesian resistances had to be grasped sympathetically and with considerable relativism: "We don't know how to judge others without comparing them to ourselves; and surely divine wisdom consists in weighing each according to its own measure."[12]

Leenhardt's growing relativism caused him to question seriously the notion of religious "conversion." He criticized (privately) the naiveté of Loyalty Islands colleagues like Philadelphe Delord. Delord, a veteran evangelist and innovator

in the treatment of leprosy, was one of those missionaries who knew how to sway an audience with tales of dramatic transformations. He believed in the existence of simple peoples, desirous of the faith. Their "paganism" was for him merely a sort of natural state, not a living culture rooted in a complex reality. Leenhardt was increasingly critical of this approach. Rather than imagine a people yearning for the gospels, it is better, he said, simply to see "various tribes, looking for a support."[13] As a veteran, Leenhardt went further. In the native people's adherence to a religion, he wrote to his wife, prestige plays a key role: they become Protestant in English colonies and Catholic in French. Conversion is for them a means of becoming involved in the white world. Adoption of a new religion can be a method of observation of the white. And finally, it can spring from a "need to react against the deadly breath of civilization." Religious adherence in this case involves a "judgement" of one culture by another. Moreover, the *natas'* message had been essentially this-worldly, a promise of better explanation, prediction, and control of a changing environment. Christianity's other-worldly significance, concentrated in personal communion with a transcendent God, was not so easily accepted.[14] Adherence to the practical religion of the *natas* did not necessarily entail even an elementary acquaintance with Christ.

As a consequence of such views, Leenhardt had difficulty in adopting the modes of discourse proper to his profession. His mother prodded him repeatedly to include more "touching stories" and "edifying conversations" in his reports. Anyone who has leafed through mission journals will know the sort of thing she wanted. But Leenhardt could not bring himself to adopt a language he felt to be fundamentally meaningless. Only with difficulty could he write using "the little touch which creates sympathy." In early 1905, he expressed the radical opinion that, since his arrival, he had seen no real conversions at all, only mass and individual "adherences."[15] He could be mordant in his deflation of colleagues:

> how dangerous it is to always portray the march of the Kingdom of God as if it advanced overstriding all contingencies. It makes me think of Delord moving an audience with a Caledonian woman's story about how the prayer of a *nata* had swayed a pagan chief. But at the same time, the *nata* had sent 2 [other] chiefs as delegates with 25F of persuasion. The prayer stands, but so does the contingency—and the chief is still pagan.[16]

Leenhardt's mother, in pressing him to recount stories like Delord's, wrote not simply as an orthodox believer but also as a fund raiser. Sentimental stories brought in donations; her son's infrequent, long, and rather dryly descriptive reports did not. At one point Leenhardt promised his parents he would write more "sentimentalism." But he added in exasperation: "I gave myself dispassionately to this work. Why can't Christians learn to give—dispassionately?"[17] Leenhardt was chided, too, by Alfred Boegner, president of the Paris mission society, for not writing the right kind of reports for the Mission Journal, not including enough of his personal experience. The missionary replied: "It must therefore be the case that to interest people in a mission you've got to be able to interest them in yourself. But I feel myself incapable of doing for us what Delord does so well." And he added, once more, his plea for dispassion.[18] Important issues of evangelical method were at stake. The Delord, Coillard style of mission, centring on the romantic figure of the evangelist, seemed dangerous to Leenhardt. It diverted attention from the real work, which was the encouragement of indigenous churches. His own reports tended to leave himself out of the picture and to describe political and cultural circumstances in the Grande Terre, including frequent portraits of individual Melanesian Christians.

Leenhardt, like many a missionary, was torn between the real needs of his work and the demands of his publicity. He had somehow to avoid sacrificing the former to the latter. And this choice involved struggle, for missionary practice was deeply enmeshed in the fantasy systems of European religious sentimentality. Many evangelists never really chose between their audience in the metropole and their audience in the bush. Leenhardt felt the attraction of "pure" primitivism. Small-scale, anti-clerical Christianity had always been his ideal, and in the back hills he rediscovered "the true *canaque* of before, . . . who has not rubbed against the White. He is more savage, a hundred times better, and in him one sees the lost soul to be brought home so much more clearly than among the poor natives who have been made corrupt and cynical [*désabusés*]."[19] But Leenhardt had to resist this taste for the primitive. He did not question the need for education and change, and traditional socio-religious structures were, he thought, collapsing. Thus his greatest energies were devoted to students and *natas*. These, he thought, were minds in transition, searching for a new conception of themselves which could be guaranteed only through a personal relation with divinity. The conversion process, as Leenhardt analyzes it in a number of subsequent works, consists of an interrelated series of movements: from concrete toward abstract modes of thought and expression, from a diffuse, participatory consciousness toward self-consciousness, from the affective domain of myth toward detached observation and analysis. The process must not, however, be accomplished in simple imitation of whites. It must develop as "some kind of appropriate civilization, affirming itself gradually."[20] In religious terms conversion was the emergence of an internalized moral conscience based on an intimate communion with Christ. True conversion was never collective.

To encourage the necessary individual experience, Leenhardt urged his students to write down as best they could their life stories—to testify to themselves. The missionary and ethnologist learned a great deal from these documents. For example, in a notebook written by Eleisha Nebay at Guilgal in November 1911 we learn that the Christian God appeared to the young convert as a new father *and* mother. Eleisha testifies also to a new feeling, something he had not experienced before becoming a *nata*-in-training. Previously, "there seemed to be only one man in my heart . . ."

> At that time my eyes saw well what they saw and my heart was direct [*droit*]. After a few years in God's work, I've found there to be two men within me, disputing in eloquence every day till the present. I used to wonder whether the first state was God's will. I prayed to him ceaselessly to take the other away. I'm opening myself, telling you what isn't clear to me; but that's how it seemed in my heart.[21]

The conception of conversion as struggle within a divided heart has its origin in the literature of the early Church. To Leenhardt in colonial Melanesia it was a hopeful sign, indicating that his students were growing in self consciousness. People like Eleisha, he thought, would henceforth be able to separate themselves out from the flux of events, making clear choices. This would make resistance to colonial temptations possible, an active selection of alternative moral values within the new, ambiguous context. Other readers of Eleisha Nebay's notebook may be less content with what appears as the birth of modern self-alienation. And indeed, Leenhardt was aware of the danger that the newly individualized Christian person might develop into an experience of separations, without healing communions. The person, he believed, must not abandon myth for rationality, becoming severed from passionate involvements with land and kin. If conversion involved a process of separation and self-discrimination, it

had also to be based on translation, a knowing search for equivalents and mediations uniting the old and new, pagan and Christian, mythic and rational.

Leenhardt believed at first that the Melanesian experience of divinity could be brought directly over into Christianity. In 1905 he began experimenting with using the *bao* (a spirit, ancestor, or corpse) to clarify in the native language the "visions" spoken of in the gospels. The development of his translation researches will be treated more fully below. It is worth noting here that for Leenhardt this kind of activity represented a form of questioning which sometimes verged on rebellion. For example, after describing in a letter his use of the *bao* in teaching, he added: "Mama shouldn't think I'm playing the rebel. The thing is too serious here, and why rebel when there's no one to scandalize?"[22] But of course there was someone to scandalize, for Leenhardt, at the antipodes, remained a member of the French Protestant extended family. His father had told him to devise a "simplistic theology" for his students.[23] Leenhardt's problem was to do more—to purify as well as to simplify the Christianity he was teaching. His faith had to be conceived as concretely as possible: this was a prerequisite of communication. The immediate aim was subtle and effective evangelization; but more than just that was at stake. The idea of a cross-culturally translatable Christianity coincided with the sort of lived religion and morality which the young missionary was seeking for himself. From the start he was worried about the need for absolute sincerity in his classes. He was free to follow his feelings, but at the same time he felt uneasy about the great leeway he enjoyed and the resultant dangers of teaching a heterodoxy. "My entire difficulty," he wrote, "is to teach them nothing that I don't believe myself."[24]

In 1913 he sent a report to his Society in Paris for publication in its Journal.[25] In it he hinted at the supple method of evangelization

he had for some time been practising. The article was composed in Leenhardt's best "missionary style"; "From Shadows into the Light" was
its title. It described halting and apparently
rather quaint attempts by *natas* and Do Neva
students to grasp the true message of Christ.
Various strange native prayers and mistaken
concepts are portrayed and explained. Then the
concept of "God" is discussed. God had to have
a vernacular name, Leenhardt argued, or rather
He had to co-opt the generic term for the traditional gods and spirits. Otherwise, as a new and
foreign term, the Christian God might be simply added to the roster of deities as *primus inter
pares*. Other missionaries, for example Patteson,
and Codrington of the English Melanesian Mission, had opted for the European term "God."
They feared the inevitable misunderstandings
involved in the adaptation of a pagan name. But
Leenhardt believed that a certain confusion was
part of any process of change and education;
and unless native terms could be brought to new
significances there would be no real conversion.

Thus the Christian God had to appropriate the
essence of Melanesian spirits by taking possession
of their generic name, *Bao*. In the process of co-
optation, Leenhardt suggested, Christianity was
in fact recovering a religious essence which pre-
existed the magical gods and spirits, an affective,
communal essence that he later identified with
totemism and worship of the landscape. This approach to conversion, amounting in some ways to
a reversion, was dangerously close to heterodoxy.
Where did the Christian missionary draw the line
in making use of archaic concepts and terms?

It is interesting to see, from the private letters, that Leenhardt had already censored his article. Writing to his father he revealed that he
had begun with an account which would have
been much more specific and controversial than
the one he finally sent. In the original version he
had discussed openly

> the heart of the question . . . which is to de-
> termine: is God the revelation man has of

Spirit with which we are in relation, and
which man then personifies according to his
mentality in various spirits etc . . . , until he
even succeeds in systematizing and hierarchizing these spirits; or is God much more
transcendant, not discoverable by man?

God is either "immanent or transcendant"; and
if he is the former . . .

> If Jehovah is really that which is visible since
> the creation . . . then the pagans must have
> an obscure revelation of God at the heart of
> their beliefs. This is a minimum of experi-
> ences upon which the preaching of the
> Gospel can be based. And thus we shouldn't
> reject the entire jumble of their gods in order
> to give them a new god with a foreign name;
> rather we should search for the word in their
> language, even the strangest word, into which
> can be translated the visible experience of
> God.[26]

The *natas*, he adds, had already been doing this,
"openly adopting the pagan name." Leenhardt
sympathized, but he felt himself to be walking a
fine line.

We cannot know exactly what Leenhardt felt
he should exclude from his article, or just how
he recast its style. But we can compare a passage
he allowed to remain with a later analysis of the
same passage. He quotes a prayer overheard on
the lips of a Melanesian Protestant: "Oh God
who is wholly long, you came to our Néporo
and Asana families; then you stretched yourself
out again and arrived in Monéo, and again
stretching yourself you came to Paci." In the article as printed Leenhardt cited this curious
prayer merely as a poetic image for the gospel's
progress throughout the land. But the "long
god" meant something much more profound to
a Melanesian. It evoked the elemental flux, or
life force, emanating from the totem and passing into the present generations through the
blood of the maternal lineage. If the Christian

God was called "wholly long" it meant that it had appropriated this potent myth. In a lecture given much later at the Paris Ecole des Missions Leenhardt describes the relation of the "long god" to the totemic flow of "life" and adds that "this god who stretches out may make us smile when we don't understand paganism. But when we are familiar with the "long god," the image is a moving one, touching the Missionary's heart."[27] This was the sort of comment Leenhardt could not permit himself in his original article, where the "*dieu long*" remained a picturesque image. In 1913 Leenhardt was still unsure of his missionary-ethnology. He asked his father whether it was permissible to affix pagan names and properties to the Christian God. And the question posed once more the basic theological problem for Leenhardt: that of mediating an apparent choice between immanence and transcendence.

> . . . so that according to whether God is transcendent or immanent (I mean glimpsed as such, for I think he is both) we translate using the foreign name or the pagan name; and who knows whether we're being orthodox or heterodox?

Was God in effect already present in Melanesian language and experience? Or did He have to be imported? Leenhardt's instincts were all on the side of immanence, but he needed encouragement:

> I wish father would tell me what he thinks of all this; because I wrote that article as a search, and seeing that I was heading straight for heterodoxy, I began again and turned it into edification. But if Father tells me I'm on the right track, I'll feel a lot more courage in searching for God among the pagans.[28]

In the ambiguous freedom of his mission work, Leenhardt had to develop enough self-confidence to see God for himself in strange contexts. This was a problem of personal identity, or "sincerity" in the language of Leenhardt which was that of Rousseau. However the romantic route of introspection and confession made no claim on the activist. He looked for his "god among the pagans," among the others— and in this he opened himself personally to the conversion process.

"Inverse acculturation" was Leenhardt's way of describing, later, in an ethnological context, a desirable colonial reciprocity in which the European would learn from the Melanesian.[29] Before an audience of young evangelists he put it rather differently. The missionary, he insists, keeps his mind open—but not in order to be influenced by primitivism so much as to be, simply, a purer Christian and man.

> The missionary is called to bring the Gospel of Jesus Christ and not the Gospel of whites. His purpose is not the founding of a white church. In remaining perfectly loyal to the mandate given him by God, not men, he must become a man, and not the representative of a civilization. Otherwise . . . his message will not be that of pure Gospel; it will contain a mixture of voices . . . [30]

The purity required of the missionary was not a form of dogma or divine inspiration. It was an attitude of openness—a poetic negative capability. "The Gospel of Jesus," the veteran said in his lecture, "adapts itself to all peoples." As an evangelist Leenhardt had to learn to recognize true translation when it was already at work in an unfamiliar idiom.

The *nata* Joané Nigoth had already produced a Houailou version of the Gospel of Matthew. The translation of the remaining New Testament was a collective enterprise spanning more than 15 years which became, for Leenhardt, an intense focus for ethnolinguistic research. A letter sets out his procedure:

> Just a word while waiting for Boesoou, my old teacher with whom I can't manage to find

a few quiet hours to work on translations. By now he's used to the work and gives the correct word fairly quickly. For two hours a week I read completed chapters to the students, and it's very interesting to see them satisfied by a good word which makes clear in their minds something they hadn't understood; or protesting sometimes against a word which doesn't satisfy them. After their verdict I give the rough draft to Apou to copy . . . [31]

It was often almost impossible to find meaningful equivalents for Christian religious concepts, and Leenhardt went to great lengths to avoid imposing a foreign expression. It was important not to be in a hurry. He would try to hold an open mind and keep discussing a troublesome idea whenever he could, in classes and sermons, until some Houailou-speaker arrived spontaneously at a meaningful rendition.

An example of how the process sometimes worked is given in Leenhardt's article of 1922 on translating the New Testament. He was having difficulty with the rendering of a key concept in the Epistle to the Romans.

> While I was seeking for the meaning of the term "propitiatory," I heard a native Christian explain the text of Romans 3:25 with these words, which I translate literally, "God has made Jesus an objects *of sacrifice, and the healing and propitiatory leaf* is his blood for those who have faith." This confusing and awkward expression is translated in Caledonian by a very short word, "Demo." Its original significance is "leaf cicatrization, or living leaf, the ideas of healing and of life being connected. But this should not lead us to think that it is the leaf which cicatrizes; in that case the phrase would be "cicatrizing leaf," "*De Pemo.*" The leaf is only the vehicle for a virtue transmitted through the benevolence of a divinity in the course of a sacrifice. Without this sacrifice or an offering, the leaf does not act. This virtue, originally given to a leaf, must have been extended later to other objects, for the word designating it has a generic sense and is applied to all objects provoking or soliciting divine influence. In this very primitive idea, the medicinal value of the leaf has not been grasped; the leaf is effective only by virtue of its propitiatory value. When *Canaques* applied this word to Jesus Christ, they perceived that the death of Christ modified the relations between man and God, and took away their sin, as these leaves in sacrifices formerly altered their condition and took away their sufferings. This is perceived from a wholly simple and concrete standpoint.[32]

Leenhardt goes on to suggest that the Melanesian—who propitiates a god or totem using the *demo* leaf as part of his everyday activities of fishing or gardening, etc.—probably grasps the expiatory role of Christ in a manner that is more alive than that of many Christians, tied to a juridical mode of comprehension.

In the same context, Leenhardt tells how he finally arrived at a term which would express the idea of redemption. Previous missionaries had interpreted it in terms of exchange—an exchange of life, that of Jesus for ours. But in Melanesian thinking more strict equivalents were demanded in the exchanges structuring social life. It remained unclear to them how Jesus's sacrifice could possibly redeem mankind. So unclear was it that even the *natas* gave up trying to explain a concept they didn't understand very well themselves and simply employed the term "release." So the matter stood, with the missionary driven to the use of cumbersome circumlocutions, until one day during a conversation on I Corinthians 1:30 Boesoou Erijisi used a surprising expression. The term *nawi* which he employed referred to the custom of planting a small tree on land cursed either by the blood of battle or some calamity. "Jesus was thus the one who has accomplished the sacrifice and has planted himself like a tree, as though to absorb all the misfortunes of men and to free the world from its taboos." Here at last was a concept which seemed to render that of redemption, while reaching deeply enough into living modes of thought. "The idea was a rich one, but how could I be sure I understood it right?" The key test was in the reaction of students and *natas* to his provisional version. They were, he reports, overjoyed with the deep translation.

Often enough, Melanesian terms seemed to express the elemental meaning of the Bible more truly than the French or the Greek, both of which were less concrete tongues than the original language of the gospels. Thus Leenhardt's intercultural translation was more than a simple scriptural exegesis. His "primitivizing" of the gospel restored to it a rich, immediate context and concrete significance. An example of the kinship between the Biblical and the Melanesian, which Leenhardt would elaborate again and again throughout his ethnological career, was the term for "word" or "speech" (French, *parole*, Houailou, *no*). "In the beginning was the Word . . ." was first translated by the Loyalty missionaries using the Greek, and pronouncing it in native fashion. "In the beginning the logos."

Canaques are intelligent people: I've never heard them using words which have no meaning. But when a *Canaque* speaks French, he translates his thoughts as best he can. He has no trouble at all expressing himself concerning the man who has conceived good things, has said them, done them, or even accomplished the three acts at once: "The word [*parole*] of this man is good." Thought, speech, and action are all included in the Caledonian term *No*. Thus in speaking of an adulterous man, one may say: "He has done an evil word." One may speak of a chief whose character is uncertain, who does not think, organize, or act correctly, as—"His word is not good." The expression "the Word of God," which we limit to divine discourse or literature, here includes the thoughts and acts of God. "God spoke and it was done." We need search no farther; we translate using

No this term of such richness—the *Logos* of the first verses of John that the native attempts to transpose into French using "*parole*." The term for Word takes on a broad, living meaning, worthy of the God whose creative will it must make intelligible. Things become clearer. The native has no trouble seeing the word becoming action, the word made flesh, the word as phenomenon.[33]

The opening of the Book of John was particularly effective in Melanesian vernacular. Another "improved" passage was Matthew 19:6, *New English Bible:*

"Have you never read that the Creator made them from the beginning male and female?"; and he added, "For this reason a man shall leave his father and mother, and be made one with his wife; and the two shall become one flesh. It follows that they are no longer two individuals: they are one flesh. What God has joined together, man must not separate."

These words were "more expressive in Houailou."[34] Leenhardt was discovering that the vernacular abounded in locutions of duality and plurality. These were substantives, and they did not imply the additive combination of separate parts. Rather, they were one flesh, as with husband and wife. It was also true for other couplings, grandfather and grandson, nephew and maternal uncle, the relation of homonyms. What in Western languages would be seen as composites would in Houailou be expressed as ensembles, substantial entities or "images."[35]

For Leenhardt, translation was part of the creative interpenetration of two cultures, a liberation and revivification of meanings latent in each. In the process it was essential not simply to find accurate expressions, but to locate and use *meaningful* expressions. In this concern he anticipated modern, ethnolinguistic approaches to Bible translation, the search for "dynamic equivalences."[36] Imposed terminology had no place in real translation. Spontaneously borrowed and adapted foreign words were accepted, after scrutiny. Archaic expressions, words which once had sense but had been abandoned, were left to their fate. On the other hand, "those expressions which spring from the native mind in an attempt to formulate new concepts revealed by the knowledge of the gospel or by contact with [Western] civilization, exhibit a great variety. And their value is far greater; for these are not artificial words, but truly living words."[37]

Leenhardt is attempting here to grasp a moving language. He values those usages which, although they might appear corrupt when judged against an imagined, static, primitive standard, are in reality the most vital elements of a parlance. He works within a dynamic conception of culture. Rather than simply transferring meanings from one cultural code to another, a situation of dialogue is created in which the language of all parties is enriched. As opposed to the ethnographer, who typically concentrates on making an alien expressive system understandable, Leenhardt works at making himself and his belief system understood—to others and, in the process, to himself. A context of exchange is initiated. By contrast, scientific ethnology runs the risk of overemphasizing the univocal translation of exotic cultures and languages, as if they were inert texts (*langues*) rather than evolving expressivities (*paroles*). Perhaps in order to translate "them" into "us," one must be prepared to translate "us" into "them." The missionary's summary of the translator's role is relevant—in some degree—to all ethnographic encounters:

> The work of the translator is not to interrogate his native helpers, as if compiling human dictionaries, but rather he must solicit their interest, awaken their thinking [. . .] He does not create a language; this is composed by the native himself; it is the product and translation of his thoughts. And the translator, he who has initiated this thinking, merely

transcribes the words he has aroused, overheard, seized upon—fixing them in writing.[38]

The translator seizes a moment of intercultural "thinking." He is participant and midwife in language's perpetual process of rebirth in the encounter with other languages.

The importance of this process for Leenhardt was two-fold. First, in cooperation with Melanesians, he hoped to preserve an endangered expressivity, not as a static ethnological document, but in words which would be "acts of life inspired by experience." Living New Caledonian culture required living languages. Secondly, for himself and his own culture, Leenhardt uncovered in the translation process a purified and concretized Christianity.

> The missionary has once more experienced the power of the Gospel, and now the natives have helped him in better understanding this power. He perceives that if psychological and theological terms are abstract and indefinite, words as they spring from the experience of the believer are concrete and precise. He realizes that the religious fact expressed in abstract terms is without active value and constitutes merely a dead formula whose spirit has departed. [. . .] Christianity will appear to [the missionary] stripped of the various historical garments which conceal it from the eyes of so many in Europe. And [he] will glimpse the entire beauty of the Gospel, light and life-force for those who seek it with simplicity.[39]

Thus the translator's credo. As Leenhardt conceived the process involved, there could be no simple importation of a Western divinity into a Melanesian religious landscape. For the European, "God" would take on unexpected forms. He watched and listened: "*Para bao we kei pai ae para rhe we ke mi roi powè.*" (Tous les dieux à cause les hommes, d'autre part tous les totems à cause venir selon femmes.) A phrase "overheard in the mouth of a *Canaque*" provided Leenhardt with a key to the complex structure of New Caledonian religion.[40] "Gods come from men, totems proceed from women."

The *natas,* as we have seen, had translated the Christian "God" as "*Bao.*" Perhaps it was disconcerting for their young missionary when he discovered that *Bao* could be a term for cadaver. (He was probably not as confused, however, as his missionary predecessors on Lifou who for a time had translated "Bible" as "container of the Word," until they discovered that the islanders also called their penis sheath "container of the word.")[41] Leenhardt considered all translations to be provisional; he let *Bao* stand, and began looking into the term's wide variety of connotations. *Bao,* he found, could be a magical spirit of recent origin used in magic and sorcery, like the "red god," *doki.*[42] *Bao* could be a human corpse, or even a very old person, still alive; it could also be an ancestor deceased in recent memory; it could be a more distant ancestor, founder of an island or region; it could be an almost forgotten deity, remembered by a single exaggerated trait or identified with an element of nature or geography. Finally, *bao* could refer to a totem which had become confused with an ancestor and was thus also a "god." *Bao,* Leenhardt discovered, was generally identified with the male ancestral lineage, heritage of the clan and the chief. Its properties were masculine, its virtue was "power." Leenhardt observed that the *bao* most actively worshipped were magical manifestations—spirits of fairly recent origin, linked to present occasions. As he understood better the common usages of *bao,* he worried that the Christian deity's status might be that of one more magical "god." It might—like the *doki,* recently imported from Lifou—fail to express really ancient mythic attachments. How could the missionary-translator be sure that *Bao,* the Christian god, would penetrate to the deepest strata of Melanesian feeling and belief?

Leenhardt was at first much impressed with the power in New Caledonian life of the *bao* ancestor-gods. This was most manifest in the au-

thority of chiefs, representatives of the masculine clan lineage, and mediators with the *bao.* But as he became more sensitive to local custom, he discovered that in practice the chiefs often deferred to uterine kin, members of clans from which the paternal clan received its wives. The maternal uncle, or *kanya,* had to be given gifts at births, deaths, *pilou* festivals, marriages, to ensure the counter gift of female life.[43] But the *kanya* did not hold power in himself any more than the chief did. The latter was spokesman, *parole,* of the clan ancestors; the former was representative of the maternal line. The *chef* incarnated the heritage of masculine "power," the *kanya* of feminine "life." An elemental living force flowed as blood from mother to child; its original source was the totem, or *rhë.* The totem was an animal, plant, or mineral, peculiar to a clan and recognized by a system of ritual gestures and sacrifices.[44] Prior to Leenhardt's identification of *rhë* as "totem," New Caledonian culture had been classified as nontotemic. The missionary now had to explain the coexistence of two parallel sources of authority, *bao*-chief, and totem-*kanya.* At first he hypothesized a society in transition from matriarchy to patriarchy. But after further research he dropped these terms, and with them abandoned a theoretical stance tending to explain incongruous elements in a culture as survivals, or evidences of past historical stages. Nineteenth-century evolutionism frequently posited that culture in its early periods had passed from matriarchy to patriarchy. However Leenhardt rejected the notion of opposed, successive states. He found that in New Caledonia duality was structural, with opposition best understood as complementarity. He came to see the lineages of "power" and "life," male and female, in reciprocal union. The missionary, in looking hard at Melanesian religion, had done more than derive a simple equivalent for "God." He had identified a coherent socio-religious system.[45]

Although Leenhardt admired the aesthetic balance of the Melanesian sociomythic order, he nonetheless judged it to be no longer viable. New modes of thought were required, to deal with new conditions. The mythic landscape in which the deeper forms of ancestor worship and totemic identification had found expression was shattered. A new person, less externalized, more centred in an individually defined ego would have to develop. (This Western person, Lévi-Strauss has remarked, seems to have as "totem" his own personality.)[46] Leenhardt's concern was with the spiritual health of this new individual, the quality of "life" available to it. He did not wish to encourage the development of a belief system reduced to merely technical, magical, or rational manipulation of an objective environment. Deeper attachments were needed. Leenhardt identified these affective attitudes primarily with totemic myth as well as with older forms of ancestor-nature worship. It seemed to Leenhardt that acculturation was likely to result in a shift away from myth in the direction of magic, the latter involving a more instrumental attitude toward the world. But he did not wish the Christian *Bao* to be simply a powerful new tool for the understanding and control of immediate events. This would be to encourage shallowness of belief and to promote the development of sorcery and messianism, unstable means of socio-religious problem solving.

Beneath the changing repertoire of *bao*-gods lay the more authentic attachments of myth, geographic and totemic. Something of these forces would need to be co-opted into the new, personal "God" if modes of mythic participation were to co-exist with, not simply be replaced by, techniques of rational manipulation. Thus, the missionary could be delighted, even moved, to hear an old man participating in a Christian festival address a temperance commitment to "his mountains."[47] Much of this religious essence might be excluded in naming "God" *Bao*. The Supreme Being might be thought of as just another lesser god, magical, this worldly, and merely useful for dealing with the white world. There was a risk of excluding the entire female-

totemic "side" of the traditional socio-religious structure. The first Loyalty Islands *natas* had tried to use the name "Jehovah," but their New Caledonian converts preferred "*Bao*," and Leenhardt respected their instinct, though he knew the translation to be imperfect.[48] The *bao* concept would have to be reunderstood, not as a generic term but capitalized, as a personal name. And mythic depth might be added to it through the annexation of as much totemic language as was possible. Leenhardt was encouraged by his discovery that *bao* was, traditionally, a highly adaptable concept. It could apply not merely to a corpse, recent ancestor, or magical divinity, but its masculine "power" could sometimes fuse spontaneously with the feminine-totemic principle of "life." It sometimes happened that a mythic founding father might in collective memory become identified with a totem. Leenhardt had also discovered an encouraging composite usage of *bao,* the "long god" which we have already mentioned. Here was a masculine "god" being associated with the curving flow of the female lineage. If such "totem-god" associations could naturally occur, there was hope for a similar mediation in the person of the Christian *Bao*. "God" could be a "long god," a source of both "power" and "life."

The religious language of Leenhardt's Houailou *New Testament (Peci Arii)* is drawn from a broad range of sources. Totemic expressions abound.[49] The new *Bao* is characterized in language drawn from the expressive systems of myth, of social morality, of magic. The Christian God had to embrace the totality of Melanesian life. It had to co-opt the all-encompassing "peaceful abode" ("*séjour paisible,*" Houailou *maciri*) so effectively incarnated in the traditional village, with its symbolic male and female alleyways inserted in a living, mythic landscape.[50] Leenhardt tried to preach in a concrete local language, expressive of wholeness and quality. He wrote to his father that he was teaching the Melanesians that "the god to whom they give boiled yams and from whom they ask an abundant harvest (*maciri,* the kingdom, same word as kingdom of heaven, *maciri, re néko*) is the same whose hand they now ask for, to help them walk in righteousness."[51] But to appeal to the traditional "peaceful abode" was to invoke immanent spatial attachments, relationships mythical, ecological and social, not habitually thought of as "a" god. This quotation is from an early letter; Leenhardt would become more sophisticated in his translations. But the general aim revealed to his father remained: somehow a localized, immediate mythic experience had to be encompassed by the "person" of a transcendent deity.

In adopting the language of totemic myth in order to evoke the Christian Bao, and in identifying Him with *maciri,* the "peaceful abode" and traditional village, Leenhardt in effect broadened the God of European orthodoxy in two crucial ways. In translating his deity the missionary made "Him" more androgynous, a totem-*bao* of feminine "life" as well as masculine "power." He also rendered God less transcendent, expressing Him through myths of immediate social and religious experience—this worldly and participative.[52]

The Houailou translation of the *New Testament* fairly successfully incarnates Leenhardt's religious ideal. But it was quite another thing to achieve as precise and nuanced a translation in the actual beliefs of Melanesian Protestants. When Leenhardt and his wife returned to New Caledonia in 1938, they found evidence that many *natas* were preaching the Christian *Bao* as if it were "added" onto traditional religion.[53] The missionary's successors had de-emphasized the use of Houailou in religious instruction and ritual and were not as sophisticated as he had been in detecting when Christianity was in danger of slipping either into a syncretist or merely magical-instrumental status. It is difficult today to know precisely how much of the mythic depth Leenhardt strove to preserve in the language of New Caledonian Christianity in fact survives. French is the island's *lingua franca,* and

the young have largely forgotten the old religious words.

On the other hand, there are solid indications that an immanent attachment, at once social, mythic, and ecological, to land and habitat has in fact survived to a significant degree in Christian New Caledonia. And a passing first-hand acquaintance with Protestantism on the Grande Terre has persuaded the present author at least (in the absence of any detailed study) that there is more to "modernization" here than meets the eye. There are still, for example, Protestants who, during their regional church festivals, "pass along the young girl," in the form of a symbolic gift, back and forth between clans united by ancient exchanges of uterine blood (life). Moreover, the desire for a return of expropriated ancestral habitats is the most constant and profound current of political agitation among the island's Melanesians. If Leenhardt's specific Houailou translations have been superseded by events beyond his control, there has been no rejection of the spirit in which they were collectively made. For the missionary, in any event, there were no final versions. Authenticity was a process—the translation of cultures, creative and humanly indeterminate.

NOTES

1. K. O. L. Burridge, "Missionary Occasions," in J. Boutilier, D. Hughes, and S. Tiffany (eds.), *Mission, Church and Sect in Oceania* (Ann Arbor 1978), 1–30.

2. Colin Turnbull, *The Lonely African* (New York 1962), 105–20, 123–4.

3. Maurice Leenhardt, *Gens de la Grande Terre* (Paris, revised ed., 1952), "Deuxième avant-propos," 8.

4. Maurice Leenhardt, *Do Kamo, Person and Myth in the Melanesian World* (Chicago 1979), Intro. by Vincent Crapanzano; "Centenaire de Maurice Leenhardt," special number, *Journal de la Société des Océanistes,* XXXIV: 58–59 (1978); see also Leenhardt issue of *Objets et Mondes, la revue du Musée de l'Homme,* XVII: 2 (1977); Roselène Dousset-Leenhardt, "Maurice Leenhardt," *L'Homme,* XVII (1977), 105–15.

5. James Clifford, "Maurice Leenhardt: Ethnologist and Missionary," PhD dissertation, Harvard University (Cambridge 1977).

6. On Leenhardt's political work see: Clifford, op. cit., ch. 4; Jean Guiart, "Maurice Leenhardt, missionaire et sociologue," *Le Monde Non Chrétien,* XXXIII (1955), 52–71; and "Maurice Leenhardt inconnu: l'homme d'action," *Objets et Mondes,* XVII: 2 (1977), 75–85; *Journal de la Société des Océanistes,* XXXIV: 58–59, (1978), 9–42.

7. See J. Guiart, *Destin d'une église et d'un peuple: étude monographique d'une oeuvre protestante missionaire* (Paris 1959).

8. The bulk of Leenhardt's papers are in the hands of M. R. H. Leenhardt, 59 Rue Claude Bernard, Paris 5e. All unpublished documents, usually cited by date unless otherwise specified, are from this collection. Some letters and journals (1917, 1922–1923) are held by Mme R. Dousset-Leenhardt, 10 Rue de Tournon, Paris 6e. The Archives of the Former Société des Missions Evangéliques are housed in the Bibliothèque du Département Evangélique Français d'Action Apostolique (DEFAP), 102 Bd Arago, Paris 14e.

9. M. Leenhardt, *Le Mouvement éthiopien en Sud de l'Afrique, de 1896 à 1899* (Cahors 1902); repr. Académie des Sciences d'Outre-Mer (Paris 1976).

10. "Consecration de Maurice Leenhardt, Montpellier, 1902," TS, Leenhardt Papers (hereinafter LP).

11. This was recognized by his Marist competitors: see Father Provincial, "Rapport de Visite," 16 Oct. 1913, pp. 21–2, 25, Rome, Archives Pères Maristes, Océanie, Nouvelle-Calédonie, 208; however, development of a Melanesian priesthood has been slow and confined to the post-World War Two period. A full comparison of Protestant and Catholic evangelical practices is beyond the scope of this essay.

12. Maurice Leenhardt (hereinafter ML)—Parents, undated fragment, probably 1905, LP.

13. ML—Parents, 2 June 1903, LP.

14. ML—Jeanne Leenhardt, 13 Oct. 1919, LP. Leenhardt's thinking on conversion appears to anticipate recent "intellectualist" views of the process. See primarily Robin Horton, "African Conversion," *Africa,* XLI (1971), esp. 93–101. Horton distinguishes between (a) traditional religious systems which combine the experience of "communion" with "explanation-prediction-control" of the world's "space-time events" and (b) Christianity, which tends to abandon day-to-day control functions and concentrates on communion with a personal God. In Leenhardt's view, as

in Horton's, full Christianization entails a general revolution in the ways a person communes with and manipulates his world. A consistently Christian ethic would thus result in what Burridge (op. cit., 17) calls a social situation of "generalized individuality." However, Leenhardt, as his thought developed in the conclusion of *Do Kamo* at least, strongly rejected any reduction of experience to an "individual" personal configuration.

15. ML—Parents, 10 Oct., 20 Nov. 1903, 22 Mar. 1905, LP.

16. ML—Parents, 31 Aug. 1911, LP.

17. ML—Parents, 6 Feb. 1904, LP.

18. ML—Boegner, 13 Feb. 1904, Paris, Archives of the Société des Missions Evangéliques (hereinafter SME).

19. ML—Parents, 13 Sept. 1904, LP.

20. ML, "Expériences sociales en terre canaque," *Revue du Christianisme Social,* n.s. (Oct.–Nov. 1921), 786–802, repr. in *Le Monde Non Chrétien,* LXVI (1963), 18. See also ML, *Le catéchumène canaque,* Cahiers Missionaires, no. 1 (Paris 1922); *Do Kamo . . . ,* chs 11 and 12.

21. "Cahier d'Eleisha Nebay, 1911," trans. from the Houailou by R.-H. Leenhardt, LP.

22. ML—Parents, 1905, no month or day, LP.

23. Franz Leenhardt—Maurice, 24 Dec. 1902, LP.

24. ML—Parents, 1905, no month or day, LP.

25. *Journal des Missions Evangéliques,* II (1913), 309–13.

26. ML—Parents, 25 Oct. 1913, LP.

27. "La notion de dieu chez les mélanésiens," TS, n.d. (Lecture notes for a class at the SME school, Paris, probably late 1930s.) On the "dieu long" see ML, *Notes d'ethnologie Néo-Calédonnienne* (Paris 1930), 187, 233–4.

28. ML—Parents, 25 Oct. 1913, LP.

29. ML, *Gens . . . ,* 8.

30. ML, "Ethnologie," TS, n.d. (Lecture notes for a class at the SME school.)

31. ML—Parents, 19 Mar. 1915, LP; for details on Boesoou Erijisi, Leenhardt's remarkable ethnographic informant, see R.-H. Leenhardt, "Un Sociologue Canaque," *Cahiers d'Histoire du Pacifique,* IV (1976), 19–53.

32. ML, "Notes sur la traduction du Nouveau Testament en langue primitive," *Revue d'Histoire et de Philosophie Religieuse,* (May-June 1922), 216–17.

33. Ibid., 212; for a full discussion of "the Word" in Houailou usage, see ML, *Do Kamo . . . ,* chs 9 and 10.

34. ML—Parents, 4 June 1912, LP.

35. On Houailou duals and plurals see esp. ML, "La Personne mélanésienne," *Annuaire de l'Ecole Pratique des Hautes Etudes,* 5ᵉ Section, 1941–42 (Melun 1942), 5–17; idem, *Langues et dialectes de l'Austro Mélanésie* (Paris 1946), Intro., xxxiii–xxxix.

36. See, particularly, E. A. Nida and C. R. Taber, *The Theory and Practice of Translation* (Leiden 1969), 22–32, which sets out principles developed by Nida in a distinguished career as linguist and Bible translation theorist.

37. ML, "Notes sur la traduction du Nouveau Testament," 196.

38. ML, "La Bible en mission," *Evangile et Liberté,* XXI (Oct. 1934).

39. ML, "Notes sur la traduction . . . ," 218.

40. ML, *Notes d'ethnologie . . . ,* 234.

41. ML, "Modes d'expression en sociologie et en ethnologie," *Synthèse,* X, Proc. 6th International Significal Summer Conference (n.d., 1951?), 262. For an account of discovering that *bao* = cadaver, see *Do Kamo . . . ,* 80.

42. See ML, *Notes d'ethnologie . . . ,* 239.

43. See the very beautiful ritual discourses to and by the *kanya* in ML, *Documents néo-calédoniens* (Paris 1932), 341–51.

44. See ML, *Notes d'ethnologie . . . ,* 179–212; ML—Parents, 24 May 1914, LP.

45. ML, *Notes d'ethnologie . . . ,* 77–9, and 98 fn, where he traces the development of his thinking beyond evolutionism to the recognition of a reciprocal system. See also ML, "Observation de la pensée religieuse d'un peuple océanien et d'un peuple bantou," *Histoire générale des religions* (Paris 1948), I, 53; for the system of social exchanges see *Notes d'ethnologie,* ch. 5. (The kinship system, for ML, was not separate from myth.)

46. C. Lévi-Strauss, *La pensée sauvage* (Paris 1962), 285.

47. ML—Jeanne Leenhardt, 17 Aug. 1918, LP.

48. ML, "Notes sur la traduction . . . ," 210–11.

49. See the list of terms drawn from totemism provided by Pierre Métais in his valuable analysis of ML's translation: "Sociologue parce que linguiste," *Journal de la Société des Océanistes,* X (1954), 42, 44. On Christian appropriation of totemic terms see also ML's report in *Annuaire de l'Ecole Pratique des Hautes Etudes,* 5ᵉ Section, (1949–50), 31.

50. ML, *Gens . . . ,* ch. 1.

51. ML—Parents, 1904, no day or month, LP.

52. On the Christian God (Christ) as unity of male "power" and feminine "life," see ML, "Quelques éléments communs aux formes inférieures de la religion," M. Brillant and R. Aigran (eds) *Histoire des religions* (Paris 1953), 109; also ML—Parents, 25 Oct. 1919, LP.

53. Jeanne Leenhardt—children, 1 Feb. 1939, LP.

38

Donna Haraway
1944–

Donna Haraway received her M.Phil. and Ph.D. from Yale University. Haraway's training as a scientist enables her to fuse the specialized knowledge of science and the history of science with a sociological and feminist discourse. "Biological and biosocial disciplines," she explains, "have been important parts of belief and value systems which may function as expressive control or may be reclaimed for other ends." It has been the effort of Haraway in a process of reclaiming scientific discourse for the ends of feminism. Her major works include *Crystals, Fabrics, and Fields: Metaphors of Organicism in Twentieth-Century Developmental Biology* (1976); *Primate Visions: Gender, Race and Nature in the World of Modern Science* (1989); and *Simians, Cyborgs, and Women: the Reinvention of Nature* (1991), in which "A Cyborg Manifesto: Science, Technology, and Socialist-Feminism in the Late Twentieth Century" is also reprinted.

Haraway's "A Cyborg Manifesto: Science, Technology, and Socialist-Feminism in the Late Twentieth Century" is an effort to appropriate the resources of contemporary sciences and technologies in the construction of "an ironic political myth faithful to feminism, socialism, and materialism." The icon of Haraway's new feminist mythology is the cyborg, a half-organic half-mechanical offspring of modern science. The cyborg, situated on the boundary of organism and machine, does not participate in Western mythologies. The cyborg, Haraway argues, is a post-gender, post-Marxist, post-Western, non-oedipal creation whose exclusion from traditional epistemologies makes it a viable image of new subjectivity for feminists. Not bound by patriarchal, imperialist, and teleological polarities, it defies "original unity" in the Western humanist sense of the term. "The cyborg," writes Haraway, "would not recognize the Garden of Eden."

The consciousnesses of gender, race, and class, Haraway explains, are the products of the "terrible historical experience" of the Western tradition. In her critique of formations of identity in traditional Marxism and feminism, Haraway discusses how the unifying emphasis of each has caused it to develop a unified subjectivity based on the exclusion or marginalization of biological reproduction, sex, and race (in traditional Marxism) and labor, social reproduction, and race (in some forms of feminism). A new feminist subjectivity, Haraway contends, must be composed on new principles. Feminist subjectivity in a postmodern world must identify itself with simulation instead of representation, surface instead of depth, stress management instead of hygiene, AIDS instead of tuberculosis, replication instead of reproduction, Lacan instead of Freud, robotics instead of labor, artificial intelligence instead of the mind, Star Wars instead of World War II, and the informatics of domination instead of white capitalist patriarchy.

In "A Cyborg Manifesto," Haraway claims that a possible feminist entry into the postmodern circuit of "informatics of domination" may be found in the new sciences of communications and biotechnology. The intense emphasis on the flow of information in these sciences depends on the language of microelectronic coding. This coding, Haraway explains, operates on a new linguistic system of "copies without originals," of signifiers without signifieds, a linguistic system grounded in what Jean Baudrillard has called "pure simulacra." It is through this new language, with its possibilities for almost infinite interfacing, that feminists may construct new social relations, new sexualities, and new ethnicities.

Haraway concludes with a construction of a "cyborg myth" that integrates women and machines into a new fiction. She offers two possible fictions in the world of "cyborg identity": the fiction of women of color and the fiction of science fiction. For outsider women such as Audre Lorde, author of *Sister Outsider,* Haraway explains that the ideas of writing and language, so crucial to the technology of the cyborg, have always been a matter of survival. Science fiction, in which cyborgs abound, challenges many of Western culture's traditional images of gender, race, class, and human identity. These fictions are two of the first "cyborg myths" with which, Haraway argues, feminists must replace the reductionist dualisms, the totalizing polarities, and the god-goddess mythologies of the Western tradition.

A Cyborg Manifesto: Science, Technology, and Socialist-Feminism in the Late Twentieth Century[1]

AN IRONIC DREAM OF A COMMON LANGUAGE FOR WOMEN IN THE INTEGRATED CIRCUIT

This chapter is an effort to build an ironic political myth faithful to feminism, socialism, and materialism. Perhaps more faithful as blasphemy is faithful, than as reverent worship and identification. Blasphemy has always seemed to require taking things very seriously. I know no better stance to adopt from within the secular-religious, evangelical traditions of United States politics, including the politics of socialist feminism. Blasphemy protects one from the moral majority within, while still insisting on the need for community. Blasphemy is not apostasy. Irony is about contradictions that do not resolve into larger wholes, even dialectically, about the tension of holding incompatible things together because both or all are necessary and true. Irony is about humour and serious play. It is also a rhetorical strategy and a political method, one I would like to see more honoured within socialist-feminism. At the centre of my ironic faith, my blasphemy, is the image of the cyborg.

A cyborg is a cybernetic organism, a hybrid of machine and organism, a creature of social reality as well as a creature of fiction. Social reality is lived social relations, our most important political construction, a world-changing fiction. The international women's movements have constructed "women's experience," as well as uncovered or discovered this crucial collective object. This experience is a fiction and fact of the most crucial, political kind. Liberation rests on the construction of the consciousness, the imaginative apprehension, of oppression, and so of possibility. The cyborg is a matter of fiction and lived experience that changes what counts as women's experience in the late twentieth century. This is a struggle over life and death, but the boundary between science fiction and social reality is an optical illusion.

Contemporary science fiction is full of cyborgs—creatures simultaneously animal and machine, who populate worlds ambiguously natural and crafted. Modern medicine is also full of cyborgs, of couplings between organism and machine, each conceived as coded devices, in an intimacy and with a power that was not generated in the history of sexuality. Cyborg "sex" restores some of the lovely replicative baroque of ferns and invertebrates (such nice organic prophylactics against heterosexism). Cyborg replication is uncoupled from organic reproduction. Modern production seems like a dream of cyborg colonization work, a dream that makes the nightmare of Taylorism seem idyllic. And modern war is a cyborg orgy, coded by C^{3}I, command-control-communication-intelligence, an $84 billion item in 1984's US defence budget. I am making an argument for the cyborg as a fiction mapping our social and bodily reality and as an imaginative resource suggesting some very fruitful couplings. Michel Foucault's biopolitics is a flaccid premonition of cyborg politics, a very open field.

By the late twentieth century, our time, a mythic time, we are all chimeras, theorized and fabricated hybrids of machine and organism; in short, we are cyborgs. The cyborg is our ontology; it gives us our politics. The cyborg is a condensed image of both imagination and material reality, the two joined centres structuring any possibility of historical transformation. In the traditions of "Western" science and politics—the tradition of racist, male-dominant capitalism; the tradition of progress; the tradition of the appropriation of nature as resource for the productions of culture; the tradition of reproduction of the self from the reflections of the other—the relation between organism and machine has been a border war. The stakes in the border war have been the territories of production, reproduction, and imagination. This chapter is an argument for *pleasure* in the confusion of boundaries and for *responsibility* in their construction. It is also an effort to contribute to socialist-feminist culture and theory in a postmodernist, non-naturalist mode and in the utopian tradition of imagining a world without gender, which is perhaps a world without genesis, but maybe also a world without end. The cyborg incarnation is outside salvation history. Nor does it mark time on an oedipal calendar, attempting to heal the terrible cleavages of gender in an oral symbiotic utopia or post-oedipal apocalypse. As Zoe Sofoulis argues in her unpublished manuscript on Jacques Lacan, Melanie Klein, and nuclear culture, *Lacklein,* the most terrible and perhaps the most promising monsters in cyborg worlds are embodied in non-oedipal narratives with a different logic of repression, which we need to understand for our survival.

The cyborg is a creature in a post-gender world; it has no truck with bisexuality, pre-oedipal symbiosis, unalienated labour, or other seductions to organic wholeness through a final appropriation of all the powers of the parts into a higher unity. In a sense, the cyborg has no origin story in the Western sense—a "final" irony since the cyborg is also the awful apocalyptic *telos* of the "West's" escalating dominations of abstract individuation, an ultimate self untied at last from all dependency, a man in space. An origin story in the "Western," humanist sense depends on the myth of original unity, fullness, bliss and terror, represented by the phallic mother from whom all humans must separate, the task of individual development and of history, the twin potent myths inscribed most powerfully for us in psychoanalysis and Marxism. Hillary Klein has argued that both Marxism and psychoanalysis, in their concepts of labour and of individuation and gender formation, depend on the plot of original unity out of which difference must be produced and enlisted in a drama of escalating domination of woman/nature. The

cyborg skips the step of original unity, of identification with nature in the Western sense. This
is its illegitimate promise that might lead to subversion of its teleology as Star Wars.

The cyborg is resolutely committed to partiality, irony, intimacy, and perversity. It is oppositional, utopian, and completely without innocence. No longer structured by the polarity of
public and private, the cyborg defines a technological polis based partly on a revolution of social relations in the *oikos,* the household. Nature
and culture are reworked; the one can no longer
be the resource for appropriation or incorporation by the other. The relationships for forming
wholes from parts, including those of polarity
and hierarchical domination, are at issue in the
cyborg world. Unlike the hopes of Franken-
stein's monster, the cyborg does not expect its
father to save it through a restoration of the garden; that is, through the fabrication of a heterosexual mate, through its completion in a finished whole, a city and cosmos. The cyborg does
not dream of community on the model of the
organic family, this time without the oedipal
project. The cyborg would not recognize the
Garden of Eden; it is not made of mud and cannot dream of returning to dust. Perhaps that is
why I want to see if cyborgs can subvert the
apocalypse of returning to nuclear dust in the
manic compulsion to name the Enemy. Cyborgs
are not reverent; they do not remember the cosmos. They are wary of holism, but needy for
connection—they seem to have a natural feel for
united front politics, but without the vanguard
party. The main trouble with cyborgs, of course,
is that they are the illegitimate offspring of mili-
tarism and patriarchal capitalism, not to mention state socialism. But illegitimate offspring
are often exceedingly unfaithful to their origins.
Their fathers, after all, are inessential.

I will return to the science fiction of cyborgs
at the end of this chapter, but now I want to signal three crucial boundary breakdowns that
make the following political-fictional (political-
scientific) analysis possible. By the late twentieth

century in United States scientific culture, the
boundary between human and animal is thoroughly breached. The last beachheads of
uniqueness have been polluted if not turned
into amusement parks—language, tool use, social behaviour, mental events, nothing really
convincingly settles the separation of human
and animal. And many people no longer feel the
need for such a separation; indeed, many
branches of feminist culture affirm the pleasure
of connection of human and other living creatures. Movements for animal rights are not irrational denials of human uniqueness; they are a
clear-sighted recognition of connection across
the discredited breach of nature and culture. Biology and evolutionary theory over the last two
centuries have simultaneously produced modern
organisms as objects of knowledge and reduced
the line between humans and animals to a faint
trace re-etched in ideological struggle or professional disputes between life and social science.
Within this framework, teaching modern Christian creationism should be fought as a form of
child abuse.

Biological-determinist ideology is only one
position opened up in scientific culture for arguing the meanings of human animality. There is
much room for radical political people to contest the meanings of the breached boundary.[2]
The cyborg appears in myth precisely where the
boundary between human and animal is transgressed. Far from signalling a walling off of people from other living beings, cyborgs signal disturbingly and pleasurably tight coupling.
Bestiality has a new status in this cycle of marriage exchange.

The second leaky distinction is between ani-
mal-human (organism) and machine. Precyber-
netic machines could be haunted; there was always the spectre of the ghost in the machine.
This dualism structured the dialogue between
materialism and idealism that was settled by a
dialectical progeny, called spirit or history, according to taste. But basically machines were
not self-moving, self-designing, autonomous.

They could not achieve man's dream, only mock it. They were not man, an author to himself, but only a caricature of that masculinist reproductive dream. To think they were otherwise was paranoid. Now we are not so sure. Late twentieth-century machines have made thoroughly ambiguous the difference between natural and artificial, mind and body, self-developing and externally designed, and many other distinctions that used to apply to organisms and machines. Our machines are disturbingly lively, and we ourselves frighteningly inert.

Technological determination is only one ideological space opened up by the reconceptions of machine and organism as coded texts through which we engage in the play of writing and reading the world.[3] "Textualization" of everything in poststructuralist, postmodernist theory has been damned by Marxists and socialist feminists for its utopian disregard for the lived relations of domination that ground the "play" of arbitrary reading.[4] It is certainly true that postmodernist strategies, like my cyborg myth, subvert myriad organic wholes (for example, the poem, the primitive culture, the biological organism). In short, the certainty of what counts as nature—a source of insight and promise of innocence—is undermined, probably fatally. The transcendent authorization of interpretation is lost, and with it the ontology grounding "Western" epistemology. But the alternative is not cynicism or faithlessness, that is, some version of abstract existence, like the accounts of technological determinism destroying "man" by the "machine" or "meaningful political action" by the "text." Who cyborgs will be is a radical question; the answers are a matter of survival. Both chimpanzees and artefacts have politics, so why shouldn't we (de Waal, 1982; Winner, 1980)?

The third distinction is a subset of the second: the boundary between physical and non-physical is very imprecise for us. Pop physics books on the consequences of quantum theory and the indeterminacy principle are a kind of popular scientific equivalent to Harlequin romances as a marker of radical change in American white heterosexuality: they get it wrong, but they are on the right subject. Modern machines are quintessentially microelectronic devices: they are everywhere and they are invisible. Modern machinery is an irreverent upstart god, mocking the Father's ubiquity and spirituality. The silicon chip is a surface for writing; it is etched in molecular scales disturbed only by atomic noise, the ultimate interference for nuclear scores. Writing, power, and technology are old partners in Western stories of the origin of civilization, but miniaturization has changed our experience of mechanism. Miniaturization has turned out to be about power; small is not so much beautiful as pre-eminently dangerous, as in cruise missiles. Contrast the TV sets of the 1950s or the news cameras of the 1970s with the TV wrist bands or hand-sized video cameras now advertised. Our best machines are made of sunshine; they are all light and clean because they are nothing but signals, electromagnetic waves, a section of a spectrum, and these machines are eminently portable, mobile—a matter of immense human pain in Detroit and Singapore. People are nowhere near so fluid, being both material and opaque. Cyborgs are ether, quintessence.

The ubiquity and invisibility of cyborgs is precisely why these sunshine-belt machines are so deadly. They are as hard to see politically as materially. They are about consciousness—or its simulation.[5] They are floating signifiers moving in pickup trucks across Europe, blocked more effectively by the witch-weavings of the displaced and so unnatural Greenham women, who read the cyborg webs of power so very well, than by the militant labour of older masculinist politics, whose natural constituency needs defence jobs. Ultimately the "hardest" science is about the realm of greatest boundary confusion, the realm of pure number, pure spirit, C^3I, cryptography, and the preservation of potent secrets. The new machines are so clean and light. Their engineers are sun-worshippers mediating a new scientific revolution associated with the night dream of post-industrial society. The diseases evoked by these clean machines are "no more" than the minuscule coding changes of an antigen in the immune system, "no more" than the experience of stress. The nimble fingers of "Oriental" women, the old fascination of little Anglo-Saxon Victorian girls with doll's houses, women's enforced attention to the small take on quite new dimensions in this world. There might be a cyborg Alice taking account of these new dimensions. Ironically, it might be the unnatural cyborg women making chips in Asia and spiral dancing in Santa Rita jail [a practice at once both spiritual and political that linked guards and arrested anti-nuclear demonstrators in the Alameda County jail in California in the early 1980s] whose constructed unities will guide effective oppositional strategies.

So my cyborg myth is about transgressed boundaries, potent fusions, and dangerous possibilities which progressive people might explore as one part of needed political work. One of my premises is that most American socialists and feminists see deepened dualisms of mind and body, animal and machine, idealism and materialism in the social practices, symbolic formulations, and physical artefacts associated with "high technology" and scientific culture. From *One-Dimensional Man* (Marcuse, 1964) to *The Death of Nature* (Merchant, 1980), the analytic resources developed by progressives have insisted on the necessary domination of technics and recalled us to an imagined organic body to integrate our resistance. Another of my premises is that the need for unity of people trying to resist world-wide intensification of domination has never been more acute. But a slightly perverse shift of perspective might better enable us to contest for meanings, as well as for other forms of power and pleasure in technologically mediated societies.

From one perspective, a cyborg world is about the final imposition of a grid of control on the planet, about the final abstraction embodied in a Star Wars apocalypse waged in the name of defence, about the final appropriation of women's bodies in a masculinist orgy of war (Sofia, 1984). From another perspective, a cyborg world might be about lived social and bodily realities in which people are not afraid of their joint kinship with animals and machines, not afraid of permanently partial identities and contradictory standpoints. The political struggle is to see from both perspectives at once because each reveals both dominations and possibilities unimaginable from the other vantage point. Single vision produces worse illusions than double vision or many-headed monsters. Cyborg unities are monstrous and illegitimate; in our present political circumstances, we could hardly hope for more potent myths for resistance and recoupling. I like to imagine LAG, the Livermore Action Group, as a kind of cyborg society, dedicated to realistically converting the laboratories that most fiercely embody and spew out the tools of technological apocalypse, and committed to building a political form that actually manages to hold together witches, engineers, elders, perverts, Christians, mothers, and Leninists long enough to disarm the state. Fission Impossible is the name of the affinity group in my town. (Affinity: related not by blood but by choice, the appeal of one chemical nuclear group for another, avidity.)[6]

FRACTURED IDENTITIES

It has become difficult to name one's feminism by a single adjective—or even to insist in every circumstance upon the noun. Consciousness of exclusion through naming is acute. Identities seem contradictory, partial, and strategic. With the hard-won recognition of their social and historical constitution, gender, race, and class cannot provide the basis for belief in "essential" unity. There is nothing about being "female" that naturally binds women. There is not even such a state as "being" female, itself a highly complex category constructed in contested sexual scientific discourses and other social practices. Gender, race, or class consciousness is an achievement forced on us by the terrible historical experience of the contradictory social realities of patriarchy, colonialism, and capitalism. And who counts as "us" in my own rhetoric? Which identities are available to ground such a potent political myth called "us," and what could motivate enlistment in this collectivity? Painful fragmentation among feminists (not to mention among women) along every possible fault line has made the concept of *woman* elusive, an excuse for the matrix of women's dominations of each other. For me—and for many who share a similar historical location in white, professional middle-class, female, radical, North American, mid-adult bodies—the sources of a crisis in political identity are legion. The recent history for much of the US left and US feminism has been a response to this kind of crisis by endless splitting and searches for a new essential unity. But there has also been a growing recognition of another response through coalition—affinity, not identity.[7]

Chela Sandoval (n.d., 1984), from a consideration of specific historical moments in the formation of the new political voice called women of colour, has theorized a hopeful model of political identity called "oppositional consciousness," born of the skills for reading webs of power by those refused stable membership in the social categories of race, sex, or class. "Women of color," a name contested at its origins by those whom it would incorporate, as well as a historical consciousness marking systematic breakdown of all the signs of Man in "Western" traditions, constructs a kind of postmodernist identity out of otherness, difference, and specificity. This postmodernist identity is fully political, whatever might be said about other possible postmodernisms. Sandoval's oppositional consciousness is about contradictory locations and heterochronic calendars, not about relativisms and pluralisms.

Sandoval emphasizes the lack of any essential criterion for identifying who is a woman of colour. She notes that the definition of the group has been by conscious appropriation of negation. For example, a Chicana or US black woman has not been able to speak as a woman or as a black person or as a Chicano. Thus, she was at the bottom of a cascade of negative identities, left out of even the privileged oppressed authorial categories called "women and blacks," who claimed to make the important revolutions. The category "woman" negated all non-white women; "black" negated all non-black people, as well as all black women. But there was also no "she," no singularity, but a sea of differences among US women who have affirmed their historical identity as US women of colour. This identity marks out a self-consciously constructed space that cannot affirm the capacity to act on the basis of natural identification, but only on the basis of conscious coalition, of affinity, of political kinship[8] Unlike the "woman" of some streams of the white women's movement in the United States, there is no naturalization of the matrix, or at least this is what Sandoval argues is uniquely available through the power of oppositional consciousness.

Sandoval's argument has to be seen as one potent formulation for feminists out of the worldwide development of anti-colonialist discourse; that is to say, discourse dissolving the "West" and its highest product—the one who is not animal, barbarian, or woman; man, that is, the author of a cosmos called history. As orientalism is deconstructed politically and semiotically, the identities of the occident destabilize, including those of feminists.[9] Sandoval argues that "women of colour" have a chance to build an effective unity that does not replicate the imperializing, totalizing revolutionary subjects of previous Marxisms and feminisms which had not faced the consequences of the disorderly polyphony emerging from decolonization.

Katie King has emphasized the limits of identification and the political/poetic mechanics of identification built into reading "the poem," that generative core of cultural feminism. King criticizes the persistent tendency among contemporary feminists from different "moments" or "conversations" in feminist practice to taxonomize the women's movement to make one's own political tendencies appear to be the *telos* of the whole. These taxonomies tend to remake feminist history so that it appears to be an ideological struggle among coherent types persisting over time, especially those typical units called radical, liberal, and socialist-feminism. Literally, all other feminisms are either incorporated or marginalized, usually by building an explicit ontology and epistemology.[10] Taxonomies of feminism produce epistemologies to police deviation from official women's experience. And of course, "women's culture," like women of colour, is consciously created by mechanisms inducing affinity. The rituals of poetry, music, and certain forms of academic practice have been pre-eminent. The politics of race and culture in the US women's movements are intimately interwoven. The common achievement of King and Sandoval is learning how to craft a poetic/political unity without relying on a logic of appropriation, incorporation, and taxonomic identification.

The theoretical and practical struggle against unity-through-domination or unity-through-incorporation ironically not only undermines the justifications for patriarchy, colonialism, humanism, positivism, essentialism, scientism, and other unlamented -isms, but *all* claims for an organic or natural standpoint. I think that radical and socialist/Marxist-feminisms have also undermined their/our own epistemological strategies and that this is a crucially valuable step in imagining possible unities. It remains to be seen whether all "epistemologies" as Western political people have known them fail us in the task to build effective affinities.

It is important to note that the effort to construct revolutionary standpoints, epistemologies as achievements of people committed to changing the world, has been part of the process showing the limits of identification. The acid tools of postmodernist theory and the constructive tools of ontological discourse about revolutionary subjects might be seen as ironic allies in dissolving Western selves in the interests of survival. We are excruciatingly conscious of what it means to have a historically constituted body. But with the loss of innocence in our origin, there is no expulsion from the Garden either. Our politics lose the indulgence of guilt with the *naïveté* of innocence. But what would another political myth for socialist-feminism look like? What kind of politics could embrace partial, contradictory, permanently unclosed constructions of personal and collective selves and still be faithful, effective—and, ironically, socialist-feminist?

I do not know of any other time in history when there was greater need for political unity to confront effectively the dominations of "race," "gender," "sexuality," and "class." I also do not know of any other time when the kind of unity we might help build could have been possible. None of "us" have any longer the symbolic or material capability of dictating the shape of reality to any of "them." Or at least "we" cannot claim innocence from practising such dominations. White women, including socialist feminists, discovered (that is, were forced kicking and screaming to notice) the non-innocence of the category "woman." That consciousness changes the geography of all previous categories; it denatures them as heat denatures a fragile protein. Cyborg feminists have to argue that "we" do not want any more natural matrix of unity and that no construction is whole. Innocence, and the corollary insistence on victimhood as the only ground for insight, has done enough damage. But the constructed revolutionary subject must give late-twentieth-century people pause as well. In the fraying of identities and in the reflexive strategies for constructing them, the possibility opens up for weaving something other than a shroud for the day after the apocalypse that so prophetically ends salvation history.

Both Marxist/socialist-feminisms and radical feminisms have simultaneously naturalized and denatured the category "woman" and consciousness of the social lives of "women." Perhaps a schematic caricature can highlight both kinds of moves. Marxian socialism is rooted in an analysis of wage labour which reveals class structure. The consequence of the wage relationship is systematic alienation, as the worker is dissociated from his (sic) product. Abstraction and illusion rule in knowledge, domination rules in practice. Labour is the pre-eminently privileged category enabling the Marxist to overcome illusion and find that point of view which is necessary for changing the world. Labour is the humanizing activity that makes man; labour is an ontological category permitting the knowledge of a subject, and so the knowledge of subjugation and alienation.

In faithful filiation, socialist-feminism advanced by allying itself with the basic analytic strategies of Marxism. The main achievement of both Marxist feminists and socialist feminists was to expand the category of labour to accommodate what (some) women did, even when the wage relation was subordinated to a more comprehensive view of labour under capitalist patriarchy. In particular, women's labour in the household and women's activity as mothers generally (that is, reproduction in the socialist-feminist sense), entered theory on the authority of analogy to the Marxian concept of labour. The unity of women here rests on an epistemology based on the ontological structure of "labour." Marxist/socialist-feminism does not "naturalize" unity; it is a possible achievement based on a possible standpoint rooted in social relations. The essentializing move is in the ontological structure of labour or of its analogue, women's activity.[11] The inheritance of Marxian humanism, with its pre-eminently Western self, is the difficulty for me. The contribution from these formulations has been the emphasis on the daily responsibility of real women to build unities, rather than to naturalize them.

Catherine MacKinnon's (1982, 1987) version of radical feminism is itself a caricature of the appropriating, incorporating, totalizing tendencies of Western theories of identity grounding action.[12] It is factually and politically wrong to assimilate all of the diverse "moments" or "conversations" in recent women's politics named radical feminism to MacKinnon's version. But the teleological logic of her theory shows how an epistemology and ontology—including their negations—erase or police difference. Only one of the effects of MacKinnon's theory is the rewriting of the history of the polymorphous field called radical feminism. The major effect is the production of a theory of experience, of women's identity, that is a kind of apocalypse for all revolutionary standpoints. That is, the totalization built into this tale of radical feminism achieves its end—the unity of women—by enforcing the experience of and testimony to radical non-being. As for the Marxist/socialist feminist, consciousness is an achievement, not a natural fact. And MacKinnon's theory eliminates some of the difficulties built into humanist revolutionary subjects, but at the cost of radical reductionism.

MacKinnon argues that feminism necessarily adopted a different analytical strategy from Marxism, looking first not at the structure of class, but at the structure of sex/gender and its generative relationship, men's constitution and appropriation of women sexually. Ironically, MacKinnon's "ontology" constructs a non-subject, a non-being. Another's desire, not the self's labour, is the origin of "woman." She therefore develops a theory of consciousness that enforces what can count as "women's" experience—anything that names sexual violation, indeed, sex itself as far as "women" can be concerned. Feminist practice is the construction of this form of consciousness; that is, the self-knowledge of a self-who-is-not.

Perversely, sexual appropriation in this feminism still has the epistemological status of labour; that is to say, the point from which an analysis able to contribute to changing the world must flow. But sexual objectification, not alienation, is the consequence of the structure of sex/gender. In the realm of knowledge, the result of sexual objectification is illusion and abstraction. However, a woman is not simply alienated from her product, but in a deep sense does not exist as a subject, or even potential subject, since she owes her existence as a woman to sexual appropriation. To be constituted by another's desire is not the same thing as to be alienated in the violent separation of the labourer from his product.

MacKinnon's radical theory of experience is totalizing in the extreme; it does not so much marginalize as obliterate the authority of any other women's political speech and action. It is a totalization producing what Western patriarchy itself never succeeded in doing—feminists' consciousness of the non-existence of women, except as products of men's desire. I think MacKinnon correctly argues that no Marxian version of identity can firmly ground women's unity. But in solving the problem of the contradictions of any Western revolutionary subject for feminist purposes, she develops an even more authoritarian doctrine of experience. If my complaint about socialist/Marxian standpoints is their unintended erasure of polyvocal, unassimilable, radical difference made visible in anticolonial discourse and practice, MacKinnon's intentional erasure of all difference through the device of the "essential" non-existence of women is not reassuring.

In my taxonomy, which like any other taxonomy is a re-inscription of history, radical feminism can accommodate all the activities of women named by socialist feminists as forms of labour only if the activity can somehow be sexualized. Reproduction had different tones of meanings for the two tendencies, one rooted in labour, one in sex, both calling the consequences of domination and ignorance of social and personal reality "false consciousness."

Beyond either the difficulties or the contributions in the argument of any one author, neither Marxist nor radical feminist points of view have tended to embrace the status of a partial expla-

nation; both were regularly constituted as totalities. Western explanation has demanded as much; how else could the "Western" author incorporate its others? Each tried to annex other forms of domination by expanding its basic categories through analogy, simple listing, or addition. Embarrassed silence about race among white radical and socialist feminists was one major, devastating political consequence. History and polyvocality disappear into political taxonomies that try to establish genealogies. There was no structural room for race (or for much else) in theory claiming to reveal the construction of the category woman and social group women as a unified or totalizable whole. The structure of my caricature looks like this:

socialist feminism—structure of class//wage
labour//alienation
labour, by analogy reproduction, by extension
sex, by addition race
radical feminism—structure of gender//sexual
appropriation//objectification
sex, by analogy labour, by extension reproduction, by addition race

In another context, the French theorist, Julia Kristeva, claimed women appeared as a historical group after the Second World War, along with groups like youth. Her dates are doubtful; but we are now accustomed to remembering that as objects of knowledge and as historical actors, "race" did not always exist, "class" has a historical genesis, and "homosexuals" are quite junior. It is no accident that the symbolic system of the family of man—and so the essence of woman—breaks up at the same moment that networks of connection among people on the planet are unprecedentedly multiple, pregnant, and complex. "Advanced capitalism" is inadequate to convey the structure of this historical moment. In the "Western" sense, the end of man is at stake. It is no accident that woman disintegrates into women in our time. Perhaps socialist feminists were not substantially guilty of producing essentialist theory that suppressed women's particularity and contradictory interests. I think we have been, at least through unreflective participation in the logics, languages, and practices of white humanism and through searching for a single ground of domination to secure our revolutionary voice. Now we have less excuse. But in the consciousness of our failures, we risk lapsing into boundless difference and giving up on the confusing task of making partial, real connection. Some differences are playful; some are poles of world historical systems of domination. "Epistemology" is about knowing the difference.

THE INFORMATICS OF DOMINATION

In this attempt at an epistemological and political position, I would like to sketch a picture of possible unity, a picture indebted to socialist and feminist principles of design. The frame for my sketch is set by the extent and importance of rearrangements in world-wide social relations tied to science and technology. I argue for a politics rooted in claims about fundamental changes in the nature of class, race, and gender in an emerging system of world order analogous in its novelty and scope to that created by industrial capitalism; we are living through a movement from an organic, industrial society to a polymorphous, information system—from all work to all play, a deadly game. Simultaneously material and ideological, the dichotomies may be expressed in the following chart of transitions from the comfortable old hierarchical dominations to the scary new networks I have called the informatics of domination:

Representation	Simulation
Bourgeois novel, realism	Science fiction, postmodernism
Organism	Biotic component
Depth, integrity	Surface, boundary
Heat	Noise
Biology as clinical practice	Biology as inscription
Physiology	Communications engineering
Small group	Subsystem
Perfection	Optimization
Eugenics	Population Control
Decadence, *Magic Mountain*	Obsolescence, *Future Shock*
Hygiene	Stress Management
Microbiology, tuberculosis	Immunology, AIDS
Organic division of labour	Ergonomics/cybernetics of labour
Functional specialization	Modular construction
Reproduction	Replication
Organic sex role specialization	Optimal genetic strategies
Biological determinism	Evolutionary inertia, constraints
Community ecology	Ecosystem
Racial chain of being	Neo-imperialism, United Nations humanism
Scientific management in home/factory	Global factory/ Electronic cottage
Family/Market/ Factory	Women in the Integrated Circuit
Family wage	Comparable worth
Public/Private	Cyborg citizenship
Nature/Culture	Fields of difference
Co-operation	Communications enhancement
Freud	Lacan
Sex	Genetic engineering
Labour	Robotics
Mind	Artificial Intelligence
Second World War	Star Wars
White Capitalist Patriarchy	Informatics of Domination

This list suggests several interesting things.[13] First, the objects on the right-hand side cannot be coded as "natural," a realization that subverts naturalistic coding for the left-hand side as well. We cannot go back ideologically or materially. It's not just that "god" is dead; so is the "goddess." Or both are revivified in the worlds charged with microelectronic and biotechnological politics. In relation to objects like biotic components, one must think not in terms of essential properties, but in terms of design, boundary constraints, rates of flows, systems logics, costs of lowering constraints. Sexual reproduction is one kind of reproductive strategy among many, with costs and benefits as a function of the system environment. Ideologies of sexual reproduction can no longer reasonably call on notions of sex and sex role as organic aspects in natural objects like organisms and families. Such reasoning will be unmasked as irrational, and ironically corporate executives reading *Playboy* and anti-porn radical feminists will make strange bedfellows in jointly unmasking the irrationalism.

Likewise for race, ideologies about human diversity have to be formulated in terms of frequencies of parameters, like blood groups or intelligence scores. It is "irrational" to invoke concepts like primitive and civilized. For liberals and radicals, the search for integrated social systems gives way to a new practice called "experimental ethnography" in which an organic object dissipates in attention to the play of writing. At the level of ideology, we see translations of racism and colonialism into languages of development and under-development, rates and constraints of modernization. Any objects or persons can be reasonably thought of in terms of disassembly and reassembly; no "natural" architectures constrain system design. The financial districts in all the world's cities, as well as the export-processing and free-trade zones, proclaim this elementary fact of "late capitalism." The entire universe of objects that can be known scientifically must be formulated as problems in communications engineering (for the managers) or theories of the text (for those who would resist). Both are cyborg semiologies.

One should expect control strategies to concentrate on boundary conditions and interfaces, on rates of flow across boundaries—and not on the integrity of natural objects. "Integrity" or "sincerity" of the Western self gives way to decision procedures and expert systems. For example, control strategies applied to women's capacities to give birth to new human beings will be developed in the languages of population control and maximization of goal achievement for individual decision-makers. Control strategies will be formulated in terms of rates, costs of constraints, degrees of freedom. Human beings, like any other component or subsystem, must be localized in a system architecture whose basic modes of operation are probabilistic, statistical. No objects, spaces, or bodies are sacred in themselves; any component can be interfaced with any other if the proper standard, the proper code, can be constructed for processing signals in a common language. Exchange in this world transcends the universal translation effected by capitalist markets that Marx analysed so well. The privileged pathology affecting all kinds of components in this universe is stress—communications breakdown (Hogness, 1983). The cyborg is not subject to Foucault's biopolitics; the cyborg simulates politics, a much more potent field of operations.

This kind of analysis of scientific and cultural objects of knowledge which have appeared historically since the Second World War prepares us to notice some important inadequacies in feminist analysis which has proceeded as if the organic, hierarchical dualisms ordering discourse in "the West" since Aristotle still ruled. They have been cannibalized, or as Zoe Sofia (Sofoulis) might put it, they have been "techno-digested." The dichotomies between mind and body, animal and human, organism and machine, public and private, nature and culture, men and women, primitive and civilized are all in question ideologically. The actual situation of women is their integration/exploitation into a world system of production/reproduction and communication called the informatics of domination. The home, workplace, market, public arena, the body itself—all can be dispersed and interfaced in nearly infinite, polymorphous ways, with large consequences for women and others—consequences that themselves are very different for different people and which make potent oppositional international movements difficult to imagine and essential for survival. One important route for reconstructing socialist-feminist politics is through theory and practice addressed to the social relations of science and technology, including crucially the systems of myth and meanings structuring our imaginations. The cyborg is a kind of disassembled and reassembled, postmodern collective and personal self. This is the self feminists must code.

Communications technologies and biotechnologies are the crucial tools recrafting our bodies. These tools embody and enforce new social relations for women world-wide. Technologies and scientific discourses can be partially understood as formalizations, i.e., as frozen moments, of the fluid social interactions constituting them, but they should also be viewed as instruments for enforcing meanings. The boundary is permeable between tool and myth, instrument and concept, historical systems of social relations and historical anatomies of possible bodies, including objects of knowledge. Indeed, myth and tool mutually constitute each other.

Furthermore, communications sciences and modern biologies are constructed by a common move—*the translation of the world into a problem of coding,* a search for a common language in which all resistance to instrumental control disappears and all heterogeneity can be submitted to disassembly, reassembly, investment, and exchange.

In communications sciences, the translation of the world into a problem in coding can be illustrated by looking at cybernetic (feedback-controlled) systems theories applied to telephone technology, computer design, weapons deployment, or data base construction and maintenance. In each case, solution to the key questions rests on a theory of language and control; the key operation is determining the rates, directions, and probabilities of flow of a quantity called information. The world is subdivided by boundaries differentially permeable to information. Information is just that kind of quantifiable element (unit, basis of unity) which allows universal translation, and so unhindered instrumental power (called effective communication). The biggest threat to such power is interruption of communication. Any system breakdown is a function of stress. The fundamentals of this technology can be condensed into the metaphor C^3I, command-control-communication-intelligence, the military's symbol for its operations theory.

In modern biologies, the translation of the world into a problem in coding can be illustrated by molecular genetics, ecology, sociobiological evolutionary theory, and immunobiology. The organism has been translated into problems of genetic coding and read-out. Biotechnology, a writing technology, informs research broadly.[14] In a sense, organisms have ceased to exist as objects of knowledge, giving way to biotic components, i.e., special kinds of information-processing devices. The analogous moves in ecology could be examined by probing the history and utility of the concept of the ecosystem. Immunobiology and associated medical practices are rich exemplars of the privilege of coding and recognition systems as objects of knowledge, as constructions of bodily reality for us. Biology here is a kind of cryptography. Research is necessarily a kind of intelligence activity. Ironies abound. A stressed system goes awry; its communication processes break down; it fails to recognize the difference between self and other. Human babies with baboon hearts evoke national ethical perplexity—for animal rights activists at least as much as for the guardians of human purity. In the US gay men and intravenous drug users are the "privileged" victims of an awful immune system disease that marks (inscribes on the body) confusion of boundaries and moral pollution (Treichler, 1987).

But these excursions into communications sciences and biology have been at a rarefied level; there is a mundane, largely economic reality to support my claim that these sciences and technologies indicate fundamental transformations in the structure of the world for us. Communications technologies depend on electronics. Modern states, multinational corporations, military power, welfare state apparatuses, satellite systems, political processes, fabrication of our imaginations, labour-control systems, medical constructions of our bodies, commercial pornography, the international division of labour, and religious evangelism depend intimately upon electronics. Microelectronics is the technical basis of simulacra; that is, of copies without originals.

Microelectronics mediates the translations of labour into robotics and word processing, sex into genetic engineering and reproductive technologies, and mind into artificial intelligence and decision procedures. The new biotechnologies concern more than human reproduction. Biology as a powerful engineering science for re-designing materials and processes has revolutionary implications for industry, perhaps most obvious today in areas of fermentation, agriculture, and energy. Communications sciences and biology are constructions of natural-technical objects of knowledge in which the difference between machine and organism is thoroughly blurred; mind, body, and tool are on very intimate terms. The "multinational" material organization of the production and reproduction of daily life and the symbolic organization of the production and reproduction of culture and imagination seem equally implicated. The boundary-maintaining images of base and superstructure, public and private, or material and ideal never seemed more feeble.

I have used Rachel Grossman's (1980) image of women in the integrated circuit to name the situation of women in a world so intimately restructured through the social relations of science and technology.[15] I used the odd circumlocu-

tion, "the social relations of science and technology," to indicate that we are not dealing with a technological determinism, but with a historical system depending upon structured relations among people. But the phrase should also indicate that science and technology provide fresh sources of power, that we need fresh sources of analysis and political action (Latour, 1984). Some of the rearrangements of race, sex, and class rooted in high-tech-facilitated social relations can make socialist-feminism more relevant to effective progressive politics.

THE "HOMEWORK ECONOMY" OUTSIDE "THE HOME"

The "New Industrial Revolution" is producing a new world-wide working class, as well as new sexualities and ethnicities. The extreme mobility of capital and the emerging international division of labour are intertwined with the emergence of new collectivities, and the weakening of familiar groupings. These developments are neither gender- nor race-neutral. White men in advanced industrial societies have become newly vulnerable to permanent job loss, and women are not disappearing from the job rolls at the same rates as men. It is not simply that women in Third World countries are the preferred labour force for the science-based multinationals in the export-processing sectors, particularly in electronics. The picture is more systematic and involves reproduction, sexuality, culture, consumption, and production. In the prototypical Silicon Valley, many women's lives have been structured around employment in electronics-dependent jobs, and their intimate realities include serial heterosexual monogamy, negotiating childcare, distance from extended kin or most other forms of traditional community, a high likelihood of loneliness and extreme economic vulnerability as they age. The ethnic and racial diversity of women in Silicon Valley structures a microcosm of conflicting differences in culture, family, religion, education, and language.

Richard Gordon has called this new situation the "homework economy."[16] Although he includes the phenomenon of literal homework emerging in connection with electronics assembly, Gordon intends "homework economy" to name a restructuring of work that broadly has the characteristics formerly ascribed to female jobs, jobs literally done only by women. Work is being redefined as both literally female and feminized, whether performed by men or women. To be feminized means to be made extremely vulnerable; able to be disassembled, reassembled, exploited as a reserve labour force; seen less as workers than as servers; subjected to time arrangements on and off the paid job that make a mockery of a limited work day; leading an existence that always borders on being obscene, out of place, and reducible to sex. Deskilling is an old strategy newly applicable to formerly privileged workers. However, the homework economy does not refer only to large-scale deskilling, nor does it deny that new areas of high skill are emerging, even for women and men previously excluded from skilled employment. Rather, the concept indicates that factory, home, and market are integrated on a new scale and that the places of women are crucial—and need to be analysed for differences among women and for meanings for relations between men and women in various situations.

The homework economy as a world capitalist organizational structure is made possible by (not caused by) the new technologies. The success of the attack on relatively privileged, mostly white, men's unionized jobs is tied to the power of the new communications technologies to integrate and control labour despite extensive dispersion and decentralization. The consequences of the new technologies are felt by women both in the loss of the family (male) wage (if they ever had access to this white privilege) and in the character of their own jobs, which are becoming capital-intensive; for example, office work and nursing.

The new economic and technological arrangements are also related to the collapsing welfare state and the ensuing intensification of demands on women to sustain daily life for themselves as well as for men, children, and old people. The feminization of poverty—generated by dismantling the welfare state, by the homework economy where stable jobs become the exception, and sustained by the expectation that women's wages will not be matched by a male income for the support of children—has become an urgent focus. The causes of various women-headed households are a function of race, class, or sexuality; but their increasing generality is a ground for coalitions of women on many issues. That women regularly sustain daily life partly as a function of their enforced status as mothers is hardly new; the kind of integration with the overall capitalist and progressively war-based economy is new. The particular pressure, for example, on US black women, who have achieved an escape from (barely) paid domestic service and who now hold clerical and similar jobs in large numbers, has large implications for continued enforced black poverty *with* employment. Teenage women in industrializing areas of the Third World increasingly find themselves the sole or major source of a cash wage for their families, while access to land is ever more problematic. These developments must have major consequences in the psychodynamics and politics of gender and race.

Within the framework of three major stages of capitalism (commercial/early industrial, monopoly, multinational)—tied to nationalism, imperialism, and multinationalism, and related to Jameson's three dominant aesthetic periods of realism, modernism, and postmodernism—I would argue that specific forms of families dialectically relate to forms of capital and to its political and cultural concomitants. Although lived problematically and unequally, ideal forms of these families might be schematized as (1) the patriarchal nuclear family, structured by the dichotomy between public and private and accompanied by the white bourgeois ideology of separate spheres and nineteenth-century Anglo-American bourgeois feminism; (2) the modern family mediated (or enforced) by the welfare state and institutions like the family wage, with a flowering of a-feminist heterosexual ideologies, including their radical versions represented in Greenwich Village around the First World War; and (3) the "family" of the homework economy with its oxymoronic structure of women-headed households and its explosion of feminisms and the paradoxical intensification and erosion of gender itself. This is the context in which the projections for world-wide structural unemployment stemming from the new technologies are part of the picture of the homework economy. As robotics and related technologies put men out of work in "developed" countries and exacerbate failure to generate male jobs in Third World "development," and as the automated office becomes the rule even in labour-surplus countries, the feminization of work intensifies. Black women in the United States have long known what it looks like to face the structural underemployment ("feminization") of black men, as well as their own highly vulnerable position in the wage economy. It is no longer a secret that sexuality, reproduction, family, and community life are interwoven with this economic structure in myriad ways which have also differentiated the situations of white and black women. Many more women and men will contend with similar situations, which will make cross-gender and race alliances on issues of basic life support (with or without jobs) necessary, not just nice.

The new technologies also have a profound effect on hunger and on food production for subsistence world-wide. Rae Lessor Blumberg (1983) estimates that women produce about 50 per cent of the world's subsistence food.[17] Women are excluded generally from benefiting from the increased high-tech commodification of food and energy crops, their days are made more arduous because their responsibilities to provide food do not diminish, and their repro-

ductive situations are made more complex. Green Revolution technologies interact with other high-tech industrial production to alter gender divisions of labour and differential gender migration patterns.

The new technologies seem deeply involved in the forms of "privitization" that Ros Petchesky (1981) has analysed, in which militarization, right-wing family ideologies and policies, and intensified definitions of corporate (and state) property as private synergistically interact.[18] The new communications technologies are fundamental to the eradication of "public life" for everyone. This facilitates the mushrooming of a permanent high-tech military establishment at the cultural and economic expense of most people, but especially of women. Technologies like video games and highly miniaturized televisions seem crucial to production of modern forms of "private life." The culture of video games is heavily orientated to individual competition and extraterrestrial warfare. High-tech, gendered imaginations are produced here, imaginations that can contemplate destruction of the planet and a sci-fi escape from its consequences. More than our imaginations is militarized; and the other realities of electronic and nuclear warfare are inescapable. These are the technologies that promise ultimate mobility and perfect exchange—and incidentally enable tourism, that perfect practice of mobility and exchange, to emerge as one of the world's largest single industries.

The new technologies affect the social relations of both sexuality and reproduction, and not always in the same ways. The close ties of sexuality and instrumentality, of views of the body as a kind of private satisfaction- and utility-maximizing machine, are described nicely in sociobiological origin stories that stress a genetic calculus and explain the inevitable dialectic of domination of male and female gender roles.[19] These sociobiological stories depend on a high-tech view of the body as a biotic component or cybernetic communications system. Among the many transformations of reproductive situations is the medical one, where women's bodies have boundaries newly permeable to both "visualization" and "intervention." Of course, who controls the interpretation of bodily boundaries in medical hermeneutics is a major feminist issue. The speculum served as an icon of women's claiming their bodies in the 1970s; that handcraft tool is inadequate to express our needed body politics in the negotiation of reality in the practices of cyborg reproduction. Self-help is not enough. The technologies of visualization recall the important cultural practice of hunting with the camera and the deeply predatory nature of a photographic consciousness.[20] Sex, sexuality, and reproduction are central actors in high-tech myth systems structuring our imaginations of personal and social possibility.

Another critical aspect of the social relations of the new technologies is the reformulation of expectations, culture, work, and reproduction for the large scientific and technical work-force. A major social and political danger is the formation of a strongly bimodal social structure, with the masses of women and men of all ethnic groups, but especially people of colour, confined to a homework economy, illiteracy of several varieties, and general redundancy and impotence, controlled by high-tech repressive apparatuses ranging from entertainment to surveillance and disappearance. An adequate socialist-feminist politics should address women in the privileged occupational categories, and particularly in the production of science and technology that constructs scientific-technical discourses, processes, and objects.[21]

This issue is only one aspect of enquiry into the possibility of a feminist science, but it is important. What kind of constitutive role in the production of knowledge, imagination, and practice can new groups doing science have? How can these groups be allied with progressive social and political movements? What kind of political accountability can be constructed to tie women together across the scientific-technical

hierarchies separating us? Might there be ways of developing feminist science/technology politics in alliance with anti-military science facility conversion action groups? Many scientific and technical workers in Silicon Valley, the high-tech cowboys included, do not want to work on military science.[22] Can these personal preferences and cultural tendencies be welded into progressive politics among this professional middle class in which women, including women of colour, are coming to be fairly numerous?

WOMEN IN THE INTEGRATED CIRCUIT

Let me summarize the picture of women's historical locations in advanced industrial societies, as these positions have been restructured partly through the social relations of science and technology. If it was ever possible ideologically to characterize women's lives by the distinction of public and private domains—suggested by images of the division of working-class life into factory and home, of bourgeois life into market and home, and of gender existence into personal and political realms—it is now a totally misleading ideology, even to show how both terms of these dichotomies construct each other in practice and in theory. I prefer a network ideological image, suggesting the profusion of spaces and identities and the permeability of boundaries in the personal body and in the body politic. "Networking" is both a feminist practice and a multinational corporate strategy—weaving is for oppositional cyborgs.

So let me return to the earlier image of the informatics of domination and trace one vision of women's "place" in the integrated circuit, touching only a few idealized social locations seen primarily from the point of view of advanced capitalist societies: Home, Market, Paid Work Place, State, School, Clinic-Hospital, and

Church. Each of these idealized spaces is logically and practically implied in every other locus, perhaps analogous to a holographic photograph. I want to suggest the impact of the social relations mediated and enforced by the new technologies in order to help formulate needed analysis and practical work. However, there is no "place" for women in these networks, only geometrics of difference and contradiction crucial to women's cyborg identities. If we learn how to read these webs of power and social life, we might learn new couplings, new coalitions. There is no way to read the following list from a standpoint of "identification," of a unitary self. The issue is dispersion. The task is to survive in the diaspora.

Home: Women-headed households, serial monogamy, flight of men, old women alone, technology of domestic work, paid homework, reemergence of home sweatshops, home-based businesses and telecommuting, electronic cottage, urban homelessness, migration, module architecture, reinforced (simulated) nuclear family, intense domestic violence.

Market: Women's continuing consumption work, newly targeted to buy the profusion of new production from the new technologies (especially as the competitive race among industrialized and industrializing nations to avoid dangerous mass unemployment necessitates finding ever bigger new markets for ever less clearly needed commodities); bimodal buying power, coupled with advertising targeting of the numerous affluent groups and neglect of the previous mass markets; growing importance of informal markets in labour and commodities parallel to high-tech, affluent market structures; surveillance systems through electronic funds transfer; intensified market abstraction (commodification) of experience, resulting in ineffective utopian or equivalent cynical theories of community; extreme mobility (abstraction) of

marketing/financing systems; interpenetration of sexual and labour markets; intensified sexualization of abstracted and alienated consumption.

Paid Work Place: Continued intense sexual and racial division of labour, but considerable growth of membership in privileged occupational categories for many white women and people of colour; impact of new technologies on women's work in clerical, service, manufacturing (especially textiles), agriculture, electronics; international restructuring of the working classes; development of new time arrangements to facilitate the homework economy (flex time, part time, over time, no time); homework and out work; increased pressures for two-tiered wage structures; significant numbers of people in cash-dependent populations world-wide with no experience or no further hope of stable employment; most labour "marginal" or "feminized."

State: Continued erosion of the welfare state; decentralizations with increased surveillance and control; citizenship by telematics; imperialism and political power broadly in the form of information rich/information poor differentiation; increased high-tech militarization increasingly opposed by many social groups; reduction of civil service jobs as a result of the growing capital intensification of office work, with implications for occupational mobility for women of colour; growing privatization of material and ideological life and culture; close integration of privatization and militarization, the high-tech forms of bourgeois capitalist personal and public life; invisibility of different social groups to each other, linked to psychological mechanisms of belief in abstract enemies.

School: Deepening coupling of high-tech capital needs and public education at all levels, differentiated by race, class, and gender; managerial classes involved in educational reform and refunding at the cost of remaining progressive educational democratic structures for children and teachers; education for mass ignorance and repression in technocratic and militarized culture; growing anti-science mystery cults in dissenting and radical political movements; continued relative scientific illiteracy among white women and people of colour; growing industrial direction of education (especially higher education) by science-based multinationals (particularly in electronics- and biotechnology-dependent companies); highly educated, numerous élites in a progressively bimodal society.

Clinic-hospital: Intensified machine-body relations; renegotiations of public metaphors which channel personal experience of the body, particularly in relation to reproduction, immune system functions, and "stress" phenomena; intensification of reproductive politics in response to world historical implications of women's unrealized, potential control of their relation to reproduction; emergence of new, historically specific diseases; struggles over meanings and means of health in environments pervaded by high technology products and processes; continuing feminization of health work; intensified struggle over state responsibility for health; continued ideological role of popular health movements as a major form of American politics.

Church: Electronic fundamentalist "super-saver" preachers solemnizing the union of electronic capital and automated fetish gods; intensified importance of churches in resisting the militarized state; central struggle over women's meanings and authority in religion; continued relevance of spirituality, intertwined with sex and health, in political struggle.

The only way to characterize the informatics of domination is as a massive intensification of insecurity and cultural impoverishment, with common failure of subsistence networks for the most vulnerable. Since much of this picture interweaves with the social relations of science and technology, the urgency of a socialist-feminist politics addressed to science and technology is plain. There is much now being done, and the grounds for political work are rich. For example, the efforts to develop forms of collective struggle for women in paid work, like SEIU's District 925, [Service Employees International Union's office workers' organization in the US] should be a high priority for all of us. These efforts are profoundly tied to technical restructuring of labour processes and reformations of working classes. These efforts also are providing understanding of a more comprehensive kind of labour organization, involving community, sexuality, and family issues never privileged in the largely white male industrial unions.

The structural rearrangements related to the social relations of science and technology evoke strong ambivalence. But it is not necessary to be ultimately depressed by the implications of late twentieth-century women's relation to all aspects of work, culture, production of knowledge, sexuality, and reproduction. For excellent reasons, most Marxisms see domination best and have trouble understanding what can only look like false consciousness and people's complicity in their own domination in late capitalism. It is crucial to remember that what is lost, perhaps especially from women's points of view, is often virulent forms of oppression, nostalgically naturalized in the face of current violation. Ambivalence towards the disrupted unities mediated by high-tech culture requires not sorting consciousness into categories of "clear-sighted critique grounding a solid political epistemology" versus "manipulated false consciousness," but subtle understanding of emerging pleasures, experiences, and powers with serious potential for changing the rules of the game.

There are grounds for hope in the emerging bases for new kinds of unity across race, gender, and class, as these elementary units of socialist-feminist analysis themselves suffer protean transformations. Intensifications of hardship experienced world-wide in connection with the social relations of science and technology are severe. But what people are experiencing is not transparently clear, and we lack sufficiently subtle connections for collectively building effective theories of experience. Present efforts—Marxist, psychoanalytic, feminist, anthropological—to clarify even "our" experience are rudimentary.

I am conscious of the odd perspective provided by my historical position—a PhD in biology for an Irish Catholic girl was made possible by Sputnik's impact on US national science-education policy. I have a body and mind as much constructed by the post-Second World War arms race and cold war as by the women's movements. There are more grounds for hope in focusing on the contradictory effects of politics designed to produce loyal American technocrats, which also produced large numbers of dissidents, than in focusing on the present defeats.

The permanent partiality of feminist points of view has consequences for our expectations of forms of political organization and participation. We do not need a totality in order to work well. The feminist dream of a common language, like all dreams for a perfectly true language, of perfectly faithful naming of experience, is a totalizing and imperialist one. In that sense, dialectics too is a dream language, longing to resolve contradiction. Perhaps, ironically, we can learn from our fusions with animals and machines how not to be Man, the embodiment of Western logos. From the point of view of pleasure in these potent and taboo fusions, made inevitable by the social relations of science and technology, there might indeed be a feminist science.

CYBORGS: A MYTH OF POLITICAL IDENTITY

I want to conclude with a myth about identity and boundaries which might inform late twentieth-century political imaginations. I am indebted in this story to writers like Joanna Russ, Samuel R. Delany, John Varley, James Tiptree, Jr., Octavia Butler, Monique Wittig, and Vonda McIntyre.[23] These are our story tellers exploring what it means to be embodied in high-tech worlds. They are theorists for cyborgs. Exploring conceptions of bodily boundaries and social order, the anthropologist Mary Douglas (1966, 1970) should be credited with helping us to consciousness about how fundamental body imagery is to world view, and so to political language. French feminists like Luce Irigaray and Monique Wittig, for all their differences, know how to write the body; how to weave eroticism, cosmology, and politics from imagery of embodiment, and especially for Wittig, from imagery of fragmentation and reconstitution of bodies.[24]

American radical feminists like Susan Griffin, Audre Lorde, and Adrienne Rich have profoundly affected our political imaginations—and perhaps restricted too much what we allow as a friendly body and political language.[25] They insist on the organic, opposing it to the technological. But their symbolic systems and the related positions of ecofeminism and feminist paganism, replete with organicisms, can only be understood in Sandoval's terms as oppositional ideologies fitting the late twentieth century. They would simply bewilder anyone not preoccupied with the machines and consciousness of late capitalism. In that sense they are part of the cyborg world. But there are also great riches for feminists in explicitly embracing the possibilities inherent in the breakdown of clean distinctions between organism and machine and similar distinctions structuring the Western self. It is the simultaneity of breakdowns that cracks the matrices of domination and opens geometric possibilities. What might be learned from personal and political "technological" pollution? I look briefly at two overlapping groups of texts for their insight into the construction of a potentially helpful cyborg myth: constructions of women of colour and monstrous selves in feminist science fiction.

Earlier I suggested that "women of colour" might be understood as a cyborg identity, a potent subjectivity synthesized from fusions of outsider identities and in the complex political-historical layerings of her "biomythography," *Zami* (Lorde, 1982; King, 1987a, 1987b). There are material and cultural grids mapping this potential, Audre Lorde (1984) captures the tone in the title of her *Sister Outsider*. In my political myth, Sister Outsider is the offshore woman, whom US workers, female and feminized, are supposed to regard as the enemy preventing their solidarity, threatening their security. Onshore, inside the boundary of the United States, Sister Outsider is a potential amidst the races and ethnic identities of women manipulated for division, competition, and exploitation in the same industries. "Women of colour" are the preferred labour force for the science-based industries, the real women for whom the world-wide sexual market, labour market, and politics of reproduction kaleidoscope into daily life. Young Korean women hired in the sex industry and in electronics assembly are recruited from high schools, educated for the integrated circuit. Literacy, especially in English, distinguishes the "cheap" female labour so attractive to the multinationals.

Contrary to orientalist stereotypes of the "oral primitive," literacy is a special mark of women of colour, acquired by US black women as well as men through a history of risking death to learn and to teach reading and writing. Writing has a special significance for all colonized groups. Writing has been crucial to the Western myth of the distinction between oral and written cultures, primitive and civilized mentalities, and more recently to the erosion of that distinction in "postmodernist" theories attacking the phallogocentrism of the West, with its worship of the monotheistic, phallic, authoritative, and singular work, the unique and perfect name.[26] Contests for the meanings of writing are a major form of contemporary political struggle. Releasing the play of writing is deadly serious. The poetry and

stories of US women of colour are repeatedly about writing, about access to the power to signify; but this time that power must be neither phallic nor innocent. Cyborg writing must not be about the Fall, the imagination of a once-upon-a-time wholeness before language, before writing, before Man. Cyborg writing is about the power to survive, not on the basis of original innocence, but on the basis of seizing the tools to mark the world that marked them as other.

The tools are often stories, retold stories, versions that reverse and displace the hierarchical dualisms of naturalized identities. In retelling origin stories, cyborg authors subvert the central myths of origin of Western culture. We have all been colonized by those origin myths, with their longing for fulfilment in apocalypse. The phallogocentric origin stories most crucial for feminist cyborgs are built into the literal technologies—technologies that write the world, biotechnology and microelectronics—that have recently textualized our bodies as code problems on the grid of C^3I. Feminist cyborg stories have the task of recording communication and intelligence to subvert command and control.

Figuratively and literally, language politics pervade the struggles of women of colour; and stories about language have a special power in the rich contemporary writing by US women of colour. For example, retellings of the story of the indigenous woman Malinche, mother of the mestizo "bastard" race of the new world, master of languages, and mistress of Cortés, carry special meaning for Chicana constructions of identity. Cherríe Moraga (1983) in *Loving in the War Years* explores the themes of identity when one never possessed the original language, never told the original story, never resided in the harmony of legitimate heterosexuality in the garden of culture, and so cannot base identity on a myth or a fall from innocence and right to natural names, mother's or father's.[27] Moraga's writing, her superb literacy, is presented in her poetry as the same kind of violation as Malinche's mastery of the conqueror's language—a violation, an illegitimate production, that allows survival. Moraga's language is not "whole"; it is self-consciously spliced, a chimera of English and Spanish, both conqueror's languages. But it is this chimeric monster, without claim to an original language before violation, that crafts the erotic, competent, potent identities of women of colour. Sister Outsider hints at the possibility of world survival not because of her innocence, but because of her ability to live on the boundaries, to write without the founding myth of original wholeness, with its inescapable apocalypse of final return to a deathly oneness that Man has imagined to be the innocent and all-powerful Mother, freed at the End from another spiral of appropriation by her son. Writing marks Moraga's body, affirms it as the body of a woman of colour, against the possibility of passing into the unmarked category of the Anglo father or into the orientalist myth of "original illiteracy" of a mother that never was. Malinche was mother here, not Eve before eating the forbidden fruit. Writing affirms Sister Outsider, not the Woman-before-the-Fall-into-Writing needed by the phallogocentric Family of Man.

Writing is pre-eminently the technology of cyborgs, etched surfaces of the late twentieth century. Cyborg politics is the struggle for language and the struggle against perfect communication, against the one code that translates all meaning perfectly, the central dogma of phallogocentrism. That is why cyborg politics insist on noise and advocate pollution, rejoicing in the illegitimate fusions of animal and machine. These are the couplings which make Man and Woman so problematic, subverting the structure of desire, the force imagined to generate language and gender, and so subverting the structure and modes of reproduction of "Western" identity, of nature and culture, of mirror and eye, slave and master, body and mind. "We" did not originally choose to be cyborgs, but choice grounds a liberal politics and epistemology that imagines the reproduction of individuals before the wider replications of "texts."

From the perspective of cyborgs, freed of the need to ground politics in "our" privileged position of the oppression that incorporates all other dominations, the innocence of the merely violated, the ground of those closer to nature, we can see powerful possibilities. Feminisms and Marxisms have run aground on Western epistemological imperatives to construct a revolutionary subject from the perspective of a hierarchy of oppressions and/or a latent position of moral superiority, innocence, and greater closeness to nature. With no available original dream of a common language or original symbiosis promising protection from hostile "masculine" separation, but written into the play of a text that has no finally privileged reading or salvation history, to recognize "oneself" as fully implicated in the world, frees us of the need to root politics in identification, vanguard parties, purity, and mothering. Stripped of identity, the bastard race teaches about the power of the margins and the importance of a mother like Malinche. Women of colour have transformed her from the evil mother of masculinist fear into the originally literate mother who teaches survival.

This is not just literary deconstruction, but liminal transformation. Every story that begins with original innocence and privileges the return to wholeness imagines the drama of life to be individuation, separation, the birth of the self, the tragedy of autonomy, the fall into writing, alienation; that is, war, tempered by imaginary respite in the bosom of the Other. These plots are ruled by a reproductive politics—rebirth without flaw, perfection, abstraction. In this plot women are imagined either better or worse off, but all agree they have less selfhood, weaker individuation, more fusion to the oral, to Mother, less at stake in masculine autonomy. But there is another route to having less at stake in masculine autonomy, a route that does not pass through Woman, Primitive, Zero, the Mirror Stage and its imaginary. It passes through women and other present-tense, illegitimate cyborgs, not of Woman born, who refuse the ideological resources of victimization so as to have a real life. These cyborgs are the people who refuse to disappear on cue, no matter how many times a "Western" commentator remarks on the sad passing of another primitive, another organic group done in by "Western" technology, by writing.[28] These real-life cyborgs (for example, the Southeast Asian village women workers in Japanese and US electronics firms described by Aihwa Ong) are actively rewriting the texts of their bodies and societies. Survival is the stakes in this play of readings.

To recapitulate, certain dualisms have been persistent in Western traditions; they have all been systemic to the logics and practices of domination of women, people of colour, nature, workers, animals—in short, domination of all constituted as others, whose task is to mirror the self. Chief among these troubling dualisms are self/other, mind/body, culture/nature, male/female, civilized/primitive, reality/appearance, whole/part, agent/resource, maker/made, active/passive, right/wrong, truth/illusion, total/partial, God/man. The self is the One who is not dominated, who knows that by the service of the other, the other is the one who holds the future, who knows that by the experience of domination, which gives the lie to the autonomy of the self. To be One is to be autonomous, to be powerful, to be God; but to be One is to be an illusion, and so to be involved in a dialectic of apocalypse with the other. Yet to be other is to be multiple, without clear boundary, frayed, insubstantial. One is too few, but two are too many.

High-tech culture challenges these dualisms in intriguing ways. It is not clear who makes and who is made in the relation between human and machine. It is not clear what is mind and what body in machines that resolve into coding practices. In so far as we know ourselves in both formal discourse (for example, biology) and in daily practice (for example, the homework economy in the integrated circuit), we find ourselves to be cyborgs, hybrids, mosaics, chimeras. Biological organisms have become biotic systems, communications devices like others. There is no fundamental, ontological separation in our formal knowledge of machine and organism, of technical and organic. The replicant Rachel in the Ridley Scott film *Blade Runner* stands as the image of a cyborg culture's fear, love, and confusion.

One consequence is that our sense of connection to our tools is heightened. The trance state experienced by many computer users has become a staple of science-fiction film and cultural jokes. Perhaps paraplegics and other severely handicapped people can (and sometimes do) have the most intense experiences of complex hybridization with other communication devices.[29] Anne McCaffrey's pre-feminist *The Ship Who Sang* (1969) explored the consciousness of a cyborg, hybrid of girl's brain and complex machinery, formed after the birth of a severely handicapped child. Gender, sexuality, embodiment, skill: all were reconstituted in the story. Why should our bodies end at the skin, or include at best other beings encapsulated by skin? From the seventeenth century till now, machines could be animated—given ghostly souls to make them speak or move or to account for their orderly development and mental capacities. Or organisms could be mechanized—reduced to body understood as resource of mind. These machine/organism relationships are obsolete, unnecessary. For us, in imagination and in other practice, machines can be prosthetic devices, intimate components, friendly selves. We don't need organic holism to give impermeable wholeness, the total woman and her feminist variants (mutants?). Let me conclude this point by a very partial reading of the logic of the cyborg monsters of my second group of texts, feminist science fiction.

The cyborgs populating feminist science fiction make very problematic the statuses of man or woman, human, artefact, member of a race, individual entity, or body. Katie King clarifies how pleasure in reading these fictions is not largely based on identification. Students facing Joanna Russ for the first time, students who have learned to take modernist writers like James Joyce or Virginia Woolf without flinching, do not know what to make of *The Adventures of Alyx* or *The Female Man,* where characters refuse the reader's search for innocent wholeness while granting the wish for heroic quests, exuberant eroticism, and serious politics. *The Female Man* is the story of four versions of one genotype, all of whom meet, but even taken together do not make a whole, resolve the dilemmas of violent moral action, or remove the growing scandal of gender. The feminist science fiction of Samuel R. Delany, especially *Tales of Nevèrÿon,* mocks stories of origin by redoing the neolithic revolution, replaying the founding moves of Western civilization to subvert their plausibility. James Tiptree, Jr, an author whose fiction was regarded as particularly manly until her "true" gender was revealed, tells tales of reproduction based on nonmammalian technologies like alternation of generations of male brood pouches and male nurturing. John Varley constructs a supreme cyborg in his arch-feminist exploration of Gaea, a mad goddess-planet-trickster-old woman-technological device on whose surface an extraordinary array of post-cyborg symbioses are spawned. Octavia Butler writes of an African sorceress pitting her powers of transformation against the genetic manipulations of her rival (*Wild Seed*), of time warps that bring a modern US black woman into slavery where her actions in relation to her white master-ancestor determine the possibility of her own birth (*Kindred*), and of the illegitimate insights into identity and community of an adopted cross-species child who came to know the enemy as self (*Survivor*). In *Dawn* (1987), the first instalment of a series called *Xenogenesis,* Butler tells the story of Lilith Iyapo, whose personal name recalls Adam's first and repudiated wife and whose family name marks her status as the widow of the son of Nigerian immigrants to the US. A black woman and a mother whose

child is dead, Lilith mediates the transformation of humanity through genetic exchange with extra-terrestrial lovers/rescuers/destroyers/genetic engineers, who reform earth's habitats after the nuclear holocaust and coerce surviving humans into intimate fusion with them. It is a novel that interrogates reproductive, linguistic, and nuclear politics in a mythic field structured by late twentieth-century race and gender.

Because it is particularly rich in boundary transgressions, Vonda McIntyre's *Superluminal* can close this truncated catalogue of promising and dangerous monsters who help redefine the pleasures and politics of embodiment and feminist writing. In a fiction where no character is "simply" human, human status is highly problematic. Orca, a genetically altered diver, can speak with killer whales and survive deep ocean conditions, but she longs to explore space as a pilot, necessitating bionic implants jeopardizing her kinship with the divers and cetaceans. Transformations are effected by virus vectors carrying a new developmental code, by transplant surgery, by implants of microelectronic devices, by analogue doubles, and other means. Laenea becomes a pilot by accepting a heart implant and a host of other alterations allowing survival in transit at speeds exceeding that of light. Radu Dracul survives a virus-caused plague in his outerworld planet to find himself with a time sense that changes the boundaries of spatial perception for the whole species. All the characters explore the limits of language; the dream of communicating experience; and the necessity of limitation, partiality, and intimacy even in this world of protean transformation and connection. *Superluminal* stands also for the defining contradictions of a cyborg world in another sense; it embodies textually the intersection of feminist theory and colonial discourse in the science fiction I have alluded to in this chapter. This is a conjunction with a long history that many "First World" feminists have tried to repress, including myself in my readings of *Superluminal* before being called to account by Zoe

Sofoulis, whose different location in the world system's informatics of domination made her acutely alert to the imperialist moment of all science fiction cultures, including women's science fiction. From an Australian feminist sensitivity, Sofoulis remembered more readily McIntyre's role as writer of the adventures of Captain Kirk and Spock in TV's *Star Trek* series than her rewriting the romance in *Superluminal*.

Monsters have always defined the limits of community in Western imaginations. The Centaurs and Amazons of ancient Greece established the limits of the centred polis of the Greek male human by their disruption of marriage and boundary pollutions of the warrior with animality and woman. Unseparated twins and hermaphrodites were the confused human material in early modern France who grounded discourse on the natural and supernatural, medical and legal, portents and diseases—all crucial to establishing modern identity.[30] The evolutionary and behavioural sciences of monkeys and apes have marked the multiple boundaries of late twentieth-century industrial identities. Cyborg monsters in feminist science fiction define quite different political possibilities and limits from those proposed by the mundane fiction of Man and Woman.

There are several consequences to taking seriously the imagery of cyborgs as other than our enemies. Our bodies, ourselves; bodies are maps of power and identity. Cyborgs are no exception. A cyborg body is not innocent; it was not born in a garden; it does not seek unitary identity and so generate antagonistic dualisms without end (or until the world ends); it takes irony for granted. One is too few, and two is only one possibility. Intense pleasure in skill, machine skill, ceases to be a sin, but an aspect of embodiment. The machine is not an *it* to be animated, worshipped, and dominated. The machine is us, our processes, an aspect of our embodiment. We can be responsible for machines; *they* do not dominate or threaten us. We are responsible for boundaries; we are they. Up till now (once upon

a time), female embodiment seemed to be given, organic, necessary; and female embodiment seemed to mean skill in mothering and its metaphoric extensions. Only by being out of place could we take intense pleasure in machines, and then with excuses that this was organic activity after all, appropriate to females. Cyborgs might consider more seriously the partial, fluid, sometimes aspect of sex and sexual embodiment. Gender might not be global identity after all, even if it has profound historical breadth and depth.

The ideologically charged question of what counts as daily activity, as experience, can be approached by exploiting the cyborg image. Feminists have recently claimed that women are given to dailiness, that women more than men somehow sustain daily life, and so have a privileged epistemological position potentially. There is a compelling aspect to this claim, one that makes visible unvalued female activity and names it as the ground of life. But *the* ground of life? What about all the ignorance of women, all the exclusions and failures of knowledge and skill? What about men's access to daily competence, to knowing how to build things, to take them apart, to play? What about other embodiments? Cyborg gender is a local possibility taking a global vengeance. Race, gender, and capital require a cyborg theory of wholes and parts. There is no drive in cyborgs to produce total theory, but there is an intimate experience of boundaries, their construction and deconstruction. There is a myth system waiting to become a political language to ground one way of looking at science and technology and challenging the informatics of domination—in order to act potently.

One last image: organisms and organismic, holistic politics depend on metaphors of rebirth and invariably call on the resources of reproductive sex. I would suggest that cyborgs have more to do with regeneration and are suspicious of the reproductive matrix and of most birthing. For salamanders, regeneration after injury, such as the loss of a limb, involves regrowth of structure and restoration of function with the constant possibility of twinning or other odd topographical productions at the site of former injury. The regrown limb can be monstrous, duplicated, potent. We have all been injured, profoundly. We require regeneration, not rebirth, and the possibilities for our reconstitution include the utopian dream of the hope for a monstrous world without gender.

Cyborg imagery can help express two crucial arguments in this essay: first, the production of universal, totalizing theory is a major mistake that misses most of reality, probably always, but certainly now; and second, taking responsibility for the social relations of science and technology means refusing an antiscience metaphysics, a demonology of technology, and so means embracing the skilful task of reconstructing the boundaries of daily life, in partial connection with others, in communication with all of our parts. It is not just that science and technology are possible means of great human satisfaction, as well as a matrix of complex dominations. Cyborg imagery can suggest a way out of the maze of dualisms in which we have explained our bodies and our tools to ourselves. This is a dream not of a common language, but of a powerful infidel heteroglossia. It is an imagination of a feminist speaking in tongues to strike fear into the circuits of the supersavers of the new right. It means both building and destroying machines, identities, categories, relationships, space stories. Though both are bound in the spiral dance, I would rather be a cyborg than a goddess.

NOTES

1. Research was funded by an Academic Senate Faculty Research Grant from the University of California, Santa Cruz. An earlier version of the paper on genetic engineering appeared as "Lieber Kyborg als Götrin: für eine sozialistisch-feministische Unterwanderung der Gentechnologie," in Bernd-Peter Lange and Anna Marie Stuby, eds., Berlin: Argument-Sonderband 105, 1984, pp 66–84. The cyborg manifesto grew from my "New machines, new bodies, new communities: political dilemmas of a cyborg feminist," "The Scholar and the Feminist X: The Question of Technology," Conference, Barnard College, April 1983.

The people associated with the History of Consciousness Board of UCSC have had an enormous influence on this paper, so that it feels collectively authored more than most, although those I cite may not recognize their ideas. In particular, members of graduate and undergraduate feminist theory, science, and politics, and theory and methods courses contributed to the cyborg manifesto. Particular debts here are due Hilary Klein (1989), Paul Edwards (1985), Lisa Lowe (1986), and James Clifford (1985).

Parts of the paper were my contribution to a collectively developed session, "Poetic Tools and Political Bodies: Feminist Approaches to High Technology Culture," 1984 California American Studies Association, with History of Consciousness graduate students Zoe Sofoulis, "Jupiter space"; Katie King, "The pleasures of repetition and the limits of identification in feminist science fiction: reimaginations of the body after the cyborg"; and Chela Sandoval, "The construction of subjectivity and oppositional consciousness in feminist film and video." Sandoval's (n.d.) theory of oppositional consciousness was published as "Women respond to racism: A Report on the National Women's Studies Association Conference." For Sofoulis's semiotic-psychoanalytic readings of nuclear culture, see Sofia (1984). King's unpublished papers ("Questioning tradition: canon formation and the veiling of power"; "Gender and genre: reading the science fiction of Joanna Russ"; "Varley's *Titan* and *Wizard:* feminist parodies of nature, culture, and hardware") deeply informed the cyborg manifesto.

Barbara Epstein, Jeff Escoffier, Rusten Hogness, and Jaye Miler gave extensive discussion and editorial help. Members of the Silicon Valley Research Project of UCSC and participants in SVRP conferences and workshops were very important, especially Rick Gordon, Linda Kimball, Nancy Snyder, Langdon Winner, Judith Stacey, Linda Lim, Patricia Fernandez-Kelly, and Judith Gregory. Finally, I want to thank Nancy Hartsock for years of friendship and discussion on feminist theory and feminist science fiction. I also thank Elizabeth Bird for my favourite political button: "Cyborgs for Earthly Survival."

2. Useful references to left and/or feminist radical science movements and theory and to biological/biotechnical issues include: Bleier (1984, 1986), Harding (1986), Fausto-Sterling (1985), Gould (1981), Hubbard *et al.* (1982), Keiler (1985), Lewontin *et al.* (1984), *Radical Science Jour-*

nal (became *Science as Culture* in 1987), 26 Freegrove Road, London N7 9RQ; *Science for the People,* 897 Main St, Cambridge, MA 02139.

3. Starting points for left and/or feminist approaches to technology and politics include: Cowan (1983), Rothschild (1983), Traweek (1988), Young and Levidow (1981, 1985), Weizenbaum (1976), Winner (1977, 1986), Zimmerman (1983), Athanasiou (1987), Cohn (1987a, 1987b), Winograd and Flores (1986), Edwards (1985). *Global Electronics Newsletter,* 867 West Dana St, #204, Mountain View, CA 94041; *Processed World,* 55 Sutter St, San Francisco, CA 94104; ISIS, Women's International Information and Communication Service, PO Box 50 (Cornavin), 1211 Geneva 2, Switzerland, and Via Santa Maria Dell'Anima 30, 00186 Rome, Italy. Fundamental approaches to modern social studies of science that do not continue the liberal mystification that it all started with Thomas Kuhn, include: Knorr-Cetina (1981), Knorr-Cetina and Mulkay (1983), Latour and Woolgar (1979), Young (1979). The 1984 Directory of the Network for the Ethnographic Study of Science, Technology, and Organizations lists a wide range of people and projects crucial to better radical analysis; available from NESSTO, PO Box 11442, Stanford, CA 94305.

4. A provocative, comprehensive argument about the politics and theories of "postmodernism" is made by Fredric Jameson (1984), who argues that postmodernism is not an option, a style among others, but a cultural dominant requiring radical reinvention of left politics from within; there is no longer any place from without that gives meaning to the comforting fiction of critical distance. Jameson also makes clear why one cannot be for or against postmodernism, an essentially moralist move. My position is that feminists (and others) need continuous cultural reinvention, postmodernist critique, and historical materialism; only a cyborg would have a chance. The old dominations of white capitalist patriarchy seem nostalgically innocent now: they normalized heterogeneity, into man and woman, white and black, for example. "Advanced capitalism" and postmodernism release heterogeneity without a norm, and we are flattened, without subjectivity, which requires depth, even unfriendly and drowning depths. It is time to write *The Death of the Clinic.* The clinic's methods required bodies and works; we have texts and surfaces. Our dominations don't work by medicalization and normalization any more; they work by networking, communications redesign, stress management. Normalization gives way to automation, utter redundancy. Michel Foucault's *Birth of the Clinic* (1963), *History of Sexuality* (1976), and *Disci-*

pline and Punish (1975) name a form of power at its moment of implosion. The discourse of biopolitics gives way to technobabble, the language of the spliced substantive; no noun is left whole by the multinationals. These are their names, listed from one issue of *Science:* Tech-Knowledge, Genentech, Allergen, Hybritech, Compupro, Genen-cor, Syntex, Allelix, Agrigenetics Corp., Syntro, Codon, Repligen, MicroAngelo from Scion Corp., Percom Data, Inter Systems, Cyborg Corp., Statcom Corp., Intertec. If we are imprisoned by language, then escape from that prisonhouse requires language poets, a kind of cultural restriction enzyme to cut the code; cyborg heteroglossia is one form of radical cultural politics. For cyborg poetry, see Perloff (1984); Fraser (1984). For feminist modernist/postmodernist "cyborg" writing, see HOW(ever), 871 Corbet Ave, San Francisco, CA 94131.

5. Baudrillard (1983). Jameson (1984, p. 66) points out that Plato's definition of the simulacrum is the copy for which there is no original, i.e., the world of advanced capitalism, of pure exchange. See *Discourse* 9 (Spring/Summer 1987) for a special issue on technology (cybernetics, ecology, and the postmodern imagination).

6. For ethnographic accounts and political evaluations, see Epstein [1991], Sturgeon (1986). Without explicit irony, adopting the spaceship earth/whole earth logo of the planet photographed from space, set off by the slogan "Love Your Mother," the May 1987 Mothers and Others Day action at the nuclear weapons testing facility in Nevada none the less took account of the tragic contradictions of views of the earth. Demonstrators applied for official permits to be on the land from officers of the Western Shoshone tribe, whose territory was invaded by the US government when it built the nuclear weapons test ground in the 1950s. Arrested for trespassing, the demonstrators argued that the police and weapons facility personnel, without authorization from the proper officials, were the trespassers. One affinity group at the women's action called themselves the Surrogate Others; and in solidarity with the creatures forced to tunnel in the same ground with the bomb, they enacted a cyborgian emergence from the constructed body of a large, non-heterosexual desert worm.

7. Powerful developments of coalition politics emerge from "Third World" speakers, speaking from nowhere, the displaced centre of the universe, earth: "We live on the third planet from the sun"—*Sun Poem* by Jamaican writer, Edward Kamau Braithwaite, review by Mackey (1984). Contributors to Smith (1983) ironically subvert naturalized identities precisely while constructing a place from

which to speak called home. See especially Reagon (in Smith, 1983, pp. 356–68). Trinh T. Minh-ha (1986–87).

8. Hooks (1981, 1984); Hull *et al.* (1982). Bambara (1981) wrote an extraordinary novel in which the women of colour theatre group. The Seven Sisters, explores a form of unity. See analysis by Butler-Evans (1987).

9. On orientalism in feminist works and elsewhere, see Lowe (1986); Said (1978); Mohanty (1984); *Many Voices, One Chant: Black Feminist Perspectives* (1984).

10. Katie King (1986, 1987a) has developed a theoretically sensitive treatment of the workings of feminist taxonomies as genealogies of power in feminist ideology and polemic. King examines Jaggar's (1983) problematic example of taxonomizing feminisms to make a little machine producing the desired final position. My caricature here of socialist and radical feminism is also an example.

11. The central role of object relations versions of psychoanalysis and related strong universalizing moves in discussing reproduction, caring work, and mothering in many approaches to epistemology underline their authors' resistance to what I am calling postmodernism. For me, both the universalizing moves and these versions of psychoanalysis make analysis of "women's place in the integrated circuit" difficult and lead to systematic difficulties in accounting for or even seeing major aspects of the construction of gender and gendered social life. The feminist standpoint argument has been developed by: Flax (1983), Harding (1986), Harding and Hintikka (1983), Hartsock (1983a, b), O'Brien (1981), Rose (1983), Smith (1974, 1979). For rethinking theories of feminist materialism and feminist standpoints in response to criticism, see Harding (1986, pp. 163–96), Hartsock (1987), and H. Rose (1986).

12. I make an argumentative category error in "modifying" MacKinnon's positions with the qualifier "radical," thereby generating my own reductive critique of extremely heterogeneous writing, which does explicitly use that label, by my taxonomically interested argument about writing which does not use the modifier and which brooks no limits and thereby adds to the various dreams of a common, in the sense of univocal, language for feminism. My category error was occasioned by an assignment to write from a particular taxonomic position which itself has a heterogeneous history, socialist-feminism, for *Socialist Review*. A critique indebted to MacKinnon, but without the reductionism and with an elegant feminist account of Foucault's paradoxical conservatism on sexual violence (rape), is de Lauretis (1985; see also 1986, pp. 1–19). A theoretically elegant feminist social-historical examination of family violence, that insists on women's, men's, and children's complex agency without losing sight of the material structures of male domination, race, and class, is Gordon (1988).

13. This chart was published in 1985. My previous efforts to understand biology as a cybernetic command-control discourse and organisms as "natural-technical objects of knowledge" were Haraway (1979, 1983, 1984). The 1979 version of this dichotomous chart appears in this vol., ch. 3; for a 1989 version, see ch. 10. The differences indicate shifts in argument.

14. For progressive analyses and action on the biotechnology debates: *Gene Watch, a Bulletin of the Committee for Responsible Genetics,* 5 Doane St, 4th Floor, Boston, MA 02109; Genetic Screening Study Group (formerly the Sociobiology Study Group of Science for the People), Cambridge, MA; Wright (1982, 1986); Yoxen (1983).

15. Starting references for "women in the integrated circuit": D'Onofrio-Flores and Pfafflin (1982), Fernandez-Kelly (1983), Fuentes and Ehrenreich (1983), Grossman (1980), Nash and Fernandez-Kelly (1983), Ong (1987), Science Policy Research Unit (1982).

16. For the "homework economy outside the home" and related arguments: Gordon (1983); Gordon and Kimball (1985); Stacey (1987); Reskin and Hartmann (1986); *Women and Poverty* (1984); S. Rose (1986); Collins (1982); Burr (1982); Gregory and Nussbaum (1982); Piven and Coward (1982); Microelectronics Group (1980); Stallard *et al.* (1983) which includes a useful organization and resource list.

17. The conjunction of the Green Revolution's social relations with biotechnologies like plant genetic engineering makes the pressures on land in the Third World increasingly intense. AID's estimates (*New York Times,* 14 October 1984) used at the 1984 World Food Day are that in Africa, women produce about 90 per cent of rural food supplies, about 60–80 per cent in Asia, and provide 40 per cent of agricultural labour in the Near East and Latin America. Blumberg charges that world organizations' agricultural politics, as well as those of multinationals and national governments in the Third World, generally ignore fundamental issues in the sexual division of labour. The present tragedy of famine in Africa might owe as much to male supremacy as to capitalism, colonialism, and rain patterns. More accurately, capitalism and racism are usually structurally male dominant. See also Blumberg (1981); Hacker (1984); Hacker and Bovit (1981); Busch and Lacy

(1983); Wilfred (1982); Sachs (1983); International Fund for Agricultural Development (1985); Bird (1984).

18. See also Enloe (1983a, b).

19. For a feminist version of this logic, see Hrdy (1981). For an analysis of scientific women's story-telling practices, especially in relation to sociobiology in evolutionary debates around child abuse and infanticide, see this vol., ch. 5.

20. For the moment of transition of hunting with guns to hunting with cameras in the construction of popular meanings of nature for an American urban immigrant public, see Haraway (1984–5, 1989b), Nash (1979), Sontag (1977), Preston (1984).

21. For guidance for thinking about the political/cultural/racial implications of the history of women doing science in the United States see: Haas and Perucci (1984); Hacker (1981); Keller (1983); National Science Foundation (1988); Rossiter (1982); Schiebinger (1987); Haraway (1989b).

22. Markoff and Siegel (1983). High Technology Professionals for Peace and Computer Professionals for Social Responsibility are promising organizations.

23. King (1984). An abbreviated list of feminist science fiction underlying themes of this essay; Octavia Butler, *Wild Seed, Mind of My Mind, Kindred, Survivor,* Suzy McKee Charnas, *Motherliness;* Samuel R. Delany, the Nevèrÿon series; Anne McCaffery, *The Ship Who Sang, Dinosaur Planet;* Vonda McIntyre, *Superluminal, Dreamsnake;* Joanna Russ, *Adventures of Alyx, The Female Man;* James Tiptree, Jr., *Star Songs of an Old Primate, Up the Walls of the World;* John Varley, *Titan, Wizard, Demon.*

24. French feminisms contribute to cyborg heteroglossia. Burke (1981); Irigaray (1977, 1979); Marks and de Courtivron (1980); *Signs* (Autumn 1981); Wittig (1973); Duchen (1986). For English translation of some currents of francophone feminism see *Feminist Issues: A Journal of Feminist Social and Political Theory,* 1980.

25. But all these poets are very complex, not least in their treatment of themes of lying and erotic, decentred collective and personal identities. Griffin (1978), Lorde (1984), Rich (1978).

26. Derrida (1976, especially part II); Lévi-Strauss (1961, especially "The Writing Lesson"); Gates (1985); Kahn and Neumaier (1985); Ong (1982); Kramarae and Treichler (1985).

27. The sharp relation of women of colour to writing as theme and politics can be approached through: Program

for "The Black Woman and the Diaspora: Hidden Connections and Extended Acknowledgments," an International Literary Conference, Michigan State University, October 1985; Evans (1984); Christian (1985); Carby (1987); Fisher (1980); *Frontiers* (1980, 1983); Kingston (1977); Lerner (1973); Giddings (1985); Moraga and Anzaldúa (1981); Morgan (1984). Anglophone European and Euro-American women have also crafted special relations to their writing as a potent sign: Gilbert and Gubar (1979), Russ (1983).

28. The convention of ideologically taming militarized high technology by publicizing its applications to speech and motion problems of the disabled/differently abled takes on a special irony in monotheistic, patriarchal, and frequently anti-semitic culture when computer-generated speech allows a boy with no voice to chant the Haftorah at his bar mitzvah. See Sussman (1986). Making the always context-relative social definitions of "ableness" particularly clear, military high-tech has a way of making human beings disabled by definition, a perverse aspect of much automated battlefield and Star Wars R&D. See Welford (1 July 1986).

29. James Clifford (1985, 1988) argues persuasively for recognition of continuous cultural reinvention, the stubborn non-disappearance of those "marked" by Western imperializing practices.

30. DuBois (1982), Daston and Park (n.d.), Park and Daston (1981). The noun *monster* shares its root with the verb *to demonstrate.*

WORKS CITED

Athanasiou, Tom, "High-tech Politics: The Case of Artificial Intelligence," *Socialist Review* (1987) 92:7–35.

Bambara, Toni Cade, *The Salt Eaters* (New York: Vintage/Random House, 1981).

Baudrillard, Jean, *Simulations,* P. Foss, P. Patton, P. Beitchman, trans. (New York: Semiotext[e], 1983).

Bird, Elizabeth, "Green Revolution Imperialism, I & II," papers delivered at the University of California, Santa Cruz, 1984.

"The Black Woman and the Diaspora: Hidden Connections and Extended Acknowledgments," an International Literary Conference, Michigan State University, October 1985.

Bleir, Ruth, *Science and Gender: A Critique of Biology and Its Themes on Women* (New York: Pergamon, 1984).

———, ed., *Feminist Approaches to Science* (New York: Pergamon, 1986).

———, "The Situation of Lesbianism as Feminism's Magical Sign: Contests for Meaning and The U.S. Women's Movement, 1968–72," *Communication* (1986) 9(1):65–92.

Kingston, Maxine Hong, *China Men* (New York: Knopf, 1977).

Klein, Hilary, "Marxism, Psychoanalysis, and Mother Nature," *Feminist Studies* 15(2); 255–78.

Knorr-Cetina, and Michael Mulkay, eds., *Science Observed: Perspectives on the Social Study of Science* (Beverly Hills: Sage, 1983).

———, *The Manufacture of Knowledge* (Oxford: Pergamon, 1981).

Kramarae, Cheris, and Paula Treichler, *A Feminist Dictionary* (Boston: Pandora, 1985).

Lange, Bernd-Peter and Anna Marie Stuby, eds., *1984* (Berlin: Argument-Sonderband, 1984) 66–84.

Latour, Bruno, and Steve Woolgar, *Laboratory Life: The Social Construction of Scientific Facts* (Beverly Hills: Sage, 1979).

Lerner, Gerda, ed., *Black Women in White America: A Documentary History* (New York: Vintage, 1973).

Lewontin, R.C., Steven Rose, and Leon J. Kamin, *Not in Our Genes: Biology, Ideology, and Human Nature* (New York: Pantheon, 1984).

Lorde, Audre, *Sister Outsider* (Trumansberg, NY: Crossing, 1984).

Lowe, Lisa, "French Literary Orientalism: The Representation of "Others" in the Texts of Montesquieu, Flaubert, and Kristeva," University of California at Santa Cruz, PhD thesis (1986).

Mackey, Nathaniel, "Review," *Sulfur* (1984) 2:200–5.

"Many Voices, One Chant: Black Feminist Perspectives," *Feminist Review* (1984) 17, special issue.

Markoff, John, and Lenny Siegel, "Military Micros," Paper Presented at Silicon Valley Research Project Conference, University of California at Santa Cruz, 1983.

Marks, Elaine and Isabelle de Courtivron, eds., *New Feminisms* (Amherst: University of Massachusetts Press, 1980).

Microelectronics Group, Microelectronics: Capitalist Technology and the Working Class (London: CSE, 1980).

Mohanty, Chandra Talpade, "Under Western Eyes: Feminist Scholarship and Colonial Discourse," *Boundary* (1984) 2,3(12/13):333–58.

Moraga, Cherrie, and Gloria Anzaldua, eds., *This Bridge Called My Back: Writings by Radical Women of Color* (Watertown: Persephone, 1981).

Morgan, Robin, ed., *Sisterhood Is Global* (Garden City, NY: Anchor/Doubleday, 1984).

Nash, June and Maria Patricia Fernandez-Kelly, eds., *Women and Men and the International Division of Labor* (Albany: State University of New York Press, 1983).

Nash, Roderick, "The Exporting and Importing of Nature: Nature -A ppreciation as a Commodity, 1850-- 1980," *Perspectives in American History* (1979) 3:5174–60.

National Science Foundation, *Women and Minorities in Science and Engineering* (Washington: NSF, 1988).

Obrien, Mary, *The Politics of Reproduction* (New York: Routledge & Kegan Paul, 1981).

Ong, Aihwa, *Spirits of Resistance and Capitalist Discipline: Factory Workers in Malaysia* (Albany: State University of New York Press, 1987).

Ong, Walter, *Orality and Literacy: The Technologizing of the Work* (New York: Methuen, 1982).

Park, Katherine, and Lorraine J. Datson, "Unnatural Conceptions: The Study of Monsters in Sixteenth- and Seventeenth-Century France and England," *Past and Present* (1981) 92:20–54.

Perloff, Marjorie, "Dirty Language and Scramble Systems," *Sulfur* (1984) 11:178–83.

Piven, Frances Fox and Richard Coward, *The New Class War: Reagan's Attack on the Welfare State and Its Consequences* (New York: Pantheon, 1982).

Preston, Douglas, "Shooting Paradise," *Natural History* (1984) 93(12):14–19.

Reagon, Bernice Johnson, "Coalition Politics: Turning The Century," in Smith (1983) 356–68.

Reskin, Barbara and Heidi Hartmann, eds., *Women's Work, Men's Work* (Washington: National Academy of Sciences, 1986).

Rich, Adrienne, *The Dream of a Common Language* (New York: Norton, 1978).

Rose, Hilary, "Hand, Brain, and Heart: A Feminist Epistemology for the Natural Sciences," *Signs* (1983) 9(I):73–90.

———, "Women's Work: Women's Knowledge," in *What Is Feminism? A Re-Examination,* eds., Juliet Mitchell and Ann Oakley (New York: Pantheon, 1986), pp. 161–83.

Rose, Stephen, *The American Profile Poster: Who Owns What, Who Makes How Much, Who Works Where, and Who Lives with Whom?* (New York, Pantheon, 1986).

Rossiter, Margaret, *Women Scientists in America* (Baltimore: Johns Hopkins University Press, 1982).

Rothschild, Joan, ed., *Machina ex Dea: Feminist Perspectives on Technology* (New York: Pergamon, 1983).

Russ, Joanna, *How To Suppress Women's Writing* (Austin: University of Texas Press, 1983).

Sachs, Carolyn, *The Invisible Farmers: Women in Agricultural Production* (Totowa: Rowman & Allenheld, 1983).

Said, Edward, *Orientalism* (New York: Pantheon, 1978).

Schielbinger, Linda, "The History and Philosophy of Women in Science: A Review Essay," *Signs* (1987) 12(2):305–32.

Science Policy Research Unit, "Microelectronics and Women's Employment in Britain," University of Sussex, 1982.

Signs, Autumn, 1981.

Smith, Barbara, ed., *Home Girls: A Black Feminist Anthology* (New York: Kitchen Table, Woman of Color Press, 1983).

Smith, Dorothy, "A Sociology of Women," in *The Prism of Sex,* eds. J. Sherman and E.T. Beck (Madison: University of Wisconsin Press, 1979).

———, "Women's Perspective as a Radical Critique of Sociology," *Sociological Inquiry* (1974) 44.

Sofia, Zoe, "Exterminating Fetuses: Abortion, Disarmament, and the Sexo-Semiotics of Extra-terrestrialism," *Diacritics* 14(2):47–59.

Sontag, Susan, *On Photography* (New York: Dell, 1977).

Stacey, Judith, "Sexism by a Subtler Name? Postindustrial Conditions and Postfeminist Consciousness," *Socialist Review* (1987) 96:7–28.

Stallard, Karin, Barbara Ehrenreich, and Holly Sklar, *Poverty in the American Dream* (Boston: South End, 1983).

Sturgeon, Noel, "Feminism, Anarchism, and Non-violent Direct Action Politics," University of California at Santa Cruz, PhD qualifying essay, 1986.

Sussman, Vic, "Personal Tech. Technology Lends a Hand," *The Washington Post Magazine, 9* (1986) November, pp. 45–56.

Traweek, Sharon, *Beamtimes and Lifetimes: The World of High Energy Physics* (Cambridge, MA: Harvard University Press, 1988).

Trinh T. Minh-ha, ed., "She, the Inappropriate/d Other," *Discourse* 8 (1986–1987).

Weizenbaum, Joseph, *Computer Power and Human Reason* (San Francisco: Freeman, 1976).

Wilford, John Noble, "Pilot's Helmet Helps Interpret High Speed World," *New York Times* (1 July 1986), pp. 21,24.

Wilford, Denis, "Capital and Agriculture, A Review of Marxian Problematics," *Studies in Political Economy* (1982) 7:127–54.

Winner, Langdon, *Autonomous Technology: Technics out of Control as a Theme in Political Thought* (Cambridge, MA: MIT Press, 1977).

———, *The Whale and the Reactor* (Chicago: University of Chicago Press, 1986).

Winograd, Terry and Fernando Flores, *Understanding Computers and Cognition: A New Foundation for Design* (Norwood, NJ: Ablex, 1986).

Wittig, Monique, *The Lesbian Body,* David LeVay, trans. (New York: Avon, 1975) (orig. 1973).

"Women and Poverty," *Signs,* special issue (1984) 10(2).

Wright, Susan, "Recombinant DNA Technology and Its Social Transformation, 1972–82," *Osiris,* 2nd Series, (1986) 2:303–60.

———, "Recombinant DNA: The Status of Hazards and Controls," *Environment* (1982, July/August) 24(6):12–20,51–53.

Young, Robert M. and Les Levidow, eds., *Science, Technology and the Labour Process,* 2 vols. (London: CSE and Free Association Books, 1981, 1985).

———, "Interpreting the Production of Science," *New Scientist* (1979) 29:1026–8.

Yoxen, Edward, *The Gene Business* (New York: Harper & Row, 1983).

Zimmerman, Jan, ed., *The Technological Woman: Interfacing with Tomorrow* (New York: Praeger, 1983).

Credits

PHOTO CREDITS

Index

Abrams, M. H., 51
Academic criticism/critique, 67, 281, 641
Academic world. *See also* Academic criticism/critique; Teaching
  and cultural studies, 641, 647, 648
  Derrida's views of, 345–363
  and feminism, 572
  and humanism, 116
  and literary studies, 3–4, 57–57, 204–205
  and theory, 119
Acker, Kathy, 241, 566
Aesthetics, 10, 16, 21, 30, 31, 35, 42, 87, 88, 89, 90, 94, 119, 120, 123, 648. *See also* Cultural studies
  and African-Americans, 130, 131, 135
  critique of, 90
  and ethics, 93, 642
  ideology of, 90, 107, 651
  politics of, 90
  and theory, 87–99, 104–105, 106, 107, 109, 110, 112
  as a variety of the social, 472
African-Americans
  and academic hierarchy, 130
  and aesthetics, 130, 131, 135
  and Black Power movement, 131
  and critique of essentialism, 133–134
  and feminism, 228–229, 710, 715, 718
  and postmodern critique of identity, 132–133
  and postmodernism, 130–135
  and rhetoric and reader response, 192–199, 228–229
  and theory, 161–162
African-American literary criticism, history of, 54–56
After the New Criticism (Lentricchia), 30
Ahmad, Aijaz, 5, 12, 28, 29, 88, 90, 92, 95, 96, 97, 135–156, 175, 323, 459, 461, 462, 642, 650
Alice's Adventures in Wonderland (Carrol), 537–564, 567
Allegories of Reading (De Man), 168, 326
Allegory, 73–74
Althusser, Louis, 118, 140, 311, 319, 326, 328, 378–379, 381, 401, 460, 659, 660, 664, 671–673, 675
Anatomy of Criticism (Frye), 30, 39, 92, 139, 143, 162, 260, 396

"Apostrophe, Animation, and Abortion" (Johnson), 168, 176, 221–235
Appadurai, Arjun, 552–555
Archetypal criticism, 22, 394–397
Aristotle, 4, 10, 165, 170–171, 346, 347, 350, 353, 360, 368, 458
Armstrong, Nancy, 3, 5, 22, 95, 255, 460, 465, 466, 467, 536–537, 537–564, 567, 569, 641, 642
Arnold, Matthew, 4–5, 7, 20, 22, 23, 24, 41–42, 49, 52, 59, 60, 61, 62, 115, 116, 119, 120, 121, 122, 125, 154, 643, 644
Art
  as aesthetic communication, 473–474
  and criticism, 40–49
  definitions of, 642
  fallacious views of, 472–473
  as object, 500–501
  as practice, 500–501
  and public, 40–49
  as social, 460, 472
Austen, Jane, 149, 163, 547, 601
Austin, J. L., 181, 319, 326, 332–336, 337–339, 340, 645
Authorship, 321, 327, 365–376

Babbitt, Irving, 27, 61
Bachelard, Gaston, 171
Bacon, Sir Francis, 81–82, 510
Bakhtin, Mikhail, 10, 13, 14, 90, 95, 153, 169, 258, 262, 458, 460, 461, 462, 465, 470, 471–488. *See also* Vološinov, V. N.
Baldick, Chris, 6
Balibar, Etienne, 461
Barthes, Roland, 13, 22, 23, 30, 88, 89, 147, 153, 170, 237, 240, 253, 255, 256, 259, 260, 280, 281–283, 300, 309, 327, 378, 384, 385–386, 658–659, 661, 662
"Base and Superstructure in Marxist Cultural Theory" (Williams), 490–501
Bate, Walter Jackson, 119, 120, 122
Baudelaire, Charles, 221–223, 224, 230, 232–233
Baudrillard, Jean, 147, 237, 649–650
Baym, Nina, 207
Belsey, Catherine, 3, 30, 90, 255, 256, 262, 319, 321, 323–324, 325, 326, 328, 377–378, 378–392, 396–397,

401, 460, 461, 467, 565–566, 567, 569, 645
Benhabib, Syla, 89
Benjamin, Walter, 458, 461–462, 465
Benstock, Shari, 26
Bentham, Jeremy, 121
Benveniste, Emile, 229, 262, 379, 380
Beyond the Culture Wars: How Teaching the Conflicts Can Revitalize America (Graff), 3–4, 57, 176
Bhabha, Homi K., 95, 152–153
Bhagavad Gita, 70–71
Binswanger, Ludwig, 171–172
Biological criticism, 566, 698, 708
Birmingham Center for the Study of Popular Culture, 646, 647–648
"Black Critics and the Pitfalls of Canon Formation" (West), 50–56
Black Formalism, 55–56
Blacks. *See* African-Americans
Blake, William, 141
Blanchot, Maurice, 116–118, 285
Bleich, David, 173, 174, 175, 201
Bloom, Allan, 57, 150, 162
Bloom, Harold, 139, 143, 144, 151, 202, 212
Body
  history of, 620, 622
  as situation, 616
  as socially mediated, 583
"Body and Cinema: Some Problems for Feminism, The" (Kuhn), 573–575
Bolter, David Jay, 170, 239, 241, 246–247, 249
Booth, Wayne, 14, 197–198, 199, 200–201, 203
Borch-Jacobsen, Mikkel, 631
Borges, Jorge Luis, 247, 248
Brantlinger, Patrick, 646
Brief and True Report of the New Found Land of Virginia, A (Harriot), 503, 504–515, 521, 529
Brooks, Cleanth, 29, 51, 119, 144, 394
Brooks, Gwendolyn, 176, 224–225, 226, 228
Brooks, Peter, 442–443
Brown, John, 141
Burke, Kenneth, 142, 167, 169, 171, 463
Bush, Douglas, 183
Butler, Judith, 571–572, 575, 611–612, 612–623